A Directory of

ULSTER DOCTORS

(who qualified before 1901)

Volume I

A Directory of
ULSTER DOCTORS
(who qualified before 1901)

Volume I

compiled by
R.S.J. CLARKE

ULSTER HISTORICAL FOUNDATION

Ulster Historical Foundation is pleased to acknowledge support for this publication given by the Ulster Medical Society, the Ireland, Empire and Education Project at Trinity College, Dublin and the individual donors and subscribers. All contributions have made this publication possible.

First published 2013
by Ulster Historical Foundation
49 Malone Road, Belfast, BT9 6RY
www.ancestryireland.com
www.booksireland.org.uk

Except as otherwise permitted under the Copyright, Designs and Patents Act 1988, this publication may only be reproduced, stored or transmitted in any form or by any means with the prior permission in writing of the publisher or, in the case of reprographic reproduction, in accordance with the terms of a licence issued by The Copyright Licensing Agency. Enquiries concerning reproduction outside those terms should be sent to the publisher.

© R.S.J. Clarke

ISBN: 978-1-909556-02-7   (2 Volume Set)
ISBN: 978-1-909556-03-4   (Volume I)
ISBN: 978-1-909556-04-1   (Volume II)

Printed by Bell & Bain Limited
Design by Cheah Design

CONTENTS

Volume I

FOREWORD	vii
INTRODUCTION	xi
ACKNOWLEDGEMENTS	xl
LIST OF ABBREVIATIONS	xlii
BIOGRAPHIES OF THE DOCTORS A–L	1

FOREWORD

'Now, what I want is Facts' says Gradgrind in *Hard Times*, and no-one has collected more facts of local medical historical interest than has Richard Clarke, sometime Professor of Anaesthetics at Queen's University, Belfast, and for the past seventeen years Honorary Archivist to the Royal Victoria Hospital in Belfast. And not only facts for medical historians but facts for other historians as well through, for example, his ambitious project of compiling or editing the presently some thirty volumes of the Ulster Historical Foundation's series *Gravestone Inscriptions*[1]. Professor Clarke, however, has always harboured a wider vision which, on his retirement from Queen's in 1994, he promoted to a Grand Design – to compile a 'biographical archive' of the Ulster 'medical profession' from the eighteenth, nineteenth and earlier twentieth centuries, and to include 'any who were born, educated, worked or died in the nine counties of Ulster': this would be 'of value to local historians as well as … for medical and family history'. This was in part prompted by the example of the publication of the Succession Lists (including biographical material) of the clergy of the Established Church in Ireland by diocese up to and beyond its Disestablishment (1869) which have provided much useful material for national as well as for church and local historians. Despite the duties of the Archive Office, the *Gravestone Inscriptions*, a book-length biography[2], lectures, talks and articles, and the magisterial bicentennial history of the Royal Victoria Hospital[3], Professor Clarke has now in the present compendious work completed his Grand Design.

This is a prodigious achievement, truly a *tour de force*. What seemed at first a 'mission impossible' has become a triumphant 'mission accomplished'. For depth, scope, detail and scholarly rigour it has no peer among Irish compilations, though Croly's pioneer *Medical Directory*[4], the biographical 'indexes' of William Wilde, Percy Kirkpatrick and John Widdess[5], and the contemporary 'biographical encyclopaedias' of Irish surgeons (by Barry O'Donnell)[6] and of 'medical travel authors' (by Edward Martin)[7] among others, are justifiably important. Moreover, the present work has been accomplished against long odds. Professor Clarke had no specifically dedicated assistants; for much of the period covered there was little or no worthwhile professional regulation let alone central registration, and no consistent criteria for admission to the ranks of the 'medical profession'. Until the early nineteenth century when the traditional demarcation lines were blurred by the emergence of the 'surgeon-apothecary' as a prototyped general practitioner, the profession was structured much as in Tudor times on the three core estates of physician (who treated internal diseases), surgeon (who treated external conditions) and apothecary (who compounded medications and offered advice), each of which had its professional bodies and position in society. Their education and training were, however, haphazard though as the century progressed the latter two estates had newly established diplomas which at first supported, then supplanted traditional apprenticeship. Regulation, however, remained ineffective until the mid-century: physicians, surgeons and apothecaries jostled with various other groups (who were liberally contaminated with quacks and charlatans) all bundled together, for national census purposes, under the rubric of '[others] ministering to health' (broadly those later to be variously termed 'paramedicals', 'professions allied to medicine', and recently simply 'other medical professionals') in a splintered 'extended profession'. Anything approaching a comprehensive ascertainment of those eligible for Professor Clarke's 'medical profession' required the laborious mining of many sources as disparate as universities, the medical and surgical royal colleges and the societies of apothecaries, the Army and Naval Medical Service lists, medical directories and registers, biographies, local histories including those of hospitals, apprenticeship records and others, and the staples of the local historians' diet (newspapers, Public Record Office papers, probate and wills registers, estate papers, private archives and many others), enhanced by opportunistic forays and the favours of serendipity.

As the century progressed, however, and especially after the Medical Acts of 1858 and 1886 with their central regulation and registration, the publishing of more comprehensive and detailed *Directories* and *Registers*, and with the unitary structure of medical education in place by end-century with the common undergraduate curriculum and approved licensing bodies (certain professional bodies and universities with medical schools) which held 'qualifying examinations' for registerable degrees and diplomas as evidence of competence in the 'effective practice of medicine, surgery and midwifery', and with changes in the demands of society and in the law, ascertainment of 'medical practitioners' became less tedious and more efficient through official sources and publications. Professor Clarke, however, never slackened in his search for 'completeness' and continued to scour possible source material as remorselessly as he had for the earlier periods. As a final trial, much of the data handling and the screening of sources predated the digital age. By way of compensation Professor Clarke had only the freedom from meeting deadlines which allowed him to drink very deeply indeed at those wells of information. It must have taken all his legendary commitment and determination to bring this formidable enterprise to its successful conclusion.

The descriptions of sources, methodologies, definitions and the other technical aspects of the study are the models of clarity and detail to be expected from such a seasoned compiler and cataloguer. Moreover, the author is a gifted narrator and synthesiser and his 'Introduction' also includes a coherent and informative *résumé* of 'Medical Training and Qualifications' and 'Medical Practice' over the entire period, as well as important events which could, and often did, have a bearing on them, such as the Great Famine. Among other sections is one on 'Ulster Women in the Medical Profession', who numbered over the period just twenty-two! The biographies of nearly 6,000 entries are as full as the facts allow, run from being (necessarily) brief to (justifiably) several hundred words and, helpfully, are clearly referenced citing both primary and secondary sources. There are some 200 illustrations, four detailed appendices and an imposing bibliography comprising, in commendable detail, alphabetically-ordered lists headed General and Unpublished Sources, Personal Communications, and Published Books and Papers. Gradgrind would have been well satisfied.

Who stands to benefit from this Aladdin's cave of Professor Clarke's modestly-titled *Directory*? The author identifies special interest groups as 'local historians' and those interested in 'medical and family history'; but there will be a wider interest, and for good reasons. Apart from the professional historian there is an increasing activity of what one might call 'the amateur historian' sparked by greater and more accessible data banks, digital sourcing techniques and increased publication outlets including the Internet. Most local historical societies in Ulster thrive: some e.g. the Glens of Antrim Historical Society, publish a periodical *The Glynns*; the Ulster Genealogical and Historical Guild and the Ulster Historical Foundation publish the journal *Familia* (the Foundation also publishes longer local historical works); the *Ulster Medical Journal* in a tri-annual print-run of over 800, invariably includes at least one article on local medical history; and in 1993 the *Journal of Medical Biography*, an 'international quarterly … focused on the lives of those in or associated with medicine' was added to them. Better, more abundant and more easily accessed data both stimulate and feed this growing interest, and this holds for the contemporary trend of 'medical history' to consider medicine from the viewpoint of the patient and the public, as it does for that traditionally focused on the practitioner and the profession: indeed by involving more interest-groups it enhances it. 'Amateur' medical historians are fast learning that they contribute most significantly when they simply ferret out facts and tell a story no matter how unspectacular this may seem – *histoire* in French and *Geschichte* in German both mean both 'history' and 'a story', an impressive *imprimatur* for their activities – rather than aspire to the higher aims of the professionals who concern themselves with analysis, interpretation, revision and memorable narrative mainly using facts others provide.

This *Directory* is therefore a rich source for many working not just in the medical historical but also cognate fields; but not for all of them. The numerically-minded might look for more 'statistics'; those of a carping disposition might criticise points of methodology and presentation; not only the social scientist may regret the absence of family exploration in depth. If they do they miss the point; this compilation is a *Directory*; it was not intended to perform the functions they require or aspire to the discipline of the rigorous research project, but only to supply information which may be of value to others pursuing their various interests. For example, the relationship, if any, between medical practitioners of similar family name especially if from the same or neighbouring districts, would probably repay further study, as would such matters as the aggregation of rural doctors especially in the eighteenth and nineteenth centuries in growing conurbations rather than being more diffusely spread, and whether this could be related to the fact that the dispensary doctor, did most of his 'rounds' on horseback which, incidentally, he had to supply himself out of his (mid-nineteenth century) 'average' emoluments of some £70– £80 p.a.![8] Optimists might hope that such a study could be extended to other parts of Ireland. Professor Clarke has packed much information into many rooms and the doors lie unlocked, ready to be opened.

Many will benefit from Professor Clarke's labours. At some 1,350 pages this *Directory* is unlikely to inhabit many private bookshelves, though it would grace those that it did, but it certainly should those of universities, hospitals, medical schools and societies, medical professional and regulatory bodies, public libraries, other relevant research bodies such as those dealing with migratory and population dynamics and such other repositories, and not necessarily those confined to an Irish or a medical readership, whose *clientele* will benefit from it. It is not a work complete in itself but one which also points the way others could follow. The arrival of the digital age makes this suggestion realistic and no longer merely fanciful.

Peter Froggatt
August 2013

References
1. Clarke, R.S.J., *Gravestone Inscriptions: County Down*, vols 1–21, Belfast, 1966–1998, County Antrim, vols 1–4, Belfast, 1977–2004 and *Belfast*, vols 1–4, 1982–1991.
2. Clarke, R.S.J., *A Surgeon's Century: The Life of Sir Ian Fraser, DSO, FRCS*, Belfast, 2004.
3. Clarke, R.S.J., *The Royal Victoria Hospital, Belfast: A History 1797–1997*, Belfast, 1997.
4. Croly, H., *The Irish Medical Directory*, Dublin, 1843 (1st edition); 1846 (2nd edition).
5. Froggatt, P., 'Eighteenth century Irish medical biography; neglected sources', *Journal of the Irish Colleges of Physicians and Surgeons* 1991; **20**: 106–07.
6. O'Donnell, Barry (ed.), *Irish Surgeons and Surgery in the Twentieth Century*, Dublin, 2008.
7. Martin, J.A., *A Biographical Encyclopaedia of Medical Travel Authors*, vols 1–6, Lampeter, 2010.
8. Froggatt, P., 'The response of the medical profession to the great famine', Chapter 6 in E. Margaret Crawford (ed.) *Famine, The Irish Experience, 900–1900*, Edinburgh, 1989.

INTRODUCTION

Scope of the Directory
This Directory was planned as an attempt to create a biographical archive of the medical profession such as exists for the Church of Ireland clergy and Presbyterian ministers (see Bailie and Kirkpatrick, 2005; Barkley, 1986 and 1987; Leslie, various; and McConnell, 1951). However, unlike the clergy, the profession had no corporate organization keeping its records until the Medical Act of 1858, and even this was confined to details of medical qualifications. The medical profession, like the Church, has played a considerable part in the history of the community, and therefore, the record is of value to local historians, as well as its more obvious interest for medical and family history. Like the Church, the medical profession has spread all over the world, which adds to its interest but contributes greatly to the difficulty of collecting names and biographical details.

The Directory aims to include all 'doctors' who qualified in medicine before 1901, who were born, educated, worked or died in the nine counties of Ulster. The term 'doctor' in the period before medical registration (1859) includes physicians, surgeons and apothecaries, all of whom could practise medicine in some form, but with physicians at the top of the hierarchy. Medical students, where there is no evidence that they qualified or practised medicine, have been omitted. The geographical and temporal limitations adopted here were simply to give a reasonable prospect of completion by one person, though a study of this kind is never truly complete. It is to be hoped that others will extend the work over the whole island of Ireland and possibly extend the time span.

Many who were born or educated in Ulster left to work in England, the Empire or with the navy, army or Indian Medical Service. In addition, some from outside the province went to school or university in Ulster and left immediately afterwards. In short, many who are included here will be thought to have little connection with the province of Ulster, but the very diversity of the group is probably a feature of life in Ireland and Scotland and runs contrary to the view that people in past centuries lived and died within the same parish. It has always been the case that to gain advancement in the medical profession, one has to be prepared to travel or even to emigrate permanently and a medical qualification opens the door to many other fields (e.g. Augustine Henry, botanist, and Charles Lever, writer).

The information included starts with the name (with alternative spellings), dates and main places of work. Then follows, where possible, date and place of birth, name and occupation of father and mother; names of medical brothers and close relations; schools; places of medical education; qualifications in chronological order; details of career and residence chronologically; honours; presidencies of learned societies; publications (listing only books); major nonmedical interests (such as politics); date and place of marriage(s) with wife's name, parentage and dates of birth and death; names of medical children; date and place of death (and cause of death where unusual or a major infection such as tuberculosis or typhus); place of burial; details of portraits, busts or memorials; place and date of probate or grant of administration. Finally, there is an abbreviated list of sources of information, published and unpublished. The object is to provide names and biographical details for those studying medical, family or local history. The references are intended not only to indicate the sources used but where further information may be obtained. The information is as accurate as could be obtained, and sources such as registered dates of birth, marriage and death and the Medical Register, have been used, wherever possible. Townland names have been standardized according to the Census of Ireland Townland Index (1877). Inevitably most entries do not include all the above items, but it seemed preferable to include as full biographies as was practicable rather that to pare them down to the minimum obtainable about all.

Sources of Information

The names of doctors are derived largely from the standard lists, such as Irish *Street Directories* (1807 onwards), *Croly's Medical Directories* (1843 and 1846), *Irish Medical Directories* (1852–60) and from 1859, the *Medical Register* and *Medical Directory*. One of the largest sources of additional names with an identification of origin is Peterkin and Johnston's *Medical Officers in the British Army, 1660–1898*, but there are large numbers in Crawford's *Roll of the Indian Medical Service, 1815–1930*, as well as the published registers of Members of the Royal College of Physicians of London (*Munk's Roll*) and Fellows of the Royal College of Surgeons of England (Plarr), though the place of origin of doctors is not always recorded in any of the above. The manuscript admission registers of Queen's College, Belfast (as it was until 1908) have contributed a large number of the names and all who qualified in medicine, with or without a degree from Queen's College, are included here. The published registers of Trinity College, Dublin (Burtchaell and Sadleir's *Alumni Dublinenses*, 1924 and 1935) have contributed names of doctors for the period up to 1860 and the registers for Glasgow (Addison, 1898 and 1913) and St Andrew's (Smart, 2004) Universities have provided their medical graduates. A biographical list of students of Leyden University has also been published (Innes Smith, 1932) and a short list of students of Padua (Brockliss) is available (see below).

Some doctors' names may have been included twice where they worked in places far apart or there is not enough information to identify them as the same person.

The lists of students attending the medical school in the Collegiate Department of the Royal Belfast Academical Institution (RBAI) or 'Inst' (1835–49) are fragmentary and contain no details about the individual. Only two detailed school admission registers for Ulster covering the period of this Directory, have been published – those for the Royal School, Armagh (Ferrar, 1933), and for the Methodist College, Belfast (Fry, 1984). The relevant years of these have been combed for pupils who became doctors and have provided further names, particularly of those who left the province after school (for instance to go to Trinity College, Dublin).

A large number of biographies and local histories have provided additional names in the period before medical registration began. Indexes of wills and administrations, published (e.g. Eustace, Thrift or Vicars) or in the Record Offices of Belfast or Dublin often give the occupation and have provided many names for the period before 1858. Doctors were often witnesses to wills of family or neighbours and their names are included in will abstracts (e.g. Archibald McNeale, apothecary, of Belfast c 1720). Some doctors we know of because of their marriages, such as Mr Arrott of Comber who married a Miss Beggs in 1798 and a Dr Edward Atkinson of Armagh who married Mary Macartney in 1785, but we know nothing of their qualifications or career. We know of Joseph Aickin because he recorded his experiences of the Siege of Londonderry in a long poem and Dr William Alexander of Belfast, 'a practitioner of some reputation at the beginning of the 18th century' because he is mentioned in the Drennan Letters (Agnew, 1998). We are more likely to know of those doctors who were born in Ulster but went away to seek fame in Dublin or London. These include names such as Patrick Maxwell, physician to Charles I, Joseph Black, who became professor of chemistry in Edinburgh in 1766, Sir Hans Sloane (1660–1753), founder of the British Museum, and James Curry (c 1762–1819) who became a physician of Guy's Hospital, London. There were also the two notable naval figures, Dr Leonard Gillespie and Sir William Beatty, and Dr James McHenry, senior, who was a soldier and secretary to Washington during the War of American Independence. Finally, we might never have heard of two doctors, Dr James Cord of Killinchy and Dr Lynn of Randalstown, if they had not been executed for their parts in the 1798 rising. However, such sources listed above can never provide a full list of earlier doctors and it is acknowledged that others will eventually fill out the many possible omissions.

The above sources also provide details of the doctors' medical careers but most of the work in compiling this Directory has been in trying to add personal details of their life. The date of birth is usually stated in the school and Queen's College admission records and in the more complete biographies, but often we have only the age at admission to school or university, or age at death. This gives, at best, only an approximate year of birth and, at worst, can be several years out, with conflicting information from different sources. The date of birth can, of course, be obtained from the civil registration records which began for Ireland in 1864, but unless the individual has an uncommon name and the exact place of birth is known, firm identification is impossible. For those born before 1864 there are often church registers of birth but the same difficulties apply. Likewise, information on parentage can usually only be obtained from an earlier biography or a register of births. The school attended is usually stated on the Queen's University admission register but, as has been said, only a few detailed school registers have been published. Registers for Rathmines School, Dublin, and for many schools in England have provided information when a lead was obtained from the university admission registers. The published lists of pupils at Belfast's 'Inst' (Fisher and Robb) and Portora Royal School are also of corroborative value.

The unpublished admission records of Queen's College, Belfast, are clearly of particular value for this study. Records of universities other than Queen's College, Belfast, often add biographical details, once the bare names are known. Those of Dublin, Glasgow and St Andrew's have been mentioned. Edinburgh University has published a list of its medical graduates, with country of origin and subject of MD thesis (see under Edinburgh University and Kirkpatrick (1889)) in the bibliography, but few libraries (other than QUB) have a copy. Records may also be consulted in Edinburgh University library which has detailed records of the students from c 1833. The admission records in the Manuscript Department of the Library of Trinity College, Dublin, are of value for the period after the published *Alumni Dublinenses*.

Details of career can usually be worked out from the *Medical Directory* but not all doctors supplied complete details to it and dates of moves and appointments are at best approximate. The various *Medical Directories* from 1852 to 1913 have a valuable though incomplete obituary section. The list of names in the *Medical Register* is more complete, but in the early years not all doctors took the trouble to register. The Army and Indian Medical Service lists give much detail but often omit crucial facts such as place of origin or date of death. Information about marriage and children has been particularly difficult to obtain, since there is usually no lead to it from medical sources. However, whatever information could be found has been included.

The date of death has been obtained from the will calendar records of Belfast, Dublin, Edinburgh or London, or from the General Register Office of these cities. Since most doctors leave a will, the former sources are the most convenient, but, particularly in the nineteenth century, some doctors died soon after qualifying, leaving no will. The Certificate of Death is clearly the most reliable record of date and place of death and also gives age, home address, cause of death, name of person registering the death and (in Ireland only) marital status. It should be remembered that information from the General Register Office of births, marriages and deaths for England and Wales can only be provided on certificates and in a study of this kind the overall cost is significant. Information from the General Register Offices in Belfast, Dublin and Edinburgh can be obtained in various forms. The information is not always accurate as regards age at death (and therefore date of birth) since it depended on the knowledge of the person registering the death. It is clear that the average age at death was much younger than at present, but causes of death have not been studied in detail. Finally, the place of burial has been given where known, though in a few cases the listing of a person's name on a gravestone may not mean that he is actually buried there.

Newspapers provide a source of information limited only by the time taken to search them. The *Belfast News Letter* (*BNL*) is available in the Linen Hall Library in an almost complete run from 1738, and this has been combed for marriage and death records of doctors in the period before civil registration. Indexes to the *Ballymoney Northern Herald* (Beck 2002), *Coleraine Chronicle* (Beck, 2003) and *Londonderry Sentinel* (Beck, 2006) are a newer source and one can only hope for more. All newspapers have frequent references to marriages and deaths of doctors' children, but these have not generally been included.

Portraits are only available for the minority who became celebrated but as many portraits and photographs as was practicable have been included.

Medical Training and Qualifications – Eighteenth Century and earlier
Many doctors before the nineteenth century had no recognizable qualification, such as MD or Licentiate of a Royal College or Apothecaries Hall, but had served an apprenticeship to a prominent surgeon, trained for the army or navy, or simply attended in a hospital (Brockliss et al, 2005). They could then practise without difficulty in the country towns, being described as physician, surgeon or apothecary (the last two often combined) or inaccurately, as MD.

The province of Ulster was far removed from the capital of Ireland and from centres of learning in this period and the routes for Ulster men to obtain a medical qualification were limited. There was no medical school in Ulster, and Trinity College, Dublin accepted only members of the Church of Ireland until 1795. In addition, its medical school was only founded in 1711 and teaching was quite haphazard throughout the century (Kirkpatrick, 1912). In fact there were few medical students of any denomination and only some 19 Ulster graduates from Trinity in the period before 1800 (Burtchaell and Sadleir, 1924). This contrasts with 76 who graduated in Scotland and 65 who graduated on the continent of Europe, mainly in Rheims (Table I). Those wanting a medical qualification from Dublin could also go to the Kings' and Queens' College of Physicians, the Royal College of Surgeons or the Apothecaries' Hall, but only the Royal College of Surgeons (opened in 1784) gave teaching to medical students. No less than 66 apothecaries from Ulster were licensed at the Apothecaries' Hall in Dublin during the last ten years of the eighteenth century, and these were also allowed to practice medically. In fact, when Dr William Drennan, with his Edinburgh MD, went to practice in Newry in 1783, he complained to his sister about the competition from them (Agnew, 1998).

Most Ulster students went to the universities of Glasgow or Edinburgh and the Royal Colleges in these cities. In spite of the greater distance from Ireland

(and many students would have had to walk across Scotland), the majority went to Edinburgh rather than Glasgow, presumably because of its more distinguished teachers, trained under Boerhaave of Leyden.

Dr William Drennan kept up a steady correspondence with his sister, Martha McTier, throughout much of his life (Agnew, 1998), including his student years, 1776–8. He had come over from Belfast, taken an arts degree in Glasgow and had no doubt that Edinburgh was the best place to study medicine. Drennan's description of his own life in his second year of medicine (letter, 16 November 1777) certainly does not fit in with the dissolute student image (even accepting that he was writing to his sister).

> I rise a little after six in the morning and am resolved (not with one of my Belfast resolutions) to continue this custom. I strike my flint, blow my tinder, and light my match; ... and after preparing for my classes, at about 8 o'clock, if it be a good morning I give stretch to my legs for half an hour in the meadow which lies near my lodging – [after which] I return to take my academical breakfast of bread and milk, and then issue out to the labours of the day. From nine till one I am tossed about with the wind of doctrine through the different parts of the University; from 9 till 10 at the practice; from 10 till 11 at chemistry (my second attendance at both), from 11 till 12 at the materia medica, a class which treats of medicines, their nature, use and application; from 12 till 1 at the Infirmary, from which I derive much more benefit than when last here, and after another walk and some dinner in the evening have some select friends whom I make as drunk as they can be with tea and warm water.

By his third year he was able to say 'I am now grown perfectly callous to the distresses of the Infirmary ... I cannot say, however, that I have yet arrived to that pitch of scientific insensibility which Munro recommends to his students when he defines surgery to be performing a piece of dissection on a living body' (letter, 8 February 1778). Perhaps Drennan's most telling remarks are 'It is greatly the fashion here to despise the students. A student of medicine is a term of contempt, but an Irish student of medicine is the very highest complication of disgrace' (letter, 8 February 1778). He does not explain the reason for this contempt, and some of the students' bad reputation may have been well founded, but he goes on 'We had a fever here which is now gone off – it was said, though I believe without reason, to arise from the Infirmary. Three or four students were attacked and one of them died.' This sounds more like people looking for a scapegoat than any evidence-based assessment.

The end result of all this work was an MD, obtained for a thesis on a chosen subject and three extensive vivas. All was carried out in Latin and Drennan refers (letter, 23 November 1777) to 'one Brown who spawns young physicians and surgeons, in order to speak Latin, and get a thesis written by his instructions', help which pushed up the cost of the degree from £25 to £40. After his final exam he writes 'I spoke confidently and, though not in elegant, at least in good medical Latin, as well at least as some of my examiners'. His thesis title may be translated as 'The use of venesection or bleeding in continuous fever', which probably means typhus, as distinct from intermittent fevers such as malaria.

Table I
Number of medical graduates, born in Ulster or who came to Ulster later, grouped by university of first medical degree

University	Year of primary medical qualification*		
	−1800	1801–50	1851–1900
Trinity College, Dublin	19	73	273
Queen's College, Belfast	–	–	969
Other Irish universities	–	–	69
Edinburgh University	45	221	94
Glasgow University	23	245	96
Other Scottish universities#	8	33	56
English universities	1	2	23
European universities+	65	4	8
Totals	145	519	1554

* In some cases a College licentiate, followed by a degree later
\# Approximately 35 per cent from Aberdeen and 65 per cent from St Andrew's
\+ Largely from Rheims

The practice of obtaining degrees from Aberdeen and St Andrew's began in the eighteenth century. In most cases these were secondary qualifications obtained by people who already had a medical Licentiate or training as a naval surgeon and were recommended by a testimonial from one or two respected physicians. It did not imply any further course of study or any examination until 1826.

It would appear that only one Ulster doctor took an English degree in the eighteenth century, and even later they were mainly degrees following another qualification. Scarcely any took the examinations of the Royal Colleges in London, though they did train in London hospitals for the Navy Board exams.

Finally, many went to the great medical schools of Europe – Leyden, Padua, Orange and Rheims. Those attending Leyden have attracted particular interest (Froggatt, 1993), thanks to the publication of its matriculation list in 1875 and the monumental labour of Innes Smith in producing his *English-Speaking*

Students of Medicine at the University of Leyden (1932). The University of Leyden was founded by William the Silent in 1574 as a reward to the citizens for having withstood a prolonged siege by the Spanish forces and its great attraction for Protestants was that it did not require a *Declaratio Fidei* of allegiance to the Catholic faith and in fact took students of any religion (including Jews). As with other medical schools, many who attended for study there actually obtained their degree elsewhere. Latin was still the universal language for teaching and therefore students could move freely from country to country. It appears that approximately 233 Irish students attended Leyden up to 1817, when the last Irish student graduated. Of these some 30 appear to have been from Ulster, including the last, Joseph Taylor. It is, however, difficult to be certain of the exact origin of the students as the terms *Angli, Scoti, Hiberni, Scoto-Hiberni*, etc, are used somewhat loosely and town of origin is rarely given (except for John Catherwood who was 'Belfastensis – Hibernensis'). About half of these 30 had also studied at Trinity College but did not take a degree. The period of most distinction at Leyden was when Herman Boerhaave (1701–38) was professor of medicine, and he was one of the greatest medical teachers ever. His students went on to influence medicine and medical teaching throughout the British Isles. The university to benefit most from Boerhaave's students was Edinburgh and all five of the medical professors at the new university (founded in 1726) had studied under him. This in turn contributed to the distinction of Edinburgh's medical degree and induced Irish students to study there in the later years of the eighteenth century, in preference to Dublin or Glasgow.

Fewer Irish Catholics studied at Leyden since Rheims, Montpellier, Cahors, Padua and many others were open to them, and the majority of English-speaking students at these universities were in fact Irish (Innes Smith). Padua separated Protestants from Catholics by giving the former a degree from the 'Collegio Veneto Artista'. The list has been published and includes only eight Irish before 1806, of whom only one (Henry Leslie) is said to have been a Scoto-Hibernus (Morpurgo, 1927). Oliver Goldsmith probably attended the medical schools of both Leyden and Padua, but did not take a degree from either. French universities granted degrees only to Catholics, but the Principality of Orange was under Dutch rule and from it Hans Sloane obtained his MD in 1683. It was not, in fact a very prestigious university and was constantly being harassed by the kings of France, but it suited Sloane's grand tour better than Leyden or Padua (de Beer, 1953).

It must be stressed again, in spite of all the concentration on qualifications from Universities and Royal Colleges, that the number of unqualified and unlicensed practitioners of medicine in this period, was much greater.

Medical Training and Qualifications, 1800–50
After 1800 the number of doctors in Great Britain and Ireland increased greatly, but there were still the same three groups of medical practitioners, those with

degrees, those with licentiates and those without paper qualifications. The last group was swollen by the numbers of surgeons required by the army and navy, most of whom were discharged for general practice after 1815. However, taking this fifty year period as a whole, the number obtaining degrees and licentiates had risen to approximately equal the number without and by 1850 virtually all practising doctors had a medical qualification.

Trinity College, Dublin, was now accepting all religious denominations and there was some rise in numbers of medical students attending, although the Scottish universities had an even bigger rise (Table I). The balance between Glasgow and Edinburgh had shifted in favour of the former and the reasons for this are, perhaps, to be seen in some comments by John Creery Ferguson (the future Professor of Medicine at Queen's College, Belfast) in a letter of 24 November 1824 (Belf PRO 1918/2): 'The School of Medicine here is by no means such as I was led to suppose, nor does it at all merit the character it has obtained, being on the whole inferior to Dublin.' 'There is such a crowd of students that should I add myself to the number I should learn nothing.' 'The professors are not worth the fees', and we must remember that all the fees went personally to the professor. (In Belfast also, a professor who was a good teacher could earn a lot, and later in the century, the Professor of Anatomy, Peter Redfern, was said to be the highest earning professor in the University (Moody and Beckett, 1959), leaving the considerable sum of £96,000 at his death in 1912. J.C. Ferguson never did take an Edinburgh degree but after six months moved on to Paris, which was much cheaper. St Andrew's was the next most popular university in Scotland and scarcely any students now took their primary degree on the continent of Europe after the break caused by the Napoleonic wars.

Throughout the century and indeed until World War II, many went to Paris, Vienna and Berlin for post-graduate education. There is a brief diary of Dr John Miller Pirrie (extracts in the Office of Archives, RVH), later physician in the Belfast General Hospital, during post-graduate studies in Paris and Heidelberg. He had graduated MB in Dublin but then wanted to broaden his mind. Some features which distinguish his visit to Paris from the modern post-graduate's visit to America are:

1 He had to take French lessons daily and even started to learn German.
2 He dined well with a bottle of champagne and claret (shared) each evening.
3 He played a lot of whist.
4 He attended church services and soon learned to understand the sermons in French.

On the medical side he attended a range of hospitals with lectures, clinics and operations. This was still in the era before anaesthesia and he reports on seeing amputations, operations for hare lip, drainage of abscesses, a high forceps delivery on a patient with eclampsia, many cataracts and several unspecified operations. He does not comment on the horrors, but one wonders whether this was because he was uncaring or (more likely) to avoid distress to his readers at home. After six months in Paris he moved on to Heidelberg and comments that on his first day there were 'no less than four duels among the German students, fought with Schlagers' (duelling swords). Unfortunately he appears to have been too busy with work in Germany to continue with the diary.

When the Belfast Academical Institution (later RBAI) was founded in 1810, it was intended as both school and college. In fact, the school opened in 1814 and the college in 1815 (for details see Fisher and Robb (1913), Jamison (1959), and Froggatt (1976, 1978)), but the only medical subjects taught there were Professor James Lawson Drummond's anatomy and botany. Only in 1835 was it possible to open a complete medical school with additional chairs in midwifery, materia medica, chemistry, surgery and medicine. Inst was not able to award degrees in any subject, though it gave a General Certificate in the arts subjects, which was sufficient for the Presbyterian ministry. However, with theoretical knowledge from Inst and practical experience obtained in the Fever Hospital (which had been teaching students since 1820), students were able to transfer to other universities or colleges for medical qualifications. Unfortunately we have only incomplete lists of students who attended Inst's medical faculty and we cannot be certain how many obtained a medical qualification. Inst suffered from chronic lack of funding, which affected mainly the medical school, and the sustained antagonism of the orthodox wing of the Presbyterian church, which affected mainly the arts faculty. Eventually, the government was persuaded to set up a new Queen's College in Belfast which was opened in 1849, at the same time as the Queen's Colleges of Cork and Galway, and the Collegiate Department of Inst was forced to close. Those students who were enrolled for medical courses at Inst were allowed credit for years completed, provided they passed the matriculation examination of Queen's College and attended the new college for at least one year. Initially the university only provided lecture facilities and students still had to study practical anatomy in the old dissecting room at Inst until 1863.

The Royal College of Surgeons in Ireland and its medical school were founded in 1784 and very quickly developed its teaching schools of anatomy and surgery, but such was the need for surgeons in the army and navy during the Napoleonic Wars, that private medical schools soon began to be formed (Widdess, 1967). The first of these opened in 1804, but the most famous, the Ledwich School, dates from 1809. It was followed in 1812 by the Hardwicke School which became the Richmond School and in 1824, the Carmichael College. The schools had many students from Ulster over the years until in 1888 they were amalgamated into the Royal College of Surgeons, with which they had always had close ties and which granted the students an actual licence to practice.

Medical Training and Qualifications, 1850–1900

During the second half of the nineteenth century the balance of qualifications changed again. Virtually all new graduates practising medicine had a degree or licentiate by 1850 and this was made compulsory by the Medical Act of 1858. By the same Act the General Medical Council was set up and empowered to keep a *Register* of all qualified medical practitioners, which has been published from 1859 to the present day. Only a few, who were in practise before 1820 or who did not wish to practise in the United Kingdom, failed to register. In 1861 the annual *Medical Directory* for the United Kingdom first came out with more information about each doctor, but inclusion in it has always been a personal choice, and the regional divisions used until recently, clearly has advantages and disadvantages.

During this period an increasing proportion of those training in medicine took university degrees rather than College diplomas. However, the Colleges' position was regularized by an amending Medical Act of 1886 which stated that all doctors had to be qualified in medicine, surgery and midwifery. A surprising result of this was that the Licentiate of the Apothecaries' Hall was recognized as a full medical qualification, but it also led to the cooperation of the two Dublin Colleges of Medicine and Surgery in a 'conjoint' diploma.

The university scene in Ireland was transformed by the opening in 1849 of the three Queen's Colleges of Belfast, Galway and Cork. Although they had wide local autonomy, they could not grant degrees and were incorporated into the Queen's University in Ireland (QUI) for this purpose. Students could move freely from one Queen's College to another in different years, and indeed could take part of their course in another university provided they brought a certificate from the professor or lecturer of the previous medical school. In 1882 the Queen's Colleges became part of the Royal University of Ireland (RUI), which became the degree-granting body, and in 1908 the autonomous Queen's University of Belfast (QUB) was created by the Irish Universities Act.

When Queen's College, Belfast, opened, the majority of Ulster medical students naturally studied medicine here, rather than travel to Scotland (Table I). However, a surprising number now studied at Trinity College, Dublin. As a largely residential university it would probably have attracted the more affluent students, as well as those from the south and west of the province who were less attracted to Belfast than those in Antrim and Down.

We know more about the origins and careers of Ulster doctors in this period than in those earlier, largely because most of them went to Queen's College, Belfast, and its records have been well preserved. The majority of medical students came from country areas, being the sons of small farmers, shopkeepers, Presbyterian ministers and doctors. Of these only a few had been to the established schools in Armagh, Downpatrick, Dungannon, Foyle or Portora. The great majority had attended small private schools run by a clergyman acting as schoolmaster for his sons and a few boys in the congregation. Many of the country boys attended the larger schools in Belfast – RBAI, Belfast Academy and the Diocesan Seminary, and RBAI supplied 25–30 per cent of medical students during the nineteenth century. These boys would usually have lived with relatives or lodged nearby and this practise continued when they moved on to the University. The education which the boys received at school was often very restricted, particularly in the sciences and it is not surprising that many continued with French, English and Mathematics at the university, as well as the basic sciences of chemistry, physics, botany and zoology. Poor school education led to a considerable proportion of all students entering the university below the age of 17, but while this number was 18 per cent in 1850, it had fallen to 5 per cent twenty years later.

It was necessary to pass a matriculation examination before proceeding to a degree and at the opening of the university about a third of all students were non-matriculated. However, over the first three decades the proportion declined as the arts students came to regard a BA degree as essential and non-matriculated students in all faculties were debarred from scholarships. In addition, the General Medical Council was steadily pressurising the University to insist on matriculation as an indicator of general education outside medicine.

The first medical students of QCB were awarded the degree of MD after a four-year course and would often take an additional licentiate in surgery from one of the Royal Colleges. However, in 1865 students who undertook an additional examination in operative surgery could obtain the MCh and in 1871 the Diploma in Midwifery was introduced for those who took an examination in midwifery. The General Medical Council from its establishment in 1858 pressed the College to change to MB as the primary qualification and the advent of the Royal University of Ireland in 1882 established the MB BCh BAO as the norm. However, throughout the decade some still graduated MD (RUI) as their first degree, though after a longer period of study.

The parents of most medical students would not have been wealthy and many students worked part-time during the term or took a term or a year off to earn money at some stage of the course. This was particularly the case if the father died while the student was at university, and it can be seen from the records that many did, and in such instances the widow might move to Belfast to combine the needs of education and lower living costs. The full course for the medical degree at Queen's College was four years but a student could sit the examinations of one of the Royal Colleges in Dublin, Glasgow, Edinburgh or London in three years, so there was a great temptation to take this short-cut and start to earn a living. The other possible fate of the medical student was, of course, to drop out completely, either for financial reasons or inability to pass examinations. A broad survey of the first twenty-five years of the medical school shows that approximately 50 per cent graduated MD, 20 per cent obtained another medical qualification, and 30 per cent never reached the Medical Register.

Roman Catholic students in Ulster were, of course, able to enter the medical schools in all universities and colleges along with Protestants, throughout the nineteenth century. However, with the opening of the three 'godless colleges' of Belfast, Cork and Galway in 1849 there was pressure from both Catholic religious leaders and nationalist elements, for Catholic students to be educated separately, with a common ethos (Froggatt, 1991). A Catholic University of Ireland was therefore established in Dublin in 1854, with its medical school in Cecilia Street in 1855. From this time a small but steady flow of Catholic students of Ulster studied medicine in Cecilia Street, though initially far more went to all three of the Queen's Colleges. Students, after study in these colleges, then went on to take degrees and diplomas with the various medical institutions (QUI, RUI, RCSI and Apothecaries' Hall). Numbers of students attending Cecilia Street remained small until the formation of the Royal University of Ireland in 1882, but after this date numbers grew, until by 1900 it had the largest and most able medical entry in Ireland. In this stage of success and confidence it was merged into University College, Dublin in 1908.

Medicine in Ulster before 1800
There is clearly not as much information as one would like about this period, but we have names and can get a broad picture of their work. This falls into general medical practice and hospital medicine, though the two were always combined until the twentieth century. Medicine in the armed services will be considered later.

General medical practice was always carried out where groups of people lived and in earlier times this was not necessarily in large cities such as Dublin. It was reported by van Helmont in his *Confessio Authoris*, published in 1648 and quoted by Fleetwood (1951, p 25) that 'The Irish nobility had in every family a domestic physician, whose recommendation was not that he came loaded from the college with learning, but that he was able to cure disorders, which knowledge they have from their ancestors by means of a book belonging to particular families …'. The Cassidys or O'Cassidys were the hereditary physicians of the Maguires and include Finghin (died 1322), Gilla na nAingel (died 1355), Tadhg (died 1450), Feoris (died 1504) and Feidhlimidh (died 1520) (Fleetwood, 1951, p 29). There were also Thomas O'Cassidy (*q.v.*) of county Fermanagh c 1500 and Patrick Cassidy (*q.v.*) who was buried in Devenish in 1720. Other names in Ulster that emerge are the MacDonlevy family (*q.v.*) of county Donegal in the seventeenth century, Nial O'Glacan (*q.v.*) of Donegal who practised in Spain and France and died in 1655 and Owen O'Sheil (*q.v.*) who died near Letterkenny c 1650.

Another source of information for the seventeenth century is a visitation of licensed physicians in the diocese of Connor of 1694, which gives 17 names in small towns ranging from Coleraine, Ballymoney and Portrush in the north to Lisburn and Carrickfergus in the south, although two of the physicians listed are recorded elsewhere as working in Belfast (Belf PRO, Tenison Groves, T808/9895). Again, we see that in this period there were doctors in the rural areas and they were recognised for their profession.

Legal deeds in the 1708–45 period (Eustace, 1956) record the names as witnesses or executors of six surgeons or apothecaries in the counties of Cavan, Down and Tyrone, and the small town of Belfast. The next volume covering 1746–85 (Eustace, 1954) has the names of a further 14 physicians, surgeons and apothecaries in a similar range of places – Strabane, Londonderry, Magherafelt, Antrim, Belfast and Markethill. The remainder of the century (Ellis and Eustace, 1984) has a further nine physicians, surgeons and apothecaries from Londonderry, Belfast, Cavan, Antrim and Strabane.

Newry was one of the more affluent towns of the province and when Dr William Drennan (q.v.) went there in 1782 there were already six apothecaries and a number of physicians.

Having emphasized the wide distribution of doctors, it can also be seen that the funeral register of First Belfast Presbyterian Church records 18 doctors during the short period of 1712–36 (Agnew, 1995). Towards the end of the century Belfast was becoming more prosperous and there were opportunities for an even higher concentration of doctors as recorded by Benn in his *History of the Town of Belfast* (1877), Malcolm in his *History of the General Hospital, Belfast* (1851) and Strain in his *Belfast and its Charitable Society* (1961). This was the era of Drs Robert Apsley, John Bankhead, Richard Devlin, William Drennan, Bartholomew Fuller, Alexander Henry Haliday, William Haliday, H.M. Hull, Richard McClelland, Robert McCluney, Alexander McDonnell, James McDonnell, John Mattear, Alexander Ross, James Ross, Samuel Martin Stephenson, Robert Stevenson and John Campbell White (all q.v.).

Hospital care in Ulster was non-existent during the centuries from the dissolution of the monasteries to the late eighteenth century. Care was essentially at home, with such nursing as could be afforded and the advice of a visiting doctor. Hospitals were opened first in the larger cities of southern Ireland, with Cook Street Hospital, Dublin in 1718, Dr Steevens' Hospital, Dublin in 1720, Cork's North Charitable Infirmary in 1721 and the Meath Hospital, Dublin in 1753. However, the need was felt for wider distribution of hospitals and in 1766 an Act was passed for 'Erecting and Establishing Public Infirmaries in this Kingdom'. It then became the responsibility of the Church dignitaries and prominent citizens of each area to establish hospitals as they thought appropriate, funded by the grand juries. Hence we have the Down County Infirmary in Downpatrick (Parkinson, 1967), the Antrim County Infirmary in Lisburn (Board minutes) and the Armagh Infirmary (Weatherup, 2001), all of which opened in 1767, with the Tyrone County Infirmary in Omagh about the same time, though the first building only came in 1796 (Wilmot, 1988). Building of the City and County Infirmary in Londonderry started in 1791, although a Poor House and Infirmary had existed within the walled city from about 1710 (Johnston, 1960). These hospitals were to have a County Surgeon who had served a regular apprenticeship to a practising surgeon of not less than five years and to have undergone an examination before a Board consisting of the Surgeon-General of the Forces and other Dublin surgeons. This Board was thus the first examining body for surgeons in Ireland, though it became unnecessary with the establishment of the Royal College of Surgeons in Ireland and was abolished in 1796. There was also an apothecary in these infirmaries who combined his hospital work with running a shop, but in total, the hospitals were very basic nursing homes and offered few medical posts for the first hundred years of their existence.

Hospital care in Belfast began a little later on a voluntary basis, with the Belfast Charitable Society, which opened its Poor House in 1774, with an Infirmary for the sick inmates of the Poor House (Strain, 1961). It also provided some dispensary services for the poor in their own homes. However, the need to establish this on a firmer basis led to the opening of a General Dispensary for Belfast in the Poor House in 1792. This, in turn, led to the opening of a General Dispensary and Fever Hospital in a house in Factory Row (now Berry Street), Belfast in 1797 (Malcolm, 1851; Clarke, 1997). These were voluntary hospitals and the attending physicians and surgeons were unpaid and in the early days, the leading Belfast physicians were all involved. The other early hospital in Belfast was the Lying-in Hospital, opened by a group of charitable ladies in 1794 in Donegall Street, with the doctors of the town providing attendance when requested.

Ulster Doctors and the United Irishmen (Table II)
One of the major Irish political events of the late eighteenth century was the formation of the United Irishmen. The origins of this socio-political movement may be summarised as a desire for Irish political independence, more favourable conditions for Irish trade and the cause of Catholic emancipation. In Ulster, particularly counties Antrim and Down, these had a particular appeal for the liberal or 'New Light' wing of Presbyterianism, but also included some members of the Church of Ireland. Inevitably some of the medical profession were involved, but in general, while they sympathised with the aims of the movement, attended meetings, and allowed them in their houses, they stopped short of taking up arms. A total of twenty have been identified and some of these were arrested and threatened into withdrawing from the movement, William Drennan being by far the most prominent. Dr James Cord of Killinchy was the only one to be hanged for actively taking part in the 1798 rising, although Dr Lynn of Randalstown was hanged for banditry. Dr James McDonnell was rather ambivalent and was criticised for not helping to resuscitate Henry Joy McCracken after he was hanged and for contributing to the reward for the capture of Thomas Russell in 1803.

Table II
Ulster Doctors and the United Irishmen

Acheson, Robert, doctor and Presbyterian minister, arrested in 1798 but released.
Agnew, —, doctor and publican, of Templepatrick; U.I. meeting held in his house 1798 but he escaped.
Caldwell, James, surgeon, of Magherafelt; United Irishman c 1793 but moved to London; died c 1814.
Cord, James, of Killinchy; led a troop at Battle of Saintfield June 1798; hanged 1798.
Crawford, Alexander, of Lisburn; U.I. 1794; imprisoned in Kilmainham Gaol; died 1820.
Dease, William, of Cavan and Dublin; PRCSI; United Irishman; died 1798.
Drennan, William, of Belfast, Newry and Dublin; founder member of United Irishmen 1791.
Jackson, James, of Newtownards; a senior officer of the Newtownards men.
Johns(t)on, James, apprenticed in Belfast and became United Irishman c 1797; left to join Navy 1798.
Johnston, Samuel Shannon; surgeon with the Yeomanry 1798, but sympathised with the United Irishmen.
Lynn, —, of Randalstown; United Irishman 1798; hanged for banditry after rising 1800.
Macartney, James; started a branch of United Irishmen in Armagh 1792, but withdrew 1795.
McDonnell, James, of Belfast; early member of United Irishmen 1792 but withdrew.
Musgrave, Samuel, of Lisburn; imprisoned 1796 and 1803 for sympathies with United Irishmen.
Reynolds, James, of Cookstown and Dublin; sent as United Irishman to Kilmainham 1793; emigrated.
Tennent, Robert; planter in West Indies and philanthropist; sympathised with United Irishmen.
Thompson, David, of Ballyrush [?]; attended meetings of United Irishmen 1797–8.
Todd, Nathaniel, United Irishman; involved in rising 1798; emigrated to USA; died there 1823.
Warden, David Bailie, of county Down; colonel in United Irishmen; imprisoned but emigrated.
White, John Campbell, of Belfast; implicated in 1798 rising; emigrated to USA c 1800.

Medical practice in the early nineteenth century
The Poor Relief Act of 1838 established a workhouse system for Ireland and the main group of new hospitals was the Workhouse Infirmaries attached to each of the workhouses in the province, and opened largely between 1841 and 1843. These were managed by the Poor Law Guardians of the Union, with the Board of Commissioners in Dublin having overall responsibility. The largest of these Infirmaries in Ulster was in Belfast, opened in 1841 with only six beds,

though these were soon increased to over one hundred. The first medical officer was Dr Thomas Andrews (*q.v.*) who was at the same time attending physician to the Belfast Fever Hospital and Professor of Chemistry at the RBAI. The Infirmary was followed in 1847 by a new Fever Hospital, under the charge of Dr Seaton Reid (*q.v.*), to take the pressure off the old Fever Hospital, which then became the Belfast General Hospital. The other new hospital of the period was the Belfast Asylum, which was opened in 1829 (Malcolm, 1851). Outside Belfast, infirmaries were also opened in Londonderry and Magherafelt during the 1840s. It must be said that the Poor Relief Act did not come into full operation until 1845, the year in which the Famine started. This coincidence may have been valuable for the relief of the starving, but it did nothing to popularise the workhouses, which were thereafter associated in Ireland with famine and death.

Table III
Distribution of physicians, surgeons and apothecaries by counties in Ulster from Croly's Directory of 1846

County	Towns (with doctors)	Doctors
Antrim	29	148*
Armagh	20	65
Cavan	17	59
Donegal	27	60
Down	40	96
Fermanagh	12	33
Londonderry	18	61
Monaghan	14	40
Tyrone	22	72
Total	199	534

*including 67 in Belfast

This was the era of directories, first street directories and later medical directories, so that we now get a much clearer picture of the number and distribution of doctors across Ulster. Belfast was particularly well served and Joseph Smyth's *Directory* of 1807 (Adams, 1991) lists eight physicians and eleven surgeons/apothecaries in the city, while his 1808 *Directory* adds another four army surgeons, presumably stationed in Belfast. *Bradshaw's Directory of Down and Armagh*, compiled in 1819, lists eleven physicians, fifteen surgeons and eight apothecaries in Belfast. *Pigot's Directory* of 1824 is probably the earliest to cover the whole Province, with no less than 363 doctors in 74 Ulster towns, 34 being in Belfast (as in Bradshaw). Croly's first *Irish Medical Directory* of 1843 and 1846 take this further and in 1846 there were 534 doctors (of all kinds) spread over the 199 towns and villages of the nine counties (Table III). At first sight this might seem a very large number of doctors but when the only transport was the horse, doctors had to be widely and thinly spread, and of course, the rural population of Ireland was much higher before the Famine.

It is not possible to say precisely when a widespread dispensary system was initiated (Fleetwood, 1951; Russell, 1983). It seems that some landlords formed friendly societies for the relief of their sick tenants and in 1805 they received Government grants for this. The arrangements were haphazard in the early years of the century, but by 1833 there were 452 scattered throughout Ireland. The dispensaries were financed from local subscriptions, fines imposed by the local Petty Sessions, and Grand Jury Presentments and extracts from the Ballygawley minute books give a heart-warming picture of how much the work of Dr Samuel Philips (*q.v.*) during the famine era was appreciated (Gillespie, 1966).

The Great Famine
This casts such a shadow over medicine in the nineteenth century that its effects and management are worth considering for Ireland generally (MacArthur, 1951; Woodham-Smith, 1962; Froggatt, 1995) and later for the Ulster counties (Kinealy and Parkhill, 1997). The famine was the result of a potato blight which affected the crop, mildly in 1845, and severely in 1846, 1847 and 1848. There had been recurring famines in Ireland over the centuries, but they had generally lasted for only one season, whereas the repeated years of crop failure and the epidemic of fever which accompanied them, made the Great Famine a unique disaster. Even in 1843, J.G. Kohl, a German traveller, described the Irish peasants as more poorly housed than he had seen anywhere in Europe. A large number had only seasonal employment and they were almost totally dependent on the potato which they grew in a patch of land beside their miserable cabins. Any animals reared and other crops grown by small farmers and labourers, were mainly to pay the rent rather than to feed the family. As a result, when the potato crop failed, whole families felt that there was nothing to do but leave home and make for the nearest town. Out of an Irish population of 8.2 million in 1841, at least one million had died of starvation and fever by the 1851 census and a further one million had emigrated, an overall population decline of approximately 20 per cent (Froggatt, 1995; Killen, 1995).

Every famine in these islands was accompanied by fever which consisted of the two separate conditions, typhus and relapsing fever, both louse-borne, and often simultaneous, though their identity and mode of transmission were not understood until many years later. Relapsing fever, which was often associated with jaundice, was less often fatal than typhus (MacArthur, 1948). The whole situation of large groups of people crowded into small houses, then taking shelter huddled together on the road, and eventually in overcrowded workhouses, inevitably led to almost universal infection among the poor. Typhus was endemic in Ireland throughout most of the nineteenth century and was the more deadly of the two fevers. Surprisingly, it was more prevalent and deadly in the prosperous households, perhaps because the poor had an acquired immunity to the disease. Cholera, typhoid fever, bacillary dysentery and smallpox were also frequent before and after the acute famine period and an infectious ophthalmia which left many sufferers blind, was noted frequently in the workhouses.

Government's response to the Famine was notoriously inadequate. There were the dispensaries and dispensary doctors, as listed by Croly (1846), but the doctors were poorly paid and particularly at risk from the fever, often having several attacks of it. The Fever Act of March 1846 established a Central Board of Health, with Sir Robert Kane, Sir Philip Crampton and Dr Dominic John Corrigan as medical members, but only the last of these was a serious worker in the field and the Board became thoroughly unpopular with the profession. They did set up 'temporary fever hospitals', which could consist of anything from the old Royal Hospital, Kilmainham, to a few army tents. However, the Board decreed that doctors attending patients in these fever hospitals and dispensaries should only be paid 5 shillings a day. Dr John Oliver Curran (*q.v.*), Professor of the Practice of Medicine at the Apothecaries' Hall, ostentatiously refused the 5 shillings fee and worked without reward at the Dublin Dispensary, only to die of fever in September 1846.

The Famine in Ulster
Until recently it was widely assumed that the Famine had little impact on the province of Ulster, but detailed analysis shows that this was certainly not true (Killen, 1995; Kinealy and Parkhill, 1997). Using the earlier criteria of population decline between the 1841 and 1851 censuses, the figures show Munster as the worst affected (22.5 per cent), followed by Connaught (19.9 per cent), Ulster (15.7 per cent) and Leinster (15.3 per cent). The decline in the rural population was in fact, larger than these figures suggest, because there was a rise in that of Dublin and the larger towns, notably Belfast with a 33 per cent rise, but in general the figures for each county do give an indication of the severity of the famine as a cause of death and emigration. The worst declines were seen in Monaghan (29 per cent), Cavan (28 per cent), Fermanagh (25 per cent), Tyrone (18 per cent) and Armagh (16 per cent). Counties with smaller population declines were Londonderry (14 per cent), Donegal (13 per cent), Down (11 per cent) and Antrim (9 per cent).

The medical situation in Belfast was graphically described by Malcolm (1851), after the disastrous return to Belfast of the *Swatara* in May 1847 with a large number of passengers stricken with fever.

The Union Infirmary was enlarged by nearly 90 beds, and a shed was erected on the grounds of the General Hospital. The old Cholera buildings, and, in short, every available spot, were filled with patients. Still it was not enough. The plague was striking down its victims at the rate of 50 per day, and, with the addition of the College Hospital, which was now opened, the total number of cases on the 29th of May was 1,149 – a number very nearly twice the annual average of previous ordinary years.

The epidemic began to subside in mid-July, so that on the 13th of November the General Hospital ceased to receive fever patients and the Barrack Street Hospital was closed in December, the Workhouse and its fever hospital being then able to cope with the numbers. Malcolm gives a figure for admissions to the three hospitals for the year as 13,676, with an unknown number of private cases treated at home. It may be said again that the Belfast Union Infirmary (now Belfast City Hospital), was part of the Belfast Workhouse, being opened in 1841 and supplemented in 1847 by a Union Fever Hospital, a separate building on the same site (now Gardner Robb House).

The medical aspects of the Famine in individual counties are worth looking at. County Monaghan had the largest population decline but it had built up the highest population density with many underemployed labourers and a miserable standard of living; in addition, at least some of the decline was due to assisted emigration in the early 1840s (Duffy, 1997). The neighbouring county of Cavan had similar problems (Gallogly, 1997), and it was also notable for the burning of the temporary fever hospital at Belturbet in April 1847. This had just been opened by Dr William Maxwell Wade (*q.v.*), but people in the neighbourhood had a blind fear that infection from it would be spread round the town. Presumably common sense eventually prevailed as the hospital was reopened in June and had 77 patients by July. Fermanagh was another county badly affected (Cunningham, 1997), but Tyrone was much less so (Grant, 1997). Nevertheless, during Christmas week 1846, 23 inmates of Omagh workhouse, including 16 children, died, and by February 1847 the Board ordered that the workhouse should take no new admissions for the next few weeks.

Workhouses all over Ulster were overcrowded but the case of Lurgan, with a large workhouse covering the northern half of county Armagh, stands out. MacAtasney (1997) has analysed the Board of Guardians' minute books and other related papers in the Public Record Office of Northern Ireland (BG 22/A/4 and 22/A/5) and they reveal an appalling mixture of indifference and incompetence in 1846 and 1847, for which none of the staff escape blame. The workhouse opened in 1841 and for the first few years was less than a quarter full. Then came the Famine and very soon demand outstripped the number of beds and problems arose, requiring an inspection from Dublin. The dismissal of the medical officer, Dr Robert Bell (*q.v.*), was demanded in the summer of 1846, but the Guardians supported him and he stayed on. However in the first week of January 1847 the number of deaths was 18, in the second 36 and in the third it was 55, the sequence leading to a letter to Robert Bell from the Commissioners in Dublin asking for a detailed report. Dr Bell replied blaming the high mortality on the extreme sickness of those entering the workhouse. He suggested also that many famine victims who were dying came to the workhouse for the sake of a free coffin! He also blamed the deaths on the damp bedding and poor drying facilities and suggested that now that these were being improved, figures for deaths would decline – a hope contradicted by the ever rising death rate into February 1847. The figure of 95 in the week ending 6 February was the highest in Ulster, the next highest being Enniskillen with 30 deaths. Later in the year Robert Bell was shamed into resigning, to be replaced by Dr William Ross MacLaughlin (*q.v.*), and the general chaos in the workhouse is indicated by the fact that it had seven masters between May 1845 and May 1847, perhaps explaining the dirt of the wards, the reuse of unwashed clothes after patients had died, the delay in removing dead bodies from the dormitories, and the appalling food.

The remaining counties of Ulster had similar problems but to a less marked degree. In Londonderry most of the workhouses exceeded their limits of inmates in 1847 and a severe epidemic of fever developed in the winter of 1847–8 (Parkhill, 1997). In Ballyshannon workhouse, county Donegal, there was a similar situation (Begley and Lally, 1997) and a temporary fever hospital was set up in July 1847. At this stage Dr Barclay Sheil (*q.v.*) who was a relative of Dr Simon Sheil (*q.v.*), medical officer to the workhouse, complained that the Ballyshannon Guardians refused to pay the expense. Altogether, one has the impression that the figures for population decline in Donegal underestimate the suffering from famine and disease in this county. Down may not have been as severely affected as central and west Ulster but the poverty around Newtownards was considerable, and not helped by the statements and actions of the Third Marquess of Londonderry, who was largely an absentee landlord (McCavery, 1997). Certainly between 1841 and 1851 the population of Newtownards fell by 14 per cent and in 12 of its townlands fell by over 20 per cent. The actual potato blight was probably the same in county Antrim as elsewhere and in spite of better management, resources were still strained (Dallat, 1997). There were seven workhouses in the county, Antrim, Ballycastle, Ballymena, Ballymoney, Belfast, Larne and Lisburn and of these only Ballycastle exceeded its limit. Ballycastle also needed a temporary fever hospital which was situated in an old salt store, possibly because salt was regarded as a possible cure for the fever. Altogether, care of the starving and those who developed fever, cholera and dysentery would have stretched any country at that time in the context of current 'health care policies'.

Medicine in Ulster after 1850

Hospital medicine in this era expanded considerably and staffing grew proportionately. Belfast, in 1850, had its General Hospital, the Union Infirmary and Fever Hospital, the Maternity Hospital and the Asylum. These were followed in 1860 by Malone Place, in 1873 by the Samaritan and two Childrens' Hospitals, the Belfast Hospital for Sick Children in King Street (Calwell, 1973), and the Ulster Hospital for Children (later 'and Women') in Chichester Street (Marshall and Kelly, 1973). The Belfast Hospital for Sick Children moved in 1879 into a new building in Queen Street and in 1932 to the Falls Road, beside the Royal Victoria Hospital, itself becoming 'Royal' in 1948. The Ulster Hospital moved in 1891 to Templemore Avenue, where it was bombed in 1941, to be rebuilt on a new site and reopened in 1962. The Ophthalmic Hospital in Great Victoria Street was opened in 1867 and the Benn Hospital for eye, ear, nose and throat diseases, in 1871 (Allison, 1969). The Throne Hospital on the Antrim Road was founded in 1872 (opened in 1874) specifically for convalescents, to take the pressure off the acute beds in the Belfast General Hospital and it was expanded in 1885 to take in patients with tuberculosis (Clarke, 1997). However this aspect was superseded in 1897 by the Forster Green Hospital in the old Fortbreda House at Knockbreda (Wallace, 2009). The Mater Infirmorum Hospital, was opened in 1883 by the Sisters of Mercy on the Crumlin Road as another general hospital (Casement, 1969). Outside Belfast there was a similar pattern with voluntary hospitals and workhouse infirmaries, with asylums rather later, the Downshire Hospital, Downpatrick, opening in 1868 and Holywell Hospital, Antrim, in 1898.

The dispensary system, which had been operating irregularly from the early nineteenth century, was put on a firm footing by the Medical Charities Act of 1851 and official dispensary districts were formed. There was one doctor for each dispensary district (more in Belfast), and dispensary and doctor were often the same as before 1851. However, the dispensary districts were managed by committees composed of Guardians and ratepayers and eventually under the same management as the infirmaries and fever hospitals (Fleetwood, 1951; Russell, 1983).The doctor received a small salary and treated free any patient with a ticket indicating his poverty (a system much abused), as well as conducting smallpox vaccination, certifying lunatics and providing medical care in prisons. The remainder of the doctor's income came from the fees of those who could afford to pay. In 1878 the Public Health Act added the status of district Medical Officer of Health to the role of Dispensary Medical Officer, with an additional increase in salary, and in 1898 the Dispensary Committees were abolished and their duties transferred to the Boards of Guardians. A rather grim picture of the dispensary doctor's life is given by Dr William Lyle of Newtownstewart ($q.v.$) (Lyle, 1937) and essentially this system lasted until the National Health Service was formed in 1948.

Table IV
Ulster Women in the Medical Profession

Adams, Charlotte (c 1870–1901); born Tullylish; studied medicine in London; LRCP LRCS Edin 1895.

Allman, Dora Elizabeth (1871/2–1953); born Cork; studied medicine at QCC; MB (RUI) 1898; medical officer to Armagh District Asylum.

Beatty, Elizabeth (1857–1924); born Ballymena; studied medicine at QCB; LRCP LRCS Edin 1899.

Bell, Elizabeth Gould (1862–1934); born Newry; studied medicine at QCB; MB (RUI) 1893.

Bell, Margaret Smith (1864–1906); born Newry; studied medicine at QCB; LRCPI LRCSI 1894.

Chestnutt, Emily Frances (1866–1937); born Kerry; studied medicine at QCB; LRCP LRCS Edin 1896.

Collier, Georgina (1875–1942); born Lisburn; studied medicine at QCB; LRCP LRCS Edin 1897.

Crawford, Anne Helen (b 1873), born Coleraine; studied medicine at QCB; MB (RUI) 1899.

Crooks, Emily Martha (1875–c 1954); born Larne; studied medicine at QCB, MB (RUI) 1899.

Dickson, Emily Winifred (1866–1944); born Dungannon; studied medicine at RCSI; LKQCPI LRCSI 1891.

Horner, Mary Campbell (c 1870–1941); born Limavady; studied medicine in Glasgow; LRCP & S Edin 1894.

Huston, Alexandrina Crawford (b 1874); born Randalstown; studied medicine at QCB; MB (RUI) 1899.

McCall, Eva (1869–1951); born Belfast; studied medicine in Glasgow, MB (Glas) 1898; MD 1901.

McIlroy (Dame) Anne Louise (1878–1968), born Ballycastle, studied medicine in Glasgow, MB (Glas) 1898; first Professor of Obs & Gyn at the Royal Free Hospital.

McMordie, Sarah Brown (d c 1910); studied medicine in Edinburgh; LRCP LRCS Edin 1895.

Macrory, Elizabeth (1869–1958); born Belfast, studied medicine at Edinburgh & QUB, MB (Edin) 1900.

Montgomery, Eleanor Agnes (1871–1954); born Bangor; studied medicine in Edinburgh; LRCP & S Edin 1895.

Neil, Harriette Rosetta (1855–1942); born Belfast; studied medicine at QCB; MB (RUI) 1894.

Powell, Lilian Ann (1867–1939); born Kingstown, county Dublin studied medicine at QCB, MB (RUI) 1895.

Stewart, Martha Maud (b 1865); born Newry; studied medicine at QCB, LRCP LRCS Edin 1895.

Tate, Isobel Addy (1875–1917); born Portadown; studied medicine at QCB; MB (RUI) 1899.

White, Sara Elizabeth (1855/6–1938); born Tanderagee; studied medicine in London 1891; MB (Lond) 1896.

Ulster Women in the Medical Profession (Table IV)

The history of the acceptance of women into the medical profession in Ireland has been described by Mary Logan (1990). The first move in Queen's College, Belfast was made as early as 1870 when it was decided that women could attend lectures if the professor agreed. However, various obstacles were set up during the next twelve years, including a bar on obtaining scholarships, before they were permitted to attend arts lectures, and it was not until 1889 that they were allowed to attend medical lectures. The first women to do so were the two sisters Elizabeth Gould Bell and Margaret Smith Bell, and Harriette Rosetta Neil. In the same year the medical staff of the Belfast Royal Hospital agreed that there would be no restriction on women attending the wards.

There were only 22 women who qualified before 1901 and were born, studied or worked in Ulster, and of these, only 16 were born in the province, only 12 studied at Queen's College, Belfast and only six graduated from Queen's. The first two to graduate were Elizabeth Bell and Emily Dickson in 1893 and Emily Dickson was able to become the first woman FRCSI in the same year. Once qualified in university or college, women had no difficulty with medical registration as they had been eligible since the first issue of the Medical Register in 1859. Listing the positive landmarks tends to hide the great difficulties for women in obtaining recognition at all stages, with bodies like the British Medical Association, the Physiological Society and the Royal Society of Medicine, all slow to admit women members. This was more striking at a time when, in 1889, the Women's Medical College of Pennsylvania had been in existence for 37 years and there were about 37 women doctors in the USA.

Most of these women went into general practice, but some went into the mission field and some into gynaecology or mental health. Probably the most distinguished was Dame Anne Louise McIlroy, daughter of a general practitioner of Ballycastle, who became a gynaecological surgeon in Glasgow, worked with the RAMC during World War I, receiving the Croix de Guerre and later was appointed the first professor of Obstetrics and Gynaecology at the Royal Free Hospital, London. Isobel Addy Tate also worked with the RAMC during the War but tragically died of typhoid fever in Malta in 1917. Women were not then allowed in the RAMC and she is the only woman on the Queen's University war memorial in front of the University. Altogether women made up in enterprise and courage what they lacked in numbers.

Ulster doctors whose main work was outside medicine (Table V)

Many doctors obtained a medical qualification and used it as a way of entry into a related field such as natural history or indeed moved into a quite unrelated field. Many of these qualified before medical registration began (1859), but even after this date they often did not register as doctors and do not appear in the *Medical Directory* as they saw no value in recording this qualification. A large group was ordained as Church of Ireland clergy or Presbyterian ministers, the most distinguished, probably, being Bishop Reeves, the historian of the mediaeval church in Ireland.

Robert Lloyd Praeger produced a useful biographical volume called *Some Irish Naturalists* (1949) covering a wide span of time and field of interests, and many of those included have medical qualifications. He started his collection with personal friends and colleagues but many such as Robert Templeton pre-date his lifetime. Professor Sir John Biggart gave a lecture in the same year entitled 'Parergon' which deals with the theme of work that is done over and above the daily round. He discusses doctors in the wider world who have made contributions to literature and other fields and he certainly taught that 'The wider your education, the greater the knowledge of self, the more easily will you make contact with the sentient entity that is your patient, and the better a practitioner you will be.'

Table V
Ulster doctors whose fame or principal work was outside medicine

Abraham, James Johnston	Writer
Adair, 'Robin'	Subject of a romantic ballad
Agnew, Sir James Willson	Prime Minister of Tasmania
Allman, George Thomas	Professor of Botany at TCD
Allman, William	Rector of Mevagh and Kilmacrenan
Andrews, Thomas	Professor of Chemistry, QCB
Armstrong, Sir Alexander	Explorer and naturalist
Babington, William	Founder of the Royal Geological Society
Black, Joseph	Professor of Chemistry in Glasgow and Edinburgh
Bredon, Sir Robert Edward	Diplomat (Chinese Custom Service)
Bryson, Samuel Maziere	Notable collector of Irish manuscripts
Burke, William	Minister of First Ramelton Presbyterian Church
Colvill(e), Rev Alexander	Non-Subscribing Presbyterian minister of Dromore
Crawford, Adair	Professor of Chemistry in Woolwich
Crone, John Smith	Writer and biographer
Cunningham, Robert Oliver	Professor of Natural History and Geology, QUB
Dickie, George	Professor of Botany, Aberdeen
Dill, Edward Marcus	Minister of Coagh and Cork Presbyterian Churches
Drennan, William	United Irishman
Drummond, James Lawson	Professor of Anatomy, Physiology and Botany, RBAI

Elliott, Robert	Rector of Altadesert, Middletown and Tullyallen
Gore, William Crampton	Artist
Hancock, Thomas	Quaker, writing on the 1798 Rising
Henry, Augustine	Botanist and Professor of Forestry in Dublin
Irvine, James Fergus	Minister of Largy Presbyterian Church
Irvine, William	Brigadier in United States Army
Johnson, James	Writer and polemicist
Kirkpatrick, Thomas Claude Percy	Medical historian
Knowles, James Sheridan	Writer
Lever, Charles James	Writer
McAdam, James	Minister of Lislooney Presbyterian Church
McCready, Edward McConkey	Rector of Magheradroll Church
McCreight, Daniel Chambers	Founding member of the Royal Botanic Society of London
MacLear, Sir Thomas	Astronomer, of South Africa
Martin, Henry Newell	Professor of Biology and Physiology, Baltimore, USA
Morgan, Sir Thomas Charles	Writer and socialite
Parke, Thomas Heazle	Explorer
Reeves, Rev William	Bishop of Down and Connor, and Dromore, and historian
Simpson, Maxwell	Professor of Chemistry in Dublin
Sloane, Sir Hans	Naturalist and collector
Steele, William Edward	Botanist
Stephenson, Rev Samuel Stephenson	Non-Subscribing Presbyterian minister and physician
Telfair, Charles	Botanist and 'sugar baron'
Templeton, Robert	Naturalist
Tennent, Robert	Philanthropist
Walker, David	Medical officer to expeditions and naturalist
Warden, David Baillie	United Irishman and traveller
White, John	Botanist

Surgeons in the Naval Medical Service (Appendix I)
The armed forces in the period up to the end of the Napoleonic Wars contained naval, army and Indian medical services. The choice of service for the young doctor probably depended largely on family connections, influencing the decision as to whether to set up practise near home or to join the service where friends or relatives could help advancement. The training and career in both army and naval medical services are discussed in detail by Brockliss, Cardwell and Moss (2005) and they make it clear that the army was the preferred branch, at least until 1805, because of relatively better pay, status among their colleagues

and opportunities for social intercourse. They do suggest, however, that the poor status of the naval surgeon and consequent difficulties in recruitment to the service during the Napoleonic Wars, may have been exaggerated to help their case for equality with military surgeons.

The great majority of men entering the naval medical service had no medical qualification but attended hospitals and apprenticeships in London, Edinburgh or Dublin. The trainee then had to undergo an oral examination from the Royal College of Surgeons in these cities and, if successful, was accepted as an assistant surgeon into the Naval Medical Service. Later he had to undergo a second oral examination for promotion to full surgeon. The duties of a naval surgeon were largely treating minor ailments and injuries, but he had a small sick berth which could be increased in size if there was an epidemic of fever or during a naval engagement. The normal ship's complement was a surgeon and his assistant or mate, though we know that on HMS *Victory* at the Battle of Trafalgar there was William Beatty, with two surgeons under him and a third added on the evening of the battle. His work was largely that of a physician but during a naval engagement he might have to perform more surgery than he would do during the whole remainder of his life. He would be posted first to a small ship and gradually over the years work his way up to a ship of the line, with at some stage the higher rank of fleet surgeon. From there, he would either be placed on permanent half pay or, for a very few, be given a hospital post on shore as physician or inspector of the hospitals and fleet.

Ulster doctors who served in the Naval Medical Service before 1900 are listed in Appendix I. All have probably not been identified because of the lack of a published register, but out of the total of 368 about 134 served before and during the Napoleonic Wars, a much higher figure than that for the Army Medical Service in this period. The most distinguished of these were Leonard Gillespie and Sir William Beatty (Brockliss, Cardwell and Moss, 2005; Clarke, 2006), but others included James Johnston, David McBride, Richard McClelland, Sir George Magrath, Andrew Marshall, David Moore and Sir James Prior. While some surgeons continued to serve in the navy for their full career, many retired to country towns around Ulster and Pigot (1824) lists 16 retired naval surgeons.

After 1815 there was inevitably a decline in naval recruitment and it would appear that the army and Indian army became relatively more attractive. However, the Naval Medical Service still included such figures as the explorer and director general Sir Alexander Armstrong, who wrote the *Personal Narrative of the Discovery of the North-West Passage* (1857). There was also Dr Samuel Browne who, after being discharged from the navy for drunkenness, went on to do notable work for ophthalmology in Belfast and subsequently became Mayor of Belfast, chief sanitary officer for the town, and first superintendent medical officer of health.

Surgeons in the Army Medical Service (Appendix II) **and the Indian Medical Service** (Appendix III)

The army surgeons during the eighteenth century, were better paid, had smarter uniforms and mixed more in the social life of garrison towns than their naval counterparts, making it apparently the more attractive service to join. However, in spite of this Brockliss and his colleagues do not believe that they differed in terms of their social or educational background, both being largely drawn from the merchant, professional and small landowning classes. The Ulster surgeons in the Army Medical Service, are listed in Appendix II and number 361, only 86 of whom were in the pre-1815 era, showing that the navy had the greater attraction at this time. The first on the main list is Robert or Robin Adair (c 1711–70) who is really only known because of the romantic ballad associated with him. The most notable was probably Sir Robert Alexander Chermside, who joined in time to serve in the Peninsular War and the battle of Waterloo, earning a host of distinctions before he died in his bed at the age of 73. (This name, unique to the Portaferry area, appears to have died out in Ulster, but had no less than six doctors in the nineteenth century.)

Two of the Ulster surgeons who took part in the wars of the nineteenth century were not actually in the army at all. Dr Alexander Leslie Gracey, having just graduated from Edinburgh, was a civil surgeon attached to the British and Turkish armies in the Crimean War. Dr (later Sir) William MacCormick played a similar role in the Franco-Prussian War, attached to the Red Cross. However, there were prominent surgeons in the Army Medical Service who were recognised before the end of their career – Sir Walter George Augustus Bedford, Sir Robert Edward Bredon (diplomat with the Chinese Custom Service), Sir Robert Porter, and our only medical VC of the century, Valentine Munbee McMaster, who won his VC during the Indian Mutiny. The Army Medical Service was re-formed into the Royal Army Medical Corps in 1898, partly in response to considerable dissatisfaction with the status of the army surgeons, and partly to obtain adequate study leave and generally update the surgical care, which had been so much criticized during the Crimean War. In the protracted negotiations the British Medical Association played a considerable part.

The Indian Medical Service (Crawford, 1930) dates from the early seventeenth century and was divided into three regional 'establishments' – Bombay, Madras and Bengal, in order of formation. After 1896 all entries were into the General establishment. It would appear that the 120 Ulster doctors who served in it were similarly represented in all three of the regional establishments. Only eight of these enrolled before 1815, but in the nineteenth century notable figures included Sir Richard Havelock Henry Charles who reached high rank in the Indian administration. Sir Robert McCarrison and Sir John Wallace Dick Megaw made outstanding contributions in the field of tropical medicine. We must also remember people like James Graham who had served for 37 years in the IMS and was wantonly shot when out driving with his daughter in Sialkot during the Indian Mutiny.

Doctors who died from infections probably contracted in the course of their work (Appendix IV)

The cause of death, even when known accurately, has not routinely been included in these medical biographies but deaths caused by accident, tuberculosis or infectious fevers have been noted throughout. Those due to fevers and probably contracted in the course of a doctor's work, are of particular interest. Cholera was recorded more often in the earlier part of the nineteenth century, particularly during the 1832 epidemic, and typhoid in the latter part. Typhus, often described simply as fever, was often acquired from patients, and was responsible for 30 deaths in doctors between 1836 and 1843. It became prominent again during the Great Famine, but the total death rate among Ulster doctors in the three famine years, is hard to determine with accuracy. Altogether about 350 doctors and 'pupils' in Ireland died during the three years 1845–7, nearly half of them from fever (Cusack and Stokes, 1847 and 1848), and there were probably about 80 from Ulster. This figure fits in with the number of doctors' names which disappear between Croly's lists of the 1843–6 period and the advent of the Irish Medical Directories in 1852, though this is a fairly crude indicator. We have some actual names, such as Dr Alfred Anderson (*q.v.*) who died of typhus fever at the Belfast General Hospital on 3 October 1847 aged 24, and the 22 who can be identified are listed in Appendix IV. A particularly high mortality from typhus was noted in doctors who contracted the fever, perhaps because they had less acquired immunity than their patients. As Sir Peter Froggatt had stated (Froggatt, 1995 and 1999), 'the medical profession emerged from the Famine with credit' (as well as the clergy of all denominations, it must be said). Wilde (1849) brilliantly documented the common thread of danger, tragedy, suffering, stoicism, courage, and compassion. The great majority of these doctors left behind widows and children who were totally without financial provision. Cusack and Stokes (1847) also make the interesting point that mortality among doctors during the Famine was higher than among Wellington's army officers during the Peninsular War, taking injuries and disease together.

Tuberculosis (phthisis) was also a common killer of young adults, including doctors, until the advent of antibiotics, but it is difficult to relate the onset to the doctor's work.

ACKNOWLEDGEMENTS

This *Directory of Ulster Doctors* is the result of sixteen years of work and I am grateful to the many people who have given me access to material along the way. In terms of numbers of doctors, the greatest help has been from Queen's University, Belfast, which has allowed me to examine the manuscript Admission Registers of the old Queen's College. The earlier admission records of Trinity College, Dublin are in print but the staff of the manuscript department of the Library of Trinity College also made their records available. I owe a debt of gratitude to Robert Mills, Librarian of the Royal College of Physicians of Ireland, for giving me access to their unique collection of *Medical Directories* and *Registers* and to the Kirkpatrick Archive. Mary O'Doherty of the Royal College of Surgeons in Ireland has also helped with access to some of their material. More recently I have been in the Linen Hall Library regularly, using both the heavy files and the microfilms of the *Belfast News Letter* and I am most grateful to the staff for their ready help.

The staff of the Public Record Office of Northern Ireland and the National Archives of Dublin and Edinburgh, have been helpful with their various types of records, particularly regarding wills and church registers. I have also used the General Register Offices in London (now online), Edinburgh, Dublin and Belfast, for records of birth, marriage and death and have found all four valuable and accessible sources of primary information. (London being the most expensive and Edinburgh the cheapest, to access!)

The large number of private individuals who have helped me with information is listed in the bibliography, and I am particularly grateful to Dr Brian Trainor, Simon Elliott and Paul Hitchings for the steady flow of help over many years.

Images of as many as possible of the doctors in the text have been included and Marion Magee of the Department of Medical Illustration of the Royal Victoria Hospital, has prepared most of the material for the illustrations. Sources of these images have included the Queen's University of Belfast, the Royal Victoria Hospital, the National Museums of Northern Ireland, the Ulster Medical Society, the Royal Belfast Academical Institution, the Royal College of Physicians of Ireland, the Royal College of Surgeons in Ireland, the National Library of Ireland, the Rotunda Hospital, Dublin, the National Maritime Museum, Greenwich, the Natural History Museum, South Kensington, and the Royal Free Hospital, London (as indicated in the List of Illustrations). Many published sources have been used but the greatest number of photographic images have been taken from Young and Pike's *Belfast and the Province of Ulster in the 20th Century* (1909).

Publication has been in the hands of the Ulster Historical Foundation, with which I have had a long and happy association, and I am particularly grateful to Fintan Mullan for his care and attention to the final production, and Jill Morrison of Cheah Design for her thoroughness and professionalism during the design stage.

Sir Peter Froggatt has seen the work in its final stages and has most generously provided a Foreword.

The administrative costs of obtaining and collating the material for publication have been borne by me, but I am grateful to the Ulster Medical Society and to Drs Steven and Anne Haigh, Drs Barry and Susan Kelly, Drs John S. and John I. Logan, and Christopher Shepard of the Ireland, Empire and Education Project at Trinity College, Dublin (through the Irish Research Council for Humanities and Social Sciences) for generous donations towards the cost of publication.

R.S.J. Clarke
August 2013

LIST OF ABBREVIATIONS

Aber	Aberdeen
Adm Reg	Admission Register
AMS	Army Medical Service
(b)	(births)
BA	Bachelor of Arts
BAO	Bachelor of the Art of Obstetrics
BCh	Bachelor of Surgery
Belf	Belfast
Belf Fev Hosp, Ann Rep	*Belfast Fever Hospital, Annual Reports*
Belf Lit Soc	*Belfast Literary Society, 1801–1901, Historical Sketch*
Belf PRO	Public Record Office of Northern Ireland
BMA	British Medical Association
BNL	*Belfast News Letter*
c	*circa* (about)
Camb	Cambridge
CM	Master of Surgery
(d)	(deaths)
DAB	*Dictionary of American Biography*
DIB	*Dictionary of Irish Biography*
DPH	Diploma of Public Health
Dub	Dublin
Edin	Edinburgh
Edin Univ	*List of Graduates in Medicine in the University of Edinburgh*
fl c	*floruit circa* (= lived about)
FLS	Fellow of the Linnean Society
FRCSE	Fellow of the Royal College of Surgeons of England
FRCS Edin	Fellow of the Royal College of Surgeons of Edinburgh
FRCSI	Fellow of the Royal College of Surgeons of Ireland
FRS	Fellow of the Royal Society
FZS	Fellow of the Zoological Society
Glas	Glasgow
GRO	General Register Office
hon causa	*honoris causa* (honorary)
HMS	His (Her) Majesty's Ship
IMS	Indian Medical Service
LAH Dub	Licentiate of the Apothecaries' Hall, Dublin
LFPS Glas	Licentiate of the Faculty of Physicians and Surgeons of Glasgow
LGI	*Landed Gentry of Ireland*
LKQCPI	Licentiate of the Kings and Queens College of Physicians of Ireland
LM	Licentiate of Midwifery
Lond	London

LRCP Lond	Licentiate of the Royal College of Physicians of London
LRCSE	Licentiate of the Royal College of Surgeons of England
LSA Lond	Licentiate of the Society of Apothecaries, London
(m)	marriages
MA	Master of Arts
MB	Bachelor of Medicine
MD	Doctor of Medicine
Med Dir	*Medical Directory*
Med Reg	*Medical Register*
MP	Member of Parliament
MRCS	Member of the Royal College of Surgeons
MRIA	Member of the Royal Irish Academy
Nat Arch	National Archives
NLI	National Library of Ireland
Oxford DNB	*Oxford Dictionary of National Biography*
pers com	personal communication
PPR	Principal Probate Registry
PRO	Public Record Office
QCB	Queen's College, Belfast
QUB	Queen's University of Belfast
QUI	Queen's University in Ireland
(*q.v.*)	(*quod vide*) (which see or refer to)
RBAI	Royal Belfast Academical Institution
RCPI	Royal College of Physicians of Ireland
RCSI	Royal College of Surgeons in Ireland
Rot Hosp Dub	Rotunda Hospital, Dublin
RUI	Royal University of Ireland
RVH	Royal Victoria Hospital, Belfast
sic	*sic* (= literally correct)
SS	Steamship
TCD	Trinity College, Dublin
TCD Cat	*Trinity College, Dublin, Catalogue of Graduates*
TCD Reg	*Trinity College, Dublin, Register of Graduates*
UHF	Ulster Historical Foundation
UMJ	*Ulster Medical Journal*
UMS	Ulster Medical Society
will cal	Calendar of Wills

A

ABERNETHY, WILLIAM RUSSELL (1857/8–1920), Ballygawley, county Tyrone;
born 1857/8; studied medicine at the Carmichael School, Dublin; LM Rot Hosp Dub; LRCP LRCS Edin 1893; LFPS Glas 1893; medical officer to Kilmainham Smallpox Hospital, Dublin; medical officer to Ballygawley Dispensary District and registrar of births and deaths; JP; married Prudence Phillips; father of Dr William Russell Abernethy, junior, of Ballygawley, MB (QUB) 1919; died 29 July 1920 at Ballygawley. [Belf GRO (b, son) and (d); *Med Dir*].

ABERNETHY, — (*fl c* 1845), Dromara, county Down;
general practitioner and medical officer to constabulary, in Dromara c 1845. [Croly (1843–6)].

ABRAHAM, JAMES JOHNSTON (1876–1963), London;
born 16 August 1876 in Coleraine, county Londonderry, eldest son of William Abraham JP, tea merchant, of county Fermanagh and Kingsgate Street, Coleraine, and Elizabeth Ann Morrison of Toberdoney, county Antrim; educated at Coleraine Academical Institution; studied arts and medicine at Trinity College, Dublin, and the London Hospital; BA (TCD) 1898; MB BCh BAO 1900; LM Rot Hosp Dub 1900; FRCSE 1909; MD and MA 1912; Litt D (TCD) (*honoris causa*) 1946; house surgeon at the West London Hospital 1901–06; ship's surgeon on SS *Clytemnestra* 1906–07; general practitioner in county Clare; resident medical officer to the London Lock Hospital 1907; assistant surgeon to the Princess Beatrice Hospital; of 6 Adelphi Terrace, London; medical officer with the Serbian, Egyptian and Portuguese armies 1914–18, with the rank of lieutenant-colonel; Knight of St Sava of Serbia 1915; DSO 1918; CBE 1919; surgeon to Kensington Hospital and London Lock Hospital; prolific writer on medical history and autobiography, including *A Surgeon's Log* (1911), *The Night Nurse* (1913) and *A Surgeon's Journey* (1957), as well as other books under the *nom de plume* of James Harpole; of 30 Camden Hill Court, London W8; president of the Irish Medical Graduates' Association 1939–50; chairman of Heinemann's Medical Publications and of the library committee of the Athenaeum; Vicary Lecturer of the Royal College of Surgeons of England 1943; married 21 April 1920 in St Martin's in the Fields Church, London, Lillian Angela Francis (who died 4 January 1969), eldest daughter of Dr Alexander Francis of 9 Henrietta Street, Cavendish Square, London; died 9 August 1963 at Camden Hill Court; probate London 6 November 1963. [Abraham (1957); *BMJ* obituary (1963); *DIB* (2009); Kirkpatrick Archive; *Lancet* obituary (1963); Lond GRO (m); Lond PPR, will cal; Martin (2003) and (2010); *Med Dir*; Newmann (1993); Robinson and Le Fanu (1970)].

ABRAHAM, ROBERT (1859–98), Aughnacloy, county Tyrone;
born 6 June 1859 at Aughnacloy, son of Joseph Abraham, merchant, of Aughnacloy; studied medicine at Queen's College, Belfast, from 1878; LKQCPI and LM 1884; MD MCh (RUI) 1885; LRCSI 1885; medical officer to Ballymagran Dispensary

District and constabulary; unmarried; died 14 January 1898 at 30 North Parade, Belfast; probate Armagh 1 March 1898. [Belf PRO, will cal; Dub GRO (d); *Med Dir*; QCB, adm reg].

ACHESON, GEORGE HENRY (d c 1895), Gilford, county Down and Greymouth, New Zealand;
son of Robert Acheson, farmer, of Drumiller, county Down; studied medicine in Glasgow; LM Anderson's College 1850; LFPS Glas 1852; FFPS 1854; LM Coombe Hosp Dub 1856; general practitioner in Gilford; emigrated to Hokitika, New Zealand c 1873; general practitioner, of Greymouth, New Zealand from c 1878; married 24 October 1851 in Fourtowns Presbyterian Church, county Down, Jane Heron of Tullymore, county Down, daughter of the Rev Thomas Heron, minister of Ballygoney Presbyterian Church, county Londonderry; died c 1895. [*Med Dir*; UHF database (m)].

ACHESON, HAMILTON (*fl c* 1845), Enniskillen, county Fermanagh;
LAH Dub 1827; MRCSE 1829; general practitioner, of Enniskillen c 1845. [Apothecaries (1829); Croly (1843–6)].

ACHESON, HOWARD WILLIAM (1859/60–1929), Castlereagh, county Roscommon, and Cavan;
born 1859/60; studied medicine at the Royal College of Surgeons in Ireland; LKQCPI and LM 1881; LRCSI 1881; surgeon to the Union Steamship Company; general practitioner in Castlereagh c 1885; surgeon to the Cavan County Infirmary and medical officer to the post office and constabulary, from c 1890, of Infirmary House, Cavan; retired to Farnham Street, Cavan, 1923; moved to 40 Ulverton Road, Dalkey c 1929; married —; died 27 November 1929 at 40 Ulverton Road; probate Dublin 13 February 1930. [Dub GRO (d); Dub Nat Arch, will cal; *Med Dir*; O'Donnell (2008)].

ACHESON, JOHN (1857–1931), Naval Medical Service and Armagh;
born 30 November 1857 at Tassagh, county Armagh, son of John Acheson, farmer, of Tassagh; educated at the Cathedral School, Armagh; studied medicine at Queen's College, Belfast, from 1875; MD Dip Mid MCh (QUI) 1879; joined the Naval Medical Service c 1880 as assistant surgeon; retired to Roughan House, Lislea, Armagh c 1900; unmarried; died 3 September 1931 at Roughan House; administration Belfast 17 November 1931. [Belf GRO (d); Belf PRO, will cal; *Med Dir*; QCB, adm reg].

ACHESON, JOHNSTON HAMILTON (1787–1864), Naval Medical Service, and Enniskillen, county Fermanagh;
born 1787; MRCSE 1815; FRCSE 1844; joined the Naval Medical Service as assistant surgeon c 1803; surgeon 1804; retired on half pay; surgeon, of Enniskillen c 1845; retired to Misken Terrace, Dalkey, c 1850; of Hill View, Dalkey, c 1860; married Frances Anne —; died 8 July 1864 at Hill View; probate Dublin 11 August 1864. [Belf PRO, will cal; Croly (1843–6); *Med Dir; NMS* (1826); Plarr (1930)].

ACHESON (ACHISON), ROBERT (1763–1824), Coleraine, county Londonderry, Glenarm, county Antrim, and Belfast;
> born 1763 in Clough, county Antrim, son of James Acheson of Clough and Elizabeth Reid; studied medicine at Edinburgh University 1788–9 but obtained no degree and practised for a while in Coleraine before studying for the presbyterian ministry; ordained 1792; 'New Light' minister of Glenarm 1792–9; arrested in June 1798 by the army on a charge of complicity in rebellion but released in an exchange of prisoners; re-joined the insurgents and was charged with 'traitorously assembling with a body of rebels', but acquitted after pressure from Colonel Leslie of Glasslough; resigned 1799 to become minister of Cliftonville Presbyterian Church, Belfast 1799–1824; married 1788 his cousin Elizabeth Smith of Coleraine (who was born 1758/9 and died 22 December 1828); died 21 February 1824; both buried in Knockbreda graveyard. [Bailie (1982); Blair (1993); Clarke, *County Down*, vol 2 (2nd ed, 1988); Dickson (1960); *DIB* (2009); Edin Univ; McConnell (1951); McKillop (1987); Wilsdon (1997)].

ADAIR, ARTHUR JOHN (1867–1900), Londonderry;
> born 17 March 1867 in Bindon Street, Ennis, son of Arthur Charles Adair, county surveyor, and Sarah Magee; educated at Dover College, Kent; studied arts and medicine at Trinity College, Dublin, from 1886; BA (TCD) 1891; MB BCh 1893; general practitioner, of 21 Crawford Square, Londonderry; surgeon with the Cunard Steamship Company on the SS *Aurania* when it was chartered for troop transport to and from South Africa; unmarried; died 19 May 1900 at sea, of dysentery; buried in Londonderry; probate Londonderry 20 June 1900. [Belf PRO, will cal, will; *BMJ* obituary (1900); Dub GRO (b) and (d); *Med Dir*; TCD adm reg; *TCD Cat*, vol II (1896)].

ADAIR, ROBERT ('ROBIN') (c 1711–90), Army Medical Service, Dublin and London;
> born c 1711, 'probably a native of Ballymena, Co Antrim' (Widdess); trained as a surgeon in Dublin and went to London 1738, walking from Holyhead to London; on finding a coach overturned gave medical and other assistance and was given 100 guineas, also gaining entry into London society; became a member of the Company of Barber Surgeons 1738; joined the Army Medical Service as staff surgeon to the Forces in Flanders 1742, also studying at Leyden University from 1742; chief surgeon to the Hospital for the Forces in Great Britain and Inspector of the Regimental Infirmaries in 1756 and 1760; practised as a surgeon in London; master of the Company of Surgeons 1767–8; surgeon to the King and to Chelsea Hospital 1773; honorary member of the Dublin Society of Surgeons 1780 and of the new Royal College of Surgeons in Ireland 1784; surgeon general of His Majesty's Forces 1786; resigned 1789; hero of the song 'Robin Adair', written by Lady Caroline Keppel, second daughter of William Anne [sic] Keppel, 2nd Earl of Albemarle, when their romance was blocked by her family sending her to Bath; the family later relented and they married 22 February 1758; she died October 1769 of tuberculosis; died 16 March 1790; engraving by Lemuel Abbott in the RCSI and two portraits by Sir Joshua Reynolds. [Burke, *Peerage* (1938); *DIB* (2009); Kirkpatrick Archive; Martin (2010); O'Brien, Crookshank and Wolstenholme (1984); Peacock (1883); Peterkin and Johnston (1968); Innes Smith (1932); Underwood (1978); Widdess (1948 and 1967)].

ADAIR, ROBERT (d 1829), Ballymena, county Antrim;
surgeon and apothecary, of Mill Street, Ballymena, c 1824; died 12 July 1829, 'much and deservedly regretted by the poor'. [*BNL* 17 July 1829 (d); Pigot (1824)].

ADAIR, THOMAS McCORMAC (1861–1947), Belfast;
born 21 May 1861, at Ballygraffan, Comber, county Down, son of William Adair, farmer; educated at University Classes, Donegall Pass, Belfast; studied medicine at the Royal College of Surgeons, Edinburgh and, from 1891, at Queen's College, Belfast; LRCP LRCS Edin 1895; LFPS Glas 1895; general practitioner, of 34 and 40 Botanic Avenue, Belfast; physician to Claremont Street Hospital, Belfast; published poetry; JP; retired to Benmount, Stewartstown Road, Dunmurry; married —; died 25 January 1947 at Benmount. [Belf GRO (d); *Med Dir*; QCB, adm reg].

ADAIR, WILLIAM (d 1832), Ballymena, county Antrim;
surgeon, of Ballymena; died 11 December 1832 'in the prime of life'. [*BNL* 21 December 1832 (d)].

ADAM, EDWARD (1838–1904), Liverpool, Lancashire;
born 5 December 1838, son of John Adam of West Cove, county Kerry; educated privately; studied medicine at Queen's College, Belfast, from 1854; MRCSE 1857; LKQCPI and LM 1863; MKQCPI 1880; MD (St Andrews) 1886 (by examination); general practitioner, of 154 Islington, Liverpool c 1875, of 95 Shaw Street c 1885 and of Prince's Avenue, Prince's Road, Liverpool c 1900; died 19 December 1904; probate London 13 February 1905. [Lond PPR, will cal; *Med Dir*; QCB, adm reg; Smart (2004)].

ADAMS, ALEXANDER MILLAR (1861–1924), Garvagh, county Londonderry;
born 2 February 1861 in Garvagh, son of John Adams, farmer, of Longland, Cottage, Garvagh; educated at Coleraine Academical Institution; studied medicine at Queen's College, Belfast, from 1876; LRCP and LM LRCS Edin 1883; general practitioner in Garvagh, county Londonderry; married 1 October 1884 in Portstewart Presbyterian Church, Jane Elizabeth Henderson, daughter of Thomas Henderson of Garvagh; father of Dr Thomas Alexander Adams of Garvagh, MB (Edin) 1910; died 4 October 1924 at Garvagh probate Londonderry 11 January 1926. [Belf GRO (d) (b, son); Belf PRO, will cal; Dub GRO (m); *Med Dir*; QCB adm reg].

ADAMS, ARCHIBALD (*fl c* 1824), Kilrea, county Londonderry;
surgeon, of Kilrea, c 1824. [Pigot (1824)].

ADAMS, ARCHIBALD (1849–1900), Naval and Indian Medical Services;
born March 1849 at Omagh, son of Andrew Archibald of Terraquin House, Omagh, and Mary Jane —; brother of Dr Charles Adams, IMS (*q.v.*); educated at Omagh Academy; studied medicine at the Royal College of Surgeons in Ireland and from 1869, at Queen's College, Belfast; MD MCh (QUI) 1872; FRCSI 1886; joined the Naval Medical Service as assistant surgeon 1872; transferred to the Indian Medical Service (Madras establishment) as surgeon 1875; surgeon major 1887; surgeon lieutenant-colonel 1895; served in the Ashanti War 1873–4; author of *The Western*

Rajaputana States (1899); married — Abbott, daughter of Lieut-Col H.B. Abbott; died 20 May 1900 at Mount Abu, India. [*BMJ* obituary (1900); Crawford (1930); Kirkpatrick Archive; *Lancet* obituary (1900); Martin (2010); *Med Dir*; QCB adm reg].

ADAMS, CHARLES (1852–1921), Indian Medical Service;
born March 1852, son of Andrew Adams of Terraquin and Mary Jane —; brother of Dr Archibald Adams (*q.v.*) and Dr Martha Adams (MB CM Glas 1901); educated in Omagh and Dublin; studied arts and medicine at Trinity College, Dublin, from 1873; BA (TCD) 1875; MB BCh 1880; Dip State Med 1885; FRCSI 1887; joined the Indian Medical Service (Madras establishment) as surgeon 1881; surgeon major 1893; surgeon lieutenant-colonel 1901; served in Burma 1895–7 (medal with clasp); lived latterly at Roseman Villa, Rosetta Park, Belfast; married —; only son Auriol Adams killed in action during World War I; died 30 March 1921 at 28 Breezehill, Donaghadee; buried in Cappagh Church of Ireland Graveyard, county Tyrone; probate Belfast 27 May 1921 and London 23 July 1921. [Belf PRO, will cal, will; Crawford (1930); Dub GRO (d); Lond PPR, will cal; McGrew (1998); *Med Dir*; TCD adm reg; *TCD Cat*, vol II (1896)].

ADAMS, CHARLOTTE (c 1870–1901), Rajasthan, India;
born c 1870; of Tullylish, Gilford, county Down; studied medicine at the London School of Medicine for Women; LRCP LRCS Edin 1895; LFPS Glas 1895; MD (Brux) 1900; lady superintendent of the Jasnant Hospital for Women, Jodhpur, Rajasthan, from c 1900; died 1901 in India. [*Med Dir*].

ADAMS, GEORGE FORBES (1831–70), Army Medical Service;
born 2 November 1831; LRCSI 1854; joined the Army Medical Service as staff assistant surgeon 1858; attached to 3rd Foot 1860; staff surgeon 1861; retired on half pay 1868 to 2 Winton Road, Leeson Park, Dublin; unmarried; died 12 June 1870 at 2 Winton Road; probate Dublin 30 July 1870. [Belf PRO, will cal; Dub GRO (d); *Med Dir*; Peterkin and Johnston (1968)].

ADAMS, GEORGE HILL (1810/11–65), Portglenone, county Antrim, Victoria, Australia, and London;
born 1810/1, youngest son of William Adams of Portglenone; studied medicine at Edinburgh University; MD (Edin) 1832 (thesis 'De tetano'); general practitioner, of Portglenone c 1837, also of Geelong, Victoria; finally of 21 Devonshire Terrace, Notting Hill, London c 1860; died 6 January 1865 at 5 Mill Terrace, Notting Hill, London, of a fever caught in Smyrna. [*Coleraine Chronicle* 21 January 1865 (d); Edin Univ; Lewis (1837); Lond GRO (d); *Londonderry Sentinel* 10 February 1865 (d); *Med Dir*].

ADAMS, HUGH THOMAS (1845–c 1879), Portglenone, county Antrim;
born 15 January 1845 at Portglenone, son of James White Adams of Portglenone; educated at RBAI; studied medicine at Queen's College, Belfast from 1863; MD MCh (QUI) 1869; LM KQCPI 1869; general practitioner in Portglenone; died c 1879. [*Med Dir*; QCB adm reg].

ADAMS, JAMES (1780–1840), Army Medical Service, Athboy, county Meath, and Dublin;
born 1780, third son of William Adams of Castletown House, county Cavan, and Olivia Wildridge; brother of Dr Neason Wildridge Adams (*q.v.*); LSA 1819; MRCSE; MD (St Andrews) 1822 (on testimonials); joined the Army Medical Service as surgeon's mate 1804; assistant surgeon 1804; staff surgeon 1810; surgeon with the 4th Ceylon Rangers 1813; retired 1816; general practitioner, of Athboy and later Dublin; married 2 September 1816 Maria Adams, daughter of Samuel Adams; died 3 September 1840 in Dublin. [Burke *LG GBI* (1894); Peterkin and Johnston (1968); Smart (2004)].

ADAMS, JAMES (d c 1861), Shercock, county Cavan;
studied medicine in Dublin; LM Dublin 1832; MRCSE 1833; LAH Dublin 1834; medical officer to Shercock Dispensary District and constabulary; died c 1861. [Croly (1843–6); *Med Dir*].

ADAMS, JAMES COWAN (1871–1951), Belfast;
born 9 August 1871, son of Samuel Adams, farmer, of Kilcreen, county Antrim and Elizabeth Jane Gaston of Duneaney; brother of Dr William Adams, LRCP LRCS Edin 1903; educated at Ballymoney Intermediate School; studied medicine at Queen's College, Belfast, from 1888; MB BCh BAO (RUI) 1894; MD (QUB) 1911; general practitioner, of 186 and 212 Ravenhill Road, Belfast; pioneer worker on causation of duodenal ulcer; married 24 August 1897 in Brookhill Avenue Presbyterian Church, Belfast, Elizabeth Martin (who was born 1871 and died 17 November 1955), daughter of Robert Martin, pawnbroker, of Coleraine; father of Dr James Cowan Adams, junior, MB (QUB) 1924, and Dr Vera Elizabeth Mary Adams, MB (QUB) 1930, who married Dr James McMaster junior, MB (QUB) 1929, son of Dr James McMaster, senior (*q.v.*); died 25 August 1951 at the Musgrave and Clark Clinic, Belfast; probate Belfast 22 October 1951. [Adams (1974); Belf GRO (d); Belf PRO, will cal; Dub GRO (b); Kennedy (1987); *Med Dir*; QCB adm reg; UHF database (m)].

ADAMS, JOHN (1846–c 1883), Belfast and Ballyclare, county Antrim;
born 22 December 1846, at Bruslee, county Antrim, son of the Rev Isaac Adams, minister of Ballylinney Presbyterian Church, county Antrim, and Elizabeth Dundee; educated by the Rev A. Russell of Franklin Place, Belfast; studied medicine at Queen's College, Belfast, from 1862; LFPS Glas 1869; general practitioner, of 25 Shankill Road c 1870–78 and of Bruslee, Ballyclare c 1878–83; died c 1883. [*Med Dir*; QCB, adm reg].

ADAMS, JOHN JAMES (1849–1941), Monaghan and Antrim;
born 14 November 1849 at Broughshane, county Antrim, son of Thomas Hugh Adams of Ashville, Antrim; brother of Dr Robert Adams of Antrim (*q.v.*); educated at RBAI; studied arts and medicine at Queen's College, Belfast, from 1868; MD (QUI) 1875; MCh Dip Mid 1877; resident medical superintendent and apothecary of County Monaghan Infirmary; general practitioner of Ashville, Antrim, from c 1880; coroner for county Antrim from 1886; JP; retired c 1933; unmarried; died 14 January 1941 at Ashville; buried in First Broughshane Presbyterian Graveyard;

probate Belfast 7 April 1941. [Belf GRO (d); Belf PRO, will cal; *BMJ* obituary (1941); Kirkpatrick Archive; *Med Dir*; QCB, adm reg].

ADAMS, JOSIAH (1824/5–1900), Dundalk, county Louth, and Cootehill and Shercock, county Cavan;
born 1824/5; studied medicine at Cecilia Street, Peter Street and Ledwich Schools, Dublin; LM Mid West Lying-in Hospital 1846; LAH Dub 1848; resident apothecary and house surgeon to the Louth Hospital, Dundalk; medical officer to Tullyvin Dispensary District, of Killaliss, Cootehill; unmarried; died 30 June 1900 at Killaliss; probate Cavan 24 August 1900. [Belf PRO, will cal; Dub GRO (d); *Med Dir*].

ADAMS, NEASON WILDRIDGE (1776–1859), Bailieborough, county Cavan;
born 1776, second son of William Adams of Castletown House, county Cavan, and Olivia Wildridge; brother of Dr James Adams (*q.v.*); LAH Dub 1799; general practitioner, of Northlands, near Bailieborough, county Cavan; married 2 April 1802 his first cousin Isabella Adams (who died 18 December 1855 on the Island of Achill), daughter of Samuel Adams; died 29 August 1859 at Kingstown, county Dublin; buried in Knockbride Parish Graveyard, county Cavan; probate Dublin 20 December 1859. [Apothecaries (1829); *BNL* 25 December 1855 (d) and 31 August 1859 (d); Belf PRO, will cal; Burke *LG GBI* (1894).

ADAMS, ROBERT (*fl c* 1796), Cookstown, county Tyrone;
LAH Dub 1796; apothecary, of Cookstown. [Apothecaries (1829)].

ADAMS, ROBERT (1837–74), Army Medical Service;
born 23 March 1837 near Portrush, county Antrim, son of James Adams of Ballywillin, Portrush; educated at Coleraine Academy; studied medicine at Queen's College, Belfast, from 1855, and Glasgow University; LRCS Edin 1859; MD (Glas) 1860; joined the Army Medical Service as assistant staff surgeon 1860; on half pay July 1861–January 1862; transferred to 81st Foot 1862; staff surgeon 1865; retired to Portrush; unmarried; died 10 April 1874 at Woolwich, Kent; administration Dublin 24 September 1874. [Addison (1898); Belf PRO, will cal; Lond GRO (d); *Med Dir*; Peterkin and Johnston (1968); QCB adm reg].

ADAMS, ROBERT (1859–89), Antrim;
born 17 March 1859, son of Thomas Hugh Adams of Ashville, Antrim; brother of Dr John James Adams (*q.v.*); educated at Monaghan Model School; studied medicine at Queen's College, Belfast, from 1878; LRCP LRCS Edin 1885; general practitioner, of Ashville, Antrim; married Mary — (who was born February 1828 and died November 1915); died 8 November 1889 at 7 Hall Gate, Doncaster, Yorkshire; buried in Broughshane First Presbyterian Graveyard; administration Belfast 20 January 1890. [Belf PRO, will cal; gravestone inscription; Lond GRO (d); *Med Dir*; QCB adm reg].

ADAMS, THOMAS (d before 1825), Randalstown, county Antrim;
surgeon, of Randalstown; married Anne — (who died 6 December 1824 in Belfast); died before 1825. [*BNL* 10 December 1824 (d)].

ADAMS, WILLIAM O'BRIEN (1803–79), Dublin and Kingstown, county Dublin; born 24 December 1804, son of Allen Adams, solicitor, and Jane King; nephew of Dr James Adams (*q.v.*) and Dr Neason Wildridge Adams (*q.v.*); educated by Mr Fea; studied arts and medicine at Trinity College, Dublin, from 1821; BA (TCD) 1825; MB 1828; FKQCPI 1832; MA 1858; assistant master of the Rotunda Hospital, Dublin 1831–4; general practitioner, of 22 Adelaide Street, Kingstown c 1870; married (1) 30 September 1835 Louisa Jane Adams (who died 15 August 1840), daughter of Captain Richard Adams; (2) 18 November 1845 in St George's Church of Ireland Church, Dublin, Elizabeth Barry (who died 30 November 1861), daughter of John Barry of Cloneen, King's County; died 1 December 1879 at 22 Adelaide Street; buried in Dean's Grange Cemetery, Dublin; probate Dublin 14 January 1880. [Belf, PRO, will cal; Burke *LG GBI* (1894); Burtchaell and Sadleir (1924); Cameron (1916); Dub GRO (m) and (d); Kirkpatrick Archive; Kirkpatrick and Jellett (1913); *Med Dir*].

ADAMSON, JAMES (1842/3–1920), Fence Houses, county Durham; born 1842/3, son of John Adamson, farmer, of Ballydugan, Moira, county Down, and Elizabeth Ann —; brother of Dr John George Adamson (*q.v.*); educated at Waringstown Select School; studied medicine at Queen's College, Belfast, from 1860 and at Glasgow University; MD (Glas)1869; LRCS and LM Edin 1869; general practitioner of Hetton House, Fence Houses, county Durham; medical officer and medical officer of health to Hetton-le-Hole District; president of Sunderland and North Durham Medical Society and Northumberland and Durham Medical Society; medical superintendent of Houghton and Hetton Joint Smallpox Hospital; superintendent of St John's Ambulance Brigade; married —; died 13 February 1920 at Hetton House; probate Durham 29 March 1920. [Addison (1898); Lond PPR, will cal, will; *Med Dir*; QCB adm reg].

ADAMSON, JOHN GEORGE (1847–90), Bellaghy, county Londonderry, and Lurgan, county Armagh;
born 23 March 1847 at Lurgan, son of John Adamson, farmer, of Ballydugan, Moira, county Down, and Elizabeth Ann —; brother of Dr James Adamson (*q.v.*); educated at RBAI from 1860; studied medicine at Queen's College, Belfast 1868–72; MA (Glas) 1867; MD MCh (QUI) 1872; medical officer to Bellaghy Dispensary District and constabulary; medical officer to Lurgan Workhouse and Fever Hospital and consulting sanitary officer in Lurgan from 1877; JP; married 16 October 1873 in the house of Matthew Bell (Presbyterian service), Frances Mary Bell, daughter of Matthew Bell, merchant, of English Street, Armagh; died 12 June 1890 at High Street, Lurgan; buried in Newmills Presbyterian Graveyard, county Down; probate Armagh 9 August 1890. [Addison (1898); Belf PRO, will cal; Dub GRO (m) and (d); Fisher and Robb (1913); gravestone inscription; Kirkpatrick Archive; *Med Dir*; QCB, adm reg].

ADAMSON, — (*fl c* 1866), Monaghan;
general practitioner and medical officer to Monaghan Infirmary c 1866; not in *Medical Register* or *Medical Directory*. [McCann (2003)].

ADDERLEY, ALEXANDER (1762/3–1835), Kilkeel and Warrenpoint, county Down;
born 1762/3; surgeon, of Kilkeel and Warrenpoint c 1800 and 1819; married Mary Moore (who was born 1751/2 and died 2 May 1833), daughter of Charles Moore of Ballynahatten, Kilkeel; died 13 July 1835 at home in Kilkeel. [*BNL* 17 May 1833 (d) and 21 July 1835 (d); Bennett (1974); Bradshaw (1919)].

ADDERLEY, ALEXANDER (1794–1829), Naval Medical Service;
born 1794; joined the Naval Medical Service as assistant surgeon; married 5 July 1819 Jane Russell of Newry, county Down; died 21 December 1829. [*BNL* 9 July 1819 (m) and 1 January 1830 (d)].

ADDERLEY, — (*fl c* 1826), Loughgall, county Armagh;
surgeon, of Loughgall; married Jane — (who died 1 March 1857 at Kingstown, county Dublin); daughter born 25 January 1826. [*BNL* 3 February 1826 (b) and 10 March 1857 (d)].

ADRAIN, JAMES (1862–1951), Larne, county Antrim, and Ardglass, county Down;
born 1 January 1862 at Raloo, county Antrim, son of James Adrain, land agent, of Magheramorne; studied medicine at Queen's College, Belfast, from 1885; MB BCh BAO (RUI) 1889; general practitioner of Main Street, Larne; medical officer to Ardglass Dispensary District from 1926; retired c 1940; married 18 January 1898 in First Belfast Presbyterian Church, Mary Whyte Porter, daughter of the Rev John Scott Porter, minister of First Belfast (Non-Subscribing) Presbyterian Church, and Margaret Marshall (eldest daughter of Dr Andrew Marshall (*q.v.*)); died 31 December 1951; probate Belfast 24 January 1952. [Belf GRO (d); Belf PRO, will cal; Dub GRO (m); Kirkpatrick Archive; *Med Dir*; QCB adm reg].

AFFLECK, JOHN (*fl c* 1801), Stewartstown, county Tyrone;
LAH Dub 1801; apothecary, of Stewartstown. [Apothecaries (1829)].

AGNEW, JAMES (1754–1843), Ballyclare, county Antrim;
born 1754; CM [?]; surgeon, of Ballyclare; died 11 December 1843. [*BNL* 15 December 1843 (d); Croly (1843–6)].

AGNEW, JAMES WILLIAM (1787/8–1823), Ballyclare, county Antrim;
born 1787/8; surgeon, of Ballyclare c 1814; married 11 November 1814 in Larne, Ellen Stewart of the Curran, Larne; father of Sir James Willson Agnew (*q.v.*); died 20 August 1823 in Ballyclare 'after a few days' illness'; 'a man of very extensive knowledge, unbending integrity and unbounded philanthropy'. [*BNL* 15 November 1814 (m) and 26 August 1823 (d)].

AGNEW, SIR JAMES WILLSON (1815–1901), Sydney, New South Wales and Hobart, Tasmania;
born 2 October 1815 in Ballyclare, county Antrim, son of Dr James William Agnew (*q.v.*) of Ballyclare and Ellen Stewart of Larne; educated at RBAI from 1829; studied medicine at University College, London, and at Paris and Glasgow; MRCSE 1838;

MD (Glas) 1839; emigrated to Sydney, Australia on the *Wilmot* 1839, arriving January 1840; general practitioner in Sydney 1840; assistant surgeon on the agricultural establishment in Hobart 1841–5; assistant and later colonial surgeon to the General Hospital in Hobart 1845–77; one of the founders of the Tasmanian Royal Society; JP 1862; member of the Legislature Council of Tasmania with various offices 1877–80 and 1884–7; prime minister of Tasmania 1886–7; KCMG 1894; author of *The last of the Tasmanians* (1888); married (1) 27 April 1846 Louisa Mary Fraser (who died 10 March 1868), daughter of Major J. Fraser of the 78th Highlanders; (2) 19 November 1878 Blanche Parsons (who died 16 December 1891), daughter of William Legge of Tipperary and widow of the Rev Dr Parsons of Hobart; died 8 November 1901 at Hobart; buried in the Comelian Bay Cemetery, Hobart; portrait by Tennyson Cole in the Hobart Art Gallery. [Addison (1898) and (1913); Crone (1928); *DIB* (2009); Fisher and Robb (1913); Newmann (1993); *Oxford DNB* (2004)].

AGNEW, JOHN (d c 1836), Knocknaroy, county Tyrone;
surgeon, of Knocknaroy; died c 1836; administration Armagh Diocesan Court 1836. [Dub Nat Arch, Armagh Dio Admins index].

AGNEW, SAMUEL (1848–1924), Lurgan, county Armagh;
born 5 May 1848 at Moira, county Down, son of William John Agnew, grocer, of Moira; educated at RBAI from 1862; studied arts and medicine at Queen's College, Belfast, from 1863; BA and MD (QUI) 1871; MCh and LM 1872; medical officer to Lurgan No 1 Dispensary District and medical superintendent officer of health; chairman of the Municipal Technical Committee, of Bengal Place, Lurgan; married (1) —; (2) 15 September 1887 in Trinity Church of Ireland Church, Belfast, Mary Douglas, daughter of John Douglas, merchant, of Lurgan; died 31 January 1924 at High Street, Lurgan; probate Belfast 12 June 1924. [Belf GRO (d); Belf PRO, will cal; Fisher and Robb (1913); *Med Dir*; QCB adm reg; UHF database (m); Young and Pike (1909)].

AGNEW, — (*fl c* 1798), Templepatrick, county Antrim;
'doctor' of Templepatrick, but also kept a public house; United Irishman; a meeting of the United Irishmen was held in his house 5 June 1798, before the Battle of Antrim, and the two field guns used in the battle were first brought to his house; later managed to escape when the soldiers came to look for him, but they burned his house. [Young (1893), pp 20–1].

AICKEN, MICHAEL HUGH (1868–1933), Belfast;
born 6 October 1868 at 2 New Durham Street, Belfast, son of Michael Aicken, pawnbroker, and Elizabeth Smith; educated at St Malachy's College, Belfast; studied medicine at Queen's College, Belfast, 1888–93; MB BCh BAO (RUI) 1893; general practitioner, of 148 Divis Street, Belfast, from c 1895; JP; member of Belfast City Council; unmarried; died 28 October 1933 at 2 Ardmoulin Street; probate Belfast 14 February 1934. [Belf GRO (b) and (d); Belf PRO, will cal; Kirkpatrick Archive; *Med Dir*; QCB adm reg].

AICKEN (AICKIN), THOMAS HENRY (d c 1860), Belfast;
son of John Aicken; LAH Dub 1839; LM (QCB) 1855; general practitioner, of Marlborough Street, Dublin c 1845 and of 38 Ann Street, Belfast c 1846–60; married 11 December 1845 in Holywood Church of Ireland Church, Agnes Casement, eldest daughter of Hugh Casement, merchant, of Moat House, county Down; died c 1860. [*BNL* 12 December 1845 (m); Croly (1843–6); Dub GRO (m); *Med Dir*].

AICKIN (AICKEN), JOHN BLACKER (1797/8–1865), Belfast;
born 1797/8; LAH Dublin 1830; MRCSE 1831; house surgeon to Belfast Fever Hospital and attending dispenser 1824–33; medical officer to constabulary; of 29 Cornmarket, 5 Adelaide Place c 1851–5 and later of 3 Mount Pleasant, Belfast; married Jane — (who died 18 March 1855 'after a prolonged illness' at 5 Adelaide Place); father of Dr William Graves Aickin (*q.v.*); died 29 August 1865 at 3 Everton Terrace, Crumlin Road; buried in Shankill Graveyard. [*BNL* 21 March 1855 (d) and 30 August 1865 (d); Clarke, *Belfast*, vol 1 (1982); Croly (1843–6); Dub GRO (d); Malcolm (1851); *Med Dir*; QCB adm reg].

AICKIN, JOSEPH (*fl c* 1689), Londonderry;
surgeon, of Londonderry throughout the siege of 1688–9; author of *Londerias or a Narrative of the Siege of Londonderry … 1689*. [Aickin (1699); Milligan (1951)].

AICKIN, P. B. (*fl c* 1750), Naval Medical Service and Carrickfergus, county Antrim;
joined the Naval Medical Service as assistant surgeon c 1750; married Jane — (who died 17 February 1839 in Carrickfergus); eldest daughter, Elizabeth, born 1778/9, lived in West Street, Carrickfergus and died 28 June 1855; died before 1839; buried in Carrickfergus Old Graveyard. [*BNL* 22 February 1839 (d) and 6 July 1855 (d, daughter); Rutherford and Clarke, *County Antrim*, vol 3 (1995)].

AICKIN (AICKEN), WILLIAM (1795/6–1837), Belfast;
born 1795/6; surgeon to No. 4 Dispensary District and apothecary, of 31 Corn Market, Belfast, 1824–6; one of the doctors who presented an inscribed gold box to Dr S.S. Thomson in 1834; married 3 April 1828 in Dublin, Jane Thompson, daughter of William Thompson of Dublin; died 15 April 1837 at his home in Corn Market, 'a gentleman well known and universally beloved' (*BNL*), buried in Clifton Street Graveyard (gravestone lost). [*BNL* 11 January 1828 (m) and 21 April 1837 (d); Malcolm (1851); Merrick and Clarke, *Belfast*, vol 4 (1991); Pigot (1824); Thomson presentation box (1834)].

AICKIN, WILLIAM (GRAVES) (1832/3–1908), Belfast;
born 1832/3, son of Dr John Blacker Aickin (*q.v.*); educated at RBAI; studied medicine at Queen's College, Belfast, from 1849, and the Royal College of Surgeons in Ireland; MD (QUI) 1855; LAH Dub 1855; MRCSE 1856; general practitioner, of 6 Chichester Street, 6 Murray's Terrace, and later 93 Victoria Street, Belfast, and medical officer to constabulary, fire brigade, Edgar Home and Female Penitentiary; retired to 2 York Villas, Sandown Park, Belfast c 1906; married Margaret —; died 16 April 1908 at Sandown Park, Belfast; buried in Belfast City Cemetery. [Belf City Cem, bur reg; Dub GRO (d); *Med Dir*; QCB adm reg].

AIKEN, ACHESON (1867–1930), Irvinestown, county Fermanagh;
born 26 November 1867 at Kesh, son of James Aiken, shopkeeper, and Isabella Black; studied medicine at the Royal College of Surgeons in Ireland; LM Rot Hosp Dub; LRCPI and LM, LRCSI and LM 1892; medical officer and medical officer of health to the Clonelly and Pettigo Dispensary Districts, the Vaughan Charter School and constabulary; married Mary Jane —; died 14 September 1930 at Drumadravy, Irvinestown; probate Londonderry 12 December 1930. [Belf GRO (b) and (d); Belf PRO, will cal; Kirkpatrick Archive; *Med Dir*].

AIKEN, WILLIAM JAMES (1871–1961), Bradford and Baildon, Yorkshire;
born 1 July 1871 in Scotch Street, Dungannon, county Tyrone, son of John Aiken, provision merchant, of Scotch Street, and Margaret Smith; educated at Dungannon Royal School; studied medicine at Queen's College, Belfast, from 1891 and in Edinburgh; LRCP LRCS Edin 1898; LFPS Glas 1898; general practitioner, of 2 Hustler Terrace, Bradford, and also of Mount Royal, Baildon; retired c 1948 to Whernside, Baildon Road, Baildon; married 27 June 1906 in Third Ballymena Presbyterian Church, Marion Elizabeth McCaughey, daughter of Hugh McCaughey, merchant, of Broughshane; died 9 February 1961; probate York 1 June 1961. [Dub GRO (b); Kirkpatrick Archive; Lond PPR, will cal; *Med Dir*; QCB adm reg; UHF database (m)].

AINSWORTH, JAMES (1820/21–59), Callao, Peru;
born 1820/1, only son of Thomas Ainsworth of Belfast; MD (St Andrews) 1850 (by exam); LRCSI; surgeon, in the British Hospital in Callao c 1851–9; died 13 June 1859 at Ballyvista, near Callao. [*BNL* 19 August 1859 (d); Smart (2004)].

AIRD, IVIE (d c 1960), Bangor, county Down, and Sydney, New South Wales;
son of Ivie Aird, farmer, of Bangor; studied medicine at Edinburgh University; MB BCh (Edin) 1899; DPH (QUB) 1920; medical officer to Liverpool Dispensary District, the Booth and other steamship companies and the Post Office; general practitioner in Bangor c 1902–14, first of Oriel House, and then of Annandale, Bangor; emigrated c 1914 to Cummock, New South Wales; of Beach Street, Clovelly, Randwick, Sydney, from c 1921; retired c 1951 to 43 Denning Street, South Coogee, Sydney; married 10 July 1905 in Newington Presbyterian Church, Belfast, Ella Margaret Armstrong, daughter of James Armstrong, engineer, of Bangor; died c 1960. [*Med Dir*; UHF database (m)].

ALCOCK, HENRY (1803/4–85), Kilnaleck, county Cavan;
born 1803/4; LAH Dub 1828; MRCSE 1830; LM Rot Hosp Dub 1831; medical officer to Mount Nugent Dispensary District and to Kilnaleck Dispensary District and constabulary; retired to 2 Eblana Avenue, Kingstown, county Dublin; unmarried; died on 1 October 1885 at Eblana Cottage; probate Dublin 19 March 1886. [Belf PRO, will cal; Croly (1843–6); Dub GRO (d); *Med Dir*].

ALEXANDER, JAMES (1793/4–1811), Naval Medical Service;
born 1793/4, son of James Alexander of Gortmessan, Strabane, county Tyrone, and Elizabeth —; brother of Dr Joseph Alexander of the Naval Medical Service (*q.v.*);

joined the Naval Medical Service as assistant surgeon; died 21 March 1811 at his father's house in Gortmessan; buried in Grange graveyard, Strabane. [*BNL* 29 March 1811 (d); Hitchings, Paul, pers com; Roulston (2010); *Shamrock* newspaper 25 March 1811 (d); Todd (1993)].

ALEXANDER, JAMES (1802/3–29), Armagh;
born 1802/3, possibly son of Dr William Alexander of Rathfriland (*q.v.*); LAH Dub 1823; surgeon and apothecary, of Thomas Street, Armagh; died 17 February 1829 in Rathfriland; buried in First Rathfriland Presbyterian Graveyard. [Apothecaries (1829); *BNL* 27 February 1829 (d); gravestone inscription; Pigot (1824)].

ALEXANDER, JAMES ACHESON (1812–89), Belfast;
born 1812, son of Thomas Alexander, farmer, and Anne Anderson; LFPS Glas 1845; general practitioner, of 67 Corporation Street, Belfast; councillor for Dock Ward 1863–81 and alderman 1872–81; finally of Dunturkey, Ballymena, county Antrim; married 23 August 1848 in Linenhall Street Presbyterian Church, Belfast, Margaretta McKay, widow of the Rev James Whiteside McKay, minister of Ballynure Presbyterian Church, and daughter of Andrew Boyd of Bruslee, Ballyclare; died 18 December 1889 at Dunturkey; buried in Old Ballylinney Graveyard; probate Belfast 10 January 1890. [*BNL* 29 August 1848 (m); Belf PRO, will cal, will; gravestone inscription; Dub GRO (m); McConnell (1951); *Med Dir*].

ALEXANDER, JOHN (*fl c* 1750), Belfast;
eldest son of the Rev Samuel Alexander, minister of Castlereagh Presbyterian Church, and Jane Park; surgeon and apothecary, of Belfast c 1750. [Jones (1977); McConnell (1951)].

ALEXANDER, JOHN (1796–1851), Rathfriland, county Down;
born 1796, possibly son of Dr William Alexander (*q.v.*); LAH Dub 1828; surgeon and apothecary, of Rathfriland c 1819 and 1845; died 7 December 1851; buried in First Rathfriland Presbyterian graveyard; probate Prerogative Court 1852. [Apothecaries (1829); *BNL* 15 December 1851 (d); Belf PRO, prerog wills index; Bradshaw (1819); Croly (1843–6); gravestone inscription; Pigot (1824)].

ALEXANDER, JOHN, (*fl c* 1845), Ballygawley, county Tyrone;
FRCSI 1844; medical officer to Ballygawley Dispensary District 1839–45; probably died c 1850. [Croly (1843–6); Gillespie (1966)].

ALEXANDER, JOHN (d 1863), Naval Medical Service and Cincinnati, USA;
youngest son of John Alexander of Caw, Londonderry (related to the Alexanders of Gortmessan); joined the Naval Medical Service; retired to Londonderry and emigrated to Cincinnati, USA; married 26 March 1853 in St Paul's Church, Cincinnati, Catherine Atkins (who died 26 January 1854), only daughter of John Atkins of county Cork; died 20 August 1863 in Cincinnati. [Hitchings, Paul, pers com; *Londonderry Sentinel* 29 April 1853 (m), 24 February 1854 (d) and 8 September 1863 (d)].

ALEXANDER, JOHN (1865–1924), Dublin, Ramelton, county Donegal, and Cape Province, South Africa;
born 1 May 1865, son of Robert John Alexander of Clarendon Street, Londonderry, and Frances Patton (who was niece of Dr David Patton RN (*q.v.*)); brother of Dr Walter Scott Alexander (*q.v.*) and of Rosa Scott Alexander who married Dr Richard Whytock Leslie (*q.v.*); studied medicine at Trinity College, Dublin; LM Combe Hosp Dub 1889; MB BCh BAO (RUI) 1890; surgeon on SS *Armenia* (Anchor Line) 1891; of 24 Morehampton Road, Dublin 1892–4 and of Ramelton 1894; emigrated to South Africa 1895; of French Hoek, Paarl, Cape Colony c 1895–1903 and of Rosedene, Ceres, Cape Province c 1903–24; married Louise Henrietta Fletcher of Caledon (who was born c 1878 and died 23 August 1953), daughter of William Alfred Slade Fletcher; died 10 February 1924 in Cape Town. [Hawbaker (2008); *Med Dir*].

ALEXANDER, JOSEPH (d 1816), Naval Medical Service;
son of James Alexander of Gortmessan, Strabane, county Tyrone, and Elizabeth —; brother of Dr James Alexander of the Naval Medical Service (*q.v.*); joined the Naval Medical Service as assistant surgeon; died 31 October 1816 at his father's house in Gortmessan. [*BNL* 8 November 1816 (d); *Londonderry Journal* 5 November 1816 (d)].

ALEXANDER, ROBERT (1837/8–65), Londonderry and Strabane, county Tyrone;
born 1837/8, son of Robert Alexander of Sandville, Strabane, and Mary Cunningham; studied medicine at Edinburgh University 1857–62, also at the Royal College of Surgeons in Ireland and the Ledwich School, Dublin; MD (Edin) 1862 (thesis 'On jaundice'); LRCSI 1863; house surgeon to the City and County Hospital, Londonderry; unmarried; died 2 October 1865 of tuberculosis at Sandville. [Dub GRO (d); Edin Univ; *Londonderry Sentinel* 3 October 1865 (d); *Med Dir*; Roulston (2010)].

ALEXANDER, ROBERT (1858–1943), Lisburn, county Antrim;
born 19 February 1858 at Annahilt, county Down, son of Robert Alexander, farmer, of Annahilt; educated at RBAI; studied medicine at Queen's College, Belfast, 1875–80; LM Dublin; MD Dip Mid (QUI) 1880; MCh 1881; medical officer to Knocknadona Dispensary District, of Brookhill, Lisburn from c 1885; retired to Amphora, 276 Seacliffe Road, Bangor, c 1920; married 15 July 1896 in First Bangor Presbyterian Church, Mary Staveley Priestley (who died 25 February 1957), daughter of James Priestley, merchant, of Bangor; died 1 June 1943 at Seacliffe Road; buried in Loughaghery Presbyterian Graveyard; probate Belfast 10 May 1944. [Belf GRO (d); Belf PRO, will cal; Clarke, *County Down*, vol 18 (1979); *Med Dir*; QCB adm reg; UHF database (m)].

ALEXANDER, SAMUEL (d 1863), Cincinnati, Ohio;
born in county Antrim; emigrated to USA; died 7 June 1863 at Cincinnati. [*Coleraine Chronicle* 18 June 1863 (d)].

ALEXANDER, SAMUEL (1862–1903), Belfast;
  born 1862 at Umgall, Templepatrick, county Antrim, son of Samuel Alexander, farmer, of Umgall; educated at RBAI; studied medicine at Queen's College, Belfast, from 1880; MD (RUI) 1885; BCh BAO 1888; general practitioner, of 24 Shankill Road, Belfast, from c 1890 and finally of 56 Crumlin Road; married Mary E. —; died 25 February 1903 at 56 Crumlin Road, Belfast; administration Belfast 1 April 1903. [Belf PRO, will cal; Dub GRO (d); *Med Dir*; QCB adm reg].

ALEXANDER, WALTER SCOTT (1868–1923), Ramelton, county Donegal, Napier and Villiersdorp, South Africa, and Chatham Islands, South Pacific;
  born 12 March 1868 in Londonderry, son of Robert John Alexander, ironmonger, of Clarendon Street, Londonderry, and Frances Patton, who was niece of Dr David Patton (*q.v.*); brother of Dr John Alexander of Cape Province (*q.v.*) and of Rosa Scott Alexander who married Dr Richard Whytock Leslie (*q.v.*); educated at Londonderry Academical Institution; studied arts and medicine at Trinity College, Dublin, from 1885; BA (TCD) 1889; MB BCh BAO 1890; general practitioner, of Ramelton c 1892–9; emigrated to South Africa c 1899; general practitioner, of Napier, Cape Province c 1899–1907 and Villiersdorp c 1907–23; civil surgeon with South African Field Force and additional district surgeon at Hope Town, Cape Province; medical officer in Chatham Islands 1921–3; married c 1898 at Napier, Bredasdorp, Cape Province, Adeline de Moldrup Baumann (who was born c 1878 and died 5 January 1959); died 24 January 1923 at Waitangi, Chatham Islands; buried in Te One Cemetery, Chatham Islands. [Hawbaker (2008); *Med Dir*; TCD adm reg; *TCD Cat*, vol II (1896)].

ALEXANDER, WILLIAM (d 1716), Belfast;
  doctor of medicine, of Belfast; 'a practitioner of some reputation at the beginning of the 18th century' (Esler); witness to a will in June 1716; died July 1716; at his funeral 19 'cloakes' were hired, an indication of the high respect with which the deceased was held. [Agnew (1995); Esler (1884); Eustace, vol I (1956)].

ALEXANDER, WILLIAM (1750/1–1827), Rathfriland, county Down;
  born 1750/1; surgeon and apothecary, of Rathfriland from c 1783; married — (who was born 1763/4 and died 23 September 1850); died 21 November 1827; buried in First Rathfriland Presbyterian Graveyard; '… in his declining years, when from weak health he was unable to undertake long journeys, frequently were the private conveyances of individuals sent to convey him to their assistance in a way which might be least injurious to himself'; 'his children saw in him, not the stern, rigid and despotic parent, but the kind protector …' (*BNL*); probate Prerogative Court 1828. [*BNL* 27 November 1827 (d) and 1 October 1850 (d); Belf PRO, prerog wills index; Bradshaw (1819); gravestone inscription; Pigot (1824)].

ALEXANDER, WILLIAM (1787/8–1830), Naval Medical Service;
  born 1787/8; joined the Naval Medical Service as assistant surgeon 1808; retired to Londonderry; married 10 December 1827 Anne Simpson of Londonderry; died 6 May 1830 'after a long and painful illness'. [*BNL* 14 December 1827 (m) and 11 May 1830 (d); *Londonderry Sentinel* 8 May 1830 (d); *NMS* (1826)].

ALEXANDER, WILLIAM (1799/1800–39), Londonderry;
born 1799/1800; surgeon, of Ferryquay, Street, Londonderry c 1823; married —; eldest daughter, Catherine Alexander, married 13 July 1840 Edward Moore of Londonderry; died 3 February 1839; buried in Grange graveyard, Strabane. [*BNL* 24 July 1840 (m, daughter); Pigot (1824); Roulston (2010); Todd (1993)].

ALEXANDER, WILLIAM (1840–1908), Army Medical Service;
born 18 April 1840, son of Thomas Alexander of Rathfriland; educated at RBAI; studied medicine at Queen's College, Belfast, from 1861; MD (QUI) 1865; LRCS Edin 1865; joined the Army Medical Service as assistant staff surgeon 1865; surgeon major 1878; served in Rathfriland in 1872 and in Egypt in 1882; retired as brigade surgeon (lieutenant-colonel) 1885; employed when on the retired list at Piershill; married Maria Adams; died 11 August 1908 at Mindoro, Park Avenue, Portobello, Midlothian; confirmation of will Edinburgh 9 September 1908. [Edin GRO (d); Edin Nat Arch, will cal; *Med Dir*; Peterkin and Johnston (1968); QCB, adm reg].

ALEXANDER, WILLIAM (1845–1919), Liverpool, Lancashire, and RAMC;
born 29 April 1845 at Holestone, Doagh, county Antrim, son of James Alexander of Holestone; educated at Doagh School; studied medicine at Queen's College, Belfast, from 1866; MD (with gold medal and exhibition) MCh (QUI) 1870; FRCSE 1877; resident medical officer to the Workhouse, Liverpool 1870–75 and visiting surgeon 1875–89; general practitioner, of 100 and 102 Bedford Street, Liverpool, c 1880; honorary surgeon to the Royal Southern Hospital, Liverpool 1889–1910; of 31 Rodney Street, Liverpool c 1905 and finally of 'Holestone', Tower Road, North Heswall, Cheshire; founder and superintendent medical officer for the Home for Epileptics, Maghull; lieutenant-colonel to 1st Western General Hospital, RAMC during World War I; author of many papers on surgery and epilepsy; married —; father of Dr David Moore Alexander, pathologist, MB (Vict Coll Manch) 1901, who died 18 March 1915 aged 37; died 9 March 1919 at Heswall; probate London 17 June 1919. [*BMJ* obituary (1915) and (1919); Lond PPR, will cal; *Med Dir*; Plarr (1930); QCB, adm reg].

ALISTER, JAMES (1855–1907), Crumlin, county Antrim, and Glasgow;
born 14 February 1855 at Lisburn, county Antrim, son of Robert Alister, coal merchant, of Lisburn, and Margaret Little; educated at Lisburn Academy; studied medicine at Queen's College, Belfast, from 1874; LRCP Edin and LM; LRCS Edin and LM 1883; medical officer and medical officer of health for Crumlin Dispensary District; medical officer to constabulary and certifying factory surgeon; general practitioner in Glasgow from c 1900; of 7 Havelock Terrace, Paisley Road, Glasgow c 1902; married 10 July 1893 in Muckamore Presbyterian Church, county Antrim, Susan Rea, daughter of Thomas Rea, merchant, of Muckamore; died 18 February 1907 at 6 Brighton Terrace, Govan, Lanarkshire. [Edin GRO (d); *Med Dir*; QCB adm reg; UHF database (m)].

ALLAN, ROBERT HONEYMAN (1871–1913), Monaghan, Belfast and Traedyrhiw, Glamorgan;
> born 12 April 1871 at Ballymena, county Antrim, son of John Allan, seedsman, of Ballymena, and Martha Giffen; educated at RBAI; studied medicine at Queen's College, Belfast, from 1889; MB BCh BAO (RUI) 1895; of 24 Church Street, Ballymena, c 1895; resident surgeon to Monaghan County Infirmary c 1896; general practitioner, of 1 Orrington, Lisburn Road, Belfast, from c 1900; finally of 1 Glantaff Road, Traedyrhiw; married 15 November 1898 in Richview Presbyterian Church, Belfast, Jane Aiken Giffen, daughter of James Giffen, merchant, of Belfast; died 18 October 1913; probate London 18 November 1913. [Dub GRO (b); Lond PPR, will cal; *Med Dir*; QCB adm reg; UHF database (m)].

ALLAN, WILLIAM (1854–c 1889), Gambia, East Africa:
> born 14 October 1854 at Dundalk, county Louth; educated at the Educational Institution, Dundalk; studied medicine at Queen's College, Galway and, from 1875, at Queen's College, Belfast; LRCSI 1879; colonial surgeon to the Gambia from c 1880; died c 1889. [*Med Dir*; QCB adm reg].

ALLEN, ALEXANDER (*fl c* 1800), Naval Medical Service;
> joined the Naval Medical Service as assistant surgeon; married Mary — (who died 20 April 1841 in Caledon, county Armagh); father of Ann Elizabeth Allen who married 17 October 1820 Dr John Crozier of Caledon (*q.v.*); died before 1821. [*BNL* 24 October 1820 (m, daughter) and 14 May 1841 (d); *Londondery Sentinel* 15 May 1841 (d)].

ALLEN, ALFRED (1856–99), Ulceby, Lincolnshire;
> born 19 April 1856 at Killinawas, county Longford, son of James Allen of Killinawas, near Edgeworthstown; educated at Carboy School, Galway; studied medicine at Queen's College, Belfast, from 1873; MD MCh Dip Mid (QUI) 1876; general practitioner, of Cleethorpe Road, Great Grimsby, Lincolnshire c 1877 and of Keelby, Laceby, Lincolnshire from c 1879; unmarried; died 30 June 1899 of phthisis at Breany, county Longford; probate Dublin 7 June 1900 and London 17 July 1900. [Belf PRO, will cal; Dub GRO (d); Lond PPR, will cal; *Med Dir*; QCB adm reg].

ALLEN, ANDREW (d c 1854), Naval Medical Service and Fintona, county Tyrone;
> joined the Naval Medical Service as assistant surgeon; general practitioner in Fintona c 1845; married —; second daughter, Margaret, born c 1826 and died 11 September 1855 at Fintona; died c 1854. [*BNL* 22 September 1855 (d, daughter); Croly (1843–6)].

ALLEN, CHARLES (1853–1912), London and Southend, Essex;
> born 11 August 1853 at Ballyglassin, county Longford, son of James Allen of Ballynascraw, county Longford; educated at Longford School; studied medicine at Queen's College, Galway, and, from 1873, at Queen's College, Belfast; LSA Lond 1884; general practitioner in London from c 1885, of Zingari Terrace, Upton Park

c 1895, of 34 Propect Hill, Walthamstow, c 1900 and then Eastwood Road, Seven Kings, Ilford; medical officer to Southend Dispensary, of 2 Whitelands Villas, Southchurch Road, Southend, from c 1900; married Marie —; died 7 May 1912; probate London 19 June 1912. [Lond PPR, will cal; *Med Dir*; QCB adm reg].

ALLEN, CHARLES DUNSCOMBE (1845–83), Glenarm, county Antrim, Bagenalstown, county Carlow, and Dublin;
   born January 1845, son of the Rev Robert Dunscombe Allen, curate of Layde (Cushendall), county Antrim, and rector of Castlerickard, county Meath, (whose father was Robert Allen, surgeon RN, of Devon) and Frances Elizabeth Wade of Fairfield House, county Galway; educated by his father; studied arts and medicine at Trinity College, Dublin, from 1862 and at the Royal College of Surgeons in Ireland; BA (TCD) 1869; MB 1870; LRCSI and LM 1870; medical officer to Glenarm Dispensary District and constabulary, c 1872–6; medical officer and public vaccinator to Bagenalstown Dispensary District, from 1876; lived finally at Bachelors' Hall, Rathfarnham, county Dublin; married 1872 Elizabeth Hannah Gerrard (who was born 1848/9 and died 5 February 1940); died 28 June 1883 of phthisis, at 8 St Anne's Villas, Notting Hill, London; probate Dublin 30 August 1883. [Belf PRO, will cal; Kirkpatrick Archive; Leslie (1937) (for brother) and (1993); Lond GRO (d); *Med Dir*; TCD adm reg; *TCD Cat*, vol II (1896)].

ALLEN, JAMES (d 1831), Stewartstown, county Tyrone;
   LAH Dub 1799; surgeon and apothecary, of Stewartstown c 1824; married Sarah — (who was born 1775/6 and died 17 January 1853); died February 1831. [Apothecaries (1829); *BNL* 22 February 1831 (d); *Londonderry Sentinel* 4 February 1853 (d); Pigot (1824)].

ALLEN, JAMES (*fl c* 1817), Tempo, county Fermanagh;
   general practitioner, of Tempo Dispensary from c 1817. [Maguire (1993), p 27].

ALLEN, JAMES, senior (*fl c* 1800–20), Newtownstewart, county Tyrone;
   surgeon and apothecary, of Newtownstewart; married —; father of Dr James Allen, junior (*q.v.*), who was born c 1800. [Dingle, Mary, pers com].

ALLEN, JAMES, junior (c 1800–56), Newtownstewart, county Tyrone, Launceston and Hobart, Tasmania, and Melbourne, Australia;
   born c 1800 in Newtownstewart, son of Dr James Allen (*q.v.*); apprenticed as a surgeon and apothecary to his father 1820–27; emigrated to Australia 1832 on the emigrant ship *Rubicon*; apothecary in Launceston Hospital 1832–3; colonial medical officer in Hobart 1833–7; returned home to Newtownstewart 1837–9 and then returned to Australia; of West Creek, near Melbourne 1842; married 21 February 1842 in the Congregational or Independent Chapel, Collins Street, Melbourne, Maria Amelia Robinson, daughter of George Augustus Robinson, commandant of Flinders Island, Tasmania; general practitioner, of Clarke Island, Bass Strait c 1842–56; drowned 1856 in an accident, while rowing between Preservation and Clarke Islands. [Dingle, Mary, pers com].

ALLEN (ALLAN), JAMES (*fl c* 1845), Caledon, county Tyrone;
MRCSE; general practitioner in Caledon c 1846; married Mary Moore (who married secondly 22 March 1845 Dr Robert Todd Huston of Tynan (*q.v.*)), daughter of Captain Moore of Drummond; daughter born 1843; died 25 February 1844 in Caledon [*cf* Croly, 1846]. [*BNL* 24 November 1843 (b) and 12 March 1844 (d); Croly (1843–6)].

ALLEN, JAMES YOUNG (*fl c* 1836), Cookstown and Strabane, county Tyrone;
surgeon, of Cookstown c 1836 and of Strabane c 1840; married 10 August 1836 in Derryloran Church of Ireland Church, Rebecca Walsh of Gortalowry House, Cookstown; daughter born November 1840. [*BNL* 27 November 1840 (b, daughter); Derryloran Mar Reg (PRONI MIC/15/1)].

ALLEN (or ALLAN), JOHN (1768/9–1857), Comber, county Down;
born 1768/9; LAH 1829; surgeon and apothecary and medical officer to constabulary, of Comber c 1845; married 3 April 1809 in the house of James Cowan, Esq, Ballylentogh, Hillsborough, Jane Graham (who was born 1779/80 and died 4 April 1854), daughter of William Graham of Lisnastrean, Drumbeg, county Down; died 11 January 1857; both buried in Comber graveyard; will dated 24 December 1855 proved in Prerogative Court 20 February 1857. [Apothecaries (1829); *BNL* 7 April 1809 (m), 5 April 1854 (d) and 12 January 1857 (d); Belf PRO, prerog wills index and D438/95; Clarke, *County Down*, vol 5 (1984); Croly (1843–6); *Med Dir;* Pigot (1824)].

ALLEN, JOHN GOWER (1847/8–1925), Loughgall and Armagh, county Armagh;
born 1847/8, son of Alexander Dawson Allen of The Retreat, Armagh; educated at Royal School, Armagh 1864–7; studied arts and medicine at Trinity College, Dublin, the Ledwich School and Meath Hospital, Dublin; LRCSI 1871; LKQCPI 1872; LM Rot Hosp Dub 1872; assistant medical officer to Loughgall Dispensary District; resident physician from 1873 to The Retreat Private Lunatic Asylum, Armagh and later medical superintendent; JP for county Armagh; married Eleanor Leeper, daughter of Dr John Leeper (*q.v.*) of Keady; died 16 June 1925 at The Retreat, Armagh; probate Belfast 20 November 1925. [Belf PRO, will cal; Ferrar (1933); *Med Dir*; Young and Pike (1909)].

ALLEN, JOHN STEWART (1810/1–58), London and Abergavenny, Monmouthshire;
born 1810/1, son of Henry Allen of Belfast; MRCSE 1833; LSA Lond 1838; LRCP Lond 1844; resident surgeon to St Marylebone Infirmary, London; physician and superintendent of the Joint Counties Asylum, Abergavenny; unmarried; died 9 January 1858 at the Asylum, Abergavenny; buried in Abergavenny and also commemorated in Knockbreda graveyard, county Down; administration Llandaff 8 February 1858. [*BNL* 16 January 1858 (d); Clarke, *County Down*, vol 2 (2nd ed, 1988); Lond GRO (d); Lond PPR, will cal; *Med Dir*].

ALLEN, JOSEPH (d 1814), Larne, county Antrim;
general practitioner of Larne; married Mary — (who died 12 February 1837); died 17 March 1814, 'He is sincerely regretted by those few who knew him ... His timidity and diffidence of being considered assuming prevented his cultivating that extensive circle of acquaintance that would from knowledge, produce a general regret in his professional practice. The poor always unsolicited found a friend and his practical farming on improved systems was an example of much advantage to that neighbourhood'. [*BNL* 22 March 1814 (d) and 17 February 1837 (d)].

ALLEN, ROBERT (d 1847), Demerara, British Guiana;
son of Robert Allen, merchant, of Belfast; Government Hospital Surgeon of Kaoo Island, Essequibo River, Demerara; died 1 March 1847. [*BNL* 13 April 1847 (d)].

ALLEN, ROBERT (1868–1908), Belfast;
born 19 July 1868 in Brownlow House, Lurgan, son of William Moore Allen, gardener, of Brownlow House, and Jane Elizabeth Allen [sic]; studied medicine at Galway, Edinburgh and Dublin; MB BCh (RUI) 1893; FRCSI 1898; studied physiology and laryngology as a travelling scholar, in Berlin; demonstrator and lecturer in anatomy at Queen's College, Galway; resident medical officer at Galway Hospital; surgeon in Belfast from 1895; attending assistant surgeon at Ulster Eye, Ear and Throat Hospital from 1903; of 13 Clifton Street, Belfast c 1904 and 5 Queen's Elms, Belfast c 1907; married Eda Kinkead of Galway; died 2 December 1908 at Queen's Elms, of pneumonia; buried in Seagoe Municipal Cemetery; probate Belfast 11 January 1909. [Allison (1969); Belf GRO (b); Belf PRO, will cal; *BMJ* obituary (1908); gravestone inscription; Kirkpatrick Archive; *Med Dir*].

ALLEN, ROBERT AUSTEN (1829–76), Army Medical Service;
born 23 December 1829 at Stewartstown, county Tyrone, third son of the Rev Robert Allen, minister of Stewartstown Presbyterian Church, and Sarah Jane Little of Stewartstown; brother of Dr Samuel Allen (*q.v.*); MRCSE 1852; LSA Lond 1853; MD (Glas) 1853; joined the Army Medical Service as assistant staff surgeon 1858; attached to 71st Foot 1861; staff surgeon 1865; surgeon major 1873; married 18 January 1859 Mary Franklin Risk, daughter of Andrew Risk of Manweny, county Donegal; died 4 December 1876 at Rawalpindi, India. [Addison (1898); Burke *LGI* (1912); McConnell (1951); *Med Dir*; Peterkin and Johnston (1968)].

ALLEN, SAMUEL (1777/8–1835), Tandragee, county Armagh, Carrickfergus and Dervock, county Antrim;
born 1777/8; studied medicine at Edinburgh University; MD (Edin) 1809 (thesis 'De rubeola'); physician, of Tandragee c 1810–19; physician and inspector of gaol at Carrickfergus c 1818–20; inherited his father's property at Lisconnan, near Dervock, 1820 and retired from medical practice; married —; son born February 1813, one of 8 children; died 9 October 1835 'after a painful and lingering illness'. [*BNL* 16 February 1813 (b) and 13 October 1835 (d); Edin Univ; Jackson (2011)].

ALLEN, SAMUEL (1826–74), Stewartstown, county Tyrone, and Southend, Essex;
born 23 June 1826, second son of the Rev Robert Allen, minister of Stewartstown Presbyterian Church, and Sarah Jane Little of Stewartstown; brother of Dr Robert Austen Allen (*q.v.*); studied arts at Glasgow University; matriculated 1843; BA (Glas) 1846; MD [?]; not in *Medical Register* or *Medical Directory*, but described as 'doctor of medicine' at probate; finally of Bolton Villas, Cliff Town, Southend; married 23 July 1863 Elizabeth Gibson (who died 23 May 1884), eldest daughter of Samuel Gibson; died 20 November 1874 at Bolton Villas, of phthisis; probate London 16 March 1875. [Addison (1898) and (1913); Burke *LGI* (1912) (under 'Little'); Lond GRO (d); Lond PPR, will cal, will; McConnell (1951)].

ALLEN, THOMAS (1810/1–1891), Brighton, Sussex;
born 1810/1, son of lieutenant — Allen and Mary Dill of Springhill, county Donegal; studied medicine at Edinburgh University; MD (Edin) 1832 (thesis 'De rheumatismo acuto'); CM (Glas) 1833; LRCS Edin 1834; of Loughgall, county Armagh; general practitioner, of 16 Regency Square, Brighton; married 20 October 1840 in Brighton Church of England Church, Maria Robinson, third daughter of the Rev W. Beauclerc Robinson of Irvington, rector of Litlington, Sussex; father of Dr Marcus Henry Allen of Brighton, MRCSE LSA Lond 1871; died 3 June 1891 at 16 Regency Square; probate London 23 June 1891. [Addison (1898); Dill (1892); Edin Univ; Lond GRO (d); Lond PPR, will cal; *Londonderry Sentinel* 7 November 1840 (m); *Med Dir*].

ALLEN, WILLIAM ROBERT (1852–c 1889), West Hartlepool, county Durham;
born 21 December 1852 at Tullynamullen, county Antrim, son of Richard Allen, farmer, of Tullynamullen; studied medicine at Queen's College, Belfast from 1878; LRCP LRCS Edin 1882; general practitioner, of 12 Scarborough Street, West Hartlepool; died c 1889. [*Med Dir*; QCB adm reg].

ALLEN, — (*fl c* 1845), Rathfriland, county Down, and East India Company;
general practitioner of Rathfriland; working with East India Company in 1845. [*Downpatrick Recorder* 23 May 1846].

ALLEY, WILLIAM (d 1838), Doagh, county Antrim;
MD [?]; of Doagh; died 1 October 1838 at his home in Doagh. [*BNL* 9 October 1838 (d)].

ALLINGHAM, EDWARD (1841–90), Bristol, London and Dublin;
born 22 May 1841 in Ballyshannon, county Donegal, second son of William Allingham, bank manager, of Ballyshannon, and his second wife, Isabella Johnston; step brother of the poet William Allingham who was the eldest son of William Allingham and his first wife Margaret Crawford; studied arts and medicine at Trinity College, Dublin, from 1859; BA (TCD) 1862; MB 1874; LAH Dub 1874; general practitioner, of 1 Meridian Terrace, Horfield, and 128 City Road, Bristol, c 1875–83, of 9 Upton Park Road, Forestgate and 26 Mansfield Road, Haverstock Hill,

London, c 1885–6 and of 15 Mountjoy Street, Dublin, c 1888–9; lived finally at 93 Falls Road, Belfast; author of *New and Original Poems* (1890); married Bridget Drummond (who died 18 July 1914 at 159 Springfield Road, Belfast); died 22 December 1890 at 93 Falls Road, from cardiac failure due to 'too free use of narcotic poison – habitually taking chloral hydrate and laudanum' (Coroner); probate Dublin 26 October 1897. [Belf PRO, will cal; Burtchaell and Sadleir (1935); Dub GRO (d); Hitchings, Paul, pers com; *Med Dir*].

ALLINGHAM, EDWARD HERRICK (1805–c 1856), Indian Medical Service and Dromahair, county Leitrim;
born 25 October 1805 at Ballyshanon, county Donegal, son of John Allingham of Portnason, county Donegal; LRCSI 1829; joined the Indian Medical Service (Bengal establishment) as assistant surgeon 1830; absent on sick leave from 1831 and struck off register 1839; medical officer to Dromahair Dispensary District and constabulary from before 1837; married December 1832 Catherine Potter, daughter of Samuel Potter of Mount Potter, county Galway; died c 1856 at Dromahair. [Crawford (1930); Croly (1843–6); Hitchings, Paul, pers com; Lewis (1837); *Med Dir*].

ALLISON, ANDREW (*fl c* 1781), Coleraine, county Londonderry;
surgeon, of Coleraine; witness to will of Dr Joseph Beers (*q.v.*) in 1781. [Eustace, vol II (1954)].

ALLISON, CHARLES WARKE (1854–97), Dungiven, county Londonderry;
born October 1854 in county Londonderry, son of Samuel Allison, farmer, of Magilligan; brother of Dr William Allison (*q.v.*) and Dr Hazlett Allison (*q.v.*); educated at Belfast Seminary; studied arts and medicine at Queen's College, Cork 1871–4 and Belfast 1874–5; BA (QUI) 1874; MD 1878; LRCS Edin and LM 1878; general practitioner, of Dungiven; married 29 November 1883 at Ballymaglin in the house of the bride's brother, Eleanor Fleming, daughter of William Fleming, farmer, of Ballymaglin, county Antrim; father of Dr — Allison; died 22 April 1897 at Dungiven; administration Londonderry 2 June 1897. [Belf PRO, will cal; Dub GRO (m) and (d); *Med Dir*; QCB adm reg].

ALLISON, HAZLETT (1851–1925), Indian Medical Service;
born 30 April 1851 at Magilligan, county Londonderry, son of Samuel Allison, farmer, of Magilligan; brother of Dr William Allison of Claudy (*q.v.*) and Dr Charles Warke Allison of Dungiven (*q.v.*); educated by Robert A. Brandon MA; studied medicine at Queen's College, Belfast, and the Royal College of Surgeons in Ireland 1866–71; MD and MCh (QUI) 1871; LM Glas 1872; joined the Indian Medical Service (Madras establishment) as surgeon 1873; surgeon major 1885; surgeon lieutenant-colonel 1893; retired to Portrush, county Antrim, 1903; married 25 June 1891 in Craigs Church of Ireland Church, Ballymena, county Antrim, Mary Hunter Woods, daughter of Michael Woods, accountant, of Craigs; died 15 November 1925 at 15 Salisbury Terrace, Portrush; probate Belfast 19 February 1926. [Belf GRO (d); Belf PRO, will cal, will; Crawford (1930); Kirkpatrick Archive; *Med Dir*; QCB adm reg; UHF database (m)].

ALLISON, SAMUEL HAZLETT BROWNE (1866–1936), Killaloo, county Londonderry;
>born 10 November 1866, son of Dr William Allison (*q.v.*) of Killaloo, and Mary Browne; educated at Londonderry Academical Institution; studied arts at Queen's College, Belfast, 1883–6 and medicine at Edinburgh University; BA (RUI) 1886; MB MCh (Edin) 1894; medical officer and medical officer of health to Claudy and Park Dispensary Districts and certifying factory surgeon, of Millfield, Killaloo; married Mable Elizabeth Anne Valence; died 2 August 1936 at Millfield; probate Londonderry 8 March 1937. [Belf GRO (b) and (d); Belf PRO, will cal, will; Kirkpatrick Archive; *Med Dir;* QCB adm reg].

ALLISON, WILLIAM (1834/5–1906), Limavady and Cumber, county Londonderry;
>born 1834/5, son of Samuel Allison, farmer, of Magilligan, county Londonderry; brother of Dr Hazlett Allison (*q.v.*) and Dr Charles Warke Allison of Dungiven (*q.v.*); MD (Edin) 1856 (thesis 'On the signs of pregnancy'); LRCS Edin and LM 1856; general practitioner of Limavady; medical officer to Claudy and Park Dispensary Districts and constabulary; retired to Millfield, county Londonderry; married 8 September 1863 in Upper Cumber Presbyterian Church, Mary Browne, daughter of the Rev William Browne, minister of Upper Cumber; father of Dr Samuel Hazlett Browne Allison (*q.v.*); died 14 July 1906 at Lettermuck, Claudy; probate Londonderry 5 November 1906. [Belf PRO, will cal, will; *Coleraine Chronicle* 19 September 1865 (m); Dub GRO (m) and (d); Edin Univ; *Londonderry Sentinel* 15 September 1863 (m); *Med Dir*].

ALLMAN, DORA ELIZABETH (1871–1955), Armagh;
>born 25 July 1871 in Bandon, county Cork, daughter of Samuel Allman, school inspector, of North Main Street, Bandon, and Anne Elizabeth Nicol; studied medicine at Queen's College, Cork; MB BCh BAO (RUI) 1898, first woman doctor to graduate in Queen's College, Cork; assistant medical officer to the Armagh District Asylum; retired c 1937 to Karavanagh, 52 Sandymount Avenue, Dublin; unmarried; died 25 February 1955 at Karavanagh; probate Dublin 19 April 1955. [Dub GRO (b) and (d); Dub Nat Arch, will cal, will; *Med Dir*].

ALLMAN, GEORGE JAMES (1812–98), Dublin and Edinburgh;
>born February 1812 in Cork, eldest son of James Allman, distiller, of Bandon, county Cork; educated at RBAI 1824–9; studied arts and medicine at Trinity College, Dublin, 1835–45; BA (TCD) 1839; MB 1843; FRCSI 1844; MD 1847; MD (Oxon) 1847; professor of Botany at Trinity College, Dublin, 1844–56, of 91 Lower Mount Street, Dublin; FRS 1854; regius professor of Natural History at Edinburgh 1856–70, of 10 Hope Street, Edinburgh; president of Linnean Society 1874–83 and of the British Association 1879; Cunningham Medal of the Royal Irish Academy 1878; died 24 November 1898 at Ardmore, Station Road, Parkstone, Poole, Dorset; buried in Poole Cemetery; probate London 14 February 1899 and Dublin 14 April 1899. [Belf PRO, will cal; Burtchaell and Sadleir (1924); Croly (1846); Crone (1928); Fisher and Robb (1913); Foster (1888); Kirkpatrick Archive; Lond GRO (d); Lond PPR, will cal; *Med Dir;* Newmann (1993); *Oxford DNB* (2004); Praeger (1949)].

ALLMAN, THOMAS (1847/8–1915), Westport, county Mayo;
born 1847/8, son of the Rev Dr William Allman, junior (*q.v.*), rector of Mevagh and of Kilmacrenan, county Donegal and Elizabeth Charlotte Georgina Hill; studied medicine at Trinity College, Dublin; LRCSI 1870; LKQCPI and LM 1870; medical officer to Islandeady Dispensary District, of Westport, from 1871; married 9 June 1878 Charlotte Isabella Anne Cather, daughter of the Reverend John Cather, Archdeacon of Tuam; died 10 November 1915 at 9 Winton Road, Rathmines, Dublin; probate Ballina 24 January 1916. [Belf PRO, will cal; Dub GRO (d); Kirkpatrick Archive; Leslie (1929); *Med Dir*].

ALLMAN, WILLIAM, junior (1820/21–95), Carrigart, county Donegal;
born 1820/1 in Dublin, son of the Rev William Allman, senior, MD, professor of Botany, TCD; studied arts and medicine in Trinity College, Dublin 1834–40; BA (TCD) 1839; MB 1840; LKQCPI 1841; LM Rot Hosp Dub 1841; MD 1843; appears not to have practised medicine; ordained 1845; curate of Milford (Raphoe) 1845–7; perpetual curate of Drum 1847–8; chaplain at Croix, West Indies 1848; curate of Clondehorkey 1849–64; rector of Mevagh 1864–73; rector of Kilmacrenan 1873–95; married 5 November 1845 in St Peter's Church of Ireland Church, Dublin, Elizabeth Charlotte Georgina Hill, daughter of Thomas Hill, surgeon, of Dublin; father of Dr Thomas Allman of Westport (*q.v.*); died 6 August 1895 at Kilmacrenan Glebe, buried in Kilmacrenan churchyard; administration (with will) Londonderry 13 March 1896. [Belf PRO, will cal; Burtchaell and Sadleir (1924); Dub GRO (m) and (d); Leslie (1929) and (1940); *Med Dir*].

ALLWORTHY, SAMUEL WILLIAM (1866–1952), Darlington, Durham, RAMC and Belfast;
born 16 December 1866, son of Edward Allworthy of 64 York Street, Belfast, merchant, and Hanna Hamilton; educated at RBAI from 1882; studied arts and medicine at Trinity College, Dublin, from 1883; BA (TCD) 1886; MB 1887; BCh 1888; MA and MD 1890; Dip State Med 1892; general practitioner in Darlington for a short time; attending physician Belfast Hospital for Diseases of the Skin (Benn) from 1893; major in RAMC and specialist in radiology and dermatology during World War I; suffered from severe injuries to his hands from overexposure to radiation, resulting in amputation of several fingers; MRIA and Member of Senate of QUB and TCD; president of the BNHPS 1940–44, and of the Ulster Photographic Society 1906–10; alderman of the city of Belfast; chairman of the Belfast Water Commissioners, and JP; of 32 Crumlin Road, Belfast, c 1895, of The Manor House, Antrim Road, c 1900 and 3 Winston Gardens, Belfast from c 1945; married Marion Bennet Macaldin, daughter of James Macaldin of Belfast; died 13 September 1952 at the Musgrave and Clark Clinic, Belfast; probate Belfast 15 January 1953. [Belf GRO (b); Belf PRO, will cal; *BMJ* obituary (1952); Deane (1921); Hall (1970); Kirkpatrick Archive; McCaw (1944); *Med Dir*; TCD adm reg; *TCD Cat,* vol II (1896); Young and Pike (1909)].

ANDERSON, ADAM (1851/2–82), Quito, Equador, and Birkenhead, Cheshire;
born 1851/2; studied medicine at Queen's College, Galway, Coombe Hospital, Dublin and the Royal Infirmary, Edinburgh; LRCP, LRCS and LM Edin 1878;

working in Quito, Equador 1879–81 and in Birkenhead 1881; married —; died 10 January 1882 of phthisis, at Curryfree, Londonderry; buried in Old Glendermott Graveyard, county Londonderry. [Dub GRO (d); *Med Dir*; Todd (1988)].

ANDERSON, ALFRED (1822/3–47), Belfast;
born 1822/3; resident surgeon to the General Hospital, Belfast; died of typhus fever 3 October 1847; buried in Clifton Street Graveyard, Belfast; memorial in RVH. [Allison (1972); *Belf Gen Hosp, Ann Rep* (1848); Merrick and Clarke, *Belfast*, vol 4 (1991)].

ANDERSON, ALEXANDER TODD (1819/20–66), Naval Medical Service;
born 1819/20; joined the Naval Medical Service as surgeon; retired; not in *Medical Directory* or *Medical Register*: unmarried; died 19 September 1866 at Springtown Cottage, Londonderry, after ten years of paralysis. [Dub GRO (d); *Londonderry Sentinel* 21 September 1866 (d)].

ANDERSON, CHARLES JAMES (or JAMES CHARLES) (d c 1875), Kilkeel, county Down, and Zoowomba, Queensland;
studied medicine at the Original Medical School, Dublin; LM Coombe Hosp Dub 1847; LRCSI 1851; LKQCPI 1858; medical officer to Kilkeel and Annalong Dispensary Districts and to Admiralty; member of the Belfast Clinical and Pathological Society c 1859–61; emigrated c 1872 to Russell Street, Zoowomba, Queensland, Australia; married c 1857 —; daughter born 15 December 1858 at Kilkeel; died c 1875. [*Belf Clin Path Soc, Transactions*; *BNL* 20 December 1858 (d); *Med Dir*].

ANDERSON, DAVID ALEXANDER (1863–1923), Cockfield, county Durham;
born 7 April 1863 at Fallagloon, county Londonderry, son of Samuel Alexander of Fallagloon; educated privately; studied medicine at Queen's College, Belfast, from 1879; LRCP LRCS Edin 1894; LFPS Glas 1894; medical officer and public vaccinator to Cockfield Dispensary District, Butterknowle, Darlington from c 1895; married —; father of Dr Samuel Eric Hill Anderson, MB (Durham) 1921; died 24 November 1923 at Cockfield; administration Durham 10 January 1924. [Lond GRO (d); Lond PPR, will cal; *Med Dir*; QCB adm reg].

ANDERSON, DESPARD (1840/1–76), Moira, county Down;
born 1840/1; studied medicine at the Carmichael School, Dublin; LM Rot Hosp Dub 1864; LKQCPI and LM 1866; LRCSI 1866; acting assistant surgeon to Liverpool North Dispensary; medical officer to Moira Dispensary District and registrar of births and deaths; married —; died 25 July 1876 at Moira; probate Dublin 29 January 1877. [Belf PRO, will cal; Dub GRO (d); *Med Dir*].

ANDERSON, FORSTER (d c 1772), Cootehill, county Cavan;
son of Samuel Anderson, apothecary, of Cootehill (*q.v.*); apothecary, of Cootehill; married c March 1754 Margaret Adams (who married (2) Ralph Brunker of Drum, county Monaghan), daughter of Allen Adams; died c 1772; will dated 26 February 1771; probate Prerogative Court 1774. [IGRS Library, Swanzy MSS p 32, Exchequer Bill dated 3 July 1779; Vicars (1897)].

ANDERSON, FRANCIS (1813–98), Indian Medical Service;
born December 1813, probably in Ulster, son of Drummond Anderson; studied medicine at Edinburgh University; MRCS 1834; MD (Edin) 1837 (thesis 'De ischuria renalis'); joined the Indian Medical Service (Bengal establishment) as assistant surgeon 1837; surgeon 1850; surgeon major 1859; deputy inspector general 1861; served in Marwar Field Force 1839, First Sikh War 1845–6, and Mudki, Firuzshahr and Sobraon (medal with two clasps); retired 1866; married 6 October 1852 in Tullylish Church of Ireland Church, Helen Nicholson (who was born 1830/1 and died 30 August 1858 at Ferozepore, India), eldest daughter of Rawdon Nicholson of Stramore House and Loughans, Banbridge, county Down; died 10 February 1898 at 25 Lansdowne Crescent, Kensington, London. [*BNL* 11 October 1852 (m) and 20 October 1858 (d); Crawford (1930); Dub GRO (m); Edin Univ; Lond GRO (d); *Londonderry Sentinel* 15 October 1852 (m)].

ANDERSON, HENRY (*fl c* 1820), Belfast;
surgeon, of Belfast; married 22 May 1820 Elizabeth Mary Hyndman, daughter of Thomas Hyndman of Antigua, West Indies. [*BNL* 23 May 1820 (m)].

ANDERSON, HENRY (1856–c 1900), Sheffield, Yorkshire and Manchester, Lancashire;
born 5 February 1856 at Ahoghill, county Antrim, son of Joseph Anderson, linen merchant, of Ballymena; educated at RBAI; studied arts and medicine at Queen's College, Belfast, from 1874; BA (QUI) 1878; MA 1879; MD (RUI) 1884; general practitioner, of 647 Queen's Road, Sheffield, c 1885; of Thornton View, Clayton, Manchester c 1885–92 and of Veremont House, Ashton New Road, Manchester, from c 1892; died c 1900. [*Med Dir*; QCB adm reg].

ANDERSON, HENRY STEWART (1872–1961), Royal Army Medical Corps;
born 15 April 1872 at Lisburn, county Antrim, fourth son of the Rev Samuel Anderson, perpetual curate of Upper Falls, county Antrim, and Eliza Foley; educated at St Columba's College, Dublin; studied medicine at Queen's College, Belfast, from 1894; LRCP LRCS Edin 1898; LFPS Glas 1898; resident clinical assistant in Belfast Royal Hospital; joined the RAMC as lieutenant 1899; captain 1902; major 1911, lieutenant-colonel 1915; served in South Africa 1899–1902, India 1902–05, Malta 1905–09 (at the time of the Messina earthquake), BEF France 1914–15 (invalided), hospital ship *Britannic* 1915–16, Egypt 1917–21; commanding officer Citadel Military Hospital, Cairo, 1918; CMG 1918; retired 1924; of Scio House, Putney Heath, London SW15; married 1910 Cicely Mary Steele; died 24 May 1961 at Scio House, Roehampton; probate London 8 August 1961. [Belf GRO (b); *BMJ* obituary (1961); Drew (1968); Hunter (1923); Leslie (1993); Lond GRO (d); Lond PPR, will cal; *Med Dir*; QCB adm reg].

ANDERSON, HUGH (1821/2–66), Ballymoney, county Antrim;
born 1821/2; studied medicine at Glasgow University; LM Glas 1843; CM (Glas) 1845; general practitioner, of Ballymoney; unmarried but left an illegitimate daughter, Ann Anderson (or Cassidy), living with her mother in Carryreagh, county

Down; died 26 April 1866 at Linenhall Street, Ballymoney; probate Belfast 25 May 1866. [Addison (1898); Belf PRO, will cal; *Coleraine Chronicle* 5 May 1866 (d); Dub GRO (d); *Med Dir*].

ANDERSON, ISAAC HENRY (1848–1929), Belfast and Naval Medical Service;
born 27 June 1848 at 68 Joy Street, Belfast, son of James Anderson of Colin View House, Belfast; studied medicine at Queen's College, Belfast, from 1864; MD (QUI) 1869; LRCS Edin and LM 1871; resident clinical assistant and resident surgeon at Belfast General Hospital, 1869–70; lived first at Colin View House, Lisburn Road, Belfast; joined the Naval Medical Service 1871; staff surgeon 1883; fleet surgeon 1892; served on HMS *Salamis* in the Egyptian war of 1882 (medal and Khedive's bronze star); served at Suakin in 1884 and on HMS *Defiance* 1890; in charge of Simonstown Hospital in 1894; retired in 1902 as Deputy Inspector General to live at Roman Villa, Twyford, Hampshire; married Marcia Helena —; died 2 February 1929 at Roman Villa; probate London 22 April 1929. [*Belf Gen Hosp, Ann Rep*; *BMJ* obituary (1929); Kirkpatrick Archive; *Lancet* obituary (1929); Lond GRO (d); Lond PPR, will cal, will; *Med Dir*; QCB adm reg].

ANDERSON, JAMES (*fl c* 1819), Belfast;
physician, of Belfast; married 14 September 1819 in the Abbey of Luce, Scotland, Jane Learmont, daughter of the Rev William Learmont, minister of Old Luce. [Addison (1913); *BNL* 28 September 1819 (m)].

ANDERSON, JAMES (*fl c* 1833), Indian Medical Service;
born May 1809 in Belfast [?]; studied medicine at Edinburgh University; MD (Edin) 1828; MRCS 1831; joined the Indian Medical Service (Bengal establishment) as assistant surgeon 18 April 1833; surgeon 1848; surgeon major 1859; served in the SW Frontier, operations against the Kols 1832, in the 2nd Sikh or Punjab War 1848–9, also Ramnagar, Sadullapur, Chilianwala and Gujarat; retired 1866; married 12 November 1833 at Calcutta, Veronica Scott Hills, eldest daughter of A. Hills of Edinburgh; died in London 3 January 1891. [*BNL* 6 May 1834 (m); Crawford (1830)].

ANDERSON, JAMES FISHER (1850–1934), Belfast, Newtownards, county Down, and New South Wales, Tasmania and Victoria, Australia;
born December 1850 at Killylea, county Armagh, son of John Anderson of Killylea and Anne Fisher; educated at Armagh Royal School 1868–9; studied medicine at Queen's College, Belfast, from 1870; LRCP LRCS Edin 1874; LAH Dub 1877; resident surgeon in Belfast Royal Hospital 1874–6; general practitioner in Newtownards c 1876; emigrated to Australia c 1878; general practitioner in Coleraine, Victoria c 1879–85, in Lislooney, Cootomundra, New South Wales, c 1885–1895, in Longford, Tasmania, c 1895–1905, and in Woodend, Victoria c 1910; retired c 1923; died 24 May 1934 at Woodend, Victoria; commemorated in Lislooney Presbyterian Graveyard, Tynan. [*Belf Roy Hosp, Ann Rep*; Ferrar (1933); gravestone inscription; *Med Dir*; QCB adm reg].

ANDERSON, JOHN (1800/1–28), Monaghan;
 born 1800/1; LAH Dub 1822; apothecary and surgeon, of the Diamond, Monaghan c 1824; died 1 May 1828 in Monaghan; administration Clogher Diocesan Court 1828. [Apothecaries (1829); *BNL* 13 May 1828 (d); Dub Nat Arch, Clogher Dio Admins index; Pigot (1824)].

ANDERSON, JOHN (d 1838), Kingscourt, county Cavan;
 general practitioner, of Kingscourt; died 13 February 1838. [*BNL* 23 February 1838 (d)].

ANDERSON, JOHN ALBERT (1844–1910); Army Medical Service;
 born 24 June 1844, son of William Anderson of Cavan; educated at India Ville, Portarlington; studied medicine at Queen's College, Belfast, from 1861; MD (QUI) 1866; LRCSI 1866; joined the Army Medical Service 1867; served with 18th Hussars from 1868; surgeon-major 1879; retired as brigade-surgeon (lieutenant-colonel) 1887; employed on retired list at Shornecliff, Kent; lived finally at Dial House, Tunbridge Wells; married Clara Ellen —; died 9 May 1910 at Les Islettes, Parame, France; probate London 8 July 1910. [Lond PPR, will cal, will; *Med Dir*; Peterkin and Johnston (1968); QCB adm reg].

ANDERSON, JOSEPH (1858–c 1884), Naval Medical Service;
 born 6 September 1858 at Breen, county Tyrone, son of John Anderson, farmer, of Breen; educated at Londonderry Academy; studied medicine at Queen's College, Belfast, from 1876; MD Dip Mid (QUI) 1880; MCh 1881; joined the Naval Medical Service as surgeon 1881; died c 1884. [*Med Dir*; QCB adm reg]

ANDERSON, JOSEPH HERBERT (1865–1940), Armagh and London;
 born 17 September 1865 in Armagh, son of Joseph Anderson, merchant, of Greenhurst, Armagh; educated at the Armagh Royal School 1880–83; studied medicine at Queen's College, Belfast, from 1885; MB BCh BAO (RUI) 1890; LAH Dub 1891; general practitioner, of Seven Houses, Armagh c 1895; moved to London c 1900; of 46 Tuffnell Park Road, Holloway c 1907 and of 63 Cartwright Gardens, London, from c 1909; unmarried; died 5 November 1940 at the Homeopathic Hospital, London; administration Llandudno 30 June 1941. [Ferrar (1933); Lond PPR, will cal, letters of administration; *Med Dir*; QCB adm reg].

ANDERSON, MARMADUKE (1787/8–1824), Rathfriland, county Down;
 born 1787/8; surgeon and apothecary, of Rathfriland c 1819, 'a man endowed with great mental abilities and literary acquirements'; died 3 November 1824. [*BNL* 18 November 1824 (d); Bradshaw (1819); *Freeman's Weekly Journal* (1824); Kirkpatrick Archive; Pigot (1824)].

ANDERSON, RICHARD JOHN (1848–1914), Newry, county Down, Belfast and Galway;
 born 29 July 1848 at Ballybot (Newry), county Armagh, second son of Robert Anderson, pawnbroker, of Newry, and Elizabeth Harcourt; brother of Dr Robert Anderson of Newry (*q.v.*); educated at Newry; studied arts and medicine at Queen's

College, Belfast, from 1866, and London; BA (QUI) 1869; MA (gold medal, 1st class hons) 1870; MD (1st class hons and many prizes) 1872; MRCSE and LM 1872; medical officer to Newry No 2 Dispensary District from 1873 and registrar of births and deaths, of 3 Windsor Hill, Newry; assistant in Physiology and demonstrator in Anatomy, Queen's College, Belfast, c 1875, living at Connaught Terrace and 58 Wellington Park, Belfast; demonstrator and later lecturer at Queen's College, Galway 1875–83; professor of Natural History, Mineralogy and Geology at Galway from 1883; JP; author of *Some Aspects of Mimicry* (1897), *Heredity* (1898) and *Flora of Connaught* (1905) as well as many papers on zoology; married 23 September 1889 at Fortwilliam Park Presbyterian Church, Belfast, Hannah Perry, BA (an early woman graduate), daughter of Samuel Perry, decorative painter; she was a founder of the Connaught Women's Suffrage League in 1913, trained as a doctor in Galway after his death, graduating MB BCh BAO (NUI) 1918 and practised in London for 20 years; died 24 July 1914; buried in St Patrick's graveyard, Newry; administration Dublin 5 August 1915. [Belf PRO, will cal; *DIB* (2009); Dub GRO (m); gravestone inscription; Kirkpatrick Archive; *Med Dir*; QCB adm reg; Young and Pike (1909)].

ANDERSON, ROBERT (d c 1782), *Stag*, privateer;
surgeon on the *Stag*, privateer; died c 1782; administration Armagh Diocesan Court 1782. [Dub Nat Arch, Armagh Dio Admins index].

ANDERSON, ROBERT (1855–83), Newry, county Down;
born 1855 in Newry, son of Robert Anderson, pawnbroker, of Newry, and Elizabeth Harcourt; brother of Professor Dr Richard John Anderson of Belfast and Galway (*q.v.*); educated at Newry School; studied medicine at Queen's College, Belfast from 1876, and Jervis Street Hospital, Dublin; LRCP Edin 1880; MD (QUI) 1881; general practitioner, of 10 Sandys Street, Newry; unmarried; died 26 May 1883 at 10 Sandys Street. [Dub GRO (d); *Med Dir*; QCB adm reg].

ANDERSON, SAMUEL (d c 1756), Cootehill, county Cavan;
apothecary, of Cootehill; married Jane —; father of Forster Anderson, apothecary, of Cootehill (*q.v.*); died c 1756; probate Prerogative Court 1758. [IGRS Library, Swanzy MSS p 32, Exchequer Bill dated 3 July 1779; Vicars (1897)].

ANDERSON, WILLIAM (*fl c* 1805), Belfast;
druggist and apothecary, of 47 and 86 High Street, Belfast. [*Belfast Street Directories* (1807) and (1808)].

ANDERSON, WILLIAM (*fl c* 1824), Curragh, county Londonderry;
LAH Dub 1824; apothecary, of Curragh. [Apothecaries (1829)].

ANDERSON, WILLIAM WALLACE (1843–91), Milford, county Donegal, Newtownhamilton, county Armagh, and Glasgow;
born 16 January 1843 at Saintfield, county Down, son of Samuel Anderson, farmer, of Lisdoonan, Saintfield, and Mary —; educated at the Belfast Seminary; studied arts and medicine at Queen's College, Belfast, from 1861 and at Belfast General Hospital; MD (QUI) 1867; LRCS Edin and LM 1867; medical officer to Milford

Workhouse and Fever Hospital, Milford and Kilmacrenan Dispensary District, constabulary and coastguards; medical officer for Newhamilton Dispensary District and Bridewell, c 1875–86 and registrar of births and deaths; of 7 Whitehill Terrace, Dennistoun, 470 Gallowgate Street, and 48 Duke Street, Glasgow 1886–91; author of various medical papers; married 28 November 1871 in Regent Street Reformed Presbyterian Church, Newtownards, Sarah M. Graham, daughter of Hugh Graham, gentleman; died 1 July 1891 in Glasgow; probate Glasgow 6 October 1891 and Dublin 17 December 1891. [Belf PRO, will cal; *Med Dir*; QCB adm reg; UHF database (m)].

ANDREWS, ALEXANDER (d before 1849), Naval Medical Service;
of Belfast; joined the Naval Medical Service as assistant surgeon; married —; father of Jane Andrews who married 7 August 1848 Dr Cunningham Mulholland (*q.v.*); died before 1849. [*BNL* 18 August 1848 (m, daughter)].

ANDREWS, J.K. (*fl c* 1855), Larne, county Antrim;
MB [?]; of Larne; married —; son born 12 December 1855. [*BNL* 21 December 1855 (b)].

ANDREWS, THOMAS (*fl c* 1845), Buncrana, county Donegal;
LRCSI; accoucheur of the Victoria Lying-In Hospital, Dublin; medical officer to Buncrana Dispensary District, c 1845; possibly died c 1850. [Croly (1843–6)].

ANDREWS, THOMAS (1813–85), Belfast;
born 19 December 1813 at 3 Donegall Square South, Belfast, eldest son of Thomas John Andrews, linen merchant, of Belfast and Elizabeth R. Stevenson; educated at RBAI from 1826–8 and worked for a time in his father's business; studied chemistry in Glasgow and Paris (in the laboratory of Prof Dumas), and medicine in Trinity College, Dublin, and Edinburgh; MD (Edin) 1835 (thesis 'On the circulation and the properties of the blood'); LRCS Edin 1835; MRIA 1839; FRS 1849; FRS Edin 1870; LLD (Edin) (*hon causa*) 1871, of TCD 1873 and of Glas 1877; DSc (QUI) 1879; professor of chemistry, RBAI 1835–45; attending physician to Belfast General Hospital and medical officer to the Belfast Union Infirmary 1838–46; consulting physician 1846–85; during the famine of 1846–7 laboured among patients with typhus; vice-president Queen's College, Belfast 1845–79; professor of chemistry, Queen's College, Belfast 1849–79; president of Belfast Literary Society 1866–7; president of the British Association for the Advancement of Science 1876; of Lennoxvale, Malone Road 1849–85; retired 1879 and was commemorated at Queen's College by the Andrews Studentship; author of *Suggestions for Checking the Hurtful Use of Alcoholic Beverages by the Working Classes* (1867), *The Church in Ireland* (1869) (advocating its disestablishment), various memoirs on the *Heat of Combination* and many other scientific papers; married 18 September 1842 Jane Hardie Walker, only daughter of Major Walker of the 42nd Highlanders; father of Mary Katherine Andrews (1851/2–1914), a prominent geologist in Belfast; died 26 November 1885; buried in Belfast City Cemetery, Falls Road, with a granite obelisk memorial; portrait by Richard Hooke in Queen's University, Belfast, and terracotta head in the Whitla Medical Building; probate Belfast 6 January 1886. [Addison (1898); *Belf Lit Soc* (1901); *BNL*

(23 September 1842) (m); Belf PRO, will cal; Biggart (1949); Black (1995); Burke *LGI* (1958); Burtchaell and Sadleit (1924); Coakley (1992); Craig (1985); Croly (1843–6); Crone (1928); *DIB* (2009); Edin Univ; Hartley (2006), p 147; *Lancet* obituary (1885); *Med Dir*; Martin (2003); Moody and Beckett (1959); Newmann (1993); *Oxford DNB* (2004); Tait and Crum Brown (1889); Whitla (1901)].

ANNESLEY, JAMES FERGUSON ST. JOHN (1864–1917), Liverpool, Lancashire, Derrylin, county Fermanagh, and RAMC;
 born 24 June 1864 at Newforge, Malone, county Antrim, second son of the Rev James Blair Annesley, Rector of Drumkeeran, county Fermanagh, and Canon of Clogher, and Elizabeth Fergusson; educated at Armagh Royal School 1876–81; studied medicine at Queen's College, Belfast, from 1881; MD MCh MAO (RUI) 1888; surgeon to Liverpool Corporation Waterworks; medical officer and medical officer of health to Derrylin Dispensary District and constabulary; joined RAMC 1916; captain 1917; married Geraldine Clara —; died 19 May 1917 as a result of a flying accident in Norfolk (coroner); probate London 24 September 1917. [*BMJ* obituary (1917); Dub GRO (b); Ferrar (1933); Kirkpatrick Archive; Leslie (1929); Lond GRO (d); Lond PPR, will cal; *Med Dir*; QCB adm reg].

ANNESLEY, SIR JAMES H. (c 1774–1847), Indian Medical Service;
 born c 1774 in county Down, son of the Hon Marcus Annesley; studied medicine at Trinity College, Dublin, and the Royal College of Surgeons in Ireland; MRCSE 1795; FRCSE 1843; joined the Indian Medical Service (Madras establishment) 1799 and arrived in India 1800; invalided home 1805; returned in 1807 as garrison surgeon at Masulipatam; in charge of 78th Regiment during the Java Expedition of 1811 and commanded the field hospital at Cornalis; served with Madras European Regiment 1812–17; superintending surgeon to the advanced divisions of the army during the last Mahratta and Penderee War 1817–18; garrison surgeon at Fort St George 1818–24; returned home 1824 and was presented with a piece of plate valued at 100 guineas for services at the Madras Roads in 1823; author of *Sketches of the most prevalent Diseases of India*, 2 vols (1825); returned to India in 1829 and produced a twelve-volume *Report on Diseases of India*; appointed to the Medical Board in 1833 and later president; retired home in 1838; Knight Bachelor 1844; FSA 1844; lived latterly at 6 Albany, Piccadilly, London; died 14 December 1847 at Florence. [Balfour (1923); *BNL* 18 January 1848 (d); Crawford (1930); Plarr (1930)].

APSLEY, ROBERT (1738/9–1806), Naval Medical Service and Belfast;
 born 1738/9; joined the Naval Medical Service as assistant surgeon; served on HMS *Hind* c 1765–75, which captured a Spanish galleon filled with a valuable cargo c 1773; made freeman of Belfast 1767; general practitioner in Belfast from c 1775; physician to the Belfast Charitable Institute 1774–7 and probably later; 'seldom heard of but supported mostly by his private fortune' in 1788 (Martha McTier); medical attendant at the Belfast Lying-in Hospital in 1794; physician to the Belfast Dispensary 1794; married Ann McCleverty of the Glynn (who was born 1746/7 and died 8 June 1785); died 28 June 1806, described then as 'one of the oldest surgeons in the Royal Navy' (*BNL*); buried in Knockbreda graveyard. [Agnew (1998); *BNL* 1 July 1806 (d); Benn, vol 2 (1880); Chart (1931); Clarke, *County Down,* vol 2

(1988); Kirkpatrick Archive; McKillop (2000); Malcolm (1851); *Memorials of the Dead*, vol XI, p 148; Strain (1961); Young (1892)].

ARBUCKLE, JAMES (c 1700–46/7), Dublin;
born c 1700, probably in county Down (or Glasgow); studied arts and medicine in Glasgow and from 1721 in Leyden; MA (Glas) 1720 [?]; MD (Glas) 1724 [?]; LKQCPI 1729; physician in Dublin and often confused with a namesake who was a poet and essayist (see Kirkpatrick); married Eleanor Wilson, daughter of Francis Wilson of Dublin and Longford, and Jane Johnston; died 1746/7; will dated 18 December 1746 proved in Prerogative Court 11 August 1747. [Belf PRO T 403/1 and T 403/76; Crone (1928); Eustace, vol 1 (1956); Kirkpatrick Archive; Newmann (1993); Innes Smith (1932); Vicars (1897)].

ARCHDALL, GORDON (d 1876), Fivemiletown, county Fermanagh, Bundoran, county Donegal, London and Queensland, Australia;
son of Robert Archdall of Archdall Lodge, county Donegal; LKQCPI and LM 1866; MRCSE 1866; medical officer of Fivemiletown Dispensary District, of Archdall Lodge, Bundoran; later medical registrar in the London Hospital, of 10 Bolton Row, Mayfair; emigrated to Australia c 1874; married Auguste —; died 28 January 1876 at Maryborough, Queensland; probate London 20 November 1877 and Dublin 3 April 1882. [Belf PRO, will cal, will; Lond PPR, will cal; *Med Reg*].

ARCHDALL, HENRY MERVYN GRAY (1840–88), Indian Medical Service;
born 1 December 1840, eldest son of Henry Gray Archdall, JP, of Brookville, county Fermanagh; LRCP Edin 1863; LRCSI 1863; of Upper Leeson Street, Dublin; joined the Indian Medical Service (Madras establishment) 1868; surgeon 1873; surgeon major 1880; married 13 June 1867 in St Stephen's Green Church of Ireland Church, Dublin, Lilly Victoria Betty, eldest daughter of Stewart Betty of Enniskillen, and Elizabeth Welsh; died 21 September 1888 at Madras. [Crawford (1930); Leslie (1940); *Londonderry Sentinel* 18 June 1867 (m); *Med Dir*].

ARCHDALL, THOMAS GRAY (1843–78), Army Medical Service, Dublin and New South Wales, Australia;
born 9 January 1843 in county Fermanagh; LRCP and LM LRCS Edin 1865; joined the Army Medical Service as staff assistant surgeon 1866; resigned 1868; of 69 Upper Leeson Street, Dublin c 1869–74 and of 6 Haigh Terrace, Kingstown c 1875; emigrated to Murrumburragh c 1875; died 21 October 1878 at Murrumburragh; probate Dublin 31 January 1880. [Belf PRO, will cal; *Med Dir*; Peterkin and Johnston (1968)].

ARCHER, FRANCIS (1803–75), Belfast and Liverpool, Lancashire;
born 23 April 1803, son of Samuel Archer, bookseller, of 37 High Street, Belfast; educated at RBAI 1818–20, including studying anatomy; MRCSE 1825; a founder member of the BNHPS in 1821; moved to Liverpool as general practitioner and surgeon to Kirkdale Gaol c 1830; president of the Liverpool Natural History Society in 1838; of 49 Rodney Street, Liverpool c 1870 and later of Little Crosley Road; married Frances Fletcher, daughter of Joseph Fletcher of Liverpool; died 5 April 1875

in Liverpool; probate Liverpool 22 April 1875. [Deane (1921); Lond PPR, will cal; *Med Dir*; Newmann (1993)].

ARCHER, JONATHAN (d 1840), Crumlin, county Antrim;
surgeon, of Crumlin; died 9 May 1840 after only about a months work 'of a fever contracted by too great a devotedness to the interests of his patients'; buried in the family burying ground at Hillsborough. [*BNL* 15 May 1840 (d)].

ARCHER, THOMAS (1855–1935), Army Medical Service;
born 21 December 1855 at Caledon, county Tyrone, son of John Archer of Caledon; educated at RBAI; studied medicine at Queen's College, Belfast, 1872–6; MD MCh Dip Mid (QUI) 1876; joined the Army Medical Service as surgeon captain 1881; surgeon major 1893; served in the Sudan 1898 and South Africa 1899–1902; lieutenant-colonel 1901; retired 1904, employed part-time at Lydd, Kent; served in RAMC during World War I; married —; died 15 February 1935 at Lydd; probate London 11 March 1935. [*BMJ* obituary (1935); Kirkpatrick Archive; Lond PPR, will cal; *Med Dir*; Peterkin and Johnston (1968); QCB adm reg].

ARDAGH, ARTHUR (1810/11–61), Rathmullan, county Donegal and Belfast;
born 1810/1, son of the Rev Arthur Ardagh, vicar of Moyglare, county Meath; MRCSE 1837; medical officer to Verner's Bridge Dispensary District c 1846; general practitioner, of Rathmullan; of 7 Lower Crescent, Belfast, from c 1860; married 6 August 1833 Charlotte Mary Morris, eldest daughter of Captain John Reid Morris, RN; died 28 April 1861 at 7 Lower Crescent; buried in Dundonald Parish Graveyard; probate Dublin 13 June 1861. [*BNL* 16 August 1833 (m); Belf PRO, will cal; Clarke, *County Down*, vol 2, (2nd ed 1988); Croly (1843–6); *Londonderry Sentinel* 3 May 1861 (d); *Med Dir*].

ARMSTRONG, SIR ALEXANDER (1818–99), Naval Medical Service;
born in 1818 in Craghan, county Fermanagh, son of Alexander Armstrong of Craghan Lodge; studied medicine at Trinity College, Dublin, and Edinburgh University; MD (Edin) (hons) 1841 (thesis 'On the diagnosis of the diseases of the heart, lungs and their investing membranes'); LRCS Edin 1841; MRCP and FRCP Lond 1860; joined the Naval Medical Service as assistant surgeon 1842, working at Haslar; appointed to HMS *Polyphemus* 1842; in medical charge of a party landed in Turkey for the exploration of Xanthus 1843, and for his scientific observations he received the thanks of the trustees of the British Museum and for his sanitary arrangement won the approval of the commander in chief; appointed to the royal yacht in 1846; surgeon 1849; surgeon and naturalist to the arctic expedition under Sir Robert John Le Mesurier McClure on HMS *Investigator* 1849–54, in search of Sir John Franklin and Francis Crozier of Banbridge, and was very successful in the prevention of scurvy on the voyage; author of *Personal Narrative of the Discovery of the North-West Passage* (1857), for which he was awarded the Gilbert Blane gold medal, and *Observations on Naval Hygiene* (1858); served in the Crimean War in 1854–5 and in the Baltic and North America field 1855–6; deputy inspector-general of hospitals and fleets at Malta 1858; in medical charge of a hospital in Malta 1859–64; inspector general 1866; director general of the medical department of the Navy

1869–71, living in the Albany or at 'The Elms', Sutton-Bonnington near Kegworth; retired 1871; military KCB 1871; FRS 1873; JP for Middlesex; honorary physician to the Queen; married 16 August 1894 in St James's Parish Church, Westminster, Charlotte King-Hall, widow of Sir William King-Hall and daughter of Samuel Campbell Simpson; died 4 July 1899 at 'The Elms'; probate Nottingham 14 August 1899; portrait in Haslar Hospital, Gosport. [*BMJ* obituary (1899); Crone (1928); *DIB* (2009); Edin Univ; Ireland (1988); *Lancet* obituary (1899); Lond GRO ((m) and (d); Lond PPR, will cal; Martin (2010); *Med Dir*; *Munk's Roll*, vol 4; Newmann (1993); Nugent (2003); *Oxford DNB* (2004)].

ARMSTRONG, JAMES (1815/6–70), Armagh;
born 1815/6; studied medicine in Dublin and St Andrews; LAH Dublin 1841; MRCSE 1842; MD (St Andrew's) 1861 (by examination); apothecary to the Armagh County Infirmary, County Gaol and District Lunatic Asylum, of English Street, Armagh; unmarried; died 29 May 1870 at English Street; probate Armagh 17 June 1870. [Belf PRO, will cal; Croly (1843–6); Dub GRO (d); *Med Dir*; Smart (2004)].

ARMSTRONG, JAMES JEKELL (1829–c 1857), Army Medical Service;
born 13 July 1829 at Belturbet, county Cavan; joined the Army Medical Service as assistant surgeon to the 2nd Dragoon Guards 1852; resigned 1855; died c 1857. [Peterkin and Johnston (1968)].

ARMSTRONG, JOHN (*fl c* 1824), Clones, county Monaghan;
studied medicine at Edinburgh University; MD (Edin) 1820 (thesis 'De haematemesi'); surgeon, of the Diamond, Clones c 1824. [Edin Univ; Pigot (1824)].

ARMSTRONG, JOHN (1845/6–82), Irvinestown, county Fermanagh;
born 1845/6; studied medicine at the Ledwich School, Dublin; LRCSI 1867; LKQCPI and LM 1869; medical officer to Irvinestown No 2 Dispensary District and constabulary; general practitioner, of Trillick, county Tyrone; married —; died 23 May 1882 in Trillick. [Dub GRO (d); *Med Dir*].

ARMSTRONG, JOHN STREAN (1817–71), Belfast, Shorncliffe, and Newtownards, county Down;
born 1817, son of James Armstrong, merchant, of Belfast; LM Belfast 1846; MRCSE 1849; LKQCPI and LM 1860; apothecary to Belfast General Dispensary 1845–6; medical officer to the General Dispensary and assistant surgeon to the Ophthalmic Institute, Belfast; of Clarendon Place, Belfast c 1855; medical officer to the Female Hospital, Aldershot Camp and Shorncliffe Hospital; physician and surgeon to the Newtownards Ophthalmic Institute, medical inspector of recruits, surgeon to the Royal North Down Militia and general practitioner, of Brooklands and Francis Street, Newtownards, from c 1856; married 19 October 1852 in Drumbo Church of Ireland Church, Margaret Thompson (who was born 1828/9), fourth daughter of John Thompson, engraver, of Ballylesson, county Down; died 1 February 1871 at Newtownards; administration Belfast 29 March 1871. [*BNL* 25 October 1852 (m), 23 April 1855 (b) and 9 September 1857 (b); Belf PRO, will cal; Dub GRO (d); *Med Dir*; UHF database (m)].

ARMSTRONG, JOSEPH (*fl c* 1842), Kingscourt, county Cavan;
MD [?]; general practitioner, of Kingscourt; not in *Medical Directory* or *Medical Register;* married 8 February 1842 in her father's house, Elizabeth Williamson, eldest daughter of John Williamson, merchant, of Bailieborough, county Cavan; possibly died c 1850. [*BNL* 15 February 1842 (m)].

ARMSTRONG, MEREDITH (1797/8–1866), Armagh;
born 1797/8; LAH Dub 1823; LRCS Edin 1824; general practitioner in Armagh, apothecary to the county gaol and medical attendant to the constabulary; unmarried; died 12 October 1866 at Beresford Row, Armagh; probate Armagh 31 October 1866. [Apothecaries (1829); Belf PRO, will cal; Croly (1843–6); Dub GRO (d); *Med Dir*].

ARMSTRONG, ROBERT YOUNG (*fl c* 1796), Cavan;
certified by the Board of Surgeons (Surgeon-General and surgeons from Steeven's and Mercer's Hospitals) in 1796, surgeon in Cavan County Infirmary. [Fleetwood (1983); Geary (2002)].

ARMSTRONG, THOMAS (1767/8–1840), Clones, county Monaghan;
born 1767/8; surgeon, of the Diamond, Clones from c 1795; 'a highly respectable medical practitioner and a member of the Primitive Wesleyan Society' (*Londonderry Sentinel*); married Anne — (who was born 1768 and died 11 January 1844 in Clones); died 20 November 1840. [*BNL* 27 November 1840 (d) and 16 January 1844 (d); *Londonderry Sentinel* 28 November 1840 (d) and 20 January 1844 (d); Pigot (1824)].

ARMSTRONG, WILLIAM (d 1833), Naval Medical Service and Brookeborough, county Fermanagh;
son of a postmaster in Brookeborough; joined the Naval Medical Service as assistant surgeon on HMS *Marlborough*; surgeon 1815; retired as general practitioner in Brookeborough; poet; letters presented in PRONI; married 1 March 1822 in Aghavea Church of Ireland Church, Eliann Glen of Maguiresbridge, county Fermanagh; died 8 October 1833 at Lisnaskea. [*BNL* 22 October 1833 (d); Belf PRO, T679/83; Johnston, J., pers com; *Londonderry Sentinel* 19 October 1833 (d); *NMS* (1826)].

ARMSTRONG, WILLIAM (d 1860), Muff, county Donegal, Culmore, county Londonderry, and Collooney, county Sligo;
eldest son of William Armstrong, surgeon, of Sligo [?]; LRCSI 1817; MD (Edin) 1826 (thesis 'De febre puerperali'); LM Rot Hosp Dub; physician of Foyle Street, Londonderry c 1838–40; medical officer to Muff Dispensary District and constabulary, of Culmore, county Londonderry, c 1845; later medical officer to Collooney Dispensary District; married 14 November 1829 in Aghavea Church of Ireland Church, county Fermanagh, Frances Haire, daughter of Hamilton Haire of Glasdrumman [where ?]; died 15 August 1860 at his home in Collooney. [*BNL* 20 November 1829 (m), 20 January 1832 (b), 15 January 1833 (b), 19 October 1838 (b) and 20 March 1840 (b) and 21 August 1860 (d); Croly (1843–6); Edin Univ; Kirkpatrick Archive; *Londonderry Sentinel* 21 November 1829 (m); *Med Dir*].

ARMSTRONG, WILLIAM (d c 1857), Lisburn, county Antrim, and Stroud, Gloucestershire;
son of the Rev William Armstrong, Methodist minister; LM Glas 1837; MRCSE 1839; surgeon, earlier from Lisburn; of Stroud c 1843; married 17 March 1843 in Stroud Parish Church, Gloucestershire, Mary Ann Stevens, eldest daughter of the Rev J. Stevens, Methodist minister; died c 1857. [*BNL* 28 March 1843 (m); Lond GRO (m); *Med Dir*].

ARMSTRONG, WILLIAM CRAWFORD (1837/8–1901), Stewartstown, county Tyrone;
born 1837/8 at Portstewart, county Antrim; apprentice 1850–54; studied medicine at Edinburgh University 1854–61 and Royal College of Surgeons, Edinburgh; MD (Edin) 1861 (thesis 'On the symptoms and treatment of cholera'); LRCS and LM Edin 1861; general practitioner, of Arnie Hill, Stewartstown; unmarried; died 8 March 1901 at Brackavilla, Coalisland; probate Armagh 31 May 1901. [Belf PRO, will cal; Dub GRO (d); Edin Univ; *Med Dir*].

ARMSTRONG, WILLIAM LEWIS (1872–1928), Belfast, Hartlepool, county Durham, and Garstang, Lancashire;
born 30 May 1872 at Clanickny, county Monaghan, son of Thomas Armstrong, gentleman, of Louisville, Alexandra Park, Belfast; educated at Belfast Mercantile Academy; studied arts and medicine at Queen's College, Belfast, from 1890; MB BCh BAO (RUI) 1898; clinical assistant to Samaritan Hospital, Belfast; house surgeon to Hartlepool Hospital; general practitioner, of West End House, Great Eccleston, Garstang, c 1910; married Mary Jane —; died 16 August 1928; administration London 13 November 1928. [Lond PPR, will cal; *Med Dir*; QCB adm reg].

ARMSTRONG, — (d 1835), Gortin and Sixmilecross, county Tyrone;
son of Matthew Armstrong of Gortin; surgeon; died 2 January 1835 'in consequence of his horse falling on the frost, while riding near Sixmilecross'. [*BNL* 13 January 1835 (d); *Londonderry Sentinel* 10 January 1835 (d)].

ARNOLD, HOWARD (1848–92), Yardley-Hastings, Northamptonshire, and Liverpool, Lancashire;
born 6 October 1848 in Belfast, son of John Arnold of 10 Lower Crescent, Belfast; educated at RBAI; studied medicine at Queen's College, Belfast 1866–72; LRCP LRCS and LM Edin 1872; surgeon to Cunard and other steamship companies; general practitoner of Yardley-Hastings, c 1878 and then of 109 Park Road, Liverpool c 1881; died 13 February 1892 at 109 Park Road, having 'poisoned himself with prussic acid whilst labouring under temporary insanity' (Coroner's verdict). [Lond GRO (d); *Med Dir*; QCB adm reg].

ARNOLD, HUGH (d 1870), Ballynahinch, county Down;
son of John Arnold of Bellfield House, Spa, county Down, and Sarah —; CM and LM (Glas) 1825; LAH Dub 1827; surgeon and apothecary, of Ballynahinch; married 10 September 1827 Elizabeth Bailie, eldest daughter of William Bailie, merchant, of

Ballynahinch; died 4 January 1870 at Ballynahinch; buried in Magheradrool graveyard; probate Belfast 15 February 1870. [Addison (1898); Apothecaries (1829); *BNL* 14 September 1827 (m) and 19 January 1852 (d, mother); Belf PRO, will cal; Clarke, *County Down*, vol 9 (1972); *Med Dir*].

ARNOLD, ISAAC (1784/5–1831), Newtownards, county Down;
born 1784/5; surgeon and apothecary, of Movilla, Newtownards c 1824; married Agnes — (who was born 1780/1 and died 14 January 1853 at her son's home in Liverpool); father of James Arnold, surgeon, of Liverpool (*q.v.*); died 12 October 1831 at Movilla 'after a long and severe illness which he bore with truly Christian patience and resignation …'; buried in Movilla graveyard, Newtownards. [*BNL* 18 October 1831 (d) and 21 January 1853 (d); Clarke, *County Down*, vol 11 (1974); Pigot (1824)].

ARNOLD, JAMES (1819–66), Liverpool, Lancashire;
born 1819; educated in Belfast; studied medicine at Edinburgh University; MRCSE 1841; FRCSE 1861; surgeon, of Abercromby Square and later of 1 Rosevale, Great Homer Street, Liverpool; died 10 March 1866 at 1 Rosevale; probate Liverpool 8 August 1866. [Lond PPR, will cal; Plarr (1930)].

ARNOLD, WILBERFORCE (1838–91), Belfast;
born 12 February 1838, son of John Arnold of 45 High Street, and 19 Clarendon Place, Belfast, and Susanna —; educated at RBAI; studied medicine at Queen's College, Belfast, from 1855; MRCSE 1858; LKQCPI 1860; resident medical officer to Belfast Hospital for Contagious and Acute Medical Diseases; honorary physician to Rescue House, Belfast, and to the students, Presbyterian College, Belfast; general practitioner, of 19 Clarendon Place, Belfast from 1858 and of Crescent House, University Road, Belfast c 1872–91; moving force for founding the Presbyterian Orphan Society in 1866; JP; author of various books and papers; married Grace Jane Steven; father of Dr Wilberforce John James Arnold (*q.v.*); died 23 March 1891 at Crescent House; buried in Balmoral Cemetery, Belfast; probate Belfast 13 May 1891. [Belf PRO, will cal; Clarke, *Belfast*, vol 3 (1986); Dewar (1900); Dub GRO (d); *Med Dir*; QCB adm reg; *The Witness*].

ARNOLD, WILBERFORCE JOHN JAMES (1867–1925), Belfast and St Helena;
born 22 April 1867 at 19 Fountainvale Terrace, Belfast, eldest son of Dr Wilberforce Arnold J.P. (*q.v.*) and Grace Jane Steven; educated at Methodist College, Belfast, 1878–84; studied arts and medicine at Queen's College, Belfast, from 1884; BA (hons) (RUI) 1887; MB BCh BAO 1894; DPH (Oxon) 1913; resident medical officer at the Cottage Hospital, Aberdare, South Wales; civil surgeon with the RAMC during the Boer War 1899–1903, in St Helena; colonial surgeon to St Helena 1903–25; major RAMC during World War I 1914–20; member of Executive Council of St Helena and acting governor; CMG 1925; died 29 January 1925; buried in St Paul's Cathedral Churchyard, St Helena; probate London 4 May 1926. [*BMJ* obituary (1925); Dub GRO (b); Fry (1984); Kirkpatrick Archive; Lond PPR, will cal; *Med Dir*; QCB adm reg; Royle (1990); Royle and Cross (1995)].

ARROTT, DAVID (1798/9–1823), Belfast;
born 1798/9, son of Dr Samuel Arrott of Belfast, (*q.v.*); surgeon, of Belfast; died August 1823 after a short illness, of erysipelas in the face. [*BNL* 26 August 1823 (d)].

ARROT(T), SAMUEL (1776/7–1844), Comber, county Down, and Belfast;
born 1776/7, son of the Rev. David Arrott, minister of Markethill Presbyterian Church (antiburgher) and — Patton; LAH Dub 1796; apothecary and surgeon, of Comber 1798, and of 8 High Street, Belfast, 1819, and 41 Lower Chichester Street; name appears frequently as collector for the hospital (1820); guarantor for the housekeeper (1822) and surgeon in charge of No 6 Dispensary District (1822–31); one of the doctors who presented an insribed gold box to Dr S.S. Thomson in 1834; married 3 February 1798 Jane Beggs (who was born 1768/9 and died 28 July 1833), daughter of the Rev James Beggs of Belfast; father of Dr David Arrott (*q.v.*), of Elizabeth Arrott who married 28 February 1826 the Rev James Seaton Reid, distinguished Presbyterian historian, and of Jane Arrott who married 13 October 1835 the Rev George Bellis; died 5 January 1844. [Allen (1951); Apothecaries (1829); *Belfast Fever Hospital, Minutes, Annual Reports*; *BNL* 5 February 1798 (m), 26 August 1823 (d, son), 2 August 1833 (d), 16 October 1835 (m) and 9 January 1844 (d); *Belfast Street Directories*; Malcolm (1851); Pigot (1824); Stewart (1950); Thomson presentation box (1834)].

ARTHURE, THOMAS (d 1822), Newry, county Down;
second son of Benedict Arthure of Seafield, county Dublin; studied medicine at Edinburgh University; MD (Edin) 1804 (thesis 'De pneumonia'); physician, of Newry; married May 1808 in the house of Robert Hutcheson of Dorset Street, Dublin, Frances Anne Armstrong, daughter of Francis Armstrong of Dublin; died 22 March 1822 (according to a great-grandson, as noted in the Edinburgh University card-index). [*BNL* 10 May 1808 (m); Edin Univ; Farrar (1897)].

ARTHURS, JOHN (1824/5–55), Ballymena, county Antrim;
born 1824/5; MD [?]; surgeon and medical officer to Ballymena Dispensary District; died 11 August 1855 in Ballymena, after a brief illness. [*BNL* 15 August 1855 (d); *Coleraine Chronicle* 18 August 1855 (d); *Londonderry Sentinel* 24 August 1855 (d); *Med Dir*].

ASHE, ISAAC (1834–91), Warrenpoint, county Down, Letterkenny, county Donegal and Dundrum, county Dublin;
born 29 November 1834 in county Dublin, eldest son of the Rev Isaac Ashe, rector of Baronstown and of Kildress, county Armagh, and Jane Ellis; studied arts and medicine at Trinity College, Dublin, from 1852 and at the Richmond Hospital; BA (TCD) 1860; LM Rot Hosp Dub 1861; MB and MCh (with prizes and exhibitions) 1862; MD 1874; LKQCPI and LM 1878; FKQCPI 1880; resident medical officer in the Richmond and Dublin Hospitals; medical officer to Warrenpoint Dispensary District; medical officer to Letterkenny Fever Hospital, Dispensary District and constabulary; visiting physician and later resident medical superintendant to Donegal County Lunatic Asylum; living c 1871 at Sprackburn House, Letterkenny but in 1875 at 3 Bayview Terrace, Londonderry; medical officer to the State Lunatic

Asylum, Dundrum, county Dublin by 1886; married Sarah Gore, daughter of Henry Gore; died 19 November 1891 at the Asylum; buried in Mount Jerome Cemetery, Dublin; probate Dublin 8 December 1891. [Belf PRO, will cal; Burtchaell and Sadleir (1935); Dub GRO (d); Fleming (2001); *Lancet* obituary (1891); Leslie (1911); *Med Dir*].

ASKIN, THOMAS CUMING (1864–1933), Liverpool, Lancashire, Huntington and Alderton, Suffolk;

born 11 March 1864 in Rathmines, son the Rev William Booker Askin, rector of Harold's Cross, Dublin, and Elizabeth Cuming of Armagh, daughter of Dr Thomas Cuming (*q.v.*); educated at Armagh Royal School 1876–82; captain of first XI and XV in 1882; studied arts and medicine at Trinity College, Dublin 1882–9; BA (TCD) 1886; MB MD 1889; assistant master to the National Lying-in Hospital, Dublin; house physician to Northern Hospital, Liverpool; house surgeon to the County Hospital, Huntingdon; medical officer to 1st and 2nd District Woodbridge Union; general practitioner in Alderton, Suffolk, 1892–1926; admiralty surgeon and agent; medical officer to Warner's Almshouse; MBE c 1919; retired 1926 to 17 Overstrand Mansions, Battersea Park, London; married Nellie Maud —; died 18 May 1933 at the Knaresborough Nursing Home, Knaresborough Place, Earls Court, London; probate London 31 July 1933. [*BMJ* obituary (1933); Ferrar (1933); Fleming (2001); Kirkpatrick Archive; Leslie and Wallace (2001); Lond PPR, will cal; *Med Dir*; TCD adm reg; *TCD Cat,* vol II (1896); *TCD Register* (1933)].

ASTON, DAVID (b 1796/7);

born 1796/7 at Armagh, son of John Aston, apothecary (*q.v.*); educated by Mr Staunton; studied arts and medicine at Trinity College, Dublin, from 1813; BA (TCD) 1818; MA MB 1824. [Burtchaell and Sadleir (1924)].

ASTON, JOHN (*fl c* 1792), Richhill, county Armagh;

LAH Dub 1792; apothecary, of Richhill; married —; father of Dr David Aston (*q.v.*). [Apothecaries (1829); Burtchaell and Sadleir (1924)].

ATKIN, JAMES (1815/6–94), Ballyjamesduff, county Cavan, and Oldcastle, county Meath;

born 1815/6; brother of Dr John Myers Atkin of Virginia (*q.v.*); LAH Dub 1840; MRCSE 1841; LM Coombe Hosp Dub; LKQCPI and LM 1860; general practitioner in Ballyjamesduff c 1845; medical officer to the Cholera Hospital 1849; of Oldcastle c 1858; medical officer to the 40th Regiment from c 1870; married —; died 10 December 1894 at Oldcastle; administration Dublin 29 January 1895. [Belf PRO, will cal; Croly (1843–6); Dub GRO (d); *Med Dir*].

ATKIN, JOHN MYERS (1799/1800–89), Virginia, county Cavan;

born 1799/1800; brother of Dr James Atkin of Oldcastle (*q.v.*); studied arts and medicine at Trinity College, Dublin, and Edinburgh University; LM Lying-in Hospital, Edinburgh 1825; LRCS Edin 1828; MD (Edin) 1825 (thesis 'De apoplexia sanguinea'); LKQCPI and LM 1859; medical officer to Virginia Fever Hospital 1842–9, to Virginia temporary fever hospital 1847–8 and to cholera patients 1849;

medical officer to Virginia and Crossbane Dispensary Districts and constabulary 1829–74; retired to Oldcastle, county Meath 1874; unmarried; died 8 September 1889 at Oldcastle; administration Dublin 22 November 1889. [Belf PRO, will cal; Croly (1843–6); Dub GRO (d); Edin Univ; *Med Dir*].

ATKIN, WILLIAM (1814/5–72), Ballyhaise, county Cavan;
born 1814/5; LM Rot Hosp Dub 1838; LAH Dublin 1838; MRCSE 1843; LKQCPI 1859; medical officer to temporary fever hospital; medical officer to Ballyhaise Dispensary District and to constabulary and public vaccinator; unmarried; died 5 September 1872 at Virginia; administration Dublin 13 March 1873. [Belf PRO, will cal; Croly (1843–6); Dub GRO (d); *Med Dir*].

ATKINSON, CHARLES (*fl c* 1848–75), Dublin, Ballybay, county Monaghan, and Toomebridge and Carnlough, county Antrim;
LM Rot Hosp Dub 1848; LAH Dub 1852; LFPS Glas 1858; of 51 Upper Baggot Street, Dublin c 1852–5; of Ballybay c 1856–9; surgeon to Toomebridge Dispensary c 1859–60; of 8 Newcomen Terrace, Dublin c 1858–75; of Carnlough c 1875; [may have had Dublin and provincial addresses simultaneously]; married —; daughters born 1859 and 1860; died c 1875. [*BNL* 4 March 1859 (b, daughter) and 9 October 1860 (b, daughter; *Med Dir*].

ATKINSON, EDWARD (d 1823), Armagh;
studied medicine at Rheims University; MD (Rheims) 1780; general practitioner, of English Street, Armagh c 1785 and 1819; married 1785 Mary Macartney (who died November 1817 of typhus fever), daughter of James Macartney of Rosebrook, county Armagh, and sister of Dr James Macartney (*q.v.*) of Dublin; died 21 April 1823 at his home in English Street 'ranked at the head of the medical profession of this city'. [Agnew (1998); *BNL* 18 April 1817 (d) and 21 April 1823 (d); Bradshaw (1819); Brockliss; Burke *LGI* (1912) (under 'Olphert')].

ATKINSON, HUGH LATIMER (1859–1916), London;
born 4 April 1859 at Bannfoot, Lurgan, county Armagh, son of Hugh Atkinson, teacher, of Bannfoot; brother of Dr Thomas William Atkinson (*q.v.*); educated privately; studied arts and medicine at Queen's College, Belfast, from 1883; BA(RUI) 1886; MB BCh BAO 1891; general practitioner, of 211 Deptford Lower Road, London, and later of 211 Lower Road, Rotherhithe, London; married 14 June 1893 in Glencraig Church of Ireland Church, county Down, Evangeline R.M. McKee (who was born 1863/4), daughter of James McKee, merchant; died 1 January 1916 in Creek Road, Deptford, as a result of a collision between his 'motor-brougham' and a motor bus; probate London 23 February 1916. [Kirkpatrick Archive; Lond PPR, will cal; *Med Dir*; QCB adm reg; UHF database (m)].

ATKINSON, JAMES LAW (1856–97), Ballyshannon, county Donegal;
born May 1856, fourth son of John Atkinson of Cavangarden, county Donegal, and Ellen Mecredy of Carnew, county Down; studied medicine at the Royal College of Surgeons in Ireland; LRCSI 1880; LKQCPI and LM 1881; general practitioner, of the Terrace, Ballyshannon; married 16 September 1889 in Kilbarron Church of

Ireland Church, county Donegal, Margaret Rogers (who was born 1864/5), daughter of William Rogers of Ballyshannon; died 17 March 1897 at Ballyshannon; buried in Ballyshannon Church of Ireland graveyard; probate Londonderry 14 June 1897. [Belf PRO, will cal; Burke *LGI* (1958); Dub GRO (m) and (d); gravestone inscription; *Med Dir*].

ATKINSON, JOHN (1810–37), Newbliss, county Monaghan;
born 1810, third son of Thomas Atkinson of Anaghbawn, county Monaghan, and Sarah Philips of Drumcall; CM (Glas) 1830; medical officer to Newbliss Dispensary; died 5 February 1837 at Newbliss, of typhus fever. [Addison (1898); *BNL* 10 February 1837 (d); Burke *LGI* (1912); *Londonderry Sentinel* 4 March 1837 (d)].

ATKINSON, THOMAS WILLIAM (1855–1919), Rotherhithe, London, and Catford, Kent;
born 12 April 1855 at Bannfoot, Lurgan, county Armagh, son of Hugh Atkinson, teacher, of Bannfoot; brother of Dr Hugh Latimer Atkinson (*q.v.*); educated privately; studied arts and medicine at Queen's College, Belfast, from 1882; BA (RUI) 1885; MB BCh BAO 1893; general practitioner in London from 1893, living at 211 Lower Road, Rotherhithe c 1895 and 78 Bromley Road, Catford, Kent; married 17 June 1896 in Walthamstow Parish Church, Ada Mary Maud, daughter of William Albert Maud, merchant, of Airedale Lodge, Walthamstow; died 8 November 1919; probate London 30 December 1919. [Kirkpatrick Archive; Lond GRO (m); Lond PPR, will cal; *Med Dir*; QCB adm reg; Young and Pike (1909)].

ATKINSON, WILLIAM (1852–1916), Clapham, London;
born 13 August 1852 at Magherafelt, county Londonderry, son of William Atkinson, farmer, of Magherafelt; educated at Moneymore Academy; studied medicine at Queen's College, Galway, and from 1876, at Queen's College, Belfast; MD (QUI) 1879; MRCSE 1883; medical officer and public vaccinator to Clapham Dispensary District; of 15 Clapham Park Road, London, from c 1880, 95 High Street, Clapham, from c 1890 and 1 The Sweep, Clapham Common, c 1905; married Violet Mary —; died 21 March 1916 at 2 The Sweep; administration London 1 May 1916. [Lond GRO (d); Lond PPR, will cal; *Med Dir*; QCB adm reg].

ATTHILL, LOMBE (1827–1910), Geashill, King's County, and Dublin;
born 3 December 1827 in county Fermanagh, sixth son of the Rev William Atthill, prebendary of Clogher and rector of Magheraculmoney, county Fermanagh, and Henrietta Margaret Eyre Maunsell; brother of Dr Robert Atthill (*q.v.*) and Jemima Grace Atthill, who was mother of Dr George Lombe St George (*q.v.*); educated in Maidstone, Kent, and at Portora Royal School, Enniskillen; apprenticed to Mr Maurice Collis, surgeon to the Meath Hospital, Dublin, 1844; studied arts and medicine at Trinity College, Dublin, 1844–9; LRCSI and LM 1847; BA MB (TCD) 1849; LKQCPI 1857; FKQCPI 1860; MD 1865; medical officer to the Fleet Street Dispensary, Dublin 1847–50 and to Geashill Dispensary, King's County, 1849–50; general practitioner, of Upper Mount Street, Dublin, from 1850; gynaecologist to the Adelaide Hospital, Dublin 1868–75; assistant master of the Rotunda Hospital, Dublin, 1851–4 and master 1875–82; an early advocate of cleanliness and asepsis in

obstetrics and surgery; president of the KQCPI 1888–9; retired 1903; living at Monkstown Castle, county Dublin; author of *Clinical Lectures in Diseases peculiar to Women* (1871) and many medical papers, also *Recollections of an Irish Doctor* (1911); married (1) 2 April 1850 in St Peter's Church of Ireland Church, Dublin, Elizabeth Dudgeon (who died 1870), daughter of James Dudgeon, insurance agent, of Upper Fitzwilliam Street, Dublin; (2) 1 June 1872 in St Anne's Church of Ireland Church, Dublin, Mary Duffey, widow of John Duffey, and daughter of Robert Christie, merchant, of Manchester; died 14 September 1910 at Strood, Rochester, Kent; buried in Mount Jerome Cemetery, Dublin; portrait by Sarah Purser in RCPI; probate Dublin 11 October 1910. [Atthill (1911); Belf PRO, will cal; *BMJ* obituary (1910); Burke *LG GB I* (1925); Burtchaell and Sadleir (1924); Crone (1928); Cunningham (1993); *DIB* (2009); Dub GRO (m x 2); Kirkpatrick Archive; Kirkpatrick and Jellett (1913); Leslie (1929); Leslie and Swanzy (1936); *Med Dir*; Newmann (1993); O'Brien, Crookshank and Wolstenholme (1984); *Portora Register* (1940); Widdess (1963)].

ATTHILL, ROBERT (1819/20–1839), Army Medical Service;
born 1819/20 in county Tyrone, second son of the Rev William Atthill, prebendary of Clogher and rector of Magheraculmoney, county Fermanagh, and Henrietta Margaret Eyre Maunsell; brother of Dr Lombe Atthill (*q.v.*) and Jemima Grace Atthill, who was mother of Dr George Lombe St George (*q.v.*); studied arts at Trinity College, Dublin, from 1826; BA (TCD) 1831; joined the Army Medical Service as staff assistant surgeon 1837; died 16 May 1839 in Jamaica. [*BNL* (23 July 1839) (d); Burtchaell and Sadleir (1924); Leslie (1929); *Londonderry Sentinel* 20 July 1839 (d); Peterkin and Johnston (1968)].

AUCHENLECK, JAMES (*fl c* 1765), Naval Medical Service;
born c 1740, third son of James Auchenleck, junior, of Thomastown, county Fermanagh, and Susanna Corry of Lisanock; joined the Naval Medical Service; died without issue. [Burke *LGI* (1912)].

AUCHINLECK, HUGH ALEXANDER (1849–1929), Dublin;
born 10 June 1849 at Liscreevaghan, Strabane, son of Hugh Auchinleck, solicitor, of Dublin and Strabane, and Margaret Burgoyne; nephew of William Auchinleck, FRCS, president of the RCSI in 1829; educated at Potterton's School, Newry; studied medicine at the Carmichael School and Jervis Street and Coombe Hospitals, Dublin; LAH Dublin 1873; LRCP LRCS Edin 1874; LRCSI 1879; FRCSI 1881; lecturer in Forensic Medicine at the Carmichael School 1875–89 and professor of Medical Jurisprudence RCSI 1889–1920; physician to Mercer's Hospital 1890–98, having been appointed by the governors against the wishes of the medical staff; of 7 Harcourt Street, Dublin from c 1900; married 11 July 1883 in All Saints' Church, Dublin, Rhoda Elizabeth Johnston (who died 1 May 1918), eldest daughter of Robert James Johnston of Liscreevaghan, Strabane, and Northampton; died 24 March 1929 at 122 Leinster Road, Rathmines; buried in Mount Jerome Cemetery, Dublin. [Cameron (1916); Kirkpatrick Archive; Lyons (1991); Martin (2003); *Med Dir*].

AUCHINLECK, JOHN (*fl c* 1796), Strabane, county Tyrone;
LAH Dub 1796; apothecary, of Strabane. [Apothecaries (1829)].

AUCHINLECK, JOHN (d 1885), Naval Medical Service;
joined the Naval Medical Service as surgeon; died 3 November 1885; commemorated in Clonallon Graveyard, Warrenpoint, county Down. [Gravestone inscription].

AUCHINLECK, WILLIAM (1787–1848), Dublin;
born 19 May 1787, fourth son of Hugh Auchinleck, solicitor, of Dublin and of Mulvin, county Tyrone; uncle of Hugh Alexander Auchinleck, FRCS (*q.v.*); indentured to surgeon Gerard Mechlin of Dublin; studied medicine at the Royal College of Surgeons in Ireland and Mercer's Hospital; LRCSI and MRCSI 1810; FRCSI; surgeon to Mercer's Hospital, Dublin, of 42 Lower Dominick Street, Dublin; president of the RCSI 1829; lecturer in surgery at Trinity College, Dublin; successfully removed the 'inferior maxillary bone' in 1842, the first surgeon in Dublin to do so; married Margaret Stewart, daughter of James Stewart; father of Dr John Stewart Auchinleck of London; died 26 December 1848, suddenly, at 42 Lower Dominick Street; buried in St Michan's Churchyard, Dublin; probate Prerogative Court 1849. [Cameron (1916); Dub Nat Arch, Prerog Wills index; *Londonderry Sentinel* 6 January 1849 (d); Widdess (1967)].

AUSTIN, JOHN JOHNSTON (1858–1915), Larne, county Antrim and Belfast;
born 12 July 1858 in Ahoghill, county Antrim, son of James Johnston Austin, grocer, of Ahoghill; educated at RBAI; studied medicine at Queen's College, Belfast, from 1877; LM KQCPI 1882; MD MCh (RUI) 1882; general practitioner, of Larne until c 1889 and then of Clifton Street Belfast; president of the Ulster Medical Society 1909–10 and 1910–11; married —; died 3 December 1915 at 7 Clifton Street; buried in Belfast City Cemetery; probate Belfast 7 January 1916. [Belf City Cem, bur reg; Belf PRO, will cal; Dub GRO (d); *Lancet* obituary (1915); *Med Dir*; QCB adm reg].

AUSTIN, ROBERT MACKAY (1829–51), Ayr, Ayrshire;
born 1829, third son of Andrew Austin of Milltown, Strabane, county Tyrone, later of Coleraine, county Londonderry, and finally of Ayr, and Margaret Mackay; studied medicine and trained as a doctor; died 2 December 1851 at Waterloo Cottage, Ayr. [*BNL* 12 December 1851 (d); Belf PRO, T6083/2 ('Records of the family of the Orrs of Aghadowey'; Hitchings, Paul, pers com].

AUTERSON, FRANCIS (1825/6–1905), Magherafelt, county Londonderry;
born 1825/6 at Coolsara, Desertmartin, county Londonderry, son of — Auterson and — Kelly; educated by his uncle, the Rev Samuel Auterson, parish priest of Kilrea, and at McCloskey's School, Tergarvil, Maghera; studied medicine at RBAI and the Royal College of Surgeons in Ireland; MRCSE 1859; LRCP Edin 1867; LM Coombe Hosp Dub 1870; general practitioner in Magherafelt and farmer; JP for county Londonderry; married —; died 5 October 1905 at Ramsey Street, Magherafelt; probate Londonderry 13 December 1905. [Belf PRO, will cal; Dub GRO (d); Maitland (1916); *Med Dir*].

AUTERSON, JOHN (1837/8–1905), Draperstown, county Londonderry, and Cookstown, county Tyrone;
> born 1837/8; studied medicine at Royal College of Surgeons in Ireland; LFPS Glas 1865; LRCP Edin 1868; general practitioner in Draperstown c 1871–4 and Cookstown c 1874–1905; unmarried; died 7 August 1905 at Cookstown; probate Armagh 11 September 1905. [Belf PRO, will cal; Dub GRO (d); *Med Dir*].

AYRE, WILLIAM (1746/7–1812), Ballycastle, county Antrim;
> born 1746/7; general practitioner, of Ballycastle; married —; died 16 February 1812, 'an honest man, an affectionate husband and a tender parent'. [*BNL* 3 March 1812 (d)].

B

BABINGTON, JOHN H. (*fl c* 1840–47), Coleraine, county Londonderry;
medical officer to Coleraine Union c 1845–7 with surviving correspondence on the Great Famine in the PRO NI; commented (13 October 1845) 'whole fields looking last week most luxuriant and untainted, this week are unfit for man or beast' … 'such being the state of crops, a great scarcity of food must be looked forward to'; subsequently involved in running soup kitchens and raising funds; married —; son born 14 November 1841. [*BNL* 23 November 1841 (b, son); Belf PRO, T2890/4 and others; Burke *LGI* (1958); Parkhill (1997)].

BABINGTON, JOHN JAMES (1815–47), Cavan;
born 1815, son of John James Babington of Cavan and Frances Boileau; brother of Dr William Babington of Cavan (*q.v.*); apothecary in Cavan and to Cavan Union Workhouse; died 22 May 1847 'of fever caught in the discharge of his duties'. [*BNL* 28 May 1847 (d); Holdrege (1982)].

BABINGTON, MARCUS HILL (1875–1968), Royal Army Medical Corps;
born 25 September 1875 at 34 Waterloo Place, Londonderry, son of Humphrey Babington, merchant, and Elizabeth Jane Rossborough; studied medicine at Edinburgh; LRCP LRCS Edin 1898; LRFPS Glas 1898; DPH Cambridge 1924; joined the RAMC as lieutenant 1899; captain 1902; major 1911; lieutenant-colonel 1915; colonel 1926; served in South Africa 1899–1902, India 1902–05, Malta 1908–13, Scutari 1913, BEF France 1914–19; commanding officer 2nd General Hospital 1915–19; served in India 1919–23, Malta 1926–8 and BAOR 1928–9; specialist in bacteriology; DSO 1917; retired 1930; lived finally at 85 Cliftonville Road, Belfast; married —; died 12 December 1968 at 85 Cliftonville Road; probate Belfast 10 June 1969 and London 2 July 1969. [Belf GRO (b); Belf PRO, will cal; *BMJ* obituary (1969); Drew (1968); *Med Dir*; Lond PPR, will cal].

BABINGTON, THOMAS HENDERSON (1813–69), Portstewart, Coleraine and Londonderry, county Londonderry;
born 15 May 1813 in county Londonderry, eleventh son of the Rev Richard Babington, rector of Lower Cumber, and Mary Boyle; studied arts and medicine at Trinity College, Dublin, from 1828; BA (TCD) 1832; MB 1834; LRCSI 1834; accoucheur of the Dublin Lying-In Hospital (Rotunda); FRCSI 1844; MD 1861; general practitioner of Portstewart c 1840; medical officer to the Coleraine Union Workhouse from c 1843; surgeon to the County Londonderry Infirmary and gaol, 1854–69; author of various medical papers, including an important description of caisson disease (1863); Mayor of Londonderry 1868; married 15 January 1840 in Portstewart Church of Ireland Church (by his brother, the Rev David Babington) Alice Amelia Ackers, youngest daughter of Thomas Ackers of Toxteth Park, Liverpool; died 2 August 1869 at 13 Pump Street of typhus fever; buried in Derry Cathedral Graveyard; probate Londonderry 2 October 1869. [Babington and Cuthbert (1863); *BNL* 17 January 1840 (m); Belf PRO, will cal; Burke *LGI* (1958); Burtchaell and

Sadleir (1924); *Coleraine Chronicle* 7 August 1869 (d); Croly (1843–6); Dallat (1990); Dub GRO (d); Kirkpatrick Archive; Leslie (1937); *Londonderry Sentinel* 18 January 1840 (m) and 3 August 1869 (d); *Med Dir; Memorials of the Dead,* vol IX, p 320–1].

BABINGTON, WILLIAM (1756–1833), Naval Medical Service, and London;
born 21 May 1756 in Portglenone, county Antrim, second son of the Rev Humphrey Babington, curate of Ahoghill, and Dorothea Battle; apprenticed to a doctor in Londonderry; studied medicine at Guy's Hospital, London; MD (Aber) 1795; LRCP Lond 1796; FRCP 1827; MD (*hon causa*) (TCD) 1831; assistant surgeon to Haslar Naval Hospital 1777–81; apothecary 1781–95 and physician to Guy's Hospital 1795–1811; founder member and, in 1822, president of the Geological Society; author of *Sylabus of the Course of Chemical Lectures at Guy's Hospital* (1789), *A Systematic Arrangement of Minerals founded on the joint Consideration of their chemical, physical and external Characters* (1795), *A New System of Mineralogy in the Form of a Catalogue* (1799) and 4 volumes of manuscript papers in King's College Library, London; FRS 1805; his chief interests were in chemistry and mineralogy rather than medicine and he was the founder of the Royal Geological Society, but he had a large and lucrative medical practice; retired to Devonshire Street, London; married 21 July 1787 Martha Elizabeth Hough; father of 2 medical sons, one of whom was Dr Benjamin Guy Babington of Guy's Hospital, MD (Cantab) 1830, and a daughter Martha Babington who married Dr Richard Bright, MD (Edin) 1813; died 29 April 1833 at Devonshire Street; buried in St Mary's, Aldermanbury; portrait by J. Tannock (1820) in the Geological Society, London, memorial by Behnes (1837) in St Paul's Cathedral and a bust by Behnes ((1839) in the Royal College of Physicians. [Biggart (1949); Brockliss, Cardwell and Moss (2005); Burke *LGI* (1958); *DIB* (2009); Leslie (1993); Martin (2003); *Munk's Roll,* vols 2 and 3; Newmann (1993); *Oxford DNB* (2004)].

BABINGTON, WILLIAM (1810–88), Cavan;
born 1810 in county Cavan, son of John James Babington, tobacconist, and Frances Boileau; educated at Portora Royal School, Enniskillen; studied arts and medicine at Trinity College, Dublin from 1826; BA (TCD) 1831; MB 1834; practised in London c 1836 and Cornwall c 1840; apothecary to the Cavan County Infirmary and Workhouse, of Fortview Cottage, Cavan c 1845; married Elizabeth Smith; died 2 January 1888 at Fortview; probate Cavan 13 March 1888; buried in Old Cavan Burying Ground. [Belf PRO, will cal; Burtchaell and Sadleir (1924); *Coleraine Chronicle* 29 May 1847 (d); Croly (1843–6); Dub GRO (d); Holdrege (1982); *Med Dir; Portora Royal School Register* (1940)].

BABINGTON, WILLIAM E. (d 1834), Edinburgh;
youngest son of H. Babington of Londonderry; surgeon; died 15 March 1834 at the house of William A. Reeves in Edinburgh. [*BNL* 1 April 1834 (d); *Londonderry Sentinel* 29 March 1834 (d)].

BACE, WILLIAM GODFREY (d 1842), Army Medical Service;
son of — Bace, assistant quartermaster general in Ireland; studied medicine at Edinburgh University; MD (Edin) 1832 (thesis 'De delerio tremente'); joined the

Army Medical Service 1833, serving with the 45th Foot; with the 26th Foot from 1838; married 6 November 1840 in Coleraine Church of Ireland Church, Elizabeth Wrixton, youngest daughter of Captain — Wrixton, late of the 5th Dragoon Guards and grandson of Colonel Beatty, HEICS; died 12 August 1842 in China. [*BNL* 10 November 1840 (m); Edin Univ; *Londonderry Sentinel* 7 November 1840 (m); Peterkin and Johnston (1968)].

BAGOT, EDWARD (1832/3–1901), Enniskillen, county Fermanagh;
born 1832/3 in county Kildare, son of the Rev John Bagot; studied arts and medicine at Trinity College, Dublin, from 1847 and the Royal College of Surgeons in Ireland; BA (TCD) 1852; LM Rot Hosp Dub 1853; LRCSI 1853; LKQCPI 1854; FRCSI 1866; medical officer to Malin Dispensary District and constabulary; admiralty surgeon and agent and medical officer to lightkeepers, Inistrahull; medical officer to Enniskillen Fever Hospital, Union Infirmary and constabulary; retired to Ilfracombe, Devonshire c 1870; married —; died 7 July 1901 at 1 Prince Arthur Terrace, Leinster Square, Rathmines, Dublin; probate London 5 October 1901 and Dublin 3 March 1902. [Belf PRO, will cal; Burtchaell and Sadleir (1935); Dub GRO (d); *Med Dir*].

BAILEY, HUNT JOHNSON (1832–93), Army Medical Service;
born 14 May 1832 in Queen's County; LRCS and LM Edin 1858; joined the Army Medical Service as staff assistant surgeon 1859; attached to 58th Foot 1864; staff surgeon 1867; retired on half pay 1870; married —; died 30 September 1893 at 6 Cliftonville, Belfast; buried in Belfast City Cemetery. [Belf City Cem, bur reg; *Med Dir*; Peterkin and Johnston (1968)].

BAILEY, JAMES BATTERSBY (1851–99), Belfast, Twerton, Somerset, and Hopesay, Shropshire;
born 17 June 1851 at Bailieborough, county Cavan, son of James L. Bailie of 10 Mount Charles, Belfast; brother of Dr William Frederick Bailie (*q.v.*); educated at Portora Royal School, Enniskillen; studied medicine at Queen's College, Belfast, from 1867; MD (QUI) 1872; LRCS and LM Edin 1872; general practitioner, of 10 Mount Charles, Belfast c 1872–5; medical officer, medical officer of health and public vaccinator for Bath District, of Twerton, c 1875–8; general practitioner, of Fir Lodge, Hopesay c 1878–94; retired to Probate Villa, Kendal, Westmoreland c 1894, to 49 Alleyne Park West, Dulwich, Surrey, and later to 6 Granville Place, Kensington; married Louise Florence —; died 2 June 1899 after taking an overdose of chloral hydrate while of unsound mind, at the Grosvenor Hotel, Buckingham Palace Road, London; administration London 17 June 1899. [Kirkpatrick Archive; Lond GRO (d); Lond PPR, will cal; *Med Dir*; *Portora Register* (1940); QCB adm reg].

BAILEY, WILLIAM FREDERICK (1861–1917), Army Medical Service and South Africa;
born 9 November 1861 at Naas, county Kildare, son of James L. Bailey, Inspector in RIC, of 10 Mount Charles, Belfast; brother of Dr James Battersby Bailie (*q.v.*); educated at Methodist College, Belfast, from 1868; studied medicine at Queen's College, Belfast, from 1879; MD MCh (RUI) 1884; joined the Army Medical Service as surgeon captain 1886; served in Zululand 1888; retired with gratuity 1896 to

47

practice in Cape Town; died 1917 in Natal, South Africa. [Fry (1984); *Med Dir*; Peterkin and Johnston (1968); QCB adm reg].

BAILIE, ANDREW (*fl c* 1739), Stewartstown, county Tyrone;
apothecary, of Stewartstown; witness to a will 1739. [Eustace, vol I (1956)].

BAILIE, H.M. (*fl c* 1824), Larne, county Antrim;
apothecary, of Larne, c 1824. [Pigot (1824)].

BAILIE, HUGH WILLIAM (1862–1933), Belfast;
born 10 March 1862 at Seaforde, county Down, son of John Bailie, farmer, of Seaforde; educated at RBAI; studied medicine at Queen's College, Belfast, from 1881 and Edinburgh; LRCP LRCS Edin 1888; LFPS Glasgow 1888; DPH RCPSI 1905; general practitioner, of 47 Ormeau Terrace c 1890–1907; superintendent medical officer of health for the City of Belfast 1906–26 and made an outstanding contribution to the public health of the city over his 20 year term of office (Blaney); of 'Ashby', 138 Malone Road, 1907–33; lecturer and examiner in Public Health for the Queen's Unversity, Belfast 1907–27; alderman for Cromac Ward; retired 1926; married Anne Adelaide —; died 19 April 1933 at Rendlesham, East Suffolk; administration Belfast 17 July 1933. [Belf PRO, will cal; Blaney (1988); Lond GRO (d); *Med Dir*; QCB adm reg; Wilson (1934)].

BAILLIE, MATTHEW (d 1828), Army Medical Service;
son of Lieutenant-General Baillie; joined the Army Medical Service as hospital assistant 1825; assistant surgeon with the 92nd Foot 1826; transferred to 79th Foot 1827; died 6 February 1828 in Belfast after a few days' illness. [*BNL* 8 February 1828 (d); Peterkin and Johnston (1968)].

BAIRD, ANDREW (1757–1843), Naval Medical Service;
born 1757 at Aughtermoy, Donemana, county Tyrone, son of William Baird of Thorny Hill, Creaghcor, Strabane, county Tyrone, and Martha —; brother of Dr Archibald Baird (*q.v.*); joined the Naval Medical Service as assistant surgeon; served with Admiral St Vincent on HMS *Ville de Paris* from before 1800; private physician to Sir John Jervis who was created Earl St Vincent in 1797; appointed physician to the Baltic Fleet when St Vincent became First Lord of the Admiralty 1801; was presented with a silver two-handled cup inscribed 'As a mark of esteem for his humane attention to the gallant officers and men who were wounded off Boulogne on the 16th of August 1801, from their Commander in Chief, Vice-Admiral of the Red Horatio, Lord Viscount Nelson, Duke of Bronte, etc'; Chief Inspector of Naval Hospitals and Senior Physician of the Fleet 1800–06 and in correspondence with Nelson on the seamen's health; described by St Vincent as 'the most valuable man in the Navy'; MD (Aberdeen) 1801; retired c 1810 to 2 Clarges Street, Picadilly, London; attended St Vincent during his last illness in 1822; elected FRS 1828; unmarried; died 17 July 1843 at Clarges Street; buried in Brompton Cemetery; will dated 10 June 1843 (copy in PRO NI), proved London 17 August 1843. [Belf PRO, EDOL/1851; Brockliss, Cardwell and Moss (2005); Dawson (1932); Elliott, Simon, pers com; Montgomery, Robert, pers com; *NMS* (1826); Roulston (2010)].

BAIRD, ARCHIBALD (1761/2–86), Strabane, county Tyrone;
born 1761/2, son of William Baird of Thorny Hill, Creaghcor, Strabane, county Tyrone, and Martha —; brother of Dr Andrew Baird RN (*q.v.*); apprenticed in Londonderry in 1778; general practitioner, of Strabane; died 10 May 1786; buried in Grange graveyard, Strabane. [Elliott, Simon, pers com; Roulston (2010); Todd (1993)].

BAIRD, JOHN (*fl c* 1843), Naval Medical Service;
great-nephew of Dr Andrew Baird, RN (*q.v.*) joined the Naval Medical Service as assistant surgeon; executor of Dr Andrew Baird's will, dated and proved 1843 and was left Andrew Baird's letters and manuscripts. [Belf PRO, EDOL/1851; Roulston (2010)].

BAIRD, JOHN (1809/10–57), Cloughfin, Carrigans, county Donegal;
born 1809/10, son of James Baird, gentleman; general practitioner, of Cloughfin; married 23 October 1856 in Strabane Church, Fanny Simms (who married (2) 20 March 1863 in Donaghmore Church of Ireland Church, Francis Arthur Doyle, second son of Timothy Doyle of Craig, county Kilkenny), seventh daughter of Nicholas Simms, hotel-keeper of the Abercord Arms in Strabane; died 20 October 1857 in Strabane, 'suddenly, of disease of the heart'. [*BNL* 26 October 1857 (d); *Coleraine Chronicle* 24 October 1857 (d); Dub GRO (m, widow); Elliott, Simon, pers com; *Londonderry Sentinel* 31 October 1856 (m) and 23 October 1857 (d) and 24 March 1863 (m); Roulston (2010)].

BAIRD, SAMUEL JAMES (1861/2–1930), Eglinton, county Londonderry;
born 1861/2; studied medicine at Glasgow University; MB CM (Glas) 1885; LM FPS Glas 1887; resident surgeon to the City and County Infirmary, Londonderry; medical officer to Eglinton Dispensary District from 1886; married Jane Robinson —; died 28 March 1930 at Eglinton; probate Londonderry 31 July 1930. [Addison (1898); Belf GRO (d); Belf PRO, will cal; Kirkpatrick Archive; *Med Dir*].

BAIRD, WILLIAM (c 1809–70), Donemana, county Tyrone;
born c 1809, son of William Baird, farmer, of Aughtermoy, county Tyrone; LFPS Glas 1830; medical officer to Donemana Dispensary District and constabulary; of Aughtermoy, where he owned 12 acres of land; subscribed to a relief fund after damage to the chapel in Killenny (in the parish of Donagheady) in 1833 and contributed to the Dunnamanagh Famine Relief Fund in 1847; married (1) 10 August 1837 in First Donagheady Presbyterian Church, Mary Jane McCrea (who died 20 December 1843), second daughter of James McCrea of Glencush; (2) 16 November 1847 in Burt Presbyterian Church, county Donegal, Margaret Porter (who was born 1811 and died 14 June 1886), youngest daughter of William Porter, farmer, of Carrowan, county Donegal; died 18 September 1870 at Aughtermoy, county Tyrone; buried in Grange graveyard; probate Londonderry 25 October 1870. [*BNL* 18 August 1837 (m) and 5 January 1844 (d); Belf PRO, will cal; Croly (1843–6); Dub GRO (m) and (d); Elliott, Simon, pers com; *Londonderry Sentinel* 19 August 1837 (m), 6 January 1844 (d) and 20 November 1847 (m); *Med Dir; Return of Owners of Land … in Ireland* (1876); Roulston (2010); Todd (1993)].

BAIRD, WILLIAM JAMES (1859–1937), Bury, Lancashire;
born 2 October 1859 in Limavady, son of Thomas H. Baird, factory manager, of Florence Terrace, Londonderry; educated at Londonderry Academy; studied medicine at Queen's College, Belfast, from 1880, also at Edinburgh and Manchester; BA (RUI) 1888; LRCP LRCS Edin 1892; LFPS Glas 1892; general practitioner, of 57 Manchester Road, Bury, from c 1894 and of 'Springwells', Bury, from c 1900; retired to Riblehurst, Fairhaven, Lytham St Annes c 1932 and to 1 Headley Parade, Langley Vale, Epsom, Surrey c 1935; married Evaleen Mary —; died 9 March 1937 at 1 Headley Parade; administration (with will) London 10 June 1937. [Lond GRO (d); Lond PPR, will cal; *Med Dir*; QCB adm reg].

BAKER, RICHARD (*fl c* 1845), Ballinagh, county Cavan;
MRCSE 1837; LAH Dub; medical officer to Ballinagh Dispensary District and constabulary c 1845. [Croly (1843–6)].

BALBIRNIE, HUGH DE VAUX (1845–1901), Sheffield, Yorkshire;
born 17 September 1845 in Glasgow, son of Dr John Balbirnie of 3 Clarkson Street, Sheffield; brother of Dr John Patrick Balbirnie (*q.v.*); educated at Heversham Grammar School; studied medicine at Queen's College, Belfast, from 1870; MD MCh (QUI) 1874; physician to St Joseph's House, Walkley; general practitioner in Sheffield, of Howard Hill, Walkley c 1885, of 3 Clarkson Street c 1895 and of 23 Harcourt Road c 1900; died 16 September 1901 at Sheffield Royal Infirmary. [Lond GRO (d); *Med Dir*; QCB adm reg].

BALBIRNIE, JOHN PATRICK (1842–98), Staveley, Westmoreland;
born 12 July 1842 at Leamington Priors, son of Dr John Balbirnie of 3 Clarkson Street, Sheffield; brother of Dr Hugh de Vaux Balbirnie (*q.v.*); educated at Heversham Grammar School; studied medicine at Queen's College, Belfast, from 1871; LRCP LRCS Edin 1876; general practitioner in Stavelely, Westmoreland; married Fanny —; died 17 February 1898 from blood poisoning due to an accidental injury to his leg, at 64 Nelson Street South, Manchester; probate Carlisle 15 April 1898. [Lond GRO (d); Lond PPR, will cal; *Med Dir*; QCB adm reg].

BALDRICK, JAMES (d 1861), Ramelton, county Donegal;
studied medicine at Glasgow University; LM; CM (Glas) 1834; MD 1835; medical officer to Fanad Dispensary, of Mossmount, Ramelton; medical officer to constabulary; unmarried; died 6 April 1861 at Mossmount; administration Londonderry 3 May 1861. [Addison (1898); Belf PRO, will cal; Croly (1843–6); Kirkpatrick Archive; *Londonderry Sentinel* 12 April 1861 (d); *Med Dir*].

BALDWIN, GODFREY WILLIAM WALLER DE COURCY (d c 1909), Belfast;
LRCP LRCS Edin 1889; LFPS Glas 1889; general practitioner, of 6 Cliftonville Place, Belfast; died c 1909. [*Med Dir*].

BALDWIN, HENRY SCHOFIELD (1838–81), Blackburn, Lancashire;
born August 1838 in Lancashire, son of — Baldwin of Sedgley Park, Staffordshire; educated at Sedgely Park School; studied medicine at Queen's College, Galway, from

1862, and at Queen's College, Belfast, from 1863; LM Rot Hosp Dub; MD (QUI) 1866; MRCSE 1867; surgeon in charge of invalids in HMS *Renown* from Madras to Netley Hospital; general practitioner, of 1 Paradise Lane, King Street, Blackburn, from 1868; died 19 April 1881 at 116 Montague Street, Blackburn; probate Lancaster 11 July 1881. [Lond GRO (d); Lond PPR, will cal; *Med Dir*; QCB adm reg].

BALFOUR, WILLIAM (d c 1800), Londonderry;
surgeon, of Londonderry city; married Letitia McElwee, with children by her before marriage (who died 10 December 1816); died c 1800; will dated 1799 proved in Prerogative Court 27 November 1800. [*BNL* 13 December 1816 (d); Ellis and Eustace, vol III (1984)].

BALL, JOHN (d 1863), Enniskillen, county Fermanagh;
LAH Dub 1839; LM Coombe Hosp Dub 1840; general practitioner, of Enniskillen; commissioner of affidavits for county Fermanagh; unmarried; died 23 April 1863; probate Armagh 22 May 1863. [Belf PRO, will cal, will; *Med Dir*].

BALL, THOMAS (1839/40–92), Belfast;
born 1839/40; studied medicine at Queen's College, Cork, and the Ledwich School, Dublin; LAH Dub 1866; LM Coombe Hosp Dub 1866; LRCP Edin and LM 1869; general practitioner with a Medical Hall at 21 Donegall Place, Belfast from c 1870; of 12 College Square East c 1887 and later of 32 University Road, Belfast; married Mary E. — (who was born 1821/2, died 13 July 1892 and was buried in Milltown Cemetery, Belfast); died 7 December 1892 at 32 University Road; buried in Belfast City Cemetery; probate Belfast 6 January 1893. [Belf City Cem, bur reg; Belf PRO, will cal; Dub GRO (d); *Med Dir*; Merrick and Clarke, *Belfast*, vol 2 (1984)].

BALNAVES, ANDREW (*fl c* 1819–35), Killybegs, county Donegal;
physician, of Killybegs; married —; father of Catherine Balnaves who was born c 1819 and died July 1833 of fever which her father caught in the exercise of his profession and which affected all the family. [*BNL* 2 August 1833 (d)].

BAMBER, CHARLES JAMES (1855–1941), Indian Medical Serivice;
born 14 July 1855 at Chittagong, India, son of Henry Bamber; educated at Bradford Grammar School; studied medicine at St Batholomew's Hospital, London; MRCSE LRCP Lond 1878; DPH (Camb) 1892; joined the Indian Medical Service (Bengal establishment) as surgeon 1878; surgeon major 1890; lieutenant-colonel 1898; colonel 1910; served on the North-West Frontier 1881 and in Burma 1886–7; in Punjab civil service from 1887; surgeon in Rawalpindi 1893–8; sanitary commissioner to the Punjab Government 1900–10; inspector general of Civil Hospitals in the Punjab 1910–15; MVO 1911; author of *The Plants of the Punjab* (1917); retired to 'Haine', St Lawrence-in-Kent; died 9 January 1941 at the Downshire Mental Hospital, Downpatrick, county Down. [Belf GRO (d); Crawford (1930); Kirkpatrick Archive; *Med Dir*].

BAMPFIELD, WILLIAM (d 1845), Army Medical Service and Armagh;
joined the Army Medical Service as surgeon's mate 1804; assistant surgeon to 58th Foot 1808; served in the Peninsula War; regimental surgeon in the Mediterrean 1813; surgeon to 81st Foot 1813; half pay March–May 1816; half pay with De Meuron's Regiment 1824; full pay with 32nd Foot July 1824; married —; died in Armagh 16 April 1845; administration Armagh Diocesan Court 1845. [Dub Nat Arch, Armagh Dio Admins index; Ferrar (1933); Peterkin and Johnston (1968)].

BANKHEAD, CHARLES (1767/8–1859), Ballycarry, county Antrim, Brighton, Sussex and Florence;
born 1767/8 at Antrim, son of the Rev John Bankhead, minister of Ballycarry Presbyterian Church, and Jane Martin; brother of Dr John Bankhead (*q.v.*); educated in Londonderry; studied medicine at Edinburgh University; MD (Edin) 1790 (thesis 'De hysteria'); LRCP Lond 1807; surgeon to the Londonderry Militia; in business in Brighton from c 1807; private physician to Lord Castlereagh who expired in his arms; physician extraordinary to the Prince Regent 1816 and physician extraordinary to King George III 1821; surgeon in Florence; married 6 May 1835 in Ballymena, Penelope Ann Bankhead, only daughter of William Bankhead of Belfast; probably father of Charles Bankhead, diplomat (*DNB*); died 26 November 1859 in Florence (aged 91). [*BNL* 12 May 1835 (m); *Blackwood Pedigrees*, vol 23; Edin Univ; McConnell (1951); *Med Dir*; *Munk's Roll*, vol 3; *Oxford DNB* (2004) (for Charles Bankhead, junior); Presbyterian Historical Society].

BANKHEAD, JOHN (d 1815), Belfast;
son of the Rev John Bankhead, minister of Ballycarry Prebyterian Church, and Jane Martin; brother of Dr Charles Bankhead (*q.v.*); attending surgeon to the Belfast Dispensary in 1794 and to the Fever Hospital in 1797 for a few months; surgeon, apothecary and practitioner in midwifery, of 92 High Street and William Street South, Belfast, 1807-8; married — (who died 22 April 1811); died 12 June 1815 at Marybrook, near Carrickfergus. [*BNL* 30 April 1811 (d) and 20 June 1815 (d); *Belfast Street Directory* 1807 and 1808; Malcolm (1851); Strain (1961)].

BANKHEAD, — (*fl c* 1840), Demerara;
general practitioner, of Demerara; married —; son born c 1840 and died 26 July 1849 in Holywood, county Down. [*BNL* 31 July 1849 (d, son)].

BANKS, ALFRED (1852–79), Donegal;
born 1852 in Dublin, youngest son of Benjamin Banks, poor law commissioner; studied arts and medicine at Trinity College, Dublin, from 1870; BA (TCD) 1874; MB MCh 1875; LM KQCPI 1875; medical officer to Donegal Dispensary District, of The Vicarage, Donegal; married Anne —; died 7 February 1879 of typhus fever at The Vicarage; administration Dublin 10 July 1879. [Belf PRO, will cal; *BMJ* obituary (1879); Dub GRO (d); Kirkpatrick Archive; *Med Dir;* TCD adm reg; *TCD Cat*, vol II (1896)].

BANNEN, — (*fl c* 1819), Banbridge, county Down;
surgeon, of Banbridge c 1819. [Bradshaw (1819)].

BARBER, ALEXANDER (d 1906), Coleraine, county Londonderry, and New South Wales;
> studied medicine at the Ledwich School and Mercer's Hospital, Dublin; LRCSI 1870; LM Coombe Hosp Dub 1870; LAH Dub 1871; MD (Brussels) 1886; general practitioner, of 10 Church Street, Coleraine c 1871–9; emigrated to Sydney, New South Wales c 1880; of Hillgrove, NSW c 1890–1900 and at Tullaghmurry House, Penrith, NSW c 1900–06; died 13 August 1906. [*Med Dir*].

BARBER, ROBERT ALEXANDER (1856–1927), Sheffield;
> born 1 August 1856 at Lisnagree, county Armagh, son of William J. Barber, farmer, of Lisnagree; educated at Tannyoky School, Poyntzpass; studied medicine at Queen's College, Belfast, from 1877; MD MCh (RUI) 1883; LM RCPI 1884; BAO 1891; general practitioner, district medical officer and certifying factory surgeon, of Grange House, Dronfield, Sheffield c 1885, of The Knott, Dronfield, c 1895 and of Fairview, Dronfield c 1905; JP c 1910; of Hounscliffe, Unstone, Sheffield c 1920; married Harriett Ann —; died 18 April 1927 at Hounscliffe; probate London 7 July 1827. [Kirkpatrick Archive; Lond GRO (d); Lond PPR, will cal; *Med Dir*; QCB adm reg].

BARBOUR, JOHN HUMPHREY (1873–1944), Royal Army Medical Corps;
> born 11 August 1873 at Huyton, Liverpool, son of Humphrey Barbour, mercantile agent, of 1 Hamilton Villas, Ballyholme, county Down; educated at Shrewsbury School, Shropshire; studied medicine at Queen's College, Belfast, from 1893; MB BCh BAO (RUI) 1900; civil surgeon at home 1900; joined the RAMC as lieutenant 1901; captain 1904; major 1913; served in South Africa 1901–2, Halifax, Nova Scotia 1903–5, India 1908–13, World War I 1914–19, India 1920–23, mentioned in despatches 1915 and 1919; British and foreign war medals; died 20 October 1944; probate Llandudno 6 February 1945. [Drew (1968); Kirkpatrick Archive; Lond PPR, will cal; *Med Dir*; QCB adm reg].

BARBOUR, WILLIAM JAMES (1828–c 1876), Lisburn, county Antrim, and Quincey, Illinois, USA;
> born 1828, third son of William Barbour of Lisburn and Elizabeth Kennedy; studied medicine at the Royal College of Surgeons in Ireland and from 1850, at Queen's College, Belfast; LRCSI 1849; general practitioner in Lisburn; emigrated to USA before 1860; general practitioner, of Quincey, Illinois; married Sarah Taylor; died c 1876. [*Lisburn Fam Hist Soc*, vol 1 (2000), pp 147–8; *Med Dir*; QCB adm reg].

BARCLAY, JOSEPH (d 1819), Armagh;
> of Moy, county Tyrone; LAH Dub 1802; LRCSI; apothecary and surgeon to the Armagh County Infirmary 1806–19; married —; died 4 October 1819 at Armagh; buried in St Patrick's Cathedral Graveyard, Armagh. [Apothecaries (1829); *BNL* 12 October 1819 (d); Ferrar (1933)].

BARKER, FREDERICK CHARLES (1846–1908), Indian Medical Service;
> born 22 May 1846 in Dublin, son of Dr William Barker of 21 Hatch Street, Dublin; educated at the Dublin Collegiate Institute; studied medicine at the Royal College of Sugeons in Ireland and, from 1864, at Queen's College, Belfast; LRCSI 1866; LM

Rot Hosp Dub 1867; MD (QUI) 1868; FRCSI 1873; joined the Indian Medical Service (Bombay establishment) as assistant surgeon 1869; surgeon 1873; professor of Pathology at Grant Medical College, Bombay, 1873–4; civil surgeon in Surat 1877–8; surgeon major 1881; surgeon lieutenant-colonel 1891; retired 1900; married Kathleen Anne —; died 10 July 1908 at Corbeyrier-sur-Aigle, Switzerland; probate London 15 August 1908. [*BMJ* obituary (1908); Crawford (1930); Kirkpatrick Archive; Lond PPR, will cal; *Med Dir*; QCB adm reg].

BARKLEY, GEORGE (1849–1917), Frizington, Cumberland, and Sheffield and Scarborough, Yorkshire;
born 3 January 1849 at Maghera, county Londonderry, son of James Barkley of Maghera; educated at RBAI; studied arts and medicine at Queen's College, Belfast, 1866–72; BA (QUI) 1871; MD MCh 1872; general practitioner, of Frizington, c 1875, of Kiverton Park, Sheffield c 1880, and 68 Victoria Road, Scarborough c 1890; retired 1910 to 12 Langdale Road, Scarborough; married —; died 15 May 1917; probate York 29 September 1917. [Lond PPR, will cal, will; *Med Dir*; QCB adm reg].

BARKLEY, JAMES (1870–1935), Belfast, Wimbledon and Cheam, Surrey, and Royal Army Medical Corps;
born 29 June 1870 at Maghera, county Londonderry, son of Hugh Graham Barkley, linen merchant, of Maghera, and Mary Lynd; brother of Dr William Barkley, MB (RUI) 1901, of London; educated at Coleraine Academical Institution and at Methodist College, Belfast, 1887–9; studied arts and medicine at Queen's College, Belfast, from 1889 and at Edinburgh; LRCP LRCS Edin 1899; LFPS Glas 1899; of Maghera, county Londonderry c 1900; house surgeon and extern house surgeon, at Royal Victoria Hospital, Belfast, house surgeon at Union Infirmary, Belfast; civil surgeon with RAMC and South African Field Force November 1900–July 1901; general practitioner in Wimbledon, of Athbeagh, 31 Melrose Avenue, Wimbledon Park c 1905; moved c 1914 to Athbeagh, Sandy Lane, Cheam, Surrey; served in World War I, with rank of lieutenant-colonel; DSO; retired c 1925 to 80 Via Umberto I, Alassia, Italy, and later to 41 Gloucester Street, Westminster, London; married Aileen Sarah —; died 28 October 1935 at Tilbury Hospital, Chadwell St Mary, Essex; administration London 4 April 1936. [Drew (1968); Dub GRO (b); Fry (1984); Lond GRO (d); Lond PPR, will cal; *Med Dir*; QCB adm reg].

BARNES, ARCHIBALD FERGUSSON (1835/6–77), Ballyjamesduff, county Cavan, Dublin and Inman Line;
born 1835/6; studied medicine at the Royal College of Surgeons in Ireland; LRCSI and LM 1860; Lic Med 1863; LRCP Edin and LM 1869; medical officer to Ballyjamesduff and Termon Dispensary Districts; general practitioner of Kenilworth Square, Rathgar, Dublin c 1873–7; surgeon to Inman Royal Mail Steamship Company and SS *Great Eastern* c 1877; of 2 Duke Street, Liverpool; died 28 December 1877. [*Med Dir*].

BARNES, ERNEST (1870–1958), Failsworth, Manchester;
born 3 November 1870 at Cheetham Hill, Manchester, son of the Rev Joseph Barnes, rector of Failsworth, Manchester; educated at Manchester Grammar School; studied

medicine at Queen's College, Belfast, from 1889, and Aberdeen University; MB MCh (Aber) 1894; resident house surgeon to Ancoats Hospital, Manchester; medical officer and public vaccinator to Failsworth, to the Post Office, police and Education Board, of 4 Pole Lane, Failsworth; retired c 1955; author of various medical publications; died 20 November 1958; probate Manchester 3 February 1859. [Crockford (1899); Lond PPR, will cal; *Med Dir*; QCB adm reg; Watt (1935)].

BARNES, RICHARD GEREN (1864–1931), Manchester and Urmiston, Lancashire, and Leeds, Yorkshire;

born 17 December 1864 at Cookstown, county Tyrone, son of the Rev George Barnes, Methodist minister, of Ballycastle, county Antrim; educated at Methodist College, Belfast, from 1874; studied medicine at Queen's College, Belfast, from 1881; LRCP LRCS Edin 1893; LFPS Glas and LM 1893; general practitioner of Pendleton Lodge, Patricroft, Manchester, c 1895, of Lauriston, Harehills Road, Leeds c 1905, of The Firs, Urmiston, c 1910–25 and of 'Oakfield', Crofts Bank Road; general practitioner and medical officer to Tenterden Union Infirmary c 1925–31, also public vaccinator and surgeon to the constabulary; married Ethel Maud —; died 1 October 1931; administration London 10 November 1931. [Fry (1984); Lond PPR, will cal; *Med Dir*; QCB adm reg].

BARNETT, HENRY CALVERT (1832–97), Belfast, Liverpool and Western Australia;

born 10 February 1832, third son of Richard Barnett, dentist, of Belfast (*q.v.*) and Sarah Craig Milford; brother of Dr Richard W. Barnett (*q.v.*) and Dr John Milford Barnett (*q.v.*); educated by Dr Molony of Carrickfergus; studied medicine at Queen's College, Belfast, from 1851; LM Dub 1854 MRCSE 1854; LRCP Edin 1860; surgeon with P & O Shipping Line c 1855; general practitioner, in Foochow, China c 1856; sailed for USA 1859 to practise there; travelled to Australia 1861 on the *Flower of the Forest* but returned to England c 1862; travelled as ship's surgeon (with his wife) to Australia on the *Lady Louisa*; colonial surgeon at York, Western Australia 1867–72 and at Freemantle from 1872; superintendent of Freemantle Lunatic Asylum; registrar of births, marriages and deaths; member of the first Medical Board in Western Australia from 1894; JP; married (1) 13 March 1867 Anne Lee Copplestone (who was divorced from lieutenant Thomas Leetham); divorced 1877 but remarried each other 1878 and she died 1879 aged 51; (2) 25 November 1880 Emily Winn Stephens; died 3 November 1897, following an overdose of sedative, probably taken accidentally; buried in Freemantle Cemetery. [*Med Dir*; QCB adm reg; Taylor, Margaret, pers com].

BARNETT, HENRY NORMAN (1872–1952), Belfast and Bath;

born 16 September 1872 at Holywood, son of Charles William Barnett, linen manufacturer and merchant, of Thornhill, Knock and Helen Mackenzie of Aberdeen; educated at Belfast Royal Academy and Brighton; studied medicine at Queen's College, Belfast, from 1891, also at Edinburgh and London; LRCP LRCS Edin 1898; LFPS Glas 1898; FRCS Edin 1903; served in South African War (Transport Service) 1899–1901; in private surgical practice at 1 College Square East, and Thornhill, Knock, Belfast; anaesthetist to Royal Victoria Hospital and Belfast Hospital for Sick

Children 1910–14; lieutenant-colonel in World War 1 in command of Field Ambulance Units; consulting surgeon to Bath ENT Hospital and to Bath, Somerset and Wiltshire Education Authorities from c 1916, of 27 The Circus, Bath; author of many medical papers; married Jane Eleanor —; died 24 April 1952 at South Lynn, Weston Road, Bath; probate Bristol 25 July 1952. [Calwell (1973); Lond GRO (d); Lond PPR, will cal; *Med Dir*; QCB adm reg; Young and Pike (1909)].

BARNETT, JOHN BOLTON (1830–62), Balla, county Mayo;
born 1830, eldest son of the Rev John Barnett, minister of First Moneymore Presbyterian Church, and Grace Bolton of Lisburn; MRCSE 1853; medical officer to Balla Dispensary District; died 8 September 1862 at 82 Lower Gloucester Street, Dublin. [*Londonderry Sentinel* 12 September 1862 (d); McConnell (1951); *Med Dir*].

BARNETT, JOHN MILFORD (1830–1913), Indian Medical Service;
born 28 September 1830 in Belfast, son of Richard Barnett, dentist, of Belfast (*q.v.*), and Sarah Craig Milford; brother of Dr Richard W. Barnett (*q.v.*) and Dr Henry Calvert Barnett (*q.v.*); studied arts and medicine at Trinity College, Dublin, and Edinburgh University; LM Coombe Hosp Dub 1850; MD (Edin) 1852 (thesis 'On necrosis'); MRCSE 1852; joined the Indian Medical Service (Bombay establishment) as assistant surgeon to the Bombay Artillery 1853; surgeon 1865; shipwrecked in a cyclone off Bombay 1854; served with Persian Expediton under Outram and Havelock, taking part in the forced march on Boorazjoon and the battle of Khoorshab, where he was wounded; served through the Indian Mutiny 1857; surgeon major 1865; retired to Croft House, Holywood, county Down 1868; moved in 1888 to 54 Elmwood Avenue, Belfast and c 1898 to St Leonard's and later to 21 Amherst Road, Bexhill-on-Sea, Sussex; married (1) 1859 Mary Elizabeth Catherine Johnston (who died 16 February 1875), daughter of John Johnston of Ashley Lodge, county Down; (2) 28 September 1875 in Clifton Parish Church, Selina Isabella Boyd, daughter of General Brooke Boyd of St Leonards, Sussex; father of Dr Kennet Bruce Barnett (*q.v.*); died 24 January 1913; probate London 1 March 1913. [*BMJ* obituary (1913); Crawford (1930); Edin Univ; Kirkpatrick Archive; Lond GRO (m); Lond PPR, will cal; *Med Dir*; Merrick and Clarke, *Belfast*, vol 4 (1991); Young and Pike (1909)].

BARNETT, KENNET BRUCE (1867–1941), Army Medical Service;
born 22 September 1867 at Holywood, county Down, son of major John Milford Barnett IMS (*q.v.*) and Mary Elizabeth Catherine Johnston; educated at Methodist College, Belfast, from 1878 and Heversham Grammar School, Kendal; studied medicine at Queen's College, Belfast, from 1885; MB BCh BAO (RUI) 1892; FRCSI 1904; joined the Army Medical Service as surgeon lieutenant 1894; surgeon captain 1897; major 1905; lieutenant-colonel 1915; served in the Tirah campaign, North West Frontier 1897–8 and in World War I; retired 1919; living c 1935–40 at Oakwood, Ledborough Lane, Beaconfield, Bucks; married —; died 31 August 1941 at Oakwood; probate Llandudno 17 October 1941. [*BMJ* obituary (1941); Dub GRO (b); Fry (1984); Kirkpatrick Archive; Lond GRO (d); Lond PPR, will cal, will; *Med Dir*; Peterkin and Johnston (1968); QCB adm reg].

BARNETT, OLIVER (1830–85), Army Medical Service;
born 30 November 1830 at Clogher, county Tyrone, son of Thomas Barnett of Clogher; educated at the Cathedral School, Armagh; studied medicine at Queen's College, Belfast, 1850–53; LRCSI 1853; joined the Army Medical Service as staff assistant surgeon 1854; attached to 6th Dragoons 1856; staff surgeon 1864; transferred to 12th Lancers 1864 and to the 11th Hussars 1865; brigade surgeon 1880; deputy surgeon general 1883; surgeon general 1885; seconded while serving on the staff of three Viceroys and Governors General of India, 1873–80; CIE 1881; served in Egypt in 1882 and in Sudan in 1885; married 20 June 1866 in Clontarf Church of Ireland Church, county Dublin, Elizabeth Isabella Irvine, third daughter of Dr Gerard Irvine (*q.v.*) of Irvinestown and 2 Holly Brook Terrace, Clontarf; died 24 July 1885 at 18 Barnett Lodge, Eastbourne; administration London 6 August 1885. [Dub GRO (m); Lond PPR, will cal; *Londonderry Sentinel* 26 June 1866 (m); *Med Dir*; Murphy (2002); Peterkin and Johnston (1968); QCB adm reg].

BARNETT, RICHARD (c 1731–73), Belfast;
born c 1731; apothecary, of Belfast c 1760–70; married Margaret Orr; father of Richard Barnett (*q.v.*), who was baptised in Rosemary Street Presbyterian Church 16 March 1767; died 21 June 1773. [Taylor, Margaret, pers com].

BARNETT, RICHARD (1767–1848), Belfast;
baptised 16 March 1767 in Rosemary Street Presbyterian Church; son of Dr Richard Barnett, apothecary (*q.v.*), and Margaret Orr; reputed to have been a doctor in Belfast; married 30 September 1792, in Lanark, Scotland, Helen Jamieson; father of Richard Barnett, dentist (*q.v.*); died 1848. [Taylor, Margaret, pers com].

BARNETT, RICHARD (c 1801–67), Belfast;
born 1801/2, son of Dr Richard Barnett (*q.v.*) and Helen Jamieson of Lanark; dentist and member of Ulster Medical Society (listed as MD); of 1 Wellington Place, Belfast, and 1 Ardmore Terrace, Holywood; married 14 February 1828 in Fisherwick Presbyterian Church, Belfast, Sarah Craig Milford (who was born c 1810 and died 2 January 1890), third daughter of John Milford of Belfast; father of Dr Richard W. Barnett (*q.v.*), Dr John Milford Barnett (*q.v.*) and Dr Henry Calvert Barnett (*q.v.*); died 29 January 1867; buried in Clifton Street Graveyard, Belfast; probate Belfast 22 February 1867. [*BNL* 15 February 1828 (m); Belf PRO, will cal; Dub GRO (d); Merrick and Clarke, *Belfast,* vol 4 (1991); UMS list; Taylor, Margaret, pers com].

BARNETT, RICHARD W. (1828–1907), Belfast and Holywood, county Down;
born 4 December 1828 in Belfast, eldest son of Richard Barnett, dentist (*q.v.*), and Sarah Craig Milford; brother of Dr John Milford Barnett (*q.v.*) and Dr Henry Calvert Barnett (*q.v.*); studied medicine at RBAI and Belfast General Hospital 1845–6 and at Edinburgh University 1846–9; MD (Edin) 1849 (thesis 'On apoplexy'); MRCSE 1852; of Pau, Pyrenees, France c 1860; general practitioner of 11 Wellington Place, and 74 Pakenham Place, Belfast and lived later at 4 Ardmore Terrace, Holywood; married 27 June 1860 in Bradley Church of England Church, Staffordshire, Adela Sarah Whieldon, daughter of the Rev Edward Whieldon of Cheadle, Staffordshire;

father of Sir Richard Whieldon Barnett, MP; died 4 December 1907 at 4 Ardmore Terrace; probate Belfast 28 January 1908. [*BNL* 30 June 1860 (m); Belf PRO, will cal, will; Dub GRO (d); Edin Univ; Lond GRO (m); *Med Dir*; Taylor, Margaret, pers com].

BARNETT, — (d 1832), Belfast;
member of the Belfast Medical Society; died 1832. [Malcolm (1851)].

BARNHILL, JAMES (d 1823), Naval Medical Service;
son of James Barnhill of Backfence, Strabane, county Tyrone; joined the Naval Medical Service as assistant surgeon on HMS *Gloucester*; died 24 February 1823 off Barbadoes 'of a decline'. [*Strabane Morning Post* 29 April 1823 (d)].

BARNSLEY, RICHARD (1816/7–47), Belfast;
born 1816/7, son of Richard Barnsley, merchant, of Bridge Street, Lisburn, county Antrim; studied medicine at Glasgow University; MD (Glas) 1838; LRCSI; surgeon, of 11 College Square, Belfast and of Ballyrainey House, Comber 1845; married 25 July 1839 in Drumbo Church of Ireland Church, Mary Halliday, second daughter of Robert Halliday of Belfast; died 20 May 1847 at 11 College Square; buried in Lisburn Cathedral Graveyard. [Addison (1898); *BNL* 26 July 1839 (m), 24 October 1845 (d, daughter) and 25 May 1847 (d); *Lisburn Fam Hist Soc*, vol 2 (2005)].

BARR, JAMES (1805/6–87), Coleraine, county Londonderry;
born 1805/6, second son of James Barr, innkeeper, of New Row, Coleraine; studied medicine at Edinburgh; LRCS and LM Edin 1828; surgeon, of New Row, Coleraine; churchwarden of St Patrick's Church of Ireland Church 1844; town commissioner; medical officer to Maghera Dispensary c 1845; (1) Elizabeth Nevin (who was born 1811/2 and died 1871), daughter of James Nevin of Kilmoyle, county Antrim; (2) Sarah J. Hill of Drumnaquill, county Londonderry; father of Dr Samuel James Barr of Liverpool, MB BCh BAO (QUB) 1941; died 10 January 1887. [Coleraine C of I Church Records; Croly (1843–6); Dub GRO (d); *Med Dir*; Mullin (1969)].

BARR, SIR JAMES (1849–1938), Glasgow and Liverpool, Lancashire;
born 25 September 1849 at Cumber, county Londonderry, eldest son of Samuel Barr, JP, of Claremont, county Tyrone, and Elizabeth Townley; educated in Londonderry; studied medicine at Glasgow University; MB (Glas) 1873; LRCS Edin and LM 1873; MD 1882; MRCP Lond 1897; FRCP 1902; LLD (Toronto) 1906; LLD (Liverpool) 1912; resident house physician to Glasgow Royal Infirmary and Liverpool Northern Hospital; general practitioner in Everton, Liverpool, from 1877; physician to Stanley Hospital, Liverpool; medical officer to Kirkdale Prison; reported unsympathetically on prison conditions in Ireland in 1885, causing much political agitation and animosity to himself; visiting physician to Royal Northern Hospital, Liverpool, from 1887; visiting physician to Liverpool Royal Infirmary 1897; medical visitor to Brook Lunatic Asylum; president of the Liverpool Medical Institute 1904 and Lancashire & Cheshire Branch of BMA; lieutenant-colonel RAMC during World War I; Fellow of the Royal Society of Edinburgh; Knight Bachelor 1905; CBE 1920; Knight of

Grace of the Order of St John of Jerusalem; DL for Lancashire; of Domingo Grove, Everton, and 72 Rodney Street, Liverpool; retired to Hindhead Brae and later 16 Wildroft Manor, Putney Heath, Surrey c 1928; married 12 July 1882 in Holy Trinity Church, Walton-on-the-Hill, Lancashire, Isabella Maria Woolley (who died in September 1938), daughter of Jeremiah Woolley of Liverpool; died 16 November 1938 at 16 Wildcroft Manor; probate Liverpool 10 January 1939; 'a vigorous, pugnacious man with a strong Ulster accent, impervious to criticism and incapable of moderation' (*Munk's Roll*). [Addison (1898); *BMJ* obituary (1938); Burke, *Peerage* (1938); Kirkpatrick Archive; Lond GRO (m); Lond PPR, will cal; *Med Dir*; *Munk's Roll*, vol 4; Young and Pike (1909)].

BARR, ROBERT McDOWELL (1791/2–1867), Naval Medical Service and Maghera, county Londonderry;
   born 1791/2; joined the Naval Medical Service as assistant surgeon 1823; medical officer to Maghera and Swatra Dispensary District and constabulary from c 1827; unmarried; died 16 April 1867 at Maghera; probate Londonderry 11 May 1867. [Belf PRO, will cal; *Coleraine Chronicle* 20 April 1867 (d); Croly (1843–6); Dub GRO (d); *Londonderry Sentinel* 19 April 1867 (d); Maitland (1988); *Med Dir*].

BARRON, JAMES (1856–87), Belfast;
   born 1856 at Lyle Hall, Ballynalough, county Antrim, son of Humphrey Barron, farmer, of Ballynalough; brother of Dr John Barron (*q.v.*); studied arts and medicine at Queen's College, Belfast, from 1871; BA (QUI) 1874; MD (hons) MCh (QUI) 1879; house surgeon to the Royal Hospital, Belfast 1882–3; assistant surgeon to the Extern Department 1883–5; surgeon to the Ulster Hospital; medical officer to No 1 District of Belfast 1885–7; in private surgical practice in Belfast at 143 Donegall Street, Belfast; died 2 April 1887 of typhus fever at 143 Donegall Street; buried in Carmavy Graveyard, Templepatrick; probate Belfast 22 April 1887. [Belf PRO, will cal; *BMJ* obituary (1887); Carmavy (1993); Dub GRO (d); *Lancet* obituary (1887); *Med Dir*; QCB adm reg; Whitla (1901)].

BARRON, JOHN (1860–1918), Belfast;
   born 20 October 1860 in Ballynalough, county Antrim, son of Humphrey Barron of Ballynalough; brother of Dr James Barron (*q.v.*); educated at RBAI from 1880; studied medicine at Queen's College, Belfast, from 1880; LM KQCPI 1885; MD MCh (RUI) 1885; medical officer and registrar of births and deaths to No 2 Dispensary District, Belfast, of 147 North Street and then of 43 Clifton Street, Belfast; married —; died 10 February 1918 at 2 Benvista, Antrim Road, Belfast; buried in Belfast City Cemetery; administration Belfast 21 June 1918. [Belf City Cem, bur reg; Belf PRO, will cal; Dub GRO (d); Fisher and Robb (1913); *Lancet* obituary (1918); *Med Dir*; QCB adm reg].

BARRON, THOMAS (*fl c* 1845), Ballybay, county Monaghan;
   MRCSE 1836; accoucheur of the Anglesey Lying-in Hospital, Dublin; general practitioner in Ballybay c 1845. [Croly (1843–6)].

BARRON, — (d 1823), Banbridge, county Down;
general practitioner, of Banbridge; died 2 May 1823; 'his extensive and successful practice as a medical man, with a good disposition refined by early education ... acquired him the esteem ... of a large circle ...' [*BNL* 16 May 1823 (d)].

BARRY, JOHN B. (*fl c* 1844–60), Indian Medical Service and Calcutta, India;
of Comber; MRCS 1844; civil medical officer at Tezpur; joined the Indian Medical Service c 1849 (Bengal establishment, supplementary list); later in practice at 13 Government Place, Calcutta c 1860–70; married 22 January 1851 Emily Jane Parker, third daughter of J.P. Parker of Calcutta; son and daughter born 1858 and 1860 in Mountpottinger, Belfast; probably died c 1870 in Calcutta. [*BNL* 16 May 1851 (m), 23 November 1858 (b) and 16 February 1860 (b); Crawford (1930); *Med Dir*].

BARTLEY, ACHESON GEORGE (1836–c 1900), Army Medical Service;
born 1 September 1836 in Monaghan, son of Joseph Bartley of Corleyfin, Ballybay, county Monaghan; educated at the Rev John Bleckley's Academy; studied arts and medicine at Queen's College, Belfast, from 1853; MA (QUI) 1857; MD 1861; MRCSE 1862; DPH (Camb) 1883; joined the Army Medical Service as staff assistant surgeon 1862; posted to 101st Foot 1864; staff surgeon 1867; posted to Royal Artillery 1868; surgeon major 1876; served in Afghan War 1878–80; retired on half pay 1882; retired with rank of brigade surgeon 1883; living at 180 Albion Road, Stoke Newington, London, c 1895; married 21 September 1869 in Trory Church of Ireland,Church, county Fermanagh, Elizabeth Baynes, eldest daughter of John Baynes of Halifax, Yorkshire, and niece of Edward Irwin, JP, of Derrygore, county Fermanagh; died c 1900. [*Londonderry Sentinel* 28 September 1869 (m); *Med Dir*; Peterkin and Johnston (1968); QCB adm reg].

BARTLEY, GEORGE (d c 1801), Monaghan town;
MD [?]; general practitioner, of Monaghan town; married — (who died 25 June 1818 in Blessington Street, Dublin, 'after a long and protracted illness'); died c 1801; probate Prerogative Court 1801. [*BNL* 7 July 1818 (d); Vicars (1897)].

BARTLEY, WILLIAM (1856–1936), Ballybay, county Monaghan;
born 1856 in county Cavan, third child of William Bartley, house contractor, of Balieborough, county Cavan, and Elizabeth Ryder; educated at Bailieborough Model School; studied medicine at the Carmichael School, and from 1877, at Trinity College, Dublin; scholar and exhibitioner of Queen's College, Galway; BA (TCD) 1880; MD MCh (RUI) 1884; LM Coombe Hosp Dub 1884; BAO 1890; general practitioner in Ballybay and medical officer to the Post Office; retired c 1934 to 58 Maryville Park, Malone Road, Belfast; married 17 June 1914 in St Anne's Church of Ireland Church, Dublin, Elizabeth Dorcas Campbell of 17 Kildare Street, Crossmolina, county Mayo, daughter of James Campbell, farmer; died 18 December 1936 at the San Remo Nursing Home, 81 University Street, Belfast; buried in Ballybay Presbyterian Churchyard; probate Belfast 15 October 1937. [Belf GRO (d); Belf PRO, will cal; Dub GRO (m); McNeill, Thomas, pers com; *Med Dir*; TCD adm reg; *TCD Cat*, vol II (1896)].

BARTON, TRAVERS BOYNE (1855–83), Lifford, county Donegal;
   born 1855 in Drogheda, county Louth, son of James Barton of Farndreg, county Louth, civil engineer; studied medicine at Trinity College, Dublin, from 1872; BA (TCD) 1876; MB 1877; LM Rot Hosp Dub 1877; LRCSI 1877; MD 1880; house surgeon to the West Kent General Hospital; resident surgeon in Adelaide Hospital, Dublin; surgeon with P & O Steamship Company; surgeon to county Donegal Infirmary from 1881, of Lifford, county Donegal; unmarried; died 24 April 1883 in a drowning accident at Prehen, county Londonderry; administration Londonderry 27 June 1883. [Belf PRO, will cal; Dub GRO (d); Kirkpatrick Archive; *Med Dir;* TCD adm reg; *TCD Cat,* vol II (1896)].

BASKIN, JAMES CHARLES (d c 1914), Lurgan, county Armagh, and Dromore, county Down;
   studied medicine at Royal College of Surgeons in Ireland; LRCSI and LM, LRCPI and LM 1898; assistant house surgeon to the Taunton and Somerset Hospital and civil surgeon to the troops; general practitioner, of Hill House, Lurgan c 1901–6 and of Ballykeel House, Dromore, c 1906–14; died c 1914. [*Med Dir*].

BASKIN, JOSEPH LOUGHEED (1869–1941), Salisbury, Wiltshire, London and RAMC;
   born 1869 at Enniskillen, son of the Rev Charles Baskin, minister of Ballynafeigh Methodist Church, Belfast; educated at Armagh Royal School 1879–81; studied medicine at Edinburgh University, London and Cork; LRCP LRCS Edin 1897; LFPS Glas 1899; MD (Bruxelles) (grande distinction) 1911; medical superintendent of Fisherton Asylum, Salisbury; neurologist at Maudesley Hospital, London (6 months); senior neurologist to the Ministry of Pensions Hospital, Orpington and the Ashurst Hospital (12 months); joined the RAMC as captain and served in France 1915–17; severely wounded at Messines (1917) and invalided out; subsequently 'travelling' but c 1935 of Warming Hall, Aylesbury, Buckinghamshire; married Kathleen —; died 30 August 1941 at the Warneford Hospital, Oxford; administration Oxford 17 January 1942. [Ferrar (1933); Lond PPR, will cal; *Med Dir*]

BATE, ABRAHAM WILLIAM (1841–1906), Army Medical Service;
   born 4 May 1841, of Burton Port, county Donegal; studied medicine at the Royal College of Surgeons in Ireland; LRCSI 1860; MD (St Andrew's) 1862 (by examination); joined the Army Medical Service as assistant staff surgeon 1865; surgeon 1873; surgeon major 1877; served in Sudan in 1885 (medal with clasp and Khedive's bronze star); retired with honorary rank of brigade surgeon (surgeon lieutenant-colonel) 1885; returned to Trinity College, Dublin to study arts and medicine; BA (TCD) 1890; MB BAO 1891; BCh 1892; FRCSI 1894; general practitioner, of 50 Northumberland Road, Dublin c 1895 and later of 'Tregenna', Sundridge Park, Bromley, Kent; married Kate —; died 22 October 1906 at 'Tregenna'; administration London 10 November 1906. [*BMJ* obituary (1906); Lond GRO (d); Lond PPR, will cal; *Med Dir*; Peterkin and Johnston (1968); Smart (2004); TCD adm reg; *TCD Cat*, vol II (1896)].

BATE, ALBERT LOUIS FREDERICK (1862–1924), Army Medical Service;
born 5 October 1862, son of Henry A. Bate of Dublin; educated at Methodist College, Belfast, from 1871; studied medicine at the Ledwich School and Rotunda Hospital, Dublin; LRCSI 1884; LRCPI and LM 1885; FRIPH; joined Army Medical Service as surgeon captain 1886; major 1899; lieutenant-colonel 1906; colonel 1914; served in South African War 1899–1902 in Natal and Zululand and was in command of the stationary hospitals at Machadodorph (received Queen's and King's medals with two clasps on each); served in World War 1 1914–18 (mentioned in despatches); retired to Fern Glen, Hampton Court Road, Kingston-on-Thames; CMG 1916; died 20 February 1924 in Queen Alexandra's Military Hospital, Millbank, London. [Fry (1984); Lond GRO (d); *Med Dir*; Peterkin and Johnston (1968)].

BATEMAN, SAMUEL (1854–1929), Middlesborough, Yorks;
born 23 August 1854 at Maralin, county Down, son of John Bateman of Feney, Maralin and Sarah —; educated at Kilkinamurry Academy; studied medicine at Queen's College, Belfast, from 1872; MD MCh (QUI) 1876; house surgeon and later honorary surgeon to the North Riding Infirmary, Middlesborough; retired to Drumnabreeze, Maralin, county Down c 1900; unmarried; died 28 November 1929 at Drumnabreeze; buried in Moira graveyard; probate Belfast 1 July 1930. [Belf GRO (d); Belf PRO, will cal; Clarke, *County Down*, vol 18 (1979); Kirkpatrick Archive; *Med Dir*; QCB adm reg].

BATTYE, JOHN HOWARD (1853–1905), London;
born 12 April 1853 in Pimlico, London, son of Dr Richard Faucett Battye; educated at Merchant Taylor's School, London; studied medicine at King's College, London, and from 1878, at Queen's College, Belfast; MRCSE 1877; LRCP Lond 1878; MD (QUI) 1880; general practitioner, of Belgrave Road, Westminster, London from c 1880; married Jemima —; died 20 September 1905; probate London 11 November 1905. [Lond PPR, will cal; *Med Dir*; QCB adm reg].

BAXTER, FRANCIS HASTINGS (1819–88), Army Medical Service and Dublin;
born 26 May 1819 at Enniskillen; LAH and LM Dublin 1840; MRCSE 1841; MD (St Andrew's) 1844 (by examination); FRCSE 1857; joined the Army Medical Service as assistant surgeon to 54th Foot 1845; staff surgeon, 2nd class, 1854; transferred to 6th Dragoon Guards 1855 and to 12th Dragoons 1860; surgeon major 1865; staff surgeon 1869; served in Crimea, being decorated with the Medjidie Order (5th class); retired on half pay with rank of deputy inspector general 1870; surgeon to the Royal Hibernian Military School, Phoenix Park, Dublin; retired to Ivy Lodge, Cheltenham; married Anne Margaret —; died 19 March 1888 at Ivy Lodge; administration Gloucester 25 April 1888. [Lond PPR, will cal; *Med Dir*; Peterkin and Johnston (1968); Plarr (1930); Smart (2004)].

BEAMISH, BENJAMIN (1860–1937), Longton, Lancashire, Datchet, Buckinghamshire, and Newry, county Down;
born 1 December 1860 in Cork city, fourth son of Dr William Beamish, MB (Edin) 1836, of Mount Beamish, Bandon, and Ellen Prudence Gregory; educated at Kingstown School; studied medicine at Royal College of Surgeons in Ireland; LRCPI

and LM, LRCSI and LM 1887; LM Rot Hosp Dub; general practitioner in Longton, c 1887–91 and in Datchet c 1892–94; physician and surgeon to Newry Fever and General hospitals from 1894; civil surgeon in medical charge of the troops at the Station Hospital, Newry; of 10 Trevor Hill, Newry c 1905; retired c 1913 to Eglinton Lodge, Dalkey, county Dublin; served in RAMC during World War I with rank of captain; moved to 'Elsinore', Malahide c 1923; married 21 March 1888 in Monkstown Church of Ireland Church, county Dublin, Florence Vance (who died in 1943), youngest daughter of Thomas Vance of Blackrock House, county Dublin; father of Dr Desmond William Beamish, LRCPI LRCSI 1913, RAMC; died 4 January 1937; probate Dublin 24 May 1937. [Burke *LGI* (1958); Crossle (1909); Dub GRO (m); Dub Nat Arch, will cal; Kirkpatrick Archive; *Med Dir*].

BEARD, THOMAS (1854–1922), Towcester, Northamptonshire, Bungay, Suffolk, London and Stirling;
born 17 June 1854 at Athy, county Kildare, son of Richard Beard of Athy; educated at the Diocesan School, Wexford; studied medicine for 4 years at the Ledwich School, Dublin, and from 1877, at Queen's College, Belfast; LSA Lond 1883; LRCPI and LM 1889; LRCS Edin 1890; general practitioner, of Towcester c 1885 and Bungay c 1895; medical officer in charge of troops at the Military Prison and Ordanance Depot, Stirling, of 8 Glebe Crescent, Stirling, from c 1896; surgeon captain in Army Medical Reserve and 2nd Hertfordshire Regiment (VR), of 120 Wrottesley Road and 4 Holland House, Harlesden, London, c 1905; medical officer to 3rd London Brigade of Royal Field Artillery; major RAMC (Territorials) c 1918; retired to Woodstock Cottage, Kelsall, Saxmundham, Kent, c 1920; married Anne Augusta Wolseley; died 20 April 1922; administration (with will) London 6 July 1922. [Lond PPR, will cal, will; *Med Dir*; QCB adm reg].

BEATT, WILLIAM (1866/7–96), Cavan, and Rawtenstall, Lancashire;
born 1866/7; LRCP LRCS Edin 1892; LFPS Glas 1892; general practitioner, of Keadew Lodge, Cavan c 1893–6, and finally of 18 Kay Street, Rawtenstall; married Marie —; died 5 July 1896 at Rawtenstall ('accidentally suffocated and killed by falling face down on the hearth rug whilst drunk'); administration Lancaster 20 July 1896. [Lond GRO (d); Lond PPR, will cal; *Med Dir*].

BEATTIE, HENRY OSBORNE (d c 1922), Rathfriland, county Down, and Pittsburg, Pennsylvania, USA;
studied medicine at the Ledwich School, Dublin; LRCSI 1883; LM Coombe Hosp Dub; medical officer with the Mediterranean, African and Atlantic Steamship Services on SS *India*; general practitioner, of Rathfriland c 1892–6; emigrated to USA c 1896; general practitioner, of 222 Sheridan Avenue, 5718 Margaretta Street, and 5941 Whitfield Street, Pittsburg, from c 1897; surgeon to various companies in Pittsburg; died c 1922. [*Med Dir*].

BEATTIE, HUGH (d 1846), Conlig, county Down;
of Comber, county Down; LRCS Edin 1818, as advertised in the *BNL*; surgeon, of Conlig; died 18 November 1846 at Conlig. [*BNL* 31 March 1818 and 24 November 1846 (d)].

BEATTIE, JAMES (d 1814), Ballycastle, county Antrim;
general practitioner, of Ballycastle; died 26 January 1814; '… in the dawn of his manhood … to a talent of the first rate description in his profession, he added all that could be acquired by study for so young a man …'. [*BNL* 1 February 1814 (d)].

BEATTIE, JAMES (1860–c 1947), Butterknowle, county Durham;
born November 1860 at Caugherty; educated at the Belfast Seminary; studied medicine at Queen's College, Belfast, from 1879; LRCP LRCS Edin 1887; LFPS Glas 1887; general practitioner and medical officer of health for Staindrop District c 1890–1908, of Woodlands, Butterknowle, county Durham; retired to 'The Garth', Old Eldon, county Durham c 1937 and to Cotherstone, Barnard Castle c 1941; died c 1946–7. [*Med Dir*; QCB adm reg].

BEATTIE, ROBERT (*fl c* 1819), London;
son of Thomas Beattie of Lisburn; MD [?]; physician, of London; married 13 April 1819 Rebecca Anne Wilkinson, eldest daughter of Captain Wilkinson, of the 60th Rifle Battalion. [*BNL* 4 May 1819 (m)].

BEATTIE, ROBERT (1848/9–1931), Loughborough, Leicestershire, and Dewsbury, Yorkshire;
born 1848/9 at Ballymena, county Antrim, son of John Beattie of Ballygarvey, Ballymena; educated at Ballymena Academy; studied medicine at Queen's Colleges, Belfast and Galway, 1872–76; MD MCh (QUI) 1876; Dip Mid 1879; MRCSE 1882; medical officer to Loughborough Infirmary and Dispensary District; medical officer of health to Soothill Upper and honorary surgeon to Dewsbury Infirmary; of Ardmore House, Dewsbury, from c 1880 and of 'Normanhyrst', Dewsbury, from c 1906; married Jane — (who died 19 May 1928 at 20 Carshalton Road, Blackpool); father of Dr Thomas Mace Beattie, LMSSA Lond 1927; died 23 April 1931 at 'Normanhyrst'; probate London 6 August 1931. [Lond GRO (d); Lond PPR, will cal, will; *Med Dir*; QCB adm reg].

BEATTIE (BEATTY), SAMUEL (1860/1–1921), Pitlochry, Perthshire;
born 1860/1, son of Nathaniel Beatty of Ahoghill, county Antrim; studied medicine at Trinity College, Dublin, and Edinburgh Unversity and the Royal College of Surgeons, Edinburgh; MB MCh (Edin) 1886; clinical assistant at Edinburgh Royal Infirmary and junior demonstrator in pathology at Edinburgh University; general physician, of Craigatin, Pitlochry, from c 1890; medical officer to Pitlochry Parish, post office and to the Irving Memorial Nursing Home; certifying factory surgeon; president of the Perthshire Branch of the BMA; chairman of Pitlochry School Management Committee; married Verbor Borikae (Agnese Nansen Ulliesweane) Douglas; died 16 June 1921 at Craigvar, Pitlochry; confirmation of will Perth 30 September 1921. [*BMJ* obituary (1921); Edin GRO (d); Edin Nat Arch, will cal; Kirkpatrick (1889); Kirkpatrick Archive; *Med Dir*].

BEATTIE, WILLIAM (*fl c* 1811), Dervock, county Antrim;
surgeon, of Dervock; married 4 September 1811 Jane Stuart, daughter of Archibald Stuart of Portrush, county Antrim. [*BNL* 17 September 1811 (m)].

BEATTIE (BEATTY), WILLIAM (d 1843), Ballymena, county Antrim;
MD [?]; surgeon and apothecary, of Mill Street, Ballymena c 1824; a daughter, Elizabeth Jane Beattie, married 6 July 1847; died 27 May 1843 at Ballymena of a lingering illness. [*BNL* 2 June 1843 (d) and 10 July 1847 (m, daughter); *Coleraine Chronicle* 10 July 1847 (m, daughter); Pigot (1824)].

BEATTIE, WILLIAM THOMAS (1858/9–1928), Ballygawley, county Tyrone;
born 1858/9; studied medicine at the Royal College of Surgeons in Ireland; LRCSI 1881; LM Rot Hosp Dub; LKQCPI 1883; general practitioner, of Ballygawley; married —; died 24 July 1928 at Ballygawley; probate Londonderry 2 November 1928. [Belf GRO (d); Belf PRO, will cal; *Med Dir*].

BEATTY, ELIZABETH (1857–1924); Dublin and Kwangning, China;
born 30 January 1857 at Ballymena, county Antrim, daughter of the Rev John Beatty, minister of Roseyards Presbyterian Church, county Antrim; educated at The Ladies' School, Ballymena; studied medicine at Queen's College, Belfast, from 1894; LRCP LRCS Edin 1899; LFPS Glas 1899; general practitioner in Dublin; medical missionary with the Presbyterian Missionary Society, in Kwangning, China 1906–17; retired to Whitehead, county Antrim, and then Berkley, California; died 16 January 1924 at Berkley. [Boyd (1908); *Irish Times* 13 August 1924 (d); Kelly (2010); Kirkpatrick Archive; *Med Dir*; QCB adm reg].

BEATTY, GUY (d c 1917), Tempo, county Fermanagh, South Africa and Nigeria;
studied medicine at Edinburgh University; MB MCh (Edin) 1894; LDS RCSI 1905; general practitioner, of Tempo c 1896–1900; civil surgeon with South African Field Force c 1900; general practitioner, of Highgate, Princes Street, Port Elizabeth, Cape Colony c 1903–9; medical officer with West African Medical Staff, Nigeria, c 1909–17; died c 1917. [*Med Dir*].

BEATTY, JAMES (1786–1854), Enniskillen, county Fermanagh;
born 1786; studied medicine at Edinburgh University; MD (Edin) 1808 (thesis 'De consensu'); assistant surgeon to Fermanagh militia 1810; superintendent of Enniskillen Cholera Hospital 1832; general practitioner, of Enniskillen c 1845; married —; father of Prudentia Beatty (who was born 1814/5 and died 21 October 1835 of smallpox); died 17 December 1854 at Omagh; probate Prerogative Court 1856. [*BNL* 25 December 1854 (d); Belf PRO, prerog wills index; Croly (1843–6); Dub GRO (m); Edin Univ; Leslie (1929); *Med Dir*; *Strabane Morning Post* 27 October 1835 (d)].

BEATTY, JAMES (1870–1947), Dublin, Manchester, Lancashire, Northampton, RAMC and Cardiff;
born 7 July 1870 in Ballymena, county Antrim, son of James Beatty, druggist; educated at Coleraine Academical Institution; studied arts and medicine at Trinity College, Dublin, from 1888; scholar 1891; BA (TCD) 1892, with gold medal; MB (hons) BCh BAO 1895 with many scholarships and prizes; MD 1896; MB (Lond) (hons in medicine) 1899; DPH RCPSI 1901; MA 1902; house surgeon and physician to Dr Steeven's Hospital, and demonstrator in anatomy to Trinity College,

Dublin, c 1897; general practitioner, of 28 Harcourt Street, Dublin c 1898–1901; senior assistant to the medical officer of health for Manchester c 1901–3; medical officer of health and superintendent of Infectious Diseases Hospital and Hospital for Consumption, Northampton, of 26 Derngate, Northampton c 1903–20; temporary captain in RAMC during World War I; lecturer in dermatology and assistant lecturer in pharmacology to the Welsh National School of Medicine, Cardiff, and dermatologist to Cardiff Royal Infirmary and Hamadryad Hospital, of 121 Queen Street, Cardiff c 1920–27; of 84 Cathedral Road, Cardiff c 1927–47; president of the Cardiff Medical Society; author of papers on tuberculosis, dermatology and public health; retired 1937; died 16 October 1947 in Cardiff. [*BMJ* obituary (1947); Dub GRO (b); *Med Dir*; TCD adm reg; *TCD Cat*, vols II (1896) and III (1906)].

BEATTY, JOHN (b c 1763), Dublin and Cavan;
born c 1763, second son of the Rev John Beatty, vicar of Garvaghy, county Down, by his first wife Abigail Young of Killashandra; studied medicine at Trinity College, Dublin, 1786–8; MD (St Andrews) 1788 (by examination and testimonials); physician, of Molesworth Street, Dublin, and of Dingens, county Cavan; married November 1792 Mary Betagh, fourth daughter of Henry Betagh, solicitor, of York Street, Dublin; father of the Rev John Beatty, rector of Donacloney, county Down, who was father of Dr Thomas Berkley Beatty, IMS (*q.v.*). [Farrar (1897); Smart (2004); Swanzy (1933)].

BEATTY, JOHN WILLIAM (1856–1942), Army Medical Service;
born 15 June 1856 in Dublin, son of John Beatty, carpet manufacturer, of Stillorgan, Dublin; educated at Parsonstown School; studied medicine at the Royal College of Surgeons in Ireland and, from 1878, at Queen's College, Belfast; LM Rot Hosp Dub 1876; LKQCPI and LM 1876; LRCSI 1876; MD (QUI) 1879; joined the Army Medical Service as surgeon captain 1881; surgeon major 1893; served in Egypt 1882 and Ashanti 1895–6; retired 1899 to Highdown Avenue, Worthing, Sussex; died 4 June 1942 at the Myrtles Nursing Home, Farncombe Road, Worthing; probate Llandudno 29 July 1942. [Lond PPR, will cal; *Med Dir*; Peterkin and Johnston (1968); QCB adm reg].

BEATTY, MARTYN (MARTIN) CECIL (1875–1945), Army Medical Service;
born 30 March 1875 at Donaghadee, county Down, son of the Rev John Beatty, minister of Ballycopeland Presbyterian Church, county Down, and Mary Moorehead; brother of Dr Robert Moorhead Beatty (*q.v.*); educated at RBAI; studied medicine at Queen's College, Belfast, from 1894; MB BCh (Edin) 1900; DPH 1903; joined the Army Medical Service as lieutenant 1901; captain 1904; major 1913; temporary lieutenant-colonel 1915–18; lieutenant-colonel 1923; served in South Africa 1902, India 1903–9, France 1914–16, East Africa 1916–19, Egypt 1920–21, India 1921–4, BAOR 1924–9; retired 1930; of the Laurels, Broadway, Worcestershire from c 1935; married Dorothy Mary —; died 1 June 1945 at Evesham Hospital, Worcestershire; probate Llandudno 17 August 1945. [Barkley (1986); Drew (1968); Kirkpatrick Archive; Lond PPR, will cal; *Med Dir*; QCB adm reg].

BEATTY, ROBERT (1796–1821), Indian Medical Service;
born 29 September 1796, fifth son of Thomas Beatty, tanner, of Lisburn, and Elizabeth Higginson; joined the Indian Medical Service (Bombay establishment) as assistant surgeon 1819; married Rebecca Wilkinson of Ballinderry, daughter of Captain — Wilkinson of the 8th Veterinary Battalion; died 5 January 1821 at Surat, Bombay. [*BNL* 31 July 1821 (d); Belf PRO, T 1289/3; Crawford (1930); *Lisburn Fam Hist Soc*, vol I (2000)].

BEATTY, ROBERT MOORHEAD (1865–1947), Belfast and Heckmondwike, Yorkshire;
born 6 January 1865 at Ballycopeland, county Down, son of the Rev John Beatty, minister of Ballycopeland Presbyterian Church, and Mary Moorhead; brother of Dr Martyn Cecil Beatty (*q.v.*); educated at Methodist College, Belfast, from 1883; studied arts and medicine at Queen's College, Belfast, from 1883; BA (RUI) 1886; MB BCh BAO 1893; resident medical officer at Rotunda Hospital, Dublin; civil surgeon to Station Hospital, Victoria Barracks, Belfast; house surgeon and house physician, Belfast Royal Hospital; assistant pathologist to Royal Victoria Hospital, Belfast 1903–4; pathologist to Forster Green Hospital and honorary attending assistant physician to Belfast Hospital for Sick Children 1901–7; medical officer to Liversedge Dispensary District 1908–36, of Westfield House, Heckmondwike; author of various medical papers, married —; died 24 December 1947 at Westfield House, Heckmondwike; probate London 19 May 1948. [Barkley (1986); Belf GRO (b); Calwell (1973); Fry (1984); Kirkpatrick Archive; Lond GRO (d); Lond PPR, will cal, will; *Med Dir*; QCB adm reg].

BEATTY, THOMAS BERKELEY (1827–1916), Indian Medical Service;
born 4 November 1827 in county Armagh, youngest son of the Rev John Beatty, rector of Donaghcloney, county Down, and Charlotte Wakefield Nicholson of Stranmore House, county Down; grandson of Dr John Beatty of Dublin (*q.v.*) and first cousin of Brigadier General John Nicholson of the Indian Mutiny; educated by Mr Jones; studied arts and medicine at Trinity College, Dublin, from 1845; BA (TCD) 1850; LRCSI 1850; MB MD 1861; FRCSI 1861; joined the Indian Medical Service (Bombay establishment) as assistant surgeon 1851; surgeon 1864; surgeon major 1871; deputy surgeon general 1876; surgeon general 1880; retired 1885; married (1) 16 March 1854 in Karachi, India, Jane Woodbourne, eldest daughter of Colonel Woodbourne, CB, brigadier commanding the station at Karachi; (2) 17 October 1861 in St Peter's Church of Ireland Church, Dublin, Sarah Augusta Ellis (minor), daughter of Dr George Ellis of 91 Lower Leeson Street, Dublin; (3) — Capper; father of Dr Thomas Edward Bellingham Beatty, MB (TCD) 1919, RAMC; died 28 November 1916 at Monkstown, county Dublin; probate Dublin 18 January 1917. [*BNL* 3 May 1854 (m); Belf PRO, will cal; *BMJ* obituary (1917); Burtchaell and Sadleir (1924); Crawford (1930); Dub GRO (m) and (d); Kirkpatrick Archive; Swanzy (1933)].

BEATTY, WALLACE (1853–1923), Dublin;
born 13 November 1853 in Halifax, Nova Scotia, son of James Beatty, engineer, and Sarah Jane Burke of Kilmarron Rectory, county Monaghan; educated at

Dungannon Royal School; studied arts and medicine at Trinity College, Dublin 1872–9; scholar 1875; BA (TCD) 1876; MB BCh 1879; LM Rot Hosp Dub 1881; LRCPI 1885; MD 1886; MKQCPI 1886; FKQCPI 1887; house surgeon to St Mark's Ophthalmic Hospital, Dublin; medical officer to the Dublin Throat and Ear Hospital; demonstrator of anatomy in the Carmichael College and later lecturer in pathology and medicine; senior assistant physician and later physician (and dermatologist) to the Adelaide Hospital; honorary professor of dermatology, TCD; author of many medical papers; of 38 Merrion Square, Dublin from c 1900; married 2 June 1888 Frances Eleanor Edge (who died 30 April 1908), daughter of Samuel Edge of Grantstown House, Queen's County; father of Dr John Edge Beatty; died 8 November 1923 at 38 Merrion Square; memorial in the Adelaide Hospital; probate Dublin 7 December 1923. [*BMJ* obituary (1923); Cameron (1916); Dub Nat Arch, will cal; Kirkpatrick Archive; *Med Dir;* TCD adm reg; *TCD Cat*, Vol. II (1896)].

BEATTY, SIR WILLIAM (1773–1842), Naval Medical Service;
born April 1773 in Londonderry, eldest son of James Beatty of H M Customs, Londonderry, and Ann Smyth; probably apprenticed to his uncle Dr George Smyth (*q.v.*) c 1755; continued to study medicine in London c 1789–91; examined and joined the Naval Medical Service 1791 as surgeon's mate; appointed surgeon to HMS *Dictator* 1791, *Iphigenia* 1791, *Hermione* 1793 in West Indies, *Flying Fish* 1793, *Alligator* 1794, *Amethyst* 1795, *Pomona* 1795 where he had an argument with Captain Fitzroy and was court martialled but acquitted; *Alcmene* 1796–1801 (with valuable prizes); served at the Nile engagement 1798 and the evacuation of King Ferdinand and Lord and Lady Hamilton 1799; served on HMS *Resistance* and *Leash* 1801, *Spencer* 1803 and *Victory* 1804–6; attended Admiral Nelson at his death, carried out a post mortem and preserved his body for burial in Westminster Abbey; MD (Aberdeen) (on testimonials) 1806; appointed physician to the Fleet c 1806; MD (St Andrew's) (on testimonials) 1817; LRCP Lond 1817; FRS 1818; author of *An Authentic Narrative of the Death of Lord Nelson* (1807); resident physician to Greenwich Hospital 1822–39; Knight 1831; unmarried; died 25 March 1842 at 43 York Street, Portman Square, London; buried in Kensal Green Cemetery (no memorial); portrait by Arthur William Devis (c 1806) in National Maritime Museum. [Allison (1941); Brockliss, Cardwell and Moss (2005); Clarke (2006); Clippingdale (1915); *DIB* (2009); Lond GRO (d); *Munk's Roll*, vol 3; *NMS* (1826); *Oxford DNB* (2004); Smart (2004)].

BEATTY, — (*fl c* 1815), Lisnaskea, county Fermanagh;
general practitioner, of Lisnaskea c 1815; married 17 November 1815 in Lisnaskea Church of Ireland Church, Susan Rennick of Lisnaskea. [Lisnaskea C of I Mar Reg (Belf PRO, D/2896/1/2)].

BEATTY, — (d before 1839), Lisburn, county Antrim;
general practitioner, of Lisburn; married —; daughter born c 1804 and died 13 April 1838 at Ballynahinch; died before 1839. [*BNL* 24 April 1838 (d, daughter)].

BEAUMONT, JOHN (*fl c* 1780), Rathfriland, county Down;
general practitioner, of Rathfriland; married —; father of — Beaumont who was born 1780/1, married S. Dunlop, surgeon (*q.v.*) and died 3 May 1860. [*BNL* 8 May 1860 (d, daughter)].

BECK, FREDERICK EMMET (1843/4–96), Belfast;
born 1843/4, son of Dr John Woods Beck (*q.v.*) of 128 North Street, Belfast; brother of Dr John Fritz Beck (*q.v.*) and Dr Walter Beck, LRCP LRCS Edin 1902; educated at Belfast Academy; studied arts and medicine at Queen's College, Belfast, from 1859; LM QCB 1861; LRCP Edin and LM 1867; LRCS Edin and LM 1867; LAH Dub 1867; MRCP Edin 1877; FRCP Edin 1878; general practitioner, of 113 North Street, Belfast c 1871, 5 Clarence Place (c 1875) and Fitzroy House, Botanic Avenue c 1885–96; married Margaret Orr; died 31 October 1896 at Fitzroy House; buried in Belfast City Cemetery; probate Belfast 16 December 1896. [Belf City Cem, bur reg; Belf PRO, will cal; Dub GRO (d); *Med Dir*; QCB adm reg; Whitla (1901)].

BECK, JOHN FRITZ (1842/3–1900), Milford, county Donegal;
born 1842/3, son of Dr John Woods Beck (*q.v.*) of 128 North Street, Belfast; brother of Dr Frederick Emmett Beck (*q.v.*) and Dr Walter Beck, LRCP LRCS Edin 1902; educated at Belfast Academy; studied arts and medicine at Queen's College, Belfast, from 1859; BA (QUI) 1864; MA 1865; MD MCh 1868; ordained minister of Milford Reformed Presbyterian Church 1870; married —; died 29 March 1900 at Urbalshinny, Milford. [Dub GRO (d); *Med Dir*; Presb Hist Soc; QCB adm reg].

BECK, JOHN WOODS (1819–86), Belfast;
born 1819; studied medicine at RBAI from 1835, at Glasgow University and Belfast General Hospital; LM Belf 1836; LM Glas 1838; CM (Glas) 1839; MD (Glas) 1840; LAH Dub 1841; medical officer to the Belfast Dispensary 1841–7; general practitioner at 128 and 130 North Street, 53 Bentinck Street, 11 Canning Street and Claremont Street, Belfast, from 1840; married c 1840 —; father of Dr John Fritz Beck (*q.v.*), Dr Frederick Emmett Beck (*q.v.*) and Dr Walter Beck, LRCP LRCS Edin 1902; died 2 May 1886 at Claremont Street, Belfast; buried in Belfast City Cemetery; probate Belfast 2 June 1886. [Addison (1898); Belf City Cem, bur reg; Belf PRO, SCH 524/1A; Belf PRO, will cal; Croly (1843–6); Dub GRO (d); Malcolm (1851) *Med Dir;* Whitla (1901)].

BECKETT, ALEXANDER (1831/2–88), Victoria, Australia, Moneymore, county Londonderry;
born 1831/2, son of Philip Beckett, farmer; studied medicine at Glasgow University; LM Glasgow Lying-in Hospital 1848; MD (Glas) 1852; honorary medical officer to Beechworth Hospital, Victoria, Australia; general practitioner at Moneymore; married 9 December 1869 in First Donaghadee Presbyterian Church, Sarah Ekin, daughter of John Ekin, farmer, of Coagh, county Tyrone; died 23 January 1888 at Moneymore; probate Londonderry 23 February 1888. [Addison (1898); *Coleraine Chronicle* 18 December 1869 (m); Belf PRO, will cal; Dub GRO (m) and (d); *Londonderry Sentinel* 14 December 1869 (m); *Med Dir*].

BECKETT, JOHN C. (d 1841), Falmouth, Jamaica;
>of Drumart, Ballymoney, county Antrim; died 12 October 1841 at Aberdeen Pen, Falmouth, Jamaica. [*BNL* 28 December 1841 (d); *Londonderry Sentinel* 8 January 1842 (d)].

BEDFORD, SIR WALTER GEORGE AUGUSTUS (1858–1922), Army Medical Service;
>born 24 October 1858 at Rathmullan, county Donegal, son of Vice-Admiral George Augustus Bedford; studied medicine at Durham University and St Bartholomew's Hospital, London; MD (Durham) 1880; MRCSE 1880; DCL (*hon causa*) (Durham) 1920; joined the Army Medical Service as surgeon (surgeon captain) 1881; surgeon major RAMC 1893; lieutenant-colonel 1901; colonel 1908; staff officer to the principal medical officer in the South African Field Force 1899–1901; principal medical officer in South China 1908–11 and in London 1912–13; retired on half pay 1912–4 when he returned as surgeon general; adjutant at the Aldershot Depot; director of medical services to the Mediterranean and Egyptian Expeditionary Forces 1915–16; CMG 1901; CB (military) 1916; retired with rank of major-general 1918; KCME 1918; of The Holt, Eynsham, Oxford; married 29 December 1880 in St Bartholomew's Parish Church, Lewisham, Harriette Adelaide Drakeford, daughter of the Rev David James Drakeford; died 8 January 1922 at Eynsham; probate London 15 February 1922. [*BMJ* obituary (1922); Kirkpatrick Archive; *Lancet* obituary (1922); Lond GRO (m); Lond PPR, will cal; *Med Dir*; Peterkin and Johnston (1968)].

BEERS, JAMES (SHAW) (d 1851), Ballymoney, county Antrim;
>studied medicine at Glasgow University; CM (Glas) 1832; accoucheur of the Lying-in Hospital, Glasgow; general practitioner in Ballymoney c 1845; married 14 September 1835 in Billy Church, county Antrim, Jane Hill, daughter of Samuel Hill of Ballylough, Bushmills; died 19 March 1851 at Ballylough. [Addison (1898); *BNL* 22 September 1835 (m); *Coleraine Chronicle* 29 March 1851 (d); Croly (1843–6); *Londonderry Sentinel* 28 March 1851 (d)].

BEERS, JOSEPH (d 1781), Ballymoney, county Antrim;
>surgeon, of Ballymoney; married Elizabeth —; died 1781; probate 1782, abstract in Registry of Deeds, Dublin. [Eustace, vol II (1954)].

BEGGS, SAMUEL THOMAS (1873–1958), Belfast, Burnley and Manchester, Lancashire and RAMC;
>born 7 February 1873 at 4 Brook Street, Mountpottinger, Belfast, son of James Beggs, clerk, of Brook Street and Margaret McMurtray; studied medicine at Queen's College, Belfast, from 1891; MB BCh BAO (hons) (RUI) 1896; MD (QUB) 1911; DPH 1919; house surgeon and house physician to the Royal Victorial Hospital, Belfast; demonstrator in physiology at Queen's College, Belfast; clinical assistant to Ulster Hospital for Children and Women and the Samaritan Hospital, Belfast; civil and military surgeon to the Victoria Barracks, Belfast; surgeon to Bangor Homes of Rest and Dromore Cottage Hospital; of 30 Lonsdale Terrace, Carlisle Circus, Belfast; moved as general practitioner c 1906 to 96 Manchester Road, Burnley; medical

officer in charge of recruiting, Burnley; captain RAMC Reserve of Officers c 1910; served in RAMC in World War I with rank of major; medical officer of health of Middleton, Manchester, c 1923; retired c 1943 to live at 12 Broadway, Morecambe, Lancashire, and later at 33 Albert Road, 6 Queen's Road and 52 Ashton Road, Southport; married —; died 20 February 1958 at the Royal Southern Hospital, Liverpool; buried in Belfast City Cemetery; probate Liverpool 15 May 1958. [Belf City Cem, bur reg; Belf GRO (b); Lond GRO (d); Lond PPR, will cal, will; *Med Dir*; QCB adm reg].

BELL, CHARLES (*fl c* 1798), Ballynure, county Antrim;
LAH Dub 1798; apothecary, of Ballynure. [Apothecaries (1829)].

BELL, DOLWAY (1799/1800–65), Glenavy, county Antrim;
born 1799/1800; studied medicine at Glasgow University; LFPS and LM Glas 1854; medical officer to Glenavy Dispensary District, of Bellgrove, Glenavy; married 23 December 1854 in Soldierstown, county Antrim, Martha Heastie, daughter of John Heastie of Aghalee; died 18 February 1865 at Bellgrove; buried in Glenavy Roman Catholic Graveyard; probate Belfast 27 April 1865. [*BNL* 31 December 1824 (m); Belf PRO, will cal; Croly (1843–6); gravestone inscription; *Med Dir*].

BELL, ELIZABETH GOULD (1862–1934), Belfast and Malta;
born 24 December 1862, daughter of Joseph Bell, clerk of the Union, of Killeavy Castle and Springhill, county Armagh, and Margaret Smith; sister of Dr Margaret Bell (*q.v.*); studied arts and medicine at Queen's College, Belfast, from 1887, and Belfast Royal Hospital; one of the first five women medical students in Belfast; MB BCh BAO (RUI) 1893; general practitioner, of 41 and later 83 Great Victoria Street and 4 College Gardens, Belfast, 1925; worked in Malta during World War I; medical offier to the Malone Place Hospital, Riddell Hall and Belfast Corporation 'Baby Club', Belfast c 1922–6; married 2 March 1896, in Fitzroy Presbyterian Church, Belfast, Dr Hugh Fisher (*q.v.*) of 75 Great Victoria Street (1895); died 9 July 1934 at 4 College Gardens; probate Belfast 27 August 1934. [Belf GRO (d); Belf PRO, will cal; Belfast Royal Hospital, register of students; Bewley (2005); *BMJ* obituary (1934); Calwell (1986); Kirkpatrick Archive; Logan (1990); McClelland and Hadden (2005); *Med Dir*; QCB adm reg; UHF database (m)].

BELL, GEORGE WASHINGTON (*fl c* 1824), Newry, county Down;
surgeon and chemist, of Hill Street, Newry c 1824; married 10 September 1819 in Kiltullagh, county Roscommon, Charlotte Chesney, fourth daughter of Alexander Chesney of Prospect, county Down; died 11 May 1829 'in the prime of life and height of his usefulness … blessed with professional talents of the very first order'. [*BNL* 21 September 1819 (m) and 19 May 1829 (d); Pigot (1824)].

BELL, HENRY (1844/5–1922), Bangor, county Down;
born 1844/5 (or 1841/2) at Ballymaconnell, county Down, son of Archibald Bell, sea captain, of Groomsport; educated at RBAI; studied medicine at Queen's College, Belfast, 1867–70, also at London, Edinburgh and Dublin; LRCP and LRCS Edin 1870; surgeon to the Ocean Steamship Company; surgeon to the 75th Regiment;

general practitioner, of Sandy Row, Bangor (c 1885) and later of Chislehurst, Ranfurly Avenue, Bangor; married 3 September 1892, in Mountpottinger Presbyterian Church, Belfast, Mary Jane Hill, daughter of Henry J. Hill, bookkeeper, of Strandtown; died 10 December 1922 at Chislehurst; buried in Bangor Abbey graveyard; probate Belfast 31 January 1923. [Belf GRO (d); Belf PRO, will cal; Kirkpatrick Archive; *Med Dir*; Merrick and Clarke, *County Down*, vol 17 (1978); QCB adm reg; UHF database (m)].

BELL, JAMES (d 1826), Army Medical Service and Belfast;
joined the Army Medical Service as surgeon's mate in Grenada 1779; surgeon to 67th Foot 1791; apothecary on Foreign Service 1795; retired on half pay 1799; surgeon, of 65 Waring Street, Belfast, in 1807–8; surgeon to the Belfast Dispensary 1809; lived finally at 'Bellville', Ballymacarrett, county Down; married 3 June 1804 Mary Tisdall, widow; died 23 January 1826; 'in the line of his profession he was much esteemed'; will dated 9 January 1826, probate Down Diocesan Court 4 February 1826 (abstract in Registry of Deeds, Dublin). [*Belfast Directory* 1807, 1808; *BNL* 29 June 1804 (m) and 27 January 1826 (d); Ellis and Eustace, vol III (1984); Malcolm (1851); Peterkin and Johnston (1968)].

BELL, JOHN (d 1792), Army Medical Service and Sierra Leone;
uncle of Dr William Byrtt (*q.v.*); joined the Army Medical Service as surgeon to the 94th Foot 1780; retired on half pay when regiment was disbanded 1783; joined 5th Foot in 1784; resigned 1787; later physician general to Sierra Leone; author of a valuable early work on military hygiene and diet; married July 1786 Sarah Lewis (who was born 1764/5 and died 9 October 1854, being buried in Clifton Street Graveyard, Belfast), daughter of James Lewis of The Grove, Belfast, presumably while stationed in Belfast; died May 1792. [Agnew (1998); *BNL* 1 June 1792 (d) and 13 October 1854 (d); Farrar (1897); Merrick and Clarke, *Belfast*, vol 4 (1991); Peterkin and Johnston (1968)].

BELL, JOHN C. (d 1836), Belfast;
MD [?]; house surgeon and apothecary to the Belfast Fever Hospital in 1835; performed a Caesarean section in 1823, as reported in the *BNL;* married Sarah — (who was born 1764/5 and died 9 October 1854); died 20 October 1836 of typhus fever. [*Belf Fev Hosp, Ann Rep*; *BNL* 11 March 1823 (news); Malcolm (1851); Merrick and Clarke, *Belfast*, vol 4 (1991)].

BELL, JOHN JAMES (c 1871–1948), Belfast and Bradford, Yorkshire;
born c 1871, son of Benjamin Bell, farmer; studied medicine at the Royal College of Surgeons in Edinburgh; LRCP LRCS and LM Edin 1894; LFPS Glas 1894; FRCSI 1905; FRCS Edin 1905; general practitioner, of 41 Fitzwilliam Street, Belfast c 1895 of 39 Antrim Road, Belfast c 1903 and of Royd House, Manningham Lane, Bradford, from c 1905; surgeon to the Waddilone Samaritan Hospital for Women from c 1911; president of Bradford Medico-Chirurgical Society 1922–3; of Ploverfield, The Drive, Ben Rhydding, Yorkshire from c 1928; retired c 1935; married 10 September 1903, in St Anne's Church of Ireland Church, Belfast, Anne

Emma Wright (who was born 1870/1), daughter of Charles Wright, farmer; died 13 August 1948; probate London 24 November 1948, leaving the unusually large sum of £180,495. [Dub GRO (m); Kirkpatrick Archive; Lond PPR, will cal; *Med Dir*; UHF database (m)].

BELL, MARGARET SMITH (1864–1906), Belfast and Manchester;
born 3 July 1864 at Springhill, Newry, daughter of Joseph Bell, clerk of the Union, of Killeavy Castle and Springhill, county Armagh, and Margaret Smith; sister of Dr Elizabeth Gould Bell (*q.v.*); studied arts and medicine at Queen's College, Belfast, from 1887, and at Belfast Royal Hospital; one of the first five women medical students in Belfast; LRCPI and LM 1894; LRCSI and LM 1894; general practitioner at 334 Oxford Road, Manchester 1893–1906; married 9 October 1901, in Warrenpoint Presbyterian Church, county Down, Dr Joseph Douglas Boyd (*q.v.*); mother of Dr Douglas Priestley Bell Boyd, MB (QUB) 1931, radiologist, of Belfast; died 21 August 1906 at 17 Claremont Street, Belfast; buried in Killeavy graveyard, county Armagh. [Belf GRO (b); Belfast Royal Hospital, register of students; *BMJ* obituary (1906); Dub GRO (d); Kirkpatrick Archive; Logan (1990); *Med Dir*; QCB adm reg; UHF database (m)].

BELL, RICHARD (d before 1852), Naval Medical Service;
brother of Dr Thomas Bell, surgeon RN (*q.v.*); joined the Naval Medical Service as assistant surgeon; died before 1852. [*BNL* 14 April 1852 (d, brother James)].

BELL, ROBERT (*fl c* 1807), Newry, county Down;
surgeon and apothecary, of Newry; advertised for an apprentice June 1807; married —; father of Dr Robert Henry Bell (*q.v.*). [*BNL* 30 June 1807 (advert) and 12 October 1819 (d, son)].

BELL, ROBERT (1786/7–1855), Lurgan, county Armagh;
born 1786/7; CM (Glas) 1811 [?]; LAH Dub 1829; accoucheur of the Glasgow Lying-in Hospital; surgeon and apothecary, of Lurgan 1824; medical officer to Lurgan Union Workhouse from its opening in 1841; heavily criticized (with the Board of Guardians and others) in Stevens' report on deaths in the Workhouse in May 1846 but refused to resign; questioned on the deaths in January 1847 and criticized in another report in February 1847 for the standard of hygiene, sanitation and food and did resign later in that year; married Mary — (who was born 1794/5 and died 6 February 1874); died 25 April 1855 in Lurgan after a long illness, 'an old and highly esteemed inhabitant of Lurgan'; probate Prerogative Court 1855. [*BNL* 2 May 1855 (d); Belf PRO, BG 22/A/4, p 426; Belf PRO, prerog wills index; Bradshaw (1819); Croly (1843–6); gravestone inscription; Kirkpatrick Archive; MacAtasney (1997); *Med Dir*; Pigot (1824)].

BELL, ROBERT (1858–1902), Pomeroy, county Tyrone;
born 25 November 1854 at Annahilt, county Down, son of William Bell, farmer, of Annahilt; educated at Annahilt National School; studied medicine at Queen's College, Belfast, from 1877; MD MCh (RUI) 1884; medical officer to Pomeroy

Dispensary District; married Margretta Meharry —; died 29 December 1902 at Pomeroy; probate Armagh 23 February 1903. [Belf PRO, will cal; Dub GRO (d); Kirkpatrick Archive; *Med Dir*; QCB adm reg].

BELL, ROBERT HENRY (d 1819), Army Medical Service;
son of Dr Robert Bell of Newry (*q.v.*); joined the Army Medical Service as hospital mate, General Service, 1810; assistant surgeon to 86th Foot (Royal County Down Regiment) 1811; on half pay 1818; died 17 March 1819 at Madras; buried in St Mary's Cemetery, Madras. [*BNL* 12 October 1819 (d); Peterkin and Johnston (1968)].

BELL, THEODORE (1863–1922), Warrenpoint, county Down;
born 1863 in Dublin, son of Alexander Bell, solicitor; educated at Wesley College, Dublin; studied arts and medicine at Trinity College, Dublin, from 1881; BA (TCD) 1885; LM Rot Hosp Dub 1886; MB BCh 1887; MD 1892; medical officer to constabulary and certifying factory surgeon; of Coolbawn and later 'Seaport', Warrenpoint; served in World War I with rank of captain; married Alicia Rosa —; died 14 March 1922 at Seaport, Warrenpoint; probate Belfast 28 June 1922. [Belf GRO (d); Belf PRO, will cal; *Med Dir;* TCD adm reg; *TCD Cat*, vol II (1896)].

BELL, THOMAS (d 1839), Naval Medical Service;
joined the Naval Medical Service as assistant surgeon; married — (who was born 1751/2 and died 22 August 1846 at Castlederg, county Tyrone); died May 1839 at Ballygawley, county Tyrone. [*BNL* 31 May 1839 (d) and 14 April 1852 (d, brother James); *Londonderry Sentinel* 1 June 1839 (d) and 5 September 1846 (d); *Londonderry Standard* 11 September 1846 (d)].

BELL, THOMAS (d c 1838), Newry, county Down;
surgeon, of Tullyvallen, Newry; died c 1838; administration Armagh Diocesan Court 1838. [Dub Nat Arch, Armagh Dio Admins index].

BELL, THOMAS (*fl c* 1824), Naval Medical Service and Stranorlar, county Donegal;
brother of Dr Richard Bell, surgeon RN (*q.v.*); MD (Edin) 1794 (thesis 'De pneumonia'); joined the Naval Medical Service as assistant surgeon 1805; surgeon, of Stranorlar c 1824 and of Talbot Street, Dublin c 1852. [*BNL* 14 April 1852 (d, brother James); Edin Univ; *NMS* (1826); Pigot (1824)].

BELL, THOMAS GILLESPIE (1855–1916), Gilford, county Down, Bournemouth, Hampshire, and Branksome, Dorset;
born 27 July 1855 at Armagh, son of Matthew Bell, merchant, of 28 English Street, Armagh; educated at Armagh Royal School 1873–5; studied medicine at Queen's College, Belfast (with prizes), from 1878; Malcolm Exhibition, Belfast Royal Hospital, 1881; MD MCh (RUI) 1882; LM KQCPI 1884; general practitioner, of Gilford, c 1886–90, of Bournemouth c 1890–95 and of 38 Poole Road, Branksome, c 1895–1916; died 18 December 1916; administration Blandford 31 March 1917, 20 October 1933 and 17 April 1943. [*Belf Roy Hosp, Ann Rep*; Ferrar (1933); Lond PPR, will cal; *Med Dir*; QCB adm reg].

BELL, THOMAS VESEY (1854/5–1931), Enniskillen, county Fermanagh and Durham;
> born 1854/5; studied medicine at the Ledwich School, Dublin; LRCSI 1877; LKQCPI and LM 1878; MKQCPI 1885; general practitioner, of Enniskillen from c 1880; moved c 1900 to county Durham; general practitioner in Middleton-St-George, Darlington, of Spring Grove Villa; medical officer to the post office and to Ropner and Cook's Memorial Homes; of 'Whinfield', Middleton-St-George from c 1910; married Ellen Irwin —; died 1 December 1931 at 'Whinfield', Middleton-St-George; probate Durham 27 January 1932. [Lond GRO (d); Lond PPR, will cal; *Med Dir*].

BELL, WILLIAM JOHN (d 1820), Sierra Leone;
> of Magherafelt, county Londonderry; colonial surgeon in Sierra Leone c 1819–20; married Anne Dawson (who married secondly 19 November 1845 John Travis Hamilton, chemist), daughter of Arthur Dawson, gentleman; died 1 June 1820 of fever. [*BNL* 25 August 1820 (d) and 25 November 1845 (m, widow); Dub GRO (m, widow)].

BENNETT, JOHN (1866–c 1940), Hyde, Cheshire;
> born 23 July 1866 at Lisdoonan, county Down, son of John Bennett, pawnbroker, of 3 The Mount, Mountpottinger, Belfast; educated at RBAI; studied medicine at Queen's College, Belfast, from 1884; MB BCh BAO (RUI) 1890; general practitioner, of Hyde; medical officer of health for Hyde 1900–19, of 19 Mottram Road, Hyde c 1895, and of Chapel Street, Hyde from c 1900; married —; father of Dr John Barry Bennett, MB ChB (Manch) 1922; died c 1940. [*Med Dir*; QCB adm reg].

BENNETT, JOHN BOYLE (1808–80), Clonakilty, county Cork and New Zealand;
> born 1808, son of John Bennett, grocer and later postmaster, of Clonakilty; studied medicine; MD [?]; probably general practitioner in Clonakilty for some years; trained for the Methodist ministry; stationed at Belfast 1834–36 and at Dublin 1837–39; resigned in May 1839 following a charge of 'intemperance'; returned to ministry in 1841; stationed at Enniskillen 1841–2; invited to go to London as an editor of the British Methodist newspaper *The Watchman* c 1842; emigrated to New Zealand as editor of the *New Zealander* c 1847–53; registrar of births, deaths and marriages for Auckland in 1853 and registrar general for New Zealand 1854–66; a noted speaker in London and New Zealand and remained actively involved in Methodist affairs; author of religious pamphlets; married Horatio Marian Carlisle (who died 16 September 1881); died 15 June 1880 at Wellington, New Zealand. [Crookshank, vol 3 (1888)].

BENNETT, THOMAS (1869–1941), Bantry, county Cork, and Bangor, county Down;
> born 1869; studied medicine at Edinburgh University; LRCP LRCS Edin and LM 1892; LRFPS Glas 1892; LAH Dub 1895; general practitioner, of Bantry, county Cork c 1895–1913, of Bella Vista, 9 Gray's Hill, Bangor c 1913–41; married Ellen —; retired c 1941 to Barry's Hall, Timoleague, county Cork; died 27 December 1941 at Timoleague; buried at Clonakilty. [Dub GRO (d); Kirkpatrick Archive; *Med Dir*].

BENNETT, WILLIAM HALLARAN (1859–92), Army Medical Service;
born 2 September 1859 in Belfast, son of lieutenant-colonel Robert Bennett; educated at Jersey Collegiate School; studied arts and medicine at Trinity College, Dublin, from 1876; BA (TCD) 1880; MB BCh 1882; LM KQCPI 1882; joined the Army Medical Service as surgeon captain 1885; retired to Longford; unmarried; died 29 July 1892 at Longford (verdict of suicide at inquest); administration Dublin 28 September 1892. [Belf PRO, will cal; Dub GRO (d); *Med Dir*; Peterkin and Johnston (1968); TCD adm reg; *TCD Cat*, vol II (1896)].

BENNIS, GEORGE (b 1662/3), Enniskillen, county Fermanagh;
born 1662/3 at Moymore, county Clare, son of Augustine Bennis, gentleman; educated by Mr Carrig; studied arts and medicine at Trinity College, Dublin, from 1685; scholar 1687; BA (TCD) 1688; MA MB 1691; MD 1699; headmaster of Portora Royal School, Enniskillen 1692–1700. [Burtchaell and Sadleir (1924); Dundas (1913); Leslie, Crooks and Moore (2006); *Portora Register* (1940)].

BERESFORD, RALPH (1858–1912), Sheffield and Bradford, Yorkshire;
born 6 July 1858 at Nottingham, son of Thomas Beresford of Prince of Wales Road, Norwich, commission agent and merchant; educated at Mr Lewis's School, Norwich; studied medicine at Queen's College, Belfast, from 1877, also at the Middlesex and National Dental Hospitals; LSA Lond 1883; MRCSE 1894; assistant house surgeon at Sheffield Jubilee Hospital; general practitioner, of 78 Eccleshall Road, Sheffield, c 1885, of 151 Manningham Lane, Bradford c 1895; of The Priory, Sudbury, Suffolk, c 1905; died 3 September 1912 at Penlee Nursing Home, Walmer Villas, Manningham. [Lond GRO (d); *Med Dir*].

BERNARD, HENRY WILLIAM (1864–1941), Sutton, county Dublin, RAMC, ship's surgeon and Portrush, county Antrim;
born 14 February 1864 at 'Laranda', Grosvenor Road, Rathmines, Dublin, son of George Bernard, solicitor, of 'Laranda', and Nannie Lynas [?]; educated at Rathmines School from 1878; studied arts and medicine at Trinity College, Dublin, from 1882; BA (TCD) 1886; MB BCh BAO 1897; perhaps living abroad until c 1910; of The Burrow, Sutton, county Dublin; captain (temporary) in RAMC during World War I 1916–9; surgeon with New Zealand Shipping Company c 1919–22; general practitioner, of Old Rock Ryan, Portrush c 1922–6; retired c 1926 to Dublin, living at 5 Trafalgar Terrace, Seapoint Avenue c 1940; unmarried; died 30 December 1941 at 'Lenco', Sutton, county Dublin; probate Dublin 26 November 1942. [Dub GRO (d); Dub Nat Arch, will cal; Figgis and Drury (1932); Kirkpatrick Archive; *Med Dir*; TCD adm reg; *TCD Cat*, vol II (1896)].

BERNARD, WALTER (1827–1912), Army Medical Service and Londonderry;
born 1 May 1827 at Newmarket, county Cork, son of Walter Bernard, army officer; studied medicine at Park Street and Peter Street Hospital, Dublin; MRCSE 1852; LM Rot Hosp Dub 1852; LKQCPI 1858; FKQCPI 1876; joined the Army Medical Service as chief surgeon to the 3rd Division and principal medical officer to 2nd Division of the Army Works Corps, Crimea, in 1854–5 and attended the wounded on the field of Inkerman; won silver medal of Royal Humane Society for saving an

officer's life in 1855; surgeon to the SS *Pacific*; consulting and visiting physician to Londonderry Lunatic Asylum and consulting physician to the Fever and EENT Hospitals and Infirmary, Londonderry; of Great James's Street and 14 Queen Street, Londonderry; responsible for rebuilding the Grianan an Aileach in 1874–8; living c 1910 at Ardaravan, Buncrana; married 28 August 1856 in Booterstown Church of Ireland Church, Dublin, Elizabeth Catherine Eames (who was born 1837/8), eldest daughter of Dr William James Eames, senior (*q.v.*), of Dawson Court, Booterstown, and Londonderry; died 6 December 1912 at Buncrana; probate Dublin 2 August 1913. [Belf PRO, will cal; *BMJ* obituary (1912); Dallat (1990); Dub GRO (m) and (d); *Londonderry Sentinel* 5 September 1856 (m); *Med Dir*].

BERRY, JOHN (d c 1877), Waringstown, county Down, and Belfast;
son of Joseph Berry, farmer; LM Anglesey Hospital, Dublin 1842; LFPS Glas 1851; assistant surgeon to Lurgan Fever Hospital and Infirmary; medical officer to Donacloney, Tullylish and Waringstown Dispensary Districts, factory and constabulary; general practitioner in Belfast c 1864–77, of 125 Peter's Hill, 112 Divis Street and 137 Donegall Street, Belfast; married 26 June 1851 in St Anne's Church of Ireland Church, Belfast, Phoebe Shaw Brown (who was born 1830/1), daughter of James Brown of Belfast; died c 1877. [*BNL* 27 June 1851 (m); Dub GRO (m); *Med Dir*].

BERRY, MATTHEW WEST (d c 1894), Belfast and London;
studied medicine at Ledwich School, Dublin; LM Anglesey Hospital, Dublin 1854; MRCSE 1856; surgeon to Anglo-Luso, Brazilian, and Cunard Services; general practitioner, of 4 Pennington Place (c 1862) and 137 Donegall Street, Belfast (c 1875); moved c 1877 to general practice at Woodburn House, 238 Hornsey Road, Holloway, then to 81 Highbury Quadrant, London, to 46 Tachbrook Street, Pimlico and 284 King's Road, Chelsea; married 26 October 1868 in St Mary Magdalene's Church of Ireland Church, Belfast, Georgina Jane Thompson (who was born 1841/2 and died 25 September 1893), youngest daughter of Robert Thompson of Castleton, county Antrim; died c 1894. [*Coleraine Chronicle* 31 October 1868 (m); *Med Dir*; Stewart (1994)].

BETHUNE, GEORGE (*fl c* 1731);
'Scot-Hib'; studied medicine at Rheims University; MD (Rheims) 1731. [Brockliss]

BETTY, HENRY (1843/4–70), Maguiresbridge, county Fermanagh;
born 1843/4; studied medicine at Ledwich School, Dublin; LRCSI 1865; LRCP Edin and LM 1866; medical officer to Lisbellaw Dispensary District; of Cappy House, Gola, Enniskillen; unmarried; died 25 August 1870 of phthisis at Cappy. [Dub GRO (d); *Med Dir*].

BETTY, MOORE MONTGOMERY (1870–1926), Enniskillen, county Fermanagh;
born 17 November 1870 at Derrygiff, county Fermanagh, son of Moore Betty of Derrygiff, and Angelina Montgomery; studied medicine at the Royal College of Surgeons in Ireland; LRCPI and LM 1894; LRCSI and LM 1894; LM Coombe Hosp Dub; FRCSI 1912; resident medical officer to the Meath Hospital, Dublin;

medical officer to the Enniskillen Union and Fever Hospitals and Post Office; of 32 Darling Street, Enniskillen c 1920; married Gertrude Lemon, only daughter of Robert Lemon of Enniskillen; died 19 July 1926 at Portobello Nursing Home, Dublin; probate Belfast 8 December 1926. [Belf GRO (b); Belf PRO, will cal; Dub GRO (d); Kirkpatrick Archive; *Med Dir*].

BETTY, WILLIAM (1800/1–53), Lowtherstown, county Fermanagh;
born 1800/1; MRCSE 1825; accoucheur of the Dublin Lying-in Hospital (Rotunda); medical officer to Lowtherstown (Irvinestown) and Ballinamallard Dispensary Districts c 1845; inherited an apothecary's shop in Enniskillen from his cousin, Hugh Collum, apothecary, in 1847; married 18 December 1834 in Newtownbutler Church, Belinda Redmond, eldest daughter of William Redmond of Enniskillen; died 16 August 1853 at Lowtherstown; probate Prerogative Court 1853. [*BNL* 23 December 1834 (m); Belf PRO, LPC/1210; Belf PRO, prerog wills index; Croly (1843–6); *Londonderry Sentinel* 27 December 1834 (m) and 26 August 1853 (d)].

BICKERSTAFFE, ROGER (1853–c 1892), Argentina;
born 28 June 1853 at Liverpool, son of the Rev Roger Bickerstaff, vicar of Lydiate, Lancashire and late of Killead, county Antrim, and Camilla Isabella —; educated by Dr Molony of Carrickfergus; studied medicine at Queen's College, Belfast, from 1871; MD MCh Dip Mid (QUI) 1875; of Colonia Florencia, Bella Vista, Corientes, Argentina c 1885; died c 1892. [Leslie (1993); *Med Dir*; QCB adm reg].

BIGGER (or **BIGGAR**), **DAVID** (1843/4–77), Portadown, county Armagh;
born 1843/4; studied medicine at Glasgow University; MB (Glas) 1868; LRCS Edin & LM 1868; MD (Glas) CM 1870; medical officer to Tartaraghan Dispensary District and registrar of births and deaths; married Margaret —; died 26 June 1877 at Seagoe (drowned on the river Bann when his boat overturned); buried in Drumcree churchyard; administration Armagh 12 July 1877. [Addison (1898); *BMJ* obituary (1877); Kirkpatrick Archive; Dub GRO (d); *Med Dir*].

BIGGER, SIR EDWARD COEY (1861–1942), Belfast and Dublin.
born 23 September 1861 in Belfast, sixth son of Joseph Bigger of Carnmoney and Mary Jane Ardery of Banbridge; brother of Dr Samuel Ferguson Bigger (*q.v.*) and Francis Joseph Bigger, the antiquarian; educated at the Mercantile Academy, Belfast; studied medicine at Queen's College, Belfast, 1879–83; MD MCh (RUI) 1883; LM KQCPI 1883; Dip State Med RCPSI 1894; general physician, of 10 Carlisle Terrace, Carlisle Circus from c 1885; visiting physician to the Belfast Fever Hospital 1892–1900 and the Ulster Hospital for Children and Women; medical commissioner on the Local Government Board of Ireland from 1900; alderman in the Belfast City Council; crown representative on the GMC; chairman of the Central Midwives Board of Ireland 1918–42; chairman of the General Nursing Council of Ireland; Knight Bachelor 1921; elected Member of the Irish Senate 1925–36; of 'Lisnacran', Glenageary, county Dublin; married 5 August 1886 in Fortwilliam Presbyterian Church, Belfast, Margaret Coulter Warwick (who died 5 February 1925), daughter of Dr William Warwick of Belfast (*q.v.*); father of Prof Joseph Warwick Bigger of Trinity College, Dublin, MB BCh BAO (TCD) 1916; died 1 June 1942 at

'Lisnacran'; buried in Mallusk graveyard, county Antrim; probate Belfast 26 November 1942. [Belf PRO, will cal; *BMJ* obituary (1942); *DIB* (2009); Dub GRO (m); *Irish Times* obituary (1942); Kirkpatrick Archives; *Lancet* obituary (1942); Martin (2003); *Med Dir*; QCB adm reg; Sibbett (1997)].

BIGGER, SAMUEL FERGUSON (1834–1931), Indian Medical Service;
born 4 October 1854 in Belfast, son of Joseph Bigger of Carnmoney and Mary Jane Ardery of Banbridge; brother of Sir Edward Coey Bigger (*q.v.*) and Francis Joseph Bigger, the antiquarian; studied medicine at Liverpool University; MRCSE 1875; LSA Lond 1877; MB (Lond) 1884; joined the Indian Medical Service (Bengal establishment) as surgeon 1877, attached to the 3rd Punjab Cavalry; surgeon major 1891; surgeon lieutenant–colonel 1898; served in the Afghan War 1879–80 including the capture of Zawa and operations in the Kuram Valley (medal), the Chin-Lusha Expedition 1889–90 (despatches, medal with clasp), the Wariston Expedition 1894–5 and the Tirah Expedition including the action at Dargai (despatches, medal and two clasps); retired 1903 to Ellersley Villas, Bray, county Wicklow; married Evelyn Alice —; died 2 February 1931 in Bray; probate Dublin 23 April 1931. [*BMJ* obituary (1931); Crawford (1930); Dub Nat Arch, will cal; Kirkpatrick Archive; *Lancet* obituary (1931); *Med Dir*].

BIGGER, WILLIAM GRIMSHAW (1861–1922), London, and Mitcham, Surrey;
born 7 April 1861 at Londonderry, son of William J. Bigger, merchant, of Riverview, Londonderry; educated at RBAI; studied arts and medicine at Queen's College, Belfast, and medicine at St Thomas's Hospital, London, 1878–85; BA (QUI) 1881; MD MCh (RUI) 1885; MRCSE 1885; LSA Lond 1885; clinical assistant to the Hospital for Women, Soho, and the Evelina Hospital for Children; medical officer for Brixton Dispensary District, of 6 Queen's Park Gardens, Streatham Common c 1886 and of Aberfoyle, Streatham Common c 1890; general practitioner, of The Croft, Commonside East, Mitcham, Surrey from c 1916; married —; father of Dr Walter Grimshaw Bigger, LRCP Lond, MRCSE 1913, and Dr Charles Edgar Bigger, LRCP Lond, MRCSE 1926; died 27 January 1922; probate London 8 May 1922. [Lond PPR, will cal; *Med Dir*; QCB adm reg].

BINDON, JOHN VEREKER (1814/5–75), Saintfield, county Down, Moneygall, King's County, Coalisland, county Tyrone, and New Zealand;
born 1814/5; studied medicine at the Royal College of Surgeons in Ireland and Trinity College, Dublin; Licence in Pharmacy RCSI 1839; LRCSI and LM Rot Hosp Dub 1840; FRCSI 1844; LM RCSI 1864; medical officer to Saintfield Dispensary District and constabulary; to Moneygall and Toomavara Dispensary Districts and constabulary, King's County, 1841–50; and to Coalisland Dispensary District; emigrated to Kawa-kawa, Bay of Islands, New Zealand, c 1870; married —; son born 1 August 1855; died 31 March 1875 in Guy's Hospital, London. [*BNL* 10 August 1855 (b, son); Lond GRO (d); *Med Dir*].

BINGHAM, HENRY (1848–98), Belfast;
born 26 May 1848 at Crossgar, county Down, son of Samuel Bingham, farmer, of Crossgar; educated at Belfast Royal Academy; studied medicine at Queen's College,

Belfast, 1873–8; MD (QUI) 1878; Dip Mid 1879; LRCSE 1893; general practitioner, of the Lodge, Mount-pottinger, Belfast; married 25 November 1879 in College Square Presbyterian Church, Letitia McConnell, daughter of John McConnell, pawnbroker; died 29 March 1898 at Mountpottinger; buried in Belfast City Cemetery; probate Belfast 1 June 1898. [Belf City Cem, bur reg; Belf PRO, will cal; Dub GRO (m) and (d); *Med Dir*; QCB adm reg; UHF database (m); Whitla (1901)].

BINGHAM, JOHN (d 1829), Rostrevor, county Down;
MD [?]; general practitioner, of Rostrevor, county Down c 1819; married (after 1794) Martha Moore (who died June 1803), widow of Ross Moore of Carlingford, and third daughter of Edward Corry, MP for Newry, and Catherine Bristow; married —; died 4 July 1829; probate Prerogative Court 1829. [*BNL* 21 July 1829 (d); Belf PRO, Corry pedigree T618/333; Belf PRO, prerog wills index; Bradshaw (1819)].

BINGHAM, PATRICK (1811/2–38), Belfast and Haiti, West Indies;
born 1811/2; of Belfast; medical officer in Haiti; died September 1838. [*BNL* 25 December 1838 (d)].

BINGHAM, WILLIAM BREWSTER (1795/6–1848), Downpatrick, county Down;
born 1795/6, younger son of James Bingham of Rademon, county Down, and — Brewster of Scotland; educated by the Rev Moses Neilson of Rademon, and then worked as assistant teacher in Dr Bruce's Academy in Belfast; studied medicine at Edinburgh University from c 1819 but was also thr first medical student pupil in Belfast Fever Hospital in 1821; MD (Edin) 1823 (thesis 'De venesectione in febribus continuis'); FRCSE 1844; physician, of Irish Street, Downpatrick 1823–35, and of Scotch Street from 1835; physician to the Downpatrick Fever Hospital 1833–47; retired 1847 following an attack of fever; married 27 October 1831 at Downpatrick, Mary Rowan (who married secondly 14 March 1854 Dr William Ponsonby Deverell (*q.v.*)), eldest daughter of John Rowan of Downpatrick; died 23 September 1848 at Downpatrick; buried in Rademan graveyard; probate Prerogative Court 1848. [*BNL* 1 November 1831 (m), 29 September 1848 (d), 3 October 1848 (d) and 15 March 1854 (m, widow); Belf PRO, prerog wills index; *Belf Street Dirs*; Croly; *Downpatrick Recorder* 4 and 11 September 1847, 8 July 1848 and 10 September 1848; Dub GRO (m); Edin Univ; Lewis (1837); Malcolm (1851); Parkinson (1967); Pigot (1824); Pilson (1838)].

BIRCH, GEORGE (*fl c* 1766–1814), Indian Medical Service and Moneyrea, county Down;
son of John Birch of Birchgrove, Gilford, county Down, and Jane Ledlie of Carnan, county Tyrone; brother of the Rev James Jackson Birch and the Rev Thomas Ledlie Birch, both of whom were presbyterian ministers and the latter of whom was a United Irishman; joined the Indian Medical Service (Bombay establishment) as surgeon 1766; surgeon at Basra 1770; retired to Ireland 1782; presented a clock to First Saintfield Presbyterian Church when his brother Thomas was a minister; general practitioner and landowner, of Ballybeen House, Moneyrea, county Down; appointed JP for county Down in 1789; commanded the Newtownards Yeomanry Cavalry during the battle of Saintfield when two of his sons were United Irishmen fighting

against him; later used his influence to plead for the lives of his brother and sons; in 1800 accompanied the Moderator to interview Lord Castlereagh and press for an increase in the Regium Donum; married in India, Catherine Charlotte Walder (nee Quinn), a widow; died 1814; probate Prerogative Court 1814. [Belf PRO, prerog wills index; Birch (2011); Crawford (1930); McClelland (1963a)].

BIRNIE, GEORGE (1790/1–1845), Naval Medical Service, Larne, county Antrim, and Belfast;
   born 1790/1; LAH Dub 1819; LRCSE; joined the Naval Medical Service as assistant surgeon; served on HMS *Antelope* in the Carribean c 1816–7, where he had an attack of yellow fever and wrote a paper on this; surgeon 1819; served on HMS *Conway* c 1821 and on HMS *Blenheim* c 1837, when the ship was transporting convicts to Australia; apothecary and surgeon, of Larne c 1824 and later of 21 York Street, Belfast; died 8 October 1845 at 21 York Street; buried in Rashee Old Graveyard, county Antrim. [Apothecaries (1829); *BNL* 10 October 1845 (d); Croly (1843–6); Malcolm (1851); *NMS* (1826); Pigot (1824); Richmond (2007)].

BIRT, THOMAS (*fl c* 1838), Cushendall, county Antrim;
   surgeon, of Cushendall; married March 1838 at Armoy, Alice Walsh, sister of the Rev Luke Walsh, parish priest of Culfeightrin, county Antrim. [*BNL* 13 March 1838 (m)].

BITTLES, ADAM (d c 1782), Charlestown, South Carolina, USA;
   emigrated to USA; surgeon, of Charlestown; died c 1782; administration Armagh Diocesan Court 1782. [Dub Nat Arch, Armagh Dio Admins index].

BLACK, CHRISTOPHER STRONG (1818/9–91), Belfast, and Holywood, county Down;
   born 1818/9, son of Henderson Black, JP, of Belfast; studied medicine at Glasgow University, Richmond Hospital, Dublin, and Royal College of Surgeons in Ireland; LM Cumberland Street Hospital, Dublin 1837; LRCSI and LM 1839; MD (Glas) 1840; medical attendant for cholera to poor patients during the epidemic; general practitioner, of 44 Upper Queen Street, Belfast c 1846; senior medical officer to Belfast General Dispensary, of 53 Victoria Place c 1852–8, at Claremont, Holywood c 1872, and of 8 Royal Terrace, Belfast, from c 1880; married 30 June 1853 in St Anne's Church of Ireland Church, Belfast, Mary Murray, youngest daughter of Francis Murray, merchant, of Belfast; died 4 March 1891 at 8 Royal Terrace; probate Belfast 3 April 1891. [Addison (1898); *BNL* 1 July 1853 ((m); Belf PRO, will cal; *Coleraine Chronicle* 2 July 1853 (m); Dub GRO (m) and (d); *Londonderry Sentinel* 8 July 1853 (m); *Med Dir*].

BLACK, JAMES BIRCH (1819/20–c 1895), New Brighton, Cheshire, and Queenstown, county Cork;
   born 1819/20, son of James B. Black of Dromara, county Down; educated at RBAI; studied medicine at Queen's College, Belfast, from 1855; MRCSE 1858; LRCP Edin 1869; senior surgeon on the Inman Line RMSS *City of Brussels*; general practitioner of Magazine Park, New Brighton, Cheshire c 1869–80 and of Willmount,

Queenstown c 1880–88; retired 1888; married 5 December 1860 in Hazlewood Church, Prescott, Lancashire, Anne Higginson, eldest daughter of Richard Higginson; died c 1895. [*BNL* 8 December 1860 (m); *Med Dir*; QCB adm reg].

BLACK, JOHN (*fl c* 1802), Randalstown, county Antrim;
LAH Dub 1802; served as an apprentice apothecary to Dr William Black of Newry (*q.v.*); apothecary, of Randalstown; died 22 August 1815 at Kilkenny, in the prime of life, after an illness of ten days. [Apothecaries (1829); *BNL* 15 September 1815 (d); *Newry Telegraph* 12 September 1815 (d)].

BLACK, JOHN GREER (1858–1914), Army Medical Service;
born 7 November 1858 at Letterloan, county Londonderry; MD (QUI) 1881; MCh (RUI) 1882; joined the Army Medical Service as surgeon (surgeon captain) 1886; surgeon major RAMC 1898; served in South Africa 1900–02; retired 1906; unmarried; died 1 March 1914 at 5 Landsowne Crescent, Portrush; probate Dublin 1 May 1914. [Belf PRO, will cal; Dub GRO (d); *Med Dir*; Peterkin and Johnston (1968)].

BLACK, JOSEPH (1728–99), Glasgow and Edinburgh;
born 16 April 1728 in Bordeaux, fourth son of John Black, wine merchant from Belfast, and Margaret Gordon; educated in Belfast from the age of 12; studied arts and medicine at Glasgow University 1746–52 and Edinburgh University 1752–4; MD (Edin) 1754 (thesis 'De humore acido a cibis orto, et magnesia alba', a classic paper in chemistry); MFPS Glas 1757; FRCP Edin 1767; physician in Edinburgh 1754–6; lecturer and professor of Chemistry at Glasgow 1756–60; professor of Medicine at Glasgow 1757–66 and professor of Chemistry at Edinburgh 1766–99; identified carbon dioxide and the principles of latent and specific heat; influenced James Watt in his studies of steam engines; author of *Lectures on the Elements of Chemistry* (1803), published in many editions, but few scientific papers; unmarried; died 6 December 1799 (*DNB*) at Nicholson Street, Edinburgh; buried in Greyfriars Churchyard, Edinburgh; portrait by Sir Henry Raeburn (c 1790) in Glasgow University. [Addison (1913); Agnew (1996); *BNL* 20 December 1799 (d); Benn (1877); Biggart (1949); Edin Univ; Esler (1884); Frackleton (1953); Garvin and O'Rawe (1993); Malcolm (1851); Newmann (1993); *Oxford DNB* (2004); Riddell (1920); Ward (1903)].

BLACK, MOSES (1849–c 1875), Strangford, county Down;
born 29 August 1849, son of the Rev Moses Black, minister of Kilmore Presbyterian Church, and — Sloane of Drumbo; educated at RBAI; studied medicine at Queen's College, Belfast, from 1865; MD (QUI) 1871; MCh Dip Mid (QUI) 1872; medical officer to Strangford Dispensary District; died c 1875. [McConnell (1951); *Med Dir*; QCB adm reg].

BLACK, ROBERT JAMES (1854/5–1929), Greenwich, Kent;
born 1854/5 at Ballymoghan, Magherafelt, son of Andrew Black, farmer, of Ballymoghan; educated at Moneymore School; studied medicine at Queen's College, Galway, 1877–80, at Queen's College, Belfast, from 1880, and in Edinburgh; LRCP

LRCS Edin 1895; LFPS Glas 1895; general practitioner of 24 and 52 South Street, Greenwich, from c 1898; public vaccinator for South Deptford; died 30 July 1929 at 69 Vincent Square, Westminster; probate London 12 September 1929. [Lond PPR; will cal; *Med Dir*; QCB adm reg]

BLACK, ROBERT JOHN (1828–79), London;
born 1828, son of John Black, merchant, of Belfast; educated at Belfast Academy; studied medicine at Queen's College, Belfast, 1847–52; also at Trinity College, Dublin, and the Richmond Hospital; LM RBAI; LRCSI 1848; MD (QUI) 1852; LSA Lond 1857; resident surgeon at the Belfast General Hospital; honorary surgeon to the N. Islington Dispensary District; of Blenheim Terrace, De Beauvoir Square, London 1854–5; general practitioner of Donegall House, Green Lanes, Highbury, and 373 Euston Road, Islington; married 4 August 1853 in Fisherwick Presbyterian Church, Belfast, Rosalinda Blow (who was born 1832/3), second daughter of William N. Blow, merchant, of Albion Place, Belfast; died 2 January 1879 at Donegall House; probate London 6 February 1879. [*BNL* 5 August 1853 (m), 9 August 1854 (b) and 22 November 1855 (b); Lond GRO (d); Lond PPR; will cal; *Med Dir*; QCB adm reg; UHF database (m)].

BLACK, SAMUEL (1762–1832), Newry, county Down;
born 1762 at Marymount, Lurganbane, county Down; son of James Black, landowner and linen merchant, and Mary Cullen; studied medicine at Edinburgh University 1782–6; MD (Edin) 1786 (thesis 'De ascensu vaporum spontaneo'); MRIA 1796; LKQCPI 1816; physician, of 7 Marcus Square, Newry, from 1788 (blue plaque on his house); pioneer worker on angina pectoris; author of *Clinical and Pathological Reports* (1818); published four cases of angina pectoris, with his own dissection of the coronary arteries, in 1795, 1805 and 1819, including important observations on the predisposing factors, also a paper on the typhus epidemic in Newry of 1817; married 8 September 1801 at Springfield, Dromore, Margaret Maitland of Springfield, Dromore (who was born 1773/4 and died 6 June 1846), daughter of Adam Maitland and Margaret Waddell; died 6 July 1832 at 7 Marcus Square; buried in St Patrick's graveyard, Newry; will dated 20 February 1828 (copy in PRO NI) probate Prerogative Court 1833. [Agnew (1998); *BNL* 15 September 1801 (m); Belf PRO, D/379/3; Belf PRO, prerog wills index; Bradshaw (1819); Clarke, *County Down*, vol 21 (1998); *DIB* (2009); Edin Univ; Evans (1991) and (1995); Farrar (1897); Newmann (1993); *Newry Examiner* 11 July 1832 (d); Pigot (1824); Proudfit (1985); Siegel (1963)].

BLACK, THOMAS (c 1769–1829), Rostrevor and Newry, county Down;
born c 1769, son of Thomas Black of Drummaul, Randalstown, county Antrim; brother of Dr William Black of Newry (*q.v.*); surgeon and apothecary of Forest Brook, Rostrevor and Newry; married 3 April 1789 — Hale of Drumnavaddy, Seapatrick (who was born 1767/8 and died 12 September 1816 at Forest Brook); father of Margaret Black who married Dr William Jones, surgeon RN (*q.v.*); died 18 April 1829 at Forest Brook. [*BNL* 7 April 1789 (m), 17 September 1816 (d), 19 March 1819 (m, daughter) and 28 April 1829 (d); Bradshaw (1819); Farrar (1897); *Newry Telegraph* 24 April 1829 (d)].

BLACK, THOMAS (1803–94), Newry, county Down, and Sydney and Melbourne, Australia;
born 1803, eldest son of Dr William Black of Newry (*q.v.*); educated at RBAI; studied medicine at Glasgow University; CM (Glas) 1826; emigrated to Sydney, Australia, in 1833; moved to Melbourne, Victoria, in 1841; founder of the Medical Society of Victoria and of the Bank of Victoria; died 15 September 1894; portrait in the Bank of Victoria. [Addison (1898); Clarke, *County Down*, vol 21 (1998); *Newry Telegraph* 25 May 1883 and 23 October 1894 (d)].

BLACK, THOMAS HENRY (1814/5–64), Newry, county Down;
born 1814/5, son of Adam Black, gentleman; LAH Dub 1838; LM Rot Hosp Dub 1840; MRCSE 1840; surgeon under Relief Committee during the great famine 1846–7; medical officer to Newry and Crobane Dispensary Districts; surgeon and apothecary of Newry; married 5 September 1854 in Loughbrickland Presbyterian Church, county Down, Elizabeth Brown (who was born 1836/7), daughter of Samuel Brown, farmer, of Brownhill, Banbridge; died 30 March 1864 at Marcus Square, Newry; probate Belfast 25 May 1864. [*BNL* 13 September 1854 (m); Belf PRO, will cal; Croly (1843–6); Dub GRO (m) and (d); *Med Dir*; *Newry Telegraph* 14 September 1854 (m); UHF database (m)].

BLACK, WILLIAM (1749/50–after 1823), London;
born 1849/50, probably at Drumadoney, Dromara, county Down; one of the 'lives' in a lease in the Downshire estates of 12 May 1755; later physician of London in 1823. [Belf PRO, D/671/A4/18 and 19; McCabe, John, pers com].

BLACK, WILLIAM (c 1760–1835), Newry, county Down;
born c 1760, second son of Thomas Black of Drummaul, Randalstown, county Antrim; brother of Dr Thomas Black of Rostrevor (*q.v.*); studied medicine at Glasgow University 1779–82; MD (Glas) 1782; physician, of Rockview, North Street, Newry from 1782; married Jane Irwin (who was born 1760/1 and died 4 September 1836, buried in St Patrick's Graveyard Newry), elder daughter of Dr — Irwin of Mount Irwin, Tynan, county Armagh; father of Dr Thomas Black of Australia (*q.v.*), Dr William Black of Ballymena (*q.v.*) and Jane Black who married 31 December 1830 Michael Smith, son of the Rev Dr Brabazon Smith of Donaghmore (*q.v.*); died 27 May 1835; buried in St Patrick's Graveyard, Newry. [Addison (1898) and (1913); *BNL* 7 January 1831 (m, dau); Bradshaw (1819); Clarke, *County Down*, vol 21 (1998); *Newry Telegraph* 2 June 1835 (d); Pigot (1824)].

BLACK, WILLIAM (1808/9–88), Ballymena, county Antrim;
born 1808/9, younger son of Dr William Black of Newry (*q.v.*); studied medicine at Glasgow University; CM (Glas) 1830; LAH Dub 1841; general practitioner of Mill Street, Ballymena, and surgeon to constabulary; married 19 April 1833 Mary Anne Harrison McCullough (who was born 1811/2 and died 23 July 1834 in Ballymena), youngest daughter of John Shaw McCullough of Drogheda; died 27 October 1888; buried in Drummaul Graveyard, Randalstown; probate Belfast 7 January 1889.

[Addison (1898); *BNL* 29 July 1834 (d); Belf PRO, will cal; Croly (1843–6); gravestone inscriptions; *Med Dir*; *Newry Examiner* 24 April 1833 (m)].

BLACKETT, EDWARD RALPH (1835–93), Southwold, Suffolk;
born 1835, son of John Blackett of Ballyne, Pilltown, county Kilkenny; educated privately; studied arts from 1848 at Trinity College, Dublin and medicine at the Royal College of Surgeons in Ireland; BA (TCD) 1853; LM Rot Hosp Dub 1854; LRCSI 1855; LSA London 1857; acting assistant surgeon in army 1855–6; house surgeon in Suffolk General Hospital 1857–60; medical officer to Southwold Dispensary, Suffolk, from 1862, and medical officer and public vaccinator to the 8th District of Blything Union, of Wangford, Suffolk; married Laura Jane —; died 18 June 1893; probate Ipswich 22 Septembet 1893. [Burtchaell and Sadleir (1935); Kirkpatrick Archive; Lond PPR, will cal; *Med Dir*; QCB adm reg].

BLACKLEY, TRAVERS ROBERT (1800/1–c 1874), Louth and Armagh;
born 1800/01 in Dublin, son of John Blackley, merchant; studied arts at Trinity College, Dublin, and medicine at the Royal College of Surgeons in Ireland; BA (TCD) 1822; FRCSI 1824; surgeon in County Louth Infirmary; retired before 1846, living at Beechhill, Armagh; living at Ashtown Lodge, Castleknock, county Dublin c 1859; living abroad from c 1862; author of *Hints Relative to the Present State of the Medico-Chirurgical Profession in Dublin* (1839); married (1) —; (2) 24 April 1855, in Rosemary Street First Presbyterian Church, Belfast, Jane Montgomery, daughter of Robert Montgomery, merchant, of Belfast; died c 1874. [Burtchaell and Sadleir (1924); Croly (1843–6); Dub GRO (m); *Med Dir*; UHF database (m)].

BLACKWOOD, ALEXANDER O'REILLY (1861–94), Queenstown, county Cork, and Ballywalter, county Down;
born 27 May 1861 at Holywood, county Down, son of John O'Reilly Blackwood of Ballymenoch, Holywood, and his second wife Sarah Anne Skelly of Donaghadee; educated at Hillbrook School, Holywood; studied medicine at Queen's College, Belfast, from 1879; LRCP LRCS Edin 1886; general practitioner, of Glenmore, Queenstown, c 1886; moved c 1890 to Ballywalter; died 14 September 1894 at Yeovil, Somerset. [Blackwood pedigrees, vol 51; *Med Dir*; QCB adm reg].

BLACKWOOD, ARTHUR (1862–1906), Liverpool;
born 10 May 1862, son of William Blackwood, draper, of Lakeview, Milford, county Donegal, and Anna Maria Montgomery of Ray, county Donegal; brother of Anna Maria Blackwood who married Dr William Henrie Crawford Clarke (*q.v.*); educated at Milford National School; studied medicine at Queen's College, Belfast, from 1880; MD MCh and Diploma of Obstetrics (RUI) 1884; surgeon to the Pacific Steam Navigation Company; resident medical officer to the Liverpool Parish Infirmary; general practitioner, and public vaccinator to No 1 and 2 Districts of Liverpool; of 100 Bedford Street; married 13 April 1892 Ruth Shearson Barrow, 2nd daughter of Edward Shearson Barrow FRCS of Golborne, Lancashire; died 6 April 1906 at 100 Bedford Street; probate Liverpool 28 May 1906. [Blackwood pedigrees, vol 71; *BMJ* obituary (1906); Kirkpatrick Archive; Lond PPR, will cal; *Med Dir*; QCB adm reg].

BLACKWOOD, PINKSTAN, senior (1735–76), London;
born 1 May 1735, son of John Blackwood of Bangor, merchant and Agnes Pinkstan; physician in London; had a liason with Elizabeth Powell and was father of Dr Pinkstan Blackwood, junior (*q.v.*); died October 1776; buried in St James's, Picadilly. [Belf PRO, D2961/2/2/6; Blackwood pedigrees, vol 51].

BLACKWOOD, PINKSTAN, junior (1776–1864), Belfast, Downpatrick, county Down, and Brussels;
born 11 November 1776, probably in London, baptised 17 November in St James's, Piccadilly, probably son of Pinkstan Blackwood, surgeon, of London (*q.v.*), and Elizabeth Powell; LAH Dub 1803; surgeon to North Down Militia; elected member of Belfast Literary Society 1801 and addressed it in March 1803; surgeon to the Down County Infirmary 1811–12; lived in Brussels for much of his life and finally at his brother's rectory in Middleton Tyas, Yorkshire; married 11 November 1800 Mary Hamilton (who died 23 August 1864 at Ryhope, Durham), daughter of John Hamilton of Ballyalloly, county Down; died 6 October 1864 at Middleton Tyas; probate York 26 October 1864. [Apothecaries (1829); *BNL* 14 November 1800 (m); Belf PRO, D2961/2/2/6; Blackwood pedigrees, vol 51; Farrar (1897); Lond PPR, will cal].

BLACKWOOD, WILLIAM (1773/4–1838), Letterkenny, county Donegal;
born 1773/4; surgeon and merchant, of Letterkenny c 1837; married —; father of Martha Blackwood who married Dr James Rankin, RN (*q.v.*); died 8 January 1838 at Letterkenny. [*BNL* 23 January 1838 (d); *Londonderry Sentinel* 23 September 1837 (m, daughter)].

BLACKWOOD, — (d 1806), Letterkenny, county Donegal;
died 15 April 1806 after a short illness; 'successful in his profession and conciliating in his manner, he gained the esteem of an extensive circle …' [*BNL* 25 April 1806 (d)].

BLADEN, ISAAC N. (*fl c* 1828), Stewartstown, county Tyrone;
surgeon, of Stewartstown; married August 1828 in Dungannon, Sarah Jane Garrett, daughter of Henry Garrett of Dungannon. [*BNL* 15 August 1828 (m)].

BLAIN, JOHN (1806/7–48), Urbana, Maryland, USA;
born 1806/7, youngest son of Andrew Blain of Ballynahinch, county Down; emigrated to USA; surgeon, of Urbana; died 24 June 1848 at Urbana. [*BNL* 1 December 1848 (d)].

BLAIR, BRICE (BRYCE) (1811/2–73), Ballymena, county Antrim, and Coagh and Moneymore, county Londonderry;
born 1811/2; MRCS Eng 1835; LM Anglesey Hospital 1835; studied medicine at Glasgow University; MD (Glas) 1837; LAH Dub 1840; resident surgeon to Anglesey Hospital, Dublin; physician to Ballymena Workhouse; medical officer to Coagh Dispensary District and constabulary and registrar of births and deaths; married 13 June 1839 Ellen Dunseath (who was born 1817 and died 13 January 1845), youngest

Dr Robert ('Robin') Adair (c 1711–90),
oil painting by *Lemuel Abbott*
(reproduced courtesy of the Royal College
of Surgeons in Ireland)

Dr Samuel Agnew (1848–1924)

Dr John Gower Allen (1847/8–1925)

Prof George James Allman, MD (1812–98)

Dr Samuel William Allworthy (1866–1952)

Prof Richard John Anderson (1848–1914)

Prof Thomas Andrews, MD (1813–85), oil painting by *Richard Hooke* (reproduced courtesy of the Queen's University of Belfast)

Dr Thomas William Atkinson (1855–1919)

Dr Lombe Atthill (1827–1910), oil painting by *Sarah Purser* (reproduced courtesy of the Royal College of Physicians of Ireland)

Dr Hugh William Bailie (1862–1933)

Mr Henry Norman Barnett, FRCS (1872–1952)

Dr John Milford Barnett (1830–1913)

Sir James Barr, FRCP (1849–1938)

Sir William Beatty, surgeon RN (1773–1842), oil painting by *Arthur William Devis* (reproduced courtesy of the National Maritime Museum, Greenwich)

Sir Edward Coey Bigger, MD (1861–1942)

Prof Joseph Black (1728–99), engraving

Dr Samuel Black (1762–1832), gravestone

Dr John St. Clair Boyd (1858–1918)

Dr George Bracken (1858–1929)

Sir Robert Edward Bredon, MB (1846–1918)

Dr Richard King Brown (1864–1942)

Dr James Browne (1857–1929)

Sir John Walton Browne, MD (1844–1923)

Dr Samuel Browne, senior, surgeon RN (1809–90)

Dr John Samuel Bryars (1861–1915)

Prof William Burden, MD (1798–1879), oil painting, artist unknown (reproduced courtesy of the Queen's University of Belfast)

Prof Sir John William Byers, MD (1853–1920)

Dr William Calwell, senior (1859–1943)

Dr William John Cameron (1853–1929)

Mr Robert Campbell, FRCS (1866–1920)

Dr Fleetwood Churchill (1808–78), oil painting by *Sir Thomas Alfred Jones* (reproduced courtesy of the Royal College of Physicians of Ireland)

Dr James Alexander Clarke (1868–1951)

daughter of Thomas Dunseath of Ballymena; died 18 March 1873 at Moneymore; administration (with will) Londonderry 14 August 1873. [Addison (1898); *BNL* 18 June 1839 (m) and 28 January 1845 (d); Belf PRO, will cal; Croly (1843–6); Dub GRO (d); Kirkpatrick Archive; *Med Dir*].

BLAIR, CRAWFORD (1821–76), Ballynure, county Antrim;
   born 1821; studied medicine at Queen's College, Belfast, and Anderson's College, Glasgow; LFPS Glas 1852; medical officer to Ballynure Dispensary District 1852–72 and registrar of births and deaths; married Janet Orr (who was born 1824 and died 1872); father of Dr William Park Blair (*q.v.*) and Mary Agnew Blair who married Dr Samuel McNair (*q.v.*); died 25 May 1876 at Ballynure; buried in Raloo graveyard; administration (with will) Belfast 2 October 1876. [Belf PRO, will cal; Dub GRO (d); *Med Dir*; Rutherford and Clarke, *Antrim*, vol 2 (1981)].

BLAIR, D. (*fl c* 1826), Islandmagee, county Antrim;
   surgeon, of Islandmagee; married 12 May 1826 — Knox, niece of Robert Knox, merchant, of Belfast. [*BNL* 16 May 1826 (m)].

BLAIR, JAMES (*fl c* 1742), Ballymena, county Antrim;
   doctor of physick, of Ballymena; witness to a will dated 1742. [Eustace, vol II (1954)].

BLAIR, RANDAL (1791/2–1837), Larne, county Antrim;
   born 1791/2; surgeon in Larne; involved in treating patients in the cholera epidemic of February 1833; married Susanna — (who was born 1797 and died 17 January 1836); died 3 April 1837 in Larne; buried in Larne Old Graveyard; probate Connor Diocesan Court (see transcript of will in PRO NI). [*BNL* 22 January 1836 (d) and 11 April 1837 (d); Belf PRO, T/502/36; McKillop (2000); Rutherford and Clarke, *County Antrim*, vol 4 (2004)].

BLAIR, WILLIAM (1812/3–36), Berbice, British Guiana;
   born 1812/3 in Larne; surgeon; medical officer in Berbice c 1835–6; died 30 November 1836 of 'brain fever', '… a young man of the most amiable disposition …' [*BNL* 3 February 1837 (d)].

BLAIR, WILLIAM PARK (1856–1902), Ballynure, county Antrim;
   born 24 August 1856 at Ballynure, county Antrim, son of Dr Crawford Blair (*q.v.*) and Janet Orr; educated at Belfast Academy; studied medicine at Queen's College, Belfast, from 1873 and Glasgow Royal Infirmary; LRCP Edin 1879; LFPS Glas 1879; medical officer to Ballynure Dispensary District; married Lizzie Crawford —; died 31 August 1902 at Ballynure; probably buried in Old Ballynure Graveyard; administration Belfast 17 October 1902. [Belf PRO, will cal; Dub GRO (d); *Med Dir*; QCB adm reg; Rutherford and Clarke, *County Antrim*, vol 2 (1981) and vol 3 (1995)].

BLAIRE, JAMES (*fl c* 1812), Raphoe, county Donegal;
   LAH Dub 1812; apothecary, of Raphoe. [Apothecaries (1829)].

BLAKE, CHARLES JOSEPH (1868–97), Headford, county Galway;
born 17 March 1868 at Tuam, county Galway, son of Mark Blake, gentleman, of Tuam; educated at the Jesuit's College, Galway; studied medicine at Queen's College, Belfast, from 1875 and at the Ledwich School and Mercer's Hospital, Dublin; LRCP LRCS Edin 1882; LM Coombe Hosp Dub; resident pupil at the Fever Hospital, Dublin; medical officer to Headford Dispensary District and constabulary; unmarried; died 28 April 1897 at Headford, from a head injury due to an accident; administration (with will) Tuam 7 August 1897. [Belf PRO, will cal; Dub GRO (d); *Med Dir*; QCB adm reg].

BLAKELY, EDMUND BREAKEY (1842–90), Dublin and USA;
born 15 February 1842 at Dromorebrague, Banbridge, county Down, son of Isaac Blakely, farmer, of Dromorebrague, and Martha —; educated at Banbridge School; studied medicine at Queen's College, Belfast, from 1863; LRCP and LM LRCS and LM Edin 1868; demonstrator in anatomy and later lecturer in botany at the Carmichael School of Medicine, Dublin, of 17 North Frederick Street, c 1870 and of 76 Blessington Street c 1878; emigrated to USA; died 16 February 1890; commemorated in Loughbrickland Presbyterian graveyard. [Gravestone inscription; *Med Dir*; QCB adm reg].

BLAKELY SAMUEL (1824/5–1902), Aughnacloy and Fivemiletown, county Tyrone;
born 1824/5 at Boardmills, county Down, son of William Blakely, farmer; educated at RBAI; studied medicine at Queen's College, Belfast, from 1848; LM RBAI 1849; LFPS Glas 1852; MRCSE 1859; MD (Aberdeen) 1860; LM KQCPI 1863; medical officer to Aughnacloy Dispensary District and Jackson's Almshouse; medical officer to Fivemiletown Dispensary District and constabulary and registrar of births and deaths; married 26 November 1863, in First Ramelton Presbyterian Church, Catharine Hay Davidson, daughter of Samuel Davidson, merchant, of Ramelton; father of Dr William Edmund Blakely (*q.v.*) and Dr Sydney Herbert George Blakely, MB (RUI) 1902; died 14 December 1902 at Fivemiletown; probate Dublin 15 May 1903. [Belf PRO, will cal; *Coleraine Chronicle* 5 December 1863 (m); Dub GRO (m) and (d); *Londonderry Sentinel* 1 December 1863 (m); McCann (2003); *Med Dir*; QCB adm reg].

BLAKELY, WILLIAM EDMUND (1864–1932), Fivemiletown, county Tyrone;
born 29 August 1864 at Aughnacloy, county Tyrone, son of Dr Samuel Blakely (*q.v.*); brother of Dr Sydney Herbert George Blakely, MB (RUI) 1902; studied medicine at Queen's College, Belfast, and the Royal College of Surgeons in Ireland; LRCP LRCS Edin 1893; LFPS Glas 1893; medical officer and medical officer of health to the Fivemiletown Dispensary District and constabulary; of Lismoyle, Fivemiltown; unmarried; died 3 March 1932 at Lismoyle; administration Belfast 21 June 1932. [Belf GRO (d); Belf PRO, will cal; *Med Dir*; QCB adm reg].

BLAK(E)NEY, SAMUEL (1798/9–1828), Donaghadee, county Down;
born 1798/9; surgeon, of Donaghadee c 1824; died 2 January 1828 in Donaghadee; buried in Donaghadee graveyard. [*BNL* 18 January 1828 (d); Clarke, *County Down*, vol 16 (1976); Pigot (1824)].

BLA(Y)NEY, ALEXANDER JOSEPH McAULEY (1869–1925), Dublin;
born 24 November 1869 at Cushendall, county Antrim, son of Alexander Blaney, sea captain, of Cushendall, and Ann Jane McAuley; brother of Dr Neil John Bla(y)ney, surgeon, of Maryborough, Queen's County (*q.v.*); educated at St Malachy's College, Belfast; studied medicine at the Catholic University of Ireland, Dublin; MA (RUI) 1891; MB BCh BAO 1893; FRCSI 1898; house surgeon to the Mater Misericordiae Hospital, Dublin; demonstrator in anatomy to the Catholic University; of 5 Donegall Terrace, Antrim Road, Belfast; professor of biology in University College, Dublin; surgeon to the Mater Misericordiae Hospital and assistant professor of surgery to the Catholic University; visiting surgeon to St Patrick's College, Maynooth; of 15 Merrion Square North, Dublin; author of various surgical papers; married (1) —; (2) 1 September 1920 in the Roman Catholic Chapel of St Patrick's Hospital, Cork, Mary Stanton, daughter of John Stanton, solicitor, of 5 Alexandra Place, Cork; father, by (2) of Dr Alexander John Edward Blayney, MB (NUI) 1942, anaesthetist at the Mater Misericordiae Hospital, Dublin; died 12 July 1925 on Portmarnock Golf Links; administration Dublin 12 January 1926. [Dub GRO (b), (m) and (d); Dub Nat Arch, will cal; *Med Dir;* O'Donnell (2008)].

BLA(Y)NEY, NEIL JOHN (1873/4–1919), Maryborough, Queen's County;
born 1873/4, son of Alexander Blaney, sea captain of Cushendall, and Ann Jane McAuley; brother of Dr Alexander Joseph McAuley Bla(y)ney (*q.v.*); studied medicine at the Catholic University of Ireland; MB BCh BAO (RUI) 1897; resident surgeon and physician to the Mater Misericordiae Hospital, Dublin; surgeon to the Queen's County Infirmary and physician to the Queen's County Sanatorium, Maryborough, from c 1905; married Eileen M. —; died 26 February 1919 at New Park Villa, Maryborough; probate Dublin 11 October 1919. [Dub GRO (d); Dub Nat Arch, will cal, will; *Med Dir*; O'Donnell (2008)].

BLECKLEY, THOMAS MACDOUGALL (1828–82), Army Medical Service;
born 13 December 1828 in Monaghan, son of the Rev John Bleckley, minister of Monaghan Presbyterian Church, and his second wife — Mollan; studied arts and medicine at Trinity College, Dublin, from 1842; BA (TCD) 1847; MB 1852; LRCSI 1853; MD 1865; MA 1870; FKQCPI (hon) 1874; joined the Army Medical Service as assistant staff surgeon to 14th Foot, 1854 and served in the Crimean War 1855 including the siege and fall of Sebastopol; staff surgeon 1863; transferred to 46th Foot 1865 and served in Bengal; Inspector-General of Hospitals for India; served in the Ashanti campaign 1873; CB (military) 1874; retired on half pay with rank of brigadier 1880; of Lorne House, Upper Norwood, London; married 10 October 1865 in St Stephen's Church of Ireland Church, Dublin, Lily Hamilton, eldest daughter of Andrew Hamilton of 6 Somerset Place, Raglan Road, Dublin; died 23 November 1882 at Upper Norwood; administration London 13 June 1883. [Burtchaell and Sadleir (1924); *BMJ* obituary (1882); *Coleraine Chronicle* 14 October 1865 (m); Lond PPR, will cal; McConnell (1951); *Med Dir*; Peterkin and Johnston (1968); Widdess (1963)].

BLEWITT, JAMES (c 1870–1945), Belfast;
born c 1870; studied medicine at the Catholic University of Ireland, Dublin, and the Surgeon's Hall, Edinburgh; LRCP LRCS Edin 1896; LFPS Glas 1896; general practitioner and Admiralty Surgeon and Agent, of 4 the Mount, Belfast c 1910 and later of 12 College Square North, 114 Newtownards Road and 108 Marlborough Park; married —; died 22 October 1945 at the Musgrave and Clark Clinic, Belfast; probate Belfast 1 October 1946. [Belf GRO (d); Belf PRO, will cal; *Med Dir*].

BLIZARD, JOHN McCANCE (1819/20–62), Belfast and Liverpool, Lancashire;
born 1819/20 in Belfast, son of Conway Blizard; studied medicine at RBAI from 1835, at Dublin 1838–9 and at Edinburgh University 1839–43; MD (Edin) (thesis 'De pneumonia') 1843; LM Dub 1847; MRCSE 1847; physician, of 1 Wellington Place, Belfast, c 1849–53 and of 202 Grove Street, Liverpool c 1853–62; married 16 May 1848 in Cheriton Parish Church, Kent, Jane McCance (who died 31 December 1858 at 202 Grove Street), eldest daughter of John McCance of Suffolk, county Antrim; died 22 March 1862 at Ashton Street Asylum, Liverpool; probate Liverpool 16 April 1862. [*BNL* 26 May 1848 (m), 2 February 1849 (b, son) and 1 January 1859 (d); Belf PRO, SCH 524/1A/; *Belfast Street Directories*; Edin Univ; Lond GRO (m) and (d); Lond PPR, will cal; *Med Dir*].

BLUE, CHARLES (1869–1915), Brighouse, Bradford and Skelton-in-Cleveland, Yorkshire, and Lewisham, London;
born 15 June 1869 at Clarence River, New South Wales; educated at Sullivan Upper School, Holywood; studied medicine at Queen's College, Belfast from 1888; MB BCh BAO (RUI) 1895; of St Moffatt's Terrace. Holywood, c 1895; general practitioner, of 'The Poplars', Rastric Common, Brighouse c 1896–8, of Lynthorne Road, Frizinghall, Bradford c 1898–1902, of Boosbeck, Skelton-in-Cleveland c 1902–05, and of St Kilda, Lewisham Park, London c 1905–15; married Alice Mary —; died 11 July 1915 at 49 Catford Hill, Catford, Kent; probate London 30 August 1915. [Kirkpatrick Archive; Lond PPR, will cal, will; *Med Dir*; QCB adm reg].

BOAK, JAMES (d before 1832), Strabane, county Tyrone;
general practitioner, of Ballylaw, Strabane; married — (who died 19 May 1831 at Ballylaw); died before 1832. [*BNL* 7 June 1831 (d)].

BODKIN, JOHN CHARLES (1859/60–93), Chinese Imperial Maritime Customs;
born 1859/60 at Bovevagh, county Londonderry, son of John Bodkin, farmer, of Bovevagh; educated at Moneymore Academy; studied medicine at Queen's College, Belfast, 1876–80; MD (hons) MCh Dip Mid (QUI) 1880; joined Chinese Imperial Maritime Customs in Chefoo, China c 1881; died 1893. [*Med Dir*; QCB adm reg].

BODKIN, WILLIAM (1843–1906), Chelmsford, Essex;
born 29 March 1843 at Desertmartin, county Londonderry, son of John Bodkin of Desertmartin; educated at Cookstown Academy; studied medicine at Queen's College, Belfast, from 1863; LRCS LRCP Edin 1866; MD MCh (QUI) (with prizes) 1867; LM Glas 1867; general practitioner, of The Cloisters, Chelmsford, Essex; married —; father of Dr Herbert Alfred Bodkin, LRCP Lond, MRCSE 1905, of

Bloemfontein, South Africa; died 20 October 1906; probate London 19 January 1907. [London PPR, will cal, will; *Med Dir*; QCB adm reg].

BOLTON, REUBEN (1844–1900), Belfast and Bangor, county Down;
born 12 April 1844 at Castlecaulfield, county Tyrone, son of Dr Robert Henry Bolton (*q.v.*) and his first wife, Mary Anne Crawford; educated at the Belfast Seminary; studied medicine at Queen's College, Belfast, from 1859; MD MCh (QUI) 1865; LM RCSE 1866; LAH Dub 1866; surgeon to the Allan Line of Steamers; apothecary in Great Georges' Street, Belfast, from 1867 and at 9 Trinity Street and later in 147 York Street, Belfast; apothecary to the Belfast Hospital for Sick Children 1873–5; general practitioner in Main Street, Bangor, from 1875; medical officer to Bangor Dispensary District, constabulary and Cottage Hospital from 1878; JP; married (1) 23 November 1870 in Rosemary Street Presbyterian Church, Belfast, Mary Anne Leck, daughter of William Leck, muslin manufacturer; (2) 27 December 1877 in Great James's Street Presbyterian Church, Londonderry, Rachel McKillip, daughter of John McKillip, agent, of Londonderry; died 20 November 1900 at 3 Catherine Place, Bangor; buried in Bangor Abbey Graveyard; probate Belfast 13 February 1901. [Belf PRO, will cal; Bolton, Benjamin, pers com; Calwell (1973); Dub GRO (m) x 2 and (d); Kirkpatrick Archive; *Med Dir*; Merrick and Clarke, *County Down*, vol 17 (1978); *Newtonards Chronicle* 24 November 1900 (d); QCB adm reg].

BOLTON, ROBERT HENRY (1778–1866), Naval and Army Medical Services, Dungannon, county Tyrone, Newry, county Down, and Belfast;
born 21 November 1778 (Peterkin) or c 1786 (other records); brother of Thomas Bolton AMS (died 1821) and nephew of Abraham Bolton AMS (died 1818); joined the Naval Medical Service as assistant surgeon on HMS *Orion* 1805–06 and present at the battle of Trafalgar, being awarded medal and clasp; joined the Army Medical Service as surgeon's mate 1807; assistant surgeon to 62nd Foot 1809; served in the Peninsular War; regimental surgeon in Mediterranean 1813; half pay 1815; MD (Edin) 1818 (thesis 'De haematemesi'); surgeon to 78th Foot 1823; retired on half pay 1826; surgeon in Dungannon, and medical officer to constabulary c 1830–50, in Newry c 1850–59 and finally of 28 Fleet Street, Belfast; married (1) 14 August 1820 in Ballyshannon Church, Mary Anne Crawford (who died 30 April 1844, 18 days after the birth of Reuben), daughter of William Crawford of Ballyshannon; (2) Letitia Waddell (nee Patterson) (who was born 1810/1 and died 22 May 1874 in Belfast), widow of James Waddell, surveyor; father, by his first marriage, of Dr Reuben Bolton (*q.v.*); died 8 July 1866 in Bangor; buried in Bangor Abbey graveyard; probate Belfast 20 August 1866 and 11 September 1874. [*BNL* 25 August 1820 (m); Belf PRO, will cal; Bolton, Reuben (Ben), pers com; Edin Univ; Merrick and Clarke, *County Down*, vol 17 (1978); Peterkin and Johnston (1968)].

BOLTON, SAMUEL JOHN (1864–1951), Kilrea and Aghadowey, county Londonderry;
born 28 July 1864 at Kilrea, county Londonderry, son of Sloan Bolton, farmer, of Kilrea; educated at Londonderry Academical Institution; studied medicine at Queen's College, Belfast, from 1884; LRCP LRCS Edin and LM 1891; LFPS Glas 1891;

general practitioner in Kilrea 1890–1915; medical officer to Aghadowey Dispensary District 1915–35, of Beechcroft, Aghadowey; JP; retired 1935 to live at Glenshane, 80 Strand Road, Portstewart; married 28 November 1895 in Magherafelt Presbyterian Church, Isabella Kirkland, daughter of George Kirkland, farmer; father of Dr Sloan McIlrath Bolton, MB (QUB) 1921, and Dr Samuel Ernest Bolton, MB (QUB) 1926; died 12 December 1951 at Portstewart; buried in Second Kilrea Presbyterian Graveyard; probate Belfast 17 April 1953. [Belf GRO (d); Belf PRO, will cal; Bolton, Gordon, pers com; Dub GRO (m); *Med Dir*; QCB adm reg].

BOLTON, THOMAS (b 1691/2);
born 1691/2 in Dublin, son of the Reverend John Bolton, Dean of Derry, and Dorcas Tomlinson of Drogheda; educated at Derry Diocesan School (Foyle College); studied arts and medicine at Trinity College, Dublin, from 1708; BA (TCD) 1712; studied medicine at Leyden University from 1715; MD (Rheims) 1715; MB MD (TCD) 1737. [Burtchaell and Sadleir (1924); Kirkpatrick Archive; Leslie (1937); Innes Smith (1932)].

BOND, WILLIAM JAMES (1853–98), Brill, Buckinghamshire;
born 1853, son of Joseph Bond, farmer, of Disertowen, county Londonderry, and Elizabeth Hamilton (who was sister of Dr William James Hamilton, RN (*q.v.*); studied medicine at Glasgow University 1870–05; MB ChB (Glas) 1875; LRCS and LM Edin 1875; general practitioner, of Waterloo House, Brill, from c 1875; married 20 September 1877 in St Peter's in the East Church, Oxford, Adelaide Pargeter (who was born 1857/8), daughter of William Pargeter, farmer, of Yeat Farm, Wotton Under Wood, Buckinghamshire; died 28 November 1898 at Brill; administration Oxford 18 January 1899. [Lond GRO (m) and (d); Lond PPR, will cal; *Med Dir*; Todd (2008)].

BOOMER, JOHN McWATTERS (1842–1920), Venezuela, and Lisburn, county Antrim;
born 13 July 1842 at Old Park, Lisburn, son of Henry Boomer of Old Park; educated at Lisburn Academy; studied medicine at Queen's College, Belfast from 1859, Trinity College, Dublin and Edinburgh University; LRCP LRCS Edin 1873; government medical officer, Jamaica c 1878; civil surgeon, Zulu War; surgeon to the Chile and the Gold Mining Companies, Venezuela; retired to Clonlee, Lisburn, c 1890; unmarried; died 14 December 1920 at Clonlee. [Dub GRO (d); *Med Dir*; QCB adm reg].

BOOTH, BRABAZON SHEILS (1829–1909), India, and Newry, county Down;
born 7 December 1829; studied medicine at Trinity College, and the Richmond Hospital, Dublin; MRCSE 1857; LKQCPI and LM 1872; assistant surgeon to Calcutta Native Hospital 1858–64; civil surgeon at Tirhoot, India, 1864–74; physician to Newry Fever Hospital 1874–94; living at 3 Trevor Hill, Newry, 1874–95 and later at 13 Downshire Road, Newry; married on 24 January 1867 Barbarina Elizabeth Wilson, eldest daughter of James Wilson of Underwood, Pembrokeshire; died 7 January 1909 at 13 Downshire Road, Newry; buried in St Patrick's graveyard, Newry (no memorial); probate Belfast 5 April 1909. [Belf PRO, will cal; Dub GRO (d); *Med Dir*].

BOSQUET, FRANCIS (*fl c* 1720), Lisburn, county Antrim;
    medical doctor of Lisburn c 1711–26; 3 sons graduated at Trinity College, Dublin. [Burtchaell and Sadleir (1924)].

BOTHWELL, GEORGE GRANVILLE, senior (1840/1–91), Guildford, Surrey, Greenwich, Kent, Leighton Buzzard, Bedfordshire, and Topsham, Devon;
    born 1840/1, son of George Bothwell, gentleman, of Dungannon; studied medicine at Ledwich School and Mercers' Hospital, Dublin; LAH Dub 1859; LM Coombe Hosp Dub; MRCSE 1861; LM RCSE 1863; LSA Lond 1863; LRCP Edin 1867; resident medical officer to the Guildford and West Surrey Dispensary 1862–70, but also described as 'of Rathmullan' c 1863; medical officer to Royal Kent Dispensary District and surgeon to Royal Navy c 1870–05, living in Greenwich; moved c 1875 to Leighton Buzzard; medical officer and public vaccinator from c 1880 to Topsham Dispensary District, of Broadway House, Topsham; married 25 March 1863 in Killygarvan Church of Ireland Church, county Donegal, Mary Ellen de Burgh, widow of Dr Walter de Burgh, who had died 18 November 1862, and daughter of William Coleham [?] Mayne, government officer, of Rathmullan, county Donegal; father of Dr George Granville Bothwell, junior, MB (Aberdeen) 1892; died 1 January 1891 at the Devon and Exeter Hospital; probate Exeter 10 March 1891. [Dub GRO (m); Kirkpatrick Archive; Lond GRO (d); Lond PPR, will cal; *Med Dir*].

BOURKE, GEOFFREY JAMES (1850/1–1917), Shercock, county Cavan;
    born 1850/1; studied medicine at Royal College of Surgeons in Ireland; LM Coombe Hosp Dub 1875; LRCSI 1875; LAH Dub 1875; medical officer to Shercock Dispensary District and constabulary from 1875; coroner for county Cavan and certifying factory surgeon; married Mary Clare J. —; died 21 April 1917; probate Cavan 18 July 1917. [Belf PRO, will cal; Dub GRO (d); Kirkpatrick Archive; *Med Dir*].

BOWDEN, CHARLES (c 1777–1810), Downpatrick, county Down;
    born c 1777, second son of Hugh Bowden of Ballyward, county Down and Eliza Moore; apothecary to Down County Infirmary from 1803 and its second surgeon after the death of William Waring (*q.v.*) in 1808; elected member of Belfast Literary Society and addressed it 1803–05 (resigned 1806); married 21 July 1808 Elizabeth Simms of Belfast (who died 3 February 1818 at Carrickfergus); died 14 September 1810 at the early age of 33, buried in Ballyhalbert graveyard. [*Belf Lit Soc*; Belf PRO, D2961/2/2/6; *BNL* 22 July 1808 (m) and 10 February 1818 (d); Bennett (1974); Clarke, *County Down*, vol 15 (1975); Malcolm (1851); Parkinson (1967); Pilson (1838).]

BOWDEN, GEORGE (1823/4–59), Castleshane and Clontibret, county Monaghan;
    born 1823/4, second son of Hugh Bowden, gentleman, of Portaferry; studied medicine at the Royal College of Surgeons in Ireland and Glasgow University; LM Rot Hosp Dub; LRCSI 1847; MD (Glas) 1848; medical officer to Castleshane and Monaghan Dispensary Districts and surgeon to the military in Monaghan from c 1849; of Andrea Cottage, Clontibret; author of various medical papers; married 10 July 1849, in Ballyhemlin Non-subscribing Presbyterian Church, county Down,

Ann Allen (who was born 1825/6), daughter of Alexander Allen, gentleman; drowned 26 October 1859 in Redwharf Bay, Anglesea, in the wreck of the *Royal Charter*; commemorated in Ballyhalbert graveyard. [Addison (1898); *BNL* 17 July 1849 (m); Clarke, *County Down*, vol 15 (1975); *Med Dir*; UHF database (m)].

BOWEN, ARTHUR WINNIETT NUNN (1873–1964), Royal Army Medical Corps; born 13 January 1873 at Portaferry, county Down, youngest son of George Edward Bowen, land agent, of Portaferry; studied medicine at Cambridge University and Guy's Hospital, London; LRCPI and LM, LRCSI and LM 1894; resident surgeon at Meath Hospital, Dublin; joined RAMC as lieutenant 1897; captain 1900; major 1909; lietentant-colonel 1915; served in World War I 1914–18; DSO 1917; CBE c 1919; lived finally at Ranviles Nursing Home, Ranviles Lane, Fareham, Hampshire; married 22 November 1917 in St Margaret's, Westminster, Edith Sanders Phillips (who was born 1886/7), widow of captain W.C.O. Phillips, and daughter of Samuel Alfred Einem Hickson, RNVR; died 4 February 1964; probate Winchester 9 July 1964. [Kirkpatrick Archive; Lond GRO (m) and (d); Lond PPR, will cal; *Med Dir*; Peterkin and Johnston (1968)].

BOWEN, EDWARD (1778/9–1867), Taughboyne, county Donegal; born 1778/9; surgeon in Dublin 'when he had the good fortune to be setting the late Marquis of Abercorn's leg after a carriage accident, which his Lordship had sustained. Subsequently entering Holy Orders he was presented by his patron to the above rectory' [Taughboyne] (Leslie); ordained deacon 1807 [no degree!]; married —; father of Jane Bowen who married John Maginniss of Burt House, county Donegal, son of Sir John Maginniss (*q.v.*); died 18 August 1867 at Bagay, Killea, county Donegal; probate Londonderry 5 September 1867. [Belf PRO, will cal; Dub GRO (d); Leslie (1940)].

BOWEN, WILLIAM H. (*fl c* 1840), Downpatrick, county Down; apothecary to the Down County Infirmary, Downpatrick March 1839–April 1840; required to resign because he married in 1839. [Parkinson (1967)].

BOWMAN, HENRY O. (*fl c* 1846), Carrickfergus, county Antrim, and Bishop Wearmouth, county Durham; third son of Davys Bowman of Carrickfergus; MD [?]; married 1 September 1846 at Bishop Wearmouth, Elizabeth Catherine Kidson, third daughter of John P. Kidson, solicitor, of Sunderland. [*BNL* 18 September 1846 (m)].

BOWMAN, JAMES (*fl c* 1750), Quebec, Canada; eldest son of Whitney Bowman of Carrickfergus and Eleanor Fleming; his sister Letitia Bowman married Robert McGowan and was mother of Dr John McGowan (*q.v.*); MD [?]; emigrated to Quebec, Canada. [Jones (1977)].

BOWMAN, ROBERT (1842–98), Indian Medical Service; born 8 May 1842 at Armagh, son of Robert Bowman, banker; educated at Armagh Royal School 1853–7; LKQCPI 1863; LRCSI 1863; joined the Indian Medical Service (Bombay establishment) as assistant surgeon in 1866; surgeon 1873; surgeon major 1878; brigade surgeon 1889; surgeon colonel 1893; served in Abyssinian Campaign 1867–8 (medal); retired to Charlemont Place, Armagh; married Maud M. —; died 12 July 1898 at Charlemont Place; buried in St Mark's, Armagh; probate Armagh 9 August 1898. [Belf PRO, will cal; Crawford (1930); Dub GRO (d); Ferrar (1933); *Med Dir*].

BOYD, HENRY JOHNSTON (1857–1925), Hillsborough, county Down;
born 4 April 1857 at Hillsborough, son of Dr William Boyd of Hillsborough (*q.v.*); educated at RBAI; studied medicine at Queen's College, Belfast, 1875–80; LRCP LRCS Edin 1880; medical officer to Hillsborough Dispensary District and certifying factory surgeon, of Park House, Hillsborough; JP; married 9 June 1886, in Aghalee Church of Ireland Church, county Antrim, Anne Best (who was born 1863/4), daughter of Robert Best, farmer, of Aghalee; father of Dr William Stanley Boyd, MB (QUB) 1913; died 29 March 1925 at 81 University Street, Belfast; buried in Hillsborough graveyard; probate Belfast 14 July 1925. [Belf GRO (d); Belf PRO, will cal; *BMJ* obituary (1925); Clarke, *County Down*, vol 18 (1979); Kirkpatrick Archive; *Med Dir*; QCB adm reg; UHF database (m)].

BOYD, HUGH (*fl c* 1845), Dromara, county Down;
CM (Glas) [?]; general practitioner in Dromara c 1845. [Croly (1843–6)].

BOYD, JAMES (1834/5–98), Newcastle-upon-Tyne, Northumbedrland;
born 1834/5, son of William Boyd of 73 North Queen Street, Belfast; educated at RBAI; studied medicine at Queen's University, Belfast, from 1853; LM (QUI) 1855; LRCS Edin and LM 1859; LRCP Edin and LM 1869; general practitioner, of 26 Elswick West Terrace, Rye Hill, Newcastle-on-Tyne from c 1871; author of various medical papers; married Jane King of Belfast (who was born 1826/7 and died 17 July 1886), daughter of Robert King and Margaret —; died 18 October 1898 at Somerset Place, Newcastle; probate Newcastle-upon-Tyne 8 December 1898. [Clarke, *Belfast*, vol 3 (1986); Lond GRO (d); Lond PPR, will cal, will; *Med Dir*; QCB adm reg].

BOYD, JOHN (*fl c* 1770), Armagh;
apothecary, of Armagh, c 1770; married —. [Clarkson, Leslie, pers com].

BOYD, JOHN (1797/8–1841), Ballycastle, county Antrim;
born 1797/8; surgeon and apothecary, of Main Street, Ballycastle, c 1824; died 12 February 1841 of fever in Ballycastle; 'as a medical man he stood high in his profession and his benevolence knew no bounds' (*BNL.*). [*BNL* 19 February 1841 (d); *Londonderry Sentinel* 20 February 1841 (d); Pigot (1824)].

BOYD, JOHN (*fl c* 1845), Coleraine, county Londonderry;
surgeon in Coleraine; MP for the Borough of Coleraine and JP, of Dundoan House, Coleraine, c 1845. [Croly (1843–6)].

BOYD, JOHN CRAIG (1844/5–1920), Strabane, county Tyrone;
born 1844/5, son of William Craig; educated at Portora Royal School from 1857; studied arts and medicine at Trinity College, Dublin, from 1862; BA (TCD) 1866;

MB 1869; MCh 1870; general practitioner in Strabane and Lifford; superintendent medical officer of health and sanitary officer for Strabane Rural District from 1874; medical officer to Strabane Union Workhouse 1875–1919; surgeon to Donegal County Infirmary; married Phyllis C. —; father of Madeline Boyd, matron of Riddell Hall, Belfast 1934–60; died 14 August 1920 at Lifford. [Dub GRO (d); Kirkpatrick Archive; McClelland and Hadden (2005); *Med Dir*; O'Donnell (2008); *Portora School Register*; TCD adm reg; *TCD Cat*, vol II (1896)].

BOYD, JOHN McALISTER (1867–1938), Wigan, Lancashire;
born 13 November 1867 at Aghadowey, county Londonderry, son of John Boyd, national schoolteacher, of Cullycapple, Aghadowey; educated at Coleraine Academical Institution and Magee College, Londonderry; studied arts and medicine at Queen's College, Cork, from 1885 and Queen's College, Belfast, from 1893; BA (RUI) 1891; MB BCh 1897; general practitioner of Drumcroon Park Road, Wigan, from 1898; president of the Wigan Medical Society; married 28 December 1898 in First Killyleagh Presbyterian Church, county Down, Margaret Elizabeth Furey, only daughter of Francis Furey, merchant, of Killyleagh; died 11 March 1938 at Liverpool; probate Liverpool 4 June 1938. [*BMJ* obituary (1938); Kirkpatrick Archive; Lond PPR, will cal; *Med Dir*; QCB adm reg; UHF database (m)].

BOYD, JOHN ST. CLAIR (1858–1918), Belfast;
born 9 December 1858 at Cultra House, Holywood, county Down, only son of John Kane Boyd, joint owner of Blackstaff Mill, of Ballynahinch and Cultra House, Holywood; educated at Methodist College, Belfast, from 1868; studied medicine at Queen's College, Belfast, and Belfast Royal Hospital, from 1880, and also in Edinburgh and Paris; MD MCh (RUI) 1886; BAO 1888; trained as a surgeon in Edinburgh Royal Infirmary 1886, and Birmingham Hospital for Women 1887–8; assistant surgeon to the Belfast Hospital for Sick Children 1888–91; visiting gynaecologist to the Ulster Hospital for Children and Women, Belfast 1889–1905 and to the Samaritan Hospital from 1892–1905; performed the first hysterectomy in Ulster in the Ulster Hospital on 18 July 1889; attending surgeon to the Forster Green Hospital; of 19 Victoria Place and 'Chatsworth', 12 Malone Road, Belfast; first president of the Belfast Branch of the Gaelic League 1895 and for some years, and was a generous financial donor; retired 1907 due to ill health; married 1 November 1887 at Deddingston Church of Scotland Church, Helen A.C. MacAdam (who was born 1859/60), daughter of Stevenson MacAdam, PhD, of Edinburgh; died 10 July 1918 at 'Chatsworth'; buried in Belfast City Cemetery, with a fine Celtic cross memorial; probate Belfast 18 November 1919. [Belf City Cem, bur reg; *BNL* 11 July 1918 (d); Belf PRO, will cal; Blaney (1984), (1986) and (1996); Calwell (1973); Campbell (1963a); *DIB* (2009); Edin GRO (m); Fry (1984); Hartley (2006), p 141; *Lancet* obituary (1918); Marshall (1959); *Med Dir*; Newmann (1993); *Northern Whig* 1918 (d); QCB adm reg].

BOYD, JOHN STEWART (1844/5–76), ship's surgeon, and Wigton, Cumberland;
born 1844/5, son of William Boyd of Sandholes, county Tyrone; educated at Cady School, county Tyrone; studied medicine at Queen's College, Belfast from 1860, also

at Queen's College, Galway; LRCP and LM, LRCS and LM Edin 1866; clinical assistant in Belfast General Hospital; of Sandholes, Dungannon c 1869; surgeon in the West India Royal Mail Company's Service c 1870; general practitioner in Wigton, Cumberland from c 1870; died 31 July 1876 at Wakewaam, British Guiana. [*Med Dir*; QCB adm reg].

BOYD, JOSEPH DOUGLAS (1867–1954), Oldham and Manchester, Lancashire;
born 4 February 1867 at Ballymoney, county Antrim, son of John Boyd, merchant, of Forttown, Ballymoney; educated at Ballymoney Intermediate School; studied medicine at Queen's College, Belfast, from 1885; MB BCh BAO (RUI) 1895; general practitioner, of 6 Manchester Road, Tyldesley, and Boothstown, near Manchester c 1897–1900, of 199 Lees Road, Oldham c 1900–06, and of 334 Oxford Road, Manchester from c 1906; retired c 1947 to 34 Charlotte Street, Ballymoney; married 9 October 1901, in Warrenpoint Presbyterian Church, county Down, Dr Margaret Smith Bell (*q.v.*); father of Dr Douglas Priestley Bell Boyd, MB (QUB) 1931; died 11 December 1954 at 56 Rugby Road, Belfast; probate Belfast 13 June 1955. [Belf PRO, will cal; *Med Dir*; QCB adm reg; UHF database (m)].

BOYD, MARCUS (*fl c* 1763), Limavady, county Londonderry;
general practitioner, of Limavady; photocopy of his case-book of 1763 is in the PRO NI. [Belf PRO, T3657].

BOYD, MARGARET SMITH;
See BELL, MARGARET SMITH

BOYD, ROBERT (1808–83), London, and Wells, Somerset;
born 1808, son of William Boyd, captain in the Downshire Militia; MRCSE 1830; MD (Edin) 1831 (thesis 'De anatomia cordis'); LRCP Lond 1836; FRCP 1852; assistant apothecary to Marylebone Workhouse Infirmary, London c 1836–45; lecturer on medicine and resident physician 1845–50; physician and superintendent to the Lunatic Asylum, Wells c 1850–68; retired to run a private asylum at Southall Park, London, c 1868–83; of 1 Bolton Road, Mayfair; president of the Medico-Psychological Association 1870; pioneer in the care of the insane in the workhouse rather than moving them to distant County Asylums; author of many medical papers; married 23 September 1847 in Downpatrick Church of Ireland Church, Isabella Keown (who was born 1814), youngest daughter of Richard Keown, solicitor, of Ballydugan House, Downpatrick; died 14 August 1883 while trying to save his patients from a fire; probate London 13 September 1883. [*BNL* 28 September 1847 (m); *BMJ* obituary (1883); Dub GRO (m); Edin Univ; *Lancet* obituary (1883); Lond PPR, will cal; *Munk's Roll*, vol 4; *Oxford DNB* (2004); Pilson (1838)].

BOYD, ROBERT (1865–1925), Portadown, county Armagh, and Belfast;
born 22 March 1865 at Forttown, Ballymoney, county Antrim, son of James Boyd, farmer, of Forttown, and Martha Hunter Forsythe of Fort Town; studied medicine at Queen's College, Belfast, from 1885; MB BCh BAO (RUI) 1891; MD 1903; resident surgeon to Belfast Infirmary; general practitioner, of Thomas Street,

Portadown c 1895–8 and of The Lodge, Mountpottinger and Connsbrook House, Holywood Road, Belfast, from 1898; married 12 June 1897 Elizabeth Lamont Jellie (who was born 1870 and died 26 March 1924), daughter of Robert Jellie of Moneyrea, county Down; father of Dr Clarence James Boyd of Malaya, MB (QUB) 1924; died 7 April 1925 at Connsbrook House; probate Belfast 17 August 1925. [Belf GRO (d); Belf PRO, will cal; Bennett (1974); Kirkpatrick Archive; *Med Dir*; QCB adm reg].

BOYD, ROBERT JAMES (d c 1936), Stockport, Lancashire, Stewartstown, county Tyrone, and New Zealand;
   studied medicine at Queen's College, Galway or Cork (not Belfast); MD MCh (RUI) 1886; BAO 1889; medical officer to Stockport Dispensary District, of 44 Middle Hill Gate and 11 Greek Street, Stockport c 1890–95 and of Stewartstown c 1895–1905; emigrated c 1906 to 254 Upper Willis Street, Wellington, New Zealand; medical superintendant Taihape Hospital c 1911–21, of Eltham c 1922, of Whangarei c 1924, and medical superintendent of Raetihe Hospital c 1925–29, living at 53 Broadway, Palmerston North; died c 1936. [*Med Dir*].

BOYD, SAMUEL (1823/4–56), Portaferry, county Down;
   born 1823/4, son of Hugh Boyd, merchant, of Portaferry; LRCS Edin 1845; surgeon, of Portaferry; married 3 August 1848, in Portaferry Presbyterian Church, Sophia Moreland (who was born 1824/5), daughter of James Moreland, innkeeper, of Portaferry; died 22 March 1856 in Portaferry; buried in Ballyphilip graveyard, Portaferry. [*BNL* 8 August 1848 (m) and 26 March 1856 (d); Clarke, *County Down*, vol 13 (1975); *Med Dir*; UHF database (m)].

BOYD, SAMUEL BURNSIDE (1849–1929), Ballymoney, county Antrim;
   born 15 April 1849 at Drunkendult, Ballymoney, son of David Boyd of Drunkendult and Jane McElderry; educated at Coleraine Academical Institution; studied medicine at Queen's College, Belfast, from 1866; MD (QUI) 1870; LRCS Edin 1870; general practitioner in Ballymoney; medical officer for Ballymoney Dispensary District from 1878; unmarried; uncle of Dr Samuel Burnside Boyd Campbell of the Royal Victoria Hospital, MB (Edin) 1912, and Dr John Stewart Campbell, MB (QUB) 1924; died 3 March 1929 at Victoria Street, Ballymoney; probate Belfast 9 May 1929. [Belf GRO (d); Belf PRO, will cal, will; Burns (1988); Kirkpatrick Archive; *Med Dir*; Mullin (1969); QCB adm reg].

BOYD, THOMAS (1851–1923), Army Medical Service;
   born 30 November 1851 in Ballina, county Mayo; LRCSI and LM 1874; LKQCPI 1875; joined the Army Medical Service as surgeon 1877; surgeon major 1889; surgeon lieutenant-colonel 1897; served in Egypt 1882 and was present at the battle of Tel-el-Kebir, receiving the medal with clasp and Khedive's bronze star; also in the Sudan 1884–5 and in the Nile expedition, where he was in charge of the field hospital at Absarat; retired 1897; employed in Armagh after retirement; unmarried; died 21 March 1923 in Ballina; probate Ballina 22 November 1924. [*BMJ* obituary (1923); Dub GRO (d); Dub Nat Arch, will cal; *Med Dir*; Peterkin and Johnston (1968)].

BOYD, THOMAS (*fl c* 1843–60), Arvagh, county Cavan;
LAH Dub 1820; LM Coombe Hosp Dub 1846; apothecary and medical officer to constabulary in Arvagh c 1843–60; died c 1860. [Apothecaries (1829); Croly (1843–6); *Med Dir*].

BOYD, WILLIAM (*fl c* 1824), Naval Medical Service, and Stewartstown, county Tyrone;
joined the Naval Medical Service as assistant surgeon; surgeon 1812; retired to Stewartstown before 1824. [*NMS* (1826); Pigot (1824)].

BOYD, WILLIAM (1829–84), Hillsborough, county Down;
born 1829, son of William Boyd, farmer, of Moira, county Down; educated at RBAI; studied medicine at Queen's College, Belfast, from 1851; LFPS Glas 1855; general practitioner, of Hillsborough; married 11 May 1854 in Hillsborough Church of Ireland Church, Maria Phenix (who was born 1826/7 and died 6 March 1906), daughter of James Phenix, farmer, of the Maze; father of Dr Henry Johnston Boyd (*q.v.*); died 12 July 1884; buried in Hillsborough graveyard; probate Belfast 8 September 1884. [Belf PRO, will cal, will; Clarke, *County Down*, vol 18 (1979); *Med Dir*; QCB adm reg; UHF database (m)].

BOYDE, JOSEPH (*fl c* 1766), Armagh;
apothecary (honorary) to the Armagh Charitable Infirmary c 1766–70; of Irish Street, Armagh; married —; daughter Mary born c 1733. [Beale (2000); *BNL* 24 February 1825 (d, daughter); Weatherup (2001)].

BOYDE, SAMUEL (1812/3–46), Dromore, county Down;
born 1812/3; surgeon, of Dromore; died 7 February 1846 at Dromore. [*BNL* 13 February 1846 (d)].

BOYES, JOHN FREDERICK (1840/1–1926), Borough, Yorkshire, and Hastings and Brighton, Sussex;
born 1840/1 at Holywood [county Down?], son of James Marlow Boyes, officer in the army; educated by Mr Ryan; studied medicine at Trinity College, Dublin, from 1857; LM Rot Hosp Dub 1860; BA (TCD) 1861; MB MCh 1862; general practitioner of Borough, Yorkshire c 1870–75, of Magdalen Terrace, Bohemia Road, Hastings c 1875–80, of 8 Goldstone Villas, Cliftonville, Brighton c 1880–90, of 66 Claredon Villas, Hove c 1890–1900 and of Seaview House and Woodbine, Bagot, Jersey c 1900–20; retired to 7 Wellswood Park, Torquay c 1920; married Sophia Abigail —; died 21 February 1926 at 7 Wellswood Park, after falling from a window (Coroner); probate London 16 April 1926. [Burtchaell and Sadleir (1935); Lond GRO (d); Lond PPR, will cal; *Med Dir*].

BOYLE, ALEXANDER (1793/4–1833), Coleraine, county Londonderry;
born 1793/4; surgeon and apothecary, of Coleraine c 1824; married —; son married in 1865; died 30 May 1833 in Coleraine. [*BNL* 7 June 1833 (d); *Londonderry Sentinel* 15 June 1833 (d) and 23 February 1866 (m, son); Pigot (1824)].

BOYLE, DANIEL O'CONNELL (1841/2–86), Omagh, county Tyrone, and Multyfarnham, county Westmeath;
> born 1841/2, son of Daniel Boyle, merchant, of Omagh; studied medicine at Dr Steevens' Hospital, Dublin; LM Rot Hosp Dub 1862; LRCSI 1870; LRCP Edin 1871; LM RCSI 1871; general practitioner at 8 George's Street, Omagh, county Tyrone c 1871; medical officer to Multyfarnham and Crooked Wood Dispensary Districts, Wilson's Hospital and the constabulary from c 1880; of Rivervale, Multyfarnham, county Westmeath; married 4 June 1873 at Loreto Convent, Omagh, Ellen Frances Harkin (who was born 1841/2), third surviving daughter of John Harkin of Omagh; died 10 January 1886 of tuberculosis at Multyfarnham; probate Mullingar 20 March 1886. [Belf PRO, will cal; Dub GRO (m) and (d); McGrew (2001) (m); *Med Dir*].

BOYLE, EDWARD PATRICK (1830–54), Army Medical Service;
> born 1830, son of Daniel Boyle of county Tyrone and Anne —; joined the Army Medical Service as staff assistant surgeon in 1854; served in the Crimean War; died 8 December 1854 of cholera, at the battle of Inkerman; commemorated in St Mary's Roman Catholic Graveyard, Killyclougher, county Tyrone. [McGrew (1998) and (2001) (d); Peterkin and Johnston (1968)].

BOYLE, THOMAS (1850–78), Maghera, county Londonderry;
> born 8 May 1850, at Maghera, county Londonderry, son of Dorrington Boyle of Maghera; educated at RBAI and Magee College, Londonderry; studied medicine at Queen's College, Belfast, from 1870; LRCP LRCS Edin 1876; general practitioner in Maghera; unmarried; died 17 April 1878, of phthisis, at Ballymacilcurr, Maghera. [Dub GRO (d); *Med Dir*; QCB adm reg].

BOYLE, WILLIAM (d 1785), Dungannon, county Tyrone;
> surgeon and apothecary, of Dungannon; married Anne — (who died 23 June 1818 in Coleraine at the home of her son-in-law Archibald McIlwain); died 30 July 1785 at Dungannon; administration Armagh Diocesan Court 1788. [*BNL* 5 August 1785 (d) and 30 June 1818 (d); Dub Nat Arch, Armagh Dio Admins index].

BRABAZON, PHILIP EMANUEL (1811/2–56), Downpatrick, county Down;
> born 1811/2, eldest son of Charles Francis Brabazon, solicitor, of Neillstown, county Dublin; studied arts and medicine at Trinity College, Dublin, from 1827; BA (TCD) 1832; LRCSI; FRCSI; surgeon to the Down County Infirmary 1841–56, also to Downpatrick Gaol and constabulary; married 5 March 1844 in St George's Church of Ireland Church, Dublin, Letitia Hudson, elder daughter of Edward Hudson of Loughbrickland, county Down, and Gardiner's Place, Dublin; died 26 August 1856; memorial tablet in Downpatrick Cathedral and portrait in Downpatrick Masonic Hall. [*BNL* 19 March 1844 (m) and 18 September 1856 (d); Belf PRO, D2961/2/2/6; Burtchaell and Sadleir (1924); Clarke, *County Down*, vol 7 (1993); Croly (1843–6); *Downpatrick Recorder* 8 July 1848; *Med Dir*; Parkinson (1967); Pilson (1934)].

BRACKEN, GEORGE (1858–1929), Lurgan, county Armagh;
born 20 March 1858 at Blacklion, county Cavan, son of William C. Bracken, JP, of Blacklion; brother of Dr William Henry Bracken (*q.v.*); educated at Methodist College, Belfast, 1870–76; studied arts at Queen's College, Belfast, from 1876 and arts and medicine at Trinity College, Dublin, from 1879; BA (QUI)1879; MA 1880; Scholar (TCD) 1883; BA (TCD) 1883; MB BCh BAO 1889; worked in America for a year c 1890; general practitioner in Lurgan; retired to Glen Dhu, 575 Old Park, Belfast; unmarried; died 26 December 1929 at Glen Dhu; probate Belfast 1 April 1930. [Belf GRO (d); Belf PRO, will cal; Fry (1984); Kirkpatrick Archive; *Med Dir*; QUB; TCD adm reg; *TCD Cat*, vol II (1896); Young and Pike (1909)].

BRACKEN, WILLIAM HENRY (1855–85), Army Medical Service;
born 2 May 1855 at Tuam, Blacklion, county Cavan, son of William C, Bracken, JP, of Blacklion; brother of Dr George Bracken (*q.v.*); educated at Methodist College, Belfast, from 1869; studied medicine at Queen's College, Belfast, and the Royal College of Surgeon in Ireland 1872–77; MD (QUI) 1877; MCh 1879; medical officer to the City of Dublin Hospital; joined the Army Medical Service as surgeon 1880; died 16 April 1885 at Pietermaritzburg, Natal. [Fry (1984); *Med Dir*; Peterkin and Johnston (1968); QCB adm reg].

BRADFORD, ROBERT DICKIE (1855/6–1937), ship's surgeon, Pontypool, Monmouthshire, and Rillington and Aldborough, Yorkshire;
born 1855/6 at Carnbeg, Dundalk, county Louth, son of Thomas Bradford, farmer, of Carnbeg; educated at RBAI; studied arts and medicine at Queen's College, Belfast, from 1873; LRCP LRCS Edin and LM 1882; surgeon to the African Mail Steamship Company, Anchor Line and New South Wales Emmigration Service; general practitioner, of Pontypool c 1885 and Rillington c 1895; medical officer and public vaccinator to Aldborough Dispensary District, Yorkshire; certifying factory surgeon; admiralty surgeon and agent; of The Elms, Skirlaugh, Hull; married Anne —; died 6 August 1937; probate York 27 September 1937. [Lond PPR, will cal; *Med Dir*; QCB adm reg].

BRADLEY, DAVID (1854–1914), Hebden Bridge, Yorkshire, and Blackburn, Lancashire;
born 15 August 1854 at Magherafelt, county Londonderry, son of Joseph Bradley of Magherafelt; educated at Magherafelt School; studied medicine at Queen's College, Belfast, from 1872; MD (QUI) 1876; MCh 1879; general practitioner, of Hebden Bridge, Yorkshire, from c 1880 and of Blackburn, Lancashire, from c 1900, of 6 Bank Top and later 45 King Street, Blackburn; married Elizabeth —; died 7 November 1914; administration London 12 December1914. [Lond, PPR, will cal; *Med Dir*; QCB adm reg].

BRADLEY, HUGH (*fl c* 1824), Randalstown, county Antrim;
apothecary, of Main Street, Randalstown c 1824. [Pigot (1824)].

BRADLEY, JAMES (1836–c 1916), Naval Medical Service;
born 1836, son of Alexander Bradley of Saintfield, county Down; educated by the Rev David Maginnis; studied medicine at Queen's College, Belfast 1857–60; LRCS Edin 1860; joined the Naval Medical Service as assistant surgeon c 1862; served on HMS *Asia* c 1871–2, HMS *Nimble* c 1862–4, HMS *Caradoc* c 1864–9, HMS *Liverpool* c 1869–71, Royal Hospital, Haulbowline c 1872–3; surgeon on HMS *Agincourt* 1873–4; staff surgeon, 2nd class on HMS *Duke of Wellington* c 1874–5, staff surgeon 1875; served on HMS *Lily* 1876–9, on HMS *Gannet* 1879–84; fleet surgeon 1884; retired c 1890; died c 1916. [*Med Dir*; QCB adm reg].

BRADLEY, JOHN THOMAS (1870–c 1941), Kilrush, county Clare, Seychelles, and Bangor, county Down;
born 21 November 1870 at Kilrush, son of John James Bradley, shopkeeper, auctioneer, and valuer, of 72 Moore Street, Kilrush; educated in Kilrush and at University classes, Donegall Pass, Belfast; studied arts and medicine at Queen's College, Belfast, from 1894; Gold Medal in Practical Midwifery, Clifton Street Maternity Hospital, Belfast 1898–9; LRCP LRCS Edin 1899; LFPS Glas 1899; MD (Bruxelles) 1909; general practitioner of Kilrush, assistant medical officer to Seychelles and from c 1926; later chief medical officer; OBE 1932; Chevalier de L'Ordre de Pius IX; Chevalier of the Order of the Crown of Italy; author of a *History of the Seychelles*; retired c 1934 to Shalom, Mahe, Seychelles; died c 1941. [*Med Dir*; QCB adm reg].

BRADLEY, JONATHAN KIDD (1843–72), Kilmoganny, county Kilkenny;
born 1843, son of Jonathan Bradley of Castlecomer, county Kilkenny; educated at the Wesleyan Connectional School, Dublin; studied medicine at Queen's College, Belfast, from 1860; LRCSI 1864; LKQCPI and LM 1868; medical officer to Kilmoganny Dispensary District, of Kell's Grange, Stoneyford, county Kilkenny; married —; died 4 July 1872 at Kilmoganny, following a leg injury. [Dub GRO (d); *Med Dir*; QCB adm reg].

BRADLEY, MICHAEL McWILLIAMS (1841/2–1906), Jarrow-on-Tyne, county Durham;
born 1841/2 at Killeylough, Maghera, county Londonderry, son of a farmer; assistant to Dr Arthur Connor of Glasgow; studied medicine at Glasgow University; MB CM (Glas) 1870; LRCP Edin and LM 1874; MD 1876; medical officer of health to Jarrow-on-Tyne, Durham, and medical officer to Jarrow Dispensary District; author of papers on midwifery; married Elizabeth Mary —; died 25 May 1906 at Tamnaharrie Park, Warrenpoint; buried in Jarrow; probate Durham 24 December 1906. [Addison (1898); *BMJ* obituary (1906); Dub GRO (d); Kirkpatrick Archive; Lond PPR, will cal; *Med Dir*].

BRADSHAW, WILLIAM LUCKNOW (1858–1928), Yarmouth, Norfolk, Stockton-on-Tees, Durham, and High Wycombe, Buckinghamshire;
born 1858 at 19 Harcourt Street, Dublin, son of Dr Robert Bradshaw, LRCSI 1850, LKQCPI 1859, of Sierra Leone and Carrick-on-Shannon, county Leitrim; brother

of Dr Albert Bradshaw, LRCP LRCS Edin 1888, LFPS Glas 1888, of Smethwick, Staffordshire; educated at Alston College, England; studied medicine at the Royal College of Surgeons in Ireland, the Apothecaries' Hall, Dublin, and from 1876, at Queen's College, Belfast; LRCP Edin 1884; LFPS Glas 1888; DPH RCPSI 1906; general practitioner, of 22 Wellesley Road, Great Yarmouth, c 1885 and of 2 Victoria Terrace, Stockton-on-Tees c 1895; medical officer and public vaccinator to the 3rd District, Chipping Wycombe, and medical officer of health for High Wycombe from c 1900; medical superintendent of Wycombe Isolation Hospital and honorary surgeon to Wycombe Cottage Hospital; retired to 'Sherbrook', 7 Christchurch Road, Bournemouth c 1910; married Emma Kathleen —; died 30 March 1928 at 7 Christchurch Road; probate London 15 June 1928. [Kirkpatrick Archive; Lond GRO (d); Lond PPR, will cal, will; *Med Dir*; QCB adm reg].

BRADY, ANDREW (1795/6–1866), Ardlougher, county Cavan;
born 1795/6; LAH Dub 1858; general practitioner, of Ardlougher c 1824; medical officer to the Dispensary and constabulary c 1845; unmarried; died 4 April 1866 at Ardlougher; probate Cavan 28 April 1866. [Belf PRO, will cal; Dub GRO (d); *Med Dir;* Pigot (1824)].

BRADY, BERNARD (*fl c* 1709), Cavan;
of Cavan; studied medicine at Rheims University; MD (Rheims) 1738. [Brockliss].

BRADY, CHARLES (*fl c* 1738), Cavan;
of Cavan; studied medicine at Rheims University; MD (Rheims) 1709. [Brockliss].

BRADY, GEORGE FRAZER (FRASER) (1819/20–77), Rutland, England and Falcarragh, county Donegal;
born 1819/20, eldest son of Hugh Brady of Lifford, county Donegal; studied medicine at Trinity College, Dublin, City of Dublin and Mercers' Hospitals and Edinburgh University; MRCSE 1839; FRCSE 1858; medical officer to Rutland Dispensary District; medical officer to Dungloe, Templecrone, Gweedore and Burtonport Dispensary Districts and constabulary; assistant surgeon to County Donegal Infirmary; J.P. for county Donegal and surgeon and agent for the Admiralty; co-author of a vivid account of condition in Arran Island in January 1847; married 7 February 1850 in St Anne's Church of Ireland Church, Dublin, Fanny Russell, third daughter of James Russell, JP, of Dunlewey House, county Donegal; died 15 March 1877 at Falcarragh; probate Londonderry 8 May 1877. [Belf PRO, will cal; Croly (1843–6); Dub GRO (d); Kirkpatrick Archive; *Londonderry Sentinel* 8 February 1850 (m); *Med Dir*; Plarr (1930)].

BRADY, JOHN (*fl c* 1845), Cavan;
studied medicine at Edinburgh University; MD (Edin) 1825 (thesis 'De rheumatismo acuto'); general practitioner in Cavan town c 1845; married 11 April 1835 in Enniskillen, Mary Joyce, youngest daughter of Captain Joyce, JP; possibly died c 1850. [*BNL* 21 April 1835 (m); Croly (1843–6); Edin Univ].

BRADY, JOHN (1840–1908), Belfast;
born 5 December 1840 at Ballymacombs, Bellaghy, county Londonderry, son of John and Mary Brady of Ballymacombs; educated by J. Paisley of King Street, Belfast; studied medicine at Queen's College, Belfast, from 1859; MRCSE 1865; general practitioner at 11 Victoria Street, Belfast c 1870–90 and then at 59 Great Victoria Street; retired to Ballynease, Portglenone; married —; died 3 February 1908 at Ballynease; administration (with will) Londonderry 19 September 1908. [Belf PRO, will cal; Dub GRO (d); *Med Dir*; QCB adm reg].

BRADY, NICHOLAS (1766/7–1823), Belfast;
born 1766/7 in Antrim town; LAH Dub 1793; surgeon, apothecary and practitioner in midwifery, c 1807–19 of 31 High Street, 34 Ann Street, and 47 Ann Street, Belfast; died 26 January 1823. [Apothecaries (1829); *Belfast Street Directory* (1807, 1808, 1819); *BNL* 31 January 1823 (d)].

BRADY, PATRICK (d 1771/2), Knockfad, county Cavan;
physician, of Knockfad; will dated 1771; died 1771/2; probate Kilmore Diocesan Court 1772. [Smythe-Wood (1975)].

BRADY, PATRICK (*fl c* 1824), Kilmacrieve, county Cavan;
LAH Dub 1824; apothecary, of Kilmacrieve. [Apothecaries (1829)].

BRADY, TERENCE (*fl c* 1824), Pettigo, county Fermanagh;
apothecary, of Pettigo c 1824. [Pigot (1824)].

BRADY, THOMAS J (1801–64), Dublin;
born 1801 at Carrickmacross, county Monaghan, son of James Brady, merchant; educated by Mr O'Reilly; studied medicine at Trinity College, Dublin, from 1821; BA (TCD) 1826; MB 1828; LKQCPI 1829; FKQCPI 1832; lecturer in medical jurisprudence in the Original School of Medicine and first professor in 1839; vice-president of KQCPI 1853; physician to Cork Street Fever Hospital; medical officer to Newgate, Smithfield and Lusk Prisons; of 9 Upper Temple Street, Dublin; married 1839 Anna Maria Molloy, daughter of major Brian Molloy of Milicent, county Kildare; died 16 March 1864 at 9 Upper Temple Street, Dublin; buried in Glasnevin Cemetery. [Burtchaell and Sadleir (1924); Cameron (1916); Dub GRO (d); *Med Dir*].

BRADY, THOMAS CLARK (1827–71), Army Medical Service;
born 20 February 1827 in county Donegal; MRCSE 1850; joined the Army Medical Service as assistant surgeon to 57th Foot 1852; staff surgeon 1854; served in the Crimea; Chevalier of the Legion of Honour 1856; transferred to 8th Foot 1863; retired on half pay 1869; died 12 July 1871 at Geneva. [*Med Dir*; Peterkin and Johnston (1968)].

BRAMPTON, CHARLES (d 1839), New Brunswick, Canada;
of Strabane, county Tyrone; MD [?]; emigrated to Canada; died 2 July 1839 at John's, New Brunswick, Canada. [*Londonderry Sentinel* 31 August 1839 (d)].

BRAND, WILLIAM THOMAS (1863–c 1913), Cambridge, Pocklington, Yorkshire, Hanley, Staffordshire, and Canada;
> born 23 January 1863 at Lawrencetown, county Down, son of Thomas Brand, farmer, of Florida Manor, Killinchy, county Down; educated at Kilmood School; studied arts and medicine at Queen's College, Belfast, from 1883; MB BCh BAO (RUI) 1888; general practitioner, of 10 Wentworth Terrace, Huntingdon Road, Cambridge c 1895, of Providence Villa, Pocklington, Yorkshire c 1905, and of Old Hall Cottage, Hanley, Staffordshire c 1910; emigrated to Canada; married 7 December 1888 in Killinchy Presbyterian Church, Matilda Elizabeth Coulter, daughter of John Coulter, miller, of Balloo, county Down; died c 1913. [*Med Dir*; QCB adm reg; UHF database (m)].

BRANGAN, JOHN (1871–1927), Kells, county Meath;
> born January 1871 at Ardcath, county Meath, son of Edward Brangan, farmer, of Ardcath; educated at St Malachy's College, Belfast; studied medicine at Queen's College, Belfast, from 1895 and the Catholic University of Ireland, Dublin; LRCP LRCS Edin 1899; LFPS Glas 1899; medical officer and medical officer of health for Kilskeer, from 1900, of Kells; coroner for North Meath; JP for county Meath; a keen breeder of racehorses; married Caroline —; father of Dr Eileen Brangan, MB (TCD) 1924, of Kells, and Dr Patrick Brangan, MB (TCD) 1927, of Kells; died 14 February 1927 at Headford Place, Kells; administration Dublin 26 April 1927. [Dub Nat Arch, will cal; *Med Dir*; QCB adm reg].

BRANGIN, THOMAS (d 1813), Antrim, county Antrim;
> surgeon, of Antrim; married 22 January 1809 Mary Ramage of Mullans, Ballymoney, county Antrim (who died 17 August 1810 at Antrim); died 12 April 1813 at Antrim. [*BNL* 24 January 1809 (m), 28 August 1810 (d) and 20 April 1813 (d)].

BRANNIGAN, HENRY COOKE (1854–1902), Liverpool, Lancashire, and Queensland, Australia;
> born 1854 at Ballina, county Mayo, son of the Rev Michael Brannigan, minister of Ballinglen Presbyterian Church, Ballina, and — Dobbin; brother of Dr Robert Allen Brannigan (*q.v.*) and Dr John Henderson Brannigan (*q.v.*); educated at RBAI; studied medicine at Queen's College, Belfast, from 1872; LRCP LRCS Edin 1877; MD MCh (RUI) 1883; general practitioner in Liverpool with his brother Robert, of 109 Upper Parliament Street from c 1880; emigrated to Australia c 1890; civil surgeon in Zulu and Sekukuni Campaigns; resident surgeon to Mount Morgan Hospital, Queensland 1896–1900; resident medical superintendant of the Plague Hospital, Rockhampton, Queensland c 1900–02; died 1902. [Barkley (1986); *Med Dir*; QCB adm reg].

BRANNIGAN, JOHN HENERSON (1857–1933), Venice, Liverpool, Lancashire, ship's surgeon and Army Medical Corps;
> born 28 December 1857, son of the Rev Michael Brannigan, minister of Ballinglen Presbyterian Church, Ballina, county Mayo, and — Dobbin; brother of Dr Robert Allen Brannigan (*q.v.*) and Dr Henry Cooke Brannigan (*q.v.*); educated at RBAI; studied arts and medicine at Queen's College, Belfast 1875–9; LRCP LRCS Edin 1879; living in Venice c 1880; general practitioner with his brother in Liverpool

c 1881; surgeon with P&O Steamship Company c 1882; joined the Army Medical Service as surgeon captain 1885; surgeon major 1897; served in the Zhob Valley 1890, North West Frontier 1897–8 and South Africa 1899–1902; retired 1905 but returned to the army 1915–18; of Fircroft, Englefield Green, Surrey c 1925; married Marie Cecilia —; died 21 April 1933; probate London 7 June 1933. [Barkley (1986); Lond PPR, will cal; *Med Dir*; Peterkin and Johnston (1968); QCB adm reg].

BRANNIGAN, ROBERT ALLEN (1851–1922), Liverpool, Lancashire;
born 12 February 1851 at Ballina, county Mayo, son of the Rev Michael Brannigan, minister of Ballinglen Presbyterian Church, Ballina, county Mayo, and — Dobbin; brother of Dr Henry Cooke Brannigan (*q.v.*) and Dr John Henderson Brannigan (*q.v.*); educated at RBAI; studied medicine at Queen's College, Belfast 1871–6; MD MCh (QUI) 1876; senior resident medical officer to Brownlow Hill Infirmary, Liverpool, and assistant house surgeon to the South Dispensary, Liverpool; general practitioner in Liverpool with his brother Henry, of 109 Upper Parliament Street from c 1880; married Bessie —; died 30 March 1922 at Carmen de Mata Moras, Granada, Spain; probate London 20 June 1922. [Barkley (1986); Lond PPR, will cal; *Med Dir*; QCB adm reg].

BRATTON, WILLIAM (1866–1923), Consett, county Durham;
born 9 December 1866 at Seskinore, Omagh, county Tyrone, son of John Bratton, farmer, of Seskinore; educated at Omagh Intermediate School; studied medicine at Queen's College, Belfast, from 1886; LRCP LRCS Edin 1894; LFPS Glas 1894; general practitioner, of Consett from c 1900; retired to Milltown, Seskinore; unmarried; died 6 October 1923 at Milltown; probate Belfast 14 December 1923 and London 21 December 1923. [Belf PRO, will cal, will; Lond PPR, will cal; *Med Dir*; QCB adm reg].

BREADON, JOSHUA (JOSEPH) (*fl c* 1828–45), Fivemiletown, county Tyrone;
LAH Dub 1828; apothecary and surgeon, of Fivemiletown c 1845. [Apothecaries (1829); Croly (1843–6); Maguire (1993), p 27].

BREAKEY, JOHN (1828/9–1911), Naval Medical Service;
born 1828/9, son of John Breakey of Ballybay, county Monaghan; educated at RBAI; studied medicine at Queen's College, Belfast 1849–53; MRCSE 1851; MD (QUI) 1853; assistant house surgeon in the General Hospital 1851–2; house surgeon 1852–3; joined the Naval Medical Service 1854; surgeon on HMS *Bulldog* c 1865 and on HMS *Serapis* c 1870; staff surgeon on HMS *Flora* c 1875; fleet surgeon in Haslar Royal Hospital c 1880; fleet surgeon c 1885; deputy inspector general of hospitals and fleets c 1885; inspector general c 1890; retired c 1892; lived finally at 58 Carlisle Mansions, Victoria Street, Westminister; married (1) 9 April 1861 in St George's Church, Hanover Square, London, Jane Kennedy Miller (who died 20 February 1868), only child of Arthur Kennedy Miller of Whitehouse, Belfast, and Margaret —; (2) —; father of Mary Breakey who married Dr William Rogerson White, MB (TCD) 1871, RN; died 21 October 1911 at 58 Carlisle Mansions; administration (with will) London 4 January 1912. [*Belf Gen Hosp, Ann Rep*; *Coleraine Chronicle* 13 April 1861

(m); Lond GRO (d); Lond PPR, will cal, will; *Med Dir*; Merrick and Clarke, *Belfast*, vol 4 (1991); QCB adm reg].

BREDON, ALEXANDER (1802/3–66), Portadown, county Armagh;
born 1802/3; studied medicine in Dublin and at Glasgow University; LAH Dub 1827; LM Dub Lying-in Hosp (Rotunda) 1828; MRCSE 1829; MD (Glas) 1837; medical officer to Portadown and Tullyhappy Dispensary Districts and Fever Hospital and constabulary; of Ballintaggart House, Portadown; married 10 December 1844 in Lurgan Church of Ireland Church, Catherine Breadon, daughter of Joseph Breadon, assistant surgeon RN; father of Sir Robert Edmund Bredon (*q.v.*), Dr Alexander Macaulay Bredon (*q.v.*) and Hester (Hessie) Jane Bredon who married Sir Robert Hart of the Chinese Custom Service; died 14 May 1866 at Millicent Terrace, Portadown; buried in Drumcree Parish Churchyard; probate Dublin 12 February 1867. [Addison (1898); *BNL* 17 December 1844 (m); Belf PRO, will cal; Bell (1985); Croly (1843–6); Dub GRO (d); *Med Dir*].

BREDON, ALEXANDER MACAULAY (1849–1915), Portadown, county Armagh;
born 14 July 1849 in Portadown, son of Dr Alexander Bredon (*q.v.*); brother of Dr Robert Edward Bredon (*q.v.*) and Hester (Hessie) Jane Bredon who married Sir Robert Hart of the Chinese Custom Service; educated at Dungannon Royal School; studied arts and medicine at Trinity College, Dublin, from 1867; BA; MB MCh (TCD) 1873; MCh 1874; LM KQCPI 1876; general practitioner in Portadown and later at 15 Aberdeen Walk, Scarborough, Yorkshire; married —; died 5 April 1915 at 50 Aberdeen Walk, Scarborough; probate Dublin 23 June 1915 and London 7 July 1915. [*BNL* 31 July 1849 (b); Belf PRO, will cal; Clarke, *County Down*, vol 5 (1984); Kirkpatrick Archive; Lond GRO (d); Lond PPR, will cal; *Med Dir*; TCD adm reg; *TCD Cat,* vol II (1896)].

BREDON, SIR ROBERT EDWARD (1846–1918), Army Medical Service and China;
born 4 February 1846 at Portadown, son of Dr Alexander Bredon (*q.v.*) of Portadown, county Armagh and Catherine Bredon; brother of Dr Alexander Macaulay Bredon (*q.v.*) and Hester (Hessie) Jane Bredon who married Sir Robert Hart; educated in Portadown and at the Royal School, Dungannon; studied medicine at Trinity College, Dublin, from 1862 and at the Richmond Hospital, Dublin; BA MB MCh (TCD) 1866; LM Rot Hosp Dub 1866; LRCSI 1867; joined the Army Medical Service as staff assistant surgeon 1867; attached to 97th Foot 1867; served in England, Ireland and West Indies; resigned 1873 and joined Chinese Customs Service; deputy inspector general Imperial Martime Customs 1898–1909; acting inspector general with rank of Provincial Lieutenant Governor in absence of Sir Robert Hart; was present with his wife and daughter during the siege of Peking in 1900; CMG 1903; KCMG 1904; many decorations from China, Japan, Norway, Sweden, Denmark, Russia and Prussia; married 1879 Lily Virginia Banks, youngest daughter of Thomas Crane Banks of San Francisco; died 3 July 1918 at Peking; probate Shanghai 1918 and London 19 March 1919. [Bell (1985); *BMJ* obituary (1918); Kirkpatrick Archive; Lond PPR, will cal; *Med Dir*; Peterkin and Johnston (1968); TCD adm reg; *TCD Cat,* vol II (1896); Young and Pike (1909)].

BREEN, HENRY (1863/4–92), Ballyconnell, county Cavan, and Derrylin, county Fermanagh;
born 1863/4; studied medicine at the Ledwich School and Mercer's and St Mark's Hospitals, Dublin; LM Coombe Hosp Dub 1884; LRCSI 1884; LRCP Edin 1888; general practitioner, of Cross House, Ballyconnell; medical officer, medical officer of health and public vaccinator to Derrylin Dispensary District, county Fermanagh; unmarried; died 8 January 1892 of phthisis at Carrowcarlin, Derrylin. [Dub GRO (d); *Med Dir*].

BREEZE, CHARLES KIRKPATRICK (d c 1880), Saintfield, county Down and San Francisco, USA;
studied medicine at Glasgow University; MRCSE 1851; medical officer to Kilmood Dispensary District c 1851–6; medical officer to Saintfield Dispensary District and constabulary c 1856–70; emigrated to San Francisco c 1870; died c 1880. [Lyttle (2003); *Med Dir*].

BRENNAN, BERNARD (*fl c* 1824), Castleblayney, county Monaghan;
surgeon, of Castle Street, Castleblayney c 1824; married 13 July 1823 Frances Olive, youngest daughter of William Olive. [*BNL* 1 August 1823 (m); Pigot (1824)].

BRERETON, RALPH WESTROP (1846/7–1924), Naval Medical Service;
born 1846/7; studied medicine at Trinity College, Dublin; LKQCPI and LM LRCSI 1869; joined the Naval Medical Service c 1871 as assistant surgeon with home address of Falcarragh, county Donegal; surgeon c 1880 serving on HMS *Tyrion*; staff surgeon c 1883; retired as fleet surgeon c 1892; lived finally at 3 Cherryvalley Park, Belfast; unmarried; died 24 August 1924 at D'Olier, 3 Cherryvalley Park; probate Belfast 28 November 1924. [Belf GRO (d); Belf PRO, will cal; *Med Dir*].

BRICE, ALEXANDER (1801/2–81), Armagh, county Armagh;
born 1801/2; LAH Dub 1829; apothecary and general practitioner in Armagh; married —; died 10 June 1881 in English Street, Armagh; probate Armagh 28 August 1881. [Belf PRO, will cal; Croly (1843–6); Dub GRO (d); *Med Dir*].

BRICE, FREDERICK AUGUSTUS (*fl c* 1795), Cavan;
LAH Dub 1794; apothecary and surgeon, of Cavan; married February 1795 Eliza Jane Moore of Dromore. [Apothecaries (1829); *BNL* 6 February 1795 (m)].

BRICE, WILLIAM HENRY (1832–62), Army Medical Service;
born 6 March 1832 in Cavan; LRCSI 1853; joined the Army Medical Service as staff assistant surgeon to 28th Foot 1854; died 2 July 1862 at Purandhar, Bombay. [Kirkpatrick Archive; Peterkin and Johnston (1968)].

BRICE, WILLIAM MOORE (1798/9–1870), Cavan, county Cavan;
born 1798/9; LAH Dub 1820; apothecary in Cavan town and to Fever Hospital and gaol; married Ann —; father of Elizabeth Maria Brice who married Dr William Malcomson (*q.v.*); died 17 November 1870 in Main Street, Cavan; probate Cavan

7 December 1870. [Apothecaries (1829); Belf PRO, will cal, will; Croly (1843–6); Dub GRO (d); *Med Dir;* Pigot (1824)].

BRIEN EDWARD HENRY (d c 1860), Naval Medical Service, and Ballyshannon, county Donegal;
> joined the Naval Medical Service as assistant surgeon 1794; surgeon 1797; retired on half pay; apothecary, of Ballyshannon, c 1824–60; married — (who died 16 April 1834 in Ballyshannon); died c 1860. [*BNL* 29 April 1834 (d); Croly (1843–6); *Londonderry Sentinel* 10 May 1834 (d); *Med Dir; NMS* (1826); Pigot (1824)].

BRIEN, ROBERT (1787–1853), Naval Medical Service, and London;
> born 16 June 1787 in Enniskillen, county Fermanagh; studied medicine in Dublin; joined the Naval Medical Service 1806 as assistant surgeon to HMS *Pomona*; distinguished himself during an epidemic on board ship and was promoted to surgeon 1808; served on HMS *Brazen*, HMS *Polyphemus,* HMS *Hyperion*, HMS *Bann* and HMS *Cherub*, around Africa, West Indies, Newfoundland and Southern USA; resigned 1817; MD (St Andrews) 1812 [not in Smart]; MRCSE 1820; general practitioner, of Spencer Street, Clerkenwell c 1817–35, of Myddleton Square 1835–45 and of 26 St Mary's Road, Islington c 1845–53; one of the founders of the Infant Orphan Asylum, Wanstead; died 8 May 1853 at 26 St Mary's Road. [*Med Dir*; *NMS* (1826)].

BRIEN, SAMUEL (1760/1–1835), Ballymena, county Antrim;
> born 1760/1; surgeon, of Ballymena; died February 1835. [*BNL* 17 February 1835 (d)].

BRIGHAM, JOHN KING (1844–1926), Farnham, Surrey, and London;
> born 10 July 1844 in Donegal, son of James Brigham of Donegal; educated at RBAI; studied arts and medicine at Queen's College, Belfast, from 1862 and medicine also at the Royal College of Surgeons in Ireland; BA (QUI) 1865; MA 1867; MD MCh 1871; general practitioner 1872, of 4 Downing Street, Farnham, Surrey; medical officer on the Australian Mail Packet Service c 1875; general practitioner, of 33 West Hill, Maplehurst, Sydenham, London c 1885; consulting physician to the Home for Sick Children and Dispensary for Women, Lower Sydenham; of 5 Thorpewood Avenue, Sydenham, from c 1910; retired c 1922 to Silversea, Herbert Road, Milton, Hants; married Mary —; died 3 March 1926 at Silversea; administration London 26 March 1926. [Kirkpatrick Archive; Lond GRO (d); Lond PPR, will cal; *Med Dir*; QCB adm reg].

BRITTON, JOHN (*fl c* 1830), Ballyshannon, county Donegal;
> MD [?]; no record in any of the Medical Directories; married 30 March 1830 in Ballyshannon Church of Ireland Church, Mary Chinnery Folingsby, second daughter of Joseph Folingsby, collector of customs at Ballyshannon, and Eleanor Chinnery; daughter born in Ballyshannon 24 March 1831. [*BNL* 2 April 1830 (m) and 8 April 1831 (b, dau); Burke, *Dictionary of the Peerage and Baronetage of the British Empire*, 23rd edition (1861); *Londonderry Sentinel* 10 April 1830 (m)].

BRITTON, JOHN (1836/7–1910), Strabane, county Tyrone;
born 1836/7, son of the Rev Alexander Britton, minister of Bready Reformed Presbyterian Church, county Tyrone; studied medicine at Glasgow University; MD (Glas) 1857; LRCS Edin and LM 1857; FRCS Edin 1879; general practitioner of Hazelwood, Strabane; married 15 November 1883 in Donegall Street Presbyterian Church, Belfast, Margaret Henry Magill, daughter of the Rev George Magill, minister of Cliftonville Presbyterian Church, Belfast; died 11 October 1910 at Derry Road, Strabane; probate Londonderry 24 March 1911. [Addison (1898); Belf PRO, will cal; Dub GRO (d); Loughridge (1970); *Med Dir*; UHF database (m)].

BRONTE, ALEXANDER (1866–c 1948), South Africa, Buenos Aires, Argentina, and Auckland, New Zealand;
born 10 July 1866 at Drumiller, Dromore, county Down, son of John Bronte, farmer, of Drumiller and later chemist, of Wellington, New Zealand, and Mary Bingham; educated privately; studied medicine at Queen's College, Belfast, from 1884; LRCP LRCS Edin 1893; LFPS Glas 1893; resident medical officer to Glasgow Royal Infirmary c 1895; civil surgeon to the South African Field Force c 1901; general practitioner, of Buenos Aires c 1905, and of Pukekohe and Takapuna, Auckland, from c 1909; retired c 1932, to 33 Ewen Street, Takapuna, and to 6 Hinemaru Street, Rotorua c 1946; died c 1948. [Dub GRO (b); *Med Dir*; QCB adm reg].

BROOKE, ALEXANDER (*fl c* 1724), Cavan;
apothecary, of Cavan; witness to a will 1724. [Eustace, vol I (1956)].

BROOKE, ARTHUR (d 1702), Lisburn, county Antrim;
son of Dr Francis Brooke (*q.v.*), surgeon, of Lisburn; surgeon, of Lisburn; married Mary Workman, daughter of Thomas Workman of Maghon, county Armagh; died 1702; will dated 7 November 1702 proved in Prerogative Court 19 December 1702. [Belf PRO, Burke's Pedigrees, vol 12, pp 85 and 88; Vicars (1897)].

BROOKE (BROOKS), FRANCIS (d 1694), Lisburn, county Antrim;
chirurgeon, of Lisburn; married —; father of Dr Arthur Brooke (*q.v.*); died 1694; buried 14 November 1694 in Lisburn Cathedral Graveyard; will dated 25 January 1689 proved in Prerogative Court 6 March 1695. [Belf PRO, Burke's Pedigrees, vol 12, pp 85 and 88; Carmody (1926); *Lisburn Fam Hist Soc,* vol 2 (2005), pp 28 and 133; Vicars (1897)].

BROOKE, WILLIAM (b 1769), Dromavana, county Cavan, Dublin, and Culmaine, county Monaghan;
born 1769 in Longford, second son of the Rev William Brooke, DD, rector of Longford, and of Dromavana; studied medicine at Trinity College, Dublin, from 1784 and later at Edinburgh University; MD (Edin) 1789 (thesis 'De rheumatismo'); general practitioner, of Dromavana, Dublin, and Culmaine House; married Angel Perry, daughter of Captain Edward Perry of county Tyrone. [Burke *LGI* (1912); Burtchaell and Sadleir (1924); Edin Univ].

BROTCHIE, THEODORE RAINY (1847–1900), Liverpool, Lancashire, and Belfast;
born 22 March 1847 at Kintore, Scotland, son of John Brotchie; studied medicine at Aberdeen University; MB CM (Aberdeen) 1871; MD 1877; of 27 Constitution Street, Aberdeen 1871; general practitioner of 54 Roscommon Street, Liverpool, c 1875–80 and of 96 and 102 Richmond Terrace, Great Victoria Street, Belfast, c 1880–1900; married Gertrude —; died 22 April 1900 at Wyke House, Isleworth, Middlesex; probate Belfast 23 May 1900. [Belf PRO, will cal; Johnston (1906); Lond GRO (d); *Med Dir*].

BROWN, DANIEL (*fl c* 1824), Belfast;
apothecary, of 62 Donegall Street, Belfast c 1824. [Pigot (1824)].

BROWN, DAVID (1872–1939), Tiensin, North China;
born 5 March 1872 at Mount Pottinger, Belfast, son of Robert Brown, headmaster of the National School, Wingfield Lodge, Bloomfield, Belfast; educated at Belfast Model School and RBAI; studied medicine at Queen's College, Belfast, from 1891; MB BCh BAO (RUI) 1898; resident surgeon to Belfast Union Infirmary; surgeon to the Chinese Government Railways, from c 1900, of 28 Victoria Road, Tiensin; retired c 1930 to Chalet Delphine, Boulevard Edouard Badouin, Juan-les-Pins, France; of The Priory, North Bersted, Sussex c 1938; died 9 July 1939; administration (with will) London 27 February 1940, Singapore 12 June 1940, Shanghai 9 August 1940 and Hong Kong 26 September 1940. [Lond PPR, will cal; *Med Dir*; QCB adm reg].

BROWN, FERGUS MALCOLM (1848–c 1897); Belfast, Northampton, and New South Wales, Australia;
born 24 December 1848 at Oakworth, Yorkshire, son of Thomas Brown of Stewartstown, county Tyrone; educated at Cookstown Academy; studied medicine at Queen's College, Belfast, from 1866; LRCP Edin 1871; LFPS Glas 1871; of 1 and 3 Peter's Hill, Belfast c 1871; general practitioner in Wansford, Northamptonshire c 1875; emigrated to Australia c 1880; general practitioner, of Richmond, New South Wales c 1883 and of Cootamundra, NSW c 1890; died c 1897. [*Med Dir*; QCB adm reg].

BROWN, FRANCIS G.S. (d 1840), London;
only son of Samuel Brown of Coleraine; finished his course of studies as a physician April 1840 and died 12 July 1840 of consumption, in London. [*Londonderry Sentinel* 8 August 1840 (d)].

BROWN, GEORGE (*fl c* 1783), Baltimore, Maryland, USA;
of Ballymena, county Antrim; qualified as a doctor; emigrated to USA 1783; general practitioner in Baltimore; married Ann Davison, daughter of John Davison of Drumnasole, county Antrim. [Irvine (1982), pp 45 and 48].

BROWN, GEORGE (d c 1812), Londonderry;
apothecary, of Londonderry; married —; father of Dr Thomas Campbell Brown (*q.v.*); died c 1812; will dated 4 November 1811 (original in Belf PRO) proved in

Derry Diocesan Court 28 September 1812. [Belf PRO, D/2035/3/2; *Londonderry Sentinel* 18 January 1840 (d, son); Thrift (1920)].

BROWN(E), GEORGE (1771/2–1847), Naval Medical Service, and Claudy, county Londonderry;
born 1771/2; joined the Naval Medical Service as assistant surgeon; surgeon 1795; retired to Claudy; medical officer to constabulary c 1845; married — Stephenson; died 4 August 1847 in the house of his brother-in-law, James Stephenson of Portrush, county Antrim; probate Prerogative Court 1847. [*BNL* 13 August 1847 (d); Belf PRO, prerog wills index; *Coleraine Chronicle* 7 August 1847 (d); Croly (1843–6); *Londonderry Sentinel* 7 August 1847 (d); *NMS* (1826)].

BROWN, HENRY (1841–c 1885), Northallerton, Yorkshire;
born 21 April 1841 in Belfast, son of James Brown of 34 Mill Street, Belfast; educated at the Belfast Seminary; studied medicine at Queen's College, Belfast 1862–6; LRCP and LM, LRCS and LM Edin 1866; general practitioner of Northallerton from c 1868; surgeon to Northallerton Cottage Hospital; author of various medical papers; died c 1885. [*Med Dir*; QCB adm reg].

BROWN, JAMES (*fl c* 1757), Belfast;
apothecary, of Belfast; married 22 May 1759 in Shankill Church of Ireland, Belfast, Elinor Stewart. [Gillespie and O'Keefe (2006)].

BROWN, JAMES McCULLAGH (1865–1914), Gilford, Helen's Bay, and Knock, county Down;
born 9 December 1865 at Ballymena, county Antrim, son of James Brown, MA, inspector of National Schools, of Lurgan, county Armagh; educated at Lurgan College; studied medicine at Queen's College, Belfast, from 1884; MB BCh BAO (RUI) 1890; general practitioner, of Gilford, c 1890–1904, of Helen's Bay c 1904–08; of Rathlee, Green Road, Knock, c 1908–14; unmarried; died 18 February 1914 at Rathlee; probate Belfast 29 April 1914. [Belf PRO, will cal; Dub GRO (d); *Med Dir*; QCB adm reg].

BROWN, RICHARD KING (1864–1942), London;
born 16 February 1864 at Athlone, son of Rev Samuel Edgar Brown, minister of Ballywalter, Athlone and Clough Presbyterian Churches and Mary Anne King of Dublin; educated at Ranelagh School, Dublin, and Coleraine Academical Institution; studied medicine at Queen's College, Belfast, from 1883 and University College Hospital, London; BA (RUI) 1886; MB BCh BAO 1891; MD (Gold Medal) 1903; DPH RCPSE 1894; resident clinical assistant to Belfast Royal Hospital; in private medical practice in SE London 1896–1901; medical officer of health and bacteriologist for Bermondsey, London from 1901; lecturer in Public Health, Guy's Hospital, from 1906; an early worker on actinotherapy and editor of the *British Journal of Physical Medicine*; of 12 Asylum Road, Peckham from c 1912 and 69 Grove Park, Denmark Hill from c 1922; retired c 1928; married 10 February 1892 in Belmont Presbyterian Church, Belfast, Sarah Elizabeth Smith, widow, daughter of

William Smith, railway agent, of Armagh and USA; died 28 April 1942 at Goring-by-Sea, Sussex; probate Llandudno 31 July 1942. [*BMJ* obituary (1924); Dub GRO (m); Kirkpatrick Archive; Lond PPR, will cal; *Med Dir*; QCB adm reg; Young and Pike (1909)].

BROWN(E), THOMAS CAMPBELL (1788–1839), Indian Medical Service;
born 16 February 1788, only son of Dr George Brown, surgeon, of Londonderry (*q.v.*); MD (Edin) 1808 (thesis 'De apoplexia'); MRCS 1811; joined the Indian Medical Service (Bengal establishment) as assistant surgeon with the 74th Native Infantry 1811; surgeon 1823; served in Java, including the capture of Java 1811; married Leonora Raffles (who was born 1783/4 and died 5 July 1855 at home in Shipquay Street, Londonderry), eldest daughter of Benjamin Raffles and Anne Lyde, and younger sister of Sir Thomas Stamford Raffles, founder of Singapore; died 22 October 1839 at Jodhpur. [*BNL* 21 January 1840 (d) and 7 July 1855 (d); Crawford (1930); Edin Univ; *Londonderry Sentinel* 18 January 1840 (d) and 6 July 1855 (d); *Londonderry Standard* 22 January 1840 (d); *Oxford DNB* (2004) (for Raffles)].

BROWN, WILLIAM (1789/90–1839), Army Medical Service, Indian Medical Service, and Newry, county Down;
born 1789/90, MD (Edin) 1811 (thesis 'De animi motu'); joined the Army Medical Service as surgeon's mate 1812, becoming assistant surgeon to 24th Dragoons; on half pay with East India Company (Bengal establishment) 1819; 'struck off' and joined 87th Foot 1820; surgeon to 45th Foot 1827 and 52nd Foot 1833; died 7 October 1839 at Newry; buried in St Patrick's Graveyard, Newry. [*BNL* 7 October 1839 (d); Clarke, *County Down*, vol 21 (1998); Crawford (1930); Edin Univ; Peterkin and Johnston (1968)].

BROWNE, ABRAHAM WALKER (1854–1939), Army Medical Service;
born 6 September 1854 in Ireland; LRCSI 1875; LKQCPI and LM 1876; joined the Army Medical Service as surgeon 1877; surgeon major 1889; surgeon lieutenant-colonel 1897; served in Afghan War 1878–80 and Egypt 1884; retired on half pay 1900 and retired fully 1903; employed in Armagh in 1907 on the retired list; brevet colonel 1917; CBE c 1919; retired c 1920 to Cooleen, St Kevin's Park, Dublin; married —; died 25 July 1939 at Cooleen, St Kevin's Park; probate Dublin 9 December 1939 and Belfast 18 January 1940. [Belf PRO, will cal; Dub GRO (d); Dub Nat Arch, will cal; *Med Dir*; Peterkin and Johnston (1968)].

BROWNE, ALFRED VALENTINE (1859–c 1909), Belfast;
born 21 December 1859 at Lagan Cottage, Belfast, son of Edward Valentine Browne, surveyor of customs, of Mountpottinger, Belfast; educated at RBAI; studied medicine at Queen's College, Belfast, from 1876; LRCP LRCS Edin 1885; general practitioner, of Connsbrook Avenue and later of 209 Lorne Terrace, Mountpottinger, Belfast; married 12 May 1900 in St Patrick's Church of Ireland Church, Ballymacarrett, Poppie Wightman, daughter of James Wightman, merchant, of Belfast; died c 1909. [*Med Dir*; QCB adm reg; UHF database (m)].

BROWNE, ANDREW LANG (1848–1930), Army Medical Service;
born 24 October 1848 at Dundalk, son of Dr John Browne of Dundalk; brother of Dr William Agnew Browne (*q.v.*); educated at Dundalk Grammar School; studied medicine at Queen's College, Belfast, 1868–71; MD MCh (QUI) 1871; joined the Army Medical Service as assistant surgeon 1872; surgeon major 1884; surgeon lieutentant-colonel 1892; brigade surgeon lieutenant-colonel 1896; retired 1899 but returned as colonel during the Boer War October 1902 and during World War I; married Edith Margaret —; died 6 October 1930 at Park Lodge Nursing Home, Bath Road, Reading; probate London 31 December 1930. [Lond PPR, will cal; *Med Dir*; Peterkin and Johnston (1968); QCB adm reg].

BROWNE, DAVID GRAHAM (1847–c 1889), Alfreton, Derbyshire, and Melbourne, New South Wales;
born 1 January 1847 in Belfast, son of William Browne of Springfield Terrace, Falls Road, Belfast; educated privately; studied arts and medicine at Queen's College, Belfast, from 1862; BA (QUI) 1866; MD MCh 1871; Dip Mid 1874; general practitioner of Pinxton near Alfreton, Derbyshire, from c 1871; emigrated c 1885 to Melbourne; died c 1889. [*Med Dir*; QCB adm reg].

BROWNE, DAVID JOHN (1845/6–1930), Londonderry;
born 1845/6; studied medicine at Ledwich School, Dublin; LM Coombe Hosp Dub 1868; LKQCPI and LM 1869; LRCSI 1869; clinical assistant in Mercer's Hospital, Dublin; medical officer to Letterkenny Union Workhouse; medical officer to Waterside Infirmary and Fever Hospital; general practitioner, of 36 Bishop Street, later 22 and 28 Pump Street and Clarendon Street, Londonderry; married —; died 19 July 1930 at 49 Clarendon Street; probate Londonderry 9 January 1931. [Belf GRO (d); Belf PRO, will cal; *Med Dir*].

BROWNE, DAVID SAMUEL (1869–1908), Portaferry, county Down, Belfast, and Seychelles;
born 25 March 1869 at Mullaghglass, Newry, county Armagh, son of James Browne, farmer, of Mullaghglass; educated at Mullaghglass School; studied medicine at Queen's College, Belfast, from 1887 and Edinburgh University; LRCP and LRCS Edin 1891; LFPS Glas and LM 1891; medical officer and medical officer of health to Portaferry Dispensary District, medical officer to coastguards and constabulary c 1891–1900; general practitioner, of 10 Crumlin Road Belfast c 1907; assistant medical officer of Seychelles Islands June–November 1908; married 5 August 1896 in Portaferry Presbyterian Church, Elizabeth Donnan, daughter of Henry Donnan, merchant, of Portaferry; died 2 November 1908 at Victoria, Mahe, Seychelles; probate Dublin 6 August 1909. [Belf PRO, will cal; *Med Dir*; *Newtownards Chronicle* 7 November 1908 (d); QCB adm reg; UHF database (m)].

BROWNE, EDWARD GEORGE (1863–1952), Army Medical Service;
born 28 March 1863 at Killymaddy House, Dungannon, county Tyrone, son of William Browne, farmer, of Killymaddy House and Anna —; nephew of Dr James Browne, RN (*q.v.*); brother of Dr Thomas John Browne (*q.v.*), Dr Samuel Cairns

Browne (*q.v.*) and Dr Theodore Dickson Browne (*q.v.*); LRCSI 1884; LM KQCPI 1886; DPH RCPSI 1907; joined the Army Medical Service as surgeon 1887; major 1899; lieutenant-colonel 1911; colonel 1915; served in Chitral 1895 and World War I 1914–18; CB (military) 1916; CMG c 1919; retired as major-general; living finally at The Lindens, Farnborough Park, Hamphire; married Mabel Hathway, youngest daughter of major-general Hamilton Robert Hathway, BSC, of The Croft, Hampton Park, Hereford; died 17 January 1952 at The Lindens; probate London 23 April 1952. [Kirkpatrick Archive; Lond GRO (d); Lond PPR, will cal; *Med Dir*; Peterkin and Johnston (1968); Simpson, F., pers com].

BROWNE, EDWARD VALENTINE (later **VALENTINE EDWARD**) (1845–c 1906), New South Wales and Victoria, Australia;
born 5 June 1845 at Waringstown, county Down, son of Edward Browne of 3 Ross's Terrace, Falls Road, Belfast; educated by the Rev George H. Wilson; studied medicine at Queen's College, Belfast from 1862; LRCSI 1872; BA MB (TCD) 1873; emigrated to Australia c 1874; general practitioner in Sydney, New South Wales c 1875, and later of 32 Lonsdale Street, Melbourne, Victoria; died c 1906. [*Med Dir*; QCB adm reg; *TCD Cat,* vol II (1896)].

BROWNE, ELLIOTT SANDERSON (1851/2–1943), Londonderry and London;
born 1851/2; studied medicine at the Royal College of Surgeons in Ireland, and the City of Dublin and Coombe Hospitals; LRCSI 1873; LM RCSI 1874; LKQCPI 1874; house surgeon to Londonderry City and County Infirmary and Fever Hospital; moved c 1877 to Putney, London and various other addresses, then 5 Cavendish Mansions, Langham Street, and c 1914 to 146 Great Portland Street; retired c 1925 and moved c 1927 to The Birches, Farnham Lane, Haslemere, Surrey; died 8 May 1943 at Stoneycroft Nursing Home, Hindhead, Surrey; probate Llandudno 24 July 1943. [Lond GRO (d); Lond PPR, will cal; *Med Dir*].

BROWNE, GEORGE (1864–1938), Ballynahinch, county Down;
born 10 January 1864 at Ballynahinch, son of Andrew Browne, clerk; brother of Dr Andrew Edwin Browne, LRCPI LRCSI 1910, of Ormeau Road, Belfast; educated at the Belfast Semimary; studied medicine at Queen's College, Belfast 1881–6; MD MCh MAO (RUI) 1886; of Galwally, Castlereagh, county Down, c 1886; surgeon with various shipping lines; medical officer and medical officer of health for Ballynahinch Dispensary District, medical officer to the constabulary and railways and certifying factory surgeon from c 1901; of Railway Street, Ballynahinch; married 10 December 1895 in the Spa Presbyterian Church, Agnes Gordon, daughter of William Gordon, farmer, of Magheratimpany, county Down; died 1 May 1938 at Ballynahinch; buried in Second Ballynahinch Presbyterian Graveyard; probate Belfast 17 August 1938. [Belf GRO (d); Belf PRO, will cal; Kirkpatrick Archive; *Med Dir*; QCB adm reg; UHF database (m)].

BROWNE, JAMES (d 1838), Ballymena, county Antrim;
surgeon, of Ballymena; died 23 October 1838 'after a lingering illness'; buried in Clough Graveyard. [*BNL* 30 October 1838 (d)].

BROWNE, JAMES (c 1796–1880), Naval Medical Service and Dungannon, county Tyrone;

born c 1796, son of James Browne of Killymaddy House, Dungannon, and Mary —; brother of William Brown of Killymaddy House who had four medical sons, Dr Thomas John Brown (*q.v.*), Dr Samuel Cairns Brown (*q.v.*), Dr Theodore Dickson Browne (*q.v.*) and Dr Edward George Brown AMS (*q.v.*); studied medicine at the Royal College of Surgeons of England, Trinity College, Dublin and Glasgow University; MRCSE 1822; MD (Glas) 1829; FRCSE 1844; joined the Naval Medical Service 1823; retired as fleet surgeon, to Dungannon; unmarried; died 28 March 1880 at Northland Row, Dungannon; buried in Benburb Churchyard, county Tyrone; probate Armagh 19 May 1880. [Addison (1898); Belf PRO, will cal; Dub GRO (d); *Med Dir*; *Memorials of the Dead*, vol II, p 365; *NMS* (1826); Plarr (1930); Simpson, F., pers com].

BROWNE, JAMES (1857–1929), Dublin, York and London;

born 24 November 1857 at Drumnabuoy, Strabane, county Tyrone, son of Samuel Browne, farmer, of Drumnabuoy; educated at Strabane Academy; studied medicine at Queen's College, Belfast, from 1875; MD (RUI) 1885; BCh 1895; resident medical officer in Jervis Street Hospital, Dublin; general practitioner in York 1886, in London, at Witton House, Hill Top, West Bromwich 1896 and 49 Belgrave Road, SW 1908; also medical officer of Pimlico Dispensary District; married Mary Gladys —; died 11 March 1929 at 49 Belgrave Road; probate London 10 July 1929. [Kirkpatrick Archive; Lond PPR, will cal; *Med Dir*; QCB adm reg; Young and Pike (1909)].

BROWNE, JAMES ANDERSON (1872–1911), Belfast;

born 24 June 1872 at 14 College Square East, Belfast, son of Sir John Walton Browne (*q.v.*) of 14 College Square East and Fanny Anderson; educated at Clifton College and St Peter's School, York; studied medicine at Trinity College, Dublin, 1892–3 and Queen's College, Belfast, from 1883; LRCPI and LM, LRCSI and LM 1898; junior clinical assistant to Moorfields Ophthalmic Hospital, London; assistant ophthalmic surgeon to the Belfast Ophthalmic Hospital, of 10 College Square North, Belfast c 1900–10; and finally of Lismore, Windsor Avenue, Belfast; died 4 July 1911 of alcoholism and delerium tremens at the Alexandra Military Hospital, London; probate Belfast 18 August 1911. [Belf PRO, will cal; *BMJ* obituary (1911); Dub GRO (b); Kirkpatrick Archive; Lond GRO (d); *Med Dir*, QCB adm reg].

BROWNE, JAMES ARTHUR (1865–1940), Belfast, London, and Newport and Saffron Walden, Essex;

born 28 December 1865 in Belfast, son of James Browne, woollen merchant of 1 Wilmont Place, Belfast, and Mary Ann Gibson of Ballywalter; educated at RBAI; studied arts and medicine at Queen's College, Belfast, from 1884 and at Trinity College, Dublin and Vienna; BA (RUI) 1887; MB BCh BAO 1890; LM Rot Hosp Dub 1890; surgeon in Belfast for 18 months; medical officer to the Bloomsbury Lying-in Hospital, London; general surgeon, of 61 Guildford Street, Russell Square c 1892–1908; surgeon to the Saffron Walden Hospital; medical officer to the Newport Post Office and Saffron Walden Union, of Belmont House, Newport c 1908–40; surgeon to Red Cross Hospitals in France 1914–15 and Saffron Walden 1916–18; married 12 September 1893 in University Road Methodist Church, Belfast, Anna Threekeld Mary Gorman, daughter of the Rev William Gorman, methodist minister, of 33 College Street, Belfast; died 10 July 1940; administration London 15 August 1940. [Dub GRO (m); Fry (1984); Kirkpatrick Archive; Lond PPR, will cal; *Med Dir*; QCB adm reg; UHF database (m); Young and Pike (1909)].

BROWNE, SIR JOHN WALTON (1844–1923), Belfast;
born 5 October 1844 in Belfast, son of Dr Samuel Browne, senior (*q.v.*) and Charlotte Walton; brother of Dr Samuel Browne, junior (*q.v.*); studied arts and medicine at Queen's College, Belfast; 1860–67; BA (QUI) 1863; MD 1867; MRCSE and LM 1867; house surgeon to Belfast General Hospital; medical officer to Belfast Dispensary District; assistant surgeon to Belfast Ophthalmic Hospital 1880–87 and visiting surgeon 1887–1923; attending ophthalmic (later general) surgeon at the Royal (Victoria) Hospital, Belfast 1875–1912; honorary surgeon to the Ulster Hospital for Children and Women 1882–1923; of 4 College Square East and Lismore, Windsor Avenue, Belfast; president of Ulster Medical Society 1880–81 and North of Ireland Branch of BMA; gave annual winter oration at Belfast Royal Hospital 1885 and 1903; chairman of the Royal Victoria Hospital medical staff 1899–1912; author of many medical papers; retired 1912; deputy lieutenant for Belfast 1913; Knight Bachelor 1921; married (1) 6 July 1871 in Belmont Presbyterian Church, Belfast, Frances Anderson, daughter of David Anderson of Strandtown, Belfast, and Matilda Grant; (2) —; father of Dr James Anderson Browne (*q.v.*); died 18 December 1923 at Lismore; buried in Belfast City Cemetery; probate Belfast 13 March 1924. [Belf City Cem, bur reg; Belf PRO, will cal; *BMJ* obituary (1923); Hunter (1936); Kirkpatrick Archive; *Lancet* obituary (1923); Marshall and Kelly (1973); *Med Dir*; O'Donnell (2008); QCB adm reg; UHF database (m); Young and Pike (1909)].

BROWN(E), JOSEPH (1819/20–84), Naval Medical Service and Stranorlar, county Donegal;
born 1819/20 in county Tyrone, son of Benjamin Browne, farmer; LRCS Edin 1840; MD (St Andrew's) 1854 (by examination); FRCS Edin 1858; LRCP Edin 1859; joined the Naval Medical Service as assistant surgeon 1842; surgeon 1851; volunteered to go to Jamaica during cholera epidemic in 1850–51; Baltic Medal; retired 1851 to Corcam House, Stranorlar; honorary member of Surgical Society of Ireland; also general practitioner, of Clarendon Street, Londonderry; married 21 October 1851 in Donaghmore Presbyterian Church, Stranorlar, Rachel Craig, youngest daughter of John Craig, farmer, of Killygordon, county Donegal; died 10 April 1884 at Corcam House; probate Londonderry 23 May 1884. [*BNL* 24 October 1851 (m); Belf PRO, will cal; Croly (1843–6); Dub GRO (m) and (d); *Med Dir;* Smart (2004)].

BROWNE, RICHARD JEBB (1774/5–1832), Army Medical Service and Newry;
born 1774/5; joined the Army Medical Service as surgeon's mate to the 15th Regiment of Foot 1794; assistant surgeon to the 59th Foot 1804; surgeon 1806; staff surgeon 1812; on half pay 1814–15; retired on half pay 1827 and was attached to the

staff of the Northern Recruiting District, living in Newry; served in Dominica 1794, Walcheren and the Peninsular War but not at Waterloo; married 1811 in Newry, Mary Reid (who was born 1780/1 and died 6 May 1871), daughter of Samuel Reid, Seneschal of Newry; died 19 May 1832 in Newry of cholera; buried (with his wife and children) in Saint Patrick's graveyard, Newry; memorial in St Mary's Church of Ireland Church, Newry. [*BNL* 8 March 1811 (m) and 25 May 1832 (d); Bennett (1974); Clarke, *County Down*, vol 21 (1998); *Londonderry Sentinel* 26 May 1832 (d); Peterkin and Johnston (1968)].

BROWNE, ROBERT (*fl c* 1845), Newry, county Down;
LRCSI; general practitioner, of Newry c 1845. [Croly (1843–6)].

BROWNE, SAMUEL, senior (1809–90), Naval Medical Service and Belfast;
born 1809, son of the Rev Solomon Browne, minister of Castledawson Presbyterian Church; studied medicine at the Royal College of Surgeons in Ireland; LKQCPI 1830; MRCSE 1851; LM KQCPI 1859; MKQCPI 1881; joined the Naval Medical Service as surgeon's mate 1830; surgeon 1839; served afloat in West Indies, North America, Atlantic and Mediterranean stations; court martialled for drunkenness 1841; opened eye dispensary in Belfast 1845; attending surgeon to Belfast General Hospital from 1851; of 19 College Square East; retired 1875; honorary consulting surgeon to Belfast Hospital for Sick Children 1873–90; sixth president of the Belfast Clinical and Pathological Society 1858–9; Mayor of Belfast 1870; Chief Sanitary Officer for Belfast 1876 and first superintendent medical officer of health 1880–90; JP; married Charlotte Walton; father of Sir John Walton Browne (*q.v.*) and Dr Samuel Browne, junior (*q.v.*); lived in his latter years at 'Lindisfarne', Strandtown, county Down; died 26 August 1890 at 'Lindisfarne'; buried in Belfast City Cemetery; portrait by Richard Hooke in Belfast City Hall; plaster bust in the Ulster Medical Society rooms; probate Belfast 12 September 1890. [Allison (1969) and (1972); Belf City Cem, bur reg; *Belf Clin Path Soc Trans* 1858–9; Belf PRO, will cal, will; Blaney (1988); Calwell (1969) and (1973); McConnell (1951); *Med Dir*; Whitla 1901)].

BROWNE, SAMUEL, junior (1850–1925), Naval Medical Service and Warwick;
born 7 August 1850 in Belfast, son of Dr Samuel Browne (*q.v.*) and Charlotte Walton; brother of Sir John Walton Browne (*q.v.*); educated at Belfast New Academy; studied medicine at Queen's College, Belfast 1867–72 and at Edinburgh; MD MCh (QUI) 1872; DPH RCP Edin 1883; joined the Naval Medical Service as assistant surgeon on HMS *Duke of Wellington* in Portsmouth Harbour 1873; served in Gold Coast c 1873–4 and later Plymouth Hospital; various periods of sick leave c 1874–81 due to gonorrhoea and fractured fibula but had many favourable references from senior officers; served on HMS *Antelope* 1880–81; resigned 1882 on grounds of 'urgent private affairs'; medical officer to HM Prison, Warwick 1884–1901; medical officer of health for Leamington 1890–1910; medical officer to 8th battalion of the Royal Warwickshire Regiment from c 1910; married Ada Elizabeth Simpson, daughter of George Simpson; died 7 March 1925 at Esher, Surrey; probate London 13 May 1925. [*BMJ* obituary (1925); Kirkpatrick Archive; *Irish Times* obituary (1925); Lond PPR, will cal; Lond PRO, ADM 104/28 (393); QCB adm reg].

BROWNE, SAMUEL CAIRNS (1855/6–87), Naval Medical Service;
born 1855/6 at Killymaddy House, Dungannon, county Tyrone, son of William Browne, farmer, of Killymaddy Houseand Anna Elizabeth —; nephew of Dr James Browne RN (*q.v.*); brother of Dr Thomas John Browne (*q.v.*), Dr Theodore Dickson Browne (*q.v.*) and Dr Edward George Browne (*q.v.*); educated at Coleraine Academical Institution; studied medicine at the Royal College of Surgeons in Ireland; LRCSI 1879; LRCP Edin and LM 1880; resident surgeon to the City of Dublin Hospital; joined the Naval Medical Service as assistant surgeon 1881; served in China during the Franco-Chinese War, where he may have caught malaria; staff surgeon on HMS *Cambridge* 1886–7 and HMS *Tay* 1887; with home address of Killymaddy House; unmarried; died 1 August 1887 of 'pneumonia' at the Royal Naval Lunatic Hospital, Yarmouth, Norfolk; buried in Benburb Churchyard; probate Armagh 26 October 1887 and London 28 November 1887. [Belf PRO, will cal; Lond GRO (d); Lond PPR, will cal; *Med Dir; Memorials of the Dead*, vol II, p 365; Simpson, F., pers com].

BROWNE, SAMUEL HASLETT (1850–1933), Naval Medical Service and Indian Medical Service;
born 19 January 1850 at Buncrana, county Donegal, son of the Rev William Browne, minister of Buncrana Presbyterian Church, and — Haslett of Foyle View, county Londonderry; educated at RBAI; studied medicine at Queen's College, Belfast 1866–70; MD MCh (QUI) 1870; MRCP London 1896; joined the Naval Medical Service as assistant surgeon 1870; transferred to the Indian Medical Service (Bengal establishment) as surgeon 1874; surgeon major 1876; surgeon lieutenant-colonel 1894; colonel 1903; served in Afghanistan 1878–80; inspector general of the Civil Hospitals of Bengal; principal of the Medical College, Lahore; honorary surgeon to the viceroy of India; CIE 1896; retired 1906; lived finally at Craig Dhu Varen, Portrush; unmarried; died 8 July 1933; probate Belfast 24 January 1936. [Belf PRO, will cal; *BMJ* obituary (1933); Crawford (1930); Kirkpatrick Archive; McConnell (1951); *Med Dir*; QCB adm reg].

BROWNE, THEODORE DICKSON (1859–1931), Benburb, county Tyrone;
born 1859 at Killymaddy House, son of William Browne, farmer, of Killymaddy House and Anna Elizabeth —; nephew of Dr James Browne RN (*q.v.*); brother of Dr Thomas John Browne (*q.v.*), Dr Samuel Cairns Browne (*q.v.*) and Dr Edward George Browne (*q.v.*); studied medicine at the Carmichael School, Dublin; LRCSI 1884; LRCPI and LM 1885; medical officer to Benburb Dispensary District; married Hilda Mabel Geraldine West of Glenaul House, Benburb, county Tyrone (who was born 1868 and died 21 October 1911); died 4 May 1931 at Northland Row, Dungannon; both buried in Benburb Churchyard; probate Belfast 20 July 1931. [Belf GRO (d); Belf PRO, will cal; *Med Dir*; Simpson, F., pers com].

BROWNE, THOMAS (1841–1926), Naval Medical Service;
born 1841, son of Samuel Browne, farmer, of Ballymena, county Antrim, and Agnes Dall; educated at Ballymena Academy; studied medicine at Queen's College, Belfast 1857–62; MD (QUI) (1st class hons)1862; LRCS Edin 1862; joined the Naval Medical Service as assistant surgeon 1863; deputy inspector general 1893; inspector

general 1899; medical officer to the Naval Mental Hospital, Great Yarmouth, from 1880, becoming superintendent; superintendent of the Royal Naval Hospital, Bermuda 1894–7 and deputy superintendent at the Royal Naval Hospital, Plymouth 1897–9; retired 1899; author of various medical papers; a keen golfer, he is said to have introduced the term 'bogey' (after colonel Bogey) for the par score; married 8 March 1871 in North Berwick, East Lothian, his cousin Agnes Robertson Dall (who was born 1846/7), daughter of James Dall, merchant and JP, of Park House, North Berwick, and Ann Pagan; died 29 January 1926 at 7 Carlton Road North, Weymouth, Dorset; probate London 25 March 1926. [*BMJ* obituary (1926); Edin GRO (m); Kirkpatrick Archive; *Lancet* obituary (1926); Lond GRO (d); Lond PPR, will cal; *Med Dir*; QCB adm reg].

BROWNE, THOMAS JOHN (1850–1943), Dungannon, county Tyrone, Dalysfort, Galway, Queenstown, county Cork, and Dublin;
born 1850 at Killymaddy House, Dungannon, county Tyrone, son of William Browne, farmer, of Killymaddy House; nephew of Dr James Browne RN (*q.v.*); brother of Dr Samuel Cairns Browne (*q.v.*), Dr Theodore Dickson Browne (*q.v.*) and Dr Edward George Browne AMS (*q.v.*); educated in Newry; studied arts and medicine at Trinity College, Dublin, from 1866; BA MB (TCD) 1871; LRCS Edin and LM 1873; house surgeon to Liverpool Northern Dispensary; surgeon with the Pacific Steamship Navigation Company c 1875; general practitioner, of Dungannon c 1877–89; medical officer of health, public vaccinator and registrar of births and deaths to Dungannon Dispensary District; general practitioner, of Dalysfort c 1889–90, of Middleton Park, Queenstown c 1890–1911, and of 'Atherstone', Temple Road, Dublin, c 1911–18; medical officer to the Local Government Board; retired c 1918 to 4 De Vesci Terrace and later to 11 Windsor Terrace, Kingstown, county Dublin; moved c 1927 to 49 St Ronan's Road, Southsea, Hampshire; married 24 April 1878 in Warrenpoint Presbyterian Church, county Down, Sara Sinclair, daughter of William Sinclair, merchant, of Warrenpoint; died 22 May 1943 at the Royal Victoria Hospital, Boscombe, Hampshire, 'due to war operations'; probate Llandudno 4 November 1943. [Lond GRO (d); Lond PPR, will cal; *Med Dir*; Simpson, F., pers com; TCD adm reg; *TCD Cat*, vol II (1896); *TCD Reg*; UHF database (m)].

BROWNE, WILLIAM (1815/6–80), Naval Medical Service and Londonderry;
born 1815/6, son of Thomas Browne, gentleman, of Londonderry; studied medicine at Trinity College, Dublin, Park Street School and Edinburgh University; MD (Edin) 1836 (thesis 'On gout'); FRCSI 1844; LM Edin; joined the Naval Medical Service as surgeon; surgeon in charge RN Hospital of Ascension; medical officer of health for the City of Londonderry, registrar of births and deaths and Government Inspector of Emigrants for the Port of Londonderry; lived at Pump Street, Londonderry, and later at Ronaragh, Fahan, county Donegal; married 11 November 1851 in Christ's Church, Marylebone, London, Florinda Watt, daughter of Andrew Alexander Watt, distiller, of Londonderry; died 11 October 1880 at Ronaragh; administration (with will) Londonderry 20 December 1880. [*BNL* 14 November 1851 (m); Belf PRO, will cal; Dub GRO (d); Edin Univ; Lond GRO (m); *Londonderry Sentinel* 14 November 1851 (m); Hitchings, Paul, pers com; *Med Dir*].

BROWNE, WILLIAM AGNEW (1841/2–91), Bowen, Queensland;
> born 1841/2, son of Dr John Browne of Dundalk; brother of Dr Andrew Lang Browne (*q.v.*); educated at Dundalk Grammar School; studied medicine at Queen's College, Belfast, from 1880; MD (QUI) 1863; LRCSI and LM 1863; surgeon with P & O Company c 1866; emigrated to Australia c 1870; general practitioner in Bowen and medical officer to Bowen Hospital, Queensland; died January 1891. [*Med Dir*; QCB adm reg].

BROWNE, WILLIAM JAMES (1850–1918), Londonderry, and Letterkenny, county Donegal;
> born 4 February 1850 at Ballyeglish, Moneymore, county Londonderry, son of Robert Browne of Moneymore; educated at Moneymore Academy; studied medicine at Ledwich School, Dublin; LM Coombe Hosp Dub 1873; LRCSI 1875; LRCP Edin and LM 1876; resident surgeon to Londonderry County Infirmary and City Fever Hospital; medical officer to Church Hill Dispensary District and constabulary and certifying factory surgeon, of Mount View, Drumbologue, Letterkenny, from 1876; died 14 April 1918 at Mountview; probate Londonderry 21 June 1918. [Belf PRO, will cal; Dub GRO (d); Kirkpatrick Archive; *Med Dir*, QCB adm reg].

BROWNE, WILLIAM RICHARD (1850–1924), Indian Medical Service;
> born 23 May 1850 in Hobart, Tasmania, son of Captain — Browne of Hoffe House, Stirling; educated privately; studied medicine at the Carmichael School, Dublin and, from 1870–71, at Queen's College, Belfast; MD MCh (QUI) 1871; joined the Indian Medical Service (Madras establishment) as assistant surgeon 1873; surgeon major 1885; surgeon lietunant-colonel 1893; colonel 1903; surgeon general 1904; served at the suppression of the Rumpa Rebellion 1879–80; CIE 1906; retired 1908; married Ethel Rosa —; died 16 September 1924 at Rougemont, Switzerland; probate London 19 November 1924. [*BMJ* obituary (1924); Crawford (1930); Kirkpatrick Archive; Lond PPR, will cal; *Med Dir*; QCB adm reg].

BROWNLEE, JOSEPH JOHN, senior (1852–1929), Christchurch, New Zealand;
> born 9 August 1852 at Derryland, county Armagh, son of John Brownlee of Derryland, educated at the Model School, Belfast; studied medicine at Queen's College, Belfast, 1879–83; Malcolm Exhibition (1882) and Coulter Exhibition (1883), Belfast Royal Hospital; MD (RUI) Dip Obst 1883; MCh 1884; MAO 1888; DPH RCPSI 1898; surgeon on the SS *Aberdeen*; emigrated to Christchurch, New Zealand c 1885; of 83 Cashel Street, Christchurch c 1905; medical officer to the Educational Board, Christchurch c 1912–20, of 256 Cashel Street, Christchurch; married — McKee; father of Dr Joseph John Brownlee, junior, of Christchurch, MB (NZ) 1927, FRCSE 1934; died 13 October 1929. [*Belf Roy Hosp, Ann Rep*; Kirkpatrick Archive; *Med Dir*; QCB adm reg].

BROWNLEE, ROBERT (d c 1828), Fernisky, county Antrim;
> surgeon, of Fernisky; died c 1828; administration Connor Diocesan Court 1828. [Dub Nat Arch, Connor Dio Admins index].

BROWNLEES, JOHN KIRKPATRICK (later known as **KILPATRICK**) (1868–1929), Larne, county Antrim and London;
> born 8 July 1868 at Aghafatten, Ballymena, son of James Brownlees of Aghafatten, farmer and publican, and Elizabeth Kirkpatrick; educated at Ballymena Intermediate School; studied medicine at Queen's College, Belfast, from 1886; LRCP and LRCS Edin 1893; LFPS Glas 1893; surgeon in the mercantile marine; medical officer to Glenwherry Dispensary District; of Main Street, Larne; moved to London c 1907 as general practitioner, certifying factory surgeon, lecturer in physiology, etc, at the Collegiate Schools, Winchmore Hill, c 1907–15; served in the London Irish Rifles and RAMC during World War I becoming a captain; of The Chestnuts, Winchmore Hill from 1917; also surgeon to the constabulary from 1918 and medical officer and public vaccinator to Edmonton Union from 1922; married (1) 28 October 1897 at Reidstown House, Glenwhirry, Jane Andrews, daughter of William Henry Andrews, farmer, of Glenwhirry; (2) Emily Maude —; died 7 February 1929 at Roseneath Nursing Home, Winchmore Hill; probate London 22 March 1929. [Belf GRO (b); Dub GRO (m); Lond GRO (d); Lond PPR, will cal, will; *Med Dir*; QCB adm reg; UHF database (m)].

BROWNLOW, NATHANIEL (1820/1–61), Banbridge, county Down;
> born 1820/1, youngest son of Hugh Brownlow of Banbridge; studied medicine at Glasgow University; MD and CM (Glas) 1842; general practitioner of Rathfriland Street, Banbridge; died 22 May 1861 at Rathfriland Street; buried in First Banbridge Presbyterian Graveyard; probate Belfast 27 June 1861. [Addison (1898); Belf PRO, will cal; Clarke, *County Down*, vol 20 (1889); Croly (1843–6); *Med Dir*].

BROWNRIGG, GEORGE HANNAY (1809/10–33), Bangor, county Down, and British Guiana;
> born 1809/10, probably in Bangor, county Down; studied medicine at Edinburgh University; MD (Edin) 1830); (thesis 'De peritonaei dissectione'); medical officer in Berbice, British Guiana; died 20 July 1833 in Berbice of 'inflamation of the brain'; probate Down Diocesan Court 1835. [*BNL* 15 November 1833 (d); Belf PRO, Down Dioces Wills index; Edin Univ].

BROWNRIGG, THOMAS HENRY (1850/1–1922), Moira, county Down;
> born 1850/1; studied medicine at the Ledwich School, Dublin; LRCP LRCS and LM Edin 1875; resident at Mercer's Hospital, Dublin; medical officer and medical officer of health to Moira Dispensary District and constabulary, of Fairmount House, Moira (c 1905); JP; married —; father of Anna Martha Brownrigg who married 26 October 1910 in Moira Church of Ireland Church, Dr James Erskine MacFarlane; died 24 April 1922 at Gortnamoney, Moira; probate Belfast 16 June 1922. [Belf GRO (d); Belf PRO, will cal; *Med Dir*; UHF database (m)].

BRUCE, ALEXANDER (1801/2–58), Belfast, London and Antrim;
> born 1801/2; LM Edin 1831; LRCS Edin 1832; LAH Dub 1841; surgeon in London and was bequeathed all the surgical instruments of his friend Dr James Bell (*q.v.*) in 1826, who stated that he was formerly of Belfast; surgeon and apothecary, of Antrim c 1843; died 1 May 1858 at Antrim; buried in Muckamore Graveyard. [*BNL* 3 May

1858 (d); *Coleraine Chronicle* 8 May 1858 (d); Croly (1843–6); Ellis and Eustace, vol III (1984); gravestone inscription; *Med Dir*].

BRUCE, JOHN (*fl c* 1789–1824), Antrim;
apothecary and surgeon, of Main Street, Antrim c 1789 and 1824, married November 1789 Hannah — of Antrim; father of Ann Jane Bruce who married 17 November 1811 William Morris of the Londonderry Militia. [*BNL* 27 November 1789 (m) and 26 November 1811 (m, daughter); Pigot (1824)].

BRYANS, JOHN (1850–96), Pettigo, county Fermanagh;
born 7 January 1850 at Killyneill, county Monaghan, son of John James Bryans, farmer, of Killyneill; brother of Dr Robert Bryans (*q.v.*); educated at Armagh College; studied medicine at Queen's College, Belfast, from 1866; MD MCh Dip Mid(QUI) 1872; LAH Dub 1872; medical officer to Clonelly and Pettigo Dipensary Districts; living in Tullyhommon; married Jessy —; died 26 August 1896 at Tullyhommon. [Dub GRO (d); Kirkpatrick Archive; *Med Dir*; QCB adm reg].

BRYANS, ROBERT (1863–95), Monaghan and South Africa;
born 13 April 1863 at Killyneill, county Monaghan, son of John James Bryans, farmer, of Killyneill; brother of Dr John Bryans (*q.v.*); educated at Monaghan Collegiate School; studied medicine at Queen's College, Belfast, from 1882; MB MCh (RUI) 1887; LM KQCPI 1888; general practitioner, of Killyneill House, Monaghan; emigrated to South Africa c 1894; died March 1895 at Umzinta, South Africa. [*Med Dir*; QCB adm reg].

BRYARS, JOHN SAMUEL (1861–1915), Belfast;
born 17 July 1861 at Bessbrook, county Armagh, son of William Bryars, school teacher, of Bessbrook and Belfast, and Mary Jane Kingon; educated at McQuiston National School; studied medicine at Queen's College, Belfast, from 1877 and Edinburgh Royal Infirmary; LRCP and LRCS Edin 1886; LFPS Glas 1886; general practitioner, of 53 Thornton Street and 'Ulidia', West Hartlepool c 1887–92, of 227 Newtownards Road, Belfast c 1893–5, of 155 Albertbridge Road c 1895–8 and of 239 Mountpottinger Road c 1898–1915; chairman of Belfast Board of Guardians 1908; married 26 November1891 at Loughside House, Hamilton, Jessie Paterson, daughter of Gavin Paterson, calenderer, of Glasgow, and Jannet Harvie; father of Dr William Bryars of Berkeley, Gloucester, MB BCh BAO (QUB) 1916; died 21 November 1915 at 239 Mountpottinger Road; buried in Belfast City Cemetery. [Belf City Cem, bur reg; *BMJ* obituary (1915); Dub GRO (d); Edin GRO (m); Kirkpatrick Archive; *Med Dir*; QCB adm reg; Young and Pike (1909)].

BRYCE, ROBERT (1802–62), Belfast;
born 22 December 1802, son of the Rev James Bryce, minister of Aghadowey (Killaig) Presbyterian Church, and Catherine Annan of Auchtermuchty; brother of Dr William Bryce (*q.v.*); MD CM (Glas) 1836; general practitioner, of 63 Donegall Street, Belfast; unmarried; died 23 October 1862 at 63 Donegall Street; buried in Killaig Graveyard, Aghadowey; probate Dublin 19 March 1863. [Addison (1898); Bailie and Kirkpatrick (2005); Belf PRO, will cal; *Coleraine Chronicle* 25 October

1862 (d); Croly (1843–6); gravestone inscription; Kirkpatrick Archive; *Londonderry Sentinel* 31 October 1862 (d); *Med Dir*].

BRYCE, WILLIAM (1821/2–1914), Edinburgh and Dalkeith, Midlothian;
born 1821/2, son of the Rev James Bryce, minister of Aghadowey (Killaig) Presbyterian Church, and Catherine Annan; brother of Dr Robert Bryce (*q.v.*); studied medicine at Edinburgh University and the Royal College of Surgeons in Ireland; MD (Edin) 1853 and gold medal (thesis ('On the medical topography of the Lake District of the North of England'); general practitioner, of 75 High Street, Edinburgh c 1860; surgeon to the Queen's Light Infantry Militia; abroad c 1862–6; of Edinburgh Road, Dalkeith c 1866–70, of 13 East Maitland Street, Edinburgh c 1870–72, of 31 Charlotte Square, Edinburgh c 1872–98 and of 34 Greenhill Gardens Edinburgh c 1898–1914; vice-president of the Obstetrical Society of Edinburgh; married 29 July 1857 at Eskbank House, Midlothian, Bessie Darling Hastie, eldest daughter of Thomas Hastie of Corsehope died 21 February 1914 at Edinburgh; confirmation of will Edinburgh 7 May 1914. [Bailie and Kirkpatrick (2005); *Coleraine Chronicle* 15 August 1857 (m); Edin GRO (d); Edin Nat Arch, will cal; Edin Univ; *Londonderry Sentinel* 21 August 1857 (m); *Med Dir*].

BRYSON, EDWARD (1789/90–1838), Antrim;
born 1789/90; surgeon and apothecary to Antrim Dispensary c 1824; died 19 May 1838, '... largely endowed with natural talents of the first order, which had been highly cultivated by a liberal education and an extensive and close course of study. In his profession he was eminently distinguished for science and skill. In domestic life he was amiable, charitable and benevolent to all classes and as a patriot he was enthusiastic and consistent in claiming and conceding equity of rights to all'. [*BNL* 25 May 1838 (d); Pigot (1824)].

BRYSON, JAMES (1823/4–53), Newry, county Down;
born 1823/4, probably son of the Rev Alexander Bryson, minister of Fourtowns Presbyterian Church, Newry; MRCSE; married 25 March 1845 Mary Wilson, eldest daughter of Samuel Wilson of Great Edward Street, Belfast; died 17 March 1853; buried in Fourtowns Presbyterian Graveyard. [Bailie and Kirkpatrick (2005); *BNL* 28 March 1845 (m); gravestone inscription].

BRYSON, JOSEPH WALLACE (1807–55), Belfast;
born 20 June 1807, second son of Dr Samuel Maziere Bryson (*q.v.*) and Alice Standfield; brother of Dr Samuel Bryson (*q.v.*); educated at RBAI from 1818; studied medicine at Edinburgh University from 1825; LRCS Edin 1828; MD (Edin) 1831 (thesis 'De neuralgia'); general physician at 98 High Street, Belfast, with his father and brother, and attending surgeon to the Belfast Fever Hospital 1833–36; one of the doctors who presented an inscribed gold box to Dr S.S. Thomson in 1834; later of 32 York Street; married 25 June 1839 Olivia Baldwin Mulligan of Franklin Place, Belfast; father of James Bryson, linen merchant, who was father of Dr Samuel Bryson, MB (Glas) 1915; died 8 March 1855 at 32 York Street. [*BNL* 28 June 1839 (m) and 9 March 1855 (d); Blaney (1984) and (1996); Edin Univ; Fisher and Robb (1913); *Med Dir*; Thomson presentation box (1834)].

BRYSON, ROBERT (*fl c* 1818), Poyntzpass, county Armagh;
surgeon, of Poyntzpass; married (1) 17 September 1818, Sarah Bennet, eldest daughter of George Bennet of Poyntzpass; (2) 27 January 1824 Eleanor Gawn, eldest daughter of James Gawn of Donegore. [*BNL* 22 September 1818 (m) and 17 February 1824 (m)].

BRYSON, ROBERT (*fl c* 1830), Carnmoney, county Antrim;
general practitioner in Carnmoney; his son John Alexander Bryson entered RBAI, aged 16, in 1841; Robert died before 1841. [Belf PRO, SCH 524/1A/7].

BRYSON, SAMUEL (1810–58), Belfast;
born Nov 1810, third son of Dr Samuel Maziere Bryson (*q.v.*) and Alice Standfield; brother of Dr Joseph Wallace Bryson (*q.v.*); educated at RBAI from 1817; studied medicine at Edinburgh University; LRCS Edin 1834; MD (Edin) 1835 (thesis 'On peritonitis'); appointed district medical officer to the Belfast Dispensary and Fever Hospital 1836 and practised medicine at 98 High Street, Belfast, 1839–c 1851; married Mary Ann Hull, a 'minor'; died 29 May 1858 at 4 Spencer Terrace East, Spencer Road, Albert town, London; administration London 26 June 1858 and Dublin 27 March 1860. [*BNL* 2 June 1858 (d); Belf PRO, will cal; Blaney (1984) and (1996); Crone (1928); Deane (1921); Edin Univ; Fisher and Robb (1913); Newmann (1993)].

BRYSON, SAMUEL MAZIERE (1776–1853), Belfast;
born 9 March 1776 in Holywood, county Down, twenty-first son of the Rev. James Bryson, minister of the 2nd Presbyterian Congregation, Rosemary Street, Belfast and 4th Congregation, Donegall Street; studied medicine in Edinburgh; LRCS Edin c 1800; LAH Dub 1806; had a business in drugs, oils and colours which he dissolved when he became a licensed apothecary; practised as an apothecary and physician, of 50, 90 and 98 High Street, Belfast 1806–48; an early member of the revived Belfast Medical Society in 1822; also assistant surgeon to the 32nd Regiment (not in Peterkin and Johnston); formed a notable collection of Irish manuscripts, now in the Belfast Public Library; author of *Remains of the Irish Bards*; one of the doctors who presented a gold box to Dr S.S. Thomson in 1834; retired 1848 to 'Cluan', Ballymacarrett; married 3 October 1805 Alice Stanfield of Belfast (who was born c 1769 and died 17 April 1840), father of Dr Joseph Wallace Bryson (*q.v.*) and Dr Samuel Bryson (*q.v.*); died 28 February 1853 at 'Cluan'; buried in the Priory Graveyard, Holywood (no headstone); probate Prerogative Court 1853. [Apothecaries (1829); *Belfast Directory* (1807) and (1808); *BNL* 11 October 1805 (m), 1 October 1806 (advert) and 4 March 1853 (d); Belf PRO, prerog wills index; Blaney (1984) and (1996); *DIB* (2009); Esler (1884); Malcolm (1851); Newmann (1993); Pigot (1824); Thomson presentation box (1834)].

BRYSON, THEOBALD MATHEW (1844–1909), Limavady, county Londonderry
born 31 July 1844 at Sistrakeel, Ballykelly, county Londonderry, son of Bryan Bryson of Sistrakeel, and Mary Mullan of Terrydoo, county Londonderry; educated at the Fishmongers' School, Ballykelly; studied medicine at Queen's College, Belfast, from 1862, and the Royal College of Surgeons in Ireland, City of Dublin Hospital and County Dublin Infirmary (Meath Hospital), also Glasgow University; LFPS Glas

1868; LRCP Edin and LM 1874; general practitioner and coroner, of Main Street, Limavady; JP; inherited the farm at The Maine from his wife's father in 1899; married 3 September 1872 at the O'Kane family home, Mary Jane O'Kane (who was born c 1833 and died 1913), younger daughter of John O'Kane of The Maine and Jane Haslett of Drumnecy; father of Michael Bryson who was father of Dr John O'Kane Bryson, MB (UCD) 1931, of Sheffield, Yorkshire, and of Mary Jane Bryson who married Dr Michael Higgins of Dungiven (*q.v.*); died 25 May 1909 at Main Steet, Limavady; buried in Tamlaght Finlagan Old Graveyard; probate Londonderry 28 July 1909. [Belf PRO, will cal; Dub GRO (d); Higgins (2007); *Med Dir*; Mullin (1983); QCB adm reg].

BRYSON, W. ALLEN (or **ALLAN**) (1832–74), Army Medical Service;
born 11 December 1832 at Strannywham, Dobbsland, Kilroot, son of Robert Bryson, farmer, of Dobbsland, and Mary —; studied medicine at Glasgow University; LRCS Edin 1854; MD (Glas) 1854; joined the Army Medical Service as assistant surgeon to the 97th Regiment of Foot 1854; surgeon major 1865; staff surgeon 1870; on half pay 1871; served in Crimea, at the siege and fall of Sevastopol 1850, the affair of the Quarries 1855 and the assault of the Redan 1855; medal and clasp and Turkish medal; later in Ceylon and India; died on the steamship *Indus* on his passage home from India 8 March 1874, buried at sea, commemorated in Kilroot graveyard; bequeathed his savings to the Belfast Royal Hospital, the largest gift in the 19th century (£2,975), with commemorative tablet in RVH; probate London 14 May 1874. [Addison (1898); *BNL* March 1874 (d); Logan, J.I., pers com; Lond PPR, will cal; *Med Dir*; Peterkin and Johnston (1968); Rutherford and Clarke, *County Antrim,* vol 2 (1981)].

BUCHANAN, ANDREW (1861–1939), Indian Medical Service;
born 17 May 1861 at Killyclogher, Omagh, county Tyrone, son of John Buchanan, farmer, of Killyclogher; brother of Dr James Buchanan (*q.v.*); studied medicine at Queen's College, Belfast, and St Bartholomew's Hospital, London 1878–82; BA (1st class Hons and Gold Medal) (QUI) 1881; MA 1882; Malcolm Exhibition, Belfast Royal Hospital, 1884; MD MAO (RUI) 1885; MCh 1886; joined the Indian Medical Service (Bengal establishment) as surgeon 1887; major 1899; lieutenant-colonel 1907; served on the North-East Frontier, Chin Lushai, 1889–90 (medal with clasp); civil surgeon and superintendent of the gaol, Sangor; author of papers on the diseases of India; retired 1921 to St Jacques, Guernsey; died 26 March 1939. [*BMJ* obituary (1939); Crawford (1930); Kirkpatrick Archive; *Med Dir*; QCB adm reg].

BUCHANAN, GEORGE (*fl c* 1756–70), Strabane, county Tyrone;
apothecary, of Strabane c 1756 (witness to a will); bequeathed land in Londonderry city 1769 and executor of a will 1770; [possibly married Ann — (who was born 1856/7 and died 10 August 1838 in Fintona)]. [*BNL* 28 August 1838 (d); Eustace, vol II (1954)].

BUCHANAN, GEORGE (1799/1800–41), Downpatrick, county Down;
born 1799/1800, son of — Buchanan, apothecary, of Dublin, and — Wright; LRCSI; medical officer to Rostrevor Dispensary District c 1824; surgeon and apothecary to

the Down County Infirmary, Downpatrick 1829–41, in succession to the alcoholic Dr James Hartwell (*q.v.*), also surgeon to the County Gaol; responsible for the move in 1831 from the old Infirmary building in Barrack Lane to a new site on the hill above Pound Lane; contributed to Ordnance Survey Memoir of Downpatrick in 1834; married 11 December 1824 Anna Wright (who died 3 May 1851), eldest daughter of Richard Wright, of Pembroke Place and Lower Ormond Quay, Dublin; died 19 October 1841 of typhus fever; buried in Downpatrick Church of Ireland Graveyard. [*BNL* 26 October 1841 (d) and 7 May 1851 (d); Belf PRO, D2961/2/2/6; Clarke, *County Down*, vol 7 (2nd ed, 1993); Day and McWiliams (1992); Malcolm (1851); Parkinson (1967); Pigot (1824); Pilson (1838); Wilson (1995)].

BUCHANAN, JAMES (1864–1942), Calabar, West Africa and Watford, Hertfordshire;
 born 23 January 1864 at Killyclogher, county Tyrone, son of John Buchanan, farmer, of Killyclogher; brother of Dr Andrew Buchanan (*q.v.*); educated at Omagh Model School; studied medicine at Queen's College, Belfast from 1882, with various scholarships, and at University College, London; MB BCh MCh BAO (RUI) 1888; house surgeon at Tyrone County Infirmary; medical officer of health for Old Calabar c 1890; medical officer to Watford Dispensary District, Watford Schools and the Union Infirmary; general practitioner, of 66 Queen's Road, Watford c 1895 and of 'Holmwood', Station Road, Watford c 1905; clinical assistant to the ENT Department, Tottenham Hospital; president of the West Herts Medical Society; later of 2 Dellfield Close, Watford; died 17 December 1942 at Killyclogher; probate Llandudno 27 April 1943. [Lond PPR, will cal; *Med Dir*; QCB adm reg].

BUCHANAN, JOHN (*fl c* 1824), Monaghan;
 physician, surgeon and apothecary, of the Diamond, Monaghan c 1824; married Elizabeth — (who was born 1754/5 and died 17 November 1835 in Monaghan); died before his wife. [*BNL* 27 November 1835 (d); Pigot (1824)].

BUCHANAN, LEWIS (1850–1921), Arvagh, county Cavan;
 born 21 July 1850 at Carrick House, Ballyjamesduff, county Cavan, son of Robert Buchanan, farmer, and Jane Grey; educated at Kingstown and Rathmines School, Dublin; studied arts and medicine at Trinity College, Dublin, from 1867; BA (TCD) 1875; LLB 1878; LM RCPI 1878; LRCS Edin 1878; medical officer and medical officer of health to Arvagh Dispensary District and constabulary from 1878; JP; married —; died 2 May 1921 at Arvagh. [Dub GRO (d); Figgis and Drury (1932); Kirkpatrick Archive; *Med Dir*; TCD adm reg; *TCD Cat*, vol II (1896)].

BUCHANAN, — (d 1832), possibly Belfast;
 married — (who died 4 March 1834 in Cromac Street, Belfast); died July 1832 of cholera. [*BNL* 14 March 1834 (d)].

BUCHANNON, JOHN (d c 1813), Army Medical Service;
 'assistant surgeon with English army in Portugal'; died c 1813; administration Clogher Diocesan Court 1813. [Dub Nat Arch, Clogher Dio Admins index].

BUCKENHAM, JOHN (1832/3–1908), Belfast, Brandon, Suffolk and Cambridge; born 1832/3, son of Wiliam Buckenham of Brandon, Suffolk; educated at Brandon; studied medicine at Queen's College, Belfast, from 1854; LM QCB 1856; MRCSE 1858; LRCP Edin 1860; general practitioner, of 1 Victoria Street, Belfast; moved to Brandon, Suffolk 1862; medical officer to Cambridge No 2 (later No 1) Dispensary District, prison and workhouse from c 1867, of Huntingdon House, Cambridge; married —; died 19 July 1908 at 112 Castle Street, Cambridge; probate Peterborough 22 September 1908. [Lond GRO (d); Lond PPR, will cal; *Med Dir*; QCB adm reg].

BURDEN, HENRY, senior, (1835–93), Belfast;
born 1835 at 16 Alfred Street, Belfast, younger son of Prof William Burden (*q.v.*) and Margaret Mitchell; educated at RBAI; studied arts and medicine at Queen's College, Belfast, from 1850, but interrupted by a period as apprentice to a Mr McGill, and working in Liverpool; BA (with hons and Gold Medal) (QUI) 1859; MD 1860; MRCSE 1860; MA 1861; Diploma of State Medicine RCPI 1890; MRIA; demonstrator in anatomy at Queen's College, Belfast, 1860–65; assistant physician to Belfast Lying-in Hospital 1865–8, of 8 Alfred Street, Belfast; president of Belfast Literary Society 1869–70; started a course of lectures on natural science at RBAI in 1870 and one of the Board of Masters in the school from 1876, teaching a wide range of subjects in physics; resigned 1883; gave annual winter oration at Belfast Royal Hospital 1887; first pathologist to the Belfast Royal Hospital 1888–92; president of Ulster Medical Society 1888–9; married on 5 August 1862 Anne MacCormac (who was born 1838/9 and died May 1871), daughter of Prof Henry MacCormac (*q.v.*); father of Dr Henry Burden junior, FRCS (*q.v.*); died 18 February 1893 at Wymstay Gardens, London; probate Belfast 27 March 1893. [*Belf Lit Soc* (1901); Belf PRO, will cal; *BMJ* obituary (1893); Burden (1889); Deane (1921); Dub GRO (d); Fisher and Robb (1913); Hunter (1936); Kirkpatrick Archive; *Lancet* obituary (1893); *Med Dir*; Newmann (1993); QCB adm reg; Strain (1967); Whitla (1901)].

BURDEN, HENRY, junior (1867–1953), London and Indian Medical Service;
born 26 April 1867 at 8 Alfred Street, Belfast, son of Dr Henry Burden, senior, (*q.v.*) and Anne MacCormac; educated at home; studied medicine at St Thomas's Hospital, London; MRCSE LRCP Lond 1892; FRCSE 1893; house surgeon at St Thomas's, the Royal Free and Stockwell Fever Hospitals; joined Indian Medical Service (Bengal establishment) as surgeon lieutenant 1894; surgeon captain 1897; major 1905; CIE 1911; lieutenant-colonel 1913; served on the NW Frontier, Tirah Campaign, Middle East and India; retired with rank of colonel 1921 to Heatherland, Budleigh Salterton; married 29 July 1924 Ellen Muriel Darby, widow of John Darby, daughter of George Frederick Adams, civil engineer; died 18 January 1953 at his home Pine Grange, Bath Road, Bournemouth; probate London 27 February 1953. [Crawford (1930); Lond GRO (m); Lond PPR, will cal; *Med Dir*; QCB adm reg; Robinson and Le Fanu (1970); *Times* obituary (1953)].

BURDEN, WILLIAM (1798–1879), Newry, county Down, and Belfast;
born 1798 in India, only child of Dr Henry Burden; of Huguenot descent from three generations of doctors; sent home to Belfast c 1810, when his father and mother died, to live with his three aunts, the Misses Burden; educated at Belfast Academy;

apprenticed to Messrs Vance and Stockdale for some years; studied medicine at the Belfast Fever Hospital and Glasgow University; MD CM (Glas) 1830; general practitioner, of Newry c 1830–33 and then in Belfast; one of the doctors who presented an inscribed gold box to Dr S.S. Thomson in 1834; physician to the Belfast Lying-in Hospital 1837–69; professor of Midwifery, RBAI 1840–49; professor of midwifery, Queen's College, Belfast 1849–67; lived at 16 Alfred Street, Belfast c 1835–67, 'Glendivis', Belfast, 1867–71, at Prospect, Ballynafeigh, from 1871 and later at Nyree Villa, Holywood; married 1829 Margaret Mitchell (who died May 1871 at 'Glendivis'), eldest daughter of Alexander Mitchell, civil engineer; father of Dr Henry Burden, senior (*q.v.*); died 4 April 1879 at Nyree Villa; buried in Belfast City Cemetery; portrait in Queen's University, Belfast; probate Belfast 30 April 1879. [Addison (1898); Belf City Cem, bur reg; Belf PRO, will cal; Croly (1843–6); Deane (1921); Hartley (2006), p 68; Kirkpatrick Archive; Macafee (1942) (1958) and (1975); Moody and Beckett (1959); Newmann (1993); O'Brien, Crookshank and Wolstenholme (1984); Thomson presentation box (1834)].

BURGESS, ANDREW (1862–1920), Liverpool, Lancashire, and Lincoln;
born 13 September 1862 at Ballycreely, county Down; educated at RBAI; studied medicine at Queen's College, Belfast, from 1879; BA (RUI) 1885; MA 1888; MD BCh BAO 1889; general practitioner, of 107 Arundel Avenue, Liverpool c 1895; medical officer to the First District, Lincoln, from c 1900, of 123 Canwick Road, Lincoln; died 29 February 1920 at The Red House, Nettleham Road, Lincoln; probate Lincoln 29 April 1920. [Lond PPR, will cal; *Med Dir*; QCB adm reg].

BURGESS, ROBERT (1852–1928), Coagh, county Tyrone;
born 7 March 1852 at Castleblaney, county Monaghan, son of James Burgess of Castleblaney; educated at RBAI; studied medicine at Queen's College, Belfast, 1868–73; LRCP LRCS Edin 1873; medical officer to Coagh Dispensary District and constabulary and certifying factory surgeon; JP; president of the Coagh Cooperative Dairy Society 1893–1918; married —; father of Dr Charles Herbert Burgess of Cheshire; died 10 December 1928 at Coagh; probate Londonderry 8 February 1929. [Belf GRO (d); Belf PRO, will cal; Kirkpatrick Archive; *Med Dir*; QCB adm reg].

BURKE, MATTHEW RICHEY (1812/3–37), Army Medical Service;
born 1812/3, eldest son of Captain Burke of Glenarm, county Antrim; joined the Army Medical Service 1836 as staff assistant surgeon to the 76th Foot, attached to HMS *Kite*; died 6 August 1837 at Up Park Camp, Kingston, Jamaica, of a 'malignant fever'. [*BNL* 10 October 1837 (d); *Londonderry Sentinel* 14 October 1837 (d); Peterkin and Johnston (1968)].

BURKE, WILLIAM (d 1765), Lurgan, county Armagh;
surgeon and apothecary, of Lurgan; died 6 September 1765, from the effects of a fall from his horse. [*BNL* 10 September 1765 (d)].

BURKE, WILLIAM (1778–1842), Dublin;
born in 1778 at Ramelton, county Donegal, son of the Rev William Burke, minister of First Ramelton Presbyterian Church; educated by his father; studied arts at Trinity

College, Dublin, from 1798, as a sizar; BA (TCD) 1803; ordained minister of First Ramelton in June 1804 in succession to his father who died on 9 January 1803; resigned in October 1805 and returned to Trinity College to study medicine; MB (TCD) 1813; LKQCPI; general practitioner, of Sweetmount, Dundrum, county Dublin; married — Burrowes, daughter of the Rev John Burrowes of Prospect House, Blackrock; his only son William Nassau Burke died October 1836 aged 19 'while zealously engaged in acquiring medical information by giving attendance to patients of the South-Eastern Dispensary in Dublin'; died 4 April 1842 at Sweetmount. [*BNL* 19 April 1842 (d); Burtchaell and Sadleir (1924); Leslie and Wallace (2001); *Londonderry Sentinel* 22 October 1836 (d, son) and 16 April 1842 (d); McConnell (1951)].

BURKITT, JOHN COLLEY SMYTH (1859/60–1929), Whitwick, Leicester;
born 1859/60, son of Canon George Burkitt, rector of Kilcooley, county Tipperary; brother of Dr William Arthur Handcock Burkitt (*q.v.*); educated at Methodist College, Belfast, from 1875; studied medicine at Queen's College, Cork, and Carmichael School, Dublin; MD MCh (RUI) 1884; DPH RCSI 1891; FRIPH; general practitioner and medical officer of health in Whitwick; medical officer to Mount St Bernard's Abbey, Whitwick, and to the 4th District, Ashby-de-la-Zouche Union; major in Leicestershire Imperial Yeomanry during World War I; of The Old Vicarage, Whitwick c 1920; retired c 1927 to live at Warneford House, Ravenstone, Leicestershire; married —; died 23 November 1929 at Warneford House; probate London 25 February 1930. [Fry (1984); Kirkpatrick Archive; Lond GRO (d); Lond PPR, will cal; *Med Dir*].

BURKITT, WILLIAM ARTHUR HANDCOCK (1862/3–1926), Goulburn, New South Wales;
born 1862/3 in Kilkee, county Clare, son of Canon George Burkitt, rector of Kilcooley, county Tipperary; brother of Dr John Colley Smyth Burkitt (*q.v.*); educated at Methodist College, Belfast, from 1875; studied medicine at Queen's College, Cork, the Carmichael School, Dublin, and from 1881, at Trinity College, Dublin; BA MB BCh BAO (TCD) 1889; emigrated to Australia c 1892; general practitioner at Goulburn, New South Wales, and surgeon at Goulburn Hospital, of Belmore Square, Goulburn; married —; died 7 September 1926 at the Empire Nursing Home, Vincent Square, London. [Fry (1984); Kirkpatrick Archive; Lond GRO (d); *Med Dir*; TCD adm reg; *TCD Cat*, vol II (1896)].

BURLEIGH, FRANCIS (*fl c* 1845), Castlefin, county Donegal;
LAH Dub; apothecary in Castlefin, county Donegal, c 1845; married —; a son Francis died 28 July 1832 aged 3½ years. [Croly (1843–6); *Londonderry Sentinel* 11 August 1832 (d, son)].

BURLEIGH, GEORGE (1770/1–1826), Naval and Army Medical Service;
born 1770/1, son of John Burleigh of county Antrim and Mary Jackson; joined the Naval Medical Service 1792, as surgeon's mate on HMS *Brunswick* and fought in the battles on 28, 29 May and 1 June 1794; transferred to the South Essex Fencibles and fought in the 1798 Rising; joined the Army Medical Service as assistant surgeon

to the 38th Foot 1802; with the 4th Royal Garrison Battalion 1803–4; returned to 38th Foot; transferred to the Royal Waggon Train 1805; taken prisoner by a French Privateer and held in Calais and Valenciennes, 1805–13; surgeon to the 2nd Ceylon Regiment 1814; served in the Kandian Insurrection of 1817–18; retired on half pay 1822; married Rebecca Kingsley (who was born 1776/7 and died 21 November 1855 at Jaffna); died 8 April 1826 at Jaffna, Ceylon; memorial tablet in the Dutch Church at Jaffna. [Kirkpatrick Archive; Peterkin and Johnston (1968); Wolfe (1893)].

BURLEIGH, PATRICK (*fl c* 1795), Limavady, county Londonderry;
LAH Dub 1795; physician and apothecary, of Limavady. [Apothecaries (1829); Pigot (1824)].

BURNEY, GEORGE (*fl c* 1824), Larne, county Antrim;
apothecary, of Larne c 1824. [Pigot (1824*)*].

BURNS, ALEXANDER (1861–1922), Shorncliffe, Kent, and Belfast;
born 11 June 1861 at Magheragall, Lisburn, county Antrim, son of William Burns, grocer, of 18 Bristol Street, Belfast; educated at the Working Men's Institute; studied medicine at Queen's College, Belfast, from 1890; MB BCH BAO (RUI) 1896; civil surgeon to the Shorncliffe Station Hospital 1900; general practitioner, of 37 Lisburn Road, Belfast c 1905; anaesthetist to the Samaritan Hospital, Belfast; captain in RAMC during World War I; of 94 Castlereagh Street, Belfast c 1920; married Anne —; died 18 December 1922 at Richmond Nursing Home, Belfast 'following an operation for appendicitis'; administration (with will) Belfast 13 April 1923. [Belf GRO (d); Belf PRO, will cal; Kirkpatrick Archive; *Med Dir*; QCB adm reg].

BURNS, FREDERICK JAMES (1861–1925), Naval Medical Service;
born 18 January 1861 at Castleblaney, county Monaghan, son of James Burns, proprietor of the *Newry Reporter*, of 2 Downey Terrace, Warrenpoint; educated at Castleblaney Classical School; studied medicine at Queen's College, Galway, from 1880, and Belfast from 1881; MD (RUI) 1884; MCh 1885; joined the Naval Medical Service 1886; fleet surgeon from c 1900; surgeon commander from c 1919; retired c 1922 to 36 Belsize Square, Middlesex; died 3 August 1925 at Belsize Square; probate London 8 October 1925. [Lond PPR, will cal, will; *Med Dir*; QCB adm reg].

BURNS, JAMES McTIER, (d 1859), Dunolly, Victoria;
originaly from Newtownards; studied medicine at Glasgow University; MD (Glas) 1852; emigrated to Australia c 1855 general practitioner of Dunolly; unmarried; died 15 December 1859 at Dunolly; administration Dublin 1 December 1860. [Addison (1898); Belf PRO, will cal].

BURNS, JOHN (*fl c* 1819), Tanderagee, county Armagh;
surgeon and apothecary, of Tanderagee c 1819. [Bradshaw (1819)].

BURNS, JOHN (c 1812–80), Tanderagee, county Armagh;
born c 1812; studied medicine in Glasgow University; CM (Glas) 1834; surgeon and apothecary, of Tanderagee; unmarried; died 27 October 1880 at Tanderagee,

having choked on a piece of meat under the influence of excess of alcohol; administration Armagh 19 November 1880. [Addison (1898); Belf PRO, will cal; Dub GRO (d); Kirkpatrick Archive; *Med Dir;* Pigot (1824)].

BURNSIDE, DOUGLAS MASSY (1875–1906), South Africa, Belfast, and Brynmawr, Breckonshire;
 born 21 April 1875, son of the Rev Samuel Douglas Burnside, minister of Carryduff Presbyterian Church, and Frances Isabella Massy of county Tipperary; brother of Dr William Charles Massy Burnside, LRCP LRCS (Edin) 1903, of Belfast; educated at University Classes; studied medicine at Queen's College, Belfast, from 1891; LRCP LRCS Edin 1899; LFPS Glas 1899; civil surgeon during the South African War 1899–1902; general practitioner, of 13/15 Mount Charles, Belfast c 1903 and of Brynmawr c 1904–06; surgeon to William's Collieries, Brynmawr; married Frances —; died 29 April 1906 at Brynmawr; administration (with will) Belfast 27 June 1906. [Barkley (1986); Belf PRO, will cal; *BMJ* obituary (1906); Burke *LGI* (1912); Kirkpatrick Archive; *Med Dir*; QCB adm reg].

BURNSIDE, JAMES (1788/9–1862), Naval Medical Service, and Londonderry and Muff, county Londonderry;
 born 1788/9 at Drummaneny, county Londonderry; MRCSE; joined the Naval Medical Service as assistant surgeon 1810; retired on half pay; surgeon of Waterside, Londonderry c 1824; medical officer to Muff Dispensary c 1845; married 16 October 1819 in First Glendermott Presbyterian Church, Sophia Burnside, daughter of David Burnside of Ardmore, county Londonderry; died 9 September 1862 at Eglinton, county Londonderry; probate Londonderry 6 October 1862. [*BNL* 22 October 1819 (m); Belf PRO, will cal, will; Croly (1843–6); *Londonderry Journal* 19 October 1819 (m); *Londonderry Sentinel* 12 September 1862 (d); *Med Dir*; *NMS* (1826); Pigot (1824)].

BURNSIDE, THOMAS (d 1798), Newtownstewart, county Tyrone;
 studied medicine at Edinburgh University; MD (Edin) 1786 (thesis 'De phrenitide idiopathica'); 'an eminent physician' of Newtownstewart; died September 1798. [Edin Univ; Kirkpatrick Archive].

BURNSIDE, THOMAS (d 1837), Millview, county Tyrone;
 MD [?]; died March 1837 'at an advanced age' at his sister's residence, near Millview. [*BNL* 28 March 1837 (d); *Londonderry Sentinel* 8 April 1837 (d)].

BURROUGHS, LEWIS (d c 1786), Londonderry;
 'doctor' of the Diocese of Derry; died c 1786; probate Derry Diocesan Court 1786. [Thrift (1920)].

BURROWS, ADAM CLARKE (1863–1938), Carlisle, Cumberland;
 born 16 November 1863 at Waterford, son of William Burrows, merchant, of Carrickfergus, county Antrim; brother of Dr James Rogers Burrows (*q.v.*); studied medicine at Queen's College, Belfast, from 1883; LRCP LRCS Edin 1890; LFPS Glas 1890; general practitioner, of 35 Cecil Street, Carlisle, from c 1891, and later

of 4 Wilfred Street, Portland Square, Carlisle; honorary medical officer to the Carlisle and Cumberland Branch of the USPCC; retired c 1918 to Etterley House, then to Milton House, Great Corby, and later to the Beeches, Wetheral, Cumberland; died 8 June 1938 at Beckfoot, Silloth, Cumberland; probate Carlisle 20 August 1938. [Lond PPR, will cal; *Med Dir*; QCB adm reg].

BURROWS, JAMES ROGERS (1858–1901), Army Medical Service;
born 3 May 1858, son of William Burrows, merchant, of North Lodge, Carrickfergus, county Antrim; educated at Methodist College, Belfast, from 1873; studied medicine at Queen's College, Belfast, from 1879; BA (RUI) 1882; MD MCh 1885; joined the Army Medical Service as surgeon captain 1886; major 1898; served in Sudan 1878; married 4 March 1886 at the home of Robert Green, Carrickfergus, Elizabeth Green, daughter of Robert Green, gas director; died 15 April 1901 at Calicut, India. [Dub GRO (m); Fry (1984); *Med Dir*; Peterkin and Johnston (1968); QCB adm reg; UHF database (m)].

BURTON, BINDON JOHN (1818/9–92), Ballinderry and Aghalee, county Antrim;
born 1818/9; studied medicine at Royal College of Surgeons in Ireland, and the Richmond and Meath Hospitals, Dublin; LM West Hospital, Dublin 1846; MRCSE 1848; medical officer to Ballinderry Dispensary District 1849–50; medical officer to Aghalee Dispensary District 1851–9 and to constabulary; retired 1875; married —; died 9 July 1892 at Crumlin; buried in Aghalee Parish Graveyard. [Dub GRO (d); gravestone inscription; *Med Dir*].

BURY, PERCY BELLAMY (1855–90), Naval Medical Service;
born March 1855 ed St Ives, Huntingdonshire, son of J. Bury; educated at Rossall School, Lancashire; studied medicine at Queen's College, Belfast, from 1877, also at Edinburgh University, and St Thomas's Hospital, London; MB MCh (Edin) 1882; joined the Naval Medical Service c 1885; retired to 4 Park Side, Cambridge; unmarried; died 1 January 1890 at 4 Park Side; administration London 13 February 1890. [Kirkpatrick (1889); Lond PPR, will cal; *Med Dir*; QCB adm reg].

BUTLER, GARRET (d 1860), Drumuskey, county Fermanagh and New Orleans, USA;
MRCSE 1852; general practitioner, of Drumusky, Maheraveely, county Fermanagh; emigrated to USA; general practitioner, of 122 Camp Street, New Orleans; died 16 September 1860 in New Orleans; administration (with will) Dublin 4 June 1861. [Belf PRO, will cal; *Med Dir*].

BUTT, EDWARD ORMISTON (1857–1935), Army Medical Service;
born 4 March 1857 at Whiteabbey, county Antrim, son of John Gillis Butt manager of the Northern Bank, Virginia, county Cavan; educated at Methodist College, Belfast, from 1870 and RBAI; studied medicine at Queen's College, Belfast, from 1874 and the Royal College of Surgeons in Ireland; LM Rot Hosp Dub 1877; FRCSI 1884; DPH 1888; LRCPI LRCSI 1893; joined the Army Medical Service as captain 1881; major RAMC 1893; lieutenant-colonel 1901 and colonel 1909; retired on half pay 1913 and retired fully 1914; of 11 Roslin Road, Bournemouth c 1930;

married —; died 12 November 1935 at 15 Boscombe Spa Road, Bournemouth; probate London 15 January 1936. [*BMJ* obituary (1935); Fry (1984); Lond PPR, will cal, will; *Med Dir*; Peterkin and Johnston (1968); QCB adm reg].

BYERS, ISAAC MANDALE (1870–1923), Belfast, ship's surgeon, St Anne's-on-the-Sea, Lancashire, and RAMC;

born 3 March 1870 at Mouhan, county Armagh, son of Samuel Byers, land commissioner, of Mouhan; educated at RBAI; studied medicine at Queen's College, Belfast, from 1888; MB BCh BAO (RUI) 1899; of Markethill, county Armagh; house physician and house surgeon and extern house surgeon to Royal Victoria Hospital, Belfast c 1900–02; medical officer to P & O Steamship company; general practitioner in St Anne's-on-the Sea, Lancashire, from c 1908, of 1 Stanley Villa, 24 St Anne's Road; captain in RAMC during World War I; married Maud M.H. —; died 28 October 1923 at 24 St Anne's Road; probate Belfast 18 March 1924 and London 26 March 1924. [Belf PRO, will cal; Lond GRO (d); Lond PPR, will cal; *Med Dir*; QCB adm reg].

BYERS, SIR JOHN WILLIAM (1853–1920), Belfast;

born 10 November 1853 in Shanghai, only son of the Rev John Byers, presbyterian missionary, and Margaret Morrow, founder and first principal of Victoria College, Belfast; educated at RBAI; studied medicine at Queen's College, Belfast, the London Hospital and Rotunda Hospital, Dublin; BA (QUI) (1st class hons) 1874; MA 1875; MD (1st class hons) MCh (hons) 1878; MRCSE 1879; LM KQCPI 1879; physician to Belfast Hospital for Sick Children 1879–93; attending physician, setting up the new gynaecology department, Belfast Royal Hospital 1883–1900; of Lower Crescent, Belfast; gave annual winter oration at Belfast Royal Hospital 1886 and 1915; professor of midwifery, Queen's College, Belfast 1893–1920; attending gynaecologist to the Royal Victoria Hospital, Belfast 1900–19; chairman of medical staff of the Royal Victoria Hospital 1915–18; on staff of Belfast Maternity Hospital 1902–20; Knight Bachelor 1906; author of many papers on midwifery; president of the Belfast Literary Society 1885–6; president of the Ulster Medical Society 1893–4; president of the BNHPS 1908–11; an authority on Ulster folk-lore and dialect, publishing many papers on these subjects; married 10 September 1902 at 17 Wellington Park, Belfast, Frances (Fanny) Reid, daughter of James Reid, merchant, of Netherleigh, Belfast; died 20 September 1920 at his home, Dreenagh House, Lower Crescent; buried in Belfast City Cemetery; portrait by Henrietta Rae in QUB; probate Belfast 4 February 1921. [Belf City Cem, bur reg; *Belf Lit Soc* (1901); *BNL* September 1920 (d); Belf PRO, will cal; *BMJ* obituary (1920); Calwell (1973); Crone (1928); Deane (1921); *DIB* (2009); Dub GRO (m); Hartley (2006), p 46; Hunter (1936); Kirkpatrick Archive; *Lancet* obituary (1920); Macafee (1942); *Med Dir*; Moody and Beckett (1959); Newmann (1993); O'Brien, Crookshank and Wolstenholme (1984); QCB adm reg; UHF database (m); Young and Pike (1909)].

BYRNE, HUGH F. (*fl c* 1847), Belfast and New Yotk, USA;

surgeon, of Belfast; emigrated to USA; married 4 September 1847 in New York, Catherine Marshall Clindinning, fourth daughter of William Clindinning of Belfast. [*BNL* 5 October 1847 (m)].

BYRNE, JOSEPH (1847/8–1911), Londonderry;
born 1847/8; studied medicine at the Catholic University, Carmichael School and Jervis Street Hospital, Dublin; LM Rot Hosp Dub; LKQCPI 1872; LRCSI 1872; MKQCPI 1880; FRCSI 1886; general practitioner at 21 and 24 Pump Street, Londonderry; married —; died 18 January 1911 at Pump Street; probate Dublin 23 February 1911. [Belf PRO, will cal; Dub GRO (d); *Med Dir*].

BYRNE, PATRICK (1802/3–56), Annaclone, county Down;
born 1802/3; surgeon, of Glaskerbeg, Aghaderg; married Catherine —; father of Rose Byrne who married 7 January 1858 in Loughbrickland Roman Catholic Church, Edward Lavery of Trainview, Moira; died 29 June 1856; buried in Annaclone Roman Catholic Graveyard. [*BNL* 15 January 1858 (m, daughter); gravestone inscription].

BYRNE, — (fl c 1818), Tanderagee, county Armagh;
married 25 June 1818 at Tanderagee, Elizabeth Hood, second daughter of William Hood. [*BNL* 30 January 1818 (m)].

BYRTT, WILLIAM (1786–1845), Army Medical Service and Belfast;
born 25 April 1786, son of William Byrtt and Juliana Lewis; nephew of Dr John Bell (*q.v.*) and Sarah Lewis; joined the Army Medical Service as assistant surgeon to 20th Foot, 1808; surgeon to 28th Foot 1813; served in the Penisular War; on half pay April 1820 to October 1823 when he joined the 24th Foot; retired on half pay 1835; returned to Belfast and served on committee of Belfast Fever Hospital 1838–45; married 23 January 1833 in St Anne's Church of Ireland Church, Belfast, Mary Ann Harriet Lewis (who was born 1805/6 and died 29 September 1847), daughter of James Lewis of Donegall Street, Belfast; died 9 October 1845 in Belfast; buried in Clifton Street Graveyard with memorial tablet in Christ Church, Belfast. [Agnew (1898); *Belf Fev Hosp, Ann Rep*; *BNL* 25 January 1833 (m); Clarke, *Belfast*, vol 1 (1966); Malcolm (1851); Merrick and Clarke, *Belfast*, vol 4 (1991); Peterkin and Johnston (1968)].

C

CADMAN, ARTHUR WELLESLEY (1852–1928), London;
born 16 June 1852 in Manchester, son of Joseph Cadman, tea merchant, of Derby; studied medicine at Owen's College, Manchester and, from 1878, at Queen's College, Belfast; BSc (Manch); LKQCPI 1880; MRCSE 1882; FRCSE 1894; house surgeon in Manchester Royal Infirmary; lecturer in applied anatomy and demonstrator in anatomy at King's College, of 1 Mornington Crescent, London c 1885, at 20 Devonshire Street, Portland Place, London, c 1895, at 19 Wickham Road, Brockley, c 1905, and at 2 Linden Gardens c 1915; retired c 1925 to Wonford House Hospital, Exeter; died 11 August 1928 at Sidmouth. [*Med Dir*; Plarr (1930); QCB adm reg].

CAHEY, — (d 1788), Londonderry;
doctor, of Bogside Street, Londonderry; died 25 November 1788. [*BNL* 28 November 1788 (d)].

CAHILL, MARK FRANCIS (1869–1935), Dublin, Newcastle-upon-Tyne, Northumberland, and Belfast;
born 15 November 1869 at 66 Dame Street, Dublin, son of Dr Mark Cahill, LRCP LRCS Edin 1860, of 66 Dame Street and Minnie Kennedy; brother of Dr Frank Kennedy Cahill, LRCPI LRCSI 1901, of Dublin and Colonel Robert John Cahill, MB (RUI) 1903, DSO, RAMC, of England; studied medicine at the Royal College of Surgeons in Ireland, Durham University and Baltimore; LRCSI and LM, LRCPI and LM 1891; MB (Durham) 1899; FRCSI 1901; assistant physician to the Children's Hospital, Dublin; assistant medical officer to Newcastle-on-Tyne Public Dispensary; general practitioner, of 93 Shankill Road, Belfast; barrister-at-law, Gray's Inn, London 1922; of 3 University Square, Belfast c 1905–30 and 6 Crescent Gardens c 1930–35; married Lula Priscilla —; died 12 January 1935 at 6 Crescent Gardens, Belfast; probate Belfast 7 February 1935. [Belf GRO (d); Belf PRO, will cal; Dub GRO (b); Kirkpatrick Archive; *Med Dir*].

CAIRNES, THOMAS (1674/5–c 1721), Dunmore, county Tyrone;
born 1674/5, fifth son of William Cairnes of Killyfaddy, county Tyrone, and Jane Holland; studied medicine at Leyden, Netherlands, from 1704; MD (Utrecht) 1705 (thesis 'De pleuritide et peripneumonia' in British Library); inherited the townlands of Dunmore and Altanorla, county Tyrone; married his cousin Mary Elliot, daughter of William Elliot; the will of his uncle David Cairnes of Londonderry refers to 'their low condition and poverty', and 'the very ill and unjust doings and carriage of her husband towards her, which I will here say no more of'; father of a natural son but no legitimate issue; died in or before 1721. [Lawlor (1906), p 111; Innes Smith (1932)].

CAIRNS, ALEXANDER (1766/7–99), Donaghadee, county Down;
born 1766/7; of Comber, county Down; LAH Dub 1792; apothecary and surgeon, of Donaghadee; married — Lusk (who was born 1750/1 and died 2 August 1817 at

Ballywalter), daughter of Arthur Lusk 'who circumnavigated the globe under Lord Anson'; died 11 October 1799 at Donaghadee; probate Down Diocesan Court 1817. [Apothecaries (1829); *BNL* 22 October 1799 (d) and 12 August 1817 (d); Belf PRO, Down Diocesan Wills index].

CAIRNS, DALWAY E. N. (*fl c* 1866), Duneight, county Down, and Lisburn, county Antrim;

general practitioner, of Duneight c 1839, and later of Largymore and Sloane Street, Lisburn; married — Peel, daughter of Mark Peel of Ballinderry; father of Dalway Cairns who died 10 July 1839 and of Margaret Susanna Cairns who died 13 October 1866 aged 19, both of tuberculosis. [*BNL* 16 July 1839 (d, son); Dub GRO (d, daughter); *Lisburn Fam Hist Soc*, vol I (2000)].

CAIRNS, EDWARD (1864–1936), Belfast;

born 24 May 1864 at Cherryvalley, county Down, son of John Cairns, farmer, of Cherryvalley, and Mary Ann Robinson; studied medicine at Queen's College, Belfast, from 1887; LRCPI and LM, LRCSI and LM 1893; general practitioner, of 4 Hillside Terrace, Ballysillan, of 23 and 85 Cliftonville Road, Belfast; married Elizabeth Ann —; died 15 March 1936 at 85 Cliftonville Road; administration 2 June 1936. [Belf GRO (d); Belf PRO, will cal; Dub GRO (b); *Med Dir*; QCB adm reg].

CAIRNS, JOHN (1792–1827), Ballywalter, county Down;

born 1792 in Ballywalter; surgeon, of Ballywalter; probably unmarried; died 26 December 1827; 'possessed of eminent ability in his profession … his days passed away in the bosom of innumerable well-wishers'. [*BNL* 11 January 1828 (d)].

CAIRNS, THOMAS (1867–1939), Northampton;

born 6 October 1867 at Halifax, Yorkshire, son of the Rev John Cairns, minister of Ballina Presbyterian Church, and Jane Steen; nephew of Dr Edward Cairns (*q.v.*); educated at Ballina Intermediate School; studied medicine at Queen's College, Galway, also at Queen's College, Belfast, from 1890 and in Edinburgh and Glasgow; LRCPI and LM, LRCSI and LM 1895; general practitioner, of White Lodge, Leicester Parade, Northampton; medical officer to Northampton School Board; later of 1 Abington Park Crescent, Northampton; married Edith Marion —; died 15 March 1939 at Northampton General Hospital; probate London 5 July 1939. [Barkley (1986); *BMJ* obituary (1939); Kirkpatrick Archive; Lond PPR, will cal; *Med Dir*; QCB adm reg].

CALDWELL, ALFRED GEORGE (1870–1950), Edinburgh, Transvaal, South Africa, RAMC, Southampton, Hampshire and London;

born 29 December 1870 at 28 Gayfield Square, Edinburgh, son of William Caldwell, lithographer, of Edinburgh and later of 4 Elmwood Avenue, Belfast, and Margaret Munro; educated at Daniel Stewart's Institute, Edinburgh; studied medicine at Queen's College, Belfast, from 1889; MB BCh BAO (RUI) 1894; MD 1900; DPH RCPSE 1904; general practitioner, of 8 South Gray Street, West Mayfield, Edinburgh c 1895; assistant medical officer to the SE and SW Fever Hospitals, London from c 1900, of 197 Mitcham Road, Tooting; medical officer in Krugersdorp, Transvaal c 1910; DCMS (tropical diseases), Ministry of Pensions, East Midlands; temporary captain (RAMC) c 1914–18; moved to Southampton c 1925; senior assistant medical officer to the Port of Southampton, of 10 Banister Road c 1935; retired c 1945 to Flat 5, 2 Harpenden Road, St Albans; married —; died 3 December 1950 at Hazeldene Nursing Home, Peter Street, St Albans, Herts; probate London 9 March 1951. [Edin GRO (b); Kirkpatrick Archive; Lond PPR, will cal, will; *Med Dir*; QCB adm reg].

CALDWELL, GEORGE (d 1887), Dublin, Rostrevor, county Down, Belfast, and Birmingham, Warwickshire;

LRCSI 1849; demonstrator of anatomy in the Apothecaries' Hall and assistant demonstrator in the Carmichael Medical School; surgeon to the Institute for Diseases of the Eye and Ear and for General Diseases, Summer Hill, Dublin; general practitioner, of Rostrevor c 1850, and of 98 High Street, Belfast, c 1855; general practitioner, of 34 Worcester Street, and of Emdale, 108 Upper Mary Street, Birmingham, and of Llanfairfechan, Carnarvonshire, from c 1860; author of a pamphlet 'On Bronchitis and Inflamation of the Lungs' (1868); married Rose —; died 25 March 1887 at Emdale; probate Worcester 29 April 1887. [Lond PPR, will cal; *Med Dir*].

CALDWELL (CALLWELL), GEORGE MACARTNEY (1773/4–1824), Naval Medical Service;

born 1773/4 in Newtownards, son of the Rev Hugh Caldwell, perpetual curate of Newtownards, and Anne Winder of Bangor; joined the Naval Medical Service as assistant surgeon; later surgeon; lost in HM Sloop *Arab*, January 1824 off the north-west coast of Ireland; memorial in Newtownards Parish Church. [Clarke, *County Down*, vol 11 (1974); Leslie and Swanzy (1936); *Strabane Morning Post* 20 January 1824 (d)].

CALDWELL, JAMES (d 1814), Magherafelt and Coleraine, county Londonderry, and London;

surgeon, of Magherafelt and United Irishman, c 1793; moved to London 1803–04 but returned to Magherfelt and Coleraine; married — (who died in 1793); died 25 May 1814; administration Derry Diocesan Court 1814. [Agnew (1998); *BNL* 7 June 1814 (d); Dub Nat Arch, Derry Dio Admins index].

CALDWELL, JAMES (1859–1908), Barnsley, Yorkshire;

born 17 March 1859 at Rateen, county Fermanagh, son of John Caldwell, farmer, of Rathmackin, county Tyrone; educated at RBAI; studied medicine at Queen's College, Belfast, from 1881; MD BCh BAO (RUI) 1890; general practitioner, of Hoyland Common, Barnsley; married Eveline Alice —; died 22 July 1908; probate Wakefield 31 August 1908. [Lond PPR, will cal; *Med Dir*; QCB adm reg].

CALDWELL, JOHN (1751–1839), Magherafelt and Londonderry, county Londonderry;

born 1751/2, son of Joseph Caldwell of Magheragar, county Tyrone; brother of Dr Joseph Caldwell RN (*q.v.*); studied medicine at Edinburgh University; MD (Edin) 1780 (thesis 'De hysteria'); presumably the same John Caldwell, physician, who was involved in a fight with David Chambers in Magherafelt in January 1803; in court the jury found him guilty of assault and (perhaps harshly) he was sentenced to two months in gaol in Londonderry; following this, he sold property in Magherafelt and presumably left the town; physician, of 3 Pump Street, Londonderry c 1824; married Mary Lecky (who was born 1762 and died 29 December 1839), elder daughter of Hugh Lecky of Agivy and Bushmills, county Antrim, and Matilda Hutchinson of Ballymoney; died 10 June 1839 at Coolkeiragh House, the home of his son-in-law, Richard Young (who married his only child, Elizabeth Caldwell); buried in Londonderry Cathedral burying ground. [*BNL* January 1803 (law report) and 18 June 1839 (d); Burke *LGI* (1912) (Lecky and Young of Coolkeiragh); Dub Reg of Deeds 712.98.487233; Edin Univ; Kirkpatrick Archive; *Londonderry Sentinel* 15 June 1839 (d), 5 October 1849 (m, sister Helen) and 4 January 1840 (d); *Memorials of the Dead*, vol X, p 114; Pigot (1824)].

CALDWELL, JOSEPH (*fl c* 1820), Naval Medical Service;
son of Joseph Caldwell of Magheragar, county Tyrone; brother of Dr John Caldwell of Londonderry (*q.v.*) and of Helen Caldwell who married 4 September 1849 Armour Matthews of Dooghary, county Tyrone, nephew of Dr Robert Matthews of Drumquin (*q.v.*); joined the Naval Medical Service as assistant surgeon. [*Londonderry Sentinel* 5 October 1849 (m, sister)].

CALDWELL, SAMUEL (1848/9–1911), Virginia, county Cavan;
born 1848/9; studied medicine at Ledwich School and Mercers' Hospital, Dublin; LKQCPI and LM 1871; LRCSI 1871; medical officer to Virginia Dispensary District; retired to Drumsheil, Cootehill; unmarried; died 21 September 1911 at Drumsheil; probate Cavan 19 March 1912. [Belf PRO, will cal; Dub GRO (d); *Med Dir*].

CALDWELL, THOMAS (d 1807), Aughnacloy and Omagh, county Tyrone;
born 1767/8; LAH Dub 1794; apothecary and surgeon, of Aughnacloy and later of Omagh; died 19 December 1807. [Apothecaries (1829); McGrew (2001)].

CALDWELL, THOMAS CATHCART (1875–c 1920), South Africa, Portrush, county Antrim, Belfast and Queensland, Australia;
born 20 January 1875 in Main Street, Portrush, son of James Crofton Caldwell, commission agent, of Portrush and Martha Hunter; studied medicine at Edinburgh University; MB BCh (Edin) 1899; DPH Edin and Glas 1903; Diploma of Tropical Medicine, Liverpool, 1905; civil surgeon to South African Field Force 1900–02; general practitioner, of Causeway View Terrace, Portrush, c 1904; of Mosella, Osborne Park, Belfast, c 1910; emigrated to Goodna, Queensland, Australia c 1912; died c 1920. [Belf GRO (b); *Med Dir*].

CALDWELL, WILLIAM HAMILTON (1850/1–1901), Coleraine, county Londonderry;
born 1850/1 at Aghadowey, county Londonderry, son of William Caldwell, farmer, of Aghadowey; educated at Killeague School, Aghadowey; studied medicine at Queen's College, Belfast, from 1874; MD MCh Dip Mid (QUI) 1880; general

practitioner and medical officer of health for Coleraine, of Waterside, Coleraine; married 5 August 1891 in Coleraine Methodist Church, Martha Rodgers, daughter of Samuel Rodgers, jeweller, of Coleraine; died 25 October 1901 in Coleraine. [Dub GRO (m) and (d); *Med Dir*; QCB adm reg].

CALDWELL, — (*fl c* 1856), Kells, county Antrim;
general practitioner, of Kells; married Jane Wilson (who married (2) 23 June 1857 in First Antrim Presbyterian Church, Thomas Kinnear), daughter of Henry Wilson, farmer, of Kells; died before 1857. [*BNL* 26 June 1857 (m); Dub GRO (m); *Londonderry Sentinel* 3 July 1857 (m)].

CALDWELL, — (1784/5–1857), Coleraine, county Londonderry;
born 1784/5; general practitioner, of Coleraine; married Elizabeth Ann — (who was born 1783/4 and died 24 November 1866 at Waterside, Killowen, Coleraine); died 22 February 1857 at Kells, county Antrim. [*Coleraine Chronicle* 28 February 1857 (d) and 1 December 1866 (d); Dub GRO (d); *Londonderry Sentinel* 30 November 1866 (d)].

CALLAN, JOHN (*fl c* 1730), Clogher;
of Clogher; studied medicine at Rheims University; MD (Rheims) 1730. [Brockliss].

CALVERT, JOSEPH WHITE (1849–89), Liverpool, Lancashire and American Steamship Company;
born 15 January 1849 at Whitehouse, county Antrim, youngest son of Joseph Calvert of Whitehouse and Sarah —; educated by the Rev G.H. Wilson of Belfast; studied medicine at Queen's College, Belfast, from 1865; LRCS Edin 1871; house surgeon to the Belfast General Hospital 1871–2; surgeon to Walton Prison, Liverpool; medical officer to the American Steamship Company c 1885; died 7 September 1889; commemorated in Carnmoney Graveyard. [Kirkpatrick Archive; *Med Dir*; QCB adm reg; Stewart (1994)].

CALWELL, WILLIAM (1850–1922), Wellington, Shropshire;
born 1850 at Ballyreagh, son of Andrew Calwell of Ballyreagh; educated at RBAI; studied medicine at Queen's College, Belfast, from 1868; LRCP LRCS Edin 1876; general practitioner of Springfield, Wellington, Shropshire, and surgeon to the Wellington Dispensary; married Isabel —; died 29 August 1922 at Springfield; probate Shrewsbury 19 October 1922. [Lond PPR, will cal, will; *Med Dir*; QCB adm reg].

CALWELL, WILLIAM, senior (1859–1943), Belfast;
born 26 June 1859, youngest son of Robert Calwell, merchant, of Annadale House, county Down, and Jane McDonnell; educated at RBAI; studied medicine at Queen's College, Belfast, from 1876, and St Thomas's Hospital, London; BA (QUI) 1880; MA 1881; MD MCh (RUI) 1883; LM KQCPI 1883; consulting surgeon to the Ulster Hospital for Children and Women 1887–1941; first 'registrar' to Belfast Royal Hospital 1894–5; assistant physician to Royal Hospital, Belfast 1895; gave annual winter oration at Royal Victoria Hospital 1898 and 1917; attending physician to

Royal Victoria Hospital 1900–24 with a special interest in dermatology and neurology; Lord Chancellor's Medical Visitor in Lunacy; consulting physician to County Antrim Infirmary, Belfast Charitable Institute and Throne Hospital; president of the Ulster Medical Society 1904–05 and 1905–06; lived at 1 College Square North, 56 Wellington Park, and 6 College Gardens, Belfast; OBE 1919; retired 1924; married 13 September 1892 in Holywood Church of Ireland Church, Helen Agnes Anderson (who was born 1868/9), daughter of lieutenant-colonel Robert Anderson of Richmond, Yorkshire; father of Dr Helen Marjorie Calwell, MB (QUB) 1919, who married 8 September 1920 in Knockbreda Church of Ireland Church, Robert Norman McNeill of Belfast, barrister; died 10 May 1943 at Wellington Park, Belfast; probate Belfast 20 January 1944. [*Belf Lit Soc* (1901); Belf PRO, will cal; Calwell (1979); Kirkpatrick Archive; Marshall and Kelly (1973); *Med Dir*; QCB adm reg; UHF database (m) x 2; Young and Pike (1909)].

CALWELL, WILLIAM, junior (1870–1958), Belfast;
born 10 May 1870 at Ballylesson, Glynn, county Antrim, son of Robert Calwell, builder, of 198 Old Park Road and Dock Street, Belfast, and Isabella Gault, who was sister of Dr Hugh Gault of Belfast (*q.v.*), brother of Dr Robert Bryson Calwell, MB (RUI) 1905, of 166 Crumlin Road, Belfast, Dr Gault Caldwell, MB (RUI) 1907, of 132 Ravenhill Road, Belfast, Dr Sarah Elizabeth Calwell, MB (QUB) 1912, of 71 Duncairn Gardens, Belfast, and Dr David Calwell, MB (QUB) 1913; educated at Belfast Model School; studied medicine at Queen's College, Belfast, from 1891; MB BCh BAO (RUI) 1897; general practitioner at 71 Duncairn Gardens c 1905 and 100 York Street, Belfast; married Amelia Taylor, daughter of William Taylor, partner in William Mullan and son, booksellers; father of Dr Isobel Calwell (Mrs Agnew), MB (QUB) 1927, of 69 Duncairn Gardens, Belfast, Dr Hugh Gault Calwell, MB (QUB) 1929, of Tanganyika and honorary archivist to the Royal Victoria Hospital, Belfast, Dr Margaret Gault Calwell (Mrs Gibson), MB (QUB) 1932, of Liverpool and Dr Robert Calwell, MB (QUB) 1939, of 100 York Street and the Planting Head, Whitehead; died 28 August 1958 at the Royal Victoria Hospital, Belfast; probate Belfast 18 January 1960. [Belf PRO, will cal; *Med Dir*; QCB adm reg; RVH, Office of Archives, papers; Walker and McCreary (1994)].

CAMAC, JAMES (1794/5–1870), Dervock, county Antrim;
born 1794/5, son of John Camac of The Garry, county Antrim, and Nancy Nevin of Kilmoyles; LFPS and LM Glas 1814; accoucheur of Glasgow Lying-in Hospital; medical officer to Dervock Dispensary District, constabulary and Liscolman Spinning Factory; married Isabella Rowan (who was born 1796/7 and died 12 September 1827); father of Dr Peter Gamble Camac (*q.v.*); died 8 May 1870 at Dervock. [*BNL* 28 September 1827 (d); Bennett (1974); Croly (1843–6); Dub GRO (d); gravestone inscription; *Med Dir*; Mullin (1969)].

CAMAC(K), PETER GAMBLE (1824/5–1912), Derrykeighan, Dervock, county Antrim;
born 1824/5, son of Dr James Camac (*q.v.*); studied medicine at Glasgow University; MD (Glas) 1845; CM 1877; general practitioner in Derrykeighan, Dervock; assistant medical officer to Ballymoney Fever Hospital from 1847; married 4 August 1849 in

Roseyards Presbyterian Church, Ballymoney, Jane Camac (a first cousin, who was born 1830/1 and died 26 December 1912), second daughter of Thomas Camac, farmer, of The Garry; father of Mary Matilda Camac who married Dr Robert John Roulston of East London, South Africa (*q.v.*), of Agnes Nevin Camac who married Dr Robert Craig Miller (*q.v.*) of Dervock, and Isabella Camac who married Dr James Laughlin Nevin (*q.v.*) of Ballymoney; died 10 June 1912 at Derrykeighan; probate Dublin 19 October 1912. [Addison (1898); Belf PRO, will cal; Bennett (1974); Burns (1988); *Coleraine Chronicle* 11 August 1849 (m); Dub GRO (d); gravestone inscription; *Londonderry Sentinel* 11 August 1849 (m); *Med Dir*; Mullin (1969); UHF database (m)].

CAMAC, ROBERT JOHN (1854–1900), Ballymoney, county Antrim;
born 22 August 1854, at Dervock, county Antrim, elder son of Robert Camac, merchant, of Dervock, county Antrim, and Hester Patrick of Mostragee; brother of Dr Samuel James Camac (*q.v.*); nephew of Dr James Camac (*q.v.*); educated at Coleraine Academical Institution; studied medicine at Queen's College, Belfast, from 1870; MD MCh (QUI) 1876; general practitioner, of High Street, Ballymoney; married 7 January 1882 in Second Broughshane Presbyterian Church, Matilda Parkhill (who died 4 June 1930), third daughter of Robert Parkhill, farmer, of Coldagh, Ballymoney; father of Dr James Camac of Church Gresley, Derbyshire, MB BCh BAO (QUB) 1919, who became partner of his uncle, Dr Robert Alexander Parkhill (*q.v.*); died 12 June 1900 at Coldagh; administration Belfast 27 August 1900. [Belf PRO, will cal; Bennett (1974); Dub GRO (d); *Med Dir*; Mullin (1969); QCB adm reg; UHF database (m)].

CAMAC, SAMUEL JAMES (1860–c 1906), Ballycastle, county Antrim, and New South Wales, Australia;
born 24 April 1860, at Dervock, younger son of Robert Camac, merchant, of Dervock, county Antrim, and Hester Patrick of Mostragee; brother of Dr Robert John Camac (*q.v.*); educated privately; studied medicine at Queen's College, Belfast, from 1878 and at Edinburgh; LRCP LRCS Edin 1884; general practitioner in Ballycastle; emigrated c 1895 to New South Wales; general practitioner, of Ultime, NSW; married 2 November 1886 in Ramoan Church of Ireland Church, Ballycastle, Madeline Stuart, daughter of Dr James Hamilton Stuart (*q.v.*) of Ballycastle; died c 1906. [Bennett (1974); *Med Dir*; Mullin (1969); QCB adm reg; UHF database (m)].

CAMERON, WILLIAM JOHN (1853–1929), London;
born 27 January 1853 at Craigywarren, Ballymena, county Antrim, son of James Cameron, farmer, of Craigywarren; educated at the Classical School, Ballymena and RBAI; studied medicine at Queen's College, Belfast, from 1880, the Royal College of Science, St Thomas's Hospital and London University; MB (Lond) 1892; headmaster of the classical department in Belfast Academy for 2 years in the middle of his medical course; consulting surgeon, of 'Two Oaks', Balham Park Road, London; surgeon to the Anti-Vivisection Hospital, Battersea; married 26 December 1885 Mary Louisa Haddon, daughter of William Haddon of Torquay; died 1 April 1929 at 17 Balham Park Road, London; probate London 31 May 1929. [Lond GRO (d); Lond PPR, will cal; *Med Dir*; QCB adm reg; Young and Pike (1909)].

CAMPEL, ROBERT (1659/60–1720), Magherally, county Down;
born 1659/60, 'chirurgeon' of Kilmacrew, Magherally; married Euphan —, (who was born 1666/7 and died 30 May 1702); died 19 June 1720; buried in Magherally Parish Graveyard. [Clarke, *County Down*, vol 20 (1989)].

CAMPBELL, ARTHUR ROBERT (1853–82), Indian Medical Service;
born 6 January 1853 at Hawick, Scotland, son of Robert Campbell of 3 Ormond Terrace, Rathmines, Dublin; educated at Glasgow High School; studied medicine at Queen's College, Belfast, from 1872; MD (QUI) 1874; LRCS Edin 1874; general practitioner, at Hemsworth, Pontefract, Yorkshire c 1875; joined the Indian Medical Service (Bombay establishment) as surgeon 1879; married 17 April 1875 in Donnybrook Church of Ireland Church, Dublin, Lucy Lee Bapty, eldest daughter of Frederic Bapty, merchant, of Dublin; died 2 April 1882 at Nimach, North India. [Crawford (1930); Dub GRO (m); Kirkpatrick Archive; *Med Dir*; QCB adm reg].

CAMPBELL, DAVID CLARKE (1860–1936), Crossgar and Annahilt, county Down, and Lisburn, county Antrim;
born 15 October 1860 at Ballymacarn, Ballynhinch, county Down, son of William Campbell, farmer, of Ballymacarn; educated at RBAI; studied medicine at Queen's College, Belfast, from 1879; MD (RUI) MCh MAO 1887; general practitioner, of Saintfield c 1888–92; medical officer to Crossgar Dispensary District and constabulary and certifying factory surgeon c 1892–1902; medical officer to Annahilt Dispensary District and constabulary and certifying factory surgeon c 1902–10; honorary surgeon to Dromore Cottage Hospital from 1902; JP for county Down; medical officer and medical officer of health for Lisburn Dispensary District c 1910–33; retired c 1933 to 11 Brooklyn Avenue, Bangor; married —; died 13 January 1936 at 11 Brooklyn Avenue; probate Belfast 12 May 1936. [Belf GRO (d); Belf PRO, will cal; Kirkpatrick Archive; *Med Dir*; QCB adm reg].

CAMPBELL, EDWARD (1766–c 1820);
born 1766 at Omagh, county Tyrone, son of John Campbell, gentleman, of Omagh; educated by Dr Murray; studied arts at Trinity College, Dublin 1782–7, BA (TCD) 1787; studied medicine at Edinburgh 1787–90 and at Leyden, Netherlands 1790–02; MD (Leyden) 1792 (thesis 'De haemorrhagia' in Leyden) 1792; LRCP Lond 1807; MA (TCD) 1811; incorporated at Oxford 1811; MB (Oxon) 1812; name last appears in the Royal College of Physicians register in 1820. [Burtchaell and Sadleir (1924); Foster (1888); *Munk's Roll*, vol 3; Innes Smith (1932); Underwood (1978)].

CAMPBELL, EDWARD McCLURE (1865–1933), Cambridge;
born 13 January 1865 in Lisburn, county Antrim, son of Dr John Campbell of Lisburn (*q.v.*); educated at RBAI; studied medicine at Queen's College, Belfast, from 1883; LRCP LRCS and LM Edin 1894; LFPS Glas 1894; general practitioner, of 5 Warkworth Villas, Warkworth Street, Cambridge, c 1895, of 12 Lindewood Road from c 1906, and of Beechwood House, 41 Hills Road, from c 1912; married 5 December 1894 in Lisburn Cathedral, Matilda Beatrice Bell (who was born 1865/6), daughter of William Laughry Bell, linen merchant, of Lisburn; father of Dr Edward

Cormier Campbell, MRCSE LRCP Lond 1930, of Cambridge; died 3 May 1933; probate Peterborough 24 July 1933. [Lond PPR, will cal, will; *Med Dir*; QCB adm reg; UHF database (m)].

CAMPBELL, EMILY FRANCES
See CHESTNUT, EMILY FRANCES

CAMPBELL, GEORGE (1768/9–1826), Naval Medical Service and Coagh, county Tyrone;
born 1768/9; joined the Naval Medical Service as assistant surgeon 1796; retired to his farm in Coagh; unmarried; died 16 September 1826 in Coagh; will dated 11 September 1826 ('sick in body but sound in mind') proved in Armagh Diocesan Court 7 July 1832 (original will and papers in PRO NI). [*BNL* 22 September 1826; Belf PRO, D1118/14/C/9/A–B; *NMS* (1826)].

CAMPBELL, HENRY (1868–1917), Cardiff, Glamorgan;
born 12 March 1868 at Newtowncrommelin, county Antrim, son of John Campbell, farmer, of Newtowncrommelin; older brother of Dr Frederick William Campbell, MRCSE LRCP Lond 1912, of Cardiff; educated at Methodist College, Belfast [?]; studied medicine at Queen's College, Galway, and from 1887, at Queen's College, Belfast; LRCP LRCS Edin 1893; LFPS Glas 1893; MD (Durham) 1908; general practitioner, of 'Glenariff', 349 Cowbridge Road, Cardiff from c 1900 with his brother; honorary surgeon to Cardiff Race Club; married Edith Ellen —; died 19 June 1917; administration London 26 September 1917. [*BMJ* obituary (1917); Kirkpatrick Archive; Lond PPR, will call; *Med Dir*; QCB adm reg].

CAMPBELL, JAMES (*fl c* 1796), Lisburn, county Antrim;
LAH Dub 1796; apothecary, of Lisburn. [Apothecaries (1829)].

CAMPBELL, JAMES (*fl c* 1826), Belfast;
surgeon, of Belfast [?]; married 20 September 1826 Rose Anne Shaw, second daughter of John Shaw of Belfast; died 25 March 1831 in London. [*BNL* 22 September 1826 (m) and 5 April 1831 (d)].

CAMPBELL, JAMES (d 1851), Omagh, county Tyrone, and London;
LRCSI; surgeon, of Gortmore, Omagh c 1845; moved to London; died 1851; probate Prerogative Court 1851. [Belf PRO, prerog wills index; Croly (1843–6)].

CAMPBELL, JAMES (1794/5–1853), New York, USA;
born 1794/5, son of the Rev Robert Campbell of Killeeshil, county Tyrone (who was presumably the Rev Robert Campbell, curate of Boho, county Fermanagh, and later of Carrickmacross, county Monaghan); emigrated to USA; died 1853 in New York. [*BNL* 20 April 1853 (d); Leslie (1928)].

CAMPBELL, JAMES DAVIS (*fl c* 1791–1824), Armagh;
LAH Dub 1791; MD [?]; apothecary and physician, of Vicar's Hill, Armagh c 1819 and 1824. [Apothecaries (1829); Bradshaw (1819); Pigot (1824)].

CAMPBELL, JARVIS (b 1836/7), Ahoghill, county Antrim;
born 1836/7, son of Dr John Campbell (*q.v.*); LM Belf Lying-in Hosp 1876; surgeon, of Ahoghill [not in *Medical Directory*]; married 13 February 1864 in Connor Church of Ireland Church, county Antrim, Christina Harper (who was born 1839/40), eldest daughter of Robert Harper, farmer, of Slaght, Connor. [*Ballymena Observer* 15 July 1976 (news); Dub GRO (m); *Londonderry Sentinel* 19 February 1864 (m)].

CAMPBELL, JOHN (d 1804), Carrickfergus, county Antrim;
surgeon, apothecary and burgess of Carrickfergus; died April 1804. [*BNL* 6 April 1804 (d)].

CAMPBELL, JOHN (d 1828), Belfast;
surgeon, apothecary and practitioner in midwifery, of 68 and 76 Donegall Street, Belfast c 1807–19, also 8 Donegall Street and 30 High Street c 1824; married Elizabeth Anne — (who was born 1754/5 and died 30 April 1836); father of John Campbell who was born 1785/6; died 4 July 1828. [*Belfast Directories*, 1807, 1808 and 1819; *BNL* 8 July 1828 (d), 6 May 1836 (d) and 27 May 1836 (d, son); Malcolm (1851); Pigot (1824)].

CAMPBELL, JOHN (*fl c* 1834–64), Belturbet, county Cavan;
surgeon, probably of Belturbet; married c 1834 —; father of Dr Jarvis Campbell (*q.v.*). [Dub GRO (m, son); McCabe, John, pers com].

CAMPBELL, JOHN (1807–32), Blackwatertown, county Armagh;
born 1807; surgeon, of Blackwatertown; died 5 December 1832 of cholera, 'literally killed by over-exertion at the commencement of disease in Blackwatertown'. [*BNL* 14 December 1832 (d)].

CAMPBELL, JOHN (1818/9–67), Lisburn, county Antrim;
born 1818/9; MRCSE 1842; LAH Dub 1842; MD (St Andrew's) 1850 (by examination); medical officer to Lisburn Workhouse, Fever Hospital and constabulary and to the Manor and Temporary Fever Hospitals, Lisburn; performed a Caesarean section operation under chloroform anaesthesia on a woman in a 'wretched cabin' near Dromore, county Down, on 18 May 1849; county coroner; married Sarah McClure (who died 16 January 1914 at Island House, Lisburn); father of Dr Edward McClure Campbell (*q.v.*); died 6 September 1867 at Market Square, Lisburn; buried in Blaris graveyard, and also commemorated in Lisburn Cathedral Graveyard; probate Belfast 25 October 1867. [*BNL* 7 September 1867 (d) and 19 January 1914 (d); Belf PRO, will cal; Clarke, *County Down*, vol 5 (1984); Croly (1843–6); Dub GRO (d); *Lisburn Fam Hist Soc*, vol 2 (2005); *Med Dir*; O'Sullivan (1990); Smart (2004)].

CAMPBELL, SIR JOHN (1862–1929), Belfast;
born 18 February 1862 at Templepatrick, elder son of the Rev Robert Campbell, minister of Templepatrick Old Presbyterian Congregation, and Elizabeth Simpson; brother of Dr Robert Campbell (*q.v.*); educated in Holywood and at RBAI; studied arts and medicine at Queen's College, Belfast, from 1880, also at the London

Hospital, Paris and Vienna; BA (RUI) 1883; MA (with first class hons) 1884; Coulter Exhibition, Belfast Royal Hospital, 1887; MD MCh MAO 1887; MRCSE 1888; FRCSE 1891; LLD (RUI) (*hon causa*) 1909; demonstrator in anatomy at Queen's College, Belfast 1888–91; assistant surgeon Belfast Hospital for Sick Children 1891–2; attending surgeon (gynaecologist) Samaritan Hospital from 1892 and later to the Belfast Maternity Hospital; first Irish surgeon to close a perforating gastric ulcer, July 1897; president of the Ulster Medical Society 1902–03 and 1903–04; surgeon to British Red Cross Hospital, Wimereux, France, during World War I; MP for Queen's University, Belfast (NI Parliament) 1922–9; knight bachelor 1925; author of *Obstetrics and Gynaecology* (1908) and *A Textbook of Treatment* (1908) and papers on obstetrics and gynaecology; lived at Crescent House, University Road, Belfast and later at Culloden, Craigavad; married in 1902 Dr Emily Frances Fitzsimons, nee Chestnut (*q.v.*); father of Mr William Stewart Campbell, MB (QUB) 1932, FRCS, gynaecologist; died 31 August 1929 at Culloden; buried in Templepatrick Old Graveyard; probate Belfast 7 March 1930. [*Belf Lit Soc* (1901); Belf GRO (d); Belf PRO, will cal; *Belf Roy Hosp, Ann Rep*; *BMJ* obituary (1929); Calwell (1973); Crone (1928); *DIB* (2009); Dub GRO (b) (son); gravestone inscription; Hunter (1936); Kirkpatrick Archive; *Lancet* obituary (1929); *Med Dir*; Mitchell (1900); Moody and Beckett (1959); Newmann (1993); Plarr (1930); QCB adm reg].

CAMPBELL, JOHN (c 1872–c 1953), Plumbridge, county Tyrone, and towns in England, Wales and Scotland;
born c 1872; studied medicine at the Royal College of Surgeons in Ireland and the Meath and Coombe Hospitals, Dublin; LRCPI and LM 1894; LRCSI and LM 1894; medical officer in Castleton, Lancashire, Plumbridge, Tyrone, Swinefleet, Reeth and Richmond, Yorkshire, Tow Law, Durham, Chesterfield, Derbyshire, Langholm, Dunfriesshire, Pontycymmer, Glamorgan, Wraysbury, Buckinghamshire, and Larkfield Lodge, Hampton Hill, Middlesex, between 1896 and 1948; retired c 1948; died c 1953. [*Med Dir*].

CAMPBELL, JOHN ALEXANDER (1843–89), Army Medical Service;
born 10 January 1843; probably from Dungiven, county Londonderry; studied medicine at Dr Steeven's Hospital, Dublin; LM Dr Steeven's Hosp Dub; LRCP LRCS Edin 1864; joined the Army Medical Service as staff assistant surgeon 1865; on half pay 1875–8; surgeon major 1880; retired 1888 to 50 Lady Margaret Road, Kentish Town, London; died 18 March 1889 at 50 Lady Margaret Road; probate London 18 April 1889. [Lond PPR, will cal; *Med Dir*; Peterkin and Johnston (1968)].

CAMPBELL, LOFTUS (d c 1897), Enniskillen, county Fermanagh, and New South Wales, Australia;
LRCSI 1883; LRCP Edin 1885; of Derrykean, Enniskillen; emigrated to Australia c 1890; general physician, of Barraba, New South Wales; died c 1897. [*Med Dir*].

CAMPBELL, MARCUS DILL (b 1839), Ramelton, county Donegal, and India;
born 1839, third son of Samuel Campbell of Glenleary, Ballymagowan, Kerrykeel, Fanad, county Donegal, and Mary Dill of Springfield, Tamney, county Donegal; brother of Dr Samuel Campbell (*q.v.*); studied medicine at Glasgow University; BA

(Glas) 1845; MA 1846; MD 1850; general practitioner, of Ramelton; unmarried; died in India. [Addison (1898); Meade (1979)].

CAMPBELL, MICHAEL (1810/1–46), East Indies;
born 1810/1; studied medicine at Edinburgh University; MD (Edin) 1833; (thesis 'De ascite'); medical officer at Comercully [?], East Indies; died 21 November 1846 at Comercully. [*BNL* 2 February 1847 (d); Edin Univ].

CAMPBELL, RICHARD, (1857–c 1922), London;
born 4 September 1857 at Millisle, county Down, son of John Campbell, farmer, of Ballyhaskin, educated at RBAI; studied medicine at Queen's College, Belfast, from 1874, and at the Glasgow Royal Infirmary; MD (QUI) 1880; MCh 1881; LM KQCPI 1882; moved to London c 1883, of 83 Virginia Road, Shoreditch, from c 1885 and also of 20 Navarino Road, Dalston c 1890; died c 1922. [*Med Dir*; QCB adm reg].

CAMPBELL, ROBERT (*fl c* 1807–10), Greyabbey, county Down;
surgeon, of Greyabbey; treated a patient with dropsy and ascites in 1808–10 and removed 140 gallons of fluid over 16 months; married in May 1807 — McVee of Whitechurch. [*BNL* 24 April 1810; Farrar (1897)].

CAMPBELL, ROBERT (b 1849), New York;
born 10 January 1849 in New York, son of Andrew Campbell of 404 Fourth Avenue, New York; educated at New York College; studied medicine at the College of Physicians and Surgeons in New York and, from 1869, at Queen's College, Belfast; MD (QUI) 1872; presumably returned to New York. [QCB adm reg].

CAMPBELL, ROBERT (1866–1920), Chester and Belfast;
born 1 August 1866, second son of the Rev Robert Campbell, minister of Templepatrick Old Presbyterian Congregation, and Elizabeth Simpson; brother of Sir John Campbell MD (*q.v.*); educated at Roughfort and RBAI; studied arts and medicine at Queen's College, Belfast, from 1884; BA (hons) (RUI) 1887; Coulter Exhibition, Belfast Royal Hospital, 1891; MB BCh BAO (hons) 1892; MRCSE LRCP Lond 1893; FRCSE 1896; demonstrator in anatomy, Queen's College, Belfast 1892–3; house surgeon at St Thomas's Hospital, London 1893–4; resident physician to Chester Infirmary 1894–6; assistant surgeon to the Belfast Hospital for Sick Children 1897 and attending surgeon 1898–1920; pioneer in the outpatient surgery of inguinal hernia in children; assistant surgeon to the Royal Victoria Hospital 1900–12 and attending surgeon 1912–20; gave annual winter oration at Royal Victoria Hospital 1901; surgeon to the Ulster Volunteer Force Hospital, Belfast 1915–18; president of the Ulster Medical Society 1916–17; married Amy Isobella MacTaggart of Eltham, matron of the Belfast Hospital for Sick Children (who died 1 April 1935); lived at 21 and 63 Great Victoria Street, Belfast and 2 College Gardens; died 6 September 1920, buried in Templepatrick Old Graveyard; commemorated by memorial there and by an Ulster Medical Society Oration, with a portrait-medal by Rosamond Praeger; probate Belfast 3 December 1920. [*Belf Lit Soc* (1901); Belf PRO, will cal; *Belf Roy Hosp, Ann Rep*; *BMJ* obituary (1920); Calwell (1991); Campbell

(1963b); gravestone inscription; Hunter (1936); Kirkpatrick Archive; *Lancet* obituary (1920); *Med Dir*; O'Brien, Crookshank and Wolstenholme (1988); O'Donnell (2008); Plarr (1930); QCB adm reg].

CAMPBELL, SAMUEL (1832–1910), Naval Medical Service;
born 3 January 1832, second son of Samuel Campbell of Glenleary, Ballymagowan, Kerrykeel, Fanad, county Donegal, and Mary Dill of Springfield, Tamney, county Donegal; brother of Dr Marcus Dill Campbell (*q.v.*); studied medicine at Glasgow University from 1851; MD (Glas) 1856; LRCS Edin 1856; joined the Naval Medical Service as assistant surgeon 1856, serving on HMS *Victory* for a few months and then on HMS *Plumper*, which was being fitted up as a surveying ship to work in British Columbia; set up a shore hospital in Esquimalt but worked mainly as a surveyor up the Fraser River and along the coast; returned to Woolwich for leave 1864; returned to surveying work on HMS *Nassau* 1866, this time to the Straits of Magellan and Patagonia; also involved there in botanical studies with Dr Robert Oliver Cunningham (*q.v.*); had geographical features in British Columbia and Patagonia named after him; promoted to surgeon 1867; returned to England 1869 and was appointed to HMS *Ocean* 1869 and to HMS *Sylvia* 1870, for service in China; returned home again 1877 and transferred to HMS *Implacable* and HMS *Northumberland*; retired to Fanad because of ill health 1880; unmarried; died 20 February 1910 at Ballymagowan, Fanad; buried in Rossnakill graveyard, county Donegal. [Addison (1898); Dub GRO (d); Meade (1979); *Med Dir*].

CAMPBELL, SAMUEL HENRY (c 1822–1901), Portrush, county Antrim;
born c 1822, son of James Campbell, gentleman; studied medicine at Glasgow University; MD (Glas) 1844; CM 1862; LFPS Glas and LM 1864; medical officer to Portrush Dispensary District, the constabulary and coastguard service, of Mark Street Cottage, Portrush; married 28 March 1848 in Lissan Church of Ireland Church, county Tyrone, Anne Louisa Dunn (who was born 1825/6 and died 21 July 1858 at Hill Street, Stoke-on-Trent; buried in Ballywillan graveyard), eldest daughter of Thomas Dunn of Muff, Cookstown, surgeon RN (*q.v.*); died 10 December 1901 at 68 Main Street, Portrush. [Addison (1898); *BNL* 4 April 1848 (m) and 4 August 1858 (d); *Coleraine Chronicle* 1 April 1848 (m); Dub GRO (m) and (d); *Londonderry Sentinel* 6 August 1858 (d); *Med Dir*].

CAMPBELL, SAMUEL MARCUS DILL (1875–1953), Dovercourt, Essex;
born 8 January 1875 at Glenleary, county Donegal, son of David Campbell, farmer, of Glenleary; educated at Dungannon Royal School; studied medicine at Queen's College, Belfast, from 1895 and at Edinburgh University; MB BCh (Edin) 1900; moved to Dovercourt, Essex, c 1907; medical officer and public vaccinator, 1st and 2nd Districts, Tendering Union, Essex, from c 1910; honorary surgeon to Fryatt Memorial Cottage Hospital, Dovercourt, Essex; of Glenleary, Dovercourt c 1914–48, and of The Windmill House, Ramsey c 1948–53; married Olive Jane —; father of Dr Marcus Samuel Campbell, MB (QUB) 1934, of Dovercourt; died 8 December 1953 at The Windmill House; probate Ipswich 22 July 1954. [Lond GRO (d); Lond PPR, will cal; *Med Dir*; QCB adm reg].

CAMPBELL, THOMAS VINCENT (1863–1930), Mysore, India;
born 1863 at Londonderry; studied medicine at Edinburgh University; MA (Edin) 1884; MB CM 1888; medical missionary at Jammalamadugu, South India, from 1890, with a home address of Ballynagard House, Londonderry; in charge of the London Mission Hospital at Chikka Ballapur, Mysore, India; awarded the Kaisar-I-Hind medal in 1908; married Dr Florence Gertrude Longbottom, MB (Lond) 1891, of Halifax, Yorkshire; died 16 December 1930. [Kirkpatrick (1889); Kirkpatrick Archive; *Lancet* obituary (1930); *Med Dir*].

CAMPBELL, WILLIAM (d c 1791), Bunnoe, county Cavan;
of Bunnoe; probate Prerogative Court 1791. [Vicars (1897)].

CAMPBELL, WILLIAM WILSON (d 1858), Dublin and Portstewart, county Londonderry;
MD; LRCSI; FRCSI; accoucheur of Dublin Lying-in Hospital (Rotunda); assistant master of Rotunda Hospital, 1834–7; general practitioner, of The Castle, Portstewart c 1846; JP; MRIA; died 19 January 1858 at The Castle. [Croly (1843–6); Kirkpatrick Archive; Kirkpatrick and Jellett (1913); *Med Dir*].

CANNING, JOHN (*fl c* 1829–40), Garvagh, county Londonderry;
MD [?]; physician and surgeon, of Garvagh; married 17 November 1829, in the bride's home, Margaret Moore, (who subsequently married on 21 August 1849 Dr Hugh Glenholme of Magherafelt (*q.v.*)), daughter of Samuel Moore of Clintagh, county Londonderry; died before 1846 (not in Croly's *Directory*). [*BNL* 1 December 1829 (m) and 28 August 1849 (m); *Coleraine Chronicle* 25 August 1849 (m) *Londonderry Sentinel* 28 November 1829 (m)].

CANNING, WILLIAM (1869–1932), Cardiff, Glamorgan, and Rockcorry and Clones, county Monaghan;
born 24 January 1869 at Newtownhamilton, county Armagh, son of Patrick Canning, merchant, of Newtownhamilton, and Elizabeth —; educated at St Malachy's College, Belfast; studied medicine at Queen's College, Belfast, from 1886; MB BCh BAO (RUI) 1897; general practitioner, of Cardiff; medical officer to Rockcorry Dispensary District and constabulary 1900–28 and to Clones Dispensary District, from c 1930, of Altmore House, Clones; unmarried; died 19 March 1932 at the Diamond, Clones; buried in Newtownhamilton Roman Catholic Graveyard. [Dub GRO (d); gravestone inscription; Kirkpatrick Archive; *Med Dir*; QCB adm reg].

CANNON, PATRICK (d 1860), Kilteevock and Letterkenny, county Donegal;
LM Rot Hosp Dub 1840; LRCSI 1841; medical officer of Kilteevock Dispensary District, c 1842–8; general practitioner, of Rosemount, Letterkenny c 1848–60; died 18 May 1860 at Rosemount. [Croly (1843–6); Kirkpatrick Archive; *Londonderry Sentinel* 25 May 1860 (d); *Med Dir*].

CANNON, PHILIP (*fl c* 1837), Ballymena, county Antrim;
probably son of Philip Cannon; general practitioner, of Castle, Ballymena c 1834 and 1837; married 9 August 1834 in Ahoghill Church of Ireland Church, Sarah

Mary Stafford, second daughter of Lennox Stafford of Gracehill, county Antrim, captain in 27th Foot. [*BNL* 12 August 1834 (m); Lewis (1837)].

CANTRELL, THOMAS JOSEPH (*fl c* 1852–85), Belfast;
son of James Cantrell, chemist, of Belfast; LAH; apothecary and surgeon and member of the Ulster Medical Society; formed the company of Cantrell and Cochrane, with Henry Cochrane of Dublin (later Alderman Sir Henry Cochrane), in Belfast in 1852; sank artesian wells in Belfast to obtain pure water which was aerated to produce 'soda water'; also founded the Ulster Medical Hall, Castle Place, Belfast, in 1852, which became Davidson & Leslie, Pharmaceutical Chemists, in 1869; 'in failing health' in 1885 and the partnership with Cochrane was dissolved; married 5 September 1855 in St Anne's Church of Ireland Church, Belfast, Mary Anne Hanlon, daughter of James Hanlon, merchant. [Dub GRO (m); *Industries of the North* (1986); UMS list].

CARBERRY, EDWARD OLIVER BAMFORD (1872–1962), Naval Medical Service;
born 15 May 1872 at Georgetown, British Guiana, son of Edward Carberry, barrister; educated at Christ's Hospital; studied arts and medicine at Queen's College, Galway, from 1889 and medicine at Queen's College, Belfast, from 1895; MB BCh BAO (RUI) 1897; house physician in the City of London Chest Hospital; joined the Naval Medical Service 1900 as staff surgeon, with home address at Hillcroft, Winchester, Hampshire; fleet surgeon c 1915; OBE (military division) 1919; temporarily transferred to RAF as lieutenant-colonel c 1920; retired as surgeon captain RN c 1925 to Drostre House, Tal-y-Llyn, Breconshire; of 11 Herbert Park, Dublin, from 1930 and of The Forge, Upton-on-Severn, and Raffdene, Wills Road, Malvern, Worcestershire from c 1939 and finally to Froome House, Mordiford, near Hereford c 1960; died 25 May 1962 at Clanmere Nursing Home, near Malvern; probate Bristol 5 September 1962. [Kirkpatrick Archive; Lond PPR, will cal; *Med Dir*; QCB adm reg].

CAREW, EDWARD JOHN (*fl c* 1840), Belfast;
LAH Dublin 1834; general practitioner, of 17 Academy Street, Belfast; probably died before 1850. [*Belfast Street Directories*].

CAREY, JAMES MAHER (d 1860), Carlow and Kildare;
MRCSE 1842; LM Rot Hosp Dub 1842; LAH Dub 1846; general practitioner of Tullow Street, Carlow, c 1852–3; medical officer to Newbridge and Kildare Dispensary District c 1853–60; died 1860 probably at Warrenpoint. [*Med Dir*].

CARGIN, JOHN SIDNEY (1874–1911), Belfast and Chester;
born 28 September 1874 at Dromore, county Down, son of Alexander Cargin, draper, of Bridge Street, Dromore; educated at Lurgan College; studied medicine at Queen's College, Belfast, from 1893; MB BCh BAO (RUI) 1900; MD 1905; of 27 Wellington Park, Belfast c 1905; general practitioner, moved c 1907 to Holland House, Seabank Road, Liscard, Cheshire; died 6 October 1911 at Chester General Infirmary, following a car accident; buried in First Dromore Presbyterian graveyard; administration Chester 4 December 1911. [Clarke, *County Down*, vol 19 (1983); Lond GRO (d); Lond PPR, will cal; *Med Dir*; QCB adm reg].

CARLETON, F. (*fl c* 1854), Draperstown, county Londonderry;
general practitioner, of Draperstown c 1854; father of Dr Patrick Maurice Carleton (*q.v.*). [QCB adm reg (for son)].

CARLETON, PATRICK MAURICE (1854–c 1936), Army Medical Service and Londonderry;
born 24 March 1854 at Draperstown, county Londonderry, son of Dr F. Carleton (*q.v.*) of Draperstown; educated at Belfast Academy; studied medicine at Queen's College, Belfast, from 1872; MD (QUI) and LM 1877; MCh 1878; joined the Army Medical Service as surgeon captain 1880; surgeon major RAMC 1892; served in Burma in 1892–3, in South Africa 1900; retired as major 1901; barrister-at-law, Inner Temple; of Cloverhill House, Maghera, county Londonderry; JP for county Londonderry; retired c 1937; died c 1947. [*Med Dir*; Peterkin and Johnston (1968); QCB adm reg].

CARLI(S)LE, HUGH (c 1794–1860), Belfast;
born c 1794 at Armagh (or Newry), son of Hugh Carlile, merchant, and his first wife Sarah Ogle; educated at Dr Andrew O'Beirne's School, Carrickfergus; studied arts and medicine at Trinity College, Dublin 1812–17; BA (TCD) 1817; MB 1837; MA MD 1849; demonstrator in anatomy and assistant to his uncle James Macartney, professor of anatomy and physiology at Trinity College, Dublin, 1832–7; one of the proprietors and professor of anatomy and physiology of the Park Street School of Medicine, Dublin 1837–49; professor of anatomy and physiology, Queen's College, Belfast, 1849–60; brought with him from Park Street the anatomy museum which Queen's College bought for £250; author of various medical papers; married 5 October 1829 Sarah Jane Boyd nee Macartney (who died 26 July 1855 at Prospect Terrace, Belfast), widow of Hugh Boyd; died 22 February 1860 at Holywood, county Down; buried in St Patrick's Church of Ireland Graveyard, Newry; portrait in Queen's University, Belfast; probate Dublin 12 April 1860. [*BNL* 1 August 1855 (d) and 24 February 1860 (d); Belf PRO, T618/ 326, T618/ 333; Belf PRO, will cal; Black (1995); Burtchaell and Sadleir (1924); Cameron (1916); Clarke, *County Down*, vol 21 (1998); Harrison (1980); Kirkpatrick Archive; *Med Dir*; Moody and Beckett (1959); Roddie (1987)].

CARLISLE, JAMES (1847–1928), Annacloy, county Down, and Belfast;
born 19 March 1847 at Drumgiven, Crossgar, son of Robert Carlisle, farmer; studied medicine at Queen's College, Belfast, from 1864; LFPS Glas and LM 1869; general practitioner, certifying factory surgeon and medical officer to the constabulary, of Annacloy, Crossgar; retired first to Cargagh, near Downpatrick, and then to 20 Ashley Gardens, Belfast c 1923; married 30 June 1868 in Kilmore Presbyterian Church, county Down; Ellen Morrison, daughter of Samuel Morrison, farmer, of Ballylone, county Down; died 20 December 1928 at Ashley Gardens; probate Belfast 7 February 1929. [Belf GRO (d); Belf PRO, will cal; Kirkpatrick Archive; *Med Dir*; QCB adm reg; UHF database (m)].

CARLI(S)LE, NEWTON (d 1839), Castlewellan, county Down and Coburg, Canada; LAH Dub 1828; apothecary, of Castlewellan; emigrated to Canada; married —; died April 1839 of apoplexy in Coburg near Toronto. [Apothecaries (1829); *BNL* 9 July 1839 (d); Croly (1843–6)].

CARLISLE, SAMUEL BURNS (1865–1927), Dromore, county Down;
born 4 March 1865, son of Henry Carlisle, farmer, of Ballylone, Ballynahinch; educated at Ballynahinch Intermediate School; studied medicine at Queen's College, Belfast, from 1881; LRCP LRCS Edin 1890; LRFPS Glas 1890; general practitioner in Dromore; married 23 June 1896 at Rockmore Cottage, Ballynahinch, Ellen Russell, daughter of Hans Russll, farmer, of Rockmore Cottage; father of Dr Samuel Burns Carlisle, junior; died 17 December 1927 at Church Road, Dromore; administration Belfast 29 August 1928. [Belf GRO (d); Belf PRO, will cal; Dub GRO (m) *Med Dir*; QCB adm reg; UHF database (m)].

CARLISLE, WILLIAM HENRY (1857–1942), Belfast and Bangor, county Down;
born 17 February 1857 in Belfast, son of David Carlisle, master painter, of 29 Lincoln Avenue, Belfast; educated at Nelson Street School; studied medicine at Queen's College, Belfast, from 1881; LRCP LRCS Edin 1890; LFPS Glas 1890; general practitioner, of 29 Lincoln Avenue c 1895 and Duncairn Gardens, Belfast c 1900–18; of 76 Donaghadee Road, Bangor, c 1918–42; married —; died 21 December 1942 at Bangor Cottage Hospital. [Belf GRO (d); *Med Dir*; QCB adm reg].

CARMALT, THOMAS BARRY (1816/7–46), Antigua, West Indies;
born 1816/7, son of Lieutenant Thomas Carmalt, RN, of Brook Hill, Londonderry, and later 7 Ardgowan Street, Greenock, Renfrewshire, and Jane —; medical officer in Antigua; married 23 January 1845 in St Luke's Church, St John's, Antigua, Anne Sanderson, second daughter of the Hon Thomas Sanderson, Speaker of the House of Assembly, and Master in Chancery, Antigua; died 4 February 1846 at St John's, Antigua. [*Londonderry Sentinel* 1 March 1845 (m) and 21 March 1846 (d)].

CARMICHAEL, THOMAS (1843–c 1900), Malabar, India;
born 18 November 1843 at Cairncastle, county Antrim, son of Rev James Carmichael, minister of Cairncastle Presbyterian Church, county Antrim; educated at RBAI; studied medicine at Queen's College, Belfast, from 1860; MD (QUI) 1866; LRCS Edin 1866; medical officer at Vithray, South Wyniad, Malabar, from c 1870; died c 1900. [*Med Dir*; QCB adm reg].

CARNAGHAN
See KERNAHAN

CARNEY, JAMES (1827/8–80), Ballybay, county Monaghan, and Berbice, British Guiana;
born 1827/8; LFPS Glas 1855; LRCP Edin 1867; general practitioner in Ballybay; working in Berbice, British Guiana briefly c 1876; unmarried; died 10 November 1880 at Market Street, Coothill, county Cavan; probate Dublin 20 December 1881. [Belf PRO, will cal; Dub GRO (d); *Med Dir*].

CARNSTON, WILLIAM (*fl c* 1866), Aughnamullen, county Monaghan; general practitioner, of Aughnamullen, c 1856–76. [McCann (2003)].

CARPENTER, EDGAR GODFREY BOYD (1865/6–1943), Hull, Yorkshire, Cairo, Egypt, Naval and Army Medical Services and Orient Steamship Company; born 1865 in the 'North of Ireland', son of the Rev Henry George Carpenter of Liverpool and Alice Catherine Ball of Killybegs, county Donegal; nephew of the Rev William Boyd Carpenter, Bishop of Ripon; educated at Blundell's School, Tiverton, Devon; studied medicine at St Bartholomew's Hospital, London; LRCP Lond MRCSE 1889; DPH Camb 1895; FRCSE 1900; assistant house surgeon at the East Suffolk and Ipswich Hospital and at the Royal Infirmary, Hull; resident surgeon to the Kasr-el-Aini Hospital, Cairo and sub-director of public health at Alexandria; surgeon in the Royal Navy during World War I, serving in a merchant cruiser and later in HMS *Glasgow*; transferred to RAMC as temporary captain in 1917, serving on Salisbury Plain and Southhampton and after the war winding up VAD hospitals in south-west England; ship's surgeon with the Orient Steamship Company for nine years travelling to and from Australia; retired c 1930 and lived at York House, London Road, Worcester; returned to work with the local medical board during World War II; became ill in 1941 and moved to the Isle of Man in 1942; died 1 April 1943 at Noble's Hospital, Douglas; probate Llandudno 2 June 1943. [Leslie (1940); Lond PPR, will cal; *Med Dir*; Power and Le Fanu (1953)].

CARR, JOHN MITCHELL (d c 1909), Tullamore, King's County, Newtownhamilton, county Leitrim, and Cootehill, county Cavan; studied medicine at the Ledwich School, Dublin; LRCS Edin 1878; LRCP Edin 1880; general practitioner in Tullamore c 1880–95 and in Newtownhamilton c 1895–1903; medical officer to Tyllyvin Dispensary District, Cootehill, county Cavan c 1903–09; died c 1909. [*Med Dir*].

CARRE, FENWICK (1845/6–1915), Bellaghy, county Londonderry and Ramelton and Letterkenny, county Donegal; born 1845/6, son of the Rev Henry Carre, rector of Glencolumbkill and (later) prebendary of Inver, county Donegal, and Jane Inch; brother of Dr George Edward Carre (*q.v.*); studied medicine at the Ledwich School, Meath and Mercers' Hospitals and Trinity College, Dublin; MRCSI 1866; LKQCPI and LM 1866; FRCSI 1871; medical officer to Bellaghy Dispensary District c 1871–4 and to Ramelton Dispensary District and Fever Hospital from c 1874; medical officer to Letterkenny Dispensary District, Fever Hospital, constabulary and troops and vistor and consulting physician to the county Donegal Lunatic Asylum, living at Sprackburn House, Letterkenny, c 1905; JP; unmarried; died 3 April 1915 at Sprackburn House; probate Dublin 1 June 1915. [Belf PRO, will cal; Bellaghy Hist Soc (2003); Dub GRO (d); Leslie (1940); *Med Dir*].

CARRE, GEORGE EDWARD (1833/4–1929), Ramelton, county Donegal, Castlebar, county Mayo, and Omagh, county Tyrone; born 1833/4, son of the Rev Henry Carre, rector of Glencolumbkill and (later) prebendary of Inver, county Donegal, and Jane Inch; brother of Dr Fenwick Carre (*q.v.*); studied medicine at the Ledwich School, Royal College of Surgeons in Ireland, Meath, Mercers, and Sir Patrick Dun's Hospitals and Trinity College, Dublin; BA (TCD) 1858; MB 1858; LRCSI 1858; LM Rot Hosp Dub; medical officer to Ballinamore Dispensary District; medical officer to Ramelton Dispensary District and Fever Hospital c 1865, of Ayr Hill, Ramelton; consulting and visiting physician to Donegal District Lunatic Asylum from 1870; medical officer to Letterkenny Dispensary District and Fever Hospital and constabulary from 1873; resident medical superintendant to the District Lunatic Hospital, Castlebar, from 1874; resident medical superintendent to the District Lunatic Asylum, Omagh, from 1880; retired c 1914 to Noel Lodge, Silchester Road, Glenageary, county Dublin; married 3 April 1861 Emily Sophia Box of Dublin; father of Dr Henry Carre (*q.v.*); died 22 January 1929 at Noel Lodge; probate Belfast 2 May 1930. [Belf PRO, will cal, will; Burtchaell and Sadleir (1935); Kirkpatrick Archive; Leslie (1940); *Med Dir*].

CARRE, HENRY (1871–1947), Omagh, county Tyrone, Gortnavel, Shrewsbury, Shropshire, and Glasgow, Lanarkshire;
born 8 December 1871 at Ayr Hill, Ramelton, son of Dr George Edward Carre (*q.v.*); studied medicine at the Royal College of Surgeons in Ireland and Trinity College, Dublin; LRCPI and LM 1893; LRCSI and LM 1893; medical officer to the District Lunatic Asylum, Omagh c 1893–6; clinical clerk to the Royal Asylum, Gortnavel, c 1896; junior assistant medical officer to Salop and Montgomery County Asylum, Bicton Heath, Shrewsbury c 1896–8; assistant medical officer and later medical superintendent to the Barony Parochial Asylum, Woodilee, Lenzie, Glasgow, c 1898–1938; retired c 1938 to Broadwood, Gifford, East Lothian; married Elizabeth Tennent Montgomerie-Fleming; died 14 June 1947 at Broadwood; confirmation of will Haddington, 20 August 1947. [Dub GRO (b); Edin GRO (d); Edin, Nat Arch; Kirkpatrick Archive; *Med Dir*].

CARROL, MAJOR (d 1812), Army Medical Service;
joined the Army Medical Service as surgeon to the East Indiaman *Nottingham* 1784; surgeon's mate 1795; surgeon to the York Rangers 1796; on half pay June–July 1797; staff surgeon 1803; retired on half pay 1808; died 21 April 1812 at Market Hill, county Armagh. [Peterkin and Johnston (1968)].

CARROLL, EDMUND RAYMOND (1872/3–1907), ship's surgeon and Belfast;
born 1872/3; studied medicine at Edinburgh and Queen's College, Cork; LRCP LRCS Edin 1889; LFPS Glas 1889; surgeon on SS *India* and SS *Cloncurry*; general practitioner of 89 Springfield Terrace, Dunville Park, Belfast; unmarried; died 24 October 1907 at 89 Falls Road, Belfast; administration Dublin 18 December 1907. [Belf PRO, will cal; Dub GRO (d); *Med Dir*].

CARROLL, JOHN (d 1860), Virginia, county Cavan, and Glenties, county Donegal;
son of Terence Carrol of Virginia; LM Anglesey Hospital, Dublin 1847; LRCSI 1851; medical officer to Virginia Workhouse and Dispensary, also of Glenties, county Donegal; unmarried; died 27 December 1860 at Virginia; administration Dublin 29 April 1861. [Belf PRO, will cal; *Med Dir*].

CARROLL, WILLIAM (1835–1926), US army and Philadelphia, USA;
born 24 February 1835 in Rathmullan, county Donegal, eldest child of Thomas Carroll, weaver, shoemaker and farmer, and Elizabeth McClure of Rathmullan; brother of three medical doctors in the USA; emigrated with family to Philadelphia in 1838 and later moved to Keene, Coshocton county, Ohio; educated in Keene; apprenticed in harness-making in Pittsburg from 1850; strong freemason, becoming Knight Templar at Mount Vernon, Ohio in 1857; studied medicine at Jefferson Medical College, Philadelphia; MD 1863; joined the US army as assistant surgeon 1863, serving in the civil war; surgeon captain in 1866 and, after combating a cholera epidemic among the soldiers, promoted to lieutenant colonel; resigned 1867 to practise medicine at 617 South 16th Street, Philadelphia; became a friend of John Mitchel and John Martin 1869, accompanied John Mitchel to Ireland in 1874 and presided at a large memorial service in their honour after their deaths in 1875; joined the Clan na Gael c 1872 and was chairman 1875, but broke with them in 1880 over Parnell's views and policy disagreements; involved also with the Irish Republican Brotherhood and Americal politics, as a Republican; married 1884 Anna Davidson (who died 1896), daughter of a Scottish immigrant; died 3 May 1926. [*DIB* (2009)].

CARROLL, — (*fl c* 1786–8), Dromore, county Down;
surgeon and apothecary, of Dromore; advertised for an apprentice apothecary in May 1788, with a note that 'he has for hire a neat hearse, with or without horses'; married 12 February 1786 at Dromore, — Spears. [*BNL* 17 February 1786 (m) and May 1788 (advert)].

CARSE, ROBERT FREDERICK (1862–1927), Liverpool, Lancashire and ship's surgeon;
born 16 June 1862 at Creevagh, county Tyrone, son of the Rev Stewart Carse, minister of Carland Presbyterian Church, Dungannon, and — Davis of Belfast; educated at Dungannon; studied medicine at Queen's College, Belfast, and the Ledwich School, Dublin 1881–91; MD BCh BAO (RUI) 1891; DPH Camb 1895; Malcolm Exhibition (Royal Hospital, Belfast); assistant surgeon to the South Dispensary, Liverpool; surgeon to the African Royal Mail, American and Cunard Steamship Companies; general practitioner, of 170 Upper Parliament Street, Liverpool, from c 1900; retired to Langton Hall Private Hotel, Bournemouth; married Jeannie Black; died 9 November 1927; probate London 26 January 1928. [Lond PPR, will cal; *Med Dir*; QCB adm reg].

CARSON, ALEXANDER (1824/5–59), London;
born 1824/5, son of Dr George Ledlie Carson of Coleraine (*q.v.*); MRCSE 1850; surgeon, of 121 Cock Hill, Ratcliffe, East London; married Anne —; died 3 January 1859 at Cock Hill of epilepsy, after four day's illness; administration London 15 April 1859. [*BNL* 10 January 1859 (d); Lond GRO (d); Lond PPR, will cal; *Londonderry Sentinel* 14 January 1859 (d); *Med Dir*].

CARSON, ALEXANDER TERTIUS (c 1839–91), Articlave, county Londonderry, Portrush, county Antrim, and Toronto, Canada;
born c 1839 at Coleraine, county Londonderry, eldest son of Dr James Crawford Ledlie Carson (*q.v.*); studied medicine with his father and at Trinity College, Dublin, 1857–8 and at Edinburgh University, 1858–61; MRCSE 1861; MD (Edin) 1862 (thesis 'On inflamation of the breast during lactation'); LAH Dub 1862; LM Edin and Rot Hosp Dub 1863; MCPS Ontario 1882; medical officer to Articlave Dispensary District from 1863 and to Portrush Dispensary District from 1873; moved c 1882 to 12 Gerrard Street East, Toronto, Canada c 1888; retired c 1890 to Ardhill, county Londonderry; married 23 April 1868 in Second Glendermott Presbyterian Church, Jane Stevenson, second daughter of Robert Stevenson, JP, of Ardhill, county Londonderry; died 31 August 1891 in Heidelberg, Germany; administration Dublin 29 January 1892. [Belf PRO, will cal; *Coleraine Chronicle* 25April 1868 (m); Edin Univ; Kirkpatrick Archive; *Londonderry Sentionel* 24 April 1868 (m); *Med Dir*].

CARSON, GEORGE LEDLIE (1802/3–38), Coleraine, county Londonderry, and Portrush, county Antrim;
born 1802/3; son of the Rev Alexander Carson, minister of Tobermore Presbyterian Church, county Londonderry; brother of Dr James Crawford Ledlie Carson (*q.v.*); LAH Dub 1828; apothecary, of Coleraine; married —; father of Dr Alexander Carson of London (*q.v.*); died 3 February 1838 at his home in Coleraine of fever caught during his attendance on some of his patients; 'as a medical practitioner he was esteemed for his knowledge and skill' (*BNL*). [Apothecaries (1829); *BNL* 2 March 1838 (d); Dub GRO (m, daughter); *Londonderry Sentinel* 26 May 1854 (m, daughter) and 14 January 1859 (d, son); McConnell (1951)].

CARSON, JAMES CRAWFORD LEDLIE (1815/6–86), Coleraine, county Londonderry;
born 1815/6, son of the Rev Alexander Carson, minister of Tobermore Presbyterian Church, county Londonderry; brother of Dr George Ledlie Carson of Coleraine (*q.v.*); studied medicine at Trinity College, Dublin, the Royal College of Surgeons in Ireland, Digges Street School, Glasgow University, Glasgow Infirmary and the Eye Infirmary; LM Anglesey Hospital, Dublin 1834; MD CM (Glas) 1837; LAH Dub 1841; of Ballymena 1837; medical officer to Coleraine Workhouse and Fever Hospital and certifying factory surgeon; JP 1875; married 4 October 1837 at Springvale, county Londonderry, Elizabeth Greer (who was born 23 March 1805 and died 2 June 1873), eldest daughter of the Rev Thomas Greer, minister of First Dunboe Presbyterian Church, county Londonderry, and Elizabeth Caldwell; father of Dr Alexander Tertius Carson (*q.v.*); died 2 June 1886 at Bannfield, Coleraine; probate Londonderry 25 June 1889. [Addison (1898); *BNL* 10 October 1837 (m); Belf PRO, will cal; Croly (1843–6); Dub GRO (d); Edin Univ; Greeves (1973); Kirkpatrick Archive; *Londonderry Sentinel* 26 May 1854 (m); McConnell (1951); *Med Dir*].

CARSON, JOHN (d 1860), Cavan;
  LAH Dub; apothecary, of Main Street, Cavan c 1856–60; married Anna Maria —; died 4 May 1860 at Main Street, Cavan; probate Cavan 15 June 1860. [Belf PRO, will cal; Kirkpatrick Archive; *Med Dir*].

CARSON, JOHN (1844/5–89), Dowra, county Cavan;
  born 1844/5; studied medicine at Trinity College, Dublin, the Royal College of Surgeons in Ireland and Adelaide Hospital, Dublin; LKQCPI 1868; LRCSI 1868; LM 1869; general practitioner of Corard House, Dowra, county Cavan; moved c 1888 to Taff's Well, Cardiff; died 6 June 1889 at Taff's Well with delerium tremens and liver failure. [Lond GRO (d); *Med Dir*].

CARSON, JOHN HENRY (1860–1937), Portrush and Crumlin, county Antrim, and Salford, Lancashire;
  born 19 September 1860 at Killough, county Down, son of Thomas Carson, farmer, of Ballylig, Killough; educated at the Belfast Seminary; studied medicine at Queen's College, Belfast, from 1877; LRCP LRCS Edin 1888; LFPS Glas 1888; general practitioner, of Portrush, county Antrim; medical officer of health for Crumlin Dispensary District; general practitioner, Salford, Lancashire, from c 1900; medical officer to the Day Industrial School, Manchester c 1905, of 72 Crosslane and 48 The Crescent, Salford; civil surgeon to the 7th Lancashire Fusilliers; retired c 1926 to 'Syringa', Newcastle, county Down; married 19 April 1893 in Legacurry Presbyterian Church, county Down, Elizabeth Morrow, daughter of Robert Morrow, farmer, of Legacurry; died 29 November 1937; probate Belfast 8 April 1938. [Belf PRO, will cal; *Med Dir*; QCB adm reg; UHF database (m)].

CARSON, RICHARD BERESFORD (1832–70), Army Medical Service;
  born 1 September 1832 at Croghan Castle, county Cavan, second son of George Carson of Croghan, and Catherine Hudson; educated at Armagh Royal School 1849–51; studied arts and medicine at Trinity College, Dublin, from 1851; BA (TCD) 1856; MB 1857; MRCSE 1858; joined the Army Medical Service as staff assistant surgeon 1858; posted to 2nd Foot 1859; staff surgeon 1861; unmarried; died 23 May 1870 in London. [Burtchaell and Sadleir (1935); Ferrar (1933); *Med Dir*; Peterkin and Johnston (1968); Swanzy (1903)].

CARSON, ROBERT, (*fl c* 1777), Belfast;
  apothecary, of Belfast; married 2 March 1777 — Shanks of Lisburn. [*BNL* 28 March 1777 (m)].

CARSON, WILLIAM (1818/9–80), Trillick, county Tyrone, and Lisbellaw, county Fermanagh;
  born 1818/19 in Dublin, son of William Flynn, merchant; educated by Mr Flynn; studied arts in Trinity College, Dublin from 1836 and medicine in Glasgow University; accoucheur of the Coombe Lying-in Hospital and Dublin Lying-in Hospital (Rotunda) 1841; LRCSI, LM and L Pharmacy, 1841; MD (Glas) 1842; FRCSI 1846; BA (TCD) 1847; medical officer to Trillick and Lisbellaw Dispensary

Districts and Fever Hospital from c 1846; ordained c 1850; rector of Cappoquin and of Ardmayle (Cashel) from c 1855; unmarried; died 22 October 1880 at Ardmayle Vicarage; administration (with will) Dublin 8 December 1881. [Addison (1898); Belf PRO, will cal; Burtchaell and Sadleir (1924); Croly (1843–6); Dub GRO (d); Kirkpatrick Archive; *Med Dir*].

CARSON, WILLIAM (*fl c* 1845), Cavan;
MRCSE 1842; general practitioner in Cavan town c 1845. [Croly (1843–6].

CARSWELL, ROBERT (1802/3–33), Rostrevor, county Down;
born 1802/3, son of Joseph Carswell of Carrick, Loughbrickland, county Down; died 20 June 1833 at his father's house in Rostrevor. [*BNL* 22 July 1833 (d)].

CARTER, ALBERT EDWARD (1841–79), Liverpool, Lancashire;
born 9 November 1841, fourth son of the Rev Henry Carter, rector of Carrickfergus and of Ballintoy, county Antrim, and Maria Theresa Bayley; brother of Dr Sidney Herbert Carter (*q.v.*); studied medicine at the Ledwich School, Dublin; LRCSI 1865; LRCP Edin and LM 1867; resident medical officer to Toxteth Park Infirmary and Fever Hospital, Liverpool; senior resident surgeon to the North Dispensary, Liverpool, of 5 Hemans Street and 52 Upper Parliament Street, Liverpool c 1870–09; married 22 October 1873 in Monkstown Church of Ireland Church, Dublin, Maria Jeanette Thompson, daughter of Joseph Thompson of New York; died 8 January 1879 of typhus fever. [Leslie (1993); *Med Dir*].

CARTER, GERALD BAYLEY (1872–c 1925), Royal Army Medical Corps;
born 1 January 1872 at Moy, county Tyrone, son of the Rev Henry Bryan Carter, curate of Loughgall, county Armagh, and later rector of Derryloran (Cookstown), and Elizabeth Beresford Jackson; brother of Dr James Edward Carter (*q.v.*); educated at Dungannon Royal School; studied arts and medicine at Trinity College, Dublin, from 1890; BA (TCD) 1895; MB BCh BAO 1896; joined the Royal Army Medical Corps as lieutenant 1898; captain 1901; major 1909; retired with gratuity 1911; living c 1924 at Balaclava, Melbourne, Australia; died c 1925. [*Med Dir*; Peterkin and Johnston (1968); TCD adm reg; *TCD Cat*, vol II (1896) and III (1906)].

CARTER, JAMES EDWARD (1865–1923), Army Medical Service;
born 23 April 1865 at Levalleglish, Loughgall, county Armagh, son of the Rev Henry Bryan Carter, curate of Loughgall and later rector of Derryloran (Cookstown), and Elizabeth Beresford Jackson; brother of Dr Gerald Bayley Carter (*q.v.*); educated at Dungannon Royal School; studied arts and medicine at Trinity College, Dublin, from 1883; BA (TCD) 1888; MB BCh BAO 1889; joined the Army Medical Service as surgeon captain 1891; wounded in South African War 1899–1900; on half pay December 1901–October 1905; major 1905; retired 1913; served in World War I 1914–18; lived finally at The Lion Hotel, Machynlleth, Montgomeryshire; unmarried; died 25 July 1923 at the Hospital, Machynlleth; probate London 16 October 1923. [Belf GRO (b); Kirkpatrick Archive; Lond PPR, will cal; will; *Med Dir*; Peterkin and Johnston (1968); TCD adm reg; *TCD Cat*, vol (1896)].

CARTER, ROBERT A.J. (1861–c 1885);
   born 26 January 1861 at Georgetown, Demerara, son of Joseph Carter of Georgetown; educated at RBAI; studied medicine at Queen's College, Belfast from 1879; MD MCh (RUI) 1884; died c 1885. [*Med Dir*; QCB adm reg].

CARTER, SIDNEY HERBERT (1848–1926), Liverpool, Lancashire. Bristol, Gloucestershire, and Army Medical Service;
   born 14 March 1848 in county Antrim, sixth son of the Rev Henry Carter, rector of Carrickfergus and of Ballintoy, county Antrim, and Maria Theresa Bayley; brother of Dr Albert Edward Carter (*q.v.*); studied arts and medicine at Trinity College, Dublin; BA (TCD) 1868; MB 1871; LRCS Edin and LM 1871; house surgeon to Liverpool Workhouse, Infirmary and Fever Hospital 1871–2; assistant medical superintendent of Bristol Lunatic Asylum 1872–4; joined the Army Medical Service as surgeon 1874; surgeon major 1886; surgeon lieutenant-colonel RAMC 1894; brigade surgeon lieutenant-colonel 1897; served in Afghan War 1878–80, Egypt 1882, NW Frontier 1897–98 and South Africa 1899–1901; retired 1903; lived finally at 19 St Nicholas Road, Brighton; married Henrietta Balmer; died 15 October 1926 at 19 St Nicholas Road; probate London 23 December 1926. [*BMJ* obituary (1926); Kirkpatrick Archive; Leslie (1993); Lond GRO (d); Lond PPR, will cal; *Med Dir*; Peterkin and Johnston (1968); TCD adm reg; *TCD Cat*, vol II (1896)].

CARY, TRISTRAM (1830–1907), Australia, Claudy, county Londonderry, Moville, county Donegal, and London;
   born 4 January 1830, son of Anthony Thomas Grayson Cary and Charlotte Slacke of Slackegrove, county Monaghan; studied medicine at Edinburgh University; LFPS Glas 1851; LRCSI and LM 1859; MD (St Andrews) 1860 (by examination); practised briefly in Australia; medical officer to Claudy Dispensary District 1861–c 1875; general practitioner of Moville, c 1875–80; moved c 1880 to Edenbridge, Kent; moved c 1884 to 48 St Thomas's Road, Victoria Park, London, and c 1892 to Cromwell House, Gunnersbury, Middlesex; married 1 June 1852 Dorothy Maria Oakes (who died 10 February 1914), fourth daughter of Sir Henry Thomas Oakes, Bart, of Mitchem Hall, Surrey; died 10 December 1907 at Hedge Road, Brentford. [*Burke's Peerage* (1938); Kirkpatrick Archive; Lond GRO (d); *Med Dir*; Smart (2004); Young (1929)].

CASEMENT, BRABAZON NEWCOMEN (1852–1910), Ballycastle and Ballymena, county Antrim, and Sydney, New South Wales;
   born 19 August 1852, son of John Casement of Magherintemple, county Antrim, and Charlotte Newcomen of Camla House, county Roscommon; educated at Dungannon Royal School; studied arts and medicine at Trinity College, Dublin, from 1869; scholar 1874; BA (TCD) 1875; MB 1877; MRCSE 1878; general practitioner, of Ballycastle c 1879–80 and Clonavon Terrace, Ballymena c 1880–83; emigrated to Australia c 1884; of Kempsey, Sydney, from c 1884; married 15 September 1880 Henrietta Louisa Burke, daughter of the Rev Thomas James Burke, rector of Babcary, county Somerset; died February 1910. [Addison (1898); Burke, *LGI* (1912); *Med Dir*; TCD adm reg; *TCD Cat*, vol II (1896)].

CASEMENT, GEORGE (1745–1834), Naval Medical Service and Larne, county Antrim;
born 1745, son of Hugh Casement of county Antrim and Elizabeth Higginson of Magheragall, county Antrim; joined the Naval Medical Service as assistant surgeon; served on HMS *Hind* c 1765–75, which captured a Spanish galleon filled with valuable cargo c 1773; settled at Inver, Larne and was one of the jurors who found William Orr guilty of treason in September 1797 (on very flimsy evidence); he was subsequently attacked in revenge for his role and managed to escape a threat to his life in June 1798 (a long letter by him reproduced by McKillop); married (1) Elizabeth —; (2) Matilda (or Martha) Montgomery (who died 11 April 1840), daughter of Hugh Montgomery; died 4 October 1834; buried in St Cedma's Parish Graveyard, Larne. [Burke *LGI* (1912); McKillop (2000); Rutherford and Clarke, *Antrim*, vol 4 (2004); Young (1893)].

CASEMENT, JOHN (b 1825/6), Dublin;
born 1825/6 in county Antrim, son of Roger Casement; educated privately; studied arts and medicine at Trinity College, Dublin, from 1844; LM Rot Hosp Dub 1847; LRCSI 1848; BA MB (TCD) 1849; MA 1865; physician to Dubliin General Dispensary c 1850; general practitioner, of 5 and 6 Upper Mount Street, Dublin c 1852; died c 1853. [Burtchaell and Sadleir (1924); *Med Dir*].

CASSIDY, JAMES (d 1850), Dungannon, county Tyrone;
apothecary and surgeon in Dungannon c 1845; died 15 July 1850 in Dungannon. [*BNL* 19 July 1850 (d); Croly (1843–6)].

CASSIDY, JOHN BRADLEY (1792/3–1855), Inistioge, county Kilkenny, and Maghera, county Londonderry;
born 1792/3; LRCS Edin 1825;; LAH Dub 1828; general practitioner, of Inistioge from c 1830, and of Maghera, c 1845; married Anna Lamont (who was born 1802/3 and died 16 November 1838 at Maghera), second daughter of Captain Lamont; died June 1855 at Maghera. [*BNL* 23 November 1838 (d) and 29 June 1855 (d); *Coleraine Chronicle* 30 June 1855 (d); Croly (1843–6); *Londonderry Sentinel* 24 November 1838 (d); *Med Dir*].

CASSIDY, JOHN PAUL (1869/70–1922), Holloway and Queen's Park, London;
born 1869/70, second son of Anthony Cassidy of The Graan, Enniskillen, county Fermanagh; studied medicine at the Royal College of Surgeons in Ireland, the Catholic University of Ireland, and the Mater Misericordiae Hospital, Dublin; LRCPI and LM 1895; LRCSI and LM 1895; DPH Dub 1910; general practitioner, of 92 St James's Road, Holloway c 1896–8, of 359a New North Road, Islington c 1898–1900, of 1 Millman Road, Queen's Park, London c 1900–13, and of 7 Brondesbury Road, Kilburn c 1913–22; assistant school medical officer to Willesden Council; married Lilian —; died 14 June 1922 at 7 Brondesbury Road; buried in Glasnevin Cemetery, Dublin; probate Dublin 28 July 1922 and London 5 August 1922. [Dub Nat Arch, will cal; Kirkpatrick Archive; Lond PPR, will cal; *Med Dir*].

CASSIDY, PATRICK (d 1720), Devenish, county Fermanagh;
'doctor', of Devenish; died 27 September 1720; buried in Devenish Island Graveyard. [*Memorials of the Dead*, vol VII, p 586].

CASSIDY
See also O'CASSIDY

CASTLES, HENRY (1875–1904), Distington, Cumberland;
born 1 June 1875 at Maralin, county Down, son of Joseph Castles, merchant, of Maralin; educated at Lurgan Model School; studied medicine at Queen's College, Belfast, from 1875; MD (QUI) 1880; general practitioner, of Distington, Cumberland c 1885; died 5 March 1904; administration Carlisle 4 August 1904. [Lond PPR, will cal; *Med Dir*; QCB adm reg].

CATHCART, JAMES (1812/3–76), Ballybay, county Monaghan;
born 1812/3; studied medicine at Glasgow University and Dublin Infirmary; CM and LM (Glas) 1835; medical officer for cholera, district vaccinator and general practitioner in Ballybay; unmarried; died 8 August 1876 at Ballybay. [Addison (1898); Croly (1843–6); Dub GRO (d); *Med Dir*].

CATHCART, MARTIN (1784–1856), Army Medical Service;
born 22 March 1784; joined the Army Medical Service as surgeon's mate 1808; assistant surgeon with the York Light Infantry Volunteers 1809; surgeon 1815; transferred to 60th Foot 1817, to the 38th Foot 1818, and to the 7th Dragoon Guards 1832; retired on half pay to Gortnamoyagh, Garvagh, county Londonderry, 1843; died 3 December 1856 at Gortnamoyagh House; probate Prerogative Court 1857. [*BNL* 13 December 1856 (d); Belf PRO, prerog wills index; Kirkpatrick Archive; Peterkin and Johnston (1968)].

CATHCART, THOMAS CHARLES DUFFIN JOHNSTON (1860–1939), Belfast;
born 6 November 1860 at Kells, county Antrim, son of John Cathcart, farmer, of Kells; educated privately; studied medicine at Queen's College, Belfast, from 1878, and the Carmichael School, Dublin; LRCP LRCS Edin 1889; LFPS Glas 1889; general practitioner, of Ruperta House, 297 Newtownards Road and 8 Kirkliston Drive, Belfast; married —; died 7 April 1939 at 8 Kirkliston Drive; buried in Belfast City Cemetery; probate Belfast 5 June 1939. [Belf City Cem, bur reg; Belf GRO (d); Belf PRO, will cal; Kirkpatrick Archive; *Med Dir*; QCB adm reg].

CATHER, WILLIAM (1762/3–1836), Naval Medical Service and Omagh, county Tyrone;
born 1762/3; joined the Naval Medical Service as assistant surgeon; retired 1793; surgeon, of Omagh c 1824; died 30 July 1836 at Omagh; probate Prerogative Court 1836. [Belf PRO, prerog wills index; *Londonderry Standard* 9 August 1836 (d); McGrew (1998) and (2001); *NMS* (1826); Pigot (1824); *Strabane Morning Post* 9 August 1836 (d)].

CATHERWOOD, HUGH (*fl c* 1716), Kirkistown, county Down;
surgeon, of Kirkistown; witness to a will 1716. [Eustace, vol I (1956)].

CATHERWOOD, JOHN (b 1685/6), Bristol;
born 1685/6, of Belfast; studied medicine at Leyden from 1710; MD (Utrecht) 1710 (thesis 'De apoplexia' in British Library); practised for a time in Bristol; author of *A New Method of Curing Apoplexy*, London (1715). [Innes Smith (1932)].

CATHERWOOD, WILLIAM ALISTER (1843–1901), Army Medical Service;
born 25 November 1843, son of Dr William Hutcheson Catherwood (*q.v.*) of Donaghadee; educated at RBAI from 1858; studied medicine at Queen's College, Belfast, and Edinburgh 1858–65; LRCP LRCS Edin 1864; MD (QUI) 1865; joined the Army Medical Service as assistant surgeon 1865; surgeon major 1877; lieutenant-colonel 1884; surgeon colonel 1894; surgeon general 1898; served in the Ashanti War 1873–4 (medal and clasp) and the Egyptian War of 1882–4, being present at the battle of Tel-el Kebir (medal and clasp and Khedives's star); served in the Sudan Expedition; married —; died 24 September 1901 at Nainital, India; memorial tablet in Donaghadee Parish Church. [Clarke, *County Down*, vol 16 (1976); Fisher and Robb (1913); *Med Dir*; Peterkin and Johnston (1968); QCB adm reg].

CATHERWOOD, WILLIAM HUTCHESON (*fl c* 1815–45), Donaghadee, county Down;
studied medicine at Edinburgh University; MD (Edin) 1815 (thesis 'De nostalgia'); of Ballyvester, Donaghadee; medical officer to Donaghadee Dispensary District and surgeon and agent for the Naval Medical Department, c 1824 and 1845; married 22 May 1816 in First Donaghadee Presbyterian Church Isabella Cochrane of Donaghadee, widow; father of Dr William Alister Catherwood (*q.v.*); four of his daughters died between 1854 and 1860. [*BNL* 24 May 1816 (m), 28 May 1854 (d, dau), 4 May 1858 (d, dau), 26 July 1858 (d, dau) and 3 August 1860 (d, dau); Croly (1843–6); Edin Univ; McConnell (1951); Pigot (1824)].

CAVIN, WILLIAM (1788/9–1872), Coleraine, county Londonderry;
born 1788/9, third son of Mathew Cavin of Maghera; studied arts at Glasgow and later medicine at Edinburgh Univesity; MA (Glas) 1813; MD (Edin) 1830 (thesis 'De phthisi pulmonali'); LRCS Edin 1830; first a licentiate in the Irish Presbyterian church in 1817 but became a general practitioner in Coleraine; married Anne Newtown (who died 12 November 1842 in Coleraine), only daughter of Henry Newtown of Coleraine; died 4 March 1872 at Ferryquay Street, Coleraine; probate Londonderry 12 April 1872. [Addison (1898) and (1913); *BNL* 22 November 1842 (d); Belf PRO, will cal; Croly (1843–6); Dub GRO (d); Edin Univ; *Londonderry Sentinel* 26 November 1842 (d); *Med Dir*].

CHAIN, ALEXANDER (1839–1907), Liverpool, Lancashire;
born 1839, son of William Chain of Rathfriland; educated at Rathfriland Academy; studied medicine at Queen's College, Belfast, from 1857; LM Belfast Lying-in Hospital 1860 (prize in midwifery); LRCS Edin and LM 1861; LRCP Edin and LM

1867; general practitioner, of 6 (later 44) Juvenal Street, Liverpool; died 4 February 1907 at 44 Juvenal Street; probate Liverpool 25 March 1907. [Lond GRO (d); Lond PPR, will cal; *Med Dir*; QCB adm reg].

CHAIN, ROBERT (1797/8–1864), Banbridge, county Down;
born 1797/8; LM; LRCS Edin 1822; LAH Dub 1827; apothecary and surgeon in Banbridge; unmarried; died 3 December 1864 of typhus fever at Banbridge; administration Dublin 10 January 1865. [Apothecaries (1829); Belf PRO, will cal; Croly (1843–6); Dub GRO (d); *Med Dir*; Pigot (1824)].

CHAMBERS, JAMES (d 1727), Letterkenny, county Donegal;
surgeon, of Letterkenny; died 1827; will dated 28 June 1727 (abstract in PRO NI) proved in Raphoe Diocesan Court 1727; asks to be buried in Leck Churchyard. [Belf PRO, T808/3121; Thrift (1920)].

CHAMBERS, JAMES (1853–1923), Fintona, county Tyrone;
born 30 October 1853 at Ballylough, Banbridge, county Down, son of James Chambers, farmer and county cess collector, of Banbridge; educated at Ballylough National School and Banbridge Academy; studied medicine at Queen's College, Belfast, from 1874 and at Edinburgh; LRCP LRCS Edin 1881; general practitioner, of Brookwood, Fintona; JP; married —; father of Dr James Chambers, junior; died 3 June 1923 at Fintona; probate Londonderry 13 May 1924. [Belf GRO (d); Belf PRO, will cal; Kirkpatrick Archive; *Med Dir*; QCB adm reg].

CHAMBERS, JAMES (1858–1938), Belfast, Dublin, Montrose, Forfar, Roehampton and London;
born 16 August 1858 at Ballymaguire, Stewartstown, county Tyrone, son of John Chambers, farmer, of Stewartstown; educated at RBAI; studied arts and medicine at Queen's College, Belfast, from 1874 and at the Richmond and Rotunda Hospitals, Dublin; BA (QUI) 1879; MA 1882; LKQCPI 1885; MD MCh (RUI) 1886; demonstrator in anatomy, Queen's College, Belfast; resident physician to the Hampstead and Highfield Private Asylums, Dublin; assistant medical superintendent to the Royal Asylum, Montrose, and the Cumberland and Westmoreland Asylum; resident medical superintendent to The Priory, Roehampton from 1892; of 6 Mansfield Street, 16 Queen Anne Street and 26 Devonshire Place, Cavendish Square, London; president of the medico-psychatric association; lecturer in mental diseases to the Middlesex Hospital Medical School; honorary consultant in mental disease to the London Military Hospitals; physician to the Special Hospital for Officers, Latchmere House; retired c 1932 to Estia, Highdown Road, Roehampton; married Evelyn Mary —; died 7 June 1938; probate London 16 August 1938. [Lond GRO (d); Lond PPR, will cal; *Med Dir*; QCB adm reg].

CHAMBERS, JOHN (1845/6–c 1896), Indianapolis, USA;
born 1845/6 at Rathfriland, son of David Chambers of Drumnascamph, Rathfriland; educated at Rathfriland Academy; studied medicine at Queen's College, Belfast, from 1862; MD MCh (QUI) 1868; joined Cunard Steamship Company c 1870;

emigrated to USA 1875; professor of anatomy in the Indiana Medical College, of 105 North Alabama Street, Indianapolis; died c 1896. [Kirkpatrick Archive; *Med Dir*; QCB adm reg].

CHAMBERS, JOHN BROOK (d c 1793), Letterkenny, county Donegal;
surgeon, of Letterkenny; died c 1793; probate Raphoe Diocesan Court 1793. [Thrift (1920)].

CHAMBERS, SIR JOSEPH (1864–1935), Naval Medical Service;
born 25 November 1864 in county Cavan, second son of Thomas Chambers, JP, land agent, of Tandragee House, Bailieborough, county Cavan; educated at Rathmines School, Dublin, from 1876; studied arts and medicine at Trinity College, Dublin, from 1882; BA (TCD) 1886; MB BCh 1887; MD (*honoris causa*) 1924; FRCPI (hon) 1924; played rugby for Ireland in 1886 and 1887; joined the Naval Medical Service as assistant surgeon 1889; fleet surgeon c 1900; served in the South African War 1899–1902 and World War I 1914–18; surgeon in charge of Plymouth Naval Hospital 1922; vice-admiral and director general of the Medical Department of the Royal Navy 1923–7; honorary physician to the King 1925; KCB 1926; married 22 December 1908 in St Bridget and St Martin's Church of England Church, City of London, Irene Tanner (born 1877/8), daughter of Robert C. Tanner of Chester; died 22 September 1935 at Harrogate, Yorkshire. [*BMJ* obituary (1935); Figgis and Drury (1932); Kirkpatrick Archive; *Lancet* obituary (1935); Lond GRO (m); *Med Dir*; TCD adm reg; *TCD Cat*, vol II (1896); Widdess (1963)].

CHAMBERS, ROBERT (1749/50–90), Downpatrick, county Down;
born 1749/50; apothecary, of Downpatrick; supplied medicines to Downpatrick Gaol in 1790 and was apparently still supplying them in 1802, but his wife may have continued the business in his name; (his only son Brice was a minor in 1790); died June 1790; will dated 28 April 1790 (abstract in PRO NI) proved in Down Diocesan Court 28 August 1790. [Belf PRO, Down Diocesan Wills index; Belf PRO, T808/2974; Pilson (1934); Stranney (2008)].

CHAMBERS, ROBERT (1820/1–66), Castlewellan, county Down;
born 1820/1, son of James Chambers, farmer, of Dree, Dromara, county Down; CM (Glas) 1845; general practitioner in Castlewellan; unmarried; died 13 July 1866 at Downpatrick Infirmary; administration Belfast 25 June 1867. [Addison (1898); Belf PRO, will cal; Dub GRO (d); *Med Dir*].

CHAMBERS, ROBERT (1842/3–1911), London;
born 1842/3; studied medicine in Dublin and Edinburgh; LRCS Edin 1868; LKQCPI 1870; of 10 Holford Square, London, c 1875; physician to the Church Army Training Homes and Shafesbury Institute and London Medical Mission c 1875, of 10 Holford Square, London; superintendent of the Marylebone Medical Mission, of 43 Carlisle Street, Edgeware Road, from c 1885; retired c 1909 to 'Westwood', Ravenhill Park, Belfast; married Fanny —; died 28 August 1911 at 'Westwood'; administration Belfast 6 November 1911. [Belf PRO, will cal; Dub GRO (d); *Med Dir*].

CHAMBERS, SAMUEL (*fl c* 1869), Keady, county Armagh;
  general practitioner, of Keady [not in *Medical Register* or *Medical Directory*]; married 10 November 1869 in Fisherwick Place Presbyterian Church, Belfast, Mary Sophie McKee, eldest daughter of the Rev James McKee of 39 Rugby Road, Belfast. [*Coleraine Chronicle* 13 November 1869 (m)].

CHAMBERS, WILLIAM (*fl c* 1824), Ballynahinch, county Down;
  apothecary, of Ballynahinch c 1824; married — (who was born 1752/3 and died 12 May 1824). [*BNL* 18 May 1824 (d); Pigot (1824)].

CHAMBERS, WILLIAM (1826/7–98), Shercock, county Cavan, and Banbridge, county Down;
  born 1826/7, son of James Chambers, farmer, of Ballylough county Down; educated at RBAI; studied medicine at Queen's College, Belfast, from 1857; and Belfast General Hospital; LM Belfast Lying-in Hospital 1861; MD (St Andrews) 1862 (by examination); LRCS Edin and LM 1863; medical officer to Shercock Dispensary District and Bailieborough Union Workhouse c 1871–4; general practitioner, of Banbridge c 1874–98, of Rose Hall, Laurencetown; married 15 July 1875 in Rostrevor Presbyterian Church, Elizabeth McAlister, daughter of Andrew McAlister, farmer, of Donacloney; died 19 July 1898 at Drumnascamph, near Banbridge; administration Belfast 13 August 1898. [Belf PRO, will cal; Dub GRO (d); Kirkpatrick Archive; *Med Dir*; QCB adm reg; Smart (2004); UHF database (m)].

CHANCELLOR, WILLIAM (1865–1925), Banbridge, county Down, Belfast, and Birmingham, Warwickshire;
  born 9 January 1865 at Strabane, county Tyrone, son of the Rev James Alexander Chancellor, minister of Bready Reformed Presbyterian Church, and Professor of Theology in Belfast, and — Thompson; studied arts and medicine at Queen's College, Belfast, from 1881; BA (RUI) 1883; MB BCh BAO 1893; medical officer to Banbridge Union Infirmary and certifying factory surgeon, of Bridge Street, Banbridge; of Queen's Crescent, North Queen Street, Belfast c 1895; general practitioner of 622 Stratford Road, Birmingham c 1917 and later of 43 Washwood Heath Road, Saltley, Birmingham; died 24 April 1925 at 43 Washwood Heath Road; administration Birmingham 19 June 1925. [Kirkpatrick Archive; Lond GRO (d); Lond PPR, will cal; Loughridge (1970); *Med Dir*; QCB adm reg].

CHARLES, DANIEL ALLEN (1850–86), Bellaghy, county Londonderry;
  born 18 June 1850 at Cookstown, county Tyrone, son of Dr David Hughes Charles (*q.v.*); brother of Prof John James Charles (*q.v.*), Dr Thomas William Cranstoun Charles (*q.v.*) and Sir Richard Havelock Henry Charles (*q.v.*); educated at Cookstown Academy; studied medicine at Queen's College, Belfast, 1870–75; MD MCh Dip Mid (QUI) 1875; medical officer to Bellaghy Dispensary District 1875–83; retired 1883 & was presented with illuminated address; married Anna —; died 2 January 1886 at Cookstown; probate Armagh 9 February 1886. [Belf PRO, will cal; *Bellaghy Hist Soc* (2003); Dub GRO (d); Kirkpatrick Archive; Martin (2003); *Med Dir*; QCB adm reg].

CHARLES, DAVID HUGHES (1818–99), Cookstown, county Tyrone;
born 19 September 1818, son of John Charles of Moor Cottage, Beltonaneane, county Tyrone; brother of Dr Richard Charles (*q.v.*); studied medicine at Dublin, Glasgow and Edinburgh Universities; LM Glas 1840; LRCS Edin 1843; MD (Glas) 1843; general practitioner, of Loy House, Cookstown; JP; married 19 August 1843 Anne E. Allen (who died June 1897), second daughter of John Allen; father of Prof John James Charles (*q.v.*), Dr Thomas William Cranstoun Charles (*q.v.*), Dr Daniel Allen Charles (*q.v.*), Sir Richard Havelock Henry Charles (*q.v.*) and Marie Charles who married Dr George K. Given (*q.v.*); died 21 August 1899 at 17 Bradmore Road, Oxford; probate Armagh 4 December 1899. [Addison (1898); Belf PRO, will cal; *Burke's Peerage, Baronetage and Knightage* (1938); Lond GRO (d); *Med Dir*].

CHARLES, HENRY RICHARD (1809–73), New York, and Cookstown, county Tyrone;
born 1809 at Moor House, Beltonanean, county Tyrone; LM Anglesey Hosp Dub 1835; studied medicine at the Royal College of Surgeons in Ireland and Glasgow University; MD (Glas) and CM 1836; physician and surgeon in New York c 1837–44 and then of Cookstown and medical officer to constabulary; married Mary —; died 24 November 1873 at Cookstown; probate Armagh 22 December 1873. [Addison (1898); Belf PRO, will cal; Croly (1843–6); Dub GRO (d); Kirkpatrick Archive; *Med Dir*].

CHARLES, JOHN JAMES (1845–1912), Belfast, Cork and Dublin;
born 13 December 1845 in Cookstown, county Tyrone, eldest son of Dr David Hughes Charles of Loy House, Cookstown (*q.v.*); brother of Dr Daniel Allen Charles (*q.v.*), Dr Thomas William Cranstoun Charles (*q.v.*) and Sir Richard Havelock Henry Charles (*q.v.*); educated by Mr John Smyth of Cookstown; studied medicine at Queen's College, Belfast, from 1861, University College Hospital, London, Edinburgh and Paris Universities; MD (hons) MCh (QUI) 1865; BA 1867; MA (with 2 gold medals) 1868; LRCS and LM Edin 1871; DSc (*hon causa*) 1882; assistant lecturer on comparative anatomy, Edinburgh, demonstrator and lecturer in anatomy, Queen's College Belfast 1869–75; of 25 Crescent Terrace, Belfast 1871 and 11 Fisherwick Place, Belfast 1874; professor of anatomy and physiology at Queen's College, Cork 1875–1907; of 1 Alexandra Place, Cork in 1895; a concise and clear lecrurer and a strict disciplinarian; author of various medical papers; retired in 1907 to 8 Clyde Road, Dublin; married (1) 1 July 1873 in Agherton Church of Ireland Church, Portstewart, county Londonderry, Harriet Madeline Godfrey (who died 10 June 1874), daughter of William Wellington Godfrey, customs officer, of Portstewart, county Londonderry, and Botanic Road, Belfast; (2) 21 December 1880 Georgina E. Smith, daughter of George Smith of Newmarket, county Cork; father by first wife of Dr Godfrey Eustace Charles, and by second wife of Dr John James Percival Charles; died 10 August 1912 at 19 Lansdowne Crescent, Portrush; left money for a fund to award a 'Charles Medal' of the Cork Medical School; probate Dublin 14 December 1912. [*BNL* 19 December 1845 (b); Belf PRO, will cal; *BMJ* obituary (1912); Clarke, *County Down*, vol 21 (1998); Crawford (1930); *DIB* (2009); Dub GRO (m) and (d); Dub Nat Arch, will; Kirkpatrick Archive; *Med Dir*; Newmann (1993); O'Rahily (1949); QCB adm reg].

CHARLES, RICHARD (1800–63), Angelica, New York, USA;
   born 24 May 1800, eldest son of John Charles of Moor Cottage, Beltonanean, county Tyrone, seneschal of Omagh; brother of Dr David Hughes Charles (*q.v.*); studied at Glasgow University, matriculating in 1819; CM 1820; emigrated to USA; general practitioner in Angelica, New York State; died 24 April 1863 at Angelica. [Addison (1898) and (1913); *Coleraine Chronicle* 30 May 1863 (d)].

CHARLES, SIR RICHARD HAVELOCK HENRY (1858–1934), Indian Medical Service and London;
   born 10 March 1858, sixth son of Dr David Hughes Charles (*q.v.*) of Cookstown; brother of Prof John James Charles (*q.v.*), Dr Daniel Allen Charles (*q.v.*) and Dr Thomas William Cranstoun Charles (*q.v.*); studied medicine at Queen's College, Cork, University College, London, Paris, Berlin and Vienna; MD MCh (1st class hons and gold medal) (QUI) 1881; FRCSI 1891; LLD (QUB) (*hon causa*) 1923; joined the Indian Medical Service (Bengal establishment) as surgeon 1882, with first place in the examination and various prizes; served in the Afghan Boundary Commission 1884–6; professor of anatomy in Lahore Medical College and surgeon to the Mayo Hospital, Lahore 1886–94; author of papers on anatomy; surgeon major 1894; surgeon lieutenant-colonel 1902; professor of anatomy in Calcutta Medical College and surgeon to the Medical College Hospital 1894–1908; accompanied the Prince and Princess of Wales on their tour of India 1905–06; KCVO 1906; honorary FRCSE and gold medal 1906; Arnot gold medal 1907; lieutenant-colonel 1908 on retirement; sergeant surgeon to King George V 1910–28; served on the Medical Board of the India Office 1907–23, accompanied King George V and Queen Mary on their tour of India 1911–12; GCVO 1912; president of the Board 1913–23 and medical adviser to the Secretary of State for India; dean of the London School of Tropical Medicine 1916; of 9 Manchester Square, London; major-general 1913; KCSI 1923; Knight of the Order of St John of Jerusalem; baronet 1928; married 19 April 1886 Gertrude Seton Gordon (who died 9 July 1923), youngest daughter of Adam Annand Gordon of Aberdeen and London; died 27 October 1934; probate London 12 December 1934. [*BMJ* obituary (1934); *Burke's Peerage* (1938); Crawford (1930); Crone (1928); *DIB* (2009); Kirkpatrick Archive; Lond PPR, will cal; *Med Dir*; Newmann (1993)].

CHARLES, THOMAS WILLIAM CRANSTOUN (1848–94), Belfast and London;
   born 29 January 1848 at Cookstown, son of Dr David Hughes Charles of Cookstown (*q.v.*); brother of Prof John James Charles (*q.v.*), Dr Daniel Allen Charles (*q.v.*) and Sir Richard Havelock Henry Charles (*q.v.*); educated at Cookstown Academy; studied medicine at Queen's College, Belfast, from 1864; MD MCh (QUI) 1869 with first class honours and gold medal; resident physician to Belfast Fever Hospital; demonstrator and assistant lecturer in chemistry at Queen's Collge, Belfast c 1870–75; medical officer organising an ambulance service for the wounded in the Turko-Serbian War of 1876; demonstrator in physiology and medical registrar at St Thomas's Hospital, from 1876; later joint lecturer in anatomy and physiology and subsequently lecturer in practical physiology; of 9 Albert Mansions, Victoria Street, and of Crofton Lodge, Coventry Park, Streatham, London c 1885; author of many books, including *Elements of Physiological and Pathological Chemistry* (1884), and papers; married —; died 24 January 1894 at 2 Edinburgh Mansions, Victoria Street,

following a small overdose of morphine (inquest verdict: accidental death); administration London 5 March 1894. [*BMJ* obituary (1894); Lond GRO (d); Lond PPR, will cal; *Med Dir*; QCB adm reg].

CHARTRES, JOHN (1843/4–94), Lisnaskea, county Fermanagh;
born 1843/4 in county Fermanagh, son of John Chartres; studied arts and medicine at Trinity College, Dublin, from 1862 and at the Carmichael School; BA (TCD) 1868; MB 1872; general practitioner in Lisnaskea; married Elizabeth Jane —; died 14 August 1894 at Lisnaskea; probate Dublin 13 June 1895. [Belf PRO, will cal; Dub GRO (d); *Med Dir*; TCD adm reg; *TCD Cat*, vol II (1896)].

CHARTRES, WILLIAM (d c 1880), Strangford, county Down;
LRCSI 1873; LM Rot Hosp Dub 1874; LKQCPI 1874; medical officer to Strangford Dispensary District, of Blackcauseway House; moved to Ville d'Hiver, Arachon, France c 1878; died c 1880. [*Med Dir*].

CHEVERS, NORMAN (1818–86), London, Belfast and Indian Medical Service;
born 27 April 1818, son of Forbes McBean Chevers, surgeon RN, and Anne Telman of Newhouse, Kent; educated at St George's School, Haslar; studied medicine at Guy's Hospital, London and Glasgow University; LSA Lond 1839; MD (Glas) 1839; MRCS 1841; FRCS 1878; pathologist at Guy's Hospital c 1839–48; of Belfast 1848; joined the Indian Medical Service (Bengal establishment) as assistant surgeon 1848; surgeon 1862; surgeon major 1868; CIE 1881; retired 1876; author of *Diseases of the Heart and Aortic Aneurysm* (1851), *On Preserving Health of European Soldiers in India*, in 4 parts (1858–60) and *Commentary on Diseases of India* (1886); married 25 May 1848 in St Anne's Church of Ireland Church, Belfast, Emily Ann Victor (who was born 1828/9), daughter of John George Victor, captain RN, of Belfast; died 2 December 1886 at 32 Tavistock Road, London; buried in Kensal Green; probate London 15 December 1886. [Addison (1898); *BMJ* obituary (1886); *BNL* 26 May 1848 (m); Brockliss, Cardwell and Moss (2005); Crawford (1930); Dub GRO (m); Lond PPR, will cal; Plarr (1930); UHF database (m)].

CHERMSIDE, JAMES (*fl c* 1780), Portaferry, county Down;
apothecary, of Portaferry c 1780; married —; father of Dr Thomas Chermside, senior (*q.v.*). [Pilson (1934)].

CHERMSIDE, ROBERT (1746/7–1803), Portaferry, county Down;
born 1746/7; surgeon, of Portaferry; married Elizabeth Jackson (who was born 1756/7 and died 1 June 1830); father of Sir Robert Alexander Chermside (*q.v.*); died 17 November 1803 in Portaferry 'after a tedious illness'; probate Down Diocesan Court 1803; buried in Ballyphilip graveyard, Portaferry. [*BNL* 22 November 1803 (d) and 22 June 1830 (d); Belf PRO, Down Dio Wills index; Clarke, *County Down*, vol 13 (1975)].

CHERMSIDE, ROBERT (1804/5–42), Warrenpoint, county Down;
born 1804/5 in Portaferry; MD (Edin) 1828 (thesis 'De diabete'); general practitioner, of Warrenpoint; married — (daughters born in 1834 and 1838); died

1 September 1842; probate Prerogative Court 1842. [*BNL* 16 December 1834 (b), 23 February 1838 (b), 29 June 1838 (d) and 9 September 1842 (d); Belf PRO, prerog wills index; Edin Univ].

CHERMSIDE, SIR ROBERT ALEXANDER (1787–1860), Army Medical Service;
born 1787 in Portaferry, county Down, third son of Dr Robert Chermside of Portaferry (*q.v.*); joined the Army Medical Service as assistant surgeon with the 7th Hussars 1810; surgeon with the 10th Hussars 1815; served in the Peninsula War and and Waterloo; studied medicine at Edinburgh University; MD (Edin) 1817 (thesis 'De aqua frigida'); LRCP Lond 1821; FRCP Lond 1843; settled in Paris 1821, retired from army on half pay 1823; commuted half pay 1831; Knight of the Hanoverian Guelphic Order 1831; Knight Bachelor 1835; Knight Commander of the Hanoverian Guelphic Order 1840; Knight of St John of Jerusalem; Knight of the Red Eagle of Prussia; Chevalier of the Legion d'Honneur; physician to the British Embassy at Paris and physician extraordinary to HRH Duchess of Kent; lived finally at Beaumont Street, Oxford; married 15 May 1821 in Edinburgh, Jane Meriel Williams (who died 1852), only daughter of Robert Williams of Cerne Lodge, Dorsetshire; died 8 September 1860 in Beaumont Street; probate Oxford 30 October 1860. [*BNL* 29 May 1821 (m); Crone (1928); Edin Univ; Kirkpatrick Archive; Lond PPR, will cal; Martin (2003); *Munk's Roll*, vol 3; Newmann (1993); *Oxford DNB* (2004); Peterkin and Johnston (1968)].

CHERMSIDE, SAMUEL WILLIAM (d 1842), Army Medical Service;
born in Portaferry, county Down, son of Dr Robert Chermside (*q.v.*); studied medicine at Edinburgh University c 1816–19; MD (St Andrew's) 1814 (on testimonials); joined the Army Medical Service as assistant surgeon with the 11th Foot 1818; on half pay 1819; with 7th Royal Veteran Battalion 1819; on half pay 1821; returned to 11th Foot 1824; surgeon with 23rd Foot (Royal Welsh Fusilliers) 1839; retired on half pay 1841; died 14 January 1842; buried in Ballyphilip graveyard, Portaferry. [*BNL* 21 January 1842 (d); Clarke, *County Down*, vol 13 (1975); Newmann (1993); Peterkin and Johnston (1968); Smart (2004)].

CHERMSIDE, THOMAS, senior (1780/1–1852), Portaferry, county Down;
born 1780/1, son of Dr James Chermside, apothecary, of Portaferry (*q.v.*); surgeon and apothecary, of Portaferry; married Jane — (who was born 1785/6 and died 24 February 1846); father of Dr Thomas Chermside, junior (*q.v.*); died 20 May 1852; buried in Ballyphilip graveyard, Portaferry; probate Down Diocesan Court 1852 (copy of will in PRO NI). [*BNL* 3 March 1846 (d) and 26 May 1852 (d); Belf PRO, Down Dio Wills index; Belf PRO, T662/197; Clarke, *County Down*, vol 13 (1975); *Med Dir*; Pigot (1824); Pilson (1934)].

CHERMSIDE, THOMAS, junior (1809/10–57), Portaferry, county Down;
born 1809/10, son of Dr Thomas Chermside, senior, of Portaferry (*q.v.*); LAH Dub 1828; MD (Glas) 1841; general practitioner of Portaferry; married 8 June 1848 in Portaferry Presbyterian Church, Margaret Bowden (who was born 1821/2 and died 27 October 1849), daughter of Hugh Bowden, merchant, of Portaferry; died 22 May 1857 in Portaferry; buried in Ballyphilip graveyard, Portaferry. [Addison (1898);

Apothecaries (1829); *BNL* 13 June 1848 (m), 13 November 1849 (d) and 26 May 1857 (d); Clarke, *County Down*, vol 13 (1975); *Coleraine Chronicle* 17 June 1848 (m); *Med Dir*; Pilson (1934); UHF database (m)].

CHERRY, GEORGE (*fl c* 1824), Armagh;
surgeon, of Scotch Street, Armagh c 1824. [Pigot (1824)].

CHERRY, MOSES (*fl c* 1725), Belfast;
'doctor'; given freedom of Belfast 1725. [Young (1892)].

CHESTNUT, EMILY FRANCES (1866–1937), Belfast;
born 23 December 1866 in county Kerry, daughter of the Rev William Wallace Chestnut, minister of Tralee Presbyterian Church, and Elizabeth Stewart; educated at Tralee Ladies' School; married (1) 24 October 1889 in Tralee Presbyterian Church, the Rev James Henry Fitzsimons, missionary, who died abroad c 1890; studied medicine at Queen's College, Belfast, from 1891; LRCP LRCS Edin 1896; LFPS Glas 1896; general practitioner and anaesthetist (for her second husband), of Clounalour, Antrim Road, of Crescent House, University Road, Belfast and of Tralee, county Kerry; married (2) 25 June 1902 Sir John Campbell (*q.v.*); died 20 May 1937 at Culloden, Craigvad, county Down; administration Belfast 26 October 1937. [Belf GRO (d); Belf PRO, will cal; *BMJ* obituary (1937); Dub GRO ((b) and (m); *Med Dir*; QCB adm reg].

CHESTNUTT, JOSEPH WALLACE (c 1837–86), Ahoghill, county Antrim;
born c 1837, son of John Chestnutt, farmer, of Ballymoney, county Antrim; educated at Belfast Academy; studied arts and medicine at Queen's College, Belfast, from 1857; BA (QUI) 1860; MD 1865; LRCS Edin and LM 1865; LM Lying-in Hospital, Cork; MA (RUI) 1882; medical officer and registrar of births and deaths to Ahoghill Dispensary District; married (1) 6 October 1869 in First Cookstown Presbyterian Church, Anne Smyth, daughter of J.A. Smyth, esquire, of Cookstown; (2) 25 November 1875 in Second Ahoghill Presbyterian Church. Mary Raphael Buick, third daughter of the Rev Frederick Buick, minister of Trinity Presbyterian Church, Ahoghill, and — Raphael; died 7 July 1886 at Ahoghill; buried in Trinity Presbyterian Graveyard, Ahoghill; probate Belfast 23 August 1886. [Belf PRO, will cal; *Coleraine Chronicle* 9 October 1869 (m); Dub GRO (d); gravestone inscription; *Med Dir*; QCB adm reg; Stewart (1950); UHF database (m)].

CHILD, ROBERT (c 1612–54), New England, Kent and Belfast;
born c 1612, son of John Child of Northfleet, Kent; studied arts at Corpus Christi College, Cambridge from 1628; BA (Cantab) 1631; MA 1635; studied medicine at Leyden 1635 and Padua from 1636; MD (Padua) 1638; emigrated to New England 1644; in trouble there because of his theological views; convicted of sedition, fined and imprisoned; left for England 1647 but the ship's captain was warned that there was a Jonah on board and when a storm arose his papers were thrown overboard; settled in Kent and devoted himself to science and alchemy; moved to Ulster 1652; died 1654 near Belfast. [Morpurgo (1927); Innes Smith (1932); Venn (1922)].

CHILD, WARWICK LONG (1856–95), London;
born 14 September 1856 at Manchester, son of J.G.T. Child, merchant, of 8 Belsize Park, London; studied medicine at Queen's College, Manchester, and from 1878, at Queen's College, Belfast; MRCSE 1878; MD and LM (QUI) 1881; junior house surgeon at Ancoats Hospital, Manchester; general practitioner, of 'Silverhowe', 2 College Park Villas, Harrow Road, London, from c 1883; married Mary Ocland —; died 15 March 1895; administration (with will) London 11 June 1895. [Lond PPR, will cal; *Med Dir*; QCB adm reg].

CHILLICK, JAMES (1800–61), Clareview, county Fermanagh;
born 1800; died 30 December 1861 at Clareview, the home of his brother-in-law, John Humphreys. [*Londonderry Sentinel* 3 January 1862 (d); *Med Dir*].

CHIPP, E.T. (*fl c* 1863), Belfast;
surgeon; of Belfast c 1863; married —; sons educated at RBAI. [Fisher and Robb (1913)].

CHIRMSIDE, — (*fl c* 1850), Portaferry, county Down;
general practitioner, of Portaferry c 1850; died aged 37; buried in Ballyphilip graveyard, Portaferry (worn gravestone). [Clarke, *County Down*, vol 13 (1975)].

CHRISTAL, JOHN (d c 1927), Cootehill, county Cavan, and San Francisco;
studied medicine at the Ledwich School, Dublin; LRCSI 1875; LKQCPI and LM 1876; general practitioner, of Cootehill, county Cavan c 1885; emigrated to USA c 1890; general practitioner of 789 Mission Street, San Francisco, c 1895 and of 612 Hyde Street c 1905, of 1536 Webster Street c 1910, of 1271 Pine Street c 1915–20, and of 1377 Fulton Street c 1925; died c 1927. [McCann (2003); *Med Dir*].

CHRISTIAN, JAMES STANLEY (1813/4–71), Castleshane, county Monaghan, and London;
born 1813/4; MRCSE 1837; LRCP Lond 1841; FRCSI 1844; medical officer to Castleshane Dispensary District and constabulary c 1846; general practitioner, of 1 Ovington Terrace, Brompton Road, London c 1870; died 17 October 1871 at 7 Prince of Wales Terrace, Kensington; probate London 29 November 1871. [Croly (1843–6); Lond GRO (d); Lond PPR, will cal; *Med Dir*].

CHRISTIAN, THOMAS (*fl c* 1840), county Antrim;
general practitioner; married 16 June 1840 Eleanor Dickson (who died 23 August 1858), eldest daughter of the Rev Stephen Dickson, prebendary of Cairncastle, county Antrim. [*BNL* 23 June 1840 (m); Leslie (1993)].

CHRISTIE, DAVID (1836/7–1917), Carrigart, county Donegal;
born 1836/7; studied medicine at Glasgow University and Anderson's College, Glasgow; LRCP Edin 1863; LFPS Glas and LM 1863; surgeon on the sailing ships *Stadacona* and *Minnehaha* in 1865–6, the last of the emigrant saling ships from Londonderry to America; medical officer to Dunfanaghy Union Workhouse; medical

officer to Rosguill Dispensary District, coastguards and constabulary 1868–1900; author of various medical papers; retired 1906; married —; died 29 August 1917 at Carrigart; probate Dublin 2 October 1917. [Belf PRO, will cal; Dub GRO (d); Kirkpatrick Archive; *Lancet* obituary (1917); Lucas (1962); *Med Dir*].

CHURCH, ELWOOD (d 1855), Kilrea, county Londonderry;
surgeon; died 23 June 1855 at Kilrea. [*BNL* 3 July 1855 (d)].

CHURCH, JOHN (c 1752/3–1844), Russian army;
born 1752/3; served for 30 years as surgeon major in the service of the Russian Emperor; retired to Ballymaclary, Limavady; married —; died 10 October 1844 at Ballymaclary. [*BNL* 5 November 1844 (d); Hitchings, Paul, pers com; *Londonderry Sentinel* 2 November 1844 (d)].

CHURCH, ROBERT (*fl c* 1795), Limavady, county Londonderry;
surgeon, of Ballymaclary, Limavady; married 11 August 1795 in St Patrick's Church of Ireland Church, Coleraine, Catherine Kennedy. [Coleraine, St Patrick's C of I mar reg; Hitchings, Paul, pers com].

CHURCHILL, FLEETWOOD (1808–78), Dublin;
born 21 February 1808 in Nottingham, third son of Fleetwood Churchill, a businessman of Nottingham, and Hannah Page; apprenticed to a general practitioner in Nottingham and indentured to surgeon Willaim Forbes of Camberwell, London; studied medicine in London, Edinburgh, Dublin and Paris; MD (Edin) 1831 (thesis 'De peritonitide'); LKQCPI 1832; FKQCPI 1851; MD (TCD) 1851; obstetrician and gynaecologist in Dublin 1832–75; co-founder, with Dr Robert Duffield Speedy, of the Western Lying-in Hospital 1835 (closed 1853); a founding member of the Sanitary Association 1850; lecturer in midwifery in Digge's Street and Carmichael School of Medicine; professor of midwifery in the School of Physic, Trinity College, Dublin 1856–64; of 15 St Stephen's Green, Dublin; president of Obstetrical Society; president of the KQCPI 1867–8; president of the Pathological Society; author of *Diseases of Women and Children* (1838), *Operative Midwifery* (1841) and *Diseases of Children* (1849); retired in 1875 to live with his daughter, Mary Ferrier Churchill who had married the Rev William Henry Meade, at Ardtrea, county Tyrone, and presented his library to the RCPI; married in 1832 Janet Rebecca Ferrier; father of Dr Fleetwood Churchill, junior, LRCSI 1853, of Dublin, Dr Alexander Ferrier Churchill, MB (TCD) 1861, AMS, Dr Charles Fleetwood Churchill, MB (TCD) 1863, AMS, and Dr George Fleetwood Churchill, MB (TCD), AMS; died 31 January 1878 at the Rectory, Ardtrea, the home of his daughter; buried in Ardtrea churchyard; 'probably the best-known doctor in his specialty in the United Kingdom, other than J.Y. Simpson of Edinburgh' (*Oxford DNB*); portrait in RCPI by Sir Thomas Alfred Jones; probate Dublin 18 March 1878. [Belf PRO, will cal; *BMJ* obituary (1878); Burtchaell and Sadleir (1935); Cameron (1916); *DIB* (2009); Dub GRO (d); Edin Univ; Fleetwood (1983); Grimshaw (1878); Kirkpatrick Archive; Kirkpatrick and Jellett (1913); Leslie (1911); *Med Dir*; O'Brien, Crookshank and Wolstenholme (1984); *Oxford DNB* (2004) Widdess (1963)].

CINNAMOND, ROBERT (1770/1–1832), Naval Medical Service;
born 1770/1, son of Robert Cinnamond of Magheragall, county Antrim; joined the Naval Medical Service as assistant surgeon; surgeon 1795; died 21 October 1833 [*BNL*] or 19 October 1832 [*Mem Dead*]; buried in Trummery graveyard, county Antrim. [*BNL* 25 October 1833 (d); *Memorials of the Dead*, vol XI, p 398; *NMS* (1826)].

CLANNY, WILLIAM REID (1776–1850), Naval Medical Service and Bishopwearmouth, county Durham;
born 1776 in Bangor, county Down; studied medicine at Edinburgh University; MD (Edin) 1803 (thesis 'De asphyxia'); joined the Naval Medical Service as assistant surgeon and was present at the battle of Copenhagan (1801); retired 1802; invented a safety lamp for miners in 1812, several years before Sir Humphrey Davy, for which he received gold and silver medals from the Society of Arts in 1816 and 1817, and a public presentation at Sunderland, county Durham; author of *An Analysis of the Mineral Waters of Batterby* (1807), *Hypreanthraxis* (1832) (on cholera) and *Priority of Invention of the Safety Lamp* (1844); married 14 March 1802 in Edinburgh, Margaret Mitchell, daughter of an East India Company official; died 10 January 1850 at 1 Bridge Street, Bishopwearmouth. [Crone (1928); Edin Univ; Lond GRO (d); McCoy (1985); *Med Dir;* Newmann (1993); *Oxford DNB* (2004)].

CLARE, JOHN HAMILTON (*fl c* 1845), Bangor, county Down;
MRCSE 1838; accoucheur of the Dublin Lying-in Hospital (Rotunda); general practitioner in Bangor, county Down c 1845. [Croly (1843–6)].

CLARENDON, SAMUEL ALKER (1815/6–1900), Bryansford, county Down;
born 1815/6 in Dublin, son of Thomas Clarendon; educated at the Luxemburgh School; studied arts and medicine at Trinity College, Dublin, from 1832; BA (TCD) 1837; LRCPI 1838 and LM Rot Hosp Dub 1838; MB 1839; FRCSI 1845; medical officer to Bryansford Dispensary District, constabulary and coastguard; retired c 1890 to 36 Mountjoy Square, Dublin; unmarried; died 16 January 1900 at 36 Mountjoy Square; probate Dublin 6 March 1900. [Belf PRO, will cal; Burtchaell and Sadleir (1924); Dub GRO (d); *Med Dir*].

CLARK, BENJAMIN (c 1760–93), Abbeville, South Carolina;
born c 1760 in Ballybay, county Monaghan, fourth son of the Rev (Dr) Thomas Clark (*q.v.*), minister of Cahans Presbyterian Church, and Elizabeth Nesbitt; emigrated to join his father in the USA in 1764 and settled in Abbeville; married — Cochran; died c 1793 in Abbeville. [Nesbitt (1999)].

CLARK, CHARLES (d 1873), Dublin, London, Naval Medical Service and Adelaide, South Australia;
born in 'the north of Ireland' (Plarr); educated at Redemon Academy, county Down; qualified as a medical student by passing an examination in latin and greek at the Apothecaries' Hall 1825; apprenticed to Dr James Murray of Belfast 1826–c 1831; studied medicine at the Royal College of Surgeons in Ireland and Trinity College,

Dublin 1833–5; MRCSE 1836; LKQCPI 1860; FRCSE 1862; assistant inspector of anatomy (under Sir James Murray) in Dublin; travelled to the Cape and India 1836; general practitioner in Hampstead Road, London 1837; surgeon to the West India Steam Packet Service; passed examination by the Navy Board and joined HMS *Actaeon* at Barbados 1842, traveling extensively; retired 1843 and emigrated to Australia; general practitioner in Brighton, Adelaide; died 23 December 1873 at Brighton. [*Med Dir*; Plarr (1930)].

CLARK(E), HENRY BOLTON (1825–95), Upperlands, county Londonderry, US Army, Eastwood, Nottinghamshire and Adelaide, Australia;
born 20 November 1825 in Dublin, fifth son of Alexander Clark of Ampertain House, Upperlands, and Sarah Newport; younger brother of Dr Jackson Newport Clark (*q.v.*); educated by Mr Fredlesius; studied arts and medicine at Trinity College, Dublin, from 1833 (no degree); MRCSE 1849; LM Rot Hosp Dub 1852; general practitioner of Upperlands, surgeon in United States Army; civil surgeon with British Army during Crimean War 1854–5; surgeon on SS *State of Pennsylvania* c 1875; general practitioner of Eastwood, c 1878; emigrated to Adelaide, South Australia c 1880; married 27 November 1883 in St Paul's Church, Adelaide, Rosetta Lane (who died 2 April 1905), daughter of Dr Alexander Lane (*q.v.*) of Aghadowey; died 24 July 1895. [Burke's *Irish Family Records* (1976); Burtchaell and Sadleir (1924); Hitchings, Paul, pers com; *Med Dir*].

CLARK, JACKSON (NEWPORT) (1815–78) Upperlands, county Londonderry;
born 8 Febuary 1815 in county Londonderry, third son of Alexander Clark of Ampertain House, Upperlands, and Sarah Newport; older brother of Dr Henry Bolton Clark (*q.v.*); educated by Mr McCloskey; studied arts and medicine at Trinity College, Dublin, from 1831, Royal College of Surgeons in Ireland and Richmond Hospital; BA (TCD) 1836; LRCSI 1837; LM Rot Hosp Dub 1837; MD (Glas) 1838; general practitioner in Upperlands, Maghera; unmarried; died 20 April 1878 at Upperlands. [Addison (1898); *Burke's Irish Family Records* (1976); Burtchaell and Sadleir (1924); Dub GRO (d); Kirkpatrick Archive; *Med Dir*].

CLARK, JOHN HENRY (1862–1950), ship's surgeon, and Bellaghy and Kilrea, county Londonderry;
born 5 September 1862, fourth son of William Clark, linen merchant, of Ampertain House, county Londonderry, and Marianne Elizabeth Paul Newport; nephew of Drs Jackson Newport Clark (*q.v.*) and Henry Bolton Clark (*q.v.*); educated by Dr Ford; studied arts and medicine at Trinity College, Dublin, from 1881; BA (TCD) 1886; LM Rot Hosp Dub 1888; MB BCh BAO 1888; MD 1889; medical officer to the London Provident Dispensary; surgeon to the Anchor Line Steamship Company; medical officer to Bellaghy Dispensary District; general practitioner, of Clougheen, Kilrea; married 10 November 1892 Mary Violet Moore (who was born 1872/3 and died 12 April 1965), eldest daughter of Thomas Moore of Flowerfield, Portstewart, county Londonderry; died 12 December 1950; probate Belfast 28 June 1951. [Belf PRO, will cal; *Burke's Irish Family Records* (1976); *Med Dir*; TCD adm reg; *TCD Cat*, vol II (1896)].

CLARK, THOMAS (1720–92), Ballybay, county Monaghan;
born 5 November 1720 in Paisley, Scotland; studied medicine and divinity at Glasgow University c 1744–5, while he was chaplain to a gentleman's family in Galloway; LFPS Glas 1748; minister of Cahans (Ballybay) Presbyterian Church (Seceeders) 1751–64; probably practised medicine occasionally in Monaghan, and did later in Long Cane; imprisoned for two months for refusal to take the oath in the usual form 1754; seems to have been aggressive and critical of his Monaghan flock, being described as 'peculiarly odd and uncouth'; author of various religious works; emigrated on 10 May 1764 with 300 other Presbyterians, sailing from Narrow Water to New York; settled first at Salem, New York 1764–82; moved to South Carolina, serving congregations at Cedar Spring, Little Run and Long Cane 1782–92; married c 1752 Elizabeth Nesbitt (who was born 1730 and died 17 December 1862; buried at Cahans), daughter of Thomas Nesbitt of Drumaconner; died 26 December 1792 (found dead sitting in his chair); buried in Cedar Springs Cemetery, Abbeville. [Nesbitt (1999); Stewart (1950)].

CLARK, THOMAS (1832–91), Army Medical Service;
born 11 December 1832, youngest son of Thomas Clark of Belfast and Mary —; LRCSI 1853; joined the Army Medical Service 1854 as assistant surgeon to 33rd Foot; staff surgeon 1864; transferred to 69th Foot 1867; retired on half pay with honorary rank of brigade surgeon 1880; served in Crimea and Indian Mutiny; died 23 December 1891 at the Bethelem Hospital, London; commemorated in Clifton Street Graveyard, Belfast; probate London 20 February 1892. [Lond PPR, will cal; *Med Dir*; Merrick and Clarke, *Belfast*, vol 4 (1991); Peterkin and Johnston (1968)].

CLARK, WILLIAM (*fl c* 1826), Magherascouse, county Down;
surgeon, of Magherascouse; married 24 February 1826 Elizabeth Frazer (who died 23 September 1843), youngest daughter of Richard Frazer of Ravara, county Down. [*BNL* 3 March 1826 (m) and 3 October 1843 (d)].

CLARKE, ADAM (1844/5–1912), Tempo, county Fermanagh;
born 1844/5; studied medicine at Royal College of Surgeons in Ireland; LM Rot Hosp Dub 1865; LKQCPI and LM 1866; LRCSI 1866; medical officer to Tempo Dispensary District and constabulary, registrar of births and deaths and public vaccinator; married Elizabeth —; died 16 October 1912 at Tempo; administration Dublin 16 June 1913. [Belf PRO, will cal; Dub GRO (d); *Med Dir*].

CLARKE, ANDREW (*fl c* 1807–20), Trinidad and Belmont, county Donegal;
general practitioner, of Trinidad c 1807 and of Belmont c 1820; married —; father of William Hislop Clarke who entered Trinity College, Dublin 1821. [Burtchaell and Sadleir (1924); Kirkpatrick Archive].

CLARKE, ANDREW (1845/6–82), Victoria, Australia;
born 1845/6 in Clones, county Monaghan, son of Andrew Clark, merchant; educated at Dungannon Royal School; studied medicine at Trinity College, Dublin, from 1864 and Sir Patrick Dun's and the House of Industry Hospitals, Dublin; Scholar 1867;

BA (TCD) 1868; MB MCh 1873; LM Rot Hosp Dub 1873; resident surgeon at the Richmond Hospital; emigrated to Linton, Victoria, Australia c 1875 and moved to Maryborough, Victoria c 1877; died 19 March 1878 at Ararat, Victoria; administration (with will) Dublin 8 December 1887. [Belf PRO, will cal; *Med Dir*; TCD adm reg; *TCD Cat*, vol II (1896)].

CLARKE, ANDREW CAMPBELL (1805/6–76), Coleraine, county Londonderry;
born 1805/6; LRCS Edin 1831; LAH Dub 1841; surgeon, of 10 Church Street, Coleraine, from 1838; married c 1838 Margaret —; died 17 April 1876 at 10 Church Street; administration Londonderry 3 February 1877. [Belf PRO, will cal; Dub GRO (d); Kirkpatrick Archive; *Med Dir*].

CLARKE, ARNOLD (1844–84), Carrickmacross, county Monaghan;
born 14 April 1844 in Cavan, son of Thomas Clarke of Killinkere, county Cavan; educated by the Rev John King of Bellases, Coleraine; studied medicine at Queen's College, Belfast, from 1863; LRCP and LRCS Edin 1871; general practitioner, of Corvalley, Carrickmacross, c 1875; married —; died 28 July 1884 at Ballybay; administration Armagh 11 February 1885. [Belf PRO, will cal; Dub GRO (d); *Med Dir*; QCB adm reg].

CLARKE, CHARLES GRANVILLE (1852/3–1920), Bessbrook, county Armagh, and London;
born 1852/3; studied medicine at Bellevue, New York, Paris and Dublin; MD (Bellevue College, NY) 1880; LRCPI and LM 1882; general practitioner, of Bessbrook, county Armagh; moved to Downs Park Road, Clapton, London, c 1906, to Dumsmure Road, Stamford Hill, c 1909 and to 8 Chardmore Road, Stoke Newington c 1912; died 27 August 1920 at 8 Chardmore Road; probate London 3 December 1920. [Lond GRO (d); Lond PPR, will cal; *Med Dir*].

CLARKE, FRANCIS (1808–77), Middletown, county Armagh, Blackrock, county Dublin, Mountrath, Queen's County, and Dunfanaghy, county Donegal;
born 1808 in Portarlington, Queen's County, son of the Rev Richard Clarke, chaplain of Portarlngton Church of Ireland Church; studied arts and medicine at Trinity College, Dublin, from 1824 and at Park Street, Dublin; BA (TCD) 1829; MRCSE 1831; accoucheur of the Anglesey Lying-in Hospital; MA MB 1832; FRCSI 1844; LM 1860; MRIA; medical officer of Middletown Fever Hospital, county Armagh, and of Blackwatertown and Benburb Dispensary Districts, county Tyrone, and constabulary c 1840–55; medical officer of Blackrock c 1860, and of Mountrath Dispensary District and Fever Hospital 1862–6; medical officer of Dunfanaghy Dispensary District and Fever Hospital 1866–76; retired 1876 to 3 Ormond Road, Rathmines, Dublin; married 15 May 1839 in St Peter's Church of Ireland Church, Dublin, Rebecca Clarke (who died 16 November 1858), daughter of Jonathan David Clarke of Merrion Square South, Dublin, and La Bergerie, Portarlington; father of Dr Francis Edward Clarke (*q.v.*); died 4 October 1877 at 3 Ormond Road; probate Dublin 18 January 1878. [*BNL* 21 May 1839 (m) and 18 November 1858 (d); Belf PRO, will cal; Burtchaell and Sadleir (1924); Croly (1843–6); Leslie and Wallace (2009); *Med Dir*].

CLARKE, FRANCIS EDWARD (c 1847–1910), Oughterard, county Galway, and Boyle, county Roscommon;

born c 1847, eldest son of Dr Francis Clarke of Dunfanaghy, county Donegal (*q.v.*); educated privately; studied medicine at Trinity College, Dublin, from 1864 and the Meath and Sir Patrick Dun's Hospitals, Dublin; BA (TCD) 1867; MB 1868; MRCSE 1868; LM Rot Hosp Dub 1868; MA 1872; LKQCPI and LM 1873; MD 1873; MRIA 1876; LLB and LLD 1877; medical officer to Oughterard Dispensary District c 1875; ordained deacon 1878 and priest 1879 (Kilmore); curate of Killashee 1878–9; rector of Killinagh 1879–83 and of Boyle (Elphin) 1883–1910; precentor of Elphin 1892–1904; archdeacon of Elphin 1904–10; married 28 October 1869 in South Molton Church, Devonshire, Lucy Elizabeth Flexman (who was born 1841/2), eldest daughter of Dr James Flexman, surgeon, of South Molton; died 9 March 1910; buried in Boyle Churchyard; commemorated by three windows in the church. [Leslie and Crooks (2008); Lond GRO (m); *Londonderry Sentinel* 5 November 1869 (m); *Med Dir*; TCD adm reg; *TCD Cat*, vol II (1896)].

CLARKE, FREDERICK (1824–59), Army Medical Service;

born 9 June 1824 at Limavady, county Londonderry, eldest son of the Rev Edward Marmaduke Clarke, curate of Clonleigh (Lifford, county Donegal), and later rector of Upper Badoney (Newtownstewart, county Tyrone); LRCSI; joined the Army Medical Service as assistant surgeon 1848, attached to 25th Foot 1849; transferred to 13th Foot 1852 and 24th Foot 1853; staff surgeon 2nd class 1857; died 3 January 1859 at Cork barracks. [*BNL* 12 January 1859 (d); *Coleraine Chronicle* 22 January 1859 (d); Leslie (1937); *Londonderry Sentinel* 14 January 1859 (d); Peterkin and Johnston (1968)].

CLARKE, GEORGE (1824/5–58), Naval Medical Service;

born 1824/5; brother of Dr Robert Clarke, Naval Medical Service (*q.v.*); of Port Hall, county Donegal; joined the Naval Medical Service as surgeon; died 30 April 1858 in Paris; buried in Montparnasse Cemetery and commemorated in Grange graveyard, Strabane. [*Coleraine Chronicle* 8 May 1858 (d); *Londonderry Sentinel* 14 May 1858 (d); Todd (1993)].

CLARKE, GEORGE (1855–1925), Belfast and India;

born 6 May 1855 in Belfast, son of John Clarke, druggist, of Wellington Place, Belfast, and Plasmerdyn, Holywood; educated at Foyle College, Londonderry; studied medicine at Queen's College, Belfast, from 1876; MD MCh (RUI) 1883; LRCP LRCS Edin 1883; general practitioner of 13 Wellington Park, Belfast; in Sileuri, Cachar, Bengal, India c 1895–1905; director of Messrs John Clarke & Co, wholesale chemists; returned to 13 Wellington Park c 1905; unmarried; died 20 February 1925 at 13 Wellington Park; buried in Belfast City Cemetery; administration Belfast 29 June 1925. [Belf City Cem, bur reg; Belf GRO (d); Belf PRO, will cal; Kirkpatrick Archive; *Med Dir*; QCB adm reg].

CLARKE, GEORGE (1862–94), Portadown, county Armagh;

born 8 February 1862 at Tandragee, county Armagh, son of Thomas Clarke, farmer, of Drumcree and Tandragee; educated at Lurgan College; studied medicine at

Queen's College, Belfast, from 1879; MD MCh (RUI) 1884; LM KQCPI 1885; general practitioner, of Church Place, Portadown; married 2 July 1890 in Portadown Methodist Church, Elizabeth Bathhurst of Rosemount Terrace, Belfast, daughter of William Bathhurst; died 24 June 1895; administration Dublin 18 December 1895. [Belf PRO, will cal; Dub GRO (m); Kirkpatrick Archive; *Med Dir*; QCB adm reg].

CLARKE, HUGH (*fl c* 1781), Cavan;
of Cavan; studied medicine at Rheims University; MD (Rheims) 1781. [Brockliss].

CLARKE, HUGH ALEXANDER (1855–1939), Liverpool;
born 21 November 1855, son of David Clarke, farmer, of Gloonan, Gracehill, county Antrim, brother of Dr William Robert Clarke (*q.v.*) of Liverpool; educated at RBAI; studied arts, law and medicine at Queen's College, Belfast, from 1872, and University College, Liverpool; BA (QUI) 1875; MA 1877; MD MCh (RUI) 1885; general practitioner, of 94 Durning Road, Liverpool c 1886 and of 2 Beech Street, Liverpool c 1895; honorary physician to Liverpool Hospital for Consumption and visiting physician to Liverpool City Hospital East, of 1 Deane Road, Liverpool; retired c 1934; married —; died 24 June 1939 at 1 Deane Road; probate Liverpool 13 September 1939. [Lond GRO (d); Lond PPR, will cal; *Med Dir*; QCB adm reg].

CLARKE, JAMES (1793/4–1822), Moneymore, county Londonderry;
born 1793/4, only son of William Clarke of Springvale, near Moneymore; general practitioner; died 11 June 1822 'after a lingering illness' with 'unremitting attention to the poor of his neighbourhood, to whose health his abilities and purse were principally devoted'. [*BNL* 5 July 1822 (d)].

CLARKE, JAMES (1852–1901), Indian Medical Service;
born 27 February 1852 in Belfast, son of Dr John Clarke of 99 Donegall Street, Belfast (*q.v.*); educated at RBAI from 1868; studied medicine at Queen's College, Belfast, from 1870; MD MCh Dip Mid (QUI)1877; FRCSI 1893; DPH Camb 1893; returned to Queen's College in 1878–9 to study 'dissections'; joined the Indian Medical Service (Bengal establishment) as surgeon 1880; surgeon major 1892; surgeon lieutenant-colonel 1900; served on North-East Frontier, Akha, 1883–4; died 15 February 1901 at Sialkot, Lahore. [Crawford (1930); Fisher and Robb (1913); *Med Dir*; QCB adm reg].

CLARKE, JAMES (1861/2–1929), Ballyjamesduff, county Cavan;
born 1861/2, eldest son of the Rev James Clarke, rector of Castlewellan, county Down, and Sarah Louisa Pratt of Gawsworth, county Cork; studied arts and medicine at Trinity College, Dublin, from 1882; BA (TCD) 1885; MB 1887; BCh 1889; LM Coombe Hosp Dub; of The Rectory, Castlewellan c 1887; medical officer to the Cariboo District, British Columbia c 1890; general practitioner, of Ballyjamesduff and medical officer and public vaccinator to Termon Dispensary District c 1895–1919, of the Cottage, Mullagh, Kells, county Meath; married 16 April 1896 in Oldcastle, county Meath, Adelaide A.E. King, daughter of the Rev Joseph King, rector of Munterconnaught, county Cavan, and sister of Dr Francis Joseph George King of Shilelagh, county Wicklow (*q.v.*); died 13 October 1929 at

Morehampton Road, Dublin; administration Dublin 17 December 1929. [Dub GRO (m); Dub Nat Arch, will cal; Kirkpatrick Archive; Leslie and Crooks (2008); *Med Dir*; Swanzy (1933); TCD adm reg; *TCD Cat*, vol II (1896)].

CLARKE, JAMES ALEXANDER (1868–1951), Carrickfergus, county Antrim;
born 16 September 1868 at Ballyagan, Garvagh, county Londonderry, son of Robert Clarke, farmer, of Ballyagan, and Anne Boyce; educated at Coleraine Academical Institution; studied medicine at Queen's College, Cork; MB BCh BAO (RUI)1895; general practitioner in West Street, Carrickfergus from c 1900 and High Street from c 1906; living finally at 'Ordsall', Downshire Park, Carrickfergus; married Mary Elizabeth —; died 7 March 1951 at 'Ordsall', Carrickfergus; probate Belfast 14 August 1951. [Belf GRO (d); Belf PRO, will cal; Dub GRO (b); Kirkpatrick Archive; *Med Dir*; Young and Pike (1909)].

CLARKE, JOHN (*fl c* 1800), Belfast;
surgeon, of Belfast c 1774; surgeon to the Poor House in 1775, 1813 and 1827 [possibly two of the same name]; married Catherine Sarah Dickson, sister of Margaret Dickson who married Dr Alexander Ross (*q.v.*); executor of the will of Margaret Ross, dated 1774, proved 1786. [Ellis and Eustace, vol III (1984); Strain (1961)].

CLARKE, JOHN (1815/6–1908), Templepatrick, county Antrim, and Belfast;
born 1815/6; studied medicine at Trinity College, Dublin, and Edinburgh University, Edinburgh Infirmary and Jervis Street Hospital; MRCSE 1840; surgeon, of Templepatrick, c 1846; surgeon to Belfast General Dispensary until 1857; general practitioner, of 99 Donegall Street, Belfast c 1870 and of 162 York Street c 1885; married 7 December 1840 in Edinburgh, Margaret Grey Burns (who was born 1820/1 and died 3 October 1861), third daughter of David Burns, writer; father of Dr James Clarke (*q.v.*); died 25 October 1908 at 4 Donegall Terrace, Antrim Road; buried in Movilla graveyard, Newtownards. [*BNL* 15 December 1840 (m); Clarke, *County Down*, vol 11 (1974); Croly (1843–6); Dub GRO (d); *Med Dir*].

CLARKE, JOHN (1830–64), Army Medical Service;
born 14 September 1830 at Ballymena, county Antrim; MD (King's College, Aberdeen) 1860; joined the Army Medical Service as staff assistant surgeon 1853, attached to the 95th Foot from 1854; staff surgeon 1860; transferred to 10th Foot 1862 and to 15th Foot 1864; served in the Crimea and the India Mutiny; died 4 September 1864 in Bermuda. [Peterkin and Johnston (1968)].

CLARKE, JOHN CLELLAND (1849/50–98), Coleraine, county Londonderry, and Bolton, Lancashire;
born 1849/50; brother of Dr Alexander Carson Clarke, MD (Edin) 1862; studied medicine at Edinburgh University; MB (Edin) (2nd class hons) 1871; MRCSE 1871; LSA Lond 1871; general practitioner in Coleraine; moved to 41 Long Causeway, Farneworth near Bolton c 1880; died 16 February 1898 of typhoid fever, at 41 Long Causeway; administration London 4 May 1898 and 9 January 1901. [Kirkpatrick (1889); Lond GRO (d); Lond PPR, will cal; *Med Dir*].

CLARKE, JOHN HENRY (1816/7–71), Kilkeel, county Down;
born 1816/7; studied arts and medicine at Trinity Collge, Dublin, from c 1833; BA (TCD) 1836; LRCSI 1838; MB MA 1839; medical officer in Manilla, Philipines; general practitioner and registrar of births and deaths for Kilkeel; married Elizabeth Dillon; died 5 June 1871 at Kilkeel; administration (with will) Dublin 18 April 1872. [Belf PRO, will cal; Burtchaell and Sadleir (1924); Dub GRO (d); Kirkpatrick Archive; *Med Dir*].

CLARKE, JOHN PATRICK (1851/2–1945), Castleblaney, county Monaghan;
born 1851/2; studied medicine at the Catholic University of Ireland; LRCSI 1876; LKQCPI and LM 1877; LAH Dub 1877; medical officer to Castleblaney Dispensary District, of York House, Castleblaney; married —; died 30 November 1945 at York House, Castleblaney. [Dub GRO (d); *Med Dir*].

CLARKE, JOSEPH (1758–1834), Dublin;
born 8 April 1758 at Tamnadoey, Desertlin parish, county Londonderry, second son of James Clarke, farmer; brother of Martha Clarke who married James Collins and was mother of Dr Robert Collins (*q.v.*) of Dublin; educated locally; studied arts at Glasgow University 1775–6 and medicine at Edinburgh University 1776–79; MD (Edin) 1779 (thesis 'De putretini in typho'); LRCPI 1785; visited Lausanne, Switzerland, and London 1780; moved to Dublin 1781 to visit his grand-uncle Dr George Maconchy, a leading obstetrician; assistant master of the Rotunda 1783–6 and master 1786–93; outstanding obstetrician who did much to reduce infant mortality; Hon FRCPI 1807; author of *A Treatise on Human Milk* (1786), *Observations on the Puerperal Fever* (1790) and *Remarks on the Causes and Cure of some Diseases of Infancy* (1793), as well as detailed accounts of 10,383 hospital deliveries and 3,878 private deliveries; of Sackville Street, Dublin, until 1802 and of 114 Rutland Square West 1802–34; retired 1829; married 7 April 1786 Isabella Cleghorn (who died 7 May 1847), niece of Professor George Cleghorn; father of Barbara Clarke who married Dr Robert Collins (*q.v.*), his biographer who was later master of the Rotunda; father of Dr James Clarke of Dublin, physician to the Rotunda Hospital, who died 5 October 1820 from typhus contracted in the Dublin House of Industry; died 10 September 1834 at Moray Place, Edinburgh, the home of his nephew Mr Learmont, while attending a meeting of the British Association; 'he had intended to even read a paper there, but finding himself, through increasing illness, unequal to the task, he handed it over to his friend Dr Jackson to read in his stead' [*BNL*]; buried in Moneymore Graveyard, county Londonderry; portrait by Martin Cregan (1836) in the Rotunda Hospital, Dublin. [*BNL* 19 September 1834 (d); Collins (1849); Collins, John, pers com; Crone (1928); *DIB* (2009); Edin Univ; Kirkpatrick and Jellett (1913); *Memorials of the Dead*, vol VIII, p 380; Newmann (1993); O'Brien, Crookshank and Wolstenholme (1984); O'Doherty (2002); *Oxford DNB* (2004); Widdess (1963)].

CLARKE, JOSEPH (1805/6–88), Naval Medical Service and Kilrea, county Londonderry;
born 1805/6; studied medicine at Edinburgh University; MD (Edin) 1827 (thesis 'De apoplexia'); LRCS Edin 1827; joined the Naval Medical Service as assistant

surgeon; retired to Kilrea; medical officer to Union and Mercer's Company's Dispensary, Kilrea, and constabulary; married 27 December 1838 in Bovevagh Presbyterian Church, Mary Kyle, second daughter of Arthur Kyle of Dungiven; died 21 April 1888 in Kilrea; probate Dublin 6 September 1888. [Belf PRO, will cal; Croly (1843–6); Dub GRO (d); Edin Univ; *Londonderry Sentinel* 29 December 1838 (m); *Med Dir*].

CLARKE, JOSEPH (1814/5–78), Bailieborough, county Cavan;
born 1814/5; LAH Dub 1836; LM Anglesey Hosp Dub 1837; LRCS Edin 1839; MRCSE 1855; LKQCPI and LM 1861; medical officer to Bailieborough Dispensary District, Model School and constabulary; married Elizabeth —; died 10 April 1878 at Bailieborough; probate Dublin 6 June 1878. [Belf PRO, will cal; Croly (1843–6); Dub GRO (d); *Med Dir*].

CLARKE, JOSEPH (d c 1868), Belfast;
studied medicine at RBAI from 1835, also at Dublin, Edinburgh and Glasgow; accoucheur of Edinburgh 1838; LAH Dub 1843; apothecary and surgeon, of 8 Castle Place, Belfast; medical officer for emigrant ships to USA and Australia; emigrated c 1865 and died abroad c 1868. [Belf PRO, SCH 524/1A; *Med Dir*].

CLARKE, JOSEPH (1854/5–93), Bailieborough, county Cavan;
born 1854/5; LRCSI and LM 1875; LKQCPI 1877; general practitioner in Bailieborough; unmarried; died 20 February 1893 at Bailieborough; administration Cavan 10 March 1893. [Belf PRO, will cal; Dub GRO (d); *Med Dir*].

CLARKE, ROBERT (d c 1886), Dunmurry, county Antrim;
son of the Rev William Clarke of Templepatrick; educated at RBAI 1831–5; studied medicine there 1835–9; MRCSE 1839; general practitioner of Dunmurry; died c 1886. [Belf PRO, SCH 524/1A/; Fisher and Robb (1913); *Med Dir*].

CLARKE, ROBERT (1815/6–57), Naval Medical Service;
born 1815/6; brother of Dr George Clarke, Naval Medical Service (*q.v.*); joined the Naval Medical Service as assistant surgeon; married Flora — (who was born 1827/8 and died 1 January 1900); died 29 December 1857 at Maghereagh, near Strabane; buried in Grange graveyard, Strabane. [*Coleraine Chronicle* 2 January 1858 (d); *Londonderry Sentinel* 1 January 1858 (d); Todd (1993)].

CLARKE, ROBERT MORRISON (1872–1958), Belfast;
born 2 December 1872 at Francis Street, Newtownards, county Down, son of James Clarke of Francis Street, woollen draper, and Lilley Morrison; educated at Methodist College, Belfast 1888–9; studied medicine at Queen's College, Belfast from 1889; MB BCh BAO (RUI) 1896; pathologist and assistant medical officer to Wadsley Asylum, Yorkshire; general practitioner in Belfast, of 2 Belgravia, Lisburn Road from c 1900; temporary captain RAMC during World War I; moved to 'St Keyne', Myrtlefield Park c 1926; married —; died 8 April 1958 at 35 Myrtlefield Park; probate Belfast 25 June 1958. [Belf GRO (b) and (d); Belf PRO, will cal; Fry (1984); *Med Dir*; QCB adm reg].

CLARKE, SAMUEL (1847/8–75), Clones, county Monaghan;
born 1847/8; studied medicine at the Royal College of Surgeons in Ireland; LKQCPI and LM 1869; LRCSI and LM 1869; surgeon in the mercantile marine; medical officer of Drum Dispensary, Clones; unmarried; died 1 August 1875 at Whitehall Street, Clones of phthisis. [Dub GRO (d); McCann (2003); *Med Dir*].

CLARKE, THOMAS (1846–1940), Liverpool;
born 16 May 1846 at Ahoghill, county Antrim, son of David Clarke; educated at RBAI; studied medicine at Queen's College, Belfast 1863–71; MD (QUI) 1871; MCh Dip Mid 1875; general physician in Gracehill, Ballymena c 1875; surgeon to the Pacific Steam Navigation Company; moved to Liverpool c 1880; medical officer to Liverpool Dispensary districts; resident medical officer to Liverpool Parish Infirmary (three years); of 94 (Worston House) Durning Road, Liverpool from c 1885 and also of 60 Castle Street; honorary physician to Liverpool Hospital for consumption and Delamere Sanatorium; JP; married —; father of Dr Thomas Courtenay Clarke, MB (Liverpool) 1911; died 13 September 1940; probate Liverpool 2 December 1940. [Lond PPR, will cal, will; *Med Dir*; QCB adm reg].

CLARKE, WILLIAM (d 1858), Dunfanaghy, county Donegal;
of Dundrum, county Tipperary; studied medicine at Glasgow University; MD (Glas) 1846; LRCS Edin 1846; lecturer in materia medica at the Peter Street Medical School, Dublin; general practitioner, of Dunfanaghy; JP; married Christina — (who moved to Belturbet, county Cavan, after William's death); died 15 April 1858; administration Londonderry 29 May 1858. [Addison (1898); *BNL* 24 April 1858 (d); Belf PRO, will cal; *Med Dir*].

CLARKE, WILLIAM GEORGE (1828–58), Army Medical Service;
born 4 February 1828 at Ballymena; joined the Army Medical Service as assistant surgeon to the 35th Foot 1852; died 23 April 1858 in the East Indies. [Peterkin and Johnston (1968)].

CLARKE, WILLIAM HENRIE CRAWFORD (1864/5–1936), Dublin, ship's surgeon, and Milford, county Donegal;
born 1864/5, son of Thomas Clarke, farmer, of Milford, and his first cousin Elizabeth Clarke; educated at Raphoe Royal School; studied medicine at the Royal College of Surgeons in Ireland; LM Rot Hosp Dub 1888; LRCPI and LM, LRCSI and LM 1888; resident surgeon to the Meath Hospital and the City of Dublin Hospital; ship's surgeon; medical officer to Kilmacrennan and Milford Dispensary Districts 1893–1935 and Milford Union Workhouse and Fever Hospital 1893–1922; married 31 July 1902 in Milford Presbyterian Church, Anna Maria Blackwood, daughter of William Blackwood of Milford, and sister of Dr Arthur Blackwood (*q.v.*); died 28 August 1936 at Milford; buried in Milford Church of Ireland Graveyard; probate Dublin 26 November 1936. [*BMJ* obituary (1936); Clarke, Arthur, pers com; Dub GRO (m) and (d); Dub Nat Arch, will cal; Kirkpatrick Archive; *Med Dir*].

CLARKE, WILLIAM ROBERT (1864–1917), Morley, Yorkshire;
: born 18 February 1864 at Gracehill, county Antrim, son of David Clarke, farmer, of Gracehill; brother of Dr Hugh Alexander Clarke (*q.v.*) of Liverpool; educated at RBAI; studied arts and medicine at Queen's College, Belfast, from 1882; BA (RUI) 1885; LSA Lond 1892; LMSSA 1907; general practitioner and surgeon to West Riding police, of Alma House, Commercial Street, Morley, and later of Studley House, Morley; married Margaret Dudne —; died 17 December 1917; probate London 21 March 1918. [Lond PPR, will cal, will; *Med Dir*; QCB adm reg].

CLELLAND, HUGH (d 1799), county Fermanagh;
: surgeon to the Fermanagh Militia; died January 1799 at Roundwood, county Wicklow. [*BNL* 29 January 1799 (d)].

CLELLAND, JOHN (1812/3–37), Hillsborough, county Down;
: born 1812/3; surgeon, of Hillsborough; died 6 September 1837 of fever. [*BNL* 15 September 1837 (d)].

CLEMENTS, FRANCIS HENRY (d 1919), Clogher, county Tyrone, Stalybridge, Cheshire, and Manchester, Lancashire;
: brother of Dr Samuel David Clements of Leeds, LRCP LRCS Edin LFPS Glas 1897; MB BCh (RUI) 1892; of Carrigallen, county Leitrim, c 1893–4; general practitioner, of Corbo, Clogher c 1895–1902, of 47 Mottram Road, Stalybridge c 1902–05; general practitioner and medical officer to Outpatients Department, Ancoats Hospital, Manchester, of 37 Downing Street, Manchester, c 1905–19; died 5 November 1919; probate London 19 February 1920. [Lond PPR, will cal, will; *Med Dir*].

CLEMENTS, JOHN EDMUND (1875–1946), Indian Medical Service;
: born 25 February 1875 at Maryborough, Queen's County, son of W.J. Clements, inspector's assistant of national schools; educated at Methodist College, Belfast, from 1888; studied medicine at Queen's College, Belfast, from 1893; MB BCh BAO (RUI) 1899; DPH (QUB) 1911; clinical assistant to Royal Victoria Hospital, Belfast; of 4 Bellevue Park, Belfast; joined the Indian Medical Service (General establishment) as lieutenant in 1902; captain 1905; major 1913; lieutenant-colonel 1921; served in China (medal) in 1900; superintendent of jails at Agra; retired 1930 as lieutenant-colonel to Riva Bella, Roseville Street, Jersey; finally of Tudor Court Hotel, 58/60 Cromwell Road, London; married 25 March 1902 in St Thomas's Church of Ireland Church, Belfast, Jean Stevenson (who died 1 November 1947), daughter of John Stevenson, manufacturer; died 3 March 1946; probate London 27 July 1946. [Crawford (1930); Fry (1984); Kirkpatrick Archive; Lond PPR, will cal; *Med Dir*; QCB adm reg; UHF database (m)].

CLEMENTS, ROBERT (1848–1900), Belfast, Dublin and Galway;
: born 23 February 1848 at Beragh, county Tyrone, son of David Clements of Beragh; educated at Clogherney School, Beragh; studied medicine at Queen's College, Galway, Queen's College, Belfast (1870–73) and the General Hospital, Belfast; MD

(QUI) 1873; LRCS Edin and LM 1874; resident medical officer to the Union Hospital for Contagious and Acute Medical Diseases, Belfast; general practitioner in Belfast, of 16 York Street c 1875; visiting physician (midwifery) to the Ulster Hospital for Children and Women from 1881, of 7 Clifton Street, Belfast c 1885; medical inspector with the Local Government Board, Custom House, Dublin, from c 1890 and working with the Local Government Board in Maryville, Galway from c 1895; married (1) 9 November 1875 in St Paul's Church of Ireland Church, Belfast, Phoebe Wilson, daughter of William Wilson of Belfast; (2) Elizabeth —; died 9 June 1900; probate Tuam 5 January 1901. [Belf PRO, will cal; Dub GRO (d); *Med Dir*; QCB adm reg; UHF database (m); Whitla (1901)].

CLEMENT(S), WILLIAM (1707/8–82), Dublin;
born in 1707/8 at Carrickmacross, county Monaghan, son of Thomas Clement(s), merchant; educated by Mr Foulds of Carrickmacross; studied arts and medicine at Trinity College, Dublin, from 1722; Scholar 1724; BA (TCD) 1726; MA 1731; Fellow 1733; MB 1747; MD 1748; lecturer in Botany, TCD, 1733–63; lecturer in natural philosophy 1745–59; Donegal lecturer 1750–59; vice-provost 1853–63; Regius Professor of Physic, 1761–81; MP for TCD 1761 and for Dublin 1771; married —; died 15 January 1782. [Burtchaell and Sadleir (1924); Kirkpatrick (1912)].

CLEMENTS, — (*fl c* 1771), Dungannon, county Tyrone;
surgeon, of Dungannon; married March 1771 — Newton of Cuckold's Hill. [*BNL* 2 April 1771 (m)].

CLIBBORN, CUTHBERT JOHN (1846–1914), Belfast;
born 10 January 1846, son of Cuthbert John Clibborn, JP, of Moate, county Westmeath and Jane Holmes of Moorock, King's County; studied medicine at Trinity College, Dublin, from 1864; LM Rot Hosp Dub; BA (TCD) 1867; MB MCh 1869; of 13 Leeson Park, Dublin c 1871; medical officer to the Local Government Board, Belfast, from c 1897, of 76 University Street, Belfast; retired 1910 to Rosemount, Moate, county Westmeath; JP for county Wicklow; married (1) 2 November 1871 in St Thomas's Church of Ireland Church, Dublin, Mary Groves Cathrew, minor, daughter of Graves Cathrew, barrister, of 36 Upper Gloucester Street, Dublin; (2) 15 December 1910 Edith Frances Nugent, widow of John Nugent of Rosemount, third daughter of William Fetherstonhaugh of Grouse Lodge, county Westmeath; died 4 January 1914; probate Mullingar 20 February 1914. [Belf PRO, will cal; Burke *LGI* (1912); Dub GRO (m); Kirkpatrick Archive; *Med Dir;* TCD adm reg; TCD Cat, vol II (1896)].

CLINDENNIN, WILLIAM (*fl c* 1828), Killashandra, county Cavan;
LAH Dub 1828; apothecary, of Killashandra. [Apothecaries (1829)].

CLOKEY, JOHN GETTY (1865–1910), Belfast;
born 3 October 1865 in Belfast, son of Thomas Clokey, presbyterian town missionary, of 15 Landscape Terrace, Belfast; educated at RBAI and Belfast Model

School; studied medicine at Queen's College, Belfast, from 1885, and Dublin; MB BCh BAO (RUI) 1894; general practitioner, of 'Albertville', Crumlin Road, and 15 Landscape Terrace, Belfast; married 9 July 1901 in Eglinton Street Presbyterian Church, Belfast, Margaret McConnell, daughter of Francis McConnell, clerk, of Belfast; died 12 March 1910 at 'Albertville'; buried in Belfast City Cemetery; administration Belfast 6 April 1910. [Belf City Cem, bur reg; Belf PRO, will cal; Dub GRO (d); *Med Dir*; QCB adm reg; UHF database (m)].

CLOSE, JOSEPH KINNEAR (1865–1940), Indian Medical Service;
born 22 December 1865, at Carrickfergus, son of the Rev William Close, minister of Loughmorne Reformed Presbyterian Church, Carrickfergus; educated at Rockview Intermediate School, Carrickfergus; studied medicine at Queen's College, Belfast, from 1881; MD MCh MAO (RUI) 1886; joined the Indian Medical Service (Bengal establishment) as surgeon 1887; major 1899; lieutenant-colonel 1907; colonel 1918; served on the North East Frontier 1888; honorary surgeon to the King c 1922; retired 1922; lived finally at 2 Vineyard Hill Road, Wimbledon Park, Surrey; married Sarah Bruney —; died 29 May 1940; probate London 4 July 1940. [Crawford (1930); Lond PPR, will cal; *Med Dir*; QCB adm reg].

CLOSE, WILLIAM (d 1834), Old Calabar, West Africa;
son of William Close of New Forge, near Magheralin, county Down; medical officer in Old Calabar; died 5 July 1834 at Old Calabar. [*BNL* 18 November 1834 (d)].

CLOTWORTHY, DAVID (1816/7–41), Dromore, county Down;
born 1816/7; surgeon, of Dromore; died 3 February 1841 of fever, at Dromore, 'universally esteemed by all who knew him'. *BNL* 12 February 1841 (d)].

CLOUGHER, JOHN (1791/2–1813), Spain;
born 1791/2, son of Thomas Clougher of Derrycaw [?], county Armagh; surgeon; 'appointed to the medical department in Spain, from which he was permitted to return to his native country, for the restoration of his health, but was prematurely cut off'; died 1 June 1813 at the Buck Inn, near Portsmouth. [*BNL* 25 June 1813 (d)].

CLUFF, JAMES STANTON (1862–c 1910), Manchester;
born 18 September 1862 at Cookstown, county Tyrone, son of Richard Cluff, JP, cabinet maker, of Kildress House, Cookstown, and Frances Jenkins; brother of Dr William Cluff (*q.v.*); educated at Cookstown Academy; studied medicine at Queen's College, Belfast, from 1880; LRCP LRCS Edin 1890; LFPS Glas 1890; general practitioner, of High Bank House, Openshaw, Manchester, c 1895; died c 1910. [*Med Dir*; QCB adm reg].

CLUFF, THOMAS (1811/2–39), Lurgan, county Armagh;
born 1811/2; surgeon, of Lurgan; died 20 January 1839 in Lurgan of enteritis; 'affability of manners, kind disposition and unaffected simplicity, added to his honesty and attention to the sick, endeared him to all who knew him'. [*BNL* 29 January 1839 (d)].

CLUFF, WILLIAM, (1868–1941), Manchester;
born 12 March 1868 at Loy, Cookstown, county Tyrone, son of Richard Cluff, JP, cabinet maker, of Loy and later of Kildress House, Cookstown, and Frances Jenkins; brother of Dr James Stanton Cluff (*q.v.*); educated at Coleraine Academical Institution; studied medicine at Queen's College, Belfast from 1886; MB BCh BAO (RUI) 1890; general practitioner, Rostrevor, county Down; of High Bank House, Openshaw, Manchester c 1895; retired to 'Grianan', Rostrevor c 1930; married — Leeper of Cookstown; died 9 February 1941 at 'Grianan'; administration Belfast 18 July 1941 and Llandudno 5 August 1941. [Belf GRO (d); Belf PRO, will cal; Dub GRO (b); Kirkpatrick Archive; Lond PPR, will cal; *Med Dir*; QCB adm reg].

CLUGSTON, WILLIAM ALEXANDER (1831/2–96), Ballyclare, county Antrim;
born 1831/2, son of William Clugston, farmer, of Ballyclare; studied medicine at Queen's College, Belfast from 1849, Belfast General Hospital, Edinburgh University from 1850 and the Royal Infirmary; MD (Edin) 1853 (thesis 'On disease of the heart'); LRCS Edin and LM 1853; medical officer to Doagh Dispensary District, constabulary and registrar of births and deaths; married 24 June 1862 in Regent Street Reformed Presbyterian Church, Newtownards, Isabella Cosh (who was born 1836/7), daughter of Samuel Cosh, builder; died 15 January 1896 at Ballyclare; probate Belfast 12 February 1896. [Belf PRO, will cal; Dub GRO (m) and (d); Edin Univ; *Med Dir*; UHF database (m)].

COANE, JAMES (1853–c 1894), Hamilton, Victoria, Australia;
born 18 September 1853 at Higginstown, Ballyshannon, county Donegal; educated at Mr North's School, Rathmines, Dublin; studied medicine at Queen's College, Belfast, from 1879; LRCP Edin 1881; LRCSI 1881; emigrated to Hamilton, Victoria, Australia c 1883; died c 1894. [*Med Dir*; QCB adm reg].

COATES, JOHN (1826–95), Army Medical Service and Hythe, Kent;
born 6 December 1826 at Downpatrick; LRCSI 1847; MD (Glas) 1848; joined the Army Medical Service as assistant surgeon to the 26th Foot 1850; staff surgeon 2nd class 1856; transferred to 24th Foot 1865; surgeon major 1869; staff surgeon 1873; retired with rank of brigade surgeon 1881 and was for some years in medical charge of the School of Musketry at Hythe, Kent; died 15 March 1895 at Hythe; probate Canterbury 12 June 1895. [Addison (1898); Lond GRO (d); Lond PPR, will cal; *Med Dir*; Peterkin and Johnston (1968)].

COATES, JOHN MARTIN (1832–95), Indian Medical Service;
born 6 July 1832, son of Henry Coates of Portaferry; educated at RBAI; studied medicine at Queen's College, Belfast, from 1851; MD (QUI) 1855; joined the Indian Medical Service (Bengal establishment) as assistant surgeon 1855; surgeon 1867; surgeon major 1873; brigade surgeon 1881; served through Indian Mutiny, 1857; sanitary commissioner for Bengal; president and professor of medicine in Calcutta Medical College for many years; retired in 1890 as brigade surgeon; author of *Vocabulary of Seven Languages of Dialects of Chota Nagpore* (1875); married 1863 Sophia Harper, daughter of Martin Harper of Belfast; father of Dr — Coates of

London; died 18 July 1895 in Calcutta of cholera. [Crawford (1930); *Newtownards Chronicle* 27 July 1895 (d); QUB].

COATES, STANLEY BERESFORD (1854–1936), Belfast, and Donaghadee, county Down;
born 30 March 1854 in Belfast, son of John Coates, solicitor, of 43 Arthur Street and 41 Chichester Street, Belfast; educated by the Rev Dr Russell of Belfast; studied medicine at Queen's College, Belfast, from 1870; LRCS Edin and LM 1874; LRCP Edin 1875; DPH RCSI 1890; junior and senior resident surgeon to Royal Hospital, Belfast 1874–6; medical officer of health to the Port of Belfast and superintendent medical officer of health Belfast R District; visiting physician (midwifery) to the Ulster Hospital for Children and Women from 1881; of 93 Great Victoria Street from c 1880, of 5 Shaftesbury Square from c 1890 and of Craigmore, Donaghadee from 1920; married 10 December 1878 at St Thomas's Church of Ireland Church, Elizabeth Coates (two Coates brothers married two Coates sisters), daughter of Foster Coates, railway secretary, of Hunter Villa, Upper Windsor Avenue, Belfast; father of Dr Foster Coates, MB (RUI) 1905, physician to the Royal Victoria Hospital, Belfast; died 9 March 1936, at Warren Road, Donaghadee; probate Belfast 11 June 1936. [Belf GRO (d); Belf PRO, will cal; Belf Roy Hosp, Ann Rep; Dub GRO (m); Kirkpatrick Archive; Marshall (1959); *Med Dir*; QCB adm reg].

COATES, THOMAS J. (1826/7–55), Strathblane, Stirlingshire;
born 1826/7, eldest son of John Coates of the Crescent, Belfast, secretary to the Grand Jury of County Antrim; general practitioner, of Strathblane; died 12 September 1855 at Strathblane. [*BNL* 17 September 1855 (d); *Coleraine Chronicle* 22 September 1855 (d); *Londonderry Sentinel* 21 September 1855 (d)].

COCHRAN, JACKSON WRAY (*fl c* 1814), Naval Medical Service;
MRCSE; of Articlave, county Londonderry; joined the Naval Medical Service as assistant surgeon on HMS *Tiger* 1814. [*Londonderry Journal* 19 April 1814 (news)].

COCHRAN, JOHN (1825/6–56), Brooklyn, New York;
born 1825/6, second son of George Cochran of Killylane, county Londonderry; general practitioner; died 15 August 1856 at Brooklyn. [*Coleraine Chronicle* 6 September 1856 (d); *Londonderry Sentinel* 5 September 1856 (d)].

COCHRANE, JOHN (d 1801), Garvagh, county Londonderry;
MD [?]; general practitioner, of Garvagh; died December 1801; buried in Desertoghill Churchyard. [*Memorials of the Dead*, vol VI, p 388].

COCHRANE, JOHN JAMES (1856–93), ship's surgeon, Monaghan, and Pinchbeck, Lincolnshire;
born 1856 in Virginia, county Cavan, son of Adam Cochrane, farmer; studied medicine at Trinity College, Dublin; BA (TCD) 1878; MB 1883; BCh 1884; LM Coombe Hosp Dub; surgeon on SS Lake *Huron*; resident surgeon to Monaghan County Infirmary c 1886; general practitioner, of Swan Park, Monaghan; general

practitioner, medical officer and medical officer of health to Pinchbeck District, Lincolnshire; married Anne —; died 21 March 1893 at Pinchbeck; administration Lincoln 4 July 1893. [Lond GRO (d); Lond PPR, will cal; *Med Dir*; TCD adm reg; *TCD Cat*; vol II (1896)].

COCHRANE, ROBERT (1852/3–1910), Coleraine, county Londonderry;
born 1852/3; studied medicine at Queen's College, Galway; LRCSI and LM 1880; general practitioner, of Blackhill, Coleraine; married —; died 3 December 1910 at Aghadowey. [Dub GRO (d); *Med Dir*].

COCHRANE, ROBERT STRANGMAN (1852–1900), Longford;
born 1852 at Cootehill, county Cavan, son of Gore Gregory Cochrane, banker; educated at Armagh Royal School 1864–70; studied arts and medicine at Trinity College, Dublin 1871–5; LRCSI and LM 1874; BA MB (TCD) 1875; FRCSI 1884; general practitioner at Longford; medical officer to Longford Workhouse and constabulary; unmarried; died 11 September 1900 at Longford; administration (with will) Dublin 8 October 1900. [Belf PRO, will cal; Dub GRO (d); Ferrar (1933); Kirkpatrick Archive; *Med Dir*; TCD adm reg; *TCD Cat*, vol II (1896)].

COCKBURN, JAMES (DUNDAS) (1814–99), Army Medical Service;
born 12 March 1814 at Drumhome, Ballyshannon, county Donegal; joined the Army Medical Service as staff assistant surgeon to the 30th Foot 1836; transferred to the Royal Horse Guards 1843; surgeon to the First Life Guards 1848; surgeon major 1858; retired on half pay with rank of Deputy Inspector General 1863, to live at Cowlinge, Suffolk; died 20 January 1899; administration London 7 March 1899. [Lond PPR, will cal; Peterkin and Johnston (1968)].

COCKBURN, WILLIAM (d 1842), Ballintra, county Donegal;
youngest son of Abner Cockburn of Ballintra; qualified in medicine 1842; died 22 August 1842 of consumption, at his brother's house in Callowhill, county Cavan [?]; buried in Drumholm Graveyard, Ballintra. [*BNL* 30 August 1842 (d); *Londonderry Sentinel* 10 September 1842 (d)].

COFFEY, CHARLES (d 1851), Naval Medical Service;
son of Dr Robert Coffey, professor of Surgery at RBAI (*q.v.*); joined the Naval Medical Service as assistant surgeon c 1840; died 20 October 1851 on HMS *Pilot* on his passage from Hong Kong to Singapore. [*BNL* 24 December 1851 (d)].

COFFEY, RICHARD (1873–1952), Barrow-in-Furness, Lancashire, and RAMC;
born 2 October 1873, son of Robert Coffey of Coolshannagh House, Monaghan, clerk of the Asylum, and Margaret Elizabeth —; studied medicine at the Royal College of Surgeons in Ireland; LRCPI and LM 1894; LRCSI and LM 1894; LM Rot Hosp Dub 1894; general practitioner, with his uncle, Dr Alexander Mallagh (*q.v.*), of Michaelson Road, 46 Church Street. and 21 Storey Square, Barrow-in-Furness c 1895–1951; served in RAMC 1914–18, in field hospitals in France and later in Territorials (TD 1925); DSO 1918; married —; died 6 September 1952 at 21 Storey

Square; administration Lancaster 18 October 1952. [*BMJ* obituary (1952); Kirkpatrick Archive; Lond PPR, will cal; *Med Dir*].

COFFEY, ROBERT (1796–1847), Belfast;
born 1796 in county Antrim; studied medicine in Edinburgh and/or Glasgow; LRCS Edin 1819; LAH Dub 1820; MD (Glas) 1833; member of Committee of Management of Belfast Fever Hospital and surgeon to various Dispensary Districts in Belfast from 1823; an early member of the revived Belfast Medical Society in 1822; apothecary, of 49 Ann Street c 1824; attending surgeon to the Fever Hospital 1827–36 and consulting surgeon 1836–47; one of the doctors who presented an inscribed gold box to Dr S.S. Thomson in 1834; professor of surgery at RBAI 1837–47 (third professor but effectively the first, in spite of opposition from Presbyterian church); presented with an illuminated address by medical student class of 1838–9; president of the Faculty of Medicine at RBAI 1839–40; living at 59 Donegall Street, Belfast in 1839; married 22 May 1820 — Blackwood of Belfast; father of Dr Charles Coffey, Naval Medical Service (*q.v.*); died 5 January 1847 at Botanic Road, Belfast, buried in Clifton Street Graveyard, Belfast; portrait (anonymous). [Addison (1898); Allison (1972); Apothecaries (1829); *BNL* 23 May 1820 (m), 8 January 1847 (d) and 24 December 1851 (d, son); *Belfast Street Directory*; Calwell (1977); Croly (1843–6); Fisher and Robb (1913); Froggatt (1996b); Malcolm (1851); Merrick and Clarke, *Belfast*, vol 4 (1991); O'Brien, Crookshank and Wolstenholme (1984); Pigot (1824); Thomson presentation box (1834)].

COGHRAN, BRICE (*fl c* 1750), Downpatrick, county Down;
apothecary, of Irish Street, Downpatrick; married —; father of Hanna Coghran who married 15 August 1765 Richard Caddel of Downpatrick. [Pilson (1934)].

COLBY, DANIEL (d c 1734), Mountcharles, county Donegal;
surgeon, of Mountcharles; will dated 1734 proved in Diocese of Raphoe. [Thrift (1920)].

COLE, JOHN MARTIN COATES (1858–c 1916), Isle of Man and Curacoa;
born 1 February 1858 in Glasgow, son of John Cole, draper, of the Diamond, Clones; educated at Clones National School; studied medicine at Queen's College, Belfast, from 1876; LM KQCPI 1884; MRCSE 1886; MD (Carrabobo) 1901; MD (Durham) 1907; general practitioner, of 5 Douglas Street, Peel, Isle of Man, c 1886; medical officer of Aruba, Curacao, West Indies, c 1895 and of Maracaibo, Venezuela c 1907; honorary medical officer to Chiquinquira Hospital c 1907; died c 1916. [*Med Dir*; QCB adm reg].

COLEMAN, SAMUEL (1797/8–1867), Kells, county Antrim;
born 1797/8; studied medicine at Glasgow University; MD (Glas) 1841; general practitioner in Kells; unmarried; died 13 January 1867 in Wellington Street, Ballymena; administration Belfast 8 October 1867. [Addison (1898); Belf PRO, will cal; Dub GRO (d); *Med Dir*].

COLEMAN, THOMAS (*fl c* 1824), Carrickmacross, county Monaghan; apothecary, of Carrickmacross c 1824. [Pigot (1824)].

COLHOUN (CALHOUN), ROBERT BELL (d 1845), Fork Hill, county Armagh; son of William Colhoun of county Donegal; studied medicine at Edinburgh University; MD (Edin) 1839 (thesis 'On absorbtion'); of Belmont, Fork Hill; married 18 October 1842 in St Thomas's Church of Ireland Church, Dublin, Sophia Elizabeth Macklin, youngest daughter of George Macklin, of Great Chesterford, Essex, and of Esker, county Galway; died 26 April 1845 of apoplexy, at Portadown. [*BNL* 21 October 1842 (m) and 9 May 1845 (d); Edin Univ; *Londonderry Sentinel* 22 October 1842 (m)].

COLHOUN, — (d 1793), St Johnstown, county Donegal; doctor; died April 1793 near St Johnstown. [*BNL* 16 April 1793 (d)].

COLLEN, GEORGE DENBIGH (1868–1954), Dublin, Belfast and London; born 1868, in Australia, son of John Collen, builder; educated at Armagh Royal School; studied arts and medicine at Trinity College, Dublin, from 1886; BA (TCD) 1890; MB BCh 1893; MD 1897; general practitioner in Dublin, of 5 Clanwilliam Place, Dublin (c 1895), and 70 Upper Leeson Street (c 1904); civil surgeon with the South African Field Force and the Station Hospital, Devonport; general practitioner, of 15 Lisburn Road, Belfast, c 1907; moved to 39 Carleton Road, London c 1909, to 71 Charlwood Street, London, c 1925, 1 Templeton Place c 1930, 25 Pembridge Gardens c 1940, 11 Clanricarde Gardens c 1947 and finally of the Limes Nursing Home, Jacob's Post, Ditchling, Sussex; died 21 March 1954; probate Lewes 25 May 1954. [Ferrar (1933); Lond PPR, will cal; *Med Dir*; TCD adm reg; *TCD Cat*, vol II (1896)].

COLLIER, GEORGINA (1875–1942), Wimbledon, London; born 17 July 1875 at Lisburn, daughter of the Rev Robert Collier, Methodist minister, sister of Dr John Thomas Collier (*q.v.*), Dr Robert James Collier (*q.v.*), Dr Samuel Ruddell Collier (*q.v.*), and Dr William Arthur Collier (*q.v.*); educated by Mr Hoare of Lisburn; studied medicine at Queen's College, Belfast, from 1893; LRCP LRCS Edin 1897; LFPS Glas 1897; general practitioner, of 135 Hartfield Road, and of Dorset Lodge, 160 Kingston Road, Merton Park, Wimbledon from c 1900; retired c 1946; of 4 St Aubyn's Court, Raymond Road, London c 1952; married 11 April 1900 in West Ham Methodist Church, London, Dr Joseph Harvey (*q.v.*); died 10 October 1955 at Jason Hall Nursing Home, Wimbledon; administration Liverpool 6 January 1956. [*Lancet* obituary to J.T. Collier (1931); Lond GRO (m); Lond PPR, will cal; *Med Dir*; QCB adm reg].

COLLIER, JOHN THOMAS (1853–1931), Lincoln; born 1 March 1853 at Belturbet, county Cavan, son of the Rev Robert Collier, methodist minister; brother of Dr Robert James Collier (*q.v.*), Dr Samuel Ruddell Collier (*q.v.*), Dr William Arthur Collier (*q.v.*) and Dr Georgina Collier (*q.v.*); educated at Methodist College, Belfast, from 1868; studied medicine at Queen's College, Belfast, from 1873; Malcolm Exhibition, Belfast Royal Hospital, 1876;

Coulter Exhibition, 1877; LM Rot Hosp Dub 1878; MD (QUI) 1878; MCh 1880; general practitioner, of 9 West Parade, Lincoln, from c 1885; retired c 1912 to Helens Court, Tyson Road, Forest Hill, London; moved c 1924 to Helens Court, 10 Carlisle Road, Hove, Sussex; author of various medical papers; married Melinda —; died 17 November 1931 at 10 Carlisle Road; probate London 30 December 1931. [Fry (1984); Kirkpatrick Archive; *Lancet* obituary (1931); Lond GRO (d); Lond PPR, will cal; *Med Dir*; QCB adm reg; RVH, Office of Archives].

COLLIER, ROBERT JAMES (1859–1920), London;
born 1 December 1858 at Ballyclare, county Antrim, son of the Rev Robert Collier, methodist minister, brother of Dr John Thomas Collier (*q.v.*), Dr Samuel Ruddell Collier (*q.v.*), Dr William Arthur Collier (*q.v.*) and Dr Georgina Collier (*q.v.*); educated at Methodist College, Belfast, from 1870; studied medicine at Queen's College, Belfast, from 1884, and Edinburgh; LRCP and LRCS Edin 1891; LFPS Glas 1891; general practitioner in London, of Grosmont House, Manor Park, London c. 1895; and of 753 Romford Road from c 1914; married 20 August 1895 in University Road Methodist Church, Louisa Sidley Gray, daughter of William Gray of 8 Mount Charles, Belfast; died 22 September 1920 at 4 Lorelei, Bangor; probate Belfast 21 January 1921. [Belf PRO, will cal; Dub GRO (d); Fry (1984); Kirkpatrick Archive; *Med Dir*; QCB adm reg; UHF database (m)].

COLLIER, SAMUEL RUDDELL (1863–1941), Belfast and London;
born 1 October 1863 at Brookeborough, county Fermanagh, son of the Rev Robert Collier, methodist minister, brother of Dr John Thomas Collier (*q.v.*), Dr Robert James Collier (*q.v.*), Dr William Arthur Collier (*q.v.*) and Dr Georgina Collier (*q.v.*); educated at Methodist College, Belfast from 1874; studied medicine at Queen's College, Belfast 1881–6; Coulter Exhibition, Belfast Royal Hospital, 1886; MD MCh MAO (RUI) 1886; general practitioner, of Clarence Villa, Hartfield, Wimbledon c 1895; moved to 'Somers', Wimbledon Hill c 1905 and then to 85 Worple Road, Wimbledon; moved c 1936 to 48a Saxon Road, Hove and finally to 36 Chaucer Road, Bedford; married —; died 29 August 1941 at 36 Chaucer Road; probate Llandudno 31 December 1941. [Belf Roy Hosp, Ann Rep; Fry (1984); Lond GRO (d); Lond PPR, will cal; *Med Dir*; QCB adm reg].

COLLIER, WILLIAM ARTHUR (1866/7–1949), Belfast and London;
born 1866/7 at Dunkineely, county Donegal, son of the Rev Robert Collier, methodist minister, brother of Dr John Thomas Collier (*q.v.*), Dr Robert James Collier (*q.v.*), Dr Samuel Ruddell Collier (*q.v.*) and Dr Georgina Collier (*q.v.*); educated at Methodist College, Belfast, from 1877; studied medicine at Queen's College, Belfast, from 1886, and St Thomas's Hospital, London; LRCP LRCS Edin 1892; LFPS Glas and LM 1892; medical officer of Westminster Dispensary District 1892–c 1920, of 36 Great Smith Street, Westminster, London from c 1892 and of 6 Vincent Square, Westminster from c 1910; retired c 1939 to 34 Derek Avenue, Hove, Sussex; married —; died 11 July 1949 at 'Little Bellan', West End Bay, Lancing, Sussex; probate Lewes 31 September 1949. [Fry (1984); Lond GRO (d); Lond PPR, will cal; *Med Dir*; QCB adm reg].

COLLINS, CLARKE (1808–40), Belfast;
born 1808, fifth son of James Collins, merchant, of Cookstown, county Tyrone, and Martha Clarke (who was sister of Dr Joseph Clarke (*q.v.*) of Dublin); LRCSI; surgeon, of Ship Street, Belfast; unmarried; died October 1840 in Belfast; buried with his parents in Moneymore Graveyard. [Collins, John, pers com; *Memorials of the Dead*, vol VIII, p 380].

COLLINS, FREDERICK HENRY (1854–1907), Manchester, Lancashire;
born 24 June 1854 at Belfast, fifth son of William Magill Collins, solicitor, of Notting Hill, Belfast, and Anne Lynd; nephew of Dr Robert Collins (*q.v.*) of Belfast; educated at Methodist College, Belfast, from 1868; studied medicine at Queen's College, Belfast, from 1872; MD MCh Dip Mid (QUI) 1876; LRCSI 1876; resident house officer to Meath Hospital, Dublin; house surgeon from 1877 and later consulting physician to the Hulme Dispensary, Manchester; general practitioner in Manchester from c 1880, of 7 Bath Street, Hulme, c 1885, of 16 St Ann's Passage c 1895, of Bridge House, Wilmslow Road, Didsbury and 97 Withington Road, Whalley Range, Manchester c 1905; married Dinah —; died 17 February 1907 at Bridge House, Didsbury; administration (with will) London 5 April 1907. [*BMJ* obituary (1907); Collins, John, pers com; Fry (1984); Kirkpatrick Archive; Lond GRO (d); Lond PPR, will cal; *Med Dir*; QCB adm reg].

COLLINS, JAMES (1735/6–1806), Cookstown, county Tyrone;
born 1735/6 in Cookstown, probably son of James Collins, merchant, of Cookstown; married Jane — (who was born 1783/4 and died 19 December 1826); died 4 May 1806; buried in Donaghenry graveyard. [Collins, John, pers com; gravestone inscription].

COLLINS, JAMES (d c 1824), Cookstown, county Tyrone;
surgeon, of Loy, Cookstown; died c 1824; administration Armagh Diocesan Court 1824. [Dub Nat Arch, Armagh Dio Admins index].

COLLINS, JAMES VANCE (1856/7–1924), Laghey, county Donegal;
born 1856/7; LKQCPI and LM 1884; LRCSI 1884; medical officer to Laghey Dispensary District; married Harriet —; died 16 April 1924 at Laghey; probate London 8 August 1924 and Belfast 5 October 1924. [Belf PRO, will cal; Dub GRO (d); Lond PPR, will cal; *Med Dir*].

COLLINS, JOHN (b 1772), Cookstown and Charlemont, county Tyrone;
born 1772, fourth son of John Collins of Cookstown and nephew of Dr James Collins (*q.v.*), surgeon, of Cookstown; LAH Dub 1794; surgeon and apothecary, of Cookstown and Charlemont; married 1795 Elizabeth Pillar (who was born 26 September 1773 and died March 1843; buried in Shankill Graveyard, Belfast), daughter of James Pillar of Charlemont and Arabella English; father of Dr John Collins (*q.v.*) of Texas; died before 1828. [Apothecaries (1829); Clarke, *Belfast*, vol 1 (1982); Collins, John, pers com; Dub Nat Arch, Armagh mar lic bonds].

COLLINS, JOHN (1811–90), Athens, Texas, USA;
born 24 August 1811 in Cookstown, county Tyrone, third son of Dr John Collins (*q.v.*) of Cookstown, and Elizabeth Pillar; educated by Mr Henderson; studied at Trinity College, Dublin, from 1828 but did not graduate; emigrated to USA c 1839 and possibly graduated in medicine at Jefferson Medical College, Philadelphia; general practitioner briefly in Philadelphia and later in Athens, Texas; married (1) — Wingate (c 1815–c 1845); (2) Arminda Winifred Derden; died 1890. [Burtchaell and Sadleir (1924); Collins, John, pers com].

COLLINS, JOHN SHEILL (1860–93), Belfast, ship's surgeon, Manchester, Lancashire, Hull, Yorkshire, Keelby, Lincolnshire, and Sydney, Australia;
born 24 May 1860 at Belfast, son of William Collins, wholesale druggist, of Victoria Street, Belfast; educated at Methodist College, Belfast, from 1868 and Dulwich College, London; studied medicine at Queen's College, Belfast, from 1876; MD Dip Mid (QUI) 1880; MRCSE 1881; general practitioner, of 2 Chlorine Place, Belfast c 1881–4; surgeon to Royal Mail Steamship Company c 1884; house physician to Manchester Royal Infirmary c 1884–5; assistant house surgeon to Hull Royal Infirmary c 1885–6; general practitioner, of Keelby, Lincolnshire, c 1886–9; emigrated to Sydney, New South Wales, c 1889, where he died in 1893. [Fry (1984); *Med Dir*; QCB adm reg].

COLLINS, ROBERT (1800–68), Dublin;
born 1800, third son of James Collins, merchant, of Cookstown, county Tyrone, and Martha Clarke (who was sister of Dr Joseph Clarke (*q.v.*), Master of the Rotunda Hospital, Dublin); brother of Dr Clarke Collins (*q.v.*); first cousin of Dr Robert Collins (*q.v.*) of Belfast; studied medicine at Glasgow University; MD (Glas) 1822; LKQCPI 1824; FKQCPI 1839; MD (TCD) (*hon causa*) 1839; obstetrician in Dublin; Master of the Rotunda 1826–33, 'the most distinguished Master of the century' (Coakley); continued Dr Joseph Clarke's methods of cleanliness, fumigation and good ventilation to virtually eradicate puerperal sepsis, by methods which influenced Semmelweis in Vienna; designed a new type of obstetric forceps in 1830 and helped to introduce the use of the obstetric stethoscope, following J.C. Ferguson's work (*q.v.*); President of the KQCPI 1847–8; of Rutland Square, Dublin, c 1833, and of 2 Merrion Square North c 1852; also of Ardsallagh, Navan, county Meath, and Garvery Lodge, county Fermanagh; author of *A Practical Treatise on Midwifery* (1835), *Observations on Professor Hamilton's Deviations from the Ordinary Mode of Stating Practical Results* (1838) and *A Short Sketch of the Life and Writings of the late Joseph Clarke* (1849); married (1) his first cousin Barbara Clarke (who was born 1790 and died 13 May 1833), daughter of Dr Joseph Clarke (*q.v.*); (2) 16 August 1849 in Tamney Church of Ireland Church, county Dublin, Mary Kennedy (who was born 24 November 1800 and died 1 June 1891), daughter of the Rev John Pitt Kennedy, rector of Balteagh, county Londonderry, and sister of Dr Evory Kennedy (*q.v.*); died 11 December 1868 at Ely Place, Dublin; buried in Coolock Graveyard, county Dublin; probate Dublin 4 February 1869. [Addison (1898); Belf PRO, will cal; Burtchaell and Sadleir (1924); Coakley (1992); Collins, John, pers com; Dub GRO (m); Kirkpatrick and Jellett (1913); Leslie (1937); *Londonderry*

Sentinel 24 August 1849 (m) and 15 December 1868 (d); *Med Dir*; *Memorials of the Dead*, vol XI, p 431].

COLLINS, ROBERT (1812/3–52), Belfast;
born 1812/3 in Dublin or Cookstown, county Tyrone, second son of Joshua Collins and Maria Magill; brother of William Magill Collins who was father of Dr Frederick Henry Collins (*q.v.*); studied medicine at Glasgow Univeristy; MD (Glas) 1833; LKQCPI; general practitioner, of 2 and 4 Brunswick Street, Belfast, c 1838–46 and 20 Queen Street, Belfast c 1846–52; physician to Belfast Skin Diseases Dispensary; married 31 July 1837 Elizabeth Dunlop (who was born 12 December 1810 and died 7 July 1898; buried in Drumbo C of I Graveyard), daughter of Major Charles Dunlop of Edenderry House, county Down, and brother of Dr James Dunlop RN (*q.v.*); died 7 May 1852 in Queen Street, Belfast; buried in Shankill Graveyard, Belfast (no surviving inscription). [Addison (1898); *BNL* 4 August 1837 and 10 May 1852 (d); Clarke, *County Down*, vol 18 (1979); Collins, John, pers com; Croly (1843–6); *Med Dir*].

COLLINS (COLLYNS), WILLIAM TENISON (1817/8–50), Keady, county Armagh;
born 1817/8, son of John Collins, wine merchant; LAH Dub; accoucheur, Anglesey Lying-in Hospital, Dublin; apothecary in Keady; medical officer to constabulary and public vaccinator, c 1845; married (1) —; (2) 12 January 1846 in Armagh Brague Church of Ireland Church, Emma Jane Magee, third daughter of Dr Samuel Magee of Keady (*q.v.*); died 25 October 1850 in Newtownhamilton, county Armagh. [*BNL* 16 January 1846 (m) and 1 November 1850 (d); Croly (1843–6); Dub GRO (m); *Med Dir*].

COLLIS, MAURICE HENRY (1824/5–69), Dublin;
born 1824/5, son of the Rev Robert Fitzgerald Collis, perpetual curate of Tamlaght O'Crilly Lower, county Londonderry, and later rector of Kilconnell, Clonfert, and Maria Bourke; educated at Dungannon Royal School; studied arts and medicine at Trinity College, Dublin, from 1842; BA (TCD) 1847; LRCSI 1847; MB 1848; FRCSI 1850; MD 1867; apprenticed to his uncle Maurice Collis, president of the RCSI; demonstrator of anatomy at the RCSI; surgeon to the Meath Hospital from 1851; of 11 Lower Fitzwilliam Street, Dublin c 1852 and later of 25 Lower Baggot Street; lecturer in surgery to the Peter Street School of Medicine from 1853 and also at the Carmichael School; author of many medical papers; married (1) Frances Diana — (who died 16 June 1850 in Merrion Square, Dublin); (2) 10 August 1852 in Malahide Church of Ireland Church, county Dublin, Sarah Marcella Lyster Jameson, daughter of William Jameson, FRCS; father of Dr Robert William Collis, LRCSI 1877, LKQCPI 1878, of Denver, Colorado, USA; died 28 March 1869 at 25 Lower Baggot Street, following a septic wound while operating; buried in Mount Jerome Cemetery, Dublin; administration (with will) Dublin 25 June 1869. [*BNL* 28 June 1850 (d); Belf PRO, will cal; *BMJ* obituary (1869); Burtchaell and Sadleir (1924); Cameron (1916); Dub GRO (m); Kirkpatrick Archive; *Lancet* obituary (1869); Leslie (1927); Martin (2003); *Med Dir*].

COLLUM, HUGH (d 1847), Enniskillen, county Fermanagh;
LAH Dub 1824; apothecary to the workhouse, Enniskillen, and the County Coroner; of Main Street, Enniskillen c 1824; unmarried with one illegitimate child; died 22 May 1847 in Enniskillen, of typhus fever; probate Prerogative Court 19 June 1847; original will in PRO NI; bequeathed his apothecary's business to his cousin, William Betty (*q.v.*). [Apothecaries (1829); *BNL* 1 June 1847 (d); Belf PRO, LPC/1210; Belf PRO, prerog wills index; Croly (1843–6); *Londonderry Sentinel* 29 May 1847 (d); Pigot (1824)].

COLLUM, JOHN (*fl c* 1816), Enniskillen, county Fermanagh;
LAH Dub 1816; apothecary, of Enniskillen. [Apothecaries (1829)].

COLLUM, ROBERT (1814–1900), Indian Medical Service and Surbiton, Surrey;
born January 1814 in Enniskillen, county Fermanagh; studied medicine in Dublin and Glasgow; LM Dub 1836; MRCSE 1836; MD (Glas) 1837; MRCP Lond 1859; joined the Indian Medical Service (Bombay establishment) as assistant surgeon in 1838; surgeon 1851; attached to Sir C. Napier's staff during the conquest of Sind, surgeon to the Field and General Hospitals; when the ship on which he set out for Sind was stricken by cholera and 64 out of 200 soldiers died, he not only looked after the sick but also acted as pilot of the vessel; surgeon to the Ameers of Sind for 7 years; superintendent of the Medical Department at Aden; assay master to the Bombay Mint; civil surgeon and superintendent of the Agency Jail of Hazaribagh; retired 1858; physician accoucheur to the Paddington Maternity Hospital and physician to the Western General Dispensary; general practitioner in Surbiton, Surrey, of Croy, and later of Sutherland House, Surbiton; member of the consulting commission of the India Office; honorary physician to the Metropolitan Convalescent Institute; died 12 January 1900 at home in Surbiton; buried in Kensal Green Cemetery, London; probate London 10 March 1900. [Addison (1898); *BMJ* obituary (1900); Crawford (1930); Lond PPR, will cal; *Med Dir.*]

COLSTON, RALPH (*fl c* 1845), Lisnaskea, county Fermanagh;
apothecary, of Lisnaskea c 1845. [Croly (1843–6)].

COLTHEART, SAMUEL (*fl c* 1742), county Tyrone;
of county Tyrone; studied medicine at Rheims University; MD (Rheims) 1742. [Brockliss].

COLVAN (COLVEN, COLVIN), JOHN (1789/90–1860), Armagh;
born 1789/90, son of John Colvan, baker, of Armagh; studied medicine at Trinity College, Dublin, and the Royal College of Surgeons in Ireland; LM TCD; MRCSE 1816; accoucheur of the Westminster Lying-in Institution 1816; LAH Dub 1827; LKQCPI and LM 1829; FRCSI 1844; surgeon to Armagh County Infirmary and gaol 1817–18 and 1822–3; medical officer to the Temporary Fever Hospital, Armagh 1817–18 and 1847; physician to the Cholera Hospital 1832–3; wrote to Chief Secretary in 1833 commenting bitterly on the method of appointment to county infirmaries; physician and surgeon to Armagh City Fever Hospital for 30 years; of

Scotch Street, Armagh c 1819 and of English Street c 1845; medical superintendent of Armagh Dispensary and Infirmary; retired to Carnmine Cottage, Newry, county Down; married 30 July 1841 in St Mary's Church of Ireland Church, Newry, Deborah Coulter, eldest daughter of John Coulter of Carnmeen; died 13 December 1860 at Carnmeen Cottage; probate Dublin 6 June 1863. [Apothecaries (1829); *BNL* 1 October 1830 (d, father), 6 August 1841 (m) and 17 December 1860 (d); Belf PRO, will cal; Bradshaw (1819); Croly (1843–6); Geary (2002); Lewis (1837); *Med Dir*; Weatherup (2001)].

COLVILL(E), ALEXANDER (1699–1777), Dromore, county Down;
born 1699, son of the Rev Alexander Colville, minister of Newtownards Presbyterian Church and later of Dromore; studied divinity and medicine at Edinburgh and Glasgow universities [The son dropped the 'e' c 1724.]; MA (Edin) 1715; MD (Glas) 1728; licenced by the Presbytery of Cupar-Fife 1722; non-subscriber and therefore ordained privately in London 1724, causing a split in the congregation, though the majority supported him; joined himself and followers to the expelled Presbytery of Antrim 1730; a new meeting house built for him and his Non-Subscribing Presbyterian congregation in Dromore; practised as minister and doctor and also raised a troop of dragoons in 1745 to counter unrest caused by the Young Pretender; author of various religious pamphlets; married —; died 23 April 1777 of apoplexy at Dromore; buried in Dromore. [Addison (1898); *BNL* 25 April 1777 (d); Crone (1928); Dickson (1898); McConnell (1951); Martin (2003); Newmann (1993); *Oxford DNB* (2004)].

COLVILLE, JAMES (1865–1933), Belfast;
born 2 October 1865 at Belfast, son of James M. Colville, merchant, of Marlborough Park, Belfast; educated at RBAI; studied medicine at Queen's College, Belfast, from 1884; BA (RUI) 1888; MB BCh BAO 1893; MD 1895; of 25 University Road c 1895; medical registrar to the Royal Victoria Hospital, Belfast; honorary physician to Ulster Hospital, Belfast; assistant physician to Belfast Hospital for Sick Children 1908–12; president of the Ulster Medical Society 1918–19; of 11 University Square, Belfast, 1904–07 and of 7 University Square 1907–33; married —; died 6 October 1933 at 7 University Square; probate Belfast 14 August 1934. [Belf GRO (d); Belf PRO, will cal; Calwell (1973); Hunter (1936); *Med Dir*; QCB adm reg; Strain (1967); Wilson (1934)].

COMINS, WILLIAM (d 1838), Army Medical Service and Belfast;
joined the Army Medical Service as surgeon on the Irish Establishment 1795; physician to the Belfast Poor House 1802; for many years stationed in Belfast and Athlone; surgeon and deputy inspector-general of hospitals 1803, of Arthur Street, Belfast; addressing the Belfast Literary Society 1809–16; commisioned for general service 1824; retired on half pay 1826; died 19 May 1838. [Adams (1991); *Belf Lit Soc* (1901); *BNL* 25 May 1838 (d); Peterkin and Johnston (1968); Strain (1961)].

CONAN, JOHN (1820/1–99), Plumbridge, county Tyrone;
born 1820/1; studied medicine at Trinity College, Dublin; MRCSE 1846; LM Rot Hosp Dub 1853; FRCSI 1856; medical officer to Plumbridge Dispensary District

and constabulary; married —; died 4 August 1899 at Plumbridge. [Dub GRO (d); *Med Dir*].

CONDON, FREDERICK WILLIAM (1870/1–1914), Ballyshannon, county Donegal;
born 1870/1; LM Rot Hosp Dub 1891; LRCPI and LM 1891; LRCSI and LM; FRCSI 1894; resident physician to Government Hospitals, Dublin; medical officer to Ballyshannon Union Hospital and constabulary, consulting sanitary officer to Ballyshannon Union, visiting surgeon to the Sheil Hospital, Ballyshannon and certifying factory surgeon; of The Mall, Ballyshannon; maried Mary F. —; died 15 June 1914 at The Mansion, Beckenham Park, Beckenham, Kent; buried in Ballyshannon; administration Dublin 25 September 1914. [Belf PRO, will cal; Kirkpatrick Archive; Lond GRO (d); *Med Dir*].

CONDON, JAMES DAVID (1842/3–1914), Ballyshannon, county Donegal;
born 1842/3; studied medicine at the Royal College of Surgeons in Ireland; LKQCPI 1863; LRCSI and LM 1863 LM Coombe Hosp Dub 1863; MRCPI 1891; medical officer to Ballyshannon Dispensary District, of Ivy College, Ballyshannon; married 21 September 1868 in the Church of the Assumption, Rathmines, Frederica Augusta Brown, daughter of William Pierce Brown of Wilton Hall. Limerick; died 27 January 1914 at Ballyshannon. [Dub GRO (d); *Londonderry Sentinel* 29 September 1868 (m); *Med Dir*].

CONDON, WILLIAM RICHARD (1855/6–1905), Shronell, county Tipperary;
born 1855/6 at Shronell, county Tipperary, son of Richard Condon, DVC, gentleman farmer, of Shronell; studied arts and medicine at Queen's College, Galway, Queen's College, Cork and from 1878, Queen's College, Belfast; LRCP LRCS Edin 1884; general practitioner, of 2 Derby Terrace, Nelson Street, Tipperary, and later of Shronell, county Tipperary; married —; died 19 October 1905 at Shronell. [Dub GRO (d); *Med Dir*; QCB adm reg].

CONDON, — (d 1847), Enniskillen, county Fermanagh;
general practitioner, of Enniskillen; died 1847 of typhus fever. [Cunningham (1997)].

CONDY, ALEXANDER (d 1818), Strabane, county Tyrone;
LAH Dub 1804; apothecary, of Strabane; married —; father of Anne Elizabeth Condy who married 20 February 1834 William Cook(e) of Strabane; died 22 December 1818. [Apothecaries (1829); *BNL* 1 January 1819 (d) and 4 March 1834 (m, daughter); *Strabane Morning Post* 25 February 1834 (m, dau)].

CONLON, THOMAS PETER (1858/9–1945), Monaghan;
born 1858/9 at Channonrock, county Louth; studied medicine at the Catholic University of Ireland; LRCPI and LM, LRCSI and LM 1894; resident medical superintendent of the District Asylum, Monaghan; retired c 1937 to Drumbear, Monaghan; married —; father of Dr Thomas Joseph Conlon of Enniscorthy, LRCPI and LRCSI 1931; died 4 May 1945 at Monaghan County Hospital; probate Dublin 23 November 1945. [Dub GRO (d); Dub Nat Arch, will cal; Kirkpatrick Archive; *Med Dir*].

CONNELLY, PATRICK (*fl c* 1802), Ballynaught, county Cavan;
LAH Dub 1802; apothecary, of Ballynaught. [Apothecaries (1829)].

CONNIN, FRANCIS (*fl c* 1824), Ballynahinch, county Down;
apothecary, of Ballynahinch c 1824. [Pigot (1824)].

CONNOLLY, HUGH (*fl c* 1835), Middletown, county Armagh;
surgeon, of Middletown; married 8 September 1835 Catherine Kelly, fourth daughter of James Kelly. [*BNL* 25 September 1835 (m)].

CONNOLLY, JOHN (*fl c* 1818), Monaghan;
LAH Dub 1818; apothecary, of Monaghan. [Apothecaries (1829)].

CONNOLLY, JOSEPH (1840/1–81), Belfast;
born 1840/1, son of John Connolly of Castle Street, Armagh; studied medicine at Queen's College, Belfast, from 1858; MRCSE 1862; LM KQCPI 1863; LKQCPI 1867; general practitioner, of 49 Cromac Street, Belfast; unmarried; died 6 June 1881 of phthisis and laryngitis, at 13 Derby Street, Belfast. [Dub GRO (d); *Med Dir*; QCB adm reg].

CONNOR, GEORGE WASHINGTON (1872–1936), Newry, county Down;
born 30 August 1872 at Seaview Cottage, Warrenpoint, fourth son of Dr Samuel Connor of Newry and Warrenpoint (*q.v.*) and Margaret McIlwaine; educated at Coleraine Academical Institute; studied medicine at the Middlesex and Royal Dental Hospitals, London; MRCSE LRCP Lond 1896; LDS RCSE 1896; house surgeon to the Dental Hospital, London; honorary dental surgeon to Newry Hospital; dental surgeon, of 77 Hill Street, Newry and Seaview Cottage, Warrenpoint; married 17 August 1915 Winifred Beatrice Haslett; father of Dr George Haslett Connor, MB BCh BAO (QUB) 1942, and Ida Mary Connor who married Leonard Walker RN and was mother of Dr Frederick George Connor Walker, MB BCh BAO (QUB) 1938; died 7 August 1936 at Seaview Cottage; probate Belfast 3 February 1937. [Belf GRO (b) and (d); Belf PRO, will cal; Bennett (1974); Kirkpatrick Archive; *Med Dir*].

CONNOR, JAMES STEWART (1803/4–80), Moira, county Down;
born 1803/4; LFPS Glasgow 1835; LM Glasgow 1852; medical officer to the Fever Hospital, Belfast; general practitioner, of Moira, medical offcer to the constabulary and public vaccinator; married —; children born 1852 and 1855; died 24 May 1880 at Moira. [*BNL* 2 August 1852 (b) and 23 October 1855 (b); Croly (1843–6); Dub GRO (d); Kirkpatrick Archive; *Med Dir*].

CONNOR, JOHN COLPOYS (1867–1936), Army Medical Service;
born 13 August 1867 at Stoneyford, Lisburn, county Antrim, son of John Connor, farmer, of Stoneyford; brother of Dr Samuel Connor (*q.v.*) of Victoria, Australia; educated at RBAI; studied arts and medicine at Queen's College, Belfast, from 1883; MB BCh BAO (RUI) 1889; joined the Army Medical Service as surgeon captain 1891; major 1903; lieutenant-colonel 1913; temporary colonel (ADMS) 1916; served in South Africa 1899–1902 and World War I 1914–18; CMG 1917; retired

c 1925 to Uplands, Hythe, Kent; married Evelyn —; died 16 November 1936; probate London 12 August 1937. [Lond PPR, will cal; *Med Dir*; Peterkin and Johnston (1968); QCB adm reg].

CONNOR, PATRICK (1773/4–1882), Newry, county Down;
born 1793/4; studied medicine at Glasgow and Edinburgh University; CM (Glas) 1817; MD (Edin) 1826 (thesis 'De sanguinis in typho mittendi utilitate'); LAH Dub 1856; apothecary and general practitioner of 3 Bridge Street, Newry; married 10 March 1830 in St Mary's Church of Ireland Church, Newry, Magdalene ('Meady') Townsley, (who died 10 July 1839 and was buried in St Patrick's Church of Ireland Graveyard, Newry), daughter of Samuel Townsley of Newry; died 9 July 1882 at Bridge Street; probate Armagh 28 August 1882. [Addison (1898); *BNL* 16 March 1830 (m) and 19 July 1939 (d); Belf PRO, will cal; Clarke, *County Down*, vol 21 (1998); Croly (1843–6); Dub GRO (d); Edin Univ; *Med Dir*].

CONNOR, SAMUEL (1836–94), Newry, county Down;
born 30 April 1836, son of John Connor, farmer; uncle of Dr Samuel Connor of Australia (*q.v.*); LM Belf Lying-in Hosp 1857; LRCS and LM Edin 1858; LAH Dub 1861; apothecary and general practitioner at 39 Hill Street (c 1860–75), 19 Hill Street (c 1886) and Seaview Cottage, Warrenpoint; JP; married 24 December 1862 in Rostrevor Presbyterian Church, Margaret McIlwaine (who died 29 January 1913 aged 75), daughter of John McIlwaine of Kilkeel; father of Dr Samuel Graham(e) Connor (*q.v.*) and Dr George Washington Connor (*q.v.*); died 14 April 1894 at Hill Street; buried in Newry Presbyterian Graveyard; administration (with will) 14 September 1894. [Bassett (1886), p 80; Belf PRO, will cal; Bennett (1974); Clarke, *County Down*, vol 21 (1998); Dub GRO (d); *Med Dir*; UHF database (m)].

CONNOR, SAMUEL (1861–1927), Coleraine, Victoria, Australia;
born 17 June 1861, fourth son of John Connor, farmer, of Stoneyford, county Antrim; brother of Dr John Colpoys Connor (*q.v.*); nephew of Dr Samuel Connor of Newry (*q.v.*); educated at Stoneyford National School and RBAI from 1875; studied medicine at Queen's College, Belfast, from 1876, but worked in his uncle's shop in Newry for 11 months, 1877–8; MD Dip Mid (QUI) 1881; assistant to Dr Henry McBride of Gilford (*q.v.*) for four months in 1881–2; surgeon on SS *Superb* from London to Melbourne 1882; general practitioner in Coleraine, Victoria, surgeon to the militia and honorary surgeon to Hamilton Hospital; JP; married —; died September 1927 in Coleraine. [Fisher and Robb (1913); Geary (1995); *Med Dir*; QCB adm reg].

CONNOR, SAMUEL GRAHAM(E) (1865–1941), Newry, county Down, and London;
born 28 August 1865 in Hill Street, Newry, son of Dr Samuel Connor (*q.v.*) of Newry and Margaret McIlwaine; brother of Dr George Washington Connor (*q.v.*); educated at Coleraine Academical Institution; studied medicine at Queen's College, Cork, London University and Edinburgh University; MB MCh (Edin) 1889; general practitioner of Newry; moved to practice in London c 1905; manager of the Metropolitan Asylums Board and chairman of the Westminister Board of Guardians

and Central London Sick Asylum; certifying factory surgeon; of 42 Oxford Street, London c 1907, of 21 Dryden Chambers, 119 Oxford Street c 1925 and of 75 Bedford Court Mansions c 1935; married Florence Mary Lulman, daughter of A. Lulman; died 16 February 1941 at 79 Hill Street, Newry; buried in Newry Presbyterian Graveyard. [Belf GRO (d); Bennett (1974); Clarke, *County Down*, vol 21 (1998); Dub GRO (b*); Med Dir*; Young and Pike (1909)].

CONOLLY, SAMUEL RUSSELL (1823/4–98), Killinchy, county Down;
born 1823/4; studied medicine at the RBAI, Queen's College, Belfast, from 1850, and Belfast General Hospital; LM (QUB) 1852; LFPS Glas 1853; general practitioner, of Ballymacreely, Killinchy; married Sarah —; died 21 April 1898 at Ballymacreely; administration Belfast 27 June 1898. [Belf PRO, will cal; Dub GRO (d); *Med Dir*; QCB adm reg].

CONRY, THOMAS (1836/7–85), Naval Medical Service;
born 1836/7, son of Captain Robert Conry; educated by S. McCutcheon of Longford; studied medicine at Queen's College, Belfast, from 1857; MRCSE 1865; joined the Naval Medical Service; assistant surgeon on HMS Agincourt c 1871; surgeon in Bermuda c 1874; with Royal Marine Artillery Hospital in Portsmouth c 1876; staff surgeon c 1877; on HMS *Hector* c 1879; died 15 November 1885 at Melville Hospital, Chatham, Kent. [Lond GRO (d); *Med Dir*; QCB adm reg].

CONSIDINE, PATRICK OSWALD (1851–1912), Port Elizabeth, South Africa;
born 4 September 1851 at Port Elizabeth, son of William Considine, merchant, of Port Elizabeth; educated at Grey's College, Port Elizabeth; studied medicine at Queen's College, Belfast, from 1873; LM Rot Hosp Dub; LRCSI 1877; MD (QUI) 1878; general practitioner in Port Elizabeth from c 1880; died 1912 at Port Elizabeth. [*Med Dir*; QCB adm reg].

CONWAY, JOHN (*fl c* 1801), Cookstown, county Tyrone;
LAH Dub 1801; apothecary, of Cookstown. [Apothecaries (1829)].

CONWELL, ANTHONY (1792–1830), Indian Medical Service;
born 24 April 1792, son of Patrick Conwell; MRCSE 1818; joined the Indian Medical Service (Bombay establishment) as assistant surgeon 1819; surgeon 1826; present at the capture of Kittur 1824; married Jane —; died 5 July 1830 at Liverpool, Lancashire; commemorated in Eglish Graveyard, county Londonderry. [Crawford (1930); Larkin (1981a) and (1981b)].

CONWELL, EDWARD (1779–1806), Army Medical Service;
born 1779, son of John Conwell of Ballymulligan, Magherafelt, county Londonderry; brother of Dr Michael Conwell RN (*q.v.*) and Dr William Eugene Edward Conwell IMS (*q.v.*); educated for the priesthood, like his uncle the Rev Henry Conwell, who became Bishop of Philadelphia, but failed to secure a place in an Irish College abroad; joined the Army Medical Service, first as hospital mate, and in 1804 as assistant surgeon to the 46th Foot; died 16 December 1806 in Dominica, West Indies;

commemorated in Eglish Graveyard. [Larkin (1981a) and (1981b); Peterkin and Johnston (1968).

CONWELL, JOHN (1810–35), Indian Medical Service;
born March 1810, son of Hugh Conwell; MRCS 1832; joined the Indian Medical Service (Madras establishment) as assistant surgeon 1832; died 31 January 1835 at Capetown, South Africa; commemorated in Eglish Graveyard. [Crawford (1930); Larkin (1981a) and (1981b)].

CONWELL, MICHAEL (1772/3–1808), Naval Medical Service;
born 1772/3, son of John Conwell of Ballymulligan, Magherafelt, county Londonderry; brother of Dr Edward Conwell AMS (*q.v.*) and Dr William Eugene Edward Conwell IMS (*q.v.*); joined the Naval Medical Service and served in China and the Far East; died 1808 on his way home from the Far East; commemorated in Eglish Graveyard. [Larkin (1981a) and (1981b)].

CONWELL, WILLIAM EUGENE EDWARD (1785–1836), Indian Medical Service;
born September 1785 in county Londonderry, son of John Conwell of Ballymulligan, Magherafelt; brother of Dr Michael Conwell RN (*q.v.*) and Dr Edward Conwell AMS (*q.v.*); apprenticed to a doctor in Dungannon and later to a doctor in London, always under conditions of great poverty, while he worked for the MRCS; studied medicine at the Royal College of Surgeons of England and at Paris University; MD (Paris) (thesis 'L'emploi en medicine de l'huile de croton tiglium'); MRCSE 1806; LRCSE 1807; B Lit and B Sc (Paris); LLB and MRIA; also studied at Trinity College, Dublin, but took no degree; joined the Indian Medical Service (Madras establishment) as assistant surgeon 1806; surgeon 1821; senior surgeon 1836; author of various medical papers, notably on the treatment of yellow fever; died 18 May 1836 at Bangalore and was buried there; commemorated in Eglish Graveyard, county Londonderry. [Burtchaell and Sadlier (1924); Crawford (1930); Kirkpatrick Archive; Larkin (1981a) and (1981b)].

COOK, HENRY DAVID (1847–1901), Indian Medical Service;
born 2 May 1847 in Calicut, India, son of Henry David Cook of Calicut; educated at RBAI; studied medicine at Queen's College, Belfast, and Edinburgh University 1864–9; MB MCh (Edin) 1869; joined the Indian Medical Service (Madras establishment) 1870 as assistant surgeon; surgeon 1873; surgeon major 1882; retired 1900; died 16 December 1901 at Bedford. [Crawford (1930); Kirkpatrick (1889); *Med Dir*; QCB adm reg].

COOKE, ALEXANDER HALDAIN (HALDANE), (1835/6–70), Belfast;
born 1835/6, son of the Rev Henry Cooke, minister of Donegore and Killyleagh Presbyterian Churches and of May Street, Belfast, and Ellen Mann; educated at Belfast Academy; studied medicine at Queen's College, Belfast, from 1854; MRCSE 1859; assistant house surgeon to Belfast General Hospital 1856–7; general practitioner, of 19 Ormeau Road, Belfast, and assistant surgeon to Antrim Militia; unmarried; died 19 August 1870 of phthisis, at Tonaghmore, Saintfied. [*DIB* (2009) (for father); Dub GRO (d); Kirkpatrick Archive; *Med Dir*].

COOKE, JAMES (1840/1–77), Manchester;
born 1840/1, son of James Cooke of Kensingston Cottage, Malone, Belfast and later of 19 Sydney Street, Oxford Road, Manchester; educated at Belfast Academy; studied medicine at Queen's College, Belfast, from 1858; MRCSE 1863; LKQCPI and LM 1867; general practitioner, of 241 St George's Place, Stockport Road, Manchester from c 1870; married Harriet —; died 3 December 1877 of phthisis, at Over, Cheshire. [Lond GRO (d); *Med Dir*; QCB adm reg].

COOKE, JAMES (1861–c 1920), Canterbury, New Zealand;
born 29 March 1861 in Belfast, son of James Cooke, merchant tailor, of 2 Woodstock Road, Belfast; educated at RBAI; studied medicine at Queen's College, Belfast, from 1877; MD (RUI) 1882; LRCS Edin 1884; emigrated to New Zealand c 1885; general practitioner, of Lincoln, Canterbury, New Zealand; died c 1920. [*Med Dir*; QCB adm reg].

COOKE, JOHN GALWEY (GALWAY) (1859/60–1938), Londonderry;
born 1859/60, son of the Rev Ambrose Cooke, rector of Thomastown, county Kilkenny, and Maria Chapman; educated in Kingstown, county Dublin; studied arts and medicine at Trinity College, Dublin, from 1879; BA (TCD) 1885; MB BCh 1887; LM Rot Hosp Dub; house surgeon, assistant surgeon and surgeon to the City and County Infirmary, Londonderry 1887–1920; OBE c 1920; of 67 Clarendon Street, Londonderry, from c 1920; retired c 1936; unmarried; died 24 March 1938 at 17 Clarendon Street, Londonderry; probate Londonderry 28 June 1938. [Belf GRO (d); Belf PRO, will cal; *BMJ* obituary (1938); Dallat (1990); Kirkpatrick Archive; Leslie (1933); *Med Dir*; TCD adm reg; *TCD Cat*, vol II (1896)].

COOKE, RICHARD WOODS (1811/2–47), Kilkeel, county Down;
born 1811/2; studied medicine at Edinburgh University; MRCSE 1834; MD (Edin) 1835 (thesis 'Practical remarks on some injuries of the head'); LRCSI 1843; accoucheur of the Anglesey Lying-in Hospital, Dublin; medical officer to Kilkeel and Annalong Dispensary Districts; married 19 January 1842 in Ballybay Church, Kate Woods, third daughter of William Woods of Frankford, King's County; died 17 July 1847 (drowned); buried in Kilhorne Church of Ireland graveyard, Annalong. [*BNL* 28 January 1842 (m); Clarke, *County Down*, vol 10 (1973); Croly (1843–6); Edin Univ; Kirkpatrick Archive; Malcolm (1851)].

COOPER, DAVID MIDDLETON (*fl c* 1850), Randalstown, county Antrim;
born in Randalstown; emigrated to USA; practised as a physician but not in the British *Medical Directory* or *Medical Register*; married 23 September 1850 in Christ Church, St Louis, Missouri, Fanny Fallon, eldest daughter of Major B.O. Fallon. [*BNL* 11 October 1850 (m); *Coleraine Chronicle* 12 October 1850 (m)].

COOTE, CHARLES (1816/7–93), Monaghan, Kinvarra, county Galway, and Kilrush, county Clare;
born 1816/7, second son of Major Coote of Cootehill, county Cavan; studied medicine at Jervis Street, the City of Dublin, Sir Patrick Dun's and the Rotunda Hospitals; LAH Dub 1840; apothecary and surgeon to the Monaghan Militia c 1858;

of The Diamond, Monaghan; apothecary to Kinvarra Dispensary District; moved c 1874 to Kilrush, county Clare; married 18 July 1842 Maria (L of A) or Matilda (*BNL*) Fitzpatrick, second daughter of Henry Fitzpatrick of Whitehill, county Wicklow; died 16 September 1893 in the High Street, Kilrush; administration Limerick 27 November 1893. [*BNL* 29 July 1842 (m) and 23 December 1858 (b, daughter); Belf PRO, will cal; Dub GRO (d); McCann (2003); *Med Dir*].

COOTE, RICHARD (d 1856), Dunkineely, county Donegal;
youngest son of Sir Charles Coote, Bart; LRCSI; surgeon to Dunkineely Dispensary; married 22 July 1843 in St Mary's Church, Dublin, Mary Hay, eldest daughter of Alexander Hay of Villa, county Galway; died 27 September 1856 at his home, Holybroke, county Donegal. [*BNL* 15 August 1843 (m); *Londonderry Sentinel* 3 October 1856 (d); *Med Dir*].

COOTE, WILLIAM (*fl c* 1845), Cootehill, county Cavan;
studied medicine at Glasgow University; MD (Glas) 1833; FRCSI; general practitioner in Cootehill c 1845. [Addison (1898); Croly (1843–6)].

COPE, BARCLAY (d 1757), Drumglass, county Tyrone, and Loughgall and Ballymore, county Armagh;
fifth son of the Rev Anthony Cope, rector of Ardearn, county Roscommon, and archdeacon of Elphin, and Elizabeth Cope of Loughgall; brother of Dr Henry Cope, MD (TCD) 1717, Regius Professor of Physic at TCD; studied arts and medicine at Trinity College, Dublin; MB and MD 1718; subsequently ordained in the Diocese of Armagh and appears not to have practiced medicine; rector of Drumglass and Tullaniskin, county Tyrone 1720–23; prebendary of Loughgall 1724–41; prebendary of Ballymore 1757; died 1757. [Burtchaell and Sadleir (1924); Leslie (1911); Leslie and Crooks (2008)].

COPELAND, EDWARD (1822/3–90), Lisbellaw and Florence Court, county Fermanagh;
born 1822/3; studied medicine at the Carmichael School and Richmond Hospital; LRCSI 1846; surgeon to the Westmeath Regiment of Militia; surgeon to the Lisbellaw Dispensary District, Fever Hospital and constabulary; medical officer to the Florence Court Dispensary District, of Drumlaghy, Florence Court; unmarried; died 8 July 1890 at Drumlaghy; administration Dublin 31 July 1890. [Belf PRO, will cal; Dub GRO (d); *Med Dir*].

CORBETT, CHARLES (*fl c* 1866), Monaghan town;
surgeon, of Monaghan Infirmary c 1866. [McCann (2003)].

CORBETT, JAMES (d c 1873), Rathfriland, county Down;
son of Samuel Corbett, farmer; studied medicine at Glasgow University and in Dublin; CM (Glas) 1826; LAH Dub 1827; surgeon and apothecary in Dromore Street, Rathfriland c 1845; married (1) 1 February 1833 in Newry, — Lacy, widow of Alexander Lacy, master of the brig *Samuel*; (2) 28 January 1852 in First Rathfriland Presbyterian Church, Elizabeth Mitchell, daughter of John Mitchell, farmer, of

Grallagh, county Down; died c 1873. [Addison (1898); apothecaries (1829); *BNL* 8 February 1833 (m); Croly (1843-6); *Med Dir*; UHF database (m)].

CORBETT, THOMAS (1806/7-90), Londonderry;
born 1806/7; LFPS Glas 1824; LAH Dub 1830; LM Coombe Hosp Dub 1840; medical officer to Londonderry Dispensary District No 2 and certifying factory surgeon, of 20 Shipquay Street, Londonderry c 1886; married Martha Denham, daughter of the Rev Joseph Denham of Killashandra, county Cavan, and Elizabeth Cromley of Clones; died 3 March 1890 at Shipquay Street. [Dub GRO (d); *Med Dir; Memorials of the Dead*, vol XI, p 13].

CORBITT, JOSEPH ALBERT (1867-1932), India, Bangor, county Down, Portadown, county Armagh, ship's doctor and Liverpool, Lancashire;
born 14 September 1867 at Moira, county Down, son of George Corbitt, farmer, of Gilford, county Down; educated at Methodist College, Belfast, from 1879; studied medicine at Queen's College, Belfast, from 1886; MB BCh BAO (RUI) 1893; of 126 Ellenborough Terrace, Mount Pottinger, Belfast, c 1895; district surgeon to North Cachar, India and West Dooars, Jalpaiguri, India; surgeon to the Cottage Hospital and Ordnance Survey, Bangor, county Down; general practitioner, of 56 Hanover Street, Portadown, from c 1900; of 39 Thomas Street, Portadown c 1908; medical officer with the Cunard Steamship Company, Westport, from c 1910; of 5 Galloway Road, Waterloo, Liverpool c 1930; married (1) Isabella Caroline — (who was born 1870/1 and died 12 January 1905; buried in Magherlin Old Graveyard); (2) 9 January 1913 in Christ Church Church of Ireland Church, Belfast, Mary Anne Hall, daughter of Thomas John Hall, farmer; died 20 September 1932 at 3 South View, Waterloo; probate Liverpool 15 December 1932. [Clarke, *County Down*, vol 19 (1983); Dub GRO (m); Fry (1984); Lond GRO (d); Lond PPR, will cal; *Med Dir*; QCB adm reg; UHF database (m)].

CORCORAN, GEORGE (*fl c* 1824), Kilnaleck, county Cavan;
LAH Dub 1824; apothecary, of Kilnaleck; died 16 September 1852 at Ballymahon, county Longford. [Apothecaries (1829); *BNL* 24 September 1852 (d)].

CORD (CHOORDE), JAMES(1766/7-98), Killinchy, county Down;
born 1766/7; general practitioner in Killinchy; led a troop of Killinchy insurgents at the battle of Saintfield 'riding a whitish beast, a drawn sword in his hand and a cockade in his hat'; tried by court martial at Downpatrick 21-23 June 1798, condemned and hanged on 23 June 1798; buried in Killinchy Presbyterian Graveyard. [Allen (2004); Clarke, *County Down*, vol 6 (1971); Hill, Turner and Dowson (1998); Wilsdon (1997)].

CORDNER, LOUIS MAXWELL (1844-1902), Belfast, Aughnacloy, county Tyrone and New Zealand;
born 14 June 1844 at Deramore, Belfast, sixth son of the Rev Edward James Cordner, curate of Derriaghy, and Maria Purdon (daughter of Dr Henry Purdon, senior (*q.v.*)); educated at Rossall School, Fleetwood, Lancashire 1858-61; studied medicine at the Ledwich School, Dublin and from 1863, at Queen's Colllege, Belfast; LKQCPI and

LM 1866; LRCSI 1866; house surgeon to West Ham, Stratford and Essex Dispensary; resident medical officer to Belfast Hospital for Acute Medical and Contagious Diseases c 1872; general practitioner in Aughnacloy from c 1875; emigrated to Rakaia, Canterbury, New Zealand 1888; died 1902. [King (1890); Leslie (1993); *Med Dir*; QCB adm reg].

CORE, WILLIAM SCOTT (1846–1906), Belfast;
born 30 November 1846 at Caledon, county Armagh, son of John Core of the Royal Irish Fusiliers, Omagh; educated at the Belfast Seminary; studied medicine at Queen's College, Belfast, from 1863, and at the Belfast General Hospital; MD (QUI) 1867; LRCS Edin 1868; surgeon to the White Star Line; resident medical officer to the Belfast Union Infirmary; general practitioner in Belfast, of 261 York Street and Abbotsford Place, Belfast; married 26 April 1872 in St Paul's Church of Ireland Church, Belfast, Hannah Bond, daughter of Hugh Bond, teacher, of Strandtown; died 21 April 1906 at 261 York Street. [*BMJ* obituary (1906); Dub GRO (d); Kirkpatrick Archive; *Med Dir*; QCB adm reg; UHF database (m)].

CORKEY, WILLIAM (1871–1927), Glenanne, county Armagh, and Brynamman, Glamorgan;
born 10 December 1871 at Ballylane, county Armagh, son of Robert Corkey of Ballylane; educated at Newry Intermediate School; studied medicine at Queen's College, Belfast, from 1889, and Edinburgh; LRCP LRCS Edin 1894; LFPS Glas 1894; MD (Bruxelles, hons) 1898; general practitioner, of Lisdrumchor, Glenanne, county Armagh, from c 1900; general practitioner in Brynamman c 1910; died 2 August 1927 at 29 Glyn Road, Brynamman; probate Carmarthen 13 October 1927. [Lond GRO (d); Lond PPR, will cal; *Med Dir*; QCB adm reg].

CORNWALL, GABRIEL (d 1784), Stewartstown, county Tyrone;
'celebrated surgeon and accoucheur'; lieutenant in the Stewartstown First Company of Militia; died 3 February 1784 at Stewartstown; administration Armagh Diocesan Court 1784. [*BNL* 6 February 1784 (d); Dub Nat Arch, Armagh Dio Admins index].

CORRY, ALEXANDER (1862–c 1925), Ballarat, Victoria, Australia;
born 1 May 1862 at Ballintrain, Sixmilecross, county Tyrone, son of Samuel Corry, farmer, of Ballintrain; educated at RBAI; studied medicine at Queen's College, Belfast, from 1880; MD MAO (RUI) 1885; emigrated to Australia; general practitioner of Mount Egerton, Ballarat; died c 1925. [*Med Dir*; QCB adm reg].

CORRY, THOMAS CHARLES STEUART (1825/6–96), Belfast;
born 1825/6, possibly in Brandon, Suffolk, elder son of Thomas Charles Stewart Corry of Rockcorry, Monaghan, MP, and his second wife Mary Britnell; educated at RBAI; studied medicine at RBAI c 1844 and King's College, London; LM Belfast 1845; MRCSE 1846; MD (King's College, Aberdeen) 1856; LRCP Edin 1859; LM RCSE 1860; LAH Dub 1891; general practitioner in Belfast from 1846; noted for his zeal in helping the sick and poor, particularly in 1846–7; campaigner for clean drinking water; senior surgeon Belfast Dispensary District and registrar of births and deaths for Belfast; founder of Corry's Mineral Water Company c 1847, which grew

to be one of the largest in the world c 1896; creator of two large dioramas about Ireland; author of *The Battle of Antrim* [8-page poem] (1875) and *Irish Lyrics, Songs and Poems* (1879); of 9 Clarendon Place c 1870; of 45 Ormeau Terrace c 1885 and finally of 1 Glenfield Place, Belfast; married (1) 8 February 1855 in St Anne's Church of Ireland Church, Belfast, Elizabeth Phoenix (who was born 1823/4), second daughter of William Phoenix, gentleman, of Banbridge; (2) 8 April 1891 in Malone Presbyterian Church, Belfast, Anne Martin, daughter of Robert Martin of Belfast; died 20 May 1896 at 1 Glenfield Place; buried in Belfast City Cemetery; probate Belfast 22 June 1896. [Belf City Cem, bur reg; *BNL* 9 February 1855 (m); Belf PRO, will cal; *DIB* (2009); Dub GRO (m) and (d); Jamieson (1959); Kirkpatrick Archive; Martin (2003); *Med Dir; Newtownards Chronicle* 2 August 1879; UHF database (m)].

CORRY, WILLIAM (1850–1900), Drumquin, county Tyrone, London and Victoria, Australia;
born 11 January 1850 at Sixmilecross, county Tyrone, son of Samuel Corry, farmer, of Ballintrain, Sixmilecross; educated at Omagh Model School; studied medicine at Queen's College, Belfast, from 1872; MD MCh Dip Mid (QUI) 1877; DPH (Camb) 1890; medical officer and medical officer of health to Drumquin Dispensary District and constabulary; JP for county Tyrone; general practitioner, of Yucca House, South Lambeth Road, London c 1890–93; emigrated to Australia c 1893; general practitioner and medical officer of health of Kingston, Victoria, of Surrey Hills, Melbourne, Victoria; died 1900. [*Med Dir*; QCB adm reg].

CORSCADDEN, GEORGE ROBERT (1848/9–1917); Ballintra, county Donegal;
born 1848/9; studied medicine at Edinburgh University and the Royal College of Surgeons in Ireland; LRCSI 1873; LRCP Edin and LM 1877; assistant house surgeon to Liverpool Dispensary District from 1874; medical officer to Ballintra Dispensary District and constabulary; retired c 1914 to Rossnowlagh; married Rebecca —; died 3 April 1917 at Drumholm, Ballintra; probate Dublin 16 June 1917. [Belf PRO will cal; Dub GRO (d); Kirkpatrick Archive; *Med Dir*].

COSGRAVE, JAMES STEELE (b 1819/20), Holywood, county Down;
born 1819/20, son of Thomas Cosgrave, farmer; surgeon, of Malone and Holywood; married 16 November 1847 in Dunmurry Presbyterian Church, Anna O'Neill, fourth daughter of John O'Neill, merchant, of Belfast; sons born 23 March 1851 in Ballylesson Cottage and 18 March 1855 in Holywood. [*BNL* 23 November 1847 (m), 28 March 1851 (b, son) and 19 March 1855 (b, son)].

COULTER, DANIEL (d 1847), Naval Medical Service;
second surviving son of Daniel Coulter of Drumconnig House, Omagh, county Tyrone; brother of Dr John Coulter RN (*q.v.*) and Dr Joseph Coulter RN (*q.v.*); joined the Naval Medical Service as assistant surgeon; served on HMS *Agincourt*; died 31 March 1847 at Penang, China. [*BNL* 30 July 1847 (d); *Londonderry Sentinel* 17 July 1847 (d); McGrew (2001)].

COULTER, JOHN (1803/4–51), Naval Medical Service;
born 1803/4, eldest son of Daniel Coulter of Drumconnig House, Omagh, county Tyrone; brother of Dr Daniel Coulter RN (*q.v.*) and Dr Joseph Coulter RN (*q.v.*); joined the Naval Medical Service as assistant surgeon; served on HMS *Bellerophon*; died 28 August 1851 at the Royal Naval Hospital, Stonehouse, Plymouth. [*BNL* 15 September 1851 (d); *Londonderry Sentinel* 19 September 1851 (d); McGrew (2001)].

COULTER, JOHN (*fl c* 1829), Cootehill, county Cavan;
LAH Dub 1829; apothecary, of Cootehill. [Apothecaries (1829)].

COULTER, JOHN GORDON (1840–72), Belfast and Bengal;
born 31 March 1840 at Dundonald, only son of the Rev John Coulter, minister of Gilnahirk Presbyterian Church and Isabella Gordon; his sister Jane married Dr William Warwick (*q.v.*); studied medicine at Queen's College, Belfast, from 1859, and the General Hospital,Belfast; MD (QUI) 1863; MRCSE 1864; worked at Aenakhall, Bengal, India, where he died on 5 Oct 1872; buried at Silchar, India; money given by friends in 1875 to fund an Exhibition in his memory at the Royal Hospital; memorial tablet in Gilnahirk Presbyterian church. [Allison (1972); *Med Dir*; Miller (1987); QCB adm reg].

COULTER, JOSEPH (1818/9–62), Naval Medical Service;
born 1818/9, youngest son of Daniel Coulter of Drumconnig House, Omagh, county Tyrone; brother of Dr Daniel Coulter RN (*q.v.*) and Dr John Coulter RN (*q.v.*); joined the Naval Medical Service as assistant surgeon; retired to Drumconnig House; died 14 October 1862. [McGrew (2001)].

COULTER, ROBERT (1838/9–67), Fintona, county Tyrone, and Scotstown, county Monaghan;
born 1838/9; studied medicine at Trinity College and the Adelaide Hospital, Dublin; LM Coombe Lying-in Hospital 1861; LRCSI 1862; LRCP Edin 1864; of Scotstown, county Monaghan; assistant medical officer to Fintona Dispensary District; medical officer to Scotstown Dispensary District and constabulary; unmarried; died 23 December 1867 at Scotstown; administration Dublin 6 March 1868. [Belf PRO, will cal; Dub GRO (d); McCann (2003); *Med Dir*;].

COULTER, WILLIAM (1848–1912), Manchester, Lancashire, and Calcutta, India;
born 31 December 1848 at Castleblaney, county Monaghan, son of the Rev George Bartley Coulter, minister of First Castleblaney Presbyterian Church and — Smith of Castleblaney; educated privately; studied medicine at Queen's College, Belfast, from 1865, and later St Thomas's Hospital, London; MD MCh (QUI) 1870; MRCSE 1871; general physician, of 15 Church Street, Manchester, from c 1871; went as physician to Calcutta c 1880; retired c 1905 to Highwick, St Albans, England; married Katherine —; died 22 April 1912 at St Albans; probate London 13 June 1912. [Lond PPR, will cal; *Med Dir*; QCB adm reg; Stewart (1950)].

COULTHARD, WILLIAM JOSEPH CAMPBELL (1871/2–1943), Maryport and Aspatria, Cumberland;
   born 1871/2; studied medicine at Edinburgh University; MB MCh (Edin) 1895; of c/o James Bowman, Main Street, Bangor, c 1895; general practitioner, of 18 Curzon Street, Maryport, Cumberland c 1896–9, and of Yarrow House and Bishop's Close and Balwinnan, King Street, Aspatria c 1900–43; married Evelyn Olive —; father of Dr William Francis Hirsch Coulthard (eldest son), MB ChB (Edin) 1927; died 4 March 1943 at 8 Eden Mount, Stanwix, Carlisle; probate Carlisle 17 April 1944. [Lond GRO (d); Lond PPR, will cal, will; *Med Dir*].

COURTENAY, EDWARD MAZIERE (1846–1912), Limerick and Dublin;
   born 1846 in county Antrim, only son of the Rev David Carlile Courtenay, perpetual curate of Ballyeaston and later vicar of Magherafelt and of Ticmacreevan, all in county Antrim, and Dorothea Brady of Dublin; nephew of Sir Maziere Brady, Bart, Lord Chancellor of Ireland; educated at Armagh Royal School 1859–63; studied medicine at Trinity College, Dublin, from 1863; BA (TCD) 1868; MB MCh 1871; assistant medical officer to Derby County Asylum; medical superintendant of Limerick Asylum 1873–90; Inspector of Lunatics, of the Lunacy Office, Dublin Castle c 1890–1911 and of Dunmore, Kingstown, county Dublin; married (1) 20 April 1887 Alice Atkins, widow of George Atkins and daughter of the Rev M. Lloyd; (2) Kathleen —; died 30 December 1912 at the Elpis Private Hospital, Dublin; probate Dublin 19 February 1913. [Belf PRO, will cal; *BMJ* obituary (1913); Dub Nat Arch, will; Ferrar (1933); Kirkpatrick Archive; Leslie (1993); *Med Dir;* TCD adm reg; *TCD Cat*, vol II (1896)].

COURTENAY, JOSHUA PASLEY (1835/6–1900), Naval Medical Service;
   born 1835/6; studied medicine at the Richmond Hospital, Dublin, and University College, London; LM Rot Hosp Dub 1855; LRCSI 1856; LKQCPI 1859; of Dunkineely, county Donegal, c 1858; joined the Naval Medical Service as assistant surgeon on HMS *Pembroke* c 1859; later surgeon and staff surgeon on HMS *Nereus* c 1876 and HMS *Curacoa* c 1887; fleet surgeon c 1882; retired c 1890; finally of the Royal Naval Lunatic Hospital, Great Yarmouth; died 8 April 1900; probate London 1 May 1900. [Lond GRO (d); Lond PPR, will cal; *Med Dir*].

COURTENAY, THOMAS (c 1812–93), Galgorm, county Antrim;
   born c 1812; studied medicine at Trinity College, Dublin, Glasgow University and Royal College of Surgeons in Ireland; MRCSE 1836; LM Dublin; MD (Glas) 1846; medical officer and registrar of births and deaths for Galgorm Dispensary District; unmarried; died 19 November 1893 at Galgorm; administration Belfast 30 January 1894 and 23 April 1894. [Addison (1898); Belf PRO, will cal; Dub GRO (d); *Med Dir*].

COUSINS, ISAAC (d c 1820), Jamaica, West Indies;
   surgeon, of Jamaica; died c 1820; administration Armagh Diocesan Court 1820. [Dub Nat Arch, Armagh Dio Admins index].

COUSINS, WILLIAM JOHN (1869–1957), Manchester, Lancashire;
born 4 March 1869 at Moira, county Down, son of Joseph Cousins, merchant, of Moira; educated at Lurgan College; studied medicine at Queen's College, Belfast, from 1891; MB BCh BAO (RUI) 1900; honorary assistant surgeon to the French Hospital, Manchester; general practitioner, of Athol House, Brook's Bar, Manchester, from c 1901 and honorary surgeon to Hulme Dispensary; married Constance —; died 31 October 1957; probate Manchester 15 January 1958. [Lond PPR, will cal; *Med Dir*; QCB adm reg].

COWAN, JAMES (1773/4–1818), Hillsborough, county Down;
born 1773/4; general practitioner, of Hillsborough; died 4 February 1818 at Hillsborough. [*BNL* 13 February 1818 (d)].

COWAN, JAMES (1871–1959), Army Medical Service;
born 6 December 1871 at Manchester, son of — Cowan of Clady, Dunadry, county Antrim; educated at RBAI; studied medicine at Queen's College, Belfast, from 1889; MB BCh BAO (RUI) 1896; joined the Army Medical Service as lieutenant in 1898; captain 1901; major 1910; lieutenant-colonel 1915; served in India 1899–1904 and 1912–20; served in West Africa 1906–07; assistant director of pathology at Aldershot 1920–22 (specialist in bacteriology); retired on grounds of ill health 1922; died 19 January 1959 at Manor Hospital, Bath, Somerset; probate London 25 June 1959. [Drew (1968); Lond PPR, will cal; *Med Dir*; QCB adm reg].

COWDEN, WILLIAM JAMES (1853–1936), Dromore, county Down;
born 6 October 1853 at Dromore, son of James Cowden, farmer, of Dromore; educated at RBAI; studied medicine at Queen's College, Belfast, 1874–9; MD (QUI) 1879; MCh (RUI) 1885; LM KQCPI 1885; medical officer to Dromore Dispensary District, honorary surgeon to the Cowan Bridge Hospital and medical officer of health to Banbridge and Dromore; of Church Street, Dromore; married 7 March 1888 in Dunmurry Presbyterian Church, Mary Elizabeth Bell, daughter of Alexander Bell, farmer, of Innisloughlin; died 10 January 1936; probate Belfast 24 September 1936. [Belf GRO (d); Belf PRO, will cal; Kirkpatrick Archive; *Med Dir*; QCB adm reg; UHF database (m)].

COWDON, JAMES (1700/1–63), Londonderry;
born 1700/1, son of — Cowdon and Jane Playfair; apothecary, of Londonderry; witness to the will of James Ash 1750; died 28 October 1763; buried in Derry Cathedral Graveyard; will proved in the Diocese of Derry 1763. [Eustace, vol II (1954); *Memorials of the Dead*, vol VIII, p 588; Thrift, vol V (1920)].

COWEN, CHARLES EDMUND (d c 1954), Leatherhead, Surrey, Cala, Cape Province, and Trans Nzola, Kenya;
studied medicine at Trinity College, Dublin; LM Rot Hosp Dub 1892; LRCPI and LM 1893; LRCSI and LM 1893; of Letterkenny c 1895; general practitioner, of Reigate Villas, Highland Park, Leatherhead, c 1895–8; emigrated to South Africa; general practitioner, of Cala, Cape Province c 1898–1928 and of Kitale, Trans Nzola c 1928–1954; died c 1954. [*Med Dir*].

COX, SAMUEL LAWRENCE (1809–65), Indian Medical Service and Aghadowey, county Londonderry;
   born 5 April 1809, son of Henry Cox of Dublin and Helen Lawrence of Coleraine, county Londonderry; MRCS 1831; joined the Indian Medical Service (Madras establishment) as assistant surgeon 1832; surgeon 1849; retired to Flowerfield, Aghadowey 1856; JP; married Emma Pearse, daughter of Dr George Pearse (*q.v.*); father of Dr Henry Lawrence Cox, AMS (born and died in India); died 2 March 1865. [Crawford (1930); Dub GRO (d); Hitchings, Paul, pers com; Peterkin and Johnston (1968)].

COYLE, EDWARD (1851/2–1925), Belfast;
   born 1851/2 in Glasgow; LSA Lond 1883; LFPS Glas and LM 1884; general practitioner, of 7 Duncairn Terrace, Antrim Road, Belfast; a writer of poetry; married —; died 5 February 1925 at the Royal Victoria Hospital, Belfast. [Belf GRO (d); Kirkpatrick Archive; *Med Dir*].

COYLE, PATRICK (*fl c* 1824), Castleblayney, county Monaghan;
   surgeon, of Broad Street, Castleblayney c 1824. [Pigot (1824)].

COYNE, BERNARD (1802–55), Cavan;
   born 1802, eldest son of Dr B. Coyne of Sligo; studied medicine at Edinburgh University; MD (Edin) 1824 (thesis 'De typho graviore'); MRCSE 1825; FRCSI 1844; medical officer to Cavan Workhouse, Dispensary District and constabulary c 1845; of 5 Farnham Street, Cavan; married 15 January 1828 in Donnybrook Church, county Dublin, Elizabeth Lennon (who died 5 March 1852 in Cavan), eldest daughter of Dr G. Lennon of Drumrany House, county Westmeath; died 20 December 1856 at 5 Farnham Street. [*BNL* 25 January 1828 (m), 10 March 1852 (d) and 25 December 1855 (d); Croly (1843–6); Edin Univ; Kirkpatrick Archive; *Med Dir*].

COYNE, JAMES (1846/7–80), Dungannon, county Tyrone and Crossmaglen, county Monaghan;
   born 1846/7; LRCSI 1871; LRCP Edin 1873; general practitioner in Dungannon c 1874 and moved in 1876 to Crossmaglen; married —; father of Dr Michael John Coyne, LRCPI LRCSI 1906, of Monaghan; died 8 June 1880 of phthisis, in Crossmaglen. [Dub GRO (d); Kirkpatrick Archive; *Med Dir*].

CRABBE, BENJAMIN (1833/4–66), Naval Medical Service;
   born 1833/4; LRCS Edin 1854; joined the Naval Medical Service c 1855; surgeon to HMS *Trident* c 1865; married Elizabeth —; died 18 March 1866 of phthisis, at Irish Street, Strabane. [*Coleraine Chronicle* 31 March 1866 (d); Dub GRO (d); *Londonderry Sentinel* 27 March 1866 (d); *Med Dir*].

CRAIG, CHARLES (1754/5–88), Connor, county Antrim;
   born 1754/5, son of John Craig; surgeon, of Kells; married Ann — (who was born 1751/2 and died 28 October 1786); died 15 March 1788; buried in St Saviour's Graveyard, Connor. [Dunlop (1995); gravestone inscription].

CRAIG, FREDERICK ALEXANDER (1865–1932), Nottingham and Londonderry;
born 9 May 1865 in Belfast, son of Alexander Craig of Craig's Engineering Works, Londonderry; brother of Dr James Craig (*q.v.*); educated at Londonderry Academical Institution (Foyle College); studied arts and medicine at Queen's College, Belfast, from 1884; MB BCh BAO (RUI) 1890; DPH RCPSI (hon) 1897; clinical assistant to Borough Asylum, Nottingham; junior assistant medical officer to Kent County Asylum, Chartham; general practitioner in Londonderry from c 1900; head of Craig's Engineering Works; of 21 Clarendon Street c 1904; of 14 Queen Street c 1909; of Ard-Cluan, Waterside, Londonderry, from c 1920; married Harriet Mary —; died 19 March 1932 at Ard Cluan; administration Londonderry 15 June 1932. [Belf GRO (d); Belf PRO, will cal; Kirkpatrick Archive; *Med Dir*; QCB adm reg; Young and Pike (1909)].

CRAIG, HENRY LESLIE (1873–1923), Ballymena, county Antrim;
born 14 November 1873 in Kirkinriola Parish, son of Robert Craig, linen manufacturer, of Kirkinriola, and Maria Hopkins; educated at Ballymena Model School; studied medicine at Queen's College, Belfast, from 1891, and Trinity College, Dublin; MB BCh BAO (RUI) 1899; assistant surgeon to Wincanton Infirmary and Hospital, Somerset; general practitioner of Kirkinriola House, Ballymena c 1904; moved to 95 Crystal Palace Road, East Dulwich, London c 1909; died 31 August 1923 at the Maudsley Hospital, Denmark Hill, London; administration (with will) London 25 September 1923. [Belf GRO (b); Lond GRO (d); Lond PPR, will cal; *Med Dir*; QCB adm reg].

CRAIG, JAMES (1860–1923), Londonderry;
born 10 July 1860 in Belfast, eldest son of Alexander Craig of Craig's Engineering Works, Londonderry; brother of Dr Frederick Alexander Craig (*q.v.*); educated at Belfast Academy and Londonderry Academical Institution (Foyle College); studied medicine at Queen's College, Belfast, from 1877; MD (QUI) 1881; MCh MAO (RUI) 1882; postgraduate experience at Liverpool University, West London Hospital, Meath Hospital and Royal College of Surgeons in Ireland; medical officer and medical officer of health to Londonderry No 2 Dispensary District; of 2 Carlisle Terrace, Londonderry; JP for Londonderry; married 6 July 1886 in Grange Presbyterian Church, Ballymena, Lillie Spence Nelson, daughter of Matthew Nelson, linen manufacturer, of Newferry, Toome, county Antrim; father of Dr Frederick William Craig, MB (Edin) 1912; died 15 May 1923 at Carlisle Terrace; probate Londonderry 2 August 1923. [Belf GRO (d); Belf PRO, will cal; Kirkpatrick Archive; *Med Dir*; QCB adm reg; UHF database (m); Young and Pike (1909)].

CRAIG, SIR JAMES (1861–1933), Dublin;
born 16 October 1861 at Castlecat, Bushmills, county Antrim, eldest son of Johnston Craig, farmer, of Castlecat, and Ellen Wallace of Castlecat; educated at Coleraine Academical Institution; studied arts and medicine at Trinity College, Dublin; BA (TCD) 1879; MB BCh 1885; MD 1891; FRCPI 1892; assistant physician to the Meath Hospital, Dublin, 1886–92 and visiting physician 1892–1910; also physician to Sir Patrick Dun's and Dr Steeven's Hospitals; of 35 York Street, Dublin (c 1895) and later of 18 Merion Square; King's Professor of Medicine, Trinity College, Dublin 1910;

vice president RCPI 1912–14; president RCPI 1919–21; knight bachelor 1921; MP for Trinity College, Dublin, 1921–33; president Royal Academy of Medicine of Ireland 1924; author of many medical papers; was responsible for the Irish Sweepstakes Bill; married 21 February 1906 in St Andrew's Presbyterian Church, Booterstown, Dublin, Kathleen Isabel Millar, daughter of Thomas Millar, merchant, of Belle Vue, Merrion, Dublin; father of Dr William Johnston Craig and Dr James Wallace Craig (twins), both MB (TCD) 1932 and both of 1 Stormont Road, Highgate, London; died 12 July 1933 at 18 Merrion Square, Dublin; buried in Dean's Grange Cemetery; portrait in TCD; probate London 28 August 1933 and Dublin 19 October 1933. [*BMJ* obituary (1933); *DIB* (2009); Dub GRO (m) and (d); Dub Nat Arch, will cal; Kirkpatrick Archive; *Lancet* obituary (1933); Lond PPR, will cal; *Med Dir*; Newmann (1993); *TCD Cat*, vol II (1896); *Who Was Who* 1929–40; Widdess (1963)].

CRAIG, JAMES ANDREW (1872–1958), Belfast;
born 20 March 1872 in Church Street, Ballymoney, county Antrim, son of James Craig, merchant, of Church Street, and Margaret Fulton; educated at Coleraine Academical Institution; studied medicine at Queen's College, Belfast, and Vienna; MB (hons) BCh BAO (RUI) 1895; MRCSE LRCP Lond 1898; FRCSE 1900; MD (*hon causa*) (QUB) 1951; resident house physician and surgeon to the Royal Southern Hospital, Liverpool 1895–8; demonstrator in anatomy, Queen's College, Belfast 1899–1901; assistant surgeon to EENT Department, RVH 1902–05 and attending surgeon 1905–45; gave annual winter oration at Royal Victoria Hospital 1906; lecturer in ophthalmology and otology, QUB 1913–37, and in otology 1939–44; chairman of RVH medical staff 1936–7; retired in 1937 but practised again 1939–45; of 103 Great Victoria Street c 1899–1908 and of 11 University Square 1908–58; president of the Ulster Medical Society 1925–6 and honorary fellow 1947; president of the Irish Ophthalmological Society; married 3 October 1917 in St Anne's Church of Ireland Church, Belfast, Alison Blanche Waldron (who was born 1881/2 and died 16 July 1952), daughter of John Robert Waldron, merchant seaman, of The Red Cottage, Hythe, Hampshire; died 26 November 1958 at the Musgrave and Clark Clinic, Belfast; probate Belfast 18 December 1958; benefactor of QUB, which established a James Craig Prize. [Belf GRO (b); Belf PRO, will cal (both); *BMJ* obituary (1958); Kirkpatrick Archive; *Lancet* obituary (1958); *Med Dir*; O'Donnell (2008); QCB adm reg; Robinson and Le Fanu (1970); Thomson (1947); UHF database (m); Young and Pike (1909)].

CRAIG, SAMUEL HORNER (1860–1952), Feeny, county Londonderry, and London;
born 8 May 1860, fourth son of George Craig of Drumcovit, Feeny, and Matilda Jane Eakin of Craigdarragh; educated at Coleraine Academical Institution; studied medicine at Edinburgh University; LRCP LRCS Edin 1886; general practitioner, of Drumcovit House, Feeny; moved to London c 1900, of 124 Stroud Green Road, Finsbury Park; retired c 1920; moved c 1926 to 68 Regency Square, Brighton, c 1929 to Burleigh Hall, King's Road, Brighton, and c 1940 to Sillwood Hall; unmarried; died 27 August 1952 at Drumcovit; probate Londonderry 16 February 1953 and London 28 February 1953. [Belf GRO (d); Belf PRO, will cal; Burke *LGI* (1958); Lond PPR, will cal; *Med Dir*].

CRAIG, WILLIAM (1869/70–1933), Sheffield, Yorkshire;
born 1869/70; studied medicine at Queen's College, Galway, and the Royal College of Surgeons, Edinburgh; LRCP LRCS Edin 1895; LFPS Glas 1895; of Daleview, Ballindrait, county Donegal c 1895; general practitioner, of 2 and 4 Norfolk Road, Sheffield c 1900–28; retired c 1928 to 'Glenties', Little Common Road, Bexhill-on-Sea, Sussex; married Evangeline Gertrude —; father of Dr David Craig, MRCSE LRCP Lond 1935, of Bexhill-on-Sea; died 6 October 1933 at the Buchanan Hospital, Hastings, Sussex; administration London 11 April 1934. [Lond GRO (d); Lond PPR, will cal; *Med Dir*].

CRAIG, — (*fl c* 1851), Belfast;
general practitioner, of Donegall Street, Belfast; married —; son born 4 June 1851. [*BNL* 8 June 1851 (b, son)].

CRANSTON, WILLIAM (1852–80), Ballybay, county Cavan;
born 18 December 1852 at Bailieborough, county Cavan, son of John Cranston of Corraweelis, county Cavan; educated at RBAI; studied medicine at Queen's College, Belfast, from 1869; LRCP LRCS Edin 1875; general practitioner in Ballybay; unmarried; died 10 February 1880 at Ballybay, as a result of an accident; administration Dublin 4 June 1880. [Belf PRO, will cal; Dub GRO (d); *Med Dir*; QCB adm reg].

CRAVEN, CLEMENT (*fl c* 1791), Monaghan;
LAH Dub 1791; apothecary, of Monaghan town. [Apothecaries (1829)].

CRAWFORD, ADAIR (1748–95), London and Woolwich, London;
born 1748 in Ballytromery, Crumlin, county Antrim, third son of the Rev Thomas Crawford, minister of Crumlin Presbyterian Church, county Antrim, and Anne Mackey of Vinecash, county Armagh; brother of Dr Alexander Crawford (*q.v.*) and Dr John Crawford (*q.v.*); studied medicine at Glasgow and Edinburgh Universities, 'universally esteemed the most ingenious student of medicine at present in this University' (Drennan); MA (Glas) 1770; MD 1780; LRCP Lond 1784; FRS 1786; began researches on 'animal heat' and combustion in 1777 and published *Experiments and Observations on Animal Heat and the Inflamation of Combustible Bodies, being an attempt to resolve these phenomena into a general law of nature* (1779); physician to St Thomas's Hospital, London; professor of chemistry at the Royal Military Academy at Woolwich; became ill and retired in 1795 to the Marquis of Landsdowne's seat near Lymington, Hants; married — (who died 15 June 1817 at Hagley, Worcestershire); father of Dr Stewart Crawford of Bath; died 29 July 1795; his 'unaffected deference to the wants of others … universally beloved …' (from a memorial which was never erected). [Addison (1898) and (1913); Agnew (1998); *BNL* 7 August 1795 (d) and 27 June 1817 (d); Crone (1928); Kirkpatrick Archive; McConnell (1951); *Memorials of the Dead*, vol III, p 201; *Munk's Roll*, vol 2; Newmann (1993); *Oxford DNB* (2004)].

CRAWFORD, ALEXANDER (1754/5–1820), Lisburn, county Antrim;
born 1754/5, son of the Rev Thomas Crawford, minister of Crumlin Presbyterian Church, county Antrim, and Anne Mackey of Vinecash, county Armagh; brother of

Dr Adair Crawford (*q.v.*) and Dr John Crawford (*q.v.*); studied medicine at Glasgow University; MA MD (Glas) 1774; general practitioner, of Lisburn; owned a vitriol factory in Lisburn, set up with Thomas Gregg and Waddell Cunningham [vitriol or sulphuric acid was used in the bleaching of linen]; built 'Roseville' on the north side of the Lagan, opposite the Island c 1780; involved in the United Irishmen from 1794 and imprisoned in Kilmainham Gaol, but presumably soon released; physician, of Lisburn c 1811; married Anne Smyly, daughter of William Smyly of Camus, county Tyrone, and Jane Armstrong; died 29 August 1820 [often stated as 1823]; 'as a man of talent and an eminent physician [he] has been long known and will be long regretted'. [Addison (1898); Agnew (1998); *BNL* 13 September 1820 (d); Burke *LGI* (1912) (Smyly); Holden (1811); Rankin (2002)].

CRAWFORD, ANNE HELEN (b 1873), Ahmedebad, India;
born 3 December 1873, daughter of Alexander Crawford, merchant, of Coleraine; educated at Coleraine Ladies' School; studied arts at Queen's College, Belfast, from 1892 and medicine from 1895; MB BCh BAO (RUI) 1899; medical missionary with the Presbyterian Missionary Society in Ahmedabad, India 1900–c 1910. [Kelly (2010); QCB adm reg].

CRAWFORD, ARTHUR WILLIAM (1870–c 1911), Newcastle, Western Australia;
born 10 October 1870 at Ballinaboy, Cloughmills, county Antrim, son of John Crawford, farmer, of Ashfield, Cloughmills; educated at Coleraine Academical Institution; studied medicine at Queen's College, Belfast, from 1890; MB BCh BAO (RUI) 1899; emigrated to Australia c 1900; general practitioner of Newcastle, Western Australia; died c 1911. [*Med Dir*; QCB adm reg].

CRAWFORD, DAVID (1759–1825), Naval Medical Service and Ballyshannon, county Donegal;
born 1759 in Donegal, second son of James Crawford of Donegal, and Mary Makelwaine of Ballyshannon; joined the Naval Medical Service as assistant surgeon; retired to property in Ballyshannon; barrack-master of Ballyshannon for many years; married 18 August 1791 Sarah Caldwell (who died 18 February 1853), daughter and heiress of the Rev Robert Caldwell; father of Dr James Crawford (*q.v.*) and Dr William Crawford (*q.v.*); died 8 November 1825 at Ballyshannon. [*BNL* 22 November 1825 (d); Burke, *LGI* (1912)].

CRAWFORD, GEORGE BROWN (1861–1923); ship's surgeon and Dublin;
born 4 September 1861 at Londonderry, son of Isaac Crawford, gentleman, of Troy Villa, Londonderry; educated at RBAI; studied medicine at Queen's College, Belfast, from 1879, also at Edinburgh University and St Thomas's Hospital, London; MD MCh (RUI) 1885; surgeon with the British Burmese Navigation Company and the steam whaler *Arctic of Dundee*; civil surgeon attached to RAMC 1899–1904, with home address at 15 Mark Street, Portrush; general practitioner, of 70 Kenilworth Square, Rathgar, Dublin, from c 1905; married 4 September 1896 in Rosbercon Church of Ireland Church, Kilkenny, Dorothea Elizabeth Thomas Boyd, youngest daughter of Thomas N. Boyd, Clerk of the Crown and Peace for county Tipperary, of

Chilcomb Park, New Ross, Wexford; died 26 July 1923 at 70 Kenilworth Square; buried in Mount Jerome Cemetery, Dublin; probate Dublin 15 October 1923. [Dub GRO (m); Dub Nat Arch, will cal; Kirkpatrick Archive; *Med Dir*; QCB adm reg].

CRAWFORD, GILBERT STEWART (1868–1953), Army Medical Service;
born 14 May 1868, son of Samuel Crawford, farmer, of Ballybogy, Ballymena, county Antrim, and Jane Stewart; studied medicine at the Royal College of Surgeons in Ireland; LM Coombe Hosp Dub; LRCP LRCS Edin 1891; LFPS Glas 1891; DPH RCS Edin 1892; DTM Liverp 1908; MD (Malta) 1910; joined the Army Medical Service as surgeon lieutenant 1892; surgeon captain 1895; major 1904; lieutenant-colonel 1914; served in North West Frontier, India 1897–8 and South Africa 1900–02; awarded commander of the Crown of Italy medal by the King of Italy after the earthquake at Messina 1908, and also the silver medal and diploma of the Italian Red Cross Society; served in World War I 1914–18; CMG 1915; commanded a Stationary Hospital during the Gallipoli operations; retired c 1919; author of various medical papers; lived latterly at 54 Victoria Road, Exmouth, Devon; married 3 October 1895 in Cullybackey Presbyterian Church, Mary Lydia Bresland, daughter of James Bresland, headmaster, of Ballymena; died 2 November 1953 at Halsdown House, Exeter Road, Exmouth; probate Exeter 4 December 1953. [Dub GRO (b); Lond PPR, will cal; *Med Dir*; Peterkin and Johnston (1968); UHF database (m)].

CRAWFORD, ISAAC (1861–1938), Tredegar, Monmouthshire;
born 15 February 1861 at Omagh, county Tyrone, son of William Crawford of the High Street, Omagh; educated at Omagh Model School; studied medicine at Queen's College, Belfast, from 1879; senior scholar in anatomy, physiology and medicine; LRCP LRCS Edin 1888; LFPS Glas 1888; general practitioner in Tredegar, Monmouthshire, from c 1890; retired c 1932 to Milnthorpe, Portishead, Somerset; died 29 December 1938; probate London 3 February 1939. [Lond PPR, will cal; *Med Dir*; QCB adm reg].

CRAWFORD, JAMES (1794–1855), Army Medical Service and Montreal, Canada;
born 20 February 1794, second son of Dr David Crawford (*q.v.*) of Ballyshannon, and Sarah Caldwell; brother of Dr William Crawford (*q.v.*); studied medicine at Edinburgh University; MD (Edin) 1820 (thesis 'De strictura in urethra'); joined the Army Medical Service as hospital mate August–December 1815 and hospital assistant 1820; assistant surgeon to the 68th Foot 1825 and the 24th Foot 1829; resigned 1836; emigrated to Montreal, Canada as surgeon; married Emma Matilda Platt, daughter of John Platt of Montreal; died 28 December 1855. [Burke *LGI* (1912); Edin Univ; Peterkin and Johnston (1968)].

CRAWFORD, JAMES (1816–57), Indian Medical Service;
born 5 March 1816, son of the Rev James Crawford, minister of Strand Presbyterian Church, Londonderry, and Margaret Law; joined the Indian Medical Service (Madras establishment) as assistant surgeon 1846, but returned home on sick leave; died 25 November 1857 at Londonderry; buried in Londonderry City Cemetery. [Bailie and Kirkpatrick (2005); Crawford (1930); *Londonderry Sentinel* 27 November 1857 (d)].

CRAWFORD, JAMES (1827/8–89), Ballymena, county Antrim, and Belfast;
born 1827/8, son of James Crawford of Belfast; educated at RBAI; studied medicine at Queen's College, Belfast, from 1849; MRCSE 1851; LAH Dub 1856; general practitioner, of Ballymena c 1871; of 128 Hughes Buildings, Belfast c 1875; of 3 Nelson Place, Belfast c 1885; married —; died 26 September 1889 at Belfast. [Dub GRO (d); *Med Dir*; QCB adm reg].

CRAWFORD, JAMES MANSFIELD (c 1852–1935), Hull, Yorkshire;
born c 1852, probably son of the Rev James Alexander Crawford, rector of Stranorlar, county Donegal; studied medicine at Edinburgh University; MB MCh (Edin) 1895; of Stranorlar Rectory c 1895; general practitioner, of Norham-on-Tweed c 1900–11, and of 157 Boulevard and 155 North Boulevard and 455 Hessle Road, Hull c 1911–34; died 11 May 1935; probate London 12 July 1935. [Leslie (1940); Lond PPR, will cal; *Med Dir*].

CRAWFORD, JOHN (1746–1813), Barbados, Demerara and Baltimore, USA;
born 3 May 1746 at Ballytrumery, Crumlin, county Antrim, son of the Rev Thomas Crawford, minister of Crumlin Presbyterian Church, county Antrim and Anne Mackey, of Vinecash, county Armagh; brother of Dr Adair Crawford (*q.v.*) and Dr Alexander Crawford (*q.v.*); studied medicine at Trinity College, Dublin c 1763 [?] but left to become a ship's surgeon; [accounts of his early life are conflicting, including possibly the Indian Medical Service]; MD (St Andrew's) 1791 (on testimonials); surgeon to British Naval Hospital in Barbados c 1778–82 and c 1783–90, and in Demerara c 1790–94; contributor to *Medical Commentaries* in 1793; studied medicine at Leyden, Netherlands, 1794; settled in Baltimore 1796 where he was physician to Baltimore City Hospital and an early exponent of vaccination; a really original thinker and was many years ahead of his time, with the concept of disease being spread by insect vectors (and was derided by his contemporaries); examiner for the University of Maryland and member of the Board of Health; freemason and Grand Master of his lodge in 1801; author of *An Essay on the Nature, Cause and Cure of a disease incident to the Liver* [? beriberi] (1772) and papers on causation of disease; married (1) c 1778 — O'Donnell (who died on the voyage home from Barbados c 1780), daughter of John O'Donnell of Trinagh Castle, county Limerick, and Deborah Anderson of county Tipperary; (s) — (who survived him); died 9 May 1813 in Baltimore; buried in Westminister Presbyterian Churchyard, Baltimore; his library was sold to the University of Maryland. [Coakley (1992); Crawford (1930); *DAB* (1932); *DIB* (2009); McConnell (1951); Martin (2010); Oliver (1936); Smart (2004); Innes Smith (1932); Wilson (1942)].

CRAWFORD, JOHN (1796–1837), Indian Medical Service;
born 1796, probably in Ballyshannon, county Donegal; MD (Edin) 1820 (thesis 'De quibusdam febris epidemiae varietatibus'); joined the Indian Medical Service (Bombay establishment) as assistant surgeon 1825; died 12 June 1837 at Dharwar, Mysore. [*BNL* 21 November 1837 (d); Crawford (1930); Edin Univ; *Londonderry Sentinel* 18 November 1837 (d)].

CRAWFORD, JOHN DUNCAN (1824–71), Indian Medical Service;
born 20 April 1824 at Ballyshannon, county Donegal, eldest son of Samuel Crawford, solicitor, of Ballyshannon, and Margaret Duncan of Dublin; educated by Mr Murphy; studied arts and medicine at Trinity College, Dublin, from 1841; LRCSI; BA MB (TCD) 1846; joined the Indian Medical Service (Bengal establishment) as assistant surgeon, 1846; surgeon 1859; surgeon major 1866; served during the Indian Mutiny 1857–8 and on the North-West Frontier; died 16 May 1871 at Dharmsala, India. [Burke *LGI* (1912); Burtchaell and Sadleir (1924); Crawford (1930); Croly (1843–6); *Med Dir*].

CRAWFORD, JOSEPH (*fl c* 1832), Ballyshannon, county Donegal;
surgeon, of Ballyshannon and surgeon to the Donegal Militia; married —; daughter born 1822; said to have died in November 1832 of cholera, with the epitaph 'a gentleman justly valued in private as well as public life for those virtues that endear man to man', but report was later contradicted. [*BNL* 28 June 1822 (b); *Londonderry Sentinel* 17 November 1832 (d); *Strabane Morning Post* 20 and 27 November 1832 (d)].

CRAWFORD, JOSEPH DAWSON (1836/7–1911), Warrenpoint, county Down, and Liverpool, Lancashire;
born 1836/7, son of John Crawford, gentleman; MRCSE 1855; LM Glasgow 1855; LRCP Edin 1859; FRCS Edin 1859; resident surgeon to the General Hospital, Nottingham; general practitioner in Warrenpoint c 1870 but moved to 40 Rodney Street, Liverpool c 1872; honorary surgeon to Liverpool Hospital for Cancer and Skin Disease fo 30 years; of 40 Rodney Street, Warrenmount, Freshfield, Liverpool c 1890; married 30 November 1858 in Rostrevor Presbyterian Church, Annabella Smyth, daughter of the Rev William Smyth, minister of Glennan Presbyterian Church, county Monaghan; died 7 February 1911 at 40 Rodney Street, following a fractured femur (coroner); probate Liverpool 13 March 1911. [*BNL* 6 December 1858 (m); Lond GRO (d); Lond PPR, will cal, will; McConnell (1951); *Med Dir*; UHF database (m)].

CRAWFORD, JOSEPH DAWSON (1867–1922), Swanley, Kent;
born 19 April 1867 at Mullaghgreenan, county Monaghan, son of Richard Crawford, farmer, of Drumbrain House, Newbliss, county Monaghan, and Sarah Jane Crawford; twin brother of Dr Richard Atkinson Crawford (*q.v.*); educated privately; studied arts and medicine at Trinity College, Dublin, from 1885; BA (TCD) 1892; LM Rot Hosp Dub 1892; MB BCh BAO 1893; MD 1901; general practitioner, of Orchard Lea, Swanley, Kent from c 1900; medical officer and public vaccinator to 3rd District, Dartford Union; medical officer to the Homes for Orphan Boys, Swanley, and the Homes for Little Boys, Farningham; JP; married Kathleen Emma —; died 4 April 1922 at Orchard Lea; probate London 27 May 1922. [Dub GRO (b); Kirkpatrick Archive; Lond GRO (d); Lond PPR, will cal; *Med Dir*; TCD adm reg; *TCD Cat*, vols II (1896) and III (1906)].

CRAWFORD, OLIVER (1794/5–1826), Dublin;
born 1794/5, son of the Rev Oliver Crawford, curate of Clonoe, near Dungannon, county Tyrone; studied medicine at Trinity College, Dublin; MD [not recorded in

B & S]; died 5 April 1826 in York Street, Dublin, of fever. [*BNL* 21 April 1826 (d); Leslie (1911)].

CRAWFORD, RICHARD ATKINSON (1867–1940), Castleshane, county Monaghan, and Swanley, Kent;
born 19 April 1867 at Mullaghgreenan, county Monaghan, son of Richard Crawford, farmer, of Drumbrain House, Newbliss, county Monaghan, and Sarah Jane Crawford; twin brother of Dr Joseph Dawson Crawford (*q.v.*); studied medicine at the Carmichael and Ledwich Schools and the Royal College of Surgeons in Ireland; LM Rot Hosp Dub; LRCSI and LM, LRCPI and LM 1891; resident medical pupil at Meath Hospital and County Dublin Infirmary; medical officer and medical officer of health to Castleshane Dispensary District and to constabulary; medical officer and public vaccinator to Swanley Dispensary District, Kent, and medical officer to the Swanley House for Orphan Boys and Farmingham House for Little Boys from 1922, of The Cedars, Swanley; married Jane Elizabeth McAskie (who died 26 July 1947), daughter of the Rev James McAskie); father of Dr Edward Sydney Atkinson Crawford, MB BCh BAO (TCD) 1925, and of Dr Richard Ronald Dawson Crawford, MB BCh BAO (TCD) 1921; died 29 February 1940; probate London 14 May 1940. [*BMJ* obituary (1940); Dub GRO (b); Lond GRO (d); Lond PPR, will cal; *Med Dir*].

CRAWFORD, SAMUEL (*fl c* 1824), Ballymoney, county Antrim;
physician, of Main Street, Ballymoney c 1824. [Pigot (1824)].

CRAWFORD, SAMUEL KIRKER (1830/1–82), Tanderagee, county Armagh;
born 1830/1, son of Samuel Crawford, farmer, of Drumkeen, Aghabog, Newbliss, county Monaghan, and Christina —; educated by the Rev Mr Lyttle; studied medicine at Queen's College, Belfast, from 1852 and at Anderson's College, Glasgow; LRCS Edin 1860; MD (St Andrews) 1862 (by examination); medical officer to Tanderagee Dispensary District and constabulary c 1870; married 2 February 1871 in Elmwood Presbyterian Church, Belfast, Sarah Futhey, daughter of James Futhey, gentleman, of Belfast and Tanderagee; died 12 December 1882 at Tanderagee; probate Armagh 16 January 1883. [Belf PRO, will cal; Dub GRO (m) and (d); Kirkpatrick Archive; *Med Dir*; QCB adm reg; Smart (2004)].

CRAWFORD, SIR THOMAS (1824–95), Army Medical Service;
born 1 March 1824 at Drumbrain, Newbliss, county Monaghan, son of Joseph Crawford of Drumbrain; studied medicine at Edinburgh University; MD (Edin) 1845 (thesis 'On the history, causes, pathology and treatment of paralysis'); MCh (RUI); LRCS Edin 1845; FRCSI (hon) 1883; FKQCPI (hon) 1884; LLD (Edin) 1884; joined the Army Medical Service as assistant surgeon to 51st Foot 1848; surgeon to 18th Foot 1855; staff surgeon 1861; surgeon major 1868; deputy inspector general 1870; surgeon general 1876; principal medical officer for forces in India 1880–82; director general of the Army Medical Service 1882; served in Burma 1852–3, Crimea 1855–6, and Indian Mutiny 1857; played a large part in improving medical care in the army between 1856 and 1889; KCB (military) 1885; honorary

surgeon to the Queen 1886; retired 1889; married (1) 6 October 1859 in St Peter's Church of Ireland Church, Dublin, Clara Frances Morrison, (who died 1860), second daughter of Richard Morrison of Leeson Street, Dublin, and Elizabeth Jones; (2) 1869 Mary Jane Edwards (who died 1895), daughter of General Clement A. Edwards, CB; father of Margaret Jane Crawford who married Dr William Henry; died 12 October 1895 at 5 St John's Park, Blackheath, Surrey; buried at Blackheath; probate London 21 December 1895. [*BNL* 8 October 1859 (m); *BMJ* obituary (1895); Burke *LGI* (1912) (Morrison of Coolegegan); Crone (1928); Eakins (1982); Edin Univ; Lond PPR, will cal, will; *Med Dir*; Peterkin and Johnston (1968)].

CRAWFORD, THOMAS WILLIAM (1782/3–1842), Ballyshannon, county Donegal;
born 1782/3; surgeon of the Donegal Regiment of Militia for many years; of Rockville, Ballyshannon; married Margaret — (who was born 1782/3 and died 4 July 1841); died 24 July 1842 at Rockville; buried with his family in Ballyshannon Church of Ireland Graveyard. [*BNL* 16 July 1841 (d) and 2 August 1842 (d); *Londonderry Sentinel* 10 July 1841 (d) and 6 August 1842 (d); *Memorials of the Dead*, vol I, p 84 and vol II, p 58; Pigot (1824)].

CRAWFORD, WILLIAM (1738/9–1800), Banbridge, county Down;
born 1738/9; surgeon and apothecary, of Banbridge, married — (who died 24 December 1816 in Banbridge); died 18 November 1800. [*BNL* 25 November 1800) (d) and 3 January 1817 (d)].

CRAWFORD, WILLIAM (1801–55), Shrewsbury, Shropshire;
born 1 May 1801, seventh son of Dr David Crawford (*q.v.*) of Ballyshannon, and Sarah Caldwell; brother of Dr James Crawford (*q.v.*); MD (Edin) 1823 (thesis 'De apoplexia'); general practitioner, of Bicton House, Shrewsbury; married 13 January 1834 at St Chad's Church, Elizabeth Hunt (who died 21 May 1867), widow of Captain Hunt of Buton House, Shrewsbury, and daughter of — Morris; died 6 October 1855 at Shrewsbury. [*BNL* 4 February 1834 (m); Burke, *LGI* (1912); Edin Univ; *Med Dir*].

CRAWFORD, — (*fl c* 1783), Strabane, county Tyrone;
doctor; married December 1783 at Strabane — Smyly. [*BNL* 9 December 1783 (d)].

CREERY, ANDREW (1843–73), Enniskillen, county Fermanagh, and Dungloe, county Donegal;
born 1843; LM Rot Hosp Dub; LRCSI 1868; LRCP Edin 1869; general practitioner, of 4 Clyde Terrace, Sandymount c 1870 and of 23 Darling Street, Enniskillen c 1871; medical officer to Dunglow Dispensary District from 1872; married —; died 30 December 1873 at Dunglow, of typhus fever; administration Dublin 6 February 1874. [Belf PRO, will cal; Dub GRO (d); Kirkpatrick Archive; *Med Dir*].

CREERY, JOHN TATE (1857/8–1933), Coleraine, county Londonderry;
born 1857/8, son of Canon Andrew Creery, rector of Kilmore, county Down, and Alice Tate; studied arts and medicine at Trinity College, Dublin, from 1875; BA

(TCD) 1879; LM Rot Hosp Dub 1880; MB BCh 1880; house surgeon to Londonderry Infirmary from 1880; medical officer to Coleraine Dispensary District, Coleraine Academical Institution, constabulary and post office from 1884; of Riverton, Coleraine; married — Stirling, daughter of Col T. Stirling; died 7 March 1933 at Riverton; buried in Aghadowey graveyard; probate Belfast 9 June 1933. [Belf GRO (d); Belf PRO, will cal; Kirkpatrick Archive; Leslie and Swanzy (1936); *Med Dir*; TCD adm reg; *TCD Cat*, vol II (1896); Wilson (1934)].

CREGAN, WILLIAM JOHN (1855–97), Liverpool;
born 26 December 1855 at Hillsborough, county Down; educated privately; studied medicine at Queen's College, Belfast, from 1876; LRCP LRCS Edin 1883; general practitioner, of East Dispensary, Richmond Row, Liverpool, c 1886, and 101 Everton Road, c 1895; died 4 November 1897; administration Liverpool 11 December 1897. [Lond PPR, will cal; *Med Dir*; QCB adm reg].

CREIGHTON, ROBERT HARRY (d 1917), Ballyshannon, county Donegal and Natal, South Africa;
eldest son of Robert Creighton, JP; studied arts and medicine at Queen's College, Belfast, and the Royal College of Surgeons in Ireland; LM Rot Hosp Dub 1889; BA (RUI) (hons) 1889; MB BCh BAO 1890; MAO 1895; senior resident student at Richmond Hospital, Dublin; surgeon to the Sheil Hospital and to the troops and constabulary, Ballyshannon; emigrated c 1906; died 3 September 1917 at Stanger, Natal, South Africa. [Kirkpatrick Archive; *Med Dir*].

CREIGHTON, ROBERT O'NEILL (b 1816/7), Cavan;
born 1816/7 in county Cavan, son of John Creighton, gentleman; studied arts and medicine at Trinity College, Dublin, from 1836; BA MB (TCD) 1840; probably died before 1860. [Burtchaell and Sadleir (1924)].

CROCKET, JOHN (*fl c* 1824, Naval Medical Service and Maghera, county Londonderry;
joined the Naval Medical Service as assistant surgeon; surgeon 1815; retired; surgeon, in Maghera c 1824. [*NMS* (1826); Pigot (1824)].

CROCKETT, EDWARD (1842/3–1918), Middlesex, Staffordshire, Lancashire and London;
born 1842/3, son of James Crockett of Maghera; educated at RBAI; studied medicine at Queen's College, Belfast, from 1860; LRCP LRCS LM Edin 1867; FRCS Edin 1881; general practitioner, of the North Dispensary, Liverpool, from c 1868; of Hampton Wick, Middlesex from c 1876; of 55 Darlington Street, Wolverhampton, Staffordshire, from c 1885; of 9 Upper Queen's Terrace, Fleetwood, Lancashire, from c 1895; moved c 1911 to 46 Sinclair Road, Kensington, London; married Edith Augusta —; father of Dr Gwendoline Mary Crockett (Mrs Cogswell); died 2 December 1918 at 46 Sinclair Road; probate London 4 January 1919. [Lond PPR; will cal, will; *Med Dir*; QCB adm reg].

CROFTON, EDWARD REGAN (1861–1901), Southhampton, Hampshire, and Bedminster, Somerset;

> born 6 February 1861 at Cleheen, Carrick-on Shannon, county Leitrim, son of Edward Crofton, farmer, of Cleheen; brother of Dr Patrick Regan Crofton (*q.v.*); educated at St Malachy's College, Belfast; studied medicine at Queen's College, Belfast, from 1880; MD (RUI) 1887; LSA Lond 1888; general practitioner, of 18 Bernard Street, Southampton c 1895; moved to 109 East Street, Bedminster, c 1898; married Kathleen —; died 16 March 1901 at 109 East Street, following an accidental fall (coroner); probate Bristol 1 May 1901. [Lond GRO (d); Lond PPR, will cal, will; *Med Dir*; QCB adm reg].

CROFTON, PATRICK REGAN (1856–1900), London and Southampton, Hampshire;

> born 12 March 1856 at Cleheen, Carrick-on-Shannon, county Leitrim, son of Edward Crofton, farmer, of Cleheen; brother of Dr Edward Regan Crofton (*q.v.*); educated at Deverill's Academy, Dublin; studied medicine at Queen's College, Belfast, from 1880; LRCP LRCS Edin 1891; LFPS Glas 1891; general practitioner, of 37 Bolina Road, Cliftonville, London; moved to 18 Bernard Street, Southampton c 1892; married Elizabeth Agnes —; died 9 January 1900 at 18 Bernard Street; probate Winchester 10 February 1900 and May 1900. [Lond GRO (d); Lond PPR, will cal, will; *Med Dir*; QCB adm reg].

CROKER, (MICHAEL) GEORGE (1815–1904), Castlewellan and Hillsborough, county Down, and Belfast;

> born 31 October 1815 in Wexford, son of John Croker of Beaufield, Wexford; educated by Mr Bayly; studied arts and medicine at Trinity College, Dublin, from 1831, also at Dr Steevens' Hospital, Dublin, and Glasgow, Edinburgh and Paris; BA (TCD) 1834; MA 1839; MD (Glas) 1840; LRCSI 1840; FRCSI 1844; LM Rot Hosp Dub; medical officer to Castlewellan Dispensary District c 1840–44; medical officer to Hillsborough District and Fever Hospital from c 1844, of Culcavey, Hillsborough; surgeon to the South Down Militia; medical officer to Ballymacarrett Dispensary District and constabulary c 1870; of Mount Pottinger, Belfast; married 13 May 1842 Kate Georgina Spaight Thomas (who died 4 March 1883), youngest daughter of the Rev Edward Thomas of Ballynacourty, county Kerry; father of Dr Walter Blundell Croker (*q.v.*); died 22 September 1904 at 115 Albertbridge Road, Belfast; buried in Hillsborough Parish Graveyard; probate Belfast 17 October 1904. [Addison (1898); Belf PRO, will cal; Burtchaell and Sadlier (1924); Clarke, *County Down*, vol 18 (1979); Croly (1843–6); *Downpatrick Recorder* 28 November 1840; Dub GRO (d); *Freeman's Journal* 1842 (m); Kirkpatrick Archive; *Med Dir*].

CROKER, WALTER BLUNDELL (1862–90), Hillsborough, county Down;
> born 9 June 1862 at Hillsborough, county Down, son of Dr George Croker (*q.v.*); educated at Hawarden Grammar School, Flintshire, and Methodist College, Belfast, from 1875; studied medicine at Queen's College, Belfast, from 1880; LRCSI and LM, LKQCPI and LM 1889; house physician to Royal Hospital, Belfast May — August 1890; home address, Mount Pottinger, Belfast; died 1 August 1890; buried

in Hillsborough Parish Graveyard; memorial tablet in the Royal Victoria Hospital. [Clarke, *County Down*, vol 18 (1979); Fry (1984); *Med Dir*; QCB adm reg].

CROMIE (CROMEY), ALEXANDER (1800–47), Clough, county Down;
born 1800, eldest son of John Cromie of Seafin, county Down, and Sarah Bell; brother of Dr Robert Cromie of Clough (*q.v.*); studied medicine at Glasgow University; MD (Glas) 1836; general practitioner of Clough; died 14 February 1847; buried in Ballyroney Presbyterian Graveyard. [Addison (1898); *BNL* 23 February 1847 (d); Blackwood Pedigrees, vol 11; gravestone inscription; Kirkpatrick Archive].

CROMIE, GEORGE (d 1731), Belfast;
son of Francis Cromie, merchant of Dublin; general practitioner in Belfast; died March 1731. [Agnew (1995)].

CROMIE, JOHN (*fl c* 1845), Kilkeel, county Down;
CM (Glas) [?]; general practitioner in Kilkeel c 1845. [Croly (1843–6)].

CROMIE, JOHN (1863–1930), Blyth, Northumberland and Auchencairn, Kircudbright;
born 15 November 1863 at Rathfriland, county Down; educated at Rathfriland Intermediate School; studied medicine at Queen's College, Belfast, from 1880 and Newcastle-on-Tyne; LRCP LRCS Edin 1885; general practitioner, of Waterloo Villa, Blyth, Northumberland c 1886–1915; medical officer to health for South Blyth UDC and Blyth River Port Sanitary Authority, medical officer and public vaccinator for Blyth; of 'Elderslie', Auchencairn c 1915–30; JP for Northumberland and Kirkcudbright; died 22 January 1930. [*BMJ* obituary (1930); Kirkpatrick Archive; *Med Dir*].

CROMIE, ROBERT (1814–1901), Clough, county Down;
born December 1814, fourth son of John Cromie, joiner, of Seafin, county Down, and Sarah Bell; brother of Dr Alexander Cromie of Clough (*q.v.*); studied medicine at Glasgow University; CM (Glas) 1834; medical officer to Clough Dispensary District; married 21 June 1849 in Bright Church of Ireland Church, county Down, Anne Jane Henry (who was born 8 April 1823 and died 31 January 1899), only child of William Henry of Grange Lodge; father of Dr Thomas Cromie of Clough (*q.v.*); died 18 December 1901 at Clough; buried in Clough Presbyterian Graveyard; probate Belfast 15 April 1902. [Addison (1898); Belf PRO, will cal, will; Blackwood Pedigrees, vol 11; Dub GRO (d); gravestone inscription; *Med Dir*; UHF database (m)].

CROMIE, THOMAS (1860–1935), Clough, county Down;
born 18 December 1860, sixth son of Dr Robert Cromie of Clough (*q.v.*); studied medicine at Queen's College, Belfast, from 1878; Coulter Exhibition, Belfast Royal Hospital, 1882; MD MCh Dip Obst (RUI) 1882; MAO 1885; medical officer to Clough Dispensary District from 1894; unmarried; died 15 June 1935 at Clough; buried in Clough Presbyterian Graveyard; probate Belfast 20 January 1936. [Belf GRO (d); Belf PRO, will cal; *Belf Roy Hosp, Ann Rep*; Blackwood Pedigrees, vol 11;

BMJ obituary (1935); gravestone inscription; Kirkpatrick Archive; *Med Dir*; QCB adm reg].

CRONE, JOHN SMYTH (1858–1945); London and RAMC;
born 25 November 1858 in Belfast, son of John Crone, publican, of 54 Pilot Street, Belfast, and Isabel —; educated at RBAI; studied medicine at Queen's College, Belfast, 1874–8, and the London Hospital; LSA Lond 1882; LKQCPI and LM 1887; general practitioner, of Kensal Lodge, Kensal Green, London Wl; assistant school medical officer for Willesden; president of the Willesden and District Medical Association; chairman of the Willesden District Council 1900–03; lieutenant in the RAMC during World War I with the 6th Battalion Middlesex Regiment; JP for Middlesex; deputy coroner for West Middlesex 1916–39; stood as Liberal candidate in Parliament for the West Willesden Division in 1918, but lost; retired c 1922; High Sheriff of Middlesex 1933–4; of 'Castlereagh', 34 Cleveland Road, Ealing; a founder of the Ulster Association in London; a founder member and president of the Irish Literary Society in London 1918–25; MRIA; author of *A Run Round Ulster* (1894), *A Concise Dictionary of Irish Biography* (1928) and *Henry Bradshaw: His Life and Work* (1931); founder and editor of *The Irish Book Lover*; married (1) 14 November 1879 in St Pancras' Church of England Church, London, Mary Hirst Smyth (who was born 1842/3 and died 29 December 1897), daughter of the Rev Thomas Smyth of Raloo, 'retired Presbyterian minister' [?]; (2) 2 January 1899 in Warrenpoint Presbyterian Church, Nina Gertrude Roe, daughter of Peter Roe, coal merchant, of Dromore Lodge, Warrenpoint; died 6 November 1945 at 34 Cleveland Road, Ealing; probate London 2 May 1946; bequeathed a large collection of Irish books, manuscripts, etc to the Belfast Central Library. [*BMJ* obituary (1945); *DIB* (2009); Dub GRO (m); Kirkpatrick Archive; *Lancet* obituary (1945); Lond GRO (m) and (d); Lond PPR, will cal; *Med Dir*; Newmann (1993); QCB adm reg; Young and Pike (1909)].

CRONIN, RICHARD (1841/2–1902), Galway, Cushendall, county Antrim, and Slane, county Meath;
born 1841/2; studied medicine at the Catholic University, Dublin, the Mater Misericordiae Hospital, Dublin, and Charing Cross Hospital, London; LFPS Glas 1868; LRCP Edin 1870; LRCSI 1870; LAH Dub 1879; resident medical officer to Mater Misericordiae Hospital; medical officer to Spiddall and Inverin Dispensary Districts, Admiralty Surgeon and agent, registrar of births and deaths, Galway and to constabulary c 1871; medical officer to Cushendall Dispensary district c 1874; medical officer to Painestown Dispensary District, Slane, from 1880, living at Conyngham Lodge; married Flora —; three of their children died in 1874 and were buried in Layde Graveyard, Cushendall; died 8 January 1902 in Slane; administration Dublin 8 February 1902. [Belf PRO, will cal; Dub GRO (d); gravestone inscription; Kirkpatrick Archive; *Med Dir*].

CROOK, — (*fl c* 1790), Lurgan, county Armagh;
general practitioner, of Lurgan; married —; daughter Emily born c 1790 and married November 1809; died before 1810. [*BNL* 28 November 1809 (m, daughter)].

CROOKS, EMILY MARTHA (1875–1937), Kirin, Manchuria, and Peking, China;
born 17 August 1875 at Model Farm, Larne, daughter of William John Crooks, schoolmaster, of Model Farm and Anne Cosgrove; educated at University Classes, Donegall Pass; studied medicine at Queen's College, Belfast, from 1884; MB BCh BAO (RUI) 1899; house surgeon to Temple Street Children's Hospital, Dublin; medical missionary with the Presbyterian Missionary Society at Kirin, Manchuria, 1902–33; member of staff of obstetric Department, Union Medical College, Peking 1930–31; retired 1933 to live at 6 Ma Hutting, Hatamen Street, Peking; died 1937 in Peking. [Belf GRO (b); Belf PRO, D2332/2 and D2332/3; Boyd (1908); Kelly (2010); *Med Dir*; QCB adm reg].

CROSKERY, HUGH (*fl c* 1856–80), Naval Medical Service, Jamaica and British Guiana;
eldest son of Hugh Croskery of Downpatrick, merchant; studied medicine at the Ledwich School, Dublin; LRCSI 1856; FRCS Edin 1878; joined the Naval Medical Service as assistant surgeon; medical officer in Chapeltown, Jamaica, in 1871; took holy orders at this time but continued in medical practice; working in British Guiana by 1882; author of various medical papers; married 19 July 1859 in Clarendon, Jamaica, Charlianna Sophia Hall, eldest daughter of the Rev Henry Hall, rector of Clarendon; died c 1890. [*BNL* 6 September 1859 (m); *Downpatrick Recorder* 16 September and 28 October 1871; *Med Dir*].

CROSKERY, ROBERT (1834/5–95), Portrush, county Antrim;
born 1834/5, son of Thomas Croskery of Downpatrick; educated by the Rev William Graham of Downpatrick; studied medicine at Queen's College, Belfast, from 1860; MRCSE 1861; LRCP Edin 1867; general practitioner in Liverpool 1866–9 and physician to Liverpool Special Cholera Hospital 1866; temporary medical officer to Mullaglass Dispensary District 1870; general practitioner in Portrush c 1875 and at Desborough, Northamptonshire c 1885, lived finally at 48 Stanley Road, Kirkdale, Liverpool; married Elizabeth —; died 23 May 1895; administration London 15 June 1895. [Lond PPR, will cal; *Med Dir*; QCB adm reg].

CROSS, RICHARD HAMILTON (c 1831–79), Strangford and Newtownards, county Down;
born c 1831(?), son of Richard Cross; educated at Bectine House Seminary, Dublin; studied medicine at Queen's College, Belfast, from 1854; LM Rot Hosp Dub 1856; MRCSE 1857; LKQCPI 1859; LM KQCPI 1861; house physician to Belfast Fever Hospital; medical officer to Strangford Dispensary District c 1866–76 and surgeon to Royal North Down Rifles Militia; general practitioner in Newtownards; married Anne —; died 8 February 1879 at Francis Street, Newtownards; buried in Movilla Cemetery; administration Belfast 19 May 1879. [Belf PRO, will cal; *Downpatrick Recorder* 15 February 1879 (d); Dub GRO (d); *Med Dir*; Napier, Christopher, pers com; QCB adm reg].

CROSS, ROBERT (1864–1937), Moy, county Tyrone, and Barnsley, Yorkshire;
born 1864 in county Tyrone; LRCSI 1884; LRCP Edin 1887; general practitioner, of Killyman, Moy c 1895; general practitioner and doctor to Maplewell Colliery, of

Mapplewell, Barnsley c 1900–37; presented with a set of cutlery in September 1937 in appreciation of his work for the community; retired to 'The Poplars', Spark Lane, Staincross, near Barnsley; married Florence —; died 27 December 1937 at 78 Clarkehouse, Road, Sheffield; probate Wakefield 22 April 1938. [*BMJ* obituary (1937); Kirkpatrick Archive; Lond PPR, will call; *Med Dir*].

CROSSEN, HENRY (1823/4–c 1880), Victoria, Australia;
born 1823/4, son of William Crossen of Whiteabbey, county Antrim; educated at Belfast Academy; studied medicine at Queen's College, Belfast, from 1849; LFPS Glas 1851; emigrated to Australia; general practitioner in Melbourne c 1870, of Echucha, Victoria; died c 1880. [*Med Dir*; QCB adm reg].

CROSSITT (or **CROSSETT**), **RICHARD** (c 1850–1915), Brecon, Wales, and Cookstown, county Tyrone;
born c 1850, at Coolshinny, Magherafelt, county Londonderry, son of Richard Crossitt, farmer, of Coolshinny; educated at Moneymore Academy; studied medicine at Queen's College, Belfast, from 1872; LRCP LRCS Edin 1876; general practitioner, of Camden Cottage, Brecon c 1877–8 and of Cookstown c 1878–1915; consulting sanitary officer to Cookstown Union; married 30 December 1879 in St Mary's Church of Ireland Church, Newry, Henrietta Stanton (who was born 1858/9), daughter of James Stanton, mechanic, of Newry; died 6 April 1915 at Long Street, Cookstown; probate Armagh 16 June 1915. [Belf PRO, will cal; Dub GRO (d); Kirkpatrick Archive; *Med Dir*; QCB adm reg; UHF database (m)].

CROSSLE, FRANCIS CLEMENTS (1847–1910), Tandragee, county Armagh, and Newry, county Down;
born 17 March 1847 at Anahoe, county Tyrone, sixth son of the Rev Charles Crossle, Rector of Kilclooney, county Armagh; educated at Dungannon Royal School; studied medicine at Queen's College, Belfast, and Belfast General Hospital, at Trinity College, Dublin, from 1864, the Royal College of Surgeons in Ireland and the Meath, Sir Patrick Dun's, City of Dublin and Rotunda Hospitals, Dublin; BA (TCD) 1868; MB MCh 1871; LM Rot Hosp Dub 1871; medical officer to Whitwell District, Worksop, Nottingham; general practitioner in Tanderagee, county Armagh 1872–5; medical officer, public vaccinator and registrar of births and deaths to No 2 Dispensary District, Newry, 1875–1900; of 10 New Street, Newry c 1885, of The Chestnuts c 1895, and of 11 Trevor Hill c 1905; author of *A History of Nelson Masonic Lodge No. XVIII, Newry* (1909); collected a large amount of historical material, now in PRONI, Dublin National Archives and Masonic Archives in Dublin; married 7 August 1872 Annie Waller Jones (who was born 1855/6 and died 19 November 1927 at Rostrevor), second daughter of Phillip Jones of Nutgrove, Rathfarnham, county Dublin; father of Dr Howard Crossle, MB (TCD) 1901, IMS; died 15 October 1910 at Trevor Hill, Newry; both buried in Jonesborough Church of Ireland graveyard; memorial tablet in St Mary's Church, Newry; probate Dublin 22 November 1910. [Belf PRO, will cal; Clarke, *County Down*, vol 21 (1998); Crossle (1909); Dub GRO (d); Fleming (2001); gravestone inscription; Kirkpatrick Archive; Martin (2003); *Med Dir*; TCD adm reg; *TCD Cat*, vol II (1896)].

CROTHERS, ROBERT (1815/6–1903), Moy, county Tyrone, Nice, France, and St Leonards-on-Sea, Hampshire;
> born 1815/6; studied medicine at Glasgow University and the Royal College of Surgeons in Ireland; CM (Glas) and LM 1839; MD (Glas) 1848; MD (QUI) 1855; MRCP Lond 1860; surgeon, of Moy c 1860 and to the Royal Tyrone Artillery Militia; of Nice, France, c 1871; of 2 Warrior Square Terrace, and St Leonards-on-Sea c 1872–90; retired to Highfield, Southborough, Kent c 1895; married Jessie — (who died 22 September 1872); died 15 June 1903 at Highfield; probate London 31 July 1903. [Addison (1898); Croly (1843–6); Kirkpatrick Archive; Lond GRO (d); Lond PPR, will cal; *Med Dir*].

CROWE, ROBERT (*fl c* 1796), Ballybay, county Monaghan;
> LAH Dub 1796; apothecary, of Ballybay. [Apothecaries (1829)].

CROWTHERS, JAMES (*fl c* 1845), Castlewellan, county Down;
> LAH Dub; apothecary in Castlewellan c 1845. [Croly (1843–6)].

CROZIER, JOHN (1785/6–1853), Caledon, county Tyrone;
> born 1785/6; studied medicine at Glasgow University; MD (Glas) 1809; medical officer to Caledon Dispensary District c 1845; married 17 October 1820 at Newtownhamilton, Ann Elizabeth Allen, only daughter of Dr Alexander Allen (*q.v.*); father of Mary Crozier who married in 1842 Dr A. Durham, IMS; died 29 July 1853. [Addison (1898); *BNL* 24 October 1820 (m) and 12 August 1853 (d); Croly (1843–6); *Londonderry Sentinel* 7 May 1842 (m)].

CROZIER, MATTHEW (*fl c* 1802), Ballynabraggett, county Down;
> LAH Dub 1802; apothecary, of Ballynabraggett. [Apothecaries (1829)].

CROZIER, RICHARD (b 1810/1), Richhill, county Armagh;
> born 1810/1, in Armagh, son of William Crozier, linen merchant; studied arts and medicine at Trinity College, Dublin, from 1828; BA (TCD) 1833; MB 1835; physician to Loughgall and Richhill Dispensaries; practising c 1859 but not in the *Medical Register*. [Burtchaell and Sadleir (1924); Croly (1843–6); *Med Dir*].

CRUMING, GEORGE (d c 1723), Belfast;
> general practitioner; freeman of Belfast 1723; died c 1723. [Young (1892)].

CRUMLEY, JAMES (1863/4–1914), Bundoran, county Donegal;
> born 1863/4; studied medicine at the Cecilia Street School of Medicine and the Catholic University of Ireland; LRCPI and LM, LRCSI and LM 1892; prosector in anatomy in the Catholic University and the Mater Misericordiae Hospital, Dublin; medical officer and medical officer of health and certifying factory surgeon to Kinlough Dispensary District, Bundoran; unmarried; died 8 March 1914 at Bundoran. [Dub GRO (d); Kirkpatrick Archive; *Med Dir*].

CULLEN, DANIEL JOSEPH (1845/6–1906), Carrickmacross, county Monaghan;
born 1845/6; studied medicine at Ledwich School, Dublin; LKQCPI and LM, LRCSI 1870; medical officer to Carrickmacross Dispensary District and Union Workhouse; married Maria E. —; a daughter married Dr Brian McCaul (*q.v.*); died 12 August 1906 at Blackrock, county Louth; probate Dublin 20 September 1906. [Belf PRO, will cal; Dub GRO (d); *Med Dir*].

CUMINE, SAMUEL SHANNON PARKINSON- (1846–1915), Killough, county Down;
born 11 February 1846 at Killough, third son of the Rev William Parkinson of Killough, curate of Ballymascanlon, county Louth; studied medicine at Queen's College, Belfast, from 1874; LFPS Glas and LM 1882; LRCP Edin 1886; general practitioner, of 93 St Mary's Terrace, Crumlin Road, Belfast c 1885; took the additional name of Cumine c 1890; general practitioner and medical officer to Shiel's Institute, Killough; married —; died 26 December 1915 at Killough; buried in family vault in Dunsford Graveyard; administration (with will) 21 June 1916. [Belf PRO, will cal; Dub GRO (d); Kirkpatrick Archive; *Med Dir*; QCB adm reg].

CUMING, BENJAMIN VEITCH (d 1860), Edenderry, King's County, Dublin and Castleblaney, county Monaghan;
son of James Cuming of Lexview, county Cavan, and Castleblaney, and Ann —; accoucheur of Townsend Street Lying-in Hospital 1834; MRCSE 1836; LAH Dub 1839; medical assistant to Edenderry Dispensary 1827–9; in Butler's Medical Hall, Dublin 1829–31; general practitioner, of Castleblaney c 1845; married 17 June 1847 in Castleblaney Church of Ireland Church, Anne Hunter, daughter of Edward Hunter, merchant, of Castleblaney; died 1860. [*BNL* 20 September 1842 (d, mother); Croly (1843–6); Dub GRO (m); *Londonderry Sentinel* 26 June 1847 (m); *Med Dir*].

CUMING, JAMES (1833–99), Belfast;
born 1833 at Markethill, county Armagh, son of Edward Cuming of Markethill; educated at St Patrick's College and briefly at Armagh Royal School; studied arts and medicine at Queen's College, Belfast 1849–55; BA (QUI) 1854; MD 1855; MA 1858; LKQCPI 1865; FKQCPI 1876; attending physician to the General Hospital, Belfast 1865–99; professor of medicine at Queen's College, Belfast, 1865–99, the first Queen's graduate to hold a Queen's College Chair and the only catholic on the academic staff throughout his thirty-four years of office (Moody & Beckett); president of Ulster Medical Society 1868–9 and 1881–2, of Belfast Literary Society 1876–7 and 1882–3 and of BMA 1884; chairman of medical staff of Belfast Royal Hospital 1880–99; gave annual winter oration at Belfast Royal Hospital 1884; chairman of the Belfast District Asylum Board; of 33 Wellington Place (c 1860) of 10 Chichester Street, Belfast, and Loughside, Greenisland, county Antrim; married 13 January 1858 in St Malachy's Roman Catholic Church, Belfast, Harriet McLaughlin (who died 19 February 1893), daughter of Francis McLaughlin, grocer and tobacconist, of Donegall Square South, Belfast; died 27 August 1899 at Greenisland; buried in Milltown Cemetery; portrait by Harry R. Douglas in Queen's

University, Belfast, and portrait in the Royal Victoria Hospital (anon); probate Belfast 22 September 1899. [*Belf Lit Soc* (1901); *BNL* 1899 (d); Belf PRO, will cal; Black (1995); Coakley (1992); Ferrar (1933); Froggatt (1986); *Med Dir*; Merrick and Clarke, *Belfast*, vol 2 (1984); Moody and Beckett (1959); O'Brien, Crookshank and Wolstenholme (1984); QCB adm reg; Whitla (1901)].

CUM(M)ING, JAMES GEORGE (1799/1800–31), Ballylesson, county Down;
born 1799/1800, son of George Cuming and Margaret —; surgeon, of Ballylesson; died 11 April 1831, '… esteemed by all who knew him'; buried in Drumbo Church of Ireland Graveyard. [*BNL* 14 April 1831 (d); Clarke, *County Down*, vol 1 (1966)].

CUMING, JOHN (d 1860), Virginia and Kingscourt, county Cavan;
LAH Dub; apothecary, of Virginia c 1845 and of Kingscourt; married Sarah —; died 5 May 1860 at Kingscourt; administration Dublin 13 Nov 1860. [Belf PRO, will cal; Croly (1843–6)].

CUMING, THOMAS (1798–1887), Armagh;
born 19 March 1798 in Armagh, son of the Rev Thomas Cuming, minister of First Armagh Presbyterian Church and Elizabeth Black; educated at Armagh Royal School 1808–15; studied medicine at Trinity College, Dublin, and Edinburgh University; LM Rot Hosp Dub 1818; MD (Edin) 1819 (thesis 'De quibusdam febris epidemicae anni 1818 sequelis'); LKQCPI 1820; MD (TCD) 1854; FKQCPI 1854; physician to Wellesley Fever Hospital, Dublin 1826–9; assistant physician to the Institute for Diseases of Children, Pitt Street, Dublin; lecturer at Richmond Hospital and Pitt Street Institute; general practitioner in Armagh from 1829 with a heavy involvement in cholera and tuberculosis; visiting physician to Armagh District Lunatic Asylum for 37 years; author of various medical papers; married 15 June 1826 Mary Black (who died before him), second daughter of the Rev Robert Black, DD, minister of First Derry Presbyterian Church, and his cousin Mary Black; father of Elizabeth Cuming who married the Rev William Booker Askin and was mother of Dr Thomas Cuming Askin (*q.v.*); died 4 September 1887 at The Mall, Armagh; probate Armagh 30 September 1887. [*BNL* 23 June 1826 (m); Belf PRO, will cal; *BMJ* obituary (1887); Cameron (1916); Croly (1843–6); Dub GRO (d); Edin Univ; Ferrar (1933); Kirkpatrick Archive; Leslie and Wallace (2001); McConnell (1951); *Med Dir*].

CUMMING, HUGH SMYTH (c 1835–63), India;
born c 1835, eldest son of the Rev Hugh Smith [*sic*] Cumming, vicar of Ballyclug, county Antrim and, from 1841 rector of Loughinisland and precentor of Down, and Elizabeth Taylor of Ballymena; medical missionary in India; died 16 August 1863 of fever at Calcutta. [Leslie and Swanzy (1936); *Londonderry Sentinel* 5 January 1864 (d)].

CUMMING, SAMUEL WILLIAM (1876/7–1939), Shercock, county Cavan, and Dudley, Worcestershire;
born 1876/7; studied medicine at Royal College of Surgeons in Ireland; LM Rot Hosp Dub; LRCPI and LM, LRCSI and LM 1900; general practitioner, of Drumlum, Shercock; moved c 1908 to Dudley; medical officer to Dudley Union

Workhouse (Institute); of Beaconsfield House, Dudley; died 14 January 1939 at the Guest Hospital, Dudley; probate Birmingham 9 March 1939. [Lond GRO (d); Lond PPR, will cal; *Med Dir*].

CUMMINS, WILLIAM (*fl c* 1845), Naval Medical Service and Castlederg, county Tyrone;
: joined the Naval Medical Service; retired on half pay; general practitioner in Castlederg c 1845; possibly died c 1850. [Croly (1843–6)].

CUNINGHAM, HERBERT WILLIAM (1868–1932), Londonderry;
: born 19 May 1868 at the Ulster Bank, Ardee, son of William Cuningham, bank manager, and Margaret Clarke; educated at Londonderry Academical Institution and Magee College, Londonderry; studied medicine at Queen's College, Belfast, from 1885; MB BCh BAO (RUI) 1892; MD 1895; house physician (and anaesthetist) at the City and County Infirmary, Londonderry; medical officer to Londonderry No 1 and Upper Liberties Dispensary District, of 35 Clarendon Street, Londonderry; medical visitor in lunacy for the Lord Chief Justice; president of the Ulster Branch of the BMA; married —; father of Dr Ronald William Cuningham of Londonderry, MRCSE LRCP Lond 1925, BCh (Camb) 1926, MB 1927; died 25 February 1932 at 35 Clarendon Street; probate Londonderry 21 April 1932. [Belf GRO (d); Belf PRO, will cal; *BMJ* obituary (1932); Dub GRO (b); Kirkpatrick Archive; *Lancet* obituary (1932); *Med Dir*; QCB adm reg].

CUNNINGHAM, B.V. (*fl c* 1847), Castleblaney, county Monaghan;
: MD [?]; general practitioner, of Castleblaney; married 17 June 1847 in Castleblaney Church, Ann Hunter, daughter of Edward Hunter of Castleblaney. [*Londonderry Sentinel* 26 June 1847 (m)].

CUNNINGHAM, CHARLES ARONAULDUS (*fl c* 1852), London;
: of Carrickfergus, county Antrim; MD [?]; later physician, of Winchester Terrace, London; married 15 September 1852 in Upton Parish Church, Buckinghamshire, Harriet Emma Burton, daughter of the Rev William Burton, rector of Faccomb-cum-Tangley, Hampshire, and later of Trelawney, Jamaica. [*BNL* 4 October 1852 (m)].

CUNNINGHAM, HUGH (1816–45), Ballyclare, county Antrim, and London;
: born August 1816 [or 1818]; surgeon, of Ballyclare and of Kingswood Place, Lambeth, London; died January [or 26 February] 1845 at Carrickfergus; buried in Ballylinney Old Graveyard. [*BNL* 11 March 1845 (d); gravestone inscription].

CUNNINGHAM, HUGH (*fl c* 1826–50), Burt, county Donegal;
: MD [?]; general practitioner, of county Donegal c 1830–50; of Castlecooly, Burt c 1837; married 22 December 1826 Anne Harvey (who died 21 June 1869 at Castlecooly, and was buried in Burt Churchyard), daughter of John Harvey of Londonderry. [*BNL* 29 December 1826 (m); Burtchaell and Sadleir (1935); Lewis (1837); *Londonderry Sentinel* 22 June 1869 (d)].

CUNNINGHAM, JAMES (1781/2–1853), Ballyclare, county Antrim;
born 1781/2; CM Glas; surgeon, of Ballyclare c 1845; married Jane — (who died 1859); died 21 November 1853; buried in Ballylinney Old Graveyard; probate Belfast 29 July 1859. [Belf PRO, will cal; Croly (1843–6); gravestone inscription].

CUNNINGHAM, JAMES (1870–c 1953), Ballybofey, county Donegal, and Kent;
born 25 March 1870 at Stranorlar, county Donegal, son of Robert Andrew Cunningham, bank manager, of Ballybofey; educated at Stranorlar Intermediate School; brother of Dr Robert Allan Cunningham (*q.v.*); studied medicine at Queen's College, Belfast, from 1887; MB BCh BAO (RUI) 1894; general practitioner of Summerhill, Ballybofey; general practitioner c 1900–23 in High Street, Borough Green, Kent, and then returned to Ballybofey; died c 1953. [*Med Dir*; QCB adm reg].

CUNNINGHAM, JOHN (*fl c* 1845), Magherafelt, county Londonderry;
surgeon in Magherafelt c 1845; possibly died c 1850. [Croly (1843–6)].

CUNNINGHAM, JOHN (1814–74), Larne, county Antrim;
born August 1814; CM (Glas) 1834; general practitioner in Larne; retired to Ballymullock, Larne; unmarried; died 18 February 1874 at Ballymullock; buried in Ballylinny Old Graveyard; probate Belfast 10 April 1874. [Addison (1898) Belf PRO, will cal; Croly (1843–6); Dub GRO (d); gravestone inscription; *Med Dir*].

CUNNINGHAM, JOHN ADAMS (1857–1910), Indian Medical Service;
born 8 April 1857 (or 29 April 1858 – Crawford) at Beragh, county Tyrone, son of Thomas Cunningham, farmer, of Beragh; educated at Omagh Model School; studied medicine at Queen's College, Belfast 1876–80; MD MCh (QUI) 1880; joined the Indian Medical Service (Bengal establishment) as surgeon 1881; surgeon major 1893; lieutenant-colonel 1901; colonel 1910; served on the North West Frontier, Tirah (medal with clasp) 1897–8; superintendent of the Lahore Lunatic Asylum and professor at Lahore Medical College; died 31 December 1910 of cholera, at Calcutta. [*BMJ* obituary (1911); Crawford (1930); Kirkpatrick Archive; *Med Dir*; QCB adm reg].

CUNNINGHAM, JOHN PHILLIPS (1827–92), Army Medical Service;
born 16 July 1827 at Carrickfergus, county Antrim; studied medicine at Edinburgh University 1846–9; MD (Edin) 1849 (thesis 'On intermittent fever'); LRCS Edin 1849; joined the Army Medical Service as assistant surgeon to the 45th Foot 1852; staff surgeon 1859; transferred to 60th Foot 1861 and to 20th Hussars 1868; surgeon major 1872; brigade surgeon 1879; deputy surgeon general 1880; served in Africa, India and China; retired with rank of surgeon general 1882 to Violet Lodge, Du Barry Avenue, Bedford; married —; father of Herbert Hugh Blair Cunningham, MRCSE LRCP Lond 1903, MD (Brux) 1904, FRCSI 1905; died 30 September 1892 at Bedford; buried in Belfast City Cemetery; probate London 9 November 1892. [Belf City Cem, bur reg; Edin Univ; Lond PPR, will cal; *Med Dir*; Peterkin and Johnston (1968)].

CUN(N)INGHAM, JOHN SNOW ALLAN (1841/2–67), Dublin;
born 1841/2; studied medicine at the Royal College of Surgeons in Ireland and Queen's College, Galway; LM Rot Hosp Dub 1861; LRCSI 1863; LKQCPI 1864; MD (QUI) 1866; resident apothecary to the City of Dublin Hospital; general practitioner of Francesca, Grosvenor Road East, Rathmines, Dublin; unmarried; died 24 December 1867 at Ballybofey, county Donegal. [Dub GRO (d); *Med Dir*].

CUNNINGHAM, PETER (*fl c* 1803), Donaghmore, county Down
LAH Dub 1803; apothecary, of Donaghmore. [Apothecaries (1829)].

CUNNINGHAM, ROBERT ALLAN (1871–1957), Royal Army Medical Corps and Kenya;
born 19 April 1871 at Navenny, Killygordon, county Donegal, son of Robert Andrew Cunningham, cashier in Northern Bank, of Navenny, Killygordon, and Matilda Brigham; brother of Dr James Cunningham (*q.v.*); educated at Stranorlar Intermediate School; studied arts and medicine at Queen's College, Belfast, from 1887, and Edinburgh; MB BCh BAO (RUI) 1896; DPH Glas 1905; house surgeon to County Donegal Infirmary; joined RAMC as lieutenant 1899; captain 1902; major 1911; lieutenant-colonel 1915; served in South Africa 1899–1902 (invalided), Malta 1902–05, India 1909–15, France 1915–16, India 1916 (invalided), Salonica 1917–18, Germany 1920; retired 1920; became c 1922 resident physician to Mount Kenya Sanatorium, Rumuruti, Kenya; retired c 1932; living at Thomson's Fall, Kenya c 1945; died 25 July 1957. [Drew (1968); Dub GRO (d); *Med Dir*; QCB adm reg].

CUNNINGHAM, ROBERT OLIVER (1841–1918), Belfast;
born 1841 at Prestonpans, East Lothian, son of the Rev W.B. Cunningham, minister of First Prestonpans Presbyterian Church; studied medicine at Edinburgh University; MD (Edin) 1864 (thesis 'On the natural history and anatomy of the solan goose'); LRCS Edin 1864; DSc (RUI) 1882; FRCS Edin 1884; went on a scientific expedition to South America 1866–9 which led to the publication of *The Natural History of the Straits of Magellan* (1871); professor of natural history and geology at Queen's College, Belfast; 1871–1902; author of papers on natural history; FGS; retired in 1902 to Paignton, Devonshire; married —; died 14 July 1918 at Westbourne Central Avenue, Paignton. [Deane (1921); Edin Univ; Kirkpatrick Archive; *Lancet* obituary (1918); Lond GRO (d); Moody and Beckett (1959); Praeger (1949)].

CUNNINGHAM, THOMAS (1823–59), Edinburgh and Currie, Midlothian, and Belfast;
born 12 May 1823, youngest son of John Cunningham, farmer and corn miller, of Glenwood House, Shankill Road, Belfast, and Jane Gault (or Galt) of Templepatrick, county Antrim; educated in Ballymena at a boarding school of the Rev Mr Matthews and at Thomas Blain's Classical and General Academy, Arthur Street, Belfast; studied medicine at the RBAI Medical School 1844–6 and Edinburgh University 1846–9; president of the Hunterian Medical Society as a student; MD (Edin) 1849 (thesis 'On the exploring needle'); worked with Professors James Syme and James Young Simpson

in the early days of anaesthesia; his correspondence with his father and brother, John, survives in Edinburgh University Library, along with other Cunningham material, all with copies in PRO NI and material relating to Simpson and Cunningham survives in Birmingham, Alabama; house surgeon to the Royal Maternity Hospital in Edinburgh 1849–50; general practitioner at Currie, 1850–58; medical inspector of factories 1854–8; returned to general practice in Belfast in summer 1858; married 15 June 1854 in Slateford, Jessie Steven Ramage, daughter of William Ramage of East Kenleith, Edinburgh; died 25 March 1859 at 10 Queen Street, Belfast; buried in Clifton Street Graveyard, Belfast (New Burying Ground). [*Belfast Morning News* 1859 (d); *BNL* 21 June 1854 (m) and 26 March 1859 (d); Belf PRO, MIC 32; Cunningham Family Bible; Currie Parish Register (m); Edin Univ and Edin Univ Lib; *Med Dir*; Reynolds Historical Library, Birmingham, Alabama; RVH, Office of Archives, copies of unpublished material].

CUNNINGHAM, WILLIAM (*fl c* 1729), Ballyrobin, county Antrim;
surgeon, of Ballyrobin; witness to a will in 1729. [Eustace, vol I (1956)].

CUNNINGHAM, WILLIAM (1793/4–1816), Groomsport, county Down;
born 1793/4; studied medicine at RBAI and Glasgow, with some surgical qualification [?]; surgeon in Groomsport; died 16 March 1816 in Belfast of smallpox caught from a patient, even though he had been inoculated against it as a child; buried in Donaghadee graveyard with a fine epitaph (stone now lost). [*BNL* 22 March 1816 (d); Clarke, *County Down*, vol 16 (1976)].

CUNNINGHAM, — (d 1829), Clonleigh, county Donegal;
son of James Cunningham of Clonleigh; died 20 December 1829 at Clonleigh, after a severe illness. [*BNL* 29 December 1829 (d)].

CUNNINGHAM, WILLIAM (*fl c* 1837), Ballyclare, county Antrim;
surgeon, of Ballyclare c 1837; married —; his son William, attended RBAI from 1837. [Fisher and Robb (1913)].

CUPPAGE, THOMAS (d 1893), Lurgan, county Armagh, Holywood, county Down, and Birkenhead, Cheshire;
studied medicine at Edinburgh and Glasgow Universities and the Carmichael School, Dublin; MD CM (Glas) 1864; LM KQCPI 1866; general practitioner, of Lurgan c 1867–85, of 1 Moffat Terrace, Holywood c 1885–92, but also of 186 Borough Road, Birkenhead c 1887–9; died 14 May 1893. [Addison (1898); *Med Dir*].

CUPPAGE, WILLIAM BURKE (1841–1928), Shrewsbury, Shropshire;
born 3 September 1841 at Lurgan, county Armagh, son of John Cuppage, JP, of Ulsterville, Belfast; educated at Dr Young's Collegiate School, Belfast and Queen's College, Galway; MD MCh (QUI) 1871; Dip Mid 1877; general practitioner, of Battle, Sussex, c 1875, of St John's Wood, London c 1885 and of Shrewsbury, Shropshire c 1895; medical officer and public vaccinator to Shawbury District; medical officer to the Post Office; physician to the Roden Convalescent Home; of Selby House,

Ellenmere Road, Shrewsbury, c 1915; retired c 1917; died 20 September 1928 at Holly Cottage, Shawbury. [Lond GRO (d); *Med Dir*; QCB adm reg].

CUPPLES, CHARLES (1791–1848), Army Medical Service and Lisburn, county Antrim;

born 1791 at Carrickfergus, county Antrim (baptised 18 July 1791 at Carrickfergus), third son of the Rev Snowden Cupples, rector of Lisburn, and Elinor Ross; studied medicine at Edinburgh University; MRCSE 1812; MD (Edin) 1821 (thesis 'De asthmate'); joined the Army Medical Service as assistant surgeon 1812; retired on half pay 1818; medical officer to Lisburn Union Workhouse and town councillor; married 31 August 1824 Antonia Legg, eldest daughter of John Legg of Carrickfergus; died 5 October 1848 at Lisburn. [*BNL* 3 September 1824 (m) and 13 October 1848 (d); Carmody (1926); Croly (1843–6); Edin Univ; Leslie (1993); *Lisburn Fam Hist Soc*, vol 2 (2005); Peterkin and Johnston (1968)].

CUPPLES, GEORGE PEPPER (d 1840), Mullahead, county Armagh;

surgeon, of Mullahead; died June 1840; probate Prerogative Court 1844. [Belf PRO, prerog wills index].

CUPPLES, THOMAS (1756–1801), Newry, county Down;

born 8 June 1756; son of William Cupples of Mullahead and Prospect House, county Armagh; brother of the Rev Snowden Cupples, rector of Lisburn; studied medicine at Edinburgh University; MD (Edin) 1777 (thesis 'De hypochondriasis causis'); general practitioner, of Newry; married —; father of Elizabeth Cupples who married in Lisburn in 1810; died 6 August 1801, 'eminently endowesd with every amiable quality …'; probate Prerogative Court 1801. [*BNL* 14 August 1801 (d); Carmody (1926); Edin Univ; Leslie (1993); *Lisburn Fam Hist Soc*, vol 2 (2005); *Memorials of the Dead,* vol VII, p 236; Vicars (1897)].

CURLING (CURLINE), WILLIAM (d 1671), Londonderry;

physician of Londonderry c 1665–71; married —; one son died December 1666 and one was born 1666/7; died December 1671; buried in Derry Cathedral graveyard. [Burtchaell and Sadleir (1924); Derry Cathedral Registers, pp 196 and 211; Ferrar (1933)].

CURRAN, HENRY (1829–72), Dublin;

born 6 March 1829 in Bridge Street, Downpatrick, second son of Waring Curran of Downpatrick and Ann Adair Pilson; educated at the Diocesan School; studied medicine at the Carmichael School, Dublin; LRCSI 1855; LKQCPI and LM 1869; medical officer to the Queen Street Dispensary and physician to the Mater Misericordiae Hospital, Dublin; unmarried; died 25 July 1872 in Blessington Street, Dublin. [Cameron (1916); Dub GRO (d); Kirkpatrick Archive; *Med Dir*].

CURRAN, JOHN OLIVER (1819–47), Dublin;

born 30 April 1819 at Trooperfield, Lisburn, only son of Dr Joseph Curran of Lisburn and the Isle of Man (*q.v.*); family moved to the Isle of Man where he was educated;

studied medicine at Glasgow University from 1833 (matriculated 1836), at Trinity College, Dublin, from 1838, at the Meath, Jervis Street and St Vincent's Hospitals, Dublin, and at Paris; MB (TCD) 1843; LKQCPI 1846; professor of medicine in the Apothecaries Hall from 1846 and physician to the Dublin General Dispensary; of Waterloo Road, Dublin; author of *Observations on Scurvy* ... (1847); outspoken critic of the management of disease in Dublin during the Famine; MRIA; died 26 September 1847 at 1 Waterloo Road, Dublin, of typhus fever; lithograph portrait by James Henry Lynch in his obituary. [Addison (1913); Burtchaell and Sadleir (1924); Cameron (1916); Crone (1928); Curran (1847); *DIB* (2009); Froggatt (1995); Newmann (1993); O'Brien, Crookshank and Wolstenholme (1984); Wilde obituary (1847)].

CURRAN, JOHN WARING (1844/5–78), Mansfield, Nottinghamshire;
born 1844/5; son of Waring Curran of Quoile Castle, Downpatrick; studied medicine at the Carmichael School, Richmond and St Vincent's Hospital, Dublin; LRCSI 1864; LKQCPI and LM 1865; FRCS Edin 1874; demonstrator in anatomy to the Carmichael School, Dublin; medical officer to Sutton Dispensary, Nottinghamshire c 1866–70; surgeon to Mansfield Hospital, Nottinghamshire and medical officer to Mansfield Dispensary District from 1870, of Wood House and 140 Stockwell Gate and Pleasley, Derbyshire; received presentation in December 1870; married Julie Amelia —; died 3 March 1878 at Mansfield Woodhouse, Nottinghamshire; administration (with will) Nottingham 3 March 1879. [*Downpatrick Recorder* 31 December1870; Lond GRO (d); Lond PPR, will cal; *Med Dir*].

CURRAN, JOSEPH (*fl c* 1820), Lisburn, county Antrim, and Isle of Man;
MRCS; surgeon, of Lisburn c 1820 and later of Mount Vernon, Isle of Man; father of Dr John Oliver Curran (*q.v.*); died 2 October 1857 at his son's home, 1 Waterloo Road, Dublin. [*BNL* 6 October 1857 (d); Burtchaell and Sadleir (1924)].

CURRELL, HUGH (1871–c 1943), Korea, and Melbourne, Victoria;
born 8 February 1871 at Carnlough, county Antrim, son of Daniel Currell, grocer, of Carnlough; educated at Carnlough National School; studied medicine at Queen's College, Belfast, from 1889; MB BCh BAO (RUI) 1897; medical missionary, with Australian Presbyterian Mission, in Chinju, via Masampo, Korea; general practitioner, of Melbourne from c 1915; died c 1943. [*Med Dir*; QCB adm reg].

CURRIE, ROBERT (*fl c* 1824), Ballyconnell, county Cavan;
physician and surgeon to Ballyconnell Dispensary c 1824; married —; father of Helen Juliet Currie who married 22 August 1843 in Ballyconnell Church, John Palmer Cobean of Woodview, county Cavan. [*BNL* 12 September 1843 (m, daughter); Pigot (1824)].

CURRIE, ROBERT (1854–1953), Ballymena, county Antrim;
born 9 April 1854 at Ballymena, son of Samuel Currie, farmer and linen manufacturer, of Tullaghgarley; educated at RBAI; studied medicine at Queen's

College, Belfast, from 1873, and Edinburgh; LRCP LRCS and LM Edin 1883; medical officer to Ballymena Dispensary District and constabulary, medical officer of health for Ballymena and visiting surgeon to Ballymena Cottage Hospital, of Linenhall Street and later of Westmead, 5 Grange Road, Ballymena; married (1) —; (2) 28 September 1897 in First Ballymoney Presbyterian Church, Mary May Steen, daughter of James Steen, farmer, of Ballymoney; died 6 April 1953 at 5 Grange Road; probate Belfast 6 October 1953. [Belf GRO (d); Belf PRO, will cal; *Med Dir*; QCB adm reg; UHF database (m)].

CURRY, JAMES (c 1763–1819), ship's surgeon, Nottingham and London;
born c 1763 in Antrim town; studied medicine at Edinburgh University; MD (Edin) 1784 (thesis 'De humorum in morbis contagiosis assimulatione'); LRCP Lond 1802; surgeon to a ship bound for the East Indies but returned home because of ill health; physician in Nottingham and to the county Hospital; physician to Guy's Hospital, London 1802; elected Corresponding Member of Belfast Literary Society 1802; author of papers on death from drowning and suffocation, and on the therapeutic use of mercury; died 26 November 1819; portrait by Simonam, engraved by Mills. [*Belf Lit Soc* (1901); Edin Univ; Kirkpatrick Archive; *Munk's Roll*, vol 3].

CUSTER, BERNARD (d 1828), Naval Medical Service;
joined the Naval Medical Service as assistant surgeon, later surgeon; died 9 November 1828 at Ashburn, Moneymore, 'a man of extensive information, generous disposition and a benevolent heart'. [*BNL* 25 November 1828 (d)].

CUTHBERT, ALEXANDER (1834–76), Waterside, Londonderry;
born 31 October 1834, son of Alexander Cuthbert of Coleraine and Margaret McCarter; educated by Mr Goudy of Coleraine; studied medicine at Queen's College, Belfast, from 1850, also at the Original Medical School and Mercer's Hospital, Dublin; LM Coombe Hosp Dub; MD (QUI) 1856; MRCSE 1856; MA 1882; house surgeon to Londonderry County Infirmary and Fever Hospital; medical officer to Glendermott Dispensary District 1860; of Murray's Row, Clooney Terrace, Waterside; co-author with Dr Thomas Henderson Babington (*q.v.*) of a paper on caisson disease (1863); built Gortfoyle House, Spencer Road, 1872; medical officer to Londonderry Workhouse and Fever Hospital 1873; superintendent medical officer of health for Londonderry 1874; married (1) 12 February 1862 in Armagh Cathedral, Harriette Elizabeth Magill (who was born 1856 and died 25 March 1863), eldest daughter of William Magill of Dunmore House, Cookstown, county Tyrone; (2) 7 November 1865 in Glendermott Church of Ireland Church, county Londonderry, Margaret Dunn (who was born 1838/9 and died 5 March 1909), daughter of Robert Dunn of Dunfield, Waterside, Londonderry; father by (2) of Alice Cuthbert who married Dr Robert Moore Fraser (*q.v.*) as his second wife; died 1 March 1876 of typhus fever, at Gortfoyle House; buried in Londonderry City Cemetery. [Babington and Cuthbert (1863); Belf PRO, will cal; *Coleraine Chronicle* 15 February 1862 (m), 28 March 1863 (d) and 11 November 1865 (m) Dub GRO (d); Kirkpatrick Archive; *Londonderry Sentinel* 27 March 1863 (d) and 10 November 1865 (m); McCormack (2002); *Med Dir*; QCB adm reg; RVH Archives, Cuthbert family tree].

CUTHBERT, WILLIAM (1765/6–1817), Londonderry city;
born 1765/6; surgeon and apothecary, of Ferryquay Street, Londonderry; married Amelia Maginniss (who was born 1760 and died 27 May 1829 in Dublin), sister of Dr Hamilton Maginniss, senior, of Londonderry (*q.v.*) and Dr William Maginniss of Coleraine (*q.v.*); father of Dr William Hamilton Cuthbert (*q.v.*); died 9 April 1817; buried in Derry Cathedral graveyard; administration Derry Diocesan Court 1817 and 1833, and Dublin 24 October 1863. [Belf PRO, will cal; Dub Nat Arch, Derry Admins index; Elliott, Simon, pers com; *Londonderry Journal* 15 September 1818; *Memorials of the Dead*, vol IX, p 123; Smythe-Wood (2007b)].

CUTHBERT, WILLIAM HAMILTON (1798–1855), Londonderry and Dublin;
born 1798 in Londonderry, son of Dr William Cuthbert of Londonderry (*q.v.*); physician, of Ferryquay, Londonderry, and later of St Georges Place, Dublin; married (1) his cousin Mary Maginniss (who died 11 April 1829 at George's Place, Dublin), daughter of Dr William Maginniss of Coleraine (*q.v.*); married (2) 1830 Mary Ann Conway; father of Emily Cuthbert who married in November 1852 Dr Charles Holmes of Donegal and Dublin (*q.v.*), LAH Dub 1826, MD (Glas) 1839; died 2 July 1855 in Dublin; buried in Mount Jerome Cemetery, Dublin. [*BNL* 10 November 1852 (m, daughter); Elliott, Simon, pers com; *Londonderry Chronicle and Weekly Mercantile Advertiser* 29 April 1829 (d); *Med Dir*].

CUTHBERTSON, WILLIAM (d 1815), Naval Medical Service;
joined the Naval Medical Service as assistant surgeon and served 'for many years'; retired to Ballycolman, Strabane, county Tyrone; died 24 April 1815 at Ballycolman. [*Strabane Morning Post* 25 April 1815 (d)].

D

DALLAS, JACOB (1763–96), Derrykeighan, county Antrim;
   born 1763/4, son of Alexander Dallas; surgeon, of Derrykeighan; died 26 August 1796; buried in Derrykeighan Old Graveyard. [Gravestone inscription].

DALTON, JOHN G. (d 1834), Killashandra, county Cavan;
   surgeon, of Killashandra; died 1 December 1834 at Killashandra. [*BNL* 12 December 1834 (d)].

DALY, CHARLES CALTHROP DE BURGH (1860/1–1947), Ningpo, China, Dublin and Blackrock, county Dublin;
   born 1860/1 in London, son of White J. Daly, civil servant; educated at Portora Royal School 1877–8; studied arts and medicine at Trinity College, Dublin, from 1878; BA (TCD) 1883; MB BCh 1883; worked in H M Colonial Service in China for 28 years and organized the Red Cross during the Chinese-Japanese and Russo-Japanese Wars; asked to return from retirement in 1910 to combat an epidemic of pneumonia in Manchuria; major RAMC; medical officer to HBM Consulate and IM Customs at Newchwang c 1910–15; of 71 Park Avenue, Sidney Parade, Dublin c 1915–23; OBE c 1918; medical superintendent, Special Surgical Hospital, Blackrock c 1920–25; of Priory Lodge, Grove Avenue, Blackrock c 1923–40; of 'Reford', Knocksinna Road, Blackrock c 1940–47; died 5 September 1947; administration (with will) Dublin 20 January 1948. [Dub Nat Arch, will cal; Duncan *et al* (2007); *Med Dir*; *Portora Royal School Register*; TCD adm reg; *TCD Cat* (1896)].

DALY, EDWARD (1816/7–91), Belfast;
   born 1816/7; studied medicine at Queen's College, Belfast, from 1849; LRCS Edin 1851; general practitioner, of 54 North Street, and 47 Laburnum Terrace, Belfast; retired to Holywood, county Down; married —; died 20 November 1891 at Glenside, Ballysillan, county Antrim; probate Belfast 21 December 1891. [Belf PRO, will cal; Dub GRO (d); *Med Dir*; QCB adm reg].

DALY, GEORGE WILLIAM (1847–1904), Liverpool, Lancashire, and Ratoath, county Meath;
   born 7 July 1847, son of John Daly of Cultromer, county Meath; educated at Navan Seminary; studied medicine at the Ledwich School, Dublin and Queen's College, Belfast, from 1865; LRCSI 1867; MD (QUI) 1869; general practitioner in Liverpool from c 1870; medical officer to the North Dispensary; returned to Ireland as medical officer to Dunshaughlin Workhouse 1872; superintendent medical officer for Dunshaughlin 1874 and medical officer to Ratoath Dispensary District from 1874; unmarried; died 7 April 1904 at Ratoath; probate Dublin 12 August 1904. [Belf PRO, will cal; Dub GRO (d); Kirkpatrick Archive; *Med Dir*; QCB adm reg].

DALZELL, WILLIAM (d 1819), Belfast;
apothecary to the Belfast Fever Hospital, 1818–19; died 20 August 1819. [Malcolm (1851)].

DANE, RICHARD MARTIN (1813–1901), Army Medical Service;
born 4 April 1813 in county Fermanagh, son of Richard Martin Dane of Killyhevlin and Anne Auchinleck of Lisgoole Abbey; educated by Mr Leney; studied arts and medicine at Trinity College, Dublin, from 1828; BA (TCD) 1833; MB 1834; LRCSI 1834; FRCSI 1846; MD 1859; joined the Army Medical Service in 1835 as staff assistant surgeon, serving with the 90th Foot; transferred to 29th Foot 1840; surgeon with the 11th Foot 1846; transferred to 63rd Foot 1847 and 29th Foot 1848; surgeon major 1855; deputy inspector general of hospitals 1858; inspector general 1868; served in Sutlej 1846 and China 1858; retired on half pay 1872; CB (Military) 1873; of Clarendon Lodge, Millbrook, Hampshire; married 1844 Sophia Elizabeth Griffiths, daughter of Colonel Charles Griffiths; father of Dr Arthur Henry Cole Dane, LRCSI LKQCPI 1874, IMS (Bombay establishment); died 27 March 1901; probate London 19 April 1901. [Burke, *LGI* (1912); *Burke's Irish Family Records* (1976); Burtchaell and Sadleir (1924); Crawford (1930) (for son); Lond PPR, will cal; *Med Dir*; Peterkin and Johnston (1968)].

DANE, WILLIAM (1808/9–47), Drumard, county Fermanagh;
born 1808/9, second son of James Dane of Drumard, and Margaret Armstrong of Enniskillen; surgeon, of Drumard; unmarried; died 2 October 1847 at Drumard; probate Prerogative Court 1847. [*BNL* 8 October 1847 (d); Belf PRO, Prerog Wills index; Burke *LGI* (1912); *Londonderry Sentinel* 9 October 1847 (d)].

DANIEL, JAMES (d 1857), Carrickmacross, county Monaghan;
surgeon, of Carrickmacross; died 1857. [*Med Dir*].

DANIEL, RICHARD (d 1805), Armagh;
studied medicine at the Royal College of Surgeons in Ireland and Mercers' Hospital, Dublin; worked to relieve Mr Shrewbridge in Armagh County Infirmary 1776; surgeon to the Infirmary 1788–1804; died 1805. [Beale (2002); Paterson (1962); Weatherup (2001)].

DANIEL, TERENCE (d 1855), Carrickmacross, county Monaghan;
surgeon, of Carrickmacross; died 1855. [*Med Dir*].

DARCUS, HENRY RICHARDSON (1838/9–c 1886), Londonderry;
born 1838/9, son of Henry Darcus of Londonderry and Anne Elizabeth Harris; educated at Foyle College; studied medicine at Queen's College, Belfast, 1858–63, and the General Hospital, Belfast, also at the Royal College of Surgeons in Ireland and Mercer's Hospital, Dublin; LM Rot Hosp Dub; LRCSI 1863; LKQCPI 1865; medical officer to the City of Londonderry Dispensary No 1 District, and constabulary; medical inspector of seamen; registrar of births and deaths and public vaccinator; of 27 Clarendon Street, London-derry; mentioned in his father's will of 1885; died c 1886. [Belf PRO, will cal (father); *Med Dir*; QCB adm reg].

D'ARCY, SAMUEL ALGERNON (1861/2–1946), Rosslea, county Fermanagh, and RAMC;
   born 1861/2, son of Francis Joshua D'Arcy, gentleman; studied medicine at the Royal College of Surgeons in Ireland and Trinity College, Dublin; LM Rot Hosp Dub; LRCPI and LM, LRCSI and LM 1889; assistant master to National Lying-in Hospital, Dublin; medical officer and medical officer of health to Rosslea Dispensary District and certifying factory surgeon; medical officer to the constabulary; of Etna Lodge, Magheranure, county Monaghan; temporary captain in RAMC during World War I; author of antiquarian papers; retired to Lismoyle, Cushendall, county Antrim c 1938; married 5 December 1891 in St Thomas's Church of Ireland Church, Belfast, Elizabeth Adelaide Whitsitt (who was born 1873), daughter of Benjamin Whitsitt, gentleman, of Belfast; died 6 November 1946 at Lismoyle, Cushendall; probate Belfast 15 July 1947. [Belf GRO (d); Belf PRO, will cal, will; Kirkpatrick Archive; *Med Dir*; UHF database (m)].

DARLEY, ARTHUR LA TOUCHE (1877–1967), Naval Medical Service and Nottingham;
   born 13 January 1877 in Belfast, son of the Rev William Shaw Darley of University Square, Belfast; educated at Methodist College, Belfast, from 1883; studied medicine at Queen's College, Belfast, from 1893; LRCPI and LM LRCSI and LM 1900; joined the Naval Medical Service c 1903; retired as surgeon commander c 1922; lieutenant-colonel RAMC; general practitioner in Nottingham living at 11 Church Street, Mansfield Woodhouse, and 1 Victoria Embankment, c 1935; retired c 1948 to Trowell Lodge, and from c 1959 to 11 Russell Drive, Wollaton, all in Nottinghamshire; also lived latterly at Sharrowhurst, Ballindean, Roodepoort, Transvaal; married —; died 1 April 1967 at Sharrowhurst; administration (with will) Nottingham 30 August 1968. [Fry (1984); Lond PPR, will cal; *Med Dir*; QCB adm reg].

DARLING, JOHN SINGLETON (1855/6–1927), Lurgan, county Armagh;
   born 1855/6 at Clonakilty, county Cork, son of John Singleton Darling, bank manager; studied arts and medicine at Trinity College, Dublin, from 1873, and at Vienna; BA (TCD) 1877; MB 1879; LM KQCPI 1879; BCh 1880; MD MCh 1909; medical officer to Lurgan Workhouse Hospital 1883–90; surgeon to Lurgan Infirmary from 1890; president of Ulster Branch of BMA; president of Ulster Medical Society 1924–5; of 11 High Street, Lurgan; married (1) —; (2) 24 May 1909 in the Ormeau Gospel Hall, Belfast, Marjorie Shillington, daughter of Henry Shillington, civil engineer, of Convention Villa, Belfast; died 8 November 1927 at 11 High Street, Lurgan; probate Belfast 5 April 1928. [Belf GRO (d); Belf PRO, will cal; *BMJ* obituary (1927); Dub GRO (m); Hunter (1936); Kirkpatrick Archive; *Lancet* obituary (1927); *Med Dir*; TCD adm reg; *TCD Cat*, vol 2 (1896); UHF database (m)].

DARNELL, CHARLES KNAPP (1869–1942), Bangor, county Down;
   born 2 February 1869 at Hillmorton, Rugby, Warwickshire, son of the Rev Daniel Charles West Darnell, curate of Welton, Northamptonshire, and Elizabeth Fisher; educated at Rugby School; studied medicine at Edinburgh University and from 1895,

at Queen's College, Belfast, LRCP LRCS Edin 1898; LFPS Glas 1898; general practitioner, of 'Greenbank', 15 Tennyson Avenue, Bangor; involved in a prolonged lawsuit which he won in 1906; married —; died 10 April 1942 at 15 Tennyson Avenue; buried in Clandeboye House graveyard; probate Belfast 14 July 1942. [Belf GRO (d); Belf PRO, will cal; *BMJ* (1906); Crockford; Kirkpatrick Archive; Lond GRO (b); *Med Dir*; Merrick and Clarke, *County Down*, vol 17 (1978); QCB adm reg].

DARTNELL, GEORGE RUSSELL (1799–1878), Army Medical Service;
born 28 July 1799; MRCSE 1822; joined the Army Medical Service 1820 as hospital assistant; assistant surgeon to the 41st Foot 1825; staff surgeon 1833; surgeon to the 1st Foot 1839; staff surgeon 1st class 1845; deputy inspector general 1850; retired on half pay 1857 to Arden House, Henley-in-Arden, Warwickshire; married —; children born c 1837 and 1844; died 22 July 1878 at Leamington. [*BNL* 16 January 1844 (b and d); Peterkin and Johnston (1968)].

DAVENPORT, JAMES (*fl c* 1835), London;
born in county Londonderry; MD [?]; general practitioner, of London; married October 1835 in Camberwell, London, Mira Nuthall, daughter of W.H. Nuthall, HEICS. [*BNL* 27 October 1835 (m); *Londonderry Sentinel* 24 October 1835 (m); *Strabane Morning Post* 27 October 1835 (m)].

DAVENPORT, JAMES (1806–98), Indian Medical Service;
born 12 July 1806; studied medicine at Edinburgh University; MD (Edin) 1827 (thesis 'De scarlatina'); MRCSI 1828; joined the Indian Medical Service (Bengal establishment) as assistant surgeon 1828; surgeon 1845; retired 1850; married 10 March 1842 in Dacca, India, Elizabeth Lamb Wilson, only daughter of lieutenant-colonel R.W. Wilson of the 65th Native Infantry; died 16 March 1898 at 'Rosenstein', Doyle Road, St Peter Port, Guernsey. [Crawford (1930); Edin Univ; Lond PPR, will cal; *Londonderry Sentinel* 14 May 1842 (m); *Med Dir*].

DAVIDGE, GEORGE MOORE (*fl c* 1834), county Cavan;
MD [?]; general practitioner, of county Cavan; married 29 September 1834 in Loughcrew Church of Ireland Church, county Meath, Charlotte Sandys, daughter of Abraham Sandys of Chesterfield, county Galway. [*BNL* 10 October 1834 (m)].

DAVIDSON, ISAAC ALEXANDER (1869–1942), Belfast;
born 23 January 1869 in Frevent, France, son of James Davidson, foreman mechanic and agent for Coombe, Barbour and Coombe, of 97 St Mary's Terrace, Crumlin Road, Belfast; cousin of Dr John Crossie Davidson (*q.v.*) and Dr Thomas Augustus Davidson (*q.v.*); educated at Methodist College, Belfast, from 1881; studied arts and medicine at Queen's College, Belfast, from 1885; BA (hons) (RUI) 1889; MB BCh BAO 1892; MD 1898; DPH (Camb) 1902; house physician and house surgeon to Belfast Royal Hospital; post-graduate student in Vienna; general practitioner, of 20 Lonsdale Terrace, Belfast; honorary anaesthetist to the Benn Ulster ENT Hospital 1902–09, to the Belfast Hospital for Sick Children 1901–04, and the Royal Victoria

Hospital; honorary assistant surgeon to the Benn Hospital 1913–39; served in RAMC during World War I as ophthalmic specialist with rank of captain; honorary ophthalmic surgeon to Ulster Hospital for Children and Women 1914–34; of 3 Laurington, Antrim Road, Belfast c 1925; president of the Irish Ophthalmological Society; married Alison Knowles —; died 15 May 1942 at Danesfort, Annadale Avenue, Belfast; probate Belfast 2 December 1942. [Allison (1969); Belf GRO (d); Belf PRO, will cal; Calwell (1973); Fry (1984); Kirkpatrick Archive; *Lancet* obituary (1942); Marshall and Kelly (1973); *Med Dir*; O'Donnell (2008); QCB adm reg].

DAVIDSON, JAMES (*fl c* 1825), Downpatrick, county Down;
LAH Dub 1825; apothecary, of Downpatrick. [Apothecaries (1829)].

DAVIDSON, JAMES WALSHE (1855–1921), Shrewsbury, Shropshire, Wigan, Lancashire, Acklington, Northumberland, London, and Wolverhampton, Staffordshire; born 15 April 1855, son of David Davidson, grocer, of Kells, county Antrim; educated at Tullynamullan School; schoolmaster in Dervock c 1874–6; studied medicine at Queen's College, Belfast, from 1876; LRCS Edin and LM 1882; of Ramoan, Ballycastle, c 1882–4; general practitioner, of 1 Wyle Cop, Shrewsbury c 1887–90, of Holly Terrace, Haigh Road, Aspull, Wigan c 1890–91, of Amble, Acklington c 1891–2, of 230 Burdet, Bow, London c 1892–4, of 91 London Road, Southwark c 1894–8 and of Snow Hill, Wolverhampton c 1898–1920; retired c 1920 to 18 Somerset Avenue, Bangor, county Down; married 7 July 1882 in Ramoan Church of Ireland Church, Ballycastle, Elizabeth Morrow McCotter, daughter of Richard McCotter, farmer, of Dervock, county Antrim; father of Dr Norman Grenville Walshe Davidson, OBE, of Glasgow; died 18 August 1921 at the Lorelei Nursing Home, 18 Somerset Avenue; buried in Connor New Cemetery, Kells; probate Belfast 26 October 1921. [Belf PRO, will cal, will; Dub GRO (m) and (d); Dunlop, Eull, pers com; *Med Dir*; QCB adm reg; UHF database (m)].

DAVIDSON, JOHN (1814/5–44), Dromore, county Down;
born 1814/5; surgeon, of Dromore; married 1 June 1836 in Dromore, Alicia Stewart (who died 14 November 1845 at her father's home), second daughter of Robert Stewart of Dromore; died 3 February 1844 of apoplexy, at his home in Dromore; administration Dromore Diocesan Court 1844. [*BNL* 1 July 1836 (m), 13 February 1844 (d) and 18 November 1845 (d); Dub Nat Arch, Dromore Dio Admins index].

DAVIDSON, JOHN (d c 1872), Newry, county Down;
studied medicine at Glasgow University; CM (Glas) 1835; general practitioner of Newry c 1860–72; died c 1872. [Addison (1898); *Med Dir*].

DAVIDSON, JOHN (d 1863), Belfast;
studied medicine at Glasgow University; MD (Glas) 1849; LFPS and LM Glas 1855; of Rich Hill, county Armagh c 1858; general practitioner and surgeon to the constabulary, of 45 Falls Road, Belfast c 1859–63; married Mary —; died 21 November 1863; administration Belfast 5 April 1864. [Addison (1898); Belf PRO, will cal; *Med Dir*].

DAVIDSON, JOHN CROSSIE (1857/8–97), Belfast;
born 1857/8, son of John Crossie Davidson of 6 Carlisle Terrace, Crumlin Road, Belfast; brother of Dr Thomas A. Davidson (*q.v.*); LRCP and LRCS Edin 1886; LFPS Glas 1886; general practitioner, of 6 Carlisle Terrace, Crumlin Road; unmarried; died 14 May 1897 at 6 Carlisle Terrace; buried in Belfast City Cemetery; administration Belfast 27 August 1897. [Belf City Cem, bur reg; Belf PRO, will cal; Dub GRO (d); *Med Dir*].

DAVIDSON, JOHN MATTHEW (1857–95), London;
born 24 June 1857 at Stoneyford, county Antrim, son of William W. Davidson, principal of Brookfield Agricultural School, near Moira; educated at Brookfield Agricultural School and Flounders College, England; studied medicine at Queen's College, Belfast, from 1879; LSA London 1883; moved to London c 1884, general practitioner, of 121 Goswell Road, London, from c 1886; later also of 324 City Road and 63 Raleigh Road; married Hannah —; died 29 January 1895 at 121 Goswell Road. [Lond GRO (d); *Med Dir*; QCB adm reg].

DAVIDSON, JOSEPH (b 1815/6), Rathfriland, county Down;
born 1815/6, son of Robert Davidson, farmer; surgeon and medical officer to constabulary in Rathfriland, c 1843–6; married (1) 29 October 1846 in Glascar Presbyterian Church, county Down, Mary McSpadden (who was born 1815/6), daughter of David McSpadden, farmer, of Ballynaskeagh, county Down; (2) 31 March 1856 in Hilltown Presbyterian Church, county Down, Margaret Waddell (widow), daughter of Hugh Hall, farmer, and widow of Dr Hugh Waddell of Hilltown (*q.v.*); probably died c 1860. [*BNL* 10 November 1846 (m) and 4 April 1856 (m); Croly (1843–6); UHF database (m) (2)].

DAVIDSON, RICHARD BAXTER (1840–89), India, and Rademon, county Down;
born 1840/1, son of John Davidson of Drumaness, county Down; educated by the Rev James Mulligan; studied medicine at Queen's College, Belfast, from 1854; MD (QUI) 1860; tea planter at Labuc, Cachar, India; afterwards agent for Mr Sharman Crawford of Rademon; general practitioner; married —; died 5 May 1889 at Rademon House as a result of falling out of a window 'in a state of somnambulism' (coroner); buried in Magheradrool graveyard, Ballynahinch; probate Belfast 7 February 1890. [Belf PRO, will cal; Dub GRO (d); *Newtownards Chronicle* 11 May 1889 (d); QCB adm reg].

DAVIDSON, THOMAS AUGUSTUS (1862/3–1928), Belfast;
born 1862/3, son of John Crossie Davidson of 6 Carlisle Terrace, Crumlin Road, Belfast; brother of Dr John Crossie Davidson (*q.v.*) and cousin of Dr Isaac Alexander Davidson (*q.v.*); LRCP LRCS Edin 1887; LFPS Glas 1887; general practitioner, of 13 Clifton Street and later 6 Carlisle Terrace, Crumlin Road, Belfast (c 1904); unmarried; died 28 March 1928 at St John's Home, Crumlin Road, after being knocked down by a tram car on 16 March (coroner); buried in Belfast City Cemetery; probate Belfast 16 July 1928. [Belf City Cem, bur reg; Belf GRO (d); Belf PRO, will cal; Kirkpatrick Archive; *Med Dir*].

DAVI(D)SON, WILLIAM (1802/3–42), Tandragee, county Armagh;
born 1802/3; surgeon, of Tandragee; died 19 January 1842 in Tandragee; probate Prerogative Court 1842. [*BNL* 1 February 1842 (d); Belf PRO, prerog wills index].

DAVIDSON, WILLIAM (*fl c* 1827), Rathfriland, county Down;
LAH Dub 1827; apothecary, of Rathfriland. [Apothecaries (1829)].

DAVIDSON, WILLIAM (*fl c* 1853), Crossgar, county Down;
surgeon, of Crossgar; married 1 September 1853 in Second Dromara Presbyterian Church, county Down, Isabella Waddell, daughter of Samuel Waddell, farmer, of Crossgar. [Dub GRO (m); UHF database (m)].

DAVIES, JOHN (d c 1928), Carrickfergus, county Antrim;
studied medicine at Edinburgh and Leeds; LRCP LRCS Edin 1898; LRFPS Glas 1898; DTM Edin 1909; DPH Edin 1910; general practitioner, of Scoutbush, Trooperslane, Carrickfergus; working with Ministry of Pensions, Northern Ireland from 1927; died c 1928. [*Med Dir*].

DAVI(E)S, WILLIAM ALEXANDER (1796/7–1877), Newry, county Down;
born 1796/7; studied medicine at Trinity College, Dublin, Dr Steeven's Hospital, Dublin, and Glasgow University; LAH Dub 1821; LM Rot Hosp Dub 1829; MRCSE 1831; MD (Glas) 1841; medical officer to the Newry Union and Workhouse Fever Hospital, constabulary and District National Model School; married 4 April 1834 in Grange Church of Ireland Church, county Armagh, Jemima McBride, second daughter of Robert McBride of Alistragh, county Armagh; father of Dr William Hancock Davis (*q.v.*), Dr George McBride Davis (*q.v.*) and Dr Richard Davis (*q.v.*) and; died 7 November 1877; buried in St Patrick's graveyard, Newry; memorial tablet in St Mary's Church of Ireland Church, Newry; probate Armagh 29 November 1877. [Addison (1898); *BNL* 11 April 1834 (m); Belf PRO, will cal; Clarke, *County Down*, vol 21 (1998); Croly (1843–6); Kirkpatrick Archive; *Med Dir*].

DAVIES, WILLIAM NAUNTON (1853/–1932), Llantrissant, Glamorganshire;
born 1853/4 at Basley, Monmouthshire, son of Dr David Williams Davies of Llantrissant, Glamorganshire; educated privately; studied medicine at Queen's College, Galway, the Ledwich School, Dublin, and from 1878, at Queen's College, Belfast; MD (QUI) 1880; MCh Dip Mid 1881; general practitioner, of The Firs and later Llantrissant House; medical officer of health, medical officer, certifying factory surgeon and public vaccinator for Llantrissant and Llantivit Vardre District; medical officer to various collieries; died 26 June 1932; probate Llandaff 14 December 1932. [Lond PPR, will cal; *Med Dir*; QCB adm reg].

DAVIS, ARTHUR NATHANIEL (1857/8–1922), London, Portsmouth, Hampshire, Dorchester, Dorset and Exminster, Devon;
born 1857/8 at Newport, county Mayo, son of Dr James Davis of Newport; educated at Cavan Royal School; studied medicine at Queen's College, Galway and, from 1876,

at Queen's College, Belfast; LRCP LRCS and LM Edin 1880; resident medical officer of Bethnal House Asylum, London; assistant medical officer of Portsmouth Asylum and Westbrook House Asylum; resident medical officer of the Dorset County Asylum c 1885–90 and medical superintendent c 1898–1900; medical superintendent of Devon County Asylum, Exminster c 1900–22, of Bath House, Exmouth; died 22 June 1922; probate London 31 July 1922. [Lond PPR, will cal; *Med Dir*; QCB adm reg].

DAVIS, GEORGE McBRIDE (1846–1909), Indian Medical Service;
born 29 March 1846 at Newry, son of Dr William Alexander Davis (*q.v.*) of Newry; brother of Dr William Hancock Davis (*q.v.*) and Dr Richard Davis (*q.v.*); educated at Newry School; studied medicine at Queen's College, Belfast, from 1861; LAH Dub 1866; MD and MCh (QUI) 1866; joined the Indian Medical Service (Bengal establishment) as assistant surgeon 1869; surgeon 1873; surgeon major 1881; surgeon lietenant-colonel 1894; surgeon colonel 1897; served on North West Frontier, Mahud Waziri 1881, first Miranzai War 1890, Hazara 1891 (medal with clasp); Waziristan Delimitation Escort 1894 as principal medical officer; DSO 1895; Tirah 1897–8; CB 1898; China 1900; Waziristan 1901–02; retired 1902; lived finally at the East India, United Services Club, St James's Square, London; died 4 October 1909 at 5 Parkview Terrace, Wimbledon; commemorated in St Patrick's graveyard, Newry; probate London 30 November 1909. [*BMJ* obituary (1909); Clarke, *County Down*, vol 21 (1998); Crawford (1930); Kirkpatrick Archive; Lond PPR, will cal; *Med Dir*; QCB adm reg].

DAVIS, HUGH ALEXANDER (1851– c 1932), Newport, county Mayo and London;
born 9 December 1851 at Newport, son of James Davis of Newport; educated at Cavan Royal School; studied medicine at Queen's College, Cork, and from 1870–72, at Queen's College, Belfast; MD MCh Dip Mid (QUI) 1872; general practitioner at Newport, Mayo, c 1873–90; superintendent medical officer of health and consulting sanitary officer to Newport from 1875; general practitioner in Tottenham, London, of 228 Northumberland Park, from c 1895; of 22 Hindes Road, Harrow, from c 1906; of 120 Haydon's Road, Wimbledon, from c 1912; married —; died c 1932. [Kirkpatrick Archive; *Med Dir*; QCB adm reg].

DAVIS, JAMES (1811/2–54), Ballybofey, county Donegal;
born 1811/2; LRCS Edin; surgeon, of Ballybofey, c 1845; died 9 July 1854 at his mother's residence in Ballybofey. [*BNL* 17 July 1854 (d); Croly (1843–6); *Londonderry Sentinel* 14 July 1854 (d)].

DAVIS, JAMES (1835–1903), Army Medical Service;
born 15 April 1835 at Newry, county Down; LAH Dub 1855; LRCSI 1856; joined the Army Medical Service as assistant surgeon to the 57th Foot 1858; transferred to the 39th Foot 1868; surgeon major 1873; brigade surgeon 1883; deputy surgeon general, afterwards surgeon colonel 1888; surgeon major-general 1894; served in New Zealand in 1861 and 1865–6; retired 1895 to Broxholme, 6 Waverley Avenue, Southsea, Hampshire; won the Royal Humane Society's medal; married —; father of Dr William John Nixon Davis (*q.v.*); died 8 November 1903 at Southsea; probate

Winchester 30 November 1903. [Lond PPR, will cal; *Med Dir*; Peterkin and Johnston (1968)].

DAVIS, JOHN HENRY (1864–1916), Belfast, Liverpool, Lancashire, and RAMC;
born 21 February 1864 at 56 York Street, Belfast, son of Robert Davis, grocer and provision merchant, of 58 Duncairn Street, Belfast; educated at Belfast Model School; studied medicine at Queen's College, Belfast, from 1886; MB BCh BAO (RUI) 1899; general practitioner, of 16 Duncairn Street, Belfast c 1910; general practitioner, of 276 Upper Parliament Street, Liverpool; lieutenant (temporary) RAMC 1914–16; died 21 June 1916 at The Accident Hospital, Garston, Liverpool, of 'injuries to head and left leg caused by accidentally colliding with an electric tram car whilst riding a motor bicycle'; buried in Belfast City Cemetery; administration Liverpool 5 June 1917. [Belf City Cem, bur reg; Kirkpatrick Archive; Lond GRO (d); Lond PPR, will cal; *Med Dir*; QCB adm reg].

DAVIS, JOSEPH (1808/9–91), Poyntzpass, county Armagh;
born 1801/2 (c of d) or 1808/9 (gravestone); studied medicine at Glasgow University; CM (Glas) 1829; surgeon, of Poyntzpass; married Elizabeth — (who was born 1807/8 and died 29 May 1847); died 12 May 1891 in Poyntzpass; buried in Acton Church of Ireland Graveyard, Poyntzpass. [Addison (1898); Dub GRO (d); gravestone inscription; *Med Dir*].

DAVIS, RICHARD (1848–80), Exminster, Devonshire;
born 13 May 1848 at Newry, son of Dr William Alexander Davis (*q.v.*) of Sugar Island, Newry; brother of Dr William Hancock Davis (*q.v.*) and Dr George McBride Davis (*q.v.*); educated by Mr Patterson of Newry; studied medicine at Queen's College, Belfast, 1866–72; LAH Dub 1872; MD MCh Dip Mid (QUI) 1872; medical officer of Devon County Asylum, Exminster; died 16 August 1880 at Exminster County Asylum, of typhoid fever; buried at Exminster and commemorated in the family grave, St Patrick's Graveyard, Newry. [Clarke, *County Down*, vol 21 (1998); Lond GRO (d); *Med Dir*; QCB adm reg].

DAVIS, ROBERT HENRY DOUGLAS (d c 1887), Killybegs, county Donegal;
studied medicine at the Royal College of Surgeons in Ireland; LM Rot Hosp Dub 1854; LRCSI 1856; medical officer to Bangor Dispensary District, county Mayo, of 3 St John's Terrace, Clontarf, county Mayo, c 1856–63; abroad c 1863–7; medical officer to Killybegs Dispensary District, constabulary and coastguards from c 1867; died c 1887. [*Med Dir*].

DAVIS, SAMUEL (d c 1836), Tandragee, county Armagh, and Barbados;
surgeon and apothecary, of Tandragee c 1824; died 29 March 1836 of dropsy, on his passage home from Barbados; administration Connor Diocesan Court 1836. [*BNL* 5 April 1836 (d); Dub Nat Arch, Connor Dio Admins index; Pigot (1824)].

DAVIS, SAMUEL (*fl c* 1845), Letterkenny, county Donegal;
general practitioner in Letterkenny c 1845; medical officer to the Revenue Constabulary. [Croly (1843–6)].

DAVIS, THOMAS (1768/9–1822), Letterkenny, county Donegal;
born 1768/9; surgeon, of Letterkenny; married —; died 10 June 1822 at Letterkenny. [*BNL* 21 June 1822 (d); *Strabane Morning Post* 25 June 1822 (d)].

DAVIS, THOMAS (1817/8–1900), Manorhamilton, county Leitrim;
born 1817/8, son of Robert Davis, farmer; studied medicine at the Carmichael School, Dublin and Glasgow University; LM Rot Hosp Dub 1838; MRCSE 1838; LAH Dub 1843; MD (Glas) 1843; surgeon superintendent to HM Emigration Service; medical officer to Lurganboy Dispensary District, Manorhamilton; medical officer to Manorhamilton Dispensary District, Union Workhouse and Fever Hospital from 1872, of Rockwood, Manorhamilton; JP; retired to Roslyn Villa, Londonderry c 1875, living from c 1877 at Spencer Road and later at 6 Crawford Square, Londonderry; married 11 April 1850 in First Derry Presbyterian Church, Alice Haslett, youngest daughter of Samuel Haslett, gentleman, of Foyleview, Londonderry; died 18 February 1900 at 6 Crawford Square; probate Londonderry 24 April 1900. [Addison (1898); *BNL* 16 April 1850 (m); Belf PRO, will cal; Dub GRO (m) and (d); Kirkpatrick Archive; *Londonderry Sentinel* 12 April 1850 (m); *Med Dir*].

DAVIS, THOMAS PLAISTED (1782/3–1825), Naval Medical Service;
born 1782/3; joined the Naval Medical Service as assistant surgeon; married 12 October 1803 Margaret Doran (who was born 1785/6 and died 30 May 1858), youngest daughter of the Rev — Doran of Moorgrove (not identified); died 20 October 1825 in Holywood, county Down; buried in Knockbreda graveyard. [*BNL* 19 October 1813 (m) and 1 November 1825 (d); Clarke, *County Down*, vol 2 (1988)].

DAVIS, WILLIAM HANCOCK (1838/9–1909), Cheadle, Staffordshire;
born 1838/9, second son of Dr William Alexander Davis (*q.v.*) of Newry; brother of Dr George McBride Davis (*q.v.*) and Dr Richard Davis (*q.v.*); educated at Newry Collegiate School; studied medicine at Queen's College, Belfast from 1858; LAH Dub 1861; MD (QUI) 1862; LRCS Edin and LM 1862; medical officer, public vaccinator and certifying factory surgeon to Checkley Dispensary District, Cheadle, Staffordshire, of Brooklands, Tean, Staffordshire; married Sarah —; died 3 March 1901; administration Litchfield 4 May 1901. [Lond PPR, will cal; *Med Dir*; QCB adm reg].

DAVIS, WILLIAM JOHN NIXON (1870–c 1963), Chicago;
born 15 May 1870 at Ferozopore, India, son of surgeon major-general James Davis (*q.v.*); educated at Armagh Royal School 1881–4; studied medicine at Trinity College, Dublin, Edinburgh University and the Royal College of Surgeons, Edinburgh; LRCP LRCS Edin 1896; LFPS Glas 1896; general practitioner in Chicago, of 7502 Saginaw Avenue, Windsor Park, Chicago, and then of 7706 Saginaw Avenue; died c 1963. [Ferrar (1933); *Med Dir*].

DAVIS, — (*fl c* 1866), Monaghan;
general practitioner, of Monaghan c 1866. [McCann (2003)].

DAVISON, FRANCIS (d c 1885), Armagh, Bury, Lancashire, and Morocco;
studied medicine at Queen's College, Galway, the Royal College of Surgeons in Ireland and Ledwich School, Dublin; LM Coombe Hosp Dub 1872; LAH Dub 1872; LRCP and LRCS Edin 1873; consultant sanitary officer for Armagh Urban District; general practitioner of Elton, Bury, from c 1876; medical officer in Saffi, Morocco, from c 1880; died c 1885. [*Med Dir*].

DAVISON, GEORGE (1857–87), Bellaghy, county Londonderry;
born 1857, son of Mark Davison of Ballyscullion, county Londonderry; studied medicine at the Royal College of Surgeons in Ireland and the Richmond Hospital, Dublin; LM Coombe Hosp Dub; LRCSI 1884; surgeon on the SS *Victoria*; general practitioner of Bellaghy 1885–7; unmarried; died 22 December 1887 of phthisis, at Ballyscullion. [*Bellaghy Hist Soc* (2003); Dub GRO (d); *Med Dir*].

DAVISON, HENRY ALEXANDER (1856–82), Armagh;
born 1856 in Armagh, second son of Henry Davison, county surveyor, of Melbourne Terrace, Armagh; educated at Armagh Royal School 1867–72; studied arts and medicine at Trinity College, Dublin 1872–6, at the Meath Hospital, Dublin and at Vienna; BA and MB (TCD) 1876; general practitioner, of 7 Melbourne Terrace, Armagh; died 26 January 1882 at The Firs, Hounslow. [Ferrar (1933); *Med Dir*; TCD adm reg; *TCD Cat,* vol II (1896)].

DAVISON, JAMES (1846–1928), Sheffield, Yorkshire, and Bournemouth, Hampshire;
born 9 March 1846 at Lisbane, Saintfield, son of Samuel Davison of Lisbane; educated at Saintfield Academy and RBAI; studied medicine at Queen's College, Belfast, from 1864; MD (QUI) 1869; MCh Dip Mid 1880; MRCP London 1889; demonstrator in anatomy at Sheffield School of Medicine; general physician and otolaryngologist, of Brotton, Saltburn-by-the-Sea, Yorkshire c 1871; of Stockbridge, Sheffield c 1875; physician to the National Sanatorium for Consumption and Diseases of the Chest, Bournemouth; physician to the ENT Department, Royal Victoria Hospital, Bournemouth; of Walderslow, Bournemouth, c 1885, of 'Streat Place', 16 Bath Road, Bournemouth c 1895, and of 1 Bryanstone Road, Bournemouth, c 1925; president of the Bournemouth Medical Society; married Sarah Lucy —; died 18 March 1928; probate London 25 April 1928. [Lond PPR, will cal; *Med Dir*; QCB adm reg].

DAVISON, JOHN ROBERT (1860–1931), Belfast;
born 25 April 1860 in Leeds, son of Robert Davison, flax spinner, Yaroslav, Russia, and of 2 Duncairn Avenue, Belfast, and Margaret Hill; educated at Coleraine Academical Institution; studied arts at Queen's College, Cork, 1877–80 and medicine at Queen's College, Belfast 1880–88; BA (QUI) 1880; MD (RUI) 1887; BCh MAO 1888; general practitioner, of 'Romanov', Ormeau Road, Belfast; married Elizabeth —; died 17 September 1931 at 'Romanov'; buried in Belfast City Cemetery; probate Belfast 13 November 1931. [Belf City Cem, bur reg; Belf GRO (d); Belf PRO, will cal; Irwin (1932); Kirkpatrick Archive; *Med Dir*; QCB adm reg].

DAVISON, SAMUEL (1811/2–84), Dromara and Crossgar, county Down;
born 1811/2; studied medicine at Glasgow University and Royal Infirmary; MD and LM (Glas) 1838; assistant apothecary to Glasgow Royal Infirmary; physician to Dromara Fever Hospital; medical officer to Crossgar Dispensary District and constabulary; also agent of the landlord of the area, William Waring; received presentation in January 1874; retired in 1880 because of ill health, but was refused a pension by the Board of Guardians; unmarried; died 15 March 1884 at Dromara; buried in First Dromara Presbyterian Graveyard; probate Belfast 2 May 1884. [Addison (1898); Belf PRO, will cal; *BMJ* (1880); Clarke, *County Down*, vol 19 (1983); Croly (1843–6); *Downpatrick Recorder* 17 January 1874 (news); Dub GRO (d); Kirkpatrick Archive; *Med Dir*].

DAVISON, WILLIAM (1792/3–1849), Glenavy, county Antrim;
born 1792/3; MD [?]; died 24 February 1849 of asthma, at Glenavy. [*BNL* 6 March 1849 (d)].

DAVISON, WILLIAM ROBERT (1858–1942), Ballymena, county Antrim;
born 1858 in county Londonderry, son of John Davidson, farmer, of county Londonderry; studied medicine at Edinburgh University and, from 1886, Queen's College, Belfast; MB MCh (Edin) 1887; DPH RCPSI 1893; MRCVS 1909; medical officer to Ballymena Workhouse, Fever Hospital and post office; general practitioner in Ballymena; of Wellington Street, Ballymena from c 1900 and of Moyola, Broughshane Road, Ballymena from c 1930; married 19 August 1889 in Glenarm Presbyterian Church, county Antrim, Anna Davison, daughter of William Davison, farmer; father of Dr John Harold Davison of Liverpool and Dr Eric Alan Davison of Abergavenny; died 8 October 1942; probate Belfast 11 December 1942. [Belf GRO (d); Belf PRO, will cal; Kirkpatrick (1889); Kirkpatrick Archive; *Med Dir*; QCB adm reg; UHF database (m)].

DAVY, WILLIAM ROBERT (1869–1921), Letterkenny, Donegal;
born 12 March 1869 at Terenure, county Dublin, son of Dr Edmond W. Davy; educated at Rathmines School, Dublin, from 1879; studied medicine at Trinity College, Dublin; LM Rot Hosp Dub 1892; LM LCh LAO (TCD) 1895; medical officer of health to Fannad Dispensary District and medical officer to the constabulary; of Croaghan House, Tamney, Letterkenny; married Evelene Rorke, daughter of T.S. Rorke of 20 Brighton Square, Dublin; died 17 March 1921 at Croaghan House. [Figgis and Drury (1932); Kirkpatrick Archive; *Med Dir*].

DAWSON, LOUIS RICHARD (1857–c 1900), Indian Medical Service;
born 25 June 1857 in Cork, son of lieutenant-colonel Richard Dawson of Gortmore, Omagh; educated privately; studied medicine at Queen's College, Belfast, from 1869; MD (hons) MCh Dip Mid (QUI) 1873; joined the Indian Medical Service (Bengal establishment) as surgeon in 1889 at Gujurat; died c 1900. [Crawford (1930); *Med Dir*; QCB adm reg].

DAWSON, RICHARD (1783/4–1808), Army Medical Service;
   born 1783/4, third son of Captain Dawson of Boveen, Dungannon, county Tyrone; joined the Army Medical Service as assistant surgeon to the 26th Foot 1804; transferred to the 5th Garrison Battalion 1806 and the 7th Foot 1807; unmarried; died 24 October 1808 at Halifax, Nova Scotia, Canada. [*BNL* 9 December 1808 (d); Peterkin and Johnston (1968)].

DAWSON, WILLIAM (1793/4–1847), Dungannon, county Tyrone;
   born 1793/4, son of Captain — Dawson of Bovain House, Dungannon; MRCSE 1815; LAH Dub 1827; MD (Erlangen) 1839; surgeon and apothecary, of Scotch Street, Dungannon c 1819 and of Market Street, Dungannon c 1824 and later of Ranaghan, Dungannon; medical officer to Dungannon Union Workhouse; married 6 December 1822 in Drumcree Church of Ireland Church, Elizabeth Carrick (see will) of Richmond, county Armagh; father of the Rev Abraham Dawson, who was father of Dr William Richard Dawson (*q.v.*); died 23 January 1847 of fever caught in the discharge of his professional duties in the Dungannon Workhouse; probate Prerogative Court 11 February 1847 (will extant in PRO NI). [Apothecaries (1829); *BNL* 13 December 1822 (m), 17 June 1845 (m, brother) and 29 January 1847 (d); Belf PRO, prerog wills index; Belf PRO, T877/527; Bradshaw (1819); *Coleraine Chronicle* 30 January 1847 (d); Croly (1843–6); *Londonderry Sentinel* 30 January 1847 (d); Pigot (1824); Swanzy (1933)].

DAWSON, WILLIAM EDWARD (1857–1909), Clacton-on-Sea, Essex and Walton-le-Soken, Essex;
   born 23 August 1857 at sea, son of a gentleman, of The Terrace, Walton-on-the-Naze, Essex; educated at Beckford Grammar School, Woodbridge, Suffolk; studied medicine at Queen's College, Belfast, from 1876; LSA Lond 1882; LKQCPI and LM 1885; house surgeon to the Victoria Hospital, Worksop; resident medical officer to Tower Hamlets Dispensary; general practitioner of Tower Lodge, Clacton-on-Sea, Essex, c 1886 and Walton-le-Soken, Essex, c 1895; medical officer in charge of troops in Sierra Leone 1901; author of many medical publications; died 19 October 1909 at Hong Kong. [*Med Dir*; QCB adm reg].

DAWSON, WILLIAM JAMES (1873–1945), Newtownhamilton, county Armagh;
   born 1873 at Rosemount, Roscrea, county Tipperary, son of William James Dawson, banker, of Rosemount, and Susan Elizabeth Molloy; educated in Clonmel and Drogheda; studied arts and medicine at Trinity College, Dublin, from 1890; BA (TCD) 1894; LM Rot Hosp Dub; MB BCh BAO 1895; MD 1902; medical officer to Newtownhamilton Dispensary District and constabulary c 1896–1945; married Eva Mary Manning (who died 5 August 1936), daughter of Dr Manning of Rathdrum, county Wicklow; died 26 September 1945 at Newtownhamilton; probate Belfast 28 August 1946. [Belf GRO (d); Belf PRO, will cal; Dub GRO (b); Kirkpatrick Archive; *Med Dir;* TCD adm reg; *TCD Cat,* vol III (1906)].

DAWSON, WILLIAM RICHARD (1864–1950), Dublin, Edinburgh, Belfast and RAMC;

born 11 September 1864 at Stramore, Gilford, county Down, son of the Rev Abraham Dawson, Dean of Dromore, and Charity Wade of Paddenstown, county Meath; grandson of Dr William Dawson (*q.v.*) of Dungannon; educated at Dungannon Royal School; studied arts and medicine at Trinity College, Dublin, from 1882; BA (TCD) 1887; LM Rot Hosp Dub 1890; MB BCh BAO 1890; MD 1891; LRCPI 1896; Stewart Scholarship in Mental Diseases 1895; certificate of the Medico-Psychological Association 1896; MRCPI 1898; FRCPI 1899; DPH 1907; demonstrator in pathology at Royal College of Surgeons in Ireland; assistant physician to Royal Edinburgh Asylum 1894; resident medical superintendent to Farnham House and Maryville Private Hospital for Mental Diseases, Finglas, Dublin 1894–1911; assistant registrar and resident medical officer to Cork Street Fever Hospital, Dublin; government inspector of Lunatic Asylums in Ireland from 1911; lieutenant-colonel RAMC (temporary) 1914–18; specialist in nervous diseases for troops in Ireland; of Claremont, Burlington Road, Dublin, c 1916 and of 7 Ailesbury Road, Dublin c 1918–21; co-editor of the *Journal of Mental Science* c 1920; MRIA 1915; author of various papers on mental disease; OBE 1919; moved c 1922 to 26 Windsor Park, Belfast; consultant neurologist to Ministry of Pensions; chief medical officer to Ministry of Home Affairs, N. Ireland 1922–9; president of the Medico-Psychological Association; later of Westlecott Manor, Swindon; married 1 September 1898 in St Peter's Church of Ireland Church, Dublin, Florence Anne Elizabeth Shekleton (who died 9 July 1948), daughter of Robert William Shekleton, QC, of 31 Fitzwilliam Square, and sister of Dr Richard Auchmuty Shekleton (*q.v.*); died 17 June 1950 in a nursing home in Swindon; buried in Lansdown Cemetery, Bath; probate Bristol 20 September 1950. [*BMJ* obituary (1950); *DIB* (2009); Dub GRO (m); Kirkpatrick Archive; Lond PPR, will cal; *Med Dir*; Swanzy (1933); TCD adm reg; *TCD Cat*, vol II (1896)].

DAY, HENRY GRATTAN GUINNESS (1857/8–1943), Dublin;

born 1857/8; studied medicine at the Royal College of Surgeons in Ireland; LRCSI 1884; LKQCPI 1886; LM Rot Hosp Dub 1887; resident surgeon in Jervis Street Hospital, Dublin; medical officer to No 3 South City Dispensary, Dublin, of 21 Lower Leeson Street, Dublin; retired c 1939 to Cavangarden, Ballyshannon; married —; died 17 December 1943 at Cavangarden; probate Belfast 31 March 1944. [Belf PRO, will cal; Dub GRO (d); *Med Dir*].

DEACON, JOHN GILLESPIE (1859–1903), Army Medical Service;

born 11 June 1859 at Kildarton, county Armagh, third son of John Gillespie Deacon, merchant, of 'The Hill', Kildarton, county Armagh, and Elizabeth Dobbin; brother of Dr William Oliver Deacon (*q.v.*) and Henrietta Adelaide Deacon who married her cousin Dr Leonard Dobbin Gamble (*q.v.*); educated at HM St George's Private School; studied medicine at Edinburgh University and, from 1876, at Queen's College, Belfast; LAH Dub 1880; MD MCh (RUI) 1883; joined the Army Medical Service as surgeon (afterwards surgeon captain) 1886; retired to Warlingham House, West Croydon, Surrey, 1894; married 4 March 1891 at Croydon, Surrey, Caroline Elizabeth Pook (who was born 1867, married (2) 2 May 1908 John Davis-Smith of Beaconsfield, Buckinghamshire, and died 30 December 1951 at Poole, Dorset), elder daughter of Frederick Pook of Thornton Heath, Surrey and Brighton, Sussex; father of Dr John Nissen Deacon, MC, MD (Lond) 1915; died 30 June 1903 at Warlingham House. [*Burke's Irish Family Records* (1976); Lond GRO (d); *Med Dir*; Peterkin and Johnston (1968); Power, Barbara, pers com; QCB adm reg].

DEACON, ROBERT (1838–74); Indian Medical Service;
born 1 March 1838 (Crawford) or 9 November 1830 (Burke), at Kildarton, county Armagh, son of John Deacon of Armagh City and 'The Hill', Kildarton, and Elizabeth Gillespie, a cousin of Leonard Gillespie RN (*q.v.*); brother of John Gillespie Deacon, who was father of Dr William Oliver Deacon (*q.v.*) and Dr John Gillespie Deacon (*q.v.*); studied medicine at the Ledwich School, Dublin; LRCS Edin 1863; LM Anglesey Lying-in Hospital, Dublin; LRCP Edin 1864; joined the Indian Medical Service (Bengal establishment) as assistant surgeon 1865; surgeon 1873; married 16 March 1866 in St Mary's Church of Ireland Church, Dublin, Henrietta Courtney of Clones, county Monaghan (who was born 4 August 1841 and died 26 October 1901), daughter of James Courtney, merchant, of 170 Great Britain Street, Dublin; died 29 January 1874 at Hazaribagh, Bengal. [*Burke's Irish Family Records* (1976); Crawford (1930); Dub GRO (m); *Med Dir;* Power, Barbara, pers com].

DEACON, WILLIAM OLIVER (1854–84), Liverpool, Lancashire, and Richill, county Armagh;
born 22 August 1854 at Kildarton, county Armagh, eldest son of John Gillespie Deacon, merchant, of 'The Hill', Kildarton, county Armagh, and Elizabeth Dobbin; brother of Dr John Gillespie Deacon (*q.v.*) and Henrietta Adelaide Deacon who married her cousin Dr Leonard Dobbin Gamble (*q.v.*); studied medicine at Edinburgh University and the Ledwich School and Adelaide and Coombe Hospitals, Dublin; LRCP LRCS and LM Edin 1876; LAH Dub 1876; surgeon to the Liverpool, Brazil and River Plate Steam Navigation Company c 1877; resident surgeon to the West Derby Hospital, Everton c 1880–83; general practitioner, of Richhill 1883–4; unmarried; died 24 January 1884 at Richhill; probate Armagh 13 February 1884. [Belf PRO, will cal; Dub GRO (d); *Burke's Irish Family Records* (1976); *Med Dir;* Power, Barbara, pers com].

DEANE, ANDREW (1846–1922), Indian Medical Service and Belfast;
born 2 December 1846 in Limavady, county Londonderry; brother of William Deane (*q.v.*); studied medicine at the Ledwich School, Dublin; LAH Dub 1868; LM Coombe Hosp Dub 1868; LRCSI 1869; FRCSI 1881; MD (Durham) 1881; joined the Indian Medical Service (Bengal establishment) as assistant surgeon 1869; surgeon 1873; surgeon major 1881; lieutenant-colonel 1895; brigade surgeon in the North-West Province of India for 11 years; residency surgeon in Jammu and Kashmir 1886–98; inspector-general of Civil Hospitals of Punjab 1898–1900; retired to Clifton, near Bristol 1900; (medical) superintendent of Royal Victoria Hospital, Belfast 1901–20; retired to 28 Cobham Road, Southend-on-Sea, Essex 1920–22; married —; father of Dr Reginald Neville Deane, MB (QUB) 1919, of London; died 29 November 1922 at Southend-on-Sea; probate London 15 February 1923. [Crawford (1930); Kirkpatrick Archive; *Lancet* obituary (1922); Lond GRO (d); Lond PPR, will cal; *Med Dir*].

DEANE, CHARLES CHATTERTON (1867–1926), Loughgall, county Armagh; born 25 May 1867 at Newlawn, county Dublin, son of Alexander Sharpe Deane, JP, and Elizabeth Hargrove; educated privately; studied arts and medicine at Trinity College, Dublin, from 1885; LM Coombe Hosp Dub 1890; BA MB BCh BAO (TCD) 1892; MD 1895; resident surgical pupil at the City of Dublin Hospital; medical officer, medical officer of health and public vaccinator to Loughgall Dispensary District; medical officer to constabulary and certifying factory surgeon; OBE c 1919; married Adelaide E. Stocker, daughter of Captain Stocker; father of Hector Charles Chatterton Deane, MB (TCD) 1921, FRCS; died 10 April 1926 at The Infirmary House, Armagh; probate Belfast 13 January 1927. [Belf GRO (d); Belf PRO, will cal; Dub GRO (b); Kirkpatrick Archive; *Med Dir*; TCD adm reg; *TCD Cat*, vol II (1896), Young and Pike (1909)].

DEANE, WILLIAM (1856–95), Indian Medical Service; born 28 March 1856, probably in Limavady, county Londonderry; brother of Colonel Andrew Deane, IMS (*q.v.*); studied medicine at the Ledwich School, Dublin; LRCSI 1879; LRCP Edin 1879; FRCSI 1892; joined the Indian Medical Service (Bengal establishment) as surgeon 1880; surgeon major 1892; served in Burma 1886–7 (medal with clasp); died 7 May 1895 at Naini Tal. [Crawford (1930); *Med Dir*].

DEASE, WILLIAM (c 1752–98), Dublin; born c 1752 at Lisney, county Cavan, younger son of Richard Dease and Anne Johnson; educated at Dr Clancy's school in Dublin; apprenticed to Michael Keogh, surgeon, of Dublin; studied medicine in Dublin and Paris; practised in surgery and obstetrics in Dublin; one of the founders of the RCSI in 1784, where he was the first professor of surgery 1785; surgeon to the United Hospitals of St Nicholas and St Catherine and to the Lock Hospital; fifth president of the RCSI 1789; visiting surgeon to the Meath Hospital from 1793; author of *Observations on Wounds in the Head* (1776), *Different Methods of Treating the Venereal Diseases* (1779) and *Observations on Midwifery* (1783) and (1798); of Meath Street, Usher's Quay and Sackville Street, Dublin; member of the Society of United Irishmen; married Elizabeth Dowdall, daughter of Sir Richard Dowdall of Portlumney, county Meath; father of Richard Dease PRCSI and Dr William Dease MRCSI; died 21 January 1798 at home in Sackville Street, possibly by suicide following a surgical mistake which caused a patient's death; a bust by John Smyth (1812) and a statue by Thomas Farrell were subsequently made for the RCSI. [Cameron (1916); *DIB* (2009); Kirkpatrick Archive; Martin (2003); Newmann (1993); O'Brien, Crookshank and Wolstenholme (1988); Ormsby (1888); *Oxford DNB* (2004); Widdess (1967)].

DEAZELEY, CHARLES (1817/8–82), Milford Haven, Pembrokeshire; born 1817/8, eldest son of John Deazeley of Corbally, county Tyrone; studied medicine at the Westminster Hospital, London; MA [?]; MRCSE 1841: demonstrator of anatomy and practical surgery; president of the Medical Society of the Westminster Hospital; surgeon, of Charles Street, Milford Haven; married 13 September 1853 in Steynton Church, Pembrokeshire, Eleanor Howard James, youngest daughter of Captain James, RN, of Milford Haven; died 22 November

1882 at Skelgagh, county Tyrone; probate London 11 January 1883. [Dub GRO (m); Lond PPR, will cal; *Londonderry Sentinel* 23 September 1853 (m); *Med Dir*].

DE BURGH, WALTER (1834–62), Sandymount, county Dublin;
born 20 November 1834, fifth son of the Rev William de Burgh, rector of Arboe, county Tyrone, and St John's, Sandymount, and his first wife, Anne Coppinger; LRCSI 1854; LKQCPI 1861; general practitioner, of Sandymount; married 28 January 1862 in Monkstown Church of Ireland Church, county Dublin, Mary Ellen Mayne, daughter of William Coleham Mayne, auditor-general of Sydney, New South Wales, Australia; she married (2) 25 March 1863 Dr George Granville Bothwell (*q.v.*); died 18 November 1862 at Rathmullan, county Donegal. [Burke *LGI* (1912); Dub GRO, (m); Fleming (2001); Leslie (1912); *Londonderry Sentinel* 21 November 1862 (d); *Med Dir*].

DE LA CHEROIS, EDMUND BOURJONVAL (1861–1901), Brighton;
born 20 January 1861 in Dublin, second son of Daniel De La Cherois of the Manor House, Donaghadee, and Ellen Leslie; educated at Armagh Royal School 1876–9; studied arts and medicine at Trinity College, Dublin 1879–86; BA (TCD) 1883; MB BCh 1886; MD 1890; general practitioner, of 1 Lower Rock Gardens, Brighton; married 7 January 1893 in All Souls Parish Church, Brighton, Caroline Fisher, daughter of Robert Adams, merchant, and widow of C. Fisher of Brighton; died 1 June 1901 at Sandford, Winscombe, Somerset as a result of a carriage accident (thrown from a trap while driving with his brother whom he was visiting); buried in Donaghadee graveyard; memorial window in Donaghadee Parish Church; administration London 26 July 1901. [*BNL* 3 June 1901 (d); Burke *LGI* (1912); Burtchaell and Sadleir (1935); Clarke, *County Down*, vol 16 (1976); Ferrar (1933); Lond GRO (m) and (d); Lond PPR, will cal; *Med Dir*; TCD adm reg; *TCD Cat*, vol II (1896)].

DELANAUZE, JOHN (d 1720), Killashandra, county Cavan;
'doctor of physic', of Killashandra; died 1720; will dated 1720 proved Kilmore Diocesan Court 1720. [Smythe-Wood (1975)].

DELAP, GEORGE GOSLETT (1873–1945), Royal Army Medical Corps;
born 13 April 1873 at Maghery, county Donegal, son of the Rev Alexander Delap, rector of Valentia Island, county Kerry, and canon of Limerick, and Anita Jane Goslett; LM Rot Hosp Dub; LRCPI and LM LRCSI and LM 1896; resident physician to the National Hospital for Diseases of the Heart, Soho Square, London; joined the Royal Army Medical Corps as lieutenant 1899; captain 1902; major 1911; lieutenant-colonel 1915; colonel 1925; served in South Africa 1899–1902, in India 1902–05, South Africa 1912–14, Mediterranean Expeditionary Force 1915–16, Mesopotania 1916–20, West Africa 1923–4, India 1925–9; DSO 1901; CMG 1918; married —; died 27 June 1945 in a nursing home in Dublin; buried on Valentia Island. [Drew (1968); Dub GRO (d); Hitchings, Paul, pers com; Kirkpatrick Archive; *Med Dir*].

DELAP, WILLIAM (*fl c* 1785), Dublin, Naval Medical Service and Ramelton, county Donegal;
> apprenticed to 'Surgeon Maxwell' of the Tyrone Infirmary; surgeon, of Dublin; joined the Naval Medical Service as assistant surgeon; general surgeon with apothecary's shop in Ramelton 1784; married 5 July 1785 Jane Moore of Ramelton. [*BNL* 12 July 1785 (m); Hitchings, Paul, pers com; *Londonderry Journal* 25 May 1784 (advert)].

DE MONTMORENCY, ARTHUR HILL TREVOR (1846–1910), Dublin;
> born 19 February 1846, fourth son of the Rev Hervey Morres, fourth Viscount Mountmorres, Dean of Achonry; educated at Armagh Royal School 1858–60 and Dungannon Royal School; studed arts and medicine at Trinity College, Dublin, from 1864; BA (TCD) 1868; MB 1873; LRCSI and LM 1873; MD 1875; general practitioner, of 'The Grange', Carrickmines, county Dublin; married 28 March 1878 Caroline Kemmis (who died July 1937), younger daughter of the Rev George Kemmis of St Helen's, Blackrock; died 1 January 1910 at 'The Grange'; probate Dublin 12 April 1910. [Belf PRO, will cal; Burke *Peerage and Baronetage* (1938); Ferrar (1933); Kirkpatrick Archive; *Med Dir;* TCD adm reg; *TCD Cat,* vol II (1896)].

DEMPSEY, SIR ALEXANDER (1852–1920), Belfast;
> born 1852 in Coldagh near Ballymoney, county Antrim, son of Bernard Dempsey of Coldagh, Ballymoney; educated at St Malachy's College, Belfast; studied medicine at the Catholic University of Ireland, and Queen's College, Galway; MD (RUI) 1874; LRCSI and LM 1874; physician and gynaecologist, of Donegall Street, 26 Clifton Street, 36 Clifton Street and later of Lisanore, Antrim Road, Belfast; a founder member of the North of Ireland Branch of the BMA and later its president; president of the Ulster Medical Society 1890–91; closely involved with the foundation of the Mater Infirmorum Hospital in 1883 and its extension which was opened in 1900; JP for Belfast 1880; knight bachelor 1911; married Jane — (who died 2 August 1905); father of Dr Alexander Joseph Dempsey; died 18 July 1920 at Coldagh, Somerton Road, Belfast; buried in Milltown Cemetery, Belfast; probate Belfast 22 November 1922. [Belf PRO, will cal; *BMJ* obituary (1920); Dub GRO (d); Hunter (1936); Kirkpatrick Archive; *Med Dir;* Merrick and Clarke, *Belfast,* vol 2 (1984); Newmann (1993); O'Donnell (2008); Young and Pike (1909)].

DEMPSEY, PATRICK JOSEPH (1850–1916), Army Medical Service;
> born 28 March 1850 at Mullaghinch, Aghadowey, county Londonderry, son of Francis Dempsey of Aghadowey; educated at St Malachy's College, Belfast; studied medicine at Queen's College, Belfast, from 1872, and the Catholic University, of Ireland; Coulter Exhibition, Belfast Royal Hospital, 1876; MD MCh Dip Mid (QUI) 1876; joined the Army Medical Service as surgeon 1878; surgeon major RAMC 1890; lieutenant-colonel 1898; served in Afghan War 1878–80 and in Burma 1886–7; retired 1905 to Clonmalier, Aghadowey, county Londonderry; unmarried; died 24 June 1916 at Mullaghinch, Aghadowey; probate Londonderry 24 June 1916. [Belf PRO, will cal; Dub GRO (d); *Med Dir;* Peterkin and Johnston (1968); QCB adm reg; RVH, Office of Archives].

DEMPSEY, PATRICK JOSEPH (1858/9–1937), Kingscourt, county Cavan;
born 1858/9; studied medicine at the Catholic University of Ireland; LRCPI and LM 1881; LRCSI 1881; LM Coombe Hosp Dub 1881; medical officer and medical officer of health to Kingscourt Dispensary District; medical officer to constabulary and certifying factory surgeon; married —; died 14 May 1937 at Kingscourt; probate Dublin 13 August 1937. [Dub GRO (d); Dub Nat Arch, will cal; *Med Dir*].

DENHAM, JOHN (1804–87), Dublin;
born 10 October 1804 in Killashandra, county Cavan, youngest son of the Rev Joseph Denham, minster of Killashandra Presbyterian Church, and his second wife Elizabeth Crowley; educated at RBAI and indentured to Ephraim McDowel of the Richmond Hospital, Dublin on 1 December 1826; studied medicine at the Royal College of Surgeons in Ireland and the Richmond and House of Industry Hospitals; MD (Edin) 1831 (thesis 'De rheumatismo acuto'); MRCSI 1831; LKQCPI 1861; FRCSI 1863; taught anatomy and physiology in the Park Street School and midwifery in the Carmichael School, Dublin, 1850–61; assistant master of the Rotunda Hospital, Dublin 1845–8 and master 1861–8; in general surgical and obstetrical practice in Dublin; president of the RCSI 1873–4; of 30 Merrion Squary, Dublin, and later of 7 Clarinda Park East, Kingstown, county Dublin; author of *Use of chloroform in 56 cases of labour* (1849); married (1) 8 December 1841 in Edinburgh, St Clair Knox (who died 4 December 1866), daughter of St Clair Stuart Knox; (2) Louisa Barclay, daughter of Samuel Purton of Cheshire and widow of Ebenezer Barclay of Aberdeen; father of Dr John Knox Denham FRCS of Donnybrook, and of Mary Denham who married Sir Henry Swanzy, ophthalmologist; died 21 January 1887 at 7 Clarinda Park East; buried in Mount Jerome Cemetery, Dublin; bust in the Royal College of Surgeons in Ireland and portrait in the Rotunda Hospital, Dublin; probate Dublin 23 April 1887. [*BNL* 11 January 1842 (m); Belf PRO, will cal; Cameron (1916); Edin Univ; Kirkpatrick Archive; Kirkpatrick and Jellett (1913); Martin (2003); *Med Dir*; *Memorials of the Dead*, vol XI, p 13; O'Brien, Crookshank and Wolstenholme (1988)].

DENHAM, THOMAS REID (1851–85), Belfast, and Wigton, Cumberland;
born September 1851 at Randalstown, county Antrim, son of the Rev William Denham, minister of Boveedy and later of Duneane Presbyterian Church, Randalstown; educated by the Rev Robert King of Ballymena; studied medicine at Queen's College, Belfast, from 1869; MD MCh Dip Mid (QUI) 1877; general practitioner, of 21 Victoria Place, Belfast; medical officer of health for Wigton District, of King Street, Wigton, c 1879–85, also medical officer and public vaccinator to Ireby District; died 15 September 1885; probate Carlisle 14 December 1885. [Barkley (1986); Lond PPR, will cal; *Med Dir*; QCB adm reg].

DENISTON, EDWARD (*fl c* 1826–8), Strabane, county Tyrone;
MRCS Edin 1826; LAH Dub 1827; apothecary, of Strabane; married 23 January 1828 Jane Kinkead, daughter of James Kinkead of Strabane. [Apothecaries (1829); *Strabane Morning Post* 22 August 1826 (news) and 29 January 1828 (m)].

DENMARK, ALEXANDER (c 1772–1836), Naval Medical Service;
born c 1772 in Belfast; joined the Naval Medical Service c 1790; surgeon's mate on HMS *Espoir* in 1795; surgeon to Haslar Hospital; physician to the Mediterranean fleet 1814; died 1836 in Torquay. [Lond PRO, Naval Records; *NMS* (1826); RVH Office of Archives].

DENNY, GEORGE ANTHONY (1842/3–73), Tralee, county Kerry;
born 1842/3, son of Willian Denny; educated at Portora Royal School, Enniskillen, from 1857; studied arts and medicine at Trinity College, Dublin, from 1860; BA (TCD) 1864; MB MA 1867; LRCSI 1868; general practitioner of Day Place, Tralee, county Kerry, and medical officer to Ardfert Dispensary District from 1870; married Cara Belinda —; died 16 February 1873 at Tralee, of typhus fever; administration Dublin 6 August 1873. [Belf PRO, will cal; Burtchaell and Sadleir (1935); Dub GRO (d); Kirkpatrick Archive; *Med Dir*; *Portora Register* (1940)].

DENNY, SAMUEL (*fl c* 1852), Naval Medical Service;
son of David Denny of Omagh; studied medicine at Edinburgh University; MD (Edin) 1848 (thesis 'On the fever in Ireland'); joined the Naval Medical Service; married 3 November 1852 at St Peter's Church, London, Susan Elizabeth Frances Renwick (who died 22 February 1862), daughter of lieutenant-colonel — Renwick. [Edin Univ; *Londonderry Sentinel* 19 November 1852 (m) and 7 March 1862 (d); McGrew (2001) (m)].

DENVIR, THOMAS (1816/7–42), Naval Medical Service;
born 1817/8, son of — Denvir of Hill Street, Newry; joined the Naval Medical Service as assistant surgeon, serving on HMS *Impregnable*; died 29 July 1842. [*BNL* 5 August 1842].

D'EVELYN, ALEXANDER McNEILL (1859/60–1933), Ballymena;
born 1859/60, third son of the Rev John William Devlin (later D'Evelyn), rector of Armoy, county Antrim; educated at Foyle College, Londonderry; studied arts and medicine at Trinity College, Dublin, from 1879; BA (TCD) 1883; MB BCh 1886; LM Rot Hosp Dub 1886; MD 1890; medical officer to a steamship company; general practitioner, of Ballymena; honorary medical officer to Ballymena Cottage Hospital, certifying factory surgeon and medical visitor in lunacy; unmarried; died 31 December 1933 at Ballymena Cottage Hospital; buried in the New Cemetery, Ballymena; administration Belfast 12 February 1934. [Belf GRO (d); Belf PRO, will cal; *BMJ* obituary (1933); Kirkpatrick Archive; Leslie (1993); *Med Dir*; TCD adm reg; *TCD Cat*, vol II (1896)].

DEVENEY, DANIEL (1803/4–69), Killybegs, county Donegal;
born 1803/4; LRCS Edin 1830; medical officer to Killybegs Dispensary District, Admiralty and constabulary; unmarried; died 19 January 1869 at Killybegs. [Croly (1843–6); Dub GRO (d); *Med Dir*].

DEVERELL, WILLIAM PONSONBY (d 1892), Rosslea, county Fermanagh, Dromore, county Down, Ravensdale, county Louth and Ardglass, county Down;
> son of William Deverell, esquire; studied medicine at the Royal College of Surgeons in Ireland and Glasgow University; LM SE Lying-in Hospital, Dublin, 1843; LRCSI and LM 1845; MD (Glas) 1846; medical officer to Rosslea Dispensary District, constabulary and Temporary Fever Hospital c 1847, to Dromore Dispensary District and constabulary c 1850–55 and to Ravensdale Dispensary District c 1855–60; of 20 Clanbrassil Terrace, Dublin c 1861; general practitioner, of Ardglass and medical officer to Shiel's Institute (almshouses), Killough c 1862–92; married 14 March 1854 in St Anne's Church of Ireland Church, Belfast, Mary Bingham, widow of Dr William Brewster Bingham (*q.v.*) and daughter of John Rowan, woollen draper, of Downpatrick; died 14 May 1892 at the Charlemont Street Private Hospital, Dublin; probate Dublin 12 June 1892. [Addison (1898); *BNL* 15 March 1854 (m); Belf PRO, will cal; Dub GRO (m); *Med Dir;* Pilson (1934)].

DEVINE, ROGER (*fl c* 1824), Cavan;
> apothecary, of Main Street, Cavan c 1824. [Pigot (1824)].

DEVLIN, HENRY WILLIAM (1835–96), Army Medical Service;
> born 1 May 1835 at Ballygawley, county Tyrone; MRCSE 1858; joined the Army Medical Service as staff assistant surgeon 1858; transferred to 44th Foot 1861 and Royal Artillery 1864; staff surgeon 1865; surgeon major 1873; retired on half pay 1878; served in Abyssinia 1868; married —; died 25 May 1896 at Blackrock, county Dublin; probate Dublin 11 September 1896. [Belf PRO, will cal; Dub GRO (d); *Med Dir*; Peterkin and Johnston (1968)].

DEVLIN, HENRY WILLIAM (d c 1955), Ballygawley, county Tyrone, and Manley, New South Wales;
> studied medicine at the Royal College of Surgeons in Ireland; LKQCPI and LM 1890; LRCSI and LM 1890; LM Rot Hosp Dub 1890; general practitioner, of Tullyglush House, Ballygawley c 1895–1920; emigrated to Australia c 1920; ship's surgeon with Burns Philip and Co, Sydney; general practitioner, of 'Odapa', Belgrave Street, Manley c 1920–30, and 21 Towns Road and 21 Strickland Street, Rose Bay c 1930–40; medical assistant to the Maryborough Clinic; retired to St Martin, Himeomea Avenue, Normanhurst, Sydney c 1940; died c 1955. [*Med Dir*].

DEVLIN, JOHN (d 1861), Maghera, county Antrim;
> MRCSE 1841; LFPS Glas 1846; general practitioner in Maghera and Bellaghy; died 12 March 1861. [*Bellaghy Hist Soc* (2003); *Med Dir*].

DEVLIN, RICHARD (*fl c* 1800), Belfast;
> apothecary to the Belfast Dispensary and Fever Hospital 1795–1806; married 12 November 1805 in St Patrick's Roman Catholic Church, Belfast, Addy McDougal. [Malcolm (1851); UHF database (m)].

DEVLIN, THOMAS (1822/3–50), Dungannon, county Tyrone;
born 1822/3; surgeon, of Dungannon c 1846–50; died 4 November 1850 'at his father's residence in Ballygawley'; administration Armagh Diocesan Court 1851. [*Coleraine Chronicle* 9 November 1850 (d); Dub Nat Arch, Armagh Dio Admins index].

DEVLIN, THOMAS PATTERSON (1853–1923), Edinburgh, Bristol, Gloucestershire, Great Yarmouth, Norfolk, and Balfour, British Columbia;
born 2 June 1853 in Belfast, son of Thomas Devlin, merchant, of Lonsdale Terrace, Crumlin Road, Belfast; educated at Belfast Academy; studied medicine at Queen's College, Belfast, from 1869; LRCP LRCS Edin 1882; LCPS Brit Col 1909; surgeon with the Cunard Steamship Company; general practitioner, of 18 Ranheilor Street, Edinburgh, c 1885, of 27 Morley Square, Bishopston, Bristol, c 1895 and of 42 King Street, Great Yarmouth c 1905; captain in the First Norfolk Volunteer Artillery 1899 and the Royal Field Artillery; emigrated to Balfour, British Columbia, 1909; major RAMC 1914–20; general practitioner and coroner, medical inspector of schools and surgeon to the Canadian Pacific Railway; author of various medical papers; died 30 October 1923 at Westminister, British Columbia. [*BMJ* obituary (1923); Kirkpatrick Archive; *Med Dir*; QCB adm reg].

DIAMOND, CHARLES (1814/5–86), Rasharkin, county Antrim;
born 1814/5; studied medicine at Glasgow Royal Infirmary and Anderson's College; LFPS Glas 1852; LM Edin 1857; LRCP Edin 1867; general practitioner, of Rasharkin and medical attendant to constabulary; married —; died 17 June 1886 at Ballylifford, Magherafelt. [Dub GRO (d); *Med Dir*].

DIAMOND, CHARLES JOHN (1849/50–81), Londonderry;
born 1849/50; LRCSI 1872; LRCP Edin 1876; general practitioner, of 4 Carlisle Road, Londonderry; married Norah —; died 16 July 1881 at Londonderry; administration London 2 November 1881. [Belf PRO, will cal; Dub GRO (d); *Med Dir*].

DICK, JOHN (d 1845), India;
son of A. Dick of Strabane, county Tyrone; died 13 November 1845, on a voyage from Calcutta to Demerara. [*Londonderry Sentinel* 4 April 1846 (d)].

DICK, JOHN (1847–71), Naseby and Otago, New Zealand;
born 1 May 1847 at Strabane, county Tyrone, son of James Dick of Knockiniller, Strabane; educated at Foyle College, Londonderry and Queen's College, Galway; studied medicine at Queen's College, Belfast, from 1866; MD (QUI) 1869; LRCSI and LM 1870; emigrated to New Zealand; medical officer to Mount Ida District Hospital, Otago, of Naseby near Otago; died 20 September 1871. [Gravestone inscription in Naseby, copied by Prof Elizabeth Trimble; Kirkpatrick Archive; *Med Dir*; QCB adm reg].

DICK, JOHN STAVELY (1865–1951), Manchester, Lancashire;
born 4 April 1865 near Lisburn, son of the Rev Thomas Houston Dick, minister of Bailiesmills Reformed Presbyterian Church, county Down, and — Graham of

Hillhead, Lisburn; educated at Londonderry Academical Institution; studied medicine at Queen's College, Belfast, from 1883; MB BCh BAO (RUI) 1893; general practitioner, of William Terrace, Harpurhey, Manchester; surgeon to Manchester and Salford Reformatory; honorary physician to Ancoats Hospital; clinical pathologist to Manchester North Hospital and to Manchester and Salford Skin Hospital; pathologist (VD) to Strangeways Prison; author of various medical publications; married —; father of Dr Thomas Bonser Staveley Dick, MB ChB (Manch) 1938; retired c 1945 to Westmoreland; died 3 December 1951 at St Nicholas' Vicarage, Great Crosby, Lancashire; administration Manchester 26 November 1952. [Lond PPR, will cal; Loughridge (1970); *Med Dir*; QCB adm reg].

DICK, ROBERT (1831–1913), Indian Medical Service;
born 1 June 1831, son of Robert Dick, farmer, of Garry, Ballymoney, county Antrim; brother of Ellen Megaw, mother of Sir John Megaw; educated by the Rev Joseph McFadden of Ballymoney; studied medicine at Queen's College, Belfast 1849–53, winning many scholarships and prizes; MD (QUI) 1853 with prize medal; MRCSE 1854; FRCSE 1867; joined the Indian Medical Service (Bombay establishment) as assistant surgeon 1855; surgeon 1867; surgeon major 1873; served in the Anglo-Persian War of 1856–7 and Indian Mutiny of 1857; retired 1876 and lived in Garry from 1874; unmarried; died 14 October 1913; buried in the Old Church Burying Ground, Ballymoney; probate Dublin 9 March 1914. [Belf PRO, will cal; Crawford (1930); gravestone inscription; Kirkpatrick Archive; *Lancet* obituary (1913); *Med Dir*; Megaw (1989); Plarr (1930); QCB adm reg].

DICKEY, ARCHIBALD ALEXANDER GEORGE (1861–1936), Ebbw Vale, Monmouthshire, and Colne and Bolton, Lancashire;
born 20 September 1861 at Carnowen, Raphoe, county Donegal, son of the Rev John Porter Dickey, minister of Carnone [sic] Presbyterian Church; educated at Raphoe Royal School; studied medicine at Queen's College, Belfast 1879–83; MD (RUI) 1883; LM KQCPI 1883; LRCSI 1885; general practitioner, of Hillside House, Ebbw Vale, c 1886; medical officer and public vaccinator to Colne Dispensary District, of Higgin House, Colne, 1890–1921; honorary medical officer to Colne Cottage Hospital; JP for Colne; MBE c 1919; medical officer and public vaccinator to Halliwell Dispensary District, Bolton from 1921, of Heysham House, Chorley Old Road, Bolton; retired to Hillside, Chorley Old Road, Bolton, c 1935 and finally to Wavecrest, 18 West End Parade, Pwllheli, Carnarvonshire; married Marion —; father of Dr H.W. Dickey of Pwllheli; died 19 January 1936; buried in Forebridge Parish Graveyard; probate London 27 February 1936. [*BMJ* obituary (1936); Kirkpatrick Archive; *Lancet* obituary (1936); Lond PPR, will cal; *Med Dir*; QCB adm reg].

DICKEY, HUGH JAMES (1864–1948), Manchester and Chalfont St Peter, Buckinghamshire;
born 25 March 1864 at Dickeystown, county Antrim, son of Robert Dickey; educated by the Rev W.J. McCracken; studied medicine at Queen's College, Belfast, from 1882; MB BCh (RUI) 1892; general practitioner, of 50 Didsbury Road, Heaton Mersey, Manchester, from c 1894; of Braeside, Chalfont St Peter, from c 1919; retired

c 1932 and moved to Walnut Tree Cottage, Firs Avenue, Felpham, Sussex c 1946; died 22 February 1948 at Chalfont St Peter; probate Manchester 21 December 1948. [Kirkpatrick Archive; Lond PPR, will cal; *Med Dir*; QCB adm reg].

DICKEY, SAMUEL (1848–c 1922), Belfast, London and Saskatchewan;
born 23 March 1848 at Ballyeaston, county Antrim, son of Thomas John Dickey, clerk, of Belfast; educated at RBAI; studied medicine at Queen's College, Galway and from 1875, at Queen's College, Belfast; MD MCh LM (QUI) 1879; general practitioner, of 9 Clifton Street, Belfast c 1885; assistant physician to Belfast Lying-in Hospital; consultant physician to the Hospital for Consumption and Chest Diseases, Belfast; moved to 54 Barry Road, East Dulwich, London, c 1890; returned to 8 Cavendish Terrace, Belfast c 1897; consultant physician to Forster Green Hospital, of 1 Ben Vista, Antrim Road, c 1900; moved c 1908 to Perdue, Saskatchewan; married 27 April 1882 at No 4 Newington, Belfast, Mary Ann Wright, daughter of Philip Wright, merchant, of Belfast; died c 1922. [Dub GRO (m); Kirkpatrick Archive; *Med Dir*; QCB adm reg; UHF database (m)].

DICKIE, GEORGE, (1812–82) Aberdeen and Belfast;
born 23 November 1812 in Aberdeen, son of John Dickie, purser RN, and Isabella Fowler; studied arts at Marishal College, Aberdeen; studied medicine at Aberdeen and Edinburgh Universities; MA (Aberdeen) 1830; MRCSE 1834; MD (Aberdeen, *hon causa*) 1841; lecturer in botany at King's College, Aberdeen 1839–49 and in materia medica 1840–44; librarian at the College 1840–44; professor of natural history, Queen's College, Belfast 1849–60; professor of botany, Aberdeen 1860–77; author of *Flora of Aberdeen* (1838), *Botanist's Guide to the Counties of Aberdeen, Banff and Kincardine* (1860), *Flora of Ulster* (1864) and other botanical works; Fellow of the Linnean Society 1863, honorary fellow of the Edinburgh Botanical Society 1879 and FRS 1881; married 27 August 1856 at 31 Union Place, Aberdeen, Agnes [or Anna (*BNL*)] Williamson Low, daughter of Alexander Low, merchant, of Aberdeen; died 15 July 1882 at 16 Alleyn Terrace, Aberdeen; confirmation of will Aberdeen 11 August 1882. [*BNL* 2 September 1856 (m); Deane (1924); Edin GRO (d); Edin Nat Arch, will cal; Martin (2010); Moody and Beckett (1959); Newmann (1993); *Oxford DNB* (2004); Praeger (1949)].

DICKSON, BENJAMIN (1782/3–1883), Naval Medical Service, and Dungannon, county Tyrone;
born 1782/3, fourth son of John Dickson of Mullycar, county Tyrone; probably apprenticed to a surgeon in Dungannon c 1803; joined the Naval Medical Service as assistant surgeon 1813; served on HMS *Bedford* (a prison hulk) and HMS *Spencer* 1813–18; on half pay 1818–21; surgeon and apothecary, of Market Street, Dungannon c 1819; served on HMS *Bann* on anti-slavery patrol 1821–3; surgeon 1824; served on other ships and finally on HMS *Samarang* 1825–31; retired on half pay 1831 to Union Place, Dungannon; married Catherine — (who died 13 June 1842 with administration of estate at Armagh 4 May 1860); died 22 February 1883 at Union Place; probate Armagh 5 May 1883. [Belf PRO, will cal; Bradshaw (1819); Croly (1843–6); Dickson, Christopher, pers com; Dub GRO (d); *Med Dir*].

DICKSON, D.M. (c 1772–c 1899), Naval Medical Service;
born c 1772, eldest son of the Rev William Steel Dickson, minister of Ballyhalbert, Portaferry and finally of Keady Presbyterian Churches, United Irishman, and Isabella Gamble; studied medicine at Edinburgh University and was elected annual president of the Hibernian Medical Society, Edinburgh 1794; joined the Naval Medical Service and died c 1799. [Dickson (1960); Latimer (1897)].

DICKSON, EDWARD THOMAS (1791/2–1869), Naval Medical Service and Jersey;
born 1791/2, son of Joshua Dickson of Magherafelt, county Londonderry; joined the Naval Medical Service as assistant surgeon; surgeon 1814; admiralty surgeon in Jersey, of 1 Grove Place, St. Helier; died 15 September 1869 in Jersey. [*Coleraine Chronicle* 2 October 1869 (d); *Med Dir*; *NMS* (1826)].

DICKSON, EMILY WINIFRED (1866–1944), Dublin and Rainhill, Lancashire;
born 13 July 1866 at 52 Scotch Street, Dungannon, county Tyrone, daughter of Thomas Alexander Dickson, linen manufacturer, privy councillor and Liberal MP for county Tyrone, of 52 Scotch Street, and Elizabeth Greer McGeagh; educated at the Ladies Collegiate, Belfast, Harold House School, London, and Milltown House, Dungannon 1879–84; studied medicine at the Royal College of Surgeons in Ireland from 1887; LKQCPI and LM, LRCSI and LM 1891; MB BCh BAO (RUI) (1st class hons and gold medal) 1893; FRCSI 1893 (first woman FRCSI); MD MAO (1896); studied also in Vienna and Berlin; assistant master of the Coombe Hospital, Dublin; gynaecologist on the staff of the Richmond Hospital, Dublin, 1894–9; general practitioner and medical officer of health; of 78 St Stephen's Green and 18 Upper Merrion Street, Dublin; presented with a silver tea set on retirement after marriage in 1899; of 8 Burlington Road, Dublin c 1910 and Castlewarden, Straffan, county Kildare c 1915; returned to work in 1915 to supplement the family's small income; assistant medical officer to the Rainhill Mental Hospital 1916; general practitioner, of Church Street, Ellesmere, Shropshire c 1917–19, of Wimbledon 1919–26; of Church Road, Tunbridge Wells, Kent 1928–30; 'travelling' c 1930–35; finally of 8 Treemain Road, Whitecraigs, Renfrewshire; returned to Rainhill Mental Hospital married 14 December 1899 in Ormond Quay Presbyterian Church, Dublin, Robert Macgregor Martin, accountant and textile manager, of Scotland and Dublin, who enlisted in the army in 1914, was later shell-shocked and unable to work, son of Joseph R. Martin; separated from her husband c 1919; mother of Dr Russell Dickson Martin, MB B Ch (Glas) 1923, who emigrated to Canada, and Elizabeth Winifred Martin ('Jane') who married 10 January 1927 Kenneth Mackenzie Clark, later Lord Clark; died 19 January 1944 at 8 Treemain Road; probate Llandudno 29 August 1944. [Bewley (2005); *DIB* (2009); Dickson, Christopher, pers com; Dub GRO (b) and (m); Edin GRO (d); Finn (2000); Kelly (2010); Lond PPR, will cal; *Med Dir; Oxford DNB* (2004)].

DICKSON, HUGH (d 1804), Portaferry, county Down;
fifth son of John Dickson, farmer, of Carnmoney; studied arts and medicine at Glasgow University; matriculated 1777; MA (Glas) 1781; MD 1784; possibly Dr Hugh Dickson, physician, of Portaferry; married — (who died 28 November

1805 'after a tedious illness'); died 7 November 1804 in Portaferry. [Addison (1898) and (1913); *BNL* 13 November 1804 (d) and 3 December 1805 (d)].

DICKSON, JAMES (1828/9–1902), Ballynahinch and Killinchy, county Down;
born 1828/9, son of James Hill Dickson of Banbridge; educated by Andrew Mullan of Banbridge; studied medicine at Peter Street School, Dublin, and Queen's College, Belfast, 1849–52; MRCSE and LM 1851; MD (QUI) 1852; medical officer to Ballynahinch Dispensary District and constabulary; JP; later of Ashville, Killinchy; married 28 March 1860, in First Killyleagh Presbyterian Church, Anna Richardson Harper (who was born 1835/6 and died 29 August 1864), younger daughter of Robert Harper of Maymore, Killyleagh, and Anne Kenning; father of Dr Robert Harper Dickson (*q.v.*); died 3 October 1902 in Dublin; both buried in Killyleagh Presbyterian graveyard; probate Belfast 4 March 1903. [*BNL* 30 March 1860 (m); Belf PRO, will cal, will; Clarke, *County Down*, vol 7 (1972); Dub GRO (m); QCB adm reg].

DICKSON, JAMES (1854–1913), Long Eaton, Derbyshire;
born 2 November 1854 at Corrgarry, Newbliss, county Monaghan, son of John Dickson, farmer, of Corrgarry; educated at Ballybay National School; studied medicine at Queen's College, Belfast, from 1874; LRCP LRCS Edin 1880; general practitioner of Long Eaton, from c 1885; retired c 1910; married Mary Isabella —; died 6 December 1913; probate Derby 24 March 1914. [Lond PPR, will cal; *Med Dir*; QCB adm reg].

DICKSON, JAMES (*fl c* 1890), Belfast and Ballynahinch, county Down;
son of T.H. Dickson, farmer; general practitioner, of Belfast and Ballynahinch; married 22 August 1890 in Fortwilliam Park Presbyterian Church, Elizabeth Edgar, daughter of the Rev David Edgar, minister of Second Ballynahinch Presbyterian Church and Professor of Divinity. [Bailie and Kirkpatrick (2005); Dub GRO (m)].

DICKSON, JAMES REID (or ROBERT) (1843–99), Broughshane, county Antrim;
born 14 April 1843, son of Thomas Dickson of Broughshane; educated at the Franklin Place Academy, Belfast; studied medicine at Queen's College, Belfast, from 1860, and at the General Hospital, Belfast; MD (QUI) 1866; MCh 1868; LM RCSE 1868; house surgeon to Belfast Union Infirmary; medical officer to Broughshane Dispensary District; married —; died 14 September 1899 at Broughshane; probate Belfast 12 January 1900. [Belf PRO, will cal; Dub GRO (d); *Med Dir*; QCB adm reg].

DICKSON, JOHN (d 1835), Dungannon, county Tyrone;
general practitioner, of Dungannon; married (probably c 1790) Anne — (who was born 1764/5 and died 21 September 1839); died 1835. [*BNL* 1 October 1839 (d); Jackson (2011)].

DICKSON, JOHN (d c 1835), Dungannon, county Tyrone;
studied medicine at Edinburgh University; MD (Edin) 1830 (thesis 'De pneumonia'); MRCS; physician and surgeon, of Northland Row, Dungannon c 1819 and 1824;

married 2 November 1830 in St Martin's Church of Ireland Church, Portadown, Mary Sinnamon, third daughter of Thomas Sinnamon; died c 1835; probate Prerogative Court 1835. [*BNL* 9 November 1830 (m); Belf PRO, prerog wills index; Bradshaw (1819); Edin Univ; Pigot (1824)].

DICKSON, JOHN DUNBAR (1853–1923), Great Marlow, Buckinghamshire;
born 22 January 1853 in Belfast, son of Henry H. Dickson of Garville Avenue, Rathgar, Dublin, and Letitia —; educated at the Brothers' Grammar School, Warrington; studied medicine at Trinity College, Dublin, and, from 1872, at Queen's College, Belfast; MD MCh Dip Mid (QUI) 1876; LRCSI 1876; LM Rot Hosp Dub 1876; house surgeon to Buckinghamshire General Infirmary and Ripon Dispensary; assistant house surgeon to Darlington Hospital; medical officer and public vaccinator to Bisham and Hurley Dispensary Districts and medical officer of health to Marlow and Wycombe from c 1880; of The Gables, Marlow, Buckinghamshire; JP 1906; married 1883 Emily Margaret Carson, daughter of David Carson of Glasgow; died 13 January 1922 at Marlow; buried in Marlow Parish Graveyard; probate London 12 April 1923. [*BMJ* obituary (1922); Kirkpatrick Archive; *Lancet* obituary (1922); Lond PPR, will cal; *Med Dir*; QCB adm reg].

DICKSON, JOHN ROBINSON (1819–82), Kingston, Ontario, Canada;
born 1819 in Dungannon, second surviving son of David Dickson and his second wife, Isabella Robinson; half-brother of Dr William Dickson (*q.v.*) and nephew of Dr Benjamin Dickson (*q.v.*); apprenticed to Dr William McClean, surgeon and apothecary of Dungannon (*q.v.*), 1830–36; studied medicine at RBAI and Anderson College, Glasgow c 1835–7; emigrated to Canada with his mother and sisters 1837; apprenticed to Dr John Hutchison for 5 years; licensed to practise medicine in Upper Canada 1841; studied medicine in New York 1841–2; MD (New York), the first MD awarded there; surgeon to Kingston General Hospital from 1846 and on the Hospital Board from 1853; established the Medical School of Queen's College, Kingston 1854 and was appointed vice-president, professor of surgery, and in 1863, dean of the Faculty of Medicine; MD (Kingston) 1863; MRCP Lond 1863; MRCSE 1863; FRCS Edin 1863; appointed surgeon to Kingston Penitentiary (after conflict with Dr John Stewart); resigned from Queen's College and, after the passing of the Upper Canada Medical Act in 1865, became first President of the new Medical Board and established a new Royal College with its FaguIty of Medicine in 1866; medical superintendent of Rockwood Lunatic Asylum, Kingston 1869–78; author of *Prison Reports* and *Asylum Reports* and various medical papers; retired 1881 to Wolfe Island; married 1839 Ann E. Benson (who was born 1813 in Fintona, county Tyrone, and died 29 December 1896), first cousin, and daughter of his mother's sister; father of Dr Anne E. Dickson of Kingston, Dr John Robinson Dickson, junior, IMS, and Dr Charles Rea Dickson of Toronto; died 23 November 1882. [Dickson, Christopher, pers com; *Med Dir*].

DICKSON, JOHN STEELE (1817–62), Belfast;
born 1818 [gravestone] or 1823 [c of m], son of Dr William Dickson (*q.v.*) of Belfast, surgeon; educated at RBAI from 1831 and Collegiate Department; General Certificate 1838; ordained presbyterian minister of Ballygawley, county Tyrone 1842;

resigned 1844 to study medicine; LFPS Glas 1848; MD (St Andrew's) 1860 (by examination); medical officer to Ballygomartin Dispensary, Belfast 1848–62; married 24 October 1849 in St Anne's Church of Ireland Church, Belfast, Sarah Mairs of Belfast (who was born 1824 and died 2 June 1910), eldest daughter of Thomas Mairs of Great George's Street, Belfast, and Greenisland, county Antrim; died 8 April 1862; buried in Knockbreda parish graveyard; administration Belfast 6 October 1862. [Barkley (1986); *BNL* 8 October 1850 (b), 16 September 1853 (b) and 28 November 1853 (d, child); Belf PRO, will cal; Clarke, *County Down*, vol 2 (2nd ed, 1988); Dub GRO (m); Fisher and Robb (1913); Kirkpatrick Archive; *Med Dir*; Smart (2004); UHF database (m)].

DICKSON, JOHN WILSON (1858–1932), Lisnaskea, county Fermanagh, and Colwyn Bay, Denbighshire;
born 1858 at Edentilone, county Tyrone, son of James Dickson of Fairview House, Edentilone; educated at Carnteel School; studied medicine at Queen's College, Belfast, from 1892 and the Royal College of Surgeons in Ireland; LRCP LRCS Edin 1900; LFPS Glas 1900; DPH RCSI 1905; general practitioner of Lisoneill House, Lisnaskea; medical officer of Pettigo Dispensary District; moved c 1923 to 4 Meirion Gardens, Colwyn Bay; retired c 1928 to The Bawn, Aughnacloy, county Tyrone; married —; father of Dr William Arthur Dickson of Derryinch, Enniskillen; died 16 June 1932 at Derryinch; probate Londonderry 22 February 1933. [Belf GRO (d); Belf PRO, will cal; Kirkpatrick Archive; *Med Dir*; QCB adm reg].

DICKSON, JOSEPH (1814/5–50), Drummully, county Cavan;
born 1814/5; MD [?]; of Drummully House; died 26 May 1850 at Castle Hamilton. [*BNL* 7 June 1850 (d)].

DICKSON, ROBERT (d 1841), Naval Medical Service, and Cookstown and Dungannon, county Tyrone;
son of the Rev Thomas Dickson, minister of Sandholes Presbyterian Church, county Fermanagh; brother of Dr Thomas Dickson, Naval Medical Service (*q.v.*); joined the Naval Medical Service as assistant surgeon; retired to Killyneddan, Cookstown; married —; father of Margaret Dickson who married 28 October 1842 in Sandholes, Forbes Seaton; died 25 September 1841 at Alder Lodge, Rock, Dungannon; administration Armagh Diocesan Court 1841. [*BNL* 1 October 1841 (d) and 1 November 1842 (m, daughter); Dub Nat Arch, Armagh Dio Admins index; *Londonderry Sentinel* 2 October 1841 (d)].

DICKSON, ROBERT (1804/5–62), Dromore, county Down;
born 1804/5, son of Robert Dickson, gentleman; educated by Mr Armstrong; studied arts and medicine at Trinity College, Dublin, from 1824; BA (TCD)1829; MB 1832; general practitioner, of Tullycairne, Dromore, also of Loughbrickland; married 3 March 1836 in Newry, Matilda Mitchel (who died 3 June 1897), daughter of the Rev John Mitchel of Newry and sister of John Mitchel, the Irish patriot; their son, John Mitchel Dickson, was father of Dr Charles Dickson, RAMC, author of *Revolt in the North* (1960); died 17 July 1862 at Tullycairne; buried in Dromore Non-Subscribing Presbyterian Graveyard; probate Belfast 10 September 1862. [*BNL* 8 March 1836

(m); Belf PRO, will cal; Burtchaell and Sadleir (1924); Clarke, *County Down*, vols 19 (1983) and 21 (1998); Croly (1943–6); Kirkpatrick Archive; *Londonderry Sentinel* 12 March 1836 (m); RVH Office of Archives, Mitchel family tree].

DICKSON, ROBERT HARPER (1861–1934), Newcastle-under-Lyme, Staffordshire; born 5 March 1861 at Ballynahinch, county Down, son of Dr James Dickson of Ballynahinch (*q.v.*) and Anna Richardson Harper; educated at RBAI; studied medicine at Queen's College, Belfast, from 1878, and the Catholic University of Ireland; LRCSI 1887; LKQCPI and LM 1887; resident surgeon at St Mark's Ophthalmic Hospital, Dublin for 2 years; medical officer to Newcastle-under-Lyme Workhouse and District and constabulary; public vaccinator; assistant ophthalmic surgeon, c 1895–1914, ophthalmic surgeon c 1914–22 and then consulting ophthalmic surgeon to the North Staffordshire Infirmary and Eye Hospital; of Nelson Place, Newcastle-under-Lyme; of 23 The Ironmarket, and Grindley House, Newcastle, from c 1920 and of 16 King Street, Newcastle from c 1932; married 1 November 1901 at Mountpleasant, Banbridge, Mary Edith Edgar, daughter of John Edgar, bleacher, of Banbridge; died 9 November 1934 at Grindley House; probate London 28 January 1935. [Dub GRO (m); Lond PPR, will cal; *Med Dir*; QCB adm reg; UHF database (m)].

DICKSON, ROBERT LOWRY (1846–95), Maguire's Bridge, county Fermanagh; born 27 March 1846 at Hollybrook, Lisnaskea, county Fermanagh, son of lieutenant-colonel Robert Lowry Dickson of the Indian Army; educated at the Royal Military College, Sandhurst; studied medicine at Queen's College, Galway, Dr Steeven's Hospital, Dublin, and from 1876, at Queen's College, Belfast; LRCP LRCS and LM Edin 1883; surgeon to the British India and Castle Mail Packet Steamship Companies; medical officer to Maguire's Bridge Dispensary District and constabulary, of Riverside, Maguire's Bridge; died 14 August 1895; administration Armagh 19 June 1896. [Belf PRO, will cal; Dub GRO (d); *Med Dir*; QCB adm reg].

DICKSON, THOMAS (LOY) (1782/3–1857), Naval Medical Service and Cookstown, county Tyrone;
born 1782/3, son of the Rev Thomas Dickson, minister of Sandholes Presbyterian Church, county Fermanagh; brother of Dr Robert Dickson, Naval Medical Service (*q.v.*); joined the Naval Medical Service as surgeon; general practitioner in Cookstown c 1846; married Sarah —; died 27 January 1857 at Tullygowan, Cookstown.(or Tullygarvan) administration Armagh 8 February 1858 [*BNL* 1 November 1842 (m, niece); Belf PRO,will cal; *Coleraine Chronicle* 7 February 1857 (d); Croly (1843–6); Pigot (1824)].

DICKSON, WILLIAM (1788/9–1835), Lisburn, county Antrim, and Belfast;
born 1788/9; surgeon, of Lisburn c 1815 and Belfast c 1820; married 6 October 1815 Miss — Steele, daughter of Adam Steele of Derriaghy, county Antrim; father of Dr John Steele Dickson (*q.v.*) and of James Dickson, medical student, who died 16 June 1851; died 22 August 1835. [*BNL* 13 October 1815 (m), 28 August 1835 (d) and 18 June 1851 (d, son); Dub GRO (m, son)].

DICKSON, WILLIAM (1794/5–1860), Naval Medical Service and Cookstown, county Tyrone;
> born 1794/5, fourth son of David Dickson, merchant, of Dungannon, and his first wife, Susanna —; nephew of Dr Benjamin Dickson, Naval Medical Service (*q.v.*) and half-brother of Dr John Robinson Dickson (*q.v.*); joined the Naval Medical Service as assistant surgeon 1812; served in the 1812 War with the United States and on HMS *Ocean* 1814; served on HMS *Camel* in 1821 when it brought home Napoleon's personal entourage, from which he acquired a pair of Napoleon's black silk stockings (now on view in a Toronto museum); retired as unfit 1839; surgeon, of Cookstown; died 20 February 1860 at his home near Armagh; buried in Lagger Hill Church of Ireland Graveyard, Loughgall. [*BNL* 25 February 1860 (d); Dickson, Christopher, pers com; gravestone inscription; *Londonderry Sentinel* 24 February 1860 (d); *NMS* (1826)].

DILL, EDWARD FRANCIS (1850–90);
> born 1850, younger son of Moses Dill of Springfield, county Donegal, and Isabella Reid; MD [?]; not in *Medical Directory* or *Medical Register*; died 1890. [*Burke's Irish Family Records* (1976)].

DILL, REV EDWARD MARCUS (1813–62), Coagh, county Tyrone, and Clonakilty, county Cork;
> born 7 March 1813, youngest son of the Rev Richard Dill, minister of Knowhead Presbyterian Church, county Donegal; brother of Jane Dill who married Dr Andrew Thompson of Londonderry (*q.v.*); first cousin of Professor Robert Foster Dill (*q.v.*); studied arts and medicine at Glasgow University; matriculated 1828; MA (Glas) 1831; MD 1834; never practised medicine but was ordained at Cookstown in 1835; minister of Coagh Presbyterian Church 1835–8; minister of Trinity Presbyterian Church, Cork 1838–46; Home Mission Agent and later Secretary of the Scottish Reformation Society; collected large sums in the USA in aid of the famine sufferers, in 1848; author of *The Mystery Solved: or Ireland's Miseries: their cause and cure* (1852) and *The Gathering Storm of Britain's Romeward Career*; minister of Clonakilty 1860–62; married 9 August 1837 Sarah Jane Robinson of Coagh; died 23 November 1862 at Fethard, county Tipperary; buried in Clonmel. [Addison (1898) and (1913); *Burke's Irish Family Records* (1976); *Coleraine Chronicle* 29 November 1862 (d); Crone (1928); Dill (1992); Kirkpatrick Archive; McConnell (1951); Newmann (1993)].

DILL, FRANCIS NESBITT (c 1816–46), Hong Kong;
> born c 1816 at Castlefin, county Donegal, son of the Rev Samuel Dill, minister of Donoughmore Presbyterian Church, county Donegal, and Hester Foster, only child of Robert Foster of Berwick Hall, Donoughmore; brother of Professor Robert Foster Dill of Belfast (*q.v.*); nephew of Dr Marcus Dill of Limavady (*q.v.*); MRCSE 1839; MD (Edin) 1840 (thesis 'On erysipelas'); assistant to Dr Marcus Dill c 1846; colonial surgeon in Hong Kong; founder of the China Medico-Chirurgical Society; unmarried; died 30 September 1846 of fever, at Victoria, Hong Kong; 'greatly beloved in the country, his death is felt as a public loss'. [*BNL* 15 January 1847 (d); *Burke's Irish Family Records* (1976); Croly (1843–6); Dill (1992); Edin Univ].

DILL, JAMES SCOTT (1850–82), Indian Medical Service;
born 31 July 1850, third son of the Rev James Reid Dill, minister of Dromore Presbyterian Church, county Tyrone, and Sarah Sproule (widow of Andrew Sproule and daughter of James Scott of Ballyarr, county Donegal); educated at RBAI; studied medicine at Queen's College, Belfast, from 1866 and the General Hospital, Belfast; MD MCh (QUI) 1872; joined the Indian Medical Service (Madras establishment) as assistant surgeon 1873; surgeon 1873; married Gertrude Greene (who was born 1855/6 and died 23 November 1940), daughter of C.H. Greene of Johnstown House, county Cavan; died 31 July 1882 at Merkara, Coorg, India. [*Burke's Irish Family Records* (1976); Crawford (1930); Dill (1992); Kirkpatrick Archive; *Med Dir*; QCB adm reg].

DILL, JOHN (1778–1871), Brighton, Sussex;
born 1778, third son of Marcus Dill of Springfield, Fanad, county Donegal, and Mary McClure of Convoy; worked on the farm at Springfield until he was aged 30; studied medicine at London; MD [?]; MRCSE 1814; surgeon to an East India Company ship; general practitioner in Brighton, of 21 Regency Square and 3 Western Cottages, Brighton; retired c 1860; married Elizabeth Hall (who died 1869), daughter of Timothy Hall of Brighton; died 26 November 1871 at 3 Western Cottages, Brighton; probate Lewes 1 March 1872. [Burke *LGI* (1958); *Burke's Irish Family Records* (1976); Dill (1992); Lond GRO (d); Lond PPR, will cal; *Med Dir*].

DILL, JOHN (1802–32), London;
born 31 May 1802, eldest son of the Rev Richard Dill, minister of Knowhead (Muff) Presbyterian Church, county Donegal; studied medicine at Glasgow and Edinburgh Universities; CM (Glas) 1824; MD (Edin) 1825 (thesis 'De inhalatione per cutem'); house surgeon and physician to the London Hospital; author of *Empiricism*; unmarried; died 8 March 1832 of typhus caught in the attendance on his professional duties; 'from his erudition and very studious habits it cannot be doubted that had his life been prolonged he would have soon attained to great medical eminence'. [Addison (1898); *BNL* 27 April 1832 (d); *Burke's Irish Family Records* (1976); Dill (1992); Edin Univ].

DILL, JOHN (1821/2–78), Liverpool and Manchester, Lancashire;
born 1821/2, son of Dr Marcus Dill of Limavady (*q.v.*) and Elizabeth Gordon; studied medicine at Trinity College, Dublin; BA (TCD) 1845; MB 1849; LRCSI 1849; LSA Lond 1849; LM Dublin; medical officer to the South Dispensary District in Liverpool; general practitioner in Manchester, of Gordon Villa, Chorlton Road; unmarried; died 14 February 1878 at 20 Half Street, Cathedral Yard, Manchester. [*Burke's Irish Family Records* (1976); Burtchaell and Sadleir (1924); Dill (1992); Lond GRO (d); *Med Dir*].

DILL, MARCUS (1784–1867), Naval Medical Service and Limavady, county Londonderry;
born 4 May 1784, sixth and youngest son of John Dill, farmer, of Springfield, Fanad, county Donegal, and Susanna McClure of Convoy, county Donegal; studied arts and

medicine at Glasgow University; matriculated 1807; joined the Naval Medical Service as assistant surgeon 1808; surgeon 1812; retired on half pay 1815; MD (Glas) 1817; MCh 1852; physician, of Main Street, Limavady from 1817; medical officer to Limavady and Ballykelly Dispensary Districts; married (1) 11 January 1820 Elizabeth Gordon (who died 18 May 1826 at Limavady), eldest daughter of Robert Gordon of Belfast and Canada; (2) 27 November 1827 Margaret Lecky, only daughter of Alderman Thomas Lecky of Eglinton, county Londonderry; father of Dr John Dill of Manchester (*q.v.*); died 22 February 1867 at Ballykelly; buried in Ballykelly New Graveyard; probate Dublin 11 April 1867. [Addison (1898) and (1913); *BNL* 28 January 1820 (m), 6 June 1826 (d) and 4 December 1827 (m); Belf PRO, will cal; *Burke's Irish Family Records* (1976); *Coleraine Chronicle* 2 March 1867 (d); Dill (1992); *Londonderry Sentinel* 26 February 1867 (m); *Med Dir*; Mullin (1983); *NMS* (1826); Pigot (1824)].

DILL, MARCUS JOHN (1817–43), Naval Medical Service;
born 1817, younger son of the Rev Francis Dill, minister of Ray Presbyterian Church and later of Clough Non-Subscribing Presbyterian Church and Isabella Hamilton of Gortaquigley, Raphoe, county Donegal; younger brother of Dr William Dill of Canada (*q.v.*); joined the Naval Medical Service as assistant surgeon on HMS *Spiteful*; unmarried died 29 November 1843 in Hong Kong of a tropical fever aged 26; buried in Hong Kong and commemorated at Downpatrick Presbyterian Graveyard; will dated 8 January 1841, proved at Prerogative Court of Canterbury 16 December 1844. [*Burke's Irish Family Records* (1976); Clarke, *County Down*, vol 7 (1972); Dill (1992); *Downpatrick Recorder*, 24 February 1844 (d); Hitchings, Paul, pers com; *Londonderry Sentinel* 9 March 1844 (d)].

DILL, RICHARD (1822–1912), Brighton and Burgess Hill, Sussex;
born 18 July 1822, son of the Rev Richard Dill, minister of Ballykelly Presbyterian Church and Jane Gordon; cousin of Dr Marcus Dill of Ballykelly (*q.v.*) who was married to a sister of Jane Gordon; studied medicine at Edinburgh University; MA MD (Edin) 1845 (thesis 'De dyspepsia') 1845; LRCS Edin 1845; took over the general practice of his uncle Dr John Dill; of 19 Regency Square, Brighton, later of Burgess Hill; married 3 July 1856 in Little Shelford, Cambridgeshire, Augusta Caroline Wale (who was born 1823/4 and died 26 April 1925), daughter of General Sir Charles Wale, KCB, of 'The Hall', Little Shelford; father of Dr John Frederick Gordon Dill of Birchwood, Sussex; MB (Camb) 1884, and of Dr Robert Charles Gordon Dill of London, MRCSE, LRCP Lond 1885; died 24 February 1912 in Brighton; probate Lewes 12 May 1912. [*BNL* 17 July 1856 (m); *Burke's Irish Family Records* (1976); Burke *LGI* (1958); Dill (1992); Edin Univ; Lond PPR, will cal; *Med Dir*].

DILL, ROBERT FOSTER (1811–93), Belfast;
born 17 April 1811 at Castlefin, county Donegal, son of the Rev Samuel Dill, minister of Donoughmore Presbyterian Church, county Donegal, and Hester Foster of Berwick Hall, Donoughmore; brother of Dr Francis Nesbit Dill (*q.v.*); nephew of Dr Marcus Dill of Limavady (*q.v.*); first cousin of the Rev Dr Edward Marcus Dill (*q.v.*); studied medicine in Dublin and Glasgow; MRCSE 1833; MD CM (Glas)

1834; general practitioner with his uncle in Limavady; moved to Belfast practising as physician and obstetrician; physician to the Belfast Lying-In Hospital 1855–61 and to Belfast General Hospital 1856–64; professor of midwifery at Queen's College, Belfast 1868–93; city coroner for Belfast 1869–93; lost an eye during a riot in Belfast; honorary obstetrician and gynaecologist to the Ulster Hospital for Children and Women 1882–92; president of the Ulster Medical Society 1879–80 and 1883–4; of 3 Fisherwick Place c 1871; a strong opponent of women in medicine; married 5 February 1841 in Downpatrick, Catherine Houghton Rentoul, (who was born c 1821 and died 21 February 1892), only daughter of Dr James Rentoul of Downpatrick; [Catherine was great great grand-daughter of Dr Seneca Hadzor (*q.v.*) and Pilson dismissively described Dr Robert Foster Dill as 'an apothecary from Newtownlimavady and without any property']; father of Juana West Dill who married Dr John McCrea senior (*q.v.*) and of Hessy Foster Dill who married William Archer Kennedy and was mother of Dr Robert Foster Kennedy, MB (QUB) 1906, a distinguished neurologist of New York; portrait by Richard Hooke in Queen's University, Belfast; died 20 July 1893 at 3 Fisherwick Place; buried in Belfast City Cemetery; probate Belfast 13 December 1893. [Addison (1898); Belf City Cem, bur reg; *BNL* 9 February 1841 (m); Belf PRO, will cal; Black (1995); *Burke's Irish Family Records* (1976); Coakley (1992); *Coleraine Chronicle* 16 October 1869 (m. daughter); Croly (1843–6); Dill (1992); Dub GRO (d); Froggatt (1985); Hunter (1936); *Lancet* obituary (1893); *Londonderry Sentinel* 13 February 1841 (m); Macafee (1942) and (1975); Marshall and Kelly (1973); Moody and Beckett (1959); O'Brien, Crookshank and Wolstenholme (1988); Pilson (1838); Whitla (1901)].

DILL, WILLIAM (b 1816), Canada;
born 1816, elder son of the Rev Francis Dill, minister of First Ray Presbyterian Church and later of Clough Non-Subscribing Presbyterian Church, county Down, and Isabella Hamilton of Gortaquigley, Raphoe, county Donegal; brother of Dr Marcus John Dill, Naval Medical Service (*q.v.*); studied medicine at Glasgow University; CM (Glas) 1839; emigrated to Canada. [Addison (1898); *Burke's Irish Family Records* (1976)].

DILLON, EDWARD CUPPLES (d 1841), Islington, London;
son of William Dillon of Lisburn, county Antrim; MD [?]; died 16 December 1841 at Islington. [*BNL* 31 December 1841 (d)].

DILLON, HUGH (1756/7–1830), Limavady, county Londonderry;
born 1756/7 (family originally from Westmeath, but more recently from Lisdillon, county Londonderry); apothecary and surgeon, of Main Street, Limavady, c 1824; married — (who was born 1759/60 and died 4 October 1817); died 6 January 1830 in Limavady; buried in Roemill Road Graveyard, Limavady. [*BNL* 15 and 29 January 1830 (d); gravestone inscription; Hitchings, Paul, pers com; *Londonderry Sentinel* 23 January 1830 (d); Pigot (1824)].

DINNING, HENRY (*fl c* 1834–45), Bailieborough, county Cavan;
MRCSE 1834; accoucheur of the Coombe Lying-in Hospital; general practitioner, of Bailieborough c 1845. [Croly (1843–6).

DINSMORE, WILLIAM (1865–1946), Backworth and Earsdon, Northumberland, Dunoon, Argyleshire, and Cambuslaing, Lanarkshire;
born 1865, son of William Dinsmore, farmer, of Loughadian, Poyntzpass, county Down, and Margaret Fisher; studied medicine at Glasgow University; MB CM (Glas) 1887; MD 1898; general practitioner, of Backworth, Northumberland, and surgeon to the Backworth Collieries; medical superintendent of Conjoint Isolation Hospital, Earsdon, c 1890–1912; general practitioner, of Craigroy, Dunoon c 1912–28 and of St Magnus, Grenville Drive, Cambuslaing c 1928–38; retired c 1938 to St Magnus, 22 Barland Drive, Giffnock, Renfrewshire; married Flora Finlayson; died 24 December 1946 at 1055 Great Western Road, Glasgow; buried in Fourtowns Presbyterian graveyard, county Down; confirmation of will Paisley 15 January 1948. [Addison (1898); Edin GRO (d); Edin Nat Arch, will cal; gravestone inscription; *Med Dir*].

DISNEY, HENRY (1863–1904), London;
born 15 January 1863, second son of the Rev James Disney, rector of Killyman Church of Ireland Church, county Tyrone, and Susan Patton of Armagh; studied arts and medicine at Trinity College, Dublin, from 1880; BA (TCD) 1884; MB 1886; LM Rot Hosp Dub 1886; MD 1889; of 10 Blenheim Road and 6 Bath Road, Bedford Park, Chiswick c 1895; married Elizabeth Maughan; died 11 September 1904 at 6 Bath Road; administration (with will) London 6 October 1904. [Fleming (2001); Lond PPR, will cal, will; *Med Dir*; TCD adm reg; *TCD Cat*, vol II (1896)].

DIVER (DIVIR), JOHN HAWKINS (d 1839), Army Medical Service and Donegal;
studied medicine at Edinburgh University; MD (Edin) 1816 (thesis 'De dysenteria'); joined the Army Medical Service as hospital mate 1811; assistant surgeon to 79th Foot 1812; on half pay 1818–25; surgeon, of Donegal c 1824; surgeon with 91st Foot 1830; died 17 July 1839 in Donegal; probate Raphoe Diocesan Court 1839. [Edin Univ; *Londonderry Sentinel* 20 July 1839 (d); Peterkin and Johnston (1968); Pigot (1824); Thrift (1920)].

DIXON, AUGUSTUS EDWARD (1860–1946), Galway and Cork;
born 1860 in Belfast, son of Wakefield H. Dixon, merchant; educated in Belfast; studied arts and medicine at Trinity College, Dublin, from 1877; BA (TCD) 1881; MB MD 1885; of Dunowen, Belfast c 1886; professor of chemistry at Queen's College, Galway; professor of chemistry and member of council at Queen's College, Cork from c 1892, of Mentone Villa, Sunday's Well, Cork c 1900 and of 1 Fernhurst Avenue, Cork c 1920; retired as emeritus professor c 1925 to 19 Hatherley Road, Sidcup, Kent; married —; died 3 March 1946 at 19 Hatherley Road; probate London 13 June 1946. [Kirkpatrick Archive; Lond GRO (d); Lond PPR, will cal; *Med Dir*; TCD adm reg; *TCD Cat*, vol II (1896)].

DIXON, CHARLES HAMPDEN (1855–83), Army Medical Service;
born 4 June 1855 in Dublin, second son of the Rev Robert Vickers Dixon, rector of Clogherny, county Tyrone, and Katherine Maclean of Dublin; educated at Portora Royal School from 1869; studied arts and medicine at Trinity College, Dublin, from 1873; BA MB BCh (TCD) 1880; joined the Army Medical Service as surgeon 1880;

died 26 September 1883 at Cairo, Egypt. [Fleming (2001); *Med Dir*; Peterkin and Johnston (1968); *Portora Royal School Register* (1940); TCD adm reg; *TCD Cat*, vol II (1896)].

DIXON, SMITH (*fl c* 1845), Warrenpoint, county Down;
MCPS Glas; LAH Dub; general practitioner in Warrenpoint and medical officer to constabulary c 1845. [Croly (1843–6].

DIXON, THOMAS (d 1836), Newtownhamilton, county Armagh;
surgeon and apothecary, of Newtownhamilton; died 25 January 1836 at Newtownhamilton; administration Armagh Diocesan Court 1841. [*BNL* 9 February 1836 (d); Dub Nat Arch, Armagh Dio Admins index].

DOAK, GEORGE (1800/1–76), Naval Medical Service and Newtownstewart, county Tyrone;
born 1800/1; joined the Naval Medical Service as assistant surgeon 1833; died 12 November 1876 at Newtownstewart. [*Med Dir*].

DOAK, MICHAEL (d c 1855), Naval Medical Service;
joined the Naval Medical Service as assistant surgeon 1812; surgeon 1814; retired to Killymore, county Tyrone; married —; father of Mary Jane Doak who was born 1844/5 and married in 1864; died c 1855; probate Prerogative Court 1855. [Belf PRO, prerog wills index; Dub GRO (m, daughter); *Londonderry Sentinel* 4 November 1864 (m, daughter); *NMS* (1826)].

DOAKE, SAMUEL (1835–1901), Army Medical Service;
born 10 December 1835, son of Samuel Doake of Kinallen, Dromore, county Down, and Mary Baxter; studied medicine at Queen's College, Belfast, from 1855; BA (QUI) 1861; MD 1862; MA 1863; LM Belfast 1863; LFPS Glas and LM 1864; joined the Army Medical Service as staff assistant surgeon 1864; on half pay November 1873–January 1875; retired on half pay 1876; medical officer to Dromara Dispensary District for a short time but resigned because of ill health; married Frances Elizabeth Rowe (who died December 1888); died 13 March 1901 at Kinallen, Dromore, county Down; buried in Dromara First Presbyterian graveyard; administration Belfast 6 May 1901. [Belf PRO, will cal; Clarke, *County Down*, vol 19 (1983); Dub GRO (d); Kirkpatrick Archive; *Med Dir*; Peterkin and Johnston (1968); QUB].

DOBBIN, FRANCIS WILLIAM (1866–1928), St Alban's, Hertfordshire;
born 4 March 1866 in Dublin, only son of the Rev Frederick Dobbin, chancellor of Cork Cathedral, and Rebecca Low of Merion Castle, county Dublin; educated at Armagh Royal School 1880–85; studied arts and medicine at Trinity College, Dublin 1885–91; BA (TCD) 1889; MB BCh BAO 1891; MD 1893; house surgeon at the Cork Eye, Ear and Throat Hospital; medical officer of health for St Alban's, Hertfordshire; retired c 1905 to Kilmeen Rectory, Ballineen county Cork; unmarried; died 17 July 1928 at Desertserges Rectory, Enniskean, county Cork. [Cole (1903); Dub GRO (d); Ferrar (1930); Kirkpatrick Archive; *Med Dir;* TCD adm reg; *TCD Cat,* vol II (1896)].

DOBBIN, JAMES (1681/2–1757), Belfast;
born 1681/2, probably in Carrickfergus, county Antrim; studied medicine at Utrecht, Netherlands; MD (Utrecht) 1720 (thesis 'De angina' in Leyden Library); married Elizabeth Coleman, with children born 1745–9; general practitioner of Belfast; died 1757; buried in St Nicholas's Church, Carrickfergus (no memorial extant); probate Prerogative Court 1757. [Eustace (1949); Gillespie and O'Keefe (2006); McSkimin (1909), pp 180 and 422; Innes Smith (1932); Vicars (1897)].

DOBBIN, JOHN (c 1765–1820), Armagh;
born c 1765, third son of Leonard Dobbin of Armagh, and Mary Oates; MD [?]; unmarried; died 22 October 1820. [Burke, *LGI* (1912)].

DOBBIN, JOHN (1829/30–80), Keady, county Armagh;
born 1829/30; studied medicine at Glasgow University; MD (Glas) 1852; LRCS Ed 1870; LM KQCPI 1870; general practitioner, of Glen House, Keady; unmarried; died 10 December 1880 of typhoid fever at Keady; buried in Second Keady Presbyterian Graveyard; probate Armagh 21 January 1881. [Addison (1898); Belf PRO, will cal; Dub GRO (d); gravestone inscription; *Med Dir*].

DOBBIN, JOHN WILSON (1832–67), Naval Medical Service;
born 1832 at Cranfield, county Antrim, third son of Alexander Dobbin of Cappagh, county Down, and Cranfield, and Susannah Wilson; uncle of Dr William Dobbin of Banbridge, county Down (*q.v.*); MRCSE 1854; joined the Naval Medical Service as assistant surgeon 1856; served on HMS *Dauntless* 1859 and finally on HMS *Icarus*; surgeon 1865; unmarried; died 31 December 1867 at East Stonehouse, Plymouth, Devonshire, of paraplegia; probate London 11 April 1868. [*Burke's Irish Family Records* (1976); Lond GRO (d); Lond PPR, will cal; *Med Dir;* Power, Barbara, pers com].

DOBBIN, JOSEPH D. (d 1839), Newtownhamilton, county Armagh;
medical superintendent of Newtownhamilton Dispensary c 1815–39; died 13 August 1839, of pulmonary consumption. [*BNL* 20 August 1839 (d)].

DOBBIN, ROY SAMUEL (1873–1939), Cairo, Egypt;
born 22 November 1873 at Bressagh, county Down, son of Alexander Dobbin and Mary Ann Ringland (Munk) or only son of Samuel Dobbin (*Irish Times*); studied arts and medicine at Trinity College, Dublin, from 1891; BA (TCD) 1896; MB BCh BAO 1899; LM Rot Hosp Dub; MD 1903; FCOG 1929; FRCP Lond 1932; resident surgeon to Dr Steeven's Hospital, Dublin, 1899–1901; pathologist to Dr Steeven's Hospital 1902–04; assistant master of the Rotunda Hospital 1905–06; professor of obstetrics and gynaecology, Royal School of Medicine, Cairo, and senior obstetric surgeon and gynaecologist to the Kasr-el-Aini Hospital; captain in RAMC to the British Expeditionary Force in France 1914–18; received the order of the Nile 1937; OBE; noted collector of rare medical books, many of which passed to the Royal College of Physicians, London; unmarried; died 20 March 1939 at Port Said, Egypt; commemorated by a hospital medal and a named ward; probate London 12 June 1939. [*BMJ* obituary (1939); *Irish Times* 1939 (d); Kirkpatrick (1924);

Kirkpatrick Archive; *Lancet* obituary (1939); Lond PPR, will cal; *Med Dir*; *Munk's Roll*, vol 5; *TCD Cat*, vol III (1906)].

DOBBIN, WILLIAM (d c 1803), Magheragall, county Antrim, and Moira, county Down;
surgeon, of Magheragall and Moira; married Elizabeth — (who was born 1768/9 and died 23 September 1843); died c 1803; administration Connor Diocesan Court 1803. [*BNL* 26 September 1843 (d); Dub Nat Arch, Connor Dio Admins index].

DOBBIN, WILLIAM (1843–1903), Maghera, county Londonderry and Banbridge, county Down;
born 19 August 1843 at Anaghlone, county Down, son of the Rev William Dobbin, minister of Second Anaghlone Presbyterian Church, and Mary Robinson of Shane's Castle, county Antrim; educated at RBAI; studied arts and medicine at Queen's College, Belfast, from 1863; BA with 1st class Hons and Gold Medal (QUI) 1864; MA (hons) 1866; MD 1867; LRCS Edin 1867; FRCSI 1886; medical officer to Maghera Dispensary District c 1871; medical officer to Banbridge Dispensary District 1874; of 6 Church Street, Banbridge, from c 1885; married January 1875 Margaret Robson (who was born 1853/4 and died 13 February 1931), daughter of John Robson of Tobermore; father of Dr John Robson Dobbin, MB BCh (Edin) 1903; died 18 October 1903 at a private hospital in Fitzroy Avenue, Belfast; probate Belfast 4 January 1904. [Belf PRO, will cal; *Burke's Irish Family Records* (1976); Dub GRO (d); Kirkpatrick Archive; Linn (1935); McConnell (1951); *Med Dir*; QCB adm reg].

DOBBIN, WILLIAM WEIR (1815/6–49), Newtownhamilton, county Armagh;
born 1815/6; LRCS Edin; LAH Dub; surgeon and apothecary, of Newtownhamilton c 1845; married 29 May 1837 at Clarkesbridge Presbyterian Church, Margaret Simpson (who died 19 December 1847 at Newtownhamilton), daughter of William Simpson of Newtownhamilton; died 1 November 1849; administration Armagh Diocesan Court 1849. [*BNL* 2 June 1837 (m), 28 December 1847 (d) and 13 November 1849 (d); Croly (1843–6); Dub Nat Arch, Armagh Dio Admins index].

DOBBS, JOHN (1659–1739);
born 1659, elder son of Richard Dobbs of Castle Dobbs, and Dorothy Williams of Clints Hill, Richmond, Yorkshire; became a Quaker and practised as a physician; disinherited by his family and the estate passed to the younger son, Richard Dobbs; married 1739 —; died 1739. [*Burke's Irish Family Records* (1976); *Lisburn Fam Hist Soc*, vol 2 (2005)].

DOBSON, GEORGE EDWARD (1844–95), Army Medical Service, and Netley, Hampshire;
born 4 September 1844 in Edgeworthstown, county Longford; educated at Portora Royal School, Enniskillen, from 1857; studied arts and medicine at Trinity College, Dublin; BA (TCD) 1866; MB MCh 1867; MA 1875; First Senior Moderator and First Gold Medallist in Experimental and Natural Science; Classical Honourman and Stearns Exhibitioner; Gold Medal of the Dublin Pathological Society 1867;

joined the Army Medical Service as staff assistant surgeon 1868; surgeon major 1880; served in India 1868–75 and South Africa 1879; collected birds on the Andaman Islands, became a distinguished zoologist and was FRS, FLS and FZS; retired as surgeon lieutenant-colonel 1888; curator of the Royal Victoria Museum, Netley, from c 1878; of 26 Norland Square, Kensington; author of a *Monograph on the Asiatic Chiroptera* [bats] (1876) and a *Catalogue of the Chiroptera* (1878) and *Medical Hints to Travellers,* published by the Royal Geographical Society, reaching a 7th edition in 1893; died 26 November 1895 at West Maling, Kent; will dated 2 August 1888 proved London 29 February 1896. [Lond PPR, will cal, will; Martin (2010); *Med Dir*; *Oxford DNB* (2004); Peterkin and Johnston (1968); *Portora Royal School Reg* (1940); Praeger (1949); *TCD Cat,* vol II (1896)].

DODD, JOHN (1860–c 1929), Mozambique and Leicester;
born 14 March 1860 at Drumadonnell, county Down, son of William Dodd, farmer, of Woodford House, Dromara; educated at RBAI; studied medicine at Queen's College, Belfast 1876–81; MD MCh (QUI) 1881; general practitioner, of 58 Humberstone Gate, Leicester c 1885 and medical officer with the Compahnia do Assucar de Mozambique, Chinde, East Africa, c 1895; general practitioner, of 14 King Street, Leicester c 1904; visiting medical officer to the North Evington Poor Law Infirmary c 1907–14; of 64 New Walk, Leicester from c 1920; died c 1929. [*Med Dir*; QCB adm reg].

DO(UG)HERTY, ARCHIBALD (*fl c* 1835–45), Garvagh, county Londonderry;
studied medicine at RBAI from 1835; MRCSI; general practitioner in Garvagh, c 1843–6; married 9 July 1844 in the house of the bride's father, Matilda Brown (who died 14 January 1892), youngest daughter of the Rev James Brown, minister of First Garvagh Presbyterian Church, and Elizabeth Adams; possibly died c 1850. [*BNL* 23 January 1844 (m); Belf PRO, SCH 524/1.9/; Bennett (1974); Croly (1843–6)].

DOHERTY, BLAYNEY, A (1799/1800–44), Antrim;
born 1799/1800; surgeon, of Antrim; died 5 March 1844 at his home in Antrim. [*BNL* 8 March 1844 (d)].

DOHERTY, CHARLES (1842/3–97), Dungloe, county Donegal;
born 1842/3; studied medicine at Queen's College, Galway, and Anderson's College, Glasgow; LRCP LRCS Edin 1888; LFPS Glas 1888; medical officer to Dungloe Dispensary District; unmarried; died 4 December 1897 at the Workhouse Fever Hospital, Glenties, of typhus fever; administration Londonderry 30 March 1898. [Belf PRO, will cal; Dub GRO (d); *Med Dir*].

DO(C)HERTY, DANIEL (1866/7–1941), Clonmany, county Donegal;
born 1866/7; studied medicine at the Royal College of Surgeons in Ireland and Anderson's College, Glasgow; LRCP LRCS Edin 1891; LFPS Glas and LM 1891; medical officer to Clonmany Dispensary District, constabulary and army; married Elizabeth —; died 12 July 1941 at Cleagh, Inishowen; probate Dublin 6 November 1941. [Dub GRO (d); Dub Nat Arch, will cal; Kirkpatrick Archive; *Med Dir*].

DOHERTY, J. (*fl c* 1845), Antrim;
CM (Glas) [?]; general practitioner in Antrim c 1845; possibly died c 1850. [Croly (1843–6)].

DOHERTY, RICHARD (1813/14–76), Londonderry and Galway;
born 1813/4, son of John Doherty, gentleman; studied medicine at Edinburgh University; MD (Edin) 1833 (thesis 'De emphysemate pulmonum'; MD (RUI) 1862; general practitioner, of Mountjoy Square, Londonderry c 1847; professor of midwifery at Queen's College, Galway c 1870; author of papers on midwifery; retired to Redcastle, county Donegal; married 3 June 1847 in Upper Moville Church of Ireland Church, Jane Moore Dougherty, daughter of Thomas Dougherty of Redcastle; died 11 January 1876; administration Dublin 6 May 1876. [*BNL* 15 June 1847 (m); Belf PRO, will cal; Dub GRO (m) and (d); Edin Univ; *Londonderry Sentinel* 12 June 1847 (m); *Med Dir*].

DOHERTY, WILLIAM (*fl c* 1840), Naval Medical Service and Moville, county Donegal;
MD [?]; joined the Naval Medical Service; of Moville; married 26 November 1840 at Omagh, Mary Harkin, fourth daughter of Thomas Harkin of Omagh. [*BNL* 4 December 1840; McGrew (2001) (m)].

DOHERTY, — (1759/60–1804), Naval Medical Service and Trillick, county Tyrone;
born 1759/60; joined the Naval Medical Service as assistant surgeon; retired to Trillick; married Elizabeth — (who was born 1761/2 and died 15 April 1842); died 7 January 1804; buried in Old Kilskeery Graveyard, near Trillick. [Gallachair (1973), p 92].

DOLAN, JOHN JOSEPH (1873/4–1905), Lisburn, county Antrim;
born 1873/4; studied medicine at the Catholic University of Ireland; LM Rot Hosp Dub 1893; LRCPI and LM, LRCSI and LM 1895; general practitioner, of 16 Seymour Street, Lisburn; unmarried; died 30 January 1905 of phthisis, at 14 Kenilworth Square, Rathmines, Dublin. [Dub GRO (d); Kirkpatrick Archive; *Med Dir*].

DOMVILLE, JAMES (b c 1770), Naval Medical Service;
born c 1770, probably in Edinburgh, son of a linen draper of Edinburgh (with Ulster connections); brought up from the age of 10 by his sister Elizabeth and her husband Dr David McAnally (*q.v.*) in Markethill, county Armagh; joined the Naval Medical Service in 1798 as surgeon's mate; subsequently rose to become Deputy Inspector General of Naval Hospitals. [McAnally (1947)].

DONAHOE (DONOHOE), PATRICK (*fl c* 1812), Killashandra, county Cavan;
LAH Dub 1812; apothecary and surgeon, of Killashandra c 1824. [Apothecaries (1829); Pigot (1824)].

DONAHOO (DONAHOE), THOMAS (c 1770–1838), Army Medical Service;
born c 1770 in county Cavan, son of James Donahoo, farmer; studied arts and medicine at Trinity College, Dublin, and St Andrew's University; BA (TCD) 1798;

MD (St Andrew's) 1809 (on testimonials); LRCP Lond 1814; joined the Army Medical Service as assistant surgeon to the 9th Dragoons 1797; surgeon to the 38th Foot 1806; staff surgeon 1812; on half pay September 1814–March 1815; physician 1815; served in Peninsular War and was principal medical officer in Brussels during the battle of Waterloo; retired on half pay 1816; died 16 February 1838 at Torquay, Devonshire. [Burtchaell and Sadleir (1924); *Munk's Roll*, vol 3; Peterkin and Johnston (1968); Smart (2004)].

DONALDSON, EBENEZER (1855–1904), ship's surgeon, Burt, county Donegal and Londonderry;
born 1855; nephew of Dr Walter Bernard of Londonderry (*q.v.*); studied medicine at Dr Steeven's Hospital, Dublin; LKQCPI and LM 1877; LRCSI 1877; surgeon with the Royal Mail Steam Packet Company; medical officer of Burt Dispensary District, c 1886; founder, with Dr Walter Bernard, of the Eye and Ear Hospital, Fountain Street, Londonderry in 1881; general practitioner, of 49 Great James' Street, Londonderry, from c 1888; married —; died 7 April 1904 at 49 Great James Street, Londonderry; probate Londonderry 9 June 1904. [Belf PRO, will cal; Dallat (1990); Dub GRO (d); Johnston (1960); *Med Dir*].

DONALDSON, GEORGE (1865/6–93), Clontibret, county Monaghan;
born 1865/6, son of Dr Robert Donaldson of Clontibret (*q.v.*); brother of Dr Robert Lockhart Smyth Donaldson (*q.v.*) and Dr William Ireland Donaldson (*q.v.*); educated in Monaghan; studied arts and medicine at Trinity College, Dublin, from 1883; BA (TCD) 1889; MB BCh BAO 1890; LM Rot Hosp Dub 1890; surgeon on SS *Scotia*, Anchor Line; general practitioner of Fort Hill, Clontibret; unmarried; died 17 April 1893 at Sir Patrick Dunn's Hospital, Dublin. [Dub GRO (d); *Med Dir*; TCD adm reg; *TCD Cat,* vol II (1896)].

DONALDSON, JOHN (d c 1761), Kiloroagh, county Tyrone;
MD (Edin) 1750 (thesis 'De nephritide'); of Dublin, and later of Kiloroagh [sic]; died c 1761; probate Prerogative Court 1761. [Edin Univ; Vicars (1897)].

DONALDSON, JOHN (1859–1943), Army Medical Service;
born 31 December 1859, probably in Burt, county Donegal; LRCP LRCS Edin 1885; LFPS Glas 1885; joined the Army Medical Service as surgeon captain in 1886; major 1898; lieutenant-colonel 1906; served in Burma 1888–9 and South Africa in 1902; retired 1914 to Wisborough Green, Sussex; married Anne Harriet —; died 2 October 1943; probate Llandudno 11 January 1944. [Lond PPR, will cal; *Med Dir*; Peterkin and Johnston (1968)].

DONALDSON, RICHARD (1823/4–76), Crossmaglen, county Armagh;
born 1823/4, son of Joseph Donaldson; LM Rot Hosp Dub 1843; LRCSI 1844; medical officer to Crossmaglen Dispensary District and constabulary from 1845; of Sytrim House, Crossmaglen; unmarried; died 4 March 1876 at Sytrim House; buried in Creggan Graveyard with memorial tablet in Creggan Parish Church, county Armagh; administration Armagh 17 June 1876. [Belf PRO, will cal; Dub GRO (d);

Kirkpatrick Archive; McMahon and O'Fiaich (1972); *Med Dir*; *Memorials of the Dead*, vol XII, p 191].

DONALDSON, ROBERT (1822/3–1916), Clontibret, county Monaghan;
born 1822/3; studied medicine at Trinity College, Dublin, the Carmichael School and the Richmond Hospital, Dublin; LM Coombe Hosp Dub 1845; MRCSE 1849; medical officer to Castleshane Dispensary District, county Monaghan, and constabulary; JP; retired to 6 Chichester Terrace, Belfast, c 1900; moved to 23 Eaton Square, Terrynure, Dublin c 1912; married —; father of Dr Robert Lockhart Smyth Donaldson (*q.v.*), Dr William Ireland Donaldson (*q.v.*) and Dr George Donaldson (*q.v.*); died 7 April 1916 at 23 Eaton Square; probate Dublin 28 June 1916. [Belf PRO, will cal; Dub GRO (d); Kirkpatrick Archive; McCann (2003); *Med Dir*].

DONALDSON, ROBERT LOCKHART SMYTH (1861–1943), Monaghan;
born 1861 in county Monaghan, son of Dr Robert Donaldson (*q.v.*); brother of Dr William Ireland Donaldson (*q.v.*) and Dr George Donaldson (*q.v.*); educated at RBAI; studied arts and medicine at Trinity College, Dublin, and Sir Patrick Dun's Hospital; BA (TCD) 1883; LM Rot Hosp Dub 1884; MB BCh BAO 1885; MD 1897; senior assistant resident medical superintendent of the District Asylum, Monaghan 1885–1910; attacked by a patient and injured in 1909; general practitioner in Greystones from c 1910, of Craan, Greystones; retired c 1918 to 6 Wilton Place, Dublin; lived finally with his daughter, wife of the Rev Richard Bird, at The Rectory, Delgany, Wicklow; married Ellen Gertrude — (who died 23 April 1942); died 18 December 1943 at The Rectory; probate Dublin 1 May 1944. [*BMJ* (1910); Dub GRO (d); Dub Nat Arch, will cal, will; Kirkpatrick Archive; Leslie and Wallace (2001); McMahon and O'Fiaich (1972); *Med Dir;* TCD adm reg; *TCD Cat*, vol II (1896)].

DONALDSON, THOMAS CAMPBELL (1863–1922), ship's surgeon and Houndslow, Middlesex;
born 16 September 1863 at Glenafton, Stranorlar, county Donegal, son of Samuel Donaldson, farmer, of Glenafton; educated at Londonderry Academical Institution; studied medicine at Queen's College, Belfast, from 1881; MD MCh (RUI) 1887; BAO 1890; surgeon to Royal Mail Steamship Company; medical officer to Harlington District, Houndslow, from c 1890; honorary surgeon to Harlington Cottage Hospital from c 1900; retired c 1920 to the Elms, Harlington, Staines; married K.E. —; died 19 October 1922 of tuberculosis at Linford Sanatorium, Ringwood. [Lond GRO (d); *Med Dir*; QCB adm reg].

DONALDSON, WILLIAM IRELAND (1863/4–1931) London and Cane Hill and Epsom, Surrey, and RAMC;
born 1863/4, second son of Dr Robert Donaldson (*q.v.*) of Clontibret, county Monaghan; brother of Dr Robert Lockhart Smyth Donaldson (*q.v.*) and Dr George Donaldson (*q.v.*); educated at RBAI; studied arts and medicine at Trinity College, Dublin, from 1880; BA (TCD) 1883; MB 1885; LM Rot Hosp Dub 1885; BCh 1886; MD 1897; resident medical and surgical assistant to Whitworth Hospital

Dublin; surgeon on SS *Lake Huron*; senior assistant medical officer to Camberwell House Asylum and London County Asylum, Cane Hill; clinical assistant to WR Asylum, Wakefield; medical superintendent to the London County Asylum, The Manor, Epsom c 1905; lieutenant-colonel RAMC during World War I; officer commanding The Manor War Hospital, Epsom; retired to 2 Abbeylands, Killiney, Dublin, c 1920 and to Fairholme, Ailesbury Park, Dublin, c 1925; unmarried; died 15 March 1931 at Fairholme; probate Dublin 12 June 1931. [*BMJ* obituary (1931); Dub GRO (d); Dub Nat Arch, will cal; Kirkpatrick Archive; *Med Dir;* TCD adm reg; *TCD Cat,* vol II (1896); *TCD Reg*].

DONNAN, WILLIAM DUNLOP (1869–1941), Holywood, county Down;
born 16 April 1869 at Colombo, Ceylon, eldest son of William Donnan of Toome; elder brother of Prof Donnan of University College, London; studied medicine at Queen's College, Belfast, from 1888; MB BCh BAO (RUI) 1893; MD with Gold Medal 1897; house physician and surgeon to the Belfast Royal Hospital; surgeon to the Anchor Line; medical officer to Castlereagh No 2 Dispensary District and constabulary; of 12 High Street, Holywood; president of the Ulster Medical Society 1917–18; author of various medical papers; commodore Royal North of Ireland Yacht Club; married 19 April 1906 in St Mathias' Church of Ireland Church, Dublin, Alice Caroline Isabella Magee, only daughter of David Magee, District Inspector RIC, of Taghmon, county Wexford; father of Dr Laurence Frederick Donnan, LMSSA Lond 1931, LRCP Edin 1932, and Dr Hilary Lorrain Donnan of Holywood, MB BCh BAO (QUB) 1932; died 15 March 1941 at 12 High Street; administration (with will) Belfast 8 May 1941 and 1 March 1950. [Belf GRO (d); Belf PRO, will cal; *BMJ* obituary (1941); Dub GRO (m); Kirkpatrick Archive; *Med Dir*; QCB adm reg; Young and Pike (1909)].

DONNELL, IGNATIUS SIMON (*fl c* 1757), Sligo and Donegal;
of Sligo and Donegal; studied medicine at Rheims University; MD (Rheims) 1757. [Brockliss].

DONNELL, JAMES (*fl c* 1795), Ballydonaghy, county Antrim;
LAH Dub 1795; apothecary, of Ballydonaghy. [Apothecaries (1829)].

DONNELLY, CHARLES (*fl c* 1853), Corbally, county Tyrone;
MD [?]; of Corbally; married September 1853 in Steynton Church, Pembrokeshire, Eleanor Howard James, youngest daughter of Captain James, RN, of Milford Haven, Pembrokeshire. [*BNL* 28 September 1853 (m)].

DONNELLY, HUGH (1875–1939), Draperstown, county Londonderry;
born 26 October 1875 at Magherafelt, county Londonderry, son of Felix Donnelly, farmer, of Magherafelt; educated at St Malachy's College, Belfast; studied medicine at Queen's College, Belfast, from 1893; MB BCh BAO (RUI) 1899; medical officer and medical officer of health to Draperstown Dispensary District; married Rose —; died 30 June 1939 at Draperstown; administration (with will) Londonderry 4 December 1939. [Belf GRO (d); Belf PRO, will cal; Kirkpatrick Archive; *Med Dir*; QCB adm reg].

DONNELLY, PATRICK (*fl c* 1713), Armagh;
of Armagh; studied medicine at Rheims University; MD (Rheims) 1713. [Brockliss].

DONNELLY, SAMUEL (1815/6–62), Naval Medical Service;
born 1815/6, eldest son of Thomas Donnelly, farmer, of Ray, Ramelton, county Donegal; joined the Naval Medical Service as assistant surgeon; retired as staff surgeon to Ramelton; RM; will dated 17 March 1842 when he was an assistant surgeon in London; died 22 December 1861 at Malvern Wells, Worcestershire; probate Londonderry 19 March 1862. [Belf PRO, will cal, will; Lond GRO (d); *Londonderry Sentinel* 3 January 1862 (d); *Med Dir*].

DONNELLY, THOMAS JOHN (1843–c 1890), Demerara, British Guiana and Omeath, county Louth;
born November 1843 in Newry, son of John Donnelly of Newry; educated by Mr O'Neill of Newry; studied medicine at the Royal College of Surgeons in Ireland, Meath Hospital, Dublin, and from 1865, at Queen's College, Belfast; LM Rot Hosp Dub 1865; LRCSI 1867; MD (QUI) 1871; medical officer in Demerara, British Guiana, from c 1875; general practitioner, of Laburnum Cottage, Omeath from c 1880; died c 1890. [*Med Dir*; QCB adm reg].

DONOGHOE, MICHAEL (1818/9–88), Killashandra, county Cavan;
born 1818/9; studied medicine at King's College, London; MRCSE 1839; accoucheur of the Westminister Lying-in Hospital, London; general practitioner in Killashandra and medical officer to the constabulary, c 1846; of Carrigallen, county Leitrim c 1859; married Sarah —; died 7 March 1888 of typhoid fever at Killahurk, county Leitrim; probate Cavan 18 May 1888. [Belf PRO, will cal; Croly (1843–6); Dub GRO (d)].

DONOUGHUE, JOHN (*fl c* 1795), Stradone, county Cavan;
LAH Dub 1795; apothecary, of Stradone. [Apothecaries (1829)].

DOONAN, JOHN ARTHUR CLARKE (1868–1924), ship's surgeon and Northwich, Cheshire;
born 13 August 1868 at Newry, county Down; educated at Wesley College, Dublin; studied medicine at Glasgow University and, from 1891, at Queen's College, Belfast; MB CM (Glas) 1896; surgeon to the Hall Line Steamship Company; medical officer, public vaccinator and certifying factory surgeon to the Northwich Dispensary; of Witton House, Northwich; medical officer to the post office and police; honorary surgeon to Victoria Infirmary; temporary lieutenant RAMC 1914–18; married Adina —; died 17 March 1924; probate London 5 June 1924. [Addison (1898); Lond PPR, will cal; *Med Dir*; QCB adm reg]

DORMAN, HENRY HOBART SEYMOUR (1868–1961), Keady, county Armagh;
born 21 December 1868 at Brookview, Whitechurch, county Cork, sixth son of the Rev Thomas Dorman, rector of St Michael's Church of Ireland Church, Cork and Charlotte Isabella Hobart; studied arts and medicine at Trinity College, Dublin, from 1883 (aged 14); BA (TCD) 1888; LM Rot Hosp Dub 1889; MB BCh BAO 1890;

MD 1891; medical officer and medical officer of health to Keady Dispensary District; medical officer to constabulary and certifying factory surgeon; of Willowbank and the Garden House, Keady; retired c 1959; married —; father of Dr Henry Hobart George Dorman of Armagh, MB BCh BAO (TCD) 1930; died 29 May 1961 at Willowbank; probate Belfast 14 September 1961. [Belf GRO (d); Belf PRO, will cal, will; Cole (1903); Dub GRO (b); *Med Dir;* TCD adm reg; *TCD Cat,* vol II (1896)].

DORRIAN, EDWARD (1812/3–53), Belfast;
born 1812/3, son of Patrick Dorrian, merchant, of Downpatrick, and Rose Murphy; brother of Dr Patrick Dorrian, bishop of Down and Connor; LAH Dub; MRCSE; accoucheur of the Dublin Lying-in Hospital (Rotunda); surgeon, of Belfast; died 23 August 1853; buried in Downpatrick Cathedral graveyard; administration Connor Diocesan Court 1854. [Clarke, *County Down,* vol 7 (1993); Croly (1843–6); Dub Nat Arch, Connor Dio Admins index].

DOUGAN, GEORGE (1847–1924), Tartaraghan and Portadown, county Armagh;
born 1847 at Red Rock, county Armagh, son of John Dougan of Ballymacully, county Armagh; educated at Armagh Royal School 1861–6; studied medicine at Queen's Colleges, Galway and Belfast; MD MCh LM (RUI) 1875; LAH Dub 1876; medical officer to Tartaraghan Dispensary District, constabulary and certifying factory surgeon, of Millicent Terrace, Portadown; married —; father of Dr George Dougan, MB BCh BAO (TCD) 1906, and Dr Frederick Roberts Dougan, MB BCh BAO (TCD) 1914, both of Portadown; died 12 April 1924 at Portadown; probate Belfast 18 July 1924. [Belf GRO (d); Belf PRO, will cal, will; Ferrar (1930); Kirkpatrick Archive; *Med Dir*].

DOUGHERTY, ARCHIBALD
See DOHERTY

DOUGHERTY, GEORGE ALEXANDER (*fl c* 1865), Londonderry;
of Londonderry; studied medicine at Glasgow University; MD (Glas) 1865; CM 1866; 'no further trace'. [Addison (1898)].

DOUGHERTY, JAMES (*fl c* 1793), Belfast;
LAH Dub 1793; apothecary, of Belfast. [Apothecaries (1829)].

DOUGLAS, ALEXANDER (*fl c* 1789), Kilrea, county Londonderry;
surgeon, of Kilrea; married December 1789 Jane McKay. [*BNL* 8 December 1789 (d)].

DOUGLAS, ALLEN EDMOND (1834/5–94), Glasslough, county Monaghan and Warrenpoint, county Down;
born 1834/5; studied medicine at the Royal College of Surgeons in Ireland, Ledwich School and Jervis Street Hospital, Dublin; LRCSI 1856; LM RCSI 1857; MD (St Andrew's) 1858 (by examination); FRCSI 1874; demonstrator in anatomy at Dr Steeven's Hospital; medical officer to Glasslough and Emyvale Dispensary Districts and Trough Fever Hospital; sanitary medical inspector, Carlingford; medical officer

to Warrenpoint and Mayo Dispensary Districts; married Teresa —; died 25 April 1894 at Coolbawn, county Down; probate Belfast 21 May 1894. [Belf PRO, will cal; Dub GRO (d); McCann (2003); *Med Dir;* Smart (2004)].

DOUGLAS, CHARLES JAMES (1856–1943), ship's surgeon, Killashandra, county Cavan, South Africa and Abingdon, Berkshire;
 born 23 September 1856; studied medicine at the Royal College of Surgeons in Ireland; LRCSI 1880; LKQCPI and LM 1881; surgeon to the Union Castle and Cunard Steamship Companies; general practitoner, of Tully House, Killashandra, county Cavan; district surgeon and health officer for Natal and surgeon to Grey's Hospital, Pietemaritzburg c 1900–04; returned to Killeshandra c 1905–22; moved to 'Tullyhunco', Oxford Road, Abingdon c 1922; retired c 1928 to 'Breffne', 53 Oxford Road, Abingdon; married Anna Maud Douglas (who died 4 January 1948), daughter of Henry Douglas; died 18 December 1943 at 53 Oxford Road; probate Oxford 20 April 1944. [Kirkpatrick Archive; Lond GRO (d); Lond PPR, will cal; *Med Dir*].

DOUGLAS, DAVID ALEXANDER (1826/7–50), Ballybentra, county Antrim;
 born 1826/7; MRCSI; surgeon; died 18 May 1850 at his mother's house in Ballybentra, of disease of the heart. [*BNL* 24 May 1850 (d)].

DOUGLAS, FRANCIS HAMMICK (1861–1927), Southsea, Hampshire, and Southend-on-Sea, Essex;
 born 20 February 1861 at Donaghadee, county Down, son of Stephen F. Douglas, captain RN, of 8 Cromwell Terrace, Belfast, and Glenghana, Southsea, Portsmouth; educated at the Royal Naval School, London; studied medicine at Queen's College, Belfast, from 1878; LRCP LRCS Edin 1887; LFPS Glas 1887; general practitioner, of 8 Alcester Terrace, Pelham Road, Southsea c 1895 and of 20 Norfolk Avenue, Southend-on-Sea c 1910; retired to the Mermaid Club, Rye, Sussex c 1917 and lived later at Twyford Abbey, Willesden, Middlesex; married Mary Louisa —; died 3 July 1927; probate London 26 August 1927. [Lond PPR, will cal; *Med Dir*; QCB adm reg].

DOUGLAS, JAMES HOLMES (1848/9–73), Londonderry;
 born 1848/9 in Londonderry, son of William Douglas, woollen draper, of Londonderry; educated privately; studied arts and medicine at Trinity College, Dublin, from 1866; BA (TCD) 1870; LRCSI; not in *Medical Directory* or *Medical Register*; unmarried; died 17 May 1873 in Main Street, Limavady, of tuberculosis. [Dub GRO (d); TCD adm reg; *TCD Cat*, vol II (1896)].

DOUGLAS(S), JOHN CUPPAGE (1778–1850), Dublin;
 born 1778 in Lurgan, county Armagh, son of a general practitioner of Lurgan; served 5 years' apprenticeship to his father; studied medicine at Trinity College, Dublin, and Edinburgh; LRCSI 1800; LAH Dub 1800; MD (St Andrews) 1803 (on testimonials); LKQCPI 1810; FKQCPI (hon) 1832; surgeon to the Militia Regiment of Foot in county Tipperary; obstetrician in Dublin; assistant master of the Rotunda Hospital 1808–12; with Joseph Clarke he 'laid the foundations of the high repute of

Dublin as a school of midwifery' (Wilde); of 16 Rutland Square East; author of various medical papers; married 23 January 1817 in Lisburn, Elizabeth Fulton (who was born 1783), second daughter of Joseph Fulton, solicitor and merchant, of Lisburn, and Ann Graham of Lisburn; died 20 November 1850 at 16 Rutland Square East; probate Prerogative Court 1850. [Apothecaries (1829); *BNL* 28 January 1817 (m); Croly (1843–6); Crone (1928); Dub Nat Arch, Prerog Wills index; Hope 1903); Kirkpatrick Archive; Kirkpatrick and Jellet (1913); Newmann (1993); O'Doherty (2002); Smart (2004); Widdess (1963)].

DOUGLAS, WILLIAM (1845–1929), ship's surgeon, Belfast and Leamington, Warwickshire;
born 13 December 1845, in Belfast, son of Alexander Douglas of 3 Windsor Terrace, Belfast; educated at Cookstown Academy; studied medicine at Queen's College, Belfast, from 1863 and Edinburgh University; MRCSE and LM 1868; MD (QUI) 1869; resident pupil at the General Hospital, Belfast; surgeon to the Cunard Line; general practitioner, of 3 Windsor Terrace, Belfast, c 1870–74; and of Livingstone Terrace, The Plains, Belfast c 1874–80; of 8 Leam Terrace, Leamington, c 1880 and 7 Clarendon Place, Leamington c 1881–1904; living at Goudhurst, Kent, c 1904 and finally at 'Lakeside', Richmond Road, Staines; married 1881 Anna Marie Fuller, youngest daughter of Captain S.J. Fuller, HEICS, of Canada; died 17 July 1929 at 'Lakeside'; probate London 19 September 1929. [*BMJ* obituary (1929); Kirkpatrick Archive; Lond GRO (d); Lond PPR, will cal; *Med Dir*; QCB adm reg].

DOUGLAS, WILLIAM S. (d 1842), Naval Medical Service and Lurgan, county Armagh;
LAH Dub 1809; joined the Naval Medical Service as assistant surgeon; apothecary and surgeon, of Lurgan; member of the Belfast Medical Society from 1825; died 8 May 1842 at his home in Lurgan. [Apothecaries (1829); *BNL* 13 May 1842 (d); Bradshaw (1819); Malcolm (1851); Pigot (1824)].

DOWDALL, EDWARD (1844/5–81), Banbridge, county Down;
born 1844/5, son of Matthew Dowdall, farmer; LFPS Glas 1868; general practitioner, of Bridge Street, Banbridge; married 22 November 1870 in Newry Roman Catholic Church, Jane Campbell, daughter of John Campbell, merchant; died 17 January 1881 at Bridge Street. [Dub GRO (d); *Med Dir*; UHF database (m)].

DOWGLASS, WILLIAM (1742/3–1812), Lurgan, county Armagh;
born 1742/3; surgeon and apothecary, of Lurgan; died 1 January 1812; 'in the arduous duties of a professional life was honoured with the esteem and confidence of a generous public'. [*BNL* 7 January 1812 (d)].

DOWLING, ARTHUR (1867/8–1947), St Helen's, Lancashire;
born 1867/8; studied medicine at Queen's College, Cork; LRCP LRCS Edin 1889; LFPS Glas 1889; house surgeon in the North Infirmary, Cork; medical officer of health of Haydock, St Helen's; civil medical officer to the Weeton and Knowsley Camps 1915–18; commanding officer of the South West Lancashire Volunteers 1914–18; JP for St Helen's; retired to Killowen, Rostrevor, county Down; married

Mary —; died 30 March 1947 at Killowen; probate Belfast 25 July 1947. [Belf GRO (d); Belf PRO, will cal; Kirkpatrick Archive; *Med Dir*].

DOWLING, EDMUND JOSEPH (1851–94), Limerick and Manchester, Lancashire;
 born 1851 at Kilrush, county Clare, son of John Dowling of 14 Thomas Street, Limerick; educated at the Jesuit Seminary, Limerick; studied medicine at Queen's College, Galway, and from 1871, at Queen's College, Belfast, also at the Carmichael School and Richmond and Jervis Street Hopitals, Dublin; LFPS Glas 1874; of 14 Thomas Street, Limerick c 1876; general practitioner, of 84 Bloomsbury, Rusholme Street, Manchester from c 1880; also of Temple Mungret, Limerick c 1893; died February 1894. [*Med Dir*; QCB adm reg].

DOWSE, RICHARD (*fl c* 1819–24), Dungannon, county Tyrone;
 surgeon and apothecary, of Church Street, Dungannon c 1819–24. [Bradshaw (1819); Pigot (1824)].

DOYLE, BERNARD (1842/3–c 1882), Castlewellan, county Down and Wellington, New Zealand;
 born 25 January 1842, son of Arthur Doyle of Gransha, Dromara, county Down; brother of Dr Patrick Doyle (*q.v.*); educated at Kilkinamurry School; studied medicine at Queen's College, Belfast, from 1860; LRCS Edin 1865; MD (QUI) 1871; MD (NZ *ad eundem*) 1876; general practitioner, of Castlewellan, county Down; emigrated to Wellington, New Zealand, c 1875; died c 1882. [*Med Dir*; QCB adm reg].

DOYLE, PATRICK (1849–c 1900), Christchurch, New Zealand;
 born 15 March 1849 at Gransha, Dromara, county Down, son of Arthur Doyle of Gransha; brother of Dr Bernard Doyle (*q.v.*); educated at Gransha School; studied medicine at Queen's College, Belfast, from 1866; MD and MCh (QUI) 1870; emigrated to Christchurch, New Zealand c 1872; general practitioner in Christchurch; died c 1900. [*Med Dir*; QCB adm reg].

DRAPES, THOMAS (c 1815–47), Kilnaleck and Mount Nugent, county Cavan;
 born c 1815; LRCSI; LAH Dub; accoucheur of the Dublin Lying-in Hospital (Rotunda); medical officer to the Ballymachugh and Drumlummon Dispensary District, of Lakeview, Kilnaleck, c 1846; married —; father of Dr Thomas Drapes of Enniscorthy; died 17 August 1847 at Lakeview, Mount Nugent, of fever. [*BNL* 27 August 1847 (d); Croly (1843–6); Kirkpatrick Archive].

DRENNAN, JOHN SWANWICK (1809–93), Belfast;
 born 3 October 1809 at Wem, Shropshire, fifth son of Dr William Drennan of Belfast (*q.v.*) and Sarah Swanwick of Wem; educated at RBAI from 1818 and by Mr Hutton; studied arts and medicine at Trinity College, Dublin, from 1826; BA (TCD) 1831; LRCSI 1834; MB 1838; MD 1854; medical officer to St Thomas's Dispensary District, Dublin; medical officer to Leeds Dispensary and lecturer in Materia Medica to Leeds School of Medicine; attending physician to Belfast General Hospital 1856–70; president of the Ulster Medical Society 1866–7; gave annual winter oration at

Belfast Royal Hospital 1867; of strong literary interests and author of poems in the 2nd (1859) edition of his father's *Glendalloch and Other Poems* and of *Poems and Sonnets* (1895); married 10 August 1853 in Princes Street Presbyterian Church, Cork, Emma Hincks, (who was born 1826 and died 26 December 1859 at 23 Chichester Street, Belfast), third daughter of the Rev Prof William Hincks of University College, Toronto, Canada; died 1 November 1893 at 39 Prospect Terrace, Belfast; buried in Clifton Street graveyard; probate Belfast 29 November 1893. [Agnew, vol 3 (1999); *BNL* 15 August 1853 (m) and 30 December 1859 (d); Belf PRO, will cal; *BMJ* obituary (1893); Burtchaell and Sadleir (1924); Dub GRO (m) and (d); Fisher and Robb (1913); *Lancet* obituary (1893); McNeill (1962); *Med Dir*; Merrick and Clarke, *Belfast*, vol 4 (1991); Whitla (1901)].

DRENNAN, ROBERT HUGH (1865/6–1917), Gravesend, Essex;
born 1865/6, youngest son of James Drennan, JP, of Carse Hill, Limavady, county Londonderry; studied medicine at Edinburgh University; MB CM (Edin) 1892; general practitioner, of Gravesend, Essex; joined RAMC as lieutenant (temporary) in 1915; captain 1916; lived finally at 56 Parrock Street, Gravesend; married Daisy Emily —; died 26 July 1917 at Gravesend; probate London 28 August 1917. [*BMJ* obituary (1917); Kirkpatrick Archive; Lond PPR, will cal; *Med Dir*].

DRENNAN, WILLIAM (1754–1820), Belfast, Newry, county Down and Dublin;
born 23 May 1754 at his father's manse in Belfast, youngest son of the Rev Thomas Drennan, minster of Belfast First Presbyterian Church [Blue Plaque on church], and Anne Lennox; educated by his father and the Rev Matthew Garnet; studied arts at Glasgow and medicine at Edinburgh; matriculated at Glasgow 1769; MA (Glas) 1772; MD (Edin) 1778 (thesis 'De venaesectione in febribus continuis'); physician in Belfast 1781–2; general practitioner in Newry 1782–9; active in the Volunteer movement and author of *Letters of Orellana, an Irish Helot* (1785); general practitioner in Dublin 1789–1807; originator of the idea and a founder member of the Society of United Irishmen in 1791 and president at intervals during 1792–3; tried for sedition in 1794 and acquitted; following this, as the movement became more involved in violence, withdrew from active participation, though still an advocate of radical politics, and returned to medical practice, mainly as an accoucheur; retired to Belfast 1807, following the death of his cousin Martha Young and a large legacy; living at Donegall Square South and Cabin Hill, Knock, a house which his sister Martha McTier had restored; a founder committee member of the Belfast Medical Society in 1806, also one of its presidents before it was dissolved in 1814; author of two collections of poems in 1815 (with a 2nd edition and additions by his sons in 1859) and 1817; the first person the use the phrase 'the Emerald Isle' as a description of Ireland (in one of his 1815 poems); one of the visitors involved in the foundation of the Belfast Academical Institution (later RBAI) who gave an inspiring speech at its opening in 1814 (see Fisher and Robb); married 3 February 1800 Sarah Swanwick, daughter of John Swanwick of Wem, Shropshire; father of Dr John Swanwick Drennan (*q.v.*) and a daughter, Sarah Drennan, who married John Andrews of Comber; died 5 February 1820; 'Possessing an ardent and disinterested love of his native country, he fearlessly advocated her course in the worst of times, and those who might differ from him in opinion on public affairs, could not withhold their admiration of those talents which

evinced on every occasion the accomplished scholar, the well-bred gentleman and the conscientious patriot.' (*BNL*); buried in Clifton Street graveyard, Belfast, with an epitaph by his son; portrait by Robert Home in private ownership in Belfast; his letters to and from his sister, Martha McTier, have survived and were published in 3 volumes, 1998–9; probate Prerogative Court 20 January 1821 (see will in PRO NI). [Addison (1898) and (1913); Agnew (1998–9); Bateson (2004); *BNL* 4 February 1820 (d); Belf PRO, D270/30; Belf PRO, prerog wills index; Crone (1928); *DIB* (2009); Drennan (1859); Edin Univ; Esler (1884); Fisher and Robb (1913); Larkin (1991); Logan (1983) and (2007); McNeill (1962); Malcolm (1851); Merrick and Clarke, *Belfast*, vol 4 (1991); Newmann (1993); O'Brien, Crookshank and Wolstenholme (1988); *Oxford DNB* (2004); Strain (1961)].

DROMGOOLE, JOHN (1798/9–1844), Collon, county Louth;
born 1798/9, son of Patrick Dromgoole of Patrick Street, Newry; 'doctor'; died 26 February 1844 at Collon. [*BNL* 1 March 1844 (d)].

DRUITT, ARTHUR BARTHOLD (1854–1904), Dunstable, Bedfordshire, and London;
born 28 July 1854 in Belfast, son of Charles Druitt of 6 Wilmont Terrace, Belfast; educated by Dr R.S. Reddy of Belfast and at Shrewsbury College; studied medicine at Queen's College, Belfast, from 1871; LSA Lond 1884; MRCSE 1886; general practitioner, of 22 High Street, Dunstable, Bedfordshire, c 1886, of 31 High Road, Balham c 1895 and of Ivanhoe, Bridge Road, Worthing c 1904; died 6 July 1904 at Ivanhoe. [Lond GRO (d); *Med Dir*; QCB adm reg].

DRUMGOOLE (DROMGOOLE), PETER (d 1777), Newry, county Down;
apothecary and wine merchant of Newry; had Henry Taylor as his apprentice before 1771; married Mary Magenis (who was born 1741/2 and died 13 July 1777), daughter of John Magenis of Cabra; died 26 December 1777; buried in St Mary's Roman Catholic Graveyard, Newry; probate Prerogative Court 1778. [*BNL* May 1771 (advert), 20 June 1777 (d) and 2 January 1778 (d); Clarke, *County Down*, vol 21 (1998); Vicars (1897)].

DRUMMOND, EDWARD (1842/3–1906), Oldham, Lancashire, and Rome;
born 1842/3, son of Thomas Drummond of Blyth, Northumberland; educated at The Gymnasium, Old Aberdeen; studied medicine at Aberdeen and Edinburgh Universities and from 1860 at Queen's College, Belfast; LM Edin 1863; MD (Edin) 1864 (thesis 'On the fibrinous concretions which occur in the heart and blood vessels during life'); MRCSE 1865; DPH Camb 1888; house surgeon at Chesterfield and North Derbyshire Hospital and later at York County Hospital; medical officer and public vaccinator to Royton and Thornham District, Oldham; surgeon to Oldham, Middleton and Rochdale Coal Company, of 'Kinderheim', St Anne's-on-Sea, Lancashire; later physician to the British Embassy and the Scottish College in Rome; author of translations from Italian and various medical papers; married Rebecca Rosina —; died 20 October 1906 at St Anne's-on-Sea; administration London 30 January 1907 and 13 June 1950. [Edin Univ; Lond PPR, will cal; *Med Dir*; QCB adm reg].

DRUMMOND, JAMES LAWSON (1783–1853), Naval Medical Service and Belfast; born May 1783 near Larne, younger son of Dr William Drummond, RN (*q.v.*) and Rose Hare; brother of the Rev William Hamilton Drummond, presbyterian minister, and of Isabella Drummond who married Dr Andrew Marshall (*q.v.*); educated at Belfast Academy; enrolled as an apprentice apothecary 1799 and joined Andrew Marshall in his apothecary's practice 1804/5 in 51 High Steet; studied surgery at the Royal College of Surgeons of England 1806–07; joined the Naval Medical Service as assistant surgeon 1806, with HMS *La Nereide*, serving in the Mediterranean; commissioned as surgeon to the *San Juan Nepomaceno* 1810; paid off 1813 and returned briefly to Belfast; studied medicine in Edinburgh; MD (Edin) 1814 (thesis 'De oculi anatomia comparativa'); returned to general medical practice at 5 Chichester Street, Belfast; attending physician to the Belfast Fever Hospital 1814–18; resigned on principle (with Dr S.S. Thomson) because he objected to the non-payment of attending medical staff and remained estranged from the Fever Hospital; professor of anatomy 1818–35, anatomy and physiology 1835–49, and botany 1835–6 at RBAI and first president or dean of the Medical Faculty at RBAI 1835–7 and 1844; of 8 College Square North 1824–53; president of the Belfast Literary Society 1815–16; one of the founders and first president of the Belfast Natural History Society 1821–2 and president again 1827–43; one of the doctors who presented an inscribed gold box to Dr S.S. Thomson in 1834; retired with a pension in 1849 following the fracture of a femur; author of *First Steps to Botany, Intended as Popular Illustrations of the Science Leading to its Study as a General Branch of Education*, (1823); *First Steps to Anatomy*, (1845); *Observations of Natural Systems of Botany*, (1849); married (1) 30 March 1824 in Rosemary Street Presbyterian Church, Belfast, Jane Getty (who was born 1890/1, died 8 February 1831 and was buried in Larne Old Graveyard), only daughter of John Getty of Donegall Street; (2) 13 October 1834 in St George's Church of Ireland Church, Belfast, Catherine Mitchell (who died on 27 December 1848), daughter of Alexander Mitchell of Newgrove; (3) 10 May 1850 in St Anne's Church of Ireland Church, Belfast, Elizabeth O'Rorke (who was born 1804/5 and died 27 November 1896), second daughter of Daniel O'Rorke of Ballybollen near Ballymena; died 16 May 1853 at 8 College Square North; buried with his third wife in the old burying ground in Ahoghill; memorial tablet in St Colmanell's Roman Catholic Church; portrait engraved from a watercolour by W.C. Day in the Ulster Museum, reproduced in Deane (1921); 'none did more to promote science and a medical school in Ulster' (Froggatt, 1996a). [*Belf Lit Soc* (1901); *BNL* 2 April 1824 (m), 11 February 1831 (d), 17 October 1834 (m) and 14 May 1850 (m); Benn (1880); Crone (1928); Deane (1921); *DIB* (2009); Edin Univ; Fisher and Robb (1913); Froggatt (1976, 1996a and 1998); McKillop (2000); Newmann (1993); O'Brien, Crookshank and Wolstenholme (1984); *Oxford DNB* (2004); Pigot (1824); Praeger (1949); Roddie (1987); Rutherford and Clarke, *County Antrim*, vol 4 (2004); Strain (1961); Thomson presentation box (1834); UHF database (m)].

DRUMMOND, JOHN (*fl c* 1842–6), Killybegs, county Donegal;
MRCSE 1842; medical officer to Killybegs and Kilcar Dispensary Districts c 1843–6; possibly died c 1850. [Croly (1843–6)].

DRUMMOND, WILLIAM (d 1787), Naval Medical Service and Ballyclare, county Antrim;
> probably born in Larne; apprenticed to Dr William Hamilton of Larne to learn surgery; joined the Naval Medical Service but paid off in 1783; surgeon in Ballyclare 1783–7; married Rose Hare; father of Isabella Drummond who married Dr Andrew Marshall (*q.v.*), of the Rev William Hamilton Drummond, Presbyterian minister and poet (1778–1865), and of Dr James Lawson Drummond (*q.v.*); died 18 May 1787 of fever. [*Belf Lit Soc*; *BNL* 18 May 1787 (d); Froggatt (1996a); McKillop (2000)].

DUDDY, GEORGE (1799/1800–67), Londonderry City;
> born 1799/1800; MRCSE; apothecary and surgeon, of Waterside, Londonderry, c 1824–45; married — (who died before him); died 4 November 1867 of paralysis, at his home in Londonderry; buried in Londonderry City Cemetery. [Croly (1843–6); Dub GRO (m); *Londonderry Sentinel* 5 November 1867 (d); Pigot (1824)].

DUDGEON, ARCHIBALD (*fl c* 1850), Naval Medical Service;
> son of William Dudgeon, farmer, of the Alt, county Donegal and Ardstraw, county Tyrone, and Isabella —; brother of Dr John Dudgeon, RN (*q.v.*), and Dr Roland Dudgeon (*q.v.*); MD [?]; joined the Naval Medical Service as assistant surgeon. [Elliott, Simon, pers com].

DUDGEON, JOHN (*fl c* 1850), Naval Medical Service;
> son of William Dudgeon, farmer, of the Alt, county Donegal and Ardstraw, county Tyrone, and Isabella —; brother of Dr Archibald Dudgeon, RN (*q.v.*), and Dr Roland Dudgeon (*q.v.*); MD [?]; joined the Naval Medical Service as assistant surgeon. [Elliott, Simon, pers com].

DUDGEON, ROBERT (1866–1908), London;
> born 10 January 1866 in Belfast, son of William Dudgeon, factory manager, of 37 College Street South, Belfast; studied medicine at Queen's College, Belfast from 1882; MB BCh BAO (RUI) 1891; general practitioner, of 1 Cadogan Terrace, Victoria Park, London, from c 1892; medical officer to 8th Dispensary District, Hackney; married Ethel Maude —; died 25 October 1908; administration London 1 December 1908. [Lond PPR, will cal; *Med Dir*; QCB adm reg].

DUDGEON, ROLAND (*fl c* 1850);
> son of William Dudgeon, farmer, of the Alt, county Donegal and Ardstraw, county Tyrone, and Isabella —; brother of Dr John Dudgeon, RN (*q.v.*), and Dr Archibald Dudgeon (*q.v.*); died soon after graduating. [Elliott, Simon, pers com].

DUDGEON, WILLIAM (1778/9–1826), Army Medical Service;
> born 1778/9; joined the Army Medical Service as surgeon's mate 1809; assistant surgeon to the 3rd West India Regiment 1810 and to the 63rd Regiment 1811; on half pay 1818–24, rejoining with the 86th Foot; on half pay 1825; married — Kerr, probably of Warrenpoint; died 26 May 1826 at Warrenpoint; buried in Clonallon

Graveyard, county Down. [*BNL* 2 June 1826 (d); gravestone inscription; Peterkin and Johnston (1968)].

DUFF, WILLIAM WALTER (1863–1936), Aghalee, county Antrim;
born 13 July 1863 at Church Hill, Moneymore, county Londonderry, son of William Duff, farmer, of Church Hill; educated at Moneymore Intermediate School; studied medicine at Queen's College, Belfast, from 1883, and Queen's College, Galway; MD BCh BAO (RUI) 1890; medical officer of health for Aghalee Dispensary District and medical officer to constabulary; retired to 'Slieve Mor', Rostrevor; married Jane —; died 12 April 1936 at 'Slieve Mor'; administration Belfast 23 July 1937. [Belf GRO (d); Belf PRO, will cal; *Med Dir*; QCB adm reg].

DUFFIN, JOHN (1831/2–57), Army Medical Service;
born 1831/2; joined the Army Medical Service as assistant surgeon to 46th Foot 1854; staff surgeon 1855; transferred to 43rd Foot 1857; served in Crimean War; died 5 May 1857 at Ballymena; buried in Kirkinriola Graveyard, Ballymena. [*BNL* 8 May 1857 (d); *Coleraine Chronicle* 16 May 1857 (d); gravestone inscription; *Londonderry Sentinel* 15 May 1857 (d); Peterkin and Johnston (1968)].

DUFFIN, ROBERT JOHN (1863–1902), Barnoldswick, Yorkshire;
born 1 August 1863 at Aghavary, Ahoghill, county Antrim, son of Thomas Duffin, farmer, of Aghavary; educated at Coleraine Academical Institution; studied medicine at Queen's College, Cork, from 1883, and Queen's College, Belfast, from 1885; MB MCh (RUI) 1887; general practitioner, of Park Road, Barnoldswick; died 25 January 1902. [*Med Dir*; QCB adm reg].

DUFFY, FRANCIS (1838/9–74), South Africa and Carrickmacross, county Monaghan;
born 1838/9; studied medicine at Queen's College, Galway, and Cecilia Street, Dublin; LM Rot Hosp Dub 1864; MD (hons) (QUI) 1864; MCh 1865; house surgeon to Provincial Hospital, Port Elizabeth, South Africa; medical officer to Donaghmoyne Dispensary District, county Monaghan; married Elizabeth —; died 23 June 1874 at Carrickmacross, of delerium tremens; administration Armagh 6 July 1875. [Belf PRO, will cal; Dub GRO (d); Kirkpatrick Archive; McCann (2003); *Med Dir*].

DUFFY, JOHN (*fl c* 1845), Ballybay, county Monaghan;
LRCS Edin; LAH Dub; general practitioner, of Ballybay c 1846. [Croly (1843–6)].

DUGGAN, J. (d 1855), Arvagh, county Cavan, and Kingstown, county Dublin;
born 1798; apothecary, of Arvagh, c 1845; probably moved to Kingstown c 1850; died 5 January 1855 at Osborne Lodge, Kingstown. [*BNL* 10 January 1855 (d); Croly (1843–6)].

DUNCAN, ALEXANDER (1869–1933), Ballymena, county Antrim, and RAMC;
born 3 October 1869 at Killyfaddy, Magherafelt, county Londonderry, son of William Duncan, farmer, of Killyfaddy, and Eliza Crusley; educated at Moneymore

Intermediate School; studied medicine at Queen's College, Belfast, from 1888, and Edinburgh University; LRCP LRCS Edin 1894; LFPS Glas 1894; house surgeon and physician to the Union Infirmary, Belfast; general practitioner in Ballymena from 1898; medical officer to Glenwhirry Dispensary District from 1903; honorary visiting medical officer to Ballymena Cottage Hospital, of Marlow House, Ballymena c 1910; captain in RAMC in World War I 1915–18 and served at Gallipoli and elsewhere; married Elizabeth Linn, daughter of George Linn; father of Dr William Linn Duncan of Belfast, MB BCh BAO (TCD) 1933; died 30 September 1933 at Waveney Road, Ballymena; probate Belfast 11 April 1934. [Belf GRO (b) and (d); Belf PRO, will cal, will; Kirkpatrick Archive; *Med Dir*; QCB adm reg].

DUNCAN, HENRY (*fl c* 1720), Belfast;
apothecary, of Belfast, c 1713–23; recorded as having William Clugston as apprentice in 1730. [Agnew (1995); Young (1892)].

DUNCAN, JAMES (*fl c* 1824), Irvinestown, county Fermanagh;
surgeon, of Irvinestown c 1824. [Pigot (1824)].

DUNCAN, THOMAS (1848–1915), Fintona, county Tyrone;
born 4 June 1848 at Killen, Ardstraw, county Tyrone, son of John Duncan of Killen; educated at Newtownstewart National School; studied medicine at Queen's College, Belfast and Galway; LRCP and LM, LRCS Edin 1872; medical officer and medical officer of health to Fintona Dispensary District; medical officer to constabulary; JP for county Tyrone; married 10 January 1872 Mary Elizabeth Motherwell, daughter of Dr John Motherwell of Castlederg (*q.v.*); father of Dr Alexander Harpur Robinson Duncan of Omagh, LRCPI and LRCSI 1903, and Dr Thomas Duncan, MC, of Liverpool, LRCPI LRCSI 2010; died 16 November 1915 at Fintona; probate Armagh 3 March 1916. [Belf PRO, will cal; Kirkpatrick Archive; *Lancet* obituary (1915); *Med Dir*; QCB adm reg].

DUNCAN, WILLIAM (*fl c* 1829–50), Belfast;
LAH Dub; studied medicine in Edinburgh University; MD (Edin) 1822; (thesis 'De paralysi'); attending physician to the Belfast Fever Hospital 1829–34; one of the doctors who presented an inscribed gold box to Dr S.S. Thomson in 1834; consulting physician 1834–40; married 28 June 1834 in St Peter's Church of Ireland Church, Dublin, Jane Dalway, youngest daughter of Noah Dalway of Bellahill, county Antrim; died probably after 1850. [*Belf Fever Hosp, Ann Rep*; *BNL* 1 July 1834 (m); Edin Univ; Malcolm (1851); Thomson presentation box (1834)].

DUNCAN, WILLIAM (1857–1905), Castledawson, county Londonderry, and Belfast;
born 28 February 1857 at Magherfelt, son of John Duncan, clerk of markets, of Larne; educated at Belfast Academy, studied medicine at Queen's College, Belfast, from 1875; LFPS Glas and LM 1884; general practitioner, of Castledawson, county Londonderry c 1885–91; general practitioner, of 271 Shankill Road, Belfast c 1891–1905; died 11 July 1905 at 271 Shankill Road. [Dub GRO (d); *Med Dir*; QCB adm reg].

DUNDAS, RICHARD THOMAS (1848/9–1914), ship's surgeon, and Enniskillen, county Fermanagh;
born 1848/9; studied medicine at the Royal College of Surgeons in Ireland; LM Rot Hosp Dub; LRCSI 1877; FRCSI 1882; LRCP Edin and LM 1889; surgeon with the Cunard Steamship Company; medical officer, medical officer of health and public vaccinator to Ely Dispensary District; medical officer to the constabulary; of Blaney House, Derrygonnelly; retired c 1913 to 34 and 46 Northumberland Avenue, Kingstown, county Dublin; married Ellen (Nellie) —; died 3 December 1914 at 46 Northumberland Avenue; probate Dublin 10 May 1915. [Belf PRO, will cal; Dub GRO (d); *Med Dir*].

DUNDEE, CHARLES (1857–1934), Ballycarry, county Antrim;
born 28 January 1857 at Bruslee, Ballyclare, county Antrim, son of John Dundee, farmer, of Bruslee; educated at the Belfast Seminary; studied medicine at Queen's College, Belfast, from 1876; MD (QUI) 1881; LRCS Edin and LM 1882; medical officer, medical officer of health and public vaccinator to Ballycarry Dispensary District; medical officer to the coastguards; lived at Redhall, Ballycarry, as doctor and farmer; married 3 June 1887 in Islandmagee Presbyterian Church, county Antrim, Anne Jane Hill, daughter of William Boyle Hill, farmer, of Kilcoan, county Antrim; father of Dr William Boyle Hill Dundee MC, MB (Edin) 1913, of Ballynure and Dr Charles Dundee, MB (Edin) 1913. of Redhall; died 13 December 1934 as a result of a car accident while he was attempting to start it by pushing (inquest); administration Belfast 5 April 1935. [Belf GRO (d); Belf PRO, will cal, will; *BMJ* (1906); Crozier (1978); Kirkpatrick Archive; *Lancet* obituary (1935); *Med Dir*; QCB adm reg; UHF database (m)].

DUNDEE, ISAAC CHICHESTER (1854–1910), India and Carnmoney, county Antrim;
born 28 June 1854, at Carnmoney, youngest son of Dr John Dundee, senior, of Carnmoney (*q.v.*) and Elizabeth McCullough; brother of Dr John Dundee, junior (*q.v.*); educated at Mr McClinton's Seminary, Belfast and RBAI; studied medicine at Queen's College, Galway and Belfast 1871–8, also at Dr Steeven's Hospital, Dublin, and Edinburgh Royal Infirmary; BA (QUI) 1874; MD 1877 (with various prizes); MCh 1878; LM KQCPI 1879; worked in India as a doctor 1879–94 and served in the army during the third Burmese war; succeeded his brother John to the Carnmoney practice in 1894 and was medical officer to Carnmoney Dispensary District 1894–1910, of Hillmount, Carnmoney; married 27 November 1895 in Carnmoney Presbyterian Church, Janet Elizabeth McKinney (1866–1965), daughter of William Fee McKinney, farmer, of Sentry Hill, Carnmoney; father of Dr Elizabeth Margaret Dundee, MB BCh BAO (QUB) 1923, Dr John Isaac Chichester Dundee, MB BCh BAO (QUB) 1923, of Belfast, Dr Joseph McKinney Dundee, MB BCh BAO (QUB) 1929, and Isobel R. Dundee who married Dr Thomas Howard Crozier, MB BCh BAO (QUB) 1921, of the Royal Victoria Hospital, Belfast; died 1 March 1910, after an accident when his trap overturned on the icy Mossley Brae; buried in Old Ballylinney Graveyard; probate Belfast 11 May 1910. [Belf PRO, will cal; Crozier (1978) and (1985); gravestone inscription; Kirkpatrick Archive; *Med Dir*; QCB adm reg; UHF database (m); Walker (1981)].

DUNDEE, JOHN, senior (1819–82), Carnmoney, county Antrim;
born 1819, son of Samuel Dundee of Bruslee, county Antrim, and Jane Sharp; studied medicine at Glasgow University; MD (Glas) and LM 1843; MCh 1852; medical officer to Carnmoney Dispensary; married 13 September 1844 Elizabeth McCullough (1817–99), daughter of — McCullough and Isabella Rosborough; father of Dr John Dundee, junior (*q.v.*) and Dr Isaac Chicester Dundee (*q.v.*); died 24 May 1882 at Ballyduff near Belfast; buried in Old Ballylinney Graveyard. [Addison (1898); Crozier (1978) and (1985); Dub GRO (d); gravestone inscription; *Med Dir*].

DUNDEE, JOHN, junior (1845–97), Carnmoney, county Antrim;
born 28 August 1845, eldest son of Dr John Dundee, senior, of Carnmoney (*q.v.*); brother of Dr Isaac Christopher Dundee (*q.v.*); educated at Belfast Academy; studied medicine and arts at Queen's College, Belfast, from 1861; LRCP LRCS Edin 1869; general practitioner, succeeding his father in 1882, of Hillmount, Carnmoney; unmarried; died 14 February 1897 of phthisis, at Ballyduff, Carnmoney; buried in Old Ballylinney Graveyard; probate Belfast 3 May 1897. [Belf PRO, will cal; Crozier (1978) and (1985); Dub GRO (d); gravestone inscription; *Med Dir*; QCB adm reg; Walker (1981)].

DUNKIN (DUNCAN), JAMES (1759/60–1828), Omagh, county Tyrone;
born 1759/60; surgeon of Omagh; died 14 October 1828; buried in Old Drumragh Graveyard, Omagh. [McGrew (1998)].

DUNLERN, DERMOTT JOHN (*fl c* 1709), Donegal;
of Donegal; studied medicine at Rheims University; MD (Rheims) 1709. [Brockliss].

DUNLOP, ALBERT (1857–c 1921), Ipswich, Queensland, Australia;
born 1857 at Limavady, county Londonderry, son of Robert Dunlop, farmer, of Limavady; educated at Coleraine Academical Institution; studied medicine at Queen's College, Belfast, from 1874; LRCP LRCS Edin 1879; resident medical officer to the Belfast Royal Hospital; emigrated to Australia; medical superintendent of Ipswich Hospital, Queensland, from c 1880; retired c 1900; of Belmont Avenue, Woolstonecroft, Sydney, from c 1915; died c 1921. [Kirkpatrick Archive; *Med Dir*; QCB adm reg].

DUNLOP, ARCHIBALD (1833/4–1902), Holywood, county Down;
born 1833/4, second son of the Rev Samuel Dunlop of Derriaghy Cottage, minister of Hillhall Presbyterian Church, and Jane Potts; brother of Dr James Clarke Dunlop (*q.v.*); educated at RBAI; studied medicine at Queen's College, Belfast, from 1851; LM; MRCSE 1855; MD (QUI) 1857; assistant house surgeon to Belfast General Hospital 1853–4 and house surgeon 1854–5; surgeon to Belfast Union Fever Hospital; acting assistant surgeon to Army Medical Staff c 1858; medical officer to Holywood Dispensary District, to coastguards and constabulary, of St Helen's, Holywood; married (1) 9 November 1861 in May Street Presbyterian Church, Belfast, Elizabeth Jane Stanton, widow of Captain W. Barron Stanton of the 91st Regiment, youngest daughter of the Rev Dr Pooley Shuldham Henry, President of

Queen's College, Belfast; (2) Elizabeth Moore, second daughter of James Moore, JP, of Craigavad, county Down; father of Dr Shuldham Henry Dunlop (*q.v.*); died 14 November 1902 at St Helen's, Holywood; probate Belfast 13 December 1902. [Belf PRO, will cal; Bennett (1974); *Coleraine Chronicle* 16 November 1861 (m); Dub GRO (d); McConnell (1951); *Med Dir*; QCB adm reg; Stewart (1950); UHF database (m)].

DUNLOP, CHARLES WILLIAM JULIUS (1864–1945), London and RAMC;
born 27 July 1864 at Edenderry House, county Down, son of Charles Dunlop of Edenderry House; studied medicine at Queen's College, Belfast, from 1880, and at the Royal College of Surgeons, Edinburgh; LRCP LRCS Edin 1893; LFPS Glas 1893; general practitioner, of 67 Pitfield Street, Hoxton, London, from c 1895, of 601 Forest Road, Walthamstow c 1905, 12a Hoe Street, Walthamstow c 1910 and 1 Third Avenue, Walthamstow c 1913; clinical assistant at the Central London Ophthalmic Hospital from c 1910; served in RAMC as ophthalmic surgeon during World War I; of 53 Middle Lane, Crouch End c 1920 and of 33 Priory Road, Hornsey from c 1935; died 21 November 1945; probate Llandudno 4 February 1946. [Lond PPR, will cal; *Med Dir*; QCB adm reg].

DUNLOP, JAMES (*fl c* 1845), Emyvale, county Monaghan;
CM Glas) [?]; general practitioner in Emyvale c 1845; possibly died c 1850. [Croly (1843–6)].

DUNLOP, JAMES (1846–1905), Naval Medical Service;
born 7 February 1846, at Edenderry House, eldest son of Charles Dunlop of Edenderry House, county Down; brother of Dr Peter Dunlop (*q.v.*) and of Elizabeth Dunlop who married Dr Robert Collier (*q.v.*); educated privately; studied medicine at Queen's College, Belfast, from 1860; LRCP LRCS and LM Edin 1867; MD (QUI) 1868; joined the Naval Medical Service as assistant surgeon on HMS *Ocean* c 1871; later fleet surgeon; married Elizabeth Peel (who died 1 January 1945 and was buried in Drumbo Church of Ireland graveyard), daughter of Jonathan Peel of Benneagh House, Crumlin; died 26 February 1905 in Naples; commemorated in Edenderry House graveyard; probate Belfast 29 June 1905. [Belf PRO, will cal; Clarke, *County Down*, vols 3 (1969) and 18 (1979); *Med Dir*; QCB adm reg].

DUNLOP, JAMES B. (d 1843), Edenderry, county Down;
second son of Major — Dunlop of the 18th Royal Irish Regiment and of Edenderry; LRCS; died 12 May 1843 at Dunleer, county Louth. [*BNL* 26 May 1843 (d)].

DUNLOP, JAMES CLARKE (1846–73), Naval Medical Service;
born 22 May 1846, son of the Rev Samuel Dunlop, minister of Hillhall Presbyterian Church, and Jane Potts; brother of Dr Archibald Dunlop (*q.v.*); educated at RBAI; studied medicine at Queen's College, Belfast, from 1863; LRCS Edin 1867; LRCP Edin 1868; joined the Naval Medical Service as assistant surgeon on HMS *Sirius*; died at sea between Kingston, Jamaica and Havana, Cuba, 16 March 1873; commemorated in Hillhall Presbyterian Graveyard; administration Belfast 10

September 1873. [Belf PRO, will cal; Clarke, *County Down*, vol 1 (1966); *Med Dir*; Presbyterian Historical Society; QCB adm reg].

DUNLOP, JOHN (d 1810), Bangor, county Down;
surgeon, of Bangor; died 22 November 1810, 'a young man possessed of many amiable qualities'. [*BNL* 27 November 1810 (d)].

DUNLOP, JOHN (1828/9–81), Ballycastle and Bushmills, county Antrim;
born 1828/9, son of Alexander Dunlop, gentleman, of Craig, county Antrim; studied medicine at the Royal College of Surgeons in Ireland, Meath Hospital, Dublin, and Hotel Dieu, Paris; LM RCSI 1849; LRCSI 1852; medical officer to Croagh Dispensary District, Ballycastle; coroner for county Antrim c 1874; married 28 March 1854 in Dunseverick Church of Ireland Church, Jane Stewart, daughter of William Stewart, JP, of Drumnagessa; died 22 May 1881 at Straidkillan, Bushmills; probate Belfast 8 July 1881. [Belf PRO, will cal; Dub GRO (d); *Med Dir*; UHF database (m)].

DUNLOP, JOSEPH (1850–1940), Ballycastle and Bushmills, county Antrim;
born 12 August 1850 at Conagher, county Fermanagh, son of William Dunlop, farmer, of Ballyness; educated at Knockanboy, Dervock, county Antrim; studied medicine at Queen's College, Belfast, from 1877; LRCP LRCS Edin 1883; medical officer to Croagh Dispensary District, Ballycastle, constabulary and coastguards, of Straidkillan, Bushmills; married 27 December 1888 in Dunluce Presbyterian Church, Elizabeth MacKenney, daughter of William James MacKenney, merchant, of Bushmills; died 10 January 1940 at Coleraine Cottage Hospital; administration (with will) 17 May 1940. [Belf GRO (d); Belf PRO, will cal; Kirkpatrick Archive; *Med Dir*; QCB adm reg; UHF database (m)].

DUNLOP, JOSEPH EVERARD (1862–1936), Dublin, London, Gillingham, Kent, and Belfast;
born 19 September 1862 at Mount Hamilton, county Antrim, son of Joseph M. Dunlop, merchant, of Mount Hamilton; educated at RBAI; studied arts and medicine at Queen's College, Belfast, from c 1881; BA (RUI) 1885; MD BCh BAO 1889; general practitioner, of 14 Lower Leeson Street, Dublin, c 1895; then based in London, but presumably abroad c 1910–25; of Clough Lodge, Shore Road, Belfast 1925–7; of 260 Canterbury Road, Gillingham, c 1927–35; retired to 369 Upper Newtownards Road, Belfast; unmarried; died 19 February 1936 at Norbrook, Knock, Belfast; his last will left his property to his solicitor, but it was contested (successfully) by his brother, J.M.M. Dunlop; probate Belfast 24 December 1936. [Belf PRO, will cal; Kirkpatrick Archive; *Med Dir*; QCB adm reg].

DUNLOP, JOSEPH SAMUEL (1855–97), ship's surgeon, Durham and Belfast;
born 1855 at Liverpool, son of Robert Dunlop, master baker, of King's Gate Street, Coleraine, county Londonderry; educated at Coleraine Academical Institution; studied medicine at Queen's College, Belfast, from 1874; LSA Lond 1879; LRCP LRCS and LM Edin 1882; resident medical officer in Belfast Royal Hospital; surgeon

on the Shire Shipping Line; general practitioner, of Leamside, Durham c 1882–94 and of 74 Farnham Street, Belfast c 1894–7; married Catherine —; died 26 December 1897 in Belfast Asylum; buried in Belfast City Cemetery. [Belf City Cem, bur reg; Dub GRO (d); *Med Dir*; QCB adm reg].

DUNLOP, PETER (1855–c 1920), Southampton, Hampshire, and London;
born 2 April 1855 at Edenderry House, son of Charles Dunlop, gentleman, of Edenderry House, county Down; brother of Fleet Surgeon James Dunlop (*q.v.*) and of Elizabeth Dunlop who married Dr Robert Collier (*q.v.*); educated privately; studied medicine at Queen's College, Belfast, from 1873; LRCP LRCS Edin 1881; general practitioner, of 141 Northam Road, Southampton c 1885 and of 180 Grove Road, Victoria Park, London, c 1895; medical officer with Elder Dempster and Co, Liverpool, from c 1900; returned to general practice in London c 1910, of 112a Hoe Street, Walthamstow c 1911 and 1 Third Avenue, Walthamstow c 1915; married 11 October 1883 in Templecorran Church of Ireland Church, Ballycarry, Ann Jane Ferguson, daughter of Thomas Ferguson, merchant, of Kilroot, county Antrim; died c 1920. [*Med Dir*; QCB adm reg; UHF database (m)].

DUNLOP, ROBERT (1796/7–1859), Bushmills, county Antrim, and New York, USA;
born 1796/7; CM (Glas) [?]; accoucheur of Glasgow Lying-in Hospital; medical officer to Bushmills Dispensary District and constabulary c 1845; emigrated to USA; died 24 January 1859 at New York. [*BNL* 23 February 1859 (d); *Coleraine Chronicle* 19 February 1859 (d); Croly (1843–6)].

DUNLOP, SAMUEL (1790/1–1818), Rathfriland, county Down;
born 1790/1; surgeon, of Rathfriland; married — Beaumont (who was born 1780/1 and died 3 May 1860 in Bangor, county Down), daughter of Dr John Beaumont of Rathfriland (*q.v.*); died 7 January 1818 of typhus fever. [*BNL* 16 January 1818 (d) and 8 May 1860 (d)].

DUNLOP, SHULDHAM HENRY (1863–c 1925), Holywood, county Down and Victoria, Australia;
born 10 August 1863 at Holywood, county Down, son of Dr Archibald Dunlop (*q.v.*) of Holywood, and Elizabeth Jane Henry; studied medicine at Queen's College, Belfast, and the Ledwich School, Dublin, 1880–86; LRCSI and LM 1886; MD MCh (RUI) 1886; house surgeon and house physician to Belfast Royal Hospital, 1885–7; general practitioner, of Holywood; emigrated to Australia c 1900; general practitioner in Berriwillock, Victoria, c 1905; consultant medical officer to Wycheproof Hospital and St Arnaud's Hospital, Victoria c 1910; general physician, of 107 Ferguson Street, Williamstown, Victoria c 1918; died c 1925. [*Belf Roy Hosp, Ann Rep*; *Med Dir*; QCB adm reg].

DUNLOP, WILLIAM MOODY (1847–86), Letterkenny, county Donegal;
born 8 September 1847 at Aghanloo, county Londonderry, son of Robert Dunlop of Aghanloo; educated at RBAI; studied medicine at Queen's College, Belfast, from 1865; LRCP LRCS LM Edin 1870, with prizes for medicine, midwifery and diseases of children; medical officer to Letterkenny Union Hospital and Workhouse and

apothecary to Letterkenny Asylum from 1870; unmarried; died 25 September 1886 at Letterkenny; probate Londonderry 25 March 1886. [Belf PRO, will cal; Dub GRO (d); Kirkpatrick Archive; *Med Dir*].

DUNLOP, — (*fl c* 1726–46), Belfast;
physician in Belfast, 'at the stone bridge' c 1726 married —; son died 1746. [Agnew (1995); Gillespie and O'Keefe (2006)].

DUNN, DAVID SIMPSON (1856–94), Marshe-by-the-Sea, Yorkshire;
born 21 September 1856, son of John Dunn, farmer, of Carrickmaddyroe, Boardmills, and Agnes —; studied arts and medicine at Queen's College, Belfast, from 1873; BA (QUI) 1876; MD and LM 1880; MCh 1883; medical officer and public vaccinator to Shelton Dispensary District, Marshe-by-the-Sea; died 21 August 1894; buried in Warboys, Hampshire, and also commemorated in Second Boardmills Presbyterian Graveyard; probate London 4 September 1894. [Belf PRO, will cal; Clarke, *County Down*, vol 2 (1988); Lond PPR, will cal; *Med Dir*; QCB adm reg].

DUNN, EDWIN LINDSAY (1865–1920), Liverpool, Lancashire, Yorkshire and Wallingford, Berkshire;
born 1865, only son of Robert Dunn of Dunnfield, Waterside, Londonderry; educated at Foyle College, Londonderry; studied arts and medicine at Trinity College, Dublin, from 1882; BA (honours in classics and Eng lit) (TCD); MB BCh (honours in anatomy) 1887; assistant house surgeon at Liverpool Children's Infirmary; assistant surgeon to Liverpool Dispensaries; assistant medical officer to the West Riding Asylum, Yorkshire; senior assistant medical officer and deputy medical superintendent to the Berkshire Asylum, Wallingford from 1894 and later medical superintendent; author of various medical papers; a keen sportsman with a continuing interest in literature; unmarried; died 12 January 1920; probate Oxford 23 March 1920. [*BMJ* obituary (1920); Kirkpatrick Archive; *Lancet* obituary (1920); Lond PPR, will cal; *Med Dir*; TCD adm reg; *TCD Cat*, vol II (1896)].

DUNN, JAMES (1766–1817), Naval Medical Service;
born 1766; joined the Naval Medical Service as assistant surgeon; married 9 November 1812 at Dullerton, Donagheady, county Tyrone, Sarah Armstrong of Dullerton (who died 12 August 1830 at Harmony Hill); died 24 December 1817 at Grove Hill. [*BNL* 20 August 1830 (d); *Londonderry Journal* 17 November 1812 (m) and 30 December 1817 (d)].

DUNN, JOHN (d 1841), Naval Medical Service;
probably from Londonderry; joined the Naval Medical Service as assistant surgeon; served on HMS *Caliope;* died 30 November 1841 off Moulmein, Burma. [*Londonderry Sentinel* 26 February 1842 (d); *Londonderry Standard* December 1841 (d)].

DUNN, JOHN (d 1829), Castlewellan, county Down;
surgeon and apothecary, of Castlewellan; involved in a minor lawsuit c 1824; died 1 March 1829 at his brother's house in Castlenavan, Loughinisland, county Down. [*BNL* 20 March 1829 (d); Castlewellan Court Book (1824); Pigot (1824)].

303

DUNN, JOHN (*fl c* 1836), Fahan, county Donegal [?];
surgeon; married 1 September 1836 in Upper Fahan Church of Ireland Church, Anne Jane Douglas, only daughter of Major Stewart Home Douglas of the 21st Royal Scots Fusiliers. [*Strabane Morning Post* 13 September 1836 (m)].

DUNN, ROBERT (1765/6–1841), Naval Medical Service;
born 1765/6, son of Oliver Dunn of Gortavea, county Tyrone, and Matilda Davison; older brother of Sir David Dunn who served with Nelson in a distinguished naval career, being knighted in 1843 and dying in 1859 at Chudleigh, Devon; joined the Naval Medical Service as assistant surgeon; surgeon 1790; surgeon to the Royal Naval Dockyard, Woolwich c 1811–41; married Catherine — (who was buried in the Old Priory Graveyard, Dungiven); died 9 April 1841 at his residence at the Royal Naval Dockyard. [*Londonderry Sentinel* 8 May 1841 (d); *Londonderry Standard* April 1841 (d); *NMS* (1826); Roulston (2010)].

DUNN, ROBERT (1791/2–1835), Naval Medical Service;
born 1791/2; of Ballygonny, Arboe, county Londonderry; joined the Naval Medical Service as assistant surgeon; surgeon 1815; married 8 January 1825 in St Anne's Church of Ireland Church, Belfast, Sarah Anne Crookshank, youngest daughter of John Crookshank of Mount Pleasant, Monaghan; died 26 November 1834 at his home near Cookstown; will dated 10 July 1832, proved London (PCC) 28 March 1835 (original will in National Archives, Kew); administration Armagh Diocesan Court 1836. [*BNL* 11 January 1825 (m) and 9 December 1834 (d); Dub Nat Arch, Armagh Dio Admins index; Elliott, Simon, pers com; Lond, Kew, Nat Arch; *NMS* (1826); *Strabane Morning Post* 25 January 1825 (m)].

DUNN, SAMUEL JAMES (1842–73), Stewarton, Ayrshire;
born 1842, son of Andrew Dunn of Mossfield [? Where]; studied medicine at Edinburgh University; LRCP LRCS Edin 1862; general practitioner, of Stewarton; unmarried; died 22 December 1873 of phthisis, in the family home at Mossfield; buried in St Michael's Graveyard, Dunnamanagh, county Tyrone; probate Londonderry 28 February 1874. [Belf PRO, will cal; Dub GRO (d); *Med Dir*; Roulston (2010)].

DUNN, THOMAS (d 1830), Naval Medical Service;
of Drumullan, Arboe, county Londonderry; joined the Naval Medical Service as assistant surgeon; surgeon 1815; married Margaret —; father of Anne Louisa Dunn who married Dr Samuel Henry Campbell of Portrush (*q.v.*); died 1830; will dated 21 January 1830, proved in London (PCC) 4 December 1830 (original in National Archives, Kew). [*Coleraine Chronicle* 1 April 1848 (m, daughter); Elliott, Simon, pers com; *NMS* (1826)].

DUNN, WILLIAM ALEXANDER (1856–1929), Belfast;
born 29 January 1856 in Manchester, son of Robert Dunn, railway agent, of 19 Donegall Quay, Belfast; educated at RBAI; studied medicine at Queen's College, Belfast, from 1874; LRCP LRCS Edin 1880; general practitioner, of 83 Ormeau

Road, Belfast; married —; died 23 January 1929 at 83 Ormeau Road; probate Belfast 19 April 1929. [Belf GRO (d); Belf PRO, will cal; *Med Dir*].

DUNNE, ALEXANDER MADILL (1847/8–95), Downpatrick and Portaferry, county Down;
born 1847/8; studied medicine at the Ledwich School, Dublin; LRCSI 1876; LRCP and LM Edin 1877; assistant surgeon to Down County Infirmary, Downpatrick 1878–82; medical officer to Portaferry Dispensary District, constabulary, Admiralty and Lightship; unmarried; died 2 December 1895 at Creagh, Cootehill, county Cavan; probate Cavan 8 June 1896. [Belf PRO, will cal; Dub GRO (d); *Med Dir*; Parkinson (1967)].

DUNNE, THOMAS (*fl c* 1802), Enniskillen, county Fermanagh;
LAH Dub 1802; apothecary, of Enniskillen. [Apothecaries (1829)].

DUNNE, WILLIAM (d 1874), Londonderry;
son of Henry Dunne, merchant; LAH Dub 1831; general practitioner in Londonderry and medical officer to constabulary; married 24 September 1856 in Holywood Church of Ireland Church, Rebecca Dupre Lindsay, daughter of Thomas Lindsay, merchant, of Holywood, county Down; died 12 February 1874; probate Londonderry 20 April 1874. [Belf PRO, will cal; *Med Dir*; UHF database (m)].

DUNWOODY, ARTHUR DAVID (1874–c 1909), Monaghan;
born 21 September 1874 at Monaghan, son of Forster Dunwoody, land agent of Monaghan; educated at Monaghan Collegiate School; studied medicine at Queen's College, Belfast, from 1893 and the Royal College of Surgeons in Ireland; LRCPI and LM, LRCSI and LM 1900; house surgeon to the Royal City of Dublin Hospital; subsequently described as 'travelling'; died c 1909. [*Med Dir*; QCB adm reg].

DUNWOODY, WILLIAM GEORGE (1869–1941), Ramsgate, Kent;
born 1869 in county Monaghan, son of Forster Dunwoody, land agent and JP, of Monaghan; educated at Monaghan Collegiate School; studied arts and medicine at Trinity College, Dublin, from 1886; BA (TCD) 1891; MB BCh BAO 1893; MD 1896; general practitioner, of Dashwood House, Ramsgate; married Elizabeth —; died 23 July 1941 at 10 West Cliff Terrace, Ramsgate; probate Llandudno 15 September 1941. [Kirkpatrick Archive; Lond GRO (d); Lond PPR, will cal; *Med Dir*; TCD adm reg; *TCD Cat*, vol III (1906); *TCD Reg*].

DURHAM, ANDREW (1813–74), Indian Medical Service;
born January 1813 in Aghaloo parish, county Tyrone; studied medicine at Glasgow University; MRCSE 1835; MD (Glas) 1836; joined the Indian Medical Service (Bombay establishment) as assistant surgeon 1836; surgeon 1849; surgeon major 1860; retired 1867 to Sylvan House, Belmont Avenue, Donnybrook, county Dublin; married 2 May 1842 [*BNL* and *LS*] or 5 August 1843 [church register] in Aghaloo Church of Ireland Church, Mary Crozier of Aghaloo, eldest daughter of Dr John Crozier of Mullaghmore (*q.v.*); father of Dr Samuel Durham of Greenock,

Renfrewshire, Scotland; died 4 August 1874 at Sylvan House; administration Dublin 27 August 1874. [Addison (1898); Aghaloo C of I mar reg; *BNL* 6 May 1842 (m); Belf PRO T/679/294; Belf PRO, will cal; Crawford (1930); Dub GRO (d); *Londonderry Sentinel* 7 May 1842 (m); *Med Dir*].

DYAS, JAMES (d c 1878), Belfast and Australia;
studied medicine in Dublin; LAH Dub 1852; apothecary, of 7 Donegall Place, Belfast, c 1852–62; emigrated to Australia c 1862; died c 1878. [*Med Dir*].

DYSART, HUGH (1750/1–1816), Portglenone, county Antrim;
born 1750/1; surgeon, of Portglenone; married Jane — (who died 29 April 1833 aged 73); died 10 November 1816. [Gravestone inscription].

DYSART, JOHN (1820/1–1907), Portglenone, county Antrim;
born 1820/1, son of John Dysart of Churchfield, Portglenone, gentleman (died 6 May 1876 – see will); MD (Glas) 1843; medical officer to Portglenone Dispensary District and constabulary and certifying factory surgeon, of Churchfield; JP; married 1 February 1844 in Third Portglenone Presbyterian Church, Eleanor Hunter Lyttle (who was born 1822/3 and died 7 February 1904), only daughter of James Lyttle of Portglenone; died 13 February 1907 at Portglenone; buried in Aughnahoy graveyard; probate Belfast 24 April 1907. [Addison (1898); *Ballymena Observer* 22 February 1907 (d); *BNL* 9 February 1844 (m); Belf PRO, will cal; Croly (1843–6); Dub GRO (d); gravestone inscription; *Londonderry Sentinel* 10 February 1844 (m); *Med Dir*].

E

EADIE, JOHN F. (1856–99), London and Yeovil, Somerset;
born 5 October 1856 at Alloa, Scotland, son of John Eadie, woollen manufacturer, of Lisbellaw, county Fermanagh; educated at Belfast Academy; studied medicine at Queen's College, Belfast, from 1872; MD (QUI) 1879; LRCS Edin 1880; surgeon to the Chelsea, Brompton and Belgrave Dispensary; medical officer and public vaccinator to the 2nd District, Yeovil, Somerset from c 1880; married Elizabeth Jane —; died 2 May 1899; probate Taunton 28 June 1899. [Lond PPR, will cal; *Med Dir*; QCB adm reg].

EAKIN, SAMUEL (1850–91), Poplar, London;
born 13 November 1850 at Donaghmoyne, Carrickmacross, county Monaghan, son of Samuel Eakin, farmer, of Donaghmoyne; educated at RBAI; studied medicine at Queen's College, Belfast, from 1876; MD MCh Dip Mid (QUI) 1880; general practitioner, of 451 Manchester Road, Cubitt Town, Poplar, London, c 1885; died 4 November 1891 at 451 Manchester Road; probate London 22 December 1891. [Lond PPR, will cal; *Med Dir*; QCB adm reg].

EAMES, CHETHAM (CHATHAM) (1834/5–58), Londonderry;
born 1834/5, third son of W.J. Eames of Londonderry; MRCSI; died 20 December 1858 at his father's house, Londonderry, after a short illness. [*BNL* 23 December 1858 (d); *Coleraine Chronicle* 25 December 1858 (d); *Londonderry Sentinel* 24 December 1858 (d)].

EAMES, JAMES ALEXANDER (1832/3–86), Army Medical Service, Letterkenny, county Donegal, and Cork;
born 1832/3, son of Dr William James Eames of Londonderry (*q.v.*); studied medicine at the Royal College of Surgeons in Ireland and the Meath Hospital, Dublin; LM Rot Hosp Dub 1853; LRCSI 1854; MD (St Andrew's) 1856 (by examination); LAH Dub 1856; FRCSI 1865; joined the Army Medical Service as assistant surgeon 1854; served in the Crimean War 1854–5 (medal and clasp and Turkish Medal for the Crimea); resigned 1855; resident medical superintendent of the District Lunatic Asylum, Letterkenny c 1856–73, and of the District Lunatic Asylum, Cork c 1873–86; author of various medical papers; married 23 October 1856 in Monkstown Church of Ireland Church, Dublin, Helen Hutton, fourth daughter of John Hutton of Richmond Hill, Monkstown; died 17 July 1886 of anthrax at the Asylum; probate Cork 14 October 1886. [*BNL* 25 October 1856 (m); Belf PRO, will cal; Dub GRO (m) and (d); Kirkpatrick Archive; *Londonderry Sentinel* 21 October 1856 (m); *Med Dir*; O'Rahilly (1949); Peterkin and Johnston (1968); Smart (2004)].

EAMES, JOSEPH (*fl c* 1859), Londonderry and ship's surgeon;
LRCSI and LM 1857; LM Rot Hosp Dub; of Ferryquay Street, Londonderry; medical officer with Black Ball Line of Australian Steam Packet Service. [Kirkpatrick Archive]

EAMES, WILLIAM JAMES, senior (1802/3–72), Londonderry;
born 1802/3; LAH Dub 1823; accoucheur of Dublin Lying-in Hospital (Rotunda); LRCP Edin 1871; general physician and apothecary to the County Gaol, of 3 Ferryquay Street, Londonderry; married —; father of Dr James Alexander Eames (*q.v.*) and Elizabeth Catherine Eames who married Dr Walter Bernard (*q.v.*); died 9 May 1872 at 14 Queen Street, Londonderry; probate Dublin 29 May 1872. [Belf PRO, will cal; Croly (1843–6); Dub GRO (m, daughter) and (d); Kirkpatrick Archive; *Med Dir*].

EAMES, WILLIAM JAMES, junior (d 1908), Naval Medical Service;
studied medicine at the Royal College of Surgeons in Ireland; LM Rot Hosp Dub 1854; LRCSI 1855; LKQCPI 1863; MKQCPI 1879; joined the Naval Medical Service as assistant surgeon; served on HMS *Gorgon* c 1863 and on HMS *Gladiator* c 1864; surgeon on HMS *Flora* c 1868 and HMS *Pembroke* c 1872; staff surgeon 2nd class on HMS *Duke of Wellington* c 1873 and HMS *Diamond* c 1875; fleet surgeon on HMS *Royal Adelaide* c 1878; deputy inspector general of hospitals and fleets 1886; retired to 'Culmore', Harlesden Road, London c 1890; physician and surgeon to Willesden Cottage Hospital c 1894; of 'Grianan Hill', Donnington Road, Willesden c 1899; of 11 Fitzgeorge Avenue, West Kensington c 1901; of 54 Boulevard Victor Hugo, Nice, France c 1905; author of various surgical papers; married 1 July 1863 at Ascension Island, Harriet Dobree Barnard, third daughter of Admiral Barnard of Stonehouse, Devon; died 18 October 1908 in Nice. [*Londonderry Sentinel* 24 July 1863 (m); *Med Dir*].

EARDLEY, HENRY EDWARD (1870–1911), Dublin, and Burtonport, county Donegal;
born 8 October 1870 at North Street, Monaghan, son of Francis Eardley, Inspector of Schools, of North Street, Monaghan, and Bessy McClarinan [?]; studied medicine at the Royal College of Surgeons in Ireland; LRCPI and LM, LRCSI and LM 1897; house surgeon and physician to St Michael's Hospital, Kingstown; resident surgical and medical pupil at the Mater Misercordiae Hospital, Dublin and prosector to the Royal College of Surgeons; medical officer to Dungloe No 2 Dispensary District; general practitioner, of Burtonport, from c 1900; married Margaret Teresa —; died 28 April 1911 at Burtonport, following a fall from a trap; administration Londonderry 20 September 1911. [Belf PRO, will cal; Dub GRO (b) and (d); Kirkpatrick Archive; *Med Dir*.]

EATON, JAMES BIRD (1849–89), Indian Medical Service;
born July 1849, son of Robert Eaton of Trillick, county Tyrone, and Anne —; brother of Robert Coleman Eaton, RAMC (*q.v.*); educated in Londonderry; studied arts and medicine at Trinity College, Dublin, from 1867; BA (TCD) 1873; MB 1874; MCh 1875; MAO 1889; joined the Indian Medical Service (Bombay establishment) as surgeon 1876; surgeon major 1888; served in Afghanistan 1879–80 (medal) and in Egypt 1882 (medal and Khedive's Star); died 15 May 1889 at Brighton; commemorated in Magheracross Graveyard, county Fermanagh. [Crawford (1930); gravestone inscription; *Med Dir*; TCD adm reg; *TCD Cat*, vol II (1896)].

EATON, ROBERT COLEMAN (1842–1902); Army Medical Service;
born 19 October 1842, eldest son of Robert Eaton of Trillick, county Tyrone, and Anne —; brother of Dr James Bird Eaton, IMS (*q.v.*); studied medicine at the Royal College of Surgeons in Ireland, the Richmond Hospital and Carmichael School, Dublin; LM Rot Hosp Dub 1863; LRCSI LKQCPI 1865; joined the Army Medical Service as staff assistant surgeon with the 16th Foot 1866; staff surgeon 1869; surgeon major 1878; surgeon lieutenant-colonel 1886; brigade surgeon lieutenant-colonel 1892; surgeon colonel 1896; served in Afghan War 1878–80; retired to St Bredale's, Jersey; died 15 March 1902 at Spezia, Italy; commemorated in Magheracross Graveyard, county Fermanagh; administration (with will) London 24 July 1902 and April 1903 and Dublin 3 June 1903. [Belf PRO, will cal; gravestone inscription; Lond PPR, will cal; *Med Dir*; Peterkin and Johnston (1968)].

EATON, USHER BEERE (1835–1903), Army Medical Service, Mitchelstown, county Cork, and Belfast;
born 12 July 1835 at Castlecomer, county Kilkenny; studied medicine at Queen's College, Cork, and the Royal College of Surgeons in Ireland; MD (QUI) 1860; LRCSI 1861; joined the Army Medical Service as staff assistant surgeon 1861; on half pay September 1861–May 1862, August 1868–February 1873 and from September 1873; resigned 1874; general practitioner, of Mitchelstown c 1880–88 and of Evelyn Lodge, Sydenham Park, Belfast, c 1888–99; retired to 37 Park Avenue, Sandymount, Dublin c 1899, and 31 Monks' Place, North Dublin; unmarried; died 15 October 1903 at the Richmond Hospital, Dublin.—;[Dub GRO (d); *Med Dir*; Peterkin and Johnston (1968)].

ECCLES, ROBERT (1851–91), Liverpool, Lancashire;
born 11 July 1851 at Larne, son of Thomas Eccles of Larne and Anne Munro Ferres; educated at RBAI; studied arts and medicine at Queen's College, Belfast, 1869–76; BA (QUI) 1872; MA 1873; MD 1875; MCh 1876; MRCSE 1876; moved to Liverpool c 1878, of 8 Balmoral Road, Fairfield, c 1880; resident medical officer to Liverpool Parish Infirmary and Bootle Hospital; honorary surgeon to St George's Hospital for Skin Diseases; general practitioner, of 314 Kensington, Liverpool, c 1885; unmarried; died 18 August 1891 at 314 Kensington from heart failure due to chloroform anaesthesia (coroner); commemorated in Larne Old Graveyard; administration Liverpool 13 November 1891. [Lond GRO (d); Lond PPR, will cal; *Med Dir*; QCB adm reg; Rutherford and Clarke, *County Antrim*, vol 4 (2004)].

ECCLES, ROBERT KERR (1844–c 1886), Toomebridge, county Antrim and Dublin;
born 12 March 1844 at Coleraine, son of the Rev W.S. Eccles, baptist minister, of Lakeview, Toomebridge; educated privately and at Belfast Academy; studied arts and medicine at Queen's College, Belfast, from 1864; MD Dip Mid (QUI) 1873; general practitioner in Toomebridge c 1873–85, and of 1 Grosvenor Square, Dublin, c 1885–7; died c 1886. [*Med Dir*; QCB adm reg].

ECCLES, WILLIAM JOHN (d 1849), Londonderry;
surgeon, probably of Londonderry; died 21 July 1849 at Coleraine. [*BNL* 31 July 1849 (d); *Coleraine Chronicle* 28 July 1849 (d)].

EDGAR, JOHN CARMICHAEL (1870–97), Manchester, Lancashire;
born 1870; MRCSE 1894; LRCP Lond 1894; general physician, of 52 Clyde Road, Didsbury, Manchester; died 8 June 1897 at Monsall Hospital, Newton, Manchester; buried in Clifton Street graveyard, Belfast. [Lond GRO (d); *Med Dir*; Merrick and Clarke, *Belfast*, vol 4 (1991)].

EDGE, ABRAHAM MATTHEWSON (1850–1922), Manchester, Lancashire;
born 18 September 1850, son of Abraham Edge of Park Field, Rusholme, Manchester; educated at Chorlton High School; studied medicine at Owen's College, Manchester, and from 1872, at Queen's College, Belfast; MRCSE 1872; MD (QUI) 1873, MRCP Lond 1878; BSc (Victoria Univ, Manchester) 1882; general practitioner, of 252 Oxford Street, Manchester, from c 1880; district surgeon and later physician to Salford Royal Hospital; consulting physician to Manchester Southern Hospital for Diseases of Women and Children and Cheetham Hospital; of 30 St Ann Street and 7 Demesne Road, Whalley Range, Manchester; president of the Manchester Medical Society; lieutenant-colonel RAMC (territorials); retired to The Cottage, 46 Rawlinson Road, Southport c 1915; married Anne Lilian —; died 27 July 1922; probate London 6 September 1922. [Lond PPR, will cal; *Med Dir*; QCB adm reg].

EDGEWORTH, HENRY (THOMAS GEORGE) (1816–82), Pettigo, county Donegal, and Longford;
born 4 August 1816 in Dublin, son of Thomas Newcomen Edgeworth of Kilshrewly and Longwood, county Longford, and his first wife, Marian Steele; studied arts and medicine at Trinity College, Dublin, from 1833, and the Richmond Hospital, Dublin; BA (TCD) 1838; LM Dublin Rot Hosp Dub 1840; LRCSI 1843; FRCSI 1844; medical officer to Pettigo Dispensary District c 1846; surgeon to Longford County Infirmary from 1850 and medical officer to the County Gaol; retired c 1880; married 20 April 1852 Amelia Considine (who died 14 December 1906), only daughter of General James Considine; died 8 March 1882 in Longford. [Burke *LGI* (1958); Burtchaell and Sadleir (1924); Crisp (1911); Croly (1843–6); Dub GRO (d): *Med Dir*].

EDWARDS, HENRY EDWARD (*fl* 18th cent), Boveva, county Londonderry;
general practitioner, of Straw House, Boveva; married —; his daughter married the Rev Francis Gray of Boveva. [Mullin (1983)].

EDWARDS, JOHN (*fl c* 1843), Tandragee, county Armagh;
general practitioner, of Salem Cottage, near Tandragee; married Margaret — (who was born 1816/7 and died 13 May 1843); father of Thomas Edwards (only son), who was born 1843; died before 1860. [*BNL* 6 June 1843 (d) and 20 October 1860 (d, son)].

EDIE, THOMAS (d 1794), Limavady, county Londonderry, and Army Medical Service;
probably born c 1740–50 in Limavady and may have practised medicine there c 1770–80; joined the Army Medical Service as surgeon to the 17th Foot 1782; based in the City of London on 11 September 1794 when he made his will (original

preserved in PRO NI); unmarried; died September/October 1794 in Guadalupe, where he was staff surgeon to the troops; probate Canterbury 3 June 1795. [Belf PRO, D/1118/14/E/3; Hitchins, Paul, pers com; Peterkin and Johnston (1968)].

EGAN, JOHN JOHNSTONE (1854–c 1888), Belturbet, county Cavan;
born 1 August 1854 at Swanlinbar, county Cavan, son of the Rev John Johnstone Egan of Killinagh Glebe, Blacklion, county Cavan; educated in Sligo; studied medicine at the Royal College of Surgeons in Ireland, Ledwich School, Meath and Mercer's Hospitals, Dublin, Belfast Royal Hospital, and Royal Infirmary, Edinburgh; LRCSI 1877; LRCP Edin 1879; LM RCSI 1880; general practitioner of Derrylane, Belturbet; surgeon with the P & O Shipping Company c 1887; died c 1888. [*Med Dir*; QCB adm reg].

EKIN, JAMES (1829–96), Army Medical Service;
born 4 January 1829 at Dungannon, county Tyrone; LSA Lond 1852; LRCSE 1852; MD (Lond) 1857; LM RCSE 1854; joined the Army Medical Service as staff assistant surgeon to the 4th Foot 1854; staff surgeon 1864; transferred to 37th Foot 1869; brigade surgeon 1879; deputy surgeon general 1882; served in Crimea 1854–6; accompanied Lord Roberts on the march from Kabul to Kandahar; served in the Egyptian War of 1882; present at the Battle of Tel-el-Kebir and received the medal with clasp of the Osmanieh and the Khedive's Star; CB (military) 1882; retired as surgeon general 1884; living at 6 Little St James' Street and 16 Fitzroy Square, London; unmarried; died 14 February 1896 at the Home Hospital, 16 Fitzroy Square; buried in Kensal Green Cemetery; probate London 30 June 1896. [Ekin, William Holland, pers com; gravestone inscription; Lond GRO (d); Lond PPR, will cal, will; *Med Dir*; Peterkin and Johnston (1968)].

EKIN, WILLIAM (d c 1852), London;
surgeon, of London; died c 1852; administration Armagh Diocesan Court 1852. [Dub Nat Arch, Armagh Dio Admins index].

EKIN, WILLIAM (1866–1908), Portglenone, county Antrim, and Sydney, New South Wales;
born 29 January 1866 at Soarn House, Cookstown, county Tyrone, son of Samuel Ellison Ekin, linen manufacturer, of Soarn House, and Jane Killen; educated at RBAI; studied medicine at Queen's College, Belfast, from 1882; MB BCh BAO (RUI) 1889; general practitioner, of Portglenone c 1895; emigrated to Australia; general practitioner, of Sydney c 1900; married Ellen Courtney; died 1908 at Oberon, New South Wales, of alcoholism. [Dub GRO (b); Ekin, William Holland, pers com; *Med Dir*; QCB adm reg].

ELLIOTT, BRERETON GEORGE (1868–1934), Liverpool and Blackburn, Lancashire, and RAMC;
born 24 March 1868, at Loughlarne, Donaghmore, Newry, second son of the Rev John Elliott, minister of Clarkesbridge, Donaghmore and Armagh Presbyterian Churches, and Jane Stewart Trimble of Castlebellingham; brother of Dr John Trimble Elliott (*q.v.*); educated at the Royal School, Armagh, from 1875; studied medicine

at the Royal College of Surgeons in Ireland; LKQCPI and LM 1890; LM Rot Hosp Dub; LRCSI and LM 1890; general practitioner, of Cherry Tree, Blackburn c 1895; of Kilbride House, Blackburn c 1900; joined East Lancashire Regiment as captain 1901 but remained a general practitioner in Blackburn; major 1915; temporary captain RAMC; medical officer to Fazakerley Sanatorium, Liverpool, from c 1922; died 13 October 1934 at Fazakerley Sanatorium; probate Lancaster 29 November 1934. [Belf GRO (b); Ferrar (1933); Kirkpatrick Archive; Lond GRO (d); Lond PPR, will cal; *Med Dir*].

ELLIOTT, CHARLES ROULSTON (1860–1936), Army Medical Service;
born 17 June 1860 at Drummurphy, county Donegal, second son of Andrew Elliott, farmer, of Drummurphy, and Sara Roulston; educated at Raphoe Royal School; studied medicine at Queen's College, Belfast, from 1878; MD MCh (RUI) 1884; MAO 1885; DPH (Camb) 1897; joined the Army Medical Service (RAMC) as surgeon captain 1887; major 1899; lieutenant-colonel 1911; colonel 1915; sanitary officer in Western Command, India; returned to Ireland as specialist sanitary officer in Cork c 1910; retained on the active list 1917; retired 1919 and settled in to Dhu Varren, Portrush, county Antrim, where he served on the Council 1924–6; after his death the Council expressed 'their high appreciation of his deep interest in the welfare of Portrush'; married 27 February 1895 his cousin Mary Elliott, only daughter of William Elliott of Strabane and sister of Dr Robert Moore Elliott (*q.v.*) and Dr Robert Hanna Elliott (*q.v.*); died 20 October 1936 at Dhu Varren; probate Belfast 22 December 1936 and London 13 January 1937. [Belf GRO (d); Belf PRO, will cal; *Coleraine Chronicle* 1936 (d); Elliott, Simon, pers com; Kirkpatrick Archive; Lond PPR, will cal; *Med Dir*; Peterkin and Johnston (1968); QCB adm reg].

ELLIOTT, GEORGE (1856–1922), Nottingham and Shrewsbury, Shropshire;
born 1 May 1856 at Raphoe, county Donegal, son of George Elliott, teacher, of Fivemiletown, county Tyrone; educated at Raphoe Royal School; studied medicine at Queen's College, Belfast, from 1880; had a long gap in his medical studied after his father's death, but returned in 1891; MB BCh BAO (RUI) 1896; general practitioner, of 14 Belgravia Avenue, Belfast, c 1897–1900; physician to the Congregational College, Nottingham, of 101 Rob Roy Terrace, Forest Road West, Nottingham c 1900–07; general practitioner, of 45 and 47 Ormeau Terrace (later 129 Ormeau Road), Belfast, c 1907–14; medical officer to Baschurch, Myddle and Hadnall Districts, Shrewsbury c 1914–22, of The Cedars, Baschurch; married Katherine Thompson —; died 7 March 1922; administration Shrewsbury 23 March 1922. [Lond PPR, will cal; *Med Dir;* QCB adm reg].

ELLIOTT, GEORGE (1859–1928), Drummurphy, county Donegal;
born 12 July 1859 at Drummurphy, county Donegal, son of John Elliott, farmer, of Drummurphy; educated at Raphoe Royal School; studied medicine at Queen's College, Belfast, from 1880; LRCP LRCS Edin 1889; LFPS Glas 1889; general practitioner, of Drummurphy c 1895 and of 42 (later 12) Broad Street, Stamford, Lincolnshire c 1897–1928; unmarried; died 28 April 1928; probate London 28 July 1928. [Lond PPR, will cal, will; *Med Dir*; QUB].

ELLIOTT, GEORGE FREDERICK (1833/4–1907), Naval Medical Service and Hull, Yorkshire;
> born 1833/4 at Strabane, county Tyrone, youngest son of William Elliott, solicitor, of Strabane; educated by Dr Darley; studied arts and medicine at Trinity College, Dublin, from 1850; BA MB (TCD) 1855; LRCSI 1855; MD 1866; MD (Oxon) 1867; MRCP Lond 1875; FRCP Lond 1883; joined the Naval Medical Service as assistant surgeon for 8 years; served in the Chinese War, being present at the capture of the Taku forts and the siege of Canton and on board HMS *Samson* during the blockade of the Baltic in the Crimean war; awarded a medal and two clasps; physician to the Stamford and Rutland Hospital from c 1864; lecturer on the Practice of Medicine to Hull Medical School from 1866; physician to Hull General Infirmary, of 10 Wright Street and later 1 Albion Street, Hull; author of many medical papers; married 25 July 1863 in Mortlake Parish Church, London, Rebecca de Castro, eldest daughter of Daniel de Castro, merchant, of Painsfield, East Skeen, Surrey; died 6 October 1907; buried in Filey parish graveyard. [*BMJ* obituary (1907); Burtchaell and Sadleir (1935); Foster (1888); Kirkpatrick Archive; Lond GRO (m); *Med Dir*; *Munk's Roll*, vol 4).

ELLIOTT, GILBERT (1800/1–79), Upper Canada, Rathmullan, county Donegal, and Plymouth, Devon;
> born 1800/1; LRCSI 1822; LM Rot Hosp Dub 1824; MD (Edin) 1824 (thesis 'De hepatitide'); FRCSI 1845; general practitioner in Upper Canada c 1856 and in Rathmullan c 1870; returned to England c 1872; of 14 Lower Durnford Street, Stonehouse, Plymouth c 1875, and finally of Sharon House, Belvedere Road, Upper Norwood, London; married Harriet —; died 16 March 1879; probate London 30 April 1879. [Edin Univ; Lond PPR, will cal; *Med Dir*].

ELLIOTT, JAMES MAY (1854/5–1907), Rathfriland, county Down;
> born 1854/5, son of George Elliott, farmer; LAH Dub 1894; LRCP LRCS Edin 1876; medical officer to Rathfriland Dispensary District, of Church Street, Rathfriland; married 26 September 1881 in Rathfriland Reformed Presbyterian Church, Mary Sarah Haslett, daughter of Joseph Haslett, draper, of Rathfriland; died 23 June 1907 at Rathfriland; probate Belfast 16 August 1907. [Belf PRO, will cal; Dub GRO (d); *Med Dir*; UHF database (m)].

ELLIOTT, JOHN (*fl c* 1850), Clogher, county Tyrone;
> general practitioner, of Clogher, c 1850; married —; father of the Rev Dr Robert Elliott (*q.v.*). [TCD adm reg].

ELLIOTT, JOHN FOSTER (1867–1917), Manchester, Lancashire, Natal, and Rostrevor, county Down;
> born 9 June 1867 at Townsend Street, Parsonstown, Westmeath, son of O.F. Elliott, manager of the Northern Bank, Monaghan, and Hester McCombe; studied medicine at Trinity College, Dublin, and the Ledwich and Carmichael Schools; LRCPI and LM 1893; LRCSI and LM 1893; surgeon with the Union Steamship Company; general practitioner in Manchester c 1895; Indian medical officer to the Immigration

Board of Natal from c 1900, of Shamrock Lodge, Verulam, Natal c 1900–10; general practitioner, of Southview, Rostrevor from c 1910; lieutenant (temporary) in RAMC 1916–17, during World War I; author of various medical papers and *Hints to Ships' Surgeons*; died 30 September 1917 at Rostrevor. [*BMJ* obituary (1917); Dub GRO (b); Kirkpatrick Archive; *Med Dir*].

ELLIOTT, JOHN TRIMBLE (1857–1935), Smithborough, county Monaghan;
born 1 October 1857 at Newtownhamilton, county Armagh, eldest son of the Rev John Elliott, minister of Clarkesbridge, Donoughmore and Armagh Presbyterian Churches, and Jane Trimble of Castlebellingham; grandson of Dr John Elliott of Castlebellingham, brother of Dr Brereton George Elliott (*q.v.*); educated at Armagh Royal School from 1875; studied medicine at Queen's College, Galway, and from 1851, at Queen's College, Belfast; LRCP LRCS Edin 1881; resident surgeon to the City and County Hospital, Londonderry; medical officer and medical officer of health to Kilmore Dispensary District 1882–1935; medical officer to constabulary; of 'Eldron', Smithborough; unmarried; died 9 September 1935 at 44 University Street, Belfast; probate Dublin 13 March 1936 and Belfast 24 July 1936. [Barkley (1986); Belf GRO (d); Belf PRO, will cal; *BMJ* obituary (1935); Dub Nat Arch, will cal; Ferrar (1933); Kirkpatrick Archive; *Lancet* obituary (1935); *Med Dir*; QCB adm reg].

ELLIOTT, JOHN WILLIAM (1843/4–93), Liverpool, Lancashire, and ship's surgeon;
born 1843/4; studied medicine at Queen's College, Cork, and the Ledwich School, Dublin; LAH Dub 1869; LM Coombe Hosp Dub 1869; LRCP LRCS Edin 1870; surgeon with the National Steamship Service c 1871 and the British and African Steamship Service c 1872; general physician, of 45 Rocky Lane, West Derby Road, Liverpool, from c 1874; died 13 May 1893 at the Lunatic Asylum, St Helen's. [Lond GRO (d); *Med Dir*].

ELLIOTT, JOHN WILSON (*fl c* 1854–6), Naval Medical Service;
son of James Wilson Elliott, gentleman; MD [?]; joined the Naval Medical Service as assistant surgeon; served on HMS *Donegal* 1829–31, *Prince Regent* 1831–2, *Carron* 1932–5, *Dolphin* 1837–8, *Zebra* 1839–41 and *Devastation* 1841–2; retired c 1855 to Tullynure Lodge, Dungannon; married (1) 15 October 1850 in Carntall Presbyterian Church, Clogher, county Tyrone, Susan Hume Ramsay (who was born 1820/1 and died 12 May 1854, being buried in Clogher graveyard), second daughter of Robert Ramsay of Sligo; (2) 11 December 1856 in Donaghmore Church of Ireland Church, Castlecaulfield, county Tyrone, Mehetabel Jane Elizabeth Carpendale, youngest daughter of the Rev Thomas Carpendale, rector of Donaghmore (Donoughmore), county Tyrone, and Lucinda Bagwell. [*BNL* 18 October 1850 (m), 17 May 1854 (d) and 15 December 1856 (m); Dub GRO (m); Leslie (1911)].

ELLIOTT, ROBERT (*fl c* 1845), Tempo, county Fermanagh;
MRCSE 1841; accoucheur of Anglesey Lying-in Hospital, Dublin; medical officer to Tempo Dispensary District and constabulary c 1843–6; possibly died c 1850. [Croly (1843–6)].

ELLIOTT, ROBERT (d 1852), Clogher, county Tyrone;
   born in Clogher; studied medicine at Glasgow University; MD (Glas) 1852; died two months after graduating. [Addison (1898)].

ELLIOTT, ROBERT (1851–1911), India, Altadesert, county Tyrone, Gaza, Palestine, Middletown, county Armagh, and Tullyallen, county Louth;
   born 1851 in Clogher, county Tyrone, son of Dr John Elliott (*q.v.*); studied arts and medicine at Trinity College, Dublin, from 1870; BA (TCD) 1877; LRCSI 1885; ordained deacon 1878 (Church of Ireland); priest 1879; CMS missionary to Bengal 1878–82; rector of Altadesert 1882–6; CMS missionary to Gaza 1886–92; rector of Middletown 1892–4 and of Tullyallen 1894–1900; associate secretary to CMS Medical Department 1900–03; retired to Mellifont, Shortlands Grove, Shortlands, Kent; married 4 October 1888 Mary Childe Royston (who died 29 August 1915), second daughter of the Right Rev Peter Sorenson Royston, Bishop of Mauritius; died 25 April 1911 at Penzance, Cornwall; probate London 14 June 1911. [Crockford (1899); Kirkpatrick Archive; *Lancet* obituary (1911); Leslie (1911) and (1948); Lond PPR, will cal; *Med Dir;* TCD adm reg; *TCD Cat,* vol II (1896)].

ELLIOTT, ROBERT ANDREW (1853/4–77), Arvagh, county Cavan and Llanymynech, Shropshire;
   born 1853/4; studied medicine at Ledwich School and Mercer's Hospital, Dublin; LKQCPI and LM 1875; LRCSI 1875; general practitioner, of Verview Cottage, Llanymynech; unmarried; died 5 May 1877 at Arvagh. [Dub GRO (d); *Med Dir*].

ELLIOTT, ROBERT HANNA (1866–97) Strabane, county Tyrone, and Benin, West Africa;
   born 26 February 1866 at Strabane, second son of William Elliott, merchant, of Strabane, and Dorcas Holmes Hanna; brother of Dr William Moore Elliott (*q.v.*) and Mary Elliott who married Dr Charles Roulston Elliott (*q.v.*), also brother of Dr Alfred Charles Elliott, MB BCh BAO (TCD) 1906; educated at Strabane Academy; studied arts and medicine at Queen's College, Belfast, from 1862; MB BCh BAO (RUI) 1890; general practitioner, of Strabane; district medical officer to the Niger Coast Protectorate (Nigeria); unmarried; died 4 January 1897 at Benin, killed in an ambush while on an unarmed mission to the King of Benin, with 6 army officers ('The Benin Massacre'); one of the survivors, Captain Boisragon, wrote of his bravery in saving the lives of two of them; probate Londonderry 4 June 1897. [Belf PRO, will cal, will; Elliott, Simon, pers com; *Med Dir*; QCB adm reg].

ELLIOTT, WILLIAM HAMILTON (1847–1930), Dublin and Londonderry;
   born 1847 in Dublin, son of Dr William Elliott; educated privately; studied arts and medicine at Trinity College, Dublin, from 1865; BA (TCD) 1869; MB 1870; LRCSI and LM 1872; MD 1875; junior surgeon at the Whitworth Hospital, Dublin; medical officer to Coolock and Drumcondra Dispensary District c 1875; of Richmond Place North, Dublin; medical officer to Glendermott Dispensary District and constabulary and certifying factory surgeon, of Silverton, Waterside, Londonderry; retired 1907; married —; died 27 February 1930 at Castlerock, county

Londonderry. [Belf GRO (d); Kirkpatrick Archive; *Med Dir;* TCD adm reg; *TCD Cat*, vol II (1896)].

ELLIOTT, WILLIAM MOORE (1865–99), Strabane, county Tyrone, and Accra, Gold Coast;
 born 17 January 1865 at Strabane, county Tyrone, eldest son of William Elliott, merchant of Strabane, and Dorcas Holmes Hanna; brother of Dr Robert Hanna Elliott (*q.v.*) and Mary Elliott who married Dr Charles Roulston Elliott (*q.v.*); educated at Strabane Academy and from 1879, at Methodist College, Belfast; studied medicine at Queen's College, Belfast; MB MCh MAO (RUI) 1887; MD 1891; FRCS Edin; general practitioner in Strabane c 1892; medical officer in Accra c 1893–8; unmarried; died 19 July 1899 at The Hall, Mountcharles, following a 'fracture of base of skull, probably instantaneous' (Coroner) in a bicycle accident. [Dub GRO (d); Elliott, Simon, pers com; Fry (1984); *Med Dir;* QCB adm reg].

ELLIOTT, WILLIAM SOLOMON (1858/9–1945), ship's surgeon, Downpatrick, county Down, Dublin and Malahide, county Dublin, and Bournemouth, Hampshire;
 born 1858/9; studied arts and medicine at Trinity College, Dublin, from 1876; LM Rot Hosp Dub 1879; BA (TCD) 1880; MB BCh 1881; surgeon on SS *Italy* and *Austrian*; assistant surgeon to Down County Infirmary 1886–7; general practitioner and surgeon to Admiralty and constabulary, of 7 Gardiner's Row, Dublin from c 1887; of 4 St James' Terrace, Malahide, county Dublin, c 1890 and of Balheary House, Swords, from c 1907; medical officer to Gratia Quies Military Hospital, Bournemouth, c 1917 but retired to Balheary House c 1918; moved to Berry Court Hotel, St Peters Road, Bournemouth c 1932; living c 1935 at Rushall House, Marlborough, Wiltshire; unmarried; died 29 April 1945 at Stoke Prior Nursing Home, 25 Poole Road, Bournemouth; probate Llandudno 1 September 1945. [Kirkpatrick Archive; Lond PPR, will cal; *Med Dir;* TCD adm reg; *TCD Cat*, vol II (1896)].

ELLIS, EDWARD (*fl c* 1662), Belfast;
 apothecary; given freedom of Belfast 1662. [Young (1892)].

ELLIS, GEORGE (d 1838), East Indies;
 of Londonderry; surgeon in the Dutch army; died 9 July 1838 at Tornate, East Indies. [*BNL* 2 April 1839 (d); *Londonderry Sentinel* 30 March 1839 (d)].

ELLIS, HUGH (*fl c* 1849), Kilrea, county Londonderry;
 of Kilrea, county Londonderry; studied medicine at Glasgow University; MD (Glas) 1849; medical officer to Tamlaght O'Crilly Dispensary District; died c 1852. [Addison (1898); *Med Dir*].

ELLIS, JOHN (1830/1–c 1871);
 born 1830/1 in county Fermanagh, son of James Ellis, farmer; educated at Portora Royal School, Enniskillen; studied arts and medicine at Trinity College, Dublin, from 1850; scholar 1855; BA MB (TCD) 1858; MA MD 1871; probably died c 1871. [Burtchaell and Sadleir (1935); *Med Dir; Portora Royal School Register* (1940)].

ELLIS, THOMAS, (1729/30–91), Monaghan and Dublin;
born 1729/30; studied arts and medicine at Trinity College, Dublin, from 1754, also Edinburgh and Leyden; BA (TCD) 1749; MB 1757; MD 1761; member of the Royal Medical Society of Edinburgh 1751; friend of Oliver Goldsmith at Edinburgh and Leyden; general practitioner in Monaghan and Dublin; clerk of the Irish House of Commons c 1785; married Mary Jones of Mary Street, Dublin; died 1791. [Burtchaell and Sadleir (1924); Kirkpatrick Archive; Innes Smith (1932); Underwood (1978)].

ELLIS, WILLIAM (*fl c* 1848), Belfast, ship's surgeon, and Liverpool, Lancashire;
son of William Ellis, teacher, of Belfast; MRCS; surgeon on the 'ill-fated' *Ocean Monarch*; of St Jude's Terrace, West Derby c 1848; married 14 November 1848; in St Peter's Parish Church, Liverpool, Mary Corrigan, daughter of John Corrigan, cork manufacturer, of Oxford Place, Vine Street, Liverpool, and daughter-in-law of John Lawrence of Liverpool. [*BNL* 28 November 1848 (m); Lond GRO (m)].

ELLISON, JOHN (1862–c 1908), Lisburn, county Antrim, and Victoria, Australia;
born 9 July 1862 in Belfast, son of John Ellison, flax spinner, of Lisburn; educated at Lisburn Academy; studied medicine at Queen's College, Belfast, 1879–83; MD (RUI) 1883; MCh 1887; general practitioner of Seymour Street, Lisburn, c 1885; emigrated to Australia c 1890; general practitioner, of Nathalia, Victoria c 1895; medical officer of health at Numurkah; consulting surgeon to Williamstown Hospital; acting public vaccinator and certifying factory surgeon c 1905, of 'St Winning', Ferguson Street, Williamstown; died c 1908. [*Med Dir*; QCB adm reg].

ELMSLIE, WILLIAM WALLACE (1854–c 1880), Brighton, Sussex;
born 29 May 1854 at Macao, China, son of Adam Wallace Elmslie of Ellenborough Park, Weston-Super-Mare, England; educated at King Edward's School, Sherborne, Dorset, 1865–70; studied medicine at Aberdeen University and, 1872–75 at Queen's College, Belfast; LFPS Glas 1875; general practitioner, of 7 Seafield Villas, West Brighton, from c 1875; died before 1887. [Bensly (1937); *Med Dir*; QCB adm reg].

ENGLISH, JOHN (1869/70–95) Keady, county Armagh;
born 1869/70; LRCP LRCS Edin 1893; LFPS and LM Glas 1893; general practitioner of Keady; unmarried; died 14 July 1895 at Keady. [Dub GRO (d); *Med Dir*].

ENGLISH, JOSEPH (1856–c 1927), New South Wales, Australia;
born 25 August 1856 at Crumlin, county Antrim, son of Joseph English, clerk of Petty Sessions, of Crumlin; brother of Dr Robert English (*q.v.*); educated at Crumlin Church School; studied medicine at Queen's College, Belfast, from 1874; LRCP LRCS Edin 1880; emigrated to New South Wales; general practitioner, of 90 Queen Street, Woolehra, Sydney c 1882–90, of Gunning, New South Wales c 1890–1900 and of Yass, New South Wales from c 1900; married 24 November 1885 in St Mary Magdalene's Church of Ireland Church, Belfast, Isabella McCay, daughter of Robert McCay, gentleman, of Ormeau Road, Belfast; died c 1927. [*Med Dir*; QCB adm reg; UHF database (m)].

ENGLISH, ROBERT (1862–89), Colonial Medical Service;
born 29 January 1862 at Crumlin, county Antrim, son of Joseph English, clerk of Petty Sessions, of Crumlin, and Isabella —; brother of Dr Joseph English (*q.v.*); educated at Crumlin School; studied medicine at Queen's College, Belfast, from 1879; MD (RUI) 1885; MCh 1886; joined the Colonial Medical Service as assistant surgeon; died 26 February 1889 at Cape Coast Castle, West Africa; commemorated in Glenavy Roman Catholic Graveyard. [Gravestone inscription; *Med Dir*; QCB adm reg].

ENGLISH, SAMUEL (1874–1951), Dromore, county Down, and Manchester and Blackpool, Lancashire;
born 9 October 1874 at Dromore, county Down, son of Robert English of Dromore; studied medicine at Glasgow University and Anderson's College, also in Berlin, Paris and Dublin; MB CM (Glas) 1895; FRCSI 1909; of Ballancy House, Dromore c 1895; surgeon to the Royal Hospital for Sick Children, Glasgow; surgeon to Manchester Jewish Hospital, of 332 Oxford Road and Winter's Buildings, 30 St Ann's Street, Manchester c 1900–20; major in surgical division of Berrington War Hospital; major in RAMC (East Lancashire Territorials); surgeon to Victoria Hospital, Blackpool c 1920–40, of 6 Brighton Parade and 184 Promenade, Blackpool; retired c 1940 to Beech Close, 92 Newmarket Road, Norwich; co-editor of the *Manchester Medical Review* and author of many medical papers; died 9 November 1951 at Beech Close; probate London 1 March 1952. [Addison (1898); Kirkpatrick Archive; Lond PPR, will cal; *Med Dir*].

ENMISON, — (*fl c* 1828), Antrim;
general practitioner; married 4 December 1828 Sarah Elizabeth Cunningham of Antrim. [*BNL* 6 January 1829 (m)].

ENTRICAN, JAMES (1864–1935), Indian Medical Service;
born 2 September 1864 at Londonderry, son of Samuel Entrican, commercial traveller, of Enniskillen; educated at Portora Royal School, Enniskillen; studied arts and medicine at Queen's College, Belfast, from 1881; BA MA (RUI) 1885; MD MCh MAO 1887; DPH (Camb) 1896; house surgeon to Manchester Ship Canal Hospital, Ellesmere Port; joined the Indian Medical Service (Madras establishment) as surgeon 1891; surgeon major 1903; surgeon lieutenant-colonel 1911; served in Burma 1891–2 and in China 1900; inspector-general of Civil Hospital, Burma; CIE 1922; retired as lieutenant-colonel 1923, to Annfield, Beckley, Sussex; married 11 November 1905 in Christ Church, Rangoon, Amy Mary Yarrow, daughter of Dr George Eugene Yarrow of London; died 14 March 1935 at Hove, Sussex; probate Lewes 24 June 1935. [*BMJ* obituary (1935); Crawford (1930); Dickson, Christopher, pers com; Kirkpatrick Archive; Lond PPR, will cal; *Med Dir*; *Portora Royal School Register* (1940); QCB adm reg].

ERSKINE, ALEXANDER McCONNELL (1868–1949), London and Goole, Yorkshire;
born 21 March 1868 at Ballycarry, county Antrim, son of Robert Erskine, farmer, of Ballycarry; educated at Rockview School, Carrickfergus; studied arts and medicine at

Queen's College, Belfast, from 1883; MB BCh BAO (RUI) 1889; DPH RCPS Lond 1897; MD 1904; clinical assistant to the Royal Westminster Ophthalmic Hospital and the Central London ENT Hospital; general practitioner, and from 1902, medical officer of health for Goole, surgeon to Goole Cottage Hospital, and medical superintendent to the Goole Fever and Smallpox Hospitals, of Anglesey Road and 144 Booth Ferry Road, Goole; married Dora Stanners Blair, daughter of Dr Robert Blair of Goole; died 21 January 1949 at Duchy House Nursing Home, Harrogate, Yorkshire; probate London 13 May 1949. [*BMJ* obituary (1949); Kirkpatrick Archive; Lond PPR, will cal; *Med Dir*; QCB adm reg].

ERSKINE, ARCHIBALD (1806–81), Newry, county Down;
born 1806, third son of the Rev Josiah Erskine, rector of Knockbride, county Cavan, and Marianne Swanzy; studied medicine in Dublin and Edinburgh; LM Dublin Lying-in Hospital (Rotunda); LRCSI 1829; MD (Edin) 1831 (thesis 'De dysenteria'); general practitioner, Sandys Place, Newry; married 8 May 1844 in St Mary's Church of Ireland Church, Newry, his first cousin Anne Elizabeth Wilson (who died 4 June 1891), eldest daughter of John Wilson of Newry, and Anne Swanzy; father of Dr John Wilson Erskine (*q.v.*); died 7 November 1881 in Newry; memorial in St Mary's Church of Ireland Church, Newry; probate Belfast 24 December 1881. [*BNL* 14 May 1844 (m); Belf PRO, will cal; Clarke, *County Down*, vol 21 (1998); Croly (1843–6); Edin Univ; Kirkpatrick Archive; *Med Dir*; *Memorials of the Dead*, vol III, p 258; Swanzy (1908)].

ERSKINE, JOHN WILSON (1848–1932), London;
born 6 April 1848, younger son of Dr Archibald Erskine (*q.v.*) of Sandys Place, Newry and Anne Elizabeth Wilson; studied arts and medicine at Trinity College, Dublin, from 1868; LRCSI 1874; BA (TCD) 1872; MB 1875; medical officer to the Chelsea, Brompton and Belgravia Dispensary Districts, of 321 King's Road, Chelsea, c 1880 and later of 145 Beaufort Street, Chelsea; retired c 1920 to Craig-a-vad, Rostrevor, county Down; married 15 March 1887 in Trinity Parish Church, Chelsea, Frederica Mellon (aged 17), daughter of Alfred Mellon, hotel manager, of 13 Anderson Street, London; died 1 August 1932 at 46 High Street, Manningtree, Essex; probate Belfast 4 October 1932. [Belf PRO, will cal; Lond GRO (m); *Med Dir*; Swanzy (1908); TCD adm reg; *TCD Cat*, vol II (1896)].

ERSKINE, ROBERT (1848–1916), Camborne, Cornwall, and London;
born 10 November 1848 at Tildarg, county Antrim, son of James Erskine, farmer, of Tildarg; educated at Donegore National School; studied medicine at Queen's College, Belfast, from 1871; MD (hons) MCh Dip Mid (QUI) 1875; MAO 1897; DPH RCPS Lond 1897; general practitioner, of Basset Road Villas, Camborne, from c 1880; surgeon to the Miners' Hospital, Redruth, Cornwall; surgeon to the West Cornwall Hospital for Women; moved to 62 Pembridge Villas, Notting Hill, London c 1900; of 25 Chepstow Place, London, c 1915 and of 63 Sussex Gardens c 1916; died 28 November 1916 at 16 Pembridge Gardens, London; probate London 19 February 1917. [Kirkpatrick Archive; Lond PPR, will cal; *Med Dir*; QCB adm reg].

ERSKINE, ROBERT JAMES (1862–1929), Belfast;
born 13 January 1862 at Aughnacloy, county Tyrone, son of James Erskine, merchant, of Aughnacloy; educated at Methodist College, Belfast, from 1876; studied medicine at Queen's College, Belfast, from 1891; LRCP LRCS Edin 1895; LFPS Glas 1895; general practitioner of 2 Templemore Avenue, Belfast, from c 1900; married —; died 23 October 1929 at 2 Templemore Avenue, Belfast. [Belf GRO (d); Fry (1984); Kirkpatrick Archive; *Med Dir*; QCB adm reg].

ESLER, ALFRED WILLIAM (1864–c 1925), Victoria and New South Wales, Australia;
born 15 December 1864 in Australia, son of Dr Robert Esler (*q.v.*) and his second wife; brought back to Belfast with his father; educated at Methodist College, Belfast, from 1874; studied medicine at Queen's College, Belfast, 1881–7; MD MCh MAO (RUI) 1887; returned to Australia to practise in Heathcote, Victoria c 1895, in Sydney c 1905 and in Williamstown, Melbourne c 1908; died c 1925. [Esler (1982); Fry (1984); *Med Dir*; QCB adm reg].

ESLER, ROBERT (1836–1919), Australia, Belfast and London;
born 17 February 1836 at Lisnamurrican, Broughshane, county Antrim, eldest son of Robert Esler, farmer, of Lisnamurrican and Martha Adams; educated at Lisnamurrican School; woollen draper c 1860; married, went out to Australia to look for gold, and returned to study medicine at Queen's College, Belfast, 1872–5; MD Ch Dip Mid (QUI) 1875; general practitioner, of 64 Packenham Place, Belfast, c 1886; physician to the Ulster Hospital for Children and Women 1876–89; president of the Ulster Medical Society 1887–8; moved to London 1889, general physician and surgeon to the P Division of the Metropolitan Constabulary, of 4 Queen's Road, Peckham; author of *A Guide to Belfast and Giant's Causeway and the North* (1884), a family history (Esler, 1892) and a history of the Ulster Medical Society (Esler, 1885); married (1) 1 May 1860 in Glenarm Presbyterian Church, Elizabeth Beattie, daughter of Robert Beattie, lapper, of Ballymena, who died in Australia; (2) —; (3) —; (4) 22 March 1883 in Whitehouse Presbyterian Church, county Antrim, Erminda Rentoul, daughter of the Rev Alexander Rentoul MD DD (*q.v.*); father of Dr Alfred William Esler (*q.v.*) (by his second wife) and Dr Alexander Esler and Dr Maberly Squire Esler (by his fourth wife); died 23 July 1919 at 1 Westcliff Gardens, Herne Bay, Kent; probate London 9 September 1919. [*BMJ* obituary (1919); Dub GRO (m x 2); Esler (1982); Hunter (1936); Kirkpatrick Archive; Lond PPR, will cal; Marshall and Kelly (1973); *Med Dir*; QCB adm reg; Young and Pike (1909)].

EUSTACE, HENRY MARCUS (1869–1927), Edinburgh and Dublin;
born 6 March 1869, second son of Dr John Eustace, MB (TCD) 1851, of Elmhurst, Glasnevin, Dublin; brother of Dr John Neilson Eustace (*q.v.*) and Dr William Neilson Eustace, LRCP LRCSI, 1902; educated at Armagh Royal School 1884–6; studied arts and medicine at Trinity College, Dublin, from 1886; BA (TCD) 1890; LM Rot Hosp Dub, 1891; MD BCh BAO 1892; MD 1894; clinical assistant to the Royal Asylum, Morningside, Edinburgh; resident medical superintendent of Hampstead and Highfield Private Lunatic Asylum, Dublin, from c 1900 and finally of Elmhurst, Glasnevin; married Mary Susan —; died 21 December 1927 at Highfield, Drumcondra; probate Dublin 22 February 1928. [Dub GRO (d); Dub

Nat Arch, will cal, will; Ferrar (1933); Kirkpatrick Archive; *Med Dir;* TCD adm reg; *TCD Cat*, vol II (1896)].

EUSTACE, JOHN NEILSON (1867–94), Dublin;
born 22 September 1867, son of Dr John Eustace, MB (TCD) 1851, of Elmhurst, Glasnevin, Dublin; brother of Dr Henry Marcus Eustace (*q.v.*) and Dr William Neilson Eustace, LRCP LRCSI, 1902; educated at Armagh Royal School 1884–5; studied arts and medicine at Trinity College, Dublin, from 1885, and the Adelaide Hospital, Dublin; BA (TCD) 1889; MB BCh BAO 1890; clinical assistant at Richmond Lunatic Asylum, Dublin, and the Royal Edinburgh Asylum; resident medical superintendent of the Hampstead and Highfield Private Lunatic Asylum, Drumcondra, Dublin from c 1881; unmarried; died 9 October 1894 at Elmhurst, Glasnevin; administration Dublin 15 November 1894. [Belf PRO, will cal; Dub GRO (d); Ferrar (1933); *Med Dir;* TCD adm reg; *TCD Cat*, vol II (1896)].

EVANS, GEORGE (1874/5–1950), Plumbridge, county Tyrone;
born 1874/5, son of David Evans, farmer; studied medicine at Glasgow University; LRCP LRCS Edin 1900; LFPS Glas 1900; of Glenties, county Donegal c 1901; medical officer to Plumbridge Dispensary District, of Glencoppagh c 1902–50; retired c 1950; married 23 September 1910 in Ballywillan Presbyterian Church, Portrush, county Antrim, Letitia Matthewson, daughter of Andrew Matthewson, farmer, of Newtownstewart; divorced c 1940; died 20 November 1950 at Glencoppagh, Plumbridge; buried in Plumbridge graveyard; probate Londonderry 27 June 1951. [Belf GRO (d); Belf PRO, will cal; Kirkpatrick Archive; *Med Dir*; Robinson, Ann, pers com; UHF database (m)].

EVANS, HENRY ECCLES (1846/7–1925), Kilkeel, county Down, and Dublin;
born 1846/7; studied medicine at Trinity College, Dublin; LRCSI 1871; LKQCPI and LM 1873; medical officer to Kilkeel Dispensary District, Irish Lights and Coastguards from 1872; general practitioner, of 33 Eccles Street, Dublin and, at the same time, of Mount Pleasant, Kilkeel; married —; died 5 November 1925 at Kilkeel; probate Belfast 21 April 1926. [Belf GRO (d); Belf PRO, will cal; *Med Dir*].

EVANS, JOHN (d 1844), Naval Medical Service and Buncrana, county Donegal;
MRCSE 1807; accoucheur of the Westminster Lying-in Hospital; MD (Edin) 1820 (thesis 'De colica biliosa inter tropica'); joined the Naval Medical Service as assistant surgeon; surgeon 1807; retired to the Cottage, Buncrana c 1840; married Rose — (who was born 1783/4 and died 26 February 1845 in Belfast); died 20 May 1844 at the Old Lodge, Buncrana, the home of his nephew S. McDowell Elliott; buried in the New Burying Ground, Londonderry. [*BNL* 28 May 1844 (d) and 4 March 1845 (d); Croly (1843–6); Edin Univ; *Londonderry Sentinel* 25 May 1844 (d); *Londonderry Standard* 29 May 1844 (d); *NMS* (1826)].

EVANS, ROBERT (1783/4–1846), Naval Medical Service and Magherafelt, county Londonderry;
born 1783/4; studied medicine at Edinburgh University; LRCSE 1810, MD (Edin) 1820 (thesis 'De apoplexia'); joined the Naval Medical Service as assistant surgeon;

surgeon 1807; physician, of Broad Street, Magherafelt c 1824; married Ann — (who was born 1792/3 and died 1 September 1869); died 30 May 1846 at Magherafelt; buried in Magherafelt Church of Ireland Graveyard; probate Prerogative Court 1847. [Belf PRO, Prerog Wills index; *Coleraine Chronicle* 6 June 1846 (d) and 11 September 1869 (d); Croly (1843–6); Edin Univ; gravestone inscription; *Londonderry Sentinel* 13 June 1846 (d); Maitland (1988); *NMS* (1826); Pigot (1824)].

EVANS, ROBERT LOCKE (1844/5–90), Foxford, county Mayo, Manchester, Lancashire, Carrickfergus, county Antrim and Liverpool, Lancashire;
born 1844/5; studied medicine at the Ledwich School, Dublin; LRCSI 1867; LKQCPI and LM 1867; general practitioner, of Belgariffe, Foxford, c 1870; of Manchester c 1875; of Grosvenor Place, Carrickfergus, c 1885 and from c 1890, of 286A Crown Street, Liverpool; died 19 October 1890 at Liverpool Northhouse, of 'excessive drinking' (coroner). [Lond GRO (d); *Med Dir*].

EVANS, WILLIAM (1829/30–c 1897), ship's surgeon, Calcutta, India, and London;
born 1829/30, son of John Evans of Belfast; educated at RBAI; studied medicine at Queen's College, Belfast 1849–52; MD (QUI) 1852; LRCS and LM Edin 1852; surgeon to the P & O Steamship Company; consulting physician to the City Mission, Indian Military Relief Fund and Municipal Commission, Calcutta; surgeon to the Calcutta Volunteer Cavalry; assistant surgeon to the 28th Middlesex Volunteers; superintendent physician to the Special Cholera Hospital, Great Oxford Street, Liverpool in the epidemic of 1866; general practitioner, of 1 College Terrace, Belsize Park, London, from c 1868; moved c 1878 to Glen Villa, Forest Gate, Essex; author of various medical papers; described as 'travelling' c 1894; married 28 August 1862 in Carnmoney Church of Ireland Church, Sarah Maria Johnston, eldest daughter of Philip Johnston of Dalriada, county Antrim; died c 1897. [*Coleraine Chronicle* 30 August 1862 (m); *Med Dir*; QCB adm reg].

EVATT, EVELYN JOHN (1810/1–c 1841), Carrickmacross, county Monaghan;
born 1810/1, fourth son of Humphrey Evatt, gentleman, of Mount Louise, county Monaghan, and Elizabeth Bayley; educated at the Feinagle School, Dublin; studied arts and medicine at Trinity College, Dublin, from 1828; BA (TCD) 1837; MB 1840; surgeon and medical officer to Carrickmacross Dispensary; married 1839 Berri Bayley, third daughter of Captain John Bayley; died 8 May 1841 of typhus fever at Carrickmacross. [*BNL* 14 May 1841 (d); Burke *LGI* (1912); Burtchaell and Sadleir (1924)].

EVATT, SIR GEORGE JOSEPH HAMILTON (1843–1921), Army Medical Service;
born 11 November 1843 in county Monaghan, son of Captain George Evatt; studied medicine at Trinity College, Dublin, and the Royal College of Surgeons in Ireland; MD (hons) (QUI) 1863; LRCSI 1863; joined the Army Medical Service as staff assistant surgeon 1865; attached to 25th Foot 1866; surgeon major 1877; surgeon lieutenant-colonel 1885; brigade surgeon lieutenant-colonel 1891; surgeon colonel 1896; surgeon general 1899; served in Perak 1876, Afghan War 1878–80, Sudan 1885, Zhob Valley 1890; retired 1903; CB (military) 1903; honorary colonel to Home Counties Division of RAMC; served again during World War I; KCB c 1919;

founder of the Medical Officers of Schools Association 1884; president of the Poor Law Medical Officers Association; author of *Medico-Military Topography of the Persian Gulf and Euphrates and Tigris Valleys* (1874), *Army Medical Organization* (3rd ed 1883) and many papers regarding the health of the soldier; contested three seats in the south of England, unsuccessfully, as a liberal candidate; of 33 Earls Court Square, Kensington; married 1877 Sophia Mary Francis Kerr, daughter of W.W. Raleigh Kerr; died 5 November 1921 at 33 Earls Court Square; probate London 10 December 1921. [*BMJ* obituary (1921); Crone (1928); Kirkpatrick Archive; *Lancet* obituary (1921); Lond GRO (d); Lond PPR, will cal; Martin (2003) and (2010); *Med Dir*; Newmann (1993); Peterkin and Johnston (1968)].

EVATT, HENRY (d c 1756), Enniskillen, county Fermanagh;
apothecary, of Cleenish, Enniskillen; died c 1756; administration Clogher Diocesan Court 1756. [Dub Nat Arch, Clogher Dio Admins index].

EVORY, GEORGE (d c 1774);
eighth child of William Evory, merchant, of Londonderry, and Margaret Gallagher; apothecary, of Londonderry; churchwarden of Derry Cathedral; married Anne Kennedy; father of Dr Thomas Evory of Dublin (*q.v.*); will dated 1774; died c 1774; probate Derry Diocesan Court. [Thrift (1920); Young (1929)]

EVORY, THOMAS (1758–1828), Dublin;
born 18 October 1758 in Londonderry, only son of George Evory, apothecary, of Londonderry (*q.v.*) and Anne Kennedy; studied medicine in Dublin and on 1 August 1775 was apprenticed to Mr William Vance, surgeon of the Meath Hospital, Dublin 1775–80; MD (Edin) 1782 (thesis 'De febre puerperarum'); LKQCPI 1785; LM KQCPI 1792; honorary physician to the Meath Hospital 1785–93; assistant master of the Rotunda Hospital, Dublin 1786–9; master of the Rotunda 1793–1800, improving conditions and reducing mortality; co-founder of the Cow-Pock Institution for vaccinating the poor; of 2 Rutland Square, Dublin 1801–28; unmarried; godfather and guardian of Dr Evory Kennedy (*q.v.*); died 10 January 1828 in Rutland Square, intestate; buried and memorial erected in St Audeon's church, Dublin. [*DIB* (2009); Edin Univ; Kirkpatrick Archive; Kirkpatrick and Jellett (1913); *Memorials of the Dead*, vol VIII, p 291; O'Doherty (2002); Ormsby (1888)].

EWING, JOHN (c 1816–89), Army Medical Service;
born 24 December 1815 or 1818, son of Joseph Ewing, AMS (*q.v.*); joined the Army Medical Service as staff assistant surgeon to the 97th Foot 1841; staff surgeon, second class 1852; attached to the 95th Foot 1857; staff surgeon 1859; attached to the 62nd Foot 1860; surgeon major 1867; served in the Crimea; retired on half pay 1876 as deputy surgeon general; of Winfield Terrace, Chester Road, Manchester, and finally of 39 Alderney Street, Pimlico, London; married 28 August 1856 in Armagh Cathedral, Margaret Kidd, only daughter of Osborne Kidd of Tullymore, county Armagh; died 27 July 1889 at 39 Alderney Street; probate London 19 August 1889. [*BNL* 1 September 1856 (m); Lond PPR, will cal; Peterkin and Johnston (1968)].

EWING, JOHN (1870–1950), Belfast;
> born 16 November 1870 at Deffrick, Dervock, county Antrim, son of James Ewing, farmer, of Deffrick; educated at Ballymoney Intermediate School; studied medicine at Queen's College, Belfast, from 1889, and Edinburgh University; LRCP LRCS Edin 1893; LFPS Glas 1893; LAH Dub 1898; general practitioner in Belfast; of 'Saxonia', Strandtown, Belfast of 2 Connsbrook Avenue c 1905, of 'Eversleigh', Strandtown c 1910, and of 'Saxonia' again c 1921; retired c 1936 to 103 Delamere Road, Ealing, London; married 2 September 1896 in Ballycastle Presbyterian Church, county Antrim, Anne Neil McAllister, daughter of Alexander McAllister, merchant, of Ballycastle; died 11 February 1950 at 103 Delamere Road; administration London 30 March 1950. [Dub GRO; Lond GRO (m) and (d); Lond PPR, will cal; *Med Dir*; QCB adm reg; UHF database (m)].

EWING, JOSEPH (1790–1868), Army Medical Service;
> born 13 June 1790, son of the Rev John Ewing, Church of England clergyman, and Anne Barclay; joined the Army Medical Service as assistant surgeon to the 90th Foot in 1809; retired on half pay 1818; re-joined with the 80th Foot in 1831; surgeon 1835; transferred to 95th Foot 1836; retired on half pay 1848; of Warrenpoint, county Down, from c 1850; married Jane Arbuthnot, daughter of the Rev — Arbuthnot of county Cavan; father of John Ewing, AMS (*q.v.*); died 29 March 1868 at Fort George, Inverness. [Edin GRO (d); *Med Dir*; Peterkin and Johnston (1968)].

EWING, ROBERT, (*fl c* 1845), Ballycastle;
> LM Glas [?]; general practitioner in Ballycastle c 1845; married 17 October 1844 in Ballycastle Presbyterian Church, Margaret McConaghy, youngest daughter of John McConaghy of Ballycastle; possibly died c 1850. [Croly (1843–6); *Londonderry Sentinel* 2 November 1844 (m)].

EWING, WILLIAM (1822/3–47), Belfast;
> born 1822/3; studied medicine at Glasgow University; MD (Glas) 1846; died 22 May 1847 at his father's house in Donegall Street, Belfast. [Addison (1898); *BNL* 25 May 1847 (d)].

Prof Robert Coffey, MD (1796–1847)

Dr Robert Collins (1800–68), artist unknown (reproduced courtesy of the Royal College of Physicians of Ireland)

Dr Samuel Grahame Connor (1865–1941)

Dr James Cord (1766/7–98), gravestone

Dr Frederick Alexander Craig (1865–1932)

Dr James Craig (1860–1923)

Mr James Andrew Craig, FRCS (1872–1958)

Dr John Crawford (1746–1813)

Dr John Smyth Crone (1858–1945)

Prof James Cuming, MD (1833–99), oil painting, artist unknown (reproduced courtesy of the Royal Victoria Hospital, Belfast)

Dr John Oliver Curran (1819–47), engraving

Dr Charles Chatterton Deane (1867–1926)

Prof William Dease (c 1752–98), statue by *Sir Thomas Farrell* (reproduced courtesy of the Royal College of Surgeons in Ireland)

Sir Alexander Dempsey, MD (1852–1920)

Prof Robert Foster Dill, MD (1811–93), oil painting by *Richard Hooke* (reproduced courtesy of the Queen's University of Belfast)

Dr William Dunlop Donnan (1869–1941)

Dr William Drennan (1754–1820),
oil painting, artist unknown
(private collection)

Prof James Lawson Drummond, MD
(1783–1853), engraving

Dr Robert Esler (1836–1919)

Prof John Creery Ferguson, MB (1802–65)

Dr Benjamin Banks Ferrar (1862–1948)

Dr David Finnegan (1873–1935)

Dr Alexander John Fleming (1856–1913)

Dr James Forsythe (1756–1849), oil painting by Samuel Hawksett [?] (photograph reproduced courtesy the Trustees of National Museums, Northern Ireland)

Prof Andrew Fullerton, FRCS (1868–1934), oil painting by *William Conor* (reproduced courtesy of the Royal Victoria Hospital, Belfast)

Dr William Gamble (1688/9–1778), c 1740, oil painting, artist unknown (photograph reproduced courtesy the Trustees of National Museums, Northern Ireland)

Dr Samuel Ferguson Gawn (1862–1927)

Dr William Gibson (1860–1945)

Dr Leonard Gillespie, surgeon RN (1758–1842), oil painting by *Charles Louis Bazin*

Dr George Kilpatrick Given (1846–1918)

Prof Alexander Gordon, MD (1818–87), oil painting, artist unknown (reproduced courtesy of the Queen's University of Belfast)

Dr Alexander Leslie Gracey (1824–86)

F

FAGAN, SIR JOHN (1843–1930), Belfast and Dublin;
born 16 July 1843 at Lismacaffrey, Rathowen, county Westmeath, eldest son of James Fagan of Lismacaffrey; educated at St Vincent's College, Castleknock, Dublin; studied medicine at the Catholic University of Ireland (Gold Medal) and later in London, Paris and Vienna; LRCSI 1865; LKQCPI and LM 1866; FRCSI 1874; surgeon in Belfast from c 1868 and the first surgeon in Belfast to give up the combination with general practice; living at 78 Donegall Street; first attending surgeon to the new Belfast Children's Hospital 1873–92 and a leading spirit in its foundation; of 1 Glengall Place from c 1880; studied practical anatomy and 'dissections' at Queen's College 1875–7; attending surgeon to the Belfast Royal Hospital 1877–97; president of the Ulster Medical Society 1884–6; gave the annual winter oration at the Belfast Royal Hospital in 1888; pioneer in introducing antisepsis into surgery in Belfast, a bold surgeon and energetic teacher but gave up surgery after a mistake in operating in 1890; JP for county Antrim; resigned from the Royal Hospital in 1897 to move to Dublin where he was appointed Inspector of Reformatory and Industrial Schools in Ireland; of Monasterevin, county Kildare; medical member of the General Prison Board from 1906; knight bachelor 1910; Deputy Lieutenant for Queen's County, of Portarlington, Queen's County 1928–30; married —; died 17 March 1930 at Craigeaverne, Portarlington; memorial tablet in Royal Belfast Hospital for Sick Children. [Allison (1972); *BMJ* obituary (1930); Calwell (1969) and (1973); *DIB* (2009); Dub GRO (d); Hunter (1936); *Lancet* obituary (1930); *Med Dir*].

FAGAN, PETER (d c 1820), Newry, county Down;
apothecary, of Newry c 1810; died c 1820. [Clarke, *County Down*, vol 21 (1998)].

FAIRCLOUGH, JOHN JAMES KENT (1855–1947), Manchester;
born 19 October 1855 at Lymm, Cheshire, son of George Fairclough of Kennedy Hall, Northerian, Cheshire; educated at Manchester Commercial School; studied medicine at Manchester School of Medicine, Glasgow University and, from 1874–7, at Queen's College, Belfast; BSc (Vict Coll); LKQCPI and LM 1876; MD MCh (QUI) 1877; MRCSE 1877; house surgeon to Chorlton Dispensary District, Manchester; medical officer to mercantile marine; general practitioner, of 414 Stretford Street, Manchester; anaesthetist to Manchester Dental Hospital; obstetric physician to No 4 District and Manchester Maternity Hospital; surgeon captain to Manchester Company of Voluntary Medical Staff Corps; major 1905; retired as lieutenant-colonel RAMC (TA); of 'Greenmount', Seymour Grove, Old Trafford c 1910 and of Kismet, Green Lane, Buxton c 1912; officer commanding 2nd Field Ambulance c 1914; married Jane —; died 15 September 1947; administration Manchester 7 November 1947. [Lond PPR, will cal; *Med Dir*; QCB adm reg].

FAIRSERVICE, JAMES (*fl c* 1845), Stewartstown, county Tyrone;
MRCSE; general practitioner of Stewartstown c 1845; possibly died c 1850. [Croly (1843–6)].

FALLOON, EDWARD LESLIE (or **SHEPPARD**) (1818/9–72), Lurgan, county Armagh, and Liverpool, Lancashire;
> born 1818/9, third son of the Rev Marcus Falloon, curate of Drumbo, county Down, and rector of Layde, county Antrim, and Maria Jane Wolseley; studied medicine at Trinity College, Dublin; MRCSE 1840; LRCP Edin 1865; surgeon, of Lurgan c 1845 and of 4 Shaw Street, Liverpool, from c 1850; assistant surgeon to the Bengal Volunteer Regiment, China Expedition (medal); author of various medical papers; married 18 April 1845 in Shankill Church of Ireland Church, Lurgan, Elizabeth Breadon, third daughter of Joseph Breadon, surgeon RN, of Lurgan, and sister of Catharine Breadon who married Dr Alexander Bredon (*q.v.*); died 13 August 1872 at Shaw Street; probate Liverpool 27 December 1872. [*BNL* 24 April 1845 (m); Bell (1985); Leslie (1993); Lond PPR, will cal; *Med Dir*; UHF database (m)].

FARLEY, GEORGE WILLIAM (1866–1922), Liverpool, Lancashire, Ballyhaise, county Cavan, and Clones, county Monaghan;
> born 11 December 1866 at Cloncorrie, Clones, son of James Farley, farmer, of Cloncorrie; educated at Clones School; studied arts and medicine at Queen's College, Belfast, from 1885; MD BCh BAO (RUI) 1891 (with scholarships and Malcolm Exhibition); surgeon to Allan Line and RMS *Assyrian*; resident medical officer to Liverpool City Fever Hospital at Parkhill; resident surgeon to Carnarvonshire and Anglesey Infirmary, Bangor, North Wales; medical officer and medical officer of health to Ballyhaise Dispensary District, medical officer to constabulary and certifying factory surgeon c 1895–1922; of Clinovic House, Clones, and later of The Retreat, Armagh; died 15 April 1922. [Belf GRO (d); *Med Dir*; QCB adm reg].

FARLEY, NATHANIEL (d 1856), Army Medical Service;
> MRCSE 1855; of Clones, county Monaghan; joined the Army Medical Service as staff assistant surgeon 1855; served in the Crimea 1855–6; died 22 July 1856. [*Med Dir*; Peterkin and Johnston (1968)].

FARRAN, — (*fl c* 1845), Carndonagh, county Donegal;
> general practitioner, of Carndonagh c 1845; possibly died c 1850. [Croly (1843–6)].

FARRELL, — (d 1869), Banbridge and Newcastle, county Down;
> surgeon, of Banbridge c 1819 and later of Newcastle; died 20 January 1869. [Bradshaw (1819); Newcastle RC Church, bur reg].

FARRELLY, THOMAS F. (1857/8–91), Kilnaleck, county Cavan;
> born 1857/8; studied medicine at Galway Infirmary and Mater Misericordiae and Coombe Hospitals, Dublin; MD MCh (RUI) 1883; LM KQCPI 1883; medical officer and medical officer of health to Kilnaleck Dispensary District and medical officer to constabulary; married Delia —; died 28 April 1891 of typhus fever at Bailieborough; administration Cavan 30 May 1891. [Belf PRO, will cal; Dub GRO (d); *Med Dir*].

FARREN, JOHN THOMAS (1874/5–1907), Ardara, county Donegal;
born 1874/5; educated at St Mungo's College, Glasgow; LRCP LRCS Edin 1899; LFPS Glas 1899; medical officer and medical officer of health to Ardara Dispensary District; medical officer to constabulary and coastguard; unmarried; died 11 March 1907 at Clonmany. [Dub GRO (d); *Med Dir*].

FARREN, NEIL (1843/4–89), Clonmany, county Donegal;
born 1843/4; studied medicine at Glasgow University; LFPS Glas 1867; LRCP Edin and LM 1869; surgeon on Liverpool and Great Western Company's SS *Colorado*; medical officer to Clonmany and later Buncrana Dispensary Districts; medical officer to constabulary, Admiralty and Royal Artillery and certifying factory surgeon; JP; married —; died 31 March 1889 at Buncrana; probate Londonderry 9 May 1889. [Belf PRO, will cal, will; Dub GRO (d); Kirkpatrick Archive; *Med Dir*].

FARRINGTON, WALTER (1866–1944), Belfast and Brynmawr, Breconshire;
born 5 September 1866 at Bewdley, Worcestershire, son of Thomas Edward Farrington, collector of inland revenue, Belfast, and Elizabeth Lowe; educated at Galway Grammar School; studied arts and medicine at Queen's Colleges, Galway, 1889–91 and Belfast, 1891–4; MB BCh BAO (RUI) 1894; general practitioner of Balmoral, Belfast; general practitioner in Wales from c 1906, of Holymount and later 43 Greenland Road, Brynmawr; married —; died 15 September 1944 at Monmouthshire County Hospital, Pontypool. [Kirkpatrick Archive; Lond GRO (b) and (d); *Med Dir*; QCB adm reg]

FAULKNER, WILLIAM IRVINE (1848–c 1881), Stoke-upon-Trent, Staffordshire, and Australia;
born 4 September 1848 at Aghnahoo, Killeter, county Tyrone, son of Irvine Faulkner of Aghnahoo; educated at Castlederg Intermediate School; studied medicine at Queen's College, Belfast, from 1865; MD MCh (QUI) 1873; Dip Mid 1875; house physician and house surgeon to North Staffordshire Infirmary, Stoke-upon-Trent c 1875; emigrated to Australia c 1876; of Kyneton, Victoria c 1878; died c 1881. [*Med Dir*; QCB adm reg]

FAUSSET, ANDREW GRIERSON (1860–c 1917), Leeds, Yorkshire, and London;
born 5 April 1860 in Armagh, seventh son of Robert D. Fausset, county inspector RIC; brother of Dr Herbert John Fausset (*q.v.*); educated at Armagh Royal School 1873–7 and Portora Royal School 1878–9; studied arts and medicine at Trinity College, Dublin, from 1879; BA (TCD) 1883; MB BCh 1885; resident medical officer to the Adelaide Hospital, and midwifery assistant to the Coombe Hospital, Dublin; assistant medical officer to the Friends Retreat, York; general practitioner of Stanningley, Leeds c 1885–91; moved to 66 Belgrave Road, London 1891; anaesthetist to the Gordon Hospital for Fistula and the National Heart Hospital c 1900; medical officer to the Pimlico Dispensary District; obstetric physician to St Peter's, Eaton Square, Maternity Charity; of 66 Belgrave Square c 1906; retired to 'The Beeches', Sandhurst, Kent c 1910 and 10 Charlbury Road, Oxford c 1915; author of various medical papers; married — Farquhar and changed his name to

Farquhar on retirement; died c 1917. [Ferrar (1933); *Med Dir*; *Portora Royal School Register*; TCD adm reg; *TCD Cat*, vol II (1896)].

FAUSSET, HERBERT JOHN (1846–1936), Dublin, London and Tamworth, Staffordshire;
born 7 October 1846 at Clones, county Monaghan, son of Robert D. Fausset, county inspector RIC; brother of Dr Andrew Grierson Fausset (*q.v.*); spent his boyhood in county Waterford with his maternal grandfather, lieutenant H.J. Clifford RN; educated at Armagh Royal School 1859–63; studied arts and medicine at Trinity College, Dublin 1863–8; BA (TCD) 1867; LM Rot Hosp Dub; MB MCh 1868; MD 1878; resident surgeon to the Richmond, Whitworth and Hardwick Hospital, Dublin; medical officer to the West District, Poplar, London, c 1870; medical officer of health to Tamworth, from c 1880, of 9 Cole Hill, Tamworth; surgeon lieutenant-colonel 2nd VB, North Staffordshire Regiment; medical officer and public vaccinator to 1st District, Tamworth Union; retired c 1927 to 'Hopwas', Tamworth; died 10 October 1936 at 'Hopwas'; probate London 17 November 1936. [*BMJ* obituary (1936); Ferrar (1933); Kirkpatrick Archive; Lond PPR, will cal; Martin (2003); *Med Dir;* TCD adm reg; *TCD Cat*, vol II (1896)].

FAWCETT, EDWARD (1847–1923), Indian Medical Service;
born 17 March 1847, son of John Fawcett of Augharoosky, county Fermanagh; LKQCPI and LM 1868; LRCSI 1868; FRCSI 1879; joined the Indian Medical Service (Madras establishment) as assistant surgeon 1869; surgeon 1873; surgeon major 1881; lieutenant-colonel 1894; served in Burma 1886–7 (medal with clasp); retired 1899; finally of 72 Vanburgh Park, Blackheath, Staffordshire; married Emily Susan Moloney (who was born 1859/60 and died 21 December 1893), daughter of George Moloney, RM, of Omagh, county Tyrone; died 1 November 1923 at Blackheath; probate London 12 December 1923. [Crawford (1930); Kirkpatrick Archive; Lond PPR, will cal; McGrew (1898); *Med Dir*].

FAWCETT, JOHN JAMES 1792/3–1827), Army Medical Service;
born 1792/3; joined the Army Medical Service as surgeon's mate 1812; assistant surgeon to 62nd Foot 1813; served in the Peninsular War 1813–14; died 29 May 1827 at Enniskillen, county Fermanagh; buried in Enniskillen Cathedral Graveyard. [Dundas (1913); *Memorials of the Dead*, vol II, p 110; Peterkin and Johnston (1968)].

FEARON, THOMAS (1842/3–73), Warrenpoint, county Down;
born 1842/3; studied medicine at the Catholic University of Ireland; LRCP; LRCS Edin and LM 1866; general practitioner, in Warrenpoint; unmarried; died 25 November 1873 at Warrenpoint of 'syncope' (coroner); administration Belfast 16 January 1874. [Belf PRO, will cal; Dub GRO (d); *Med Dir*].

FEE, WILLIAM (1809/10–47), Ballymena, county Antrim;
born 1809/10; surgeon, of Ballymena; married —; died 4 March 1847 in Ballymena, after a severe illness; buried in Ahoghill Old Graveyard. [*BNL* 12 March 1847 (d); *Coleraine Chronicle* 13 March 1847 (d); gravestone inscription].

FEGAN, DANIEL (1848–1908), Rathfriland, county Down;
born March 1845 at Banbridge, son of John Fegan of Ballynanny, Banbridge; educated by the Rev M. McKee; studied medicine at Queen's College, Belfast, from 1862; MD (QUI) 1870; LM (QUI) 1878; LFPS Glas 1896; general practitioner of Annaclone and Rathfriland; unmarried; died 29 January 1908 at Ballynarry, Loughbrickland. [Dub GRO (d); *Med Dir*; QUB].

FEGAN, RICHARD (c 1836–1927), Dunglow, county Donegal, and London;
born c 1836; studied medicine at the Royal College of Surgeons in Ireland; LM Dub Lying-In Hosp 1856; LRCSI 1857; LKQCPI 1860; MD (St Andrews) 1862 (by examination); MRCPI 1901; medical officer to Dunglow Dispensary District c 1858; medical officer to Ardara Dispensary District, constabulary and Admiralty c 1860; abroad c 1862; medical officer and public vaccinator to Charlton District, Lewisham c 1864; physician to Blackheath and Charlton Cottage Hospital; of Fairfield Cottage, Old Lewisham, and of 1 Charlton Park Terrace; later physician to the Royal Kent Dispensary; of 4 Waterside Terrace c 1880, of Templemore, Westcombe Park, Blackheath c 1885 and of 411–9 Salisbury House, London Wall c 1925; president of Irish Medical School and Graduate Association 1890; married —; father of Dr Richard Ardra Fegan of Leamington Spa, Warwickshire, MRCSE LRCP Lond 1897; died 19 December 1927. [*Med Dir;* Smart (2004)].

FENTON, BENJAMIN (*fl c* 1768–74), Strabane, county Tyrone;
apothecary, of Strabane c 1768 (witness of a will) and 1774 (executor of a will). [Dub Reg Deeds, 267.462.172867 (1768) and 319.546.216927 (1774); Elliott, Simon, pers com; Eustace, vol II (1954)].

FENTON, JOHN SAMUEL (1861–1929), Brackley, Northamptonshire;
born 10 August 1861 at Ballina Park, Ashford, county Wicklow, son of Samuel Fenton, JP, land agent, of Humewood, Baltinglass, county Wicklow; educated at Armagh Royal School 1872–7 and at Rathmines School, Dublin, from 1877; studied arts and medicine at Trinity College, Dublin, from 1879; BA (TCD) 1883; MB BCh 1884; LM KQCPI 1885; MD 1886; general practitioner at Brackley; died 4 July 1929 at Brackley; probate London 16 August 1929. [Ferrar (1933); Figgis and Drury (1932); Kirkpatrick Archive; London PPR, will cal; *Med Dir;* TCD adm reg; *TCD Cat*, vol II (1896)].

FENWICK, CHARLES (1854–1932), Killygordon, county Donegal and Exeter;
born 24 June 1854 at Devonport, county Devon, son of Charles B. Fenwick of Pillaton, Cornwall; educated at Blundell's School, Tiverton; studied medicine at Queen's College, Belfast, from 1871; LM Rot Hosp Dub; LRCP LRCS Edin 1876; house surgeon to Teignmouth Infirmary and Ripon Dispensary; medical officer and public vaccinator to Killygordon Dispensary District, from c 1880; medical officer and public vaccinator to Dunsford and Cheriton Districts, Exeter from c 1890; consulting surgeon to Mortonhampstead Cottage Hospital; moved to 18 Sylvan Road, Exeter c 1920; retired c 1925; of Salthaven, Sheldon, South Devon c 1930; married Ellen Sophia —; died 4 February 1932; probate Exeter 7 June 1935. [Lond PPR, will cal; *Med Dir*; QCB adm reg].

FERGUS, SAMUEL (1853–1941), Blackwatertown, county Armagh;
born 16 September 1853 at Portadown, county Armagh, son of Samuel Fergus, spirit merchant, of Portadown; educated at RBAI; studied medicine at Queen's College, Belfast, from 1870; MD (QUI) 1875; MCh Dip Mid 1876; medical officer and medical officer of health to Blackwatertown Dispensary District; medical officer to constabulary and certifying factory surgeon; JP; retired c 1932 to Springhill, Cumberland Road, Headingley, Leeds; married (1) 13 January 1876 at William Brereton's home, Corcreeny, Mary Brereton (who was born 1851/2 and died 9 September 1878), youngest daughter of William Brereton, farmer, of Corcreeny, Kilwarlin; (2) 12 May 1880 at Roscorry, Loughgall, Elizabeth Reid, second daughter of Robert Reid, farmer, of Roscorry, father of Dr William John Brereton Fergus of Leeds, MB BCh BAO (RUI) 1901; died 2 March 1941; probate Llandudno 15 May 1941. [Dub GRO (m x 2); gravestone inscription; Kirkpatrick Archive; Lond PPR, will cal, will; *Med Dir*; QCB adm reg; UHF database (m) (1876)].

FERGUSON, ALFRED AUBREY (1867/8–1956), Belfast;
born 1867/8; studied medicine at the Carmichael College, Dublin; LKQCPI and LM 1889; LRCSI and LM 1889; LM Rot Hosp Dub; DPH Camb 1894; general practitioner, of 208 and 246 Woodstock Road, Belfast; retired to 1 Broomhill Park Central c 1955; married Mary —; father of Dr Alfred Boyd Ferguson of Belfast, LRCP LRCS Edin 1933; died 17 January 1956 at 1 Broomhill Park Central; probate Belfast 30 July 1956. [Belf GRO (d); Belf PRO, will cal, will; *Med Dir*].

FERGUSON, HENRY SHAW (1814/5–90), Doagh, county Antrim, and Belfast;
born 1814/15; studied medicine at Glasgow University; MRCSE 1836; MD (Glas) 1837; general practitioner in Doagh, county Antrim 1838–46; honorary physician to the Ulster Hospital for Children and Women 1874–84; consulting physician to the Dispensary for Skin Diseases and surgeon to Belfast Charitable Infirmary c 1870; of 1 Fisherwick Place, and 8 Murray's Terrace, Belfast; married 7 September 1846 in Donegore Church of Ireland Church, Alicia Gunning, second daughter of Thomas Gunning; died 16 June 1890; probate Belfast 11 August 1890. [Addison (1898); *BNL* 11 September 1846 (m); Belf PRO, will cal; Croly (1843–6); Marshall and Kelly (1973); *Med Dir*; Stewart (1994); Whitla (1901)].

FERGUSON, JAMES (d c 1782), Coleraine, county Londonderry;
surgeon, of Coleraine; died c 1782; administration Prerogative Court 12 February 1782. [Belf PRO, T808/ p 4544; Dub Nat Arch, Prerog Admins index; Elliott, Simon, pers com].

FERGUSON, JAMES (c 1710–84), Belfast;
born c 1710, son of Dr John Ferguson of Belfast (*q.v.*); MD (Rheims) 1743; linen merchant and physician to the Poor House; in 1770 received £300 from the Linen Board for demonstrating the successful application of lime to the bleaching of linen and later introduced sulphuric acid for this; general practitioner in Belfast and physician to the Poor House from its opening in 1775; involved in liberal politics in Belfast and chaired a meeting in support of widening the franchise in 1783; married

(1) Sarah Clark (who died October 1760), eldest daughter of Jackson Clark, linen merchant of Maghera; a son died 1753; (2) 1761 Jane Stephenson of Killyfaddy, county Armagh (who was born 1721 and died 24 January 1804); died 22 December 1784 in Belfast, of a fever. [Agnew (1998); *BNL* 28 December 1784 (d) and 27 January 1804 (d); Benn (1877); Brockliss; Burke *LGI* (1912); Clark (1972); Elliott, Simon, pers com; *Faulkner's Dublin Journal* (1760); Gillespie and O'Keeffe (2006); Hitchings, Paul, pers com; Joy (1817); MacCarthy (1986); Merrick and Clarke, *Belfast*, vol 4 (1991); Pilson (1846); Strain (1961)].

FERGUSON, JAMES CHAMBERS (1808–79), Liverpool, Lancashire;
born 1808, son of Dr Thomas Ferguson, apothecary, of Tandragee and Dublin (*q.v.*), and Elizabeth Creery; brother of Professor John Creery Ferguson (*q.v.*); educated at the Feinaiglian Institution; studied arts and medicine at Trinity College, Dublin from 1824; BA (TCD) 1829; MA 1832; LRCSI 1832; MB 1835; general practitioner, of 95 Shaw Street, Liverpool c 1859 and later of Blackburn Place, Liverpool; married —; died 21 May 1879 at Blackburn Place; administration Liverpool 23 July 1879. [Belf PRO, D 1918/2; Burtchaell and Sadleir (1924); Lond PPR, will cal; *Med Dir*.]

FERGUSON, JAMES COLEMAN (1855/6–1914), Belfast;
born 14 August 1856 at Doagh, county Antrim, son Dr Thomas Ferguson of Doagh (*q.v.*); educated privately; studied medicine at Queen's College, Belfast, from 1880; MD MCh Dip Obst (RUI) 1884; MAO 1885; resident surgeon to Belfast Union Infirmary; medical officer, public vaccinator and medical officer of health to Belfast No 1 (later No 6) Dispensary District, of 257 Abbotsford Place, York Street; physician to Ulster Hospital for Children and Women, of 168 York Street and later 133 Glenfield Place, Belfast; married Isobel —; died 6 January 1914 at the Dispensary, Glengall Street, Belfast; buried in Donegore Church of Ireland graveyard; probate Belfast 17 February 1914. [Belf PRO, will cal; Dub GRO (d); gravestone inscription; Kirkpatrick Archive; *Med Dir*; QCB adm reg].

FERGUSON, JOHN (d c 1747), Belfast;
probably son of Dr Victor Ferguson of Belfast (*q.v.*); apothecary, of Belfast from c 1714; married (1) Mary —; (2) Agnes —; father of Dr James Ferguson of Belfast (*q.v.*); will dated 18 March 1746, probate Prerogative Court 28 April 1747. [Agnew (1995); Belf PRO, Burke's Pedigrees, vol 21, p 86; Belf PRO, T808/4541; Hitchings, Paul, pers com; MacCarthy (1986); Vicars (1897)]

FERGUSON, JOHN (d 1750), Strabane, county Tyrone;
son of the Rev Andrew Ferguson, senior, minister of Burt Presbyterian Church; brother of the Rev Andrew Ferguson, junior, who was father of Dr John Ferguson of Londonderry (*q.v.*); apothecary, of Strabane; married c 1744 Elizabeth Read (nee Hamilton), widow of the Rev. Paul Read, rector of Leckpatrick, county Tyrone; died April 1750; buried in Strabane; will dated 18 November 1748, proved 4 September 1751. [Belf PRO, T1192/1 (pedigree of Fergusons and Harveys); Eustace, vol II (1954); Hitchings, Paul, pers com; Leslie (1937); Vicars (1897)].

FERGUSON, JOHN (1732–95), Londonderry;
born 1732, son of the Rev Andrew Ferguson, junior, minister of Burt Presbyterian Church, and — Harvey of Glendermott, county Londonderry; nephew of Dr John Ferguson of Strabane (*q.v.*); general practitioner, of Londonderry; freeman of Londonderry 1754 and mayor 1778; married 23 July 1760 his second cousin Sarah Harvey, daughter of Robert Harvey and Mary Coningham; father of Sir Andrew Feguson, Bart, MP for Londonderry 1798–1800 (who voted for the Union and was created Baronet in 1801); candidate for Parliament in the year of his death; died 16 May 1795. [Belf PRO, LA/79/2AA/6 and T1192/1 (pedigree of Fergusons and Harveys); Burke, *Peerage and Baronetage* (1861); Elliott, Simon, pers com; Hitchings, Paul, pers com; Johnston (2002); McConnell (1951)].

FERGUSON, JOHN CREERY (1802–65), Dublin and Belfast;
born 22 August 1802 at Tanderagee, county Armagh, son of Dr Thomas Ferguson, apothecary, of Tanderagee and Dublin (*q.v.*) and Elizabeth Creery; brother of Dr James Chambers Ferguson (*q.v.*); educated at the Feinaiglian Institution, Dublin; studied arts and medicine at Trinity College, Dublin, 1818–24, Edinburgh University 1824–5 and Paris 1825–30 (see letters for this period in PRO NI); BA (TCD) 1823; MB 1827; LKQCPI 1827; FKQCPI 1829; MRCSI 1832; MA 1833; gave a paper to the Royal College of Physicians in Dublin in 1829 (published 1830) on the use of the fetal stethoscope to diagnose pregnancy and fetal death, and was the first person in the British Isles to hear the fetal heart; medical officer to a Cholera Hospital in Ennis in 1832; professor of the Theory and Practice of Medicine to the Apothecaries Hall, Dublin 1837–46; of 57 Rutland Square (his parents' home) 1828–34, and then of North Frederick Street; physician to Simpson's Hospital, Dublin 1836; physician to Sir Patrick Dun's Hospital, Dublin 1841; professor of the Practice of Medicine, Trinity College, Dublin 1846–9; professor of Medicine, Queen's College, Belfast, 1849–65; attending physician to the Belfast General Hospital 1853–65; gave annual winter oration at the hospital 1856; second president of the Belfast Clinical and Pathological Society 1854–5 and first president of the Ulster Medical Society 1862–3; author of *Consumption: What it is and what it is not: Its causation and remediability* (1858) and many medical papers; married (1) May 1833 Jane Clarke of Dublin; (2) Anne Tate of Rantalard, Whitehouse; died 24 June 1865 at 14 Howard Street, Belfast; buried in Balmoral Cemetery, Belfast; probate Belfast 20 July 1865. [*Belf Clin Path Soc, Trans* 1854–5; *BNL* 1865 (d); Belf PRO, D 1918/2; Belf PRO, will cal; *BMJ* obituary (1865); Burtchaell and Sadleir (1924); Cameron (1916); Clarke, *Belfast*, vol 3 (1986); Coakley (1992); *Coleraine Chronicle* 1 July 1865 (d); *DIB* (2009); Hunter (1936); Kirkpatrick Archive; Logan (1972); *Med Dir*; Moody and Beckett (1959); O'Brien, Crookshank and Wolstenhome (1988); O'Doherty (2002); Pinkerton (1981)].

FERGUSON, ROBERT (*fl c* 1819), Waringstown, county Down;
surgeon and apothecary, of Waringstown c 1819. [Bradshaw (1819)].

FERGUSON, ROBERT JAMES (1864–1931), London and Canterbury, Kent;
born 15 October 1864 in Ballymena, county Antrim, son of Robert Ferguson, grocer and baker, of Ballymena, and Matilda Jane Smyth; educated at Ballymena Intermediate School; studied medicine at Queen's College, Belfast, from 1881; MD

MCh MAO (RUI) 1887; MRCSE FRCSE 1904; general practitioner, of 245 South Norwood Hill, London; clinical assistant to the Samaritan Free Hospital and gynaecological registrar to the Kensington Hospital; surgeon to the Kensington and Fulham General Hospital; general practitioner in Canterbury from 1911; surgeon to the Kent and Canterbury Hosptial 1912–25; married 5 August 1896 in St Mary's Church of England Church, Princes Risborough, Buckinghamshire, Gertrude Kate Williams (who was born 1874/5), daughter of Thomas Williams, farmer; died 2 March 1931 at 25 New Dover Road, Canterbury; buried at St Martin's, Canterbury; probate London 9 June 1931. [Kirkpatrick Archive; Lond GRO (m); Lond PPR, will cal; *Med Dir*; Power and Le Fanu (1953); QCB adm reg].

FERGUSON, THOMAS (d 1832), Tanderagee, county Armagh and Dublin;
practised as an apothecary in Tanderagee but moved to Dublin c 1810; of 57 Rutland Square 1828–32; many of his letters to his son John are preserved in the Public Record Office of NI; married Elizabeth Creery (who was born 1778/9 and died 23 September 1857 in Tanderagee), daughter of the Rev John Creery, perpetual curate of Acton, county Armagh; father of Professor John Creery Ferguson (*q.v.*) and Dr James Chambers Ferguson (*q.v.*); died 1832, of cholera. [*BNL* 26 September 1857 (d); Belf PRO, D 1918/2; Cameron (1916); Leslie (1911); O'Doherty (2002); Pinkerton (1981)]

FERGUSON, THOMAS (1827/8–90), Doagh, county Antrim;
born 1827/8, son of Francis Ferguson, farmer; studied medicine in Belfast and Glasgow; MRCSE 1848; general practitioner in Doagh; married 23 September 1854 in First Antrim Presbyterian Church, Mill Row, Mary Coleman (who died 24 February 1890), daughter of James Coleman, farmer, of Ballybentra, Dunadry; father of Dr James Coleman Ferguson (*q.v.*); died 18 February 1890 at Doagh; buried in Donegore Church of Ireland graveyard; probate Belfast 26 March 1890. [*BNL* 4 October 1854 (m); Belf PRO, will cal; *Coleraine Chronicle* 7 October 1854 (m); Dub GRO (d); gravestone inscription; Kirkpatrick Archive; *Med Dir*; UHF database (m)].

FERGUSON, VICTOR (c 1650–1723), Belfast;
born c 1650 probably came to Ireland before 1680; army surgeon to the forces of William III; doctor of physic, of Belfast; published a pamphlet in favour of 'Non-Subscription' in 1721; married — (who predeceased him); probably father of Dr John Ferguson of Belfast (*q.v.*); will dated 5 October 1723; died October 1723; funeral from the First Presbyterian Church, Belfast; probate Prerogative Court 1729 (copy of will in National Archives, Dublin, and abstract in PRO NI). [Agnew (1996); Allen (1951), p 189; Belf PRO, Burke's Pedigrees, T559. vol 21, p 84; Belf PRO, T808 p 454; Benn, vol 2 (1880), pp 168–170; Dub Nat Arch, Prerog Will Book (1729); Hitchings, Paul, pers com; MacCarthy (1986); Vicars (1897)].

FERGUSON, WILLIAM (d 1710), Belfast;
son of George Ferguson; nephew of Dr Victor Ferguson (*q.v.*); apothecary, of Belfast; married Mary Wilson; died 1710; will dated 29 January 1710; probate Connor Diocesan Court (abstract in PRO NI). [Belf PRO, Connor Dio Wills index; Belf PRO, T808/4541; MacCarthy (1986)].

FERGUSON, WILLIAM (*fl c* 1824), Coleraine, county Londonderry;
surgeon and apothecary, of Bridge Street, Coleraine c 1824. [Pigot (1824)].

FERGUSSON, JAMES HUGH (1852–1913), Gweedore and Killygordon, county Donegal, and Londonderry;
born 17 March 1852, son of Joseph H.S. Fergusson, gentleman farmer, of Ballyarrell, Donaghmore, county Donegal; educated at Strabane Academy and Foyle College, Londonderry c 1869–72; studied medicine at Queen's College, Galway, and from 1875, Queen's College, Belfast; LRCP Edin 1880; LFPS Glas 1880; FRCSI 1894; DPH RCPSI 1896; medical officer to Gweedore Dispensary District c 1885 and Killygordon Dispensary District c 1890; medical superintendent officer of health for Londonderry, medical superintendent to Foyle Hill Isolation Hospital and port medical officer; of 3 Florence Terrace, Northland Road, Londonderry; married 22 December 1887 in Donaughmore Presbyterian Church, county Donegal; Anne Mathewson Caldwell, daughter of John Caldwell, gentleman farmer; father of Dr John Caldwell Fergusson, MBE MC; died 11 September 1913 at 3 Florence Terrace; buried in Donaghmore Church of Ireland Graveyard, Castlefin, county Donegal; administration Dublin 4 December 1913. [Belf PRO, will cal; Dub GRO (m) and (d); Fergusson, Hugh, pers com; Kirkpatrick Archive; *Med Dir*; QCB adm reg].

FERRAR, BENJAMIN BANKS (1862–1948), Armagh and RAMC;
born 1862 in Dublin, son of the Rev William Hugh Ferrar, Fellow of Trinity College, Dublin; educated at Rathmines School, Dublin, from 1871; studied arts and medicine at Trinity College, Dublin, from 1880; BA (TCD) 1885; MB BCh 1886; MD 1891; general practitioner, of 7 Beresford Row, Armagh; served in RAMC during World War I with rank of captain; fellow of the Zoological Society and MRIA; retired c 1912 as curator of the Royal Zoological Society Gardens, Phoenix Park, Dublin; of 103 Anglesea Road, Ballsbridge, Dublin, from c 1938; married Isabella Shaw-Hamilton, only daughter of the Very Reverend Robert Shaw-Hamilton, Dean of Armagh; died 8 November 1948; administration Dublin 13 January 1949. [Dub Nat Arch, will cal; Figgis and Drury (1932); Fleming (2001); Kirkpatrick Archive; *Med Dir;* TCD adm reg; *TCD Reg*; *TCD Cat*, vol II (1896); Young and Pike (1909)].

FERRAR, THOMAS (d 1837), Dublin, Sligo and Belfast;
born 24 August 1797 in Dublin, third son of William Hugh Ferrar of Limerick, Dublin, Larne and Belfast, and Maria Lloyd of Limerick; educated at Belfast Academy, then in Donegall Street; studied arts and medicine at Trinity College, Dublin, from 1815; BA(TCD) 1826; MB 1829; LRCSI 1830; LM RCSI; general practitioner in Dublin c 1834 and Sligo c 1835–6; second professor of surgery at RBAI July–November 1836 (dismissed for failing to attend meetings and give lectures); unmarried; died 2 June 1837 in Sligo. [*BNL* 9 June 1837 (d); Belf PRO, SCH 524; Burtchaell and Sadleir (1924); Froggatt (1996b)].

FERRES (FERRIS), CHARLES (1811/2–70), Larne, county Antrim;
born 1811/2, son of William Ferres of Larne; brother of Eliza Ferris who married — Kane and was mother of Dr Hugh Smiley Kane (*q.v.*), and Dr John Kane (*q.v.*); LRCS Edin 1836; surgeon in Larne and medical officer to constabulary; elected first

medical officer to the Larne Workhouse 1843; married 28 April 1836 in Crumlin, Letitia McDonald, youngest daughter of Dr James McDonald of Crumlin; father of Letitia McDonald Ferres who married Dr Cunningham Mulholland (*q.v.*) of Belfast; died 4 November 1870 in Larne; buried in St Cedma's Graveyard, Larne; administration Belfast 18 January 1871. [*BNL* 6 May 1836 (m); Belf PRO, will cal; Croly (1843–6); *Med Dir*; Rutherford and Clarke, *County Antrim*, vol 4 (2004); UHF database (m)].

FERRES (FERRIS), SAMUEL (1758/9–1827), Larne, county Antrim;
born 1758/9, son of Charles Ferris, distiller, of Larne; apothecary and surgeon of Larne c 1824; married November 1789 Dorothea Biers of Ballymoney (who was born 1767/8 and died 12 June 1818); died 28 May 1827 at Larne; both were buried in St Cedma's Graveyard, Larne. [*BNL* 20 November 1789 (m), 23 June 1818 (d) and 12 June 1827 (d); McKillop (2000); Pigot (1824); Rutherford and Clarke, *County Antrim*, vol 4 (2004)].

FERRIER, JOHN (1782/3–1841), Garvagh and Kilrea, county Londonderry;
born 1782/3; surgeon, of Garvagh c 1813 and Kilrea c 1824; married 5 June 1813 Margaret Rainey of Portglenone (who died 30 October 1833, after a son and daughter had died earlier in the same month, 'the supposed effect of a mother's unavailing sorrow for her deceased children'); died 16 May 1841 at his home in Kilrea; buried in Kilrea Churchyard; probate Prerogative Court 1841. [*BNL* 22 June 1813 (m), 22 October and 12 November 1833 (d) and 8 June 1841 (d); Belf PRO, Prerog Wills index; *Londonderry Sentinel* 5 June 1841 (d) *Memorials of the Dead,* vol VII, p 403; Pigot (1824)].

FERRIS, JOSEPH JOHN LAWRENCE (1857/8–1926), Liverpool, Lancashire, Londonderry and Belfast;
born 1857/8; studied medicine at Edinburgh University and the Royal College of Surgeons of Edinburgh; MB MCh (Edin) 1893; resident medical officer to the East Dispensary, Liverpool, Brownlow Hill Hospital, Liverpool, and the Neil Lane Military Hospital, Manchester, and 'travelling'; general practitioner, of New York; temporary lieutenant RAMC 1914–18; general practitioner, of Hawkins Street and Woodleigh, Londonderry c 1915–22; retired c 1922 to 88 University Street, Belfast; unmarried; died of phthisis 9 September 1926 at 24 Westminster Street, Belfast. [Belf GRO (d); *Med Dir*].

FFARGUSON, THOMAS (*fl c* 1680), Belfast;
apothecary; given Freedom of Belfast 1680. [Young (1892)].

FFENELY, RICHARD (*fl c* 1733), Belfast;
surgeon in Belfast in April 1733 (when a child of his died). [Agnew (1995)].

FFENNELL, JAMES RICHARD (1818–83), Army Medical Service;
born 17 February 1818; MRCSE 1840; joined the Army Medical Service as staff assistant surgeon 1841; attached to 8th Foot 1843 and 79th Foot 1850; staff surgeon, 2nd class, 1852; attached to 16th Foot 1858; surgeon major 1861; staff surgeon

1866; retired on half pay with rank of deputy inspector general 1868; married Emily —; died 20 October 1883 at Tonagh Lodge, Lisburn, county Antrim; administration Belfast 19 November 1883. [Belf PRO, will cal; Dub GRO (d); *Med Dir*; Peterkin and Johnston (1968)].

FFINER, THOMAS (*fl c* 1656), Belfast;
barber chierurgeon; given Freedom of Belfast 1656. [Young (1892)].

FIDDES, JOHN MONTGOMERY (1833–1919), Army Medical Service;
born 24 November 1833 in county Monaghan, fourth son of Edward Fiddes of Clenamully, Monaghan; studied arts and medicine at Trinity College, Dublin; LM Rot Hosp Dub 1857; BA (TCD) 1857; MB 1858; LRCSI 1858; joined the Army Medical Service as surgeon 1858 and served with Royal Artillery; surgeon major 1873; retired with rank of brigade surgeon 1886; lived latterly in the Junior United Services Club, Charles Street, London, and St James' Chambers, 2 Ryder Street, London; died 30 May 1919 in Pall Mall, London, as a result of a car accident; probate London 21 July 1919. [Burtchaell and Sadleir (1935); Kirkpatrick Archive; Lond PPR, will cal; *Med Dir*; Peterkin and Johnston (1968)].

FIDDES (FIDDIS), WILLIAM H. (d 1835), Dublin;
of Tullycreevy, Devenish, county Fermanagh; surgeon, of Dublin; married —; father of George Richard Fiddes who was born 1830/1 and entered TCD 1850; died 9 November 1835 'in the prime of life', 'of a decline'. [*BNL* 17 November 1835 (d); Burtchaell and Sadleir (1935) (for son)].

FIELDEN, VICTOR GEORGE LEOPOLD (1867–1946), Belfast and RAMC;
born 10 March 1867 at 19 South-hill Buildings, Stoke Damerel, Devon, son of Immer Fielden RN, surveyor, and Susan Elizabeth Cole; moved to Belfast with his family c 1881; educated in Glasgow and at RBAI; studied medicine at Queen's College, Belfast, from 1888; MB BCh BAO (RUI) 1892; Licentiate of the Pharmaceutical Society of Ireland (first place) 1890; MD (with gold medal) 1912; demonstrator in Materia Medica and Pharmacy 1893; anaesthetist to the Ulster Hospital for Children and Women 1898–1919; assistant anaesthetist to the Royal Victoria Hospital, Belfast 1900; attending physician (anaesthetist) to the hospital 1901–32; gave annual winter oration at Royal Victoria Hospital 1914; author of many papers on anaesthetics; served in RAMC during World War 1; retired 1932; married 19 August 1895 in St Thomas's Church of Ireland Church, Caroline Grant Ward, elder daughter of Charles Henderson Ward, solicitor, of Belfast; died 5 June 1946 at 1 Cleaver Park, Belfast; buried in Belfast City Cemetery; probate Belfast 19 December 1946. [Belf City Cem, bur reg; Belf PRO, will cal; *BMJ* obituary (1946); Hewitt and Dundee (1970); Kirkpatrick Archive; *Lancet* obituary (1946); Lond GRO (b); Marshall and Kelly (1973); *Med Dir*; QCB adm reg; UHF database (m); Young and Pike (1909)].

FILSON, ALEXANDER (1843–82), Dublin and Portaferry, county Down;
born 11 July 1843 at Portaferry, son of Dr Alexander Bell Filson (*q.v.*); studied arts and medicine at Queen's College, Belfast, from 1859, and the Carmichael School, Dublin; BA (QUI) 1862; MD 1865; LM Rot Hosp Dub 1865; MCh 1866; resident

medical officer to the House of Industry Hospital, Dublin; medical officer to Cloughey Cholera Hospital 1866; medical officer to Portaferry Dispensary District, constabulary, South Rock Lighthouse and Admiralty; married —; died 28 June 1882 at Portaferry; buried in Ballyphilip, Graveyard; probate Belfast 27 November 1882. [Belf PRO, will cal; *Downpatrick Recorder* 14 February 1880, 1 July 1882 (d) and 8 July 1882 (d); Dub GRO (b); *Med Dir*; QCB adm reg; Russell (1983)].

FILSON, ALEXANDER BELL (1796/7–1866), Portaferry, county Down;
born 1796/7; LRCS Edin 1819; LAH Dub 1829; MD (Glas) 1852; surgeon, of Portaferry from c 1822; medical officer to Portaferry Dispensary District from c 1852; reported on cholera epidemic to Poor Law Commissioners in 1853; retired 1862 and received a presentation of silver plate; married —; father of Dr Alexander Filson (*q.v.*); died 27 October 1866 at Portaferry; probate Belfast 10 January 1867. [Addison (1898); Apothecaries (1829); Belf PRO, will cal; Croly (1843–6); *Downpatrick Recorder* 3 May 1862 (news) and 3 November 1866 (d); Dub GRO (d); *Med Dir*; Pigot (1824); Russell (1983)]

FINLAY, ALEXANDER (1793/4–1887), Kilkeel, county Down, and Swanlinbar, county Cavan;
born 1793/4; LAH Dub 1824; accoucheur of the Coombe Lying-in Hospital, Dublin 1833; apothecary to Kilkeel Dispensary; general practitioner in Swanlinbar c 1846; married —; died 25 January 1887 at Swanlinbar. [Apothecaries (1829); Croly (1843–6); Dub GRO (d); *Med Dir*].

FINLAY, GEORGE (*fl c* 1814–59), Strangford, county Down;
LFPS Glas 1814; CM (Glas) 1814; surgeon, of Strangford c 1824; medical officer to Strangford Dispensary and constabulary c 1845; married 31 October 1825 in Lisburn Church of Ireland Church, Mary Frazer, second daughter of R. Frazer of Edentrillick, county Down; died c 1859. [*BNL* 4 November 1825 (m); Croly (1843–6); *Med Dir;* Pigot (1824)].

FINLAY, JAMES ALEXANDER (*fl c* 1845), Killashandra county Cavan;
BA (TCD) 1826; LRCSI; FRCSI; accoucheur of the Dublin Lying-in Hospital; general practitioner in Killashandra and medical officer to the Dispensary, of Hamilton Terrace, Killashandra c 1845; possibly died c 1850. [Burtchaell and Sadlier (1924); Croly (1843–6)].

FINLAY, JOHN (*fl c* 1828), Belturbet, county Cavan;
LAH Dub 1828; apothecary, of Belturbet; married —; daughter born 1854. [Apothecaries (1829); *BNL* 24 March 1854 (d)].

FINLAY, RICHARD (*fl c* 1733), Belfast;
surgeon in Belfast c 1733. [Agnew (1995)].

FINLAY, RICHARD (d 1855), Rockcorry, county Monaghan;
son of Francis Finlay, superviser; CM and Dip Mid (Glas) 1843; medical officer to Rockcorry Dispensary, Fever Hospital and constabulary c 1845; married 13 September

1849 in Tassagh Presbyterian Church, county Armagh, Anne Henry, eldest daughter of George Henry of Glenburn House, county Armagh; died 1855 at Glenburn. [*BNL* 18 September 1849 (m); Croly (1843-6); Dub GRO (m); *Med Dir*].

FINLAY, ROBERT (1825/6-49), Strangford, county Down;
born 1825/6; LRCSI; died 19 November 1849 at Strangford, of consumption. [*BNL* 30 November 1849 (d)].

FINLAY, THOMAS (1856-89), Dalkey, county Dublin;
born 1856; LRCSI 1879; LRCP Edin 1880; general practitioner, of Kalafat, Dalkey, county Dublin c 1886; unmarried; died 1 December 1889 at Kalafat. [Dub GRO (d); *Med Dir*].

FINLAY (FINLEY) WINSLOW (d 1860), Swanlinbar, county Cavan;
son of John Finlay, gentleman; MRCSE 1840; surgeon in Swanlinbar c 1846 and medical officer to Swanlinbar Dispensary and constabulary; married 15 October 1848 in Manorhamilton Church of Ireland Church, Isabella Armstrong, only daughter of Carter Armstrong of Lakeview, county Leitrim; died 1860. [Croly (1843-6); Dub GRO (m); *Londonderry Sentinel* 11 November 1848 (m); *Med Dir*].

FINNEGAN, DAVID (1873-1935), Bristol, Gloucestershire, and Wolverhampton and Wednesbury, Staffordshire;
born 23 November 1873 at Castleboy, county Down, youngest son of William Finnegan, farmer, of the Hospital House, Castleboy, and his cousin Jane McKinney; cousin of John Maxwell Finnegan, first secretary of Queen's University, Belfast; his father died when he was 5 and his mother when he was 6; educated at Kirkiston and Portaferry National Schools and later at University Classes, Donegal Pass, Belfast; studied medicine at Queen's College, Belfast, from 1892; MB BCh BAO (RUI) 1899; MD (QUB) 1914; medical officer to Bristol Royal Infirmary; general practitioner of Dunkley Street, Wolverhampton from c 1905 and Park House, King's Hill, Wednesbury c 1913-27; retired to 'Inisfail', Exeter Road, Moretonhampstead, Devon 1927; married (1) Johanna Jahn, daughter of a doctor from Sonnenburg, Germany, who was a governess with the family; (2) Elrida Anna Bertha Marie Jahn, sister of Johanna; died 16 August 1935 at Inisfail; buried in Wednesbury Cemetery; donated a stained glass window to Cloughey Presbyterian Church in memory of his parents and brothers in 1931; bequeathed legacies to Queen's University, Belfast, and the Royal Victoria Hospital, for a scholarship in Clinical Medicine; probate London 22 November 1935. [Anderson (1980); Lond PPR, will cal, will; *Med Dir*; QCB adm reg].

FINNY, ARTHUR BENJAMIN (1853-74), Downpatrick, county Down;
born 1853; studied medicine at Trinity College and the Meath Hospital, Dublin; LKQCPI and LM 1873; LRCSI 1873; registrar and assistant surgeon to the Down County Infirmary for about 9 months; unmarried; died 15 March 1874 at the Infirmary, of typhoid fever; buried in Downpatrick Cathedral graveyard. [*Downpatrick Recorder* 21 March 1874 (d); Dub GRO (d); *Med Dir;* Parkinson (1967)].

FINUCANE, FRANCIS (*fl c* 1828), Cootehill, county Cavan;
LAH Dub 1828; apothecary, of Cootehill. [Apothecaries (1829)].

FINUCANE, JOHN (d 1819), Armagh and Clara, King's County;
assistant surgeon in Armagh Militia; died May 1819 at Clara. [*BNL* 1 June 1819 (d)].

FISHER, HUGH (1870–1901), Belfast;
born 9 April 1870 at Belfast, son of Hugh Cumming Fisher, bank clerk, of Lennoxvale Street, Belfast; educated at Methodist College, Belfast, from 1885; studied medicine at Queen's College, Belfast, from 1887; MB BCh (RUI) 1893; general practitioner of 75 Great Victoria Street, Belfast; married 2 March 1896 in Fitzroy Presbyterian Church, Belfast, Dr Elizabeth Gould Bell (*q.v.*); died 18 October 1901 at Great Victoria Street of typhoid fever; buried in Belfast City Cemetery; administration Belfast 8 November 1901. [Belf City Cem, bur reg; Belf PRO, will cal; Dub GRO (d); Fry (1984); *Med Dir*; QCB adm reg; UHF database (m); Whitla (1901)].

FISHER, JOHN MOORE (1819/20–90), Kingston-upon-Hull, Yorkshire;
born 1819/20 at Ballykeel, Moneyrea, county Down; educated in Hull and trained as a Unitarian minister; living as schoolteacher and minister with resident pupils, at 1 York Street, Albion Street, Hull c 1850–54 and at 11 Wright Street c 1855–61; studied medicine at King's College, London c 1861–5 and at Edinburgh University 1865–8; MRCSE 1864; MD (Edin) 1868; of 29 Norfolk Street, Strand, London c 1870, of 2 Balmoral Terrace, Anlaby Road, Hull c 1876–82 and at 6 Prime (Pryme) Street, Sculcoates, Hull c 1885–90; married 27 June 1848 Harriet Blundell (who was born c 1821 in Hull); died 24 October 1890 at 6 Pryme Street; buried in Hull General Cemetery. [Edin Univ; *Hull and East Yorkshire Times* 1 November 1890 (d); Kirkpatrick (1889); Lond GRO (d); *Med Dir*].

FISHER, THOMAS WILLIAM (1863– c 1912), Chicago, USA;
born 3 February 1863 in Belfast, son of Thomas Fisher, merchant, of Cherry Ville, Belfast; educated at RBAI; studied medicine at Queen's College, Belfast, from 1879; LRCP LRCS Edin; LFPS Glas 1889; emigrated to USA; general practitioner of 620 Boulvard Place, Chicago c 1900; address listed as c/o the Rev T. McIlvern, The Manse, Caerlaverock, Dumfrieshire c 1906–12; died c 1912. [*Med Dir*; QCB adm reg].

FISHER, TURNER JOHNSTON (1852–1932), London;
born 10 June 1852 at Carrigallen, county Leitrim, son of the Rev John Fisher, minister of Carrigallen Presbyterian Church and — Elliott of Belfast; educated at RBAI; studied medicine at Queen's College, Belfast, from 1870; MD (QUI) 1875; MCh Dip Mid 1876; medical officer to 5th Dispensary District, Hackney, London, and to the General Post Office, of 48 Cassland Road and 29 Cassland Crescent, South Hackney; living finally at 'Clonsilla', 21 Bryansburn Road, Bangor, county Down; married —; died 4 February 1932 at 21 Bryansburn Road; probate Belfast 19 May 1932 and London 10 June 1932. [Belf GRO (d); Belf PRO, will cal; Lond PPR, will cal; *Med Dir*; QCB adm reg].

FITZGERALD, FRANCIS CREIGHTON (1847/8–1936), Holdsworthy, Devonshire and Newtownbutler, county Fermanagh;
>born 1847/8; studied medicine at the Royal College of Surgeons in Ireland and the Adelaide and City of Dublin Hospitals; LKQCPI and LM 1869; LRCSI 1869; medical officer to the Fourth District of Holsworthy and deputy surgeon to the Workhouse; medical officer and medical officer of health to Newtownbutler Dispensary District; medical officer to constabulary; registrar of births and deaths and consultant sanitary officer to Clones Union; married Lucinda —; died 12 August 1936 at Newtownbutler; administration Londonderry 12 October 1936. [Belf GRO (d); Belf PPR, will cal; *Med Dir*].

FITZGERALD, JAMES (1807/8–96), Newtownbutler, county Fermanagh;
>born 1807/8; studied medicine in Dublin and St Thomas's Hospital, London; MRCSE 1833; LM Coombe Hosp Dub 1833; medical officer to Newtownbutler Dispensary District; married 14 October 1835 in Newtownbutler, Sophia Irvine, only daughter of Captain Irvine of Newtownbutler; died 19 February 1896 at Newtownbutler; probate Dublin 22 August 1896. [*BNL* 27 October 1835 (m); Belf PRO, will cal; Dub GRO (d); *Med Dir*].

FITZMAURICE, JOHN (d c 1833), Belfast;
>surgeon, of 12 Hercules Street, Belfast c 1824; probate Prerogative Court 1833. [Belf PRO, Prerog Wills index; Pigot (1824)].

FITZPATRICK, FRANCIS (c 1800–65), Belturbet, county Cavan, and London;
>born c 1800, of Derryvehil, county Cavan; LAH Dub 1828; LSA Lond 1828; apothecary, of The Diamond, Belturbet c 1824 and later of 27 Upper Lisson Street, Lisson Grove, London; died 25 September 1865 at 27 Upper Lisson Street; probate London 6 October 1865. [Kirkpatrick Archive; Lond PPR, will cal, will; *Med Dir*; Pigot (1824)].

FITZPATRICK, HUGH (1810/1–41), Newry, county Down;
>born 1810/1; general practitioner, of Needham Place, Newry; married — (who died 9 February 1842 of consumption; died 2 June 1841 of typhus fever, at Needham Place; buried in St Mary's Roman Catholic Graveyard, Newry. [*BNL* 11 June 1841 (d) and 18 February 1842 (d); Newry RC Church, bur reg].

FITZPATRICK, JAMES VINCENT (1844/5–92), Dublin, Swindon, Wiltshire, and Moville, county Donegal;
>born 1844/5, son of James Fitzpatrick of Portaferry, coastguard officer; studied medicine at the Ledwich School and Mercer's, Jervis Street and Mater Hospitals, Dublin; LM Coombe Hosp Dub 1870; LRCSI 1873; LAH Dub 1875; LKQCPI 1883; medical officer in Mater Misericordiae Hospital, Dublin c 1875; assistant surgeon to the GWR Works, Swindon; medical officer and medical officer of health to Moville Dispensary District; author of various medical papers; unmarried; died 25 July 1892 at Moville of enteric fever; administration Londonderry 15 August 1892. [Belf PRO, will cal; Dub GRO (d); *Med Dir*].

FITZPATRICK, THOMAS (*fl c* 1824), Belturbet, county Cavan;
surgeon, of Belturbet c 1824. [Pigot (1824)].

FITZPATRICK, THOMAS (1832–1900), Indian Medical Service and London;
born 10 February 1832 in Virginia, county Cavan, son of James Fitzpatrick, farmer; educated at Carlow College; studied arts and medicine at Trinity College, Dublin, from 1848; LM Rot Hosp Dub 1856; BA (TCD) 1853; MB MCh 1856; FKQCPI 1860; MD 1862; MA 1864; MD (Camb) 1867; MRCP Lond 1868; joined the Indian Medical Service (Bengal establishment) as assistant surgeon 1856, but resigned and was invalided home 1859; practised in Ireland for a short time but moved to London c 1868; physician to the Western General Dispensary, of 30 Sussex Gardens, Hyde Park, from 1866; author of *Chronic Diseases of the Liver* (1856), *An Autumn Cruise in the Aegean* (1886) and *A Transatlantic Holiday* (1891); brilliant raconteur; married 4 May 1865, in Paddington Parish Church, Agnes Letitia Robinson, daughter of William Robinson, DL, of Tottenham; died 31 May 1900 at 30 Sussex Gardens; probate London 28 July 1900; commemorated by Fitzpatrick Lectureship at the Royal College of Physician in London, founded by his widow in 1901. [*BMJ* obituary (1900); Burtchaell and Sadleir (1935); Crawford (1930); Crone (1928); Kirkpatrick Archive; Lond GRO (m) and (d); Lond PPR, will cal; Martin (2010); *Med Dir*; Newman (1958); Newmann (1993); Venn (1940–54); Widdess (1963)].

FITZPATRICK, WILLIAM (*fl c* 1828), Belturbet, county Cavan;
chemist, of The Diamond, Belturbet 1824; LAH Dub 1828; apothecary, of Belturbet. [Apothecaries (1829); Pigot (1824)].

FITZPATRICK, — (d 1848), Ballyjamesduff, county Cavan;
general practitioner; died 24 June 1848 in Ballyjamesduff, of typhus fever 'caught whilst discharging the duties of his profession'. [*BNL* 4 July 1848 (d)].

FITZSIMONS, JOHN (1755–1830), Naval Medical Service and Blackwatertown, county Armagh;
born 1755/6; joined the Naval Medical Service as surgeon; retired; surgeon, of Blackwatertown c 1824; died 3 March 1830 at Blackwatertown, 'a gentleman respected by all who knew him' (*BNL*); administration Armagh Diocesan Court 1830. [*BNL* 5 March 1830 (d); Dub Nat Arch, Armagh Dio Admins index; Pigot (1824)].

FITZSIMONS, JOHN (1813/4–44), Downpatrick, county Down;
born 1813/4, son of James Fitzsimons of Whigamstown, Killough, county Down; MD (Edin) 1835 (thesis 'On continued fever'); physician, of English Street, Downpatrick; died 9 August 1844 in Downpatrick; buried in Rossglass Roman Catholic graveyard. [*BNL* 20 August 1844 (d); Clarke, *County Down,* vol 8 (1972); Edin Univ; Pilson (1934)].

FITZSIMONS, JOHN BINGHAM (1846–1912), Cork, Hereford and Lympstone, Devonshire;
born 20 April 1846 at Kilkenny, son of John Puxley Fitzsimmons of the Medical Hall, Kilkenny; educated at Nore View House, Kilkenny; studed medicine at the Royal College of Surgeons in Ireland, and Queen's Colleges, Cork and Belfast; MD (QUI) 1867; LRCSI 1867; LAH Dub 1867; LM Rot Hosp Dub 1867; medical officer to St Ann's Hill Hydropathic Establishment, Cork c 1885; general practitioner in Hereford and medical officer to Hereford Isolation Hospital, of 14 Owen Street, Hereford, c 1895; medical officer and public vaccinator to Lympstone Union, of The Cottage, Lympstone, from c 1906; married 13 August 1879 Orinda Anne Jeffares, eldest daughter of W.S. Jeffars of Kilkenny; died 12 May 1912 at The Cottage, Lympstone; probate Dublin 17 June 1912 and London 28 June 1912. [Belf PRO, will cal; Kirkpatrick Archive; Lond GRO (d); Lond PPR, will cal; *Med Dir*; QCB adm reg].

FITZSIM(M)ONS, THOMAS HENRY (1811/2–42), Downpatrick, county Down;
born 1811/2; apothecary and surgeon, of Irish Street, Downpatrick; died 24 January 1842 in Downpatrick, 'after a short illness of 36 hours'; administration Down Diocesan Court 1842. [*BNL* 4 February 1842 (d); Dub Nat Arch, Down Dio Admins index; Pilson (1934)].

FLANAGAN, JOHN WILLIAM HENRY (1851–c 1952), Army Medical Service;
born 20 January 1851 in county Fermanagh; studied medicine at the Carmichael School and Royal College of Surgeons in Ireland; LRCSI 1876; LKQCPI and LM 1877; joined the Army Medical Service as surgeon 1878; surgeon major 1890; lieutenant-colonel 1898; served in Afghanistan 1879–80 and Zhob Valley 1884; retired 1906; died c 1952. [*Med Dir*; Peterkin and Johnston (1968)].

FLANAGAN, ROBERT (*fl c* 1767), Enniskillen, county Fermanagh;
of Enniskillen; studied medicine at Rheims University; MD (Rheims) 1767. [Brockliss].

FLECK, DAVID McVEA (1868–1947), Caterham, Surrey, East Harling, Norfolk, RAMC and Westbury-on-Trym and Bristol, Gloucestershire;
born 11 January 1868 at Greenhill, Broughshane, county Antrim, son of George Fleck, farmer, of Greenhill, and Rachel McVea; educated at Ballymena Intermediate School; studied medicine at Queen's College, Belfast, from 1890; MB BCh BAO (RUI) 1897; assistant medical officer to the Caterham District Asylum c 1900; resident medical superintendent of Royal Victoria Homes, Brentry, c 1905; medical superintendent of East Counties Innebriate Reformatory, East Harling, of Brentry House, Westbury-on-Trym; captain in RAMC during World War I; general practitioner, of Wickhamdale, Stapleton, Bristol; author of various medical papers; retired c 1935 to 126 The Mount, York, but of St David's, 44 Weston Crescent, Harfield, Bristol, c 1945; married Alice Evelyn — died 8 August 1947; administration (with will) Bristol 5 November 1947. [Dub GRO (b); Kirkpatrick Archive; Lond PPR, will cal, will; *Med Dir*; QCB adm reg].

FLECK, WILLIAM (1848–1914), High Wycombe, Bucks;
    born 23 October 1848 at Ballymena, county Antrim, son of James Fleck, farmer, of Ballygelly; educated at Larne Model School; studied medicine at Queen's College, Belfast, from 1873; MD MCh (QUI) 1878; medical officer to Wycombe Workhouse and surgeon to Wycombe Cottage Hospital, of Frogmore Lodge, and later Tudor House, High Wycombe, from c 1880; JP for High Wycombe; married Ethel — died 21 January 1914; probate Oxford 5 March 1914. [Lond PPR, will cal; *Med Dir*; QCB adm reg].

FLEMING, ALEXANDER JOHN (1856–1913), Tamworth, Staffordshire, Church Stretton, Shropshire, and London;
    born 24 December 1856 in Longford, son of the Rev Robert Winning Fleming, minister of Coleraine Presbyterian Church, and — McKinstry of Armagh; educated at Coleraine Academical Institution; studied medicine at Queen's College, Belfast, from 1875, and the Carmichael School and Richmond Hospital, Dublin; LM Coombe Hosp Dub 1880; LRCSI 1881; MD MCh (QUI) 1881; general practitioner and assistant medical officer to the Cottage Hospital, Tamworth; general practitioner in Church Stretton, from c 1890; general practitioner in London from 1895, of Norton Lodge, 3 Arkwright Road, Hampstead; married 18 July 1894 in St John's Parish Church, Altrincham, Lily Huthart Brown (who was born 1866/7), daughter of Forrest Louden Brown, banker, of Bombay; died 22 December 1913; probate London 17 January 1914. [Barkley (1986); Lond GRO (m); Lond PPR, will cal; *Med Dir*; QCB adm reg; Young and Pike (1909)].

FLEMING, GEORGE (d 1790), Killymoon, county Tyrone;
    surgeon to the Killymoon Battalion of Militia; died 5 January 1790. [*BNL* 12 January 1790 (d)].

FLEMING, HANS (1813/4–87), Bailieborough, county Cavan, Carrickmacross, county Monaghan, and Omagh, county Tyrone;
    born 1813/4; studied medicine at the Royal College of Surgeons in Ireland, the Meath Hospital, Dublin, and St Andrews University; LRCSI and LM 1839; LM Rot Hosp Dub 1839; MD (St Andrew's) 1840 (by examination); medical officer to Baileborough Dispensary District and constabulary c 1846; medical officer to Carrickmacross Fever Hospital and Dispensary District; medical officer to Omagh Union Workhouse and superintendent medical officer of health from 1884, of Palisade House, Omagh; married 9 January 1845 Sarah Greer (who was born 19 October 1812 and died 15 May 1863), elder daughter of James Greer of Omagh, and Catherine Singby; father of Dr Hans Beresford Fleming (*q.v.*); died 7 October 1887 at Palisade House, Omagh; buried in New Drumragh Graveyard; probate Londonderry 9 November 1887 and London 21 November 1887. [*BNL* 21 January 1845 (m); Belf PRO, T810/250; Belf PRO, will cal; Croly (1843–6); Dub GRO (d); Kirkpatrick Archive; Lond PPR, will cal; *Londonderry Sentinel* 18 January 1845 (m) and 22 May 1863 (d); McGrew (1998) and (2001) (m) and (d); *Med Dir;* Smart (2004)].

FLEMING, HANS BERESFORD (1851/2–1916), ship's surgeon and Omagh, county Tyrone;
> born 1851/2 in Carrickmacross, county Monaghan, son of Dr Hans Fleming of Omagh (*q.v.*) and Sarah Greer; educated at Raphoe Royal School; studied arts and medicine at Trinity College, Dublin, from 1869; Lic Med 1875; LRCSI 1875; BA MB (TCD) 1876; LM 1877; surgeon to the army and to P & O Shipping Company; medical officer to Omagh Union Workhouse and constabulary and general practitioner in Omagh, of Carlisle Terrace c 1887 and later of Campsie House, Omagh; married Emily Beatrice — father of Dr Hans Fleming; died 4 August 1916 at Campsie House; buried in New Drumragh Graveyard; probate Londonderry 15 May 1917. [Belf PRO, will cal; Dub GRO (d); Kirkpatrick Archive; McGrew (1998); *Med Dir;* TCD adm reg; *TCD Cat*, vol II (1896)].

FLEMING, HENRY GILLESPIE (1822–47), Limavady, county Londonderry;
> born 14 September 1822, eldest son of William Fleming of Limavady and Margaret Edie Gillespie (who was daughter of Dr Henry Gillespie, senior (*q.v.*)); MD [?]; unmarried; died 17 January 1847 at his father's home in Limavady. [Belf PRO, D1936/2 (typescript 'Record of the Family of Gillespie'); Hitchings, Paul, pers com; *Londonderry Sentinel* 30 January 1847 (d)].

FLEMING, JAMES (d 1797), Stewartstown, county Tyrone;
> surgeon and apothecary in Stewartstown; died 16 January 1797. [*BNL* 27 January 1797 (d)].

FLEMING, JAMES (d 1799), Dungannon, county Tyrone;
> surgeon and apothecary in Dungannon; died 9 October 1799. [*BNL* 18 November 1799 (d)].

FLEMING, JAMES (d 1814), Naval Medical Service and Banbridge, county Down;
> joined the Naval Medical Service as assistant surgeon; retired c 1800 to Banbridge where he was mentioned in a local ballad on the death of the Rev James Traill Sturrock; died 8 May 1814 at Banbridge 'after a lingering and painful illness which he bore with great fortitude' (*BNL*). [*BNL* 20 May 1814 (d); Linn (1935)].

FLEMING, JOHN (1848–1911), Stockton-on-Tees, county Durham;
> born 7 December 1848 at Limavady, county Londonderry, son of William Fleming of Limavady; brother of Dr Robert Gage Fleming (*q.v.*); educated privately; studied medicine at Queen's College, Belfast, from 1865; MD (QUI) 1872; LRCS Edin 1872; medical officer for Bellarena Dispensary District c 1875; general practitioner in Stockton-on-Tees, of Middleton in Teesdale c 1876, 8 St John's Road from c 1880, North Terrace, Norton Road c 1905 and finally 27 Barrett Street, Stockton-on-Tees; married —; father of Dr John Fleming; died 9 June 1911; administration (with will) Durham 28 August 1911. [Kirkpatrick Archive; Lond PPR, will cal, will; *Med Dir;* QCB adm reg].

FLEMING, JOSEPH (1841–1915), Army Medical Service;
   born 21 March 1841 at Inch, county Donegal; studied medicine at Edinburgh University; LRCS Edin 1863; MD (Glas) 1863; FRCS Edin 1867; joined the Army Medical Service as assistant surgeon 1864; surgeon major 1876; on half pay October 1885–October 1886; brigade surgeon 1888; lieutenant-colonel 1893; served in Ashanti 1873–4, Afghan War 1878–80 and the Sudan 1885; retired 1890; lived finally at Castlequarter, Inch, county Donegal; unmarried; died 10 August 1915 at Castlequarter; probate Londonderry 25 October 1915. [Addison (1898); Belf PRO, will cal; Dub GRO (d); Kirkpatrick Archive; *Med Dir*; Peterkin and Johnston (1968)].

FLEM(M)ING, MICHAEL (d c 1850), Carrickmacross, county Monaghan;
   LAH Dub; apothecary to the Carrickmacross Dispensary and Fever Hospital c 1845; died c 1850. [Croly (1843–6); Pigot (1824)].

FLEMING, ROBERT GAGE (1847–1909), Limavady, county Londonderry, and Thornton Heath and Caterham, Surrey;
   born 13 March 1847 at Benone, Limavady, son of William Fleming of Limavady; brother of Dr John Fleming (*q.v.*); educated at Limavady Classical School; studied medicine at Queen's College, Belfast 1863–8; LRCS Edin and LM 1867; MD (QUI) 1868; general practitioner in Limavady c 1870; moved to Surrey c 1875, of 3 Wilton Terrace, Thornton Heath and later of Clyde Lodge, Caterham Valley, Surrey; married Clara —; died 19 February 1909; probate London 18 March 1909. [Lond PPR, will cal; *Med Dir*; QCB adm reg].

FLEMING, SAMUEL (*fl c* 1750);
   son of the Rev James Fleming, minister of First Lurgan Presbyterian church 1703–30 and Mary Bruce of Killleagh; studied medicine in Glasgow University; matriculated 1740; MA (Glas) 1743; MD 1750; married 1754 Mary Bruce (his cousin), daughter of the Rev Patrick Bruce, minister of Killyleagh Presbyterian Church, county Down, and Mary Hamilton. [Addison (1898) and (1913); Kirkpatrick Archive; McConnell (1951); McCreery (1875)].

FLEMING, SAMUEL (1841–72), Larne, county Antrim;
   born 21 Ocotber 1841, son of William Fleming, farmer, of Aghansillagh, Limavady, county Londonderry; educated at Cookstown Academy; studied medicine at Queen's College, Belfast, 1859–63; LRCS Edin 1863; LRCP Edin 1867; of Main Street, Limavady c 1866–7; medical officer to Larne Dispensary District 1870–72; married 1 March 1866 in Second Moneymore Presbyterian Church, Margaret Charles (who was born 1843/4 and died 11 October 1867 of Bright's disease, four months after the birth of a son), daughter of Stewart Charles, farmer, of Cookstown; died 10 March 1872 at Larne; administration Belfast 7 June 1872. [Belf PRO, will cal; *Coleraine Chronicle* 10 March 1866 (m); Dub GRO (m) and (d x 2); Hitchings, Paul, pers com; Kirkpatrick Archive; *Londonderry Sentinel* 6 March 1866 (m) and 15 October 1867 (d); *Med Dir*; QCB adm reg].

FLEMING, THOMAS MURPHY (1817/8–89), Carrickmacross, county Monaghan;
born 1817/8; studied medicine at Dr Steevens' Hospital, Dublin; LM Rot Hosp Dub 1840; MRCSE 1843; LKQCPI 1860; assistant demonstrator of anatomy to the School of Medicine, Dublin; assistant surgeon to Farney Dispensary and vaccinator to the Union; medical officer to Donaghmoyne Dispensary District, of Carrickmacross; unmarried; died 25 February 1889 at Carrickmacross; probate Armagh 2 May 1889. [Belf PRO, will cal; Dub GRO (d); *Med Dir*].

FLETCHER, PHILIP (c 1759–1844), Carrickfergus, county Antrim;
born c 1759; studied medicine at Edinburgh University; MD (Edin) 1781 (thesis 'On dysentery'); physician, of 'Mount Pleasant', Carrickfergus c 1824; married —; died 1 March 1844 at 'Mount Pleasant'; buried in Templecoran graveyard, Ballycarry. [*BNL* 8 March 1844 (d); Edin Univ; Pigot (1824); Rutherford and Clarke, *County Antrim*, vol 2 (1981)].

FLETCHER, ROBERT VICARS (1839–1903), Downpatrick, county Down, Waterford and Ballinasloe, county Galway;
born 1839, son of Robert Fletcher, gentleman; studied medicine at Dr Steevens' Hospital, Dublin; MRCP Edin and LM 1865; LRCS Edin 1865; LRCSI and LM 1869; FRCSI 1879; LKQCPI 1886; assistant medical superintendent to the Downshire Asylum, Downpatrick, from c 1870; resident medical superintendent to the District Asylum, Waterford; resident medical superintendent to the District Asylum, Ballinasloe, county Galway, from c 1875; married 19 December 1872 at 3 Marino Terrace, Ballybrack, Monkstown, county Dublin, Mary Lynch-Blosse Plunket, fourth daughter of the Rev and Hon Robert Plunket, Dean of Tuam, and sister of Isabella Plunket who married Dr George St George Tyner (*q.v.*); died 17 December 1903 at the Asylum, Ballinasloe; probate Dublin 18 February 1904. [Belf PRO, will cal; Burke *Peerage and Baronetage* 105th ed (1970); Dub GRO (m) and (d); *Med Dir*].

FLOOD, ALEXANDER (1815/6–88), Blacklion, county Fermanagh;
born 1815/6; LAH Dub 1843; medical officer to Killinagh Fever Hospital, county Cavan, constabulary and revenue constabulary; medical officer to Blacklion Dispensary District, of Danesfort, county Cavan; married —; father of Dr Samuel James Flood (*q.v.*); died 26 October 1888 at Danesfort; probate Armagh 5 January 1889. [Belf PRO, will cal; Dub GRO (d); Kirkpatrick Archive; *Med Dir*].

FLOOD, ALEXANDER (1851/2–95), Naval Medical Service and Drum, county Monaghan;
born 1851/2; studied medicine at the Ledwich School, Dublin; LKQCPI and LM LRCSI 1871; LM Coombe Hosp Dub 1887; joined the Naval Medical Service as assistant surgeon c 1872; surgeon c 1880; staff surgeon c 1885; retired c 1888; medical officer to Drum Dispensary District and constabulary; unmarried; died 15 December 1895 at Drum, following 'suffocation caused by overdose of some narcotic taken to relieve diarrhoea (accidental)' (Coroner); administration Armagh 25 February 1896. [Belf PRO, will cal; Dub GRO (d); *Med Dir*].

FLOOD, ALEXANDER WILLIAM (1849/50–1905), Naval Medical Service and Bundoran, county Donegal;
> born 1849/50; studied medicine at Queen's College, Galway, Edinburgh and Dr Steevens' Hospital, Dublin; LRCP LRCS Edin 1869; FRCS Edin 1889; joined the Naval Medical Service as surgeon 1871; resident surgeon at Haslar Hospital; resigned 1874; consulting surgeon to Reigate Cottage Hospital c 1876; general practitioner of Braemar, Bundoran c 1880; married Jessie McLeod — (who died 18 September 1923); father of Dr Richard Francis Flood (*q.v.*); died 3 September 1905 at Bundoran; probate Londonderry 23 March 1906. [Belf PRO, will cal; Dub GRO (d); Kirkpatrick Archive; *Med Dir*].

FLOOD, CHARLES (1857/8–1922), Northfleet, Kent;
> born 1857/8 at Aughalion, Ballyjamesduff, county Cavan, son of John Flood, land surveyor, of Aughalion; educated at St Patrick's College, Cavan; studied medicine at Queen's College, Belfast, from 1878 and at the Ledwich and Carmichael Schools, Dublin; LM Coombe Hosp Dub; LAH Dub 1887; LRCSI 1888; general practitioner, of The Hill and later of Du Warren House, Northfleet; medical officer, medical officer of health and public vaccinator to Northfleet Dispensary District; medical superintendent of the Isolation Hospital; married Cecilia —; died 15 November 1922; probate London 28 February 1923. [Lond PPR, will cal; *Med Dir*; QCB adm reg].

FLOOD, RICHARD FRANCIS (1870–1933), Bundoran, county Donegal;
> born 7 January 1870; eldest son of Dr Alexander William Flood (*q.v.*) of Bundoran and Jessie McLeod —; studied medicine at Edinburgh from 1892 and Belfast; LRCP LRCS Edin 1897; LFPS Glas 1897; house surgeon to the West Herts Infirmary, Horton Infirmary and Essex and Colchester General Hospital; general practitioner in Bundoran and medical officer to constabulary, of Braemar, Bundoran from c 1900; married 7 November 1907 in Ardtrea Church of Ireland Church, Catherine Charlotte Winifred Garnett (who was born 29 August 1878), third daughter of the Rev Charles Leslie Garnett, rector of Ardtrea, county Tyrone; father of Dr Charles John Stuart Flood, MB BCh BAO (TCD) 1937, of Mountmellick, county Laois, and Dr Denis Frederick Stuart Flood, MB BCh BAO (TCD) 1943, of Altringham, Cheshire; died 1 July 1933; probate Dublin 7 May 1934. [Dub Nat Arch, will cal; Fleming (2001); Kirkpatrick Archive; *Med Dir*; QCB adm reg].

FLOOD, SAMUEL (1842–1901), Army Medical Service and Omagh, county Tyrone;
> born 15 March 1842; LRCSI 1862; LRCP Edin 1863; joined the Army Medical Service as surgeon 1864; served with 109th Foot from 1873; surgeon major 1876; on half pay January 1881–January 1882; surgeon lieutenant-colonel 1885; served in Afghan War 1878–80 and Sudan 1884–5; retired with rank of brigade surgeon 1887; employed in Omagh while on the retired list; married Rebecca Dundas Rabi (who died 20 September 1939); died 14 September 1901 in Omagh; administration Londonderry 30 November 1901. [Belf PRO, will cal; Dub GRO (d); Kirkpatrick Archive; *Med Dir*; Peterkin and Johnston (1968)].

FLOOD, SAMUEL JAMES (1856–1900), Army Medical Service;
born 10 May 1856 at Danesfort, Belcoo, county Fermanagh, youngest son of Dr Alexander Flood (*q.v.*); LRCSI 1878; LRCP Edin 1879; FRCS Edin 1888; joined the Army Medical Service as surgeon captain 1880; surgeon major 1892; surgeon lieutenant-colonel 1900; served in Zhob Valley and Egypt in 1884; retired 1900 to 119 Jermyn Street, London and finally to 28 Shore Street, Holywood, county Down; married 4 April 1888 in First Omagh Presbyterian Church, Marion J. Sproule, only daughter of R. Sproule, JP, of Coolnagarde, Omagh, county Tyrone; died 5 September 1900 at 28 Shore Street, Holywood; probate Dublin 17 January 1901. [Belf PRO, will cal; Dub GRO (m) and (d); Kirkpatrick Archive; *Med Dir*].

FLOYD, JOHN (d 1845), Shiraz, Persia;
only son of John Floyd of Londonderry; medical officer of Messrs Floyd, Mills & Co; died 23 July 1845 in Shiraz, Persia. [*Londonderry Sentinel* 8 November 1845 (d)].

FLOYD, SAMUEL FERGUSON (1870–1968), Kilkeel, county Down;
born 8 January 1870 at Greencastle, county Down, son of William Floyd of Kilkeel and Charlotte Haydon; educated at Christ's Hospital, London, and RBAI; studied medicine at Queen's College, Belfast, from 1888; MB BCh BAO (RUI) 1895; LM Rot Hosp Dub 1895; general practitioner in Kilkeel; medical officer to the Mourne District Hospital, Kilkeel, and medical officer of health to Kilkeel No 1 Dispensary District; MBE c 1950; of 4 Borcha, Greencastle Street, Kilkeel; married —; died 16 September 1968 (aged 98) at the Mourne Hospital; probate Belfast 5 December 1968. [Belf GRO (b) and (d); Belf PRO, will cal; Kirkpatrick Archive; *Med Dir*; QCB adm reg].

FLYNN, FREDERICK FRANCIS (1833/4–78), Naval Medical Service and Dalkey, county Dublin;
born 1833/4 in Dublin, son of John Harris Flynn, private tutor; educated at Portora Royal School, Enniskillen; studied arts and medicine at Trinity College, Dublin, from 1853; BA (TCD) 1858; MB 1860; LRCSI 1860; joined the Naval Medical Service as assistant surgeon on HMS *Griffon* c 1864 and HMS *Nimble* c 1867; assistant resident physician to Cork Street Fever Hospital, Dublin; general practitioner, of 3 Henrietta Terrace, Dalkey, from c 1870; died 7 November 1878 at 1 Belgrave Square, Rathmines. [Burtchaell and Sadleir (1935); Kirkpatrick Archive; *Med Dir*; *Portora Royal School Register* (1940)].

FLYNN, WILLIAM EDWARD (1834/5–68), Milford, county Donegal;
born 1834/5, eldest son of the Rev Daniel Flynn, principal of the Academic Institute, Harcourt Street, Dublin; brother of Dr Thomas Pattison Flynn, Army Medical Service; studied medicine at Trinity College, Dublin, and the Royal College of Surgeons in Ireland; LRCSI 1862; LRCP Edin and LM 1863; LM Coombe Hosp Dub; assistant house surgeon to Liverpool Dispensaries; medical officer to Carrigart and Rossguill Dispensary District; married 4 July 1867 in Trenta Presbyterian Church, county Donegal, Anna Jack, eldest daughter of the Rev Sampson Jack, minister of Trenta Presbyterian Church, and — Gregg; died 8 May 1868 at Coxheath,

Rossguill; probate Londonderry 30 May 1868. [Belf PRO, will cal; *Coleraine Chronicle* 16 May 1868 (d); *Londonderry Sentinel* 9 July 1867 (m) and 15 May 1868 (d); McConnell (1951); *Med Dir*].

FOGARTY, JOHN WILLIAM (1863/4–1901), Cushendall, county Antrim;
born 1863/4; studied medicine at the Catholic University of Ireland; MB BCh BAO (RUI) 1889; resident surgeon to the Mater Miseriordiae Hospital, Dublin; general practitioner, of Cushendall; medical officer to Cushendall Cottage Hospital and Dispensary from its opening in 1885; married Anne —; died 22 September 1901 at Cushendall; probate Belfast 16 October 1901. [Dub GRO (d); McAlister (1880); *Med Dir*].

FORBES, ARTHUR LITTON ARMITAGE (1844/5–1925), Glenarm, county Antrim, Serbia, London and the Navigator Islands;
born 1844/5; LM Dub 1869; LRCP Edin 1870; LFPS Glas 1870; FRCS Edin 1884; MD (*hon causa*, Denver, USA) 1883; general practitioner in Glenarm, of Drumnasole, Glenarm; moved c 1880 to London; obstetric assistant and house physician to the Westminster Hospital and clinical assistant and house surgeon to the Ophthalmic Hospital, Moorfields; surgeon major in the Turkish Army during the Serbian Campaign 1876–7; surgeon to the German Consulate, Navigator Islands; aural surgeon to the Metropolitan Ear and Throat Infirmary; honorary surgeon to the School for Training Deaf Mutes; surgical superintendent of the New Zealand Emigration Service; author of *Deafness and its Curative Treatment* (8th ed) and *Diseases of the Nose* (3rd ed), *Two Years in Fiji* and *The Navigator Islands*, as well as various medical papers; FRGS; of 7 Welbeck Street, Cavendish Square c 1885, of 22 Old Burlington Street c 1895 of 15 Cavendish Place c 1915 and of 30 Coleherne Road c 1920; died 8 May 1925 at One Oak Cottage, Cothill, Abingdon, Berkshire; probate London 13 June 1925. [Lond GRO (d); Lond PPR, will cal; *Med Dir*].

FORBES, WILLIAM JOHN (1870–1952), Knaresborough, Yorkshire;
born 9 May 1870 at Clare, Castlederg, county Tyrone, son of Andrew Forbes, farmer, of Clare; educated at Castlederg Intermediate School; studied arts and medicine at Queen's College, Galway, 1888–91 and at Queen's College, Belfast, from 1891; MB BCh BAO (RUI) 1893; of Awold House, Clare c 1895; medical officer for Scriven and Knaresborough Districts, Post Office and Board of Education and medical officer of health for Knaresborough from 1896; general practitioner, of Beech House, Knaresborough; married 4 February 1897 in St Marks, Dundela, Church of Ireland Church, Belfast, Isabella McCormick, daughter of James McCormick, merchant, of Strandtown, Belfast; died 22 April 1952; probate London 25 June 1952. [*BMJ* obituary (1952); Kirkpatrick Archive; Lond PPR, will cal; *Med Dir*; QCB adm reg; UHF database (m)].

FORCADE, HENRY (1784/5–1835), Army Medical Service and Belfast;
born 1784/5 in Belfast; studied medicine at Edinburgh University from 1802; joined the Army Medical Service as assistant surgeon in 1803; with 40th Foot from 1806; surgeon with 83rd Foot 1810; staff surgeon 1813; served in the Peninsular War and received the 'General's particular commendation' (Malcolm); retired on half pay

1815; MD (St Andrew's) 1815 (on testimonials); attending surgeon to Belfast Fever Hospital 1819–28; surgeon to Belfast No 4 Dispensary District c 1822, of Castle Street, Belfast; a leader in helping to revive the Belfast Medical Society in 1822 and its treasurer until his death; one of the doctors who presented an inscribed gold box to Dr S.S. Thomson in 1834; died 22 July 1835 'and was highly esteemed for his professional skill and sagacity and for the kindly, honourable feelings which characterised him in his practice' (*BNL*); probate Connor Diocesan Court 1835. [*Belfast Fever Hospital, Annual Reports*; *BNL* 28 July 1835 (d); Belf PRO, Connor Dio Wills index; Esler (1884); Malcolm (1951); Peterkin and Johnston (1968); Pigot (1824); Smart (2004); Thomson presentation box (1834)].

FORDE, ROBERT (1808/9–58), Crumlin, county Antrim, Belfast, and Downpatrick, county Down;
born 1808/9, third son of the Rev Arthur Forde, vicar of Killaney, county Down, and Sarah Maclinchy, daughter of John Maclinchy of Downpatrick; LRCSI; general practitioner of Crumlin and of Belfast; surgeon to the Down County Infirmary 1856–8; married 6 November 1850 in Donagh Church of Ireland Church, Monaghan, Anne Hamilton Rowan (who died 12 October 1858), second daughter of Sydney Hamilton Rowan, governor of the Down Gaol; died 1 October 1858 at Downpatrick; buried in Dunsford Graveyard; administration Belfast 15 November 1858. [*BNL* 12 November 1850 (m) and 5 October 1858 (d); Belfast PRO, D2961/2/2/6; Belf PRO, will cal; Dub GRO (m); Kirkpatrick Archive; Leslie and Swanzy (1936); *Londonderry Sentinel* 8 October 1858 (d); *Med Dir*; Parkinson (1967); Pilson (1838)].

FOREMAN, THOMAS DUNWOODY (1842–1904), Ballynahinch, county Down, and Denton, Lancashire;
born 31 May 1842 at Drumalig, Boardmills, county Down, son of John Foreman of Drumalig; educated at the Belfast Seminary; studied medicine at Queen's College, Belfast, from 1860 (scholarship) and the General Hospital, Belfast; LRCP Edin and LM 1869; LFPS Glas 1869; general practitioner, of The Medical Hall, Ballynahinch; general practitioner of 126 Manchester Road, Denton, Lancashire from c 1880; married Isabella —; died 12 November 1904 at 126 Manchester Road; probate Manchester 19 December 1904. [Lond GRO (d); Lond PPR, will cal; *Med Dir*; QCB adm reg].

FORREST, JOHN VINCENT (1873–1953), Army Medical Service and Belfast;
born 21 March 1873 at Ayr, Scotland, son of William Forrest, merchant, of Champions Hall, Woodham Ferrers, Essex; studied medicine at Edinburgh University; MB CM (Edin) 1894; joined the Army Medical Service (RAMC) as surgeon 1895; captain 1898; major 1907; lieutenant-colonel 1915; deputy assistant director general at the war office 1913; served in South Africa 1900–02, world war I 1914–18; CMG 1916; ADMS, Dublin District; CB; medical superintendent of Royal Victoria Hospital, Belfast, 1921–31, of Glenmachan, Strandtown, Belfast; married 15 June 1927 in St Mark's Church of Ireland Church, Dundela, Belfast, Mary Gundreda Ewart, youngest daughter of Sir William Quartus Ewart, 2nd

baronet; died 10 October 1953 at Glenmachan, Belfast; probate Belfast 5 January 1954. [Belf GRO (m); *BNL* 1953 (d); Belf PRO, will cal; *Belfast Telegraph* 1930 and 1953 (d); *Burke's Peerage and Baronetage* (1978); *Lancet* obituary (1953); *Med Dir*; Peterkin and Johnston (1968)].

FORSTER, ARTHUR (d 1840), Tempo, county Fermanagh;
MD [?]; medical officer to Tempo Dispensary; died 4 April 1840. [*BNL* 14 April 1840 (d); *Londonderry Sentinel* 18 April 1840 (d)].

FORSTER, JOHN H. (d 1843), Dromore, county Down;
MD [?]; died 20 June 1843 at Dromore, of typhus fever. [*BNL* 27 June 1843 (d)].

FORSTER, SAMUEL (d 1837), Roshin, Templecrone, county Donegal;
son of — Forster of Roshin Lodge; MD [?]; died 29 June 1837 of typhus fever, at his father's residence. [*BNL* 25 July 1837 (d); *Londonderry Sentinel* 22 July 1837 (d)].

FORSTER, WILLIAM (d c 1850), Ballybofey, county Donegal;
CM (Glas) [?]; general practitioner in Ballybofey, c 1845; possibly died c 1850. [Croly (1843–6)].

FORSYTH, DAVID (1859–1911), Cockermouth, Cumberland and Lancaster, Lancashire;
born 30 January 1859 at Ballyhighey, Limavady, county Londonderry, son of Andrew Forysth, farmer, of Ballyhighey; educated at RBAI; studied medicine at Queen's College, Belfast, from 1876; MD (QUI) 1881; general practitioner, of Cockermouth from c 1882; moved c 1900 to 'The Close', Queen's Square, Lancaster; married Bertha Maude —; died 18 March 1911 at 'The Close'; probate Lancaster 27 May 1911. [Lond GRO (d); Lond PPR, will cal; *Med Dir*; QCB adm reg].

FORSYTH, JAMES (1794/5–1827), Gracehill, county Antrim;
born 1794/5; surgeon, of Gracehill; married 19 December 1820 — Freeman of Larkhill, Ballynahinch, county Down; died 4 February 1827 at Antrim of typhus fever; 'his premature death will be seriously felt as his character in the faculty stood high; it may with truth said he fell a victim to his humanity'. [*BNL* 26 December 1820 (m) and 13 February 1827 (d)].

FORSYTH, JAMES WATSON (d 1850), Bahia, Brazil;
nephew of Dr George Forsyth, senior, of Carrickfergus (*q.v.*); surgeon, of Bahia [Salvador], Brazil; died 7 March 1850 at Bahia, of yellow fever. [*BNL* 20 April 1850 (d)].

FORSYTH, ROBERT (1866–c 1958) Salford, Lancashire, and Capetown, South Africa;
born 1 May 1866 at Ballymena, county Antrim, son of Robert Forsyth, draper, of Lisburn; educated at Lisburn Intermediate School; studied medicine at Queen's College, Belfast, from 1883; BA (RUI) 1888; MB BCh BAO 1889; general practitioner, of 227 Oldfield Road, Salford c 1895; emigrated to Capetown, South

Africa; general practitioner of 52 Orange Street, Capetown from c 1900; of 16 Queen Victoria Street c 1910, 83 Parliament Street c 1915 and Langholm, Kloof Street from c 1920; of Kommetije c 1935 and of Plumstead c 1940; retired c 1945; died c 1958. [*Med Dir*; QCB adm reg].

FORSYTHE, ANDERSON (1843–1902), London;
born September 1843 at Moneymore, county Londonderry, son of John Forsythe of Moneymore; educated at Cookstown Academy; studied medicine at Queen's Colleges, Belfast and Galway, from 1862; BA (QUI) 1869; MD 1871; general practitioner in London, of 46 Rosoman Street, Clerkenwell, c 1875 and of 118 Great College Street from c 1880; retired c 1895 to 'Hazeldene', New Barnet, Herts; married Maria Harriet —; died 30 September 1902 at New Barnet; probate London 27 October 1902. [Lond PPR, will cal, will; *Med Dir*; QCB adm reg].

FORSYTHE, CHARLES (1849–1937), Articlave and Coleraine, county Londonderry;
born 1 November 1849 at Moneymore, county Londonderry, son of Adam Forsythe of Turnaface, Moneymore; educated by Mr Crooks; studied medicine at Queen's College, Belfast, from 1867; MD (QUI) 1872; LRCS Edin and LM 1873; LAH Dub 1891; medical officer to Articlave Dispensary District from 1873; visiting surgeon to Coleraine Cottage Hospital; medical officer to the Workhouse and Fever Hospital and certifying factory surgeon, Coleraine; medical officer to the Belfast and Northern Counties Railway and Coleraine Model School, of Church Street, Coleraine; of 'One Sycamore', Coleraine from c 1930 and later of Galgorm Road, Ballymena; married —; died 9 April 1937 at Galgorm Road; administration Belfast 25 August 1937. [Belf GRO (d); Belf PRO, will cal; Kirkpatrick Archive; *Med Dir*; QCB adm reg].

FORSYTH(E), GEORGE, senior (1781/2–1856), Carrickfergus, county Antrim;
born 1781/2, eldest son of James Forsythe of the parish of Killead, county Antrim; uncle of Dr James Watson Forsyth of Bahia, Brazil (*q.v.*); studied medicine at Glasgow University; MD (Glas) 1813; advertised that he was starting practice as physician and accoucheur in Carrickfergus in March 1814; medical officer to army and constabulary, of High Street, Carrickfergus c 1824, also of Rosebrook, Carrickfergus; married —; father of Dr James Forsythe of Culmore (*q.v.*) and Dr George Forsythe, junior (*q.v.*); died 27 December 1856 in High Street, Carrickfergus; probate Connor Diocesan Court 1857 (will copy in National Archives, Dublin). [Addison (1898); *BNL* 15 March 1814 (advert) and 29 December 1856 (d); Belf PRO, Connor Dio Wills index; Croly (1843–6); Dub Nat Arch, Down & Connor Will Book, 9002; Lewis (1837); *Londonderry Sentinel* 2 January 1857 (d); *Med Dir*; Pigot (1824); Rutherford and Clarke, *County Antrim*, vol 3 (1995), appendix, p 216].

FORSYTHE, GEORGE, junior (1822/3–48), Carrickfergus, county Antrim;
born 1822/3, son of Dr George Forsythe, senior; brother of Dr James Forsythe of Culmore (*q.v.*); died 4 November 1848 at Carrickfergus. [*BNL* 7 November 1848 (d)].

FORSYTH(E), GEORGE CROMPTON (1852/3–75), Culmore, county Londonderry;
> born 1852/3, son of Dr James Forsyth(e) of Culmore (*q.v.*) and Letitia Crompton; educated at Foyle College, Londonderry; studied arts and medicine at Trinity College, Dublin, from 1870; BA MB (TCD) 1874; general practitioner, of Temple Ard, Culmore; unmarried; died 6 October 1875 at Culmore, of diphtheria. [Dub GRO (d); Kirkpatrick Archive; *Med Dir;* TCD adm reg; *TCD Cat*, vol II (1896)].

FORSYTHE, JAMES (1756–1849), Newtownards, county Down, and Belfast;
> born 1756 in Ballynure, county Antrim, second son of John Forsythe and Catherine (Ceatron) McAlashender; educated at Ballyeaston; studied medicine at Edinburgh University; MD (Edin) 1782 (thesis 'De pneumonia'); physician, of Newtownards, Belfast, England and Belfast again (in partnership with Dr S.S. Thomson); of Upper Arthur Street, Belfast c 1824; retired to Holywood, county Down; 'he frequently entered into mercantile speculations, which assisted him in realising a very handsome income' (Benn); advised his patients to live in Holywood, saying that 'no place in the neighbourhood of Belfast was so favourable as a residence for invalids'; unmarried; died 12 June 1849 at Holywood (aged 93); buried in Ballynure Old Graveyard; portrait in Ulster Museum by Samuel Hawksett (c 1815–20) (?); probate Prerogative Court 3 July 1849 (original will dated 8 May 1849 in Belf PRO). [Agnew (1998); (*BNL* 15 June 1849 (d); Belf PRO, Prerog Wills index and T 810/248; *Belfast Street Directory* (1870); Benn (1880); Black (2000); Edin Univ; Esler (1884); Malcolm (1851); Pigot (1824); Rutherford and Clarke, *County Antrim*, vol 3 (1995)].

FORSYTH(E), JAMES (1813/4–83), Culmore, county Londonderry;
> born 1813/4, son of Dr George Forsyth(e), senior (*q.v.*); brother of Dr George Forsythe, junior (*q.v.*); studied medicine at Glasgow University; LM Glas 1841; MD (Glas) 1841; LRCS Edin 1841; house surgeon and apothecary to Londonderry Infirmary; medical officer to Kilderry Dispensary District and admiralty surgeon, of Temple Ard, Culmore; married (1) 29 April 1847 in Derry Cathedral, Letitia Crompton (who died 8 January 1857), youngest daughter of Adam Crompton of Londonderry; (2) 19 May 1859 in Monkstown Church of Ireland Church, county Dublin, Elizabeth Letitia Young (who died 3 September 1893), third daughter of Richard Young, JP, of Coolkeeragh House, county Londonderry, and Elizabeth Caldwell, only daughter of Dr John Caldwell of Londonderry (*q.v.*); died 7 July 1883 at Temple Ard, Culmore; probate Londonderry 10 August 1883. [Addison (1898); *BNL* 7 May 1847 (m); Belf PRO, will cal; Burke *LGI* (1912); *Coleraine Chronicle* 1 May 1847 (m) and 28 May 1859 (m); Croly (1843–6); Dub GRO (m) and (d); *Londonderry Sentinel* 1 May 1847 (m), 16 January 1857 (d) and 27 May 1859 (m); *Med Dir;* Young (1929)].

FORSYTH(E), JOHN (1796/7–1833), Antrim;
> born 1796/7; surgeon and apothecary, of Antrim; married Anne Ferguson (who was born 1775/6 and died 21 December 1880 and was buried in Donegore Graveyard), daughter of John Ferguson of Antrim; died 1833; administration Connor Diocesan Court 5 March 1836. [Dub Nat Arch, Connor Dio Wills and Admins index; gravestone inscription; Pigot (1824)].

FOSTER, CLARE (*fl c* 1820), county Fermanagh [?];
general practitioner, probably of county Fermanagh; married —; died before 1841. [*BNL* 26 January 1841 (m, daughter)].

FOSTER, EDWARD (c 1739–79), Londonderry and Dublin;
born c 1739 in county Donegal; studied medicine at Edinburgh University; MD (Edin) 1767 (thesis 'De nosocomiis'); physician, of Londonderry; of Dublin from 1771; assistant master of the Rotunda Hospital, Dublin 1772–5; author of *An Essay on Hospitals or Succinct Directions for the Situation, Construction and Administration of Hospitals* (1768) and *Principles and Practise of Midwifery* (1781); married in April 1768 — Lucas, daughter of Dr Charles Lucas, MP for Dublin City; died 1 April 1779 in Dublin; the subject of *A Biographical Sketch of the late Edward Foster, MD* by Dr William Patterson of Londonderry (*q.v.*). [Cameron (1916); Colby (1837); Edin Univ; Geary (1995); Johnston-Liik (2002); Kirkpatrick and Jellett (1913)].

FOSTER, HENRY STUART HAMILTON (1862/3–89), Londonderry;
born 1862/3; studied medicine at Glasgow University; MB MCh (Glas) 1885; general practitioner of Ballynacross, county Londonderry; unmarried; died 21 May 1889 of phthisis, at Ballynacross; probate Londonderry 19 August 1889. [Addison (1898); Belf PRO, will cal; Dub GRO (d); *Med Dir*].

FOSTER, ROBERT (1782/3–1855), Ballybofey, county Donegal;
born 1782/3; apothecary, of Ballybofey c 1824; married —; died 11 June 1855 at Ballybofey. [*BNL* 4 July 1855 (d); Pigot (1824)].

FOSTER, THOMAS (*fl c* 1845), Armagh;
LAH Dub; general practitioner, of English Street, Armagh c 1845; possibly died c 1850. [Croly (1843–6)].

FOX, JAMES (1858–96), Burnley, Lancashire;
born 21 January 1858 at Creggan, Ballygawley county Tyrone; educated at Carrickmore Clerical School; studied medicine at Queen's College, Belfast, from 1878; LRCP LRCS Edin 1891; LFPS Glas 1891; general practitioner, of Burnley c 1892–6; died 18 July 1896 of acute phthisis, at 11 Yorkshire Street, Burnley; probate London 16 October 1896. [Lond GRO (d); Lond PPR, will cal; *Med Dir*; QCB adm reg].

FOY, GEORGE MAHOOD (1845–1934), Dublin;
born 22 December 1845 at Cootehill, county Cavan, son of John Foy, merchant, of Cootehill and Jane Murphy; educated in Belfast and privately; studied medicine at Queen's College, Belfast, from 1870 and the Royal College of Surgeons in Ireland; LAH Dub 1873; LRCSI 1874; FRCSI 1874; MD (*hon causa*) (Virginia) 1897; senior lecturer in anatomy at Carmichael School of Medicine; surgeon to the Whitworth Hospital; of 80 Lower Gardiner Street c 1885 and of 7 Cavendish Row, Rutland Square East from c 1890; author of *Anaesthetics, Ancient and Modern* (1889), a biography of Crawford Williamson Long and many surgical papers; married Mary —; died 23 April 1934; buried in St George's Graveyard, Dublin. [Cameron (1916); Kirkpatrick Archive; *Med Dir*; QCB adm reg; Widdess (1967)].

FRAME, JAMES (1811–84), Comber, county Down;
born 1810/11 near Comber; studied medicine at Glasgow University; LFPS Glas 1845; medical officer to Comber Dispensary District and constabulary, certifying factory surgeon and registrar of births, marriages and deaths; medical officer for Andrews's mill; married 15 January 1840 in Comber, Mary McKibbin (who was born 1817/8 and died 24 November 1906), second daughter of James McKibbin of Maghereagh, county Antrim; died 15 May 1884 at Comber; both buried in Comber graveyard; probate Dublin 12 June 1884. [*BNL* 28 January 1840 (m); Belf PRO, will cal; Clarke, *County Down*, vol 5 (1984); Croly (1843–6); Dub GRO (d); *Med Dir*; *Newtownards Chronicle* 17 May 1884 (d)].

FRAME, JOHN (d c 1846), Comber, county Down;
surgeon, of Tullygirvin, Comber; died c 1846; probate Down Diocesan Court 1846. [Belf PRO, Down Dio Wills index]).

FRANCIS, ARTHUR BAILIE (1856–c 1920), Carrickfergus, county Antrim, Dumfries, and Melbourne, Victoria;
born 1 June 1856 at Greencastle, county Donegal, son of William Francis, coast guard officer, who retired to Newtownards, county Down; educated at C S and M Academy, Carlisle Circus, Belfast; studied medicine at Queen's College, Belfast, from 1886; LRCP LRCS Edin 1894; LFPS Glas 1894; general practitioner, of High Street, Carrickfergus c 1895; surgeon with the White Star Line; medical officer to Colvend, Southwick and Kirkbean from c 1900, of Mainsriddell, Preston Mill, Dumfries; medical officer to the Victorian Eye and Ear Hospital, Melbourne, Victoria from c 1915; author of various medical papers; died c 1920. [*Med Dir*; QCB adm reg].

FRASER, ARCHIBALD CRAIG (1857/8–1931), Drumkeeran, county Leitrim;
born 1857/8 at Lurganboy, county Leitrim, son of William Fraser, farmer, of Twiggspark, Lurganboy; brother of Dr James Fraser (*q.v.*); educated at Sligo Diocesan School; studied medicine at Queen's College, Cork, 1875–6 and Belfast, from 1876; MD (QUI) 1879; LFPS Glas 1880; medical officer to Drumkeeran Dispensary District of Lavagh, Drumkeeran; died 4 April 1931 at Lavagh; probate Dublin 30 July 1931. [Dub Nat Arch, will cal; Kirkpatrick Archive; *Med Dir*; QCB adm reg].

FRASER, ARTHUR REDDINGTON (*fl c* 1845), Markethill, county Armagh;
MRCSE 1839; general practitioner in Markethill and Mountnorris c 1845; possibly died c 1850. [Croly (1843–6)].

FRASER, JAMES (1846–99), Army Medical Service;
born 6 July 1846 at Lurganboy, county Leitrim, son of William Fraser of Lurganboy; brother of Dr Archibald Craig Fraser (*q.v.*); educated at Sligo Diocesan School; studied medicine at Queen's College, Belfast winning scholarships and prizes 1863–7; MD MCh (QUI) 1867; home address c 1875, Twig's Park, Manorhamilton, county Leitrim; joined the Army Medical Service as surgeon 1868; surgeon major 1880; surgeon lieutenant-colonel (RAMC) 1888; brigade surgeon lieutenant–colonel 1894; colonel 1898; served in South Africa 1879–81; retired to 39 Bootham, York;

married Susan Alberta —; died 9 May 1899 at York; probate London 17 June 1899. [Lond PPR, will cal; *Med Dir*; Peterkin and Johnston (1968); QUB].

FRASER, ROBERT MOORE (1865–1952), Belfast;
born 10 February 1865, at Crieff, Perthshire, elder son of James Fraser, supervisor of excise, of 10 Cameron Street, Belfast, and Catherine Ann Moore of Carndonagh, county Donegal; educated at RBAI; studied arts and medicine at Queen's College, Belfast, from 1882 and Trinity College, Dublin; BA (RUI) 1885; MB BCh BAO (RUI) 1890; MD (QUB) 1920; general practitioner in Belfast and medical officer to the Post Office, of Lorne Terrace, Mountpottinger and Gortfoyle, Knock, Belfast; of 10 Winston Gardens, Knock from c 1944; married (1) 1 February 1900 in Fortwilliam Presbyterian Church, Belfast, Margaret Boal Ferguson (who was born 26 May 1868 and died 10 November 1903), daughter of Adam Boal Ferguson, mill manager, and Mary Ann Molyneux; (2) 11 June 1907 in Dundela Presbyterian Church, Belfast, Alice Josephine Cuthbert (died 14 August 1953), daughter of Dr Alexander Cuthbert (*q.v.*) of Londonderry; father by (1) of Sir Ian Fraser of Belfast, MB BCh BAO (QUB) 1923, FRCSI 1926; died 28 January 1952 at 10 Winston Gardens; buried in Dundonald Cemetery, Belfast; probate Belfast 26 March 1952. [Belf PRO, will cal; Burke *LGI* (1958); Clarke (2004); Dub GRO (d); gravestone inscription; Kirkpatrick Archive; *Med Dir*; QCB adm reg; RVH Archive; UHF database (m x 2)].

FRAZER, HENRY (1847/8–91), Armagh;
born 1847/8; studied medicine at Glasgow University and the Royal College of Surgeons in Ireland; LKQCPI and LM 1868; LRCSI 1868; LM Rot Hosp Dub 1868; LAH Dub 1870; MD (Glas) 1881; surgeon to SS *Helvetia*; temporary medical officer to Belfast Dispensary; medical officer to Macan Asylum for the Blind, Armagh, from 1870; apothecary to county Armagh Lunatic Asylum; general practitioner of English Street, Armagh; married —; died 10 May 1891 at Seven Houses, Armagh; probate Armagh 1 October 1891. [Addison (1898); Belf PPR, will cal; Dub GRO (d); *Med Dir*].

FRAZER, SAMUEL (1857/8–1930), Woking, Surrey and Brentwood, Essex;
born 1857/8, son of Thomas Frazer, manager of the Spinning Mill, Buncrana, county Donegal; educated at Newry School, studied medicine at Queen's College, Cork, and from 1875, at Queen's College, Belfast; LAH Dub 1880; LRCP LRCS Edin 1882; general practitioner, of Woking, Surrey c 1885; medical officer of Brentwood District, Essex, of King's Road, Brentwood, from c 1890, later of Lansdowne House, of Collaton House and of 9 Avenue Road, Brentwood; medical officer to Hackney Training Schools, Brentwood; married —; died 14 July 1930 at Lower Broadmoor, Talbenny, Milford, Pembrokeshire. [Lond GRO (d); *Med Dir*; QCB adm reg].

FRAZER, THOMAS (*fl c* 1848), Naval Medical Service;
of Belfast; joined the Naval Medical Service as assistant surgeon; married Emma Georgiana Maria Watt (who was born 1819/20 and died 6 October 1848 at 73 York Street, Belfast), eldest daughter of James Duff Watt, assistant commissary general. [*BNL* 10 October 1848 (d)].

FREEMAN, ROBERT (*fl c* 1783), Cavan town;
surgeon, of Cavan town 1783 (witness to a will). [Ellis and Eustace, vol III, (1984)].

FRENCH, NICHOLAS (1848/9–1908) ship's surgeon and Strabane, county Tyrone;
born 1848/9, son of John French, supervisor; studied medicine at Trinity College, Dublin and the Ledwich School; LRCSI 1872; LRCP and LM Edin 1873; LAH Dub 1874; surgeon to the Guion Line; surgeon and apothecary, of Main Street, Strabane; married 9 September 1880 at Sion, Urney, county Tyrone, Mary Moore, second daughter of James Moore, farmer, of Mountilly, Sion; died 7 January 1908 at Woodbrook, Birnaghs, Newtownstewart. [*Belfast Street Directories*; Dooher (2000); Dub GRO (m) and (d); Kirkpatrick Archive; *Med Dir*].

FREW, ROBERT (b 1821/2), Killinchy, county Down;
born 1821/2, son of Robert Frew, farmer and miller, of Ballyministra, Killinchy; surgeon, of Ballyministra, but not in *Medical Directory* or *Medical Register*; married 17 September 1846 in Killinchy Non-Subscribing Presbyterian Church, Elizabeth Duff, daughter of Samuel Duff, farmer, of Ballybunden, county Down. [UHF database (m)].

FRIER, WILLIAM (1848–1932), Waringstown, county Down;
born 5 December 1848 at Linen Hill House, Katesbridge, county Down, son of James Frier of Ballyvaley, Banbridge; educated at Banbridge Academy; studied medicine at Queen's College, Belfast, from 1864; MD MCh (QUI) 1870; LM RCPI 1871; medical officer to Waringstown Dispensary District from 1871; married —; died 22 May 1932 at Waringstown; probate Belfast 15 August 1932. [Belf GRO (d); Belf PRO, will cal; Kirkpatrick Archive; *Med Dir*; QCB adm reg].

FRITH, BAPTIST GAMBLE (1789/90–1863), Enniskillen, county Fermanagh;
born 1789/90; studied medicine at Edinburgh University; LRCS Edin 1811; MD (Edin) 1811 (thesis 'De ictero'); FRCSI 1844; physician, of Main Street, Enniskillen c 1824 and surgeon to the County Fermanagh Militia; of Willoughby Place, Enniskillen; JP; married Letitia — (who was born 1791/2 and died 18 December 1878); died 17 July 1863 at Willoughby Place; buried in Enniskillen Parish Graveyard; probate Dublin 26 November 1863. [Belf PRO, will cal; Croly (1843–6); Dundas (1913); Edin Univ; Kirkpatrick Archive; *Londonderry Sentinel* 24 July 1863 (d); *Med Dir*; Pigot (1824)].

FRITH, BAPTIST GAMBLE (1860–1943), Hove, Sussex;
born 4 May 1860 in Newry, county Down, son of the Rev John Brien Frith of Enniskillen, perpetual curate of Camlough, county Armagh, and Jane Townley; educated at Portora Royal School, Enniskillen; studied arts and medicine at Trinity College, Dublin, from 1878; BA (TCD) 1882; MB BCh 1884; LM Rot Hosp Dub 1884; general practitioner, of 19 Palmeira Court, Hove, Sussex and later of 34 Pembroke Crescent, Hove; married —; died 30 July 1943; probate Llandudno 13 October 1943. [Leslie (1911); Lond PPR, will cal, will; *Med Dir*; *Portora Royal School Register* (1940); TCD adm reg; *TCD Cat*, vol II (1896)].

FRITH, RICHARD (d 1838), Antrim, and Enniskillen, county Fermanagh;
son of Alexander Frith of Cornagrade, county Fermanagh; assistant surgeon to the Antrim Militia; died 1 August 1838 of a decline, at his home near Enniskillen. [*BNL* 7 August 1838 (d)].

FRITH, WILLIAM (1731/2–1806), Enniskillen, county Fermanagh;
born 1731/2; apothecary, of Enniskillen; married —; died 5 December 1806. [Dundas (1913)].

FRITH, — (d c 1847), Enniskillen, county Fermanagh;
doctor, of Enniskillen; died c 1847 of fever during the Famine. [Cunningham (1997)].

FRIZELL, THOMAS (1856–c 1910), Australia;
born 26 April 1856 at Crew Bridge, Dungannon, county Tyrone, son of James Frizell, farmer, of Dungannon; educated at Dungannon Classical School; studied medicine at Queen's College, Belfast, from 1876; MD MCh (RUI) 1884; LM KQCPI 1884; emigrated to Australia c 1885; general practitioner, of Roebourne District, Western Australia c 1886 and of Strathfield, Sydney, New South Wales c 1895; died c 1910. [*Med Dir*; QCB adm reg].

FRIZELL(E), WILLIAM ALEXANDER (1850/1–1940), Londonderry;
born 1850/1; studied medicine at Carmichael School, Dublin, and Edinburgh; LRCP LRCS Edin 1888; LFPS Glas 1888; LM Rot Hosp Dub; general practitioner, of 43 Clarendon Street, and later of 3 Woodleigh Terrace, Londonderry; retired c 1927; married Harriet Louise —; died 9 March 1940 at 3 Woodleigh Terrace; probate Londonderry 23 April 1940. [Belf GRO (d); Belf PRO, will cal; *Med Dir*].

FRYER, WILLIAM FRANCIS (1825/6–1914), Oulart, county Wexford, and Fenagh, county Carlow;
born 1825/6 in Belfast; LM Coombe Hosp Dub 1846; MRCSE 1849; LAH Dub 1850; MD (Glas) 1850; medical officer to Oulart Dispensary District; medical officer to Fenagh and Myshall Dispensary District, county Carlow, of Clonburrin, Bagenalstown; married 11 December 1850 in St Andrew's Church of Ireland Church, Dublin, Elizabeth Stewart Cochran, daughter of John Mercer Cochran of 38 Dame Street, Dublin; daughter born 29 October 1851 in Donegall Street, Belfast; died 2 February 1914 at Clonburrin; probate Dublin 24 August 1914. [Addison (1898); *BNL* 3 November 1851 (b, daughter); Belf PRO, will cal; Dub GRO (m) and (d); *Med Dir*].

FRYER, WILLIAM FRANCIS (1858/9–1942), Ipswich, Suffolk;
born 1858/9; studied medicine at the Ledwich School, Dublin; LM Coombe Hosp Dub 1882; LRCP LRCS Edin 1882; LAH Dub 1883; medical officer to No 6 District of Woodbridge, Suffolk, and HM Prison, also public vaccinator, of Chesnut House, 11 Fore Street, Ipswich; married —; father of Dr Thomas Dermot Wyon Fryer, MRCSE LRCP Lond 1926, MB BCh (Cantab) 1930, of Ipswich; died 6

February 1942 at 11 Fore Street; probate Ipswich 1 June 1942. [Kirkpatrick Archive; Lond GRO (d); Lond PPR, will cal, will; *Med Dir*].

FUHR, ROBERT STRICKLAND HANNAY;
See HANNAY, ROBERT STRICKLAND

FULLER, BARTHOLOMEW (d 1800), Army Medical Service and Belfast;
joined the Army Medical Service as surgeon to 49th Foot in September 1776; served in the American War of Independence; resigned August 1786; already an apothecary and surgeon in Belfast in 1783 (Drennan letters) and is recorded as in practice 1788, 1789 and 1792; one of the founding committee of the Belfast Dispensary in April 1792; appointed attending surgeon in May 1792; married 17 May 1782 in St Anne's Church of Ireland Church, Belfast, Elizabeth Patterson of Donaghadee; died 1 January 1800; probate Prerogative Court 1800. [Agnew (1998); *BNL* 3 January 1800 (d); Belfast, St Anne's Parish Church Mar Reg; Esler (1884); Malcolm (1851); Peterkin and Johnston (1968); Strain (1961); Vicars (1897)].

FULLER, GEORGE HARRY HINGSTON (1860–c 1900), Liverpool, Lancashire, Deptford, London, Abingdon, Sussex, and South Africa;
born 14 October 1860 at Shoreham, Sussex, son of Dr Thomas Fuller, MD, of Shoreham; educated at Lancing College, Sussex; studied medicine at the Royal College of Surgeons, Guy's Hospital, London, and from 1881, at Queen's College, Belfast; MRCSE 1884; general practitioner, of 52 St Domingo's Grove, Liverpool c 1885–8, of Creek Road, Deptford c 1890, of Station Road, Abington c 1892; emigrated to South Africa c 1895; general practitioner, of Aliwal North, Cape Colony; of Faaresmith, Orange Free State, c 1896 and of Luckshoff c 1898; died c 1900. [*Med Dir*; QCB adm reg].

FULLERTON, ANDREW (1868–1934), London, Maidstone, Kent, Belfast and RAMC;
born 20 March 1868 at Wesley Street, Cavan, fourth son of the Rev Alexander Fullerton, Methodist minister, and Mary Jane Moffitt; younger brother of Dr Thomas William Archer Fullerton, IMS (*q.v.*); educated at Lurgan College; studied medicine at Queen's College, Belfast, from 1885; gold medal Belfast Hospital for Children; Coulter Medal, Belfast Royal Hospital 1890; MB BCh BAO (RUI) (1st class hons) 1890; MD 1893; FRCSI 1901; MCh (QUB) 1913; house surgeon at the Miller Hospital, London, and the West Kent General Hospital, Maidstone; honorary assistant surgeon to the Belfast Hospital for Children; surgical registrar to the Royal Victoria Hospital, Belfast 1900–02; honorary assistant surgeon 1902–11, surgeon in charge of outpatients 1911–18 and attending surgeon 1918–33; gave annual winter oration at Royal Victoria Hospital 1904 and 1923; served in RAMC during World War 1 rising to rank of colonel; mentioned in despatches three times; CMG 1916; CB 1919; president of the Ulster Branch of the BMA and of the Ulster Medical Society 1919–20; FACS (honorary) 1922; professor of Surgery at Queen's University, Belfast 1923–33; president of the Royal College of Surgeons in Ireland 1926–8 and the Association of Surgeons of Great Britain and Ireland 1931; chairman of the Royal

Victoria Hospital Medical Staff 1931–3; author of many medical papers; freemason and master of the Queen's University Lodge; of 8 University Square, Belfast from c 1907; married (1) 26 April 1897 in Holy Trinity Church, Upper Tooting, Caroline Bullock (who was born 1867/8 and died 1926), daughter of John Thornton Bullock of 48 Louisville Road, Upper Tooting; (2) 8 June 1928 in St George's Church of Ireland Church, Belfast, Norah Digby Counihan, daughter of the Rev Robert Digby French of Sandford, Dublin, and widow of Mr Randal Counihan, FRCS, of Ennis; died 22 May 1934 at 1 College Park East, Belfast; buried in Belfast City Cemetery; portrait by William Conor in RVH; probate Belfast 4 September 1934. [Belf City Cem, bur reg; Belf GRO (d); Belf PRO, will cal; *Belf Roy Hosp, Ann Rep*; *BMJ* obituary (1934); *DIB* (2009); Dub GRO (b); Fraser (1964) and (1976); Hunter (1936); Kirkpatrick Archive; *Lancet* obituary (1934); Leslie and Wallace (2001); Lond GRO (m); Lyons (1984); *Med Dir*; Moody and Beckett (1959); Newmann (1993); O'Brien, Crookshank and Wolstenholme (1988); O'Donnell (2008); QCB adm reg; Stewart (1935); Woodside (1934)].

FULLERTON, GEORGE (*fl c* 1820–30), Brisbane, Queensland, Australia;
son of the Rev Archibald Fullerton, minister of Aghadowey Presbyterian Church, county Antrim; emigrated to Australia; MD (Brisbane); member of the Legislative Council of Queensland; contributed £2,000 to found scholarships at Magee College. [McConnell (1951)].

FULLERTON, JAMES WATT (d c 1850), Fanad, county Donegal;
studied medicine at Edinburgh University; MD (Edin) 1837 (thesis 'On mortification'); accoucheur of Edinburgh Lying-in Hospital; medical officer to Clondavaddog Dispensary and constabulary c 1843–6; married 9 January 1844 Mary Jane Hay, daughter of Robert Hay of Aughadreena; died c 1850. [*BNL* 26 January 1844 (m); Croly (1843–6; Edin Univ].

FULLERTON, RICHARD (1853–88), Manchester and Sylhet, India;
born 1853 in Armagh, son of William Tierney Fullerton, diocesan architect, Armagh; educated at Armagh Royal School 1867–70; studied arts and medicine at Trinity College, Dublin, from 1872; exhibitioner 1872; BA MB BCh (TCD) 1876; medical officer of Chorlton Union Hospitals, Withington, Manchester c 1874; of Chandicherra, Munchi Kandi, Sylhet c 1885; died 26 April 1888 at the Cubbon Hotel, Bangalore. [Ferrar (1933); Kirkpatrick Archive; *Med Dir;* TCD adm reg; *TCD Cat*, vol II (1896)].

FULLERTON (FULLARTON), ROBERT (1819/20–54), Grenada, West Indies;
born 1819/20; of Garvagh, county Londonderry; MD [?]; general practitioner, of Tivoli Cottage, Grenada c 1845–54; married —; died 18 June 1854 of fever, at Tivoli Cottage, Grenada, 'where he was constantly engaged in the active practice of his profession' (*Coleraine Chronicle*). [*Coleraine Chronicle* 24 June 1854 (d); *Londonderry Sentinel* 16 June 1854 (d)].

FULLERTON, THOMAS WILLIAM ARCHER (1867–1907), Indian Medical Service;
> born 31 March 1867 at Abbeyleix, third son of the Rev Alexander Fullerton, Methodist minister, and Mary Jane Moffitt; older brother of Professor Andrew Fullerton (*q.v.*); studied medicine at the Carmichael School, Dublin, and the Royal College of Surgeons in Ireland; MB BCh BAO (RUI) 1890; FRCSI 1907; joined the Indian Medical Service (Bengal establishment) as surgeon lieutenant 1892; surgeon captain 1895; major 1904; served on the North West Frontier at Waziristan 1894–5 (medal with clasp) and Malakand 1897–8, operation in Bajour and in Mamand county, Utan Khel, Buser (medal with clasp) 1892; worked on the eradication of plague from India; received the Kaiser-I-Hind medal (first class); married 1893 Margaret Ann Meglaughlin of Gortmerron, Dungannon, county Tyrone; died 15 August 1907 at Lucknow, India, as a result of an infection acquired during a surgical operation; probate London 9 November 1907. [*BMJ* obituary (1907); Dub GRO (b); Fraser (1976); Kirkpatrick Archive; Lond PPR, will cal; *Med Dir*].

FULTON, ADAM (1866–1943), Nottingham;
> born 16 December 1866 at Cookstown, county Tyrone, son of Adam Fulton of Cookstown and Belfast; educated at RBAI; studied medicine at Queen's College, Belfast, from 1884; BA (RUI) 1888; MB BCh BAO 1893; resident clinical assistant to Belfast Royal Hospital; general practitioner, of 39 Lincoln Street, Old Basford, Nottingham, from c 1895, of 118 and 418 Nottingham Road, Old Basford, c 1900, and of 48 Grange Road, Southport, c 1920; retired to 9 Granby Terrace, Harrogate c 1930; JP for the City of Nottingham; married Nina Fox, daughter of the Rev G.E. Fox, of Swillington, Leeds; died 28 September 1943 at Eden Nursing Home, Victoria Avenue, Harrogate; probate Wakefield 22 November 1943. [*BMJ* obituary (1943); Kirkpatrick Archive; *Lancet* obituary (1943); Lond PPR, will cal; *Med Dir*; QCB adm reg].

FULTON, FREDERICK (1872–1949), Manchester, Oldham, and Chadderton Lancashire;
> born 27 March 1872 at Saintfield, county Down, son of Dr Thomas Fulton (*q.v.*) of Saintfield, and Marion Hamilton; educated at Lurgan College; studied arts and medicine at Queen's College, Belfast, from 1888; LRCP LRCS Edin 1898; LFPS Glas 1898; general practitioner, of 428 Eccles New Road, Manchester, c 1905 and of 231 Featherstall Road North, Oldham, from c 1908; of 57 Burnley Lane, Chadderton from c 1945; married Alice —; father of Dr Patrick Fulton; died 30 August 1949; probate Manchester 12 October 1949. [Lond PPR, will cal; *Med Dir*; QCB adm reg].

FULTON, HENRY (1793–1859), Indian Medical Service and Dublin;
> born 3 April 1793 at Lisburn, fourth son of Joseph Fulton of Lisburn and Ann Graham; studied medicine studied arts and medicine at Trinity College, Dublin, and medicine at Edinburgh University; MD (Edin) 1824 (thesis 'De dysenteria'); travelled in Europe and published *Travelling Sketches* and *Travelling Sketches in various Countries* (1840); studied medicine at Guy's and St Thomas's Hospitals, London and

Aberdeen University; MD (Aberdeen); joined the Indian Medical Service (Bengal establishment) as assistant surgeon 1828; resigned 1829 and retired to Ireland; general practitioner and amateur architect in Dublin, of 2 Gardener's Place and later of Clonmore, Stillorgan; married (1) 14 June 1816 Jane Finlay (died 1818) daughter of Dr Finlay of Belfast; (2) 2 September 1830 Anne Miller (died 1875), only daughter of John Miller of Dublin and Hannah Boyle; father of Dr Joseph Fulton of Dublin, LRCSI 1864; died 12 December 1859 at Clonmore; buried in Mount Jerome Cemetery, Dublin. [*BNL* 7 September 1830 (m) and 16 December 1859 (d); Burke *LGI* (1912); Crawford (1930); Edin Univ; Hope (1903); Kirkpatrick Archive; *Lisburn Fam Hist Soc*, vol 2 (2005); Martin (2010)].

FULTON, JAMES (1862–1935), Belfast;
born 3 December 1862 in Doagh, county Antrim, son of Samuel Fulton, farmer, of Doagh; brother of Dr Joseph Fulton (*q.v.*); educated by the Rev R.J. Hunt; studied medicine at Queen's College, Belfast, from 1884; MB BCh BAO (RUI) 1889; house surgeon in Belfast Fever Hospital; medical officer to Belfast No 10 Dispensary District, of 3 Laurel Bank, Woodvale Road, and from c 1933, of Woodbank, Ballygomartin Road; married 12 September 1895 in Belmont Presbyterian Church, Belfast, Mary Campbell, daughter of Alexander Campbell, merchant, of Madrid Street, Belfast; died 10 July 1935 at Woodbank; probate Belfast 19 December 1935. [Belf GRO (d); Belf PRO, will cal; Bell (1979); Kirkpatrick Archive; *Med Dir*; QCB adm reg; UHF database (m)].

FULTON, JOSEPH (1864–1940), Belfast;
born 11 February 1864 at Ballyhartfield, Doagh, county Antrim, son of Samuel Fulton, farmer, of Doagh; brother of Dr James Fulton (*q.v.*); educated at RBAI; studied medicine at Queen's College, Belfast, from 1894; LRCP LRCS Edin 1899; LFPS Glas 1899; resident medical officer and anaesthetist c 1900–05 and visiting surgeon from 1905 to Belfast Infirmary and Dufferin Hospital; of 2 Windsor Crescent, Lisburn Road, Belfast; presented an organ and pulpit to Ulsterville Presbyterian Church in 1934; retired February 1940; married 8 July 1902 in Windsor Presbyterian Church, Belfast, Jane B. Sefton, daughter of John Sefton, engineer, of Belfast; died 19 March 1940 at 19 Windsor Avenue, Belfast; 'a very kindly man. He never lost his country ways or his county Antrim speech ... He was completely without guile and generations of house surgeons took delight in his innocent and often quite outrageous remarks' (Craig); administration (with will) Belfast 10 October 1940 and 19 March 1957. [Belf GRO (d); Belf PRO, will cal; Bell (1979); Craig (1985); Kirkpatrick Archive; *Med Dir*; QCB adm reg; UHF database (m)].

FULTON, THOMAS (1837/8–96), Saintfield, county Down;
born 1837/8, son of John Fulton, farmer, of Dromore, county Down; educated at RBAI; studied medicine at Queen's College, Belfast, from 1856, at Belfast General Hospital and Glasgow University; LM (QCB) 1858; LRCS Edin and LM 1861; MD (Glas) 1863; medical officer to Saintfield Dispensary District and constabulary from 1866; JP; married (1) 9 March 1866 in Railway Street Presbyterian Church, Lisburn, Matilda Hanna (who was born 1843/4 and died 11 November 1879), daughter of John Hanna, merchant, of Ballynahinch, county Down; (2) 23 February 1883 in

First Saintfield Presbyterian Church, Marion Hamilton Thompson (who was born 1855/6 and died 20 November 1910), daughter of William Thompson, merchant, of Saintfield; father by (1) of Agnes C. Fulton who married Dr Joseph Matson (*q.v.*) of Ballykelly; died 6 October 1896 at Saintfield; buried in Saintfield First Presbyterian Graveyard; probate Belfast 16 November 1896. [Addison (1898); Belf PRO, will cal, will; Dub GRO (d); gravestone inscription; *Med Dir*; QCB adm reg; UHF database (m)].

FULTON, WILLIAM WEST (d c 1880), Loughbrickland, county Down;
studied medicine at Glasgow University; MB (Glas) 1868; LRCS Edin and LM 1868; MD 1872; surgeon in mercantile marine service; emigrated to Philadelphia, USA, 1878; of 1504 Frankfort Avenue; died c 1880. [Addison (1913); *Med Dir*].

FUREY, JOSEPH WILLIAM (1864–1942), Sheffield;
born 3 January 1864 at Killyleagh, county Down, son of Matthew Furey, farmer, of Killyleagh; studied medicine at Queen's College, Belfast, from 1887; LRCP LRCS Edin 1896; LFPS Glas 1896; general practitioner, of 1 Pear Street, Sheffield, from c 1900 and later 230 Eccleshall Road; married 18 August 1910 in First Killyleagh Presbyterian Church, Edith S. Coulter, daughter of James Coulter, farmer, of Ardigon, Killyleagh; died 4 March 1942; probate Llandudno 15 June 1942. [Lond PPR, will cal; *Med Dir*; QCB adm reg; UHF database (m)].

FYFFE, ANDREW WHITE (1857/8–1900), Sheffield;
born 1857/8 at Drumlegagh, county Tyrone, son of John James Fyffe of Drumlegagh; brother of Dr Robert James Fyffe (*q.v.*); educated at Londonderry Academical Institution; studied medicine at Queen's College, Belfast, from 1878; LSA Lond 1892; general practitioner, of 216 St Patrick's Road, Sheffield; married — (who predeceased him); died 14 December 1900 at 216 St Philip's Road; probate Wakefield 3 January 1901. [Lond PPR, will cal, will; *Med Dir*; QCB adm reg].

FYFFE, ROBERT JAMES (1873/4–1912), Sheffield;
born 1873/4, son of John James Fyffe of Drumlegagh, county Tyrone; brother of Dr Andrew White Fyffe (*q.v.*); MRCSE LRCP Lond 1900; general practitioner, of 262 St Philips Road, Sheffield from c 1900; married Rebecca Jane —; died 25 February 1912 at St Philip's Road; administration Wakefield 19 April 1912. [Lond GRO (d); *Med Dir*].

FYFFE, WILLIAM JOHNSTONE (1826–1901), Army Medical Service and Clifton, Gloucestershire;
born 24 April 1826 at Baronscourt, county Tyrone, son of John Fyffe, gentleman; educated at Londonderry; studied arts and medicine at Trinity College, Dublin, from 1842; BA MB (TCD) 1847; LRCSI 1847; MD 1856; joined the Army Medical Service as assistant surgeon to the 3rd West India Regiment 1848; surgeon 1851 and attached to 30th Foot from 1853, 13th Foot from 1858 and 5th Dragoon Guards from 1859; served in Crimean War 1854–6; assistant professor of Medicine at the Army Medical School, Netley, Hampshire 1866–73; surgeon major 1868; retired on half pay with honorary rank of deputy surgeon general 1874; general practitioner, of

2 Rodney Place, Clifton; physician to Clifton College; president of the Bath and Bristol Branch of the BMA; married 21 July 1858 in Corsindae House, Aberdeenshire, Catherine Elizabeth Mary Reid (who was born 1834/5 and died 21 August 1859 at 5 Clarendon Villas, Notting Hill, London), only child of James Reid, lieutenant RN; (2) 8 June 1862 in Clifton Church, Caroline Margaret Kingston, only daughter of Thomas Kingston of Charlton House, Somerset; died 17 May 1901 at Clifton; probate Bristol 13 August 1901. [Burtchaell and Sadleir (1924); Kirkpatrick Archive; Lond PPR, will cal; *Londonderry Sentinel* 30 July 1858 (m), 26 August 1859 (d) and June 1862 (m); *Med Dir*; Peterkin and Johnston (1968)].

G

GABBEY, JOHN (1819/20–c 1860), Holywood, county Down;
born 1819/20, son of Samuel Gabbey, engineer, of Holywood; CM (Glas) 1840; LFPS Glas 1841; surgeon, of Holywood; married 14 June 1848 in Holywood Church of Ireland Church, Rachel Ballagh (who was born 1822/3), daughter of William Ballagh of Holywood; possibly died c 1860. [*Med Dir*; UHF database (m)].

GAFFIKIN, PRUDENCE ELIZABETH (1874–1966), Glasgow, Warrington, Lancashire, Enfield, Middlesex, Dublin, London and Crawley, Hampshire
born 18 August 1874, daughter of Thomas Gaffikin of 70 Fitzwilliam Street, Belfast; sister of Dr Philip Jacob Gaffikin of Winchester; educated at Miss Brown's School, 8 Cliftonville Avenue, Belfast; studied medicine at Queen's College, Belfast, from 1894, with medal for Midwifery, Gynaecology and Diseases of Children from the Ulster Hospital, Belfast, also in Vienna; LRCP LRCS Edin 1900; LFPS Glas 1900; house surgeon at the Samaritan Hospital for Women, Glasgow; assistant medical officer of health to the County Borough of Warrington, c 1908; school medical officer for Enfield c 1909; medical superintendent of Peamount Sanatorium, Dublin, of 7 Ely Place, Dublin c 1915 but also of 2 Queen's Elms, Belfast; medical officer to Islington Child Welfare Centre from c 1925, of 76 Queen's Gate; later of 5 Gordon Place, Gordon Square (c 1931), of The Cottage, Gainsborough Gardens, Hampshire c 1935 and finally of Bon Secours Nursing Home, Crawley, Hampshire; retired c 1947; died 15 January 1966 at Bon Secours Nursing Home; probate Winchester 24 October 1966. [Lond PPR, will cal, will; *Med Dir*; QCB adm reg].

GAGE, FRANCIS TURNLY (1865–97), Antrim, and Ballycastle, county Antrim;
born 8 March 1865 in Madras, third son of General Ezekiel Gage of Rathlin Island and the Madras Staff Corps, and Maria Dobbs of Waterford; educated at Armagh Royal School, 1877–82; studied arts and medicine at Trinity College, Dublin, from 1882; LM Rot Hosp Dub; BA (TCD) 1886; MB BCh BAO 1890; admiralty surgeon and agent and surgeon for Trinity House; general practitioner of Trim, county Meath c 1891–2; general practitioner, of Riverside House, Antrim c 1893–4 and of Ballycastle c 1894–7; married 15 September 1890 in Ramoan Church of Ireland Church, Ballycastle, Catherine Stewart Moore, daughter of John Stewart Moore, gentleman, of Moyarget, county Antrim; died 3 November 1897 at Southhill, Ballycastle; administration Belfast 30 March 1898. [Belf PRO, will cal; Burke *LGI* (1912); Dub GRO (d); Ferrar (1933); *Med Dir;* TCD adm reg; *TCD Cat*, vol II (1896); UHF database (m)].

GALBRAITH, HUGH TENER (1866–c 1905), Londonderry;
born 7 October 1866 at Waterloo Place, Londonderry, son of David Galbraith, druggist, of Waterloo Place, and Matilda Tener; educated at Londonderry Academical Institution; studied medicine at Queen's College, Belfast, from 1889; LRCP LRCS Edin 1894; LFPS Glas 1894; LAH Dub 1894; general practitioner of Strand

Buildings, Londonderry, 1894–1905; died c 1905. [Dub GRO (b); *Med Dir*; QCB adm reg].

GALBRAITH, JOHN (b 1824/5);
born 1824/5, son of James Galbraith, gentleman, of Drumareeny, county Londonderry; studied medicine at Glasgow University; MD (Glas) 1845; married 23 April 1855 in Faughanvale Church of Ireland Church, county Londonderry, Rebecca Gillespie (who was born 1829/30), daughter of Major — Gillespie, farmer, of Longfield. [Addison (1898); *BNL* 23 April 1855 (m); *Coleraine Chronicle* 28 April 1855 (m); Dub GRO (m)].

GALGEY, WILLIAM (1826/7–c 1884), Belfast and Southampton, Hampshire;
born 1826/7, son of William Galgey of Clifton Terrace, Cork; educated at Belfast Academy; studied medicine at Queen's College, Belfast, from 1850; LAH Dub 1851; LM Belfast 1851; MD (St Andrew's) 1860 (by examination); general practitioner of 117 York Street, Belfast, c 1855, of 21 Victoria Place, Belfast, c 1870 and of 77 Marland Place, Southampton c 1875; died c 1884. [*Med Dir*; QCB adm reg; Smart (2004)].

GALLAGHER, FRANCIS (d c 1904), Pettigo, county Donegal, and London;
studied medicine at the Catholic University of Ireland and the Mater Misericordiae Hospital, Dublin; MB BCh BAO (RUI) 1894; resident clinical assistant to Coombe Hospital, Dublin; general practitioner, of Pettigo c 1895–8 and of 413 East India Dock Road, London c 1898–1904; died c 1904. [*Med Dir*].

GALLAGHER, HUGH MOSS (d 1860), Letterkenny, county Donegal, and Peru;
eldest son of Joseph Gallagher of Letterkenny; MD [?]; LRCSI; general practitioner of Letterkenny; died 1860 at Lamhaquqoe, Peru. [*BNL* 5 July 1860 (d); Kirkpatrick Archive; *Londonderry Sentinel* 6 July 1860 (d); *Med Dir*].

GALLAGHER, JOSEPH WILLIAM (1861/2–1904), Killybegs, county Donegal;
born 1861/2; studied medicine at the Catholic University of Ireland; LRCSI 1884; LM KQCPI 1888; LKQCPI 1890; general practitioner, of Elmwood House, Killybegs; JP for county Donegal; medical officer and medical officer of health to Killybegs Dispensary District and medical officer to constabulary; married —; died 9 August 1904 at Tullid, Killybegs; probate Dublin 26 January 1905. [Belf PRO, will cal; Dub GRO (d); *Med Dir*].

GALLIGAN, JOHN (*fl c* 1824), Belturbet, county Cavan;
apothecary, of Diamond Street, Belturbet c 1824. [Pigot (1824)].

GAMBLE, BAPTIST (1846/7–95), Enniskillen, county Fermanagh;
born 1846/7; LKQCPI and LM 1872; LRCSI 1872; general practitioner of Darling Street, Enniskillen; unmarried; died 14 December 1895 at Darling Street; probate Dublin 25 February 1896. [Belf PRO, will cal; Dub GRO (d); *Med Dir*].

GAMBLE, CHRISTOPHER (*fl c* 1845), Enniskillen, county Fermanagh;
LAH Dub; general practitioner and registrar of births and deaths for Enniskillen c 1845; died c 1860. [Croly (1843–6); *Med Dir*].

GAMBLE, EDWARD (*fl c* 1824), Enniskillen, county Fermanagh;
apothecary, of Main Street, Enniskillen c 1824. [Pigot (1824)].

GAMBLE, HUGH (1818/9–46), Naval Medical Service;
born 1818/9, son of W. Gamble of 'Solitude', Comber, county Down; joined the Naval Medical Service as assistant surgeon; retired to 'Solitude'; died 12 February 1846 at Edena Cottage, Belfast. [*BNL* 17 February 1846 (d)].

GAMBLE, JOHN (c 1770–1831), Indian and Army Medical Services and Strabane, county Tyrone;
born c 1770 in Strabane, county Tyrone; studied medicine at Edinburgh University; MD (Edin) 1793 (thesis 'De rheumatismo'); joined the Army Medical Service as surgeon with the army in Holland in 1798 and returned home; joined the Indian Medical Service (Bombay establishment) as assistant surgeon on *Scalesby Castle* 1799, but never reached Bombay and was landed sick at the Cape of Good Hope; transferred to St Helena establishment 1801; 2nd assistant surgeon in St Helena 1802; on sick leave, almost blind 1804; retired 1807; studied medicine further at Edinburgh University; author of *Sketches of History, Politics and Manners Taken in Dublin and the North of Ireland in the Autumn of 1810* (1811), *Sarsfield, An Irish Tale* (1814), *Howard, A Novel* (1815) and *Northern Irish Tales* (1818), giving 'a vivid picture of the Ulster of his day' (A.A. Campbell); unmarried; died 1831; buried in Old Leckpatrick Graveyard. [Campbell (1902); Crawford (1930); Crone (1928); *DIB* (2009); Edin Univ; Gamble (2000); Newmann (1993); Peterkin and Johnston (1968)].

GAMBLE, JOSIAS CHRISTOPHER (1778–1848), Enniskillen, county Fermanagh, Monaghan, Dublin and St Helens, Lancashire;
born August 1778, fourth son of David Gamble, farmer, of Monea, county Fermanagh; studied medicine and arts at Glasgow University; MD (Glas) 1787; matriculated 1794; MA (Glas) 1797; minister of Enniskillen Presbyterian Church 1799–1804; resigned 1804 to become a manufacturing chemist in (1) county Monaghan, (2) Dublin and (3) St Helens, Lancashire; married 16 September 1820 Hannah Gower who died 16 December 1852; father of Sir David Gamble, CB, JP; died 27 January 1848 at Green End, Sutton, Lancashire. [Addison (1898) and (1913); *Burke's Peerage and Baronetage* (1978); Dundas (1913); Lond GRO (d); McConnell (1951)].

GAMBLE, LEONARD DOBBIN (1861/2–1924) Abergavenny, Monmouthshire, and Orange Free State, South Africa;
born 1861/2 at Killylea, county Armagh, son of John Gamble of Lissagally, county Armagh, and Sarah Dobbin; studied medicine at Edinburgh University; MB MCh (hons) (Edin) 1886; clinical assistant in ophthalmology to Edinburgh Royal

Infirmary; Grierson Bursar and assistant demonstrator in anatomy and physiology at Edinburgh University; general practitioner, of Abergavenny c 1890–1914; honorary physician and surgeon to Abergavenny Cottage Hospital, of Western Villa and Leven House, Abergavenny; emigrated to South Africa c 1914; general practitioner, of Preston, Dover, Orange Free State c 1914–20 and of Vogeldraal, Frankfurt, from c 1920; married 6 September 1893 his cousin Henrietta Adelaide Deacon (who was born 20 June 1866 and died 24 June 1937), daughter of John Gillespie Deacon and Elizabeth Dobbin, and sister of Dr John Gillespie Deacon (*q.v.*); died 23 August 1924 at Abergavenny. [*Burke's Irish Family Records* (1976); Kirkpatrick (1889); *Med Dir*; Power, Barbara, pers com].

GAMBLE, SAMUEL BAPTIST (1842–93) Army Medical Service, ship's surgeon and Glasgow;
    born 8 August 1842 in county Fermanagh, son of Samuel Gamble, civil engineer; educated at Portora Royal School, Enniskillen; studied arts and medicine at Trinity College, Dublin, from 1860 and the Royal College of Surgeons in Ireland; BA MB MCh (TCD) 1866; joined the Army Medical Department as assistant surgeon 1866; retired on half pay 1876 and resigned 1877; surgeon with the Allan Line; general practitioner, of 103 Kent Road and 330 Renfrew Street, Glasgow, c 1885; died 9 March 1893; administration Glasgow 21 June 1893 and Belfast 4 July 1893. [Belf PRO, will cal; Burtchaell and Sadleir (1935); *Med Dir*; Peterkin and Johnston (1968); *Portora Royal School Register* (1940)].

GAMBLE, WILLIAM (1688/9–1778), Belfast;
    born 1688/9; possibly the William Gamble MD (Glas) 1731; physician of Belfast; died 21 July 1778 at 'Solitude', Edensleat, near Comber, county Down; buried in Comber Church of Ireland Graveyard; portrait (anon) in Ulster Museum. [Addison (1898); *BNL* 21 July 1778 (d); Black (2000); Clarke, *County Down*, vol 5 (1984); O'Brien, Crookshank and Wolstenholme (1984)].

GARDE, HENRY CROKER (1855–c 1933), Maryborough, Queensland, Australia;
    born 1855 at Cloyne, county Cork, son of the Rev Thomas William Garde, rector of Coole, of Sun Lodge, Cloyne, and his second wife Sophia Colles; educated at Middleton College; studied medicine at Queen's College, Cork, and from 1872, at Queen's College, Belfast; LAH Dub 1877; LRCP LRCS Edin 1878; FRCS Edin 1886; LM KQCPI 1886; emigrated to Maryborough, Queensland c 1886; member of the Legislative Assembly of Queensland; surgeon to Maryborough Hospital, of 138 Macquarie Street, Hobart c 1920 but retired to Maryborough; married Ada Hall, daughter of Captain Morgan Hall of the 48th Regiment; died c 1933. [Cole (1903); Kirkpatrick Archive; *Med Dir*; QCB adm reg].

GARDE, THOMAS WILLIAM (d 1907), ship's surgeon, Belfast and Toowomba, Queensland, Australia;
    son of the Rev Thomas William Garde, rector of Coole, of Sun Lodge, Cloyne, county Cork, and his first wife Eliza Sullivan; studied medicine at the Carmichael and Ledwich Schools, Dublin; LAH Dub 1870; LRCP LRCS Edin 1871; surgeon on the Cape and Natal Steam Navigation Company's SS *Mark Anthony*; resident medical

officer and apothecary to the Barrack Street Dispensary, Belfast; general practitioner, of 30 College Square North and 4 Ardmolin Place, Falls Road, Belfast; emigrated to Toowomba, Queensland c 1880; married 27 October 1875 in St Thomas's Church of Ireland Church, Belfast, Jane Hennrietta Lee, daughter of Henry Lee, gentleman, of Belfast; died 20 September 1907. [Cole (1903); *Med Dir*; UHF database (m)].

GARDINER, ARTHUR (STOKER) (1817/8–86), Dublin, Belfast, Horley, Surrey, and Bayswater, London;
> born 1817/8 at Fermoy, county Cork; brother of Dr William Stoker Gardiner of Fermoy, LAH Dub 1826, MRCSE 1830; studied medicine at Belfast Fever Hospital, Mercer's Hospital, Dublin and St Bartholomew's Hospital, London; MRCSE and LM 1839; LAH Dub 1840; MD (St Andrews) 1855 (by examination); general practitioner, of Kingstown, county Dublin c 1860, of 12 College Square East, Belfast c 1870 and of Lincoln Lodge, Horley, c 1875; later moved to 13 Colville Road, Bayswater; married (1) 1842 Margaret Jephson of Grafton Street, Dublin (who was born 1821/2 and died 31 March 1871 at 12 College Square East, Belfast, of tuberculosis), sister of Dr William Holmes Jephson, AMS; (2) c 1872 Lavinia Diana — (who was born 1837/8 and died 2 November 1874 of tuberculosis); died 21 April 1886 at St Thomas's Home, Lambeth; probate London 21 June 1886 and Dublin 24 July 1886. [Belf PRO, will cal; Dub GRO (m) and (d both wives); Gardiner, Sandra, pers com; Lond GRO (d); Lond PPR, will cal; *Med Dir;* Smart (2004)].

GARDINER, CHARLES EDWARD ROCHE (1865–1953), Congo and Dungloe, county Donegal;
> born 14 May 1865 at New Quay, Drogheda, county Louth, son of Captain Robert Gardiner, officer in RIC, of Greyfort, Sligo, and Mary Knight Roche; studied medicine at the Royal College of Surgeons in Ireland; LRCPI and LM LRCSI and LM 1888; district surgeon in the Congo Free State, and was awarded the Congo Star decoration; one of 14 who went to the Congo but only five survived; medical officer to Dungloe Dispensary District and to the constabulary; attended Dr William Smyth (*q.v.*) of Burtonport, who died in one of the many outbreaks of typhus there; author of various medical papers; retired c 1938 to 16 Crosthwaite Park East, Dun Laoghaire; moved c 1940 to 2 Kill Avenue, Dun Laoghaire; married Catherine O'Connor, daughter of Thomas O'Connor of 6 Jones Road, Dublin; died 9 February 1953 at 2 Mount Mapas Villas, Kill Avenue. [Dub GRO (b) and (d); How (1902); *Irish Times* 14 October 1937 and 20 May 1945; Kirkpatrick Archive; *Med Dir*].

GARDINER, WILLIAM (d c 1808), Kells, county Antrim;
> MD [?], general practitioner, of Kells; died c 1808; probate Prerogative Court 1808. [Vicars (1897)].

GARLAND, CHARLES (1838/9–80), Carrickmacross, county Monaghan;
> born 1838/9; studied medicine at the Catholic University of Ireland and Jervis Street, Meath, St Marks and Rotunda Hospitals, Dublin (gold medal and prize); LRCSI 1863; LKQCPI 1864; LM Rot Hosp Dub; medical officer to St Clare's Convent and Convent of Mercy, Newry, of 79 Hill Street, Newry; medical officer to Donaghmoyne Dispensary District, of Evelyn Street, Carrickmacross from c 1875; author of various

medical publications; unmarried; died 7 December 1880 at Carrickmacross; probate Armagh 4 March 1881. [Belf PRO, will cal; Dub GRO (d); *Med Dir*].

GARNER, JOHN (d 1907), Downpatrick, county Down, Tooting, London, Clonmel, county Tipperary, and Cairo, Egypt;
>studied medicine at St Thomas's Hospital, London; LRCP LRCS Edin 1894; LFPS Glas 1894; assistant surgeon to Down County Infirmary, Downpatrick 1894–5; assistant medical officer to the North-East Fever Hospital, London c 1895–6; general practitioner, of Clonmel c 1896–1905; inspector of public health for Upper Egypt, Cairo c 1905–07; died 26 October 1907. [*Med Dir*; Parkinson (1967)].

GARRAWAY, ROBERT (1751/2–1830), Dominica, West Indies;
>born 1751/2 in Londonderry; MD [?]; medical officer in Dominica, West Indies, from c 1773; representative in the Legislative Assembly and subsequently promoted to the Council Chamber of the island; died 2 December 1830 at Rousseau, Dominica. [*BNL* 22 March 1831 (d); *Londonderry Sentinel* 19 March 1831 (d)].

GASS, ANDREW BARRON (1863–1931) ship's surgeon and Carrington, Nottingham;
>born 8 June 1863 at Clones, county Monaghan, son of the Rev John Samuel Gass, minister of Clones Presbyterian Church, and — Barron of Meadowlands, Belfast; educated at Coleraine Academical Institution; studied arts at Queen's College, Galway, and from 1881, medicine at Queen's College, Belfast; BA (RUI) 1883; LRCP LRCS Edin 1889; LFPS Glas 1889; surgeon in mercantile marine; general practitioner, of 64 Ebury Road, Carrrington, and later of 1 Claremont Gardens, Sherwood Rise, Nottingham; FRGS; died 28 September 1931 at Southfields Nursing Home, Arthur Street, Nottingham; probate Nottingham 15 December 1931. [Barkley (1986); Lond PPR, will cal; *Med Dir*; QCB adm reg].

GAULT, HUGH (*fl c* 1805–24), Ballybay, county Monaghan;
>LAH Dub 1805; apothecary, of Ballybay c 1805–24. [Apothecaries (1829); Nesbitt (1999); Pigot (1824)].

GAULT, HUGH (1845–1920), Belfast;
>born 6 November 1845 at Glynn, county Antrim, son of William Gault of Glynn and Elizabeth —; brother of Isabella Gault who married Robert Calwell and was mother of Dr William Calwell, junior (*q.v.*), Dr Robert Bryson Calwell, MB (RUI) 1905, Dr Gault Calwell, MB (RUI) 1907, Dr Sarah Elizabeth Calwell, MB (QUB) 1912, and Dr David Calwell, MB (QUB) 1913; educated at Belfast Academy; studied medicine and arts at Queen's College, Belfast, from 1863; LRCP Edin 1874; general practitioner, of 150 (also 100 and 155 at other times) York Street; JP; married (1) Mary Jane — (who died June 1890); (2) Margaret — (who died 20 January 1945); died 22 April 1920 at Whitehead; buried with his family in Glynn graveyard; probate Belfast 28 May 1920. [Belf PRO, will cal; Dub GRO (d); *Med Dir*; QCB adm reg; Rutherford and Clarke, *County Antrim*, vol 2 (1981)].

GAUSSEN, DAVID PETER, (1861–1938), Dunmurry, county Antrim;
born 23 January 1861 at Ballyronan, county Londonderry, son of William M. Gaussen (of Huguenot descent), banker, of Lake Lodge, Magherafelt; educated at Hillbrook School; studied medicine at Queen's College, Belfast, from 1878 and at St Thomas's Hospital, London; LM KQCPI 1883; MD (RUI) (hons) 1883; MRCSE 1884; senior resident surgeon at the Belfast Union Infirmary; of 1 Fitzroy Crescent, University Street, Belfast; medical officer and medical officer of health to Dunmurry Dispensary District; medical officer to constabulary, public vaccinator and certifying factory surgeon; honorary physician to the Thompson Memorial Home, Lisburn, of The Hill, Dunmurry; served on the hospital ship *Britannic* during World War I; author of publications on obstetrics; president of the Ulster Medical Society 1906–07 and of the Ulster Branch of the BMA 1925–6; retired in 1927 to Mullantean, Stewartstown, county Tyrone; married Ethelind —; died 11 May 1938 at Mullantean; probate Belfast 10 August 1938. [Allison (1939); Belf PRO, will cal; *BMJ* obituary (1938); Hunter (1935); Kirkpatrick Archive; *Med Dir*; QCB adm reg; Strain (1967)].

GAUSSEN, JOHN LAIRD (1808/9–91), Crumlin, county Antrim, and Belfast;
born 1808/9; cousin of Dr David Peter Gaussen (*q.v.*); studied medicine at Dublin, Edinburgh and Paris; LM Dublin Lying-in Hospital (Rotunda) 1829; MRCSE 1830; MD (Edin) 1831 (thesis 'De abdominis sectione'); FRCSE 1859; medical officer to the Crumlin Dispensary c 1846; surgeon to the Antrim Militia 1852; general practitioner, of 26 Wellington Place, Belfast; married 15 February 1840 in Lisburn Cathedral, Anne Bradshaw, youngest daughter of Hercules Bradshaw of Culcavey Cottage, Hillsborough, county Down; died 22 February 1891 at 26 Wellington Place; administration Belfast 11 March 1891. [*BNL* 18 February 1840 (m); Belf PRO, will cal; Croly (1843–6); Dub GRO (d); Edin Univ; *Med Dir*; Plarr (1930)].

GAWN, SAMUEL FERGUSON (1862–1927), Antrim;
born 19 October 1862 at Carnarney, Kells, county Antrim, son of James Gawn, farmer, and Anna Louden McMeckin; studied medicine at Queen's College, Belfast, from 1885; LRCP LRCS Edin 1892; LFPS Glas 1892; general practitioner, of 211 Shankill Road, Belfast c 1895, and of the High Street, Antrim and medical officer to Antrim District Hospital, the constabulary and the post office c 1900–25; retired c 1925 to Cargagh, Dungannon, county Tyrone; married (1) —; (2) 16 October 1896 in Templepatrick Presbyterian Church, Agnes Finney (who was born 1867/8 and died 10 September 1965), youngest daughter of Matthew Finney, gardener, of Ballycraigy; died 22 January 1927 at Belvue, Larne Harbour; buried in Antrim New Cemetery. [Belf GRO (d); gravestone inscription; Kirkpatrick Archive; *Med Dir*; QCB adm reg; UHF database (m); Young and Pike (1909)].

GAYLEY, SAMUEL SMYTH (1846–c 1901), Borrisokane, county Tipperary, Banagher, King's County, and Sheffield;
born 6 July 1846 at Magheracreggan, Castlederg, county Tyrone, son of Andrew Gayley of Magheracreggan and Belle Park, Borrisokane; educated at Castlederg School; studied arts and medicine at the Ledwich School, Dublin and from 1864, at

Queen's College, Belfast; LRCP Edin 1884; general practitioner, of Belle Park, Borrisokane until c 1890, of 513 Attercliffe Road, Sheffield 1890–92 and of Garry Castle, Banagher, King's County c 1893–7; of 11 Mowbray Street and 149 Newhall Road, Sheffield c 1897–1901; died c 1901. [*Med Dir*; QCB adm reg].

GELSTON, JAMES JOHN PATTERSON (c 1823–63), Ballymacarrett and Comber, county Down, and Liverpool, Lancashire;
born c 1823, son of John Gelston, farmer, of Comber; LFPS Glas 1848; medical officer for cholera patients in Ballymacarrett 1848–9 and general practitioner in Comber c 1854; general practitioner in Liverpool from c 1856; of 6 Chester Street, Liverpool c 1858; married 28 June 1853 in Second Comber Presbyterian Church, Alicia Ann Jane Young (who was born 17 August 1821 and died 24 September 1866), daughter of Dr George Young and sister of Dr George Henry Young (*q.v.*); died 14 April 1863 at 6 Chester Street, of typhoid fever; probate Liverpool 3 August 1863. [*BNL* 29 June 1853 (m); Gelston, A, pers com; Lond PPR, will cal; *Med Dir*; UHF database (m)].

GELSTON, THOMAS (d 1801), Belfast;
surgeon of Belfast, with a shop selling drugs, painters' colours and materials, 'also provided with an electric apparatus in the most perfect order' in 1796; founding member of the Linen Hall Library in 1788; married Agnes Gunning (who died in 1810); died 27 December 1801; buried in Clifton Street Burying Ground. [Anderson (1888); *BNL* 1 January 1802 (d); Merrick and Clarke, *Belfast*, vol 4 (1991); Simms (1933)].

GEORGE, JOHN (1833–76), Ross, Herefordshire;
born 26 April 1833, son of Robert George of Carrickfergus and Martha —; educated by Mr Larmour of Carrickfergus; studied medicine at Queen's College, Belfast, from 1854; LRCS Edin 1866; LRCP and LM Edin 1867; medical officer to 3rd District of Ross Union and Ross Dispensary; public vaccinator and medical officer of health in Ross; unmarried; died 14 September 1876 of phthisis, in Carrickfergus; buried in Templecorran graveyard, county Antrim; administration Belfast 10 November 1876. [Belf PRO, will cal; Dub GRO (d); *Med Dir*; QCB adm reg; Rutherford and Clarke, *County Antrim*, vol 2 (1981)].

GERNON, NICHOLAS (1771/2–1848), Naval and Army Medical Services;
born 1771/2; joined the Naval Medical Service as assistant surgeon; transferred to the Army Medical Service, first as hospital mate and in 1803, as assistant surgeon to 30th Foot; superseded because he was absent without leave 1804; later of 12th Dragoon Guards; died 2 October 1848 at Wilville, Carlingford, county Down. [*BNL* 10 October 1848 (d); Peterkin and Johnston (1968)].

GERVAIS, F.K. (*fl c* 1766), Armagh;
certified by the Board of Surgeons (surgeon general and surgeons from Steevens' and Mercer's Hospitals) 1766; surgeon, of Armagh County Infirmary, but in fact Joseph Shewbridge was appointed the first county surgeon of Armagh in 1767 in response to an advertisement. [Fleetwood (1983); Paterson (1762)].

GETTY, JOHN (d 1787), Belfast;
surgeon and apothecary, probably of Belfast; died 14 August 1787. [*BNL* 17 August 1787 (d)].

GETTY, THOMAS BATESON (1800/1–60), Donaghadee, county Down;
born 1800/1, son of William Getty of Donaghadee and Susanna —; LRCS Edin 1828; medical officer to Donaghadee Dispensary c 1846; unmarried; died 6 February 1860 at Donaghadee; buried in Donaghadee Graveyard; administration Belfast 19 December 1860. [Belf PRO, will cal; Clarke, *County Down*, vol 16 (1976); Croly (1843–6); *Med Dir*].

GIBBON, JOHN GEORGE (1868–1940), Mullingar, county Westmeath;
born 23 January 1868, second son of John George Gibbon, barrister; educated at Armagh Royal School 1882–5; studied arts and medicine at Trinity College, Dublin, from 1885; BA (TCD) 1889; LM Rot Hosp Dub 1890; MB MCh BAO 1891; MD 1893; of Upwell, Wisbech, Cambridge, c 1895; medical officer at Grey's Hospital, Pietermaritzburg; civil surgeon at Mulligar to troops; general practitioner, of Lake View, Mullingar from c 1905; honorary surgeon to Westmeath County Infirmary from c 1908; author of various medical papers; retired c 1924 to Gorey, county Wexford; moved c 1927 to 21 Kenilworth Square, Rathgar, and c 1936 to 42 Rathdown Park, Terenure, Dublin; married —; died 24 January 1940 at 42 Rathdown Park; buried at Ballycarney, Ferns; probate Dublin 27 May 1940. [Dub GRO (d); Dub Nat Arch, will cal; Ferrar (1933); Kirkpatrick Archive; *Med Dir*; TCD adm reg; *TCD Cat*, vol II (1896)].

GIBBONS, DANIEL (*fl c* 1846), Ramelton, county Donegal;
studied medicine at Glasgow University; MD (Glas) 1838; general practitioner in Ramelton c 1843–6. [Addison (1898); Croly (1843–6)].

GIBSON, GEORGE (1861–1952), Donaghadee, county Down;
born 14 December 1861 at Raneese, Seskinore, county Tyrone, son of Robert Gibson, farmer, of Raneese; educated at Moneymore Intermediate School; studied medicine at Queen's College, Belfast, from 1883, and Edinburgh; LRCP LRCS Edin 1895; LFPS Glas 1895; medical officer of Donaghadee Dispensary District, of Glen Rual, 29 Shore Road Donaghadee; married —; died 15 August 1952 at Glen Rual; probate Belfast 4 June 1953. [Belf GRO (d); Belf PRO, will cal; *Med Dir*; QCB adm reg].

GIBSON, JAMES (*fl c* 1824), Castleblayney, county Monaghan;
surgeon, of Muckno Street, Castleblayney c 1824. [Pigot (1824)].

GIBSON, JAMES (*fl c* 1846–82), Mountnorris and Richhill, county Armagh, and Melbourne, Australia;
studied medicine at Glasgow University; LM 1841; MD (Glas) 1842; CM 1857; general practitioner in Mountnorris and Richhill c 1845; medical officer to Richhill Dispensary District; moved to Belfast c 1868 and emigrated to Melbourne, Australia c 1872; died 1882. [Addison (1898); Croly (1843–6); *Med Dir*].

GIBSON, JAMES (1826/7–58), Downpatrick, county Down, and New Orleans, USA;
born 1826/7, son of William Gibson of Ballygally, Downpatrick, county Down, and Elizabeth —; studied medicine at Edinburgh University; MD (Edin) 1826 (thesis 'De enteritide'); assistant surgeon in North Down Militia; emigrated to USA; died 24 August 1858 at New Orleans of yellow fever 'after a few days' illness'; commemorated in Inch graveyard, county Down. [*BNL* 16 October 1858 (d); Clarke, *County Down*, vol 7 (1993); Edin Univ].

GIBSON, JAMES HILL (1856–1912), Maida Vale, London;
born 7 May 1856 at Omagh, county Tyrone, son of George Gibson, house and land agent, of 13 Canning Street, Belfast; educated at Belfast Seminary and RBAI; studied medicine at Queen's College, Belfast, 1874–8; Malcolm Exhibition, Belfast Royal Hospital, 1877; Coulter Exhibition 1878; MD (Gold Medal), MCh (QUI) 1878; general practitioner, of 56 Maida Vale, London, and medical officer for the St John's Wood District; assistant surgeon to the Western Ophthalmic Hospital, surgeon to the Volunteer Artillery and active in the foundation of the Mary Wardell Convalescent Home; retired c 1905 to Parkstone, Dorset; married Alice —; died 14 May 1912 at Parkstone; buried in Longfleet Churchyard, Poole, Dorset; probate London 19 September 1912. [*BMJ* obituary (1912); Lond PPR, will cal; *Med Dir*; QCB adm reg].

GIBSON, JOHN KELLS (1866–1901), Randalstown, county Antrim;
born 10 November 1866 at Moneyhaw, Moneymore, county Londonderry, son of William Gibson, farmer, of Moneyhaw; educated at Moneymore Intermediate School; studied medicine at Queen's College, Belfast, from 1888; LRCP LRCS Edin 1895; LFPS Glas 1895; house surgeon at Belfast Union Infirmary; general practitioner of Randalstown; married Lizzie M. —; died 29 May 1901 at the Mount, Mountpottinger; administration Belfast 25 April 1902. [Belf PRO, will cal; Dub GRO (d); *Med Dir*; QCB adm reg].

GIBSON, JOHN McCOY (1875–1953), Glenavy, county Antrim, RAMC and Streatham, London;
born 26 September 1875 at Crossvale, Glenavy, son of James Gibson of Crossvale; educated at University Classes, Donegall Pass, Belfast; studied medicine at Queen's College, Belfast, from 1894; MB BCh BAO (RUI) 1900; DOMS Eng 1921; of Crossvale, Glenavy c 1904; clinical assistant to the Royal Eye Hospital for eight years; temporary lieutenant RAMC during World War I; later ophthalmic clinical assistant to King's College Hospital; honorary ophthalmic surgeon to Battersea General Hospital, of 124 and 9 Mitcham Lane, Streatham; married Mildred Elizabeth —; died 27 January 1953 at St James' Hospital, Balham; administration London 17 March 1953. [Lond GRO (d); Lond PPR, will cal; *Med Dir*; QCB adm reg].

GIBSON, SAMUEL (1825/6–60), Army Medical Service;
born 1825/6 in Armagh, son of Alexander Gibson, money lender; educated at Armagh Royal School; studied arts and medicine at Trinity College, Dublin, 1844–

51; BA (TCD) 1849; MB 1851; joined the Army Medical Service as staff assistant surgeon 1852; served with 63rd Foot as staff surgeon from 1854; transferred to 12th Dragoons 1858; served with the Saugor and Nerbudda Field Force in the Indian Mutiny and was present at the storming of the heights of Punwarree; unmarried; died 13 August 1860 at his father's home in Armagh; administration Armagh 25 September 1860. [*BNL* 20 August 1860 (d); Belf PRO, will cal; Burtchaell and Sadlier (1924); Ferrar (1933); *Med Reg*; Peterkin and Johnston (1968)].

GIBSON, WILLIAM (1860–1945), Belfast;
born 13 May 1860 at Fintona, county Tyrone, son of Robert Gibson, farmer, of Fintona; educated at Moneymore Intermediate School; studied medicine at Queen's College, Belfast, from 1878; MD and LM (RUI) 1882; MCh 1883; MAO 1885; medical officer to the Metropolitan District, London; general practitioner, of Mountpottinger House, 127 Albertbridge Road, Belfast; sanitary surveyor and inspector of emigrant ships, Belfast; of 114 Belmont Road from c 1932; JP; member of the Ulster Unionist Council; married 19 October 1885 at Alton Place, Portadown, Olivia Anne Stewart, daughter of Dr William Stewart (*q.v.*) of Alton Place; died 3 January 1945 at 114 Belmont Road; probate Belfast 10 December 1945. [Belf GRO (d); Belf PRO, will cal; Dub GRO (m); Young and Pike (1909)].

GIDDENS, J. EDWARD (d 1817), Army Medical Service;
trained as surgeon and apothecary with Dr Ralph Smith Obie in Dublin c 1808–11; joined the Army Medical Service as assistant surgeon 1811; on half pay 1816–17; died 20 September 1817 at Glaslough, county Monaghan, of typhus fever, contracted while visiting a patient. [*BNL* 23 September 1817 (d); Peterkin and Johnston (1968)].

GIFFEN, JAMES THOMAS MOORE (1864–1948), Jordanstown, county Antrim, and Chester;
born 5 February 1864, son of James Giffen, farmer, of Ballytweedy House, county Antrim; brother of Dr Samuel Moore Giffen (*q.v.*); educated at Antrim Intermediate School; studied medicine at Glasgow University 1882–3 and at Queen's College, Belfast, from 1883; LRCP LRCS Edin 1887; LFPS Glas 1887; FRCS Edin 1892; of Thornville, Jordanstown, county Antrim c 1895; general practitioner of 1 Richmond Place, Boughton, Cheshire; medical officer to Tarvin Union Workhouse; retired c 1925 to 'Woodseat', Hoole Road, Chester; died 11 March 1948 at 'Woodseat'; probate Chester 11 June 1948. [Lond GRO (d); Lond PPR, will cal; *Med Dir*; QCB adm reg].

GIFFEN, SAMUEL MOORE (1861–1925), Burnley, Lancashire;
born 15 February 1861 at Ballytweedy, county Antrim, son of James Moore, farmer, of Ballytweedy House; brother of James Thomas Moore Giffen (*q.v.*) educated at Belfast Royal Academy; studied medicine at Queen's College, Belfast, from 1879; LRCP LRCS Edin 1891; LFPS Glas 1891; general practitioner, of 64 and later 74 Bank Parade, Burnley; married Clara —; died 19 June 1925 at 74 Bank Parade; probate London 24 July 1925. [Lond PPR, will cal, will; *Med Dir*; QCB adm reg].

GILBERT, JONATHAN (1824/5–67), Lurgan, county Armagh;
born 1824/5, son of Jonathan Gilbert, farmer; studied medicine at Glasgow University; MD (Glas) 1843; general practitioner of Church Place, Lurgan; married 22 July 1859 in Soldierstown Church of Ireland Church, Aghalee, county Antrim, Elizabeth Kenning, fifth daughter of William Kenning, farmer, of Ryefield, Moira, county Down; died 26 February 1867 at Church Place, of typhus fever. [Addison (1898); *BNL* 25 July 1859 (m); Dub GRO (m) and (d); *Med Dir*].

GILBERT, WILLIAM FREDERICK (d c 1899), Ederny, county Fermanagh;
studied medicine at the Carmichael School, Dublin; LM Rot Hosp Dub 1878; LRCSI 1880; LKQCPI and LM 1880; general practitioner, of Clonee, Ederny, county Fermanagh, from c 1881; medical officer to Ederny Dispensary District from c 1890; died c 1899. [*Med Dir*].

GILCRIEST, THOMAS (1865/6–1950), Bootle, Lancashire, Omagh, county Tyrone, and Sligo;
born 1865/6; studied medicine at the Carmichael School, Dublin; LM Rot Hosp Dub; LKQCPI and LM 1889; LRCSI and LM 1889; assistant and later senior house surgeon to Bootle Borough Hospital 1890–04; general practitioner, of 7 Campsie Road, Omagh c 1894–7; assistant medical officer to Sligo District Asylum c 1897–1935; temporary captain RAMC 1914–18; retired c 1935 to The Cottage, Dromahair, county Leitrim; married —; died 15 July 1950; probate Castlebar 11 January 1951. [Dub GRO (d); Dub Nat Arch, will cal; *Med Dir*].

GILFILLAN (GILFELLAN), ALEXANDER (1793–1838), Naval Medical Service, and Gorticross and Glendermott, county Londonderry;
born 1793, son of Joseph Gilfillan of Gorticross, farmer (who died on the same day as Alexander); joined the Naval Medical Service as assistant surgeon 1813; sailed on HMS *Trent* with Sir John Franklin 1818 and developed snow blindness; surgeon 1822; posted to Jamaica 1827–30 where he became an alcoholic; resigned 1830; surgeon of Gorticross and Glendermott 1830–38; married 19 May 1831 in Second Glendermott Presbyterian Church, Elizabeth McCutcheon, daughter of Joseph McCutcheon of Lisneal, county Londonderry; died 26 March 1838 at Gorticross; buried in Enagh Lough Graveyard. [*BNL* 31 May 1831 (m) and 6 April 1838 (d); gravestone inscription; Lewis (1837); *Londonderry Sentinel* 28 May 1831 (m) and 31 March 1838 (d); McCormack (2010); *NMS* (1826)].

GILFILLAND, GEORGE (*fl c* 1837), Faughanvale, county Londonderry;
general practitioner, of Killylane, Faughanvale c 1837. [Lewis (1837)].

GILL, HUGH TODD (1861–1930), Oldham, Lancashire;
born 26 November 1861 at Newtownards, county Down, son of John Gill, boot warehouseman, of Banbridge, county Down; educated at Banbridge Academy; studied medicine at Queen's College, Belfast, from 1884; MB BCh BAO (RUI) 1889; general practitioner of 'Rosscrea' 202 Manchester Road, Oldham c 1890–1925; retired c 1925 to 'Rathvarna', Holywood Avenue, Old Colwyn, Wales; married

7 October 1891 in Fortwilliam Presbyterian Church, Belfast, Elizabeth Cambridge Carswell, daughter of Robert Carswell, merchant, of Belfast; died 10 September 1930; probate Wakefield 14 November 1930. [Lond PPR, will cal; *Med Dir*; QCB adm reg; UHF database (m)].

GILL, JOSEPH SCOTT (1871–1915), Castlecaulfield, county Tyrone;
born 6 July 1871 at Cullenramer House, Dungannon, county Tyrone, son of the Rev Robert Gill, minister of Lower Clonaneese Presbyterian Church; educated at Dungannon Royal School and Methodist College, Belfast 1888–9; studied medicine at Queen's College, Belfast, from 1891, and Edinburgh; LRCP LRCS Edin 1897; LFPS Glas 1897; medical officer and medical officer of health to Clonavaddy Dispensary District and certifying factory surgeon; of Ennish House, Castlecaulfield and of Glen Eber, Strandtown, Belfast; surgeon with the Allan Shipping Line c 1915; died 3 November 1915 on board the SS *Scandinavian*; probate Dublin 6 January 1916 [Barkley (1986); Belf PRO, will cal; Dub GRO (d); Fry (1984); *Med Dir*; QCB adm reg].

GILLESPEY (GILLESPIE), ADAM (1759/60–1835), Lifford, county Donegal;
born 1759/60; MD [?]; surgeon to the Donegal County Infirmary c 1792–1835; married —; died 12 December 1835 at Lifford, 'after a lingering illness'; buried in Donaghmore Graveyard. [*BNL* 22 December 1835 (d); Hitchings, Paul, pers com; *Londonderry Sentinel* 21 February 1821 (m, dau) and 19 December 1835 (d); Pigot (1824); *Strabane Morning Post* 22 December 1835 (d)].

GILLESPIE, HENRY, senior (b c 1736), Limavady, county Londonderry;
born c 1736, second son of William Gillespie of Drummaneny, county Londonderry, and Mary Quin of Campsey, county Londonderry; brother of Dr Joshua Gillespie, IMS (*q.v.*); apprenticed to John Stevenson, surgeon and apothecary, of Londonderry (*q.v.*) 1754–8; surgeon, of Limavady; lessee of the fishing rights on the river Roe (Limavady); married c 1770 Mary Moody of Fallowlee (who was born 1750/1 and died 2 January 1827; buried in Drumachose Church of Ireland Graveyard, Limavady); father of Dr William Gillespie, RN, (*q.v.*), Dr Henry Gillespie, junior, RN, (*q.v.*), Dr Thomas Edie Gillespie (*q.v.*) and of Margaret Edie Gillespie who married William Fleming of Limavady and was mother of Dr Henry Gillespie Fleming (*q.v.*); died before 1810. [*BNL* 19 January 1810 (m, dau); Belf PRO, D1936/2 ('Record of the Family of Gillespie' – typescript); Elliott, Simon, pers com; Hitchings, Paul, pers com].

GILLESPIE, HENRY, junior (1777–1801), Naval Medical Service;
born 1777, third son of Dr Henry Gillespie, senior, of Limavady, county Londonderry (*q.v.*); brother of Dr William Gillespie RN (*q.v.*) and uncle of Dr Henry Gillespie Fleming (*q.v.*); joined the Naval Medical Service as assistant surgeon; staff surgeon; served on the Egyptian Expedition of 1801; became ill and died 30 March 1801 in Limavady. [*BNL* 7 April 1801 (d); Belf PRO, D1936/2 ('Record of the Family of Gillespie' – typescript)]

GILLESPIE, JAMES (1838/9–1924), Clones, county Monaghan;
born 1838/9; studied medicine at the Royal College of Surgeons in Ireland; LRCSI 1861; Lic Med 1863; general practitioner, of the Diamond, Clones c 1863–1922; retired to 5 Belgravia Avenue, Belfast c 1922; author of various medical papers; unmarried; died 7 January 1924; buried in Belfast City Cemetery. [Belf City Cem, bur reg; *Med Dir*].

GILLESPIE, JOHN RICHARD (1871–1960), Manchuria, Cowbridge, Glamorgan, Southampton, Belfast;
born 29 December 1871 at Windsor Hill, Newry, son of William Gillespie, bank manager, of Windsor Hill, and Harriett Hewitt; educated at Newry Intermediate School; studied arts and medicine at Queen's College, Belfast, from 1890, with many exhibitions and prizes; BA (RUI) (1st class hons in experimental science) 1893; MA (1st class hons in experimental science) 1896; MB BCh BAO 1899; DPH (hons) 1909; MD (QUB) 1917; medical missionary with the Presbyterian Missionary Society 1900–01 and principal of Moukden College, Manchuria, 1901–08; deputy medical officer of health to Cowbridge Rural District, Glamorgan; medical officer to the Tuberculosis Dispensary, Southampton, and assistant medical officer of health for Hampshire c 1910–12, of Winton, West Street, Fareham, Hampshire; tuberculosis medical officer and medical inspector of midwives and nursing homes, for county Down, of Dunkeld, King's Road, Belfast c 1912–20 and of 28 Knockdene Park South from c 1920; president of the Ulster Medical Society 1946–7; author of various medical papers; married 12 March 1900 in Fisherwick Presbyterian Church, Belfast, Catherine T. Hunter, daughter of Charles Hunter, merchant, of Knock, Belfast; father of Dr James Hunter Gillespie, MB BCh BAO (QUB) 1930; died 29 July 1960 at Knockdene Park South; probate Belfast 11 October 1960. [Belf GRO (d); Belf PRO, will cal; Boyd (1908); Dub GRO (b); *Med Dir*; QCB adm reg; Strain (1967); UHF database (m)].

GILLESPIE, JOSHUA (d 1812), Indian Medical Service;
son of William Gillespie of Drummaneny, county Londonderry, and Mary Quin of Campsey, county Londonderry; brother of Dr Henry Gillespie, senior (*q.v.*); joined the Indian Medical Service (Madras establishment) 1777; surgeon 1781; head surgeon in Nizam's detachment 1793 and Circars 1797; served in 2nd Mysore War 1780–82 and 3rd Mysore War 1790–92; retired to Fallowfield, Faughanvale, county Londonderry 1799; married Catherine — (who was born 1752/3 and died 6 December 1831 in Londonderry); father of Joshua Gillespie who was Mayor of Londonderry 1834–5 and died 1859; died 4 February 1812; 'his hospitality and benevolence placed him above the general propensity in that society to grasp and accumulate wealth, otherwise he might have returned with an overgrown fortune' (*Londonderry Journal*); will dated 22 August 1808, proved 4 March 1812 (copy in PRO NI). [*BNL* 14 February 1812 (d) and 13 December 1831 (d); Belf PRO, D1936/2 ('Record of the Family of Gillespie' – typescript); Belf PRO, T805/1; Crawford (1930); Hitchings, Paul, pers com; *Londonderry Journal* 11 February 1812 (d); *Londonderry Sentinel* 10 December 1831 (d)].

GILLESPIE, LEONARD (1758–1842), Naval Medical Service;
born 20 May 1758 in Armagh, son of Leonard Gillespie of Armagh and Elizabeth Blakeley; apprenticed to a doctor in Armagh 1772 and studied under surgeons in Dublin 1776–7; examined by the Company of Surgeons in London and joined the Naval Medical Service as second mate, first rate, 1777; appointed second assistant surgeon to HMS *Royal Oak* 1777; transferred to HMS *Weasel* 1778; sailed down west coast of Africa and across to the West Indies 1778; acting surgeon 1778; transferred to HMS *Supply* 1779, which caught fire in the West Indies; transferred to HMS *Yarmouth* and later to HMS *Sandwich*; surgeon based in the Naval Hospital in St Lucia 1781–3; studied leg ulcers extensively during this period and advocated strongly Lind's views on prevention of scurvy; studied medicine at Edinburgh and St Andrews' Universities 1783–4 and at the Hotel Dieu in Paris 1784–5; returned to Armagh 1785–6 but became bored by inactivity and moved to London; rejoined the navy 1787 on HMS *Vanguard*, HMS *Monarch*, HMS *Swiftsure* and HMS *Racehorse*, and kept up his medical experience when it moored in Edinburgh; transferred to HMS *Nautilus* 1791 and returned to study medicine in Paris January 1791–January 1793, in spite of the growing turmoil; with the declaration of war in February 1793 was appointed to HMS *Majestic*; served in West Indies 1793–6; MD (St Andrews) 1795 (on testimonials); surgeon to the Naval Hospital, Fort Royal, Martinique 1797–1802; returned to Armagh and London 1802; promoted physician to the Mediterranean Fleet and adviser to Lord Nelson 1804, but resigned in the summer of 1805 (before Trafalgar) and retired in 1806; lived mainly in Paris from 1815; author of *Advice to the Commanders and Officers of His Majesty's Fleets Serving in the West Indies, on the Preservation of the Health of Seamen* (1798), *Observations on the Diseases which Prevailed on Board a Part of His Majesty's Squadron in the Leeward Island Station, Between Nov. 1794 and April 1796* (1800), and various medical papers; did not marry but lived with Caroline Heiliger in Martinique and had 1 son and 1 daughter; died 13 January 1842 in Paris; buried in Pere Lachaise Cemetery, Paris; portrait by Charles Louis Bazin (1837). [*BNL* 28 January 1842 (d); Clarke (2006); Keevil (1954); *NMS* (1826); Smart (2004)].

GILLESPIE, RICHARD (*fl c* 1805), Stewartstown, county Tyrone;
LAH Dub 1805; apothecary, of Stewartstown. [Apothecaries (1829)].

GILLESPIE, ROBERT (1832–96), Army Medical Service;
born 25 March 1832 in county Monaghan, son of James Gillespie of Clones, county Monaghan; educated by the Rev John Hamilton; studied medicine at Queen's College, Belfast, from 1849; MD (QUI) 1853; LFPS Glas 1854; joined the Army Medical Service as staff assistant surgeon 1858, serving with the 74th Foot; staff surgeon 1864; transferred to 51st Foot 1870; surgeon major 1873; on half pay October 1876–February 1877; served in Abyssinia in 1868; retired as brigade surgeon in 1883 to 8 St James's Terrace, Malahide, county Dublin; married Sarah R. —; died 7 March 1896 at 8 St James's Terrace; probate Dublin 22 April 1896. [Belf PRO, will cal; Dub GRO (d); *Med Dir*; Peterkin and Johnston (1968); QCB adm reg].

GILLESPIE, THOMAS EDIE (1784–1836), Indian Medical Service, Limavady, county Londonderry, and Castlecomer, county Kilkenny;
 born 11 December 1785, fifth son of Dr Henry Gillespie, senior, of Limavady (*q.v.*); studied medicine at Edinburgh; LRCPE; MRCSE 1807; joined the Indian Medical Service (Madras establishment) as assistant surgeon 1806; pensioned on Lord Clive's Fund 1815 and retired to Limavady; surgeon to Limavady Light Infantry; surgeon in Castlecomer and surgeon to Kilkenny Militia; presented with a silver hot water jug inscribed 'A small token of gratitude from Richard and Kate Eaton to Thomas Gillespie Esquire, MD, to whose professional skill and affectionate attention they are under Providence indebted for the life of their son, November 1833'; married 20 March 1818 in Shankill Church, county Carlow, Elizabeth Butler (who died 1840 and was buried in St Selskar's Churchyard, Wexford), daughter of Richard Butler and Grace Sadleir; died 4 June 1836 at Castlecomer; buried in Castlecomer. [Belf PRO, D1936/2 ('Record of the Family of Gillespie' – typescript); Crawford (1930)].

GILLESPIE, WILLIAM (1773–99), Naval Medical Service;
 born 1773, eldest son of Dr Henry Gillespie, senor, of Limavady, county Londonderry (*q.v.*); brother of Dr Henry Gillespie, junior, RN, (*q.v.*) and uncle of Dr Henry Gillespie Fleming (*q.v.*); joined the Naval Medical Service as assistant surgeon; lost on HMS *Amarantha,* a captured French ship which was wrecked off Jamaica, 25 October 1799. [Belf PRO, D1936/2 ('Record of the Family of Gillespie' – typescript); Hitchings, Paul, pers com].

GILLESPIE, WILLIAM HENRY (1846/7–97), Clones, county Monaghan, Castle Cary and Glastonbury, Somerset;
 born 1846/7; LKQCPI and LM 1870; LRCSI 1870; general practitioner, of Clones, county Monaghan c 1870–72 and of the County Asylum, Doncaster, c 1875; general practitioner, of the Villa, Castle Cary, Somerset c 1885; also medical superintendent of Sir George Bowle's Hospital, Butleigh, Glastonbury, Somerset c 1895; died 31 October 1897 at Sir George Bowle's Hospital. [Lond GRO (d); McCann (2003); *Med Dir*].

GILLMER, ALEXANDER (GEORGE) BIRCH (1800–22), Tullyniskey, county Down;
 born 31 January 1800, son of captain Eleazer Birch Gillmer of the East India Company and Scion Hill, Tullyniskey, and Rachel Birch; surgeon; married 14 November 1822 Ellen McConnell, daughter of Thomas McConnell of Drummiller; died 31 December 1822 following a fall from his horse on the preceding evening. [*BNL* 26 November 1822 (m) and 7 January 1823 (d); McClelland (1963b)].

GILMER, ROBERT (1844–96), Ballymena, county Antrim;
 born 26 November 1844, son of William Gilmer of Church Street, Ballymena; educated at RBAI; studied medicine at Queen's College, Belfast, from 1861 and at the General Hospital, Belfast; LRCP LRCS Edin 1872; LAH Dub 1874; medical officer to Ballymena Dispensary from 1874, of 2 Broughshane Street, Ballymena; married —; died 24 May 1896 at 2 Broughshane Street; probate Belfast 10 July 1896. [Belf PRO, will cal; Dub GRO (d); *Med Dir*; QCB adm reg].

GILMORE, ROBERT (1853–c 1889), Belfast;
born 4 June 1853 at Legaloy, Ballynure, county Antrim, son of James Gilmore, farmer, of Legaloy; educated at Ballynure National School and Belfast Academy; studied medicine at Queen's College, Belfast from 1875; LRCP LRCS Edin 1879; general practitioner, of 161 York Street, Belfast; married 21 October 1884 in Carrickfergus Methodist Church, Gretta Campbell Burrows (who was born 1860/1), daughter of William Burrows, gentleman, of North Lodge; died c 1889. [*Med Dir*; QCB adm reg; UHF database (m)].

GILMORE, SAMUEL (1830–83), Castleblaney, county Monaghan;
born 29 September 1830, at Liscalgat, Creggan, county Armagh, son of Samuel Gilmore, farmer, and Jane Coulter; studied arts and medicine at Glasgow University; BA (Glas) 1850; LRCS Edin 1858; LRCP and LM Edin 1863; applied 1852 for a renewal of his diploma 'having lost his former one by shipwreck'; medical officer to Castleblaney Workhouse and Fever Hospital from 1863; superintendent medical officer of health for Castleblaney Union from 1874; married 10 October 1863 in Warrenpoint Church of Ireland Church, Georgina Henry, daughter of John Henry, gentleman, of Warrenpoint and Castleblaney; died 1 June 1883 at Castle Square, Castleblaney; probate Armagh 16 August 1883. [Addison (1898); Belf PRO, will cal; Dub GRO (d); Kirkpatrick Archive; McNeill, pers com; *Med Dir*; UHF database (m)].

GILMORE, SAMUEL JAMES McWATTY (d c 1945), Bootham, Yorkshire, London, Swindon, Wiltshire, and Liverpool, Lancashire;
studied medicine at the Royal College of Surgeons in Ireland; LM Rot Hosp Dub 1888; LKQCPI and LM 1889; LRCSI and LM 1889; clinical assistant to St Luke's Hospital, London; assistant medical officer to Bootham Asylum and to York and Cornwall County Asylums; general practitioner, of Park House, Swindon c 1910–15, of Hamden Club, Phoenix Street, London c 1915–18, of 6 Shaw Street, Liverpool c 1918–22; 'travelling' c 1922–9; retired to 1 Crayford Road, Brighton c 1929 and to Ivydene, 13 Portland Villas, Hove, c 1935; died c 1945. [*Med Dir*].

GILMORE, THOMAS CHARLES (1840–1918), Malin, county Donegal;
born 4 March 1840 at Ballybay, county Monaghan, son of William Gilmore of Ballybay; educated at Belfast Seminary; studied medicine at Queen's College, Belfast, from 1860; MD (QUI) 1865; MCh 1867; LM KQCPI 1868; medical officer to Malin Dispensary District and constabulary, of Drumcrowie, Malin; married —; died 27 May 1918 at Drumcrowie; probate Londonderry 14 August 1918. [Belf PRO, will cal; Dub GRO (d); Kirkpatrick Archive; *Med Dir*; QCB adm reg].

GILMORE (GILMOUR), WILLIAM (*fl c* 1855–6), ship's surgeon, Aylesbury, Buckinghamshire and Ongar, Essex;
LFPS and LM Glas 1854; LRCP Edin 1860; medical officer on the screw-steamship *Royal Charter*; of Buckingham Street, Aylesbury c 1860–65 and of Fyfield, Ongar c 1865–75; retired to Woodford, Essex c 1875; married —; daughter born 22 October 1856 in Portstewart; died c 1877. [*BNL* 27 October 1856 (b); *Med Dir*].

GILMOUR, ALFRED JOHN (1851–1917), ship's surgeon, Garvagh, county Londonderry, Bishop Auckland, county Durham and Manchester, Lancashire;
born 5 October 1851 at Garvagh, county Londonderry, son of William Gilmour of Garvagh; educated at Coleraine Academical Institution; studied medicine at Queen's College, Belfast, from 1868; MD MCh Dip Mid (QUI) 1873; surgeon with Cunard Royal Mail Steamers; general practitioner in Garvagh c 1875; general practitioner of Eldon, Bishop Auckland, Durham c 1880; of 2 Higher Ardwick, Manchester from c 1882 and of Egerton Mount, 273 Wellington Road North, Heaton Chapel; married Minnie —; died 28 March 1917 at Egerton Mount; administration (with will) Manchester 27 September 1917 and Dublin 23 July 1918. [Belf PRO, will cal; Kirkpatrick Archive; Lond GRO (d); Lond PPR, will cal; *Med Dir*; QCB adm reg].

GILMOUR, JAMES (*fl c* 1838), Garvagh, county Londonderry;
surgeon, probably of Garvagh; married 28 November 1838 in Errigal (Garvagh) Church of Ireland Church, Eleanor Maria Herbert, daughter of the Rev G. Herbert, perpetual curate of Amluck. [*BNL* 14 December 1838 (m)].

GILMOUR, JOHN (1862–1911), Ballykelly, county Londonderry, and Stockport, Cheshire;
born 2 March 1862 at Ballyspallan, son of Stephen Gilmour, farmer, of Ballyspallan; educated at Londonderry Academical Institution; studied medicine at Queen's College, Belfast, from 1881; LRCP LRCS Edin 1891; LFPS Glas 1891; general practitioner, of Ballyspallan, Ballykelly c 1895 and of 84 Wellington Road South, and 44 Middle Hillgate, Stockport, Cheshire from c 1900; married Beatrice —; died 31 August 1911; administration Chester 25 October 1911. [Lond PPR, will cal; *Med Dir*; QUB].

GILTENNAN, A.A. (1818–53), Georgia, USA;
born 1818; of Belfast; emigrated to USA; MD; died 8 December 1853 at Stephenville, Wilkinson county, Georgia. [*BNL* 8 March 1854 (d)].

GIMLETTE, GEORGE HART DESMOND (1855–1930), Indian Medical Service;
born 8 September 1855, at St Aubyn, Stoke Damerel, Devonshire, son of assistant surgeon Hart Desmond Gimlette, RN; brother of surgeon rear admiral Sir Thomas Desmond Gimlette, MRCSE 1879, KCB, and Dr John Desmond Gimlette, LRCP Lond MRCSE 1890; studied medicine at St Thomas's Hospital, London, and from 1876, at Queen's College, Belfast; MRCSE 1877; LSA Lond 1877; MD MCh (QUI) 1879; joined the Indian Medical Service (Bengal establishment) as surgeon 1879; surgeon major 1891; surgeon lieutenant-colonel 1899; served in Egypt 1882, at Tel-el-Khebir (medal with clasp, bronze star); seconded to work in the cholera epidemic in Egypt in 1883; in charge of residency at Katmandu, Nepal, at the time of the revolution in 1885; residency surgeon of Baghelkand 1891–7, of Indore 1897–1901 and of Hyderabad 1901–10; CIE 1901; retired 1910; rejoined for World War I 1914–19 as principal medical officer on the hospital ship *Sicilia*, also serving in France, Gallipoli, Egypt and Iraq; author of *A Postscript to the Records of the Indian*

Mutiny (1927); latterly of 14a St James' Court, Buckingham Gate, London; unmarried; died 7 March 1930 at 5 Merton Road, Southsea, Hampshire; probate London 3 May 1930. [*BMJ* obituary (1930); Crawford (1930); Kirkpatrick Archive; *Lancet* obituary (1930); Lond PPR, will cal; *Med Dir*; QCB adm reg].

GIVAN, JOSEPH (1856–88), Ballygawley, county Tyrone;
born 26 September 1856 at Grange, Aughnacloy, county Tyrone, son of Archibald Givan, farmer, of Grange; educated at the National School and RBAI; studied medicine at Queen's College, Belfast, from 1873; LFPS Glas 1880; LAH Dub 1882; general practitioner, of Ballygawley; married —; died 23 June 1888 at Ballygawley. [Dub GRO (d); *Med Dir*; QCB adm reg].

GIVEN, DAVID KILPATRICK (1851–98), Drumquin, county Tyrone;
born 18 December 1851 at Drumlegagh, Baronscourt, county Tyrone, son of John Given of Drumlegagh; brother of Dr George Kirkpatrick Given (*q.v.*); educated at Portora Royal School, Enniskillen; studied medicine at Queen's College, Galway and from 1872, at Queen's College, Belfast; LRCP Edin 1883; LFPS Glas 1883; general practitioner of Drumquin; died 15 July 1898 at Drumnaforbe, Drumquin; probate Londonderry 25 October 1898. [Belf PRO, will cal; Dub GRO (d); *Med Dir*; QCB adm reg].

GIVEN, GEORGE KILPATRICK (1846–1918), Stranorlar, county Donegal, Gortin, county Tyrone, and London;
born 12 July 1846 at Drumlegagh, Baronscourt, county Tyrone, son of John Given of Drumlegagh; brother of Dr David Kilpatrick Given (*q.v.*); educated at Portora Royal School and RBAI; studied medicine at Queen's College, Belfast, also at the Ledwich School and Trinity College, Dublin; LM Dub; LRCP LRCS Edin 1869; medical officer to Cloghan Dispensary District, Stranorlar, and from 1872, to Gortin Dispensary District, Fever Hospital and constabulary; superintendent medical officer of health for Gortin from 1874; certifying factory surgeon and public vaccinator; JP; moved c 1908 to London; general practitioner, of 1 Grand Parade and 7 Firs Avenue, Muswell Hill; later of 39 Muswell Rise; author of various medical papers; married (1) 8 April 1880 in Derryloran Church of Ireland Church, Cookstown, Maria Elizabeth Cranstoun Charles, only daughter of Dr David Hughes Charles (*q.v.*) of Cookstown; (2) Eleanor Henry, daughter of Thomas Henry of Omagh; father of Dr David Hughes Charles Given; died 6 January 1918 at 39 Muswell Rise; probate Dublin 9 March 1918. [*BMJ* obituary (1918); Dub GRO (m); Kirkpatrick Archive; *Med Dir*; QCB adm reg; Young and Pike (1909)].

GIVEEN, GEORGE MARTIN (1864–1903), Stockport, Lancashire;
born 31 July 1864 at Blackrock, county Antrim, son of George Martin Giveen, land agent, of Blackrock; educated at Gracehill Academy; studied medicine at Queen's College, Belfast, from 1881; LRCP LRCS Edin 1886; general practitioner, of Hayfield, Stockport; married Emma Elizabeth —; died 27 May 1903; probate London 25 July 1903. [Lond PPR, will cal; *Med Dir*; QCB adm reg].

GIVIN, ROBERT DANIEL (1860–1911), Coleraine, county Londonderry, and Sydney, Australia;
> born 8 February 1860 at Shellfield House, Dervock, county Antrim, only son of Robert Givin of Shellfield House and Sarah —; educated at Coleraine Academical Institution; studied medicine at Queen's College, Cork, and from 1880 at Queen's College, Belfast, at Glasgow and Edinburgh Royal Infirmaries, also at St Thomas' Hospital, London; LRCP LRCS and LM Edin 1883; surgeon to the Niger Expedition 1883 and medical officer to the National Africa Company, River Niger; general practitioner, of Coleraine c 1885; emigrated to Australia c 1888; died 18 January 1911 in Sydney; commemorated in Carncullagh Presbyterian Graveyard, Dervock. [Gravestone inscription; *Med Dir*; QCB adm reg].

GLASGOW, BENJAMIN (d 1833), Mexico;
> son of Robert Glasgow of Cookstown, county Tyrone; surgeon in Veracruz, Mexico; died 26 November 1833 at New Orleans, [*BNL* 20 May 1834 (d)].

GLASGOW, EDWARD (d 1860), Hamilton, North Carolina, USA;
> born in Cookstown, county Tyrone; emigrated to USA as surgeon; died 8 April 1860 in Hamilton, North Carolina. [*Londonderry Sentinel* 25 May 1860 (d)].

GLENHOLME, HUGH (1804/5–61), Magherafelt, county Londonderry;
> born 1804/5; general practitioner, of Magherafelt c 1845; married 21 August 1849 — Canning, widow of Dr — Canning of Garvagh (*q.v.*); died 18 September 1861. [*BNL* 28 August 1849 (m); *Coleraine Chronicle* 25 August 1849 (m) and 28 September 1861 (d); Croly (1843–6); *Londonderry Sentinel* 31 August 1849 (m)].

GLENN, JOHN (1807/8–31), Broughshane, county Antrim;
> born 1807/8; MRCSE; died 27 November 1831 of pulmonary consumption, 'a young man of promising talent, amiable disposition and exemplary conduct'. [*BNL* 2 December 1831 (d)].

GLENNY, GEORGE (*fl c* 1853), New York, USA;
> son of Isaac Glenny of Glenville, county Down; emigrated to USA; general practitioner; married 21 September 1853 Elizabeth Campbell Norbury, second daughter of John Norbury of Upton Hall, Cheshire. [*BNL* 14 October 1853 (m)].

GLENNY, WILLIAM CHARLES WATSON (1875/6–1948), Omeath, county Louth, and Warrenpoint, county Down;
> born 1875/6, son of the Rev Robert Edmund Glenny, rector of Clonallon (Warrenpoint) and Edith Sarah Watson of Warrenpoint; elder brother of Dr Edmund Glenny, LRCPI LRCSI 1901, FRCSI 1904; educated at Methodist College, Belfast, from 1889, and St Bee's School, Westmoreland; studied medicine at Trinity College, Dublin, and the Royal College of Surgeons in Ireland; LRCPI and LM LRCSI and LM 1898; LM Rot Hosp Dub; surgical and medical resident in Jervis Street Hospital, Dublin; served in the South African War and World War I (captain RAMC); civil surgeon to Cambridge Hospital, Aldershot; general practitioner of Prospect, Omeath from c 1900; and of 1 Mereham Terrace, Warrenpoint, from c 1906; retired 1939;

JP; married 28 April 1900 in St Thomas's Church of Ireland Church, Belfast, Martha Thompson, daughter of Liddle Thompson, gentleman, of Belfast; died 7 January 1948 at 1 Mereham Terrace; probate Belfast 1 July 1948. [Belf GRO (d); Belf PRO, will cal; *BMJ* obituary (1948); Kirkpatrick Archive; *Med Dir*; Swanzy (1933); UHF database (m)].

GLOVER, JOHN HASTINGS (1870–c 1952), Bottesford, Nottingham, and Halifax, Yorkshire;
born 21 May 1870 at Magherafelt, county Londonderry, son of John Glover, solicitor, of Magherafelt; educated at Methodist College, Belfast, 1887–8; studied medicine at Queen's College, Belfast, from 1888, and Edinburgh University; MB CM (Edin) 1893; medical officer and public vaccinator to Bottesford District from c 1895; medical officer of health for Belvoir District; general practitioner, of Halifax from c 1920; deputy commissioner for medical services to Ministry of Pensions from c 1925; MPC 1925; moved c 1928 to Ministry of Pensions, Upper Mount Street, Dublin; died c 1952. [Fry (1984); *Med Dir*; QCB adm reg].

GODFREY, MITCHELL (c 1816–56), Toomebridge, county Antrim;
born c 1816; studied medicine at Glasgow University; MRCSE 1836; MD (Glas) 1837; medical officer to Toomebridge Dispensary District and constabulary, c 1843–6; retired 1852 to Yardley, Warwickshire; died 15 February 1856 at Studley, Warwickshire. [Addison (1898); Croly (1843–6); Lond GRO (d); *Med Dir*].

GORDON, ALEXANDER (*fl c* 1802), Broughshane, county Antrim;
LAH Dub 1802; apothecary, of Broughshane. [Apothecaries (1829)].

GORDON, ALEXANDER (1783–1855), Saintfield, county Down;
born 1783, son of Alexander Gordon of Saintfield, agent for the Price estates, and Jane McMechan; LAH Dub 1805; surgeon, apothecary and medical officer to constabulary in Saintfield; married 11 March 1813 Margaret Orr, daughter of David Orr of Ballygowan, county Down; father of Professor Alexander Gordon (*q.v.*) and Dr William Gordon (*q.v.*); died 14 August 1855 at Saintfield; buried in Saintfield Church of Ireland graveyard; will dated 22 December 1854 proved in Down Diocesan Court 3 September 1857. [Apothecaries (1829); *BNL* 16 March 1813 (m) and 16 August 1855 (d); Belf PRO, Down Diocesan Wills index; Belf PRO, T/618/324/VII; Clarke, *County Down*, vol 3 (1969); Croly (1843–6); Fraser (1976); Pigot (1824)].

GORDON, ALEXANDER (1818–87), Belfast;
born 1818 in Saintfield, county Down, son of Dr Alexander Gordon (*q.v.*) of Saintfield and Margaret Orr of Ballygowan; older brother of Dr William Gordon (*q.v.*) of Saintfield; studied medicine at RBAI and Edinburgh University winning several prizes; MD (Edin) 1841 (thesis 'On the granular disease of the kidney'); LRCS Edin 1841; in surgical practice in Belfast from 1841; demonstrator in anatomy at RBAI 1841–6; attending surgeon at Belfast General Hospital 1845–73; gave annual winter oration at Belfast General Hospital 1866; consulting surgeon 1873–6; professor of surgery at Queen's College, Belfast 1849–86; president of the Ulster

Medical Society 1856; president of the Belfast Pathological Society; author of many medical publications, mainly on fractures; invented the Gordon splint for Colles fracture; described as 'the most illustrious of Irish surgeons, a man of world-wide fame – an original genius – a man with an inventive creative mind' (Whitla) but this is 'hyperbole' (Fraser); and rather he was 'an indefatigable worker and an enthusiastic teacher'; lived at Upper Arthur Street, at 2 College Square North, 1 Howard Street, Belfast; retired 1886 to Ringneill, Comber, a house later occupied by Dr Robert Maitland Beath, MB (QUB) 1914; married 10 September 1852 in Rosemary Street First Presbyterian Church, Belfast, Annabella Telfair, fourth daughter of Robert Telfair, merchant, of Belfast; father of Winnie Gordon who married Dr Joshua Harrison Stallard of London and San Francisco; died 28 July 1887 at Saintfield; buried in Saintfield Church of Ireland graveyard; two portraits of him are in Queen's University, one by Richard Hooke (1878), the other probably posthumous and based on a photograph, demonstrating a Colles fracture, also a relief carving, now in the Whitla Medical Building; administration Belfast 17 February 1888. [*BNL* 13 September 1852 (m); Belf PRO, will cal; Black (1995); Clarke, *County Down*, vol 3 (1969); *Coleraine Chronicle* 18 September 1852 (m); Croly (1843–6); *DIB* (2009); Dub GRO (d); Edin Univ; Esler (1888); Fraser (1976); Jones (1977); Kirkpatrick Archive; *Lancet* obituary (1887); *Med Dir*; Moody and Beckett (1959); O'Brien, Crookshank and Wolstenholme (1988); UHF database (m); Whitla (1901)].

GORDON, ANDREW (1816/7–39), Kingston, Jamaica;
born 1816/7, third son of Andrew Gordon of Galgorm, county Antrim; MRCSE; medical officer in Kingston 1836–9; died 3 July 1839 of yellow fever in Kingston. [*BNL* 23 August 1839 (d)].

GORDON, GARDINER (*fl c* 1778), Londonderry;
MD [?]; surgeon to the First Company of Londonderry Volunteers 1778. [Day (1901)].

GORDON, GEORGE (d c 1772), Londonderry;
apothecary, of Londonderry city; leased land to Alderman Nathaniel Alexander of Boomhall 1762; married Elizabeth —; died c 1772; will dated 6 September 1771 proved in Derry Diocesan Court 24 March 1773. [Belf PRO, T618/324/XVII; Dub, Registry of Deeds 234.31.150887; Thrift (1920)].

GORDON, GEORGE ROBERT (1858–1945), Manchester;
born 2 December 1858 at Newry, county Down, son of Joseph Gordon, wine and spirit merchant, of 16–17 North Street, Newry; educated at Newry School; studied medicine at Queen's College, Galway, and from 1878, at Queen's College, Belfast; MD BCh (RUI) 1888; general practitioner of Alexandra Villa, 96 Alexander Road, Manchester and later of 'Ashfield', College Road, Whalley Range, Manchester; retired c 1938 to 'Breydon', West Road, Canford Cliffs, Bournemouth; OBE c 1944; married Alice Maude —; father of Dr Stanley Eric Gordon; died 17 December 1945; probate Manchester 12 April 1946. [Lond PPR, will cal, will; *Med Dir*; QCB adm reg].

GORDON, HANS (*fl c* 1845), Tandragee, county Armagh;
LAH Dub; general practitioner, of Tandragee c 1845; possibly died c 1850. [Croly (1843–6)].

GORDON, JAMES (1859–1928), Kilkeel, county Down;
born 4 March 1859 at Annalong, county Down, son of Alexander Gordon, merchant, of Annalong; 1859; educated at the Kilkeel Classical and Mathematical School; studied engineering and medicine at Queen's College, Belfast, from 1875 and medicine at Edinburgh; LRCS LRCP Edin 1886; LFPS Glas 1886; medical officer and medical officer of health to Kilkeel Dispensary District; medical officer to workhouse and fever hospital, of Fintamara, Kilkeel c 1887–1924 and later of Ivy Lodge; retired c 1924 to 'Roslyn', Annalong; married —; died 10 January 1928 at Annalong. [Belf GRO (d); *Med Dir*; QCB adm reg].

GORDON, JAMES, (1876/7–1955) Ballyshannon, county Donegal;
born 1876/7; studied medicine at the Catholic University of Ireland; LRCPI and LM LRCSI and LM 1898; FRCSI 1909; medical officer and medical officer of health to Ballyshannon and Cliffoney Dispensary Districts; physician to the Shiel Hospital, Ballyshannon; unmarried; died 18 June 1955 at Carrickboy, Ballyshannon; probate Dublin 3 May 1956. [Dub GRO (d); Dub Nat Arch, will cal, will; Kirkpatrick Archive; *Med Dir*].

GORDON, JAMES ALEXANDER (1853–1938), Great Yarmouth, Norfolk;
born 18 April 1853 at Belfast, son of James Gordon, mill manager, of 4 Bridge Street, Ballymena; educated at RBAI; studied medicine at Queen's College, Galway, and from 1872 at Queen's College, Belfast; LRCP LRCS and LM Edin 1877; medical officer of health to Holme Cultram District; medical officer and public vaccinator to Ludham District, of Ludham Manor, Great Yarmouth from c 1880; JP for Norfolk; retired c 1932 to Ludham House, 12 Marine Parade, Gorleston-on-Sea; married (1) Mary Ballentine (who was born 1855/6 and died 11 June 1879), daughter of George Ballentine; (2) Eleanor —; died 11 May 1938 at 12 Marine Parade; probate Norwich 23 June 1938. [Gravestone inscription; Lond PPR, will cal, will; *Med Dir*; QCB adm reg].

GORDON, JOHN (*fl c* 1791), Magherafelt, county Londonderry.
LAH Dub 1791; apothecary, of Magherafelt. [Apothecaries (1829)].

GORDON, JOHN FREDERICK (1859–1924), Maghull, Lancashire;
born 1859 in the USA, son of — Gordon, inspector of schools; studied arts and medicine at Queen's College, Belfast from 1877; BA (QUI) 1881; MD (RUI) 1886; BAO 1888; general practitioner, of Rockfield and High Pastures, Maghull; medical officer and public vaccinator for Ormshirk Third District; medical officer for the Home for Epileptics, Maghull and for Maghull Branch of Liverpool Workhouse and Post Office; died 17 June 1924; probate Liverpool 28 July 1924. [Lond PPR, will cal; *Med Dir*; QCB adm reg].

GORDON, ROBERT (1862–1945), Sheffield, Yorkshire;
born 15 December 1862 in Enniskillen, county Fermanagh, son of Thomas Gordon, grocer and hardware merchant of Enniskillen, and Elizabeth Parke of Derrygonnelly, county Fermanagh; studied medicine at Edinburgh University; MB CM (Edin) 1885; MD 1899; general practitioner, of 26 Westenholme Road and 24 Broadfield Park Road, Sheffield; retired c 1929 to Ashdene, Furzfield Road, Beaconsfield, Buckinghamshire; married 29 August 1894, in Sheffield Parish Church, Beatrice Mary Gertrude Wilks (who was born 26 October 1868 and died 6 March 1952), daughter of Edward John Wilks, ironmonger, of Sheffield; father of Dr Geoffrey Desmond Gordon, MRCSE LRCP Lond 1925, of Malaya and Beaconsfield; died 13 November 1945; probate Oxford 9 May 1946. [Lond GRO (m); Lond PPR, will cal; Kirkpatrick (1889); *Med Dir*].

GORDON, ROBERT HUNTER (or **HUNTLEY**) (1815–57), Portstewart, county Londonderry, Larne, county Antrim and Bellaghy, county Londonderry;
born 1815 in Belfast, son of John Gordon, merchant, of Belfast and Catherine Holmes of Islandmagee; studied medicine at Trinity College, Dublin; LRCS Edin 1835; FRCSI 1844; general practitioner in Portstewart and 1838–9 in Larne; medical officer to Bellaghy Dispensary 1839–57; also a poet and general writer; married 2 June 1847 in Ballyscullion (Bellaghy) Church of Ireland Church, Mabella Hemsworth Hill (who was born 1826/7 in Bellaghy Castle and died 11 September 1854), second daughter of John Hill JP, of Bellaghy Castle; died 16 September 1857 at Castledawson; probate Dublin 17 April 1858. [*BNL* 8 June 1847 (m), 13 September 1854 (d) and 17 September 1857 (d); Belf PRO, will cal; *Bellaghy Hist Soc* (2003); *Coleraine Chronicle* 5 June 1847 (m) and 16 September 1854 (d); Croly (1843–6); Donaldson (1927), p 141; Dub GRO (m); Kirkpatrick Archive; *Londonderry Sentinel* 12 June 1847 (m), 15 September 1854 (d) and 18 September 1857 (d); *Med Dir*].

GORDON, ROBERT JOHN (1858/9–c 1935), China and Manchuria;
born 1858/9 at Cooey, Tynan, county Armagh, son of Hugh Nixon Gordon, farmer, of Cooey and Sarah Elizabeth Lyons; educated at RBAI; studied arts and medicine at Queen's College, Belfast, from 1880; BA (RUI) 1883; MA 1884; MB BCh BAO 1891; medical missionary at Kwanchangtolo, Newchwang, North China c 1900, and of Chang Chun, Manchuria c 1920; retired c 1933 to Lyndhurst, Riselaw Crescent, Edinburgh; married Jessie Jarvis Graham; died 18 September 1935; confirmation of will Edinburgh 30 January 1936. [Edin GRO (d); Edin Nat Arch, will cal; *Med Dir*; QCB adm reg]

GORDON, THOMAS EAGLESON (1867–1929), Dublin;
born 4 February 1867 at Greenfield House, Urney, county Tyrone, son of George Gordon of Greenfield House, wine merchant, JP, and Martha Ramsay; brother of Dr William Gordon (*q.v.*) of Exeter; educated in Brighton; studied arts and medicine at Trinity College, Dublin, from 1884; BA (TCD) 1889; MB BCh 1890; FRCSI 1895; MCh (*jure officii*) (TCD) 1926; house surgeon in the Adelaide Hospital, Dublin; surgeon to the Royal City of Dublin Hospital for about twelve months;

attending surgeon to the Adelaide Hospital from c 1896; demonstrator of anatomy at Trinity College, Dublin; professor of surgery at Trinity College, Dublin, from 1916; president of the Royal College of Surgeons in Ireland 1928–9; author of many medical papers; married Ellen M. —; died 24 July 1929 at 23 Pembroke Road, Dublin; probate Dublin 7 October 1859. [*BMJ* obituary (1929); Dub GRO (b) and (d); Dub Nat Arch, will cal; Kirkpatrick Archive; *Lancet* obituary (1929); Lyons (1984); *Med Dir*; TCD adm reg; *TCD Cat*, vol II (1896); Widdess (1967)].

GORDON, WILLIAM (1828–90), Saintfield, county Down;
born 1828, son of Dr Alexander Gordon of Saintfield (*q.v.*) and Margaret Orr of Ballygowan; younger brother of Professor Alexander Gordon (*q.v.*); studied medicine at the Royal College of Surgeons in Ireland; LRCSI 1851; LKQCPI 1856; LSA Lond 1858; resident medical officer at the Richmond Hospital, Dublin; medical officer to Saintfield Dispensary District, of Tonaghnieve, Glassdrumman; unmarried; died 11 December 1890 at Tonaghnieve; buried in Saintfield Church of Ireland graveyard; probate Belfast 13 February 1891. [Belf PRO, will cal; Clarke, *County Down*, vol 3 (1969); Dub GRO (d); Fraser (1976); Jones (1977); *Med Dir*].

GORDON, WILLIAM (1863–1929), Exeter;
born 1863 at Strabane, county Tyrone, son of George Gordon JP, of Greenfield House, Strabane, wine merchant, and Martha Ramsay; brother of Professor Thomas Eagleson Gordon (*q.v.*) of Dublin; educated at Mr Creak's school, Brighton; studied medicine at Trinity College, Cambridge, from 1882, winning exhibitions and scholarships, and University College, London; BA (Cantab) 1885; LRCP Lond 1888; MA MB BCh 1890; MRCP Lond 1891; MD 1894; FRCP Lond 1903; physician to the Royal Devon and Exeter Hospital 1890–1928, also to the West of England Eye Infirmary and the Exeter Dispensary; had a special interest in tuberculosis in Devonshire and in climatology; played a prominent part as representative of the BMA in the creation of the RAMC in 1898; medical officer to No 1 Temporary Hospital in Exeter 1914–18; held several posts in the Royal Society of Medicine; author of many medical papers; married 8 January 1903 in Kensington Parish Church, London, Dora Mary Cruden (who was born 1880), daughter of Major George Robert Cruden of 32 Gordon Place, Kensington, London; died 1 October 1929 at Mowbray House, Heavitree, Exeter; probate Exeter 2 November 1929. [*BMJ* obituary (1929); Kirkpatrick Archive; *Lancet* obituary (1929); Lond GRO (m); Lond PPR, will cal; *Med Dir; Munk's Roll*, vol 4; Venn (1940–54)].

GORDON, WILLIAM (1867–1954), Birmingham;
born 15 March 1867 at Doughery, Banbridge, county Down, son of John Gordon, farmer, of Doughery; educated at Banbridge Academy; studied arts and medicine at Queen's College, Belfast, from 1884; LRCP LRCS Edin 1897; LFPS Glas 1897; general practitioner, of 652 and 722 Stratford Road, Birmingham from c 1900 and of 182 Wakegreen Road, Moseley, Birmingham from c 1928; retired c 1938; married Elsie Isabella —; father of Dr William Lindsay Gordon; died 19 May 1954 at 182 Wakegreen Road; probate Birmingham 20 July 1954. [Lond PPR, will cal, will; *Med Dir*; QCB adm reg].

GORDON, WILLIAM EAGLESON (1821/2–73), Lauder and Bridge of Allan, Stirlingshire;
   born 1821/2 at Strabane, county Tyrone, son of Robert Gordon, linen manufacturer, and Helen Eagleson; studied medicine at Edinburgh University; LM Edin 1841; MD (Edin) 1842 (thesis 'De pneumonia'); LRCS Edin 1842; general practitioner, of Lauder, and from 1858, of Home Hill House, Bridge of Allan; married (1) Marion Hay Forbes (who died 21 November 1862 at Bristow House, Bridge of Allan), eldest daughter of Alexander Forbes, ARSA, of Edinburgh; (2) 12 July 1865 at 29 Melville Street, Edinburgh, Emily Marianne Freer, widow of George Freer of 29 Melville Streert, late of Jamaica, and only daughter of Archibald Dick of Friar's Park, Elgin; died 15 January 1873 at Bridge of Allan; inventory (administration) Stirling 18 February 1873. [*BMJ* obituary (1873); *Coleraine Chronicle* 22 July 1865 (m); Edin GRO (d); Edin Nat Arch, will cal; Edin Univ; Kirkpatrick Archive; *Londonderry Sentinel* 28 November 1862 (d); *Med Dir*]

GORDON, WILLIAM SPEAR (1856–1911), Mullingar, county Westmeath;
   born 26 September 1856 in Mullingar, son of William Gordon, merchant, of Mullingar; educated at the Armagh Royal School 1870–75; studied arts and medicine at Trinity College, Dublin, from 1875; BA (TCD) 1879; MB BCh 1880; LM Rot Hosp Dub 1880; MA 1891; assistant medical officer to the District Lunatic Asylum, Mullingar; unmarried; died 9 August 1911 at 222 Lower Baggot Street, Dublin (a private hospital), of typhoid fever; probate Mullingar 16 November 1911. [Belf PRO, will cal; Dub GRO (d); Ferrar (1933); Kirkpatrick Archive; *Med Dir;* TCD adm reg; *TCD Cat,* vol II 1896)].

GORE, WILLIAM CRAMPTON (1871–1946), ship's surgeon, RAMC, Bray, county Wicklow, and Colchester, Essex;
   born 24 October 1871 in Enniskillen, county Fermanagh, only son of Captain William Gore of the 13th Hussars and Innismore Hall, Enniskillen; studied arts and medicine at Trinity College, Dublin; BA (TCD) 1894; MB BCh BAO 1899; LM Rot Hosp Dub; resident surgeon and medical officer in the Adelaide Hospital, Dublin; spent four months painting under Henry Tonks at the Slade School, London, in 1898 and travelled as ship's surgeon in New York, India and Italy, painting and sketching whenever possible; returned to the Slade in 1900 and virtually gave up medicine from 1901; lived for a short time with William Orpen in 21 Fitzroy Street, Dublin, and in 1905 shared a studio with Augustus John; exhibited frequently at the RHA and Royal Academy, London; full member of the RHA 1918; captain in RAMC 1914–15 and with the British Red Cross in Boulogne; of Knocklinn, Bray, c 1910–32 and at 1a The Avenue and 24 Queen's Road, 21 Creffield Road, and 72 Winnock Road, Colchester c 1932–46; paintings include landscapes, portraits and still life's, some in the Hugh Lane Gallery, Dublin and the Limerick City Gallery; married 1923 in France, Yvonne Rosalie Madeline —; died 10 January 1946 in the Essex County Hospital; portrait by Charles Lamb, RHA; will dated 30 August 1843 proved Ipswich 29 March 1846. [Lond PPR, will cal, will; Martin (2010); *Med Dir;* Snoddy (1996)].

GORMAN, EDWARD SAMUEL (1872–1944), Liverpool, Lancashire, and Birmingham, Warwickshire;
> born 10 August 1872 in Carrickfergus, county Antrim, son of William Gorman JP, general merchant; educated at RBAI; studied arts and medicine at Queen's College, Belfast, from 1890; MB BCh BAO (RUI) 1896; DPH (Camb) 1904; resident medical officer to the Northern Dispensary, Liverpool; resident surgical officer to the Birmingham Infirmary and resident medical officer to the Birmingham Fever Hospital; medical officer of health to the Perry Barr Urban District Council, of 'Tara', 51 Rookery Road, Handsworth, Birmingham; retired c 1938 to 'The Cedars', 40 Englestede Close, Handsworth Wood; married Gertrude —; died 11 August 1944; probate Birmingham 14 November 1944. [*BMJ* obituary (1944); Kirkpatrick Archive; Lond PPR, will cal; *Med Dir*; QCB adm reg].

GORMAN, JOHN (1866–1913), Manchester, Lancashire, and Bangor, county Down;
> born 15 December 1866 at the Maze, Lisburn, county Down, son of Philip Gorman, farmer, of the Maze; educated at Bangor Endowed School; studied medicine at Queen's College, Belfast, from 1890, and the Royal College of Surgeons in Ireland; LRCP LRCS Edin 1894; LFPS Glas 1894; general practitioner, of Manchester for 18 months; honorary physician to the Home of Rest, Bangor c 1896–1913; of 'Vanessa', Queen's Parade, Bangor; married 2 September 1896 in Ballyclare Methodist Church, Mary Lennon Vance, daughter of William Vance, auctioneer, of Riverside, Antrim; died 27 December 1913 at 'Vanessa'; probate Belfast 6 February 1914. [Belf PRO, will cal; Dub GRO (m) and (d); Kirkpatrick Archive; *Med Dir*; QCB adm reg; UHF database (m)].

GORMAN, PATRICK (1854/5–81), Carrickmacross, county Monaghan;
> born 1854/5; studied medicine at the Ledwich School, Dublin; LRCSI 1875; LAH Dub 1876; of Ardee, county Louth; medical officer to Raferagh Dispensary District and general practitioner, of Carrickmacross; married —; died 14 March 1881 at Mullacraghery. [Dub GRO (d); *Med Dir*].

GORMAN, THOMAS (1863–93), Carrickfergus, county Antrim;
> born 5 May 1863 in Carrickfergus, eldest son of William Gorman of Carrickfergus, merchant, and Margaret —; educated at Belfast Mercantile Academy; studied arts and medicine at Queen's College, Belfast, from 1883; BA (RUI) 1885; MB BCh BAO 1886; general practitioner in Carrickfergus; unmarried; died 9 March 1893 of typhoid fever, at Carrickfergus; buried in St Nicholas's churchyard; administration Belfast 26 April 1893. [Belf PRO, will cal; Dub GRO (d); *Med Dir*; QCB adm reg; Rutherford and Clarke, *County Antrim*, vol 3 (1995)].

GOSSELIN, WILLIAM (d c 1898), Cavan and New South Wales;
> MRCSE 1865; LRCP Edin 1866; general practitioner in Cavan c 1870; emigrated to New South Wales as general practitioner c 1880; died c 1898. [*Med Dir*].

GOUDY, ROBERT (1797/8–1837), Comber, county Down;
> born 1797/8, son of John Goudy and Elizabeth Stewart; surgeon, of Comber; died 8 April 1837 'of fever caught in the practice of his profession'; 'eminently successful

in surgical operations as well as in general practice ... the poor man's friend'; buried in Movilla Graveyard, Newtownards. [*BNL* 14 April 1837 (d); Clarke, *County Down*, vol 11 (1974)].

GOURLEY, SAMUEL (1841–1900), West Hartlepool, county Durham;
born 29 May 1841 at Shannon, Ballindrait, county Donegal, son of Samuel Gourley of Shannon; educated at Patterson's Academy, Strabane; studied medicine at Glasgow University 1860–62 and Queen's College, Belfast, 1862–3; LRCS Edin 1863; MD (Glas) 1864; LSA Lond 1865; LM RCSE 1865; LRCP Edin 1866; FRCS Edin 1873; general practitioner of West Hartlepool from c 1866; surgeon to Hartlepool Hospital and West Hartlepool Dockyard; medical officer and public vaccinator to Stranton District; assistant surgeon to the 4th Durham Artillery Volunteers; JP; married Sarah —; died 10 February 1900; probate Wakefield 18 July 1900. [Addison (1898); Lond PPR, will cal; *Med Dir*; QCB adm reg].

GOURLEY, WILLIAM (*fl c* 1795), Banbridge, county Down;
LAH Dub 1795; apothecary, of Banbridge. [Apothecaries (1829)].

GOWDY, JOHN (1761/2–1820), Castlewellan, county Down;
born 1761/2; surgeon, of Castlewellan; married Margaret Hodges of Castlewellan (who was born 1762/3 and died 24 December 1809); died 19 May 1820; buried in Kilmegan Graveyard, county Down. [Clarke, *County Down*, vol 9 (1972); *Memorials of the Dead*, vol III, p 430].

GOWDY, ROBERT (*fl c* 1824), Larne, county Antrim;
apothecary, of Larne c 1824. [Pigot (1824)].

GOWDY, WILLIAM HENRY (1797/8–1826), Castlewellan, county Down, and New Brunswick, Canada;
born 1797/8; surgeon and apothecary, of Castlewellan c 1824; emigrated to Canada; died 4 August 1826 at Magaugadrie [?], New Brunswick. [*BNL* 24 November 1826 (d); Pigot (1824)].

GRACEY, ALEXANDER LESLIE (1824–86), Crimea, and Tynemouth and Berwick-upon-Tweed, Northumberland;
born 30 August 1824 at 26 Molesworth Street, Dublin, son of James Gracey, solicitor, of Downpatrick, and Mary Leslie of Drogheda; educated in Downpatrick and by the Rev John Hassun of Swords; studied arts at Trinity College, Dublin, 1840–44; travelled in Europe with his father because of illness 1844–51; studied medicine at Edinburgh University 1851–1 winning many medals and prizes; LRCS Edin 1855; MD (Edin) 1856 (thesis 'On infanticide'); BA MA (TCD) 1858; surgeon with the Turkish and British army during the Crimean War 1855–6; returned to Edinburgh 1856 to complete his medical education; general practitioner in Tynemouth, Northumberland; surgeon to the 3rd brigade, Northern Division, Royal Artillery; unmarried; died 29 January 1886 at Verandah Terrace, 20 Church Street, Berwick-upon-Tweed; buried at Lindisfarne Priory, Holy Island, off the Northumbrian Coast; probate Newcastle-upon-Tyne 16 March 1886. [*Blackwood Pedigrees*, vol 11;

Burtchaell and Sadleir (1924); Clarke (2001); Down County Museum, unpublished papers and objects; Leslie and Swanzy (1936); Lond GRO (d); Lond PPR, will cal, will; *Med Dir*].

GRAHAM, BAPTIST GAMBLE (1838/9–1910), Kesh and Irvinestown, county Fermanagh;

born 1838/9; studied medicine at the Ledwich School and the Coombe and Mercer's Hospitals, Dublin; LM 1857; MRCSE 1858; resident accoucheur at the Coombe Hospital, Dublin; medical officer to Tempo Dispensary District, Enniskillen, and surgeon to Vaughan's Charity; medical officer to Ederney, and Irvinestown Dispensary Districts, Workhouse and constabulary, and medical officer of health to Irivinestown Union, of Eglinton Lodge, Irvinestown; married 6 August 1869 at Trory Church of Ireland Church, county Fermanagh, Anne Armstrong, second daughter of William Armstrong of Ballycassidy; died 27 November 1910 at Eglinton Lodge; probate Dublin 26 January 1911. [Belf PRO, will cal; *Londonderry Sentinel* 13 August 1869 (m); *Med Dir*].

GRAHAM, GEORGE (1875–1907), Preston, Lancashire, Godalming, Surrey, and Orange River Colony, South Africa;

born 18 October 1875 at Lagan Farm, Warrenpoint, county Down, son of Archibald Graham, farmer, of Warrenpoint, and Margaret Lindsay; educated at Clonallon Institution, Warrenpoint and Methodist College, Belfast, from 1889; studied medicine at Queen's College, Galway, from 1893 and at Queen's College, Belfast, from 1899; MB BCh BAO (RUI) 1900; general practitioner, of The Hollies, Walton-le-Dale, Preston, from c 1901 and later Godalming; emigrated to South Africa; general practitioner, of Trompsburg, Orange River Colony; died 1907. [Dub GRO (b); Fry (1984); *Med Dir*; QCB adm reg].

GRAHAM, HUGH McCLELLAND (1819/20–43), Armoy, county Antrim, and Nigeria;

born 1819/20, son of the Rev Jackson Graham, minister of Armoy Presbyterian Church, and Catherine —; MRCSE; died 10 October 1843 of fever, on the ship *James Dean* in Bonny River, Nigeria; commemorated in Armoy Presbyterian Graveyard. [*BNL* 6 February 1844 (d); gravestone inscription; McConnell (1951)].

GRAHAM, JAMES (*fl c* 1814), Broomhill, county Cavan;
LAH Dub 1814; apothecary, of Broomhill. [Apothecaries (1829)].

GRAHAM, JAMES (1797–1857), Indian Medical Service;

born 28 January 1797 [?] youngest son (16th child) of William Graham of Lisnastrean, county Down, and Phoebe Norwood; studied medicine at Edinburgh University; MD (Edin) 1819 (thesis 'De ophthalmia membranarum'); joined the East India Company (Bengal establishment), as assistant surgeon 1820; surgeon 1830; senior surgeon 1850; superintendent surgeon 1853; served in Gwalior 1843–4 (medal with clasp), and in the battles of Sobraon and Firozepore, 1846, also in the Second Sikh War 1848, including the siege of Multan; married 24 February 1825 Sarah Casement, nee Chadwick (who was born 17 March 1804 in county Tipperary and died 29 October 1838 at Cawnpore), widow of Major George Casement; shot by a mutineer, in Sialkot, near Lahore, when out driving with his daughter and died 9 July 1857; buried, with a memorial tomb, in Sialkot; probate London 5 June 1858. [*BNL* 12 February 1839 (d); Belf PRO D/812/121; Crawford (1930); Edin Univ; Harrison (1980); Lond PPR, will cal].

GRAHAM, JAMES (1852–1932), Belfast, county Antrim;
born 30 April 1852 at Boardmills, county Down, son of Joseph Graham of Boardmills; educated at RBAI; studied medicine at Queen's College, Belfast, from 1867, and the Belfast General Hospital; MD MCh Dip Mid (QUI) 1872; medical officer to the Jacksonian Almshouse, Aughnacloy, 1872; medical officer to Killough Dispensary District, public vaccinator and registrar of births and deaths from 1876; general practitioner, of 150 Donegal Pass, Belfast c 1885, of 12 University Square and of 1 Liscard Terrace, Ormeau Road, Belfast, from c 1890; surgeon to the Ulster Hospital for Children; member of the Lagan Pollution Committee from 1885 and alderman of the Belfast City Council from 1888; claimed to be the first medical man in Belfast to use carbolic acid as an antiseptic (having obtained supplies from Edinburgh); president of the Ulster Medical Society 1899–1900; coroner for Belfast c 1905; of 30 University Road, Belfast, and Benowin, Helen's Bay, county Down; responsible for the purchase of the Batt estate at Purdysburn, for fever and mental hospitals; presented with a Daimler car in 1910; JP; married —; died 15 June 1932 at 30 University Road; probate Belfast 27 September 1932. [Belf PRO, will cal; Hunter (1936); Kirkpatrick Archive; *Lancet* obituary (1932); Lowry (1933); *Med Dir*; QCB adm reg; Strain (1967)].

GRAHAM, JAMES (1864–1918), Brighouse, Yorkshire;
born 9 December 1864 at Glenwherry, county Antrim, son of William Mackey Graham, farmer, and Sarah Calwell; educated at Belfast Mercantile Academy; studied medicine at Queen's College, Belfast, from 1885; MB BCh BAO (RUI) 1894; general practitioner, of 1 High Street, Brighouse, from c 1900; married Mary Hannah —; died 7 July 1918 at 1 High Street of influenza and pneumonia; probate London 12 October 1918. [Lond GRO (d); Lond PPR, will cal; *Med Dir*; QCB adm reg].

GRAHAM, JOHN (1783–1862), Army Medical Service;
born January 1783; of Coleraine, county Londonderry; joined the Army Medical Service as hospital mate; apothecary 1809; served in the Peninsula War; MD Marischal College, Aberdeen 1815; retired on half pay 1816; physician to His Majesty's Forces in the West Indies; retired as apothecary to the Forces to King's Gate, Coleraine c 1824; later of Seville House, Tulse Hill, Lower Norwood, London; unmarried; died 17 December 1862 at Seville House; probate London 31 January 1863. [*Coleraine Chronicle* 17 December 1862 (d); Lond PPR, will cal; Peterkin and Johnston (1968); Pigot (1824)].

GRAHAM, JOHN (1828/9–62), Templepatrick, county Antrim;
born 1828/9, son of John Graham of Cargycroy, county Down; studied medicine at Edinburgh University; MD (Edin) 1852 (thesis 'On puerperal fever'); LRCS Edin

1852; medical officer to Templepatrick Dispensary District and constabulary; married Elizabeth Stavely — (who was born 1795/6 and died 9 June 1880); died 30 May 1862 at Templepatrick; probate Belfast 17 June 1862; . [Belf PRO, will cal; Clarke, *County Down*, vol 2 (1988); Edin Univ; Kirkpatrick Archive; *Med Dir*].

GRAHAM, JOHN BASS (1862–c 1905), Balmain, New South Wales;
born 13 January 1862 at Omagh, county Tyrone, son of Andrew Graham, pawnbroker, of 16 George's Street, Omagh; educated at Omagh Model School; studied medicine at Queen's College, Belfast, from 1877; MD MCh Dip Mid (RUI) 1883; emigrated to Australia c 1885; general practitioner, of Riverview, Balmain, c 1895; died c 1905. [*Med Dir*; QCB adm reg].

GRAHAM, JOHN CAMPBELL (1856–1932), Deli, Sumatra;
born 25 April 1856 in Bonn, Germany, son of the Rev William Graham, Presbyterian missionary to the Jews in Bonn; educated at the Gymnasium, Bonn; studied arts and medicine at Queen's College, Belfast, from 1875; BA (QUI) 1877; MA 1878; LRCS LRCP Edin 1880; MD (Bonn) 1881; FRCS Edin 1889; surgeon to the Deli-Maatshappij Hospital, Timbang Langkat, with the Langhat Plantation Company, Deli, Sumatra, c 1885–1920; retired c 1920 to St Agnes, Bishopstoke, Hampshire; died 17 May 1932 at the Old Manor, Salisbury; probate London 9 August 1932. [Lond PPR, will cal; McConnell (1951); *Med Dir*; QCB adm reg]

GRAHAM, JOHN SAUNDERS (1859/60–90), Ballysillan, county Antrim;
born 1859/60, son of Samuel Graham, farmer, of Carnaughlis, Dundrod, county Antrim, and Elizabeth Saunders; brother of Dr Samuel Graham (*q.v.*) and Dr William Graham (*q.v.*) of Armagh Asylum; educated at Belfast Academy; studied medicine at Queen's College, Galway 1878–9 and Queen's College, Belfast, from 1879; MD (RUI) 1882; LRCP LRCS Edin 1882; general practitioner, of Ballysillan; unmarried; died 16 October 1890; buried in Dundrod Presbyterian graveyard. [Dub GRO (d); gravestone inscription; *Med Dir*; QCB adm reg].

GRAHAM, JOSEPH (1856–c 1890), Blaenavon, Monmouthshire, Liverpool, Lancashire, and Devonport, Devonshire;
born 26 October 1856 at Cookstown, county Tyrone, son of Charles Graham, merchant, of Cookstown; educated at the French College, Blackrock, Dublin; studied medicine at Queen's College, Galway, and from 1875, at Queen's College, Belfast; LRCP LRCS Edin 1882; senior assistant surgeon to Blaenavon Steel Company c 1885; general practitioner, of 137 Park Street, Liverpool c 1886 and of 2 Trafalgar Place, Devonport c 1888; died c 1890. [*Med Dir*; QCB adm reg].

GRAHAM, JOSIAS (*fl c* 1796), county Antrim;
LAH Dub 1796; apothecary, of Glennohinney [?], county Antrim. [Apothecaries (1829)].

GRAHAM, ROBERT (d 1825), Army Medical Service;
son of Ezekiel Graham of Londonderry; joined the Army Medical Service as hospital mate; assistant surgeon with the 4th West India Regiment 1811 and 15th Foot 1813;

unmarried; died 24 March 1825 in Londonderry, 'snatched away by an excruciating disease'. [*BNL* 5 April 1825 (d); Peterkin and Johnston (1968)].

GRAHAM, ROBERT ALISTER LITTLE (1875–1907), Belfast;
born 29 March 1875 at Lisbellaw, county Fermanagh, eldest son of the Rev Thomas Saunders Graham, minister of Comber Presbyterian Church, and — Alister of Lisburn; nephew of Dr John Saunders Graham (*q.v.*), Dr Samuel Graham (*q.v.*) and Dr William Graham (*q.v.*); educated at RBAI; studied arts and medicine at Queen's College, Belfast, from 1892 and at London and Freiburg; BA (RUI) 1896; MB BCh BAO 1898; Dip Ment Dis 1899; Stewart Scholar in Mental Diseases 1900; assistant medical officer to the District Lunatic Asylum, Belfast, and demonstrator in pathological neurology at Queen's College, Belfast; assistant medical superintendent of Belfast District Lunatic Asylum; unmarried; died 13 February 1907 at the District Lunatic Asylum, of typhoid fever; buried in Dundrod Presbyterian graveyard; administration Belfast 20 March 1907. [Barkley (1986); Belf PRO, will cal; Dub GRO (d); gravestone inscription; Kirkpatrick Archive; *Med Dir*; QCB adm reg].

GRAHAM, SAMUEL (1858–1944), Belfast and Antrim;
born 1858, son of Samuel Graham, farmer, of Carnaughlis, Dundrod, county Antrim, and Elizabeth Saunders; brother of Dr John Saunders Graham (*q.v.*) and Dr William Graham (*q.v.*); studied medicine at Queen's College, Belfast, from 1878; LRCP Lond 1883; resident medical officer to Purdysburn Asylum, Belfast; assistant resident medical superintendent, Antrim Asylum, Holywell, 1887–98; resident medical superintendent 1898–1930; resigned 1930; lived latterly at Harristown House, Brannockstown, county Kildare; married 6 April 1903 at Mount Vernon, Shankill, Belfast, Jessie Lawther, daughter of Samuel Lawther, merchant, of Mount Vernon; died 28 February 1944 at Harristown House; buried in Dundrod Presbyterian graveyard; probate Belfast 9 January 1945. [Belf PRO, will cal; Dub GRO (m) and (d); *Med Dir*; Mulholland (1998); QCB adm reg; UHF database (m)].

GRAHAM, THOMAS (*fl c* 1819), Kilkeel, county Down;
surgeon, of Kilkeel c 1819. [Bradshaw (1819)].

GRAHAM, THOMAS HENRY (1796–1841), Indian Medical Service;
born January 1796, son of William Graham of Londonderry; MRCS 1816; travelled to India as surgeon on a free trader; joined the Indian Medical Service (Bombay establishment) as acting assistant surgeon 1823; confirmed 1824; surgeon 1838; married —; daughter born 21 April 1849 in Londonderry; died 9 July 1841 in Kingstown, county Dublin. [*BNL* 29 April 1840 (b, daughter) and 16 July 1841 (d); Crawford (1930)].

GRAHAM, WILLIAM (1809/10–61), Naval Medical Service;
born 1809/10, son of Thomas Graham of Rash, and Elizabeth —; MRCSE 1830; MD (Aber) 1851; LSA Lond 1853; joined the Naval Medical Service as assistant surgeon on HMS *Victory* 1832; on HMS *Raven* 1832–3; on HMS *Andromache* 1833–7; on HMS *Tartarus* 1837–9; on HMS *Seringapatan* 1839; HMS *Dee* 1839–

40; on HMS *Semiramis* 1840–42; surgeon 1841; on HMS *Apollo* 1842–9 (and HMS *Euryalus*, a convict ship to Gibraltar 1847); on HMS *Vengance* 1849–55 (including Crimean War); staff surgeon and principal naval medical storekeeper and examiner at the Royal Victoria Yard, Deptford, Kent 1855–61; awarded the Order of the Medjidie, 5th class 1858; retired to Omagh, county Tyrone c 1860; died 17 December 1861 at Omagh; buried in Cappagh Church of Ireland Graveyard; probate Dublin 22 March 1862. [Belf PRO, will cal; *Coleraine Chronicle* 21 December 1861 (d); Johnston, Margaret, pers com; Kirkpatrick Archive; *Londonderry Sentinel* 20 December 1861 (d); McGrew (1998) and (2001); *Med Dir*].

GRAHAM, WILLIAM,(1854–1906) Middleton, Manchester;
born 20 May 1854 at Drumbo, county Down, son of John Graham of Drumbo; educated at 'Belfast New Academy'; studied medicine at Queen's College, Belfast, from 1869; MD (QUI) 1874; MCh (RUI) 1883; Dip San Sci (Vict) 1890; medical officer of health for Middleton; general practitioner, of 54 Springvale, Tonge, Middleton; JP for Middleton; author of various medical papers; married Elizabeth —; died 4 January 1906; probate Manchester 8 March 1906. [Lond PPR, will cal; *Med Dir*; QCB adm reg].

GRAHAM, WILLIAM (1859–1917), Belfast and Armagh;
born 1859, son of Samuel Graham, farmer, of Carnaughlis, Dundrod, county Antrim, and Elizabeth Saunders; brother of Dr John Saunders Graham (*q.v.*) and Dr Samuel Graham (*q.v.*); educated privately; studied medicine at Queen's College, Belfast, from 1878; MD (RUI) 1882; LRCS Edin 1883; assistant medical superintendent of Belfast Lunatic Asylum, 1883–4; resident medical superintendent of Armagh Asylum 1884–96; resident medical superintendent of Belfast Lunatic Asylum 1896–1917 and managed the move from Grosvenor Road to Purdysburn; author of many medical papers; married 16 April 1888 Stella Catherine Dawson, eldest daughter of Robert Edward Dawson; died 5 November 1917 at Purdysburn House, following a fractured femur; buried in Dundrod Presbyterian graveyard; probate Belfast 18 February 1918. [Belf PRO, will cal; *BMJ* obituary (1917); Dub GRO (d); gravestone inscription; *Med Dir*; QCB adm reg].

GRAHAM, WILLIAM CALWELL (1859–90), Belfast;
born 25 May 1859 at Glenwherry, county Antrim, son of William M. Graham, farmer, of Glenwherry; educated at Great George's Street Academy, Belfast; studied medicine at Queen's College, Belfast, from 1878 and at Edinburgh; LRCP LRCS Edin 1886; general practitioner, of 64 Shankill Road, Belfast; unmarried; died 10 December 1890 at 64 Shankill Road. [Dub GRO (d); *Med Dir*; QCB adm reg].

GRAHAM, — (1772/3–1831), Magherafelt, county Londonderry;
born 1772/3; general practitioner, of Magherafelt; married — (who died 7 March 1818); father of Margaret Graham, who married Dr William Shannon of Magherafelt (*q.v.*); died 30 March 1831 'after a protracted illness'. [*BNL* 13 March 1818 (d), 13 April 1827 (m) and 5 April 1831 (d); *Londonderry Sentinel* 18 April 1831 (d)].

GRAHAM, — (1828/9–46), Dromore, county Tyrone;
born 1828/9, youngest son of Richard Graham of Rahony, Dromore, county Tyrone; 'doctor' [?]; died 3 September 1846 'after a long and protracted illness'. [*Londonderry Sentinel* 12 September 1846 (d)].

GRAHAME, ALEXANDER (1873–c 1913), Robben Island, Cape Colony;
born 9 June 1873 at Belfast, son of Jackson H. Graham, linen merchant, of Derryvolgie Avenue, Belfast; educated at Methodist College, Belfast, from 1883; studied medicine at Queen's College, Belfast, from 1891; MB BCh BAO (RUI) 1898; medical officer to Robben Island, Cape Colony, South Africa, from c 1903; died c 1913. [Fry (1984); *Med Dir*; QCB adm reg].

GRAINGER, THOMAS (1862–1931), Indian Medical Service;
born 25 December 1862, of Ballyoran, Dundonald, county Down, younger son of Robert Grainger, farmer, of Dundonald; studied medicine at Queen's College, Belfast, from 1880; Coulter Exhibition, Belfast Royal Hospital, 1884; MD (hons) MCh BAO (RUI) 1884; MAO 1885; joined the Indian Medical Service (Bengal establishment) as surgeon 1885; surgeon major 1897; surgeon lieutenant-colonel 1898; surgeon colonel 1909; CB 1911; surgeon general 1914; served on North East Frontier, Sikhim 1888, forcing of Jelapah Pass (medal with clasp); North West Frontier, Hazara 1891 (clasp); Tirah 1897–8; civil surgeon in Bengal and, for 10 years in Murshidabad; honorary surgeon to the King 1915; retired to 6 Pall Mall, Westminster, London 1917; unmarried; died 21 September 1931 at the Bolingbroke Hospital, London; buried in Dundonald Graveyard, Belfast; probate London 19 January 1932. [*Belf Roy Hosp, Ann Rep*; *BMJ* obituary (1931); Clarke, *County Down*, vol 2 (2nd ed, 1988); Crawford (1930); Kirkpatrick Archive; Lond PPR, will cal, will; *Med Dir*; QCB adm reg].

GRANT, EUGENE (1869/70–1914), Newry, county Down, and London;
born 1869/70; studied medicine at King's College, London; LRCP LRCS Edin 1898; LFPS Glas 1898; LM Coombe Hosp Dub 1898; medical officer to Newry No 2 Dispensary District and constabulary, and medical officer of health and public vaccinator, of 15 Trevor Hill, Newry; general practitioner of 24 Skinner Street, London c 1911–13 and then of 116 Farringdon Road; member of Lincoln's Inn c 1912; married Anne —; died 30 March 1914 at 116 Farringdon Road; administration London 15 April 1915 and 19 December 1915. [Lond GRO (d); Lond PPR, will cal; *Med Dir*].

GRANT, MAXIMILIAN (1833–83), Army Medical Service;
born 25 March 1833 at Armagh; studied medicine at Edinburgh University; MD (Edin) 1855 (thesis 'On aneurysm and its varieties'); LRCS Edin 1855; joined the Army Medical Service as staff assistant surgeon, attached to the 5th Foot 1857; transferred to the 18th Dragoons 1858; staff surgeon 1860; transferred to 2nd Life Guards 1863 and to the 9th Lancers 1867; staff surgeon (surgeon major) and transferred to the 7th Hussars in 1871; served in the Indian Mutiny 1857; died 24

August 1883 at Kuldanah, Manree, Bengal; probate London 8 March 1884 and November 1884. [Edin Univ; Lond PPR, will cal; *Med Dir*; Peterkin and Johnston (1968)].

GRATTAN, COPELAND (*fl c* 1824), Carrickmacross, county Monaghan;
studied medicine at Edinburgh University; MD (Edin) 1820 (thesis 'De ophthalmia'); surgeon to Carrickmacross Dispensary c 1824. [Edin Univ; Pigot (1824)].

GRATTAN, EDWARD SHAWE (1840/1–74), Liverpool, Lancashire;
born 1840/1, son of Thomas Grattan of 11 College Square East, Belfast; brother of Dr John Smith Grattan (*q.v.*); educated at RBAI; studied medicine at Queen's College, Belfast, from 1856; LM (QCB) 1861; MRCSE 1863; assistant surgeon to the Borough Gaol, Walton-on-the-Hill, Liverpool, after his brother; married Mary —; died 8 July 1874 of phthisis, at Bangor, county Down; probate Liverpool 11 August 1874. [Dub GRO (d); Lond PPR, will cal; *Med Dir*; QCB adm reg].

GRATTAN, JOHN (1800–71), Belfast;
born 1800 in Dublin; studied at the Apothecaries' Hall, Dublin; LAH Dub 1823; moved to Belfast in 1825 and founded the firm of Grattan and Company's Medical Hall, 10 and 12 Corn Market, Belfast; began manufacturing mineral waters at 68 Great Victoria Street in 1828, with the Company's own well on the premises; one of those who presented an inscribed gold box to Dr S.S. Thomson in 1834; president of the Belfast Literary Society 1843–4; author of papers on craniology and on Irish round towers; of Coolgreaney, Fortwilliam Park, Belfast; married Mary Shawe (who was born 1826/7 and died 24 November 1898); died 24 April 1871 at Coolgreaney; both were buried in Clifton Street Graveyard, Belfast; probate Belfast 21 July 1871. [*Belf Lit Soc* (1901); Belf PRO, will cal; Croly (1843–6); Deane (1921); *DIB* (2009); *Industries of the North* (1986); Merrick and Clarke, *Belfast*, vol 4 (1991); Symington (1903); Thomson presentation box (1834)].

GRATTAN, JOHN SMITH (1834–c 1881), Liverpool, Lancashire;
born 1834, son of Thomas Grattan of 11 College Square East, Belfast; brother of Dr Edward Shawe Grattan (*q.v.*); educated by Mr Liston of Armagh; studied medicine at Queen's College, Belfast, from 1849; MRCSE 1857; LKQCPI and LM 1860; assistant surgeon to Liverpool Borough Gaol; medical officer to Walton-on-the-Hill District, Liverpool, of Walton-on-the-Hill and of Mill Road, Everton c 1860–77; of 39 King Street, Belfast, 1877–8 and of Liverpool 1878–81; died c 1881. [*Med Dir*; QCB adm reg].

GRATTAN, THOMAS (c 1808–79), Belfast;
LM Coombe Hosp Dub 1831; LAH Dub 1832; practised as a dentist in 11 College Square East, Belfast; apothecary and dentist, of Scotch Street, Armagh c 1846, of 11 College Square East, Belfast c 1860 and later of 39 King Street, Belfast; died 21 February 1879 at Firmount, Belfast; probate Belfast 21 March 1879. [Belf PRO, will cal; Croly (1843–6); *Med Dir*].

GRAVES, CHARLES HENRY PHILIP DAMPIER (1859–1934), Cookstown, county Tyrone;
    born 20 June 1859 at Cookstown, county Tyrone, son of Dr Henry Graves of Cookstown (*q.v.*); educated at Newport Grammar School, Shropshire; studied medicine at Queen's College, Belfast, from 1878, and the Carmichael School, Dublin; LKQCPI and LM 1883; LRCSI 1883; MD MCh (RUI) 1884; clinical resident of the Richmond, Whitworth and Hardwick Hospitals, Dublin; medical officer and medical officer of health to Cookstown Workhouse Infirmary and Fever Hospital, medical officer to the constabulary and certifying factory surgeon, of Gortaleagh, Cookstown; retired c 1920; married 6 October 1884 in St James's Church of Ireland Church, Belfast, Eleanor Josephine Constance Purdon, daughter of Dr Charles Purdon (*q.v.*) of Belfast; died 6 August 1934 at the Royal Victoria Hospital; probate Belfast 7 December 1934. [Belf GRO (d); Belf, PRO, will cal; Martin (2003); *Med Dir*; QCB adm reg; UHF database (m)].

GRAVES, GEORGE HENRY FULLARTON (1876–c 1938), London and South Africa;
    born 7 July 1876 at Mani Tal, India, son of surgeon colonel William Graves, AMS; educated at Central Hill College, Upper Norwood, London; studied medicine at Glasgow University and from 1897, at Queen's College, Belfast; LRCP LRCS Edin 1900; LFPS Glas 1900; junior medical officer to the Scottish National Red Cross Hospital, Kroonsted, South Africa, 1900; surgeon with various steamship companies; of 4 Edith Road, West Kensington, London, c 1910, but travelling extensively from this time; temporary captain in RAMC during World War I; address given as St Serf's, Main Road, Dieppe River, Cape Province; died c 1938. [*Med Dir*; Peterkin and Johnston (1968); QCB adm reg].

GRAVES, HENRY (1820/1–93), Castledawson, county Londonderry, and Cookstown, county Tyrone;
    born 1820/1 in Kent, youngest son of Captain Thomas Graves, RN; educated at Dungannon Royal School; studied arts and medicine at Trinity College, Dublin, from 1837; BA (TCD) 1842; LRCSI FRCSI 1844; MB 1846; LM Rot Hosp Dub 1846; general practitioner in Castledawson c 1846; medical officer to Cookstown Dispensary from c 1850, of Joy Hill, Cookstown; married 7 December 1847 in St George's Church, Newcastle, Staffordshire, Mary Lee Dyer, only child of Charles Dyer, esquire, of Wootton-under-Edge, Gloucestershire; father of Dr Charles Henry Philip Dampier Graves (*q.v.*); died 25 January 1893 at Cookstown; administration Armagh 31 May 1893. [Belf PRO, will cal; Burtchaell and Sadleir (1924); *Coleraine Chronicle* 24 December 1847 (m); Croly (1843–6); Dub GRO (d); Kirkpatrick Archive; *Londonderry Sentinel* 18 December 1847 (m); Martin (2003); *Med Dir*].

GRAVES, ROBERT JAMES (1796–1853), Dublin;
    born 28 March 1796 in Dublin, fourth son of the Rev Richard Graves, Professor of Divinity at Trinity College, Dublin, and Dean of Ardagh, and Elizabeth Mary Drought; educated at Downpatrick Diocesan School, county Down, and by the Rev Ralph Wilde and Dr Leney of Blackrock; studied arts and medicine at Trinity College, Dublin, 1811–18; BA (TCD) (with gold medal) 1815; MB 1818; LRCP 1820;

FKQCPI 1827; MD 1841; visited medical schools in Denmark, Germany, France and Italy; went on grand tour of Europe in 1818 and met the painter W.M. Turner who became a close friend; physician to the Meath Hospital 1821; practised during the famine of 1822 and wrote *Report on The Famine Lately Present in Galway*; founded school of medicine in Park Street, Dublin and was involved in the building of Sir Patrick Dun's Hospital; King's Professor of the Institutes of Medicine, Trinity College, Dublin 1827–41; of 4 Merrion Square South, Dublin; edited *Dublin Journal of Medical and Chemical Science* and was author of *Rambles in Europe in 1839* (1841), *A System of Clinical Medicine* (1843) and many papers, including one on exophthalmic goitre – Graves' Disease; was the first person to describe peripheral neuritis; changed the whole pattern of bedside teaching in Dublin; president of the King's and Queen's College of Physicians in 1843–4; FRS 1849 and MRIA; married (1) December 1821 Matilda Jane Eustace (who died in 1825); (2) 1826 Sarah Jane Brinkley (who died in 1827), daughter of the Rev John Brinkley, Bishop of Cloyne; (3) 1830 Anna Grogan, daughter of the Reverend William Grogan of Slaney Park, Baltinglass; died 20 March 1853 at Cloghan Castle, Banagher, King's County; buried in Mount Jerome Cemetery, Dublin; commemorated by a statue (1877) by Albert Bruce Joy and bust by John Hogan, both in the RCPI, and by a drawing by Charles Grey in the National Library of Ireland. [*BNL* 25 March 1853 (d); Burke *LGI* (1912); Burtchaell and Sadleir (1924); Cameron (1916); Coakley (1992); Crone (1928); *DIB* (2009); Hunter (1933); Igoe (2001); Kirkpatrick Archive; Lewis (1839); *Londonderry Sentinel* 25 March 1853 (d); Lyons (1978); Martin (2010); *Med Dir*; Newmann (1993); O'Brien, Crookshank and Wolstenholme (1988); Ormsby (1888); *Oxford DNB* (2004); Widdess (1963)].

GRAY, ALEXANDER (*fl c* 1800), Newry, county Down[?];
possibly of Newry; married —; father of Dr Henry Gordon Gray of Newry (*q.v.*). [Dub GRO (m, son)].

GRAY, CHARLES EDWARD (1848–92), Naval Medical Service, Melbourne, Australia, and Brigg, Lincolnshire;
born 2 October 1848 at Glen Anne, Markethill, son of George Gray of Glen Anne; educated at Armagh Royal School 1863–4; studied arts and medicine at Trinity College, Dublin, from 1865; MB MCh LM (TCD) 1869; MD 1875; of Glenanne House, Armagh c 1873; joined the Naval Medical Service as surgeon c 1875; general practitioner, of Albert Park, Melbourne c 1885; married Kathleen Constance —; died 13 July 1892 at Brigg; probate London 30 August 1892. [Ferrar (1933); Lond PPR, will cal; *Med Dir*; TCD adm reg; *TCD Cat*, vol II (1896)].

GRAY, EDWARD WOLFENDEN ALEXANDER (1862–99), Army Medical Service;
born 28 September 1862 in Dublin, son of Dr Henry Gordon Gray (*q.v.*) of Millvale, Newry, county Down; studied arts and medicine at Trinity College, Dublin, from 1880; BA (TCD) 1884; MB BCh BAO 1885; LLB LLD 1896; LKQCPI and LM 1885; LAH Dub 1886; Dip State Med 1887; FRCSI 1888; joined the RAMC as captain 1887; major 1899; served in the Boer War 1899; died 31 October 1899 of wounds at Ladysmith. [Belf PRO, will cal, will (father); *Med Dir*; Peterkin and Johnston (1968); TCD adm reg; *TCD Cat* (1898) and (1906)].

GRAY, GEORGE (1842/3–1903), Castlewellan and Newcastle, county Down;
born 1842/3, son of George Gray of Eden, Newry; educated at Newry School; studied medicine at Queen's College, Belfast, from 1860 and at Belfast General Hospital; Malcolm Exhibition, Belfast General Hospital; MD (hons) MCh (QUI) 1866; LRCS and LM Edin 1866; LAH Dub 1866; general practitioner of Castlewellan, county Down and medical officer to constabulary; JP; moved to Newcastle c 1895; president of the NI Branch of the BMA 1896; author of various medical papers; married 2 August 1873 in Ballinasloe Church of Ireland Church, Jane Adelaide D'arcy, daughter of Thomas Richardson, JP, and widow of Charles Vesey D'arcy, JP, of Bryansford, county Down; died 27 April 1903 at Newcastle, county Down; probate Dublin 4 June 1903. [Belf PRO, will cal; *BMJ* obituary (1903); Dub GRO (m) and (d); Kirkpatrick Archive; *Med Dir*; QCB adm reg].

GRAY, HAMPTON ATKINSON (1868–1942), Armagh;
born 16 August 1868 in Armagh, son of Dr Robert Gray (*q.v.*) of Charlemont Place, The Mall, Armagh; brother of Dr Francis Audubon Gray, LRCP (Edin) 1902, who emigrated to Australia; educated at Armagh Royal School; studied arts and medicine at Trinity College, Dublin, from 1885; BA (TCD) 1891; LM Rot Hosp Dub 1892; MB BCh BAO MD 1893; DPH RCPSI 1901; medical officer and superintendent medical officer of health to Armagh Dispensary District, certifying factory surgeon and medical officer to the constabulary and post office, of 4 Charlemont Place, The Mall, Armagh; author of various medical papers; died 4 March 1942; probate Belfast 19 August 1942. [Belf PRO, will cal; Burke *LGI* (1912); Ferrar (1933); *Med Dir*; TCD adm reg; *TCD Cat*, vol II (1896)].

GRAY, HENRY GORDON (1807/8–94), Newry, county Down;
born 1807/8, son of Dr Alexander Gray (*q.v.*); studied medicine at Trinity College, Dublin, and the Royal College of Surgeons in Ireland; LAH Dub 1832; MRCSE 1834; general practitioner, of Millvale House, Newry, and medical officer to the constabulary c 1846; married (1) 6 April 1833 in Camlough, county Armagh, Mary Donnell of Newry (who died 6 August 1848 at Millvale House); (2) 5 September 1855 in St Peter's Church, Dublin, Anna Maria Wolfenden, youngest daughter of Edward Wolfenden of 40 York Street, Dublin; father of surgeon-captain Edward Wolfenden Alexander Gray (*q.v.*); died 4 April 1894 at Millvale House; probate Armagh 11 June 1894. [*BNL* 16 April 1833 (m), 15 August 1848 (d) and 8 September 1855 (m); Belf PRO, will cal, will; Croly (1843–6); Dub GRO (m) and (d); *Med Dir*].

GRAY, JAMES CAMPBELL (1857–1913), Tetford, Horncastle, Lincolnshire;
born 26 August 1857 at Finvoy, Ballymoney, county Antrim, son of Hugh Gray of Finvoy; educated at RBAI; studied medicine at Queen's College, Belfast, from 1869; LRCP LRCS Edin 1874; medical officer and public vaccinator to Tetford District, of Tetford House; died 9 December 1913; administration Lincoln 8 June 1914. [Lond PPR, will cal; *Med Dir*; QCB adm reg].

GRAY, JOHN (c 1772–1847), Naval Medical Service and Ballynacross, Magherafelt, county Londonderry;
   born c 1772; qualified as surgeon's mate at Royal College of Surgeons of England 1796 and joined the Naval Medical Service as assistant surgeon 1796–1801; served on HMS *Dolphin* 1796–7; full surgeon 1801; served throughout the Napoleonic Wars on HMS *Scourge*, HMS *Anacreon*, HMS *La Sophie*, HMS *Revolutionnaire*, HMS *Entreprenante,* HMS *Alfred* and at the capture of USS *Majestic* in 1812; studied medicine at Edinburgh University; MD (Edin) 1816 (thesis 'De dysenteria'); retired as physician and surgeon to Ballynacross; died 10 January 1847; probate Prerogative Court 1847. [Belf PRO, prerog wills index; Bodkin, A., pers com; Edin Univ; *NMS* (1826)].

GRAY, JOHN (1851/2–1913), Shrewsbury, Shropshire;
   born 1851/2; LRCSI 1875; LAH Dub 1875; house surgeon to Bridgnorth Infirmary; medical officer to Shrewsbury Dispensary and prison; of 2 Belmont, Shrewsbury c 1885 and of 36 Murivance, Shrewsbury c 1895; anaesthetist to the Eye, Ear and Throat Hospital, Shrewsbury; lived finally at 202 Cliftonville Road, Belfast; unmarried; died 7 December 1913; buried in Belfast City Cemetery; probate Belfast 16 March 1914. [Belf City Cem, bur reg; Belf PRO, will cal; *Med Dir*].

GRAY, JOHN CAUGHEY (1825–50), Army Medical Service;
   born 3 January 1825 in Belfast, son of John Gray of Belfast and Sarah —; joined the Army Medical Service as assistant surgeon to the 44th Regiment of Foot in 1849; died 14 July 1850 in Malta, of cholera 'brought on by unwearied exertions in the discharge of his duty'; commemorated in Clifton Street Graveyard, Belfast. [*BNL* 9 August 1850 (d); Merrick and Clarke, *Belfast*, vol 4 (1991); Peterkin and Johnston (1968)].

GRAY, MATTHEW DONOGHUE (1856–1939), Drumlish, county Longford;
   born 16 August 1856 at Ballyduffy, county Longford, son of Michael Gray, farmer, of Ballyduffy; educated at Summerhill College, Athlone; studied medicine at Queen's College, Belfast, from 1881 and the Catholic University, Dublin; LRCP LRCS Edin 1887; LFPS Glas 1887; medical officer and medical officer of health for Drumlish Dispensary District; coroner for North Longford from 1893; JP for Drumlish 1909; married —; father of Dr Thomas Gray of Ballinakill, Queen's County, LRCPI LRCSI 1913; died 23 January 1939 at Drumlish; buried at Ballymacormack, county Longford; probate Dublin 21 June 1939. [Dub Nat Arch, will cal; Kirkpatrick Archive; *Med Dir*; QCB adm reg].

GRAY, ROBERT (*fl c* 1823), Markethill, county Armagh;
   LAH Dub 1823; apothecary and surgeon, of Markethill; married 11 June 1831 — Young of Markethill. [Apothecaries (1829); *BNL* 17 June 1831 (m)].

GRAY, ROBERT (1845–1924), Armagh;
   born 18 October 1845 at Markethill, county Armagh, son of Robert Gray of Enagh, county Armagh, and Margaret Gray Patterson; educated at Armagh Royal School 1856–62; studied medicine at the Ledwich School, Dublin; LM Coombe Hosp Dub

1864; LRCSI 1865; LRCP Edin and LM 1867; LAH Dub 1869; LSA Lond 1869; LKQCPI and LM 1873; FRCPI 1895; medical officer from 1872 and medical officer of health to Armagh Dispensary District, of Russell Street, 1 Melbourne Terrace, and later of 4 Charlemont Place, The Mall, Armagh; visiting physician to Course Lodge Asylum; president of Northern Ireland Branch of British Medical Association; president of the Armagh Natural History and Philosophical Society; author of various medical papers; JP; retired 1915; High Sheriff 1915; married 10 July 1867 Harriet Ann Atkinson, daughter of Hampton Atkinson of Lisnadill, county Armagh; father of Dr Hampton Atkinson Gray (*q.v.*) and Dr Francis Audubon Gray, LRCP (Edin) 1902, later of Australia; died 25 April 1924 at 4 Charlemont Place; probate Belfast 28 November 1924. [Belf PRO, will cal; Burke *LGI* (1912); Ferrar (1933); Kirkpatrick Archive; *Med Dir*; Young and Pike (1909)].

GRAY, THOMAS (1875–1967), Tyldesley, Lancashire;
born 26 November 1875 at Ballynacross, Knockloughrim, county Londonderry, son of John Gray, farmer, of Ballynacross; brother of Dr William George Gray (*q.v.*); educated at Rainey School, Magherafelt; studied medicine at Queen's College, Belfast, from 1895; MB BCh BAO (RUI) 1900; civil surgeon to the South African Field Force 1900–02; medical officer and public vaccinator to Leigh Union, Lancashire; medical officer to Leigh Joint Hospitals Board, Astley, and later medical superintendent, of The Thistles, Tyldesley; president of Leigh and District Medical Society; retired c 1950; of the Paddock, Broseley Avenue, Kenyon, Lancashire, from c 1961; married Elizabeth Hope —; died 16 December 1967 at the Paddock; probate Lancaster 6 May 1968. [Lond GRO (d); Lond PPR, will cal, will; *Med Dir*; QCB adm reg].

GRAY, WILLIAM (*fl c* 1803), Dromore, county Down;
LAH Dub 1803; apothecary, of Dromore. [Apothecaries (1829)].

GRAY, WILLIAM (*fl c* 1804), Kennedies, county Armagh;
LAH Dub 1804; apothecary, of Kennedies. [Apothecaries (1829)].

GRAY, WILLIAM (1804–40), Markethill, county Armagh;
born 1804; surgeon, of Markethill; married 24 December 1834 Mary Jane Sinclair (who was born 1817/8 and died 22 September 1843), eldest daughter of Archibald Sinclair of Markethill; died 3 August 1840 at his home in Markethill; administration Armagh Diocesan Court 1840. [*BNL* 2 January 1835 (m), 11 August 1840 (d) and 29 September 1843 (d); Dub Nat Arch, Armagh Dio Admins index; gravestone inscription].

GRAY, WILLIAM GEORGE (1861–1918), Leigh, Lancashire;
born 11 March 1861 at Ballynacross, Knockloughrim, county Londonderry, son of John Gray, farmer, of Ballynacross; brother of Dr Thomas Gray of Tyldesley (*q.v.*); educated privately; studied medicine at Queen's College, Belfast, from 1879; LSA London 1888; general practitioner, of 2 Brown Street, Leigh, Lancashire, from c 1890; retired c 1916 to 7 Balmoral Road, St Anne's-on-Sea, and later to 88 Clyde

Road West, Didsbury, Lancashire; married —; died 25 December 1918 at 88 Clyde Road West; probate London 5 March 1919. [Lond PPR, will cal, will; *Med Dir*; QCB adm reg].

GRAY, — (*fl c* 1663), Dromore, county Down;
physician who attended Hugh, third Viscount Montgomery, during his last illness in Dromore, in 1663; disembowelled and embalmed him prior to his corpse being brought back to Newtownards; his normal place of practise is unclear. [Hill (1869), p 241].

GRAYDON, JAMES ALEXANDER (1849–1921), Limavady, county Londonderry, and London;
born 1849; LFPS Glas 1870; general practitioner in Limavady; surgeon with various shipping companies; moved c 1880 to London; general practitioner of 92 Burdett Road, South Grove, Bow c 1885, of 179 Bow Common Lane c 1900, of 21 South Grove, Bow c 1905 and of 103 Cadogan Terrace, Victoria Park c 1915; married —; died 5 December 1921 at 75a Devons Road, Bromley; administration London 11 January 1922. [Lond GRO (d); Lond PPR, will cal; *Med Dir*].

GRAYDON, JOHN (d c 1790), Cavanagarvan, county Fermanagh;
son of Samuel Graydon and Jane —; studied arts and medicine at Trinity College, Dublin, from 1746; scholar 1750; BA (TCD) 1752; MB 1756; physician, of Cavanagarvan; married Elizabeth Eccles; died c 1790; will dated 9 October 1756 proved in Prerogative Court 6 December 1790. [Belf PRO, Burke's Pedigrees, T559, vol 22, p 166; Burtchaell and Sadleir (1924); Vicars (1897)].

GRAYDON, SAMUEL (b 1730/1), county Fermanagh;
born 1730/1; general practitioner; married 3 July 1819 Christiana Ryan (who was born 1799/1800), only daughter of Richard Ryan of Maguires Bridge, county Fermanagh. [*BNL* 16 July 1819 (m)].

GRAYDON, SAMUEL JOHNSTON (c 1840–1907), Scottstown and Coalisland, county Tyrone, and Withington, Lancashire;
born c 1840, son of the Rev John Martin Graydon, rector of Ematris, county Monaghan, and Sarah —; studied medicine at the Ledwich School, Dublin; LRCSI 1861; MD (St Andrews) 1862 (by examination); LM RCSI 1863; medical officer to Scottstown and Coalisland Dispensaries and constabulary; general practitioner and public vaccinator, of 2 Grosvenor Terrace and Carahor, Withington; died 12 June 1907; probate Winchester 17 July 1907. [Leslie (1929); Lond PPR, will cal; *Med Dir; Memorials of the Dead*, vol XII, p 243; Smart (2004)].

GREEN(E), ARTHUR (b 1658/9), county Down;
born 1658/9 in county Down, son of Brian Green (e); educated by Mr Thomas Haslam; studied arts and medicine at Trinity College, Dublin, from 1676; BA (TCD) 1680; scholar 1681; MB 1684. [Burtchaell and Sadleir (1924)].

GREEN(E), DAVID (d c 1870), Dunkineely, county Donegal;
son of Finlay Green, merchant, of Dunkineely; LRCSI and LM 1859; medical officer to Dunkineely Dispensary District from c 1860; married 5 May 1864 in Manorcunningham Church of Ireland Church, Ellen Greene, eldest daughter of Andrew Greene, editor of *The Herald*, of the Mall, Ballyshannon, county Donegal; died c 1870, probably abroad. [Dub GRO (m); *Londonderry Sentinel* 6 May 1864 (m); *Med Dir*].

GREENE, HENRY BERTRAM BLODWELL (1864–c 1954), Wandsworth, London, and RAF;
born 18 January 1864 at Poona, India, son of William I. Greene, civil engineer, of Poona; educated at Rossall School, Fleetwood, Lancashire; studied medicine at the Royal Colleges of Physicians and Surgeons in Edinburgh, and from 1881, at Queen's College, Belfast; LM Rot Hosp Dub 1884; MRCSE 1887; LKQCPI 1887; moved to London c 1890; medical officer of Emmanuel School and St Peter's Hospital, Wandsworth; general practitioner, of 20 North Street and 307 Trinity Road, Wandsworth Common; temporary lieutenant in RAF during World War I; retired c 1931 to RAF Club, Piccadilly, as honorary squadron leader; surgeon in Merchant Naval Reserve 1941–2; of Moeraki, Esher Road, Walton-on-Thames; died c 1954. [*Med Dir*; QCB adm reg].

GREENE, REGINALD LATIMER WELLINGTON (1852–1934), Stratford-on-Avon, Warwickshire;
born 18 December 1852 at Antrim, son of the Rev William Greene, vicar of Antrim and later of Killead (who emigrated with his family in October 1872 to Staunton, Virginia) and Frances Whitla of Muckamore, county Antrim; educated at Iver Grammar School, Uxbridge, and Methodist College, Belfast 1869–70; studied medicine at Queen's College, Belfast, from 1873; LRCP LRCS Edin 1880; general practitioner, certifying factory surgeon and public vaccinator, of 41 Wood Street, Stratford-on-Avon; medical officer to Stratford-on-Avon Hospital; later of 7 Rother Street, Stratford-on-Avon; married —; died 12 May 1934 at Stratford-upon-Avon; probate Birmingham 11 August 1934. [Fry (1984); Leslie (1993); Lond PPR, will cal, will; *Med Dir*; QCB adm reg].

GREENFIELD, THOMAS KILLIPS (1858–1939), Poole, Dorset, and Holywood, county Down;
born 30 April 1858 at Craigavad, county Down; studied arts and medicine at Queen's College, Belfast from 1890, and Belfast Royal Hospital; MB BCh BAO (RUI) 1898; house physician and surgeon in the Belfast Royal Hospital 1898; general practitioner in Poole, 1899; general practitioner, of 8 High Street, Holywood, from c 1900; retired c 1920, moving to 'Woodleigh', Marino c 1925; died 17 November 1939 at Woodleigh; probate Belfast 30 May 1940. [Belf GRO (d); Belf PRO, will cal; Kirkpatrick Archive; *Med Dir*; QCB adm reg].

GREENFIELD, WILLIAM (c 1832–63), Holywood, county Down;
born c 1832, son of James Greenfield of Holywood and Susan —; educated by the Rev C J McAlister; studied medicine at Queen's College, Belfast, from 1849; MRCSE

1852; MD (QUI) 1852; general practitioner, of Holywood; unmarried; died 9 October 1863 of fever in Holywood; buried in Holywood Graveyard; administration Belfast 19 November 1863. [Belf PRO, will cal; Clarke, *County Down*, vol 4 (1969); Kirkpatrick Archive; *Med Dir*; QCB adm reg].

GREER, ARCHIBALD (1861–1946), Richhill, county Armagh;
born 30 March 1861 at Drummond, county Armagh, son of Robert Greer, farmer, of Drummond; educated at Ballynahinch National School; studied medicine at Queen's College, Belfast, from 1884; LRCP LRCS Edin 1896; LFPS Glas 1896; general practitioner, of Drummond, Richhill, from c 1900; medical officer of health to Richhill Dispensary District; died 10 November 1946; administration Belfast 26 March 1947. [Belf PRO, will cal; *Med Dir*; QCB adm reg].

GREER, ARTHUR JACKSON (1831–87), Army Medical Service;
born 25 April 1831 in county Tyrone, second son of William Jackson Greer of Rhone Hill, county Tyrone, and Margaret Ussher of Camphire, county Waterford; LRCSI 1852; joined the Army Medical Service as staff assistant surgeon in 1852; posted to 21st Foot (Royal Scots Fusiliers) 1852; staff surgeon 1860; transferred to 17th Lancers 1867; surgeon major 1872; retired on half pay with honorary rank of deputy surgeon general 1877; served in Crimea and awarded the Medjidie medal (5th class); honourably mentioned for his services during the attack on the Redan on 18 June 1855; retired to Thornton Lodge, Thornton-le-Beans, Yorkshire; married 17 January 1866 Emma Horsfall (who died 25 February 1802), eldest daughter of William Horsfall of Hornby Grange, Yorkshire; died 3 March 1887 at Thornton Lodge; probate London 11 May 1887. [Burke *LGI* (1912); Lond PPR, will cal; *Med Dir*; Peterkin and Jackson (1968)].

GREER, JOHN (1794/5–1823), Strangford, county Down;
born 1794/5; surgeon, of Strangford; married January 1822 at Seville Lodge, Strandtown, Belfast, Sarah Taylor (who was born 1804/5 and died 26 August 1890; buried in Ballylesson Graveyard), daughter of John Taylor of Knockbracken; died 1 April 1823 in Dublin, of typhus fever; buried in a large vault in Kilclief Graveyard, county Down; 'much lamented by the country and town of his residence, particularly the poor, from whom he never sought any remuneration, in attendance on whom he caught the contagion' (*BNL*); administration Down Diocesan Court 1823. [*BNL* 22 January 1822 (m); Clarke, *County Down*, vol 1, (1866) and vol 8 (1872); Dub Nat Arch, Down admin bonds; Greeves (1973)].

GREER, JOSEPH STIRLING (1860–1919), Crossdoney, county Cavan;
born 11 January 1860 at Mount Macgregor, Hillsborough, county Down, sixth son of the Rev Thomas Greer of Mount Macgregor, minister of Annahilt Presbyterian Church, county Down; brother of Dr Thomas Greer (*q.v.*); educated at RBAI; studied medicine at Queen's College, Belfast, from 1878, also at the Carmichael School, Dublin and the London Hospital; LRCP LRCS Edin 1887; LFPS Glas 1887; medical officer to Bellanagh Dispensary District and constabulary, visitor in Lunacy to Killashandra District and certifying factory surgeon; medical officer of health for Cavan, of The Rocks, Crossdoney; moved c 1906 to 2 Temple Terrace, Rockfort

Avenue, Dalkey; married 20 November 1889 in Kingstown Presbyterian Church, Kathleen (Kate) Geraldine Rodgers, eldest daughter of Henry W. Maxwell Rodgers; died 16 March 1919 at 2 Temple Terrace; probate Dublin 12 August 1919. [Dub GRO (d); Dub Nat Arch, will cal; Greeves (1973); Kirkpatrick Archive; McConnell (1951); *Med Dir*; QCB adm reg].

GREER, THOMAS (1847–1904), Cambridge;
born 1 April 1847 at Mount Magregor, Hillsborough, county Down, eldest son of the Rev Thomas Greer, of Mount Magregor, minister of Anahilt Presbyterian Church, county Down; brother of Dr Joseph Sterling Greer (*q.v.*), Elizabeth Greer who married Dr William Thomson (*q.v.*) of Ballycrune and was mother of Prof W.W.D. Thomson, and Samuel McCurdy Greer who married Emma Hardy, daughter of Dr Samuel Little Hardy and was father of Dr Henry Little Hardy Greer, FRCS; educated at Belfast Academy; studied arts and medicine at Queen's College, Belfast, from 1863; BA (QUI) 1863; MA 1868; MD MCh 1876; general practitioner of 16 Warkworth Street, Cambridge, from c 1880; nominated as Liberal candidate for Parliament in 1892 but not elected; married 11 July 1882 in St Thomas's Church of Ireland Church, Anna Martin, daughter of Robert Martin, merchant, of Belfast; died 21 May 1904 at 11 Warkworth Street; administration (with will) Peterborough 26 September 1904. [Greeves (1973); Kirkpatrick Archive; Lond PPR, will cal; McConnell (1951); *Med Dir*; QCB adm reg; UHF database (m)].

GREER, WILLIAM JOHN (1800/1–64), Lifford, county Donegal;
born 1800/01; LRCSI and LM 1824; MD (Edin) 1825 (thesis 'De necrosis'); FRCSI 1844; assistant surgeon to Lifford County Infirmary; medical officer to Clonleigh Dispensary District and constabulary c 1846 and to Castlefin Dispensary District c 1862; married 16 June 1836 in Argry [?], Sarah Leitch of Argry (who was born 1798/9 and died 28 October 1865); died 7 October 1864 in Lifford, of typhus fever; probate Londonderry 5 December 1864. [*BNL* 1 July 1836 (m); Belf PRO, will cal; Croly (1843–6); Dub GRO (d x 2); Edin Univ; Lewis (1837); *Londonderry Sentinel* 25 June 1836 (m), 11 October 1864 (d) and 3 November 1865 (d); *Med Dir*; *Strabane Morning Post* 21 June 1836 (m)].

GREER, WILLIAM JONES (1870–1927), Armagh, and Newport, Monmouthshire;
born 1870 at Portadown, county Armagh, son of Jones Greer, merchant, of Portadown; educated at Armagh Royal School; studied arts and medicine at Queen's Colleges, Galway from 1886, and Belfast from 1889 and the Royal College of Surgeons in Ireland; BA (RUI) 1889; LRCPI and LM 1891; LRCSI and LM 1891; FRCSI 1895; DPH RCPSI 1895; general practitioner of English Street, Armagh c 1892–96; moved to Newport, c 1900; consulting surgeon to Pontypool and Tredegar Hospitals; assistant surgeon to Blaina and Nantyglo Collieries; inpatient surgeon to Newport and Monmouthshire Hospital; major RAMC TF in 3rd General Hospital; of 19 Gold Tops, Newport; honorary surgeon to Royal Gwent Hospital, Newport; one of the first surgeons to possess an x-ray apparatus and to use it for evidence of bone injury; author of *Industrial Diseases and Accidents* and various medical papers; married —; died 3 August 1927 at Abernaht Lake Hotel, Leanwrtyd Wells,

Breconshire; probate Llandaff 18 October 1927. [*BMJ* obituary (1927); Ferrar (1933); Kirkpatrick Archive; *Lancet* obituary (1927); Lond PPR, will cal; *Med Dir*; QCB adm reg].

GREGG, SAMUEL THOMAS (1802/3–28), Lisburn, county Antrim;
born 1802/3; a Quaker; general practitioner, of Lisburn; died 20 March 1828; buried in the Friends Burying Ground, Lisburn. [*BNL* 25 March 1828 (d); *Lisburn Fam Hist Soc*, vol 2 (2005)].

GREGORY, WILLIAM (*fl c* 1810–24), Naval Medical Service and Coleraine, county Londonderry;
joined the Naval Medical Service as assistant surgeon; surgeon 1795; retired as surgeon and apothecary; medical officer to Coleraine Dispensary; of New Row, Coleraine, c 1824; married c 1810 Rose Major (who was born 1773/4 and died 24 May 1841 at Tullybrisland, the home of her brother, Thomas Major); father of Ann Gregory who married Samuel Lawrence of Bannfield, Coleraine and was mother of Dr Henry Major Lawrence (*q.v.*); died before 1835. [*BNL* 8 June 1841 (d); Hitchings, Paul, pers com; *Londonderry Sentinel* 5 June 1841 (d); *NMS* (1826); Pigot (1824)].

GREGORY, WILLIAM JAMES (1866–1921), Stranorlar, county Donegal;
born 13 February 1866 at the Glebe, Stranorlar, son of William Gregory, carpenter, of Glebe, and Elizabeth Narr; studied medicine at Edinburgh University and Queen's College, Galway; MB BCh (RUI) 1889; general practitioner, of the Glebe, Stranorlar; married Amy B. —; died 21 May 1921 at the Glebe; probate Dublin 10 September 1923. [Dub GRO (b) and (d); Dub Nat Arch, will cal; *Med Dir*].

GRETTIN, EDWARD DOMINIC (*fl c* 1859), Belfast;
surgeon, of Belfast, but not in *Medical Directory* or *Register*; married 18 October 1859 in Upper Drumgooland Roman Catholic Church, county Down, Anne Murray of Drumgooland. [UHF database (m)].

GREW, FRANCIS BLANEY (1849/50–1925), ship's surgeon and Hoboken, New Jersey;
born 1849/50 at Portadown, county Armagh, son of James Grew of Portadown; educated at St Patrick's College, Armagh; studied medicine at Queen's College, Galway, and from 1869, at Queen's College, Belfast; LRCP LRCS Edin 1875; LM KQCPI 1878; surgeon with various shipping lines; died 17 October 1925 at St Mary's Hospital, Hoboken, New Jersey, USA. [Kirkpatrick Archive; *Med Dir*; QCB adm reg].

GRIBBEN, HUGH (*fl c* 1834), Aughrim, county Londonderry;
surgeon, of Anaghorish, Aughrim; presented with a horse by the inhabitants of the townland for his 'unwearied exertions' during the epidemic of cholera, March 1834. [*BNL* 8 April 1834 (d)].

GRIBBIN, EDWARD DOMINICK (1818–88), Belfast;
born 18 May 1818, son of Edward D. Gribbin of 23 Great Edward Street, Belfast, and — Wirling; grew up with his uncle Robert Wirling at 6 Church Street, Belfast; studied medicine in Glasgow and from 1852, at Queen's College, Belfast; LFPS Glas 1849; LAH Dub 1855; LRCP Edin 1870; general practitioner and medical officer to constabulary, of 25 Great Edward Street, Belfast; re-entered QCB January 1876 to study practical anatomy; married —; died 24 May 1888 at 25 Great Edward Street; buried in Clifton Street Graveyard, Belfast; probate Belfast 20 June 1888. [Belf PRO, will cal; Dub GRO (d); *Med Dir*; Merrick and Clarke, *Belfast*, vol 4 (1991); QCB adm reg; Whitla (1901)].

GRIBBIN, HUGH A. (1837/8–c 1885), Imperial Ottoman Army, ship's surgeon, Achill, county Mayo, and Lurgan, county Armagh;
born 1837/8, son of John Gribbin of Lurganban, Dromore, county Down; educated at the Classical School, Dromore, and Glasgow College; studied medicine at the Royal College of Surgeons of Edinburgh, Trinity College, Dublin, and from 1859, at Queen's College, Belfast; LM Belf 1859; LRCS and LM Edin 1861; MD (QUI) 1862; surgeon major with Imperial Ottoman Army; surgeon to the SS *Helvetia*; medical officer to the Bangor and Ballycroy Dispensary Districts, Mayo and constabulary; medical officer to the Achill Dispensary District, Mayo, 1872, of Glenheather Lodge, Mulvanny; medical officer to Lurgan No 2 Dispensary District, of Corso Lodge, Lurgan, c 1875–85; died c 1885. [Kirkpatrick Archive; *Med Dir*; QCB adm reg].

GRIBBON, GEORGE CARSON (1836–94), Army Medical Service;
born 10 September 1836 at Coleraine, county Londonderry, son of Edward Gribbon, merchant, of Coleraine; educated by Mr Gowdy; studied arts and medicine at Trinity College, Dublin, from 1854; BA MB (TCD) 1859; LRCSI 1859; joined the Army Medical Service as staff assistant surgeon in 1859; attached to 25th Foot 1864; surgeon major 1874; brigade surgeon 1885; served in the Afghan war 1878–9 and in Suakin 1885; retired 1889 to 31 Bassett Road North, Kensington, Middlesex; married 23 May 1867 in St Andrew's Church, Montreal, Canada, Elizabeth Allan, eldest daughter of Hugh Allan of Ravenscraig, Montreal; died 12 June 1894 at Bournemouth. [Burtchaell and Sadleir (1935); *Coleraine Chronicle* 15 June 1867 (m); Lond PPR, will cal; *Londonderry Sentinel* 18 June 1867 (m); *Med Dir*; Peterkin and Johnston (1968)].

GRIER, JAMES (*fl c* 1824), Londonderry;
surgeon, of the Diamond, Londonderry c 1824. [Pigot (1824)].

GRIFFITH, PATRICK GILL (1863–1952), Hayward's Heath, Sussex, and Walton-on-Thames, Surrey;
born 26 July 1863 at Ballindine, county Mayo, eldest son of James M Griffith, farmer, of Ballindine, and Delia —; educated at Ballindine School; studied medicine at Queen's College, Belfast, from 1800 and at Queen's College, Galway; LRCP LRCS Edin 1884; MB BCh BAO (RUI) 1894;DPH (Camb)1895; general practitioner, of

Chedglow, Hayward's Heath c 1895, and of Haslemere, Walton-on-Thames c 1910; retired c 1930; died 27 March 1952 at Woodlawn, Dundrum, county Dublin; buried in Hersham Graveyard, Surrey; probate London 24 April 1952. [Kirkpatrick Archive; Lond PPR, will cal; *Med Dir*; QCB adm reg].

GRIFFITH(S), RICHARD (1809/10–62), Richmond, New South Wales, Australia; born 1809/10 in county Cavan; MD [?]; emigrated to Australia; general practitioner in Richmond; died 5 February 1862. [Kirkpatrick Archive; *Med Dir*].

GRIFFITHS, THOMAS RICHARDSON- (1860–1923), Richhill, county Armagh; born 26 February 1860 at Woolwich, London, son of colonel Thomas Richardson–Griffiths; educated at Armagh Royal School 1876–9; studied medicine at Queen's College, Galway, Edinburgh University, and from 1879, at Queen's College, Belfast; LRCP LRCS and LM Edin 1883; general practitioner, of The Hermitage, Richhill, county Armagh; medical officer to constabulary and certifying factory surgeon; unmarried; died 17 June 1923 at Richhill; administration Belfast 4 November 1925. [Belf GRO (d); Belf PRO, will cal; Ferrar (1933); *Med Dir;* QCB adm reg; Young and Pike (1909)].

GRILLS, GALBRAITH HAMILTON (1870–1954), Chester; born 17 April 1870 at Ardrossan, Scotland, son of Galbraith H. Grills, naval officer; educated at Coleraine Academical Institution; studied medicine at Queen's College, Belfast, from 1893, also at Liverpool University; MB BCh BAO (RUI) 1899; MD 1902; Diploma in Mental and Nervous Diseases RUI 1902; Gaskell Prize in Mental Diseases; medical officer to the County Asylum, Chester, from c 1902 and medical superintendent from c 1912; retired c 1945 to 92 Rednal Road, King's Norton, Birmingham and lived later at Craybrook, Whitbarrow Road, Lymm, Cheshire; married Mabel Alice —; died 16 February 1954 at Craybrook; probate Birmingham 22 April 1954. [Lond PPR, will cal, will; *Med Dir*; QCB adm reg].

GRIMSHAW, THOMAS WRIGLEY (1839–1900), Dublin; born 16 November 1839 at Whitehouse, county Antrim, son of Dr Wrigley Grimshaw, FRCSI (*q.v.*), and his cousin Alicia Grimshaw; educated at Bryce's Academy, Newry, Carrickfergus School, the Academic Institute, Harcourt Street, Dublin, and Dr Hare's School, Stephen's Green, Dublin; studied arts and medicine at Trinity College, Dublin, from 1856 and at Dr Steevens' and Sir Patrick Dun's Hospital; BA (TCD) 1860; MB MCh 1861; LRCSI 1862; MD 1867; LKQCPI 1867; FKQCPI 1869; Dip State Med (TCD) 1874; MA 1874; apprenticed to Professor Robert Harrison, president of the RCSI; physician to Cork Street Fever Hospital, Coombe Hospital and the Orthopaedic Hospital, Dublin; lecturer in botany, materia medica and medicine at Dr Steevens' Hospital and pressed for the establishment of a nursing school there; Registrar General of Ireland 1879–1900; superintended the census of 1881 and 1891 and was president of the Dublin Sanitary Association 1885–8 and the Statistical Society of Ireland 1888–90; president of the RCPI 1895 and 1896; CB 1897 as part of Queen Victoria's Diamond Jubilee celebrations; of Priorsland, Carrickmines, county Dublin; author of many publications including important papers on 'The value of thermometric measurements in typhus fever' (1867) (with J.C. Reynolds, R.O. Furlong and J.W. Moore) and 'On the relation between the distribution of cholera in Dublin during the epidemic of 1866, and the geological structure of the Dublin district' (1878); also *A Manual of Public Health for Ireland* (1875) and *The Prevalence of Tuberculosis in Ireland and the Measures necessary for its Control* (1899); married 11 April 1865 Sarah Elizabeth Thomas (who was born 14 August 1843 and died 29 April 1945), daughter of the Rev Thomas Felix Thomas of Newport, Isle of Wight; died 23 January 1900 at Priorsland; buried in Mount Jerome Cemetery; probate Dublin 20 February 1900. [Belf PRO, will cal; *BMJ* obituary (1900); Breathnach and Moynihan (2009); Burke *LGI* (1958); Burtchaell and Sadleir (1935); Cameron (1916); *DIB* (2009); Kirkpatrick (1924); Kirkpatrick Archive; *Med Dir*; Moore (1900); Widdess (1963)].

GRIMSHAW, WRIGLEY (1801–78), Dublin and Bray, county Wicklow;
born 31 December 1801, son of Thomas Grimshaw of Whitehouse, county Antrim, whose father had migrated from Whalley, Lancashire, and was among the first to spin cotton and print calico in Ireland; LRCSI 1828; FRCSI 1833; practised as a dentist; of 13 Molesworth Street, Dublin, and later, of Bray; author of papers on dental surgery; married (1) 20 March 1835 his cousin Alicia Grimshaw (who was born 10 November 1804 and died 10 February 1847), daughter of James Grimshaw of Whitehouse; (2) 2 June 1875 in St Stephen's Church of Ireland Church, Dublin, Elizabeth Dorothea Hamilton (who was born 28 August 1839), daughter of the Rev Richard Hamilton, vicar of Kilmersdon, Somerset; father by first wife of Dr Thomas Wrigley Grimshaw (*q.v.*); died 16 June 1878. [Burke, *LGI* (1958); Cameron (1916); Dub GRO (m); *Med Dir*].

GROVE, HUMPHREY (1741–84), Letterkenny, county Donegal;
born 1741, fifth son of William Grove of Castle Grove, Letterkenny, and Susanna Barry of Kilcarra, county Meath; MD [?]; general practitioner, of Letterkenny; married Barbara Delap (who was born 1737/8 and died 1809); died 1784. [Burke *LGI* (1912)].

GROVES, HENRY CHARLES (1864–1933), Monmouth, Wales, and Malahide, county Dublin;
born 4 July 1864 at Mullavilly Glebe, Ballynock, county Armagh, second son of the Rev Henry Charles Groves, perpetual curate of Mullavilly, county Armagh, rector of Donaghmoine, county Monaghan, and prebendary of Donavavey (Diocese of Clogher), and Kate Elizabeth Little, daughter of Tennison Little, of Cork; studied medicine at the Royal College of Surgeons in Ireland; LRCSI 1885; LKQCPI 1886; LM Rot Hosp Dub 1886; general practitioner, of Chippenham House, Monmouth c 1886–1911; medical officer to Monmouth Hospital and medical officer of health for Monmouth; general practitioner, of Kilronan, Malahide c 1911–33; married Catherine —; died 16 April 1933 at Kilronan; probate Dublin 19 July 1933. [Dub GRO (b) and (d); Dub Nat Arch, will cal; Fleming (2001); Leslie (1911) and (1929); Leslie, Crooks and Moore (2006); *Med Dir*].

GRU(E)BER, WILLIAM FREDERICK (1809/10–66), Rathmullan and Letterkenny, county Donegal;
> born 1809/10; MRCSE 1832; LAH Dub 1841; general practitioner, of Springfield, Rathmullan c 1837, and of Letterkenny; married 6 November 1833 in Ballyshannon Church of Ireland Church, Mary Anne Allingham, poetess, youngest daughter of John Allingham of Ballyshannon; died 5 January 1866 in Letterkenny; probate Londonderry 31 January 1866. [*BNL* 12 November 1833 (m); Belf PRO, will cal; Croly (1843–6); Dub GRO (d); Hitchings, Paul, pers com; Lewis (1837); *Londonderry Sentinel* 9 November 1833 (m) and 9 January 1866 (d); *Med Dir*].

GUINNESS, HENRY CRAMER (1838–1902), Army Medical Service;
> born 12 June 1838 at Clontarf, county Dublin, son of Dr Arthur Guinness of Dublin; LKQCPI LRCSI 1859; joined the Army Medical Service 1859 as assistant surgeon; posted to Royal Artillery 1864; surgeon major 1875; surgeon lieutenant-colonel 1879; served mainly in India but served in Newry c 1890–91, followed by Cyprus; retired 1893 to Wellington Lodge, Wellington Square, Cheltenham; married 20 May 1875 Emily Gore Ormsby (who died in November 1888 at Ahmadnagar, Bombay), second daughter of Charles Montague Ormsby of West Derby; died 2 January 1902 at Cheltenham; probate Gloucester 29 January 1902. [Crossle (1909); Lond PPR, will cal; *Med Dir*; Peterkin and Johnston (1968)].

GUNN, RICHARD DAVIES BARREE (1864–1911), Manchester;
> born 26 January 1864 at Seetapore, India, son of Captain Wilson Gunn of the Antrim Artillery Militia, Carrickfergus; educated at Aberdeen Gymnasium; entered Queen's College, Belfast 1881; LRCP LRCS Edin 1886; LFPS Glas 1886; general practitioner, of Grove Mound, Fairfield Road, Droylesden, Manchester; died 1 March 1911; probate London 9 May 1911. [Lond PPR, will cal; *Med Dir*; QCB adm reg].

GUNNING, JAMES DAVIS (1844–95), Army Medical Service;
> born 22 September 1844, son of James Gunning of Stranorlar, county Donegal; educated at RBAI; studied medicine at Queen's College, Belfast, from 1861; LRCP LRCS Edin 1867; joined the Army Medical Service as staff assistant surgeon 1867; posted to 1st Foot 1868; staff surgeon 1871; posted to 51st Foot 1872; surgeon major 1879; surgeon lieutenant-colonel 1887; brigade surgeon lieutenant-colonel 1893; married Anna Rebecca —; died 1 May 1895 at sea on board HMS *Malabar*; probate London 8 July 1895. [Lond PPR, will cal; *Med Dir*; Peterkin and Johnston (1968); QCB adm reg].

GUNNING, JOHN ST CLAIR (1849/50–96), Ramsgate, Kent, and Enniskillen, county Fermanagh;
> born 1849/50; studied medicine at the Ledwich School, and Meath Hospital, Dublin; LAH Dub 1868; LRCSI 1870; LRCP Edin 1879; resident medical officer to the Ramsgate and St Lawrence Royal Dispensary from 1872; medical officer of Seaman's Infirmary, Ramsgate, and assistant surgeon to the Kent and Canterbury Hospital; assistant surgeon and apothecary to County Fermanagh Infirmary; medical officer to Enniskillen Union Workhouse and Fever Hospital; of Darling Street,

Enniskillen c 1871; unmarried; died 17 March 1896 at Darling Street; probate Armagh 25 April 1896. [Belf PRO, will cal; Dub GRO (d); Kirkpatrick Archive; *Med Dir*].

GUNNING, ROBERT CARDWELL (1853–1930), Army Medical Service;
born 26 November 1853 at Enniskillen, county Fermanagh; studied medicine at the Ledwich School, Dublin; LKQCPI and LM 1876; LRCSI 1876; joined the Army Medical Service as surgeon 1877; surgeon major 1889; surgeon lieutenant-colonel 1897; served in South Africa 1901–02; retired 1904; rejoined during World War I 1914–18; later of Hilldrop Villa, Epson Road, Croydon, Surrey, and of 1 Birdhurst Rise, Croydon; died 7 October 1930; probate London 27 November 1930. [Lond PPR, will cal; *Med Dir*; Peterkin and Johnston (1968)].

GUTHRIE, JAMES (1850–88), Esher, Surrey;
born 17 April 1850 at Greysteel, county Londonderry, son of William Guthrie of Greysteel; educated at Londonderry Academical Institution; studied medicine at Queen's College, Belfast, from 1869; LRCS Edin 1873 MD (QUI) 1874; general practitioner, of Ashley Lodge, Esher, c 1885; died 28 November 1888 at Pebble Cottage, Esher; probate London 9 February 1889. [Lond PPR, will cal; *Med Dir*; QCB adm reg].

GWYNNE, WILLIAM (1829/30–69), Ipswich, Norfolk, and Southampton, Hampshire;
born 1829/30 in county Antrim, third son of the Rev Stephen Gwynne, treasurer of the diocese of Connor, and Mary Stevens of Belfast; educated by Mr Darley; studied arts and medicine at Trinity College, Dublin, from 1848; LRCSI and LM Rot Hosp Dub 1854; BA MB (TCD) 1857; MA 1861; general practitioner, of Nicholas Street, Ipswich, from c 1860; finally of Holly Lodge Hill, Southampton; married 21 October 1856 in St Andrew's Church of England Church, Liverpool, Laura Sothern, youngest daughter of John Sothern; died 11 August 1869 at 1 Beulah Villas, Monkton Street, Ryde, Isle of Wight; probate London 4 November 1869. [Burtchaell and Sadleir (1935); *Coleraine Chronicle* 1 November 1856 (m) and 21 August 1869 (d); Leslie (1993); Lond PPR, will cal; *Med Dir*].

H

HACKET, WILLIAM H. (1783–1854), Army Medical Service and Newry, county Down;
> born 10 May 1783; surgeon's mate in the North Downshire Militia; joined the Army Medical Service as assistant surgeon to the 15th Foot 1801; transferred to 32nd Foot 1802, to 15th Foot 1803 and 53rd Foot 1805; surgeon to 8th Foot 1808; staff surgeon 1814; on half pay 1816–25, acting as surgeon to the North Downshire Militia; deputy inspector general 1843; inspector general 1854; served at Walcheren 1809, USA 1813 (wounded at Stoney Creek) and Holland 1814; MD (St Andrews) 1817 (on testimonials); posted to Newry and erected a gravestone to his housekeeper for eight years, in Newry Presbyterian Graveyard in 1842; died 29 May 1854 in Gibraltar. [Clarke, *County Down*, vol 21 (1998); Peterkin and Johnston (1968); Smart (2004)].

HADDEN, ROBERT EVANS (1853/4–1919), Cork and Skibbereen, county Cork, and Portadown, county Armagh;
> born 14 January 1854 at Skibbereen, fourth son of Dr David Hadden, MRCSE 1840, MD (Glas) 1846, of Skibbereen; brother of Dr John Hadden, MD (QUI) 1864, of Lincolnshire, Dr George Hadden of the USA, Dr David Henry Hadden, LRCSI 1868, of Cork and Dublin, and Dr William Edward Hadden (*q.v.*) of Portadown; studied medicine at Queen's College, Cork, and the Royal College of Surgeons in Ireland; MD MCh and LM (QUI) 1878; LAH Dub 1878; prosector in anatomy at Queen's College, Cork; medical officer of health to Tullagh and medical officer to Baltimore Industrial School, of Skibbereen c 1880–c 1900; general practitioner, of Stewart Avenue, Edenderry, Portadown, from c 1902; married 23 September 1880 at Holy Trinity Church of Ireland Church, Cork, Thomasina ('Tassie') Coles Webb (who died 12 January 1912), youngest daughter of John Webb, lieutenant RN, of 13 Morrison's Quay, Cork; died 11 June 1919; buried in Seagoe Church of Ireland Graveyard; probate Armagh 15 September 1919. [Belf PRO, will cal; Dub GRO (m) and (d); Hadden, Rosalind, pers com; Kirkpatrick Archive; *Med Dir*].

HADDEN, WILLIAM EDWARD (1858–1949), Cork, Liverpool, Lancashire, ship's surgeon and Portadown, county Armagh;
> born 18 August 1858 at Skibbereen, county Cork, sixth and youngest son of Dr David Hadden, MRCSE 1840, MD (Glas) 1846, of Skibbereen; brother of Dr John Hadden, MD (QUI) 1864, of Lincolnshire, Dr George Hadden of the USA, Dr David Henry HaddenLRCSI 1868, of Cork and Dublin and Dr Robert Evans Hadden (*q.v.*) of Portadown; studied medicine at Queen's College, Cork and the Carmichael School, Dublin; LM Coombe Hosp Dub 1882; MD MCh and Dip Obst (RUI) 1882; MAO 1885; prosector and assistant demonstrator of anatomy at Queen's College, Cork; assistant house surgeon to Liverpool South Dispensary; surgeon to Dominion Steamship Company; general practitioner, of 73 Micklegate, York 1885–6; general practitioner, of Magharee House, Portadown, from 1886; retired 1930;

author of various medical papers; married 6 August 1890 at Edenderry, Rachel Robinson Robb, youngest daughter of Hamilton Robb, linen manufacturer, of Edenderry House, Portadown; father of Dr David Hamilton Hadden, MBE, RAMC, MC, Dr Edward Montgomery Hadden of Portadown, MB BCh, BAO (QUB) 1921, Dr Winifred Eileen Hadden of Portadown, MB BCh BAO (QUB) 1920 and Dr Robert Evans Haddden of Portadown, MB BCh BAO (TCD) 1926; died 12 February 1949 at Magharee; buried in Drumcree Church of Ireland Graveyard; probate Belfast 28 September 1949. [Belf GRO (d); Belf PRO; will cal; will; *BMJ* obituary (1949); Dub GRO (m); Hadden, Rosalind, pers com; Kirkpatrick Archive; *Med Dir*].

HADLEY, CLEMENT (1846–1924), Birmingham and Coventry, Warwickshire;
born 27 December 1846, second son of John Joseph Hadley of 22 Colmore Row, Birmingham; brother of Dr George Percival Hadley (*q.v.*); educated at King Edward's School, Birmingham; studied medicine at Queen's College, Belfast, from 1865 and at the General Hospital, Birmingham; MRCSE 1871; LKQCPI and LM 1880; honorary medical officer to the Birmingham Lying-in Charity; medical officer and public vaccinator to Shilton and Wolvey Districts, Birmingham, 1872–1902, of 5 Prospect Row and 89 Ashted Row, Birmingham; general practitioner, of the Cottage, Shilton, Coventry, c 1902–16; retired c 1916 to the Manse, Narborough, Leicester; married —; died 11 March 1924 at Leicester. [*BMJ* obituary (1924); *Med Dir*; QCB adm reg].

HADLEY, GEORGE PERCIVAL (1845–1909), Birmingham, Warwickshire;
born 24 February 1845, eldest son of John Joseph Hadley of 22 Colmore Row, Birmingham; brother of Dr Clement Hadley (*q.v.*); educated at King Edward's School and Sydenham College, Birmingham, 1863–5; studied medicine at Queen's College, Belfast, from 1865, and at the General Hospital, Birmingham; MRCSE 1867; LSA Lond 1868; MD (QUI) 1868; general practitioner, of Wadham House, 18 Lozells Road, Birmingham, retired c 1906; married Kezia —; father of Dr Leonard Leigh Hadley, MC, MB (Birm) 1905; died 30 March 1909; probate Birmingham 2 July 1909. [Lond PPR, will cal; will; *Med Dir*; QCB adm reg].

HADZOR, JOHN (d 1765), Army Medical Service;
son of Dr Seneca Hadzor of Downpatrick (*q.v.*); joined the Army Medical Service with the 13th Foot c 1713; ensign 1722; lieutenant and surgeon's mate in Gibraltar 1727 (appears to have been both surgeon and commissioned officer); retired 1750; died 3 December 1765; [cf probate Down Diocesan Court 1748 ??]. [Belf PRO, Down Dio Wills index; Peterkin and Johnston (1968); Pilson (1838)].

HADZOR, SENECA (d c 1746), Downpatrick, county Down;
served in the army in Spain and Gibraltar; practised in Downpatrick as a surgeon from c 1700; churchwarden of Down parish 1704; living opposite the Market Housec 1708; married —, a nun from Spain; father of Dr John Hadzor (*q.v.*) and three daughters; possibly died c 1746. [Pilson (1838); Pooler (1907); Wilson (1995)].

HAGAN, HENRY (*fl c* 1794), Lurgan, county Armagh
LAH Dub 1794; apothecary, of Lurgan. [Apothecaries (1829)].

HAGAN, — (1778/9–1815), Newry, county Down;
born 1778/9; 'doctor' of Newry; died 27 November 1815. [*BNL* 12 December 1815 (d)].

HAIRS, WILLIAM (*fl c* 1845), Londonderry;
son of William Hairs, farmer; MD (Glas) [?]; general practitioner, of Londonderry City c 1845; married (1) Jane Mildred — (who was born 1804/5 and died 27 June 1847); (2) 29 February 1848 in Derry Cathedral, Jane Rowe, daughter of John Rowe of Londonderry. [Croly (1843–6); Dub GRO (m); *Londonderry Sentinel* 3 July 1847 (d) and 4 March 1848 (m)].

HALAHAN, HENRY SAMUEL (1829/30–89), Dublin and Carrick, county Donegal;
born 1829/30; studied medicine at the Royal College of Surgeons in Ireland and the Meath Hospital, Dublin; LRCSI 1852; LKQCPI and LM 1860; assistant master of the Rotunda Hospital, Dublin, 1859–62; physician and obstetrician, of 29 Harcourt Street, Dublin; medical officer to Carrick Dispensary District, from c 1880; author of various papers on obstetrics; married —; died 5 June 1889 at Carrick; administration Dublin 2 December 1889. [Belfast PRO, will cal; Dub GRO (d); Kirkpatrick and Jellett (1913); *Med Dir*].

HALAHAN, SAMUEL HANDY (1858/9–c 1933), Enniskillen, county Fermanagh, and Edenhope and Springvale, Victoria, Australia;
born 1858/9, third son of the Rev Christopher Halahan, rector of Rossorry and Donaghmoine, county Fermanagh, and Elizabeth Catherine Dobbin; educated at Portora Royal School; studied arts and medicine at Trinity College, Dublin, from 1877; BA (TCD) 1881; MB BCh 1885; general practitioner of Rossory, Enniskillen, c 1886; emigrated to Victoria, Australia; general practitioner, of Edendhope c 1895 and of Springvale from c 1927; married —; father of Reeves Halahan of the Australian Light Horse, who died of wounds received at the Dardanelles, July 1915; died c 1933. [Leslie, Crooks and Moore (2006); *Med Dir*; *Portora Royal School Register* (1940); TCD adm reg; *TCD Cat*, vol II (1896)].

HALIDAY, ALEXANDER HENRY (1728–1802), Belfast;
born 1728 in Belfast, son of the Rev Samuel Haliday, minister of First Belfast Presbyterian Church, Rosemary Street, and Anne Dalway of Carrickfergus; brother of Robert Dalway Haliday, who was father of Dr William Haliday (*q.v.*); studied medicine at Glasgow University; matriculated 1743; MA MD (Glas) 1751; prominent physician, of 86 Donegal Street, Belfast; physician to the Poor House; corresponded with the celebrated Dr Cullen of Glasgow in 1751; involved in liberal politics in Belfast and intervened when a Hearts of Steel mob from Templepatrick burned down Waddell Cunningham's house in Belfast in 1770; he also stopped the soldiers firing on a Hearts of Steel mob at the barracks; his house in Castle Street

was the headquarters of James Caulfield, Earl of Charlemont, on his annual visits to Belfast from 1782, in connection with the Volunteer conventions; exchanged about 200 letters with him between 1780 and 1799; appointed consulting physician to the Belfast Dispensary and Fever Hospital in 1792; second president of the Belfast Reading Society 1792–8, later to become the Linen Hall Library (later bequeathed his library to the Society); married (1) 2 May 1754 in Shankill Parish Church, Belfast, Martha McCollum (who died December 1772), daughter of Randal McCollum of Belfast; married (2) 1775 Anne Edmonstone, third daughter of Campbell Edmonstone of Red Hall, county Antrim ('affable and unaffected but no way striking in looks or behavious' (Martha McTier); died 28 April 1802; buried in Clifton Street Graveyard, Belfast, his vault now sadly decayed; his will is notable for his self-deprecating references to his wife; 'probably the best known and most influential inhabitant of Belfast' (Benn). [Addison (1898) and 1913); Agnew (1998–9); Anderson (1888); *BNL* 22 December 1775 (m), 30 April and 14 May 1802 (d); Benn (1877); Blackwood's Pedigrees, vol 3; Crone (1928); *DIB* (2009); Esler (1884); Gillespie and O'Keeffe (2006); Killen (1990); Logan (2007); Malcolm (1851); Martin (2003); *Memorials of the Dead*, vol VIII, p 480; Merrick and Clarke, *Belfast*, vol 4 (1991); Newmann (1993); *Oxford DNB* (2004); Strain (1961) and (1971)].

HALIDAY, HENRY (d before 1842), Belfast
physician, of Belfast; married A. — (who died 28 March 1842 at Newlandburn House, Edinburgh); died before 1842. [*BNL* 8 April 1842 (d)].

HALIDAY, WILLIAM (1763–1836), Newry, county Down, and Belfast;
born 1763, fourth son of Robert Dalway Haliday of Castle Hill, county Down, and Elizabeth Smith of Newland, Yorkshire; nephew of Dr Alexander Henry Haliday (*q.v.*); studied arts and medicine at Glasgow University; matriculated 1779; MA (Glas) 1782; MD (Edin) (thesis 'De electricitate medica') 1786; physician in Newry, c 1799–1800; prominent physician of Belfast c 1800–36; physician to the Poor House; a founder committee member of the Belfast Medical Society in 1806 and an early president before it was dissolved in 1814; rejoined when it was revived in 1822; married February 1806 Marianne Webster (who died 1807), daughter of Gilbert Webster of Greenville, county Down, and Mary Ann Boyd; died 3 June 1836 at Clifden, near Holywood; buried in Clifton Street Graveyard, Belfast in the vault with his uncle. [Addison (1898) and (1913); *BNL* 7 June 1836 (d); Blackwood's Pedigrees, vol 3; Edin Univ; Malcolm (1851); Merrick and Clarke, *Belfast*, vol 4 (1991); Strain (1961)].

HALL, CHARLES BROMLEY (1857–1919), Liverpool, Lancashire, and Dewsbury, Yorkshire;
born 28 September 1857 at Massford, Castlecomer, county Kilkenny, son of William Hall, civil engineer, of Massford House; educated at the Wesleyan Connectional Institute, Dublin; studied medicine at Queen's College, Belfast, from 1873; MD (QUI) 1878; MCh 1880; resident medical officer to Liverpool Parish Infirmary; general practitioner, of Hirst House, Batley Carr, Dewsbury, Yorkshire; honorary surgeon to Dewsbury and District General Infirmary; medical officer and public vaccinator to Dewsbury District; of 'Massford', Birkdale Road, Dewsbury; died 1

September 1919; probate London 27 November 1919. [Lond PPR, will cal; *Med Dir*; QCB adm reg].

HALL, FRANCIS EDWARD (c 1820–c 1877), Toomebridge and Randalstown, county Antrim;
born c 1820, son of Collins Hall, farmer; LFPS Glas 1843; LM Anderson's College, Glasgow 1852; surgeon, of Antrim c 1845–50; medical officer to Toome Dispensary District and constabulary, of Taylorstown, Grange Corner, Antrim, and Randalstown, from c 1850; married 23 March 1850 in Muckamore Presbyterian Church, Elizabeth Ann Wilson, daughter of David Wilson, farmer, of Dungonnell, Killead, county Antrim; died c 1877. [*BNL* 2 April 1850 (m); Croly (1846); Dub GRO (m); *Med Dir*; UHF database (m)].

HALL, JAMES (1748/9–1822), Army Medical Service and Dromore, county Down;
born 1748/9; joined the Army Medical Service as surgeon to Colonel Ward's Regiment 1794; on half pay 1795–1803; served with 18th Foot 1803–05; married Anne — (who was born 1749/50 and died 23 April 1838); died 29 June 1822 at Dromore. [*BNL* 5 July 1822 (d) and 4 May 1838 (d); Peterkin and Johnston (1968)].

HALL, JAMES (1856–c 1920), Peel, Isle of Man, Walsall, Staffordshire, Leyton, Essex, Royston, Lancashire, and Belfast;
born 12 July 1856 at Rathkeel, county Antrim, son of William Hall, farmer, of Rathkeel, and Elizabeth Knox; educated at the Classical and Mercantile School, Ballymena; studied medicine at Queen's College, Belfast, from 1875; LRCP LRCS Edin 1880; MD (St Andrews) 1890 (by examination); general practitioner, of Peel, Isle of Man c 1886, of 30 Bridge Street, Walsall c 1890, of Brookhouse, Leyton c 1895, of Park Lane House, Royston c 1900–10, of 76 Victoria Street, Belfast c 1910–11; retired to Shirley House, Ripley, Derbyshire c 1911–20; author of various medical papers; married (1) — Jocund of the Isle of Man; married (2) — James; died c 1920. [*Med Dir*; QCB adm reg; Smart (2004)].

HALL, JAMES CAMPBELL (1851–1931), Monaghan;
born 23 October 1851 in Kilkeel, eldest son of the Rev Richard Augustus Hall, of Tully House, county Monaghan, rector of Derrygortreavy, Dungannon, county Tyrone, and Mary Henry; brother of Dr Thomas Gibson Henry Hall (*q.v.*); educated at Dungannon Royal School; studied arts and medicine at Trinity College, Dublin, from 1874; BA MB BCh (TCD) 1878; LM KQCPI 1878; Dip State Med 1878; assistant physician to Highfield and Hampstead Private Lunatic Asylum; medical officer to Scotstown Dispensary District, county Monaghan and to Monaghan Union Workhouse from 1879; physician to the Monaghan Fever Hospital; surgeon to the County Monaghan Infirmary from 1890, of Rowantree House, Monaghan; JP; DL; HS; retired 1930; a noted rose-gardener; married 9 February 1880 in St Stephen's Church of Ireland Church, Dublin, Sarah Frances Wilson, only daughter of John H.M. Wilson of Harvest Lodge, county Tipperary, and Church Hall, Essex; died 8 April 1931 at Rowantree, Monaghan buried at Drumsnatt Graveyard; memorial tablet in Monaghan County Hospital; probate Dublin 12 January 1932. [Crossle (1909); Dub GRO (m); Dub Nat Arch, will cal; Kirkpatrick Archive; *Lancet* obituary

(1931); Leslie (1911) *Med Dir;* O'Donnell (2008); TCD adm reg; *TCD Cat*, vol II (1896)].

HALL, JOHN MOORE (1864–1932), London and Bournemouth, Hampshire;
born 26 November 1864 at Hilltown, county Down, son of James Hall, farmer of Ballynanny, Hilltown; educated at the Church School, Hilltown; studied medicine at Queen's College, Belfast, from 1881; MD BCh BAO (RUI) 1889; MRCSE 1891; DPH RCPS 1892; FRCSE 1894; house surgeon at Huddersfield Infirmary; assistant superintendent at the Grove Hall Asylum, Bow, and assistant medical officer at the Hackney Infirmary, London; general practitioner in Bournemouth from c 1894; retired to 26 Linton Road, Hastings, Sussex; died 22 December 1932 at 26 Upper Maze Hill, St Leonards-on-Sea; probate Lewes 14 March 1935. [Lond PPR, will cal; *Med Dir*; Power and Le Fanu (1953); QUB].

HALL, JOHN WILLIAM (d c 1940), Portadown, county Armagh, London and Transvaal, South Africa;
studied medicine at the Ledwich School, Dublin; LM Dub 1884; LAH Dub 1885; general practitioner, of 14 High Street, Portadown c 1886; general practitioner, of 14 Huntingdon Street, Barnsbury, London c 1895; medical officer to HM Forces in South African War 1899–1902 (King's Medal with 2 clasps; Queen's Medical with 3 clasps); civil medical officer on HM Hospital Ship *Spartan*; house surgeon and anaesthetist (later surgeon) to Simmer and Jack Hospital, Germiston, Transvaal; retired to Vaalhoek Mine, Pilgrims Rest, Transvaal; JP; Commissioner for Oaths; railway medical officer; medical officer to White River Valley Medical Society; died c 1940. [*Med Dir*].

HALL, MATTHEW (*fl c* 1863), Newbliss, county Monaghan;
apothecary, of Newbliss, c 1863. [McCann (2003)].

HALL, ROBERT (*fl c* 1813), Monaghan;
LAH Dub 1813; apothecary, of Monaghan. [Apothecaries (1829)].

HALL, ROBERT (*fl c* 1845), Lisburn, county Antrim;
studied medicine at Glasgow University; CM (Glas) 1839; LAH Dub; general practitioner, of Lisburn, medical officer to the Lisburn Fever Hospital c 1845; married 29 August 1844 in Moira Church of Ireland Church, Elizabeth Ann Whitla of Ashfield, Ballinderry. [Addison (1898); *BNL* 13 September 1844 (m); Croly (1843–6)].

HALL, ROBERT (1861–1941), Belfast;
born 22 June 1861 at Hilltown, county Down, son of Hugh Hall, farmer, of The Lodge, Hilltown; educated at Hilltown; studied medicine at Queen's College, Belfast, from 1878; LRCP LRCS Edin 1886; house physician to Belfast Union Infirmary from 1886; medical officer to Belfast Union Infirmary from 1892, and later visiting physician; physician to Belfast Municipal Sanatorium; physician to UVF Hospital, Belfast; first medical superintendent to the new Belfast Municipal Sanatorium, Whiteabbey 1904–14 and medical officer 1914–41; president of Ulster Medical

Society 1921–2; of 1 Royal Terrace, Lisburn Road, Belfast, from c 1890; author of various medical papers; married Mary Ann Rodgers; father of Dr Robert ('Robin') Hall, MB (QUB) 1918, and Dr Hugh ('Hugo') Edwin Hall, MB (QUB) 1916; died 29 March 1941; probate Belfast 21 May 1942. [Belf GRO (son's b); Belf PRO, will cal; Calwell and Craig (1989); Craig (1974) and (1985); Kirkpatrick Archive; *Med Dir*; QCB adm reg; *UMJ* (anon) (1941)].

HALL, THOMAS GIBSON HENRY (d c 1918), Belturbet, county Cavan, and New Zealand;
son of the Rev Richard Augustus Hall of Tully House, county Monaghan, rector of Derrygortreavy, Dungannon, county Tyrone, and Mary Henry; brother of Dr James Campbell Hall (*q.v.*); LRCSI 1883; LKQCPI and LM 1883; emigrated to New Zealand c 1890; general practitioner, of Kamo, Auckland, c 1895 and of Whangarei from c 1900; died c 1918. [Leslie (1911); *Med Dir*].

HALL, WILLIAM (b 1683/4);
born 1683/4 in county Down, son of the Rev John Hall; educated by Mr Walker of Drogheda; studied medicine at Trinity College, Dublin, from 1699; MD (TCD) 1712. [Burtchaell and Sadleir (1924)].

HALL, WILLIAM (*fl c* 1824), Cootehill, county Cavan;
surgeon, apothecary and accoucheur, of Cootehill c 1824. [Pigot (1824)].

HALL, WILLIAM CRANSTON (1867–96), Bailieborough, county Cavan;
born 10 December 1867, son of Thomas Hall, shop-keeper, of Bailieborough, and Elizabeth Steuart; LKQCPI and LM 1891; LRCSI and LM 1891 general practitioner, of Bailieborough; unmarried; died 29 February 1896 at Bailieborough; administration Cavan 30 May 1896. [Belf PRO, will cal; Dub GRO (b) and (d); Kirkpatrick Archive; *Med Dir*].

HALLIDAY, JOHN HATCHELL (c 1820–66), Belfast;
born c 1820, son of John Halliday, flour merchant; studied medicine at Glasgow University; LRCSI 1846; MD (Glas) 1847; general practitioner, of 92 Donegall Street, Belfast; treasurer of the Belfast Clinical and Pathological Society and frequent contributor to its *Transactions*; married 28 October 1847 in St Peter's Church of Ireland Church, Dublin, Sarah Elizabeth Briscoe (who was born c 1828), third daughter of Abraham Briscoe of Rathmines, Dublin; died 14 September 1866 at 86 Donegall Street, Belfast, of phthisis; buried in Balmoral cemetery; probate Belfast 3 November 1866. [Addison (1898); *BNL* 2 November 1847 (m); *Belf Clin Path Soc Trans*; Belf PRO, will cal; Clarke, *Belfast*, vol 3 (1986); Dub GRO (d); *Med Dir*].

HALPIN, CHARLES (d 1859), Stradone, county Cavan;
LAH Dub 1824; MRCSE 1830; LM Rot Hosp Dub 1831; LRCSI 1834; LKQCPI 1843; medical officer to Stradone Dispensary, Cavan, and troops, c 1843–6; medical officer to Cavan Fever Hospital and surgeon to Cavan Military Hospital; author of various medical papers; married —; died 1859. [*BNL* 19 September 1855 (d, son); Croly (1843–6); *Med Dir*].

HAMILL, JAMES CLARKE (d 1854), Ballycastle, county Antrim, and Geelong, Australia;
>son of James Hamill, land surveyor; studied medicine at Glasgow University; MD CM (Glas) 1843; of Ballycastle, c 1844; emigrated to Australia c 1850; general practitioner, of Geelong, c 1850–54; married 24 August and 4 October 1849 in First Broughshane Presbyterian Church, Sarah Jane Wilson, daughter of Samuel Wilson, farmer, of Ballycloghan, county Antrim; father of Dr John Wilson Hamill (*q.v.*); died 30 December 1854 at Geelong. [Addison (1898); *BNL* 7 September 1849 (m) and 21 March 1855 (d); *Coleraine Chronicle* 13 October 1849 (m) and 31 March 1855 (d); Dub GRO (m); QCB adm reg; UHF database (m)].

HAMILL, JOHN WILSON (1852–1917), Worksop, Nottinghamshire and Higher Broughton, Manchester;
>born 16 October 1852 at Geelong, Australia, son of Dr James Clarke Hamill (*q.v.*) of Geelong; educated at RBAI; studied medicine at Queen's College, Belfast, from 1867 and Owen's College, Manchester; MD (QUI) 1873; MCh Dip Mid 1874; medical officer to Worksop General Dispensary, and surgeon to Worksop Cottage Hospital, c 1875, of Clowes House, Higher Broughton, Manchester, from c 1885; physician to Greengate Hospital and Dispensary, Salford, Oakhill Probationary Home, Manchester and the Retreat for Inebriated Women, the Grove, Fallowfield; examiner of lunatics to Salford Guardians; author of various medical papers; married Fanny Isabel —; died 7 January 1917; probate London 22 February 1917. [*BMJ* obituary (1917); Kirkpatrick Archive; Lond PPR, will cal; *Med Dir*; QCB adm reg].

HAMILL, ROBERT JAMES (1853–1932), London and Llanelly, Carmarthenshire;
>born 10 June 1853 at Ballymartin, son of Robert Martin, farmer, of Ballymartin; educated at the Belfast Seminary; studied arts and medicine at Queen's College, Belfast, from 1871; BA (QUI) 1874; Malcolm Exhibition, Belfast Royal Hospital 1876; LRCP and LM LRCS Edin 1877; MD 1880; MA 1882; general practitioner, of 295 Vauxhall Bridge Road from c 1880 of 49 Maxted Road, East Dulwich, from c 1899 of Clement's Inn, Strand, from c 1940, of 10 Mount Pleasant Llanelly, Carmarthenshire, from 1907; finally of 19 Gilbert Road Llanelly; died 7 July 1932; probate Carmarthen 11 August 1932. [Lond PPR, will cal; *Med Dir*; QCB adm reg].

HAMILL, SAMUEL MORRELL (1859–1943), Leicester, Burnham, Norfolk, and London;
>born 27 December 1859 at Ahoghill, county Antrim, son of John Hamill, merchant, of Ahoghill; educated at RBAI; studied arts and medicine at Queen's College, Belfast, from 1874; BA (QUI) 1877; MD MCh (RUI) 1882; assistant surgeon to Leicester Borough Fever Hospital; medical officer, public vaccinator and certifying factory surgeon to Burnham District, Westgate, Norfolk; general practitioner, of 58 Longridge Road, Earl's Court, London, from c 1918 and of 115 Coleherne Court from c 1930; died 9 January 1943; probate Llandudno 12 May 1943. [Kirkpatrick Archive; Lond PPR, will cal; *Med Dir*; QCB adm reg].

HAMILTON, ALEXANDER (c 1760–1813), Ballymoney, county Antrim;
 born c 1760; surgeon, of Ballymoney; died 9 January 1813 at Ballymoney; 'as a professional man he was eminently useful and was … one of the best informed men in his line'. [*BNL* 15 January 1813 (d)].

HAMILTON, ALEXANDER MACLEOD STAVELEY (1850–80), Liverpool, Lancashire, Leeds, Yorkshire, and Ballymoney. County Antrim;
 born 10 December 1850 at Ballymoney, county Antrim, son of Hugh McCurdy Hamilton, merchant, and clerk of Ballymoney Union for 31 years, of Church Road, Ballymoney, and Mary Staveley; educated in Coleraine Academical Institution; studied medicine at Queen's College, Belfast, from 1867; MD (QUI) 1871; MRCSE 1872; medical officer to the Infirmary, Brownlow Hill, Liverpool c 1875; medical officer to Leeds Workhouse and Industrial School c 1876–9; returned to Landhead, Ballymoney c 1879; married 21 October 1875 in Ballymoney Reformed Presbyterian Church, his first cousin Jane Adams Staveley, daughter of the Rev Alexander McLeod Staveley, minister of St John's, New Brunswick, and Kilraughts Reformed Presbyterian Churches; died 8 February 1880 at sea; his widow married (2) 19 March 1883 the Rev James Brown Armour, minister of Ballymoney Presbyterian Church; probate Belfast 10 May 1880. [Barkley (1986); Belf PRO, will cal; Bennett (1974); Loughridge (1970); *Med Dir*; QCB adm reg; UHF database (m)].

HAMILTON, ANDREW (d 1860), Londonderry and Burt, county Donegal;
 LRCP LRCS Edin 1828; MD (Edin) 1829 (thesis 'De scrofula'); general practitioner, of Sackville Street, Londonderry, and physician to the Cholera Hospital, also of Burt; married 26 January 1832 in Burt, Mary Anne Ewing of Burt; died 1 May 1860 at Burt Cottage. [*BNL* 31 January 1832 (m) and 3 May 1860 (d); Edin Univ; Kirkpatrick Archive; Lewis (1837); *Londonderry Sentinel* 28 January 1832 (m) and 4 May 1860 (d); *Med Dir*].

HAMILTON, ANDREW SMITH (1821–72), Fahan, county Donegal;
 born 1821, son of the Rev David Hamilton, minister of Fahan Presbyterian Church, and Jane Logan; studied medicine at Glasgow University; LM (Glas) 1840; MD (Glas) 1842; CM 1847; medical officer to Burt, Inch and Fahan Dispensary Districts, of Gort House, Fahan; married 16 December 1856 at Lochaline House, Morvan, Argyllshire, Mary Elizabeth Sinclair, youngest daughter of John Sinclair, landed proprietor, of Lochaline, and Catherine MacLachlan; died 29 February 1872 at Gort House; administration Londonderry 6 May 1872. [Addison (1898); Belf PRO, will cal; *Coleraine Chronicle* 27 December 1856 (m); Croly (1843–6); Dub GRO (d); Edin GRO (m); Kirkpatrick Archive; McConnell (1951); *Med Dir*].

HAMILTON, ARCHIBALD ALEXANDER (1855/6–1915), Adelaide, Australia;
 born 1855/6, youngest son of Thomas Hamilton of Grange House, Moy, county Tyrone; educated at Dungannon Royal School; studied arts and medicine at Trinity College, Dublin, from 1874; BA (TCD) 1878; MB BCh 1880; MB (Adelaide) 1883; emigrated to Australia c 1881; house physician and later honorary assistant physician to Adelaide Hospital; general practitioner, of 'The Cedars', Grote Street, Adelaide c

1885 and of Gwydir House, 25 Angus Street, Adelaide c 1895; president of the South Australian Branch of BMA; married 28 September 1880 in Christ Church, Leeson Park, Dublin, Anne Elizabeth Ringwood, daughter of the Rev Henry Taylor Ringwood, curate of Mullabrack, county Tyrone; died c 1915. [Fleming (2001); *Med Dir*; TCD adm reg; *TCD Cat*, vol II (1896)].

HAMILTON, ARTHUR (1788–1842), Army Medical Service;
born 16 June 1788; joined the Army Medical Service as assistant surgeon to the 39th Foot 1810; surgeon to the 5th Foot and 39th Foot 1825; transferred to the 45th Foot 1838; retired 1839; died 28 August 1842 at Crossgar House, county Down; buried in Kilmore Church of Ireland Graveyard; probate Down Diocesan Court 1842. [*BNL* 13 September 1842 (d); Belf PRO, Down Dio Wills Index; Clarke, *County Down*, vol 3 (1969); Peterkin and Johnston (1968)].

HAMILTON, ARTHUR BLAYNEY (1867–93), Kingstown, county Dublin;
born 29 May 1867 at Gallany, Strabane, county Tyrone, son of Richard T. Hamilton, poor law inspector, of Gallany, and Anne Blacker; educated at Portora Royal School, Enniskillen, from 1883; studied arts and medicine at Trinity College, Dublin, from 1890; BA MB BCh BAO (TCD) 1893; general practitioner, of 4 Willow Bank, Kingstown; unmarried; died 30 December 1893 at Firmount, Fortwilliam Park, Belfast, probably from tuberculosis; buried in Belfast City Cemetery. [Belf City Cem, bur reg; Dub GRO (b) and (d); *Med Dir; Portora Royal School Register* (1940); TCD adm reg; *TCD Cat*, vol II (1896)].

HAMILTON, CHARLES (*fl c* 1792), Fort Stewart, county Donegal;
LAH Dub 1792; apothecary, of Fort Stewart. [Apothecaries (1829)].

HAMILTON, CHARLES (d 1842), Army Medical Service and Portadown, county Armagh;
joined the Army Medical Service as assistant surgeon to the 72nd Foot 1809; surgeon to 54th Foot 1820; retired on half pay 1836 at Killycomain, Portadown; married 14 November 1825 in Magherafelt Church of Ireland Church, Margaret Paterson, third daughter of Thomas Paterson; died 18 December 1842 at Killycomaine House; administration Armagh Diocesan Court 1843. [*BNL* 18 November 1825 (m) and 27 December 1842 (d); Dub Nat Arch, Armagh Dio Admins index; Peterkin and Johnston (1968)].

HAMILTON, CHARLES WOLFE (c1859–1949), Marple, Cheshire, Finglass, county Dublin, and Victor Harbour, South Australia;
born 1859/60, in Castlecaulfield, county Tyrone, son of the Rev Robert Hamilton, curate of Donoughmore, county Tyrone, and rector of Dundalk and of Drumcree; [Ferrar states that he was born 1858 in county Leitrim, son of the Rev. John Hamilton, rector of Cloncare, county Leitrim]; educated at Armagh Royal School from c 1875 and in Lurgan; studied arts and medicine at Trinity College, Dublin, from 1877; BA (TCD) 1881; MB BCh 1883; MD 1894; emigrated to Australia as a general practitioner c 1884; of Gladstone and Laura, South Australia c 1885 and

of Tower Croft, Marple, Cheshire c 1885–93; surgeon to Kapunda Hospital and Gladstone Goal; of Farnham House Finglass, county Dublin c 1893–4; emigrated finally to Victor Harbour, 1896 and retired to 24 North Terrace, Adelaide; died 17 March 1949 at Victor Harbour. [Ferrar (1933); Kirkpatrick Archive; Leslie (1911); *Med Dir*; TCD adm reg; *TCD Cat*, vol II (1896); *TCD Reg*].

HAMILTON, DAVID (1858/9–1928), Fahan, county Donegal;
born 1858/9; studied medicine at the Royal College of Surgeons in Ireland; LRCSI 1882; LRCP Edin 1886; house surgeon to the Isle of Man General Hospital; medical officer to Burt, Inch and Fahan Dispensary Districts, of Gort House and later 'Ennerdale', Fahan; of Crislaghmore, Fahan, c 1895; married Elizabeth J. —; died 6 September 1928 at Figary, Fahan; probate Dublin 13 November 1928. [Dub GRO (d); Dub Nat Arch, will cal; *Med Dir*].

HAMILTON, DAVID HENNESSY (1866–92) Norton-le-Moors, Staffordshire;
born 21 December 1866 at Hill Street, Newry, son of William Robert Hamilton, druggist, of Hill Street, and Fanny Bunting Hennessy; educated at Armagh Royal School, from c 1880; studied medicine at Queen's College, Belfast, from 1883; MB BCh BAO (RUI) 1889; general practitioner, of Hillside, Norton-le-Moors; died 13 June 1892; administration Lichfield 14 October 1892. [Belf GRO (b); Ferrar (1933); Lond PPR, will cal; *Med Dir*; QCB adm reg].

HAMILTON, DAVID JOHN (1818/9–88), Cookstown, county Tyrone;
born 1818/9; brother of Dr Thomas William Hamilton (*q.v.*); MRCSE 1839; LM Dub Lying in Hosp 1839; the first medical officer to Cookstown Union Workhouse and Fever Hospital 1841–88; certifying factory surgeon; coroner for Dungannon; married 25 June 1844 in St Anne's Church of Ireland Church, Belfast, Euphemia Murray (who died 22 December 1846 at Cookstown), eldest daughter of John Murray of Belfast; died 19 January 1888 at Cookstown; probate Armagh 24 March 1888. [*BNL* 28 June 1844 (m) and 29 December 1846 (d); Belf PRO, will cal; Dub GRO (d): Johnston (1996); Kirkpatrick Archive; *Med Dir*].

HAMILTON, EDWARD WALLACE (1864–1929), London;
born 16 April 1864 at 12 St Stephen's Green West, Dublin, eldest son of Dr Edward Hamilton, MB (TCD) 1846, FRCSI, surgeon in ordinary to the Lord Lieutenant, and Elizabeth Glover; brother of Dr William Cope Hamilton (*q.v.*); educated at Armagh Royal School 1880–82; studied arts and medicine at Trinity College, Dublin, from 1881; BA MB (TCD) 1886; LRCSI 1886; general practitioner, of 100 St John's Hill, New Wandsworth, London; married Agatha Mary —; died 19 April 1929 at Fulham Infirmary following an accident; probate London 17 June 1929. [Dub GRO (b); Ferrar (1933); Lond PPR, will cal; *Med Dir;* TCD adm reg; *TCD Cat*, vol II (1896)].

HAMILTON, FRANCIS (*fl c* 1756), Belfast;
apothecary, of High Street, Belfast; lease dated 1756. [Brett (2004)].

HAMILTON, FRANCIS (d 1855), Dungannon, county Tyrone;
surgeon, of Dungannon; died 1855. [*Med Dir*].

HAMILTON, SIR HENRY (1851–1932) Indian Medical Service;
born 7 April 1851 at Raphoe, county Donegal, son of William Hamilton of Coolaghy House, Raphoe; brother of Dr James Hamilton of London (*q.v.*) studied arts and medicine at Queen's College, Belfast, from 1868; BA 1872; MD MCh Dip Mid (QUI) 1875; joined the Indian Medical Service (Bengal establishment) as surgeon 1876; surgeon major 1888; surgeon lieutenant-colonel 1896; colonel 1902; surgeon general 1907; served in Afghanistan 1878–80, action at Charasiah, operations in and around Kabul, affair at Shekhabad, march under General Roberts from Kabul to Kandahar, battle of Kandahar, mentioned in despatches, medal with three clasps and bronze star; served in Northwest Frontier, Chitral 1895, medal with clasp; served in Samara and Kurram Valley 1897–8, and in Tirah; served in China 1900, medal; GSP 1902; CB 1904; retired 1911; KCB 1913; lived finally at the Villa Noel, Mentone, Alpes Martimes, France; married (1) 1900 Violetta Williams, daughter of John Williams; and (2) 1909 Bessie Phear Woodford Locke, daughter of Henry Locke; died 21 January 1932 at Mentone; probate London 3 May 1932. [*BMJ* obituary (1932); Crawford (1930); Crone (1928); Kirkpatrick Archive; *Lancet* obituary (1932); Lond PPR, will cal; *Med Dir*; Newmann (1993); QCB adm reg].

HAMILTON, JAMES (b c 1704);
born c 1704 near Caledon, son of the Rev William Hamilton, Archdeacon of Armagh, and Catherine Leslie, educated by Mr Finlay; studied arts and medicine at Trinity College, Dublin, from 1717; BA (TCD) 1721); MB and MD 1730; studied medicine also at Leyden from 1725. [Burtchaell and Sadleir (1924); Leslie (1911); Innes Smith (1932)].

HAMILTON, JAMES (1784/5–1869), Cookstown, county Tyrone, and Auckland, New Zealand;
born 1784/5; surgeon, of Cookstown, c 1824; emigrated to New Zealand; general practitioner, of Rutland Road, Parnel, Auckland; died 8 July 1869 at Rutland Road. [*Coleraine Chronicle* 16 October 1869 (d); Pigot (1824].

HAMILTON, JAMES (1789/90–1869), Naval Medical Service and Newtownstewart, county Tyrone;
born 1789/90; LAH Dub 1808; MRCSE; joined the Naval Medical Service as assistant surgeon; surgeon 1811; Dip Mid Westminster Hospital, London; medical officer to Newtownstewart Dispensary 1842 and to Newtownstewart Dispensary District from 1852; married 1 August 1839 at Inver Church of Ireland Church, county Donegal, Patricia Babington, youngest daughter of Murray Babington of Bonny Glen; died 30 September 1869 at Newtownstewart; administration Londonderry 8 December 1873 [*BNL* 13 August 1839 (m); Belf PRO, will cal; Croly (1843–6); Dub GRO (d); *Londonderry Sentinel* 10 August 1839 (m) and 5 October 1869 (d); *Med Dir; NMS* (1826)].

HAMILTON, JAMES (1805/6–64), Dungannon, county Tyrone;
born 1805/6; LRCS Edin 1831; medical officer to Dungannon Dispensary District, Workhouse and Fever Hospital, of Northland Road, Dungannon; married 25 February 1845 in St Mary's Church of Ireland Church, Newry, Emily Wallace (who was born 1813/4 and died 16 April 1898), daughter of John Henry Wallace of Newry; died 10 March 1864 at Northland Road; administration Armagh 26 September 1866. [*BNL* 4 March 1845 (m); Belf PRO, will cal; *Coleraine Chronicle* 12 March 1864 (d); Croly (1843–6); Dub GRO (d x 2); Kirkpatrick Archive; *Londonderry Sentinel* 15 March 1864 (d); *Med Dir*].

HAMILTON, JAMES (1809/10–68), Strabane, county Tyrone;
born 1809/10; MD [?]; general practitioner and coroner, of Ballyfatton, Strabane; married Harriet —; died 2 April 1868 at Ballyfatton; probate Londonderry 13 May 1868 and 8 May 1880. [Belf PRO, will cal, will; Dub GRO (d); *Londonderry Sentinel* 3 April 1868 (d)].

HAMILTON, JAMES (*fl c* 1835–45), Ramelton, county Donegal;
MD [?]; general practitioner, of Ramelton, c 1845; married 22 October 1835 in Ramelton Church, Margaret McIlwain(e), only daughter of James McIlwain; died c 1850. [*BNL* 27 October 1835 (m); Croly (1843–6); *Londonderry Sentinel* 24 October 1835 (m); *Strabane Morning Post* 27 October 1835 (m)].

HAMILTON, JAMES (1850/1–1918), Huddersfield and Leeds, Yorkshire;
born 1850/1, youngest son of the Rev William Hamilton, minister of Edenderry Presbyterian Church, county Tyrone; brother-in-law of James Ross, senior inspector of National Schools, of Shantallow, Londonderry; studied medicine at Queen's College, Galway (scholar and exhibitioner), at the Carmichael School, Dublin, and in Glasgow; MD BCh (RUI) 1889; general practitioner, of South Parade, Huddersfield c 1895 and Chapel Hill House c 1910; died 23 September 1918 at Chapel Hill House, 27 St Michael's Road, Huddersfield; probate London 19 December 1918. [Kirkpatrick Archive; *Lancet* obituary (1918); Lond GRO (d); Lond PPR, will cal; McConnell (1951); *Med Dir*].

HAMILTON, JAMES (1852–1924), Liverpool, Lancashire, and London;
born 16 July 1852 at Raphoe, county Donegal, son of William Hamilton, farmer, of Coolaghey House, Raphoe; brother of Sir Henry Hamilton (*q.v.*); educated at Raphoe Royal School; studied medicine at Queen's College, Galway, and from 1871, at Queen's College, Belfast; MD MCh Dip Mid (QUI) 1875; medical officer to Liverpool Parish Infirmary; general practitioner, of Pelham Street and of 60 Sydney Street, Chelsea, London, from c 1880; died 11 August 1924; buried in Kensal Green Cemetery; probate London 7 October 1924. [Kirkpatrick Archive; Lond PPR, will cal; Martin (2003) *Med Dir*; *Medical Press* (1924); QCB adm reg]

HAMILTON, JAMES (c 1858–1929), Glasgow, Lanarkshire;
born c 1858, son of John Hamilton of Cushendun, county Antrim; studied medicine at Glasgow University; MB CM (Glas) 1880; FRFPS Glas 1896; assistant physician

to Victoria Infirmary, Glasgow; assistant physician and anaesthetist to Glasgow Samaritan Hospital for Women; general practitioner, of 24 Abbotsford Place, Glasgow c 1885–1900 and 1 Royal Crescent and 76 Queen's Drive, Crosshill, Glasgow, from c 1900; served in RAMC during World War I, with the 4th Scottish General Hospital; author of various medical papers; president of the Glasgow Southern Medical Society and Glasgow Medico-Chirurgical Society; died 10 June 1929 at his home; buried in Cregagh Graveyard, Cushendun. [Addison (1898); *BMJ* obituary (1929); *Independent* 11 April 1832 (d); Kirkpatrick Archive; *Med Dir*].

HAMILTON, JAMES CATHCART (1869–1947), Sunderland, county Durham;
born 15 February 1869 at Cookstown, county Tyrone, son of Henry Hamilton, timber merchant, of Cookstown; educated of Cookstown Academy; studied medicine at Queen's College, Belfast, from 1887, Edinburgh University and Royal College of Surgeons in Edinburgh; LRCP LRCS Edin 1896; LFPS Glas 1896, general practitioner, of 6 Dundas Street, Sunderland, from c 1900 and of 21 Roher Park Road, Sunderland, from c 1928; author of various medical papers; married Jean Baxter —; died 20 June 1947; probate Durham 4 September 1947. [Lond PPR, will cal; *Med Dir*; QCB adm reg].

HAMILTON, JAMES (M.) (1860–1934), Dromore, county Tyrone;
born 28 August 1860 at Meenlougher, Castlefin, county Donegal, son of A.T. Hamilton of Meenlougher; educated at Raphoe Royal School; studied medicine at Queen's College, Belfast, from 1878 and the Carmichael School, Dublin; LKQCPI LRCSI 1883; LM Rot Hosp Dub 1885; medical officer to Dromore Dispensary District, county Tyrone, from c 1890; unmarried; died 9 February 1934 at Dromore; probate Londonderry 24 September 1934. [Belf GRO (d); Belf PRO, will cal; *Med Dir*; QCB adm reg].

HAMILTON, JAMES SHARP (1875–1917), Coalville, Leicestershire;
born 1875 in Newry, county Down, son of W.R. Hamilton (*q.v.*), apothecary, of Newry; educated at Newry School; studied medicine at Queen's College, Belfast, from 1893; LRCP LRCS Edin 1898; LFPS Glas 1898; general practitioner, medical officer to the Post Office and Board of Education, of Shilton House and Belvoir Cottage, Coalville; married Agnes Mary —; died 11 April 1917; probate London 6 December 1918. [Lond PPR, will cal; *Med Dir*; QCB adm reg].

HAMILTON, JOHN (1764/5–1813), Clogher, county Fermanagh;
born 1764/5, son of John Hamilton of Killycorran, county Tyrone; FRCSI; died 10 September 1813; buried in Clogher Cathedral Graveyard. [Johnston (1972)].

HAMILTON, JOHN (*fl c* 1808–45), Aughnacloy, county Tyrone;
MFPS Glas 1808; general practitioner of Aughnacloy, c 1845. [Croly (1843–6)].

HAMILTON, JOHN (d 1850), Dungannon, county Tyrone;
surgeon; died 23 October 1850 at his father's residence in Dungannon. [*BNL* 1 November 1850 (d); *Londonderry Sentinel* 1 November 1850 (d)].

HAMILTON, JOHN, senior (c 1787–1856), Omagh, county Tyrone;
born c 1787; LAH Dub; LFPS Glas and LM 1808; MRCSI; general practitioner and surgeon, of Omagh from c 1810; married Mary — (who was born 1775/6 and died 28 June 1851); father of Dr John Hamilton, junior (*q.v.*) and Alexander Hamilton who died 11 December 1833 as a medical student; died 22 September 1856, buried in Cappagh Church of Ireland Graveyard. [*BNL* 7 July 1851 (d); *Coleraine Chronicle* 12 July 1851 (d) and 4 October 1856 (d); Croly (1843–6); *Londonderry Sentinel* 11 July 1851 (d) and 3 October 1856 (d); McGrew (1998); *Med Dir;* Pigot (1824); *Strabane Morning Post* 17 December 1833 (d, son)].

HAMILTON, JOHN, junior (1809/10–56), Omagh, county Tyrone;
born 1809/10, son of Dr John Hamilton, senior, of Omagh (*q.v.*) and Mary —; cousin of Dr Thomas Hamilton of Omagh (*q.v.*); studied medicine at Glasgow University; LM Rot Hosp Dub 1826; MRCSE 1829; MD (Glas) 1835; FRCSI 1844; general practitioner of Omagh; medical officer to Omagh Fever Hospital, Dispensary and constabulary; married 2 January 1837 Elizabeth Greer (who was born 1814/5 and died 27 June 1879), daughter of David Greer of Omagh; died 27 November 1856; buried in Cappagh Church of Ireland Graveyard. [Addison (1898); *BNL* 1 December 1856 (d); *Coleraine Chronicle* 6 December 1856 (d); Croly (1843–6); Kirkpatrick Archive; *Londonderry Sentinel* 4 December 1856 (d); McGrew (1998) and (2001) (m); *Med Dir*].

HAMILTON, JOHN (*fl c* 1845), Cookstown, county Tyrone;
LAH Dub; apothecary, of Cookstown c 1845. [Croly (1843–6)].

HAMILTON, JOHN (*fl c* 1845), Portrush, county Antrim;
general practitioner and medical officer to constabulary, of Portrush c 1845; married 10 December 1841 at Ballywillan Church, Portrush, Rebecca Rice of Portrush, fourth daughter of Thomas Rice of Coleraine; died before his daughter, Laura Louisa, who died 15 August 1862 at Coleraine. [*BNL* 17 December 1841 (m); Croly (1843–6); *Londonderry Sentinel* 22 August 1862 (d)].

HAMILTON, JOHN ECCLES (1824/5–67), Naval Medical Service and Fintona, county Tyrone;
born 1824/5, son of James Hamilton, gentleman; MRCSE 1845; LM 1857; LKQCPI 1860; LRCSE; joined the Naval Medical Service as surgeon; retired to Fintona; general practitioner, of Gartmore Cottage and, from 1864, of Castle Lodge, Fintona; married 22 June 1852 in Fintona Church of Ireland Church, Emily Buchanan, second daughter of James Buchanan of Fintona, merchant; died 11 July 1867 at Castle Lodge; probate Armagh 3 March 1868. [*BNL* 2 July 1852 (m); Belf PRO, will cal; Dub GRO (m) and (d); *Londonderry Sentinel* 25 June 1852 (m) and 16 July 1867 (d); *Med Dir*].

HAMILTON, ROBERT (1748/9–1830), Army Medical Service, Colchester, Essex and Ipswich, Suffolk;
born 1748/9 in Coleraine; studied medicine at Edinburgh University; MD (Edin) 1780 (thesis 'De nicotianae viribus in medicina'); LRCP Lond 1795; joined the Army

Medical Service as surgeon's mate to 10th Foot 1880; physician in the West Indies 1795; 'notable for his support of civil and religious liberty' and an advocate of 'the abolition of the slave trade' (*Oxford DNB*); general practitioner in Colchester and later in Ipswich; became totally blind c 1800; author of *Remarks on the Means of Obviating the Fatal Effects of the Bite of a Mad Dog, or other Rabid Animals* (1785), *The Duties of a Regimental Surgeon Considered* (2 vols) (1788), *Observations on the Marsh Remittent Fever, and on the Water Canker and Leprosy: with a Memoir of his Life* (1801) and other medical publications; married 23 December 1825 Margaret Bloomfield; died 29 May 1830 at Ipswich. [Crone (1928); Edin Univ; *Munk's Roll*, vol 2; Newmann (1993); *Oxford DNB* (2004); Peterkin and Johnston (1968)].

HAMILTON, ROBERT (1763/4–1818), Strabane, county Tyrone;
born (probably) 1763/4; surgeon; died 7 January 1818; buried in Leckpatrick Old Graveyard, Strabane (age could be 34 or 54). [Todd (1991)].

HAMILTON, ROBERT (c 1769–c 1832), Dublin;
born c 1769 'in the north of Ireland', son of a merchant; LRCSI MRCSI 1791; staff surgeon with the Irish Army March–November 1797 but was dismissed; surgeon to St Mark's Hospital, Dublin; president of the Royal College of Surgeons in Ireland 1805; 'amassed a fortune and retired to Enniskillen to enjoy it' (Cameron); married —; died c 1832. [Cameron (1916); Peterkin and Johnston (1968); Widdess (1967)].

HAMILTON, ROBERT, senior (1785/6–1864), Liverpool, Lancashire;
born 1785/6, probably at Magheraboy, Ballymoney, county Antrim; MRCS; surgeon and obstetric physician, of 1 Prince's Road, Liverpool; unmarried; uncle of Dr Robert Hamilton junior (*q.v.*), FRCSE, who appears to have shared his house and his practice; died 21 April 1864 at 1 Prince's Road; probate Liverpool 18 May 1864. [*Coleraine Chronicle* 30 April 1864 (d); Lond PPR, will cal, will; *Londonderry Sentinel* 26 April 1864 (d); *Med Dir*].

HAMILTON, ROBERT (1820–80), London and Jamaica;
born 11 November 1820 at Cluntagh, county Down, elder son of the Rev Archibald Robert Hamilton, rector of Balteagh, county Londonderry, and Jane Cotter; studied medicine at Cambridge University 1839–42; BA (Cantab) 1842; MA 1845; B es Sc (Paris) 1846; MD (Paris) 1851; MRCSE 1851; MD (Cantab) 1858; general physician to the Westminster Dispensary and NW London Free Dispensary for Sick Children; of 1 Howick Place, Victoria Street, London; member of the Board of Government, medical examiner and Commissioner for Inspection of General Hospitals and Lunatic Asylums of Jamaica; of Clifton Mount, St Andrews, Jamaica; married (1) Eleanor Anne Walkington (who died 6 July 1871), daughter of Robert Walkington; (2) 4 December 1872 Katherine Elizabeth Land, eldest daughter of Thomas Land of Spanish Town, Jamaica; died 20 May 1880 at Clifton Mount; buried at Craigton, St Andrew, Jamaica. [Burke *LGI* (1912); Leslie (1937); Lond PPR, will cal; *Med Dir*; Venn (1940–54)].

HAMILTON, ROBERT, junior (1827–1914), Liverpool, Lancashire;
born 1827, son of William Hamilton of Liverpool; nephew of Dr Robert Hamilton, senior (*q.v.*) of Liverpool; MRCSE 1849; LSA Lond 1849; FRCSE 1861; honorary surgeon to Liverpool North Dispensary and honorary assistant surgeon to Liverpool Eye and Ear Infirmary; later honorary surgeon to Liverpool South Hospital; a strong advocate of Lister's teaching on carbolic acid; of 7 Great George's Street and 1 Prince's Road, Liverpool; author of various medical papers; retired to Magheraboy, Portrush, county Antrim, a farm which he had inherited; married —; father of Dr Robert Jessop Hamilton, MRCSE 1887, of Liverpool; died 28 August 1914 at 1 Prince's Road; probate London 30 March 1915. [Lond PPR, will cal, will; Plarr (1930); *Med Dir*].

HAMILTON, SAMUEL (1857–1915), Ballynahinch, county Down;
born 1 January 1857 at Dromara, county Down, son of Andrew Hamilton, farmer, of Dromara; educated at Mr James Pyper's Academy; studied medicine at Queen's College, Belfast, from 1877; MD MCh (RUI) 1882; Dip Obst 1884; MAO; 1885; general practitioner, of Dromore Street, Ballynahinch, from c 1886; married 21 June 1890 in Seaforde Church of Ireland Church, county Down, Elizabeth Witherow, daughter of Thomas Witherow, professor of Church History, Magee College; died 4 April 1915. [Barkley (1986); Belf PRO, will cal; Dub GRO (d); *Med Dir*; QCB adm reg; UHF database (m)].

HAMILTON, SAMUEL G. (d 1851), Kilkeel, county Down, and St John, New Brunswick, Canada;
surgeon and apothecary, of Kilkeel c 1819; emigrated to Canada; died 2 July 1851 at St John, New Brunswick. [*BNL* 30 July 1851 (d); Bradshaw (1819)].

HAMILTON, THOMAS (1772/3–1854), Dungannon, county Tyrone,
born 1772/3; LRCS Edin; LAH Dub 1797; surgeon and apothecary, of Market Street, Dungannon, and medical officer to the prison, from c 1800; married c 1800 —; died 7 March 1854 in Dungannon; administration Armagh Diocesan Court 1857. [Apothecaries (1829); Bradshaw (1819); *Coleraine Chronicle* 1 April 1854 (d); Croly (1843–6); Dub Nat Arch, Armagh Dio Admins index; Dungannon Presb Church, bapt reg (PRO NI, MIC 1P/3A/1); Pigot (1824)].

HAMILTON, THOMAS (d 1868), Naval Medical Service;
son of Thomas Hamilton, merchant, of Campsie, Omagh; cousin of Dr John Hamilton, junior, (*q.v.*) of Omagh; joined the Naval Medical Service as assistant surgeon; died 26 January 1868 of yellow fever, on board HMS *Barracouta* at Port Royal, Jamaica. [*Londonderry Sentinel* 3 March 1868 (d); McGrew (2001)].

HAMILTON, THOMAS (1863–1926), Whitefield and Manchester, Lancashire;
born 7 September 1863, at Strabane, county Tyrone, son of William Hamilton, ironmonger, of Strabane; educated at Strabane Academy; studied medicine at Queen's College, Belfast, from 1881; LRCP LRCS Edin 1891; LFPS Glas 1891; general

practitioner, of Ivy House, Bury New Road, Whitefield, from c 1895; of Moville, Clifton Drive, Fairhaven, near Lytham from c 1910 and of Brentwood, Prestwick, Manchester from c 1918; married Catherine —; died 20 April 1926; probate Manchester 11 August 1926. [Lond PPR, will cal; *Med Dir*; QCB, adm reg].

HAMILTON, THOMAS THEOPHILUS (1847/8–95), Bury, Lancashire;
born 1847/8 at Loughgilly, son of John Hamilton of Loughgilly; educated at RBAI; studied medicine at Queen's College, Belfast, from 1871; LSA Lond 1883; LRCP LRCS Edin 1884; LFPS Glas 1884; general practitioner, of Mayfield House, Walmersley Road, Bury; died 5 February 1895 at Bury; probate Manchester 29 March 1895. [Lond PPR, will cal; *Med Dir*; QCB adm reg].

HAMILTON, THOMAS WILLIAM (c 1820–75), Newtownbreda, Drumbo and Ballymacarrett, county Down, and Mitcham, Surrey;
born c 1820; son of Dr James Hamilton (*q.v.* – not identified), surgeon; brother of Dr David John Hamilton (*q.v.*); studied medicine at Glasgow University; LRCSI and LM 1847; MD (Glas) 1848; house surgeon to Belfast Fever Hospital; medical officer to Newtownbreda, Drumbo and Ballymacarrett Dispensaries, Belfast; of 6 Donegall Square East; later general practitioner, of Baron Lodge, Mitcham; married 4 November 1854 in St Anne's Church of Ireland Church, Belfast, Anne Posnett, daughter of Hutcheson Posnett, gentleman, of Rose Lodge, Belfast; died 7 March 1875 at Mitcham; probate London 20 March 1875. [Addison (1898); *BNL* 13 November 1854 (m); Dub GRO (m); Lond GRO (d); Lond PPR, will cal; *Med Dir*].

HAMILTON, WALTER MOFFET (1863–1921), Patricroft and Eccles, Lancashire;
born 2 June 1863 at Saintfield, county Down, son of the Rev Samuel Hamilton, minister of First Saintfield Presbyterian Church, and his second wife, Elizabeth Breakey; educated at Lurgan College; studied medicine at Queen's College, Belfast, 1883–7; gold medal, Ulster Hospital, Belfast; MD MCh BAO (RUI) 1887; Dip State Med RCPSI 1893; general practitioner, of 456 Liverpool Road, Patricroft c 1888–93, and of Pendleton Lodge, Patricroft, from c 1893; surgeon to No 8 Section of the Manchester Ship Canal; honorary surgeon to Eccles and Patricroft Hospital from c 1898; medical officer of health for Eccles; medical officer, public vaccinator and certifying factory inspector to Barton Union; surgeon major to the 3rd Volunteer Brigade of the Lancaster Fusiliers; author of various medical papers; JP for the Borough of Eccles; married 23 September 1896 in St Mary Magdalene's Parish Church, Ashton upon Mersey, Cheshire, Florence Hardy (who was born 1873/3), daughter of Joseph Hardy, traveller, of Ashton upon Mersey; died 6 February 1921; probate Manchester 9 April 1921. [Barkley (1986); Lond GRO (m); Lond PPR, will cal; *Med Dir*; QCB adm reg].

HAMILTON, WILLIAM (1746/7–70), Downpatrick, county Down;
born 1746/7, son of Charles Hamilton of Carnacally, county Down, and Margaret —; surgeon and apothecary, of Downpatrick; died 10 June 1770; buried in Kilmore Graveyard; his shop was then sold to Dr Henry Trevor (*q.v.*). [*BNL* May 1771 (advert); Clarke, *County Down*, vol 3 (1969)].

HAMILTON, WILLIAM (1758–1807), London;
   born 1758 in Strabane, county Tyrone; studied arts at Glasgow University and medicine at Edinburgh University; MD (Edin) 1779 (thesis 'De sanguine humano'); LRCP Lond 1786; physician to the London Hospital, 1787–1807, of Old Broad Street, London; mentioned as trustee in the will (dated 26 October 1804) of Robert Coningham, formerly of Londonderry and now of Gower Street, London; died 5 May 1807 at Old Broad Street. [Edin Univ; Elliott, Simon, pers com; *Munk's Roll*, vol 2].

HAMILTON, WILLIAM (*fl c* 1765–90), Naval Medical Service, Strabane, county Tyrone, and Londonderry;
   son of Thomas Hamilton of Gortavea, county Tyrone; joined the Naval Medical Service, serving in the West Indies but resigned c 1769 because of ill health; surgeon in Gortavea, Strabane, 'earning a precarious living by inoculating children against smallpox'; applied for the post of surgeon in Lifford Hospital in 1774 and 1779 but was unsuccessful; apothecary in Londonderry c 1782 and wrote to the Earl of Abercorn in November 1783 expressing a desire to 'settle with his brother in Gortavea to keep some medicines and practise as surgeon'; did not move and was still living and working there in March 1786. [Roulston (2000) and (2010)].

HAMILTON, WILLIAM (*fl c* 1790), Londonderry;
   only son of William Hamilton, gentleman, of Londonderry; studied medicine at Glasgow University; matriculated 1774; MD (Glas) 1790; LRCS Edin; surgeon, of Ferryquay Street, Londonderry c 1824. [Addison (1898) and (1913); Pigot (1824)].

HAMILTON, WILLIAM (1782/3–1856), Oxford and Mexico;
   born 1782/3 in Dublin, eldest son of the Rev William Hamilton, rector of Clondevaddock, county Donegal (murdered 1797) and Sarah —; studied arts at Trinity College, Dublin, from 1799, and medicine at Magdalen College, Oxford, from 1808; BA (TCD) 1805; BM (Oxon) 1809; notable botanist; resident in Mexico in 1835; married Mary — (who was born 1791/2 and died 16 August 1856 at Gortmessan, Strabane, county Tyrone); died 24 May 1856 at Plymouth, Devon. [*BNL* 31 May 1856 (d) and 18 September 1856 (d); Burtchaell and Sadleir (1924); Foster (1888); Leslie (1940); *Londonderry Sentinel* 29 August 1856 (d); Praeger (1949)].

HAMILTON, WILLIAM (1867–1921), Wigan, Lancashire;
   born 27 March 1867 at Ballynabragget, Lurgan, county Armagh, son of John Hamilton, farmer, of Ballynabragget; educated at Banbridge Academy; studied arts and medicine at Queen's College, Belfast, from 1884; LRCP LRCS Edin 1895; LFPS Glas 1895; general practitioner, of 95 Wallgate, Wigan; married Viola —; died 8 November 1920; probate London 23 February 1921. [Lond PPR, will cal; *Med Dir*; QCB adm reg].

HAMILTON, WILLIAM COPE (1867–1928), Dublin;
   born 27 February 1867, second son of Dr Edward Hamilton, MD, surgeon in ordinary to the Lord Lieutenant; brother of Dr Edward Wallace Hamilton (*q.v.*);

educated at Armagh Royal School 1880–84; studied medicine at the Royal College of Surgeons in Ireland; LRCSI and LM 1892; LRCPI and LM 1892; LM Rot Hosp Dub; house surgeon in Dr Stephen's Hospital, Dublin; general practitioner, of 120 Stephens Green West, Dublin; captain in RAMC during World War I; died 7 September 1928 in the Isle of Man; administration (with will) Dublin 26 November 1928. [Dub Nat Arch, will cal; Ferrar (1933); Kirkpatrick Archive; *Med Dir*].

HAMILTON, WILLIAM FREDERICK (1857/8–1932), ship's surgeon and Donnemana, county Tyrone;
   born 1857/8, son of Dr William James Hamilton (*q.v.*); studied medicine at Glasgow University; LRCP LRCS and LM Edin 1884; surgeon on the SS *Armenia* (Anchor Line); medical officer, medical officer of health and public vaccinator to Donnemana Dispensary District from 1892; medical officer to constabulary; of Glencush House, Donnemana; retired 1924; married 25 August 1896 in Second Donagheady Presbyterian Church, Jane Margaret Katharine Clark, daughter of the Rev Frederick James Clark, rector of Donagheady and canon of Derry; died 10 September 1932 at Glencush; probate Londonderry 25 October 1932. [Belfast GRO (d); Belf PRO, will cal; Dub GRO (m); Kirkpatrick Archive; Leslie (1937); *Med Dir*].

HAMILTON, WILLIAM JAMES (1824/5–81), Naval Medical Service;
   born 1824/5, youngest son of Andrew Hamilton of Curryfree, Glendermott, county Londonderry, and Elizabeth —; brother of Elizabeth Hamilton who married Joseph Bond and was mother of Dr William James Bond (*q.v.*); studied medicine at Glasgow University; MD (Glas) 1846; LRCS Edin 1846; joined the Naval Medical Service as surgeon 1861, becoming fleet surgeon and deputy inspector general; served on HMS *Warrior*, the world's first iron battleship, launched in 1860; retired to Curryfree, Glendermot, county Londonderry; married 22 February 1853 in St George's Church, London, Caroline Anne Hunter (who was born 1826/7 and died 8 October 1913), daughter of John Hunter, surgeon, of Hart Street, Bloomsbury, London; father of Dr William Frederick Hamilton (*q.v.*); died 30 September 1881 at Curryfree; buried in Old Donagheady Graveyard; probate Londonderry 27 September 1884. [Addison (1898); Belf PRO, will cal; Dub GRO (d); *Londonderry Sentinel* 14 March 1853 (m); *Med Dir;* Todd (1992)].

HAMILTON, W.R. (*fl c* 1875–93), Newry, county Down;
   apothecary, of Newry; married —; father of Dr James Sharp Hamilton (*q.v.*) (born 1875); died before 1893. [QCB adm reg].

HAMILTON, WILLIAM ROBERT (1859–93), ship's surgeon and Clogher, county Tyrone;
   born 25 December 1859 at Creevehill, county Fermanagh, son of John Hamilton, farmer, of Creevehill; educated at Fivemiletown School; studied medicine at Queen's College, Belfast, from 1877; MD MCh (RUI) 1882; LM KQCPI 1883; surgeon on the Dominion Line; medical officer to Clogher Workhouse and Infirmary; unmarried; died 19 August 1893 at Creevehill; administration Armagh 23 May 1894. [Belf PRO, will cal; Dub GRO (d): *Med Dir;* QCB adm reg].

HAMILTON, — (*fl c* 1815), Cookstown, county Tyrone;
surgeon, of Cookstown; married 11 September 1815 Mary Jane Cloughea, eldest daughter of Thomas Cloughea of Derrycaw, county Armagh. [*BNL* 15 September 1815 (m)].

HAMMERSLEY, JOHN (1810/1–41), Belfast;
born 1810/1, only son of Lieut William Hammersley of Belfast and Jane Brown; surgeon of 3rd Garrison Battalion; died 3 April 1841 at 3 Ship Street, Belfast; buried in Knockbreda Graveyard. [*BNL* 13 April 1841 (d); Clarke, *County Down*, vol 2, (2nd ed, 1988)].

HANCOCK, THOMAS (1783–1849), Liverpool, Lancashire, London and Lisburn, county Antrim;
born 26 March 1783 in Lisburn, a Quaker, 4th son of Jacob Hancock of Lisburn and Elizabeth Phelps; educated at a Quaker school in Yorkshire; apprenticed to a surgeon and apothecary in Waterford; studied medicine in Dublin and at Edinburgh University; MD (Edin) 1806 (thesis 'De morbis epidemicis'); LRCP Lond 1809; general practitioner in London and physician to the City and Finsbury Dispensary 1809–29 and in Liverpool 1829–38 and Stannus Place, Lisburn 1838–49; author of *Researches into the Laws and Phenomena of Pestilence* … (1812), *The Law of Mercy, a Poetical Essay on the Punishment of Death* (1819) and *The Principles of Peace, as embodied in the Conduct of the Society of Friends* … (1825) containing many eye witness statements about the 1798 Rising, as well as many medical papers; married 1810 Hannah Strangman (who died in 1828), eldest daughter of Thomas Hancock Strangman of Waterford; died 16 April 1849 in Lisburn; buried in the Friends' Burying Ground, Lisburn. [*BNL* 20 April 1849 (d); Biggart (1949); Croly (1843–6); Crone (1928); *DIB* (2009); Edin Univ; Harrison (1997); *Lisburn Fam Hist Soc*, vol 2 (2005); Martin (2003); *Munk's Roll*, vol 3; Newmann (1993); *Oxford DNB* (2004); Praeger (1949)].

HANNA, HARRISON (1826/7–71), Belfast;
born 1826/7; studied medicine at Queen's College, Belfast; LM (QCB) 1851; MRCSE 1852; LM RCSE 1860; MD (Aber) 1860; general practitioner, of Peter's Hill, Belfast; married Letitia — (who was born 1817/8 and died December 1862); died 21 February 1871 at Belfast; buried in Shankill Graveyard, Belfast; probate Belfast 29 November 1871. [Belf PRO, will cal; Clarke, *Belfast*, vol 1 (1982); Dub GRO (d); *Med Dir*].

HANNA, JAMES (1839/40–c 1878), Belfast;
born 1839/40, son of David Hanna of Drumreagh, Killinchy, county Down; educated at Saintfield School; studied medicine at Queen's College, Belfast, from 1859; MRCSE 1863; general practitioner, of Peter's Hill, Belfast; died c 1878. [*Med Dir*; QCB adm reg].

HANNA JAMES (1850/1–96), Romford, Essex;
born 1850/1 at Cabra, county Down, son of John Hanna, farmer, of Cabra; educated at Newry School; studied medicine at Queen's College, Belfast, from 1879; general

practitioner, of Aberdour House, Romford, c 1885 and The Ferns, South Street, Romford c 1895; died 29 June 1896 at South Street; administration London 30 July 1896. [Lond GRO (d); Lond PPR, will cal; *Med Dir*; QCB adm reg].

HANNA, SAMUEL (1799–1867), Dublin;
born 1799 in Newry, son of James Hanna, merchant; studied arts and medicine at Trinity College, Dublin, from 1816; scholar 1819; BA (TCD) 1821; MA MB 1825; LKQCPI 1833; FKQCPI 1835; physician to Cork Street Fever Hospital and Guinness's Brewery, Dublin, of 42 Leinster Road, Rathmines; retired and lived abroad c 1864–5; lived finally at Beaumaris, Anglesey; MRIA; married — Fortesque, daughter of William Henry Fortesque of Dublin; died 22 October 1867 at Beaumaris; buried in Llanfaes Churchyard, Wales; probate Dublin 8 January 1868. [Belf PRO, will cal; Burtchaell and Sadleir (1924); Cameron (1916); *Med Dir*].

HANNA, WILLIAM (d 1863), Belfast;
LRCS Edin 1859; general practitioner, of 35 Mill Street, Belfast; died 22 May 1863 at Mill Street. [*Med Dir*].

HANNA, WILLIAM (1868–1941), Bombay, India, and Liverpool, Lancashire;
born 19 June 1868 in Belfast, son of John Hanna, draper, of Lisanor Villa, Antrim Road, Belfast; educated at Belfast Academy; studied medicine at Queen's College, Belfast, from 1886; MA (RUI) 1893; MB BCH BAO 1895; DPH Camb 1898; MD (QUB) 1912; bacteriologist with the Government in Bombay 1899–1901; assistant medical officer of health, Liverpool, 1901, medical officer to the Port and Sanitary Department, of Dale Street, Liverpool c 1910; author of *Studies in Smallpox and Vaccination* (1913) and various medical papers; lecturer and instructor in vaccination in Liverpool; married Sybil Christina —; died 13 July 1941 at David Lewis Northern Hospital, Birkenhead; probate Llandudno 18 September 1941. [*BMJ* obituary (1941); Kirkpatrick Archive; *Lancet* obituary (1941); Lond PPR, will cal; *Med Dir*; QCB adm reg].

HANNA, WILLIAM GORDON (1859–c 1910), Accrington, Lancashire;
born 9 September 1859 at Boyle, county Roscommon, son of Robert Hanna, manufacturer, of Magherfelt, county Londonderry; educated at RBAI; studied medicine at Queen's College, Belfast, from 1875; MD (QUI) 1880; Dip Obst (RUI) 1883; LM KQCPI 1883; LRCS Edin 1899; surgeon on Royal Mail Steamers; general practitioner, of 11 Abbey Street, Accrington, Lancashire c 1885 and later of Pleck House, Whalley Road, Accrington; surgeon to Accrington Collieries; died c 1910. [*Med Dir*; QCB adm reg].

HANNAY, ROBERT STRICKLAND, senior (1801/2–71), Lurgan, county Armagh, and Belfast;
born 1801/2; studied medicine in Dublin, Glasgow and Edinburgh; MRCSE 1829; MD (Edin) 1830 (thesis 'De structura arteriarum'); LAH Dub 1841; medical officer to Lurgan Dispensary, prison and constabulary, c 1845; retired to 16 Mount Charles, Belfast c 1870; married 5 September 1833 in Downpatrick, county Down, Margaret

Quaile (who died 3 October 1859 at Lurgan); father of Dr Robert Strickland Hannay, junior (*q.v.*); died 12 December 1871 at Mount Charles. [*BNL* 10 September 1833 (m) and 5 October 1859 (d); Croly (1843–6); Dub GRO (d); Edin Univ; *Med Dir*].

HANNAY, ROBERT STRICKLAND, junior (1847–c 1883), London;

born 20 April 1847 in Lurgan, county Armagh, son of Dr Robert Strickland Hannay, senior (*q.v.*); educated at RBAI from 1860; studied civil engineering, arts and medicine at Queen's College, Belfast, from 1863; MRCSE 1871; house surgeon to Belgrave Childrens' Hospital, London, and Royal Westminster Ophthalmic Hospital; general practitioner, of 34 Stanley Street, Pimlico, from c 1871; went abroad c 1873; died c 1883 abroad. [Fisher and Robb (1913); *Med Dir*; QCB adm reg].

HANNAY, ROBERT STRICKLAND (formerly **FUHR**) (1871–1948), Royal Army Medical Corps;

born 27 August 1871 at 16 Mount Charles, Belfast, as Robert Strickland Hannay Fuhr, son of Ernest Augustus Fuhr, linen merchant, of 22 Mount Charles, Belfast, and Dorothea Hannay; educated at Methodist College, Belfast, from 1887 and RBAI; studied medicine at Queen's College, Belfast, from 1887; LRCP LRCS Edin 1893; LFPS Glas 1893; adopted the surname of Hannay c 1897, joined the Royal Army Medical Corps at a lieutenant 1898; captain 1901; major 1910; lieutenant-colonel 1915; temporary colonel 1916; CMG 1917; brevet colonel 1919; colonel 1922; major general 1926; King's Honorary Surgeon 1926; CB 1926; served in South Africa, including the relief of Ladysmith, 1899–1901, India 1902–07, Mediterranean 1915–16; France (ADMS HQ) 1916–19, Egypt 1919–22 and Constantinople (DDMS Turkey) 1922–23; ADMS HQ Eastern Command 1923; DDMS HQ Scottish Command 1923; DDMS HQ Southern Command 1926–30; colonel commandant RAMC 1939–41; of Stubdale, Grasmere, Westmoreland, but lived finally at 56 Wynnstay Gardens, Kensington, London; married Kathleen Dod —; died 5 October 1948 in London; probate London 25 January 1949. [*BMJ* obituary (1948); Drew (1968); Dub GRO (b); Fry (1984); Lond PPR, will cal, will; *Med Dir*; QCB adm reg].

HAPPER, — (1762/3–1847), Tobermore, county Londonderry;

born 1762/3; general practitioner, of Tobermore; died 3 September 1847 at Tobermore. [*Coleraine Chronicle* 18 September 1847 (d)].

HARBINSON, ALEXANDER (1848–1918), Lancaster, Lancashire, and Elgin, Moray;

born June 1848 at Rathfriland, county Down, son of Robert Harbinson, farmer, of Ballynamagna, Rathfriland and Margaret Harbinson [*sic*]; educated at Newry School; studied medicine at Queen's College, Belfast, from 1866; MD (QUI) 1871; MRCSE and LM 1871; senior assistant medical officer to Lancaster County Asylum; general practitioner of Millbank, Elgin, Scotland, from 1897; author of various medical papers; JP for Elgin; married Janet Isabella Kemp; died 2 July 1918 at Millbank; confirmation of will Elgin 28 August 1918. [*BMJ* obituary (1918); Edin GRO (d); Edin Nat Arch, will cal; Kirkpatrick Archive; *Med Dir*; QCB adm reg].

HARBINSON, GEORGE CASEMENT REID (1872–1939), Belfast, and Matlock, Derbyshire;
born 15 February 1872 at the Manse, Clarkesbridge, Castleblaney, county Monaghan, son of the Rev William Hamilton, minister of Clarkesbridge Presbyterian Church, and — Reid; educated at RBAI; studied medicine at Queen's College, Belfast, from 1891; scholar in engineering and medicine; exhibition in medicine at Queen's College, Cork; MB BCh BAO (RUI) 1898; gold medal in diseases of children from Belfast Hospital for Sick Children; house surgeon at Royal Victoria Hospital; demonstrator in physiology and pathology at Queen's University, Belfast; general practitioner and physician to Smedley's Hydropathic Establishment, Matlock; author of various medical papers; married 30 July 1902 in Scarva Street Presbyterian Church, Banbridge, Mary Lawson, daughter of John Lawson, merchant, of Ormeau Road, Belfast; died 26 March 1939 at Matlock; probate Nottingham 10 August 1939. [Barkley (1986); Kirkpatrick Archive; Lond PPR, will cal, will; *Med Dir*; QCB adm reg; UHF database (m)].

HARBINSON, JAMES WILLIAM (1859–c 1935), Middle Brighton, Melbourne, Victoria;
born 5 November 1859 at Belfast, son of John H. Harbinson, jeweller, of 85 High Street and 26 University Square, Belfast; educated at RBAI; studied medicine at Queen's College, Belfast, from 1880; LRCP LRCS and LM Edin 1888; LFPS Glas 1888; emigrated to Australia; general practitioner, of 'Tanderagee', Middle Brighton, Melbourne, Victoria c 1895; author of poetry and medical papers; died c 1935. [*Med Dir*; QCB adm reg].

HARBISON, WILLIAM (d 1861), Rathfriland, county Down;
son of Robert Harbison, farmer of Ballynamagna, county Down; LFPS and LM Glas 1859; general practitioner of Rathfriland; unmarried; died 4 April 1861 of fever at Rathfriland; administration Belfast 29 April 1861. [Belf PRO, will cal; Kirkpatrick Archive; *Med Dir*].

HARCOURT, RICHARD EUGENE (1857–1921), Liverpool and Warrington, Lancashire;
born 18 March 1857 at Newark, New Jersey, USA, son of James M. Harcourt, estate agent, of Newark, but originally from county Down; studied medicine at Queen's College, Belfast, Liverpool, and King's College Hospital, London; MB BCh (RUI) 1887; BAO MD 1893; MD MS (Uruguay) 1893; MRCSE 1907; FRCSE 1907; house surgeon at the Royal Southern Hospital, Liverpool, and at the Manchester Ship Canal Hospital; medical officer to the Buenos Ayres Port Works and constabulary c 1887–97; returned to England 1898; general practitioner, of Warrington, and later of Wavertree, Liverpool, and Stoneleigh, Oakfield, Anfield; pathologist to the Liverpool Eye and Ear Infirmary from 1911 and later assistant surgeon; ophthalmic surgeon to the Bootle Education Committee, assistant surgeon to St Helen's Hospital, Liverpool and demonstrator of ophthalmic pathology in the University of Liverpool; surgeon to St Paul's Eye Hospital 1914–18; married Mary

Duncan —; died 19 May 1921 at Stoneleigh; probate Liverpool 15 August 1921. [*BMJ* obituary (1921); Kirkpatrick Archive; Lond PPR, will cal; *Med Dir*; Plarr (1930); QCB adm reg].

HARDMAN, EDWARD TOWNLEY (b 1815/6), Newbliss, county Monaghan;
born 1815/6 in Drogheda, county Louth, son of Townley Hardman, merchant; educated privately; entered Trinity College, Dublin, 1834, but did not obtain a degree; MD [?]; general practitioner, of Newbliss; married — and had a daughter Frances Hardman who married 1862 Colonel Thomas Sadleir Brereton of Rathurles, county Tipperary; probably died before 1843. [Burke *LGI* (1912); Burtchaell and Sadleir (1924)].

HARDY, CHARLES HENRY (1828/9–83), Victoria, Australia, and Dunedin, New Zealand;
born 1828/9, fourth son of Charles Hardy, merchant, of Stewartstown, county Tyrone, a major in the militia, and Mary Little of Stewartstown; brother of Dr Samuel Little Hardy (*q.v.*); studied medicine at the Royal College of Surgeons in Ireland and Glasgow University; LRCSI 1851; MD (Glas) 1851); emigrated to Australia c 1855; of Carlton, Victoria; later moved to Dunedin, New Zealand; died 24 August 1883. [Addison (1898); Burke *LGI* (1912); *Med Dir*].

HARDY, JOHN (*fl c* 1824), Aughnacloy, county Tyrone;
surgeon, of Aughnacloy c 1824. [Pigot (1824)].

HARDY, SAMUEL LITTLE (1815–68), Dublin;
born 3 October 1815 at Stewartstown, county Tyrone, eldest son of Charles William Hardy, merchant, of Coalisland, county Tyrone, a major in the militia, and Mary Little of Stewartstown; brother of Dr Charles Henry Hardy (*q.v.*); educated privately; apprenticed to Mr Ephraim MacDowel in June 1833 and studied medicine at the Richmond Hospital, Trinity College, Dublin, from 1833, the Royal College of Surgeons in Ireland and Marlborough Street Schools; LRCSI 1839; MD (Glas) 1840; FRCSI 1844; LKQCPI 1852; assistant master of the Rotunda Hospital 1842–5; physician-accoucheur (lecturer) to Dr Steeven's Hospital 1857–68 and physician to Pitt Street Hospital; lecturer in Midwifery in the Cecilia Street School; of 29 Molesworth Street and 172 Rathgar Road, Dublin; president of the Dublin Obstetrical Society; author of *Practical Observations on Midwifery* (1848) and various medical papers; married 29 December 1846 in St Anne's Church of Ireland Church, Dublin, Jemima Mary Montgomery, only daughter of Dr William Fetherstonhaugh Montgomery of Merrion, president of the KQCPI; father of Emma Hardy who married 13 April 1875 in Holy Trinity Church of Ireland Church, Dublin, Samuel McCurdy Greer and was father of Mr Henry Little Hardy Greer, MB (QUB) 1913, FRCS; died 29 October 1868 at Brooklawn, Blackrock, county Dublin. [Addison (1898); Burke *LGI* (1912); Burtchaell and Sadleir (1924); Cameron (1916); Dub GRO (m) for S.L. Hardy and Emma Hardy and (d); Kirkpatrick (1924); Kirkpatrick and Jellett (1913); Martin (2003); *Med Dir*; Widdess (1963)].

HARE, JAMES (1700/1–47), Larne, county Antrim;
born 1700/1; apothecary, of Larne; died March 1747. [Rutherford and Clarke, *County Antrim*, vol 4 (2004)].

HARKIN, ALEXANDER (1817–94), Belfast;
born 1817 at Ballymoney, county Antrim, son of Hugh Harkin of Coleraine, teacher and journalist; studied medicine at RBAI from 1835; MRCSE 1840; LAH Dub 1841; MD (King's Coll Aberd) 1859; FRCSE 1882; general practitioner, of Belfast from 1840; surgeon to Belfast Dispensary District and constabulary from 1864; JP for Belfast and county Antrim, 1864; of 8 Hercules Place, 17 Fountain Street, 1 College Square East and later 5 College Square North, Belfast; president of the Ulster Medical Society 1878–9; consulting physician to Mater Infirmorum Hospital, Belfast, from its opening in 1883; author of various medical papers; married 5 May 1851 at Gortmore, Omagh, Theresa Mary Eleanor Quin (who was born 1833/4 and died 25 September 1889), daughter of James Quin, solicitor, of Omagh; died 4 January 1894 at 5 College Square North, Belfast; buried in Milltown Cemetery, Belfast; received a long and warm obituary from Whitla; probate Belfast 29 January 1894. [*BNL* 9 May 1851 (m); Belf PRO, will cal; Casement (1969); Croly (1843–6); Dub GRO (d); Hunter (1936); Kirkpatrick Archive; *Londonderry Sentinel* 9 May 1851 (m); McGrew (2001) (m); *Med Dir*; Merrick and Clarke, *Belfast*, vol 2 (1984); Plarr (1930); Whitla (1901)].

HARKIN, JAMES CHARLES (1886–1903), Carrick, county Donegal;
born 2 June 1862 at Carndonagh, county Donegal, son of Michael Harkin, postmaster, of Carndonagh; educated locally; studied medicine at Queen's College, Galway, 1883–5 and at Queen's College, Belfast, from 1885; MB BCh BAO (RUI) 1889; general practitioner, of Carrick; died 20 November 1903 at Tullamore, King's County; probate Londonderry 6 June 1904. [Belf PRO, will cal; *Med Dir*; QCB adm reg].

HARKIN, JOHN (1842/3–72), Londonderry;
born 1842/3, son of John Harkin, gentleman, of Omagh; studied medicine at the Carmichael School and the Richmond Hospital, Dublin; MRCSE 1862; LM Coombe Hosp Dub; LRCP Edin 1864; general practitioner, of 11 Pump Street, Londonderry; married 12 September 1865 in the Church of the Three Patrons, Rathgar, Dublin, Anne Ingoldsby, youngest daughter of Terence Ingoldsby of Enniskillen, county Fermanagh, and Kenilworth Street, Rathgar, Dublin; died 2 October 1872 at 21 Pump Street; administration (with will) Dublin 13 November 1872. [Belf PRO, will cal; Dub GRO (m) and (d); Kirkpatrick Archive; *Londonderry Sentinel* 15 September 1865 (m); McGrew (2001) (m) and (d); *Med Dir*].

HARKIN, MICHAEL (d 1840), Omagh, county Tyrone;
MD (Glas) 1820; MRCSE; physician, of Omagh, c 1820–37; married 23 July 1830, Catherine Meaghan, second daughter of Francis Meaghan of Omagh; died 16 May 1840 in Omagh 'after a prolonged illness'. [Addison; *BNL* 27 July 1830 (m) and 26 May 1840 (d); Lewis (1837); *Londonderry Sentinel* 31 July 1830 (m) and 23 May 1840 (d); McGrew (2001) (m) and (d); Pigot (1824); *Strabane Morning Post* 27 July 1830 (m)].

HARKNESS, ALEXANDER (1852/3–96), Debenham, Suffolk, and London; born 1852/3, son of James Harkness, merchant, of Cultra, county Down; educated at Dr Russell's School; studied medicine at Queen's College, Belfast, from 1874; LRCP LRCS Edin 1880; general practitioner of Debenham c 1885–93 and of 4 Oak Villa, St Anne's Road, Stamford Hill, London, c 1890; finally of Hampton Hill, Middlesex; married Charlotte Susan —; died 22 May 1896 at Hampton Hill; probate London 24 June 1896. [Lond PPR, will cal; *Med Dir*; QCB adm reg].

HARMAN, EMANUEL JOHN (c 1820–89), Rathfriland, county Down, and Lurgan, county Armagh; born c 1820; studied medicine at the Catholic University of Ireland and Jervis Street Hospital, Dublin; LAH Dub 1842; LM Wellesley Inst Dub; LRCS Edin and LM 1854; medical officer to Ballyward Dispensary District, of Moneyslane, Rathfriland, c 1860; medical officer to Lurgan No 2 Dispensary District and constabulary, public vaccinator and registrar of births and deaths from c 1870, of Derryaville, Lurgan c 1870, Delta Cottage, Lurgan c 1880 and finally, of Kilvergan, Lurgan; married Fanny —; died 5 September 1889 at Kilvergan; administration (with will) Armagh 3 March 1890. [Belf PRO, will cal; Dub GRO (d); *Med Dir*].

HARPER, ARCHIBALD (1858–c 1902), Rockcorry, county Monaghan, and England; born 18 March 1858 at Unshinagh, Clones, county Monaghan, son of Archibald Harper, farmer, of Unshinagh; educated at Clones School; studied medicine at Queen's College, Belfast, from 1876; LRCP LRCS Edin 1884; general practitioner, of Nushena, Rockcorry, c 1885–1900, but appears to have moved to England c 1900; died c 1902. [*Med Dir*; QCB adm reg].

HARPER (HARPUR), HANS (1792/3–1880), Killyleagh, county Down; born 1792/3; studied medicine at Glasgow University; MD (Glas) 1819; general practitioner, of Ballywoolen and Maymore, Killyleagh; married 25 August 1821 Sarah Johnston (who was born c 1800 and died 13 December 1824 at Ballywillin), eldest daughter of Adam Johnston of Ballywoolen; died 20 February 1880 at Ballywoolen; buried in Killyleagh Presbyterian graveyard; administration (with will) Belfast 4 June 1880. [Addison (1898); *BNL* 28 August 1821 (m) and 4 January 1825 (d); Belf PRO, will cal; Clarke, *County Down*, vol 7 (1993); *Med Dir*].

HARPER (HAPPER), J. (*fl c* 1845), Ballycastle, county Antrim; apothecary, of Ballycastle c 1845; married 12 December 1844 at her father's house, Rose Anne Linton, youngest daughter of Andrew Linton of Cloughmills, county Antrim. [*BNL* 20 December 1844 (m); *Coleraine Chronicle* 28 December 1844 (m); Croly (1843–6)].

HARRIS, ANDREW (*fl c* 1886–93), Stewartstown, county Tyrone, and Magherafelt, county Londonderry; studied medicine at the Royal College of Surgeons in Ireland; LRCSI 1885; LKQCPI and LM 1886; general practitioner, of Prospect House, Stewartstown c 1886–90 and of Magherafelt, c 1890–93; died c 1893. [*Med Dir*].

HARRIS, GEORGE (d 1839), Enniskillen, county Fermanagh;
MD [?]; of Enniskillen; married 25 October 1827 in Dundalk, county Louth, Jane Martin, third daughter of Patrick Martin of Dundalk; died 24 September 1839 'after a lingering illness, borne with the greatest resignation'. [*BNL* 2 November 1827 (m) and 1 October 1839 (d)].

HARRIS, HUGH (1855/6–1919), Stewartstown, county Tyrone;
born 1855/6; studied medicine at the Royal College of Surgeons in Ireland; LRCSI 1878; LKQCPI and LM 1880; medical officer to Stewartstown Dispensary District and constabulary and medical officer of health of Stewartstown, of Prospect House, Stewartstown; author of various medical papers; married Helen MacGregor —; died 20 June 1919 at Stewartstown; probate Armagh 17 October 1919. [Belf PRO, will cal, will; Dub GRO (d); *Med Dir*].

HARRIS, JOHN (1754–1838), Naval Medical Service, Army Medical Service and Sydney, New South Wales;
born 1754, eldest son of John Harris, farmer, of Moymucklemurry, Moneymore, county Londonderry, and Ann McKee; studied medicine at Edinburgh University; joined the Naval Medical Service 1779; resigned 1789; emigrated to New South Wales 1790 and bought large land-holdings at Parramatta, Sydney; surgeon's mate before joining the Army Medical Service as surgeon to the 102nd Foot (New South Wales Corps) 1791; appointed Port Naval Officer 1802 and had various conflicts with his fellow officers; one of the rebels in the 'Rum Rebellion' of 1808, which overthrew Governor William Bligh (of the *Bounty*); retired on half pay 1811; returned to Ireland 1809–13 and resigned from the Corps; returned to Australia 1814 and settled down on a holding at Bathurst to become one of the three biggest landowners in Australia; of 'Ultimo', Sydney; married 1813 Elizabeth — (who was born 1788 and died 1837); died 27 April 1838; left no children and his large estates (valued at £150,000) passed to his brothers' and sisters' families. [*Australian Dictionary of Biography* (1966); Belf PRO, Harris papers, T3752; Cleary (1933), p 27; Ekin, William Holland, pers com; Harris (1987); Ireland (1988); Peterkin and Johnston (1968)].

HARRISON, HENRY CARY (1757/8–1835), Garvagh, county Londonderry;
born 1757/8, eldest son of the Rev Henry Harrison, curate of Dungiven and rector of Upper Badoney; surgeon; died 6 April 1835 at Garvagh; buried in Derry Cathedral. [*BNL* 21 April 1835 (d); Leslie (1937); *Londonderry Sentinel* 18 April 1835 (d)].

HARRISON, JAMES McKEAN (1866–1941), Ledbury, Herefordshire, and RAMC;
born 6 May 1866 at Mariville, Dromore, county Down, son of John Harrison of Mariville; educated at Armagh Royal School 1878–81; studied medicine at Queen's College, Belfast, from 1884; MB BCh BAO (RUI) 1890; medical officer of health for Ledbury Dispensary District, of Gloucester House, Ledbury and later of The Orchard, Ledbury; retired c 1937; lieutenant-colonel (RAMC) during World War I; author of various medical papers; lived finally at The Brown House, Culverden Park,

Tunbridge Wells; died 8 September 1941; administration (with will) Oxford 18 November 1941. [Ferrar (1933); Lond PPR, will cal; *Med Dir*; QCB adm reg].

HARRISON, JOHN WILLIAM (1809/10–85), Killough, county Down;
born 1809/10; studied medicine at the Richmond Hospital and Medical School, Dublin; LAH Dub 1827; MRCSE 1828; medical officer to Killough Dispensary District, constabulary and coastguard c 1836–76; married —; died 20 January 1885 at Killough; administration Belfast 2 March 1885. [Belf PRO, will cal; Croly (1843–6); *Downpatrick Recorder* 4 January 1876; Dub GRO (d); Kirkpatrick Archive; *Med Dir*].

HARSHAW, JOHN (1783/4–1819), Naval Medical Service and Newry, county Down;
born 1783/4, probably in Newry; joined the Naval Medical Service as assistant surgeon; married (1) 3 January 1811 — Bell, daughter of surgeon — Bell of Newry; (2) 8 June 1818 at Carnew, county Down, Anne Ker (who died 4 May 1822 at Seaview Cottage, near Belfast), third daughter of Robert Ker of Katesbridge; died 20 September 1819 at Clifton, of phthisis. [*BNL* 8 January 1811 (m), 19 June 1818 (m) and 7 May 1822 (d)].

HARSHAW, JOSEPH (1766/7–1837), Anaghlone, county Down;
born 1766/7; MD [?]; general practitioner, of Ballynafern, Anaghlone; married —; father of Agnes Harshaw who married 17 May 1842 Andrew Harshaw; died 5 January 1837 at his home. [*BNL* 31 January 1837 (d) and 20 May 1842 (m, daughter)].

HART, GEORGE SIMPSON (1868–1923), London and Atherstone, Warwickshire;
born 4 January 1868 at Drumsteeple, county Londonderry, son of the Rev John Hart, minister of Ballylagan Reformed Presbyterian Church, and Elizabeth Carlisle of Rathfriland; educated at RBAI; studied medicine at Queen's College, Belfast, from 1885; MB BCH BAO (RUI) 1891; MD 1900; clinical assistant to the Royal London Ophthalmic Hospital; medical officer of health to Ashby-de-la-Zouch, of Measham, Atherstone; married 4 August 1897 in Abersychan Parish Church, Monmouthshire, Kathleen Mulligan (who was born 1872/3), daughter of Dr John Watson Mulligan of Abersychan (*q.v.*); father of Dr John Watson Hart, LRCP Lond, MRCSE 1925; died 1 September 1923; probate Leicester 3 December 1923. [*BMJ* obituary (1923); Kirkpatrick Archive; Lond GRO (m); Lond PPR, will cal, will; Loughridge (1970); *Med Dir*; QCB adm reg].

HART(E), WILLIAM HENRY COPE (COLE) (d 1855), Downpatrick, county Down, and Lismore, Waterford;
LAH Dub; LM; apothecary and resident medical officer to Downpatrick Infirmary and Fever Hospital 1840–46; general practitioner, of Lismore c 1849–55 died 1855. [Croly (1843–6); *Med Dir*].

HARTFORD, HENRY WILLIAM (1852–1906), Christchurch, Hampshire;
born 2 July 1852, youngest son of Captain Augustus Henry Hartford of the 59th Foot, of Rose Hall, Portarlington, King's County; educated at Armagh Royal School

1870–71; studied medicine at the Royal College of Surgeons in Ireland; LRCSI 1875; LKQCPI and LM 1875; general practitioner in Christchurch, Hampshire; medical officer of health for Lymington District; medical officer of Christchurch workhouse, public vaccinator and certifying factory surgeon; married Dora Anna —; father of Dr Augustus Herbert Bibby Hartford, LRCPI LRCSI 1901; died 31 March 1906 at Square House, Hampshire; probate London 24 May 1906. [Ferrar (1933); Lond PPR, will cal will; *Med Dir*].

HARTWELL, JAMES (d 1828), Downpatrick, county Down;
son of a Dublin carpenter or builder; MRCSI; surgeon to the Royal Dublin Militia; surgeon and apothecary to the Down County Infirmary 1812–28; JP 1813; of Scotch Street, Downpatrick c 1824; 'got into drinking habits by which he impaired both his character and his health' (Pilson); married 9 June 1806 Harriet Garner (who was born 1781 and died 31 December 1861 in Dublin); daughter born in January 1809 in Londonderry; died 25 December 1828; buried in Downpatrick Cathedral graveyard. [*BNL* 13 January 1809 (b) and 2 January 1829 (d); Belf PRO, D 2961/2/6; Parkinson (1967); Pigot (1824); Pilson (1838)].

HARVEY, G. (*fl c* 1838), Crossmaglen, county Armagh;
surgeon, of Crossmaglen; married 24 March 1838 Phillipa Ussher Ball (who died 14 June 1839), eldest surviving daughter of Captain Samuel Ball of Crossmaglen. [*BNL* 30 March 1838 (m) and 25 June 1839 (d)].

HARVEY, GEORGINA
See COLLIER, GEORGINA

HARVEY, HAMILTON (*fl c* 1827–51), Dungannon, county Tyrone;
surgeon, of 3 William Place, Dungannon c 1851; married —; son, Thomas Hamilton Harvey, born c 1827 and died 9 April 1851. [*Londonderry Sentinel* 18 April 1851 (d)].

HARVEY, JAMES (1802/3–37), Indian Medical Service;
born 1802/3, son of the Rev James Harvey, minister of Redrock Presbyterian Church, county Armagh, and Jane —; MRCS 1829; joined the Indian Medical Service (Bengal establishment) as assistant surgeon 1829; died 21 May 1837 in Ireland; buried in Redrock Presbyterian Graveyard. [Bailie and Kirkpatrick (2005); Crawford (1930); gravestone inscription].

HARVEY, JOHN (1804/5–82), St Johnston, Londonderry;
born 1804/5, son of John Harvey, gentleman; studied medicine at Edinburgh University; MD (Edin) 1831 (thesis 'De enteritide') 1831; LRCS Edin 1831; medical officer and registrar of births and deaths to Killea Dispensary District; medical officer to Carrigans and Newtowncunningham constabulary; of Springfield, St Johnston, Londonderry; married 9 June 1857 in Derry Cathedral, Rosina Jane McCausland, third daughter of Marcus McCausland of East Wall, Londonderry; died 29 July 1882 at Sydney Terrace, Londonderry. [*BNL* 13 June 1857 (m); *Coleraine Chronicle* 13 June 1857 (m); Dub GRO (m) and (d); Edin Univ; *Londonderry Sentinel* 12 June 1857 (m); *Med Dir*].

HARVEY, JOSEPH (1872–1962), Wimbledon, Surrey;
born 25 May 1872 at Crossan House, Lisburn, county Down, son of William Harvey, farmer, of Crossan House; educated at Lisburn Intermediate School; entered Queen's College, Belfast, to study arts and medicine 1889; MB BCh BAO (RUI) 1897; general practitioner, of 135 Hartfield Road and Dorset Lodge, 160 Kingston Road, Merton Park, Wimbledon, from c 1900; of 4 St Aubyn's Court, Raymond Road, Wimbledon from c 1945; retired c 1950; married 11 April 1900 in West Ham Methodist Church, Dr Georgina Collier (*q.v.*); died 19 January 1962 at Wimbledon Hospital; probate London 12 March 1962. [Lond GRO (m); Lond PPR, will cal; *Med Dir*; QCB adm reg].

HARVEY, SIR LUDFORD (b 1759), London;
born 20 September 1759, fifth son of George Harvey of Malin Hall, county Donegal, and Elizabeth Hart of Kilderry, county Donegal; educated in Londonderry and later at an academy in Lothbury; apprenticed to Sir Percival Pott, surgeon, of St Bartholomew's Hospital 1777–82; surgeon to the hospital 1807–24; vice-president of the Royal College of Surgeons of England; knight bachelor 1813; married Lucy Skiner; [Burke *LGI* (1912); Elliott, Simon, pers com].

HARVEY, THOMAS (1826–58), Army Medical Service;
born 13 September 1826 at Londonderry, son of Thomas Harvey of Londonderry; joined the Army Medical Service as assistant surgeon 1852; transferred to the 6th Foot 1856; died 24 April 1858 at Raneegunge [or Rumagunge], India. [*BNL* 19 June 1858 (d); *Londonderry Sentinel* 18 June 1858 (d); Peterkin and Johnston (1968)].

HARVEY, WILLIAM, (c 1750–1819), Army Medical Service and Dublin;
born c 1750, son of the Rev Adam Harvey, rector of Camus-juxta-Mourne (Strabane) and Jane Hamilton; educated by his father; studied arts at Trinity College, Dublin, from 1766; scholar 1769; BA (TCD) 1771; studied medicine at Edinburgh University and from 1774, at Leyden; MD (Edin) 1774 (thesis 'De venenis'); president of the Edinburgh Medical Society 1774; also studied medicine at Leyden University from 1775; FKQCPI 1777; president KQCPI 1784, 1791, 1797, 1800, 1802, 1809 and 1814; physician-general to the army in Ireland from 1795; was asked to investigate the epidemic of fever in 1798; concerned in the official measures adopted regarding the introduction of vaccination in Ireland in 1801; retired on half pay 1816 and was in personal charge of the fever cases in Dr Steeven's Hospital in 1817; married Catherine Scott (who died 23 July 1817), daughter of John Scott of Ballygannon; died 12 March 1819; buried at Kilcoole, county Wicklow (memorial in the church). [Burtchaell and Sadleir (1924); Edin Univ; Kirkpatrick (1924); Leslie (1937); *Memorials of the Dead*, vol 4, p 151; Peterkin and Johnston (1968); Innes Smith (1932); Widdess (1963); Underwood (1978)].

HARVEY, WILLIAM (*fl c* 1845), St Johnston, county Donegal;
MD [?]; medical officer to St Johnston Dispensary and constabulary c 1845; possibly died c 1850. [Croly (1843–6)].

HASLETT (HAZLETT), CHARLES (1744/5–1834), Ramelton, county Donegal;
born 1744/5, son of Henry Haslett of Upper Drumneechy, county Londonderry; apothecary, of Ramelton c 1804; died 18 February 1834. [*BNL* 1 March 1834 (d); Belf PRO, T1021/25–32; Elliott, Simon, pers com].

HASLETT, JOHN COURTENAY (1856–1939), Army Medical Service;
born 16 November 1856 in Belfast, son of John Wilson Haslett, druggist, of Mervue, Duncairn, Belfast; educated at RBAI; studied medicine at Queen's College, Belfast, from 1873; MD MCh (QUI) 1878; LAH Dub 1878; LM Glas 1880; appointed honorary physician to the Ulster Hospital for Children 1880; joined the Army Medical Service as surgeon captain in 1882; surgeon major 1894; lieutenant colonel 1902; retired on half pay 1908; retired 1911; lived finally at 2 Adelaide Park, Belfast; married —; died 1 May 1939 at 2 Adelaide Park; probate Belfast 23 June 1939 and London 10 July 1939. [Belf GRO (d); Belf PRO, will cal; Kirkpatrick Archive; Lond PPR, will cal; *Med Dir*; Peterkin and Johnston (1968); QCB adm reg].

HASLETT, ROBERT WOODS (1864–1953), Liverpool, Lancashire, and Pontypool, Monmouthshire;
born 4 August 1864 at Rathfriland, county Down, son of Joseph Haslett of Rathfriland; educated at Banbridge Academy; studied arts and medicine at Queen's College, Belfast, from 1882; BA (RUI) 1885; MB (hons) BCh 1889; FRCSI 1907; resident medical officer to the Parish Infirmary, Liverpool c 1890–95; general practitioner, of Pontypool, Monmouthshire c 1905; medical officer to G.W.R. and various metal works; also certifying factory surgeon; consulting surgeon to Pontypool General Hospital, of 'St Aubyn's', 18 Gold Tops, Newport, c 1925; retired c 1928 to Tresillian, Kingsbridge, Devonshire and c 1929 to Brookmeadow, Budleigh Salterton, Devonshire; married Gladys Mildred —; died 11 April 1953; probate Exeter 17 July 1953. [Kirkpatrick Archive; Lond PPR, will cal; *Med Dir*; QCB adm reg].

HASLETT, SAMUEL TORRENS (1815/6–83), Buncrana, Laghy and Drumgowan, county Donegal;
born 1815/6, son of Samuel Haslett, gentleman; studied medicine at Trinity College, Dublin and Edinburgh University; MD (Edin) 1838 (thesis 'De hydrophobia'); LRCS Edin and LM 1838; Government assistant surgeon in Tasmania; medical officer to Buncrana Dispensary District and later to Laghy and Ballintra Dispensary Districts, of Drumgowan; retired to Sligo; married 26 November 1861 in Ballysumaghan Church of Ireland Church, county Sligo, Mary Dorcas Robinson, only daughter of Joseph Robinson of Bloomfield, county Sligo, gentleman farmer; died 28 January 1883 at Drumgowan; probate Londonderry 22 March 1883. [Belf PRO, will cal; Dub GRO (m) and (d); Edin Univ; *Londonderry Sentinel* 13 December 1861 (m); Martin (2010); *Med Dir*].

HASLETT, WILLIAM (d 1827), Jamaica;
born in Londonderry; 'doctor' in Jamaica; died 18 November 1827 in Jamaica. [*BNL* 12 February 1828 (d)].

HASSARD, ALEXANDER JASON (b 1866);
born 26 May 1866 at Willowbank, Kingstown, county Dublin, only son of Alexander Jason Hassard of Willowbank and Garden Hill, county Fermanagh, and his second wife, Frances Margaret Gilman; LRCP LRCS Edin; not in *Medical Directory* or *Medical Register*, and may have emigrated soon after qualification. [Dub GRO (b); Swanzy (1903)].

HASSARD, HENRY BOLTON (1828–92), Army Medical Service;
born 29 November 1828 at Drummully, county Fermanagh, third son of Jason Hassard, captain in 74th Highlanders, of Rockingham, county Waterford, and Elizabeth Marshall of Waterford; LRCSI 1850; joined the Army Medical Service as assistant surgeon in the Cape Mounted Constabulary 1851; staff surgeon, second class, 1858; transferred to 19th Foot 1859; surgeon major 1871; deputy surgeon general 1879; surgeon general 1884; served in Kaffir War 1851–3, at Hazara 1868, in Afghan War 1878–80; CB (Military) 1881; retired 1888 to 19 Western Parade Southsea, Hampshire; married 28 November 1860 Mary Elizabeth Brown, daughter of Robert Brown, superintending surgeon IMS; father of Dr Robert Hassard; died 2 July 1892; probate London 29 July 1892. [Lond PPR, will cal; *Med Dir*; Peterkin and Johnston (1968); Swanzy (1903)].

HASSEL, THOMAS (c 1750–97), Downpatrick, county Down;
born c 1750; surgeon with Loyal Durham Fencibles; married 23 November 1797 in Downpatrick, Anne Sharrock of Downpatrick; died 19 December 1797 at Downpatrick. [*BNL* 22 December 1797 (d)].

HASTINGS, JAMES (1851/2–1900), Portaferry, county Down;
born 1851/2 at Portaferry, county Down, son of Hugh Hastings of Portaferry; educated at RBAI; studied medicine at Queen's College, Belfast, from 1870; LRCS Edin 1875; LFPS Glas 1875; general practitioner, of Portaferry; died 10 October 1900; probate 21 December 1900. [Belf PRO, will cal; *Med Dir*; QCB adm reg].

HASTINGS, ROBERT (1819/20–68), Naval Medical Service and North Shields, Northumberland;
born 1819/20, son of Robert Hastings, farmer, of Stranorlar, county Donegal; studied medicine at Glasgow University; MD (Glas) 1840; LRCS Edin 1840; joined the Naval Medical Service as assistant surgeon; surgeon c 1860; served on HMS *Liffey* c 1863 and as staff surgeon on HMS *Castor* c 1866; married 27 June 1861 in First Londonderry Presbyterian Church, Mary Foster (who survived her husband to live in Foyle Street, Londonderry), daughter of William Foster, farmer, of Ballynacross, county Londonderry; died 24 January 1868 at Preston, North Shields, Northumberland, of typhus fever caught in the discharge of his professional duties; administration London 17 August 1868. [Addison (1898); Dub GRO (m); Lond GRO (d); Lond PPR, will cal; *Londonderry Sentinel* 28 June 1861 (m) and 28 January 1868 (d); *Med Dir*].

HASTINGS, ROSS ROBERT (1869/70–1901), Donegal and ship's surgeon;
born 1869/70 in Stranorlar, county Donegal, son of John Hastings, farmer; educated at Londonderry Academical Institution; studied arts and medicine at Trinity College, Dublin, from 1887; BA (TCD) 1893; MB BCh BAO 1894; house surgeon to Donegal County Infirmary; surgeon on SS *Staffordshire* (Bibby Line) and *Lismore Castle* (Donald Currie & Co); of Dunwiley, Stranorlar, c 1895; died c 1901. [*Med Dir*; TCD adm reg; *TCD Cat*, vol II (1896)].

HATCH, JOHN ANTHONY FREEMAN (1867–1931), Sierra Leone and Cardiff, Glamorgan;
born 8 October 1867 at Plymouth, Devonshire, son of surgeon Jeremiah Anthony Hatch RN, of Ardee Castle, county Louth; educated at Armagh Royal School 1882–4; studied medicine in Edinburgh and Dublin; LRCP LRCS Edin 1902; LFPS Glas 1902; assistant medical officer to the Sierra Leone Government Railways; anaesthetist to the Cardiff Royal Infirmary; of 'Rosemount', Gabalfa, Cardiff; captain in RAMC (Territorials) 1914–18; married Evelyne Constance —; died 30 April 1931; probate Llandaff 11 July 1931. [Ferrar (1933); Lond PPR, will cal; *Med Dir*].

HATCHELL, GEORGE WILLIAM (1841/2–1907), Westport and Castlebar, county Mayo, and Letterkenny, county Donegal;
born 1841/2; studied medicine at Trinity College, Dublin, the Royal College of Surgeons in Ireland and the Rotunda Hospital, Dublin; LRCSI 1866; LKQCPI and LM 1867; general practitioner, of the Mall, Westport, c 1875; resident medical superintendent of Letterkenny District Lunatic Asylum c 1885 and of Castlebar Lunatic Asylum from c 1900; surgeon to the South Mayo Rifles and Connaught Rangers; married Mary —; died 19 April 1907 at Asylum House, Castlebar; probate Ballina 17 June 1907. [Belf PRO, will cal; Dub GRO (d); *Med Dir*].

HATHORN, ROBERT (d 1834), Donaghadee, county Down;
surgeon, of Donaghadee c 1824; died 1 February 1834 in Donaghadee; probate Down Diocesan Court 1835. [*BNL* 14 February 1834 (d); Belf PRO, Down Dio Wills index; Pigot (1824)].

HAUGHTON, WILLIAM STEELE (1869–1951), Dublin;
born 26 September 1869 in Dublin, fourth son of Professor Samuel Haughton, professor of Geology at Trinity College, Dublin, and his cousin, Louisa Haughton; educated at the Abbey School, county Tipperary, and from 1881–8, at Portora Royal School, Enniskillen; studied arts and medicine at Trinity College, Dublin; BA (TCD) 1891; MB 1894; MD 1901; MCh (hon) 1936; demonstrator in anatomy at TCD 1894–9; assistant surgeon (mainly orthopaedic surgery) to Sir Patrick Dun's Hospital 1895–9; surgeon to Dr Steevens' Hospital 1899–1948; governor from 1917; of 16 Merrion Square North, Dublin, and later of 3 Roebuck Crescent, Clonskea; retired 1948; purchased X-ray equipment in London in 1896 and was a pioneer in the clinical use of X-rays; major in RAMC 1914–18, working in a military hospital at Blackrock, county Dublin; honorary professor of orthopaedic surgery at TCD from 1923; author of many papers on radiology and orthopaedics; married 4 August 1909 Jane Elizabeth Halahan, daughter of the Rev John Halahan, Dean of Ross; father of

Isabel Haughton who married Dr J.F. Wilde, psychiatrist, and of Dr Samuel Hewitt Haughton, surgeon in the Royal Australian Navy; died 12 October 1951 at 3 Roebuck Crescent; probate Dublin 5 March 1952. [*BMJ* obituary (1952); Coakley (1992); *DIB* (2009); Dub Nat Arch, will cal; *Med Dir; Portora Royal School Register* (1939)].

HAWORTH, STEPHEN ROCLIFFE (1861–c 1946), Staffordshire, Bridgenorth, Shropshire, South Africa and Southern Rhodesia;
 born 30 May 1861 at Easingwold, Yorkshire, son of Frank Haworth, brewer; educated at the Royal Grammar School, Newcastle-on-Tyne; studied arts and medicine at Queen's College, Belfast, from 1880; MD BCh BAO (RUI) 1891; assistant house surgeon to Staffordshire General Infirmary and house surgeon to the South Shropshire Infirmary, Bridgnorth; general practitioner, of County End, Lees, near Oldham c 1895–1905; emigrated to South Africa c 1905; general practitioner of Van Rhynsdorp, Cape Colony c 1905–10; government medical officer, of Rusapi, Southern Rhodesia c 1910–15, of Plumtree, Southern Rhodesia c 1915–28; retired c 1928 to Bulawayo; moved to St Helier, Jersey c 1932; died c 1946. [*Med Dir*; QCB adm reg].

HAWTHORN, WILLIAM A. (d 1856), New York, USA;
 son of Thomas Hawthorn of Greenan, Loughbrickland, county Down; MD [?]; emigrated to USA; died 4 August 1856 at Huntingdon, Long Island, New York. [*BNL* 28 August 1856 (d)].

HAWTHORNE, ALFRED WYNTER (1861–1941), Winston, Queensland and Carcoar, New South Wales;
 born October 1861 in Belfast, son of Dr Samuel Francis Hawthorne of Dromore (*q.v.*); brother of Dr Walter Llewellyn Hawthorne (*q.v.*) and Dr Ernest Sydney Hawthorne (*q.v.*); educated at RBAI; studied medicine at Queen's College, Belfast, from 1879; MD MCh (RUI) 1882; LM KQCPI 1882; emigrated to Australia c 1884; general practitioner of Winston, Queensland c 1885; medical officer to Carcoar Dispensary District, New South Wales, from c 1890; government medical officer and public vaccinator; retired c 1928; died 19 October 1941 at Carcoar. [Kirkpatrick Archive; *Med Dir*; QCB adm reg].

HAWTHORNE, ERNEST SYDNEY (1869–1949), Georgetown, Queensland, Romaldkirk, Yorkshire, Barnard Castle, county Durham and RAMC;
 born 16 July 1869 at Dromore, county Down, son of Dr Samuel Francis Hawthorne (*q.v.*); brother of Dr Alfred Wynter Hawthorne (*q,v,*) and Dr Walter Llewellyn Hawthorne (*q.v.*); studied medicine at the Carmichael School and Royal College of Surgeons in Ireland; LKQCPI and LM 1889; LRCSI and LM 1889; FRCSI 1900; DPH RCPSI 1906; house surgeon to St Mark's ENT Hospital, Dublin and house physician to the City Hospital, Liverpool; emigrated to Australia c 1900; surgeon to Etheridge District Hospital, Queensland; medical officer of health to Georgetown and Startfoth, Queensland; returned to Yorkshire c 1906; district medical officer and public vaccinator to Teesdale, of Romaldkirk; medical officer of health to Barnard Castle; captain (temporary) RAMC; author of various medical papers; lived finally

at the Vicarage Brampton, Cumberland; married —; died 30 December 1949 at the Vicarage; probate Carlisle 14 February 1950. [Kirkpatrick Archive; Lond GRO (d); Lond PPR, will cal; *Med Dir*].

HAWTHORNE, GEORGE STUART (1792/3–1858), Banbridge, county Down, Belfast, and Liverpool;
 born 1792/3; studied medicine at Edinburgh University; MD (Edin) 1819 (thesis 'De pneumonia'); MRCP Edin; physician, of Banbridge c 1819 and 90 Donegall Street, Belfast c 1824; attending physician to Belfast Fever Hospital 1832–6; of St Anne's Street, Liverpool c 1836–58; author of papers on the ventilation of hospitals (1832 and 1834) and The true pathological nature of cholera (1849); married Mary Anne — (who was born 1800/1 and died 21 June 1857 in Liverpool); daughter born 1834; died 16 October 1858 at his home in Liverpool. [*BNL* 17 July 1834 (b), 3 July 1857 (d) and 25 October 1858 (d); Bradshaw (1819); Malcolm (1851); *Med Dir*; Pigot (1824)].

HAWTHORNE, JOHN (1834/5–1900), Banbridge, county Down;
 born 1834/5, son of Dr William Hawthorne (*q.v.*) of Banbridge; educated by Mr Mullan of Banbridge; studied medicine at Queen's College, Belfast, from 1852 and Belfast General Hospital; LRCS Edin 1857; MD (QUI) 1861; general practitioner of Church Square Banbridge; medical officer to Banbridge Workhouse from 1872 and certifying factory surgeon; author of various medical papers; JP for county Down; married (1) 10 April 1862 in Warrenpoint Church of Ireland Church, county Down, Margaret Smyth (who was born 1832/3 and died 12 May 1897), daughter of Bryce Smyth, linen merchant, of Warrenpoint; (2) Shannon Amelia — (died 27 March 1908 of phthisis, at Dungannon); died 6 November 1900 at Banbridge; buried in Banbridge Cemetery; probate Belfast 8 February 1901. [Belf PRO, will cal; Clarke, *County Down*, vol 20 (1989); Dub GRO (d, Shannon Amelia); Kirkpatrick Archive; Linn (1935); *Med Dir*; QCB adm reg; UHF database (m)].

HAWTHORNE, SAMUEL FRANCIS (1833–92), Dromore, county Down;
 born 1833, son of Francis Hawthorne of Meenan, Loughbrickland, county Down; educated at RBAI; studied medicine at Queen's College, Belfast, from 1850; LM (QCB) 1852; LRCS Edin and LM 1854; LRCP Edin 1866; general practitioner, of Dromore, county Down; author of various medical papers; JP for county Down; married 9 December 1856 in Linen Hall Street Presbyterian Church, Belfast, Elizabeth Gray McKee (who died 23 February 1924), youngest daughter of John McKee, dentist, of Belfast; father of Dr Alfred Walter Hawthorne (*q.v.*), Dr Walter Llewellyn Hawthorne (*q.v.*) and Dr Ernest Sydney Hawthorne (*q.v.*); died 14 June 1892; probate Dublin 14 October 1892. [*BNL* 12 December 1856 (m); Belf PRO, will cal; Clarke, *County Down*, vol 19 (1983); Kirkpatrick Archive; *Med Dir*; QCB adm reg].

HAWTHORNE, WALTER LLEWELLYN (1863–c 1920), London;
 born 28 October 1863 at Dromore, county Down, son of Dr Samuel Francis Hawthorne (*q.v.*); brother of Dr Alfred Wynter Hawthorne (*q.v.*) and Dr Ernest Sydney Hawthorne (*q.v.*); educated at RBAI; studied medicine at Queen's College,

Belfast, from 1880; LRCP LRCS Edin 1893; LFPS Glas 1893; general practitioner, of 200 Cambridge Road, Kilburn, London c 1895–1900 and of the Crescent, Lucan, county Dublin, from c 1900; died c 1920. [*Med Dir*; QCB adm reg].

HAWTHORNE, WILLIAM (d 1859), Banbridge, county Down;
studied medicine at Glasgow University; CM (Glas) 1825; general practitioner, of Banbridge; married —; father of Dr John Hawthorne (*q.v.*) of Banbridge; died 1859. [Addison (1898); Croly (1843–6); UHF database (m, son)].

HAY, ALEXANDER (1819–83), Connor, county Antrim;
born 11 December 1819, eldest son of Dr Hugh Ramsay Hay (*q.v.*); brother of Dr Patrick Ramsay Hay (*q.v.*); studied medicine at Glasgow University; LM (Glas) 1839; LM (Glas) 1840; MD (Glas) 1852; medical officer, certifying surgeon, district vaccinator and registrar of births and deaths to Connor Dispensary District; married 18 June 1863 in Glenwherry Presbyterian Church, Anne Beatty Owens (who was born 31 March 1837 and died 23 October 1902), eldest daughter of Samuel Owens, merchant, of Belfast; died 8 January 1883 at Connor; buried in Ballylinny Old Graveyard; probate Belfast 5 March 1883. [Addison (1898); Belf PRO, will cal, will; *Coleraine Chronicle* 14 October 1853 (d); Dub GRO (d); gravestone inscription; *Med Dir*; UHF database (m)].

HAY, HUGH RAMSAY (1791/2–1836), Ballyeaston, county Antrim;
born 1791/2 at Crumlin; surgeon, of Ballyeaston; married Ann — (who was born 1789/90 and died 13 June 1848); father of Dr Alexander Hay (*q.v.*) and Dr Patrick Ramsay Hay (*q.v.*); died 7 May 1836 '… a most affectionate husband and indulgent father, a sincere and beloved friend, a benefactor of the poor, a firm and zealous patriot' (*BNL*); buried in Ballylinny Old Graveyard. [*BNL* 7 June 1836 (d); gravestone inscription].

HAY, PATRICK RAMSAY (1825–91), Ballymena, county Antrim;
born 14 September 1825 in Ballyclare, son of Dr Hugh Ramsay Hay (*q.v.*); brother of Dr Alexander Hay (*q.v.*); studied medicine at Glasgow University; LM (Glas) 1850; MD (Glas) 1850; CM 1852; medical officer to Glenwhirry Dispensary District, of The Nook, Moorfields, Ballymena; unmarried; died 10 October 1891 at Clatteryknowes, Ballymena; buried in Rashee Old Graveyard; probate Belfast 14 December 1891. [Addison (1898); Belf PRO, will cal; Dub GRO (d); gravestone inscription; *Med Dir;* Richmond (2007)].

HAY, ROBERT (1841–99), Naval Medical Service;
born 22 February 1841, son of William Hay of Finvoy, Ballymoney, county Antrim; educated at Belfast Academy; studied medicine at Queen's College, Belfast, from 1858; MD (QUI) 1862; MRCSE 1863; joined the Naval Medical Service as assistant surgeon on HMS *Pelorus* 1863, HMS *Asia* 1868, HMS *Implacable* 1869, HMS *Sealark* 1870, HMS *Immortalite* c 1872; surgeon to Royal Naval Hospital, Haslar 1873, HMS *Monarch* 1874; staff surgeon 1877, to HMS *Hector* 1878 and HMS *Rapid* 1879; fleet surgeon 1884; deputy inspector general 1894, of the Royal Hospital, Bermuda; married Juliet Eaton —; died 2 December 1899 at Bermuda;

probate London 27 January 1900. [*Lancet* obituary (1900); Lond PPR, will cal; *Med Dir*; QCB adm reg].

HAY, THOMAS HENRY (d c 1937), Gweedore, county Donegal, Slough, Buckinghamshire and Aberdeen;
    studied medicine at Glasgow University; MB CM (Glas) 1894; FRCSI 1909; medical officer to Gweedore Dispensary District and constabulary and certifying factory surgeon, of Bridge Cottage, later of Bunbeg, county Donegal; moved c 1923 to 33 Landsdowne Avenue, Slough, Buckinghamshire, assistant physician to Tor-na-Dee Hospital, Aberdeen c 1928–30, resident physician to Farmwood Sanatorium, Buckinghamshire c 1930–37; died c 1937. [Addison (1898); *Med Dir*].

HAY, WILLIAM (1815/6–53), Londonderry, and Burt, county Donegal;
    born 1815/6, fourth son of the Rev George Hay, minister of First Derry Presbyterian Church, and Elizabeth Thompson of Londonderry; LRCSI; surgeon, of Shipquay Street, Londonderry, c 1845; finally of Upper Bohillon, Burt; died 7 October 1853 at Glencolumbkill; buried in Glencolumbkill Graveyard, county Donegal; probate Derry Diocesan Court 1853. [*BNL* 14 October 1853 (d); Belf PRO, D/656/4; Croly (1843–6); *Londonderry Sentinel* 14 October 1853 (d); McConnell (1951); *Memorials of the Dead*, vol IV, p 22].

HAYDEN, RICHARD HENRY HUGHES (1869–1925), ship's surgeon, Brazil, and Sutherland, Cape Colony;
    born 14 September 1869 at Coolnamuck House, Carrick-on-Suir, county Tipperary, son of Edward Hayden, capitalist, of Coolnamuck House and Frances —; educated at Green's Classical School, Carrick-on-Suir; studied medicine at Queen's College, Belfast, from 1890; MD (Chicago) 1892; LRCPI and LM LRCSI and LM 1892; surgeon to Bibby and Red Cross Lines Steamship Company; medical officer, of Vaport Grangense, Manaos, Amazonas, Brazil c 1895, district surgeon to Van Rhyns Dorp and medical officer in charge of troop at Sutherland c 1900; medical officer of health to Sutherland District Council c 1910, of Commercial Street, Sutherland; JP for Sutherland; died 10 April 1925 at 'Hibernia', Goodwood, Capetown. [Kirkpatrick Archive; *Med Dir*; QCB adm reg].

HAYES, ROBERT EDMUND (1837–90), Belfast, Letterkenny, county Donegal, Lisbellaw, county Fermanagh, and Lisburn, county Antrim;
    born 1837, son of Joseph Hayes of Letterkenny, county Donegal; educated at Belfast Academy; studied medicine at Queen's College, Belfast, from 1854; LM Belf Lying-in Hospital 1856; MRCSE 1858; LRCP Edin and LM 1867; resident house surgeon to the Belfast General Hospital 1858–9; general practitioner, of Letterkenny c 1859–60; medical officer to Lisbellaw Dispensary District, constabulary and Woollen Factory, and registrar of births and death for Lisbellaw c 1860–65; general practitioner, of 50 Antrim Road, Belfast c 1866–82 and of Railway Street, Lisburn, c 1882–90; lived finally at Ravenbank, Belfast; married 8 April 1862 in St Anne's Church of Ireland Church, Belfast, Margaret Elizabeth Addy (who was born 1839/40), only daughter of the Rev Edward Addy, Methodist minister; died 7 March

1890; buried in Belfast City Cemetery. [Belf City Cem, bur reg; Crookshank (1888); Dub GRO (m); *Londonderry Sentinel* 18 April 1862 (m); *Med Dir*; QCB adm reg].

HAYES, THOMAS CRAWFORD (1843–1909), London;
> born 18 October 1843 in Banbridge, county Down, youngest son of Frederick William Hayes, owner of a threadmill; educated at Dr Forrester's School, Isle of Man; studied arts and medicine at Trinity College, Dublin (senior moderator and gold medallist), from 1861, and at King's College, London; BA (TCD) 1866; LSA Lond 1870; MB MD 1875; MRCP Lond 1872; MA 1885; FRCP Lond 1889; house physician in King's College Hospital, London; Sambrooke registrar and assistant physician–accoucheur there 1872–9; physician for diseases of woman and children 1879–96; physician–accoucheur 1896–1906; lecturer in practical obstetrics at King's College 1889–96, professor of practical obstetrics (later obstetric medicine) 1896–1906; physician to the Royal Infirmary for Women and Children, the Evelina Hospital for Children, the General Lying-in Hospital, and the Royal Free Hospital; of 17 Clarges Street, London; married Elizabeth —; died 5 April 1909 at the Calverley Hotel, Tunbridge Wells; probate London 23 September 1909. [*BMJ* obituary (1909); Kirkpatrick Archive; *Lancet* obituary (1909); Lond PPR, will cal; *Med Dir*; *Munk's Roll*, vol 4; TCD adm reg; *TCD Cat*, vol II (1896)].

HAYS, ROBERT LOWRY (1792/3–1879), Killinchy, county Down;
> born 1792/3; studied medicine at Glasgow University; MD (Glas) 1815; general practitioner, of Ballymacreely, Killinchy; married 6 November 1840 at the home of her uncle, Robert Barry of Ringneil, Isabella McEwen (who was born 1818/9 and died 28 June 1891), eldest daughter of the Rev Alexander McEwen of Lakeview, Kirkcubbin, county Down; died 10 July 1879 at The Terrace, Ballymacreely; buried in Killinchy Non-Subscribing Presbyterian graveyard; probate Belfast 22 August 1879. [Addison (1898); *BNL* 13 November 1840 (m); Belf PRO, will cal, will; Clarke, *County Down*, vol 5 (1984); Kirkpatrick Archive; *Med Dir*].

HAYS, WILLIAM (*fl c* 1845), Killinchy, county Down;
> CM (Glas) [?]; general practitioner, of Killinchy c 1845; possibly died c 1850. [Croly (1843–6)].

HAZLETON, EDWARD BENJAMIN (1857–1946) Huntington, and Sheffield, Yorkshire;
> born 5 April 1857 at Ennis, county Clare, son of the Rev Robert Hazleton MA, Methodist Minister, of Ennis, Omagh and New York; educated at Methodist College, Belfast, from 1873; studied medicine at Queen's College, Belfast from 1875; LKQCPI and LM 1884; MD (RUI) 1886; MCh 1888; general practitioner, of Stepe House, St Ives, Huntingdon c 1886, Darley Dale, Derbyshire c 1895, York House, Abbeydale Road, Sheffield c 1905 and 1 Carter Knowle Road, Sheffield c 1920; author of papers on X-Rays; retired to Grosvenor Court, Croft Road, Torquay, Devon, c 1939; of Quarry Road, Northfield, Warwickshire c 1945 and finally of 46 Park View, Hatch End, Middlesex; died 7 August 1946 at Red Hall House, Middlesex; probate London 7 August 1946. [Fry (1984); Lond PPR, will cal; *Med Dir*; QCB adm reg].

HEANEN, CHARLES (1859–c 1892), Liverpool, Lancashire;
born 10 June 1859 at Keady, county Armagh, son of John Heanen, farmer, of Keady; brother of Dr Patrick Heanen (*q.v.*); studied medicine at Queen's College, Belfast, from 1875; MD MCh (RUI) 1882; general practitioner, of 5 Liver Chambers, Tithebarn Street, Liverpool from c 1885; died c 1892. [*Med Dir*; QCB adm reg].

HEANEN, PATRICK (1869–1942), Liverpool, Lancashire;
born March 1869 at Keady, county Armagh, son of John Heanen, farmer, of Keady; brother of Dr Charles Heanen (*q.v.*); educated at Guerton Valley Academy, Liverpool; studied medicine at the Royal College of Surgeons of Edinburgh, and from 1891, at Queen's College, Belfast; LRCP LRCS Edin 1896; LFPS Glas 1896; general practitioner of 240 Stanley Road, Kirkdale, Liverpool c 1905–20 and of Greenvale, Keady from 1920; died 26 February 1942; probate Belfast 23 October 1942. [Belf PRO, will cal; *Med Dir*; QCB adm reg].

HEAP, CHARLES SYDNEY (1848–c 1880), Battle, Sussex, and Burnham, Buckinghamshire;
born 1848 in Manchester, son of William W. Heap of Gordon Street, London; educated by the Rev G.H. Wilson of Belfast; studied medicine at Queen's College, Belfast, from 1863; MRCSE 1868; LKQCPI and LM 1875; general practitioner, of Battle, Sussex c 1870 and of Burnham c 1875; died c 1880, probably abroad. [*Med Dir*; QCB adm reg].

HEARD, RICHARD (1870–1950), Indian Medical Service;
born 10 January 1870; studied arts and medicine at Trinty College, Dublin; BA (RUI) 1891; LM Rot Hosp Dub; MB BCh BAO (RUI) 1892; MD (QUB) 1912; resident surgeon to Adelaide Hospital, Dublin; joined the Indian Medical Service (Bengal establishment) as surgeon lieutenant 1893; surgeon captain 1896; surgeon major 1905; lieutenant colonel 1913; brevet colonel 1915; colonel 1920; major general 1924; served on the North West Frontier in Wazaristan with the Chitral Relief Force (medal with clasps) 1894–5; professor of midwifery and gynaecology at Lahore Medical College 1909–14; served during World War I, 1914–18; inspector general of jails in Assam; CIE 1924; surgeon general to Bengal Government from 1924; retired as major-general 1927; author of *Feeding in Infancy and Early Childhood* (1906); died 16 August 1950. [*BMJ* obituary (1950); Crawford (1930); Kirkpatrick Archive; *Med Dir;* QCB adm reg].

HEARD, ROBERT LYNN, senior (1834–1901), Army Medical Service, Londonderry, Bray, county Wicklow, and Blackrock, county Dublin;
born 15 July 1834 at Donaghadee, county Down, son of Richard Heard of Dungloe, county Donegal; educated at RBAI; studied medicine at Queen's College, Belfast, from 1851; MRCSE 1855; LKQCPI and LM 1857; FRCSI 1877; MKQCPI 1879; MD (QUI) 1880; joined the Army Medical Service as assistant surgeon 1857, attached to the 67th Foot; staff surgeon 1865; served in China 1860; resigned 1867; general practitioner, of 5 Crawford Square, Londonderry, c 1875; of Bray c 1885, and of Blackrock Lodge, Blackrock, county Dublin c 1895; married Ellen —; father of Dr Robert Lynn Heard, junior, MB (RUI) 1889; died 31 August 1901 at Blackrock;

probate Dublin 18 December 1901. [Belf PRO, will cal; *Med Dir*; Peterkin and Johnston (1968); QCB adm reg].

HEARN, GEORGE MARCUS (1834/5–90) Bawnboy, county Cavan;
born 1834/5; brother of Dr John Henry Hearn (*q.v.*); studied medicine at the Royal College of Surgeons in Ireland and the City of Dublin Hospital; LKQCPI 1860; LRCSI and LM 1860; medical officer to Bawnboy Workshouse and Ballyconnel Dispensary District, of Woodville, county Cavan; married Elizabeth Mary Adelaide Adamson, widow of the Rev Christopher Adamson and daughter of the Rev John Charles Martin, Archdeacon of Kilmore, and sister of Dr Brownlow Rudinge Martin (*q.v.*); father of Dr John George Frederick Hearn (*q.v.*); died 26 August 1890 at Woodville, of typhus fever; administration Cavan 7 January 1891. [Belf PRO, will cal; Burke *LGI* (1912); Dub GRO (d); *Med Dir*].

HEARN, JOHN GEORGE FREDERICK (1868–1912), Hazaribah, India;
born 15 January 1868 in county Cavan, son of Dr George Marcus Hearn of Woodville, county Cavan (*q.v.*) and Elizabeth Martin; educated at Drogheda Grammar School; studied arts and medicine at Trinity College, Dublin, from 1886; BA (TCD) 1891; MB BCh BAO 1893; MD 1898; working with the Dublin University Mission in Hazaribah, Chota Nagpore, India c 1895; ordained deacon 1898; lived finally at the Rectory, Killashandra; died 26 March 1912 at 84 Southbourne Road, Bournemouth, of tuberculosis; probate Cavan 25 May 1912. [Belf PRO, will cal; Crockford; Dub GRO (b); Lond GRO (d); *Med Dir; TCD Cat*; vol II (1896)].

HEARN, JOHN HENRY (1829–90), Army Medical Service;
born 20 December 1829 at Belturbet, county Cavan; brother of Dr George Marcus Hearn (*q.v.*); LFPS Glas 1854; joined the Army Medical Service as assistant surgeon to the Ordinance Medical Department in 1855; staff surgeon 1867, transferring to the 73rd Foot; served in the Crimean War 1854–6; retired on half pay 1869 to Woodville, county Cavan; unmarried; died 20 April 1890 at Woodville; administration Cavan 24 June 1890. [Belf PRO; will cal; Dub GRO (d); *Med Dir*; Peterkin and Johnston (1968)].

HEARNE, SAMUEL (*fl c* 1856), Lisnaskea, county Fermanagh;
general practitioner, of Lisnaskea; married —; daughter born 23 January 1856. [*BNL* 25 January 1856 (b)].

HEATH, RICHARD (1852–1902), Barnsley, Yorkshire, and St Leonards-on-Sea, Sussex;
born 14 August 1852 at Arklow, county Wicklow, son of William Heath of Arklow; educated at Tranmore Boarding School, county Waterford; studied medicine at Queen's College, Belfast, from 1869; MD MCh (QUI) 1873; general practitioner, of Highfield House, Barnsley c 1875, and of 29 Warrior Square, St Leonards-on-Sea, from c 1880; died 20 December 1902; probate London 23 January 1903. [Lond PPR, will cal; *Med Dir*; QCB adm reg].

HEATH, ROBERT EDWARD (1839–1922), Army Medical Service and Torbay, Devonshire;
born 1 January 1839 at Arklow, county Wicklow; son of William Heath of Arklow; educated by Mr Stapleton of 9 South Frederick Street, Dublin; studied medicine at Queen's College, Belfast, from 1855; MD (QUI) 1859; MRCSE 1860; joined the Army Medical Service as staff assistant surgeon in 1860; on half pay July 1861–January 1862; attached to 88th Foot 1862; surgeon major 1875; served at Hazara 1868; retired on half pay 1877; senior surgeon to Torbay Hospital 1877–1900; retired from this c 1900 to Bryn Adda, Grange Road, Eastbourne; married Catherine Maria —; died 9 January 1922 at Eastbourne; probate Lewes 7 February 1922. [*BMJ* obituary (1922); Kirkpatrick Archive; Lond PPR, will cal; *Med Dir*; Peterkin and Johnston (1968); QCB adm reg].

HEATHER, DAWSON DEAN (1839–70) Army Medical Service;
born 26 August 1839 in Belfast; LRCSI 1862; LM 1863 LRCP Eden 1864; joined the Army Medical Service as assistant surgeon 1864; unmarried; died 19 August 1870 at Boyle military barracks, county Roscommon by committing suicide (Coroner). [Dub GRO (d); *Med Dir*; Peterkin and Johnston (1968)].

HEBURN (HEYBURN), WILLIAM (d 1854), Belfast;
surgeon; of Belfast; married 26 October 1850 at the home of the bride's father, Margaret Ross, elder daughter of Wiilliam Ross; died 8 December 1854 in Patrick Street, Belfast. [*BNL* 29 October 1850 (m) and 11 December 1854 (d); *Med Dir*].

HEENEY, FRANCIS XAVERIUS, senior (d c 1874), Cartagena, Colombia, Belfast, and Ipswich, Queensland;
studied medicine at Glasgow University; MD (Glas) 1839; surgeon in Bolivar's Regiment of Guards (Siriadores); later Mexican consul for the port of Cartagena; general practitioner, of 4 Eglinton Terrace, Belfast c 1860–65; emigrated to Australia c 1865; general practitioner of Ipswich, Queensland; married 19 October 1837 in Rasharkin Church of Ireland Church, Henrietta Anna Dickson, daughter of the Rev William Henry Dickson, prebendary of Rasharkin, county Antrim, and Bettia Webster died c 1874. [Addison (1898); *BNL* 24 October 1837 (m); Leslie (1993); *Med Dir*].

HEENEY, FRANCIS XAVERIUS, junior (1843/4–69), Castledawson, county Londonderry;
born 1843/4, third son of James Patrick Heeney of Castledawson; brother of Dr James Patrick Heeney (*q.v.*); MRCP MRCS Edin; unmarried; died 13 November 1869 at Castledawson of typhus fever. [*Coleraine Chronicle* 20 November 1869 (d); Dub GRO (d); *Londonderry Sentinel* 16 November 1869 (d)].

HEENEY, JAMES PATRICK (1841–79), Ipswich, Queensland, and Belfast;
born 12 December 1841, son of James Patrick Heeney of Castledawson, county Londonderry; brother of Dr Francis Xaverius Heeney, junior (*q.v.*); educated at Castledawson National School; studied medicine from 1860 at Queen's College, Belfast, and later at Glasgow University; MD CM (Glas) 1872; resident medical

officer of Ispwich Hospital, Queensland 1863–70; general practitioner, of 6 Albert Terrace, and 2 Killymoon Buildings, Fall Road, Belfast c 1875; married (1) Margaret Elizabeth — (who was born 1831/2 and died 17 July 1874); (2) Elizabeth — (who was born 1838/9 and died 29 January 1919); died 24 September 1879 at 138 Albert Terrace as a result of an overdose of chloral hydrate (Coroner); administration Belfast 10 November 1879. [Addison (1898); Belf PRO, will cal; Dub GRO (d); *Med Dir*; Merrick and Clarke, *Belfast*, vol 2 (1984); QCB adm reg].

HEENEY, JOHN (d 1860), Belfast;
eldest son of James Heeney of Castledawson; died 23 January 1860 at 48 Donegall Street, Belfast. [*Coleraine Chronicle* 4 February 1860 (d); *Londonderry Sentinel* 27 January 1860 (d); *Med Dir*].

HEGAN, EDWIN (1866–1921), Upton Manor, Essex;
born 13 April 1866 at 26 Sandys Street, Newry, son of Samuel Hegan, merchant, of 6 Sandys Street; educated at Newry Intermediate School; studied arts and medicine at Queen's College, Galway, from 1883, and from 1886, at Queen's College, Belfast; MB BCh (RUI) 1891; general practitioner, of Sunnyside, 54 Terrace Road, Upton Manor from c 1895; married Gabrielle Marie Josephine —; died 11 February 1921; probate London 18 March 1921. [Lond PPR, will cal; *Med Dir*; QCB adm reg].

HEGARTY, ANDREW (1845–1923), Kilrea, Draperstown and Magherafelt, county Londonderry;
born 1845 at Kilrea, county Londonderry, son of Andrew Hegarty of Kilrea; educated by John McLoskey of Maghera; studied medicine at Queen's College, Belfast, from 1864; MD (QUI) 1868; MCh 1870; general practitioner of Kilrea from c 1870; medical officer to Draperstown Dispensary District and constabulary from c 1890 and to Magherafelt Dispensary District and constabulary from 1901; of Ardrath, Magherafelt c 1920; JP; married Jane —; father of Dr Daniel Hegarty of Magherafelt, LRCPI LRCSI 1919, Dr Andrew Hegarty, LAH Dub 1915 (killed in World War I) and Dr Patrick Nicholas Hegarty, LRCPI LRCSI 1919; died 22 November 1923; probate Londonderry 24 March 1924. [Belf PRO, will cal, will; Kirkpatrick Archive; Maitland (1916); *Med Dir*; QCB adm reg].

HEMPHILL, JAMES PATTON (1835/6–71), Liverpool, Lancashire, and Myroe, county Londonderry;
born 1835/6 in county Londonderry, son of John Hemphill, farmer; studied arts and medicine at Trinity College, Dublin, from 1854; MRCSE 1859; LRCP Edin 1863; MA (TCD) 1865; demonstrator in anatomy at Trinity College, Dublin; surgeon accoucheur to the Ladies' Charity, Liverpool; general practitioner of Wheatfield, Myroe; died 6 July 1871; buried in Ballykelly Church of Ireland Graveyard. [Burtchaell and Sadleir (1935); gravestone inscription; *Med Dir*].

HEMPHILL, WILLIAM (1830–98), Army Medical Service;
born 16 February 1830 at Castlederg, county Tyrone; studied medicine at Glasgow University; MD (Glas) 1851; joined the Army Medical Service as assistant surgeon to the 48th Foot in 1854; transferred to 66th Foot 1858; staff surgeon 1867; retired

on half pay with honorary rank of deputy surgeon general 1879; died 20 February 1898. [Addison (1898); *Med Dir*; Peterkin and Johnston (1968)].

HEMSTED, ARTHUR (1852–93), Walton-on-Thames, Surrey;
born 13 April 1852 at Seagry, son of the Rev John Hemstead of Ickford Rectory, Buckinghamshire; brother of Dr Edwin Hemsted (*q.v.*); educated at Chatham House, Ramsgate; studied medicine at Queen's College, Belfast, from 1871 and at University College, London; LRCP Lond 1877; MRCSE 1877; joined the Indian Medical Service (Bengal establishment) as surgeon 1878; resigned 1880; general practitioner, of Manor House, Walton-on-Thames; married Emily Jane —; died 21 June 1893 at Egerton, Freshwater, Isle of Wight; probate London 29 July 1893. [Crawford (1930); Lond PPR, will cal; *Med Dir*; QCB adm reg].

HEMSTED, EDWIN (1849–c 1885), Wellingborough, Northhamptonshire and Southhampton, Hampshire;
born 27 February 1849 at Seagry, son of Rev John Hemstead of Ickford Rectory, Buckinghamshire; brother of Dr Arthur Hemsted (*q.v.*); educated at Chatham House, Ramsgate, and Anderson's University, Glasgow; studied medicine at Queen's College, Belfast from 1871; MD MCh (QUI) 1873; general practitioner, of 61 Oxford Street, Wellingborough c 1875; medical officer of Freemantle and Southampton Dispensaries of Westbourne Villa, Southampton, c 1880; died c 1885. [*Med Dir*; QCB adm reg].

HEND, THOMAS (*fl c* 1824), Castleblayney, county Monaghan;
surgeon, of Market Street, Castleblayney c 1824. [Pigot (1824)].

HENDERSON, ANDREW (d c 1771), Londonderry;
apothecary, of Londonderry city; died c 1771; probate Derry Diocesan Court 1771. [Thrift (1920)].

HENDERSON, ANDREW (1800–40), Indian Medical Service;
born 11 October 1800 in Londonderry; joined the Indian Medical Service (Bengal establishment) as assistant surgeon 1831; died July 1840 in Cheybean (Charibasa), Bengal. [*BNL* 20 October 1840 (d); Crawford (1930); *Londonderry Sentinel* 17 October 1840 (d)].

HENDERSON, DANIEL (d c 1833), Drumnahaw, county Donegal;
general practitioner, of Drumnahaw, near Strabane; died c 1833; probate Derry Diocesan Court 1833. [Thrift (1920)].

HENDERSON, DANIEL (1864–c 1935), Frazerburg, South Africa;
born 1 November 1864 at Glenanne, Markethill, county Armagh, son of John Henderson, farmer and factory manager, Maytone, Mountmorris and Frances Guy; educated at Armagh Royal School from 1881; studied medicine at Queen's College, Belfast, from 1883; LRCP LRCS Edin 1887; LFPS Glas 1887; emigrated to South Africa; district surgeon and medical officer of health to Frazerburg; captain in the

South Africa Medical Corps; district surgeon to the District of Hay; died c 1935. [Belf GRO (b); Ferrar (1933); *Med Dir*; QCB adm reg].

HENDERSON, HUGH (1796/7–1867), Enniskillen, county Fermanagh;
born 1796/7; LAH Dub; apothecary, of Main Street, Enniskillen, c 1824–45; married 12 July 1833 in Colebrooke Church, county Fermanagh, Anne Armstrong, second daughter of John Armstrong of Bellahill; died 20 February 1867 at Floraville, Enniskillen. [*BNL* 23 July 1833 (m); Croly (1843–6); Dub GRO (d); *Londonderry Sentinel* 22 February 1867 (d); Pigot (1824)].

HENDERSON, JAMES (c 1865–1943), Dublin and Drumahoe, county Londonderry;
born c 1865 in county Londonderry, son of Robert Henderson, merchant, of Londonderry; educated at Londonderry Academical Institution; studied medicine at Trinity College, Dublin, from 1888; LM Rot Hosp Dub 1892; BA (TCD) 1892; MB BCh BAO 1893; MD 1897; MA 1914; assistant house surgeon, ophthalmic surgeon and aural surgeon to Dr Steeven's Hospital, Dublin; general practitioner, of Fincairn, Drumahoe; largely gave up medical practice for farming; president of the North West Agricultural Society; unmarried; died 15 September 1943 at Fincairn; probate Londonderry 28 July 1844. [Belf GRO (d); Belf PRO, will cal; Kirkpatrick Archive; *Med Dir;* TCD adm reg; *TCD Cat*, vol II (1896)].

HENDERSON, JOHN (d 1848), Naval Medical Service;
second son of James Henderson of Lisdillen, county Londonderry; joined the Naval Medical Service as assistant surgeon on HMS *Agincourt* 1811; died 24 January 1848 at Portsmouth. [*Londonderry Sentinel* 22 February 1848 (d); *NMS* (1826)].

HENDERSON, JOSEPH (1814/5–1900), Naval Medical Service;
born 1814/5 in Strabane; joined the Naval Medical Service as assistant surgeon; LRCSI 1836; MD (Aber) 1850; served on HNS *Boscawen* c 1864 and HMS *Excellent* c 1868; staff surgeon and deputy inspector general of hospitals and fleets; retired c 1871 to Ballindrait, county Donegal and to 3 Alexandra Terrace, Northland Road, Londonderry c 1895; unmarried; died 22 April 1900 at Alexandra Terrace; probate Londonderry 19 June 1900. [Belf PRO, will cal; Dub GRO (d); *Med Dir; Strabane Morning Post* 13 December 1836 (note of LRCSI)].

HENDERSON, ROBERT WILSON (1857/8–c 1953), Tredegar, Monmouthshire, and London;
born 1857/8, son of Thomas Henderson, farmer and businessman of Ballyagan, Garvagh, county Londonderry; brother of Dr Samuel Dunlop Henderson (*q.v.*); educated at Coleraine Academical Institution; studied medicine at Queen's College, Belfast, from 1878; MD MCh (RUI) 1883; LM KQCPI 1884; demonstrator of anatomy to Queen's College, Galway; general practitioner, of 'The Willows', Tredegar c 1885 and of Radclyffe, Chichele Road, Cricklewood, London c 1895; retired to White Park House, Ballintoy c 1905 but also lived c 1912–20 in Woodhouse Cliff, Hyde Park, Leeds; JP for county Antrim c 1909; died c 1953. [*Med Dir*; QCB adm reg].

HENDERSON, SAMUEL DUNLOP (1856–96), Limavady, county Londonderry, and Brighouse, Yorkshire;
>born 16 August 1856 at Garvagh, county Londonderry, son of Thomas Henderson, farmer and businessman, of Ballyagan, Garvagh; brother of Dr Robert Wilson Henderson (*q.v.*); educated at Coleraine Academical Institution; studied medicine at Queen's College, Galway, and from 1856, at Queen's College, Belfast; MD MCh (RUI) 1882; LM KQCPI 1883; general practitioner, of Main Street, Limavady, c 1885, and of Bonegate Road, Brighouse, Yorkshire, c 1895; died 9 October 1896 at Radcliffe, Chichele Road, Hendon, of chronic alcoholism with delirium tremens. [Lond GRO (d); *Med Dir*; QCB adm reg].

HENDERSON, WILLIAM (1773/4–1846), Naval Medical Service;
>born 1773/4; joined the Naval Medical Service as assistant surgeon c 1793; surgeon 1797 or 1803; retired as surgeon to Foyle View and Clooney Lodge, Londonderry; mentioned in a deed of conveyance dated 17 December 1821 and presumably retired before this; will dated 31 December 1832, died 15 March 1846 at Clooney Lodge; probate Derry Diocesan Court 27 April 1846. [*BNL* 24 March 1846 (d); Belf PRO, D/642/D31; Dub Reg Deeds, 771.205.522740; *Londonderry Standard* 27 March 1846 (d); *NMS* (1826)].

HENDERSON, WILLIAM ROBERT (1853–1907), Army Medical Service;
>born 22 December 1853 in Dublin, son of William Henderson, gentleman, of Kesh Hill, county Fermanagh; educated at RBAI; studied medicine at Queen's College, Belfast, from 1874; MD MCh (QUI) 1878; joined the Army Medical Service 1880; served in West Africa (Jebu); lived finally at Mornington, Bray, county Wicklow; died 25 June 1907; probate Dublin 1 August 1907 and London 17 August 1907. [Belf PRO, will cal; Lond PPR, will cal; *Med Dir*; Peterkin and Johnston (1968); QCB adm reg].

HENDERSON, — (d c 1827–47), Newry, county Down;
>general practitioner, of Newry; married —; son born 1807/8 and died 1827, and a son died 9 July 1847; died between 1827 and 1847. [*BNL* 14 August 1827 (d, son) and 9 July 1847 (d, son)].

HENDRICK, JOHN (1793–1855), Army Medical Service;
>born January 1793, son of William Hendrick, officer of excise, of Strabane, county Tyrone; assistant surgeon to Donegal Militia 1811–17; joined the Army Medical Service as assistant surgeon to 12th Foot 1817; on half pay 1818–23; served with 86th Foot 1823; studied medicine at Edinburgh University; MD (Edin) 1825 (thesis 'De hepatitide'); on half pay with 63rd Foot 1824–30; on full pay with 34th Foot 1830–37; 'when quartered in Galway, from his zeal and usefulness during the time cholera prevailed, received the thanks of the inhabitants, accompanied with a handsome piece of plate, previous to his going to British America'; retired on half pay 1837; died 6 April 1855. [Edin Univ; *Londonderry Sentinel* 10 August 1833 (d, father); Peterkin and Johnston (1968); *Strabane Morning Post* 6 November 1832 (cholera epidemic) and 6 August 1833 (d, father)].

HENNING, JOHN (*fl c* 1819–24), Lurgan, county Armagh;
surgeon and apothecary, of Lurgan c 1818 and 1824; married 7 November 1814 Anne Druitt of Lurgan. [*BNL* 15 November 1814 (m); Bradshaw (1819); Pigot (1824)].

HENNING, ROBERT (1816), Templepatrick, county Antrim;
surgeon and apothecary, of Templepatrick; died 20 April 1816, 'a gentleman distinguished for practical skill and success in his profession'. [*BNL* 26 April 1816 (d)].

HENRY, ALEXANDER DONALDSON (1845/6–c 1882), Kilcullen, county Kildare, Clones, county Monaghan, and Melbourne, Australia;
born 1845/6 in Clones, county Monaghan, son of Dr Richard Henry, senior (*q.v.*); brother of Dr Joseph Henry of Rochdale (*q.v.*), Dr Richard Henry, junior, of Aughnacloy and Brookeborough (*q.v.*) and Dr William Henry of Clones (*q.v.*); studied arts and medicine at Trinity College, Dublin, from 1862, and in House of Industry Hospitals; BA (TCD) 1866; MB 1867; LM Rot Hosp Dub 1867; LRCSI 1867; medical officer to Kilcullen Dispensary District from c 1868, of Liffey Bank Kilcullen, county Kildare, but also described as 'of Clones'; emigrated to Australia c 1879; general practitioner, of Melbourne, Victoria; died c 1882. [McCann (2003); *Med Dir;* TCD adm reg; *TCD Cat*, vol II (1896)].

HENRY, AUGUSTINE (1857–1930), China, Cambridge and Dublin;
born 2 July 1857 in Dundee, Angus, eldest son of Bernard Henry, flax merchant and grocer, originally of Tyanee, Bellaghy, county Londonderry, and Mary MacNamee; family moved back to Ireland, to Cookstown, county Tyrone, soon after Augustine's birth; educated at Cookstown Academy; studied arts at Queen's College, Galway 1874–8 and medicine at Queen's College, Belfast, from 1878 (Dunville scholarship); BA (RUI) (1st class hons and gold medal) 1877; MA 1878; LRCP Edin 1881; 'the best read man I met in my whole college course' (Connor); studied also in London 1878–80 and Edinburgh; encouraged to go to China by Sir Robert Hart who he had met in Belfast in 1879; medical officer with Imperial Chinese Customs under Sir Robert Hart from 1881; in Shanghai 1881–2, Hupeh Province 1882–9, Hairan 1889, home leave 1889–91, studied law at the Middle Temple, London, and was called to the Bar 1890; Shanghai and Taiwan 1891–1900; acting chief commissioner of Customs; later worked in Formosa and developed a strong interest in botany and corresponded with the Royal Botanic Gardens, Kew; returned to Britain after the Boxer Rising in 1900; helped to found the School of Forestry at Cambridge and was Reader in Forestry at Cambridge 1907–13; Professor of Forestry at the College of Science in Dublin 1913; author of *Notes on the Economic Botany of China* (1893), *The Trees of Great Britain and Ireland* (jointly with H.J. Elwes) 7 vols (1903–13), *Forests, Woods and Trees in Relation to Hygiene* (1919) and many papers; married (1) 20 June 1891 in St George's Church, Bloomsbury, London, Caroline Orridge of London (who was born c 1860 and died September 1894 of tuberculosis in Denver, USA), daughter of a London jeweller; (2) 17 March 1908 Alice Helen (Elsie) Brunton (1882–1956), daughter of Sir Lauder Brunton, physician; died 23 March 1930 at his

home, 5 Sandford Terrace, Clonskea; buried in Dean's Grange, Cemetery, Dublin; memorial plaque in Portglenone Forrest, county Antrim; plants named after him include *Acer henryi, Parthenocissus henryana,* and *Lilium henryi;* portrait (1929) by Celia Harrison, in the National Botanic Gardens, Dublin; probate Dublin 11 June 1930. [Bateson (2004); Bell (1985); *DIB* (2009); Dub Nat Arch, will cal; Edin RCP, letter; Geary (1995, quoting Dr Samuel Connor); Igoe (2001); Lond GRO (m); Martin (2010); *Oxford DNB* (2004); Pim (1984); Praeger (1949); QCB adm reg; Sturgess (1949)].

HENRY, DAVID (1866–1937), Liverpool, Lancashire;
born 20 May 1866 at Ballyblack, Newtownards, county Down, son of David Henry, farmer, of Ballyblack; educated at Newtownards Intermediate School; studied medicine at Queen's College, Belfast, from 1888; MB BCh BAO (RUI) 1897; general practitioner, of 46 Wellington Terrace, West Derby Road, Liverpool, from c 1900 and of 130 Sheil Road, Liverpool from c 1910 died 28 January 1937; probate London 11 March 1937. [Lond PPR, will cal; *Med Dir*; QCB adm reg].

HENRY, EMERSON WILSON (1844–81), Whitehaven, Cumberland;
born 28 July 1844 at Devernagh House, Newry, fifth son of the Rev Alexander Henry of Devernagh House, minister of Kingsmills Presbyterian Church, and — Stuart; educated in Newry; studied medicine at Queen's College, Belfast, from 1860; MD MCh (QUI) 1866; general practitioner in Whitehaven 1865–81; honorary surgeon to the Whitehaven and West Cumberland Infirmary and to the Whitehaven Rifle Volunteers; a prominent freemason; had a carriage accident which necessitated the amputation of one of his legs some years before his death; unmarried; died 4 December 1881 at 10 Lowther Street, Whitehaven, of blood poisoning, contracted during his professional duties; portrait by William Wilson in the Masonic Lodge, Whitehaven; administration Carlisle 21 January 1882. [*Downpatrick Recorder* 10 December 1881 (d); Kirkpatrick Archive; Lond PPR, will cal; *Med Dir*; QCB adm reg; Stewart (1950)].

HENRY, GEORGE McWILLIAMS (1856/7–1936), Halifax, Yorkshire;
born 1856/7 in county Tyrone, son of Thomas Henry, gentleman farmer; lived with an uncle in Halifax while a boy; studied medicine at University College Hospital, London; MRCSE 1880; general practitioner, of Landon House, Halifax, from c 1881; retired to 33 Orchard Road, St Annes-on-Sea; married 17 August 1882 in Harrison Road Independent Chapel, Rose Crossley (who was born 1854/5), daughter of John Crossley, machine maker, of Hopewood Hall, Halifax; father of Dr McWilliams Henry of Halifax, LRCP LRCS Edin 1909, FRCS Edin 1913; died 25 December 1936 at 33 Orchard Road; probate London 21 April 1937. [Kirkpatrick Archive; *Lancet* obituary (1936); Lond GRO (m) and (d); Lond PPR, will cal; *Med Dir*].

HENRY, HUGH (1805/6–39), Glasslough, county Monaghan;
born 1805/6; of Derryisland, Castleblayney, county Monaghan; surgeon, of Glasslough; died July 1839. [*BNL* 26 July 1839 (d)].

HENRY, JAMES (1859–1924), Ballybay, county Monaghan;
   born 23 June 1859 at Castleblaney, county Monaghan, son of Thomas Henry, merchant, of The Diamond, Monaghan; educated at Methodist College, Belfast, from 1871 and RBAI; studied medicine at Queen's College, Belfast, from 1877; MD MCh (QUI) 1882; LM KQCPI 1883; general practitioner, of Ballybay and Swan Park; medical officer and medical officer of health for Monaghan Dispensary District; medical officer to St Louis Reformatory and Industrial Schools and certifying factory surgeon; died 23 January 1924; probate Dublin 7 May 1924. [Dub Nat Arch, will cal; Fry (1984); Kirkpatrick Archive; *Med Dir*; QCB adm reg].

HENRY, JAMES FALLS (1825/6–77), Naval Medical Service, Dublin and Maghera, county Londonderry;
   born 1825/6 [?]; studied medicine at Glasgow University; MD (Glas) 1839; MRCSE 1851; joined the Naval Medical Service as assistant surgeon 1851; later surgeon in Dublin and finally in Maghera; unmarried; died 7 December 1877 at the Cottage. Maghera; administration Londonderry 14 March 1878. [Addison (1898); Belf PRO, will cal; Dub GRO (d); *Med Dir*].

HENRY, JOHN (b 1843/4), Portglenone, county Antrim;
   born 1843/4, son of Patrick Henry, farmer, of Portglenone; MD [?]; not in *Medical Directory* or *Medical Register*; married 18 June 1867 in All Saints' Roman Catholic Church, Ballymena, Catherine McLaughlin (who was born 1844/5), fifth daughter of Joseph McLaughlin, farmer, of McLaughlin's Corner, Kilrea. [*Coleraine Chronicle* 22 June 1867 (m); *Londonderry Sentinel* 25 June 1867 (m); UHF database (m)].

HENRY, JOHN JAMES (1829–1908), Army Medical Service;
   born 23 February 1829 at Cavan; LRCS Edin 1855; joined the Army Medical Service as assistant surgeon 1856; attached to the 43rd Foot 1857; staff surgeon 1864; surgeon major 1870; on half pay October 1872–April 1875; served during the Indian Mutiny 1857 and in New Zealand 1863–4; retired on half pay 1878 to the Crescent, Sandgate, Kent, and 'Strathmore', Leckhampton Road, Cheltenham, Gloucestershire; unmarried; died 2 December 1908 at 'Strathmore'; probate London 22 December 1908. [Lond PPR, will cal, will; *Med Dir*; Peterkin and Johnston (1968)].

HENRY, JOSEPH (1839/40–1903), Benala, Victoria;
   born 1839/40 at Kilkeel, county Down, son of Thomas Gibson Henry of Kilkeel and Mary Anne —; educated by Mr Ryder; studied medicine at Trinity College, Dublin, from 1857; BA (TCD) 1862; MB 1863; LRCSI 1863; emigrated to Australia; general practitioner of Benala c 1870; died 1903. [Burtchaell and Sadleir (1935); Clarke, *County Down*, vol 10 (1973); Kirkpatrick Archive; *Med Dir*].

HENRY, JOSEPH (1852–1919), Clones, county Monaghan, and Rochdale, Lancashire;
   born 9 May 1852 at Newbliss, county Monaghan, fifth son of Dr Richard Henry, senior, of Clones (*q.v.*); brother of Dr Alexander Donaldson Henry of Melbourne (*q.v.*), Dr Richard Henry, junior, of Aughgnacloy and Brookebouough (*q.v.*) and Dr

William Henry of Clones (*q.v.*); educated at Coleraine Academical Instutition; studied medicine at Queen's College, Belfast, from 1870 and the Carmichael School, Dublin; LM Rot Hosp Dub 1873; MD (hons) (QUI) 1874; LRCSI 1874; resident medical officer of the Richmond, Whitworth and Hardwick Hospitals, Dublin; general practitioner, of Clones c 1875; general practitioner, of 107 Drake Street, Rochdale c 1885 and The Crescent, Rochdale, c 1895; medical superintendent of the Rochdale Fever Hospital and medical officer of health for Rochdale; retired c 1908; married Ernestine —; father of Dr Sydney Alexander Henry of Rochdale, MRCS LRCP Lond 1905; died 30 September 1919 at 107 Drake Street; probate Manchester 25 November 1919. [Kirkpatrick Archive; Lond PPR, will cal, will; *Med Dir*; QCB adm reg].

HENRY, MATTHEW (1791/2–1812), London;
born 1791/2 in Ballymoney, county Antrim; studied medicine in Edinburgh and qualified as a surgeon; surgeon of the York Hospital [?]; moved to practice in London 1811; died 16 March 1812 in London, after 8 days' illness; 'he was a young man of great promise, really endowed with uncommon talents'. [*BNL* 31 March 1812 (d)].

HENRY, MOSES (1872–1927), Belfast;
born 3 January 1872 at Crobane House, Newry, county Down, son of James Henry, farmer, of Crobane; educated at Newry Intermediate School; studied medicine at Queen's College, Galway, and from 1896, at Queen's College, Belfast, the Catholic University of Ireland, and Edinburgh; BA (RUI) 1886; MA 1888; MB BCh BAO (RUI) 1897; civil surgeon to the Victoria Barracks, Belfast 1899–1902; general practitioner, of 7 Benvista, Antrim Road, Belfast, from 1907; served with RAMC in France during the World War; married 12 October 1906 in Trinity Street Reformed Presbyterian Church, Belfast, Frances Dick, fourth daughter of the Rev Prof James Dick of Easton Lodge, Cliftonville, Belfast; died 1 June 1927; probate Belfast 20 September 1927. [Belf PRO, will cal; Dub GRO (m); Kirkpatrick Archive; *Med Dir*; QCB adm reg; Young and Pike (1909)].

HENRY, PETER (1770/1–1846), Naval Medical Service and Maghera, county Londonderry;
born 1770/1; joined the Naval Medical Service as assistant surgeon; surgeon 1801 said to have attended Napoleon at St Helena and to have been present at his post mortem; said to have been given Napoleon's chair which is now in Castleward, county Down; retired on half pay; surgeon, of Maghera; married —; died 13 November 1846 at his home in Maghera; probate Prerogative Court 1849. [*BNL* 27 November 1846 (d); Belf PRO, prerog wills index; *Londonderry Sentinel* 28 November 1846 (d); *NMS* (1826); Pigot (1824); RVH Archives].

HENRY, RICHARD, senior (1817/8–98), Newbliss and Clones, county Monaghan;
born 1817/8; MRCSE 1836; LM Dub Lying-in Hosp (Rotunda) 1837; MD (Glas) 1848; medical officer to Newbliss Dispensary District; medical officer to Clones Dispensary District, Workhouse and Infirmary and to constabulary; married 7 December 1842 Anne Jane Donaldson, only daughter of Alexander Donaldson of Tullyvallen, county Armagh; father of Dtr Alexander Donaldson Henry (*q.v.*), Dr

Richard Henry, junior (*q.v.*), Dr Joseph Henry of Rochdale (*q.v.*) and Dr William Henry of Clones (*q.v.*); died 28 April 1898 at The Diamond, Clones; probate Dublin 25 May 1898. [Addison (1898); *BNL* 27 December 1842 (m); Belf PRO, will cal; Croly (1843–6); Dub GRO (d); Kirkpatrick Archive; McCann (2003); *Med Dir*; QCB adm reg].

HENRY, RICHARD, junior (1847–86), Aughnacloy, county Tyrone, Brookeborough, county Fermanagh, and Dublin;

born 1847, son of Dr Richard Henry, senior (*q.v.*); brother of Dr Alexander Donaldson Henry (*q.v.*), Dr Joseph Henry of Rochdale (*q.v.*) and Dr William Henry of Clones (*q.v.*); educated at Mr Rutherford's School, Clones; studied arts at Queen's College, Belfast, from 1865 and medicine at the Carmichael School and House of Industry Hospitals, Dublin; BA (QUI) 1868; MD 1871; LRCSI 1871; LM Rot Hosp Dub 1871; MA 1882; medical officer to Aughnacloy Dispensary District c 1875; medical officer and certifying factory surgeon to Brookeborough Dispensary District; finally assistant master of the Rotunda Hospital, Dublin 1881–6, of Lower Baggot Street, Dublin, and finally, of Swiss Cottage, Dundrum, county Dublin; married Anne Louisa —; died 6 November 1886 at Swiss Cottage, Dundrum, county Dublin; probate Dublin 30 Novenber 1886. [Belf PRO, will cal; Dub GRO (d); Kirkpatrick Archive; Kirkpatrick and Jellett (1913); *Med Dir;* QCB adm reg].

HENRY, ROBERT (d c 1821), Armagh;

apothecary, of Armagh; died c 1821; administration Armagh Diocesan Court 1821. [Dub Nat Arch, Armagh Dio Admins index].

HENRY, ROBERT, (1767/8–1838), Stewartstown, county Tyrone;

born 1767/8; LML (Upsala); MRCS Lond; studied medicine in Leyden from 1794; MD (Leyden) 1794 (thesis 'De spasmo tonico praecipue de trismo', dedicated to James Stewart of Killymoon); physician and surgeon, of Brigh, Stewartstown; married February 1803 Elizabeth Cuppage (who was born 1786/7 and died 2 October 1841 at Portstewart), daughter of Captain Thomas Cuppage of Ballycastle; died 6 May 1838; administration Armagh Diocesan Court 1845. [*BNL* 15 February 1803 (m) and 14 May 1838 (d) and 12 October 1841 (d); Bradshaw (1819); Dub Nat Arch, Armagh Dio Admins index; *Londonderry Sentinel* 9 October 1841 (d); Innes Smith (1932)].

HENRY, ROBERT, senior (1815/6–95), Pomeroy, county Tyrone;

born 1815/6; LRCS Edin 1835; LRCP Edin 1860; FRCS Edin 1873; medical officer to Pomeroy Dispensary District and constabulary; author of various medical papers; married (1) 17 December 1835 in Pomeroy, Letitia Whiteside, youngest daughter of James Whiteside of Lurganeden, Pomeroy; (2) 7 May 1840 at Carnteel, county Tyrone, Mary McWilliams (who died 13 November 1866), third daughter of John McWilliams of Carnteel; father of John McWilliams Henry, who died of phthisis as a medical student aged 23; died 19 January 1895 at Pomeroy; probate Dublin 25 May 1895. [*BNL* 25 December 1835 (m) and 12 May 1840 (m); Belf PRO, will cal; Croly (1843–6); Dub GRO (d); Kirkpatrick Archive; *Londonderry Sentinel* 2 January 1836 (m), 16 May 1840 (m) and 20 November 1866 (d); *Med Dir*].

HENRY, ROBERT, junior (1858/9–82), Stewartstown, county Tyrone;
born 1858/9; studied medicine at Trinity College, Dublin; LRCSI 1869; LRCP Edin and LM 1870; medical officer to Stewartstown Dispensary District and constabulary; married Florence Maude —; died 6 November 1882 at Stewartstown; administration Armagh 17 January 1883. [Belf PRO, will cal; Dub GRO (d); *Med Dir*].

HENRY, ROBERT (1859–1935), Comber, county Down;
born 21 January 1859 at Ballyblack, Comber, son of David Henry, farmer, of Ballyblack; educated at RBAI; studied medicine at Queen's College, Belfast, from 1876; MD MCh (QUI) 1881; LM KQCPI 1884; medical officer, medical officer of health and certifying factory surgeon to Comber Dispensary District from 1884 and medical officer to constabulary and to Comber Distillery; of High Street, Comber; noted Unionist and Orangeman; received presentation in 1934 for 50 years as dispensary doctor; married (1) 21 April 1897 in First Comber Presbyterian Church, Harriet M.A.K. McBurney, daughter of Thomas McBurney, farmer, of Ballyhenry; (2) 12 April 1905 in Ashley Gardens, Belfast, Rachel Reid, daughter of Robert Reid, merchant, of Ashley Gardens; father of Dr Brian Robert Henry; died 26 September 1935 at High Street, Comber; administration Belfast 17 December 1935. [Belf GRO (d); Belf PRO, will cal; *BMJ* obituary (1935); Dub GRO (m); Kirkpatrick Archive; *Med Dir*; QCB adm reg; UHF database (m, 1 and 2)].

HENRY, THOMAS (1758–1830), Randalstown, county Antrim;
born 1758, only son of the Rev William Henry, minister of Dromore and later Comber, Presbyterian Churches; studied arts and medicine at Glasgow University; matriculated 1777; minister of Dromore Presbyterian Church 1785–6; minister of Randalstown Presbyterian church (OC) 1786–1823; moderator of the General Synod 1803–04; (no record of any degree or medical qualification, but also practised as a doctor); married 14 April 1794 Eleanor Shuldham (who was born 1776 and died 17 January 1845), daughter of Pooley Shuldham of Ballymulvey, county Longford and grand-niece of Admiral Lord Shuldham; father of the Rev Pooley Shuldham Henry, first president of Queen's College, Belfast; died 30 August 1830 at Hazel Bank, Randalstown. [Addison (1898) and (1913); *BNL* 18 April 1794 (m) and 24 January 1845 (d); McConnell (1951)].

HENRY, THOMAS (*fl c* 1796), Naval Medical Service and Armagh;
studied medicine in Dublin; joined the Naval Medical Service as surgeon c 1795, attending the Royal Hospitals of Plymouth, Portsmouth and Dublin; surgeon, apothecary and practitioner of midwifery, of Thomas Street, Armagh, c 1796. [*Northern Star* 1796; Simms (1933)].

HENRY, THOMAS (1847/8–84), Pomeroy, county Tyrone;
born 1847/8, son of Robert Henry of Pomeroy; studied medicine at Queen's College, Belfast, and the Royal College of Surgeons in Ireland; LRCP LRCS and LM Edin 1881; medical officer to Pomeroy Dispensary District; unmarried; died 22 September 1884 at Pomeroy. [Dub GRO (d); *Med Dir*].

HENRY, WALTER (1791–1860), Army Medical Service;
born 1 January 1791, eldest son of John Henry, merchant, of Donegal town; educated locally; studied medicine at Trinity College, Dublin, London and Glasgow Universities; MRCSE 1811; joined the Army Medical Service as hospital mate 1811, and later in the year as assistant surgeon with the 66th Foot; surgeon 1826; staff surgeon 1839; DIG 1845; IG and retired on half pay 1855; served in the Peninsular War (Badajoz and Vittoria and capture of Bordeaux); served in India and arrived in St Helena 1817; present at the autopsy on Napoleon in St Helena 1821 and afterwards sailed for England on HMS *Consul*; served also in Ireland (Athlone, Cavan, Dublin, Limerick, Sligo, Enniskillen and Birr) 1821–7; author of *Trifles from my Portfolio* (1839) and *Events of a Military Life* (1843); married (1) 6 April 1831 Charlotte Todd (who died 1839); (2) 2 July 1834 Leah Allen Geddes; died 27 June 1860 in Canada. [*DIB* (2010); Martin (2010); Peterkin and Johnston (1968); Wilson (1971)].

HENRY, WILLIAM (*fl c* 1799), Rathfriland, county Down;
LAH Dub 1799; apothecary, of Rathfriland. [Apothecaries (1829)].

HENRY, WILLIAM (1857/8–1928), Clones, county Monaghan;
born 1857/8 in Clones, son of Dr Richard Henry, senior, of Clones (*q.v.*); brother of Dr Richard Henry, junior, of Aughnacloy, county Tyrone (*q.v.*) and Dr Joseph Henry of Rochdale (*q.v.*); educated at Dundalk Grammar School; studied arts and medicine at Trinity College, Dublin; BA (TCD) 1879; MB 1881; LRCSI 1881; medical officer and medical officer of health for Clones Dispensary District 1884–1928; medical officer to Clones Fever Hospital, of The Diamond Clones; presented with a car in 1915; married Margaret Jane — (who died 28 January 1942 in Cornwall); died 16 January 1928 at The Diamond; probate Dublin 14 April 1928. [Dub GRO (d); Dub Nat Arch, will cal; Kirkpatrick Archive; *Med Dir*; TCD adm reg; *TCD Cat*, vol 2 (1896)].

HERMAN, GEORGE ERNEST (1849–1914), London, and Cam, Gloucestershire;
born 8 February 1849, son of the Rev George Leach Herman, minister of Kilwarlin, county Down; educated privately; studied medicine at the London Hospital, from 1866, becoming resident accoucheur 1870, medical registrar in 1873 and junior resident medical officer in 1874; MRCSE 1870; LSA Lond 1870; FRCSE 1875; MB (Lond) (hons) 1879; FRCP Lond 1885; assistant obstetric physician to the London Hosptial 1876–83 and obstetric physician 1883–1903; brilliant gynaecologist and teacher; president of the Obstetrical Society of London 1893–5 and of the Hunterian Society 1896–7; retired from the London Hospital in 1903; moved to Caer Glou, Cam 1913; author of *First Lines in Midwifery* (1891), *Difficult Labour* (1894) and *Diseases of Women* (1898) and many medical papers; married 5 September 1884 in St Peter's Parish Church, Chichester, Emily Gibbings (who was born 1855/6), daughter of Thomas Gibbings, tanner, of Chichester, Sussex; died 11 March 1914; probate Gloucester 22 April 1914. [*BMJ* obituary (1914); *Lancet* obituary (1914); Lond GRO (m); Lond PPR, will cal; *Med Dir*; *Munk's Roll*, vol 4; Plarr (1930)].

HERON, ALEXANDER (1841–1923), Rathfriland, county Down;
born 4 November 1841 at Greenfield, Rathfriland, youngest son of the Rev Alexander Heron of Greenfield, minister of Ballyroney Presbyterian Church, and Mary Jane —; educated at RBAI; studied arts and medicine at Queen's College, Belfast, from 1860 and at Cork; BA (QUI) 1863; MD 1866; general practitioner, of Greenfield, Rathfriland; JP and coroner for South Down; married 23 May 1867 in Second Glendermott Presbyterian Church, Sarah Stevenson (who was born 1839/40 and died 17 April 1922), eldest daughter of Robert Stevenson, JP, of Ardkill, Glendermott, county Londonderry; father of Dr Alexander Norman Heron of Bristol (*q.v.*); died 1 February 1923 at Greenfield; buried in Ballyroney Presbyterian graveyard; probate Belfast 9 May 1923. [Belf PRO, will cal; will; *BMJ* obituary (1923); *Coleraine Chronicle* 25 May 1867 (m); gravestone inscription; Kirkpatrick Archive; *Londonderry Sentinel* 24 May 1867 (m); *Med Dir*; QCB adm reg].

HERON, ALEXANDER NORMAN (1868/9–1947), Rathfriland, county Down, and Bristol, Somerset;
born 29 April 1868 at Ballybrick, Loughbrickland, county Down, son of Dr Alexander Heron (*q.v.*) of Greenfield, Rathfriland and Sarah Stevenson; studied medicine at the Royal College of Surgeons in Ireland; LKQCPI and LM 1891; LRCSI and LM 1891; general practitioner, of Greenfield, Rathfriland, and of 2 Leopold Road, Bristol; married Elizabeth Rosalys —; father of Dr Alexander Gordon Heron of Bristol, MB (Bristol) 1924; died 25 March 1947 at 2 Leopold Road; probate Bristol 5 September 1947. [Dub GRO (b); Kirkpatrick Archive; Lond GRO (d); Lond PPR, will cal; will; *Med Dir*].

HERON, FRANCIS TURRETTIN (1871–1930), Forres, Morayshire, and Markinch, Fife;
born 28 July 1871 at Kilrea, county Londonderry, son of the Rev James Heron, minister of Kilrea and later Knock Presbyterian Church, and Margaret Turrettin of Tullyallen, county Armagh; brother of Dr Hugh Turrettin Heron (*q v*); educated at RBAI sudied medicine at Queen's College, Belfast, from 1889; MB BCh BAO (RUI) 1896; general practitioner, of Ardoyne, Forres, c 1905, and of Markinch, Fife c 1910; medical officer to Eastern Division of Markinch and to the Post Office, and certifying factory surgeon; of Fernie Bank, Markinch from c 1930; married 27 October 1897 in Loughbrickland Presbyterian Church, Emma Livingstone Buchanan, daughter of the Rev Alexander Cockburn Buchanan, minister of Loughbrickland Presbyterian Church, county Down; died 29 March 1930 at Fernie Bank; confirmation of will Cupar 28 October 1930. [Barkley (1986); Edin GRO (d); Edin Nat Arch, will cal; *Med Dir*; QCB adm reg; UHF database (m)].

HERON, HUGH TURRETTIN (1866–94), Dundalk, county Louth, and ship's surgeon;
born 20 September 1866 at Dunadry, county Antrim, son of the Rev James Heron, minister of Kilrea and later Knock Presbyterian Church, Belfast, and Margaret Turrettin of Tullyallen, county Armagh; brother of Dr Francis Turretin Heron (*q.v.*); educated at RBAI; studied arts and medicine at Queen's College, Belfast, from 1884; BA (RUI) 1887; MB BCh BAO 1891; general practitioner of 98 Park Street,

Dundalk c 1892; surgeon with Union Steamship Company c 1893; of Derryvolgie Avenue, Belfast; died 25 November 1894. [Barkley (1986); *Med Dir*; QCB adm reg].

HERON, JAMES (d 1838), Naval Medical Service and Belfast;
joined the Naval Medical Service as assistant surgeon; surgeon 1808; retired to 6 Botanic Road, Belfast; married Elizabeth — (who was born 2 March 1795 and died 2 July 1882); died 19 August 1838 in 6 Botanic Road; buried in Killyleagh Church of Ireland graveyard. [*BNL* 28 August 1838 (d); Clarke, *County Down*, vol 6 (1971); *NMS* (1826)].

HERON, JAMES MATHEWS (1866–1938), Downpatrick, county Down, RAMC and London;
born 1 November 1866 at Cultra, county Down, son of James Heron, JP, managing director of the Ulster Bank, Belfast; educated at Armagh Royal School 1881–5; studied arts and medicine at Trinity College, Dublin, from 1885; BA MB BCh BAO (TCD) 1890; MD 1893; assistant house surgeon in the East Suffolk Hospital; medical officer to Downpatrick Hospital; served with RAMC 1915–20 on East Coast Defences of England and in India; therafter he was 'travelling' and finally at 15 Seymour Street, Marylebone, London; master of the County Down Masonic Lodge; married 12 September 1899 in Downpatrick Church of Ireland Church, Anne Margaret Warner Bowlby, elder daughter of Colonel Pultney E. Bowlby; died 28 June 1938 in London; probate London 9 September 1938. [Ferrar (1933); Kirkpatrick Archive; *Med Dir;* TCD adm reg; *TCD Cat*, vol II (1896); UHF database (m); Young and Pike (1909)].

HER(R)ON, JOHN (1786/7–1826), Ballynahinch, county Down;
born 1786/7; surgeon and apothecary, of Ballynahinch; married 28 January 1823 in Ballynahinch Presbyterian Church Isabella Arnold (who was born 1805/6 and died 19 October 1826 of a decline), eldest daughter of James Arnold of Ballynahinch; died 21 July 1826 at Ballynahinch; 'as a proof of the general estimation in which he was held, his funeral was among the largest ever remembered in that town and neighbourhood'. [*BNL* 4 February 1823 (m), 1 August 1826 (d) and 27 October 1826 (d); Pigot (1824)].

HERON, THOMAS (1769–1839), Naval Medical Service;
born 1769; joined the Naval Medical Service as assistant surgeon; surgeon 1794; 'his services to his country were long and faithful'; 'his talents were devoted for the benefit of his relatives'; died 1839 in London; commemorated by a memorial in Killyleagh Church of Ireland Church. [Clarke, *County Down,* vol 6 (1971); *NMS* (1826)].

HERRICK, AUGUSTUS WILLIAM TABUTEAU-
See TABUTEAU, AUGUSTUS WILLIAM

HERRON, JAMES (1857–99), London;
born July 1857 at Rathfriland, county Down, son of Andrew Herron, farmer, of Dechomet, Rathfriland; educated at Kilkinamurry School; studied medicine at Queen's College, Belfast, from 1872; LSA Lond 1882; MD (RUI) 1883; LFPS Glas

1884; general practitioner, of 73 Southwark Bridge Road, London c 1885–99; married Sarah Elizabeth —; died 11 August 1899; probate London 26 September 1899. [Lond PPR, will cal; *Med Dir*; QCB adm reg].

HERRON, ROBERT THOMAS (1864–1930), South Africa and Armagh;
born April 1864 in Belfast, son of Robert Herron of Belfast, and Bessie Crossthuaite; educated at Armagh Royal School 1874–5; studied medicine at Durham University and Carmichael School, Dublin; LRCSI 1883; LRCP and LM Edin 1885; MRCP Edin 1904; MD (Durham) 1905; DPH RCPSI 1910; civil surgeon with HM Forces in South Africa 1901–02 (medal with 4 clasps); medical officer to Armagh Union Infirmary and Fever Hospital, of 22 English Street, Armagh c 1888–1904; proprietor of Brice's Medical Hall, Armagh; consultant sanitary officer to Armagh Rural District; physician to the Macan Asylum for the Blind; temporary major (RAMC) 1915–18, in charge of the Military Hospital and medical officer to the troops, Armagh; medical officer to Armagh Prison; author of papers on tuberculois; of 6 Victoria Street, Armagh; keen athlete, rugby player and (later) huntsman; married 4 June 1907 in St Michael and All Angels Parish Church, Kensington, London, Evelyn Maud Brice of 3 Barlby Road, Kensington (who was born 1881/2), fifth daughter of Frederick Augustus Brice, RN; died 30 December 1930 at Victoria Street, Armagh; buried in St Mark's graveyard, Armagh; probate Belfast 10 March 1931. [Belf GRO (d); Belf PRO, will cal; *BMJ* obituary (1930); Ferrar (1933); Fitzgerald and Weatherup (1993); Kirkpatrick Archive; *Lancet* obituary (1930); London GRO (m); *Med Dir*; Young and Pike (1909)].

HERRON, WALTER (1869–1903), High Wycombe, Buckinghamshire, and Belfast;
born 12 September 1869 at Dromore, county Down, son of David Herron, woollen draper, of Dromore; educated at RBAI; studied medicine at Queen's College, Belfast, from 1888; MB BCh BAO (RUI) 1895; general practitioner of Frogmoor Lodge, High Wycombe; later of Grasmere Villa, Holywood Road, Belfast; unmarried; died 26 July 1903 at the Workhouse, Belfast, of septicaemia following a wound; buried in Dromore First Presbyterian Graveyard; administration Belfast 16 September 1903. [Belf PRO, will cal; Clarke, *County Down*, vol 19 (1983); Dub GRO (d); *Med Dir*; QCB adm reg].

HETHERINGTON, CHARLES EDWARD (1847/8–1932), Downpatrick, county Down, and Londonderry;
born 1847/8 in county Westmeath, eldest son of Dr George Hetherington of Athlone, county Westmeath; brother of Dr Reynolds Peyton Hetherington (*q.v.*); educated at Portora Royal School from 1861; studied arts and medicine at Trinity College, Dublin, from 1864, and the Richmond Hospital, Dublin; BA (TCD) 1868; MB MCh 1870; LM Coombe Hosp Dub 1870; resident house surgeon and physician at Sir Patrick Dun's Hospital, Dublin; assistant surgeon and registrar to the County Down Infirmary, Downpatrick 1871–2; assistant medical superintendent of the Downpatrick Lunatic Asylum 1872–6; resident medical superintendent of the Londonderry District Asylum from 1876; retired 1919; of 13 Lawrence Hill, Londonderry, c 1925; married Adelaide —; died 25 July 1932 at 13 Lawrence Hill; probate Londonderry 14 November 1932. [Belf GRO (d); Belf PRO, will cal;

Kirkpatrick Archive; *Med Dir;* Parkinson (1967); *Portora Royal School Register* (1940); TCD adm reg; *TCD Cat*, vol II (1898)].

HETHERINGTON, REYNOLDS PEYTON (1854–1925), Army Medical Service;
born 1 September 1854 at Athlone, county Westmeath, second surviving son of Dr George Hetherington of Athlone; brother of Dr Charles Edward Hetherington (*q.v.*); educated at Portora Royal School 1868–9 and Armagh Royal School August–December 1869; studied arts and medicine at Trinity College, Dublin from 1872; BA (TCD) 1876; MB BCh 1878; LM Rot Hosp Dub 1878; MD 1897; joined the Army Medical Service as surgeon captain 1881; surgeon major 1893; lieutenant-colonel 1901; served in Egypt 1882; Sudan 1884–5, Burma 1891–2, South Africa 1899–1902; half pay from 1907; retired 1909 to Knockview, county Roscommon; married Anne Harriette —; died 16 November 1925 at 104 Lower Baggot Street, Dublin; probate Dublin 25 January 1926. [Dub GRO (d); Dub Nat Arch, will cal; Ferrar; Kirkpatrick Archive; *Med Dir*; Peterkin and Johnston (1968); *Portora Royal School Register* (1940); TCD adm reg; *TCD Cat*, vol II (1896) and vol III (1906)].

HEWISTON, THOMAS (*fl c* 1793), Belfast;
LAH Dub 1793; apothecary, of Belfast. [Apothecaries (1829)]

HEWITT, DAVID WALKER (1870–1940), Ballymoney, county Antrim, and Naval Medical Service;
born 8 June 1870 at Neas, Dungannon, county Tyrone, eldest child of John Hewitt, schoolmaster, of Kingstown, county Dublin and Anne Sophia Porter; educated at the Royal School, Dungannon; studied medicine at Queen's College, Galway, at Edinburgh and St Thomas's Hospital, London; MB BCh BAO (RUI) 1895; MRCSE FRCSE 1912; BSc 1912; general practitioner, of Cameron Place, Ballymoney; joined the Naval Medical Service as assistant surgeon 1897; fleet surgeon and assistant to the Medical Director-General 1913; surgeon captain 1915; CB (Mil) 1916; CMG 1918; senior medical officer for the North Russian Expeditionary Force; principal medical officer on hospital ship HMS *Panama* (renamed *Maine*); in charge of Royal Naval Hospital, Haslar 1920–29; surgeon rear-admiral 1924; retired 1929; married 11 February 1908 Nora Gertrude Pinkey; died 25 October 1940 at Cherrybrook, Princetown, Lydford, Devonshire; probate Llandudno 29 January 1941. [*BMJ* obituary (1940); Kirkpatrick Archive; *Lancet* obituary (1940); Lond PPR, will cal; *Med Dir*; Power and Le Fanu (1953)].

HEWITT, THOMAS (d c 1840), Killinchy, county Down;
surgeon, of 'Ardview', Killinchy, and the North Down Militia; married Mary — (who died 26 September 1835 at Killinchy); died c 1840. [*BNL* 6 October 1835 (d) and 10 June 1845 (m, daughter); Dub GRO (m, daughter)].

HICKMAN, JAMES (1855–1930), Army Medical Service;
born 26 September 1855; MA (RUI) 1877; LRCP and LM LRCS Edin 1880; joined the Army Medical Service as surgeon captain 1882; surgeon major 1894; lieutenant-colonel 1902; served in Burma 1886, Gambia 1892, Ashanti 1895–6, Sierra Leone 1898–9 and South Africa 1899–1900 (Spion Kop, Tugela Heights, Vaal Krantz,

Pieter's Hill, relief of Ladysmith; Queen's medal and 2 clasps); retired 1904; lived finally at 85 Queen's Gate, Kensington, London; married Isobel Caroline —; died 18 December 1930 at the Cancer Hospital, Chelsea; probate London 8 January 1931. [*BMJ* obituary (1930); Kirkpatrick Archive; *Lancet* obituary (1930); Lond PPR, will cal; *Med Dir*; Peterkin and Johnston (1968)].

HICKS, GEORGE ADAMS (1870–1920), Belfast;
born 1 August 1870 at Castle Street, Sligo, son of George Hicks, grocer, of Castle Street, and Marrin Merrick; educated at Santry School, Dublin; studied medicine at Queen's College, Belfast, from 1892; MB BCh BAO (RUI) 1897; MD 1904; FRCS Edin 1912; demonstrator in physiology in Queen's College; general practitioner of Belfast, from 1898; gynaecological surgeon to the Samaritan Hospital, Belfast, from 1906; of 2 College Gardens, Belfast; author of various medical papers; married —; died 24 January 1920 at 2 College Gardens of blood poisoning contracted during his professional duties; buried in Tanderagee; probate Belfast 1 April 1920. [Belf PRO, will cal; *BMJ* obituary (1920); Dub GRO (b) and (d); Kirkpatrick Archive; *Lancet* obituary (1920); *Med Dir*; QCB adm reg].

HICKSON, ROBERT (*fl c* 1813–67), Belfast;
LAH Dub 1813; LM (TCD) 1826; general practitioner, of 18 Queen Street, Belfast; living abroad c 1867; died c 1872. [*Med Dir*].

HICKY (HICKEY, HICKIE), WILLIAM (d 1677), Cavan and Dublin;
of Cavan; studied medicine at Rheims University; MD (Rheims) 1659; physician, of Dublin; married (1) c 1660 Mary Taylor (who died c 1665; probate Prerogative Court 1665), daughter of Edward Jans, alderman, of Dublin, and widow of Edward Taylor of Dublin (who died c 1650); (2) Elinor Seagrave, daughter of Henry Seagrave of Cabragh; died 1677; buried in St James's Churchyard, Dublin will dated 1 September 1677 proved in the Prerogative Court 1677. [Belf PRO, Burke's Pedigrees, T559, vol 3, pp 130 and 141; Belf PRO, D430/148–194 – scattered indentures and wills; Brockliss; Vicars (1897)].

HIGGINS, CHARLES (1804–after 1857), Paris;
born 1804, son of Edward Higgins, haberdasher, of Monaghan, and Letitia McKenna; MD [?]; Knight of the Legion of Honour; 'highly respected in the court of Napoleon III' (*Northern Standard*); died after 1857. [Moriarty (2012), *Northern Standard* 2 January 1858 (obituary for Letitia Higgins); Pigot (1824)].

HIGGINS, MICHAEL (1867–1909), Dungiven, county Londonderry;
born 20 March 1867 at Longfield, Desertmartin, county Londonderry, son of James Higgins, farmer, of Longfield; educated at Cookstown Academy; studied medicine at Queen's College, Belfast, from 1888, and the Royal College of Surgeons in Edinburgh; LRCP LRCS Edin 1896; LFPS Glas 1896; medical officer and medical officer of health to Dungiven Dispensary District, medical officer to constabulary and certifying factory surgeon 1897–1909; married 27 April 1899 in Drumsurn Old Chapel, Mary Jane Bryson, only daughter of Dr Theobald Matthew Bryson of Limavady (*q.v.*); died 28 December 1909 at Dungiven; administration Londonderry

22 February 1910. [Belf PRO, will cal; Dub GRO (m) and (d); Higgins (2007); *Med Dir*; QCB adm reg].

HIGGINS, THOMAS JAMES (1840/1–1910), Louth, Lincolnshire;
born 1840/1 at Lissan, county Tyrone, son of Robert Higgins of Lissan; educated at Cookstown Academy; studied medicine at Queen's College, Belfast, from 1862; LRCS Edin 1865; MD (QUI) 1868; house surgeon to Louth Hospital; general practitioner, of Louth, Lincolnshire from c 1870; JP for Lincolnshire; medical officer and public vaccinator for Welton District; married Hannah Riggall —; father of Dr William Robert Higgins, MB BCh (Camb) 1905, and Dr Sydney James Higgins, MRCSE LRCP Lond 1910, RAMC; died 18 March 1910; probate London 14 May 1910. [Lond PPR, will cal, will; *Med Dir*; QCB adm reg].

HIGGINSON, HENRY TALBOT (1841–91), US Army, Lisburn and Larne, county Antrim, and Bangor, county Down;
born 16 March 1841 at Lisburn, fifth son of Henry Theophilus Higginson, JP, of Carnalea, county Down, and Charlotte McConnell of Belfast; educated at Philbert's House and at Armagh Royal School 1856–7; studied medicine at Queen's College, Belfast, from 1858, the Royal College of Surgeons in Ireland, and Edinburgh University; LM Rot Hosp Dub 1861; LRCSI and LM 1862; MD (Edin) 1863 (thesis 'On light and heat'); LRCS Edin 1876; acting assistant surgeon in the US Army; medical officer to Lisburn Dispensary District 1866–c 1870; general practitioner in Larne 1870–71; general practitioner, of Bridge House, Bangor, 1871–3 and of Donaghadee 1873–5; author of various medical papers and *Notes by the Way or What I saw in my Rambles* (1890); married 21 April 1870 in Lisburn Cathedral, Isabella Watson Dobbin (who died 4 December 1890), daughter of Hugh Dobbin, gentleman, of Moira; died 30 January 1891 at Bridge House, Bangor; probate Belfast 10 July 1891. [Belf PRO, will cal; Burke *LGI* (1912); Dub GRO (m) and (d); Edin Univ; Ferrar (1933); Higginson (1890); Kirkpatrick Archive; *Lisburn Fam Hist Soc*, vol 2 (2005); *Med Dir*; QCB adm reg].

HIGNETT, LIONEL WATSON (1865–1958), Northwood, Middlesex;
born 1865; studied medicine at Edinburgh University; MRCSE LRCP Lond 1892; MB CM (Edin) 1896; DPH Camb 1909; of Donebmir, Campsie, county Londonderry c 1895; house surgeon to Liverpool Royal Infirmary; medical officer of health, medical officer and public vaccinator to Ruislip and Northwood Districts from c 1900; honorary medical officer to St Vincent's Cripples' Home, Eastcote; captain RAMC (Territorials); of Linkside, from c 1930 and later of 31 Maxwell Road, Northwood; retired c 1947 to Street Cottage, Loxwood, Sussex; died 29 January 1958 at 70 The Drive, Hove, Sussex; probate London 18 March 1958. [Lond GRO (d); Lond PPR, will cal; *Med Dir*].

HILL, ADAM (1850–1905), Bushmills, county Antrim, Glasgow, Lanarkshire, and Orkney;
born 16 November 1850 at Croaghbeg, Bushmills, son of William Hill, farmer, of Croaghbeg and Mary Steel; educated at the National School; studied medicine at Queen's College, Belfast, from 1871; LRCP LRCS Edin 1878; general practitioner,

of Croaghbeg, Bushmills, from c 1880, of 5 Camden Place, Govan Road, Glasgow, c 1895 and of Springbank, Flotta, Orkney from c 1900; medical officer to Flotta, Pharay and Cava; died 21 December 1905 at Spring Bank House, Flotta; confirmation of administration Kirkwall 11 May 1906. [Edin GRO (d); Edin Nat Arch, will cal; *Med Dir*; QCB adm reg].

HILL, DANIEL PEDEN SIMPSON (1864–1904), ship's surgeon and Larne, county Antrim;
born 16 December 1864 at Belfast, son of Edward Hill, accountant, of Ballyclare; cousin of Sir John Campbell (*q.v.*) and Dr Robert Campbell (*q.v.*); educated at Cookstown Academy; studied medicine at Queen's College, Belfast, also in Dublin and at St Thomas's Hospital, London; MB BCh BAO (RUI) 1890; surgeon to the Castle Mail Packet Steamers; general practitioner, of Larne; unmarried; died 8 April 1904; buried in Rashee Old Graveyard; probate Belfast 12 August 1907. [Belf PRO, will cal, will; *Med Dir*; QCB adm reg; Richmond (2007)].

HILL, HUGH (1776/7–1810), Newtownards, county Down;
born 1776/7, probably near Ballynure, county Antrim; LAH Dub 1798; surgeon, of Newtownards; died 23 February 1810; buried in Ballynure Old Graveyard. [Apothecaries (1829); Rutherford and Clarke, *County Antrim*, vol 3 (1995)].

HILL, JAMES (1840/1–1900), Belfast and Brisbane, Queensland;
born 1840/1, son of James Hill of Belfast; educated at Inverness Royal Academy; studied medicine at Queen's College, Belfast, from 1861, and Glasgow University; MD (Glas) 1864; LRCS Edin 1864; demonstrator of anatomy at Queen's College, Galway c 1865; general practitioner, of Mount Pottinger, Belfast c 1870; emigrated to Australia c 1880; general practitioner, of 153 Wickham Terrace, Brisbane c 1895; died 21 July 1900 at Brisbane. [Addison (1898); *Med Dir*; QCB adm reg].

HILL, NINIAN (*fl c* 1830), Belfast;
youngest son of Colonel Thomas Hill of the Bengal Artillery; MD [?]; married 24 August 1830 Anne McCracken (who died 20 June 1833 in her father's house), second daughter of John McCracken of Belfast; died before 1860. [*BNL* 31 August 1830 (m), 25 June 1833 (d) and 17 March 1860 (d, son)].

HILL, SAMUEL HAY (c 1828–50), Ballynure, county Antrim;
born c 1828, son of David Hill of Ballynure and Mary —; studied medicine at Glasgow University; MD (Glas) 1849; general practitioner of Ballynure; died 26 September 1850 at Ballymena of 'palpitations of the heart'; buried in Ballynure Old Graveyard. [Addison (1898); *BNL* 1 October 1850 (d); *Coleraine Chronicle* 5 October 1850 (d); *Londonderry Sentinel* 4 October 1850 (d); Rutherford and Clarke, *County Antrim*, vol 3 (1995)].

HILL, SAMUEL WHITEFORD (1874–1929), Larne, county Antrim;
born 9 February 1874 at Ballynure, county Antrim, son of James Hill, grocer and farmer, of Ballynure; educated at RBAI; studied medicine at Queen's College, Belfast, from 1891; MB BCh BAO (RUI) 1899; general practitioner, of Pound Street, Larne;

a keen local historian and chairman of the Larne Urban Council 1918–19; JP for Larne 1929; unofficial 'Mayor of Larne' 1928–9; married (1) 3 January 1903 in Ballynure Presbyterian Church, Elizabeth Mary Barklie, daughter of James Barklie, farmer, of Larne; (2) Isabella G. —; died 28 July 1929 at Old Walls, Castle Bromwich Road, Birmingham; probate Belfast 28 October 1929. [Belf PRO, will cal; Lond GRO (d); McKillop (2000); *Med Dir*; QCB adm reg; UHF database (m)].

HILL, THOMAS (d 1830), London;
eldest son of Adam Hill of Ballymena, county Antrim; surgeon, of London; died 14 July 1830 in London. [*BNL* 17 August 1830 (d)].

HILL, THOMAS (1824/5–93), Street, Somerset and Liverpool, Lancashire;
born 1824/5, son of Thomas Burgess Hill of Hillgrove House, Bermuda; educated privately; studied medicine at Queen's College, Belfast, from 1853; LRCS and LM Edin 1858; general practitioner and certifying factory inspector, of Street c 1860–80 and of 6 Sackville Street and 11 Kremlin Drive, Storeycraft, Liverpool c 1880–91 and finally of Westminster Road, Liverpool; married Clotilda Victoria —; died 13 March 1893; administration Liverpool 26 April 1893. [Lond PPR, will cal; *Med Dir*; QCB adm reg].

HILLYARD, WAITMAN HENRY (1864–1936), Castlewellan, county Down;
born 1864 at Castlewellan, son of George W. Hillyard, clerk of peace, of Castlewellan; studied medicine at Queen's College, Belfast from 1882; LRCP LRCS Edin 1889; LFPS Glas 1889; general practitioner, of Temple View, Castlewellan; surgeon to the constabulary and post officer; married 11 November 1897 in Banbridge, Mary Pyper, daughter of Thomas Pyper, merchant, of Banbridge; died 24 April 1936; probate Belfast 5 August 1936. [Belf PRO, will cal; Dub GRO (d); *Med Dir*; QCB adm reg; UHF database (m)].

HI(N)CKS, GEORGE, (d 1817), Army Medical Service and Belfast;
joined the Army Medical Service as assistant surgeon to the York Rangers 1804; transferred to the 44th Foot 1805 and 2nd Foot 1808; surgeon to the 92nd Foot (Highlanders) 1811; present at the battle of Waterloo 1815; died 29 November 1817 of typhus fever in Belfast, caught while visiting 'some of the numerous poor to whom he was unremitting in his attention'. [*BNL* 12 December 1817 (d); Malcolm (1851); Peterkin and Johnston (1968)].

HINDS, GEORGE (d 1851), Killashandra, county Cavan;
studied medicine at Edinburgh University; MD (Edin) 1819 (thesis 'De apoplexia'); died 23 October 1851 at Rainfield, Killashandra, 'accidentally shot whilst handling a loaded blunderbuss'. [Edin Univ; *Med Dir*].

HISLOP, JAMES ANDREW (1865–1960), ship's surgeon, Glenelg, Inverness-shire, Blackford, Perthshire, Hamilton, Lanarkshire, Assam, Ayton, Berwickshire, and Tynemouth, Northumberland;
born 17 May 1865 at Birkenhead, Cheshire, son of William Hislop, engineer, of Chupica, South America; educated at Teviot Grove Academy, Hawick, Scotland;

studied medicine at Queen's College, Belfast, from 1888; Gold Medal, Belfast Hospital for Sick Children; Malcolm Exhibition, Belfast Royal Hospital 1891; LRCP LRCS Edin 1893; LFPS Glas 1893; MD (Brux) 1903; DPH RCPS Edin 1904; surgeon with Anchor Shipping Line; general practitioner, of Bay View, Glenelg, c 1894–6; of Blackford c 1896–9; assistant medical officer of health for Lanarkshire c 1895–8, of Hamilton; visiting physician to County Smallpox Hospital; medical officer to Hathibari, Darrang, Assam c 1900–03; of Summerhill, Ayton c 1903–05; medical officer of health and school medical officer for Tynemouth from c 1909; medical superintendent of Moor Park Hospital; captain RAMC (temporary); retired c 1930 to Hartsop, Patterdale, Penrith, Westmoreland; author of various papers on tropical diseases; married — Connochie; died 31 December 1960; probate Carlisle 20 February 1961. [*Belf Roy Hosp, Ann Rep*; Lond PPR, will cal, will; *Med Dir*; QCB adm reg].

HOBSON, RICHARD J (*fl c* 1845), Antrim;
LRCSI; surgeon, of Antrim c 1845. [Croly (1843–6)].

HODGKINSON, CHARLES (*fl c* 1792), Lisburn, county Antrim,
LAH Dub 1792; apothecary, of Lisburn; married —; daughter Emily married Captain Horsburgh, HEICS, and died of dysentery in Calcutta 3 June 1825; died before 1826. [Apothecaries (1829); *BNL* 27 January 1826 (d, daughter)].

HODGES, JOHN FREDERICK (1815–99), Belfast;
born 5 December 1815 in Scotch Street, Downpatrick, county Down, only child of John Hodges, solicitor and his second cousin, Mary Hodges; father died when J.F.H. was less than one year old; educated at the Down Academy, by the Rev Samuel Craig Nelson; apprenticed to a local doctor; studied arts and medicine at Trinity College, Dublin, at Glasgow University and the University of Giessen (Germany); LFPS Glas 1837; LAH Dub 1838; MD (Giessen) 1843; MD (*hon causa*) (QUI) 1868; did not practice medicine but was essentially a chemist; professor of chemistry, RBAI, 1848–9; lecturer in medical jurisprudence at Queen's College, Belfast 1848–99 and professor of agriculture 1849–99; public analyst for county Armagh 1879; of Sandringham, Malone Road, Belfast; director of the Chemico-Agricultural Society of Ulster and editor of its journal; one of the founders of the Royal Society of Chemistry, London; received honours from many European countries; president of the Belfast Natural History and Philosophical Society 1874–7; government analyst and analyst for Belfast; JP for county Antrim; first president of the Belfast Hospital for Diseases of the Skin, Glenravel Street, founded in 1873; author of *Report on the Conversion of Diseased Potatoes into Food* (1845); *The First Book of Lessons in Chemistry in its Application to Agriculture* (1848); *Outline of the Structure and Physiology of the Animals of the Farm* (1862) and many other books and papers; married 5 April 1838 Elizabeth Benn, daughter of John Benn of Glenravel House, county Antrim, and sister of Edward and George Benn, historians and philanthropists; eldest son born 1839 and died 1847; father of John F.W. Hodges who married 6 April 1886 Mary Burden, daughter of Dr Henry Burden (*q.v.*); died 13 December 1899 in Belfast; probate Belfast 26 January 1900. [*Belf Lit Soc* (1901); *BNL* 10 April 1838 (m) and 16 April 1847 (d, son); Belf PRO, will cal; Blaney (1996); Croly (1843–6); Deane (1921);

DIB (2009); Kirkpatrick Archive; McCann (2003); McCaw (1944); *Med Dir*; Merrick and Clarke, *Belfast*, vol 4 (1991); Moody and Beckett (1959); Newmann (1993); UHF database (m)].

HODSDON, SIR JAMES WILLIAM BEEMAN (1858–1928), Edinburgh;
born 15 May 1858 at Hamilton, Bermuda, son of F. Hodson of Bermuda; educated at Sherborne School, Dorset; studied medicine at Queen's College, Belfast, from 1875, and at Edinburgh University; LRCP LRCS Edin 1880; MD MCh (QUI) 1881; MRCP FRCS Edin 1883; house surgeon to the Royal Maternity Hospital, Edinburgh, and resident physician to Royal Hospital for Children, Edinburgh; clinical assistant to Lock Ward and resident house officer, Edinburgh Royal Infirmary; senior assistant surgeon to the Edinburgh Royal Infirmary, of 30 Walker Street, Edinburgh c 1885, of 52 Melville Street c 1895; and later of 6 Chester Street; lecturer in Surgery to Edinburgh Royal Infirmary and Surgeon's Hall; president of the Royal College of Surgeons of Edinburgh 1914–17; author of many medical papers; CBE (military) 1918; KBE 1920; died 28 May 1928 on the train from London to Edinburgh. [Kirkpatrick Archive; *Lancet* obituary (1928); *Med Dir*; QCB adm reg].

HOEY, PETER JOSEPH (1831/2–65), Carrickmacross, county Monaghan;
born 1831/2; LRCSI 1854; surgeon, of Carrickmacross; unmarried; died 2 July 1865 at Carrickmacross. [Dub GRO (d); *Med Dir*].

HOGG, GEORGE ALEXANDER (1872–1933), Belfast;
born 11 June 1872 at Coalisland, county Tyrone, eldest son of William Hogg, managing director of Jennymount Mills, Belfast; educated at the Mercantile College, Belfast; studied medicine at Queen's College, Belfast, from 1891; MB BCh BAO (RUI) 1898; general practitioner, of Benvista, Antrim Road, and of 27 York Road, Belfast; member of the Masonic and Orange Orders; JP; married Agnes Elizabeth Robb, daughter of David Robb; died 17 September 1933 at 6 Upper Crescent, Belfast; probate Belfast 27 November 1933. [Belf GRO (d); Belf PRO, will cal, will; Kirkpatrick Archive; *Med Dir*; QCB adm reg].

HOGG, JAMES (1843/4–c 1908), Liverpool and Blackburn, Lancashire, ship's surgeon, Carluke, Lanarkshire, and Saltcoats, Ayrshire;
born 1843/4 at Saintfield, county Down, son of Samuel Hogg, grocer, of Saintfield; educated at Tullywest, near Saintfield; studied medicine at Queen's College, Belfast, from 1877, and Anderson's College, Glasgow; LRCP LRCS Edin 1883; general practitioner, of 44 Kirkdale Road, Kirkdale, Liverpool c 1885, and surgeon with RMS Allen Line; of 166 Montague Street, Blackburn c 1890–95; of 6 Bank Top, c/o Dr Bradford, Flakefield, Carluke c 1895–1900; of 34 Union Buildings, Ayr c 1900–03; of 6 Springvale Place Saltcoats c 1903–08; died c 1908. [*Med Dir*; QCB adm reg].

HOGG, THOMAS SIMPSON (1859–1930), Belfast;
born 3 July 1859 at Annahavil, Cookstown, county Tyrone, son of James Hogg, farmer, of Annahavil; educated at Moneymore Intermediate School; studied arts at Queen's College, Galway 1880–83, and medicine at Queen's College, Belfast, from

1883; BA (RUI) 1883; LRCP LRCS Edin 1888; LFPS Glas 1888; general practitioner of 3 and 6 Cooke Terrace, Ormeau Road, and later of 'Dunmore', Glenfield Place, Belfast; married Katherine Waggott —; died 14 January 1930 at 135 Ormeau Road; buried in Belfast City Cemetery; probate Belfast 30 April 1930. [Belf City Cem, bur reg; Belf GRO (d); Belf PRO, will cal; *Med Dir*; QCB adm reg].

HOLDEN, JOHN SINCLAIR (1837–1923), Sudbury, Suffolk;
born 27 January 1837 in Belfast, son of John Holden, rate collector, of Holywood, county Down; studied medicine at Queen's College, Belfast, from 1864; MD (QUI) 1865; LRCS Edin 1865; founder member of the Belfast Naturalists' Field Club, 1863; medical officer of health for Sudbury, Suffolk; medical officer and later honorary physician to St Leonard's Hospital, Sudbury; public vaccinator; surgeon lieutenant-colonel of the 2nd VB Suffolk Regiment; president of the Cambridge Medical Society and the East Anglian Branch of the BMA; author of various medical papers; died 13 July 1923; probate London 26 September 1923. [*BMJ* obituary (1923); Campbell (1938); Kirkpatrick Archive; Lond PPR, will cal; *Med Dir*; Newmann (1993); QCB adm reg].

HOLMES, CHARLES (1804–91), Castlefin, county Donegal;
born 23 June 1804, eldest son of Benjamin Holmes of Meenahomey, Castlefin (Donagheady), and Martha Stewart of Altrest, Donagheady; brother of Dr Daniel Stewart Holmes (*q.v.*); went to Dublin 1819 and was apprenticed to his uncle Dr Joshua Holmes (*q.v.*), of 134 Dorset Street; LAH Dub 1825; MD (Glas) 1839; elected apothecary to George's Dispensary 1829 and resigned 1847; succeeded to his uncle Joshua's practice in 1836 and, continuing in the same house, was elected Director of the Apothecaries Hall 1838 and was Governor of the Hall 1843–4; later of 6 Harcourt Street and finally of 67 Eccles Street, Dublin; married 4 November 1852 Emily Cuthbert (who was born 5 May 1820 and died 29 December 1875), eldest daughter of Dr William Hamilton Cuthbert (*q.v.*); father of Celia Mary Holmes who married Dr John Knox Denham and Margaret Emily Holmes who married Dr Whitley Bland Stokes of Dublin; died 16 March 1891 at 67 Eccles Street, Dublin; probate Dublin 8 June 1891. [Addison (1898); Apothecaries (1829); *BNL* 10 November 1852 (m); Belf PRO, will cal; Dub GRO (d); Elliott, Simon, pers com].

HOLMES, DANIEL STEWART (1805–45), Colesborne and Cirencester, Gloucestershire;
born 10 September 1805, second son of Benjamin Holmes of Meenahomey, Castlefin (Donagheady), and Martha Stewart of Altrest, Donagheady; brother of Dr Charles Holmes (*q.v.*); studied medicine in Glasgow and Dublin; LRCSE 1831; surgeon to the Poor Law Union of Colesborne and later of Cirencester; died 23 January 1845. [Elliott, Simon, pers com].

HOLMES, FRANCIS DINSMORE (1863–99), Duffield, Derbyshire;
born 2 June 1863 at Belfast, son of William P. Holmes, tea merchant, of Belfast; educated at Methodist College, Belfast, from 1869; studied arts and medicine at Queen's College, Belfast, from 1883; BA (RUI) 1884; LRCP LRCS Edin 1889; LFPS

Glas 1889; general practitioner, of Duffield House, Duffield, near Derby; married 30 August 1893 in Windsor Park, Belfast, Mary Primrose Addison Hetherington, daughter of James Hetherington, damask manufacturer, of Windsor Park; died 21 October 1899; probate Derby 5 December 1899. [Lond PPR, will cal; *Med Dir*; QCB adm reg; UHF database (m)].

HOLMES, GEORGE SMYTH (1824/5–57), Glenarm, county Antrim;
born 1824/5, son of James Holmes and Elizabeth —; studied medicine at Glasgow University; MD (Glas) 1846; general practitioner of Glenarm; died 10 September 1857 at Glenarm; buried in Ballypriormore graveyard, Islandmagee; administration Connor Diocesan Court 1857. [Addison (1898); *BNL* 15 September 1857 (d); *Coleraine Chronicle* 19 September 1857 (d); Dub Nat Arch, Connor Dio Admins index; Rutherford and Clarke, *County Antrim*, vol 1 (1977)].

HOLMES, HENRY (1846/7–92), Donemana, county Tyrone;
born 1846/7, son of John Holmes of Brosney and Elizabeth —; studied medicine at Glasgow University; MB CM (Glas) 1870; medical officer to Donemana Dispensary District, of Brookview, Donemana; married —; died 13 April 1892 at Brookview; buried in Leckpatrick Old Graveyard; probate Londonderry 30 November 1892. [Addison (1898); Belf PRO, will cal; Dub GRO (d); *Med Dir*; Todd (1991)].

HOLMES, JAMES (1803/4–34), Donaghmore, county Tyrone, and Killygordon, county Donegal;
born 1803/4; surgeon and superintendent of Donaghmore and Killygordon Dispensaries; married —; died 29 November 1834 'of a putrid sore throat' at Killygordon, county Donegal; (his brother William died two days later with the same condition). [*BNL* 9 December 1834 (d); *Londonderry Sentinel* 6 December 1834 (d); *Strabane Morning Post* 2 December 1834 (d)].

HOLMES, JAMES (1813–53), Cirencester, Gloucestershire;
born 10 March 1813, second son of Benjamin Holmes of Meenahomey, Castlefin (Donaghmore), and Martha Stewart of Altrest, Donaghady; apprenticed to his brother Dr Charles Holmes in Dublin (*q.v.*); LRCSE 1838; medical officer to the Cirencester Dispensary, living with his brother Dr Daniel Holmes until his death, after which he took over the practice; unmarried; died 30 January 1853. [Elliott, Simon, pers com].

HOLMES, JOHN (*fl c* 1831), Strabane, county Tyrone;
LM Rot Hosp Dub 1830; MRCSE 1831; surgeon, of Strabane. [*Strabane Morning Post* 14 June 1831].

HOLMES, ROBERT ANDREW KING (1844–1912), Richmond, Surrey, and Indian Medical Service;
born 16 September 1844 at Fairview, county Londonderry, son of Rev Robert Holmes, minister of Coagh Presbyterian Church, and — King; educated at Cookstown Academy, RBAI and Belfast Academy; studied arts and medicine at Queen's College, Galway, and from 1862, at Queen's College, Belfast; BA (QUI)

1866; MD 1870; MRCSE 1871; LM Coombe Hosp Dub 1871; general practitioner, of Richmond c 1872; joined the Indian Medical Service (Bengal establishment) as assistant surgeon 1872; surgeon 1873; surgeon major 1884; surgeon lieutenant-colonel 1892; retired 1899; lived finally at 21 Westgate Terrace, Kensington; married 6 October 1887 in Liverpool Presbyterian Church, Annabel Maud Patterson (who was born 1859/60), daughter of John Patterson, merchant, JP, of 16 Devonshire Road, Toxteth Park, Liverpool; died 28 January 1912 in London; probate London 15 May 1912. [Crawford (1930); Elliott, Simon, pers com; Lond GRO (m); Lond PPR, will cal; *Med Dir*; QCB adm reg].

HOLMES, SAMUEL (1788/9–1829), Army Medical Service;
born 1788/9, son of William Holmes of Coleraine and Elizabeth —; joined the Army Medical Service as hospital mate 1809; assistant surgeon to the 97th Foot 1810;, transferred to the 96th Foot; served in the Peninsular War and America 1814; author of *A Pedestrian Tour to the Falls of Niagara in Upper Canada, airing various and some perhaps rather desultory notices* (1814); half pay February 1819–December 1820; studied medicine at Edinburgh University; MD (Edin) 1820 (thesis 'De dysenteria'); transferred to 17th Dragoons 1820; half pay 1824–December 1825; surgeon to 81st Foot 1826; retired on half pay 1827; died 20 May 1829 in Coleraine, county Londonderry; buried in Coleraine graveyard; will dated 11 May 1829, probate Connor Diocesan Court 1 September 1829. [Belf PRO, T1970/4, T1970/5 and T1970/7; Edin Univ; gravestone inscription; Peterkin and Johnston (1968)].

HOLMES, SAMUEL (1803–55), Indian Medical Service;
born 2 May 1803 'in the neighbourhood of Armagh' (*BNL*); MRCS 1826; joined the Indian Medical Service as assistant surgeon 1827; surgeon 1844; died 26 April 1855 on board the *Alfred* near the Cape of Good Hope. [*BNL* 26 July 1855 (d); Crawford (1930)].

HOLMES, WILLIAM (1795/6–1823), Lisburn, county Antrim;
born 1795/6; studied medicine and qualified as a surgeon; had a short professional career, living with his father in Magheragall parish, Lisburn; died May 1823 in Lisburn of a 'disease which baffled all human aid'. [*BNL* 27 May 1823 (d)].

HOLMES, WILLIAM (1812–38), Indian Medical Service;
born November 1812, second son of the Rev William Anthony Holmes, rector of Templemore, county Tipperary, and Caroline Bond of Newbridge House, near Bath; MRCS 1836; joined the Indian Medical Service (Madras establishment) as assistant surgeon 1837; died 26 July 1838 at Bangalore, India. [*BNL* 27 November 1838 (d); Crawford (1930); Leslie (1936)].

HOLTAN, EDWARD (1832/3–73), Maguiresbridge, county Fermanagh;
born 1832/3; studied medicine at the Ledwich School, Dublin, the Royal College of Surgeons in Ireland and Mercer's and St Vincent's Hospitals, Dublin; LM Rot Hosp Dub 1863; LRCP Edin and LM 1865; LFPS Glas and LM 1865; medical officer to Maguiresbridge Dispensary District, public vaccinator and registrar of births and deaths; married —; died 12 April 1873 at Aghamore. [Dub GRO (d); *Med Dir*].

HOOD, JAMES CROCKETT (1860–c 1928), Lifford, county Donegal, and Hobart, Tasmania;
> born November 1860 at Lifford, son of William Hood, farmer, of Edenmore, Lifford; educated at Strabane Academy; studied medicine at Queen's College, Galway and from 1877 in Belfast; MD (RUI) 1883; MCh Dip Obst 1884; general practitioner, of Edenmore, Clonleigh, Lifford, c 1885; emigrated to Tasmania c 1890; general practitioner, of Sorell, Hobart c 1895; retired to Opotiki, Bay of Plenty, New Zealand c 1925; died c 1928. [*Med Dir*; QCB adm reg].

HOOD, — (*fl c* 1850), Belfast;
> surgeon, of Belfast; married —; son born and died 1850. [*BNL* 5 April 1850 (d, son)].

HOPE, FODEN PERRIN (1810/1–97), Enniskillen, county Fermanagh, and Swanlinbar, county Cavan;
> born 1810/1; LAH Dub 1836; LM Rot Hosp Dub 1845; MRCSE 1846 (or 1858); LKQCPI 1860; general practitioner of Kilsheery, Enniskillen, and Swanlinbar; married —; died 12 August 1897 at Swanlinbar; administration Cavan 14 October 1897. [Belf PRO, will cal; Dub GRO (d); *Med Dir*].

HOPKINS, JOHN BEATTY (1865/6–97), Derrylin, county Fermanagh;
> born 1865/6 in Dublin, son of Robert Hopkins, merchant; educated at Wesley College, Dublin; studied arts and medicine at Trinity College, Dublin, from 1882; BA (TCD) 1886; MB BCh 1888; MD 1889; general practitioner, of Grove Cottage, Derrylin; died 9 December 1897 at 8 Clyde Road, Didsbury, Manchester; probate Dublin 16 August 1900. [Belf PRO, will cal; Lond GRO (d); *Med Dir*; TCD adm reg; *TCD Cat*, vol II (1896)].

HORAN, PATRICK CALLAN (1837/8–81), Whitehaven, Cumberland;
> born 1837/8; probably son of Dr Thomas Horran (*q.v.*) of Cootehill, county Cavan; studied medicine at the Ledwich School, Dublin, and Royal College of Surgeons in Ireland; LRCP and LM LRCS Edin 1864; surgeon to the Whitehaven and West Cumberland Infirmary; medical officer to Whitehaven Union Workhouse, of Lower Street, Whitehaven; died 29 January 1881 at 33 Roper Street, Whitehaven; probate Carlisle 7 December 1881. [Lond GRO (d); Lond PPR, will cal; *Med Dir*].

HORAN, THOMAS (*fl c* 1822–64), Cootehill, county Cavan;
> MRCSE 1822; accoucheur of Dublin Lying-in Hospital; surgeon and accoucheur, of Market Street, Cootehill c 1824, and medical officer to Cootehill Union Workhouse; married —; probably father of Dr Patrick Callan Horan (*q.v.*); died 21 December 1864 at Cootehill; probate Dublin 4 March 1865. [Belf PRO, will cal; Croly (1843–6); Pigot (1824)].

HORNER, MARY CAMPBELL (1872/3–1941), Manchuria, North China;
> born 1872/3, daughter of John Lyle Horner, of Bovevagh, Limavady, county Londonderry; sister of Dr Thomas Lyle Horner (*q.v.*); studied medicine at Queen Margaret's College, Glasgow; LRCP LRCS Edin 1894; LFPS Glas 1894; medical

missionary with the U F Mission, Monkden, Manchuria; retired c 1927 to 22 Main Street, Limavady; unmarried; died 8 July 1941 at 22 Main Street; probate Londonderry 3 December 1941. [Belf GRO (d); Belf PRO, will cal; *Med Dir*].

HORNER, THOMAS LYLE (1846–1923), Naval Medical Service;
born 26 March 1846 at Boveva, county Londonderry, son of John Lyle Horner of Boveva; brother of Dr Mary Campbell Horner (*q.v.*); educated at Coleraine Academical Institution; studied medicine at Queen's College, Belfast, from 1863; LRCP LRCS Edin 1868; joined the Naval Medical Service as assistant surgeon c 1870 on HMS *Cossack*; surgeon c 1875; retired as deputy inspector general c 1900; lived finally at 44 Torrington Place, Plymouth; married Marian —; died 20 November 1923 at 44 Torrington Place; probate London 31 December 1923. [Lond PPR, will cal, will; *Med Dir*; QCB adm reg].

HOSKING, JAMES WITHIEL PHILLIPS (1843–c 1898), Port Chalmers, Otago, New Zealand;
born 1843 at Redruth, Cornwall, son of William Hosking, proprietor of Redruth Foundry and later manager of a mining company near Melbourne, Australia; educated at Wesley College, Taunton, Devon; studied medicine at Owen's College, Manchester, Ledwich Medical School, Dublin, and from 1874, at Queen's College, Belfast; LRCP LRCS Edin 1878; emigrated to New Zealand c 1880; general practitioner, of Port Chalmers, Otago from c 1885; died c 1898. [*Med Dir*; QCB adm reg].

HOSKINS, JOSHUA THOMAS TARRANT (1808/9–86), Clones, county Monaghan;
born 1808/9; LM Coombe Hospital Dublin 1830; LRCS Edin 1831; LAH Dub 1841; medical officer to Clones Workhouse and Clones and Rosslea Temporary Fever Hospitals; general practitioner in Clones; married 17 January 1834 Mary Clarke, daughter of Andrew Clarke of Clones; died 6 May 1886 at Clones; probate Armagh 19 June 1886. [*BNL* 28 January 1834 (m); Belf PRO, will cal; Croly (1843–6); Dub GRO (d); McCann (2003); *Med Dir*].

HOUGHTON, JAMES (1803/4–47), Dublin, Cushendun, county Antrim, and Brookeborough, county Fermanagh;
born 1803/4 in Brookeborough; studied medicine at Trinity College and the Meath Hospital, Dublin, and at Edinburgh University; MD (Edin) 1829 (thesis 'De febre intermittente'); LKQCPI; MRCSE 1830; general practitioner in Dublin for some years; medical officer to Cushendun Dispensary District and constabulary c 1830–45; medical officer to Brookeborough Dispensary District and Hospital c 1845–7; author of various medical papers; died 3 October 1847 of typhus fever 'contracted in his attendance on the poor' (memorial) and received a glowing obituary; memorial in Aghalurcher Church of Ireland Church, Colebrook, county Fermanagh. [*BNL* 15 October 1847 (d); Croly (1843–6); *Dub Quart J Med Sci* 1847; 4: 511–2; Edin Univ; *Memorials of the Dead*, vol XIII, p 12].

HOUSTON, ALEXANDER (1806/7–31), Ballindrait, county Donegal;
born 1806/7, youngest son of the Rev James Houston, minister of Ballindrait Presbyterian Church, county Donegal; brother of Dr John Houston (*q.v.*); LRCSI; died 19 May 1831 at Gortin, county Tyrone. [*BNL* 31 May 1831 (d); *Londonderry Sentinel* 28 May 1831 (d); McConnell (1951)].

HOUSTON, JAMES ALEXANDER (d 1849), New York, USA;
eldest son of the Rev Dr Houston of Ballymena, county Antrim; surgeon, of New York; married 4 September 1839 in St Mary's Church, Dublin, Anne McAulay (who died 20 April 1854 at her home in Brooklyn, New York), eldest daughter of John McAulay, merchant, of New York; died 17 September 1849 at his home in New York. [*BNL* 10 September 1839 (m), 12 October 1849 (d) and 17 May 1854 (d); *Londonderry Sentinel* 12 October 1849 (d)].

HOUSTON, JOHN (1802–45), Dublin;
born 1802 at Ballindrait, county Donegal, eldest son of the Rev James Houston, minister of Ballindrait Presbyterian Church, and Jane Taylor (sister of Dr Joseph Taylor, AMS (*q.v.*)); brother of Dr Alexander Houston (*q.v.*); brought up by his uncle Dr John Taylor (*q.v.*); educated at Dr Crawford's Academy in Strabane and in Dublin; apprenticed to Mr John Shekleton of Dublin 1819–24, who also helped him financially after Dr Taylor's death; studied medicine in Dublin and at Edinburgh University; LRCSI 1824; MD (Edin) 1832 (thesis 'De phymosi'); followed John Shekelton as curator of the RCSI Museum 1824–41; MRIA 1829; surgeon to the City of Dublin Hospital from its foundation in 1832; lecturer on surgery in the Park Street School of Medicine, the museum of which he catalogued in 1843; medical officer to several Dublin institutions; performed 2nd post mortem on Jonathan Swift in 1835; MRIA; one of the first to introduce the microscope into Dublin, seeing it as a means of staging tumours; described the valves of the rectum, 1844; author of *The Mode of Treatment in Fever* (1844) and many medical papers; died 30 July 1845 at Dalkey, following a stroke; portrait in the RCSI. [Butcher (1846); Cameron (1916); Coakley (1992)*; DIB* (2009); Edin Univ; Kirkpatrick Archive; McConnell (1951); Newmann (1993); *Oxford DNB* (2004); O'Brien, Crookshank and Wolstenhome (1984); Widdess (1967)].

HOUSTON, JOHN KNOX (1850–74), Ahoghill, county Antrim;
born 23 July 1850 at Knockbracken, county Down, son of the Rev Thomas Houston, minister of Knockbracken Reformed Presbyterian Church, and Catherine Wallace of Ballymena; uncle of Sir Thomas Houston (*q.v.*); educated at RBAI; studied medicine at Queen's College, Belfast, from 1868; MD MCh LM (QUI) 1872; medical officer to Ahoghill Dispensary District and constabulary from 1873; died 20 December 1874; buried in Knockbracken Reformed Presbyterian graveyard. [Clarke, *County Down*, vol 18 (1969); Kirkpatrick Archive; Loughridge (1970); *Med Dir*; QCB adm reg].

HOUSTON, SIR THOMAS (1868–1949), Belfast;
born 15 December 1868, at Ballyclabber, Coleraine, county Londonderry, son of the Rev James Dick Houston, minister of Ballyclabber Reformed Presbyterian Church,

and Anne Murray Anderson; nephew of Dr John Knox Houston (*q.v.*); educated at Coleraine Academical Institution; studied arts and medicine at Queen's College, Belfast, from 1887; BA (RUI) 1891; Malcolm Exhibition, Belfast Royal Hospital 1893; MB (hons) BCh BAO 1895; MD 1899; house surgeon at the Belfast Royal Hospital 1895–7; assistant gynaecologist 1897–9; assistant pathologist (haematologist) to Royal Victoria Hospital, Belfast 1900–16; gynaecologist and later pathologist to the Ulster Hospital for Children and Women 1903–20; BMA research scholar 1902–03; gave annual winter oration at Royal Victoria Hospital, Belfast, 1912; attending physician to the Forster Green Hospital, Belfast; attending physician for haematology and vaccine therapy at the Royal Victoria Hospital 1916–34, of 25 College Gardens, Belfast; physician to the St John's Ambulance Brigade Hospital at Etaples (hon major RAMC) 1914–18; OBE 1919; created the new laboratories in the Royal Victoria Hospital and started the blood transfusion service after World War I; president of the Ulster Medical Society 1920–21; Knight Bachelor 1927; retired 1934; pro-chancellor of Queen's University, Belfast, 1941; author of many medical papers; unmarried; died 21 June 1949; portrait painted by Frank McKelvey (1948) in Royal Victoria Hospital; probate Belfast 12 January 1950. [Belf GRO (b); Belf PRO, will cal, will; *Belf Roy Hosp, Ann Rep*; *BMJ* obituary (1949); Kirkpatrick Archive; *Lancet* obituary (1949); Loughridge (1970); Marshall and Kelly (1973); *Med Dir*; Nelson (1994); Newmann (1993); O'Brien, Crookshank and Wolstenholme (1984); QCB adm reg; Thomson (1948)].

HOUSTON, WILLIAM (d 1862), Sydney, New South Wales;
of Ballymena, county Antrim; MD [?]; emigrated to Australia; died 27 December 1862 at Sydney. [*Coleraine Chronicle* 11 April 1863 (d); *Londonderry Sentinel* 7 April 1863 (d)].

HOWARD, JOSEPH (d 1834), Ballybay, county Monaghan;
only child of the Rev Joseph Howard, minister of Ahoghill Presbyterian Church; general practitioner, of Ballybay; unmarried; died 23 October 1834 in Dublin,'a young man of great talent and excellent disposition and would have been an ornament to his profession' (*BNL*); buried in Ahoghill. [*BNL* 4 November 1834 (d); McConnell (1951)].

HOWARD, RICHARD (1841–1902), Arklow, county Wicklow;
born 20 April 1841 at Limerick, son of Richard Howard of Limerick; educated by the Rev Mr Elmes and Rev Mr Fitzgerald; studied medicine at the Royal College of Surgeons in Ireland, Queen's College, Galway, Dr Steeven's Hospital, Dublin and from 1862, at Queen's College, Belfast; LAH Dub 1869; general practitioner, of 46 Main Street, Arklow; married Sarah —; died 15 August 1902; probate Dublin 25 September 1902. [Belf PRO, will cal; *Med Dir*; QCB adm reg].

HOWE, JOHN HUTCHINSON GARNER (1861/2–1929), Edinburgh and Hove, Sussex;
born 1861/2 at Holywood, county Down, son of William J. Howe of Ballytrim, Killyleagh, county Down; educated at Cowley College, London; studied medicine at

Queen's College, Belfast, from c 1885; LRCP LRCS Edin 1894; LFPS Glas 1894; general practitioner, of 109 Warrender Park Road, Edinburgh, c 1895 and of Dufferin Lodge, Hove, from c 1900; surgeon RNVR during and after World War I; married Vera Domville —; died 26 December 1929; probate London 26 February 1930. [Lond PPR, will cal, will; *Med Dir*; QCB adm reg].

HOWES, SAMUEL (*fl c* 1824), Carrickmacross, county Monaghan;
apothecary, of Carrickmacross, 1824. [Pigot (1824)].

HUDSON, ALEXANDER ROBERT (1829–91), Army Medical Service;
born 16 May 1829 at Enniskillen, county Fermanagh; studied arts and medicine at Trinity College, Dublin; MRCSE 1852; BA (TCD) 1852; MB 1853; joined the Army Medical Service as assistant surgeon 1854 and posted to 6th Foot; staff surgeon (surgeon major) 1865; transferred to 47th Foot 1865 and 83rd Foot 1869; served at the Indian Mutiny 1857; retired August 1882 with honorary rank of brigadier surgeon; living at Marine Villa, Crosby Road, Liverpool; married Mary —; died 10 August 1891 at Marine Villa; probate Dublin 28 September 1891 and London 15 October 1891. [Belf PRO, will cal; Burtchaell and Sadleir (1935); Lond PPR, will cal; *Med Dir*; Peterkin and Johnston (1968)].

HUDSON, ROBERT (*fl c* 1793) Enniskillen, county Fermanagh
LAH Dub 1793; apothecary, of Enniskillen. [Apothecaries (1829)].

HUDSON, ROBERT SAMUEL (1846–83), Redruth, Cornwall;
born 3 August 1846 at Rathfriland, county Down, son of Samuel Hudson, miller, of Rathfriland; educated by Mr Samuel Moffet of Rathfriland and Mr L. Mulligan; studied medicine at Queen's College, Belfast, from 1862; MD MCh (hons) (QUI) 1868; LRCSI 1868; FRCSI 1880; house surgeon at the Royal Albert Hospital, Devonport, 1869; general practitioner at Redruth, Cornwall; married 18 February 1873 in Sandys Street First Presbyterian Church, Newry, Elizabeth Martin, daughter of David Martin, merchant, of Newry and sister of Dr Samuel Edgar Martin of Newry (*q.v.*); died 7 October 1883 at Newry; probate Bodmin 5 February 1884. [Dub GRO (d); Kirkpatrick Archive; Lond PPR, will cal, will; *Med Dir*; QCB adm reg; UHF database (m)].

HUESTON, JAMES LYLE (1847/8–1927), Maghera, county Londonderry, and Bangor-Erris, county Mayo;
born 1847/8, son of Joseph Hueston, farmer, of Rasharkin, county Antrim; studied medicine at Anderson's College, Glasgow; LFPS and LM Glas 1878; general practitioner of Maghera c 1880–1900; medical officer to Bangor-Erris Dispensary District and constabulary and medical officer of health c 1900–1925; retired to Mount Hermon, Portstewart, county Londonderry c 1925; married 3 September 1880 Mary Thomson, daughter of the Rev Andrew Thomson, minister of Third Garvagh Presbyterian Church; died 18 March 1927 at Portstewart; probate Belfast 3 October 1927. [Belf GRO (d); Belf PRO, will cal; *Med Dir*; UHF database (m)].

HUEY, DAVID (1858–1941), Bushmills, county Antrim;
born 2 January 1858 at Ballynaris, Dervock, county Antrim, son of William Huey, farmer, of Ballynaris; educated privately; studied medicine at Queen's College, Belfast, from 1878; LRCP LRCS Edin 1882; LAH Dub 1896; FRCS Edin 1924; general practitioner, of Bushmills, from c 1883; medical officer to Bushmills Dispensary District, coastguards and post office, of Bella Vista and later of Ballaghmore, Bushmills presented new X-ray equipment to the Route Hospital in 1939; married —; died 24 July 1941 at Ballaghmore; probate Belfast 5 December 1941. [Belf GRO (d); Belf PRO, will cal; *BMJ* obituary (1941); Burns (1988); Kirkpatrick Archive; *Med Dir*; QCB adm reg].

HUEY, HENRY
See TYLER, HENRY HUEY

HUEY, ISAAC MACKAY (1874–1962), South Africa and London;
born 20 September 1874 at Drumskellan, Kilderry, county Londonderry, son of William Huey, farmer, of Drumskellan, and Margaret Mulhern; studied medicine at Glasgow University; MB ChB (Glas) 1900; medical officer in charge of troopship Golconda and Civil surgeon to the South African Field Force; medical officer to Notting Hill Dispensary, London; assistant to outpatient physician, Middlesex Hospital; physician to Disabled Officers' Home; honorary anaesthetist to King George's Hospital; general practitioner, of 175 Holland Park Avenue, Kensington; retired to 7 Charlton Mansions, Holland Park, c 1948; author of various medical papers; married Ethel Halliday —; died 15 July 1862 at the Middlesex Hospital; probate Lewes 14 August 1962. [Dub GRO (b); Lond GRO (d); Lond PPR, will cal; *Med Dir*].

HUEY, ROBERT (*fl c* 1813–50), Naval Medical Service;
joined the Naval Medical Service as assistant surgeon; retired to Bushmills; married Barbara — (who was born 1778/9 and died 7 May 1865 at Bushmills); died before 1865. [*Coleraine Chronicle* 13 May 1865 (d); *Londonderry Sentinel* 12 May 1865 (d)].

HUEY, WILLIAM (d 1843), Naval Medical Service;
joined the Naval Medical Service as assistant surgeon; surgeon 1813; served for 22 years; unmarried; died 2 July 1843 at Erganagh, Castlederg, county Tyrone. [*Londonderry Standard* 12 July 1843 (d); *NMS* (1826)].

HUGGARD, WILLIAM RICHARD (1851/2–1911) London and Davos, Switzerland;
born 1851/2, son of William Huggard of 71 Main Street, Wexford; educated at the Diocesan School, Wexford; studied arts and medicine at Queen's College, Galway, and from 1873, Queen's College, Belfast; MD MCh (QUI) 1875; BA (QUI) 1876; MA 1879; MRCP Lond 1886; general practitioner in London; superintendent of the Sussex and Brandenburg House Asylums, Hammersmith; physician to the St Pancras and Northern Dispensary, London; moved to Geneva, Switzerland in 1884

and took the Swiss Federal Diploma of Medicine in 1885; physician in Davos 1885–1906; author of *Handbook of Climatic Treatment, including Balneology* (1906); British Consul in Davos; died 10 October 1911 at Kussnacht, Zurich, Switzerland; probate Dublin 1 November 1911 and London 25 November 1911. [Belf PRO, will cal; *BMJ* obituary (1911); *Lancet* obituary (1911); Lond PPR, will cal; *Med Dir*; *Munk's Roll*, vol 4; QCB adm reg].

HUGHES, WILLIAM (1840/1–1903), Naval Medical Service;
born 1840/1, son of George Hughes of 11 Irish Street, Armagh; educated at St Patrick's College, Armagh; studied medicine at Queen's College, Belfast, from 1859; MRCSE 1868; LSA Lond 1874; LKQCPI 1874; joined the Naval Medical Service c 1875 as assistant surgeon; medical superintendent to HMS *Hamadryad*, Hospital Ship, Cardiff, from 1876; died 3 May 1903. [*Med Dir*; QCB adm reg].

HUGO, EDWARD VICTOR (1865–1951), London and Indian Medical Service;
born 5 January 1865; brother of Dr James Henry Hugo (*q.v.*); educated at Foyle College, Londonderry; studied medicine at St Bartholomew's Hospital, London; MRCSE LRCP Lond 1889; MB (hons, gold medal) BS (Lond) 1890; FRCS 1906; assistant medical superintendent to Paddington Infirmary and clinical assistant to the orthopaedic department of St Bartholomew's Hospital; joined the Indian Medical Service (Bengal establishment) as surgeon lieutenant 1892; surgeon captain 1895; major 1904; lieutenant-colonel 1912; served on North-West Frontier (mentioned in despatches) 1894–5, Chitral 1895 and Chakdara 1897–8; professor of surgery at King Edward's Medical College, Lahore 1908–14 and 1918–22; senior medical officer on hospital ship *Gascon* at Dardanelles; consulting surgeon to Mesopotamian Expeditionary Force 1916; CMG 1917; retired to 79 Queen's Road, Richmond, Surrey, 1922; president of the Surrey Branch of the BMA; married 1909 Helen Frances Newton, daughter of E. Newton; died 24 December 1951 at 75 Queens Road, Richmond; probate London 19 February 1952. [Crawford (1930); Kirkpatrick Archive; Lond PPR, will cal; *Med Dir*; Power and Le Fanu (1953)].

HUGO, JAMES HENRY (1870–1943), London, Nottingham and Indian Medical Service;
born 16 July 1870; younger brother of Dr Edward Victor Hugo (*q.v.*); educated at Foyle College, Londonderry; studied medicine at St Bartholomew's Hospital, London; MRCSE LRCP Lond 1895; MB BS (Lond) 1896; DPH RCPS 1907; of 15 Beauclerc Road, The Grove, Shepherd's Bush c 1895; house surgeon to St Bartholomew's Hospital, to Nottingham General Hospital, and to Dulwich Infirmary; assistant medical officer and clinical assistant to St Saviour's Infirmary; assistant to the orthopaedic department, St Bartholomew's Hospital; joined the Indian Medical Service (general list) as surgeon lieutenant captain 1900; major 1908; lieutenant-colonel 1916; served on the North-West Frontier 1897; DSO 1898; World War I 1914–21; Legion d'Honneur 1918; retired to Guildford, Surrey 1925; died 28 February 1943 at Guildford; probate Llandudno 10 June 1943. [*BMJ* obituary (1943); Crawford (1930); Kirkpatrick Archive; Lond PPR, will cal; *Med Dir*].

HULL, H.M. (*fl c* 1792–6), Belfast;
LAH Dub 1796; first apothecary to the Belfast Dispensary 1792–5. [Apothecaries (1829); Malcolm (1851)].

HULL, THOMAS (d 1792), Comber, county Down;
surgeon, of Comber; died 9 February 1792. [*BNL* 14 February 1792 (d)].

HULL, — (*fl c* 1800), Ballinderry, county Antrim;
general practitioner, of Ballinderry; married —; eldest daughter born c 1798 and died 7 December 1855 in Hill Street, Belfast; died before 1856. [*BNL* 7 December 1855 (d, daughter)].

HUMBLE, ADAM (1716/7–62), Dublin;
born 1716/7 in county Donegal, third son of the Rev John Humble, rector of Donagh, county Donegal, and Avis Davenport of New Carthage, Culdaff; studied arts and medicine at Trinity College, Dublin, from 1733; BA (TCD) 1737; MB 1746; MD 1748; FKQCPI 1754; assistant physician to Dr Steevens' Hospital 1757–60 and physician 1760–62; president KQCPI 1759; died 1762. [Burke, *Peerage and Baronetage* (1861); Burtchaell and Sadleir (1924); Kirkpatrick (1924); Leslie (1937); Widdess 1963)].

HUME, GEORGE ALEXANDER (1819–80), Crumlin, county Antrim;
born 21 February 1819, son of Thomas Hume, farmer; studied medicine at RBAI from 1835, Glasgow University and the Royal College of Surgeons in Ireland; CM (Glas) 1838; LRCS Edin 1839; MD (Glas) 1845; medical officer to Crumlin Dispensary District and constabulary and registrar of births and deaths; coroner for county Antrim from 1867; married 27 February 1849 Christine Oakman (who was born 1816/7 and died 4 April 1898), daughter of Walter Oakman of Darraghmore, Glenavy; died 9 January 1880 at Crumlin; buried in Crumlin Presbyterian Graveyard; probate Belfast 27 February 1880. [Addison (1898); *BNL* 2 March 1849 (m); Belf PRO, SCH 524/1A/, Belf PRO, will cal; *BMJ* obituary (1880); Croly (1843–6); Dub GRO (d); gravestone inscripton; Kirkpatrick Archive; *Med Dir*].

HUME, GUSTAVUS (1732–1812), Dublin;
born August 1732, son of Robert Hume of Lisanober, county Cavan; studied medicine in Paris 1756; surgeon to Mercers' Hospital, Dublin 1758–1812, of Suffolk Street, Longford Street, and finally 63 Dawson Street, Dublin; author of *Observations on the Origin and Treatment of Internal and External Diseases and Management of Children* (1802) and *Observations on Angina Pectoris, Gout and Cow-pox* (1804); one of the surgeons to obtain the charter for the Royal College of Surgeons in Ireland in 1784; state surgeon 1791–1806; president of the RCSI 1795; speculator in land and property in Dublin and builder of several fine houses in central Dublin; laid out Hume Street and Ely Place (formerly Hume Row); married 22 October 1756 Elizabeth Travers, daughter of the Rev Boyle Travers, incumbent of St Paul's Church of Ireland Church, Dublin; father of Dr Thomas Hume of Dublin, MB (TCD) 1796,

MD 1803; died 7 February 1812 at 63 Dawson Street, Dublin; bequeathed £300 to Mercers' Hospital. [Burke *LGI* (1812) (under Macartney of Lissanoure); Burtchaell and Sadleir (1924); Cameron (1916); *DIB* (2009); Leslie and Wallace (2001)].

HUME, ROBERT (c 1807–37), Lurgan, county Armagh;
born c 1807; surgeon, of Lurgan; died 23 December 1837, of typhus fever; buried in Shankill Graveyard, Lurgan, with a large memorial; 'he fell sacrificed to his zeal in the cause of humanity, having caught the disease which terminated his valued labours in course of this gratuitous profession, attendance on the indigent sick'. [Gravestone inscription].

HUMFREY (HUMPHREY), ALEXANDER (1831–76), Army Medical Service;
born 9 August 1831 in county Donegal, third son of lieutenant-colonel Benjamin Geale Humphrey of Cavanacor, county Donegal and Mary Keys of Cavanacor; LRCSI 1853; joined the Army Medical Service as staff assistant surgeon 1854, with the 77th Foot; surgeon major 1865; with the 98th Foot 1866; served at the Crimea 1854–6; married 10 August 1865 in St Anne's Church of Ireland Church, Dublin, Mary Louisa Brabazon (who was born 28 May 1842), second daughter of the Rev John Vignoles Brabazon, curate of Drumglass, county Tyrone and rector of Rahan, county Meath; died 8 February 1876 in Malta. [Burke *LGI* (1912); *Coleraine Chronicle* 19 August 1865 (m); Fleming (2001); Kirkpatrick Archive; *Londonderry Sentinel* 15 August 1865 (m); *Med Dir*; Peterkin and Johnston (1968)].

HUMPHREYS, ALEXANDER (1757–1802), Augusta and Staunton, Virginia, USA;
born 1757 in county Armagh, sixth son of John Humphreys, merchant, of Derrynoose, Tynan, county Armagh, and Margaret Carlisle (who was sister of Dr — Carlisle of Armagh (*q.v.*); matriculated at Glasgow University 1774 and studied arts; MA (Glas) 1777; studied medicine first with Dr Carlisle and then from c 1779 at Edinburgh University; MD (Edin) c 1782 [no record of MD in Glasgow or Edinburgh]; emigrated to USA 1783 to settle with his older brother in Augusta, Virginia 1783–7; moved to Staunton, 1787, examining applicants for war pensions 1787–8; granted permission to build an elaboratory in Staunton 1788; enthusiastic teacher of medical students generally and in the dissecting room; JP 1791; trustee for the new Staunton Academy 1792 and Chairman of Board 1793; said to have carried out the first Caesarean Section in history on a living woman with mother and child surviving in 1794; married 8 April 1788 Mary Brown (who was born 14 July 1763 in Augusta, and died 28 January 1836 in South Frankfort, Kentucky), second daughter of the Rev John Brown of New Providence Presbyterian Church, and Margaret Preston; died 23 May 1802 near Staunton; buried in Trinity Churchyard, Staunton; bronze tablet erected after a ceremony on 15 April 1951. [Addison (1898) and (1913); Bell (1967); Keller (2005); Labach (2000)].

HUMPHREYS, GEORGE (*fl c* 1822) of Cavan;
LAH Dub 1822; apothecary, of Cavan. [Apothecaries (1829)].

HUMPHRIES, CHARLES JOHN (1855–1915), Belfast, and Donaghadee and Bangor, county Down;
born October 1855 at Maralin, county Down, son of Charles Humphries, schoolmaster; educated privately; studied medicine at Queen's College, Belfast, from 1878; MD (RUI) 1885; BCh BAO 1888; general practitioner, of 110 Newtownards Road, Belfast c 1885 and of 2 Templemore Avenue c 1895, of Stockbridge House, Donaghadee c 1905, of Princetown House, Bangor c 1910; retired to Thornbrook House, Duneight c 1915; married 4 June 1889 at the Methodist Manse, Scotch Quarter, Carrickfergus, Jane Alley, daughter of the Rev George Alley, Methodist minister of Carrickfergus; died 29 January 1915; buried in Belfast City Cemetery; probate Belfast 14 April 1915. [Belf City Cem, bur reg; Belf PRO, will cal; Dub GRO (m); *Med Dir*; QCB adm reg; UHF database (m)].

HUMPHRIES, SAMUEL (d 1854), Caledon, county Tyrone;
studied medicine at Glasgow University; CM (Glas) 1824, surgeon and medical officer to constabulary, of Caledon c 1845; died 3 March 1854. [*BNL* 8 March 1854 (d); Croly (1843–6); *Med Dir*].

HUMPHRYS, HUTCHINSON GOURNEY (1822/3–66), Donegal, Dublin, Derrylin, county Fermanagh, and Ballyhaise, county Cavan;
born 1822/3, eldest son of Isaac Humphrys, captain in the 62nd and 82nd Regiments of Foot; LM Combe Hosp Dub 1850; LKQCPI 1853; LRCSI 1855; of 23 Denzille Street and 91 Harcourt Street c 1851–2; house surgeon to Donegal County Infirmary; clincial assistant to Meath Hospital, Dublin; medical officer to Derrylin Dispensary District and constabulary; medical officer to Ballyhaise Dispensary District and constabulary; author of various medical papers; married 5 June 1851 in Dublin Register Office and 26 March 1852 in St Peter's Church of Ireland Church, Dublin, Matilda Jane Archer, daughter of the Rev Richard Archer, vicar of Clonduff (Hilltown), county Down, and Jane Matilda Campbell; died 5 March 1866 of pneumonia, at Bailieborough; administration Dublin 14 May 1866. [Belf PRO, will cal; Dub GRO (m) and (d); *Londonderry Sentinel* 9 March 1866 (d); *Med Dir*; Swanzy (1933)].

HUMPHRYS, ROBERT (d c 1920), Naval Medical Service;
son of John Humphrys, gentleman; LRCSI 1856; joined the Naval Medical Service c 1860 as assistant surgeon; on HMS *Molander* c 1863; surgeon 1865; on HMS *Chanticleer* c 1867; on HMS *Mersey* c 1871; staff surgeon 2nd class on HMS *Wolverene* c 1873; on HMS *Amethys*t 1874; fleet surgeon on HMS *Clyde* 1878; retired 1891; surgeon commander 1919; married 20 May 1872 in Magheraculmoney Church of Ireland Church, Frances Elizabeth Williamson, eldest daughter of the Rev Andrew Williamson, rector of Magheraculmoney, Kesh, county Fermanagh, and sister of Dr John Francis Williamson, AMS (*q.v.*); died c 1920. [Dub GRO (m); Leslie (1929); *Med Dir*].

HUNT, HENRY FITZMAURICE PHILLIPS-
See PHILLIPS, HENRY FITZMAURICE HUNT

HUNTER, ANDREW (1860/1–1939), Ballybay, county Monaghan;
   born 1860/1; studied medicine at the Ledwich School, Dublin; LRCSI 1883; LRCP and LM Edin 1884; medical officer and medical officer of health to Ballybay Dispensary District; medical officer to constabulary and certifying factory surgeon; retired to Castleblaney, county Monaghan, and later to 242 Stranmillis Road, Belfast; unmarried; died 4 February 1939 at 242 Stranmillis Road; probate Dublin 1 June 1939. [Belf GRO (d); Dub Nat Arch, will cal; *Med Dir*].

HUNTER, CHRISTOPHER (1843/4–1922), Doocharry and Carrick, county Donegal, Belcoo, county Fermanagh, and Omagh, county Tyrone;
   born 1843/4; studied medicine at Queen's College, Galway, the Royal College of Surgeons in Ireland and the Meath Hospital, Dublin; LRCP LRCS Edin 1872; LM Coombe Hospital, Dublin 1872; medical officer to Doocharry Dispensary District c 1872–5, to Carrick Dispensary District and constabulary c 1875–88, to Belcoo Dispensary District c 1885–95 and to Omagh No 2 Dispensary District and constabulary c 1895; finally of Carrickmore, county Tyrone; JP for county Fermanagh; died 14 October 1922 at Carrickmore; probate Londonderry 28 November 1922. [*BNL* 11 December 1860; Belf GRO (d); Belf PRO, will cal; Kirkpatrick Archive; *Med Dir*].

HUNTER, GEORGE (d 1860), Bailieborough, county Cavan, and Lisnaskea, county Fermanagh;
   LRCSI and LM 1844; general practitioner, of Bailieborough c 1845 and later of Lisnaskea; married Elizabeth —; died 30 November 1860 at Lisnaskea Dispensary; administration Dublin 27 June 1861. [*BNL* 11 December 1860 (d); Belf PRO, will cal; Croly (1843–6); *Med Dir*].

HUNTER, HENRY (1854–83), Georgetown, Demerara;
   born 20 November 1854 at Cullyhagan, Kilrea, county Londonderry, son of Thomas Hunter, land agent, of Kilrea; educated at RBAI; studied medicine at Queen's College, Belfast, from 1872; MD Dip Mid (QUI) 1876; LRCS Edin 1876; medical officer in Georgetown c 1877–83; married Margaret Eleanor Staveley; died 23 August 1883 at Clarence Cottage, Clacton-on-Sea; probate London 3 November 1883. [Lond PPR, will cal; *Med Dir*; QCB adm reg].

HUNTER, JAMES (1752/3–1813), Naval Medical Service and London;
   born 1752/3; joined the Naval Medical Service as assistant surgeon and served 'for many years'; surgeon, of Dean Street, Soho, London; died 25 March 1813 at Matthew Hunter's house, Derriaghy, county Antrim. [*BNL* 30 March 1813 (d)].

HUNTER, JAMES (*fl c* 1820), Strabane, county Londonderry;
   apothecary and surgeon, of Markethouse Street, Strabane c 1820; possibly died c 1822. [Dooher (2000); Pigot (1824)].

HUNTER, JAMES (d 1855), Castlewellan, county Down;
   studied medicine at Edinburgh University; MD (Edin) 1817 (thesis 'De inflamatione'); FRCSI 1844; medical officer to Castlewellan Dispensary, of

Bryansford, county Down; will dated 23 July 1853 when of 4 St Stephen's Green, Dublin c 1853; married Elizabeth — (who died 29 April 1835 at Bryansford); died 3 April 1855 at St Stephen's Green, Dublin; will dated 23 July 1853 proved 3 July 1855 (copy in PRO NI). [*BNL* 12 May 1835 (d) and 6 April 1855 (d); Belf PRO, D/671/D14/4/173; Croly (1843–6); Edin Univ; *Med Dir*].

HUNTER, JAMES (1862–c 1934), Invercargill, New Zealand;
born 14 February 1862 at Ballyhamage, Doagh, county Antrim, son of Robert Hunter, farmer, of Ballyhamage; educated at Methodist College, Belfast,1879–80; studied medicine at Queen's College, Belfast from 1880; MD MCh (RUI) 1888; LM KQCPI 1889; emigrated to New Zealand; general practitioner, of Invercargill, New Zealand; died c 1934. [Fry (1984); *Med Dir*; QCB adm reg].

HUNTER, JAMES FULLERTON (1862–1902), Manchester, Lancashire, Leeds, Yorkshire, and London;
born 17 March 1862 at Ramelton, county Donegal, son of William Henry Hunter, farmer, of New Mill, Ramelton; educated at Londonderry Academical Institution; studied medicine at Queen's College, Belfast, from 1878; MD (RUI) 1882; MCh Dip Obst 1884; MAO 1885; general practitioner, of 210 North Road, Pendlebury, Manchester, c 1885, of Earby, Leeds c 1895, of 16 Great St James' Street, Bedford Row, London, c 1900 and finally of 3 Gainsborough, Hackney Wick; married 5 August 1886 in St Nicholas' Church of Ireland Church, Carrickfergus, Charlotte Chase, daughter of Joshua Chase, schoolmaster, of Carrickfergus; died 29 September 1902 at the London Hospital; probate London 23 October 1902. [Lond PPR, will cal; *Med Dir*; QCB adm reg; UHF database (m)].

HUNTER, JOHN, senior (1784–1842), Letterkenny and Ramelton, county Donegal;
born 1784 near Strabane, county Tyrone; diploma in surgery and pharmacy of the Royal College of Physicians and Surgeons of Glasgow; opened apothecary's shop in 'Mr Nesbitt's house' [? Strabane] 7 May 1808; surgeon and apothecary, of Letterkenny c 1824; later apothecary of Ramelton, a business carried on by his widow after his death; presented with a loving cup by Lady Mary Stewart 'as a token of regard for his constant attention'; married 7 October 1812 Mary Patton (who was born c 1793 and died 17 January1856 at Burt), daughter of John Patton, brewer, of Ramelton, and Frances McNaught, and sister of Dr David Patton, RN (*q.v.*); father of Dr John Hunter, junior (*q.v.*); died 27 July 1842 in Strabane, county Tyrone, 'prematurely broken down by constant and in a great measure, gratuitous labour' (*Londonderry Sentinel*); buried in Ramelton Graveyard; probate Raphoe Diocesan Court 1842. [*BNL* 5 August 1842 (d) and 25 January 1856 (d); Elliott, Simon, pers com; Hawbaker (2008); *Londonderry Journal* 9 August 1842 (d); *Londonderry Sentinel* 6 August 1842 (d) and 25 January 1856 (d); Pigot (1824); Thrift (1920)].

HUNTER, JOHN, junior (1826–72), Buncrana, county Donegal;
born 26 July 1826, second son of Dr John Hunter, senior, of Ramelton, county Donegal (*q.v.*) and Mary Patton; studied medicine at Edinburgh University; MD (Edin) 1841 (thesis 'On cataract'); LRCS Edin and LM 1846; resident medical officer

to Londonderry Fever Hospital and medical officer to Fanad Dispensary District and constabulary; medical officer to Buncrana Dispensary District, Royal Artillery and constabulary, and certifying factory surgeon; of Seaview House, Buncrana; married 20 January 1859 in Second Omagh Presbyterian Church, Sarah Scott (who was born 18 August 1833), elder daughter of James Scott, gentleman, of Lisnamallard Lodge, Omagh, county Tyrone; died 18 November 1872 at Buncrana, of typhoid fever; administration Londonderry 30 January 1873. [*BNL* 24 January 1859 (m); Belf PRO, will cal; Dub GRO (m) and (d); Edin Univ; Hawbaker (2008); Kirkpatrick Archive; *Londonderry Sentinel* 28 January 1859 (m); McGrew (2001) (m); *Med Dir*].

HUNTER, JOHN ARNOLD (c 1871–1947), Wigton, Scotland, Whitehead, county Antrim, and Belfast;

born c 1871 at Nowchwang, China, son of Dr Joseph Molyneux Hunter (*q.v.*); educated at Methodist College, Belfast, from 1879 and RBAI; studied medicine at Queen's College, Belfast, from 1881, and Edinburgh University; MB MCh (Edin) 1896; medical officer and public vaccinator to the Parish of Kirkinner, of Beechwood, Wigtonshire, from c 1900; general practitioner, of 5 Brookville, Whitehead c 1915, of 6 Stranmillis Road, Belfast c 1920, and of Hampton Cottage, 68 Balmoral Avenue, from c 1925; married Deborah Mary Harden; father of Dr Joseph Molyneaux Hunter, MB BCh BAO (QUB) 1924, MD 1929, of 'Carrig-Nata', Portrush, county Antrim; died 19 August 1947 at 68 Balmoral Avenue, Belfast; probate Belfast 19 January 1948. [Belf GRO (d); Belf PRO, will cal; Fry (1984); Kirkpatrick Archive; *Med Dir*; QCB adm reg].

HUNTER, JOHN CHAINE (1814/5–48), Kilrea, county Londonderry;

born 1814/5; surgeon, of Tamlaght O'Crilly Dispensary; general practitioner, of Kilrea; died 11 January 1848 at his home in Kilrea, of typhus fever 'caught in the discharge of his duties'. [*BNL* 18 January 1848 (d); *Coleraine Chronicle* 22 January 1848 (d); Croly (1843–6); *Londonderry Sentinel* 22 January 1848 (d)].

HUNTER, JOSEPH MOLYNEUX (1833–84), ship's surgeon and Nowchwang, China;

born 1833, son of John Hunter of 3 Little George's Street, Belfast; educated by Samuel Bullick of Belfast; worked in business in Belfast c 1852–4; studied medicine at Queen's College, Belfast, from c 1854; LFPS Glas 1857; medical officer with Allan Line and Montreal Steamship Company on SS *Peruvian*; medical missionary in Nowchwang, China, from 1870; married 17 February 1869 in Linenhall Presbyterian Church, Belfast, Elizabeth Jane Smyth (who died 1871), daughter of Robert Smyth, merchant, of Belfast; father of Dr John Arnold Hunter (*q.v.*); died 8 May 1880 at sea; buried at sea; administration Dublin 8 August 1884 and London 28 August 1884. [Boyd (1908) and (1940); Dub GRO (m); Lond PPR, will cal; *Med Dir;* QCB adm reg].

HUNTER, MICHAEL (d 1857), Limavady, county Londonderry, and Melbourne, Victoria;

studied medicine at Glasgow University; MD (Glas) 1842; LRCS Edin 1842; of Limavady; emigrated to Australia as surgeon on SS *Broughton Hall*; general practitioner, of Melbourne; married 6 March 1845 in Ballykelly Church of Ireland Church (Tamlaght Finlagan), Adele Pierre, eldest daughter of David Frederick Petit Pierre of Neufchatel, Switzerland; died 19 May 1857 in Melbourne. [Addison (1898); *Coleraine Chronicle* 15 March 1845 (m) and 29 August 1857 (d); *Londonderry Sentinel* 22 March 1845 (m) and 28 August 1857 (d); *Med Dir*].

HUNTER, MITCHELL (1850/1–1925), Sunderland, county Durham;
born 1850/1 at Rowansgift, Castledawson, county Londonderry; MD (Miami Medical College, Cincinnati) 1871; LSA Lond 1882; general practitioner and certifying factory surgeon, of 13 Foyle Street, Borough Road, and later of 8 Park Terrace, Sunderland; surgeon to the Durham Light Infantry (Territorials); general practitioner of Magherafelt c 1905–24; retired to 56 Bryansburn Road, Bangor, county Down c 1924; married —; died 6 January 1925 at 56 Bryansburn Road. [Belf GRO (d); Kirkpatrick Archive; Maitland (1988); *Med Dir*].

HUNTER, ROBERT (1841–1901), Kilrea, county Londonderry, and Sydney, New South Wales;
born 31 March 1841 at Kilrea, son of Thomas Hunter of Kilrea; educated at Coleraine Academical Institution; studied medicine at Queen's College, Belfast, from 1861; LRCS Edin 1867; LRCP Edin 1873; general practitioner, of Kilrea c 1868–80; emigrated to Australia c 1880; general practitioner of 29 Clarence Street, Church Hill, Sydney from c 1880 and of 22 Jamieson Street, Church Hill c 1895; died 1901. [*Med Dir*; QCB adm reg].

HUNTER, ROBERT LINDSAY (1839–1900), Larne, county Antrim;
born 1 March 1839 at Cairncastle, county Antrim, son of Samuel Hunter, farmer, of Cairncastle; educated at Larne Grammar School; studied medicine at Queen's College, Belfast, from 1864 and at the City of Dublin Hospital; MD (QUI) 1868; MCh 1870; LM 1870; assistant surgeon to the International Ambulance Corps during the Franco-Prussian War; medical officer to Larne Dispensary District and constabulary; general practitioner in Larne and Admiralty Surgeon for Larne District; married 27 November 1884 in the house of Mr R. Nelson, Jane Alexander, daughter of Samuel Alexander, merchant, of Larne; died 12 January 1900; probate Belfast 2 April 1900. [Belf PRO, will cal; Dub GRO (m) and (d); *Med Dir*; QCB adm reg; UHF database (m)].

HUNTER, ROBERT SHAW (1841–c 1880), Belfast;
born March 1841 at Ballynahinch, county Down, son of James Hunter of Maybrook, Ballynahinch; educated privately; studied medicine at Queen's College, Belfast, from 1866; LRCP LRCS Edin 1873; general practitioner, of Newtownards Road, Belfast; died c 1880. [*Med Dir*; QCB adm reg].

HUNTER, SAMUEL (1810/1–66), Belfast;
born 1810/1, son of John Hunter of Aghadowey, county Londonderry; studied medicine at the Royal College of Surgeons in Ireland and Edinburgh University; LRCSI 1835; accoucheur of Dublin Lying-in Hospital (Rotunda); MD (Edin) 1837

(thesis 'A practical treatise on ruptured urethra produced by external violence – illustrated by cases'); FRCSI 1844; attending surgeon to the Belfast Fever Hospital 1841–45; general practitioner, of 3 Fountainville Terrace, Belfast; married 13 May 1841 in Dunmurry Non-Subscribing Presbyterian Church, Elizabeth Hunter, daughter of William Hunter of Dunmurry House, county Antrim; died 10 February 1866 at 3 Fountainville Terrace after 15 years of paraplegia; probate Belfast 2 March 1866. [*Belf Fev Hosp, Ann Reps*; *BNL* 18 May 1841 (m); Belf PRO, will cal; Croly (1843–6); Dub GRO (d); Edin Univ; *Londonderry Sentinel* 22 May 1841 (m); Malcolm (1851); *Med Dir*].

HUNTER, SAMUEL ROGER (1861/2–1917), Armagh and Clapham, London;
born 1861/2, son of John Hunter, architect, of Armagh; studied medicine at at the Royal College of Surgeons in Ireland and Queen's College, Cork; LM Coombe Hosp Dub 1884; MD MCh (RUI) 1884; LAH Dub 1889; surgical resident in the South Infirmary, Cork; general practitioner, of 10 Scotch Street, Armagh c 1885; medical officer to the South London Branch of Dr Barnardo's Homes, Clapham Dispensary and the Post Office, of Lynher House, Clapham, from c 1890 and finally of 2 Clapham Mansions, Nightingale Lane, Surrey; married 4 August 1886 in Gilford Methodist Church, county Down, Marion Montgomery Weir, daughter of the Rev Samuel Weir, Methodist minister, of Gilford; died 30 August 1917 at 2 Clapham Mansions; probate London 29 October 1917. [Fry (1984), girls; Lond GRO (d); Lond PPR, will cal; *Med Dir*; UHF database (m)].

HUNTER, WILLIAM (d 1829), Moy and Charlemont, county Tyrone;
surgeon and accoucheur, of Moy and Charlemont c 1824; married —; father of Dr William James Hunter (*q.v.*) and of Mary Jane Hunter who married in 1824; died 11 June 1829 at home in Moy. [*BNL* 24 May 1824 (m, daughter) and 19 June 1829 (d); Pigot (1824)].

HUNTER, WILLIAM BROWN (1844/5–1928), Jedburgh, Roxburgh, Littleport, Cambridgeshire, and Londonderry;
born 1844/5 in county Londonderry; educated in Londonderry; studied medicine at Edinburgh University; MB CM (Edin) 1866; MD 1869; general practitioner, of Jedburgh, from c 1870; medical officer of health to Littleport; general practitioner, of Londonderry, from c 1885; a moving force for opening an EENT hospital in Bridge Street, Londonderry, in 1894; retired c 1926 to 40 Hawkins Street, Londonderry; married — (who died c 1878); died 22 October 1928 at 40 Hawkins Street; probate Londonderry 30 November 1928. [Belf GRO (d); Belf PRO, will cal; Johnston (1960); Kirkpatrick (1889); Kirkpatrick Archive; *Med Dir*].

HUNTER, WILLIAM JAMES (d 1844), Naval Medical Service;
only son of surgeon William Hunter of Moy; joined the Naval Medical Service as assistant surgeon 1814; surgeon to the Royal Marine Infirmary, Woolwich; died 22 November 1844 at the Royal Marine Infirmary. [*BNL* 6 December 1844 (d); *NMS* (1826)].

HUNTER, WILLIAM JOHN (1846/7–97), London;
  born 1846/7, fourth son of James Hunter, clothier, of Kilrea, county Londonderry; studied medicine at Glasgow University and St Bartholomew's Hospital, London; LFPS Glas 1874; general practitioner, of 155 St John's Street, Clerkenwell, London c 1875, and of 10 Great Sutton Street, Goswell Road c 1885, and of 34 Aylesbury Street, Clerkenwell Road c 1895; married (1) 9 September 1874, in St Mark's Parish Church, Clerkenwell, Anne Paine (who was born 1853/4), eldest daughter of Harley Paine, hay salesman, of Clerkenwell; (2) Rose Maria —; died 11 July 1897 at 'High Bank', St James's Avenue, Brighton; administration London 12 August 1897. [Kirkpatrick Archive; Lond GRO (m) and (d); Lond PPR, will cal; *Med Dir*].

HUNTER, WILLIAM MATTHEW (1876–1958), Crumlin, county Antrim;
  born 21 September 1876 at Antrim, son of Kennedy Hunter, merchant, of Mount Oriel, Antrim; educated at RBAI; studied medicine at Queen's College, Belfast, from 1894; MB BCh BAO (RUI) 1899; house surgeon at the Royal Victoria Hospital, Belfast; medical officer to Crumlin Dispensary District and certifying factory surgeon; coroner for county Antrim; retired 1955 to 'Carncairn', 9 Malone Gardens, Dunmurry; married 10 June 1902 in First Antrim Presbyterian Church, Mary Morrison (who died 28 May 1958), daughter of William Morrison, farmer, of Crookedstone; father of Mr Kennedy Hunter, MB (QUB) 1930, FRCS, ENT surgeon to the Royal Victoria Hospital; died 8 May 1958 at Carncairn; probate Belfast 7 July 1958. [Belf PRO, wil cal; *BMJ* obituary (1958); *Med Dir*; QCB adm reg; UHF database (m)].

HURST, CHARLES (1805/6–75), Belfast;
  born 1805/6, son of Charles Hurst, merchant, of Donaghadee, county Down, and Maryann —; studied medicine at Edinburgh University; LRCS Edin 1829; MD (Edin) 1839 (thesis 'On the physical, chemical and medical properties of water'); lecturer in medical jurisprudence at RBAI; general practitioner, of Ashfield House, Ballinafeigh, Belfast; author of several medical papers; married 1 April 1851 in Newtownbreda Presbyterian Church, Mary Frazer of Locust Lodge, county Down, widow (who was born 1808/9), daughter of Joseph Singleton, merchant; died 19 January 1875 at Ashfield House; buried in Donaghadee graveyard; probate Belfast 24 February 1875. [*BNL* 2 April 1851 (m); Belf PRO, will cal; Clarke, *County Down*, vol 16 (1976); Croly (1843–6); Dub GRO (m) and (d); Edin Univ; *Med Dir*].

HURST, HUGH FRAZER (1846/7–1913), Edinburgh and Walker-on-Tyne, Northumberland;
  born 1846/7; educated by the Rev G.H. Wilson; studied arts and medicine at Queen's College, Belfast, from 1864; LRCP LRCS Edin 1874; general practitioner, of 2 Brighton Terrace, Portobello, Edinburgh, c 1875 and of Dene House, Walker-on-Tyne, from c 1880; medical officer of health to Walker-on-Tyne c 1890 and consulting surgeon to the hospital c 1905; surgeon lieutenant-colonel in the Northumberland Fusiliers (volunteers); JP for Northumberland; of Lumeah, Shaftoe, Leages, Hexham; retired to 3 Braid Crescent, Edinburgh c 1906; married Maria Smyth; died 16 January 1913 at Cluny Place, Morningside, Edinburgh; confirmation

of will Edinburgh 18 February 1913. [Edin GRO (d); Edin, Nat Arch, will cal; *Med Dir*; QCB adm reg].

HURST, JAMES TAYLOR (1793–1847), Army Medical Service and Clones, county Monaghan;

born 11 November 1793, son of the Rev James Hurst, rector of Aghabog, county Fermanagh, and Summer Taylor; studied medicine at Edinburgh University; MRCSE 1812; MD (Edin) 1817 (thesis 'De aneurismate'); accoucheur of Edin Lying-in Hospital; joined the Army Medical Service as surgeon's mate 1812; assistant surgeon to 47th Foot 1813; half pay December 1814–August 1815 and March 1816–July 1817; transferred to 33rd Foot; served in Peninsula War 1812–14; retired on half pay 1818; physician, of Clones c 1824; medical officer to Clones Fever Hospital, Dispensary and Union Workhouse; married May 1823 at Bailieborough, county Cavan, Margaret Kellett, only daughter of Young Kellett of Wilton, county Cavan; died 2 August 1847 at Clones. [Croly (1843–6); Edin Univ; Leslie (1929); Peterkin and Johnston (1968); Pigot (1824); *Strabane Morning Post* 27 May 1823 (m)].

HUSTON, ALEXANDRINA CRAWFORD (b 1874), India;

born 10 October 1874 in Randalstown, daughter of the Rev James Brown Huston, minister of Randalstown and Aghadowey Presbyterian Churches, and Anne Crawford; educated at Victoria College, Belfast; studied medicine at Queen's College, Belfast, from 1894; MB BCh BAO (RUI) 1899; worked with the Presbyterian Missionary Society in Broach, India, from c 1901; missionary in Anand, Bombay c 1925; married the Rev Hamilton Martin, missionary in India 1896–1930, who died 25 November 1935 in Portstewart, son of Robert Martin of Ballynahinch. [Barkley (1986) and (1987b); Kelly (2010); *Med Dir*; QCB adm reg].

HUSTON, CHARLES TODD (1823–75), Tynan, county Armagh;

born 1823; LM Rot Hosp Dub 1846; LRCSI and LM 1848; general practitioner, of Dartan Ree, Tynan; married 12 November 1853 in St Thomas's Church of Ireland Church, Dublin, Catherine Jane Barton (minor), second daughter of Hugh Hawthorn Barton, solicitor, of 161 Lower Gloucester Street, Dublin; died 11 May 1875 at Tynan; probate Armagh 10 September 1875. [*BNL* 16 November 1853 (m); Belf PRO, will cal, will; Brett (1999); Dub GRO (m) and (d); *Med Dir*].

HUSTON, DAVID (*fl c* 1870–72), Gosforth, Cumberland;

of Portrush, county Antrim; studied medicine at Glasgow University; MB (Glas) 1870; LRCS and LM Edin 1870; general practitioner, of Gosforth, from c 1871; died c 1872. [Addison (1898); *Med Dir*].

HUSTON, JAMES (*fl c* 1880), Rasharkin, country Antrim;

son of Joseph Hunter, farmer; surgeon, of Rasharkin; married 3 September 1880 in Rasharkin Presbyterian Church, Mary Thompson of Garvagh, daughter of the Rev Andrew Thompson of Paisley, Scotland, minister of Third Garvagh Presbyterian Church. [Bailie and Kirkpatrick (2005); UHF database (m)].

HUSTON, JAMES (1864/5–1931), Carrickfergus, county Antrim;
born 23 September 1864 at Carrickfergus, son of John Huston, farmer, of Middle Division, Carrickfergus; educated at the University, Law and Military College, Belfast; studied arts and medicine at Queen's College, Belfast, from 1885; BA (RUI) 1888; MB BCh BAO 1895; MD 1908; general practitioner, of 13 West Street, and later of Cranagh Bawn, Carrickfergus; married —; father of Dr Robert Jennings Huston of Carrickfergus; died 11 July 1931 at Governor's Place, Carrickfergus; probate Belfast 6 October 1931. [Belf GRO (d); Belf PRO, will cal; Irwin (1931); Kirkpatrick Archive; *Med Dir*; QCB adm reg].

HUSTON, JOHN (1769/70–1850), Dundrum, county Down;
born 1769/70; general practitioner; died 10 August 1850 in Dundrum. [*BNL* 20 August 1850 (d)].

HUSTON, ROBERT, senior (1759/60–1855), Coleraine, county Londonderry;
born 1759/60; LAH Dub; surgeon and apothecary, of Church Street, Coleraine c 1785–1855; member (and last survivor) of the Volunteer Yeomanry Cavalry of Coleraine and served during the 1798 rising; town commissioner for Coleraine; died 20 February 1855 at Church Street. [*Coleraine Chronicle* 3 March 1855 (d); Croly (1843–6); Pigot (1824)].

HUSTON, ROBERT, junior (1791/2–1851), Coleraine, county Londonderry;
born 1791/2; LAH Dub; apothecary and surgeon, of Coleraine c 1824–46; town commissioner for Coleraine; married Frances Macky Bowker (who was born 1800/1 and died 30 December 1847 at Rothesay House), daughter of William Bowker of Deansgate, Bolton, Lancashire; father of Alice Huston who married Dr James Stewart of Liverpool (*q.v.*), of Dr Charles Todd Huston (*q.v.*) and of Robert Huston who married 10 March 1859 Rebecca Neill, daughter of Dr Alexander Neill (*q.v.*); died 28 November 1851 at Rothsay House, Ferryquay Street, Coleraine. [*BNL* 1 December 1851 (d); *Coleraine Chronicle* 22 January 1848 (d), 29 November 1851 (d) and 12 March 1859 (m, son); Croly (1843–6); Dub GRO (m, son); *Londonderry Sentinel* 5 May 1849 (d); Pigot (1824)].

HUSTON, ROBERT FRANCIS (1871–c 1907), Belfast and South Africa;
born 10 October 1871 in Belfast, son of George Huston, flesher, of Old Park Road, Belfast; educated at Belfast Royal Academy; studied medicine at Queen's College, Belfast, from 1889; LRCP LRCS Edin 1898; LFPS Glas 1898; general practitioner, of Arvagh House, Cavehill Road, Belfast; died c 1907 in South Africa. [*Med Dir*; QCB adm reg].

HUSTON (HOUSTON), ROBERT TODD, senior (1782/3–1877), Tynan, county Armagh;
born 1782/3; FRCSI and LM 1844; army surgeon (part-time) 1816 and examiner of army recruits; assistant surgeon to the Kildare Militia; medical officer to Tynan Dispensary District and constabulary c 1837 and 1846; retired c 1850 and moved to

Evergreen Lodge, Carlow, c 1857; married 22 March 1845 in Tynan Church of Ireland Church, Mary Allan, widow of Dr James R. Allen of Caledon and only child of Captain Moore of Drummond, Aughnacloy, county Tyrone; father of Dr Robert Todd Huston, junior (*q.v.*); died 14 August 1877 at Auburn Lodge, Carlow; probate Dublin 15 January 1878. [*BNL* 28 March 1845 (m); Belf PRO, will cal; Croly (1843–6); Dub GRO (d); Lewis (1837); *Londonderry Sentinel* 29 March 1845 (m); *Med Dir*].

HUSTON, ROBERT TODD, junior (1845/6–1926), Tynan, county Armagh;
born 1845/6, son of Dr Robert Todd Huston, senior (*q.v.*); studied medicine at the Royal College of Surgeons in Ireland; LRCSI 1867; LKQCPI and LM 1867; surgeon to the Kildare Rifles; medical officer to Tynan Dispensary District and constabulary, of Dartan Ree, Tynan; married —; died 17 May 1926 at Tynan; probate Belfast 1 September 1926. [Belf GRO (d); Belf PRO, will cal; Brett (1999); *Med Dir*].

HUSTON, WILLIAM (d c 1853), Jonesborough, county Armagh;
MRCSE 1828; surgeon to the dispensary at Dartan Ree, Tynan c 1837; surgeon to Jonesborough and Meigh Dispensary c 1846; later of Culfore Cottage, Dundalk; died 1 December 1852 at Ballymascanlon, county Louth; administration Armagh Diocesan Court 1853. [*BNL* 10 January 1853 (d); Brett (1999); Croly (1843–6); Day and McWilliams, *County Armagh* (1990); Dub Nat Arch, Armagh Dio Admins index; *Med Dir*].

HUTCHESON (HUTCHINSON), HICKS (d 1863), Draperstown, county Londonderry;
LFPS Glas 1821; joined the East India Company as a surgeon [?]; later general practitioner, of Draperstown; of Waterloo Cottage, Cookstown c 1859; married 16 December 1830 in Tamlaght Church of Ireland Church, county Tyrone, Margaret Dunn of Lissan; father of Sarah Hutcheson who married Dr William Taylor of Articlave (*q.v.*); died 10 July 1863 at Draperstown; probate Londonderry 11 August 1863. [Belf PRO, will cal, will; Kirkpatrick Archive; *Londonderry Sentinel* 14 July 1863 (d); *Med Dir*; Tamlaght C of I Church mar reg].

HUTCHINSON, JOHN (1849/50–1934), Lutterworth, Leicestershire and Widness, Lancashire;
born 1849/50; of Kilrea, county Londonderry; studied medicine at Glasgow University; MB CM (Glas) 1877; MD 1879; house physician and house surgeon to the Western Infirmary Glasgow; assistant to the Lock Hospital, Glasgow; medical officer and public vaccinator to Lutterworth 2nd Dispensary District, of Claybrook Magna, Lutterworth, Leicestershire from c 1885; general practitioner and honorary physician to Widness Isolation Hospital, of Springfield, Albert Road, Widness, c 1907–13 and of Claybrook from c 1913; retired c 1925; moved to 42 Headland, Kettering, Northamptonshire c 1933; married Mary Elizabeth —; died 29 January 1934; probate London 1 March 1934. [Addison (1898); Lond GRO (d); Lond PPR, will cal; *Med Dir*].

HUTCHINSON, WILLIAM (c 1866–c 1915), Widness, Lancashire;
born c 1866; of Kilrea, county Londonderry; studied medicine at Glasgow University; MB LM (Glas) 1889; MD 1891; of Drumagarven, Kilrea c 1895; general practitioner of Springfield, Widness, c 1895–1913; described as 'travelling' from c 1910; died c 1915. [Addison (1898); *Med Dir*].

HUTTON, JAMES (*fl c* 1824), Downpatrick, county Down;
surgeon, of Irish Street, Downpatrick c 1824. [Pigot (1824)].

HUTTON, WILLIAM (*fl c* 1815), Belfast, and Cookstown, county Tyrone;
eldest son of William Hutton, merchant, of Belfast; studied arts and medicine at Glasgow University, matriculated 1811; MA (Glas) 1814; MD 1817; surgeon, of Cookstown c 1824. [Addison (1898) and (1913); Pigot (1824)].

HYNDMAN, JAMES (1819–81), Naval Medical Service and Boston, USA;
born 1819 in Londonderry; educated in Londonderry; studied medicine in Dublin and Edinburgh; joined the Naval Medical Service as assistant surgeon; resigned and emigrated to USA 1845; physician, of 46 Bowdoin Street, Boston; retired to England; died 6 May 1881 at the Brook Villa, Green Lane, West Derby, Lancashire, suddenly, from an intestinal rupture (coroner's inquest). [*Boston Transcript* 11 May 1881 (d); Elliott, Simon, pers com; Lond GRO (d)].

HYNDMAN, WILLIAM (1779/80–1841), Naval Medical Service and Hammersmith, London;
born 1779/80 at Magheracolton, Newtownstewart, county Londonderry; joined the Naval Medical Service 1804; served at Buenos Aires, Montevideo and, c 1808, near Spain; married —; died 11 February 1841 at his home at 1 Alpha Cottage, Hammersmith. [*BNL* 16 March 1841 (d); *Londonderry Sentinel* 6 March 1841 (d); *Londonderry Standard* 3 March 1841 (d)].

I

INGHAM (INGRAM), THOMAS (d 1846), Richhill, county Armagh;
    LAH Dub 1799; apothecary, of Richhill; died 21 April 1846 at his home in Mountnorris. [Apothecaries (1829); *BNL* 28 April 1846 (d)].

IRVINE, ALEXANDER (1833–79), Clonmany, county Donegal, and Irvinestown, county Fermanagh;
    born 1833, youngest son of John Irvine of Lisagore, county Fermanagh; studied medicine at the Royal College of Surgeons in Ireland and the city of Dublin Hospital; LM Coombe Hospital, Dublin, 1855; LRCSI 1857; Lic Med 1863; house surgeon and clinical clerk to the City of Dublin Hospital; medical officer to Clonmany Dispensary District and revenue constabulary; medical officer to Irvinestown Dispensary District, Fever Hospital, workhouse and constabulary, of Eglinton Lodge, Irvinestown; married 22 April 1858 in Clonmany Church of Ireland Church, Ellen Doherty, daughter of Michael Doherty of Glen House, county Donegal; died 30 December 1879 at Eglinton Lodge; probate Dublin 5 April 1880. [Belf PRO, will cal; Dub GRO (d); Kirkpatrick Archive; *Londonderry Sentinel* 30 April 1858 (m); *Med Dir*].

IRVINE, ARTHUR GERARD CHEYNE (1864–1925), Birmingham, Warwickshire, and RAMC;
    born 26 April 1864, eldest son of the Rev Arthur Benjamin Irvine, curate of Coleraine and Muff, and later rector of West Bromwich, and Louisa Caroline Brady; MRCSE 1890; LRCP Lond 1890; assistant house surgeon to West Bromwich Hospital; general practitioner of Selly Oak, Birmingham, from c 1891 and medical officer to the Post Office; temporary captain in RAMC during World War I; retired c 1920 to Berkley, Wellington College Station, Berkshire; married 1 May 1895 Charlotte Ellen Katherine Stamps, younger daughter of Thomas Stamps of Berwood, Erdington, Warwickshire; died 20 January 1925; probate London 24 February 1925. [Leslie (1937); Lond PPR, will cal; *Med Dir*; Swanzy (1903)].

IRVINE (IRWIN), CHRISTOPHER (c 1642–1714), Castle Irvine, county Fermanagh;
    born c 1642, eldest son of Dr Christopher Irvine, MD, physician general to the States of Scotland, and Margaret Wishart; MD; succeeded to the Castle Irvine estates, county Fermanagh, on the death of his uncle, Sir Gerard Irvine; High Sheriff of county Fermanagh 1690; MP for county Fermanagh 1695–9 and 1703–13; married 1704 Phoebe Blennerhassett (who died in 1710), daughter of Sir George Hume, Bart., of Castle Hume, and widow of Henry Blennerhassett of Cavendish Castle; died 9 May 1714. [Burke *LGI* (1912); Johnston-Liik (2002)].

IRVINE, CHRISTOPHER (1734/5–96), Johnstown, county Fermanagh;
    born 1734/5; MD [?]; of Johnstown, Lisnaskea; died 21 April 1796; buried in Uttony Graveyard. [Gravestone inscription; *Northern Star* 14 April 1796 (d)].

IRVINE, FRANCIS STEPHEN (1873–1962), Royal Army Medical Corps;
born 26 December 1873 at Belfast, third son of the Rev Richard Irvine, rector of St Stephen's, Belfast, of Derryvolgie, and Frances Stewart, daughter of Dr Robert Stewart (*q.v.*) of the Belfast Hospital for the Insane; brother of Dr Arthur Edmund Stewart Irvine, DSO, LRCPI, LRCSI 1905, of Dumfries, Scotland; educated at Methodist College, Belfast, from 1884; studied medicine at Queen's College, Belfast, from 1891; MB BCh BAO (RUI) 1899; joined the Royal Army Medical Corps as lieutenant 1899; captain 1902; major 1911; lieutenant-colonel 1916; brevet colonel 1924; colonel 1927; served in South Africa 1899–1902, India 1902–05, South Africa 1906–09, France 1914–15; prisoner of war August–September 1914; commandant RAMC School of Instruction and Commanding Officer Depot RAMC 1915–19; DSO 1915; served in India 1920–24; ADMS 1922–4; honorary surgeon to the Viceroy; commanding officer of Cambridge Hospital, Aldershot 1926–7; ADMS London 1927–8; DDMS Northern Command 1928–30; retired 1930–40; re-joined army 1940 as colonel; commandant 1940–46; retired 1946 as major-general; died 3 July 1962 at Queen Alexandra's Military Hospital, Millbank, London; probate London 21 August 1962. [Drew (1968); Fry (1984); Leslie (1993); Lond PPR, will cal; *Med Dir*; QCB adm reg].

IRVINE, GEORGE EDWARD (1850–c 1893), Uruguay;
born 17 March 1850 at Strangford, county Down, son of Thomas Irvine of Poyntzpass, county Armagh; educated at RBAI; studied medicine at Queen's College, Belfast, from 1867; LRCSI 1876; LRCP and LM Edin 1879; general practitioner in San Jose, Uruguay c 1885 and Montevideo c 1890; died c 1893. [*Med Dir*; QCB adm reg].

IRVINE, GERARD (1815/6–65) Irvinestown, county Fermanagh;
born 1815/6, son of Charles Irvine, farmer; studied medicine at Glasgow University; MD CM (Glas) 1836; LFPS Glas 1843; accoucheur of the Anglesey Lying-in Hospital; general practitioner of Lowtherstown (Irvinestown) c 1845; medical officer to the constabulary; of 'The Bungalow', Irvinestown; married 16 February 1847 in Kilsheery Church of Ireland Church, Rebecca Armstrong, daughter of David Armstrong, farmer, of Tattykeeran; father of Elizabeth Isabella Irvine who married Dr Oliver Barnett, surgeon, 11th Hussars (*q.v.*); died 17 November 1865 at 'The Bungalow'; administration Dublin 30 January 1866. [Addison (1898); Belf PRO, will cal; Croly (1843–6); Dub GRO (m) and (d); *Londonderry Sentinel* 21 November 1865 (d) and 26 June 1866 (m, daughter); *Med Dir*].

IRVINE, GERARD BEATTY (1863–c 1955), Indian Medical Service;
born 15 August 1863; of Lisnagore Lodge, Irvinestown, county Fermanagh; studied medicine at the Royal College of Surgeons in Ireland and the Carmichael School, Dublin; LRCSI LKQCPI and LM 1885; joined the Indian Medical Service (Bengal establishment) as surgeon 1887; major 1899; lieutenant-colonel 1907; served on North-West Frontier at Waziristan 1894–5 (medal with clasp) and at Tochi 1897–8 (medal with clasp); also in Somaliland 1903–04 (medal with clasp) and World War I 1914–18; retired 1918; CB; died c 1955. [Crawford (1930); *Med Dir*].

IRVINE, GILBERT MARSHALL (1865–1940), Mountnorris, county Armagh;
born 23 December 1865 at Mountnorris, son of Joseph James Irvine, farmer, of Mountnorris; educated at Coleraine Academical Institution; studied arts and medicine at Queen's College, Cork 1884–6, and from 1888, at Queen's College, Belfast; BA (RUI) 1888; MB BCh BAO 1895; medical officer to Mountmorris Dispensary District and constabulary; certifying factory surgeon; author of *The Lions Whelp* (a novel) and *In the Valley of Vision*; married Mary —; died 22 June 1940 at Mountnorris; probate Belfast 17 October 1940. [Belf GRO (d); Belf PRO, will cal; Kirkpatrick Archive; *Med Dir*; QCB adm reg].

IRVINE, HUGH ROBINSON (1870–1950), Belfast;
born 28 May 1870 at Hillsborough, county Down, son of Dr James Irvine (*q.v.*) of Belfast; educated at Sullivan Upper School, Holywood; studied medicine at Queen's University, Belfast, from 1888; LRCP LRCS Edin 1895; LFPS Glas 1895; of Lonsdale Villa, Strandtown, Belfast, from 1888; resident medical officer to Belfast Union Infirmary; general practitioner and medical officer to Belfast No 13 and Castlereagh No 1 Dispensary Districts; of 406 Upper Newtownards Road, Belfast; died 28 December 1950 at 406 Upper Newtownards Road; administration (with will) Belfast 23 April 1952. [Belf PRO, will cal; Belf GRO (d); Kirkpatrick Archive; *Med Dir*; QCB adm reg].

IRVINE, JAMES (*fl c* 1800), Bangor, county Down;
eldest son of Robert Irvine of Lisbane, county Down, and Mary Magee of Toddstown; surgeon, of Bangor c 1800. [Jones (1977)].

IRVINE, JAMES (1844–1902), Belfast;
born 1844 at Cabra, county Down, son of William Irvine, farmer, of Cabra; educated at Ballycrune School; studied medicine at Queen's College, Galway, and from 1861, at Queen's College, Belfast, and Belfast General Hospital; LRCP Edin 1867; LFPS Glas 1867; of Lisburn Street, Hillsborough, county Down; medical officer to Castlereagh No 3 Dispensary District, Belfast, of Llandaff Villa, Belmont Park, Sydenham, from 1872; married 1 January 1868 in Maze Presbyterian Church, Jemima Stockman, daughter of James Stockman of the Maze, county Down; father of Dr Hugh Robinson Irvine (*q.v.*); died 29 April 1902 at Belfast; probate Belfast 29 May 1902. [Belf PRO, will cal; Dub GRO (m); *Med Dir*; QCB adm reg; UHF database (m)].

IRVINE, JAMES FERGUS (1793–1872), Ballykelly, county Londonderry, and Pennsylvania and Ohio, USA;
born 1793, second son of James Irvine, farmer, of near Ballykelly; studied arts at Glasgow University from 1811; MA (Glas) 1814; licensed by the Route Presbytery 1817; emigrated to USA; studied medicine in Pennsylvania 1832; MD (Pa) 1834; first minister of the new Largy Presbyterian Church, county Londonderry 1834–46; returned to USA 1846; president of New Brighton College, Pennsylvania, and a college in Ohio 1851–65; retired 1865; died 4 May 1872 in Newark, Ohio. [Addison (1898) and (1913); Bailie *et al* (1982); McConnell (1951)].

IRVINE, JAMES PEARSON, junior (1842–80), Liverpool, Lancashire, and London; born 13 March 1842, third son of Dr James Pearson Irvine, senior, of Galgate, Lancashire; brother of Dr William Johnstone Irvine (*q.v.*); educated at the Royal Grammar School, Lancashire; studied medicine at University College, London, and from 1861, at Queen's College, Belfast, also at Liverpool Royal Infirmary; BA (Lond) 1862; BSc (hons); LRCP LRCS Edin 1864; MD 1871; MRCP Lond 1874; general practitioner, of Liverpool c 1872 and of 3 Mansfield Street, Cavendish Square, London, from 1874; assistant physician to Charing Cross Hopsital 1874–80, also lecturer in botany 1874–6 and forensic medicine 1875–80; demonstrator of morbid anatomy; physician to the Victoria Hospital for Children; married Janet —; died 15 October 1880 at 3 Mansfield Street; administration London 14 December 1880. [*Lancet* obituary (1880); Lond PPR, will cal; *Med Dir; Munk's Roll*, vol 4; QCB adm reg].

IRVINE, JOHN (*fl c* 1799–1824), Naval Medical Service and Newtownstewart, county Tyrone;
joined the Naval Medical Service as assistant surgeon; surgeon 1799; retired; surgeon, of Newtownstewart c 1824; married —; his daughter, Margaret Irvine, married 27 December 1839 Richard Yeatley of Dublin; died before 1840. [*BNL* 7 January 1840 (m, daughter); *NMS* (1826); Pigot (1824)].

IRVINE, JOHN (1784/5–1857), Naval Medical Service and Moville, county Donegal; born 1784/5; joined the Naval Medical Service as assistant surgeon 1803; surgeon 1805; MRCSE 1807; medical officer to Moville Dispensary and constabulary c 1846, of Rosebank, Moville, married Rebecca — (who died 1 June 1858 at Rosebank); died 3 July 1857 at Rosebank. [*Coleraine Chronicle* 11 July 1857 (d); Croly (1843–6); Kirkpatrick Archive; *Londonderry Sentinel* 10 July 1857 (d) and 4 June 1858 (d); *Med Times and Gazette* obituary (1857); *NMS* (1826)].

IRVINE, JOHN JAMES (1859/60–97), Clonmany, county Donegal;
born 1859/60, son of — Irvine and Ellen Doherty; LRCSI 1881; LKQCPI and LM 1882; general practitioner, of Glen House, Clonmany; unmarried; died 18 November 1897 at Glen House; buried in Clonmany Graveyard; administration (with will) Dublin 14 February 1898. [Belf PRO, will cal; Dub GRO (d); *Med Dir; Memorials of the Dead,* vol XII, p 197].

IRVINE, JOHN WILLIAM (1860–98), Patricroft and Clayton-le-Moors, Lancashire; born 26 September 1860 at San Franciso, California, son of George Irvine of Los Angeles; educated at Banbridge Academy; studied medicine at Queen's College, Belfast, from 1879; LRCP LRCS Edin 1884; general practitioner of 1 Myrtle Villas, New Lane, Patricroft, from c 1885 and later of 12 Mill Street, Clayton-le-Moors; died 12 November 1897; administration Lancaster 15 April 1898. [Lond PPR, will cal; *Med Dir;* QCB adm reg].

IRVINE, MATTHEW (*fl c* 1775), Pennsylvania, USA, and United States Army;
born near Enniskillen, county Fermanagh; brother of Dr William Irvine of Pennsylvania (*q.v.*); emigrated to USA; served in Thompson's Pennsylvania Rifle

Battalion until 1775; surgeon in General Henry Lee's Dragoons from 1778 until end of the war in 1783. [Kennedy (2005)].

IRVINE, RICHARD ALEXANDER (1858/9–1919), Oldham, Lancashire, Glasgow, Lanarkshire, and London;
   born 1858/9 at Castlederg, county Tyrone; educated at Londonderry Academy; studied medicine at Queen's College, Galway, 1877–8 and at Queen's College, Belfast, from 1878; LSA Lond 1891; chloroformist and assistant surgeon to Oldham Infirmary; clinical assistant to Glasgow Royal Infirmary; assistant medical officer to Wandworth Provident Dispensary; general practitioner, of 67 Pitfield Street, London c 1895 and of Stanmore Villas, 238 Forest Road, Walthamstow c 1905; married Jane Barnard —; died 14 February 1919; administration London 28 March 1919. [Lond PPR, will cal; *Med Dir*; QCB adm reg].

IRVINE, ROBERT (d 1900), Edinburgh and South Africa;
   son of Rev … Irvine of Londonderry [not identified]; studied medicine at Edinburgh University and the Royal College of Surgeons of Edinburgh; MB CM (Edin) 1896; house surgeon in Edinburgh Royal Infirmary; demonstrator in anatomy in the Surgeon's Hall, Edinburgh; resident surgeon at Edinburgh Royal Infirmary c 1897, of 19 Marchmont Road, Edinburgh; civil surgeon in the army during the Boer War 1900; died 26 May 1900 at Ladysmith, South Africa, of typhoid fever. [*BMJ* obituary (1900); *Med Dir*].

IRVINE, ROBERT (1866/7–1928), Mansfield, Nottinghamshire;
   born 17 May 1867, at Ballymullerty, Newtownstewart, county Tyrone, son of James Irvine, farmer, of Ballymullerty, and Matilda Margaret Moorehead; educated at RBAI; studied medicine at Queen's College, Belfast, from 1886; LRCP LRCS Edin 1895; LFPS Glas; general practitioner, of Huthwaite, Mansfield; medical officer of health for Hucknall and Huthwaite; surgeon to New Hucknall Colliery Company and Midland Railway, of 7 Market Street, Huthwaite; married Mary Florence —; died 2 September 1928 at 20 Regent Street, Nottingham; administration Nottingham 15 February 1929. [Dub GRO (b); Lond PPR, will cal; *Med Dir*; QCB adm reg].

IRVINE, THOMAS (*fl c* 1824), Castleblaney, county Monaghan;
   apothecary, of Muckno Street, Castleblaney c 1824. [Pigot (1824)].

IRVINE, WILLIAM (1741–1804), Army Medical Service, Naval Medical Service, Philadelphia, USA, and United State Army;
   born 3 November 1741 near Enniskillen, county Fermanagh; brother of Dr Matthew Irvine of Pennsylvania (*q.v.*); joined the Army Medical Service as surgeon to 12th Dragoons 1759; resigned 1760; served with the Royal Navy as surgeon c 1760–67; emigrated to Pennsylvania c 1764, where he practiced medicine; commanded 6th Pennsylvania regiment in the revolutionary war from c 1776; colonel 1777; brigadier 1779; taken prisoner at Trois Rivieres in 1776, released on parole and exchanged in 1778; a member of the court martial that tried General Lee; commanded 2nd Pennsylvania Infantry in 1778; brigadier 1779; entrusted with the defence of the North-West frontier of the United States in 1781; commandant of Fort Pitt 1781–3;

granted land by the State of Pennsylvania for his services in the War and appointed land agent in 1785; member of congress 1786–88 and 1793–5; held many state and military posts; superintendent of military stores 1800–04; married in Carlisle, Pennsylvania, Anne Callender, daughter of Captain Robert Callender; died 29 July 1804 in Philadelphia of cholera; portrait painted by Robert Edge Pine. [Crone (1928); *DAB* (1932); *DIB* (2009); Kennedy (2005); Kirkpatrick Archive; Martin (2010); Newmann (1993); *Oxford DNB* (2004); Peterkin and Johnston (1968)].

IRVINE, WILLIAM (1845–1926), Liverpool, Lancashire;
born 17 May 1845, son of Alexander Irvine of 40 York Street, Belfast; educated at Belfast Academy; studied arts and medicine at Queen's College, Belfast, from 1862; BA (QUI) 1868; MD MCh (QUI) 1869; medical officer to the Parish Infirmary, Liverpool, c 1875; physcian to Liverpool Consumption Hospital; general practitioner, of 18 Peel Street, Prince's Park, Liverpool c 1880–1920; retired c 1920 and moved c 1925 to 33 Rappart Road, Egremont, Cheshire and later to 6 Denton Drive, Wallasey, Cheshire; unmarried; died 22 July 1926 at 6 Denton Drive; probate London 10 September 1926. [Lond PPR, will cal; will; *Med Dir*; QCB adm reg].

IRVINE, WILLIAM JOHN (1852–88), Nottingham;
born 18 October 1852 at Castlederg, county Tyrone, son of Richard Irvine, farmer, of Castlederg; educated at Castlederg Academy; studied medicine at Queen's College, Galway, and from 1873, at Queen's College, Belfast; LRCS Edin 1878; general practitioner, of Oxford Villa, Alford Street South, Nottingham, c 1885; died 2 October 1888. [*Med Dir*; QCB adm reg].

IRVINE, WILLIAM JOHNSTONE (1839/40–72), Aintree and Walton-on-the-Hill, Lancashire;
born 1839/40, son of Dr James Pearson Irvine of Galgate, Lancashire; brother of Dr James Pearson Irvine, junior (*q.v.*); educated at the Royal Grammar School, Lancaster; studied medicine at Queen's College, Belfast, from 1860; LRCS and LM Edin 1862; LSA Lond 1862; general practitioner, of Warbreck Moor, Aintree, and later of Walton-on-the-Hill; unmarried; died 7 December 1872 at Walton-on-the-Hill; administration Liverpool 27 December 1872. [Lond PPR, will cal; *Med Dir*; QCB adm reg].

IRVINE, WILLIAM SKIPTON (1840/1–65), Eglinton, county Londonderry;
born 1840/1; studied medicine at Edinburgh University; MD (Edin) 1864 (thesis 'On the reciprocal relation between heart and lungs in health and disease'); LRCS Edin 1864; general practitioner, of Fawney and Tamneymore, Eglinton; unmarried; died 19 March 1865 at Londonderry County Infirmary of typhus fever; probate Londonderry 13 April 1865. [Belf PRO, will cal; *Coleraine Chronicle* 25 March 1865 (d); Dub GRO (d); Edin Univ; *Londonderry Sentinel* 21 March 1865 (d); *Med Dir*].

IRVING (IRVINE), SAMUEL (d 1806), Army Medical Service;
son of Dr Thomas Irving of Lisburn, county Antrim (*q.v.*); studied medicine at Edinburgh University 1791–3 and 1798–1800; hospital mate c 1793; joined the

Army Medical Service 1795 as surgeon to the 2nd battalion of the 29th Foot; on half pay with the 107th Foot 1795–8; MA MD (St Andrews) 1796 (on testimonials); with the 52nd Foot 1798; staff surgeon 1799; on half pay 1802–06; physician to the Forces 1806; married Jane — (who was born 1739/40 and died 7 January 1837 in the house of her son, Colonel James Irving in West Maitland Street, Edinburgh); died 20 June 1806. [*BNL* 8 July 1806 (d) and 27 January 1837 (d); *Munk's Roll* III, 29; Peterkin and Johnston (1968); Smart (2004)].

IRVING, THOMAS (d 1797), Army Medical Service and Lisburn, county Antrim;
joined the Army Medical Service as surgeon to HM 14th Regiment of Dragoons 1747 and again 1760; resigned 1774; surgeon to the Antrim County Infirmary, Lisburn for 20 years; married —; father of Dr Samuel Irving (*q.v.*); died 17 April 1797; buried in Lisburn Cathedral Graveyard; 'His high character was established equally as a man, a scholar and a Christian' (Malcolm);. [*BNL* 24 April 1797 (d); *Lisburn Fam Hist Soc*, vol 2 (2005); Malcolm (1851); Peterkin and Johnston (1968)].

IRVING, — (d 1847), Belfast;
doctor, of Belfast, member of the Belfast Medical Society; died 1847. [Malcolm (1851)].

IRWIN, EDWIN HENRY (1874–1941), Castleblaney, county Monaghan;
born 19 March 1874 in Armagh, son of James Irwin JP, tea merchant, of Scotch Street, Armagh and Martha Boyd; educated at Armagh Royal School c 1880; studied medicine at Edinburgh University; MB MCh (Edin) 1897; FRCS Edin 1904; MD 1908; general practitioner, of The Square, Castleblaney, 1898–1941; married Anna —; his library passed to Magee College, Londonderry; died 3 April 1941 at The Square; probate Dublin 29 August 1941. [Dub GRO (b) and (d); Dub Nat Arch, will cal; Ferrar (1933); Kirkpatrick Archive; *Dir Med*].

IRWIN, FITZJOHN ROBERT (1849–82), Scotstown, county Monaghan, and Kilkeel, county Down;
born 1849, fourth son of John Robert Irwin, gentleman, of Carnagh, county Armagh, and Elizabeth Emily de la Cherois Cromelin of Carrowdore; studied arts and medicine at Trinity College, Dublin, from 1865, the Ledwich School, and the Adelaide, Sir Patrick Dun's and Coombe Hospitals; BA (TCD) 1870; MB 1871; LRCSI 1871; LM RCSI 1871; medical officer to Scotstown Dispensary District, and later to Kilkeel Dispensary District; married 11 March 1880 in Newbliss Church of Ireland Church, county Monaghan, Sarah Murray-Ker, elder daughter of André Allen Murray-Ker, gentleman, of Newbliss; died 19 December 1882 at Kilkeel; probate Dublin 21 February 1883. [Belf PRO, will cal; Burke *LGI* (1912); Dub GRO (m); Kirkpatrick Archive; McCann (2003); *Med Dir;* TCD adm reg; *TCD Cat*, vol II (1896)].

IRWIN, HENRY (*fl c* 1845), Armagh;
LRCSI; FRCSI; surgeon, of Armagh, c 1845. [Croly (1846)].

IRWIN, JAMES (d 1903), Sixmilecross, county Tyrone, and Pembroke, Ontario, Canada;
>LM Dub 1857; MRCSE 1858; general practitioner, of Sixmilecross c 1870; emigrated to Canada; general practitioner, of Pembroke; died 30 June 1903, presumably in Canada. [*Med Dir*].

IRWIN, JAMES ROSS (1855–90), Whitehaven, Cumberland;
>born 15 December 1855 at Ling, county Londonderry, son of Ross Irwin, farmer, of Ling; educated at Londonderry Academical Institution; studied medicine at Queen's College, Belfast, from 1879; LRCP LRCS Edin 1882; general practitioner, of 4 Irish Street, Whitehaven, c 1885; died 13 October 1890 at Irish Street; probate Carlisle 18 November 1890. [Lond PPR, will cal; *Med Dir*; QCB adm reg].

IRWIN, JOHN WILLIAM (1860–1901), Oldham, Lancashire;
>born 30 August 1860 at Newbliss, county Monaghan, son of John Irwin, merchant, of Newbliss; educated at Monaghan Model School; studied medicine at Queen's College, Belfast, from 1880; MD (RUI) 1886; general practitioner, of 1 Werneth Hall Road, Oldham; married Sara Jane —; died 12 June 1901; administration London 14 August 1901. [Lond PPR, will cal; *Med Dir*; QCB adm reg].

IRWIN, STEWART (1866–1945) Almondsbury, Gloucestershire, and Pershore, Worcestershire;
>born 2 September 1866 at Dungannon, county Tyrone, son of W.S. Irwin, farmer, of Dungannon; educated at Dungannon Royal School; studied medicine at Queen's College, Belfast, from 1884; MB BCh BAO (RUI) 1889; house surgeon to the East Dispensary, Liverpool; surgeon to the Castle Line Steamship Company; medical officer to Almondsbury District, of Olverton, Almondsbury; general practitioner of Pensham Hill, Pershore, from c 1922; of The White Cottage, Spencer Road, New Milton, Hampshire, from c 1932 and of Cheddar, Somerset c 1941; died 30 May 1945 at Cheddar, probate Llandudno 30 July 1945. [Kirkpatrick Archive; Lond PPR, will cal; *Med Dir*; QCB adm reg].

IRWIN, THOMAS, (1756/7–1831), Warrenpoint, county Down;
>born 1756/7; surgeon, of Warrenpoint c 1819 and 1824; married Anna Maria — (who died 15 December 1845 at her home, 10 Upper Mountpleasant Avenue); died 23 September 1831; buried in St Patrick's Graveyard, Newry. [*BNL* 23 December 1845 (d); Bradshaw (1819); Clarke, *County Down*, vol 21 (1998); Pigot (1824)].

IRWIN, WILLIAM (1825/6–83), Belleek, county Fermanagh;
>born 1825/6; studied medicine at the Royal College of Surgeons in Ireland and the City of Dublin Hospital; LM South-East Lying-in Hospital, Dublin, 1847; LRCS and LM Edin 1855; surgeon to Belleek Pottery works and medical officer to Belleek Dispensary District; severely injured 1873; married —; died 7 November 1883 at Belleek; probate Armagh 23 January 1884. [Belf PRO, will cal; Dub GRO (d); Kirkpatrick Archive; *Med Dir*].

IRWIN, WILLIAM (1863–1924), Manorcunningham, county Donegal;
born 1863, of Clady, county Londonderry; studied medicine at the Ledwich School, Dublin; LM Coombe Hosp Dub; LRCP and CM Edin 1874; LRCSI 1874; resident medical officer in Adelaide Hospital, Dublin; medical officer to Manorcunningham Dispensary District from 1875; of Errity House, Manorcunningham; married Margaret Augusta —; father of Dr John A. Irwin; died 7 January 1924 at Errity; probate Dublin 3 June 1924. [Dub GRO (d); Dub Nat Arch, will cal, will; Kirkpatrick Archive; *Med Dir*].

IRWIN, WILLIAM NASSAU (1805/6–82), Castleblaney, county Monaghan;
born 1805/6; LRCSI 1829; LRCP Lond 1841; MD (St Andrews) 1864 (by examination); medical officer to Castleblaney Workhouse, Crossmaglen Dispensary District and constabulary; later of Terkeeran House, county Monaghan; married Charlotte —; died 5 September 1882 at Terkeeran House; probate Dublin 6 November 1882. [Belf PRO, will cal; Croly (1843–6); Dub GRO (d); *Med Dir*; Smart (2004)].

IRWIN, — (*fl c* 1800), Tynan, county Armagh;
surgeon, of Mount Irwin, Tynan; married —; his daughter Jane Irwin married c 1800 Dr William Black (*q.v.*) of Newry. [Clarke, *County Down*, vol 21 (1998); *Newry Telegraph* 1800 (m, daughter)].

IVERS, CHARLES FERGUSON (1823/4–82), Ballyshannon, county Donegal;
born 1823/4; LAH Dub 1854; apothecary and general practitioner, of Ballyshannon c 1870; married —; died 14 September 1882 at Ballyshannon; administration Londonderry 6 January 1883. [Belf PRO, will cal; Dub GRO (d); *Med Dir*].

IVERS, DANIEL CONWAY (d 1853), Ballyshannon, county Donegal;
MFPS Glas; LAH Dub 1827; accoucheur of Glasgow Lying-in Hospital; apothecary and surgeon, of Market Street, Ballyshannon c 1824 and c 1845; married — Ferguson (who died 15 October 1830 at Ballyshannon), daughter of Charles Ferguson of Single Street Lodge; died 28 April 1853. [Apothecaries (1829); *BNL* 6 May 1853 (d); Croly (1843–6); Pigot (1824)].

IVERS, DENIS WILLIAM (*fl c* 1730), Armagh;
of Armagh; studied medicine at Rheims University; MD (Rheims) 1730. [Brockliss].

IVERS, HUGH (1832/3–1903), Ballyshannon, county Donegal;
born 1832/3; studied medicine at Dr Steeven's Hospital, Dublin; LM Coombe Hosp Dub 1857; LRCS and LM Edin 1858; LAH Dub 1858; surgeon and apothecary, of The Medical Hall, Ballyshannon; unmarried; died 19 June 1903 at Castle Street, Ballyshannon; administration Londonderry 6 August 1903. [Belf PRO, will cal; Dub GRO (d); *Med Dir*].

IVORY, PATRICK (*fl c* 1773), Armagh;
of Armagh; studied medicine at Rheims University; MD (Rheims) 1773. [Brockliss].

J

JACKSON, ALEXANDER (1767/8–1848), Lurgan, county Armagh, and Dublin;
born 1767/8 at Aughnacloy, county Tyrone; educated at Dungannon Royal School; studied medicine at Edinburgh University; LKQCPI; general practitioner first in Lurgan and then in Dublin from 1795; FKQCPI 1824 (hon); began work at the House of Industry Hospital in Dublin c 1795; author of *Observations on the State of the Lunatic Asylum of the House of Industry in Dublin* (1809); responsible for planning of the Richmond Asylum, Ireland's first lunatic asylum, in Dublin, opened in 1815; unmarried; died 19 March 1848 at 16 Gardiner's Place, Dublin; left £8,000 for almshouses in Aughnacloy – see plaque. [*BNL* 24 March 1848 (d); *Dub J Med Sci* obituary (1848); 5: 565–6; McClelland (1988); *Med Dir*; Widdess (1963)].

JACKSON, CHARLES (1845–94), Carrickmacross, county Monaghan, and Ballyhaise, county Cavan;
born 1845; studied medicine at the Royal College of Surgeons in Ireland; LM Coombe Hosp Dub 1867; LRCSI 1869; LKQCPI 1870; medical officer to Raferagh Dispensary District, Carrickmacross; medical officer to Ballyhaise Dispensary District, of Corvally, Carrickmacross; unmarried; died 2 June 1894 at Bellturbet, county Cavan; administration Cavan 30 July 1894. [Belf PRO, will cal; Dub GRO (d); *Med Dir*].

JACKSON, HUGH (1791/2–1837), Bangor, county Down;
born 1791/2; MD [?]; of Ballywooly [?], Bangor; died 25 March 1837. [*BNL* 4 April 1837 (d)].

JACKSON, JAMES (*fl c* 1798), Newtownards, county Down;
general practitioner in Newtownards, actively involved in the 1798 rising in county Down, as a senior officer of the Newtownards men; died before 1815. [Allen (2004); *BNL* 15 December 1814 (m, daughter) Hill, Turner and Dawson (1998); Wilsdon (1997)].

JACKSON, JAMES (1848/9–c 1894), Clones, county Monaghan;
born 1848/9 in Clones, son of Henry Jackson, farmer; educated at Monaghan Diocesan School; studied arts and medicine at Trinity College, Dublin, from 1867; BA (TCD) 1872; LRCSI 1874; MB 1875; LM RCSI 1876; medical officer to Drum Dispensary District, of Cara, Clones, from 1878; died c 1894. [*Med Dir;* TCD adm reg; *TCD Cat*, vol II (1896)].

JACKSON, JOSEPH (1690–1760), Carrickfergus, county Antrim, and Limavady, county Londonderry;
born 1690; general practitioner, of Carrickfergus and later of Limavady; married —; ancestor of Andrew Jackson, seventh President of the USA; died 1760. [Kirkpatrick Archive].

JACKSON, MICHAEL (1695/6–1727), Lisburn, county Antrim;
born 1695/6; surgeon and apothecary, of Lisburn; died 1 May 1727; buried in Lisburn Cathedral Graveyard. [*Lisburn Fam Hist Soc*, vol 2 (2005)].

JACKSON, OSWALD EGBERT (1877–c 1973), Capetown, South Africa, and Salisbury, Rhodesia;
born 6 January 1877 in Belfast, son of Anthony T. Jackson, architect, of Tighnabruaich, Derryvolgie Avenue, Belfast; educated at Warwick School, Warwickshire; studied arts and medicine at Queen's College, Belfast, from 1894; MB BCh BAO (RUI) 1900; DTM Liverp 1913; MD (QUB) 1923; civil surgeon with RAMC 1901–02; surgeon to Royal Victoria Hospital, Belfast; railway medical officer in Capetown c 1904; medical officer to Joker and Abercorn Mines, Rhodesia, and district surgeon at Abercorn; later medical officer to Shamra Mine; senior government medical officer, Umtali, Rhodesia from c 1925; retired c 1938 to the Highlands, Salisbury; major Southern Rhodesia Medical Corps 1940–45; died c 1973. [*Med Dir*; QCB adm reg].

JACKSON, THOMAS (1755/6–1809), Ballybay, county Monaghan;
born 1755/6; apothecary, of Ballybay; died 15 July 1809 at his home in Ballybay; probate Prerogative Court 1809. [*BNL* 18 July 1809 (d); Vicars (1897)].

JACKSON, THOMAS (1865–1919), Indian Medical Service;
born 20 January 1865 at Mulnagore, county Tyrone, son of Hugh Jackson, farmer, of Mulnagore; educated privately; studied medicine at Queen's College, Belfast, from 1886 and Queen's College, Cork; MB BCh BAO (RUI) 1890; entered the Indian Medical Service (Bombay establishment) as surgeon lieutenant 1892; surgeon captain 1895; surgeon major 1904; surgeon lieutenant-colonel 1912; served in Sudan 1896, Dongola Campaign (medals), on North-West Frontier and Tirah 1897–8 (medal with two clasps), and in World War I 1914–18; retired 1918; died 16 October 1919 at Melbourne, Australia. [*BMJ* obituary (1919); Crawford (1930); Kirkpatrick Archive; *Med Dir*; QCB adm reg].

JACKSON, WILLIAM (d c 1745), Magherafelt, county Londonderry;
general practitioner, of Dunigrunan, Magherafelt; probate Derry Diocesan Court 1745. [Thrift (1920)].

JACKSON, WILLIAM (1813/4–74), Glenavy, county Antrim, Moira, county Down, and Lurgan, county Armagh;
born 1813/4; studied medicine at Glasgow University; LSA Lond 1829; LFPS Glas 1833; MRCSE 1855; general practitioner, of Glenavy c 1845, and of Moira c 1858; district cholera medical officer 1849; married 30 March 1832 in St Anne's Church of Ireland Church, Belfast, Margaret Alexander, daughter of John M. Alexander of Monlough, county Down; died 13 March 1874 in Lurgan; buried in Monbrief Municipal Cemetery, Lurgan. [*BNL* 3 April 1832 (m); Croly (1843–6); Dub GRO (d); gravestone inscription; Kirkpatrick Archive; *Med Dir*].

JACOB, DAVID BALDWIN (1836–1912), Maryborough, Queen's County;
born 29 April 1836, third son of Dr John Edmund Jacob of Maryborough, and Charlotte Cecilia Elizabeth Baldwin of Raheenduff, Queen's County; educated privately and at Belfast Academy; studied medicine at Queen's College, Belfast, from 1852; MD (QUI) 1856; LRCSI 1856; LM Rot Hosp Dub 1856; FRCSI 1872; surgeon to Queen's County Infirmary; visiting physician to Maryborough District Lunatic Asylum from 1864; surgeon to the County Gaol; medical officer to Maryborough Dispensary District; assistant surgeon to the Royal Queen's County Rifles; proprietor and physician to the Midland Retreat Private Asylum for the Insane; JP for Queen's County from 1864; retired c 1910 to Portleix, Maryborough; married 23 October 1857 in Cloydah Church, county Carlow, Sarah Elizabeth Fishbourne (who died 10 April 1906), eldest daughter of William Fishbourne of Forthill, county Carlow; father of Dr William Gardiner Jacob, LRCSI 1880, LKQCPI 1881, Dr Edmund Julius Jacob, LRCSI 1886, LKQCPI 1889, and a daughter Anchoretta who married Dr John Murrary Prior Kennedy, LKQCPI LRCSI 1883; died 21 July 1912 at Portleix; probate Kilkenny 18 October 1912. [Belf PRO, will cal; Burke *LGI* (1958); Dub GRO (d); Dub Nat Arch, will cal, will; Kirkpatrick Archive; *Lancet* obituary (1912); *Londonderry Sentinel* 6 November 1857 (m); *Med Dir*; QCB adm reg].

JACOB, GEORGE OGLE (b 1786), Indian Medical Service;
born 1786; joined the Indian Medical Service (Bengal establishment) as assistant surgeon 1806; surgeon 1819; served at the capture of Java 1811; retired 1827; married Mary Anne — (who was born 1795/6 and died 8 April 1868); father of Dr William Augustus Jacob, MRCS 1848, MD (Glas) 1849, IMS, and Harriet Josephine Jacob who married Dr Henry Irwin, IMS. [*BNL* 17 July 1846 (m, daughter); Crawford (1930); gravestone inscription (Tynan CI graveyard)].

JAGOE, WILLIAM HENRY (1840–93), Army Medical Service;
born 14 June 1840; joined the Army Medical Service as staff assistant surgeon 1864; assistant surgeon, on half pay 1869; retired on half pay 1873; lived latterly at Rathmines, Dublin; married —; died 11 December 1893 in Dublin; buried in Belfast City Cemetery. [Belf City Cem, bur reg; *Med Dir*; Peterkin and Johnston (1968)].

JAMES, ROBERT (1797/8–1841) Bailieborough, county Cavan;
born 1797/8; LAH Dub 1828; apothecary, of Bailieborough; married Margaret Anne — (who died 20 August 1858 at her home in Armagh); sons were born in 1830/1 and 1840/1 and both died in childhood; died 12 October 1841. [Apothecaries (1829); *BNL* 22 October 1841 (d), 2 August 1850 (d, son), 16 June 1851 (d, son) and 25 August 1858 (d)].

JAMESON, LOWTHER ALEXANDER (d 1906), Carlow, Ballyjamesduff, county Cavan, and Falkland Islands;
studied medicine at Trinity College, Dublin, and the Royal College of Surgeons in Ireland; LRCPI and LM 1892; LRCSI and LM 1892; general practitioner, of The Hermitage, Carlow c 1892–5, of Ballyjamesduff c 1895–7; medical officer, of Port Stanley and Darwin Harbour, Falkland Islands c 1897–1906; died 1906 at Darwin Harbour. [*Med Dir*].

JAMIESON, THOMAS MITCHELL (1833/4–99), Aughnacloy and Castle Caulfield, county Tyrone;
    born 1833/4; studied medicine at the Ledwich School, Dublin; LM Coombe Hospital, Dublin; LRCSI 1858; resident surgeon and clinical clerk at Mercer's Hospital, Dublin; medical officer to Clonavaddy Dispensary District from 1858, of Aughnacloy; retired to Fort Edward, Clonvaddy, Castle Caulfield; married Elizabeth —; died 8 April 1899 at Killymaddy Evans, Dungannon; administration Armagh 15 August 1899. [Belf PPR, will cal; Dub GRO (d): *Med Dir*].

JAMISON, ALEXANDER (1864–1920), Belfast;
    born 17 May 1864 at Drumaghadone, county Down, son of Alexander Jamison of Drumaghadone, county Down, and Margaret —; brother of Dr William Jamison (*q.v.*) and Dr John Jamison (*q.v.*); educated at Methodist College, Belfast, from 1883; studied arts and medicine at Queen's College, Belfast, from 1884 with many prizes and scholarships; Coulter Exhibition, Belfast Royal Hospital 1892; BA (hons) (RUI) 1887; MA 1888; MB BCh BAO 1893; assistant house surgeon to Belfast Royal Hospital; house surgeon to Hospital for Sick Children and Women, Bristol; general practitioner, of Woodstock Road, Belfast from c 1895; retired to Ballylesson, county Down; married —; died 20 January 1920 at the Royal Victoria Hospital, Belfast; buried in Dromore Non-Subcribing Presbyterian Graveyard; administration Dublin 5 May 1920 and 22 March 1946. [Belf PRO, will cal; Clarke, *County Down*, vol 19 (1983); Dub GRO (d); Fry (1984); *Med Dir*; QCB adm reg].

JAMISON, DANIEL (1865–95), Belfast;
    born 6 October 1865, youngest son of Daniel Jamison of 8 Duncairn Terrace, Belfast, and Catherine —; educated at Belfast Academy; studied arts and medicine at Queen's College, Belfast, from 1883; BA (RUI) 1886; MB BCh BAO 1890; general practitioner, of 202 Grosvenor Street, Belfast; died 31 March 1895 at 8 Duncairn Terrace, Belfast of typhus fever; unmarried; buried in Balmoral Cemetery, Belfast; administration Belfast 15 May 1895. [Belf PRO, will cal; Clarke, *Belfast*, vol 3 (1986); Dub GRO (d); *Med Dir*; QCB adm reg].

JAMISON, DAVID, senior (1812/3–92), Newtownards, county Down;
    born 1812/3; studied medicine at Edinburgh University; MD (Edin) 1834 (thesis 'On inguinal hernia'); LRCS Edin 1834; medical officer to Newtownards Dispensary District; author of various medical papers; married 24 December 1857 in Glastry Presbyterian Church, Eleanor Ferguson, daughter of George Ferguson of Ballyalicock, Newtownards; father of Dr David Jamison, junior (*q.v.*), Dr Henry George Jamison (*q.v.*) and Dr Edmund Fergus Jamison (*q.v.*); died 7 December 1892 at Francis Street, Newtownards; probate Belfast 17 February 1893. [*BNL* 26 December 1857 (m); Belf PRO, will cal; Croly (1843–6); Dub GRO (d); Edin Univ; Kirkpatrick Archive; *Med Dir*].

JAMISON, DAVID, junior (1858–1939), Newtownards, county Down;
    born 31 November 1858 in Newtownards, county Down, son of Dr David Jamison, senior (*q.v.*) of Newtownards; brother of Dr Henry George Jamison (*q.v.*) and Dr Edmund Fergus Jamison (*q.v.*); educated at Bangor Endowed School; studied

medicine at Queen's College, Belfast, from 1876; LFPS and LM Glas 1884; LAH Dub 1885; medical officer of health for Newtownards Dispensary District; general practitioner, of 39 Francis Street, Newtownards; author of various medical papers; married 3 June 1890 in First Newtownards Presbyterian Church, Margaret Bradford Moore, daughter of the Rev Hugh Moore, Presbyterian minister; father of Dr David Jamison, MB (QUB) 1914, of Newtownards; died 17 October 1939; probate Belfast 9 February 1940. [Belf PRO, will cal; *Med Dir*; QCB adm reg; UHF database (m)].

JAMISON, EDMUND FERGUS (1864–1955), Newtownards, county Down;
born 17 August 1864 at Francis Street, Newtownards, son of Dr David Jamison, senior (*q.v.*), of Newtownards, and Eleanor Ferguson; brother of Dr David Jamison, junior (*q.v.*) and Dr Henry George Jamison (*q.v.*); educated at Bangor Endowed School; studied arts and medicine at Queen's College, Belfast from 1882; BA (RUI) 1886; LRCP LRCS Edin 1895; LFPS Glas 1895; house surgeon to York Dispensary; general practitioner, of Yew Villa, Newtownards, from c 1900; retired to 11 Shandon Drive, Bangor, c 1938; died 16 September 1955; administration (with will) Belfast 20 March 1956. [Belf PRO, will cal; Dub GRO (b); *Med Dir*; QCB adm reg; Young and Pike (1909)].

JAMISON (JAMESON), GEORGE (1811/2–78), Dungannon, county Tyrone;
born 1811/2, son of James Jamison, farmer, of Drumglass, Dungannon; studied medicine at Anderson's University, Glasgow; LM Glas 1842; LFPS Glas 1844; general practitioner, of Scotch Street, Dungannon; married 14 October 1859 in First Bangor Presbyterian Church, Margaret McElroy, widow, daughter of John Robinson, farmer, of Bangor, county Down; died 4 June 1878 at Ranfurly Terrace, Dungannon; probate Armagh 2 August 1878. [Belf PRO, will cal; Dub GRO (m); Kirkpatrick Archive; *Med Dir*; UHF database, marriages].

JAMISON HENRY GEORGE (1863–1954), Liverpool, Lancashire, and London;
born 1863 at Newtownards, county Down, son of Dr David Jamison, senior (*q.v.*); brother of Dr David Jamison junior (*q.v.*) and Dr Edmund Fergus Jamison (*q.v.*); studied arts and medicine at Queen's College, Belfast, from 1878, and the Royal College of Surgeons in Ireland; BA (RUI) 1884; MD BCh BAO 1890; house surgeon to Brownlow Hill Infirmary, Liverpool; general practitioner, of Edmonton, London, c 1895; of Bellavista, Queen's Road, Broadstairs, Kent c 1906 and of Durley Dene, Palmers Green, London c 1910; returned to Yew Villa, Newtownards c 1923; retired to 5 Upper Clifton, Bangor, c 1935; unmarried; died 2 February 1954 at 5 Victoria Terrace, Bangor; probate Belfast 25 June 1954. [Belf GRO (d); Belf PRO, will cal; *Med Dir*; QCB adm reg; Young and Pike (1909)].

JAMISON, JAMES PHILIP ROBERT (1859–90), Broughshane, county Antrim;
born 5 March 1859 at Broughshane, son of James Jamison of Skerry Vale, Broughshane; educated at Coleraine and Londonderry schools; studied medicine at Queen's College, Belfast from 1879; LRCP LRCS Edin 1886; LFPS Glas 1886; general practitioner, of Skerry Vale; died 26 May 1890. [*Med Dir*; QCB adm reg].

JAMISON, JOHN (1868–1921), Belfast;
   born 12 April 1868 at Drumaghadone, Dromore, county Down, son of Alexander Jamison, farmer, of Drumaghadone; brother of Dr William Jamison (*q.v.*) and Dr Alexander Jamison (*q.v.*); educated at Banbridge Academy; studied medicine at Queen's College, Belfast, from 1884; MB BCh BAO (RUI) 1891; general practitioner, of 95 Falls Road, Belfast, from c 1900; married 21 January 1903 in Cooke Centenary Presbyterian Church, Belfast, Lavinia Gallagher (who died January 1921), daughter of John Barry Gallagher, land steward, of South Parade, Belfast; died 22 February 1921; buried in Belfast City Cemetery; administration (with will) Belfast 27 July 1921 and 28 October 1927. [Belf City Cem, bur reg; Belfast PRO, will cal; *Med Dir*; QCB adm reg; UHF database (m)].

JAMISON, THOMAS (d before 1839), Portglenone, county Antrim;
   surgeon, probably of Mullinsallagh, near Portglenone; married Rebecca — (who was born 1745/6 and died 17 July 1838 at the home of Andrew McIlrath of Mullinsallagh and was buried in Rasharkin graveyard); died before 1839. [*BNL* 31 July 1838 (d)].

JAMISON, WILLIAM (1861–1929), Dromore, county Down, Fenton, Staffordshire, and Abercynon, Glamorgan;
   born 25 May 1861 at Drumaghadone, Dromore, son of Alexander Jamison, farmer, of Drumaghadone brother of Dr Alexander Jamision (*q.v.*) and Dr John Jamison (*q.v.*); studied arts and medicine at Queen's College, Belfast, from 1881; BA (hons) (RUI) 1885; LM Coombe Hosp Dub 1888; MD BCh (RUI) 1889; resident clinical assistant to Belfast Royal Hospital; general practitioner, of Dromaghadone House, Dromore, c 1890–1900, of Market Street, Fenton, c 1900–10 and of 182/4 Abercynon Road, Abercynon, from c 1910; died 9 January 1929; administration Llandaff 19 April 1929. [Lond PPR, will cal; *Med Dir*; QCB adm reg].

JAQUES, ROBERT (1862–1953), London, Plymouth, Devonshire, and RAMC;
   born 28 February 1862 in Antrim, third son of William Jaques, taxer, and — Graves; educated privately; studied medicine at Liverpool University and King's College Hospital, London; MRCSE LRCP Lond 1900; FRCSE 1903; house surgeon at King's College Hospital 1901–03; clinical assistant and surgical registrar at the Royal Eye Hospital, Southwark 1903; ophthalmologist and honorary surgeon to Plymouth Royal Eye Hospital 1908–30; of 20 Athenaeum Street, Plymouth; advocate of nationalization of medicine as early as 1909; chairman of the Plymouth Division of BMA 1911–18 and of the South-Western Branch 1923–4; president of the Plymouth Medical Society; served in the RAMC during World War I with the rank of captain; retired 1930 to Findon House, 38 Down View Road, Worthing, Sussex; married 28 April 1906 in St Michael's Parish Church, Derby, Agatha Gabrielle Eldrid, daughter of the Rev Edwin Norton Eldrid of Derby; died 20 September 1953 at Worthing Hospital, aged 91; probate Lewes 11 December 1953. [Lond GRO (m); Lond PPR, will cal; *Med Dir*; Robinson and Le Fanu (1970)].

JARDINE, — (*fl c* 1845), Moira, county Down;
   CM Glas [?]; general practitioner of Moira, c 1845; possibly died c 1850. [Croly (1843–6)].

JAZDOWSKI, BRONISLAW (or **BRONISLAS**) **JAMES** (1838–1902), Army Medical Service;
born 1 May 1838 at Dungannon, county Tyrone; studied arts and medicine at Marischal College, Aberdeen; MA (Aber) 1857; MB (Aber) 1859; LRCS Edin 1859; joined the Army Medical Service as staff assistant surgeon 1860; attached to the 93rd Foot 1863; staff surgeon 1872; surgeon major 1875; served on the North West Frontier 1863–4, Egypt 1882 and Bechuanaland 1884–5; retired on half pay with honorary rank of brigade surgeon 1886; of 12 Charles Street, St James's Square, Westminster; inventor of a method of converting railway trucks for the conveyance of sick or wounded; died 24 November 1902 in Rome; administration (with will) 11 February 1903. [Lond PPR, will cal; *Med Dir*; Peterkin and Johnston (1968)].

JEFFARES, JAMES (1798/9–1875), Newtownbreda, county Down, and Clough, county Antrim;
born 1798/9; LM Coombe Hosp Dub 1834; MRCSE 1834; medical officer to Newtownbreda Dispensary District and later to Clough Dispensary District and constabulary, of Clough Mills cottage, Clough; unmarried; died 16 August 1875 at Drumbane, Dunaghy, Clough; probate Dublin 22 January 1876. [Belf PRO, will cal; Croly (1843–6); Dub GRO (d); *Med Dir*].

JEFFERSON, GEORGE (1869–1917), Todmorden, Yorkshire, and Stoke-on-Trent, Staffordshire;
born 29 December 1869 in Belfast, son of Ralph Jefferson, clerk, of 26 Springfield Road, Belfast; educated at Belfast Model School; studied medicine at Queen's College, Belfast, from 1893; MB BCh BAO (RUI) 1900; general practitioner of Cornholme, Todmorden, and Talke, Stroke-on-Trent; married Sarah —; died 18 April 1917 at 93 Bewsey Street, Warrington, 'following an overdose of morphia, taken to induce sleep' (coroner); buried in Belfast City Cemetery; administration London 22 August 1917 and 17 March 1919. [Belf City Cem, bur reg; Lond GRO (d); Lond PPR, will cal; *Med Dir*; QCB adm reg].

JEFFERSON, JAMES GRAHAM (1842/3–1910), Lisburn, county Antrim;
born 1842/3 at Lisburn, son of Ralph Jefferson, farmer, of Ballymacoss, Lisburn; brother of Dr John Jefferson (*q.v.*); educated at Lisburn; studied medicine at Queen's College, Belfast, from 1871; LRCP LRCS Edin 1876; senior house officer to Belfast Royal Hospital; medical officer to Lisburn Dispensary District and constabulary; medical officer of health to Lisburn Union; consulting sanitary officer to Lisburn; married Elizabeth Fairbrother —; died 16 April 1910; probate Belfast 20 June 1910. [Belf PRO, will cal; *Med Dir*; QCB adm reg].

JEFFERSON, JOHN (1845–86), Lisburn, county Antrim;
born 19 April 1845 at Ballymacoss, county Antrim, son of Ralph Jefferson, farmer, of Ballymacoss and Derriaghy; brother of Dr James Graham Jefferson (*q.v.*); educated at Lisburn Academy; studied medicine at Queen's College, Belfast, from 1861; MRCSE 1866; LRCP Edin and LM 1870; LAH Dub 1872; medical officer to Lisburn Dispensary District and constabulary, of Castle Street, Lisburn; superintendent medical officer of health from 1874; married 10 August 1877 in

Railway Street Presbyterian Church, Lisburn, Elizabeth Young, daughter of William Young, merchant, of Bow Street, Lisburn; died 12 November 1886 at Market Square, Lisburn; administration Belfast 13 December 1886. [Belf PRO, will cal; Kirkpatrick Archive; *Med Dir*; QCB adm reg; UHF database (m)].

JENCKEN, FERDINAND EDWARD (1822/3–81), Dublin and Londonderry;
born 1822/3, perhaps son of Johan Ferdinand Jencken who came to London as physician to Queen Adelaide; born blind, operated on for cataract and obtained sight of one eye in 1841; studied medicine at King's College, London and the Ecole de Medicine, Paris; MD (St Andrews) 1853 (by examination); LRCP Lond 1853; LM Rot Hosp Dub 1863; MRCSE 1869; LKQCPI and LM 1870; general practitioner, of 90 Lower Leeson Street, Dublin c 1870 and of 2 Bayview Terrace, Londonderry c 1875; author of various medical papers; retired to 22 Anglesea Place, Kingstown, county Dublin; married Anna Maria Bilhildis Jerome —; died 12 January 1881 at 22 Anglesea Place; administration (with will) Dublin 14 February 1881. [Belf PRO, will cal; Dub GRO (d); *Med Dir;* Smart (2004)].

JENNINGS, ALEXANDER (1833–80), Army Medical Service;
born 26 July 1833 at Saintfield, county Down, son of Henry Jennings of Saintfield and Belfast; nephew of Professor Alexander Gordon; educated at RBAI; studied medicine at Queen's College, Belfast, from 1849; MD (QUI) 1858; LRCSI 1858; joined the Army Medical Service as surgeon 1859; posted to Royal Artillery 1868; surgeon major 1876; served at Mauritius, Capetown and Gold Coast; author of a treatise on ophthalmia; resigned on half pay 1877; died 20 December 1880 at 46 Ulsterville Terrace; buried in Inch graveyard, county Down. [*BMJ* obituary (1880); Clarke, *County Down*, vol 7 (1993); Kirkpatrick Archive; *Med Dir*; Peterkin and Johnston (1968); QCB adm reg].

JEPHSON, ROBERT DALKEITH (1871–1904), Royal Army Medical Corps;
born 19 July 1871 at Kingstown, county Dublin, son of Robert H. Jephson of Lansdowne Road, Dublin; educated at Armagh Royal School from 1886; studied medicine at the Royal College of Surgeons in Ireland; LRCSI and LM LRCSPI and LM 1895; joined the Royal Army Medical Corps as surgeon-lieutenant 1897; captain 1900; served at the Nile in 1898 and South Africa 1899–1902; died 9 January 1904 at Rawal Pindi. [Ferrar (1933); Kirkpatrick Archive; *Med Dir*; Peterkin and Johnston (1968)].

JERICHO, — (*fl c* 1772), Belfast;
'surgeon' but probably unqualified, of Belfast; operated on Michael Adair for cataract, resulting in recovery of his sight, March 1772. [*BNL* 31 March 1772 (advert)].

JOHNS, CHRISTOPHER ARCHIBALD (1871–1935), Assam, India, and Nenagh, county Tipperary;
born 16 August 1871 at Joymount, Carrickfergus, fourth son of William Johns, barrister and solicitor, of Joymount Court, and Mary Charlotte Darby; educated at Methodist College, Belfast, 1884–5 and Sherborne School 1885–8; awarded RHS bronze medal for saving a life in Belfast Lough in 1886; studied arts and medicine at

Trinity College, Dublin, from 1888; BA (TCD) 1892, LM Rot Hosp Dub 1893; MB BCh 1894; MD 1895; DPH RCSI 1904; practised medicine in Sythet, Assam, India c 1900–05; general practitioner, of 20 Summerhill, Nenagh, county Tipperary from c 1905; married Sarah Devinish Morton (who died 28 February 1946), daughter of Dr Robert Morton of Nenagh; died 11 February 1935; probate Limerick 2 August 1935. [Bensley (1937); Dub GRO (b); Dub Nat Arch, will cal; Fry (1984); *Med Dir*; Rutherford and Clarke, *County Antrim*, vol 3 (1995); TCD adm reg; *TCD Cat*, vol II (1896)].

JOHNSON, ALEXANDER MACKEY (1857–1922), Sydney, New South Wales;
born 11 March 1857 at Killaloe, county Clare, son of Bristow Johnson, draper, of Killaloe; educated at Killaloe; studied medicine at Queen's College, Galway, 1876–7 and at Queen's College, Belfast, from 1877; MD MCh (RUI) 1883; emigrated c 1885 to Sydney, New South Wales; general practitioner, of 261 and 263 Elizabeth Street, Hyde Park, Sydney c 1900; visiting surgeon to St Margaret's Hospital; died 28 April 1922 at Sydney. [Kirkpatrick Archive; *Med Dir*; QCB adm reg].

JOHNSON, CHARLES CONWELL (1799–1832),Indian Medical Service;
born November 1799, son of Charles Johnson (formerly McShane) and Elizabeth Conwell; MRCS 1820; joined the Indian Medical Service (Madras establishment) as assistant surgeon 1822; served in Burma 1824–5; died 5 January 1832 at Wallajabad. [Crawford (1930); Larkin (1981a) and (1981b)].

JOHNSON, HENRY (1863–1920), Newark, Nottinghamshire, and Waddington, Lincolnshire;
born 6 August 1863 at Stewartstown, county Tyrone, son of Henry Johnson, farmer, of Castle Farm, Stewartstown; educated at St Malachy's College, Belfast; studied medicine at Queen's College, Belfast, from 1879, also at Anderson's College, Glasgow; LRCP LRCS Edin 1886; LFPS and LM Glas 1886; general practitioner, of Bassingham, Newark, c 1895 and of Waddington, from c 1900; married Jane —; died 5 January 1920; probate London 31 May 1920. [Lond PPR, will cal; *Med Dir*; QCB adm reg].

JOHNSON, ISAAC (d 1814), Naval Medical Service and Magherafelt, county Londonderry;
joined the Naval Medical Service as assistant surgeon; retired to Magherafelt; died 23 August 1814 in Magherafelt. [*BNL* 30 August 1814 (d)].

JOHNS(T)ON, JOHN (*fl c* 1800), Cookstown, county Tyrone;
MD [?]; married Dorothy — (who was born 1771/2 and died 24 July 1853 in the house of Robert Miller in Cookstown; died before 1853. [*BNL* 29 July 1853 (d); *Coleraine Chronicle* 30 July 1853 (d); *Londonderry Sentinel* 5 August 1853 (d)].

JOHNSON, JOHN BURNEY (1869–1939), Gilford, county Down;
born 12 April 1869 at Eden Cottage, Whiteabbey, county Antrim, son of William Johnson, clerk and accountant, of Whiteabbey; educated at RBAI; studied medicine

at Queen's College, Belfast, from 1886; MB BCh BAO (RUI) 1893; general practitioner and certifying factory surgeon, of Gilford; medical officer to the Gilford Convalescent Hospital and post office; retired c 1935; moved to 27 Belgrave Road, Monkstown, county Dublin, c 1937; died 9 July 1939 at 27 Belgrave Road; buried in Carnmoney Parish Graveyard; probate Dublin 28 August 1939. [Dub Nat Arch, will cal; Kirkpatrick Archive; *Med Dir*; QCB adm reg; Stewart (1994)].

JOHNSON, ROBERT (1779/80–1825), Naval Medical Service and Comber, county Down;
born 1779/80; joined the Naval Medical Service as assistant surgeon; surgeon, of Comber; died 19 October 1825 at his home in Comber. [*BNL* 11 November 1825 (d)].

JOHNSON, SAMUEL WILLIAM (1858–84), Ballina, county Mayo, Darlington, Yorkshire and Liverpool, Lancashire;
born 5 May 1858 at Ballina, son of Benjamin Johnston, ironmonger, of Ballina; educated at Ardnaree Academy; studied medicine at Queen's College, Belfast, from 1877, at the Carmichael School and Coombe and Mercers' Hospitals, Dublin; MD (QUI) 1881; MCh (RUI) 1882; general practitioner, of Egglestone, Darlington c 1883 and Fern House, 63 Walton Road, Liverpool; died 27 October 1884 at 63 Walton Road; probate Dublin 21 January 1885 and London 3 February 1885. [Belf PRO, will cal; Lond GRO (d); Lond PPR, will cal; *Med Dir*; QCB adm reg].

JOHNSON, THOMAS (*fl c* 1798), Ballyshannon, county Donegal;
LAH Dub 1798; apothecary, of Ballyshannon. [Apothecaries (1829)].

JOHNSON, WILLIAM (*fl c* 1769), Armagh;
born in Armagh; studied medicine at Rheims University; MD (Rheims) 1769. [Brockliss].

JOHNSON, WILLIAM (*fl c* 1836), Belfast;
MD [?]; attending physician to the Belfast Fever Hospital 1835–8; married Mabella Hudson (who was born 1793/4 and died 24 August 1836), daughter of Christopher Hudson of Mount Collyer, Belfast. [*Belf Fever Hosp, Ann Rep*; Merrick and Clarke, *Belfast*, vol 4 (1991)].

JOHNSON, WILLIAM EDWARD (1845–1908), Indian Medical Service;
born 2 November 1845 at Drumaclan, county Monaghan, son of John Johnson of Drumaclon; educated at Monaghan Diocesan School; studied medicine at Queen's College, Cork, Galway and from 1862, at Queen's College, Belfast; MD MCh (QUI) 1870; Dip Mid 1872; joined the Indian Medical Service (Madras establishment) as assistant surgeon 1872; surgeon 1873; surgeon major 1884; surgeon lieutenant-colonel 1892; surgeon colonel 1898; retired 1903 to Western Grange, Branksome Wood Road, Bournemouth; married —; died 24 November 1908 at Western Grange; probate London 17 December 1908. [Crawford (1930); Lond PPR, will cal, will; *Med Dir*; QCB adm reg].

JOHNSTON, ALEXANDER (1834–1904), Westport, county Mayo;
born 1834 in county Fermanagh, son of James Johnston, merchant; educated by Mr Nugent; studied arts and medicine at Trinity College, Dublin, from 1857; LM Rot Hosp Dub 1859; BA (TCD) 1860; LRCSI 1860; MB 1861; LM RCSI 1861; surgeon to Westport Infirmary and Fever Hospital; medical officer to Westport Dispensary District and constabulary and certifying factory surgeon; medical officer of health to Westport Union from 1874; of North Mall, Westport; died 19 November 1904 at Sidmouth, Devonshire; probate Ballina 10 January 1905. [Belf PRO, will cal; Burtchaell and Sadleir (1935); Kirkpatrick Archive; *Med Dir*].

JOHNSTON, ANDREW (1770–1833), Army Medical Service and Dublin;
born 1770, fourth and youngest son of William Johnston, architect, of Armagh, and Margaret Houston; brother of Francis Johnston, the architect; educated at Armagh Royal School; apprenticed to Mr W. Hartigan, surgeon, of Dublin July 1791; studied medicine at Mercer's Hospital and the Royal College of Surgeons in Ireland; LRCSI 1794; MRCSI 1905; joined the Army Medical Service as surgeon to the 44th Foot 1796; served in the West Indies and Egypt; retired on half pay 1802; resigned 1803 to practice in Dublin; assistant master of the Rotunda Hospital 1804–08; professor of surgical pharmacy to the RCSI 1813; president of the RCSI 1817; professor of midwifery to the RCSI 1819; married 1 July 1806 Sophia Cheney (who died 29 October 1868 aged 83), only child of George Cheney of Holywood, county Kildare; father of Dr George Johnston, MD (Edin) 1845, president KQCPI 1880–81; died 28 August 1833; buried in St George's Parish Church graveyard, Dublin. [Burke *LGI* (1912); Cameron (1916); Kirkpatrick Archive; Kirkpatrick and Jellett (1913); *Memorials of the Dead*, vol XI, p 33; Peterkin and Johnston (1968); *Weekly Irish Times* 26 October 1940].

JOHNSTON, ARTHUR (d 1857), Armagh;
of Lisburn, county Antrim; LSA Dub 1803; general practitioner, of Carrickbreda, county Armagh; married 22 May 1826 in the Anglican chapel of St John, Edinburgh and afterwards in the Roman Catholic chapel, Sarah Maria Wheeler, third daughter of Thomas Wheeler of Exeter, Devonshire; son studied at Trinity College, Dublin; died 21 February 1857; probate Prerogative Court 1857. [Apothecaries (1829); *BNL* 30 May 1826 (m); Belf PRO, prerog wills index; Burtchaell and Sadleir (1935)].

JOHNSTON, ARTHUR (1820–45), Annaclone, county Down;
born 1820; qualified in medicine 1844 [?]; died 15 January 1845 at his home in Ballynanny, Annaclone. [*BNL* 21 January 1845 (d)].

JOHNSTON, BENJAMIN (1815/6–76), Ramelton, county Donegal, and Middletown, county Cork;
born 1815/6 in Dublin, son of Benjamin Johnston, gentleman; studied arts and medicine at Trinity College, Dublin, from 1832, and the Royal College of Surgeons in Ireland; BA (TCD) 1837; LM Rot Hosp Dub 1839; LRCSI 1841; LM RCSI 1842; MB 1842; FRCSI 1845; MD 1870; clinical surgeon to Dr Steeven's Hospital, Dublin, 1841; medical officer to Ramelton Fever Hospital, Dispensary and constabulary c 1843–61; of Ayr Hill, Ramelton; medical officer to Middleton Union

Infirmary and Fever Hospital from 1861, of Riversdale, Middleton; superintendent medical officer of health from 1874; married 11 January 1843 in St Peter's Church of Ireland Church, Dublin, Emma Maturin (who was born 1812/3 and died 6 November 1890), youngest daughter of the Rev Henry Maturin, rector of Clondevadock, county Donegal; father of Dr Henry Maturin Johnston of Stranorlar, county Donegal (*q.v.*); died 2 June 1876 at Riversale; probate Dublin 17 August 1876. [Belf PRO, will cal; Burtchaell and Sadleir (1924); Croly (1843–6); Kirkpatrick Archive; Leslie (1940); *Londonderry Sentinel* 23 January 1843 (m); *Med Dir*].

JOHNSTON, BENJAMIN RIGBY (1861/2–1946), Stranorlar, county Donegal, Manchester, Lancashire, and Grasmere, Westmoreland;
born 1861/2, son of Dr Augustus Johnston of Hawkshead, Windermere, Lancashire; brother of Dr George Ainslie Johnston; studied medicine at at the Royal College of Surgeons in Ireland and the Carmichael School, Dublin; LKQCPI and LM 1884; MRCSE 1884; LM Coombe Hosp Dub 1884; MD (Bruxelles) 1895; general practitioner of Stranorlar, c 1885; assistant medical officer to Monsall Fever Hospital, Manchester; general practitioner, of Mossgrove and Rose Cottage, Grasmere; died 17 March 1946 at the Westmoreland County Hospital, Kendal; probate Carlisle 20 September 1946. [Lond GRO (d); Lond PPR, will cal; *Med Dir*].

JOHNSTON, CHARLES JAMES (1858/9–1921), Castlederg, county Tyrone;
born 1858/9 at Munnie House, Castlederg, son of Richard Johnston, farmer, of Munnie House; educated at Castlederg School, studied medicine at Queen's College, Belfast, from 1878; LRCP LRCS Edin 1892; LFPS Glas 1892; general practitioner, of Castlederg, and medical officer to Drumquin Dispensary; died 12 April 1921; probate Londonderry 22 March 1922. [Belf PRO, will cal; *Med Dir*; QCB adm reg].

JOHNSTON, DAVID (1805/6–33), Glentougher, Inishowen, county Donegal;
born 1805/6; surgeon and resident apothecary to Donegal County Infirmary; died 11 September 1833 of consumption, at Glentougher. [*BNL* 17 September 1833 (d); *Londonderry Sentinel* 14 September 1833 (d)].

JOHNSTON, DAVID (1837–98), Belfast;
born 10 November 1837 in Magherafelt, county Londonderry, son of Robert I. Johnston, farmer, of Drumrainey, Magherafelt; educated at Aughagaskin National School; studied medicine at Queen's College, Belfast, from 1861; MD (QUI) 1866; MRCSE and LM 1866; general practitioner, of 60 Old Lodge Road and later of 13 Clifton Street, Belfast; married 28 June 1876 in St James's Church of Ireland Church, Belfast, Jane Yeates, daughter of Gawn Yeates, schoolmaster, of 31 Vicinage Park, Belfast; father of Anne D. Johnston who married Dr William Porter (*q.v.*); died 6 July 1898; buried in Belfast City Cemetery; probate Belfast 24 August 1898. [Belf City Cem, bur reg; Belf PRO, will cal; Dub GRO (d); Kirkpatrick Archive; *Med Dir*; QCB adm reg; UHF database (m); Whitla (1901)].

JOHNSTON, DAVID, (1846–1914), Holywood, county Down;
born 26 August 1846 in Belfast, son of David Johnston of Holywood; educated at RBAI; studied arts and medicine at Queen's College, Belfast, from 1862; MD (QUI)

1870; MCh Dip Mid 1873; general practitioner, of Shore Street, Holywood, and later of Redcliffe, Holywood; married Clara Agnes —; father of Dr Henry Mulrea Johnston, MB BCh BAO (RUI) 1903, of Newcastle-upon-Tyne; died 11 September 1914; probate Belfast 2 November 1915. [Belf PRO, will cal, will; Kirkpatrick Archive; *Lancet* obituary (1914); *Med Dir*; QCB adm reg].

JOHNSTON, DAVID RICHMOND (1861–1917), Reading, Berkshire;
born 28 January 1861 at Moy, county Tyrone, son of the Rev Thomas Johnston, minister of Moy Presbyterian Church; educated at home; studied arts and medicine at Trinity College, Dublin, from 1878 and studied medicine Queen's College, Belfast, from 1886; BA (TCD) 1882; LRCP LRCS Edin 1889; LFPS Glas 1889; general practitioner, of 21 Queen's Road, and 101 London Road, Reading; medical officer to Huntley and Palmers Factory, Reading; medical officer to the Royal Flying Corps at Reading from 1916; died 26 February 1917 of meningitis acquired during a post mortem examination. [Barkley (1986); *BMJ* obituary (1917); *Med Dir*; QCB adm reg; TCD adm reg; *TCD Cat*, vol II (1896)].

JOHNSTON, FRANCIS (1778/9–1819), Naval Medical Service;
born 1778/9; son of William Johnston, farmer, of Aghindrumman (Aughendrummond); brother of Dr James Johnston of Enniskillen and St Angelo (*q.v.*); joined the Naval Medical Service as assistant surgeon serving on the frigate HMS *Mermaid* during the Napoleonic Wars; married Margaret Armstrong (who was born 1783/4 and died 19 March 1866), second daughter of John Armstrong of Brookeborough, county Fermanagh; died 11 January 1819 at Ballygawley, county Tyrone; buried in Clogher Cathedral Graveyard. [*BNL* 29 May 1810 (m); Johnston (1972)].

JOHNSTON, FRANCIS GRAYDON (1808/9–64), Charlton and Hyde Park, London;
born 1808/9 at St Angelo, county Fermanagh, son of Dr James Johnston of Enniskillen and St Angelo (*q.v.*); MRCSE 1828; LSA Lond 1833; general practitioner, of Charlton and 5 Craven Street, Hyde Park, London c 1860; abroad in 1861–2; married Sarah Johnston, his first cousin, daughter of the Rev John Johnston, minister of Tullylish Presbyterian Church, and sister of Dr Henry Martyn Johnston (*q.v.*); son born in London 1 February 1848; died 18 February 1864 at the home of his brother-in-law, the Rev William Johnston, Antrim Road, Belfast, of typhus fever; buried in Tullylish Presbyterian Graveyard; probate Dublin 7 May 1864. [*BNL* 4 February 1848 (b, son); Belf PRO, will cal; Clarke, *County Down*, vol 20 (1989); *Coleraine Chronicle* 27 February 1864 (d); Dub GRO (d); Kirkpatrick Archive; *Londonderry Sentinel* 23 February 1864 (d); *Med Dir*].

JOHNSTON, GEORGE (1851–1927), Tow Law, county Durham, and Sheffield, Yorkshire;
born 16 February 1851 at Desertmartin, county Londonderry, son of Joseph Johnston of Desertmartin; educated at Moneymore School; studied medicine at Queen's College, Belfast, from 1867; MD MCh (QUI) 1871; Dip Mid 1872; general practitioner, of Tow Law c 1875, of 277 St Philip's Road, Sheffield, from c 1880, also of 53 Montgomery Terrace Road and 59 Clarke Grove Road; retired c 1925;

married Emily Kate —; died 11 April 1927; probate London 13 May 1927. [Lond PPR, will cal; *Med Dir*; QCB adm reg].

JOHNSTON, GEORGE JAMESON (1866–1926), Dublin;
born 18 April 1866 at The Park, Dungannon, county Tyrone, son of Ronald Johnston, station master, of Dungannon Railway Station and Sarah Emily Ewing; educated at Dungannon Royal School; studied medicine at at Trinity College, Dublin; BA (RUI) 1891; MA MB BCh BAO 1894; FRCSI 1898; demonstrator in biology to the Royal College of Science; assistant surgeon to the Richmond Hospital, Dublin, 1895–6; honorary consulting surgeon to the Royal Hospital for Incurables, Dublin; surgeon and lecturer in surgery to the City of Dublin Hospital from 1896; professor of surgery RCSI 1912–26, of 16 Fitzwilliam Place, Dublin; temporary colonel RAMC 1914–18; author of various medical papers; married 12 August 1925 in Sandymount Church of Ireland Church, Grace Noreen Norman (who was born 1904/4 and married (2) Andrew Finlay Whitsitt of Dublin), younger daughter of Edward V. Norman, manager, of 19 Merrion View, Dublin; died 8 October 1926 at home; buried in Mount Jerome Cemetery, Dublin; probate Dublin 11 November 1926. [Cameron (1916); Dub GRO (b), (m) and (d); Dub Nat Arch, will cal; Kirkpatrick Archive; *Lancet* obituary (1926); *Med Dir*; O'Donnell (2008); Widdess (1967)].

JOHNSTON, HENRY MARTYN (1826/7–78), London and Belfast;
born 1826/7, son of the Rev John Johnston, minister of First Cootehill and later Tullylish Presbyterian Church, and his first wife Frances Jackson of Crieve House, Ballybay; brother of Sarah Johnston who married their first cousin Dr Frances Graydon Johnston (*q.v.*); LM Rot Hosp Dub; LRCSI 1850; worked as a medical officer in London; general practitioner, and medical officer to the Belfast Union Infirmary from c 1866, of 88 Donegall Street, Belfast; president of the Ulster Medical Society 1872–3; retired to Clifden Terrace, Bangor, county Down; unmarried; died 3 March 1878 of chronic phthisis, at Clifden Terrace; buried in Tullylish Presbyterian Graveyard; probate Belfast 5 April 1878. [Belf PRO, will cal; Clarke, *County Down*, vol 20 (1989); Craig (1985); Dub GRO (d); Hunter (1936); *Lancet* obituary (1878); McConnell (1951); *Med Dir*].

JOHNSTON, HENRY MATURIN (1850/1–1932), Stranorlar, county Donegal;
born 1850/1, son of Dr Benjamin Johnston of Middleton, county Cork (*q.v.*); studied medicine at Queen's College, Cork; MD (QUI) 1872; LRCSI and LM 1872; LAH Dub 1873; medical officer to Stranorlar Dispensary District, Workhouse Fever Hospital and constabulary from 1881; JP; married Amy C. —; died 9 July 1932 in Stranorlar; buried in Stranorlar; probate Dublin 20 December 1932. [Dub Nat Arch, will cal; Kirkpatrick Archive; *Med Dir*].

JOHNSTON, J. (*fl c* 1845), Newtownards, county Down;
surgeon, of Newtownards c 1845; possibly died c 1850. [Croly (1843–6)].

JOHNSTON, JAMES (1762/3–1839), Enniskillen, county Fermanagh;
born 1762/3, son of William Drummond, farmer, of Aghindrumman (Aughendrummond), Clogher, county Fermanagh, and Margaret —; brother of

Dr Francis Johnston, RN (*q.v.*); surgeon and apothecary, of Main Street, Enniskillen, and St Angelo, county Fermanagh; married Anna Maria — (who was born 1775/6 and died 4 November 1862); father of Dr Francis Graydon Johnston (*q.v.*); died 14 January 1839; probate Prerogative Court 1839. [*BNL* 22 January 1839 (d); Belf PRO, prerog wills index; Johnston (1972); Pigot (1824)].

JOHNS(T)ON, JAMES (1777–1845), Naval Medical Service, Portsmouth and London;
> born February 1777 in Ballinderry, county Londonderry (youngest son); apprenticed to Mr Young, surgeon-apothecary in Portglenone, 1792–4 and to Mr John Bankhead in Belfast 1794–6, becoming a United Irishman; went to London to complete his education and train as a surgeon; joined the Naval Medical Service as surgeon's mate 1798 and saw much active service at the Newfoundland and Nova Scotia areas; passed his second examination 1800 and was made full surgeon to serve on HMS *Cynthia* from Egypt; invalided home 1800; served on HMS *Driver* in the North Sea; after the Peace of Amiens served in the Far East 1803–06 on HMS *Caroline*; present at the disastrous expedition to Walcheren 1809; served on HMS *Impregnable* c 1814 and attended the Duke of Clarence (later William IV) during a slight attack of fever, becoming his friend; general practitioner in Portsmouth and started *The Medico-Chirurgical Review* in 1816; moved to London in 1818; MD (St Andrews) 1816 (on testimonials); LRCP Lond 1821; involved in a prolonged quarrel with Thomas Wakley of the *The Lancet* from c 1824–9, including an action for libel in which Johnson had to pay £100 in damages; physician-in-ordinary to his old shipmate King William IV, in 1830; edited *The British and Foreign Medical Review* 1836–44; author of *The Oriental Voyager* (1807), an account of his far-east service, *The Influence of Tropical Climates on European Constitutions* (1812 with later editions to 1841), *The Influence of the Atmosphere on the Health of the Human Frame* (1828), *A Tour in Ireland, with Meditations and Reflections* (1844) and other works; married in autumn 1806 Charlotte Wolfenden of Lambeg, county Antrim; father of two medical doctors; died 10 October 1845; buried in Kensal Green Cemetery; portrait by J. Wood, engraved by W. Holl. [Balfour (1923); Croly (1846); Crone (1928); *DIB* (2009); *Dub Quart J Med Sci* 1846; 1: 275–6; Froggatt (2002); Martin (2010); *Munk's Roll*, vol 3; *NMS* (1826); Newmann (1993); *Oxford DNB* (2004); Smart (2004); Sprigg (1897)].

JOHNSTON, JAMES (d 1822), Downpatrick, county Down;
> surgeon in Downpatrick; married — and had a son who died in 1821; died March 1822 in Downpatrick. [*BNL* 19 March 1822 (d); Clarke, *County Down*, vol 7 (1993)].

JOHNSTON, JAMES (*fl c* 1845), Stewartstown, county Tyrone;
> general practitioner, of Stewartstown, c 1845; possibly died c 1850. [Croly (1843–6)].

JOHNSTON, JAMES (*fl c* 1845), Hasle, county Fermanagh;
> medical officer to Hasle, and the constabulary, c 1845; possibly died c 1850. [Croly (1843–6)].

JOHNS(T)ON, JAMES (d 1852), Gilford, county Down;
CM Glas [?]; general practitioner of Gilford, c 1845; married —; father of Jane Johnston who was born 1839; died 1852. [*BNL* 25 October 1844 (d); Croly (1843–6); *Med Dir*].

JOHNSTON, JAMES (1864–89), Pontypridd, Glamorgan;
born 12 February 1864 at Recarson, Omagh, county Tyrone, son of Archibald Johnston of Recarson; educated at Omagh Intermediate School; studied medicine at Queen's College, Belfast, from 1880; MD (RUI) 1886; BAO 1888; BCh 1889; general practitioner, of Pentre, Pontypridd; died 1889. [*Med Dir*; QUB].

JOHNSTON, JAMES (1869–c 1912), Belfast and Dublin;
born 28 December 1869 at Magherafelt, county Londonderry, son of James Johnston, merchant, of 50 Wellington Park and Dundrum, Belfast; educated at RBAI; studied medicine at Queen's College, Belfast, from 1886; LRCP LRCS Edin 1895; LFPS Glas 1895; general practitioner, of Dunarnon, Belfast, from c 1896 and of 32 Elgin Road, Dublin, from c 1910; died c 1912. [*Med Dir*; QCB adm reg].

JOHNSTON, JAMES ALFRED (d c 1927), Monaghan, Southampton, Hampshire, Cape Colony, South Africa, and Dorstone, Herefordshire;
studied arts and medicine at Trinity College, Dublin, and the Royal College of Surgeons in Ireland; LM Rot Hosp Dub 1879; LKQCPI and LM, LRCSI and LM 1880; of North Mall, Westport, Mayo, c 1880–83; resident medical officer and resident surgical officer to Sir Patrick Dun's Hospital, Dublin; assistant resident medical superintendent of Monaghan and Cavan District Lunatic Asylum, Monaghan c 1883–5; general practitioner, of Richmond Lodge, Shirley, Southampton c 1885–94; emigrated to South Africa c 1895; of Middleburg, Cape Colony c 1896–1900; general practitioner, of 'Dulnain', Mount Nod Road, Streatham, London c 1900–13 and of The Hall, Dorstone c 1913–18; retired c 1918 to 'Iona', Alexandra Road, Malvern; died c 1927. [Kirkpatrick Archive; *Med Dir*].

JOHNSTON (E), JAMES JOHN (1815/6–75), Sligo;
born 1815/6, son of Dr Thomas Johnston of Lowery and Ballyshannon, county Donegal (*q.v.*), and Barbara Johnston; MRCSE 1832; LAH Dub 1836; general practitioner, of Castle Street, Sligo c 1840–78; married 15 October 1850 in St Anne's Church, Ballyshannon, Jane Allingham (who was born 1829 and was sister of the poet, William Allingham); father of Dr Thomas James William Abraham Johnston (*q.v.*); died 3 December 1875 in Sligo; probate Ballina 27 January 1876. [Belf PRO, will cal; Dub GRO (d); Hitchings, Paul, pers com; *Med Dir*].

JOHNS(T)ON, JOHN (1791/2–1829), Naval Medical Service and Armagh;
born 1791/2; uncle of Dr Samuel Johnston of Carrigart, county Donegal (*q.v.*); MD [?]; joined the Naval Medical Service as assistant surgeon; surgeon 1812; resigned and was physician and surgeon, of Barrack Street, Armagh c 1824; died 2 July 1829; buried in Armagh Church of Ireland Cathedral Graveyard; administration Armagh Diocesan Court 1829. [Dub Nat Arch, Armagh Dio Admins index; gravestone inscription; *Londonderry Sentinel* 17 August 1849 (m, nephew); *NMS* (1826); Pigot (1824)].

JOHNSTON, JOHN (1849–81), Drumquin, county Tyrone;
born 15 September 1849 at Castlederg, county Tyrone, son of Richard Johnston of Munnie, Castlederg; educated at Castlederg Classical School; studied arts and medicine at Queen's College, Belfast, from 1866; MD (QUI) 1871; MCh 1872; LFPS Glas 1872; medical officer, public vaccinator and registrar of births and deaths to Drumquin Dispensary District from 1872; married Alicia —; died 2 May 1881 of apoplexy, at Burrel's Folly, Drumquin. [Dub GRO (d); Kirkpatrick Archive; *Med Dir;* QCB adm reg].

JOHNSTON, JOHN (1872–1958), Farnworth, Lancashire;
born 14 September 1872 at Bloomfield, Belfast, son of Thomas Johnston, builder, of Bloomfield; educated at RBAI; studied medicine at Queen's College, Belfast, from 1890; MB BCh BAO (RUI) 1897; general practitioner, of Long Causeway and later Highcroft, Worsley Road, Farnworth, Lancashire; married Florence Mabel —; died 10 September 1958 at the Royal Infirmary, Bolton; probate Manchester 17 August 1959. [Lond PPR will cal; *Med Dir;* QCB adm reg].

JOHNSTON, JOHN ALEXANDER (1839/40–79), Virginia, county Cavan, and Dublin;
born 1839/40; LRCSI 1861 LKQCPI 1863; general practitioner and farmer, of Eighter, Virginia, and 84 Upper Leeson Street, Dublin; unmarried; died 17 October 1879 at Eighter House; probate Dublin 27 April 1880. [Belf PRO, will cal; Dub GRO (d); *Med Dir*].

JOHNSTON, JOHN ARMSTRONG (1829/30–63), Tempo, county Fermanagh, and Bailieborough, county Cavan;
born 1829/30; nephew of Dr James Johnston of Enniskillen and St Angelo (*q.v.*) and Dr Francis Johnston, RN (*q.v.*) and grandson of William Johnston, farmer, of Aghindrumman; LM Dub 1846; LRCSI 1850; LKQCPI 1858; assistant surgeon to Chelsea Workhouse and Dispensary, St Lukes; medical officer to Gurteen Dispensary, Boyle; medical officer to Tempo Dispensary District and constabulary; medical officer to Bailieborough Dispensary District and constabulary; author of various medical papers; married 12 March 1856 in Bailieborough Church of Ireland Church, Elizabeth Chambers (who died 25 December 1860), youngest daughter of Thomas Chambers of Bailieborough; died 7 June 1863 at Bailieborough; buried in Clogher Cathedral Graveyard; administration Dublin 10 September 1863. [*BNL* 15 March 1856 (m) and 28 December 1860 (d); Belf PRO, will cal; Johnston (1972); *Londonderry Sentinel* 12 June 1863 (d); *Med Dir*].

JOHNSTON, JOHN REID (1855–c 1882), Knocknadona, Lisburn, county Antrim;
born 3 August 1855, son of the Rev Thomas Johnston, minister of Newtownstewart, county Tyrone; educated at Londonderry Academical Institution; studied arts and medicine at Queen's College, Belfast, from 1873; MD MCh (QUI) 1878; LM KQCPI 1879; medical officer and medical officer of health to Knocknadona Dispensary District from c 1880; died c 1882. [*Med Dir;* QCB adm reg].

JOHNSTON, KENNEDY (d 1831), London;
of Magherafelt, county Londonderry; doctor, of London; died 19 July 1831. [*BNL* 30 August 1831 (d); *Londonderry Sentinel* 3 September 1831 (d)].

JOHNSTON, ROBERT (1809/10–64), Bellaghy and Castledawson, county Londonderry;
born 1809/10; MRCSE; surgeon and medical officer to Bellaghy Dispensary District; unmarried; died 5 October 1864 of spotted typhus fever, 'caught in the discharge of his duty', at the Workhouse Fever Hospital, Magherafelt; administration Dublin 29 July 1865. [Belf PRO, will cal; *Coleraine Chronicle* 15 October 1864 (d); Dub GRO (d); *Londonderry Sentinel* 11 October 1864 (d); *Med Dir*].

JOHNSTON, ROBERT (1822/3–73), Newry, county Down;
born 1822/3, son of Thomas Johnston, farmer; studied medicine at Glasgow University, Trinity College, Dublin and the Royal College of Surgeons in Ireland; MD (Glas) 1849; CM 1854; LSA Lond 1858; LAH Dub 1859; general practitioner in Newry; married 22 September 1852 in Downshire Road Presbyterian Church, Newry, Matilda Todd, eldest daughter of David Todd, merchant, of Newry; died 10 January 1873 at Newry, as a result of a fall from a horse; buried in Newry Presbyterian Graveyard; administration Belfast 9 May 1873. [Addison (1898); *BNL* 24 September 1852 (m); Belf PRO, will cal; Clarke, *County Down*, vol 21 (1998); *Coleraine Chronicle* 2 October 1852 (m); *Med Dir*; UHF database (m)].

JOHNSTON, ROBERT (1823/4–c 1878), Demerara, and Bessbrook, county Armagh;
born 1823/4, son of George Johnston, manager; studied medicine at Trinity College, Dublin, and the Royal College of Surgeons in Ireland; LM Rot Hosp Dub; LRCSI 1853; surgeon to the Government Emigration Commission 1854; assistant surgeon to Military Post Mahaica Jail, Demerara 1856 and to the Lepper Asylum and Dispensary 1857; general practitioner, of Bessbrook, and medical officer to Bessbrook Spinning Company; married 23 December 1851 in Townsend Street Presbyterian Church, Belfast, Grace Beggs (who was born 1826/7), third daughter of Hugh Beggs, miller, of Divis Street, Belfast; died c 1878. [*BNL* 5 January 1852 (m); Dub GRO (m); *Med Dir*].

JOHNSTON, ROBERT ALEXANDER (1868–1960), Alrewas, Staffordshire;
born 8 August 1868 at Ballykinlar, county Down, son of Francis Johnston, farmer, of Ballykinlar; educated at RBAI; studied medicine at Queen's College, Belfast, from 1886 and the Royal College of Surgeons in Ireland; LRCPI and LM LRCSI and LM 1900; resident medical officer for Richmond, Whitworth and Hardwick Hospitals, Dublin; general practitioner, of Alrewas; medical officer and public vaccinator for Tamworth and Lichfield Districts; temporary captain RAMC; retired c 1928 to Coleshill, Birmingham and to Hydesville, Broadway North, Walsall c 1940, to Chartley Park, Stowe-by-Chartley, Stafford c 1950, to Braeside, Thornhill Road, Streetley, Sutton Coldfield c 1951, to the Byre, Llandrindod Wells, Radnorshire c 1955; married Nellie Smith; died 27 August 1960; probate Oxford 12 October 1960. [Lond PPR, will cal; *Med Dir*; QCB adm reg].

JOHNSTON, ROBERT GRAHAM (*fl c* 1873), Maguiresbridge, county Fermanagh; studied medicine at Ledwich School, Dublin; LM Coombe Hosp Dub 1872; LRCSI 1872; LRCP and LM Edin 1873; medical officer to Maguiresbridge Dispensary District, from 1873; married Mary — (who died 1 May 1878). [Kirkpatrick Archive; *Med Dir*].

JOHNSTON, SAMUEL (1815–77), Carrigart, county Donegal, and Londonderry;
born 1815, only son of Thomas Johnston, gentleman; nephew of Dr John Johnston RN (*q.v.*); LRCSI and LM 1840; MD (Glas) 1841; general practitioner of Larganreagh, Carrigart, c 1845–50 and later of Brookhall Lodge, Londonderry; married 9 August 1849 in Carrigart Church of Ireland Church, Margaret Wilkinson (who was born in 1824/5 and died 14 April 1851, buried in Carrigart Graveyard), youngest daughter of the Rev John Wilkinson, rector of Mevagh; died 12 January 1877 at Brookhall Cottage; administration (with will) Londonderry 23 March 1877. [Addison (1898); *BNL* 21 April 1851 (d); Belf PRO, will cal; Croly (1843–6); Dub GRO (d); *Londonderry Sentinel* 17 August 1849 (m) and 18 April 1851 (d); Lucas (1962); *Med Dir*].

JOHNSTON, SAMUEL (1845–1906), Broughshane, county Antrim, and Bradford, Yorkshire;
born 22 November 1845 at Broughshane, son of Francis Johnston of Broughshane; educated at Belfast New Academy; studied medicine at Queen's College, Belfast, from 1864; LRCP LRCS Edin 1870; MD (QUI) 1872; general practitioner, of Broughshane, county Antrim c 1875 and of 47 Barkerend Road, Bradford, Yorkshire from c 1880; president of the Bradford Medico-Chirurgical Society; surgeon lieutenant-colonel (V.D.) and senior medical officer to the West Yorkshire Infantry Brigade and Regiment; died 16 January 1906 at 47 Barkerend Road; administration Wakefield 9 March 1906. [Kirkpatrick Archive; Lond PPR, will cal; *Med Dir*; QCB adm reg].

JOHNSTON, SAMUEL SHANNON (c 1749–1802), Downpatrick, county Down, and USA;
born c 1749, son of Thomas Johnston and Margaret Shannon, who were appointed porter and housekeeper of Down County Infirmary in 1767 when it was in Saul Street; probationer apothecary in the Down County Infirmary under surgeon William Waring 1770–73 and apothecary from 1773; later surgeon, of English Street, Downpatrick; served as a surgeon with the Seaforde and Kilmore Yeomanry at the Battle of Ballynahinch 13 June 1798 but was suspected of sympathy with the United Irishmen; influenced by his brother-in-law Ambrose Cramer, woollen draper of Scotch Street; emigrated with his family to the USA in the ship *Pauline* 1800; married 1794 Frances Cummine (who was born 1768/9 and died 26 June 1854 in Killough, eldest daughter of James Cummine of Killough and niece of Anne Cummine (wife of Dr William Waring); died early in 1802 and his widow and family returned to Killough. [*BNL* 10 July 1854 (d); Parkinson (1967); Pilson (1938)].

JOHNSTON, THOMAS (*fl c* 1800), Lowery, county Fermanagh, and Ballyshannon, county Donegal;
>surgeon, of Lowery and Ballyshannon; married Barbara Johnston, daughter of John Johnston of Brookhill, and Jane Weir; father of Dr James John Johnston of Sligo (*q.v.*); died before 1828. [*BNL* 13 November 1827 (m, daughter); Hitchings, Paul, pers com].

JOHNSTON, THOMAS (*fl c* 1802), Rathfriland, county Down;
>LAH Dub 1802; apothecary, of Rathfiland. [Apothecaries (1829)].

JOHNSTON, THOMAS (1796/7–1865), Naval Medical Service and Omagh, county Tyrone;
>born 1796/7 or 1801; studied medicine at St George's Hospital, London 1819 (for six months); LM Rot Hosp Dub 1825; MRCSE 1826; MD (Glas) 1841; joined the Naval Medical Service as assistant surgeon on HMS *Ringdove* 1826–8, HMS *Jason* 1828–9 and HMS *Champion* 1829–33; surgeon on HMS *Thunder* 1833–6 (in England and West Indies); on half pay from 1836 because of dyspepsia, but was able to attend Glasgow University; surgeon on HMS *Spartan* 1846–9; retired on half pay 1839 to Donaghanie, Omagh; unmarried; died 22 August 1865 at Donaghanie; buried in Edenderry Presbyterian Graveyard, Omagh; administration (with will) Londonderry 26 September 1865. [Addison (1898); Belf PRO, will cal; Dub GRO (d); Johnston, Margaret, pers com; *Londonderry Sentinel* 29 August 1865 (d); McGrew (1998) and (2001); *Med Dir*; *Tyrone Constitution*, 25 August 1865 (d)].

JOHNSTON, THOMAS JAMES WILLIAM ABRAHAM (1871–c 1943), Belfast, and Cape Province, South Africa;
>born 21 October 1871 in Sligo, son of Dr James John Johnston, surgeon, of Sligo (*q.v.*), and Jane Allingham (sister of William Allingham, the poet); educated at the Marconi Boys School, Dublin; studied medicine at Queen's College, Belfast, from 1889; MB BCh BAO (RUI) 1895; general practitioner, of 16 Chichester Avenue, Antrim Road, Belfast c 1900; emigrated to South Africa c 1906; general practitioner, of Pietersburg, Transvaal; served in South African Medical Corps during World War I; MC; of Strathbeg, Highfield Road, Rosebank, Cape Province c 1925; died c 1943. [Hitchings, Paul, pers com; *Med Dir*; QCB adm reg].

JOHNSTON, WILLIAM (1760–1832), Carrickmacross, county Monaghan, and Newry, county Down;
>born 1760, fourth son of John Johnston of Woodvale, county Armagh; studied medicine at Glasgow University; MD (Glas) 1786; general practitioner, of Carrickmacross c 1795, of Hill Street, Newry, from 1802, of Trevor Hill, Newry, from 1816; erected public baths in Newry in 1813 but they were not a financial success; retired to Dundalk, county Louth, in 1828; married in 1793 Eleanor Lindsay (who was born 1765/6 and died 14 October 1837), second daughter of the Rev Walter Lindsay; died 16 October 1832 at Dundalk; buried in Creggan graveyard. [Addison (1913); Crossle (1909); Pigot (1824)].

JOHNSTON, WILLIAM (1777/8–1813), Naval Medical Service;
born 1777/8; joined the Naval Medical Service as assistant surgeon; died 2 March 1813. [*BNL* 23 March 1813 (d)].

JOHNSTON, WILLIAM (1795/6–1865), Kesh, county Fermanagh;
born 1795/6; LSA Lond 1816; accoucheur of the Dublin Lying-in Hospital 1820; MRCSE 1820; medical officer to Kesh Dispensary District, constabulary and Tubrid Charter School from c 1826; medical officer to Ederney Dispensary District from 1852; married —; died 28 December 1865 at Kesh. [Croly (1843–6); Dub GRO (d); Kirkpatrick Archive; *Londonderry Sentinel* 2 January 1866 (d); *Med Dir*].

JOHNSTON, WILLIAM (*fl c* 1834–45), Belfast;
LRCS Edin; one of those who presented an inscribed gold box to Dr S.S. Thomson in 1834; surgeon, of Belfast c 1845. [Croly (1843–6); Thomson presentation box].

JOHNSTON, WILLIAM (1846–1900), Clay Cross, Derbyshire, and Leicester;
born 19 January 1846 in Belfast, son of Samuel Johnston of 69 Grosvenor Road, Belfast; educated at the Belfast Seminary; studied medicine at Queen's College, Belfast, from 1866; MD MCh (QUI) 1870; general practitioner, of Clay Cross c 1875 and of 64 London Road, Leicester from c 1880; died 26 December 1900; probate Leicester 27 March 1901. [Lond PPR, will cal; *Med Dir*; QCB adm reg].

JOHNSTON, WILLIAM B. (*fl c* 1836), Castledawson, county Londonderry;
surgeon, of Castledawson; married 15 April 1836 in Ballyscullion Church of Ireland Church, Bellaghy, Anna H. Hammersley, eldest daughter of William Hammersley of Lakeview. [*BNL* 22 April 1836 (m)].

JOHNSTON, W. F. (d 1832), Brookeborough, county Fermanagh;
surgeon, of Brookeborough; married —; daughter married 22 December 1840 Thomas Williams of Beacho, county Fermanagh; died 20 June 1832 at Brookeborough. [*BNL* 26 June 1832 (d) and 29 December 1840 (m, daughter)].

JOHNSTON, WILLIAM THOMAS (1853–1942), Army Medical Service;
born 2 December 1853 at Beragh, county Tyrone, son of John Johnston, merchant, of Beragh; educated at Londonderry Academical Institution; studied medicine at Queen's College, Belfast, from 1869; MD Dip Mid (QUI) 1875; LRCS Edin 1876; joined the Army Medical Service as surgeon in 1877; surgeon major 1889; surgeon lieutenant-colonel 1897; served in Egypt in 1882, also in Cyprus and China; retired in 1906 but returned during World War I 1915–18; of 'Homeville' 21 St Andrews Road, Bedford c 1920; married 11 April 1907 Eilene Hilda Macaulay Leech, elder daughter of Charles Leech; died 1 February 1942 at Patrick Street, Strabane, county Tyrone; probate Llandudno 29 June 1942. [*BMJ* obituary (1942); Burke *LGI* (1912); Kirkpatrick Archive; Lond PPR, will cal; *Med Dir*; Peterkin and Johnston (1968); QCB adm reg].

JOHNSTONE, JAMES (*fl c* 1808), Ballyshannon, county Donegal;
LAH Dub 1808; apothecary, of Ballyshannon. [Apothecaries (1829)].

JOHNSTONE, JOHN (*fl c* 1792), Ballyshannon, county Donegal;
LAH Dub 1792; apothecary, of Ballyshannon. [Apothecaries (1829)].

JOHNSTONE, JOHN (d 1853), Newtownards, county Down, ship's surgeon, and Melbourne, Australia;
of Newtownards; MD [?]; surgeon superintendent on the emigrant ship *Helen*; died 7 January 1853 at Bunguyan, near Melbourne. [*BNL* 16 May 1853 (d)].

JOHNSTONE, JOHN (*fl c* 1845), Aghadowey, county Londonderry;
surgeon of Aghadowey; married — (23 February 1825–23 February 1845); buried in Killaig Presbyterian Graveyard. [Church register].

JOHNSTONE, M. (*fl c* 1800), Ballyshannon, county Donegal;
LAH Dub 1800; apothecary, of Ballyshannon. [Apothecaries (1829)].

JOHNSTONE, SIR ROBERT JAMES (1872–1938), Belfast;
born 4 January 1872 at Greenisland, county Antrim, only son and eldest child of Charles Johnstone, landowner, and Mary McCreavy; educated at RBAI; studied arts and medicine at Queen's College, Belfast 1890–96 winning many scholarships and prizes; BA (RUI) 1893; Coulter Exhibition, Belfast Royal Hospital 1895; MB (hons) BCh 1896; FRCSE 1900; FRCOG 1929; house surgeon in Belfast Royal Hospital 1899–1900; demonstrator of anatomy and pathology at Queen's College, Belfast, followed by a period of training in London and Vienna; honorary anaesthetist to the Royal Victoria Hospital, Belfast 1900–02; of Great Victoria Street, Belfast at first and moved in 1909 to 14 University Square; assistant gynaecologist to the Royal Victoria Hospital 1902–19 and attending gynaecologist 1919–37; gave the annual winter oration at the Royal Victoria Hospital 1907; chairman of the Royal Victoria Hospital medical staff 1933–6; professor of gynaecology in Queen's College, Belfast 1920–37; surgeon to Royal Maternity Hospital, Belfast 1938; MP for Queen's University in Northern Ireland Parliament 1921–38; president of the Ulster Medical Society 1922–3; chairman of the Board of Governors of RBAI; president of the BMA 1937; knight bachelor 1938; president of the Queen's University Association 1939; retired in 1937 to Long Acre, Newcastle, county Down; author of various medical papers and humorous verses; married 8 August 1906 in Cliftonville Presbyterian Church, Belfast, Florence Warwick Magill, daughter of the Rev George Magill, minister of Cliftonville Presbyterian Church; Florence Magill's sister Helen was mother of Dr Robert William Magill Strain, MB BCh BAO (QUB) 1930, MRCPI 1949; died 26 October 1938 in Newcastle; portrait by Frank McKelvey in Queen's University (Department of O & G); commemorated by Johnstone House wing of the Royal Maternity Hospital; probate Belfast 30 March 1939. [Belf PRO, will cal; *Belf Roy Hosp, Ann Rep*; *BMJ* obituary (1938); Fraser (1987); Kirkpatrick Archive; *Lancet* obituary (1938); *Med Dir*; Moody and Beckett (1959); O'Brien, Crookshank and Wolstenholme (1988); Peel (1976); Power and Le Fanu (1953); QCB adm reg; Strain (1969); UHF database (m); *UMJ* (anon) 1939; 8: 48–50].

JOLLY, ANDREW (1852/3–97), Drum, county Cavan, Irvinestown, county Fermanagh, and Liverpool, Lancashire;
   born 1852/3, son of Andrew Jolly, farmer; studied medicine at the Carmichael School and the Richmond Hospital, Dublin; LKQCPI 1873; LRCP Edin 1873; LM Coombe Hosp Dub; medical officer to the Drum Dispensary District, Cootehill, county Cavan, from 1875; general practitioner of Irvinestown c 1876; general practitioner, of 2 Kingsley Road, Princes Park, Liverpool, c 1885 and of Smithdown Gate, Sefton Park, Liverpool c 1895; married 10 February 1880 in St Thomas's Church of Ireland Church, Belfast, Henrietta Broomfield Ker, daughter of Richard Ker, farmer, of Belfast; died 28 May 1897 at Liverpool General Hospital after an overdose of laudanum taken by misadventure (Coroner's Inquest); administration Liverpool 26 August 1897. [Dub GRO (d); Kirkpatrick Archive; *Med Dir*; UHF database (m)].

JOLLY, BENJAMIN (1811/2–70), Portarlington, Queen's County, Belturbet, county Cavan, and Letterkenny, county Donegal;
   born 1811/2; LAH Dub 1832; apothecary to the Dispensery, Portarlinton c 1840–64; apothecary in Belturbet c 1864; apothecary to Donegal Lunatic Asylum, Letterkenny c 1865–70; married —; died 24 July 1870 in Letterkenny. [Croly (1843–6); Dub GRO (d); *Med Dir*].

JONES, CONWAY (1717/8–78), Lisburn, county Antrim;
   born 1717/8, son of Valentine Jones of Lisburn; studied medicine at Edinburgh University and became a member of the Royal Medical Society 1739–40, also at Leyden University from 1741; MD (Leyden) 1743 (thesis 'De restoria vitae humanae'); general practitioner in Lisburn; married 1753 (Dublin Marriage Licence) Mary Wray Todd, daughter of William Todd of Dublin; father of G.P. Jones who studied at Glasgow University from 1773 and of William Todd Jones, United Irishman (1757–1818); died 21 November 1778 at Lisburn; will dated 25 February 1767 proved in Prerogative Court 21 January 1779. [Addison (1913); *BNL* (24 November 1778) (d); Belf PRO, Burke Pedigrees, T559, vol 24, pp 350–51; *DIB* (2009) (for son); Kirkpatrick Archive; Innes Smith (1932); Vicars (1897)].

JONES, GERVAIS BOLTON (1869–1942), ship's surgeon, Coalisland, county Tyrone, and Natal, South Africa;
   born 8 March 1869 at Tullyraw, Cookstown, county Tyrone, second son of the Rev Thomas Josiah Jones, curate of Ardtrea, county Tyrone, and later rector of Tullaniskin, county Tyrone, and Letitia Eleanor Percy of Garadice; brother of Dr Theophilus Percy Jones (*q.v.*); studied arts and medicine at Trinity College, Dublin from 1887; BA MB BCh BAO (TCD) 1892; LM Coombe Hosp Dub; surgeon on SS *Yorkshire* (Bibby Line) and SS *Boma* (British and West Africa Company) c 1893; general practitioner, of Brackaville, Coalisland, county Tyrone, c 1893–6; emigrated to South Africa c 1897; district surgeon and health officer, of 'Erin', Bergville, Natal; married 7 January 1899, Edith Sophia Greer, eldest daughter of the Rev W.H. Greer, rector of Crossboyne, county Mayo; died May 1942. [Burke, *LGI* (1912); Dub GRO (b); Fleming (2001); Leslie (1911); *Med Dir*; TCD adm reg; *TCD Cat*, vol II (1896); *TCD Reg*].

JONES, JOHN EDMUND (*fl c* 1839), Monaghan;
son of John Eccles Jones, gentleman; surgeon, of Monaghan; married 4 June 1839 in Milton-on-Thames Parish Church, Kent, Mary Anne Ayerst, eldest daughter of Francis Ayerst, gentleman, of Brompton, Kent. [*BNL* 11 June 1839 (m); Lond GRO (m)].

JONES, JOHN LANGDALE (1876–1917), Royal Army Medical Corps;
born 29 December 1876 at Aughnacloy, county Tyrone; studied medicine at the Royal College of Surgeons in Ireland; LRCPI LRCSI 1899; joined the Royal Army Medical Corps as lieutenant 1900; captain 1903; major 1912; served in Jamaica 1901–03, Ceylon 1904–08 and India 1912–17; died 12 May 1917 in India of cerebral malaria. [*BMJ* obituary (1917); Drew (1968); Kirkpatrick Archive].

JONES, THEOPHILUS PERCY (1866–1934), Army Medical Service;
born 6 January 1866 at Ardtrea, county Tyrone, eldest son of the Rev Thomas Josiah Jones, curate of Ardtrea, county Tyrone, and rector of Tullaniskin, county Tyrone, and Letitia Eleanor Percy of Garradice, county Leitrim; brother of Dr Gervais Bolton Jones (*q.v.*); studied arts and medicine at Trinity College, Dublin, from 1884; BA (TCD) 1888; MB BCh BAO 1890; joined the Army Medical Service as surgeon lieutenant 1892; surgeon captain 1895; major 1904; lieutenant colonel 1915; served on the North-West Frontier of India 1897–8, South Africa 1900–02, World War I (Gallipoli and Egypt); CMG 1916; ADMS to 42nd Division, with Mediterranean and Egyptian Expeditionary Forces; CB c 1918; retired to Lal Koti, Charlton Kings, Cheltenham; married 5 February 1896 in Bombay Cathedral, Ella Isabel Watts, youngest daughter of major E.R. Watts of the Bengal Horse Artillery; died 26 July 1934. [Fleming (2001); *Med Dir*; Peterkin and Johnston (1968); TCD adm reg;); *TCD Cat*, vol II (1896); *TCD Reg* (1937)].

JONES, WILLIAM (*fl c* 1819), Naval Medical Service and Rostrevor, county Down;
joined the Naval Medical Service as assistant surgeon; retired as surgeon to Rostrevor c 1818; married 14 March 1819 in Rostrevor Church of Ireland Church, Margaret Black, third daughter of Dr Thomas Black (*q.v.*). [*BNL* 19 March 1819 (m); Bradshaw (1819)].

JONES, WILLIAM (d c 1848), Cookstown, county Tyrone;
surgeon, of Low Cross, Cookstown; died c 1848; administration Armagh Diocesan Court 1848. [Dub Nat Arch, Armagh Dio Admins index].

JONES, WILLIAM EDMUND JAMES (1875–1956), Annahilt, county Down, and Ballymena, county Antrim;
born 24 November 1875 at Annahilt, son of William Jones, farmer, of Annahilt; studied medicine at Queen's College, Belfast, from 1890; MB BCh BAO (RUI) 1900; general practitioner, of Annahilt c 1903 and later of the Crescent and of Flixton Lodge, Ballymena; retired c 1950 to 'Cahan Croft', 39 Cushendall Road, Ballymena; married (1) 12 September 1905 in Wellington Street Christian Brethren Church, Ballymena, Mary Kane, daughter of William Kane, ironfounder, of Ballymena; (2)

Sarah —; died 23 December 1956 at 39 Cushendall Road; probate Belfast 29 April 1957. [Belf PRO, will cal, will; *Med Dir*; QCB adm reg; UHF database (m)].

JORDAN, WILLIAM GEORGE (1869–1936), Liverpool, Lancashire;
born 28 October 1869 at Hamilton's Bawn, county Armagh, eldest son of the Rev William Jordan, minister of Drumminis Presbyterian Church, county Armagh; educated at Armagh Academy and Mr Finnigan of Donegall Pass, Belfast; studied medicine at Queen's College, Belfast, from 1889; MB BCh BAO (RUI) 1897; LM Rot Hosp Dub 1897; DPH RCPSI 1904; general practitioner, of 283 Kensington, Liverpool; died 31 December 1936 at 4 Deane Road, Liverpool; probate Liverpool 1 March 1937. [Kirkpatrick Archive; Lond PPR, will cal; *Med Dir*; QCB adm reg].

JORDAN, — (*fl c* 1837);
married 18 April 1837 Elizabeth Simpson, eldest daughter of Dr Thomas Simpson of Moira (*q.v.*). [*BNL* 25 April 1837 (m)].

JOY, JOHN HOLMES (1842–1910), ship's surgeon, Valparaiso, Chile, and Tamworth, Staffordshire;
born 28 February 1842 in Dublin, youngest son of Henry Holmes Joy, QC, of Dublin; educated at Armagh Royal School 1854–7; studied arts and medicine at Trinity College, Dublin, from 1857; BA (TCD) 1862; MA MB MD MCh 1865; sailed to Chile as ship's surgeon; general practitioner in Valparaiso; general practitioner, certifying factory surgeon and medical officer to Tamworth Hospital, of The Manor House, Tamworth, from 1873; JP for Staffordshire and Warwickshire 1873; coroner for East Staffordshire from 1898; president of the Midland Medical Society and Midland Branch of BMA; author of various medial papers; married 4 November 1868 Anita Mary McKay (who pre-deceased him), second daughter of Dr John McKay of Fortwilliam, Inverness, and of Valparaiso; father of Dr Charles Holmes Joy, MB (Durham) 1896; died 4 January 1910 at Tamworth; probate London 26 April 1910. [*BMJ* obituary (1910); Burtchaell and Sadleir (1935); *Coleraine Chronicle* 9 January 1869 (m); Ferrar (1933); Kirkpatrick Archive; Lond PPR, will cal, will; *Med Dir*].

JOYCE, LANCASTER (1835/6–1909), Ballybay, county Monaghan, and Falcarragh, county Donegal;
born 1835/6; studied medicine at the Royal College of Surgeons in Ireland and the Ledwich School, Dublin; MRCSE 1859; LM Rot Hosp Dub 1861; medical officer to Shercock Dispensary District, Ballybay c 1860–74; medical officer, public vaccinator and registrar of births and deaths; to Crossroads Dispensary District, Dunfanaghy, from 1874; of Ardchicken House from c 1890; JP; married Elizabeth Frances —; died 3 January 1909 at Ardchicken House; probate Londonderry 24 June 1909. [Belf PRO, will cal; Dub GRO (d); Kirkpatrick Archive; *Med Dir*].

JOYNT, CHRISTOPHER (1828–1915), Indian Medical Service;
born 25 April 1828, son of Henry Joynt, of Ballina, county Mayo; studied medicine at Queen's Colleges, Belfast and Galway; MD (QUI) 1855; MRCSE 1856; LKQCPI

1862; FKQCPI 1880; joined the Indian Medical Service (Bombay establishment) as assistant surgeon 1856; surgeon 1868; surgeon major 1873; brigade surgeon 1879; served in Persia 1856–7 and capture of Bushire and Mahamara (medal with clasp); served in Indian Mutiny 1859–60 and Abyssina 1867–8 (medal); professor of midwifery to GM College, Bombay; PMO Quetta District 1882–3; author of various medical papers; retired to 21 Leeson Park, Rathmines, Dublin c 1885; married (1) —; (2) —; died 4 June 1915; probate Dublin 21 June 1915. [Belf PRO, will cal; Crawford (1930); Martin (2003); *Med Dir*].

JUBB, ROBERT WALTER (1873–1948), Dublin, and Dewsbury, Yorkshire;

born 5 May 1873 at Lowestoft, Suffolk, son of Walter Jubb, Board of Trade Surveyor, of 30 Cliftonville Avenue, Belfast; educated at Methodist College, Belfast, from 1891; studied medicine at Queen's College, Belfast, from 1893; LRCP LRCS Edin 1899; LFPS Glas 1899; assistant registrar and resident medical officer to Cork Street Fever Hospital and House of Recovery, Dublin; house surgeon to Bridgewater Infimary; general practitioner, of Norville, Saville Town, Dewsbury, from c 1905; clinical assistant to Women and Children's Hospital, Leeds; of 1 Headfield Road and 1 Warren Street and later of Avondale, Saville Town; married Ethel Mary — of Dewsbury; died 7 October 1948; probate London 18 May 1949. [Fry (1984); Kirkpatrick Archive; Lond PPR, will cal; *Med Dir*; QCB adm reg].

JUNK, DAVID (1857–c 1955), Manchester, Lancashire, Bradford, Yorkshire, and Queensland, Australia;

born 27 September 1857 at Sixmilecross, county Tyrone, son of the Rev Thomas William Junk, minister of Sixmilecross Presbyterian Church; studied arts and medicine at Queen's College, Belfast, from 1878; BA (QUI) 1881; MD MAO (RUI) 1886; general practitioner of Thornton House, Clayton, Manchester and Brook Street, Bradford, Yorkshire, from c 1890; emigrated to Brisbane, Queensland c 1908; general practitioner, of Qandai, South Queensland; visiting medical inspector to Berambah Aboriginal Settlement; government medical officer to Weinholtshire and Wondai; retired c 1931; died c 1955. [Barkely (1986); *Med Dir*; QCB adm reg].

JUNK, GEORGE ALEXANDER (1863–1946), St Cloud, Minnesota, and Huddersfield, Yorkshire;

born 11 November 1863, at Sixmilecross, county Tyrone, son of the Rev Thomas William Junk, minister of Sixmilecross Presbyterian Church; educated at RBAI; studied medicine at Queen's College, Belfast, from 1880; MD (RUI) 1886; emigrated to USA c 1890; general practitioner, of St Cloud, Minnesota c 1895; president of St Cloud Board of Health and city physician; attending physician to St Raphael's Hospital, Huddersfield and surgeon to Stearns County Gaol; general practitioner, of 144 Shaw Heath, Stockport, from c 1900; retired c 1939 to 142 Somerset Road, Huddersfield; died 1 December 1946. [Barkley (1986); Kirkpatrick Archive; *Med Dir*; QCB adm reg].

K

KANE, BERNARD (*fl c* 1792), Clones, county Monaghan;
LAH Dub 1792; apothecary, of Clones. [Apothecaries (1829)].

KANE, HUGH SMILEY (1838/9–72), Antrim;
born 1838/9, son of John Kane, lawyer, and Eliza Ferris; nephew of Dr Charles Ferris (*q.v.*); brother of Dr John Kane (*q.v.*); educated at Belfast Academy; studied arts and medicine at Queen's College, Belfast, from 1856; BA (QUI) 1860; MD 1862; LRCS Edin 1864; joined the Geological Survey of India (by competitive examination) and Member of the Asiatic Society of Bengal; medical officer to Antrim Dispensary District; married 23 October 1866 in Muckamore Church of Ireland Church, county Antrim, Ellen Malone, second daughter of Edmund Malone, solicitor, of Antrim; died 22 June 1872 at Cross Street, Larne 'after a brief illness'; buried in the McGarel Cemetery, Larne; administration Belfast 7 August 1872. [Belf PRO, will cal; *Coleraine Chronicle* 29 October 1866 (m); *Larne Weekly Reporter* 29 June 1872 (d); *Med Dir*; QCB adm reg; *QUB Cal*; Rutherford and Clarke, *County Antrim,* vol 4 (2004); UHF database (m)].

KANE, JOHN (1841–83), Larne, county Antrim;
born 14 July 1841 in Australia, son of John Kane, teacher, and Elizabeth Ferris; nephew of Dr Charles Ferris (*q.v.*); brother of Dr Hugh Smiley Kane (*q.v.*); educated by RBAI; studied arts and medicine at Queen's College, Belfast, from 1860; BA (QUI) 1866; LRCP LRCS Edin 1871; medical officer and medical officer of health to Larne Dispensary District and certifying factory surgeon from 1874, following his uncle, Dr Charles Ferris; married 6 April 1876 in Raloo Presbyterian Church, county Antrim, Isabella Whiteford, third daughter of the Rev James Whiteford, presbyterian minister of Raloo; died 23 September 1883 of peritonitis, at Larne; buried in McGarel Cemetery, Larne; administration Belfast 18 January 1884. [Belf PRO, will cal; *Larne Weekly Reporter* 8 April 1876 (m) and 29 September 1883 (d); *Med Dir*; QCB adm reg; Rutherford and Clarke, *County Antrim,* vol 4 (2004); UHF database (m)].

KANE, JOHN SEYMOUR (1850–c 1907), Almondsbury and Clifton, Gloucestershire;
born 1850 in Italy, son of Joseph Kane; educated at Armagh Royal School September–December 1869; studied arts and medicine at Trinity College, Dublin, from 1867; BA (TCD) 1874; MB BCh 1879; MD 1880; general practitioner, of Almondsbury c 1885 and 27 Meridian Place, Clifton, c 1895; died c 1907. [Ferrar (1933); *Med Dir;* TCD adm reg; *TCD Cat*, vol II (1896)].

KANE, THOMAS ADAM BERESFORD (1861–1938), Bishop Auckland, county Durham;
born 8 April 1861 at Richill, county Armagh, son of Woolsley Sacheverell Kane, JP, grocer and draper, of Richill; educated at Armagh Royal School; studied medicine at Queen's College, Belfast, from 1878; LRCP LRCS Edin 1884; MD (QUI) 1886;

medical officer and public vaccinator to Byers Green District, of The Old Hall, Byers Green, Bishop Auckland, surgeon Bolchrow, Vaughan and Co. collieries; later of Killowen Towers, Bishop Auckland; retired c 1928; JP for county Durham; died 6 April 1938; probate Newcastle-upon-Tyne 29 July 1938. [Ferrar (1933); Lond PPR, will cal; *Med Dir*; QCB adm reg].

KARNEY, MICHAEL (*fl c* 1845), Shercock, county Cavan;
general practitioner and medical officer to constabulary, of Shercock c 1845. [Croly (1843–6)].

KEAN, HUGH JOSEPH (1842/3–1900), Newry, county Down;
born 1842/3, son of John Kean; studied medicine at the Catholic University of Ireland in 1867, and at Queen's College, Cork, winning many prizes; MD (hons) (QUI) 1867; LRCSI 1867; resident in Jervis Street Hospital, Dublin; general practitioner of 25 Hill Street, Newry, from c 1870 and later of 6 Needham Place, Newry; of Adavoile, Newry c 1895; married 29 July 1868 in Violet Hill Roman Catholic Church, Newry, Sophia Lupton, daughter of Joseph Lupton, merchant, of Newry; father of Dr John Kean of Newry, LRCP LRCS Edin 1901; died 9 March 1900 at Adavoile; administration Armagh 10 May 1900. [Belf PRO, will cal; Dub GRO (d); Kirkpatrick Archive; *Med Dir;* UHF database (m)].

KEAN, THOMAS (1847–1901), Arran Islands, Galway;
born 26 September 1847 in Galway, son of Thomas Kean, teacher, of Galway; educated in Galway; studied medicine at Queen's College, Belfast, from 1879; LRCP LRCS Edin 1884; general practitioner of Kilronan, Arran Islands, from c 1885; married —; died 29 April 1901; probate Tuam 20 June 1901. [Belf PRO; will cal; Dub GRO (d); *Med Dir*; QCB adm reg].

KEARNEY, ANTHONY JOSEPH (1871/2–1934), Carndonagh, county Donegal, and Mullingar, county Westmeath;
born 1871/2; of Carndonagh; studied medicine at the Catholic University of Ireland; LRCPI and LM 1894; LRCSI and LM 1894; LM Rot Hosp Dub 1894; surgeon to Westmeath County Infirmary, of 6 Harbour Terrace, Mullingar; died 22 February 1934 at Mullingar County Infirmary; probate Mullingar 23 March 1934. [Dub GRO (d); Dub Nat Arch, will cal; *Med Dir*].

KEARNEY, EDWARD (1825/6–73), Carndonagh, county Donegal;
born 1825/6; studied medicine at Queen's College, Belfast; MRCSE 1857; LM Belfast Lying-in Hospital; medical officer to Carndonagh Dispensary District, Workhouse and Fever Hospital; married Sarah —; died 18 March 1873 of typhus fever at Carndonagh; administration Londonderry 22 April 1873. [Belf PRO, will cal; Dub GRO (d); *Med Dir*].

KEARNEY, JOHN BARRETT (1837/8–70), Dublin, and Clonmany, county Donegal;
born 1837/8; studied medicine at the Peter Street School, Dublin; LM Rot Hosp Dub 1855; LRCSI 1856; LKQCPI 1860; general practitioner of 19 Wellington Place,

and Gofton Hall, Finglas, Dublin, c 1858–66; general practitioner, of Clonmany c 1866–70; unmarried; died 14 February 1870 at Finglas, Dublin. [Dub GRO (d); *Med Dir*].

KEELAN, PATRICK (1836/7–92), Naval Medical Service and Hull, Yorkshire;
born 1836/7, son of Bernard Keeland of Carrickmacross, county Monaghan; educated at Carrickmacross School; studied medicine at Queen's College, Belfast, from 1854; LRCSI 1858; FRCSI 1885; MD (RUI) 1883; joined the Naval Medical Service as surgeon c 1860; staff surgeon c 1875; general practitioner, of Thornton Villa, Holderness Road, Hull c 1885; married Frances Ellen — (who died 27 January 1892; probate York 25 February 1892); died 9 May 1892; probate York 12 August 1892. [Lond PPR, will cal (both); *Med Dir*; QCB adm reg].

KEENAN, CAMPBELL BROWN (*fl c* 1845), Belfast;
MD (Glas) 1839; general practitioner, of Belfast c 1845; possibly died c 1850. [Addison (1898); Croly (1843–6)].

KEENAN, JOHN (1857/8–1936), Downpatrick, county Down, and Putney, London;
born 1857/8; studied medicine at the Carmichael School, Dublin; LRCSI 1880; LKQCPI and LM 1885; general practitioner of The Course, Downpatrick, c 1886; general practitioner, of 76 Gardner's Lane, Putney, London, from c 1890 and later of 19 Chelverton Road, Putney; retired to Kingsfield House, Downpatrick c 1925; died 25 October 1936 at Putney Lodge, Downpatrick; probate Belfast 22 December 1936. [Belf GRO (d); Belf PRO, will cal; *Med Dir*].

KEERS, SAMUEL BURNSIDE BOYD (1858–1937), ship's surgeon and Rasharkin, county Antrim;
born 23 August 1858 at Finvoy, county Antrim, son of Joseph Keers, farmer, of Finvoy; educated at Coleraine Academical Institution; studied medicine at Queen's College, Belfast, from 1878; LRCP LRCS Edin 1884; surgeon on SS *Orion*; medical officer of health to Dirraw Dispensary District; medical officer to constabulary and public vaccinator, of Donovan House, Rasharkin; retired c 1936 to 6 Station Road, Portstewart; died 31 August 1937 at 6 Station Road; probate Belfast 10 December 1937. [Belf PRO, will cal; *Med Dir*; QCB adm reg].

KEIRAN, JAMES (1818/9–74), Dublin, Enniskillen, county Fermanagh, and Belturbet, county Cavan;
born 1818/19; studied medicine at the Cecilia Street Academy and Peter Street, the Richmond and Jervis Street Hospitals, Dublin; LAH Dub 1845; LM Dub 1845; MD (St Andrews) 1850 (by examination); MRCSE 1850; general practitioner, of 17 Lower Baggott Street, Dublin, c 1848–60; abroad c 1866–8; general practitioner, of 23 Darling Street, Enniskillen c 1868–70 and of Holborn Hill, Belturbet c 1870–74; married Maria —; died 8 March 1874 at Holborn Hill, of typhoid fever; administration Dublin 28 April 1874. [Belf PRO, will cal; Dub GRO (d); *Med Dir*; Smart (2004)].

KELLETT, EDWARD (1800/1–66), Mullagh, county Cavan, and Kells, county Meath; born 1800/1; of Bailieborough, county Cavan; LAH Dub 1824; studied medicine at Edinburgh University; MD (Edin) 1838 (thesis 'On amenorrhoea'); LRCS and LM Edin 1838; accoucheur of Edinburgh Lying-in Hospital; LKQCPI and LM 1860; physician to Moynalty Temporary Fever Hospital, county Meath; medical officer to Mullagh Dispensary and constabulary c 1845; medical officer to Kells Fever Hospital and Workhouse; married —; father of Dr Edward Young Kellett (*q.v.*); died 22 February 1866 at Drunmroo, county Monaghan; administration Dublin 5 June 1869. [Apothecaries (1829); Belf PRO, will cal, Croly (1843–6 Dub GRO (d); Edin Univ; *Med Dir*; UHF database (m)].

KELLETT, EDWARD YOUNG (1831–99), Army Medical Service; born 29 May 1831 at Clones, county Monaghan, son of Dr Edward Kellett (*q.v.*); LRCSI 1851; joined the Army Medical Service as assistant surgeon 1854; attached to 68th Foot 1855; staff surgeon 1857; surgeon major 1865; served in Crimea 1854–5 and in New Zealand 1863–5; retired on half pay 1880 to 24 St David's Road, Southsea, Hampshire; married (1) 22 November 1850 in Warrenpoint Church of Ireland Church, county Down, Anne Elizabeth Watson, daughter of Leonard Watson, gentleman; (2) Jane Wilhelmina —; father of Leonard Henry Kellett, fleet surgeon, RN; died 8 October 1899 at 24 St David's Road; probate Winchester 2 November 1899. [Lond PPR, will cal, will; *Med Dir*; Peterkin and Johnston (1968); UHF database (m)].

KELLY, ANDREW JOHN GARVEY (1849/50–1907), Navan, county Meath, Liverpool, Lancashire, and Enniskillen, county Fermanagh; born 1849/50; studied medicine at the Royal College of Surgeons in Ireland and the City of Dublin Hospital; LKQCPI and LM 1883; LRCSI 1883; general practitioner, of Navan c 1884–90, of 53 Prescot Road, Liverpool c 1890–94, of 43 Darling Street, Enniskillen c 1895–1900, and of Navan c 1900–06; married Anna —; died 11 June 1907 of 'acute phthisis', at 'Boyne Villa', 30 Oakley Road, Rathmines, county Dublin. [Dub GRO (d); *Med Dir*].

KELLY CORNELIUS (d 1833), Naval Medical Service and Londonderry; joined the Naval Medical Service as assistant surgeon; surgeon 1815; resigned; surgeon, of Ferryquay Street, Londonderry c 1824; married 24 September 1818 Catherine McCormick (who was born 1793/4 and died August 1853 at 4 College Square North, Belfast), second daughter of Frederick McCormick of Burndennet; died 22 March 1833 in Ferryquay Street. [*BNL* 6 October 1818 (m), 29 March 1833 (d) and 24 August 1853 (d); Keane, Phair and Sadleir (1982); *Londonderry Sentinel* 30 March 1833 (d) and 26 August 1853 (d); *NMS* (1826); Pigot (1824)].

KELLY, DANIEL (1804/5–75), Carndonagh, county Donegal; born 1804/5 at Carndonagh; studied medicine at Glasgow University; LFPS Glas 1833; CM (Glas) 1833; worked in USA; general practitioner, of Glentaugher, Carndonagh c 1845; medical officer to Donagh Dispensary District, Workhouse and constabulary; married 27 September 1840 Bridget McIntyre, youngest daughter of Robert McIntyre of Londonderry; died 15 November 1875 at Carndonagh;

administration Londonderry 3 December 1875. [Addison (1898); *BNL* 2 October 1840 (m); Belf PRO, will cal; Croly (1843–6); Dub GRO (d); *Londonderry Sentinel* 3 October 1840 (m); *Med Dir*].

KELLY, DANIEL LUKE (d c 1890), Dublin, and Glenties, county Donegal;
LRCSI 1869; LRCP Edin 1871; general practitioner, of 33 Georges Place, Dublin c 1872–80 and of Glenties from c 1880; died c 1890. [*Med Dir*].

KELLY, DENIS (d 1777), Lisburn, county Antrim;
surgeon in Lisburn County Infirmary; died 3 February 1777 in Lisburn. [*BNL* 4 February 1777 (d)].

KELLY, EDWARD (d 1863), Ballintra and Ballyshannon, county Donegal;
MD (Edin) 1821 (thesis 'De enteritide'); accoucheur of Edinburgh Lying-in Hospital; medical superintendent of Ballintra dispensary; physician and surgeon of Castle Street, Ballyshannon c 1824; medical officer to Ballyshannon Union Workhouse and Fever Hospital from 1841; died 22 May 1863. [Croly (1843–6); Edin Univ; Johnston (1996); Kirkpatrick Archive; Pigot (1824)].

KELLY, EDWARD HENRY (1849/50–1932), Lanark, Scotland;
born 1849/50 at Dundalk, county Louth, son of Joseph Owen Kelly of Barleyfield, Dundalk; educated at Mary's College, Dundalk; studied medicine at Queen's College, Belfast, from 1869 and at the Catholic University of Ireland; MD MCh Dip Mid (QUI) 1873; medical officer to Lanark Hospital and Parish, of Strathview, Lanark, from c 1880; JP for Lanarkshire; died 23 November 1932 at Strathview. [Kirkpatrick Archive; *Med Dir*; QCB adm reg].

KELLY, J. (*fl c* 1845), Keady, county Armagh;
general practitioner, of Keady c 1845. [Croly (1843–6)].

KELLY, JOHN (d 1856), Draperstown, county Tyrone;
surgeon; died 1856 at Draperstown. [*Med Dir*].

KELLY, JOHN ALEXANDER (1861–97), Portglenone, county Antrim;
born 21 August 1861 at Glenarm, county Antrim, son of James Kelly, JP, linen manufacturer, of Ballynease, Bellaghy, county Londonderry, and Elizabeth —; educated at Methodist College, Belfast, from 1873 and RBAI; studied medicine at Queen's College, Belfast, from 1884; MB BCh BAO (RUI) 1890; general practitioner of Portglenone; died 16 January 1897; buried in Bellaghy Church of Ireland graveyard. [Fry (1984; gravestone inscription; *Med Dir*; QCB adm reg].

KELLY, JOHN THOMAS (1835/6–1912), Glenties, county Donegal;
born 1835/6; LM Rot Hosp Dub 1856; LRCSI 1857; general practitioner, of Gortnamucklagh House, Glenties c 1870; superintendent medical officer of health for Glenties from 1874, of Letterilly House, Glenties, from c 1880; unmarried; died 24 January 1912; probate Dublin 11 March 1912. [Belf PRO, will cal; Dub GRO (d); Kirkpatrick Archive; *Med Dir*].

KELLY, PETER (1843/4–81), Monaghan and Voe Walls, Shetland;
   born 1843/4, son of John Kelly, merchant, and Elizabeth Fox; studied medicine at the Carmichael School and the Richmond and Mater Misercordiae Hospitals, Dublin; LRCSI 1869; LRCP Edin 1872; general practitioner, of Monaghan c 1870–76, parish medical officer, and public vaccinator of Voe Walls c 1876–81; unmarried; died suddenly 9/10 February 1881 at 10 Shore Street, Lerwick, Shetland. [Edin GRO (d); *Med Dir*].

KELLY, THOMAS (d 1839), Killashandra, county Cavan, Monaghan, and Carlingford, county Louth;
   LAH Dub 1822; surgeon and apothecary, of Killashandra, Monaghan and Carlingford; died 22 November 1839 at Dundalk. [Apothecaries (1829); *BNL* 10 December 1839 (d)].

KELLY, THOMAS JOHN (1822/3–83), Ballyshannon, county Donegal, and Dundalk, county Louth;
   born 1822/3; studied medicine at the Royal College of Surgeons in Ireland and the Meath Hospital, Dublin; LAH Dub 1848; MRCSE 1851; LM Rot Hosp Dub; general practitioner, of Ballyshannon c 1858, and of 34 Clanbrassil Street, Dundalk c 1863–83; apothecary to Dundalk Dispensary; unmarried; died 21 February 1883 at Clanbrassil Street, Dundalk; probate Dublin 25 April 1883. [Belf PRO, will cal; Dub GRO (d); Kirkpatrick Archive; *Med Dir*].

KELLY, THOMAS TEAR (*fl c* 1848), Donaghadee, county Down;
   son of Samuel Kelly, gentleman farmer; surgeon, of Donaghadee; married 31 October 1848 in Holywood Church of Ireland Church, Mary Susan McDowell, only daughter of Major John McDowell of the Bengal Royal Artillery. [*BNL* 3 November 1848 (m); Dub GRO (m)].

KELSO, JAMES (*fl c* 1845), Portadown, county Armagh;
   general practitioner, of Portadown, c 1845. [Croly (1843–6)].

KELSO, JOHN JOHNSTON (1810/1–79), Lisburn, county Antrim;
   born 1810/1; of Lisburn c 1837; studied medicine at Glasgow University; MD (Glas)1839; LAH Dub 1840; CM 1852; general practitioner, of Lisburn; medical officer to Knocknadona Dispensary District; author of *The Plantation of Ireland* (1865) and various papers on fever; married 4 May 1840 Elizabeth Gamble, youngest daughter of George Gamble of Lisburn; died 30 January 1879 at Lisburn; administration Dublin 13 August 1879. [Addison (1898); *BNL* 19 May 1840 (m); Belf PRO, will cal; Croly (1843–6); Dub GRO (d); Lewis (1837); *Med Dir*].

KELSO, ROBERT (1812/3–49), Banbridge, county Down;
   born 1812/3; CM (Glas) [?]; general practitioner, of Banbridge c 1845; died 8 August 1849 of apoplexy at his home in Banbridge. [*BNL* 17 August 1849 (d); *Belfast Street Directory* (1843); Croly (1843–6)].

KENDAL, ALEXANDER (1768/9–1838), 'Portuguese Service';
born 1768/9; MD [?]; 'of the Portuguese Service'; died 4 March 1838 at York Street, Belfast. [*BNL* 20 March 1838 (d)].

KENDALL, ALEXANDER (d 1850), Belfast;
staff surgeon [?], of Belfast; married —; father of Alice Leckey Kendall (only child) who married 1 January 1850 the Rev Joseph Seymour Eagar, curate of Ballywillan (Portrush), county Antrim; died 27 April 1850. [Leslie (1993); Malcolm (1851)].

KENDELLAN, PATRICK (*fl c* 1765), Armagh;
of Armagh; studied medicine at Rheims University; MD (Rheims) 1765. [Brockliss].

KENNEDY, ALEXANDER (1817/8–85), Coleraine, county Londonderry, Honolulu, Sandwich Islands, and Portrush, county Antrim;
born 1817/8, youngest son of John Kennedy, farmer, of Aghadowey, county Londonderry; studied arts and medicine at Glasgow University from 1838; MA (Glas) 1841; MD CM 1846; general practitioner of Coleraine; medical officer in Honolulu; general practitioner, of Portrush; retired to Cooleen, Strandtown, county Down; married (1) —; (2) 12 April 1848 in Mosside Presbyterian Church, Ballymoney, county Antrim, Letitia Bell (who died 20 July 1857 at Yreka, Siskiyon County, California, USA, of consumption), daughter of the Rev Thomas Bell, minister of Mosside Presbyterian Church; (3) Isabella —; died 6 October 1885 at Cooleen; probate Belfast 11 January 1886. [Addison (1898) and (1913); Bailie and Kirkpatrick (2005); *BNL* 28 September 1857 (d); Belf PRO, will cal; Dub GRO (d); *Med Dir*; UHF database (m)].

KENNEDY, ALEXANDER FREDERICK (1875–1942), Portrush, county Antrim, Rhodesia, Gambia and Nigeria;
born 25 August 1875 at Ballyness House, Coleraine, county Londonderry, son of Alexander Kennedy; educated at RBAI; studied medicine at Queen's College, Belfast, from 1894; MB BCh BAO (RUI) 1900; captain in 33rd Battalion of Imperial Yeomanry, South Africa; general practitioner, of Belleview, Portrush; emigrated to Rhodesia c 1905; medical officer to Wankie Mines, Rhodesia 1908–09; medical officer of health to Bathurst, Gambia, from 1909, and later medical officer in Nigeria; retired c 1926 to 41 Eglinton Street, Portrush; OBE c 1941; died 12 June 1942; probate Belfast 22 February 1943. [Belf PRO, will cal; *Med Dir*; QCB adm reg].

KENNEDY, ANDREW (*fl c* 1816), Belfast;
LAH Dub 1816; apothecary, of Belfast; married 14 July 1806 Ann Moore of Larne; died before August 1859. [Apothecaries (1829); *BNL* 18 July 1806 (m) and 6 August 1859 (d, daughter)].

KENNEDY, DAVID LITHGOW (1847–1908), Castlederg, county Londonderry, Georgetown, British Guiana, and Loughton, Essex;
born 1847 at Rossdownie, Londonderry, son of Samuel Kennedy, clerk of the Poor Law Union; educated at Foyle College, Londonderry; studied arts and medicine at Trinity College, Dublin, from 1864; BA (TCD) 1868; MB 1871; MCh MA 1872;

LM Coombe Hosp Dub 1873; superintendent medical officer of health for Castlederg c 1873–5; medical officer for the colony and prison and medical superintendent to Kaow Island Leper Asylum, of Plaisance, East Coast, British Guiana c 1875–1900; married Catharine Emma —; died 27 January 1908 at the High Road, Loughton; administration London 11 February 1908. [Kirkpatrick Archive; Lond GRO (d); Lond PPR, will cal; *Med Dir;* TCD adm reg; *TCD Cat*, vol II (1896)].

KENNEDY, DAVID WILLIAM (d c 1900), Castleshane, county Monaghan, and Stranorlar, county Donegal;
studied medicine at the Ledwich School, Dublin; LRCSI and LM 1882; LRCP and LM Edin 1894; general practitioner, of Castleshane and later of Corlatte House, Monaghan and Tyrcallan House, Stranorlar; died c 1900, probably abroad. [*Med Dir*].

KENNEDY, EVORY (1806–86), Dublin;
born 28 November 1806 at Carndonagh, county Donegal, son of the Rev John Pitt Kennedy, rector of Donagh and Balteagh, county Londonderry, and Mary Carey of Loughesk, county Tyrone; brother of Mary Kennedy who married Dr Robert Collins (*q.v.*) and of Tristram Edward Kennedy whose daughter Caroline married Dr Edward Hugh Edwards Stack (*q.v.*); educated at Foyle College and the Diocesan School, Londonderry; studied medicine informally in Londonderry County Infirmary and at the Royal College of Surgeons in Ireland, Trinity College, Dublin, and Sir Patrick Dun's Hospital, studied also in Edinburgh 1826–7; MD (Edin) 1827 (thesis 'De febre puerperarum'); LKQCPI 1828; MD (TCD) (*hon. causa*) 1839; FKQCPI 1839; studied further in Paris and London; godson of Dr Thomas Evory (*q.v.*), of 2 Rutland Square, Dublin, and inherited his house and contents in 1832 from Thomas Evory's sister Margaret; practised as an obstetrician in Dublin from 1828; of Belgard Castle, Clondalkin, county Dublin; lecturer in midwifery at the Richmond Hospital, Dublin, from 1829; assistant master of the Rotunda Hospital 1828–31; master of the Rotunda Hospital 1833–40; fought (unsuccessfully) to prohibit the Coombe Hospital from issuing certificates to students; opened the first gynaecological ward in the Rotunda Hospital in 1835; tried, against opposition, to reduce the high maternal death rate in the Rotunda Hospital; president of the RCSI 1853–4; president of the IMA 1871; JP and DL of county Dublin; finally moved to London; author of *Obstetric Auscultation* (1833) and many medical papers; married 1835 Alicia Hamilton (who was born 1817/8 and died 28 November 1867), daughter of the Rev Richard Hamilton of Culdaff, county Donegal; grandfather of Dr Dorothy Stopford Price, pioneer of vaccination against tuberculosis; died 23 April 1886 at 20 Queensberry Place, London; buried in Mount Jerome Cemetery, Dublin; portrait by his nephew, Charles Napier Kennedy, in the Rotunda Hospital, Dublin, and smaller version in the RCPI; probate Dublin 10 July 1886 and London 26 August 1886. [Belf PRO, will cal; *BMJ* obituary (1886); Burtchaell and Sadleir (1925); Cameron (1916); Crone (1928); *DIB* (2009); Edin Univ; Kennedy family tree, published privately; Kirkpatrick Archive; Kirkpatrick and Jellett (1913); Leslie (1937); Lewis (1837); *Londonderry Sentinel* 3 December 1867 (d); Lond PPR, will cal; Newmann (1993); O'Brien, Crookshank and Wolstenholme (1984); O'Doherty (2002); Pinkerton (1981); Strickland (1969)].

KENNEDY, GILBERT (1731/2–80), Dungannon, county Tyrone;
born 1731/2; surgeon and apothecary, of Dungannon; will dated 7 March 1780; died 27 March 1780 at Dungannon. [*BNL* 31 March 1780 (d); Belf PRO, T700, p 277].

KENNEDY, HENRY (d 1804), Army Medical Service and Indian Medical Service;
second son of John Kennedy of Cultra, county Down, and Elizabeth Cole; great-grandson of Dr Hugh Kennedy (*q.v.*); joined the Army Medical Service as assistant surgeon with the 15th East Yorkshire Foot 1800; surgeon with the Royal North Down Militia 1801; joined the Indian Medical Service (Bengal establishment) as assistant surgeon 1803; served in Second Maratha War 1803; died 27 August 1804 on board the *Euphrates* at the mouth of the Ganges (near Calcutta), after an illness of 3 days. [*BNL* 5 April 1805 (d); Burke *LGI* (1912); Crawford (1930); Peterkin and Johnston (1968)].

KENNEDY, HENRY (*fl c* 1780–1805), Newry and Downpatrick, county Down;
first cousin of James Trail Kennedy, merchant, of Belfast; general practitioner in Newry, c 1783; rival to Dr William Drennan but treated him for a fever in 1783; moved to Downpatrick c 1784; visited Dublin 1805. [Agnew (1998–9].

KENNEDY, HENRY MacNEALE (b 1750/1), Monaghan;
born 1750/1 in Ireland; studied medicine at Leyden University 1775; MD (Leyden) 1775 (thesis 'De rheumatismo acuto' in Edinburgh University); LKQCPI 1785; general practitioner in Monaghan; author of *An Experimental Enquiry into the Chemical and Medicinal Properties of the Sulphurous Water at Aughnacloy* (1777). [Cameron (1916); Innes Smith (1932)].

KENNEDY, HUGH (d c 1684), Ballycultra, county Down;
native of Ayrshire; Scottish Doctor of Physic; arrived in Ulster in second half of 17th century and bought land in Ballycultra 1673; physician to the Earl of Donegall during 17th century and received a legacy from the Earl; married Mary Upton (who later married Dr John Peacock (*q.v.*)), daughter of Arthur Upton; his son John Kennedy bought the Cultra estate from the Earl of Clanbrassil in 1671; great-grandfather of Dr Henry Kennedy (*q.v.*); died c 1684; will dated 21 March 1683 proved in Prerogative Court 26 June 1685. [Belf PRO, Burke Pedigrees, T559, vol 25, p 327; Benn (1877), p 576; Burke *LGI* (1912); Carragher (2003); Esler (1884); Eustace (1949); Vicars (1897)].

KENNEDY, JAMES (1717/8–69), Downpatrick, county Down;
born 1717/8, third son of the Rev Gilbert Kennedy, minister of Dundonald Presbyterian Church, county Down and Elizabeth Lang; matriculated at Glasgow University 1735; studied medicine at Leyden from 1740; MD (Rheims) 1741; general practitioner in Downpatrick; produced an anonymous printed map of county Down in 1755 (which is highly decorative and very rare); first surgeon (honorary) to the Downe County Infirmary April–September 1767, when a paid surgeon (William Waring) was appointed; author of *Practical Observations on the Use of Goats' Whey* (1762); married 1738 his second cousin Sarah Bailie, daughter of the Rev Thomas

Kennedy, minister of Brigh (Ballyclug) Presbyterian Church, county Tyrone, and widow of Andrew Bailie of Turnishea, county Tyrone; father of the Rev Thomas Kennedy of Kilmore, who was father of Dr Richard Kennedy (*q.v.*); died 1769; will dated 6 October 1768 proved in Prerogative Court 1769 (full copy of will in PRO NI). [Addison (1913); Andrews (1997); Belf PRO, D2315/2/5; Belf PRO, D2961/2/2/6; Belf PRO, T559, Burke Pedigrees, vol 7, p 76; Belf PRO, T700, p 285; Brockliss; Cameron (1916); Leslie (1936); McConnell (1951); Parkinson (1969); Pyne (2008); Innes Smith (1932); Vicars (1897); Wilson (1995)].

KENNEDY, JAMES (1808/9–36), Newtownards, county Down;
born 1808/9, son of James Kennedy of Flush Hall, Newtownards, county Down, and Elizabeth Jane Ball; MD (Edin) 1832 (thesis 'De ascite'); died 24 December 1836; buried in Movilla Graveyard, Newtownards. [Clarke, *County Down*, vol 11 (1974); Edin Univ].

KENNEDY, JAMES (1838/9–1909), Ballyshannon, county Donegal, and Derrygonnelly, county Fermanagh;
born 1838/9; studied medicine at the Royal College of Surgeons in Ireland, the Ledwich School, Dublin, and Queen's College, Galway; LAH Dub 1864; LM Coombe Hosp Dub 1864 and Rot Hosp Dub 1865; LRCSI 1868; medical officer, medical officer of health and public vaccinator to Ballyshannon Dispensary District and workhouse; general practitioner, of Tonagh, Derrygonnelly; unmarried; died 14 June 1909 at The Infirmary, Enniskillen; probate Armagh 3 August 1909. [Belf PRO, will cal; Dub GRO (d); *Med Dir*].

KENNEDY JAMES (1848–91), Brotton and Guisborough, Yorkshire, and West Auckland, county Durham;
born 1848; of Arboe [?], county Tyrone; studied medicine at Glasgow University; MB CM (Glas) 1872; MD 1888; general practitioner, of Brotton and Guisborough, Yorkshire and West Auckland; died 17 January 1891 at Front Street, West Auckland; probate Durham 25 March 1891. [Addison (1898); Lond GRO (d); Lond PPR, will cal; *Med Dir*].

KENNEDY, JAMES MARTIN (1850–1905), Peterborough, Lincolnshire, Aberford, Yorkshire, and Burley, Hampshire;
born 16 October 1850 at Ballyjamesduff, county Cavan, son of Samuel Kennedy of Springfield, Ballyjamesduff; educated at Ballinasloe Academy; studied medicine at Queen's College, Belfast, from 1868; MD (QUI) 1876; MCh 1878; general practitioner, of Lincoln Road, Peterborough c 1885, Aberford, near Leeds c 1895, and of Durmast, Burley, c 1905; married Anne Elizabeth —; died 3 March 1905; probate London 29 May 1905. [Lond PPR, will cal; *Med Dir*; QCB adm reg].

KENNEDY, JOHN (*fl c* 1792), Rathfriland, county Down;
LAH Dub 1792; apothecary, of Rathfriland. [Apothecaries (1829)].

KENNEDY, JOHN (*fl c* 1814);
only son of James Kennedy, farmer, of Aghaderg, county Down; studied arts and medicine at Glasgow University; matriculated Glasgow 1807; MA (Glas) 1810; MD 1814. [Addison (1898) and (1913)].

KENNEDY, JOHN (*fl c* 1820), Cootehill, county Cavan;
LAH Dub 1820; apothecary, of Market Street, Cootehill c 1824. [Apothecaries (1829); Pigot (1824)].

KENNEDY, JOHN (1858–c 1906), Tasmania and Syndey, New South Wales;
born June 1858 at Newtowncrommelin, county Antrim, son of William Kennedy, merchant, of 55–56 Church Street, Ballymena; educated at RBAI; studied medicine at Queen's College, Galway, and from 1878, Belfast; MD MCh Dip Mid (QUI) 1881; emigrated to Australia c 1882; general practitioner, of Waratah, Mount Bishoff, Tasmania, and later of Athlone, Zechan, Tasmania; moved c 1900 to 'Granard', 84 Hunter Street and 'Maryville' Glebe Street, Sydney, New South Wales; died c 1906. [*Med Dir*; QCB adm reg].

KENNEDY, JOHN (1869–1942), Belfast;
born 27 October 1869 at Altnahey, Dundrod, county Antrim, son of John Kennedy, farmer, of Drumskee; educated at Tullymacarrett National School; studied medicine at Queen's College, Belfast, from 1888; LRCP LRCS Edin 1896; LFPS Glas 1896; general practitioner, of 214 and 305 Grosvenor Road, Belfast; married 19 August 1901 in Richview Presbyterian Church, Belfast, Hester Jameson, daughter of William Jameson, merchant, of Parkgate, county Antrim; died 20 November 1942 at St Catherine's, Middle Division, Carrickfergus; probate Belfast 12 March 1943. [Belf GRO (d); Belf PRO, will cal; Kirkpatrick Archive; *Med Dir*; QCB adm reg; UHF database (m)].

KENNEDY, JOHN ADOLPHUS (1871–1941), Portstewart, county Londonderry;
born 5 April 1871 at Gortnaglush, Dungannon, county Tyrone, son of the Rev Robert Kennedy, presbyterian minister, and Isabella McClelland; educated in Clones; studied medicine at Trinity College, Dublin, from 1890; BA (TCD) 1895; LM Coombe Hosp Dub 1897; MB BCh BAO 1899; MD 1904; medical officer to Portstewart Dispensary District, Cottage Hospital and constabulary, of Islay View, Portstewart; married Dr Olive Kennedy [?]; died 4 January 1941 at Hopefield Cottage Hospital, Portrush; probate Londonderry 26 September 1941. [Barkley (1987); Belf PRO, will cal; *BMJ* obituary (1941); Dub GRO (b); *Med Dir;* TCD adm reg; *TCD Cat*, vol III (1906); *TCD Reg*].

KENNEDY, JOHN H.S. (*fl c* 1853), Toomebridge, county Antrim;
MD [?]; general practitioner, of Toomebridge c 1853; married 7 December 1853 in Kingsmill Chapel, Mary Dunn, youngest daughter of Simon Dunn of Kingsmill Lodge, county Tyrone. [*BNL* 23 December 1853 (m); *Coleraine Chronicle* 24 December 1853 (m)].

KENNEDY, KENNETH WILLIAM STEWART (1865–1943), Nagpur, India;
born 10 October 1865 in county Monaghan, third son of Thomas Le Ban Kennedy, dean of Clogher, and Georgina Hester Smith of Newpark, Queen's County; educated at Armagh Royal School 1877–83; studied arts and medicine at Trinity College, Dublin, as Royal and Classics Scholar, from 1883; BA (TCD) 1888; MB MCh BAO 1891; ordained deacon 1890; priest 1891; curate of St Anne's Dublin 1890–91; founder of the Mission to Chota Nagpur, India 1891 and missionary at Hazaribagh 1892–1901; examining chaplain to the Bishop of Nagpur 1904–10 and to Chota Nagpur 1904–10 and 1915–26; bishop of Chota Nagpur 1926–c 1935, of Ranchi, Chota Nagpur; Kaisar-I-Hind Medal; rector of Rathmichael, county Dublin c 1930–43; married 1904 Mary Elizabeth Poole, daughter of the Rev Hewitt Robert Poole; died 9 December 1943 at Rathmichael Rectory; probate Dublin 10 July 1944. [Crockford (1899); Dub GRO (d); Dub Nat Arch, will cal; Ferrar (1933); Ffolliott (1958); Kirkpatrick Archive; Leslie (1929); *Med Dir;* TCD adm reg; *TCD Cat,* vol II (1896)].

KENNEDY, RICHARD (1784–1810), Kilmore, county Down;
born 1784 at Kilmore, son of the Rev Thomas Kennedy, rector of Kilmore (who later assumed the additional surname of Bailie after his mother), and Sarah Waring; educated by his father; studied arts and medicine at Trinity College, Dublin, from 1800, also at Edinburgh and London; BA (TCD) 1805; MD (Edin) 1808 (thesis 'De aqua'); died 15 June 1810 at Kilmore. [*BNL* 19 June 1810 (d); Burtchaell and Sadleir (1924); Edin Univ; Leslie (1936)].

KENNEDY, SAMUEL (*fl c* 1792–1824), Killashandra, county Cavan;
LAH Dub 1792; apothecary and surgeon, of Killashandra c 1824; married Elizabeth — (who married secondly 20 September 1833 in Killashandra Church, William S. Moneypenny of Killashandra; died in or before 1833. [Apothecaries (1829); *BNL* 8 October 1833 (m, daughter); Pigot (1824)].

KENNEDY, WILLIAM (*fl c* 1820), Hillsborough, county Down;
surgeon, of Hillsborough; married 31 January 1820 in Hillsborough, Elizabeth Jefferson, daughter of Henry Jefferson of Hillsborough. [*BNL* 4 February 1820 (m)].

KENNEDY, WILLIAM (d 1829), Naval Medical Service;
son of the Rev Charles Kennedy, minister of Maghera Presbyterian Church, county Londonderry; joined the Naval Medical Service as assistant surgeon 1824; unmarried; died 21 February 1829 in Jamaica of yellow fever. [*BNL* 5 May 1829 (d); McConnell (1951); *NMS* (1826)].

KENNEDY, WILLIAM (d 1834), Dominica, West Indies;
eldest son of Thomas Kennedy of Rathfriland; surgeon in Dominica c 1807–34; married Margaret — (who married secondly 19 May 1836 in Newry, Thomas Cunningham of Hill Street); youngest son, Terence, was born c 1829 and died in Rathfriland 3 September 1834; died 14 May 1834 in Dominica. [*BNL* 8 July 1834 (d), 26 September 1834 (d, son) and 31 May 1836 (m)].

KENNEDY, WILLIAM GEORGE (d 1857), Tarbert, county Kerry;
of Londonderry; MD CM (Glas) 1823; medical officer to Tarbert Dispensary, constabulary and militia c 1827–57; medical officer to the Cholera Hospital 1831–2 and 1848; married —; died 10 September 1857 of fever, caught in the discharge of his duties. [Addison (1898); *Coleraine Chronicle* 19 September 1857 (d); Kirkpatrick Archive; *Londonderry Sentinel* 18 September 1857 (d); *Med Dir*].

KENNEDY, WILLIAM GEORGE (d c 1931), ship's surgeon, Londonderry, Salford, Lancashire, and Victoria, British Columbia;
studied medicine at the Royal College of Surgeons in Ireland and the Carmichael School, Dublin; LRCSI 1882; LKQCPI and LM 1886; surgeon to the White Star Line; general practitioner of 40 and 48 Abercorn Road, Londonderry, from c 1884–93 and of 63 Francis Street c 1895; general practitioner, of 1 Hawthorne Street, Cross Lane, Salford c 1896–1928; medical officer to No 4 District and public vaccinator to No 2 District, Salford; emigrated to British Columbia c 1928 and retired, of 1211 North Park Street, Victoria c 1928; died c 1931. [*Med Dir*].

KENNEDY, WILLIAM SKELTON (1813/4–64), Comber, county Down;
born 1813/14; LRCSI 1838; general practitioner, of Comber; unmarried; died 27 May 1864 at Comber; administration (with will) Belfast 20 June 1864. [Belf PRO, will cal; Dub GRO (d); *Med Dir*].

KENNEDY, — (1751/2–92), Randalstown, county Antrim;
born 1751/2; general practitioner, of Duneane, Randalstown; died 16 December 1792; buried in Lower Duneane Graveyard. [Gravestone inscription].

KENNY, CHARLES ALOYSIUS (1869/70–c 1956), Kingstown, county Dublin, and Ballymahon, county Longford;
born 1869/70 at Knockagh, county Longford, son of Francis Kenny, farmer, of Castlewilder, county Longford; brother of Dr Joseph Mary Simon Kenny (*q.v.*); educated at St Vincent's College, Castleknock; studied medicine at the Catholic University of Ireland, and from 1890, at Queen's College, Belfast; LRCPI and LM, LRCSI and LM 1898; house surgeon to St Michael's Hospital, Kingstown; captain RAMC 1914–19; general practitioner, of Ballymahon; died 1955–7. [*Med Dir*; QCB adm reg].

KENNY, JAMES BERRY (1845/6–1923), Killashandra, county Cavan;
born 1845/6, son of Dr Randal Young Kenny (*q.v.*); brother of Dr William Wallace Kenny (*q.v.*) RAMC; studied medicine at the Royal College of Surgeons in Ireland and Queen's College, Cork; LKQCPI 1865; LRCSI 1868; LM Rot Hosp Dub 1868; MKQCPI 1881; medical officer to Killashandra and Newtowngore Dispensary Districts and constabulary; certifying factory surgeon; author of various medical papers; JP for county Cavan; retired c 1920 to Ardnabel, Roebuck, Clonskeagh, county Dublin; married Anna Maud Mary —; died 13 October 1923 at Ardnabel; probate Dublin 10 May 1924. [Dub GRO (d); Dub Nat Arch, will cal; *Med Dir*].

KENNY, JOSEPH MARY SIMON (1864–1947) Granard, county Longford;
born 16 July 1864 at Knockagh, county Longford, son of Francis Kenny, grazier, of Castlewilder, county Longford; brother of Dr Charles Aloysis Kenny (*q.v.*); educated at Castleknock College, Dublin; studied medicine at Queen's College, Belfast, from 1883; MB BCh BAO (RUI) 1889; LM Rot Hosp Dub; DPH RCPSI 1905; medical officer and medical officer of health to Granard Dispensary District and medical officer to Granard Hospital; retired c 1925 to Eden Vale, Longford; married —; died 29 May 1947 at Eden Vale; buried in Abbeyshrule Cemetery; probate Dublin 13 October 1947. [Dub Nat Arch, will cal, will; Kirkpatrick Archive; *Med Dir*; QCB adm reg].

KENNY, RANDAL YOUNG (1806/7–80), Killashandra, county Cavan;
born 1806/7; studied medicine at Edinburgh University and Royal Infirmary; MD (Edin) 1828 (thesis 'De podagra'); LM Dub Lying-In Hosp (Rotunda) 1829; LRCS Edin; 1829; LAH Dub 1833; medical officer to Cavan Auxillary Workhouse and Newtowngore Dispensary District; medical officer to Killashandra Dispensary District and constabulary; married —; father of Dr James Berry Kenny (*q.v.*), General William Wallace Kenny RAMC (*q.v.*) and Mary Emily Kenny who married Dr Connolly Norman (*q.v.*); died 18 July 1880 at Killashandra. [Croly (1843–6); Dub GRO (d); Edin Univ; Kirkpatrick Archive; *Med Dir*].

KENNY, THOMAS JOSEPH (b 1845), Waterford;
born 20 April 1845 at Waterford, son of Patrick J. Kenny of Waterford; educated at Waterford Collegiate School; studied arts and medicine at Queen's College, Belfast, from 1889, at Queen's College, Cork and at the Catholic University of Ireland; BA (RUI) 1893; MB BCh BAO 1896; LM Rot Hosp Dub; died c 1897. [*Med Dir*; QCB adm reg].

KENNY, WILLIAM WALLACE (1854–1929), Army Medical Service;
born 14 July 1854 at Killashandra, county Cavan, son of Randal Young Kenny (*q.v.*); brother of Dr James Berry Kenny (*q.v.*); studied medicine at Trinity College, Dublin, from 1871 and at the Royal College of Surgeons in Ireland; LRCSI 1875; BA MB (TCD) 1876; LM Rot Hosp Dub 1876; FRCSI 1889; joined the Army Medical Service as surgeon 1877; surgeon major 1889; surgeon lieutenant-colonel 1897; colonel 1904; surgeon general 1908; served in Afghan War 1879–80, Sudan 1885 and South Africa 1900; honorary surgeon to the King 1910; retired 1914 but served in World War I 1914–18; Knight of Grace, order of St John of Jerusalem; CB 1917; retired finally to 6 The Avenue, Clifton, Yorkshire; married Catherine Jane Steedman, daughter of E.B. Steedham of High Ercall Hall, Wellington, Shropshire; died 11 May 1929 at Clifton; probate York 25 June 1929. [*BMJ* obituary (1929); Kirkpatrick Archive; *Med Dir*; Peterkin and Johnston (1968); TCD adm reg; *TCD Cat*, vol II (1896)].

KEOGH, JOHN AMBROSE (1863/4–1919), Naval Medical Service;
born 1863/4, son of Michael Keogh, spirit merchant, of 10 Clarendon Place, Belfast; studied arts and medicine at Queen's College, Cork; BA (RUI) 1885; MB MCh

MAO 1886; joined the Naval Medical Service c 1890; fleet surgeon 1906; stationed in Bermuda Naval Hospital c 1914; married 25 March 1896 in St Paul's Roman Catholic Church, Belfast, Margaret O'Neill, daughter of Constantine O'Neill, spirit merchant, of 75 Falls Road, Belfast; died 5 February 1919 at the Royal Naval Hospital, Chatham; probate London 13 March 1919. [*BMJ* obituary (1919); Kirkpatrick Archive; Lond PPR, will cal, will; *Med Dir*; UHF database (m)].

KEOWN, THOMAS HERON (1813/4–76), Naval Medical Service, Killyleagh, county Down, and Belfast;
born 1813/4, son of Matthew Keown, gentleman; studied medicine at University College, London; MRCSE 1835; LSA Lond 1836; LKQCPI 1862; joined the Naval Medical Service as assistant surgeon 1841; surgeon in charge of Royal Naval Hospital, Hong Kong 1853–6; medical officer to Killyleagh Dispensary District; general practitioner of Sydenham, Belfast; author of various medical papers; married 13 August 1857 in Drumbeg Church of Ireland Church, county Down, Elizabeth Harrison, daughter of John Harrison, gentleman, of 'The Court', Hillhall, Lisburn; son born 16 June 1858 at Hillhall; died 9 December 1876 at Sydenham; administration (with will) Belfast 21 February 1877. [*BNL* 17 August 1857 (m) and 19 June 1858 (b, son); Belf PRO, will cal; Dub GRO (d); *Med Dir*; UHF database (m)].

KEOWN, WILLIAM (1808/9–23), Ardglass, county Down;
born 1808/9; surgeon, of Ardglass; died 14 June 1832 in Ardglass. [*BNL* 3 July 1832 (d)].

KERNAHAN (CARNAGHAN), — (1759/60–1834), Glenavy, county Antrim;
born 1759/60; general practitioner of Crew, near Glenavy; married —; erected a headstone in Glenavy Graveyard to his sons who were born c 1798 and 1802; another son married in 1828; died 15 June 1834 at his home. [*BNL* 5 September 1828 (m, son) and 27 June 1834 (d); gravestone inscription].

KERNAN, JAMES
See KIERNAN, JAMES

KERR, ALEXANDER (*fl c* 1824), Londonderry;
surgeon, of Ferryquay Street, Londonderry c 1824. [Pigot (1824)].

KERR, ANDREW (1765/6–1846), Newbliss, county Monaghan;
born 1765/6; younger son of the Rev Andrew Ker, rector of Aghabog, county Monaghan, and Elizabeth Montgomery of Bessmount Park; MD (Edin) 1790 (thesis 'De asthmate spasmodico'); succeded his brother Alexander to the property of Newbliss which Alexander had built in 1814, dying in that year; general practitioner, of Newbliss House c 1845; JP; died 30 May 1846 at Newbliss, childless, and the Newbliss property passed to his niece Mary Ker. [*BNL* 5 June 1846 (d); Burke *LGI* (1912); Croly (1843–6); Edin Univ; Kirkpatrick Archive; Leslie (1929); Lewis (1837)].

KERR, ANDREW WATSON (1850–1918), Ryton, county Durham;
born 26 May 1850 at Carndreen, Castlederg, county Tyrone, son of James Kerr, farmer and carpenter, of Castlefin, county Donegal; educated at Belfast Mercantile Academy; studied medicine at Queen's College, Belfast, from 1878; LSA Lond 1884; general practitioner, of Rose Villa, Crawcrook, Ryton-on-Tyne; died 7 May 1918; probate Durham 8 October 1918. [Lond PPR, will cal; *Med Dir*; QCB adm reg].

KERR, JAMES (d c 1749), Tullydraw, county Tyrone;
surgeon, of Tullydraw, Dungannon; died c 1749; probate Prerogative Court 1749. [Vicars (1897)].

KERR, JAMES (1848–c 1914) Portrush, county Antrim, Winnipeg, Canada and Washington DC, USA;
born 14 December 1848 at Portstewart, county Antrim, son of Abraham John Kerr of Roselick, Portstewart; educated at Coleraine Academical Institution; studied medicine at Queen's College, Belfast, from 1866; MD MCh (QUI) 1870; general practitioner of Portrush; surgeon with HM Transport No 12, Gold Coast Expedition 1873–4; surgeon with the Allen shipping line c 1875; superintendent of Health, Manitoba; surgeon major at North West Rebellion (Canadian Militia) 1885; professor of surgery in Manitoba, Georgetown and Columbia Universities, of 201 Donald Street, Winnipeg, c 1885; and of 816, 1711 H Street, Washington, DC c 1895; died c 1914. [*Med Dir*; QCB adm reg].

KERR, JAMES KING (1846–1920), Leytonstone, Essex, and Belfast;
born 31 October 1846 at Randalstown, county Antrim, son of James Kerr, farmer, of Randalstown; educated at RBAI; studied medicine at Queen's College, Belfast, from 1863 and St Thomas's Hospital, London; MD MCh (QUI) 1871; Dip Mid 1872; medical officer to Coagh Dispensary District and constabulary c 1873–5; general practitioner, of Holmlands, Leytonstone c 1875–91; general practitioner, of Glenaltans, Knock, Belfast c 1891–1920; JP for Belfast; alderman; chairman of the Public Health Committee from 1904; member of the Belfast Asylum Board; author of various medical papers; married 12 August 1873 in First Belfast Presbyterian Church, Charlotte McTear, daughter of George McTear, merchant, of Belfast; died 10 August 1920 at Glenaltans; portrait in City Hall, Belfast; probate Belfast 11 January 1921. [Belf PRO, will cal; Dub GRO (m); Kirkpatrick Archive; *Lancet* obituary (1920); *Med Dir*; QCB adm reg; Young and Pike (1909)].

KERR (KER), LEWIS (b 1723/4), Cavan;
born 1723/4, son of the Rev John Kerr, prebend of Donacavey, county Monaghan; educated by Dr Sheridan; studied arts and medicine at Trinity College, Dublin, from 1737; scholarship 1739; BA (TCD) 1741; MA 1744; MB 1759; master of Cavan School 1764–8. [Burtchaell and Sadleir (1924); Leslie (1929)].

KERR, WILLIAM (1864/5–1941), Armagh;
born 1864/5 at Clones, county Monaghan; studied medicine at the Catholic University of Ireland and University College, Dublin; MB MCh (RUI) 1888; general

practitioner, of Armagh; retired c 1930 to The Seven Houses, Armagh; married Kathleen Frances —; died 17 August 1941 at English Street, Armagh; probate Belfast 3 February 1942. [Belf GRO (d); Belf PRO, will cal; Kirkpatrick Archive; *Med Dir*].

KERRIGAN (KIRGAN), HUGH (d 1849), Castlederg, county Tyrone, and Graffy, county Donegal;
studied medicine at Glasgow University; CM (Glas) 1841; general practitioner, of Castlederg, c 1845; died March 1849 at Graffy, Urney, county Donegal, the home of his father. [Addison (1898); Croly (1843–6); *Londonderry Sentinel* 23 March 1849 (d)].

KERRIGAN, — (1792/3–1840), Mount Charles, county Donegal;
born 1792/3; general practitioner, of Mount Charles; died 20 December 1840 of typhus fever at Mount Charles. [*BNL* 1 January 1841 (d); *Londonderry Sentinel* 2 January 1841 (d)].

KEVIN, CHARLES (1807–75), Indian Medical Service;
born 1807, son of Bernard Kevin (formerly Cavanagh) of county Londonderry, and Mary Conwell of Ballymulderg, county Londonderry; MRCS 1832; joined the Indian Medical Service (Madras establishment) as assistant surgeon 1832; surgeon 1849; surgeon major 1860; served in operations in Kanara 1845; retired 1860 to 91 Jermyn Street, St James's, London and later to 28 Oxford Terrace, Hyde Park; died 24 January 1875 at 28 Oxford Terrace; probate London 20 February 1875. [Crawford (1930); Larkin 1981a); Lond PPR, will cal].

KEVIN, CHARLES (1847–1927), Ballyclare, county Antrim, and Belfast;
born 27 August 1847 at Garvagh, county Londonderry, son of George Kevin of 23 Eliza Street, Belfast; educated at Garvagh Wesleyan Day School; studied medicine at Queen's College, Belfast, from 1873; MD MCh Dip Mid (QUI) 1878; resident house surgeon in Belfast Royal Hospital; medical officer to Ballyclare Dispensary District; general practitioner, of 144 Donegall Pass, Belfast, from c 1880; married Anna Josephine —; father of Dr Robert George Kevin, MB BCh BAO (QUB) 1908; died 13 December 1927 at 144 Donegall Pass; buried in Belfast City Cemetery; probate Belfast 31 January 1928. [Belf City Cem, bur reg; Belf PRO, will cal, will; Kirkpatrick Archive; *Med Dir*; QCB adm reg].

KEYS, ADAM (*fl c* 1795) Glendermott, county Londonderry;
LAH Dub 1795; apothecary, of Glendermott. [Apothecaries (1829)].

KEYS, ROBERT ATCHISON (d c 1934), Edinburgh, Stranorlar and Castlefin, county Donegal, Bagillt, Flintshire, Manchester, Lancashire, Wolverhampton, Staffordshire, and London;
studied medicine at the Royal College of Surgeons of Edinburgh and Queen's College, Galway; LRCP LRCS Edin 1871; FRCS Edin 1874; resident medical officer to Toxteth Park Workhouse, General Infirmary and Fever Hospital; assistant medical officer of health for Edinburgh c 1873; medical officer to Cloghan Dispensary

District, Stranorlar, and constabulary 1874 and to Castlefin Dispensary District 1875; general practitioner, of Bagillt c 1905, of 332 Deangate, Manchester c 1910, of Wolverhampton Workhouse, New Cross, c 1915, and of 51 Manby Grove, Stratford, London c 1925; retired c 1929 to 13 Warwick Road, Stratford and 119 The Broadway, Plaistow, c 1933; died c 1934. [Kirkpatrick Archive; *Med Dir*].

KIDD, ABRAHAM (1816/7–92), Glenarm and Ballymena, county Antrim;
born 1816/7, son of Anthony Kidd, gentleman; studied medicine at the Royal College of Surgeons in Ireland and the Richmond Hospital, Dublin; MRCSE 1843; MD (Aber) 1850; LKQCPI 1857; LM KQCPI 1859; FRCS Edin 1865; medical officer to Glenarm Dispensary District; medical officer to Ballymena Fever Hospital and Union workhouse and certifying factory surgeon; general practitioner, of Ballymena; author of various medical papers; married 28 June 1870 in Ahoghill Church of Ireland Church, county Antrim, Ann Dowker Woodall, daughter of Thomas Dowker Woodall, gentleman, of Gracehill, county Antrim; died of typhus fever 12 March 1892 at Ballymena; probate Belfast 31 January 1928. [Belf PRO, will cal; Croly (1843–6); Dub GRO (d); *Med Dir;* UHF database (m)].

KIDD, ARCHIBALD NAPIER (1839–86), Armagh, ship's surgeon, and Caledon, county Tyrone;
born 6 May 1839 at Armagh, son of Dr Wiliam Lodge Kidd (*q.v.*); educated at Armagh Royal School 1849–56; studied arts and medicine at Trinity College, Dublin, from 1856; BA (TCD) 1862; LRCSI and LM 1863; LKQCPI 1865; MB 1866; FRCSI 1866; surgeon to the Montreal Ocean Steamship Company; general practitioner of The Mall, Armagh c 1870 and of Caledon c 1875; died 1 January 1886 at Caledon; probate Armagh 25 March 1886. [Belf PRO, will cal; Burtchaell and Sadleir (1935); Ferrar (1933; Leslie (1911); *Med Dir*].

KIDD, FREDERICK WILLIAM (1857–1917), Dublin and RAMC;
born 3 May 1857 at Newry, county Down, son of Frederick William Kidd, flour miller, and Lousia Sydney Macmaster; educated at Dundalk Grammar School; studied arts and medicine at Trinity College, Dublin, from 1875, also at the Carmichael School and the House of Industry Hospitals, Dublin; BA (TCD) 1880; LRCSI 1881; LM Coombe Hosp Dub 1881; MB MD 1887; LKQCPI and LM 1889; house surgeon to the Richmond and Whitworth Hospital, Dublin; master of the Coombe Hospital 1893–1900 and later consulting surgeon; gynaecologist to the Meath Hospital; professor of midwifery to the RCSI 1898–1917; president of the Leinster Branch of the BMA, the Gynaecological Section of the Irish Academy of Medicine and the Irish Medical Association 1914–16; author of many gynaecological papers; keen sportsman and rugby international; married 28 June 1888 in Newry Non-Subscribing Presbyterian Church, Anne Armstrong Crozier, daughter of the Rev John Armstrong Crozier, minister of Newry Non-Subscribing Presbyterian Church; father of Dr John Armstrong Crozier Kidd, MB BCh BAO (TCD) 1916, RAMC; died 3 September 1917; administration Dublin 12 October 1917. [Belf PRO, will cal; Cameron (1916); Kirkpatrick Archive; Martin (2003); *Med Dir*; TCD adm reg; *TCD Cat*, vol II (1896); UHF database (m); Widdess (1967)].

KIDD, GEORGE HUGH (1824–95), Dublin;
born 12 June 1824 in Armagh, son of Hugh Kidd and Elizabeth McKinstry of Keady; educated by the Rev John Bleckley in Monaghan and Dr Lyons in Newry; studied medicine at the Royal College of Surgeons in Ireland, Trinity College, Dublin, the Marlborough Street Schools, Dublin and in Edinburgh University; LRCSI 1842; FRCSI (hon) 1844; MD (Edin) 1845 with graduation medal (thesis 'On Vaccination, its protective power and the proofs of the necessity of revaccination'); MAO (*hon causa*) (TCD) 1883; medical officer to Derrylin Dispensary District 1843–4; demonstrator of anatomy in the Park Street Medical School 1845–9 and lecturer on anatomy and physiology 1849–57; of 30 and 58 Merrion Square South, Dublin; instrumental in founding the Stewart Institute for Idiotic and Imbecile Children in 1865; consulting obstetric surgeon to Richmond, Whitworth and Hardwick Hospitals, Dublin 1875; assistant master of the Coombe Hospital 1875–6 and master 1876–83 and successful in combating puerperal sepsis there; pioneer of the operation for vesico-vaginal fistula; president of the RCSI 1876–7; consulting obstetric surgeon to the House of Industry Hospital; president of the Obstetrical and Pathological Societies, Dublin and of the Obstetric section of the Irish Academy of Medicine; author of many medical papers; editor of the *Dublin Quarterly Journal of Medical Science* 1863–8; married (1) 20 July 1852 in St Andrew's Church of Ireland Church, Dublin, Frances Emily Rigby (who died 1884), second daughter of William Rigby of Suffolk Street, Dublin; (2) Ada Isabella Ham, daughter of the Rev Panton Ham; died 27 December 1895 at his home, 58 Merrion Square; probate Dublin 4 February 1896. [*BNL* 23 July 1852 (m); Belf PRO, will cal; Cameron (1916); Crone (1928); *DIB* (2009); Edin Univ; Kirkpatrick Archive; Martin (2003); *Med Dir;* Newmann (1993)].

KIDD, HUGH (*fl c* 1845), Derrylin, county Fermanagh;
MRCSE; medical officer to Derrylin Dispensary District, c 1845; possibly died c 1850. [Croly (1843–6)].

KIDD, JOHN (1803–52), Naval Medical Service and Australia;
born 1803; uncle of Dr Abraham Kidd of Ballymena (*q.v.*); studied medicine in Dublin and Edinburgh; MRCSE 1824; FRCS (by election) 1844; joined the Naval Medical Service as assistant surgeon 1823; served as surgeon on HMS *Castor;* distinguished himself as a cool and steady operator in treating the wounded during an engagement with rebel chiefs in January 1846; died January / February 1852 in Melbourne, Australia. [*BNL* 5 July 1853 (d); *Med Dir*; *NMS* (1826); Plarr (1930)].

KIDD, LEONARD (1831–84), Army Medical Service;
born 19 August 1831 at Armagh, son of Hugh Kidd, merchant; educated by Dr Brough; studied medicine at Trinity College, Dublin, from 1847; BA (TCD) 1852; MB 1859; joined the Army Medical Service as assistant surgeon with the 27th Foot 1854; staff surgeon 1866; transferred to the 51st Foot as surgeon major 1872; brigade surgeon 1879; deputy surgeon general 1883; mentioned in the General Orders for his conduct on board the troopship *Charlotte*, wrecked in Algoa Bay 20 September 1854 and at the burning of the *Eastern Monarch* at Spithead 3 June 1859; served during the Indian Mutiny 1857; employed in the Statistical Branch of the Army

Medical Department 1879, of 48 Leamington Road Villas, Westbourne Park, Paddington; married 12 October 1859 in St Mary's Church of Ireland Church, Dublin, Fanny Pakenham, third daughter of Daniel Pakenham of Dublin; died 31 October 1884 on the Island of Bermuda; probate London 23 April 1885. [*BNL* 14 October 1859 (m); Burtchaell and Sadleir (1935); Lond PPR, will cal; *Med Dir*; Peterkin and Johnston (1968)].

KIDD, LEONARD (1863–1942), Dublin, RAMC, and Enniskillen, county Fermanagh;
>born 1863 in Dundalk, county Louth, son of Frederick W. Kidd, merchant; educated in Ennis, county Clare; master at Foyle College, Londonderry, teaching modern languages; studied arts and medicine at Trinity College, Dublin, from 1881 and the Carmichael School; BA (TCD) 1885; LKQCPI and LM LRCSI 1887; MB MD BAO 1888 with gold medal in operative surgery; house surgeon at the Richmond Hospital, Dublin; assistant master of the Coombe Hospital, Dublin and resident clinical assistant at the Richmond, Whitworth and Hardwicke Hospitals; general practitioner in Enniskillen, of Green Gates, Cooper Crescent, and later of West Bridge, Enniskillen; medical officer to Portora Royal School; surgeon and later medical superintendent to Fermanagh County Infirmary, to which he devoted all his energies in modernizing during the 1920s and 1930s; president of the Ulster branch of the BMA 1906, and of the Irish Medical Association; representative on the General Medical Council 1906–42; major in RAMC with 83 General Hospital at Boulogne during World War I; DL for county Fermanagh; retired 1937; married Margaret Blanche — (who died 30 November 1937); died 2 October 1942 at Enniskillen; portrait in Portora Royal School; probate Londonderry 17 December 1942. [Belf PRO, will cal; *BMJ* obituary (1942); Kirkpatrick Archive; *Lancet* obituary (1942); *Med Dir;* O'Donnell (2008); TCD adm reg; *TCD Cat*, vol II (1896)].

KIDD, WILLIAM (1857–87), Hillsborough, county Down;
>born 3 November 1857 at Hillsborough, son of Robert Kidd of Annahilt, county Down, and Alice —; educated at RBAI; studied medicine at Queen's College, Belfast, from 1874; LRCP LRCS Edin 1883; general practitioner, of Hillsborough c 1884 and of 66 Ann Street, Belfast c 1885; unmarried; died 7 June 1887 at Hillsborough; buried in Annahilt Presbyterian Graveyard. [Clarke, *County Down*, vol 18 (1969); Dub GRO (d); *Med Dir*; QCB adm reg].

KIDD, WILLIAM LODGE (1784–1851), Naval Medical Service and Armagh;
>born 1784 at Thornhill, county Armagh, eldest son of the Rev Archibald Kidd, rector of Jonesborough, county Armagh; accoucheur of Dublin Lying-in Hospital (Rotunda); LAH Dub 1805; MRCSE 1807; MD (Edin) 1818 (thesis 'De typhi indiciis'); LAH Dub; FRCSI 1844; apprenticed to Dr Alexander Patton of Tandragee; served as a Volunteer in the Tandragee Yeomanry; assistant to an apothecary in Dublin c 1800–04; joined the Naval Medical Service as assistant surgeon in 1804, during the Napoleonic Wars; surgeon 1807; served on HMS *Tromp*, *Raleigh* and *Polorus*; served in West Indies, Walcheren, Baltic, North Sea and Adriatic; physician, of The Mall and English Street, Armagh, from c 1816; author of an important paper on typhus to the Royal Physical Society in 1817; president of the Society c 1817; noted for his care

of the victims of the cholera epidemic of 1832 and was later presented with a silver salver; inspector to the County Gaol from 1832; visiting physician to the Armagh Asylum from 1834; married (1) 3 September 1816 in Tandragee Church, Sarah Patton, eldest daughter of Dr George W. Patton (*q.v.*) of Tandragee, county Armagh; married (2) 23 January 1833 Margaret Waller (who was born 1797/8 and died 17 September 1881), widow of Colonel Charles Waller and eldest daughter of William Johnston of Armagh; father of Dr Archibald Napier Kidd (*q.v.*); died 2 April 1851 at Armagh; probate Prerogative Court 1851. [Apothecaries (1829); *BNL* 10 September 1816 (m); Belf PRO, prerog wills index; Bradshaw (1819); Cameron (1916); Croly (1843–6); Crone (1928); *Dub J Med Sci* 1951; 12: 252–6; Edin Univ; Fleming (2001); gravestone inscriptions (Armagh Church of Ireland Cathedral); Kirkpatrick Archive; Leslie (1911); Martin (2003); *Med Dir*; NMS (1826)Newmann (1993); Pigot (1824)].

KIDLEY, JOHN EDWARD (d 1852), Larne and Belfast;
son of John Kidley of Fownhope, Herefordshire; studied medicine at Edinburgh University; MD (Edin) 1824 (thesis 'De pneumonia'); general practitioner, of York Street, Belfast; in charge of an emergency cholera hospital set up in Larne in 1833; one of those who presented an inscribed gold box to Dr S.S. Thomson in 1834; died 6 April 1852; commemorated by a tablet in St Nicholas' Church, Carrickfergus; administration Connor Diocesan Court 1852. [Croly (1843–6); Dub Nat Arch, Connor Dio Admins index; Edin Univ; Kirkpatrick Archive; McKillop (2000); McSkimin (1909), p 191; *Memorials of the Dead*, vol VIII, p 235; Rutherford and Clarke, *County Antrim*, vol 3 (1995); Thomson presentation box (1834)].

K(I)ERNAN, JAMES (1795/6–1879), Enniskillen, county Fermanagh;
born 1795/6; MRCSE 1820; MD (Glas) 1835; LM Dub Lying-in Hosp (Rotunda) 1840; FRCSI 1844; general practitioner, of Enniskillen; died 12 February 1879 at Darling Street, Enniskillen; probate Dublin 13 April 1880. [Addison (1898); Belf PRO, will cal; Croly (1843–6); Dub GRO (d); Kirkpatrick Archive; *Med Dir*; Pigot (1824)].

KILLEN/KILLIN, HECTOR (1806/7–60), Downpatrick, county Down;
born 1806/7; LFPS Glas; general practitioner, of Downpatrick; died 14 April 1860; buried in Old Kilmore Graveyard. [*BNL* 21 April 1860 (d); Clarke, *County Down*, vol 3 (1995); *Med Dir*].

KILLEN, JOHN MOORE (1844/5–1926), Larne, county Antrim;
born 1844/5 at Kells, county Antrim, son of Samuel Killen, farmer, of Killead; brother of Dr Samuel Killen of Carrickfergus (*q.v.*); educated at RBAI; studied arts at Queen's College, Galway, and from 1867, medicine at Queen's College, Belfast; BA (QUI) 1866; MD 1870; LRCS Edin 1871; medical officer to Larne Hospital 1872–1924 and to Larne Dispensary District 1883–1924; married 27 April 1887 in Larne and Inver Church of Ireland Church, Elizabeth Elma McNeill, daughter of William Walsh McNeill, solicitor, of Main Street, Larne; died 28 April 1926; bronze memorial tablet in the Moyle Hospital; probate Belfast 25 October 1926. [Belf PRO, will cal; Kirkpatrick Archive; McKillop (2000); *Med Dir*; QCB adm reg; UHF database (m)].

KILLEN, SAMUEL (1842–1914), Toomebridge, Larne and Carrickfergus, county Antrim;

> born 20 October 1842 at Kells, county Antrim, son of Samuel Killen of Killead; brother of Dr John Moore Killen of Larne (*q.v.*); educated at the Chichester Street Academy, Belfast; studied medicine at Queen's College, Belfast, from 1862; LRCP LRCS Edin 1866; general practitioner of Donaghadee c 1867; medical officer to Toomebridge Dispensary District and constabulary 1868–77; general practitioner of Larne c 1877–87; medical officer and medical officer of health to Carrickfergus Dispensary District, medical officer to constabulary and admiralty surgeon, of High Street, Carrickfergus; from c 1887; married —; father of Dr Thomas Killen, MB BCh BAO (RUI) 1903, of Larne and Dr Samuel John Killen, MB BCh BAO (RUI) 1904, of Carrickfergus; died 26 August 1914; probate Belfast 11 January 1915. [Belf PRO, will cal; McKillop (2000); *Med Dir*; QCB adm reg].

KILLEN, WILLIAM MARCUS (1863–1945), Belfast;

> born 2 February 1863 at Duncairn Manse, Belfast, son of the Rev Thomas Young Killen, minister of Duncairn Presbyterian Church, and — Wilson; educated at RBAI; studied arts and medicine at Queen's College, Belfast, from 1880; BA (hons) (RUI) 1884; MD MCh MAO 1887; studied also in Dublin, London and Vienna; ENT surgeon and chloroformist to Dr William McKeown 1889–91; assistant surgeon to the Benn Hospital 1891–1904, of 9 Clifton Street, Belfast; surgeon to the ENT department of the Mater Infirmorum Hospital, Belfast; senior surgeon to the Benn Ulster ENT Hospital, Belfast 1904–34; of 32 College Gardens, Belfast, from c 1920; president of the Irish Ophthalmological Society; retired to live with his son at Aviemore, Monaghan c 1937; author of various papers on ENT surgery; married Alice Harriett Elliot; father of Dr Marcus Brice Killen of Monaghan, MB (QUB) 1929; died 1 September 1945 at Monaghan County Hospital; probate Belfast 24 January 1946. [Allison (1969; Barkley (1986); Belf PRO, will cal; *BMJ* obituary (1945); Kirkpatrick Archive; *Lancet* obituary (1945); *Med Dir*; O'Donnell (2008); QCB adm reg].

KILROY, MARK ANTHONY (1841–74), Army Medical Service;

> born 5 November 1841 in county Cavan; LKQCPI 1865; MRCSE 1865; joined the Army Medical Service as staff assistant surgeon 1867; retired on half pay 1873; died 13 August 1874, of phthisis, at 2 Versailles Road, Penge, London. [Lond GRO (d); *Med Dir*; Peterkin and Johnston (1968)].

KINCAID (KINKAID), JOHN (1752–1817), Indian Medical Service and Raphoe, county Donegal;

> born 1752; surgeon to the *Earl of Hertford* 1781–2; joined the East India Company (Madras establishment) as assistant surgeon 1782; surgeon 1790; served in the Third Maisur War 1790–92; on sick leave to China and Europe and applied for discharge on pension 1792; surgeon in Raphoe; married —; died 28 August 1817 at his home in Raphoe of typhus fever. [*BNL* 9 September 1817 (d); Crawford (1930); *Gentleman's Magazine* October 1817 p 377 (d); Kirkpatrick Archive].

KINDELL, ALEXANDER (1782–1850), Army Medical Service;
born 1782; joined the Army Medical Service as hospital mate and later assistant surgeon to the 39th Foot 1803; staff surgeon (for Portugal only, under Lieutenant-General Sir W. Carr Beresford) 1811; staff surgeon (permanent rank) 1814; half pay 1814–24; served in the Peninsular War 1811–14; retired on half pay 1831; erected a gravestone to his ancestors in Loughguile Graveyard in 1815; married 22 April 1824 at Magilligan, Elizabeth Lecky, daughter of Averell Lecky of Castle Lecky, county Londonderry; died 27 April 1850 in Belfast. [Gravestone inscription; Peterkin and Johnston (1968); *Strabane Morning Post* 4 May 1824 (m)].

KING, ALEXANDER (d 1794), Armagh;
son of Dr Gilbert King of Armagh (*q.v.*); studied medicine at Rheims University; MD (Rheims) 1765; general practitioner of Armagh; surgeon to the Armagh Charitable Infirmary c 1766; married — (who died c 1783); mentioned by William Drennan in his letters in 1785 as 'an ingenious, literary, melancholy man who is still talking of his wife though she has been dead these two years' (*Drennan-McTier Letters*); William Drennan lent him ten guineas in 1786; died 23 August 1794 at Armagh. [Agnew (1998); Beale (2002); *BNL* 25 August 1794 (d); Brockliss; Weatherup (2001)].

KING, ANDREW (d before 1826), Ballybofey, county Donegal;
LRCS Edin 1819 (at same time as his son); surgeon, of Ballybofey; married —; father of Dr John King (*q.v.*); died before March 1826. [*Londonderry Journal* 5 October 1819 (notice)].

KING, FRANCIS JOSEPH GEORGE (1861–1930), Shilelagh, county Wicklow;
born 9 December 1861 in county Cavan, eldest son of the Rev Joseph King, rector of Munterconnaught, county Cavan, and Lucy Jane Edgeworth Peacocke; educated at Armagh Royal School 1876–9; studied arts and medicine at Trinity College, Dublin, with an exhibition, from 1879; BA (TCD) 1883; MB (first place) 1884; BCh 1885; LM Coombe Hosp Dub; house surgeon to Monkstown Hospital, Dublin; medical officer to Shilelagh Workhouse and Fever Hospital and medical officer of health to Shilelagh Union, from c 1885; married Wilhelmina Louisa —; died 1 January 1930; probate Dublin 2 April 1930. [Dub Nat Arch, will cal; Ferrar (1933); Leslie and Crooks (2008); *Med Dir;* TCD adm reg; *TCD Cat,* vol II (1896)].

KING, GABRIEL (b 1695/6), Armagh;
born 1695/6; of Armagh; studied medicine at Leyden from 1719; MD (Rheims) 1719; physician, of Armagh c 1726–c 1740; author of a paper describing an ectopic pregnancy (with survival) c 1726, in *Medical Essays and Observations,* first published in Edinburgh in 1743, 5th ed 1771 (vol V). [Brockliss; King (1743); Kirkpatrick Archive; Innes Smith (1932)]. [Is this the same person as the next?].

KING, GILBERT (d 1784), Armagh;
born 1694/5; physician to the Armagh Charitable Infirmary c 1766; of Little Meeting Street, Armagh, c 1770; married —; father of Dr Alexander King (*q.v.*); died 1784. [Agnew (1998); Beale (2002); Weatherup (2001)].

KING, HENRY (*fl c* 1813–46), Army Medical Service and Castlecaulfield, county Tyrone;
> joined the Army Medical Service as surgeon's mate for general service 1813, later becoming hospital assistant; assistant surgeon with the 96th/97th Foot 1814; on half pay 1818–21; studied medicine at Edinburgh Unversity; MD (Edin) 1820 (thesis 'De febre Gibraltari'); returned on full pay to 33rd Foot 1821; retired on half pay 1831; commuted half pay 1832; general practitioner in Castlecaulfield, c 1846; JP and coroner for county Tyrone; married 10 August 1829 Hannah Beggs, eldest daughter of William Beggs of Armagh. [*BNL* 14 August 1829 (m); Croly (1843–6); Edin Univ; *Londonderry Sentinel* 11 February 1859 (m, daughter); Peterkin and Johnston (1968)].

KING, JAMES (1804/5–71), Moy, county Tyrone;
> born 1804/5; LRCS Edin 1829; acting ordnance surgeon at Charlemont from 1832; surgeon to Armagh Militia; general practitioner and medical officer to constabulary of Moy; unmarried; died 3 November 1871 at Moy ('found dead in bed' – coroner); administration Armagh 13 February 1872. [Belf PRO, will cal; Croly (1843–6); Dub GRO (d); *Med Dir*].

KING, JOHN (1797/8–1866), Donegal;
> born 1797/8, son of Dr Andrew King of Ballybofey (*q.v.*); LAH Dub 1817; LRCS Edin 1819; general practitioner, of Donegal; unmarried; died 19 January 1866 at Donegal, 'after a protracted illness'. [Croly (1843–6); Dub GRO (d); *Londonderry Journal* 5 October 1819 (advert); *Londonderry Sentinel* 23 January 1866 (d); *Med Dir*].

KING, RALPH (*fl c* 1663), Londonderry;
> general practitioner, of Londonderry; married —; son died 1663. [Derry Cathedral Registers, p 132].

KING, ROBERT (*fl c* 1804), Middleton, county Armagh;
> LAH Dub 1804; apothecary, of Middleton. [Apothecaries (1829)].

KING, THOMAS (1772/3–1841), Moy, Charlemont and Dungannon, county Tyrone;
> born 1772/3; surgeon, of Moy and Charlemont c 1824 and later of Bernagh, Dungannon; married Elizabeth — (who died 15 March 1862); died 17 September 1841 at his home in Bernagh; administration Armagh Diocesan Court 1841. [Dub Nat Arch, Armagh Dio Admins index; Jackson (2011); *Londonderry Sentinel* 21 March 1862 (d); Pigot (1824)].

KINGSBERRY, THOMAS (1687/8–1747);
> born 1687/8 near Armagh, son of Thomas Kingsberry, farmer; educated at Armagh Royal School; studied arts and medicine at Trinity College, Dublin, from 1708; scholar 1711; BA (TCD) 1712; MB 1719; MD 1721; died 10 April 1747. [Burtchaell and Sadleir (1924); *Exshaw's Magazine* (1747); Ferrar (1933)].

KINKEAD, JOSEPH (1748/9–69), Killinchy, county Down;
born 1748/9, probably son of the Rev Joseph Kinkead, minister of Killinchy Presbyterian Church; MD [?]; died 26 October 1769 aged 20. [Clarke, *County Down*, vol 6 (1971); McConnell (1951)].

KINLEY, JAMES (*fl c* 1767), Belfast;
apothecary, of High Street, Belfast; lease dated 1767. [Brett (2004)].

KIRK, THOMAS DICK (1857–1928), London and Montgomery, Wales;
born 4 July 1857 at Creevery, county Antrim, son of Samuel Kirk, farmer, of Creevery; educated at RBAI; studied medicine at Queen's College, Belfast, from 1877; LSA Lond 1882; MD MCh (RUI) 1883; BAO 1888; general practitioner, of 4 Columbia Road, London c 1895; medical officer of health for Montgomery and medical officer to Berriew District and Workhouse, certifying factory surgeon and public vaccinator; JP for Montgomeryshire; died 12 January 1928; probate London 22 May 1928. [Kirkpatrick Archive; Lond PPR, will cal; *Med Dir*; QCB adm reg].

KIRK, THOMAS SINCLAIR (1869–1940), Belfast and RAMC;
born 16 October 1869 in Fortwilliam Park, Belfast, son of Henry Kirk, linen merchant, of Belfast; educated at RBAI; studied arts and medicine at Queen's College, Belfast, from 1886; BA (RUI) 1889; MB BCh BAO 1893 [no FRCS]; medical officer to a hospital in Egypt 1893–4; house surgeon in the Belfast Royal Hospital 1894–5; practised as a surgeon in Belfast from 1895; junior attending surgeon to Belfast Children's Hospital 1895–7; senior attending surgeon 1897–1938; declined title of honorary consulting surgeon in 1938; assistant surgeon to Belfast Royal Hospital 1897–1902; attending surgeon 1902–34 (known as 'Surgeon Kirk'); gave the annual winter oration at the Royal Victoria Hospital 1899 and 1920; served in the RAMC during World War I; of 21 University Square, Belfast, 1905–40; president of the Ulster Medical Society 1908–09; chairman of the RVH medical staff 1928–31; was presented with a silver 'loving cup' on his retirement from the RVH which was returned to the hospital on his death; noted for the use of many unusual treatments involving urea, animal serum, etc, as well as the more far-seeing use of artificial limbs; married 1 August 1908 in St Anne's Church of Ireland Church, Belfast, Constance Mary Rome (who died in 1925 and was buried in St James Church of Ireland Graveyard, Kilwarlin), matron of the Belfast Children's Hospital, daughter of James Rome, banker, of Bovey Tracey, Devonshire; father of Christopher Kirk FRCS and Denzil Kirk who married Prof Thomas Walmsley, professor of anatomy, QUB; died 10 November 1940 at Belfast; memorial tablet in Children's Hospital; administration Belfast 4 April 1941. [Belf PRO, will cal; *BMJ* obituary (1940); Calwell (1973); Fraser (1987); James (1893); Kirkpatrick Archive; *Lancet* obituary (1940); *Med Dir*; O'Donnell (2008); QCB adm reg; Strain (1969); Symmers (1968); UHF database (m)].

KIRK, WILLIAM (d 1801), Naval Medical Service;
of Carrickfergus; joined the Naval Medical Service; died January 1801 on HMS *Stately*. [*BNL* 27 January 1801 (d)].

KIRK, WILLIAM (1862–c 1915), Imperial Maritime Customs, China;
   born 23 December 1862 at Newtownards, county Down, son of William Kirk, grocer and commisson agent, of Francis Street, Newtownards; educated at Newtownards Intermediate School; studied medicine at Queen's College, Belfast, from 1880; MD MCh (RUI) 1888; medical officer to the Imperial Maritime Customs, China, from c 1890; died c 1915. [*Med Dir*; QCB adm reg].

KIRKER, GILBERT (1853–1903), Naval Medical Service;
   born 14 July 1853 at Kilcross, Killead, county Antrim, son of James Kirker, farmer, of Killead; educated at Belfast Academy; studied medicine at Queen's College, Belfast, from 1872; MD (QUI) 1876; MRCSE 1877; MCh 1879; joined the Naval Medical Service; served as surgeon in the Russo-Turkish War; married Mary Anne —; died 24 November 1903; buried at Haslar; administration London 18 January 1904. [Lond PPR, will cal; *Med Dir*; QCB adm reg; RVH Archives].

KIRKHOPE, DAVID CONNOR (1871/2–1937), Belfast and Leyton, Essex;
   born 1871/2; studied medicine at Queen's College, Belfast, and Glasgow University; MB CM (Glas) 1895; MD 1906; DPH (Camb) 1907; resident assistant to the Western Infirmary, Glasgow; honorary assistant pathologist to Queen's College and Royal Victoria Hospital, Belfast, of 323 Shankill Road, Belfast; assistant medical officer of health to Leyton c 1908–14, of St Denys, Oliver Road, Leyton; medical officer of health and school medical officer to Tottenham District from 1913, of 100 Selbourne Road, Southgate; barrister-at-law at Gray's Inn; married Eliza Gray Danshen; died 25 August 1937 at 4 Dorset Square, London; probate London 16 October 1937. [Addison (1898); Kirkpatrick Archive; *Lancet* obituary (1937); Lond GRO (d); Lond PPR, will cal, will; *Med Dir*].

KIRKPATRICK, HENRY (1871–1958), Indian Medical Service and London;
   born 27 September 1871, son of the Rev George Kirkpatrick, rector of Rathgraffe, Castlepollard, county Westmeath; educated at Armagh Royal School January– December 1883 and Marlborough College 1884–9; studied arts and medicine at Trinity College, Dublin, from 1889; BA (TCD) 1893; MB BCh BAO 1894; LM Rot Hosp Dub; ophthalmic surgeon, of 54 Welbeck Street, London; joined the Indian Medical Service (General establishment) 1898; professor of ophthalmology and pathology at the Madras Medical College; superintendent of the Government Ophthalmic Hospital, Madras; ophthalmic surgeon to the Hospital for Tropical Diseases, Endsleigh Gardens, London; as surgeon lieutenant 1898; captain 1901; major 1910; lieutenant-colonel 1918; retired 1922; author of *Cataract and its Treatment* (1921), *Diseases of the Eye* (2nd ed, 1936) and papers on ophthalmology; later of Sandy Rise, Yately, Hampshire; died 11 May 1958; probate London 23 July 1958. [Crawford (1930); Ferrar (1933); Lond PPR, will cal; *Med Dir;* TCD adm reg; *TCD Cat,* vol II (1896); *TCD Reg*].

KIRKPATRICK, HUGH CUNNINGHAM (1851–1911), Army Medical Service;
   born 8 October 1851 at Ballyclare, county Antrim, son of John J. Kirkpatrick of Ballyclare; educated at the Belfast Seminary; studied medicine at Queen's College,

Belfast, from 1870; MD MCh (QUI) 1875; joined the Army Medical Service as surgeon 1877; surgeon major 1889; surgeon lieutenant-colonel 1897; served in the Afghan Wars 1879–80 and Bechuanaland 1884–5; retired 1906 to Danbury, Southsea, Hampshire; married Margaret —; died 29 June 1911 at Southsea; probate Dublin 16 September 1911 and London 27 September 1911. [Belf PRO, will cal; Lond PPR, will cal; *Med Dir*; Peterkin and Johnston (1968); QCB adm reg].

KIRKPATRICK, JAMES (1676–1743), Belfast;
born 1676, probably in Scotland, son of the Rev Hugh Kirkpatrick, minister of presbyterian churches in Lurgan, county Armagh, Dalry and Old Cummock in Scotland and Ballymoney, county Antrim; studied theology in Glasgow University; ordained minister of First Templepatrick Presbyterian Church in 1699; minister of First Belfast 1706–08 and of Second Belfast 1708–43; moderator of the Synod of Ulster 1712; an early and influential member of the Belfast Society, an association of ministers opposed to subscription to the Westminster Confession, from 1705; MD DD (Glas) 1732 and practised as both minister and physician; author of *A Sermon occasioned by the King's Death* (1702) and *An Historical Essay upon the Loyalty of Presbyterians from the Reformation to 1713* (1713) and various theological papers; married Elizabeth — (who died 15 March 1745 and was buried in Belfast Parish Graveyard); died 1743 in Dublin. [Addison (1898); Gillespie and O'Keeffe (2006); McConnell (1951); Millin (1900); *Oxford DNB* (2004)].

KIRKPATRICK (KILPATRICK, KILLPATRICK), JAMES (c 1692–1770), South Carolina, USA, ship's surgeon and London;
born c 1692 as James Kilpatrick in Carrickfergus, county Antrim, into a commercial family (names unknown); matriculated at Edinburgh University 1708 but did not graduate; returned to Ireland and practised medicine, though unsuccessfully; emigrated to South Carolina 1717 to join his uncle David Kilpatrick and practised in Charleston; physician to St Philip's Hospital there and established a pharmacy, which was the principal source of medicines for the poor; left Carolina as a ship's surgeon on an expedition against the Spanish at St Angelo, Florida; moved to London 1742 and changed name to Kirkpatrick; author of *An Essay on Inoculation Occasioned by the Small-pox being Brought into South Carolina in the year 1738* (1738 and later ed 1743), *Analysis of inoculation, comprising the history, theory and practice of it* (1754 and 3rd ed 1761) – the leading monograph on the subject – and various other papers and poetry; died 1770 in London. [*DIB* (2009); Viets (1952)].

KIRKPATRICK, JOHN (1870–c 1937), Warrington, Lancashire, and Victoria, Australia;
born 19 March 1870 at Ballymoney, county Antrim, son of James Kirkpatrick, farmer, of Ballynagashel House, Ballymoney, and Ellen Glenn Moore; educated at Ballymoney Intermediate School; studied medicine at Queen's, College, Belfast, from 1889, and the Royal College of Surgeons, Edinburgh; LRCP LRCS Edin 1899; LFPS Glas 1899; of 31 St Patrick's Square, Edinburgh 1899; civil medical officer to the station hospital, Warrington; emigrated to Australia c 1912; general practitioner, of various towns in Victoria, but finally of Mount Egerton from c 1928; married 11

December 1899 in Edinburgh, Jessie S. Lang (who was born 1873/4), daughter of Alexander Lang, coachbuilder of Edinburgh, and Margaret Reid; died c 1937. [Bennett (1974); Edin GRO (m); *Med Dir*; QCB adm reg].

KIRKPATRICK, JOSEPH (or **JOSHUA**) (1785/6–1830), Newtownards, county Down;

born 1785/6; surgeon and apothecary, of Newtownards; married 13 June 1812 Euphemia McCully (who was born 1795/6 and died 17 October 1828), third daughter of John McCully of Newtownards; died 9 February 1830; 'He was unremitting in his endeavours to alleviate the distress of those who required his professional assistance ...'; buried in Movilla Graveyard, Newtownards; probate Down Diocesan Court 1830. [*BNL* 19 June 1812 (m) and 19 February 1830 (d); Belf PRO, Down Dio Wills index; Clarke, *County Down*, vol 11 (1974); Pigot (1824)].

KIRKPATRICK, THOMAS (1804/5–67), Larne, county Antrim;

born 1804/5; studied medicine at Edinburgh University; MD (Edin) 1827 (thesis 'De dysenteria'); one of the doctors in the emergency cholera hospital set up in Larne in 1833; medical officer to Larne Dispensary District; a member of the Committee of the Larne National Schools and an advocate of giving the pupils a knowledge of the theory and practise of agriculture; appointed first inspector of Model Agricultural Schools in 1848; retired c 1864; married (1) 9 November 1831 in Larne, Jane Tweed (who was born 1814/5 and died 16 July 1843), only daughter of Joseph Tweed of Tremain; (2) 16 October 1844 in Larne, Emily Barklie, youngest daughter of Thomas Barklie of Baltimore, USA; died 20 March 1867 at Torquay, Devonshire; probate Dublin 17 June 1867. [*BNL* 11 November 1831 (m), 25 July 1843 (d) and 18 October 1844 (m); Belf PRO, will cal; *Coleraine Chronicle* 23 March 1867 (d); Croly (1843–6); Edin Univ; McKillop (2000); *Med Dir*; Rutherford and Clarke, *County Antrim*, vol 4 (2004)].

KIRKPATRICK, THOMAS PERCY CLAUDE (1869–1954), Lifford, county Donegal, Dublin and RAMC;

born 10 September 1869 at 32 Rutland Square, Dublin, second son of Dr John Rutherford Kirkpatrick, MB (TCD) 1855, FRCSI 1857, professor of Midwifery at TCD, of 32 Rutland Square and Catherine Drury; educated at Foyle College, Londonderry; studied arts and medicine at Trinity College, Dublin, from 1887 (with many prizes); BA (TCD) 1891 (first in history); MB BCh BAO MD 1895; LRCPI 1902; MRCPI 1903; FRCPI 1904; DLit (TCD) 1924; DLit (NUI, *honoris causa*) 1933; resident surgeon to County Donegal Infirmary, Lifford 1895–7; anaesthetist to Dr Steevens' Hospital, Dublin, from 1899, of 23 Lower Baggot Street, Dublin c 1899–1915 and of 11 Fitzwilliam Place, Dublin c 1915–54; lecturer in anaesthesia at TCD from c 1909 and later professor of medical history; registrar of RCPI 1910–54; attended the Royal Military Academy, Woolwich, and served in the Royal Artillery with rank of colonel; DSO; CMG; MRIA and PRIA; a lifelong collector of books and manuscripts, he left his library and biographical archive to the RCPI; author of a *History of the Medical Teaching in Trinity College, Dublin, and of the School of Physic in Ireland* (1912), with H. Jellett *The Book of the Rotunda Hospital: An Illustrated History of the Dublin Lying-in Hospital from its Foundation in 1745 to the present time* (1913), *Nursing Ethics* (1915), *The History of Doctor Steevens' Hospital, Dublin, 1720–1920* (1924), and many papers on anaesthesia and other medical subjects (see also Bourke (1954)); unmarried; died 9 July 1954 at Dr Steevens' Hospital, Dublin; probate Dublin 27 August 1954; portraits by James Sleator with the Friendly Brothers, by Leo Whelan in the RCPI, by R.B. Ganby in Dr Steevens' Hospital, a roundel in Dr Steevens' Hospital and a drawing by Sean O'Sullivan in Dr Steevens' Hospital. [Bourke (1954); *BMJ* obituary (1954); *DIB* (2009); Doolin (1954); Dub GRO (b) and (d); Dub Nat Arch, will cal; Kirkpatrick (1912); Kirkpatrick (1924); Lyons (1978); *Med Dir*; O'Brien, Crookshank and Wolstenholme (1984); O'Doherty (1998); *Oxford DNB* (2004); TCD adm reg; *TCD Cat*, vol II (1896)].

KIRKWOOD, EDWARD ALBERT (1871–1909), Belfast;
born 5 August 1871 in Belfast, son of Edward Kirkwood, farmer, of Oldpark, Belfast; educated at Belfast Mercantile Academy; studied medicine at Queen's College, Belfast, from 1891; LRCP LRCS Edin 1897; LFPS Glas 1897; general practitioner, of 129 and 190 Crumlin Road, Belfast; honorary physician to North Belfast Day Nurseries; married 7 December 1898 in Cooke Centenary Presbyterian Church, Belfast, Agnes Curry, daughter of John Curry, linen manager, of Ardoyne, Belfast; died 23 May 1909 of pulmonary tuberculosis, at 129 Crumlin Road, Belfast; probate Belfast 12 July 1909. [Belf PRO, will cal; Dub GRO (d); *Med Dir*; QCB adm reg; UHF database (m)].

KISBY, WILLIAM JOSEPH (1843/4–95), Dublin and counties Galway, Mayo, Leitrim, Sligo, Kerry, Cavan, Monaghan and Roscommon;
born 1843/4; studied medicine at the Carmichael School and Richmond Hospital, Dublin; LM Rot Hosp Dub 1863; LAH Dub 1864; LFPS and LM Glas 1865; resident medical officer and accoucheur to Cork Street Fever Hospital, Dublin; resident clinical clerk to the Richmond, Whitworth and Hardwick Hospitals, Dublin, for 3 years; apothecary to the workhouse and dispensary, county Galway c 1871; medical officer to Bangor, Dromahaire, Hollymount and Aclare Dispensary District (counties Mayo, Leitrim and Sligo) c 1870; of Waterville, county Kerry c 1871; medical officer and registrar of births, marriages and deaths to Shercock Dispensary District, county Cavan, 1872; medical officer to Ballyfarnan Dispensary District and constabulary, county Roscommon, from c 1875; of Shantonagh, Corduff and Lisnafedally, all in county Monaghan; married Elizabeth —; died 19 November 1895 at Lisnafedally, after falling about 9 feet into a stream and fracturing his skull when walking on a dark night to attend a sick patient (newspaper cutting); probate Armagh 28 February 1896. [Belf PRO, will cal; Kirkpatrick Archive; *Med Dir*].

KITSON, ROBERT RIEVES (d 1811), Naval Medical Service;
probably from county Tyrone; joined the Naval Medical Service and sailed on HMS *Saldanha* 1810–11; drowned with the shipwreck of the *Saldanha* on 4 December 1811 when it struck the rocks in Ballymastocker Bay, sailing into Lough Swilly during a violent storm. [McKeane (1994)].

KNIGHT, ALEXANDER (1822–94), Clones, county Monaghan;
> born 1822; brother of — Knight who married Dr John Riddall (*q.v.*); studied medicine at Glasgow University; LM Rot Hosp Dub 1845; LRCSI 1846; MD (Glas) 1848; physician to Monaghan County Fever Hospital; medical officer to Rosslea Dispensary District and constabulary, of Etna Lodge, Clones; married —; died 23 March 1894 at Etna Lodge; probate Armagh 23 May 1894. [Addison; Belf PRO, will cal; Dub GRO (d); Gordon, Margaret, pers com; *Med Dir*].

KNIGHT, ALEXANDER EDMOND (EDMUND) (1873–1971), Gold Coast, RAMC, Dublin, Roehampton and Manchester, Lancashire;
> born 18 July 1873 at Clones, county Monaghan, son of George Knight, Clerk of the Crown and Peace of Clones; educated at Monaghan Collegiate School; studied arts and medicine at Queen's College, Belfast, from 1891; MB BCh BAO (RUI) 1898; DPH (QUB) 1916; surgeon captain in the Gold Coast Volunteers; surgeon to the West African Medical Staff, with home address Mona Vista, Donaghadee, county Down; temporary major in RAMC 1914–18; DSO MC c 1915; principal medical officer to the Ministry of Pensions, Dublin c 1920; moved c 1927 to Baroda, Cecil Avenue, Ashton-on-Mersey; medical superintendent of Queen Mary's Hospital, Roehampton, c 1935, of 'Ravensbourne', Beaufort Road, Brooklands, Manchester; retired to Little Orchard, Court Road, Freshwater, Isle of Wight c 1939; medical superintendent of EMS Hospital, Stoke Mandeville c 1941; of 4 Maple Road, Wythenshawe, Manchester c 1950; of Ennismore House, The Birches, Portadown c 1958–61 and of the Old Manse Home, Manse Road, Bangor, county Down c 1961–7; of Mickleton House Hotel, Chipping Camden, Gloucestershire c 1967–71 and finally at 'Webbs', Stourton, Shipton-on-Stour, Warwickshire; married —; died 14 June 1971 at 'Webbs'; probate Manchester 10 September 1971. [Kirkpatrick Archive; Lond GRO (d); Lond PPR, will cal; *Med Dir*; QCB adm reg].

KNIGHT, WILLIAM JOHN ROSS (1857–c 1923), Cookstown, county Tyrone, and RAMC;
> born December 1857 at Philadelphia, USA, son of William Wright of Derrygennard, Cookstown; educated at Moneymore Academy; studied medicine at University College, Galway, and from 1874, at Queen's College, Belfast; MD (QUI) 1881; MCh (RUI) 1885; LM KQCPI 1885; general practitioner of Cookstown, from c 1885; served in RAMC during World War I; MC 1916; died c 1923. [Kirkpatrick Archive; *Med Dir*; QCB adm reg].

KNILANS (or NEELANS), ABRAHAM (d before 1777), Indian Medical Service;
> joined the Indian Medical Service (Bengal establishment) as assistant surgeon 1772; doctor, of Calcutta; died before October 1777 (Crawford); administration Derry Diocesan Court 1794. [Crawford (1930); Dub Nat Arch, Derry Dio Admins index].

KNIPE, JOHN COPELAND (1831–77), Army Medical Service;
> born 14 February 1831 at Belturbet, county Cavan; MRCSE 1854; joined the Army Medical Service as assistant surgeon 1855; attached to 88th Foot 1857; staff surgeon 1861; surgeon major 1869; transferred to 36th Foot 1869; retired on half pay 1874;

died 3 October 1877 at Morehampton Road, Dublin. [Kirkpatrick Archive; *Med Dir*; Peterkin and Johnston (1968)].

KNOWLES, GEORGE STEVENSON (1821–61), Wolverhampton, Staffordshire; born 1821 in Glasgow, but is described as 'from Ulster'; studied medicine at Edinburgh University; MD (Edin) 1851 (thesis 'On chloroform'); general practitioner, of Snowhill, Wolverhampton; died 13 July 1861 at 178 Oxford Road, Manchester. [Edin Univ; *Med Dir*].

KNOWLES, JAMES SHERIDAN (1784–1862), Belfast and London; born 12 May 1784 in Anne Street, Cork, son of James Knowles of Cork, but later headmaster of the English Department of the RBAI, and his first wife Jane Peace; first cousin of Richard Brinsley Sheridan; ran away from home and joined the Militia in 1805; MD (Aber); resident vaccinator with the Jennerian Institute, but gave up medicine c 1808 to become an actor; author of many plays: *The Elocutionist* (1813), *Caius Gracchus* (1815), first produced in Belfast, *Virginius* (1820) and *The Hunchback* (1832) which were produced in Belfast and London; taught elocution in Belfast in 1814 and when he persuaded the RBAI to appoint his father headmaster of the English School, became teacher of elocution there; when his father was dismissed in 1816 he started a private school in North Street, Belfast; moved to Glasgow 1817–22 to devote himself to the stage; described by Hazlitt as 'the first tragic writer of his time'; granted a civil list pension of £200 in 1848 and in his later years devoted himself to Baptist preaching; married (1) 25 October 1809 Maria Charteris of Edinburgh (who died 1841); married (2) — Elphinstone; father of Richard Brinsley Knowles who wrote his biography, and Jane Knowles who married Professor James Drummond Marshall (*q.v.*); died 30 November 1862 in Torquay, Devon; buried in the Glasgow Necropolis; portrait (anonymous) in RBAI and by William Trautschold (1849) in National Portrait Gallery. [Biggart (1949); *BNL* 2 May 1837 (m, daughter); Crone (1928); *DIB* (2009); Fisher and Robb (1913); Jamieson (1959); Newmann (1993); *Oxford DNB* (2004)].

KNOX, ALEXANDER (1801/2–77), Naval Medical Service, Ballycastle, county Antrim, Belfast, and Strangford, county Down;
born 1801/2; MD (Edin) 1831 (thesis 'De potestate naturae in morbis sanandis'); joined the Naval Medical Service as assistant surgeon; physician and surgeon to the Ballycastle Dispensary, Fever Hospital and Poor House until c 1840, when he had 'a severe and protracted illness' and made his study of Irish watering places; general practitioner, of 4 College Street, Belfast c 1845, and of Strangford; retired to Beechcroft, Strandtown, Belfast, c 1880; author of *Irish Watering Places* (1845), *Ballynahinch Mineral Waters* (1846), *Inquiry into the Existing State of our Knowledge of Cholera* ([?]), *A History of County Down* (1875) and various medical papers; married 1 September 1835 in Ramoan Church of Ireland Church, Ballycastle, Henrietta Greer Cuppage (who was born 1815/6 and died 3 July 1893), daughter of John Cuppage of Glenbank; died 9 November 1877 at Beechcroft; buried in Dromore Cathedral Graveyard; probate Belfast 15 February 1878. [*BNL* 8 September 1835 (m); Belf PRO, will cal; Clarke, *County Down*, vol 19 (1983); Croly (1843–6); Dub

GRO (d); Edin Univ; Kirkpatrick Archive; Knox (1845); Martin (2010); *Med Dir*; *Newtownards Chronicle* 10 November 1877 (d)].

KNOX, GEORGE (1793/4–1868), Army Medical Service and Strabane, county Tyrone;
born 1793/4, son of Thomas Knox, farmer, and Martha Lyon; joined the Army Medical Service as hospital mate and later as hospital assistant 1815; assistant surgeon to Ceylon Regiment 1825; transferred to 20th Foot 1827 and 83rd Foot and 3rd Dragoons 1837; surgeon to 6th Foot 1840; on half pay 1843; not in *Medical Register* or *Medical Directory*; surgeon, of Woodend, Strabane 1867, when his sister Jane died at his house, aged 73; unmarried; died 1 October 1868 at the Free Church Manse, Annan, Dumfriesshire. [Edin GRO (d); *Londonderry Sentinel* 29 March 1867 (d) and 6 October 1868 (d); Peterkin and Johnston (1968)].

KNOX, HUGH (1859–1925), London;
born 13 June 1859 at Hillsbrough, county Down, son of James Knox, farmer, of Annahilt, county Down; educated at RBAI; studied medicine at Queen's College, Belfast, from 1880; LRCP LRCS Edin 1893; LFPS Glas 1893; general practitioner and assistant school medical officer, of 7 and 94 Priory Park Road, Kilburn, 115 Maida Vale and 9 Steathray Gardens, Hampstead, London; married Anne —; died 30 January 1925; probate London 25 February 1925. [Lond PPR, will cal; *Med Dir*; QCB adm reg].

KNOX, JOHN (*fl c* 1845), Carrickfergus, county Antrim;
LAH Dub; apothecary to Carrickfergus Gaol c 1845. [Croly (1843–6)].

KNOX, JOHN (1848–1926), Bethnal Green, London;
born November 1848 at Rathfriland, county Down, son of John Knox of Tierkelly, Rathfriland; educated at the Chichester Street Academy, Belfast; studied medicine at Queen's College, Belfast, from 1867; MD MCh (QUI) 1871; Dip Mid 1872; honorary visiting surgeon to Queen Adelaide's Dispensary; medical officer to Bethnal House Lunatic Asylum, London c 1875; surgeon to Bethnal Green Infirmary from c 1880; general practitioner, of 254 Bethnal Green Road; retired c 1920 to Hova House, 1 Denmark Villas, Hove; married Mary Ann Elizabeth —; died 21 August 1926; probate London 22 October 1926. [Lond PPR, will cal; *Med Dir*; QCB adm reg].

KNOX, S. (*fl c* 1824), Carrickfergus, county Antrim;
surgeon, of Carrickfergus c 1824. [Pigot (1824)].

KNOX, THOMAS (*fl c* 1730), Clones, county Monaghan;
strong Calvinist and claimed descent from the Rev John Knox; physician, of Clones; married Nicola King; father of William Knox, government official and polemicist (1732–1810). [*DIB* (2009) (for son William Knox)].

KNOX, THOMAS (1851/2–1917), Lisnaskea, county Fermanagh;
born 1851/2; studied medicine at Trinity College, Dublin; LRCSI 1874; LKQCPI and LM 1875; medical officer to Lisnaskea Dispensary District, constabulary,

Workhouse and Fever Hospitals; medical officer of health to Lisnaskea, of The Cottage, Lisnaskea; married Louisa Sandels, daughter of Dr William James Sandels of Lisnaskea (*q.v.*); died 2 March 1917 at Lisnaskea; administration Armagh 24 August 1917. [Belf PRO, will cal; Dub GRO (d); *Med Dir*].

KOUGH, EDWARD (1836/7–95), Castleblaney, county Monaghan, Chertsey, Kent, and Dublin;
born 1836/6 in county Donegal, son of the Rev Thomas Kough; educated by Dr Stacpoole; studied arts and medicine at Trinity College, Dublin, from 1856; scholar of TCD 1859; BA (TCD) 1861; MA 1864; LM Rot Hosp Dub; MB 1865; MCh 1866; house physician to the Dublin Sailors' Home; medical officer to the Castleblaney Dispensary District; medical officer to Windlesham District, Chertsey, Kent c 1870; general practitioner, of Ros-y-gar, Monkstown, Dublin from 1875; married Mary E. —; died 11 November 1895; probate Dublin 10 February 1896. [Belf PRO, will cal; Burtchaell and Sadleir (1935); *Med Dir*].

KYLE, DANIEL (*fl c* 1801), Donegal, county Donegal;
LAH Dub 1801; apothecary, of Donegal town. [Apothecaries (1829)].

KYLE, DAVID (*fl c* 1824), Limavady, county Londonderry;
apothecary and surgeon, of Catherine Street, Limavady c 1824. [Pigot (1824)].

KYLE, JAMES (d 1791), Belfast;
surgeon, of Belfast; died 19 May 1791 at Ballybeen, county Down. [*BNL* 24 May 1791 (d)].

KYLE, THOMAS WILLIAM (1855–94), Measham, Leicestershire;
born 4 April 1855 at Drumnakilly, Omagh, county Tyrone, son of Robert Kyle of Drumnakilly; educated at Omagh Model School; studied medicine at Queen's College, Belfast, from 1872; MD Dip Mid (QUI) 1875; MCh 1876; general practitioner, of Measham, died 2 November 1894; probate Derby 29 January 1895. [Lond PPR, will cal; *Med Dir*; QCB adm reg].

Dr James Graham (1797–1857)

Prof Robert James Graves, FKQCPI (1796–1853), drawing by *Charles Grey* (reproduced courtesy of the National Library of Ireland, Dublin)

Dr Robert Gray (1845–1924)

Dr Thomas Richardson Griffiths (1860–1923)

Dr Alexander Henry Haliday (1728–1802), artist unknown (private collection)

Dr Robert Hall (1861–1941)

Mr Alexander Harkin, FRCS (1817–94)

Dr Augustine Henry (1857–1930)

Dr Moses Henry (1872–1927)

Dr James Mathews Heron (1866–1938)

Dr Robert Thomas Herron (1864–1930)

Dr John Houston (1802–45),
artist unknown (reproduced courtesy of
the Royal College of Surgeons in Ireland)

Sir Thomas Houston, MD (1868–1949)

Dr Edmund Fergus Jamison (1864–1955)

Dr Henry George Jamison (1863–1954)

Prof Sir Robert James Johnstone, FRCS (1872–1938)

Dr Evory Kennedy (1806–86), oil painting by *Charles Napier Kennedy* (reproduced courtesy of the Rotunda Hospital, Dublin)

Dr James King Kerr (1846–1920)

Dr Thomas Sinclair Kirk (1869–1940)

Prof Thomas Percy Claude Kirkpatrick, MD (1869–1954), oil painting by *Leo Whelan* (reproduced courtesy of the Royal College of Physicians of Ireland)

Dr James Sheridan Knowles (1784–1862), oil painting, artist unknown (reproduced courtesy of the Royal Belfast Academical Institution)

Dr Robert Rendle Louis Leathem (1869–1935)

Dr Richard Whytock Leslie (1862–1931)

Dr Charles James Lever (1806–72), drawing by *Simon Pearce* (reproduced courtesy of the National Gallery of Ireland)

Dr David Moore Lindsay (1862–1956)

Prof James Alexander Lindsay, MD (1856–1931)

Dr James Lynass (1864–1905)

Dr David MacBride (1726–78) (engraving) (reproduced courtesy of the Royal College of Physicians of Ireland)

Sir Robert McCarrison, FRCP
(1878–1960), bust by *Kathleen Scott*

Dr Michael Joseph McCartan (1857–1919)

Dr John McCaw (1858–1924)

Dr James B. McCleery (1795/6–1847),
artist unknown (reproduced courtesy of
the Ulster Medical Society, Belfast)

L

LABATT, JONATHAN (1807/8–c 1852), Dublin;
born 1807/8 in Dublin, son of Dr Samuel Bell Labatt of Dublin, LKQCPI 1802, pioneer in the introduction of smallpox vaccination in Dublin; family was of Huguenot stock and settled in Portarlington, Queen's County; brother of two medical doctors; nephew of the Rev Edward Labatt, rector of Kilcar, county Donegal; educated at RBAI 1822–3; studied arts and medicine at Trinity College, Dublin, from 1823; BA (TCD) 1828; MA 1832; FKQCPI; physician, of 67 Upper Sackville Street, Dublin c 1845 and 1851; died c 1852. [Burtchaell and Sadleir (1924); Croly (1843–6); Fisher and Robb (1913); Leslie (1940); Martin (2003); *Med Dir*; Widdess (1963)].

LAGAN, JOHN (d c 1888), Maghera, county Londonderry;
studied medicine at the Royal College of Surgeons in Ireland; LRCSI 1886; LKQCPI and LM 1886; general practitioner, of Brackaghreilly, Maghera; died c 1888. [*Med Dir*.].

LAING, ERNEST ALEXANDER RONALD (1872–1914), Alexandria, Bombay, Calcutta, Hongkong and Loddiswell, Devonshire;
born 18 February 1872 at Boyle, county Roscommon, son of James K. Laing, commercial traveller; educated at RBAI; studied arts and medicine at Queen's College, Belfast, from 1888, also at the Royal College of Surgeons in Ireland and Edinburgh; LM Rot Hosp Dub 1894; LRCP LRCS Edin 1895; LFPS Glas 1895; of Knox Street, Balina, county Mayo c 1895; medical officer to Mustafha Camp, surgeon to Station Hospital, Alexandria and Health Officer on Special Plague Duty to Government of Egypt, c 1900; medical officer in Bombay and Calcutta; assistant superintendent to Government Civil Hospital and medical officer to Government Lunatic Asylum, Hong Kong c 1900–06; medical officer in charge of Sutton Ford Isolation Hospital and Swayne's Farm Smallpox Hospital c 1906; general practitioner, of Stockadon, Loddiswell, c 1910; subsequently travelling; married Helen Best —; died 25 December 1914 at Hill House, Esher; probate London 10 February 1915. [Lond PPR, will cal; *Med Dir*; QCB adm reg].

LAING, THOMAS (1846–85), Newry, county Down;
born 16 August 1846 at Newry, son of Thomas Laing of Downshire Road, Newry; educated at RBAI; studied medicine at Queen's College, Belfast, from 1862 and the Ledwich School, Dublin; LKQCPI and LM 1870; LRCSI 1870; general practitioner, of Tudor Lodge, Newry; died 21 March 1885 at Newry; administration Belfast 15 July 1885. [Belf PRO, will cal; *Med Dir*; QCB adm reg].

LAIRD, HUGH WALLACE (d 1774), Newtownards, county Down;
surgeon and apothecary; died August 1774 at Newtownards. [*Freeman's Journal*; Kirkpatrick Archive].

LAIRD, JOHN (GEORGE) (1795/6–1868), Ballybofey, county Donegal;
born 1795/6; LAH Dub 1817; accoucheur of Dub Lying-in Hosp; general practitioner, apothecary and medical officer to constabulary, of Ballybofey c 1824–45; married —; father of Dr Samuel Laird of Dungloe (*q.v.*); died 12 August 1868 at Ballybofey; buried in Stranorlar Graveyard. [Apothecaries (1829); Croly (1843–6); Dub GRO (m, son) and (d); *Londonderry Sentinel* 20 May 1853 (m, daughter) and 14 August 1868 (d); Pigot (1824)].

LAIRD, SAMUEL (*fl c* 1765), Magherafelt, county Londonderry;
apothecary of Magherafelt, c 1765–6 (executor of will). [Eustace, vol II (1954)].

LAIRD, SAMUEL (b c 1825), Dungloe, county Donegal;
born 1825/6, son of Dr John George Laird of Ballybofey (*q.v.*); MD [?]; general practitioner, of Dungloe; married 24 May 1855 in the Sound Church, Achill Island, county Mayo, Catherine Young (who was born 1818/9), daughter of John Young of Dublin. [*BNL* 1 June 1855 (m); Dub GRO (m)].

LAKE, GERARD JOHN BAPTIST (d c 1936), ship's surgeon, Ballymena, county Antrim, and Manchester, Wigan and Preston, Lancashire;
probably born in Ballymena; studied medicine at the Carmichael College, Dublin; LRCSI 1886; surgeon on SS *Cameroons* and *Volta* (British and Africa Company); general practitioner, of Fort Hill, Ballymena, c 1891–5, of Fairfield Road, Droylsden, Manchester c 1895–1900, of Hindley Green, Wigan c 1902–08 general practitioner, of Havelock Terrace, Moor Park, Preston, c 1905–36; honorary visiting medical officer to the Little Sisters of the Poor and medical officer to the Boys' Home, Fulwood; died c 1936. [*Med Dir*].

LAMONT, AENEAS (1811/2–60), Belfast;
born 1811/2; LRCSI; FRCSI 1844; resident surgeon and apothecary to Belfast Fever Hospital 1837–8 and attending surgeon to Belfast Fever (General) Hospital 1849–55 and 1857–8; resigned because of severe illness 1858; of 60 Corporation Street, Belfast c 1858; librarian of Belfast Medical Society; died 11 November 1860 at his brother's house, Beaver Hall, Ballymacarret; buried in Clifton Street Burying Ground. [Allison (1972); *Belf Fever Hosp, Ann Rep*; *BNL* 12 November 1860 (d); Croly (1843–6); Kirkpatrick Archive; *Med Dir*; Merrick and Clarke, *Belfast*, vol 4 (1991)].

LAMPREY, RICHARD ORFORD (1840–1906), London;
born 17 August 1840 at Ballintemple Glebe, county Wicklow, son of the Rev George William Lamprey; educated at Mr Flynn's School, Dublin; studied medicine at Queen's College, Belfast, from 1858; LRCP LRCS Edin 1878; general practitioner, of 1 Granville Terrace, East Hill, Wandsworth, and later 'Burnbrae', 34 West Side, Wandsworth, London; died 13 October 1906 at St Mary's Hospital, Paddington. [Lond GRO (d); *Med Dir*; QCB adm reg].

LANE, ALBERT EDWARD BOYLE (1840–c 1886), Bellarena and Limavady, county Londonderry;
born 1840 (baptised 25 May 1840), sixth son of Dr (John) William Lane, senior, (*q.v.*) of Limavady; brother of Dr Benjamin Lane (1827–1907) (*q.v.*); studied

medicine at the Royal College of Surgeons in Ireland; LRCP Edin 1864; LFPS Glas and LM 1864; LM Rot Hosp Dub; medical officer to Bellarena Dispensary District and certifying factory surgeon; medical officer to Limavady Workhouse and Fever Hospital and consulting sanitary officer from 1876, of Main Street, Limavady; died c 1886. [Drumachose bapt reg; Hitchings, Paul, pers com; Kirkpatrick Archive; *Med Dir*].

LANE, ALEXANDER (1801/2–77), Naval Medical Service. Nova Scotia, and Coleraine, county Londonderry;

born 1801/2; studied medicine at different times at Dublin, London, Glasgow, Paris and Naples; MD (Glas) 1836; joined the Naval Medical Service in 1822 as assistant surgeon, serving on the sloop *Sparrowhawk* off Halifax, at Portsmouth and in the Mediterranean 1823–6; on the *Ramillies* in the Downs 1826; on the schooner *Speedwell* and the sloop *Fairy* at Jamaica 1828–9; on the sloop *Primrose* off Africa 1830, when he was acting surgeon and present at the capture of the Spanish slave-ship *Velos*; surgeon 1831; on the sloop *Pearl* 1831–4; on the *Herald* 1838 and the *Penelope* 1846; living at Lanesborough Villa, Mahone Bay, Nova Scotia, when his son Dr John Lane was married in 1858; retired as staff surgeon to Churchland, Clun 1860, to Ludlow, Shropshire c 1869, and to Douglas, Isle of Man c 1876; author of various medical papers; married Dorothea Stanley (who lived at Coleraine c 1835–49 and their children were baptised there, and died 5 August 1897 in her 94th year at Douglas, Isle of Man); father of Dr John William Lane, junior (*q.v.*); died 5 May 1877 at Douglas, Isle of Man. [Hitchings, Paul, pers com; *Med Dir*; *NMS* (1826)].

LANE, ALEXANDER (1812/3–87), Aghadowey, county Antrim;

born 1812/3, son of Benjamin Lane of Ballycarton, county Londonderry, JP, and Rose Dillon; younger brother of Dr (John) William Lane, senior, of Limavady (*q.v.*); studied medicine at Glasgow University; CM (Glas) 1835; MD 1836; FRCSI 1844; LKQCPI and LM 1860; medical officer to Aghadowey Dispensary District and registrar of births and deaths, of Greenfield, Aghadowey; married (1) Margaret Brown (who died 22 January 1881), daughter of Robert Brown of Northland Row, Dungannon, and Eleanor —; (2) Anne Horner (who married (2) the Rev Andrew Macafee, minister of First Omagh Presbyterian Church, and was mother of Prof C.H.G. Macafee); father of Rosetta Lane who married Dr Henry Bolton Clark (*q.v.*); died 19 October 1887 at Belleview, Aghadowey; probate Dublin 15 December 1887. [Addison (1898); Barkley (1987); Belf PRO, will cal; *Burke's Irish Family Records* (1976); *Coleraine Chronicle* 28 November 1863 (d, under Brown, Eleanor) Croly (1843–6); Dub GRO (d); Hitchings, Paul, pers com; *Med Dir*].

LANE, ALEXANDER (c 1859–c 1938), Thanet, Kent, London, Newcastle-upon-Tyne, Northumberland, and Weymouth, Dorset;

born c 1859, probably in Bellaghy, county Londonderry, eldest son of Dr John William Lane, junior (*q.v.*); studied medicine at Guy's Hospital, London; MRCSE 1880; LSA Lond 1880; FRCSI 1893; MD (Durham) 1898; general practitioner, of Minster, Thanet; surgeon, of Guy's Hospital, London c 1895–1904 but travelling abroad in 1902; surgeon, of Newcastle-upon-Tyne, of Saville Chambers and 5 Louvain Place c 1905–09; surgeon, of 7 Royal Terrace, Weymouth c 1910; retired to

Crofton Place, Yeovil, Somerset c 1937; author of various publications on electrotherapy; died c 1938. [Hitchings, Paul, pers com; *Med Dir*].

LANE, BENJAMIN (1827–1907), Dunboe, Coleraine, county Londonderry, and Army Medical Service;
born 5 June 1827 at Newtownlimavady, eldest son of Dr (John) William Lane, senior (*q.v.*), of Limavady; brother of Dr Albert Edward Boyle Lane (*q.v.*); studied medicine at the Royal College of Surgeons in Ireland; LRCSI and LM 1848; LRCP Lond 1874; accoucheur of the Coombe Lying-in Hospital, Dublin; one of the founders of the Limavady Literary Society in 1847; medical officer to Dunboe Dispensary District and constabulary c 1850–53; joined the Army Medical Service as acting assistant surgeon and then assistant surgeon to the 80th Foot in 1852; staff surgeon 1858 and surgeon to the 4th Foot 1860; surgeon major 1872; served in Burma 1852–3, first Kaffir War (1856) and the Indian Mutiny 1857–8 (mentioned in Despatches); retired as brigade surgeon 1882; married 23 April 1855 at Fort George, Inverness, Caroline Arbuthnot Ewing (who died 16 May 1903), youngest daughter of Dr Joseph Ewing (*q.v.*), Inspector General of Hospitals, Army Medical Department; father of Sir William Arbuthnot Lane, Bart, MB Lond 1881, Dr Benjamin Hugh Lane, LRCP Edin 1882, of Doncaster, and Jane Rose Lane who married lieutenant-colonel Allan Scott Roberts and was mother of Dr Cedric Sydney Lane Roberts, LRCP Lond, MRCSE 1913, CVO, FRCS 1920; died 12 June 1907 at 19 Priory Street, Cheltenham; buried in Cheltenham Cemetery; probate Gloucester 8 July 1907. [*BNL* 7 May 1855 (m); *BMJ* obituary (1907); *Coleraine Chronicle* 5 May 1855 (m); Hitchings, Paul, pers com; Kirkpatrick Archive; Lond PPR, will cal; *Med Dir*; Peterkin and Johnston (1968)].

LANE, BENJAMIN (1864/5–1922), Magilligan and Limavady, county Londonderry; born 1864/5, youngest son of Benjamin Lane, JP, of Ballycarton, county Londonderry; younger brother of Dr James Lane (*q.v.*); studied medicine at Trinity College, Dublin and the Royal College of Surgeons in Ireland; LRCSI 1884; LKQCPI and LM 1885; general practitioner, of Ballycarton, Magilligan; medical officer to Bellarena Dispensary District; coroner for county Londonderry; of Main Street, Limavady; unmarried; died 13 August 1922 at 81 University Street, Belfast; administration Londonderry 26 October 1922 and 14 September 1938. [Belf GRO (d); Belf PRO, will cal; Hitchings, Paul, pers com; Kirkpatrick Archive; *Med Dir*].

LANE, JAMES (d 1924), Magilligan, county Londonderry, and Omaha, Nebraska, USA;
second son of Benjamin Lane of Ballycarton, JP; older brother of Dr Benjamin Lane (*q.v.*); LRCSI and LM 1882; LKQCPI 1883; general practitioner, of Magilligan 1885; emigrated to USA c 1890; general practitioner of Omaha, Nebraska c 1895 and of Salt Lake City c 1910; died 18 March 1924. [Hitchings, Paul, pers com; *Med Dir*].

LANE, JOHN WILLIAM (d 1835), Naval Medical Service;
fourth son of George Lane of Woodbrook, county Tyrone; brother of Matilda Lane who married Dr (John) William Lane, senior (*q.v.*); joined the Naval Medical Service

as assistant surgeon in 1829; appointed to HMS *Warspite* on the South American Station 1831 and to HMS *Challenger* in 1833; died 13 July 1835 of fever on HMS *Blonde* in Valparaiso Harbour. [*BNL* 30 October 1835 (d); Hitchings, Paul, pers com; *Londonderry Sentinel* 24 October 1835 (d)].

LANE, (JOHN) WILLIAM, senior (1804–76), Limavady, county Londonderry;
born 24 June 1804, eldest son of Benjamin Lane, senior, of Ballycarton, county Londonderry, and Rose Dillon; studied medicine at Glasgow University; CM (Glas) 1825; LSA Lond 1827; MRCSE 1828; MD LM 1833; LAH Dub 1841; physician to the Cholera Hospital; medical officer to Limavady Fever Hospital and general practitioner, of Newtown Limavady; married in 1826 at the 'New Church of Ireland Church', Armagh, his cousin Matilda Lane (who died 2 January 1880), daughter of George Lane of Woodbrook; father of Dr Benjamin Lane of Limavady (*q.v.*), Dr Albert Edward Boyle Lane (*q.v.*) and Matilda Ann Lane who married her cousin Dr John William Lane, junior.(*q.v.*); died 13 January 1876 at Main Street, Limavady; buried in Aghanloo Graveyard, county Londonderry. [Addison (1898); *BNL* 3 March 1826 (m); Croly (1843–6); Dub GRO (d); Hitchings, Paul, pers com; *Med Dir*].

LANE, JOHN WILLIAM, junior (1837–1913), Bellaghy, county Londonderry, Bishop's Castle, Shropshire, Milford Haven, Pembrokeshire, and Douglas, Isle of Man;
born 15 March 1837 at Coleraine, county Londonderry, son of Dr Alexander Lane RN (*q.v.*) of Coleraine and Shropshire; LM Rot Hosp Dub 1856; LRCSI 1857; LM RCSI 1863; MD (St Andrews) 1863 (by examination); medical officer to Bellaghy Dispensary District and constabulary 1858–63; general practitioner, medical officer and public vaccinator, of Bishop's Castle and Welsh Street, Shropshire; 1863–c 1886; general practitioner, of Conduit, Milford Haven c 1886–90, of Murray Crescent, Milford Haven c 1890–96, and Douglas, Isle of Man c 1897–1900; retired to Appledore and 97 Goshen Street, Devonshire c 1902; married 17 March 1858 in Drumacose Church of Ireland Church, Limavady, his first cousin Matilda Ann Lane (who was born 1834/5), eldest daughter of Dr (John) William Lane, senior (*q.v.*); father of Dr Alexander Lane (*q.v.*) and Dr John George Ogilby Hugh Lane, LRCP Lond MRCSE 1895; died 10 September 1913 at 97 Goshen Street, Keyham, Devonport (the home of his sister and daughter); probate London 30 September 1913. [*Coleraine Chronicle* 20 March 1858 (m); Dub GRO (m); Hitchings, Paul, pers com; Kirkpatrick Archive; Lond PPR, will cal, will; *Londonderry Sentinel* 19 March 1858 (m); *Med Dir;* Smart (2004)].

LANE, THOMAS BAGOT (1812/3–75), Churchill, county Donegal, Ballylynan, Queen's County, Renvyle, county Galway, Baltinglass, county Wicklow and Tullow, county Carlow;
born 1812/3 in Dublin, son of Dr Thomas Bourchier Lane of Wexford and Emily Bagot; educated privately; studied medicine at Trinity College, Dublin; apprentice surgeon to Sir Philip Crompton at the Meath Hospital, Dublin, in 1829; LM Rot Hosp Dub 1837; LRCSI 1838; BA MB (TCD) 1841; FRCSI 1844; medical officer to Churchill Dispensary District 1843, of Ballylynan 1848, of Renvyle 1853, of Rathvilly, Baltinglass, 1855–60 and finally of Omragh College, Tullow; married Jane —; died 15 July 1875 at Omragh College; administration Dublin 15 December

1875. [Belf PRO, will cal; Burtchaell and Sadleir (1924); Croly (1843–6); Hitchings, Paul, pers com; *Med Dir*].

LANGAN, FRANCIS (1849/50–82), Shercock, county Cavan, and Longford;
born 1849/50; studied medicine at the Catholic University and the Meath and St Vincent's Hospitals, Dublin; LRCSI 1873; LKQCPI and LM 1874; medical officer to Kingscourt Dispensary District, of Kingscourt c 1874–6 and to Longford Dispensary District c 1876–82; unmarried; died 18 July 1882 at New Street, Longford. [Dub GRO (d); *Med Dir*].

LANGAN, JOHN EDWARD (1860–95), Ardara, county Donegal;
born 1860, son of Patrick Langan, farmer; studied medicine at the Catholic University and St Vincent's Hospital, Dublin; LRCSI 1884; LKQCPI 1886; medical officer and superintendent medical officer of health to Ardara Dispensary District; medical officer to constabulary and Admiralty; married 22 November 1887 in Kilcloony Roman Catholic Church, Ardara, county Donegal, Sarah Gallagher, daughter of William Gallagher, farmer, of Castlegoland; died 22 March 1895 at Ardara. [Dub GRO (m) and (d); *Med Dir*].

LANGLEY, PERSHOUSE WILLIAM LESLIE (1857–80), Liverpool, Lancashire;
born 6 June 1857 at Tramore, Waterford, son of Dr William Leslie Langley MD MRCS, inspector general of Army Hospitals, Tramore; educated at Waterford Diocesan School; studied medicine at Queen's College, Belfast, from 1873; MD MCh (QUI) 1878; MRCSE 1878; assistant surgeon to the South Dispensary, Liverpool; resident medical officer to the West Derby Union Hospital c 1879 died 17 May 1880 at Workhouse Mill Road, Everton, of typhus fever. [Lond GRO (d); *Med Dir*; Peterkin and Johnston (1968); QCB adm reg].

LANGSTAFF, JAMES WILLIAM (1876–1948), RAMC and Belfast;
born 19 May 1876 at Athlone, county Westmeath, son of Dr Henry Harris Langstaff, MB (TCD) 1867, of Athlone; studied medicine at the Royal College of Surgeons in Ireland; LM Rot Hosp Dub; LRCPI and LM LRCSI and LM 1898; joined the RAMC as lieutenant 1899; captain 1902; major 1911; lieutenant-colonel 1915; colonel 1926; served in South Africa 1899–1902; India 1902–04; Sierra Leone 1907–09; World War I 1914–17; India 1917–21; West Africa 1924–5; Gibraltar 1926–9; DSO 1917; retired 1929; deputy director of medical services at Gibraltar 1929–31; medical superintendent of Royal Victoria Hospital, Belfast, 1931–44; married — Ross, daughter of Sir Ronald Ross; retired to 9 Swan Court, Chelsea, London; died 12 April 1948 at the Royal National Hospital, Ventnor, Isle of Wight; will dated 16 April 1943 proved London 2 June 1948. [*BNL* 1948 (d); Drew (1968); *Lancet* obituary (1948); Lond PPR, will cal, will; Kirkpatrick Archive; *Med Dir*].

LATHAM, GEORGE AUGUSTUS (d 1840), Crumlin, county Antrim;
MD [?]; general practitioner, of Crumlin; died 12 May 1840 after a protracted illness. [*BNL* 15 May 1840 (d)].

LATHAM (LEATHAM, LEATHEM), WILLIAM (1789/90–1848), Donegal, Army Medical Service and Antrim;
> born 1789/90; MD [?]; FRCSI; assistant surgeon to the Donegal Militia 1809; joined the Army Medical Service as assistant surgeon to the 34th Foot 1816; retired on half pay from 1827 and commuted from 1830; surgeon, of Antrim c 1837; married July 1811 Florinda Ellison (who was born 1788/9 and died 18 August 1853 at Portballintrae), daughter of the Rev Dr Thomas Ellison, rector of Castlebar, county Mayo; [newspaper notices disagree on her parentage]; father of Dr William Thomas Latham (*q.v.*); died 3 November 1848 of apoplexy in Antrim. [*BNL* 9 July 1811 (m), 7 November 1848 (d) and 22 August 1853 (d); Burtchaell and Sadleir (1924); *Coleraine Chronicle* 11 November 1848 (d) and 20 August 1853 (d); Leslie and Crooks (2008b); Lewis (1837); Peterkin and Johnston (1968); Pigot (1824)].

LATHAM, WILLIAM THOMAS (1811/2–82), Dublin and Antrim and Ballymoney, county Antrim;
> born 1811/2 in county Antrim, eldest and only surviving son of Dr William Latham, surgeon (*q.v.*); educated by Mr Corley; studied arts and medicine at Trinity College, Dublin from 1829, also medicine at the Royal College of Surgeons in Ireland and Park Street, Meath, Dr Steevens' and Sir Patrick Dun's Hospitals, Dublin; BA (TCD) 1835; LRCSI 1837; LM Rot Hosp Dub 1840; FRCSI 1844; resident surgeon to the Meath Hospital and clinical assistant to the Meath and Sir Patrick Dun's Hospitals; assistant medical officer to Antrim Dispensary; medical officer to Ballymoney Dispensary District, Gaol, Infirmary and Fever Hospital 1848–78, of Charlotte Street, Ballymoney; married 21 March 1866 in Ballymoney Church of Ireland Church, Anne O'Hara (who was born 1829/30 and died 13 August 1869 at Movanagher), eldest daughter of Charles O'Hara, esquire, JP, of O'Hara Brook, county Antrim; died 7 November 1882 at Charlotte Street; probate Dublin 24 August 1887. [Belf PRO, will cal; Burke *LGI* (1912); Burns (1988); Burtchaell and Sadleir (1924); *Coleraine Chronicle* 24 March 1866 (m) and 21 August 1869 (d); Croly (1843–6); Dub GRO (d); *Londonderry Sentinel* 23 March 1866 (m); *Med Dir;* UHF database (m)].

LAUGHLIN, ALEXANDER (*fl c* 1770), Naval Medical Service, and Gortin, county Tyrone;
> joined the Naval Medical Service as assistant surgeon; surgeon, of Gortin; married Elizabeth — (who was born 1801/2 and died 16 May 1843 at Gortin 'of an inflammation of the bowels'; father of James Laughlin who was born c 1772. [*BNL* 26 May 1843 (d); *Londonderry Sentinel* 7 March 1862 (d, son)].

LAUGHLIN, ALEXANDER (*fl c* 1824), Randalstown, county Antrim;
> apothecary, of Main Street, Randalstown c 1824; married —; father of Thomas Loughlin who was born c 1825. [Pigot (1824); Pilson (1934)].

LAUGHLIN, (LOUGHLIN) ALEXANDER (1790/1–1879), Naval Medical Service, Belfast, and Gortin, county Tyrone;
> born 1790/1; studied medicine at the Middlesex Hospital, London; MRCSE 1816; joined the Naval Medical Service as assistant surgeon; surgeon 1815; apothecary, of

Belfast c 1817; medical officer to Gortin Dispensary District, constabulary and Workhouse c 1845; married (1) 2 October 1818 in Gortin, Frances Nelson, daughter of William Nelson of Strabane, county Tyrone; (2) Elizabeth — (who was born 1801/2 and died 16 May 1843 at Gortin); died 17 September 1879 at Gortin. [*BNL* 13 October 1818 (m); Burtchaell and Sadleir (1924); Croly (1843–6); Dub GRO (d); *Londonderry Sentinel* 20 May 1843 (d); *Med Dir; NMS* (1826); Pilson (1934)].

LAUGHLIN, GEORGE (*fl c* 1824), Gortin, county Tyrone;
joined the Naval Medical Service as assistant surgeon; retired; surgeon to Gortin Dispensary from 1824. [*Strabane Morning Post* 2 March 1824 (notice)].

LAUGHLIN, GEORGE (d before 1844), Dungloe, county Donegal;
MD [?]; of Dungloe; married —; a son and daughter married 1844 in Port of Spain, Trinidad, a son and daughter of Nicholas Voisin; died before 1844. [*BNL* 9 April 1844 (m); *Londonderry Sentinel* 30 March 1844 (m)].

LAVEL, CORNELIUS (*fl c* 1819), Dungannon, county Tyrone;
MD [?]; of High Street, Dungannon c 1819. [Bradshaw (1819)].

LAVENS, PATRICK HENRY (d 1842), Army Medical Service;
of Brackfield Cottage, county Londonderry; joined the Army Medical Service as hospital mate 1810; assistant surgeon to 28th Foot 1811; surgeon to 51st Foot 1816 and to 14th Dragoons 1818; died 16 January 1842, of typhoid fever, at Kirkee, near Bombay. [*BNL* 29 March 1842 (d); *Londonderry Sentinel* 26 March 1842 (d); Peterkin and Johnston (1968)].

LAVERY, PHILIP (1820/1–91), Armagh;
born 1820/1; MRCSE 1841; LKQCPI 1868; general practitioner, of Scotch Street, Armagh; married Mary —; died 29 August 1891; probate Armagh 19 October 1891. [Belf PRO, will cal; Croly (1843–6); *Med Dir*].

LAW, JAMES (*fl c* 1780–90), Banbridge, county Down;
MD [?]; captain of his own company of Banbridge Volunteers in 1780; general practitioner, of Banbridge; married 9 April 1789 Sarah Crawford (who was born 1770/1 and died 17 March 1843 and was buried in Drumbeg Churchyard). [Clarke, *County Down*, vol 3 (1969); Linn (1935)].

LAW, JOHN (d 1809), Lurgan, county Armagh, and Dublin;
studied medicine at Edinburgh University; MD (Edin) 1762 (thesis 'De asthmate recidivo spasmodico'); general practitioner, of Lurgan; attended Dr William Drennan during an attack of fever in 1783; moved to Dublin in 1790 where William Drennan soon developed a marked professional jealousy of him (Drennan Letters); died 30 April 1809 at his home in Eccles Street, Dublin, 'a humane and skilful physician' (*BNL*). [Agnew (1998); *BNL* 5 May 1809 (d); Edin Univ (1867)].

LAW, MICHAEL (d 1790), Army Medical Service and Raphoe, county Donegal;
eldest son of the Rev Samuel Law, curate of Drumragh, county Tyrone, and Anne Gourney; studied medicine at Edinburgh University; MD (Edin) 1748 (thesis 'De scorbuto'); surgeon, of Raphoe; joined the Army Medical Service as surgeon to the 20th (Inniskilling) Light Dragoons 1760; regiment disbanded and retired on half pay 1763; married Nichola — (who survived him); died 1790; will dated 11 April 1790, proved in Prerogative Court 14 September 1790. [Burke, *LGI* (1912); Dub Reg Deeds, 505.509.329742 and 786.588.532123; Edin Univ (1867); Elliott, Simon, pers com; Leslie (1937); Vicars (1897)].

LAW, SAMUEL (*fl c* 1750), Strabane, county Tyrone;
doctor of physic, of Strabane c 1750 (witness to a will); attended Mary Anne Knox after she had been shot by John Macnaghton in 1761. [Eustace, vol II (1954)].

LAW SAMUEL (d 1793), Castlewellan, county Down;
'doctor', of Castlewellan; died 7 May 1793. [Farrar (1897)].

LAW, WILLIAM FRANCIS (1857–1932), Whittingham, Lancashire, and George Town, British Guiana;
born 20 August 1857 at Laurencetown, county Down, son of William Law, linen merchant, of Glenbanna, Laurencetown; educated at Armagh Royal School 1871–4; studied arts and medicine at Trinity College, Dublin, from 1878; BA (TCD) 1881; MB 1882; MD 1885; FRCSI 1904; clinical assistant to West Riding Asylum and medical officer to Whitingham Lunatic Asylum; inspector in Government Medical Service in British Guiana from 1886, of George Town, British Guiana; medical officer of health to the port of Georgetown; retired as deputy surgeon general 1912; author of various medical papers; served with RAMC at home during World War I with rank of major; retired to 51 Claremont Street, Sandymount, county Dublin; married Sarah Alice —; died 18 March 1932; probate Dublin 12 August 1932 and London 8 September 1932. [Dub Nat Arch, will cal; Ferrar (1933); Kirkpatrick Archive; Lond PPR, will cal; *Med Dir;* TCD adm reg; *TCD Cat,* vol II (1896); *TCD Reg*].

LAW, WILLIAM KIDSTON (1852/3–1926), Coleraine, county Londonderry;
born 1852/3 in New Brunswick, Canada, son of the Rev James Law, Presbyterian minister, and Eliza Kidston of Glasgow; brother of Andrew Bonar Law, British Prime Minister; studied medicine at McGill College, Montreal; MD CM (McGill) 1877; LRCP Edin 1879; LFPS Glas 1879; FFPS 1884; general practitioner, of Coleraine; breeder of horses; married 1886 in First Coleraine Presbyterian Church, Fanny Emily Lyons, third daughter of James Lyons of Coleraine and Anne Jane Getty; father of Dr Alice Law, LRCP LRCS Edin LFPS Glas 1927, of Coleraine; died 9 April 1926 in Coleraine; probate Belfast 22 September 1926. [Belf PRO, will cal; Kirkpatrick Archive; *Med Dir;* Mullin (1969)].

LAW, — (*fl c* 1820–40), Fintona, county Tyrone;
general practitioner, of Fintona; married —; daughter born c 1826; died before 1845. [*Londonderry Sentinel* 19 April 1845 (m, daughter)].

LAWDER, EDWARD JOHN (1848/9–1922), Downpatrick, county Down, and Honiton, Devonshire;
born 1848/9; studied medicine at Trinity College, Dublin, the Royal College of Surgeons in Ireland and the City of Dublin Hospital; LRCSI and LM 1873; Lic Med. (TCD) 1874; resident assistant surgeon to Down County Infirmary 1874–5; general practitioner of Honiton c 1875; absent from the *Medical Register* c 1877–1918; died 24 August 1922 at 7 Blakesley Avenue, Ealing, London; probate London 18 October 1922. [Kirkpatrick Archive; Lond GRO (d); Lond PPR, will cal; *Med Dir*; Parkinson (1967)].

LAWLESS, GEORGE ROBERT (1859/60–1931), Sligo and Armagh;
born 1859/60; studied medicine at the Royal College of Surgeons in Ireland and Dr Steevens' Hospital, Dublin; LKQCPI 1879; LRCSI and LM 1879; FRCSI 1894; assistant medical officer to the District Asylum, Sligo c 1880–97; resident medical superintendent to the District Asylum, Armagh c 1898–1931; retired to Drumcairne, county Armagh; married Stella Harriette Beresford —; died 27 February 1931 at Braxted, Thames Dutton, Surrey; probate Belfast 21 July 1931. [Belf PRO, will cal; Lond GRO (d); *Med Dir*].

LAWRENCE, HENRY MAJOR (1845–1929), Coleraine, county Londonderry, and Hadlow, Kent;
born 6 June 1845, tenth child of Samuel Lawrence, JP, miller and spinner, of Bannfield, Coleraine, and Ann Gregory, daughter of Dr William Gregory of Coleraine (*q.v.*); studied medicine at Edinburgh; LRCP LRCS Edin 1867; general practitioner of Bannfield, Coleraine c 1870–75; medical officer and public vaccinator to the District of Tunbridge and medical officer to the London Foundlings Hospital; of Heath Cottage, Hadlow, from c 1880; married Emily Alice Hervey, daughter of Matthew Hervey of Charnwood, Melbourne, Victoria; died 15 April 1929; administration London 30 July 1929. [Hitchings, Paul, pers com; Lond GRO (d); Lond PPR, will cal; *Med Dir*].

LAWRENCE, JAMES (1844–1921), Portrush, county Antrim, and Darlington, county Durham;
born 1844 at Ballycraig, Portrush, youngest son of Charles Lawrence of Ballycraig (who was a 2nd cousin of Samuel Lawrence of Bannfield – *vid sup*); educated at Coleraine Academical Institution; studied medicine at Queen's College, Belfast, from 1866; MD MCh (QUI) 1871; MRCSE 1872; house surgeon to Darlington Hospital 1872–4; medical superintendent of the Infectious Diseases Hospital, Darlington, from 1874; physician to Darlington Fever Hospital and honorary surgeon to Darlington General Hospital; medical officer of health to Darlington Borough from 1882; of Victoria Road, Darlington, from c 1880; director of Darlington Football Club; retired c 1919 to Dunluce, Westward Ho, Devonshire; married Mary Carson Clarke of Coleraine; father of Dr Charles Andrew Lawrence, LRCP LRCS Edin 1907, and Dr Alexander Carson Clarke Lawrence, LRCP Lond MRCSE 1911; died 9 December 1921 at Dunluce; probate London 10 February 1922. [*BMJ* obituary (1921); Hitchings, Paul, pers com; Kirkpatrick Archive; Lond GRO (d); Lond PPR, will cal, will; *Med Dir*; QCB adm reg].

LAWRENCE, THOMAS (d 1714), Army Medical Service;
joined the Army Medical Service as physician to the troops at Tangier 1664; physician to Tangier Regiment 1683; physician general to the Army 1885; physician general and Director of Hospitals in Ireland 1689, including the 'great' hospital in Belfast, where in a 6 month period of 1689–90 3,762 soldiers died; later physician to Queen Anne; physician general to Land Forces 1702; served at battles of Blenheim (1704) and Malplaquet (1709); author of *Mercurius Centralis*, an account of some marine fossils found in England (1664); died 1714. [Esler (1884); Peterkin and Johnston (1968)].

LAWTHER, WILLIAM (1787/8–1849), Ballymena, county Antrim;
born 1787/8; general practitioner, of Ballymena; married —; infant daughter died in 1837; died 17 April 1849, of cholera, at Ballymena. [*BNL* 9 June 1837 (d, daughter) and 27 April 1849 (d); *Coleraine Chronicle* 21 April 1849 (d); *Londonderry Sentinel* 28 April 1849 (d)].

LAYARD, HENRY ST GEORGE (1796/7–1887), Carndonagh, county Donegal;
born 1796/7; studied medicine at Edinburgh University; LM Dub Lying-in Hosp (Rotunda) 1820; MRCSE 1823; MD (Edin) 1832 (thesis 'De dyspepsia'); FRCSI and LM 1844; medical officer to Culdaff Dispensary District, of Hollymount, Carndonagh; unmarried died 13 October 1887 at Hollymount; probate Londonderry 18 January 1888. [Belf PRO, will cal; Croly (1843–6); Dub GRO (d); Edin Univ; *Med Dir*.].

LEAHY, JAMES (c 1803–70), Templemore, county Tipperary, Cronery, county Cavan, and Meredith, Victoria;
born c 1803, possibly in county Cavan; LAH Dub 1825; accoucheur of Dublin Lying-in Hospital; MD [?] 1864; general practitioner, of Templemore; retired to Cronery c 1852; emigrated to Australia 1864; married 1829 Elizabeth Ann Langford of Ferns, county Wexford; died 1870 at Meredith, Victoria. [Croly (1843–6); *IGRS Newsletter*].

LEARY, EDWARD GEORGE (1855/6–1918), Demerara, British Guiana, and Alfreton, Derbyshire;
born 1855/6 at Minore House, Drum, Clones, county Monaghan, son of Thomas Leary of Minore House; educated at Cootehill School; studied arts at Queen's College, Galway, and from 1873, medicine at Queen's College, Belfast, and the Ledwich School, Dublin; LRCSI 1877; LKQCPI and LM 1878; medical officer to the Colonial Hospital, Demerara, c 1885 and of Tuschen House c 1895; retired c 1900; general practitioner, of Alfreton; married Lillian Maude —; died 7 October 1918; probate Derby 5 April 1919. [Lond PPR, will cal; *Med Dir*; QCB adm reg].

LEARY, SAMUEL (1832/3–89), Pettigo, county Fermanagh, Castlederg, county Tyrone, and Berbice, British Guiana;
born 1832/3, son of Thomas Leary of Cormeen, Clones, county Monaghan; educated by Mr Robotham of Drum, Clones; studied medicine at Queen's College, Belfast, from 1850; LM Anderson Univ Glas 1852; LFPS and LM Glas 1855; LKQCPI 1860; surgeon on SS *Caroline Coventry* 1855–7; general practitioner and medical officer to Pettigo and Clonelly Dispensary Districts and constabulary c 1857–68, of Forttown

House, Castlederg; medical officer at Berbice, British Guiana, from c 1868; married 5 November 1862 in Killeter Church of Ireland Church, Castlederg, Elizabeth Jane Caldwell, daughter of Audley Caldwell of Fort Town House; died 12 June 1889 at New Amsterdam, Demerara; probate Dublin 22 August 1890. [Belf PRO, will cal; *Londonderry Sentinel* 14 November 1862 (m); *Med Dir*; QCB adm reg].

LEARY, THOMAS (1838–1918), Castlederg, county Tyrone;
born August 1838; studied medicine at the Ledwich School, Dublin and Glasgow University; LM Glas 1858; LRCSI 1859; LKQCPI and LM 1870; assistant surgeon in Holyhead, Anglesey; medical officer to Castlederg Dispensary District, Workhouse, Fever Hospital and constabulary and certifying factory surgeon; JP for county Tyrone; married Ellen Berry; father of Dr William Albert Edward Leary (*q.v.*), Dr Samuel Walter Sydney Leary, MB BCh (Edin) 1904, of Durban and Dr Gerald Ferdinand Victor Leary, Mb BCh (Edin) 1907, of Castlederg; died 1 December 1918 at Castlederg; probate Londonderry 2 April 1919. [Belf PRO, will cal; Dub GRO (d); Kirkpatrick Archive; Lond GRO (b, son); *Med Dir*].

LEARY, WILLIAM ALBERT EDWARD (1871–1952), ship's surgeon and Castlederg, county Tyrone;
born 16 April 1871 at 16 Hesketh Street, Southport, Lancashire, son of Dr Thomas Leary (*q.v.*); educated at Londonderry Academical Institution; studied arts and medicine at Trinity College, Dublin, from 1887; BA (TCD) 1890; MB BCh BAO 1893; clinical resident in the Mater Misericordiae Hospital, Dublin; surgeon with the Royal Mail Steam Packet Company; general practitioner, of Castlederg; died c 1952. [*Med Dir*; TCD adm reg; *TCD Cat*, vol II (1896); *TCD Reg*].

LEATHAM, (LEATHEM) WILLIAM (1837/8–1911) Gortin and Coalisland, county Tyrone;
born 1837/8 in county Donegal, son of the Rev Moses Leatham, rector of Upper Langfield and Lower Badoney (Gortin), county Tyrone, and Catherine Stanley; studied arts and medicine at Trinity College, Dublin, from 1853, and the Ledwich School; BA (TCD) 1860; LRCSI 1860; LM Coombe Hosp Dub 1860; LM KQCPI 1876; MA 1883; medical officer to Gortin Dispensary District and Workhouse c 1867; medical officer to Coalisland Dispensary District and constabulary; author of various medical papers; JP for county Tyrone; married 24 April 1867 in Derrykeighan Church of Ireland Church, Jane Elizabeth Hamilton Hazleton, daughter of John Hazleton, gentleman, of Shrewsbury, Shropshire; died 20 February 1911 at Dungannon; probate Armagh 22 April 1911. [Belf PRO, will cal; Burtchaell and Sadleir (1935); *Coleraine Chronicle* 27 April 1867 (m); Dub GRO (m); Kirkpatrick Archive; *Lancet* obituary (1911); Leslie (1937); *Londonderry Sentinel* 26 April 1867 (m); *Med Dir*; UHF database (m)].

LEATHEM, JAMES (1837–95), Stratford, Essex, and Liverpool, Lancashire;
born April 1837, son of Andrew Leathem of Rathfriland, county Down; educated by Mr J. Moffat of Rathfriland; studied medicine at Queen's College, Belfast, from 1858 and at Charing Cross Hospital, London; MD (QUI) 1864; general practitioner, of

the Grove, Stratford, from c 1865 and of 10 Rodney Street, Liverpool, from c 1876; married —; died 2 October 1894 at 24 Daulby Street, Liverpool. [Lond GRO (d); *Med Dir*; QCB adm reg].

LEATHEM, ROBERT RENDLE LOUIS (1869–1935), London, Carlisle, Cumberland, and Belfast;
born 25 September 1869 at 9 Wellington Park, Belfast, son of John Gaston Leathem, of Northern Bank House, Belfast, and Mary Stone; educated at RBAI; studied medicine at Queen's College, Belfast, from 1886; BA (1st class hons) (RUI) 1889; MB BCh BAO 1893; resident medical officer to the North West London Hospital; house surgeon to the Cumberland Infirmary, Carlisle; general practitioner, of 10 College Gardens, Belfast; assistant physician to the Belfast Hospital for Sick Children 1899–1907 and attending physician 1907–29; a moving force in the transfer of the Children's Hospital to the Falls Road site; retired 1929 to Mountnorris, Newcastle, county Down; author of various medical papers; married 15 December 1909 in Whitehouse Church of Ireland Church, county Antrim, Wilhelmina Bell Gallaher, daughter of Thomas Gallaher, JP, chairman of Gallaher Limited, tobacco manufacturers, of Ballygolan, Whitehouse; died 20 December 1935 at Mountnorris; probate Belfast 11 March 1936. [Belf PRO, will cal; *BMJ* obituary (1936); Calwell (1973); Dub GRO (b); Kirkpatrick Archive; *Lancet* obituary (1936); *Med Dir*; QCB adm reg; UHF database (m); Young and Pike (1909) (Gallaher)].

LEATHEM, SAMUEL (1770–1811), Londonderry;
born 1770; MD [?]; of Londonderry; married Elizabeth — (who was born 1780/1 and died 18 November 1859 at 62 Lower Mount Street, Dublin); died 31 December 1811; buried in Londonderry Cathedral Graveyard. [*BNL* 10 January 1812 (d); *Londonderry Sentinel* 25 November 1859 (d); *Memorials of the Dead*, vol IX, p 124].

LEATHEM (LEATHAM), WILLIAM
See LATHAM, WILLIAM.

LEDLIE, ANDREW (1845/6–1918), Belfast;
born 1845/6 at Rathfriland, county Down, son of Robert Ledlie, farmer, of Rathfriland; educated privately; studied medicine at Queen's College, Belfast, from 1876; LSA Lond 1882; general practitioner, of 6 Strangemore Terrace, Clifton Park, Belfast; author of various medical papers; married Mary Henderson —; died 13 February 1918 at 6 Strangemore Terrace; buried in Belfast City Cemetery; probate Belfast 12 April 1918. [Belf City Cem, bur reg; Belf PRO, will cal; *Med Dir*; QCB adm reg].

LEDLIE, THOMAS (1774/5–1820), Indian Medical Service;
born 1774/5; studied medicine; Certificate of the Corporation of Surgeons 1790; joined the Indian Medical Service (Bengal establishment) as assistant surgeon 1792; surgeon 1806; served in Third Maisur War 1791–2; retired 1812; died 17 June 1820 at Antrim. [*BNL* 20 June 1820 (d); Cameron (1930)].

LEE, JAMES (1868–1942), Birkenhead, Cheshire, West Bromwich, Staffordshire, Clacton-on-Sea, Essex, and Belfast;
born 21 January 1868 at Taylorstown, Ballymena, county Antrim, son of James Lee, of Ardlea, Greenisland, county Antrim; educated at RBAI; studied arts and medicine at Queen's College, Belfast, from 1886; BA (hons) (RUI) 1890; MB CM (Edin) 1896; MD 1902; house surgeon to Birkenhead and Wirral Children's Hospital and assistant house surgeon to West Bromwich District Hospital c 1898; general practitioner, of Claremont, Clacton-on-Sea, from c 1900, 3 Mount Pleasant, Stranmillis Road, Belfast, from c 1906 and of 22 Cranmore Avenue, Belfast, from c 1925; retired c 1928 to The Bungalow, Greenisland; died 11 April 1942 at Felstead, Bryansford Gardens, Newcastle; probate Belfast 5 August 1942. [Belf PRO, will cal; Kirkpatrick Archive; *Med Dir*; QCB adm reg].

LEE, RICHARD (*fl c* 1824), Ballyshannon, county Donegal;
of Carns, Sligo; LAH Dub 1824; apothecary, of Main Street, Ballyshannon c 1824. [Apothecaries (1829); Pigot (1824)].

LEEBODY, WILLIAM (d 1854), Portadown, county Armagh;
son of William Leebody, lieutenant; MD [?]; surgeon, of Portadown c 1845; married 20 January 1847 in St Mark's Church of Ireland Church, Armagh, Elizabeth Stanley, youngest daughter of John Stanley, merchant, of Armagh; son born c 1852; died 4 December 1854 at Seagoe. [*BNL* 29 January 1847 (m) and 25 February 1856 (d, son); Croly (1843–6); Dub GRO (m); *Med Dir*].

LEEPER, GEORGE REGINALD (1856–1904), Assam, India, Ederney, county Fermanagh, and Southsea, Hampshire;
born 7 September 1856, son of the Rev Alexander Leeper, Canon of St Patrick's Cathedral, Dublin, and Catherine Porter; educated at Rathmines School, Dublin, from 1864; studied arts and medicine at Trinity College, Dublin, from 1872; BA MD (TCD) 1876; LRCSI 1876; medical officer in Assam; general practitioner, of Ederney; moved to 2 Waverley Road, Southsea; married Laura Lousia —; died 26 June 1904 at 2 Waverley Road; administration Winchester 11 August 1904. [Figgis and Drury (1932); Kirkpatrick Archive; Leslie and Wallace (2001); Lond GRO (d); Lond PPR, will cal; *Med Dir;* TCD adm reg; *TCD Cat*, vol II (1896)].

LEEPER, JAMES GEORGE
See LEPPER

LEEPER, JOHN (1810/1–80), Keady, county Armagh;
born 1810/1, son of William Leeper, farmer; brother of Dr William Waugh Leeper (*q.v.*); MRCSE 1829; LRCP Edin 1859; medical officer to Clogher Workhouse and later to Castlebellingham Dispensary District; medical officer to Keady Dispensary District and constabulary c 1845; married (1) Margaret Jane — (who was born 11816/7 and died 11 April 1854); (2) 6 December 1855 in First Keady Presbyterian Church, Sarah Blair, daughter of William Blair, farmer, of Tasso, county Armagh; father of Eleanor Leeper who married Dr John Gower Allen (*q.v.*); died 7 March 1880 at Keady; buried in First Keady Presbyterian Graveyard; probate Armagh 14

May 1880. [*BNL* 10 December 1855 (m); Belf PRO, will cal, will; Croly (1843–6); Dub GRO (m) and (d); gravestone inscription; Kirkpatrick Archive; *Med Dir*].

LEEPER, WILLIAM WAUGH (1821/2–94), ship's surgeon, Londonderry, and Loughgall, county Armagh;
   born 1821/2; brother of Dr John Leeper (*q.v.*); studied medicine at Edinburgh University and Royal Infirmary, and Trinity College, Dublin; MD (Edin) 1844 (thesis 'On general pathology of nutrition'); LRCSI and LM 1844; surgeon to the P & O steamer *Bentinck;* general practitioner, of Londonderry; medical officer to Loughgall Dispensary District and constabulary, and visiting physician to Armagh Asylum; author of various medical papers; JP for county Armagh; married Mary Jane —; died 16 May 1894 at Derrycaw, county Armagh; buried in Loughgall Parish Graveyard; probate Armagh 1 June 1894. [Belf PRO, will cal, will; Croly (1843–6); Edin Univ; *Med Dir; Memorials of the Dead,* vol III, p 369].

LEIDGE, JAMES (*fl c* 1659), Londonderry;
   'chirurgion' of Londonderry; married —; son died in March 1659 and daughter in April 1660. [Derry Cathedral Registers (1910), pp 121 and 122].

LEIGH, ALFRED GODFREY (d c 1850), Markethill, county Armagh;
   studied medicine at Glasgow University; CM (Glas) [?]; general practitioner, of Markethill c 1845; died c 1850. [Croly (1843–6)].

LEIGH, JOHN (d c 1853), Moy, county Tyrone, and Markethill and Mountnorris, county Armagh;
   son of Alexander Leigh, farmer; studied medicine at Glasgow University; CM and LM (Glas) 1836; member of the Medical Society of Glasgow; general practitioner and medical officer to constabulary, of Moy c 1846, of Derlett, Markethill c 1849 and of Mountnorris c 1852; married 5 October 1849 in Mullaghglass Church of Ireland Church, county Armagh, Jane Elizabeth Irvine, daughter of John Irvine, farmer, of Cloghinny, county Armagh; died c 1853. [Croly (1843–6); *Med Dir;* UHF database (m)].

LEIGH, WILLIAM (*fl c* 1802–45), Portadown, county Armagh;
   LAH Dub 1802; surgeon and apothecary and assistant surgeon to the Armagh Militia c 1810; of Portadown, c 1819, 1824 and 1845; married 15 August 1814 at his home in Portadown, Maria Campbell, eldest daughter of Patrick Campbell of Newry; possibly died c 1850. [Apothecaries (1829); *BNL* 16 August 1814 (m); Bradshaw (1819); Croly (1843–6); Pigot (1824)].

LEITCH, WILLIAM JOHN (1865–1935), Omagh, Clogher, Newtownstewart, and Beragh, county Tyrone;
   born 29 July 1865 at Scarvagherin, Castlederg, county Tyrone, son of John Leitch, farmer, of Scarvagherin; educated at Castlederg Intermediate School; studied medicine at Queen's College, Galway, and from 1883, at Queen's College, Belfast; LRCP LRCS Edin 1889; LFPS Glas 1889; medical officer to Omagh No 2 Dispensary District, constabulary and post office c 1890, to Clogher Infirmary

c 1893, to Newtownstewart Dispensary District c 1895 and to Sixmilecross (Beragh) Dispensary District 1899–1935; married Amelia Elizabeth Mateer; died 26 December 1935; probate Londonderry 11 December 1936. [Belf PRO, will cal, will; Kirkpatrick Archive; *Med Dir*; QCB adm reg].

LENDRICK, CHARLES RICHARD (b 1791/2);
born 1791/2 in county Antrim, son of James Lendrick; educated privately; studied arts and medicine at Trinity College, Dublin, from 1809; BA (TCD) 1813; MA 1816; MB 1818; MD 1828. [Burtchaell and Sadleir (1924)].

LENDRUM, JOSEPH (1796/7–1845), Fivemiletown, county Fermanagh;
born 1796/7; surgeon, of Fivemiletown; married Mary — (who was born 1787/8 and died 9 February 1861 at Fivemiletown); died February 1845; buried 7 February 1845 in Fivemiletown. [Fivemiletown Parish Church burial register (Belf PRO, MIC/1/6); *Londonderry Sentinel* 15 February 1861 (d)].

LENDRUM, WILLIAM HENRY (1860–97), Army Medical Service;
born 1 October 1860 at Cleen, county Fermanagh, son of John Lendrum, farmer, of Cleen, and Mary —; educated at Fivemiletown; studied medicine at Queen's College, Belfast, from 1877; MD MCh Dip Mid (QUI) 1881; MRCSE 1890; joined the Army Medical Service as surgeon captain 1883; retired with gratuity 1893; died 31 March 1897 in Hamburg. [Johnston (1972); *Med Dir*; Peterkin and Johnston (1968); QCB adm reg].

LENEY, ALEXANDER (1799–1877), Strabane, county Tyrone;
born 1799, probably son of Dr William Leney of Strabane (*q.v.*); studied medicine at Edinburgh University; LM Dub Lying-in Hosp (Rotunda) 1823; MRCSE 1823; MD (Edin) 1825 (thesis 'De febro hectica'); medical superintendent of Strabane Dispensary District, Workhouse and Fever Hospital from 1832; married 24 July 1835 at Walworth, county Londonderry, Jane Stirling (who died 15 August 1863 in Strabane), daughter of Major Stirling of Walworth; died 27 January 1877 at Strabane; will dated 10 May 1876, proved Londonderry 11 May 1877. [Belf PRO, will cal, will; Croly (1843–6); Edin Univ; *Londonderry Sentinel* 18 August 1863 (d); *Med Dir; Strabane Morning Post* 7 February 1832 (news) and 28 July 1835 (m)].

LENEY, ALEXANDER (1800/1–31), Strabane, county Tyrone, and Georgetown, Demerara;
born 1800/1; nephew of Dr William Leney of Strabane; chemist and druggist, of Strabane; medical officer to Georgetown, Demerara c 1826–31; died 20 May 1831 in Georgetown, 'fallen a victim to the ravages of that climate'. [*BNL* 22 July 1831 (d); *Strabane Morning Post* 12 July 1831 (d)].

LENEY (LINEY), WILLIAM (1766/7–1857), Strabane, county Tyrone;
born 1766/7; of Castlefinn; LAH Dub 1791; surgeon and apothecary, of Main Street, Strabane c 1820–45; married — (who died 3 April 1823); probably father of Dr Alexander Leney of Strabane (*q.v.*); died 19 April 1857 in Strabane. [Apothecaries

(1829); *BNL* 28 April 1857 (d); Croly (1843–6); Dooher (2000); *Londonderry Sentinel* 24 April 1857 (d); Pigot (1820) and (1824); *Strabane Morning Post* 8 April 1823 (d)].

LENNON, JOHN (1891–1923), Belfast;
 born 28 January 1891 at Ballylagan, county Antrim, son of Nathaniel Lennon, farmer, of Ballylagan; educated at Belfast Mercantile Academy; studied medicine at Queen's College, Belfast, from 1891; MB BCh BAO (RUI) 1896; general practitioner, of Laharna, Holywood Road, and 357 Newtownards Road, Belfast; married 26 December 1902 in Albertbridge Road Methodist Church, Belfast, Anne Abernethy Hamilton, daughter of John Hamilton, merchant, of 117 Albertbridge Road, Belfast; died 21 June 1923 in the Thompson Memorial Home, Lisburn; probate Belfast 10 October 1923. [Belf PRO, will cal, will; *Med Dir*; QCB adm reg; UHF database (m)].

LENNON, JOHN LUKE IRWIN (1841/2–77), Glasgow;
 born 1841/2 at Dromara, county Down, son of John Lennon, farmer, of Armagh, and Elizabeth Irwin; educated at St Malachy's College, Belfast, and RBAI; studied medicine at Queen's College, Belfast, from 1860; LRCP LRCS Edin 1869; general practitioner, of 318, 324 and 332 Gallowgate Street, Glasgow, c 1871; married Anne Kay; died 22 March 1877 at 580 Gallowgate, Glasgow, of pulmonary consumption. [Edin GRO (d); *Med Dir*; QCB adm reg].

LENNON, THOMAS DANIEL (d c 1900), Carlingford, county Louth, and Heywood, Lancashire;
 of Crosmaglen, county Armagh; studied medicine at the Catholic University and the Mater Misericordiae Hospital, Dublin; LRCSI 1876; LAH Dub 1882; LM Coombe Hosp Dub 1882; medical officer and medical officer of health to Carlingford Dispensary District and medical officer to constabulary and lighthouses; of Abbey View, Carlingford c 1885–90; general practitioner, of 131 York Street, Heywood c 1893–5 and then 'travelling'; died c 1900. [*Med Dir*].

LENNON, — (d before 1856), Newtownhamilton, county Armagh;
 general practitioner, of Newtownhamilton; married Elizabeth — (who married secondly 10 August 1856 in Newtownhamilton Roman Catholic Church, Peter Callan); died before 1856. [*BNL* 14 August 1856 (m)].

LENNOX, JAMES (1858–1924), Kilrea, county Londonderry;
 born 21 September 1858 at Ballymena, county Antrim, son of John Lennox, linen manufacturer, and Martha — of Kilrea (who married (2) John Thompson and was mother of the artist Hugh Thompson); educated at Coleraine Academical Institution; studied medicine at Queen's College, Belfast, from 1877; MD MCh (RUI) 1883; LM KQCPI 1884; medical officer to Kilrea Dispensary District, 1890–1924, of The Manor House, Kilrea; JP; married Florence Jane —; died 23 January 1924 at Belfast; probate Londonderry 4 July 1924. [Belf PRO, will cal; Burns (1988); Kirkpatrick Archive; Lennox (1983); *Med Dir*; QCB adm reg].

LENTAIGNE, SIR JOHN FRANCIS O'NEILL (1803–86), Dublin and Monaghan; born 21 June 1803 in Dublin, eldest son of Dr Benjamin Lentaigne, a French physician in Dublin, and Maria Therese O'Neill; educated by Mr Shine; studied arts and medicine at Trinity College, Dublin, from 1821; BA (TCD) 1825; MB 1828; LRCSI 1830; FRCSI 1844; commissioner of loan funds; inspector general of prisons, reformatories and industrial schools 1854–77; of 1 Great Denmark Street, Dublin and Tallaght, county Dublin; JP and DL for county Monaghan; High Sheriff for county Monaghan 1844; commissioner of education 1861–86; CB 1873; president of the Statistical Society 1877–8; KCB 1880; Knight of the Order of Pious IX; married 13 September 1841 Mary Magan (who died 8 May 1887), daughter and co-heir of Francis Magan, JP, of Emoe, county Westmeath; father of Sir John Vincent O'Neill Lentaigne, LRCPI 1881, FRCSI, of Dublin; died 12 November 1886 at 1 Great Denmark Street; administration (with will) Dublin 22 September 1887. [Belf PRO, will cal; Burke *LGI* (1912); Burtchaell and Sadleir (1924); Croly (1843–6); Crone (1928); *DIB* (2009); *Med Dir*; Newmann (1993)].

LEONARD, J. (1803/4–60), Enniskillen, county Fermanagh;
born 1803/4; general practitioner, of Enniskillen; died 23 June 1860. [*BNL* 28 June 1860 (d)].

LEONARD, PATRICK (*fl c* 1824–45), Enniskillen, county Fermanagh;
apothecary, of Darling Street, Enniskillen, c 1824–45; possibly died c 1850. [Croly (1843–6); Pigot (1824)].

LEPPER, JAMES (d 1851), Naval Medical Service and Buenos Aires, Argentina;
born in Strabane, county Tyrone; joined the Naval Medical Service as assistant surgeon during the Napoleonic Wars; surgeon 1809; surgeon on HMS *Euryalus* and later on HMS *Bellerophon* when Napoleon was captured and taken to England in 1815; served on HMS *Amphion* c 1818–20 and retired to Buenos Aires c 1820 when *Amphion* was stationed off Brazil; surgeon in Buenos Aires and medical adviser to President Rosa c 1820–51; died 3 February 1851 at Buenos Aires. [Lepper, Patrick, pers com; *Londonderry Sentinel* 2 May 1851 (d); *Med Dir*; *NMS* (1826)].

LEPPER, JAMES (GEORGE), senior (d c 1850), Cootehill, county Cavan, and Monaghan;
LAH Dub 1819; accoucheur of Dub Lying-in Hosp; apothecary, of Cootehill c 1824; medical officer of Monaghan Dispensary District c 1845; married c 1820 Elizabeth Cottenham [?]; father of Dr James George Leeper, junior (*q.v.*); died c 1850. [Apothecaries (1829); Croly (1843–6); Lepper, Patrick, pers com; Pigot (1824)].

LEPPER, JAMES GEORGE, junior (1824/5–54), Monaghan;
born 1824/5, son of Dr James (George) Lepper, senior (*q.v.*); accoucheur of the Western Lying-in Hospital, Dublin 1845; LAH Dub 1846; apothecary to Monaghan County Infirmary and Gaol c 1842–5; medical officer to constabulary and militia; of the Diamond, Monaghan; married —; died 19 April 1854 at his home in Monaghan, 'of inflammation of the lungs'. [*BNL* 24 April 1854 (d); Croly (1843–6); *Med Dir*].

LESLIE, DAVID (1808/9–72), Carrickmacross, county Monaghan, Tunbridge, Kent, and London;
>born 1809 at Keady, county Armagh; studied medicine at Glasgow University and Edinburgh and Paris; accoucheur of Edinburgh Lying-in Hospital; LRCS Edin 1825; MD (Glas) 1861; LSA Lond 1865; lived at Keady c 1845 but did not practice medicine; general practitioner, of Carrickmacross c 1863–5, of Tunbridge c 1865–7, of 1 Queen's Road, Wandworth c 1867–72 and finally of 140 Kensington Park Road, London; author of various medical papers; married —; died 19 October 1872 at the Middlesex Hospital, London; probate London 3 January 1873. [Addison (1898); Croly (1843–6); Kirkpatrick Archive; Lond GRO (d); Lond PPR, will cal; *Med Dir*].

LESLIE, HENRY (b 1688/9);
>born 1688/9; described as 'Hibernus, Scotus', son of Charles Leslie, studied medicine in Leyden from 1710 and at Glasgow University; MD and Phil D (Padua) 1715. [Morpurgo (1927); Innes Smith (1932)].

LESLIE, JAMES (1819/20–74), Armagh;
>born 1819/20; MRCSE 1847; LM Dub Lying-in Hosp (Rotunda); LKQCPI 1855; acting assistant surgeon to the Armagh Regiment; medical officer to Armagh Dispensary District, fever hospital and constabulary and certifying factory surgeon, of 55 Scotch Street, Armagh; married Georgina Tronson, daughter of the Rev Robert Tronson, rector of Newtownhamilton, county Armagh, and Mary Anne Miles; died 2 December 1874 at Scotch Street; probate Armagh 19 January 1875. [Belf PRO, will cal; Dub GRO (d); Fleming (2001); *Med Dir*].

LESLIE, JOHN (or JAMES) (d 1847), Armagh;
>studied medicine at Glasgow University; MD (Glas) 1840; MRCSE; LAH Dub; medical officer to Armagh Union Workhouse, of Scotch Street, Armagh, c 1843–5; died 20 March 1847 of fever caught in the discharge of his duties. [Addison (1898); *BNL* 30 March 1847 (d); Croly (1843–6)].

LESLIE, RICHARD WHYTOCK (1862–1931), Belfast;
>born 26 September 1862 at Cookstown, county Tyrone, son of the Rev John Knox Leslie, minister of Third Cookstown Presbyterian Church, and — Whytock of Dalkeith; educated at Cookstown Academy and Raphoe Royal School; studied medicine at Queen's College, Belfast, from 1881; LM Rot Hosp Dub 1885; MD MCh (RUI) 1887; LLD (RUI) (*hon causa*) 1909; attending surgeon and later physician to the Ulster Hospital for Children and Women 1891–1926, of St Heliers, Strandtown, Belfast; physician to Campbell College from 1894–1931; president of the Ulster Medical Society 1912–13; senator of the Royal University of Ireland from 1905 and of the Queen's University of Belfast; author of various medical papers; Knight of Grace of the Order of St John of Jerusalem; married 24 October 1889 in Rutland Square Presbyterian Church, Rosa Alexander (who was born 14 May 1866), elder daughter of Robert John Alexander, merchant, of Clarendon Street, Londonderry; died 22 September 1931 at 41 Malone Road, Belfast; buried in Belfast City Cemetery; probate Belfast 16 December 1931. [Belf City Cem, bur reg; Belf

PRO, will cal; *BMJ* obituary (1931); Dub GRO (m); Hawbaker (2008); Irwin (1932); Kirkpatrick Archive; *Lancet* obituary (1931); McConnell (1951); Marshall and Kelly (1973); *Med Dir*; QCB adm reg; Singleton (1999); Young and Pike (1909)].

LESLIE, — (*fl c* 1811), Stewartstown, county Tyrone;
general practitioner, of Stewartstown; married —; son born c 1811. [*BNL* 27 May 1842 (d)].

L'ESTRANGE, GUY STUART (1863–1946), Toowoomba and Brisbane, Queensland;
born 1 August 1863, son of major-general Edmund L'Estrange of Kilmonnin, Banagher, King's County; educated at Armagh Royal School 1877–81; studied medicine at Royal College of Surgeons in Ireland; LRCSI 1886; LKQCPI and LM 1886; FRCSI 1902; medical officer to P & O Steamship Company; emigrated to Australia c 1905; general practitioner, of Toowoomba, and of 108 George Street, Brisbane, c 1905–30; retired to Toowoomba c 1930; died 31 January 1946 at Toowoomba. [Ferrar (1933); Kirkpatrick Archive; *Med Dir*].

LEVER, CHARLES JAMES (1806–72), Kilrush, county Clare, Portstewart, county Londonderry, London, Brussels, Dublin and Florence;
born 31 August 1806 at 35 Amiens Street, Dublin, second son of James Lever, merchant, of Manchester and Dublin, and Judith (Julia) Candler; educated privately; visited Canada as an unqualified surgeon on an emigrant ship and while there experienced Indian and backwoods life; studied arts and medicine at Trinity College, Dublin from 1822 and at Dr Steevens' Hospital, where he began a life-long friendship with Sir William Wilde; BA (TCD) 1827; MB 1831; MD (Louvain); LLD (by diploma) 1871; experienced student life in Gottingen, Weimar, Vienna and other centres, drinking, fighting and enjoying life; medical officer during a cholera epidemic in Kilrush; medical officer to Agherton Dispensary, Portstewart [Blue Plaque on the Promenade], and in charge of a cholera hospital there 1832–7, where his wild behaviour included jumping his horse over a turf cart; later of 54 Brook Street, London; physician in Brussels 1840–42, but became more successful as a novelist with *Harry Lorrequer* (1839), *Charles O'Malley* (1841), *Jack Hinton* (1843), *Tom Burke of Ours* (1843), *The O'Donoghue* (1845), *Arthur O'Leary* (1845) and others to *Lord Kilgobbin: a Tale of Ireland in Our Own Time* (1872); edited the *Dublin University Magazine* 1842–5; friend of Thackeray, Dickens and Trollope but never produced writing of their quality; married 16 November 1831 Catherine Baker (who died 23 April 1870), daughter of W.M. Baker, master of the Royal Hibernian Marine School; died 1 June 1872 at Trieste; buried in the English Cemetery, Trieste; drawing by Simon Pearce in National Gallery of Ireland and engraving in NLI; probate London 16 October 1872. [Bateson (2004); Burtchaell and Sadlier (1924); *DIB* (2009); Downey (1906); Kirkpatrick Archive; Lond PPR; will cal; Lyons (1978); Martin (2010); Mullin (1974); O'Brien, Crookshank and Wolstenholme (1984); *Oxford DNB* (2004); Trollope, *Autobiography* (1883); Wilson (1942)].

LEVINGSTON, WILLIAM (d c 1761), Armagh;
apothecary, of Armagh; died c 1761; administration Armagh Diocesan Court 1761. [Dub Nat Arch, Armagh Dio Admins index].

LEWERS, BENJAMIN (1805/6–31), Ballybay, county Monaghan;
born 1805/6; CM (Glas) 1823; surgeon, of Ballybay c 1824; died 7 March 1831 at Anaube, county Monaghan, 'of a tedious illness'. [Addison (1898); *BNL* 25 March 1831 (d); Pigot (1824)].

LEWERS, HUGH (1861–1903), Belfast;
born September 1861 at 128 Falls Road, Belfast, son of John Lewers of 8 Falls Road, Belfast, clerk; educated at Belfast Model School; studied medicine at Queen's College, Belfast, from 1880; MD MCh (RUI) 1884; MAO 1885; general practitioner, of 128 Falls Road, Belfast, c 1885, of 257 Shankill Road, c 1895 and of 105 Everton Terrace, Crumlin Road c 1900; physician to the Ulster Hospital for Women and Children; author of 'Notes on some of the gunshot, revolver and buckshot wounds which came under my notice during the riots of 1886' and other papers; married Catherine —; died 12 November 1903; buried in Belfast City Cemetery; probate Belfast 12 January 1903. [Belf City Cem, bur reg; Belf PRO, will cal; Lewers (1887); *Med Dir*; QCB adm reg].

LEWERS, JOHN WALLACE (1815/6–72), Newtownhamilton and Markethill, county Armagh, and Drum, county Monaghan;
born 1815/6; CM (Glas) 1858; surgeon, of Newtownhamilton c 1858–60, Markethill c 1860–61 and Drum c 1861–72; married —; died 26 April 1872. [Addison (1898); Dub GRO (d); *Med Dir*].

LEWIS, CHARLES (1826/7–83), Castletown, county Cork, Markethill county Armagh, Knottingly, Yorkshire, Brentford, Middlesex, Hay, Breckonshire and Silverdale, Staffordshire;
born 1826/7; studied medicine at the Royal College of Surgeons in Ireland and St Thomas's Hospital, London; MRCSE 1852; LM RCSE 1862; LRCP Edin 1865; medical officer and registrar of births and deaths to Kilcatherine Dispensary District; medical officer to Castletown Union Workhouse c 1863–73, and to the Berehaven Mining Company; general practitioner, of Markethill c 1873–6, of Knottingly 1876–7, of Brentford 1877–9, of Hay 1879–81 and of Silverdale 1881–3; married —; died 10 January 1883 at Church Street, Silverdale. [Lond GRO (d); *Med Dir*].

LEWIS, WILLIAM MORROW (1861–c 1929), Donald, Victoria, Australia;
born 7 November 1861 at Stoneyford, county Antrim, son of Joseph Lewis, farmer, of Moneybroom, Lisburn; educated at Lisburn Intermediate School (Academy); studied medicine at Queen's College, Belfast, from 1879; MD (RUI) 1886; MCh 1887; LM KQCPI 1887; emigrated to Australia c 1890; general practitioner, of Donald, Victoria, c 1895; retired c 1925; died c 1929. [*Med Dir*; QCB adm reg].

LIDDLE, EDWARD JOHN (1873–1924), Crewe, Cheshire;
born 2 March 1873, son of Edward Liddle, merchant, of Cookstown, county Tyrone; brother of George Marcus Berkley Liddle (*q.v.*); educated at Cookstown Academy;

studied medicine at Queen's College, Belfast, from 1891; MB BCh BAO (RUI) 1896; general practitioner, of Lisgoole, Hungerford Road, Crewe, from c 1900; married Jane —; father of Dr Edward Marcus Liddle, MRCSE LRCP Lond 1924; died 11 January 1924 at the Nursing Home, Winchester; probate London 21 March 1924. [Lond PPR, will cal,will; *Med Dir*; QCB adm reg].

LIDDLE, GEORGE MARCUS BERKLEY (1871–1933), ship's surgeon, Dublin, Portadown, county Armagh, and Kilrea, county Londonderry;
born 31 May 1871 in Cookstown, county Tyrone, son of Edward Liddle, merchant, of Cookstown; brother of Dr Edward John Liddle (*q.v.*); educated at Cookstown; studied medicine at Queen's College, Belfast, from 1891; MB BCh BAO (RUI)1898; FRCS Edin 1910; DPH (Edin and Glas) 1910; DTM (Liverp) 1911; surgeon with the Pacific Steam Navigation Company; resident medical officer to the Coombe Hospital, Dublin; general practitioner, of Market Street, Portadown c 1905 and Red House, Kilrea from c 1910; finally of 9 Milton Place, Halifax, Yorkshire; unmarried; died 12 March 1933 at 9 Milton Place; probate Wakefield 12 May 1933. [Lond PPR, will cal, will; *Med Dir*; QCB adm reg].

LIGHTBURNE, EDMUND ARTHUR (1865–1901), London;
born 5 January 1865 at Newry, county Down, son of Dr Joseph Lightburne (*q.v.*) of Rosemount, Newry; educated at Newry Collegiate School; studied medicine at Queen's College, Belfast, from 1880; LRCP LRCS and LM Edin 1886; medical officer to Bromley District and to police and gas works, of 159 Bow Road, London; married Louise Josephine —; died 12 February 1901 at the West Ham Hospital, Essex; administration (with will) London 13 April 1901. [Lond PPR, will cal; *Med Dir*; QCB adm reg].

LIGHTBURNE, JOSEPH (1815/6–90), Kinnegad, county Westmeath, Brookeborough, county Fermanagh and Newry, county Down;
born 1815/6; studied medicine at Glasgow University; LM Rot Hosp Dub 1836; MD (Glas) 1839; LRCS and LM 1838; LSA Lond 1868; medical officer to Clonard and Kinnegad Dispensary Districts from 1843, to Brookeborough Dispensary District from 1855, to Bessbrook Spinning Factory 1864–8 and to Mullaghglass Dispensary District from 1868, of Millvale, Mullaghglass, Newry and of Rosemount, county Armagh; married —; father of Dr Edmund Arthur Lightburne (*q.v.*); died 5 April 1890 at Millvale; probate Armagh 6 June 1890. [Addison (1898); Belf PRO, will cal; Dub GRO (d); *Med Dir*].

LIKELY, RICHARD (1835/6–89), Ballyshannon, county Donegal;
born 1835/6, son of James Likely of Park, Kinlough, county Leitrim; LRCSI 1858; general practitioner, of Ballyshannon; married Jane —; died 28 July 1889 at Kildoney House, Ballyshannon; probate Londonderry 6 September 1889. [Belf PRO, will cal, will; Dub GRO (d); *Med Dir*].

LINCH, BERNARD (*fl c* 1731), Cavan;
probably from county Cavan; studied medicine at Rheims University; MD (Rheims) 1731. [Brockliss].

LINDEN, HENRY COOKE (1852–1916), Belfast, London, Bassingstoke, Hampshire, Bristol, Gloucestershire and Leytonstone, Essex;
>born 23 August 1852 at Holywood, county Down, son of William Linden of Belfast; educated at Wesley College, Sheffield; studied medicine at Queen's College, Galway, and from 1869, at Queen's College, Belfast; LRCP Edin 1878; LFPS Glas 1878; surgeon in Turco-Serbian campaign and Zulu War; general practitioner, of 29 Laburnum Terrace, Antrim Road, Belfast c 1879; of Martello House, Dalmeny Road, Tufnell Park, London, c 1883–90, of Fairlawn, Tadley, Basingstoke c 1890–95 and of Compton Martin, Bristol, c 1895–1902; medical officer of health to Watchet Union, Somerset; general practitioner, of Leyspring, 101 Mornington Road, Leystonstone, from c 1900; married Amy Collins —; died 10 April 1916; probate London 20 September 1916. [Lond PPR, will cal; *Med Dir*; QCB adm reg].

LINDSAY, ALEXANDER (d 1689), Londonderry;
>surgeon in Londonderry; killed in 1689 by a bomb while attending to the wounded during the siege of Derry. [Johnston (1960)].

LINDSAY, ALEXANDER (1859–1926), Burslem, Staffordshire, Leyton, Essex and London;
>born 11 July 1859 at Ramelton, county Donegal, son of Matthew Lindsay, carpenter, of Ramelton; educated at Londonderry Academy; studied medicine at Queen's College, Belfast, from 1878; MD (RUI) 1883; MCh Dip Obst 1884; MAO 1885; general practitioner, of Burslem, Staffordshire c 1895, of 347 High Road, Leyton c 1905, and of 17 Berens Road, Kensal Green, London, from c 1910; retired c 1920 to 85 Dartmouth Road, Brondesbury; died 25 February 1926; probate London 3 June 1926. [Lond PPR, will cal; *Med Dir*; QCB adm reg].

LINDSAY, DAVID MOORE (1862–1956), Dublin, London, ship's surgeon, and Salt Lake City, Utah;
>born 29 March 1862 at Castlewellan, county Down, elder son of George Lindsay, farmer, of Gracehill House, county Antrim, and Elizabeth Moore of Moore Lodge; educated at Coleraine Academical Institution and RBAI; studied medicine at Queen's College, Belfast, from 1880; LRCSI 1886; LM Rot Hosp Dub 1887; LKQCPI and LM 1888; medical officer to the Whitworth Hospital, Dublin; clinical assistant to the Golden Square Throat Hospital, London, and the Royal London Ophthalmic Hospital, Moorfields; surgeon on SS *Aurora*; emigrated to the USA c 1890; of Heber City, Utah c 1895, of 551 South Temple, Salt Lake City c 1910 and of 808 Boston Building, Salt Lake City c 1920; Fellow of the American College of Surgeons 1923; retired c 1929 to Brockley Park, Stradbally, Queen's County; MRIA; moved c 1937 to Kingswood, The Heath, Weybridge, Surrey; author of *A Voyage to the Arctic in the Whaler Aurora* (1911), *Camp Fire Reminiscences* (1912) and other publications; married 28 January 1889 Sheila (or Julia Ada) Steele, daughter of Henry Edward Steele, clerk of the Crown in Chancery, Ottawa; died 18 December 1956 at Kingswood; probate London 21 March 1957. [Bennett (1974); Lond GRO (d); Lond PPR, will cal; *Med Dir*; QCB adm reg; Young and Pike (1909)].

LINDSAY, JAMES (d 1842), Spanish Town, Jamaica;
probably from county Londonderry; medical officer to Spanish Town, Jamaica, 1842; died 27 December 1842 of yellow fever. [*Londonderry Sentinel* 11 February 1843 (d)].

LINDSAY, JAMES (*fl c* 1845), Hilltown, county Down;
LAH Dub; apothecary, of Hilltown, c 1845. [Croly (1843–6)].

LINDSAY, JAMES ALEXANDER (1856–1931), Belfast;
born 20 June 1856 at Lisnacrieve House, Fintona, county Tyrone, son of David Lindsay, business man, of Belfast and Lisnacrieve House; educated at RBAI and at Methodist College, Belfast, from 1868; studied arts and medicine at Queen's College, Belfast, from 1873; BA (RUI) (Gold Medal) 1877; MA 1878; MD MCh 1882; LM RCPI 1885; MRCP Lond 1890; FRCP 1903; also studied in Vienna; house physician to Belfast Royal Hospital 1882–3, honorary physician to Ulster Hospital for Children and Women 1883–5; assistant physician to the Belfast Royal Hospital 1883–8, attending physician 1888–1921; gave the annual winter oration at the Belfast Royal Hospital 1889 and 1916; special commissioner of *Lancet* to inquire into hygiene conditions of Sicily 1897; professor of medicine at Queen's College, Belfast 1899–1923, of 3 College Square East, and later of 3 Queen's Elms, Belfast; chairman of the RVH medical staff 1918–21; played a large part in the foundation of the school of dentistry, QUB; president of the Association of Physicians of Great Britain and Ireland, the Ulster Branch of the BMA, Belfast Literary Society 1891–2 and 1901–02 and of the Ulster Medical Society 1897–8; Bradshaw Lecturer in the Royal College of Physicians, 1909; president of the Linen Hall Library 1914–28; author of *The Climatic Treatment of Consumption* (1887), *Lectures on Diseases of the Heart and Lungs (1904), Medical Axioms, Aphorisms and Clinical Memoranda* (1923), *The Lindsay Family in Ireland*, and various medical papers; a keen golfer and presented the Lindsay cup to the Ulster Medical Society; unmarried; died 14 December 1931 at Belfast; probate Belfast 23 March 1932. [*Belf Lit Soc* (1901); Belf PRO, will cal; *BMJ* obituary (1931); Breathnach and Moynihan (2012); *DIB* (2009); Fry (1984); Hunter (1936); Killen (1990); Kirkpatrick Archive; *Lancet* obituary (1931); Marshall and Kelly (1973); *Med Dir*; Moody and Beckett (1959); *Munk's Roll*, vol 4; O'Brien, Crookshank and Wolstenholme (1984); QCB adm reg; Young and Pike (1909)].

LINDSAY, JOHN (1844–96), Belfast;
born 26 June 1844 at Ballyclare, county Antrim, son of Joseph Lindsay, manager of the Ballyclare Bleach Works; brother of Dr Joseph Lindsay (*q.v.*); educated privately; studied medicine at Queen's College, Belfast, from 1872; LRCP LRCS and LM Edin 1878; general practitioner, of Park View, 2 Templemore Avenue, Belfast; surgeon to various workers' societies in the shipyards; married —; died 10 June 1896 at Templemore Avenue. [Dub GRO (d); *Med Dir*; QCB adm reg].

LINDSAY, JOSEPH (1840–79), Belfast;
born 3 August 1840 at Ballyclare, county Antrim, son of Joseph Lindsay, manager of the Ballyclare Bleach Works; brother of Dr John Lindsay (*q.v.*); educated at Belfast Seminary; studied arts and medicine at Queen's College, Belfast, from 1858; BA

(QUI) 1863; LRCS Edin 1866; LRCP Edin and LM 1867; resident medical officer to Belfast Union Infirmary and Fever Hospital; general practitioner, of 105 York Street, Belfast; author of various medical papers; unmarried; died 1 November 1879 at 107 York Street. [Dub GRO (d); *Med Dir*; QCB adm reg].

LINDSAY, ROBERT (d 1796/7), Naval Medical Service;
of Strabane, county Tyrone; joined the Naval Medical Service as assistant surgeon on HMS *Quebec*; married Jane —; will dated 30 July 1796, proved 31 August 1797 in London (PCC) (original will in National Archives, Kew). [Elliott, Simon, pers com; Hitchings, Paul, pers com].

LINDSAY, ROBERT CHARLES WILLIAM ALEXANDER (1840–c 1882), Victoria, Australia;
born 1840/1, son of Alexander Lindsay of Fintona, county Tyrone and Londonderry; educated at Mr Hall's Seminary, Londonderry; studied medicine at Queen's College, Belfast, from 1857; LFPS Glas 1863; emigrated to Australia on the *Red Rose* and immediately went off to the goldfields in Victoria; married 18 May 1869 in Barkley Street Wesleyan Church, Ballarat, Victoria, Jane Elizabeth Williams, eldest daughter of the Rev Thomas Williams, Wesleyan minister, of Ballarat; and had 10 children, of whom 5 became famous artists; died c 1882. [*Londonderry Sentinel* 26 July 1869 (m); *Med Dir*; Nicks (1978); QCB adm reg].

LINEY, WILLIAM
See LENEY, WILLIAM

LINN, ALLAN (1799/1800–24), Donegore, county Antrim;
born 1799/1800; surgeon, of Ballysavage, Donegore; died 14 May 1824 of a rapid decline, 'a man of the most extensive knowledge … and to the poor his medical attention was generally accompanied with pecuniary aid'. [*BNL* 25 May 1824 (d)].

LINN, DAVID (d 1827), Army Medical Service and Larne, county Antrim;
joined the Army Medical Service as assistant surgeon with the 5th Light Infantry Militia 1803; on half pay c 1804 and full pay with 32nd Foot 1806; surgeon with 96th and later with 95th Foot 1811; on half pay 1818 and full pay with 62nd Foot 1824; served at Copenhagen 1807, Walcheren 1809 and Peninsular War 1808–11; retired on half pay 1825; apothecary, of Cross Street, Larne, c 1824; died 15 January 1827 at Larne. [McKillop (2000); Peterkin and Johnston (1968); Pigot (1824)].

LIPSETT, EDWARD (*fl c* 1796), Ballyshannon, county Donegal;
LAH Dub 1796; apothecary, of Ballyshannon, [Apothecaries (1829)].

LITHGOW, JAMES MACGREGOR (1857/8–1940), Leicester;
born 1857/8 at Downpatrick, county Down, son of Robert Thomas Lithgow, carriage builder, of Downpatrick; brother of Dr Robert Alexander Douglas Lithgow (*q.v.*); educated at RBAI; studied medicine at Queen's College, Belfast, from 1876; MD MCh (RUI) 1882; general practitioner, of 41 Cambridge Terrace, Humberstone Road, Leicester, and from c 1900, of Melbourne House, Highfields, Leicester; retired

c 1932 to Boskenna Cottage, Kimberley Road, Falmouth, Cornwall; married —; died 25 December 1940 at Willmead, Middle Warberry Road, Torquay. [Kirkpatrick Archive; Lond GRO (d); *Med Dir*; QCB adm reg].

LITHGOW, ROBERT ALEXANDER DOUGLAS, (1846–c 1902), New Malden, Surrey, Wisbech, Cambridgeshire, London, and Beverley, Massachusetts;
born 13 June 1846 at Downpatrick, county Down, son of Robert Thomas Lithgow, carriage builder, of Downpatrick; brother of Dr James Magregor Lithgow (*q.v.*); educated at Downpatrick Diocesan School and RBAI; studied medicine at Queen's College, Belfast, from 1862, also at Peter Street and Mercer's Hospitals, Dublin, Liverpool Royal Infirmary and Guy's Hospital, London; LSA Lond 1871; LRCP LRCS Edin 1872; MRCS Edin 1880; MD (St Andrews) 1890 (by examination); government inspector of Wisbech Port and certifying factory surgeon; general practitioner, of 4 Malden Villas, New Malden c 1873–5, 13 North Brink, Wisbech c 1875–80, 27A Lowndes Street, Belgrave Square, London, c 1880–96; name erased from Medical Register May 1897 for associating with unregistered practitioners; emigrated to USA and of Beverley, Massachusetts from c 1897; 'author of essays, poems, and numerous contributions to general literature' as well as various medical papers; married (1) Emily Mary — (who died 15 March 1895; probate London 23 April 1896); (2) Alice Clementina — (who died 25 May 1900; probate London 23 April 1901); died after 1901. [Lond PPR, will cal (Emily Mary and Alice Clemintina); *Med Dir*; QCB adm reg; Smart (2004)].

LITHGOW, — (*fl c* 1819), Coleraine, county Londonderry;
general practitioner, of Coleraine; married — (who was born 1796/7 and died 19 June 1819). [*BNL* 29 June 1819 (d)].

LITTLE, CHARLES COLHOUN (1848/9–1924), Indian Medical Service;
born 1848/9, at Letterkenny, county Donegal, son of Dr Robert Little, senior (*q.v.*), of Lifford; brother of Dr Robert Little, junior (*q.v.*); educated at Raphoe Royal School; studied medicine at Queen's College, Belfast, from 1867; LRCSI 1870; MD MCh (QUI) 1871; joined the Indian Medical Service (Madras establishment) as assistant surgeon 1872; surgeon 1873; surgeon major 1884; surgeon lieutenant-colonel 1892; colonel 1900; inspector general of dispensaries, superintendent of vaccinations and sanitary commissioner in Berars (Hyderabad) 1877–97; principal medical officer of Hyderabad Contingent 1897–9; inspector-general of jails in Burma 1899–1900, inspector general of civil hospitals in Burma 1900–05; retired 1905; of Midgham Cottage, Reading, Berkshire c 1920; married Matilda Mary —; father of Dr Gerald Lewis Colhoun Little, MB (Edin) 1907, IMS; died 21 April 1924 at 20 Seafield Road, Hove, Sussex; probate London 29 May 1924. [*BMJ* obituary (1924); Crawford (1930); Kirkpatrick Archive; Lond PPR, will cal; *Med Dir*; QCB adm reg].

LITTLE, EDWARD (STEPHEN) (1852/3–1901), London;
born 1852/3, son of Edward Little, collector of Inland Revenue, Haddington, Scotland; brother of Dr Stephen Little (*q.v.*); educated at Fauconbey Grammar School, Beccles, Suffolk; studied medicine at Queen's College, Belfast, from 1874 and St Bartholomew's Hospital, London; MD MCh Dip Mid (QUI) 1878; MRCSE

1878; general practitioner, and medical officer for Wimbledon District, of Hill Road, Wimbledon, London; retired c 1898; married Jane —; died 6 January 1901 at Worthing, Sussex; probate London 17 January 1901. [Lond PPR, will cal; *Med Dir*; QCB adm reg].

LITTLE, JAMES (*fl c* 1803), Newtownstewart, county Tyrone;
LAH Dub 1803; apothecary, of Newtownstewart. [Apothecaries (1829)].

LITTLE, JAMES (1837–1916), Armagh, Lurgan, ship's surgeon and Dublin;
born 21 January 1837 in Newry, county Down, son of Archibald Little of Newry and Mary Coulter of Carnmeen; educated at Cookstown Academy, and at Armagh Royal School 1851–3; apprenticed to Dr John Colvan, physician of Armagh (*q.v.*), and Dr Alexander Robinson, surgeon of Armagh (*q.v.*); studied medicine at the Royal College of Surgeons in Ireland from 1853 and at Edinburgh University; LRCSI 1856; MD (Edin) 1861 (thesis 'On some medico-legal questions connected with unsoundness of mind'); LKQCPI and LM 1865; FKQCPI 1867; LLD (Edin) (*hon causa*); MD (TCD, *hon causa*) 1893; medical officer to Armagh Infirmary and Lunatic Asylum; medical officer to the P & O Steamship Company 1857–60; general practitioner in Lurgan 1861–3; physician to the Adelaide Hospital, Dublin, from 1866; of 24 Lower Baggot Street, Dublin; lecturer in medicine at the Ledwich School 1868–72 and professor of medicine at the Royal College of Surgeons 1872–83; consulting physician to the Rotunda Hospital, Dublin, from 1881; president of the KQCPI 1886–7, of the Royal Academy of Medicine in Ireland, and the Association of Physicians of Great Britain and Ireland; physician to the King; MRIA; author of many medical papers and editor of the *Journal of Medical Science*; married 23 October 1871 in St Stephen's Church of Ireland Church, Dublin, Anna Murdoch, daughter of Robert Murdoch, solicitor, of 36 Lower Leeson Street, Dublin; died 23 December 1916 at 14 St Stephen's Green North, Dublin; memorial in RCPI; probate Dublin 15 February 1917. [Belf PRO, will cal; *BMJ* obituary (1916); Cameron (1916); Crone (1928); *DIB* (2009); Dub GRO (m); Edin Univ; Ferrar (1933); Kirkpatrick (1924); Kirkpatrick Archive; Kirkpatrick and Jellet (1913); *Lancet* obituary (1916); *Med Dir*; Newmann (1993); O'Brien, Crookshank and Wolstenholme (1984); Widdess (1967)].

LITTLE, JOSEPH, senior (1740–1813), Killyleagh, county Down;
born 1749 at Loughbrickland, county Down, only son of James Little, farmer, of Loughbrickland; studied arts at Glasgow University; matriculated 1762; MA(Glas)1765; minister of First Killyleagh Presbyterian Church 1768–1813; studied medicine at Edinburgh University; MD (Edin) 1780 (thesis 'De variola') returned to his ministry and acted also as a medical practitioner; married (1) — Ringland (who died of consumption six months after marriage); (2) Isabella McAlister of Loughbrickland; father of Dr Joseph Little, junior (*q.v.*); died 12 July 1813; 'as a physician he ranked high in that profession; as a divine he was instructive and entertaining' (*BNL*); buried in Killyleagh Presbyterian Graveyard. [Addison (1898) and (1913); *BNL* 23 July 1813 (d); Clarke, *County Down*, vol 7 (2nd ed,1993); Edin Univ; McConnell (1951); McCreery (1875)].

LITTLE, JOSEPH, junior (1797/8–1831), Killyleagh, county Down;
born 1797/8, eldest son of the Rev Dr Joseph Little, senior (*q.v.*); educated by Dr Leney; entered Trinity College, Dublin 1813, but did not graduate; physician, of Killyleagh c 1824; married 11 May 1825 Elizabeth Sinclair, youngest daughter of the Rev James Sinclair, minister of Glastry Presbyterian Church, county Down; father of James Sinclair Little (only son), who was born 1826/7 and died 24 March 1846 at Glasgow 'where he was prosecuting his studies for the medical profession'; died 26 February 1831 at Killyleagh. [*BNL* 20 May 1825 (m), 4 March 1831 (d) and 11 April 1846 (d); Burtchaell and Sadleir (1924); McCreery (1875); Pigot (1824)].

LITTLE, JOSHUA (d 1841), Naval Medical Service and Stewartstown, county Tyrone; joined the Naval Medical Service as assistant surgeon; retired to Stewartstown; married 17 December 1830 in Stewartstown, Mary Little, daughter of Alexander N. Little of Stewartstown; died 12 April 1841 at Stewartstown 'after a protracted illness'. [*BNL* 24 December 1830 (m) and 23 April 1841 (d); Kirkpatrick Archive; *Londonderry Sentinel* 1 January 1831 (m) and 24 April 1841 (d)].

LITTLE, ROBERT (c 1801–89), Belfast, Wolverhampton, Staffordshire, Manchester, Warwickshire, and New South Wales;
born probably in 1801 at Killyvolgan, Ballywalter, county Down, younger son of a farmer of Killyvolgan; studied medicine at Glasgow University from 1822, at the Royal College of Surgeons in Ireland and the Richmond Hospital, Dublin; MA MD (Giessen, Germany) 1824; MD CM (Glas) 1826; LAH Dub 1827; medical officer to Belfast No 4 Dispensary District 1828–30, of High Street c 1827 and of 94 and 92 Donegall Street c 1830–35; attending physician to Belfast Fever Hospital 1830–35 and consulting physician 1835–40; physician to Belfast Lying-in Charity 1830–40; lecturer in medicine at RBAI 1832–5 and professor of midwifery 1835–40; resigned 1840 following a dispute about the issuing of diplomas; treasurer and then president (dean) of the RBAI faculty of medicine 1838–9; of 9 Donegall Place c 1838 and of 59 Upper Arthur Street c 1840; general practitioner, of 9 Church Street, Wolverhampton c 1846, Darlington Street c 1850 and 9 New Bridge Street, Manchester c 1861; working at Scone, New South Wales c 1862–5; retired to 4 and 10 College Street South, Belfast c 1867; author of a book on phthisis and various medical articles; married 2 December 1830 Mary Isabella Douglas, daughter of Archibald Douglas of Randalstown; died 10 February 1889; buried in the family grave in Greyabbey graveyard. [Addison (1898); Apothecaries (1829); *BNL* 3 December 1830 (m); Clarke, *County Down*, vol 12 (1974); Dub GRO (d); *Freeman's Journal* (1830); Froggatt (1979); Froggatt and Wheeler (1983); Kirkpatrick Archive; *Med Dir*].

LITTLE, ROBERT, senior (1823/4–81), Combermore, Lifford, county Donegal;
born 1823/4 in county Monaghan, son of Robert Little, merchant; educated by Mr Mooney; studied arts and medicine at Trinity College, Dublin, from 1833; LM Rot Hosp Dub 1835; LRCSI 1837; BA MB (TCD) 1838; FRCSI 1844; medical officer to Letterkenny Dispensary, Workhouse and Fever Hospital; surgeon to Donegal County Infirmary; physician to the County Gaol; surgeon to the Prince of Wales Own Donegal Militia; author of various medical papers; married 22 July 1841 in

Conwall Church of Ireland Church, Letterkenny, Henrietta Colhoun (who was born 12 December 1813), fourth daughter of Charles Colhoun of Letterkenny; father of Dr Robert Little, junior (*q.v.*) and Dr Charles Colhoun Little (*q.v.*); died 22 July 1881 at Combermore; probate Londonderry 22 October 1881. [*BNL* 3 August 1841 (m); Belf PRO, will cal, will; Burke *LGI* (1912); Burtchaell and Sadleir (1924); Croly (1843–6); *Londonderry Sentinel* 31 July 1841 (m); *Med Dir*].

LITTLE, ROBERT (1831/2–67), Moneyglass, Castledawson, county Antrim;
born 1831/2; LM QCB 1854; MRCSE 1856; house surgeon to Belfast General Hospital; medical officer to Bellaghy Dispensary District c 1856–8; general practitioner, of Moneyglass c 1858–67; married 2 May 1860 in Castledawson Presbyterian Church, Margaret Johnston, daughter of James Johnston of Leitrim, Castledawson; died 29 November 1867 of consumption, at Moneyglass. [*BNL* 7 May 1860 (m); *Coleraine Chronicle* 19 May 1860 (m) and 14 December 1867 (d); Dub GRO (d); *Londonderry Sentinel* 11 May 1860 (m); *Med Dir*].

LITTLE, ROBERT, junior (1843/4–85), London, Wrentham, Suffolk, and Raphoe, county Donegal;
born 1843/4, son of Dr Robert Little, senior (*q.v.*); brother of Dr Charles Colhoun Little (*q.v.*); studied medicine at the Carmichael School and Richmond Hospital, Dublin; Carmichael Prize 1863; LM Rot Hosp Dub 1865; LRCSI and LM 1868; LSA Lond 1872; general practitioner, of 30 Barbican, London c 1870–72 and of Wrentham, Suffolk c 1872–6; medical officer to Raphoe Dispensary District and constabulary c 1876–85; married Alice M. — (who died 14 March 1920 at Rostrevor); died 30 March 1885 at Raphoe; administration (with will) Londonderry 20 June 1885. [Belf PRO, will cal; Dub GRO (d); Kirkpatrick Archive; *Med Dir*].

LITTLE, SAMUEL (d 1862), Naval Medical Service;
only son of John Little, ironmonger, of Londonderry; MD (Edin) 1859 (thesis 'On inguinal hernia'); LRCS Edin 1859; joined the Naval Medical Service as assistant surgeon to HMS *Vulcan*; died 7 June 1862 at Sun Kiang, China. [*Coleraine Chronicle* 30 August 1862 (d); Edin Univ; *Londonderry Sentinel* 29 August 1862 (d); *Med Dir*].

LITTLE, STEPHEN (1857–1933), Indian Medical Service;
born 8 January 1857, son of Edward Little, collector of Inland Revenue, Haddington, Scotland; brother of Dr Edward Little (*q.v.*); educated at RBAI; studied medicine at Queen's College, Belfast, from 1874, and St Bartholomew's Hospital, London; MD (hons) MCh (QUI) Dip Mid 1878; MRCP Lond 1888; joined the Indian Medical Service (Bengal establishment) as surgeon 1891; surgeon lieutenant-colonel 1899; served in Afghanistan 1879–80, on the Hissarak expedition (medal), the North-West Frontier, and Mahsud Waziri 1881; died 14 May 1933 at the Hotel Windsor, Monte Carlo; probate London 2 August 1933. [*BMJ* obituary (1933); Crawford (1930); Kirkpatrick Archive; Lond PPR, will cal; *Med Dir*; QCB adm reg].

LITTLE, — (*fl c* 1819), Banbridge, county Down;
surgeon, of Banbridge c 1819. [Bradshaw (1819)].

LITTLEJOHN, JAMES BUCHAN (d c 1952), Craven Arms, Shropshire, and Chicago, Illinois;
probably originally from Garvagh, county Londonderry; studied medicine at Glasgow University; MB CM (Glas) 1892; MD (Chicago) 1905; general practitioner, of Munslow, Craven Arms, Shropshire; emigrated to USA c 1900, first to College Springs, Iowa; professor of pathology and later of surgery in Chicago Medical School, of Steinway Hall, 17–21 Van Biren Street, and later of 17 North State Street, Chicago; author of *Notes on Histology* and *Outlines of Pathology* and various medical papers; died c 1952. [Addison (1898); *Med Dir*].

LIVINGSTON, JOHN LOCKHART (1860–1938), Hursley, Hampshire;
born 1 June 1860 at Lurgan, county Armagh, son of Robert Livingston, merchant, of Lurgan; educated at Lurgan Model School; studied medicine at Queen's College, Galway, and from 1883, at Queen's College, Belfast; MD MCh MAO (RUI) 1886; house surgeon at Bristol Hospital for Children and Women; medical officer and public vaccinator for Hursley Workhouse and District; medical officer for health for Hursley, of Home Close, Hursley; author of various medical papers; married Margaret —; died 2 April 1938 at Mayfield Nursing Home, Winchester; probate Winchester 21 April 1938. [Lond PPR, will cal; *Med Dir*; QCB adm reg].

LIVINGSTONE, SAMUEL (1779–1810), Dromore, county Down;
born 1779; surgeon; died 8 December 1810 at Dromore; 'his tender and benevolent heart rendered him a blessing to the poor'. [*BNL* 14 December 1810 (d)].

LIVINGSTON(E), WILLIAM (*fl c* 1800), Newry, county Down;
general practitioner, of Newry c 1800; married Elizabeth Sarah — (who was born 1762/3 and died 27 June 1847); his daughter, Jane Livingston, married in 1823; died before 1848. [*BNL* 11 November 1823 (m) and 6 July 1847 (d); Bennett (1974)].

LOCHRANE, EDWARD (c 1785–1880), Middletown, county Armagh;
born c 1785; studied medicine in Dublin and Edinburgh; LRCS and LM Edin 1818; general practitioner, of Middletown; married Jane — (who died 12 June 1879 aged 84); died 5 November 1880 at Middletown (aged 95); buried in Tynan Church of Ireland Graveyard. [Croly (1843–6); Dub GRO (d); gravestone inscription; Kirkpatrick Archive; *Med Dir*].

LODGE, HENRY STEWART (1835–64), Army Medical Service;
born 9 January 1835 at Carrigans, county Donegal, seventh son of the Rev William Lodge, rector of Killybegs, and Anne Story; studied arts and medicine at Trinity College, Dublin, from 1853; BA (TCD) 1858; MB 1860; LRCSI 1860; joined the Army Medical Service as assistant surgeon April 1861 but on half pay from September 1861; attached to 2nd Foot July 1862; died 31 August 1864 at Bermuda, of yellow fever; administration Dublin 29 April 1865. [Belf PRO, will cal; Burtchaell and Sadleir (1935); Leslie (1940); *Londonderry Sentinel* 30 September 1864 (d); *Med Dir*; Peterkin and Johnston (1968); Swanzy (1903)].

LOGAN, HUGH ALEXANDER (1860–1935), Rasharkin and Ballyclare, county Antrim;
 born 6 May 1860 at Lisnalinchy, county Antrim, son of Samuel Logan, farmer, of Lisnalinchy; educated at Bruslee School; studied medicine at Queen's College, Belfast, from 1879; MD (RUI) 1885; MCh 1887; LM KQCPI 1888; general practitioner, of Rasharkin c 1885–90 and of Ballyclare c 1890; member and later chairman of Ballyclare Town Council; married 22 November 1844 in Ekenhead Presbyterian Church, Shankill, Belfast, Elizabeth Wilson of Larne, second daughter of Francis Wilson, farmer, and Elizabeth Jane Ramsey; died 12 January 1935; probate Belfast 29 May 1935. [Belf PRO, will cal; *BMJ* obituary (1935); Kirkpatrick Archive; Logan, J.I., pers com; *Med Dir*; QCB adm reg].

LOGAN, JOHN SMYTH(E) (1860–c 1884), Naval Medical Service;
 born 29 July 1860 at Moira, county Down, son of John S. Logan, farmer, of Drumbane, Moira; educated at Lurgan School; studied medicine at Queen's College, Belfast, from 1877; MD MCh Dip Mid (QUI) 1881; joined the Naval Medical Service as surgeon 1882; died c 1884. [*Med Dir*; QCB adm reg].

LOGAN, THOMAS STRATFORD (1876–1918), Belfast, Wakefield, Yorkshire and Stone, Buckinghamshire;
 born 14 September 1876 at Bingley, Yorkshire, son of Dr William Logan of Belfast and Yorkshire (*q.v.*); brother of Dr Mary Ellen Margaret Logan, LRCPI LRCSI 1902, and Dr John Beatty Logan, LRCPI LRCSI 1903; educated privately; studied medicine at Queen's College, Belfast, from 1894, and Yorkshire College, Leeds; LRCP LRCS Edin 1900; LFPS Glas 1900; DPH RCPS Lond 1903; house surgeon to Royal Victoria Hospital, Belfast 1900–01, and resident medical officer to Belfast Union Infirmary; assistant medical officer to the West Riding Asylum, Wakefield, Yorkshire; deputy medical superintendent to the County Asylum, Stone 1913–18; married 20 July 1915 in Hampstead Registry Office, London, Elizabeth Susannah Maria ('Isabel') Simms (who was born 11 July 1875), daughter of Alfred Simms and Rosina Taylor of Croydon, Surrey; died 31 October 1918 at Stone; buried in St Nicholas Graveyard, Carrickfergus; probate Belfast 24 January 1919. [Belf PRO, will cal; Kirkpatrick Archive; Logan, J.I., pers com; *Med Dir*; QCB adm reg].

LOGAN, WILLIAM (1684/5–1757), Bristol, Gloucestershire;
 born 1684/5 at Lurgan, county Armagh, son of Patrick Logan; left Ireland with his father in 1689, to settle eventually in Bristol; William studied medicine at Leyden in 1710; MD (Harderwych) 1710; may have studied also at Utrecht in 1711; later became physician to the Bristol Infirmary; died 1757. [Innes Smith (1932)].

LOGAN, WILLIAM (1836–1906), Belfast, Brierley Hill, Staffordshire, and Bingley, Yorkshire;
 born 1836, son of Thomas Logan, farmer, of Straidnahanna, Ballyclare, county Antrim, and Mary Ellen Madden; educated at Straidnahanna National School; school teacher for a short time at Skilanaban, Ballyclare; studied medicine at Queen's College, Belfast, from 1857; MD (St Andrews) 1862 (by examination); MRCSE 1862; LM KQCPI 1864; general practitioner, of 223 York Street, Belfast c 1870; of

Brierley Hill, c 1868–75 and of Prospect House, Park Road, Bingley c 1875–95; retired to Carrickfergus c 1895; married Frances Stephens of Carrickfergus (who was born c 1839 and died 28 February 1919), third daughter of Stratford Stephens of Carrickfergus and Margaret Bryson of Dobbsland, Ballycarry, county Antrim; father of Dr Thomas Stratford Logan (*q.v.*), Dr Mary Ellen Margaret Logan, LRCPI LRCSI 1902, and Dr John Beatty Logan,LRCPI LRCSI 1903, (who was father of Dr John Stephens Logan, MB (QUB) 1939, physician of the Royal Victoria Hospital, Belfast); died 26 March 1906 at Knocknagalliagh, Whitehead; buried in Ballynure Old Graveyard. [Dub GRO (d); Logan, J.I., pers com *Med Dir*; Rutherford and Clarke, *County Antrim*, vol 3 (1995); Smart (2004)].

LONG, FRANCIS G. (*fl c* 1850–60), Newtowncunningham, county Donegal;
MD [?]; of Newtowncunningham; married Maria O'Donnell (who died 23 April 1858). [*Londonderry Sentinel* 30 April 1858 (d)].

LONG, JAMES (1762/3–1838), Naval Medical Service;
born 1762/3; joined the Naval Medical Service as assistant surgeon; retired to Ervey, county Londonderry; married Elizabeth — (who was born 1772/3 and died 5 January 1842 at the house of Dr James Burnside of Muff, county Londonderry (*q.v.*)); died 13 May 1838. [*Londonderry Sentinel* 19 May 1838 (d) and 8 January 1842 (d)].

LONG, JOHN (*fl c* 1845), Crumlin, county Antrim;
LAH Dub; general practitioner, of Crumlin c 1845. [Croly (1843–6)].

LOUDON, MARCUS MOORE (1860–1927), Dorchester, Berkshire, Mere, Wiltshire, London, Arundel, Sussex, and Guildford, Surrey;
born 12 August 1860 at Crindle Cottage, Myroe, county Londonderry, son of Paul Loudon, farmer, of Crindle Cottage; educated at Coleraine Academical Institution; studied medicine at Queen's College, Belfast, from 1878; MD MCh (RUI) 1884; LM KQCPI 1884; general practitioner, of Dorchester c 1885 and of Myroe c 1886; medical officer and public vaccinator to Mere Dispensary and Workhouse and certifying factory surgeon, of The Chantry, Mere c 1888–90; of 33 Hereford Road, Acton, London c 1890–91; medical officer and public vaccinator, of Carleton House and Maltravers House, Arundel c 1891–1906; general practitioner, of The Elms, Norwood Road, West Norwood, c 1906–11, of 15 Lancaster Road, West Norwood, c 1911–21 and of Oakville, Woodbriden Hill, Guildford, Surrey, from c 1921; married Florence Mary —; died 21 July 1927; probate London 7 September 1927. [Lond PPR, will cal; *Med Dir*; QCB adm reg].

LOUGH, JOHN JOSEPH (1845–1905), Liverpool, Lancashire, Dublin, Ballyjamesduff, county Cavan, and London;
born 1845 in Cavan, son of Matthew Lough, merchant; educated at Cavan Royal School; studied arts and medicine at Trinity College, Dublin, from 1863; BA (TCD) 1867; LRCSI 1868; MB 1869; house surgeon to the Liverpool Children's Infirmary and the Meath Hospital, Dublin; medical officer to Ballyjamesduff and Termon Dispensary Districts c 1875; general practitioner, of 389 City Road, London, c 1885;

died 9 December 1905 at 25 Duncan Terrace, Islington; probate London 27 January 1906. [Lond GRO (d); Lond PPR, will cal; *Med Dir;* TCD adm reg; *TCD Cat*, vol II (1896)].

LOUGHLIN, ALEXANDER
See LAUGHLIN

LOUGHNAN, MICHAEL (1847/8–1932), Gweedore and Rathmullan, county Donegal;
born 1847/8; studied medicine at the Royal College of Surgeons in Ireland and Dr Steevens' Hospital, Dublin; LKQCPI and LM 1873; LRCSI 1873; medical officer to Gweedore Dispensary District c 1874 and Rathmullan Dispensary District, constabulary and coastguards from c 1880; retired c 1919 to Bank House, High Street, Egham, Surrey, c 1923, to Westminster Bank House, Sunningdale, Berkshire and c 1928 to The Croft, Manor Road, New Milton, Hampshire; married —; died 1 September 1932 at the Croft; probate London 29 October 1932. [Lond GRO (d); Lond PPR, will cal; *Med Dir*].

LOUGHREY, RICHARD (1854–c 1915), Limavady, county Londonderry, and London;
born 20 June 1854 at Drumagosker, county Londonderry, son of William Loughrey; educated at Coleraine Academical Institution; studied medicine at Queen's College, Belfast, from 1872; LRCP LRCS Edin 1878; general practitioner, of Limavady c 1878–88; of 146 Mile End Road c 1888; died c 1914. [*Med Dir*; QCB adm reg].

LOUGHREY, WILLIAM JOHN (1856–1903), Dungiven, county Londonderry, and Forest Gate, Essex;
born 21 February 1856 at Balteagh, county Londonderry, son of Richard Loughrey, farmer, of Balteagh; educated at Dungiven Classical School; studied medicine at Queen's College, Belfast, from 1878; MD MCh (RUI) 1885; general practitioner, of Cammish, Dungiven c 1885–94 and of Stanley House, Field Road, Forest Gate, c 1894–1903; married Ellen —; died 2 February 1903 at Stanley House; administration Dublin 27 August 1903. [Belf PRO, will cal; Lond GRO (d); *Med Dir*; QCB adm reg].

LOUGHRIDGE, JOHN (d 1829), Armoy, county Antrim;
surgeon, of Armoy 1826 (witness to a will); died 6 May 1829, 'a gentleman distinguished for the more amiable qualities of universal benevolence and mildness of disposition'. [*BNL* 22 May 1829 (d); Ellis and Eustace, vol III (1984)].

LOUGHRIDGE, JOHN CARSON (1864–1941), Carnmoney and Whitewell, county Antrim;
born 9 April 1864 at Ballyvolly, county Antrim, son of Thomas Loughridge, farmer, of Ballyvolly; educated at Ballymoney Intermediate School; studied arts and medicine at Queen's Colleges, Belfast and Galway, from 1883; LRCP LRCS Edin 1892; LFPS Glas 1892; medical officer and medical officer of health to Carnmoney Dispensary

District and certifying factory surgeon, of Whitewell, Belfast; married (1) 6 July 1892 in Ballyweaney Presbyterian Church, Ballymoney, county Antrim, Agnes Hamilton, daughter of James Hamilton, farmer; (2) Margaret —; father of Dr John Carson Loughridge, junior, MB (QUB) 1917; died 5 October 1941 at Whitewell; probate Belfast 21 January 1942. [Belf PRO, will cal; *BMJ* obituary (1941); Kirkpatrick Archive; *Med Dir*; QCB adm reg; UHF database (m)].

LOVE, ALEXANDER MAYNE (1872/3–1921), Drumquin, county Tyrone, Tiptree, Essex, and Stoke-on-Trent and Longton, Staffordshire;
   born 1872/3; studied medicine at Edinburgh University; MB CM (Edin) 1895; surgeon with the Booth Steamship Company; medical officer and medical officer of health to Drumquin Dispensary District and medical officer to constabulary c 1900–16; general practitioner, of The Firs, Tiptree, Essex c 1916–17, of Stoke-on-Trent c 1917, of Longton, c 1920; married —; died 15 September 1921 at Lisnahoppin, Omagh, county Tyrone. [Dub GRO (d); *Med Dir*].

LOVE, ANDREW THOMAS (1855–1908), Castlederg, county Tyrone;
   born 16 July 1855 at Ballygawley, county Tyrone, son of Andrew Love, farmer, of Magheracreggan, Castlederg; educated at Wimbledon School, Surrey, and RBAI; studied medicine at Queen's College, Belfast, from 1873; MD MCh (QUI) 1878; general practitioner, of Magheracreggan, Castlederg, 1885 and of Rushfield, Castlederg, c 1895; married 7 January 1880 at 'Ardsalla', Fortwilliam Park, Belfast, Sara Elizabeth Rogers, daughter of John Rodgers, merchant, of Belfast; died 27 June 1908 at Castlederg. [Dub GRO (m) and (d); Kirkpatrick Archive; *Med Dir*; QCB adm reg].

LOVE, GEORGE (1795–1830), Dungiven, county Londonderry;
   born 1795; MD [?]; general practitioner, of Dungiven; married 30 October 1821 at Grove Hill, Margaret McClean, eldest daughter of Archibald McClean of Manorcunningham, county Donegal; died 26 November 1830. [*BNL* 23 November 1821 (m); *Freeman's Journal* 1830 (d); Kirkpatrick Archive; *Londonderry Sentinel* 11 December 1830 (d); Pigot (1824); Thrift (1920)].

LOVE, GILBERT (1865–1925), Norwich, Norfolk, and Marbury and Great Budworth, Cheshire;
   born 13 April 1865 at Tievenny, Strabane, county Tyrone, son of John Love, farmer, of Tievenny; educated at Strabane Intermediate School; studied medicine at Queen's College, Belfast, from 1881; medal for diseases of Women and Children, Ulster Hospital, 1886; medical and surgical assistant to Royal Hospital, Belfast; surgeon to Royal African Mail Steamship Company; honorary surgeon to Victoria Infirmary, Norwich, and honorary physician to Marbury Fever Hospital; general practitioner, of Manor House, Great Budworth, from c 1890; married (1) Mina Muir (who was born 1868 and died 24 December 1917); (2) Ann —; died 6 September 1925 after accidentally shooting himself in the leg near Downpatrick on holiday; probate London 1 January 1926. [Kirkpatrick Archive; *Lancet* obituary (1925); Lond PPR, will cal, will; *Med Dir*; QCB adm reg].

LOVE, JAMES (*fl c* 1831), Newtownstewart, county Tyrone;
surgeon, of Termon Dispensary, Newtownstewart; married 8 June 1831 in the bride's home in Newtownstewart, Mary Ann MacDonnell. [*BNL* 21 June 1831 (m); *Londonderry Sentinel* 18 June 1831 (m)].

LOVE, JAMES (1844–92), Stranorlar, county Donegal, and Castlederg, county Tyrone;
born 13 July 1844 at Lislaird, Castlederg, county Tyrone, son of the Rev Joseph Love, minister of Killeter Presbyterian Church; brother of Dr Robert Lindsay Love (*q.v.*); educated at the Rev John Bleckley's Academy, Monaghan; studied medicine at Queen's College, Belfast, from 1861 and the Royal College of Surgeons in Ireland; BA (QUI) 1865; MD 1868; LRCSE 1868; LRCP Lond 1868; medical officer to Killygordon Dispensary District and to Stranorlar Workhouse and Fever Hospital, of Lislaird, Castlederg; married Jane —; died 6 February 1892; administration (with will) Londonderry 28 June 1892. [Belf PRO, will cal; *Med Dir*; QCB adm reg].

LOVE, ROBERT (1853–c 1941), Dewsbury and Bradford, Yorkshire;
born March 1853 at Portadown, county Armagh, son of Robert Love of Timakeel, Portadown; educated privately; studied medicine at Queen's College, Belfast, from 1871; LRCP LRCS Edin 1880; general practitioner, of West Town, Dewsbury, c 1882–7 and of Wakefield Road, Bradford, c 1887–1925; retired c 1925 to The Lawns, 101 Denmark Hill, London, and from c 1934 to Durlstone Manor, Champion Hill, London; died c 1941. [*Med Dir*; QCB adm reg].

LOVE, ROBERT (1862–1929), Ahoghill, county Antrim;
born 4 March 1862 at Kilcreen, county Londonderry, son of David Love, farmer, of Kilcreen; educated at Ballymoney Intermediate School; studied medicine at Queen's College, Belfast, from 1881; LRCP LRCS Edin 1889; LFPS and LM Glas 1889; general practitioner, of Ahoghill from c 1895; medical officer to Ahoghill Dispensary District and constabulary and certifying factory surgeon; JP for county Antrim; married 18 December 1889 in Carncullagh Presbyterian Church, Ballymoney, county Antrim, Elizabeth Campbell, daughter of James Campbell, farmer, of Carncullagh, Ballymoney; died 16 May 1929 in Ballymena Cottage Hospital. [Belf GRO (d); Kirkpatrick Archive; *Med Dir*; QCB adm reg; UHF database (m)].

LOVE, ROBERT LINDSAY (1853–1937), Army Medical Service;
born 19 February 1853 at Lislaird, Castlederg, county Tyrone, son of the Rev Joseph Love, minister of Killeter Presbyterian Church; brother of Dr James Love (*q.v.*); educated at Londonderry Academical Institution; studied arts and medicine at Queen's College, Galway 1872–3 and Belfast, 1875–6; BA (QUI) 1876; MD MCh 1877; LM KQCPI 1877; joined the Army Medical Service as surgeon captain 1880; surgeon major 1892; lieutenant-colonel 1900; served in South African War 1899–1902; retired 1908; lived finally at Altwood Copse, Altwood Road, Maidenhead, Berkshire; married —; died 22 March 1937; probate London 13 April 1937. [Kirkpatrick Archive; Lond PPR, will cal; *Med Dir*; Peterkin and Johnston (1968); QCB adm reg].

LOVE, THOMAS (1796/7–1867), Virginia, county Cavan;
born 1796/7; studied medicine at Edinburgh University; MD (Edin) 1820 (thesis 'De hepatitide'); LAH Dub 1822; general practitioner, of Virginia; died 10 August 1867 at Virginia; probate Dublin 29 August 1867. [Apothecaries (1829); Belf PRO, will cal; Croly (1843–6); Dub GRO (d); Edin Univ; *Med Dir*].

LOVE, WILLIAM SPROULE (1825/6–98), Omagh, county Tyrone;
born 1825/6; studied medicine at the Royal College of Surgeons in Ireland; LM Coombe Hosp Dub 1847; MRCSE 1849; medical officer to Omagh Dispensary District and certifying factory surgeon, of 1 Castle Street, Omagh; surgeon to the Royal Tyrone Fusiliers; married (1) 12 October 1853 in Ballynahatty Presbyterian Church, Mary Margaret Sproule, only daughter of Andrew Sproule of Brookhill, Omagh; (2) Charlotte —; died 13 August 1898; probate Londonderry 14 December 1898. [Belf PRO, will cal; Dub GRO (d); *Londonderry Sentinel* 21 October 1853 (m); McGrew (2001) (m); *Med Dir*].

LOVEROCK, ROBERT GEORGE (1848/9–1906), Ballyjamesduff, county Cavan, and Newcastle, county Wicklow;
born 1848/9; studied medicine at Trinity College, Dublin, and the Royal College of Surgeons in Ireland; LKQCPI 1872; LRCSI 1872; general practitioner, of Ballyjamesduff, c 1885 and of Trudder House, Newtownmountkennedy, from c 1890; medical officer to Newcastle Dispensary District, county Wicklow, to constabulary and to Newtownmountkennedy Fever Hospital; died 17 June 1906 at Goreport, Finea, county Westmeath; probate Dublin 7 July 1906. [Belf PRO, will cal; Dub GRO (d); *Med Dir*; QCB adm reg].

LOWRY, JOHN HENRY (1857–c 1906), China;
born 29 August 1857 at Sydenham Cottage, Strandtown, county Down, son of John Lowry, merchant, of Moygara, Whitehouse, county Antrim, and Glenbank, Holywood; educated at Cheltenham College, Gloucestershire; studied medicine at Queen's College, Belfast, from 1875; LRCP LRCS and LM Edin 1880; surgeon to the Chinese Imperial Maritime Customs Service; of Hoihow, Hainan, China, c 1885 and of Wenchow, China c 1895; mandarin of fifth civil rank c 1905; married 13 September 1898 in Christchurch Church of Ireland Church, Belfast, Amelia Agnes Gillespie, daughter of George Crawford Gillespie, agent, of Belfast; died c 1906. [*Med Dir*; QCB adm reg; UHF database (m)].

LOWRY, JOHN ROBERT COLVILLE (1844–73), Indian Medical Service;
born 19 December 1844 in Dublin, fifth son of James Corry Lowry, barrister, of Rockdale, county Monaghan, and Dorinda Jones of Mount Edward, county Sligo; educated at Portora Royal School from 1860; studied arts and medicine at Trinity College, Dublin, from 1862; BA MB MCh (TCD) 1866; joined the Indian Medical Service (Bombay establishment) as assistant surgeon 1867; surgeon 1873; married 26 April 1871 in Magheragall Church of Ireland Church, Lisburn, Constance Adela Hastings Lyons, daughter of William Thomas Bristow Lyons of Old Park and Brookhill, county Antrim; died 19 July 1873 at Kulajhi, India. [Burke *LGI* (1912);

Clarke, *County Down,* vol 2 (1988); Crawford (1930); Dub GRO (m); *Med Dir; Portora Royal School Register* (1940); TCD adm reg; *TCD Cat,* vol I (1869)].

LOWRY, JOSEPH (1871–c 1952), Belfast;
born 23 April 1871 at 110 Ellenborough Terrace, Belfast, son of John Lowry, clerk; educated at Belfast Model School; studied medicine at Queen's College, Belfast, from 1889; MB BCh BAO (RUI) 1895; general practitioner, of 'Hazelwood', Bloomfield, Belfast; died c 1952. [Kirkpatrick Archive; *Med Dir;* QCB adm reg].

LOWRY, MICHAEL (1735/6–62), Killinchy, county Down;
born 1735/6; surgeon to the 62nd Regiment of Foot Militia; died 13 April 1762; buried in Killinchy graveyard. [Clarke, *County Down,* vol 6 (1971)].

LOWRY, ROBERT ROGERS (d 1811), of Killinchy, county Down;
studied medicine at Edinburgh University; MD (Edin) 1793 (thesis 'De ascite abdominale'); inspected Robert Gordon's Hospital in Aberdeen and purchased a copy of the Foundation Statutes and rules of the Hospital; general practitioner, of Ballymacashen, Killinchy; died 8 December 1811 at his home in Killinchy; probate Down Diocesan Court 1812. [*BNL* 31 December 1811 (d); Belf PRO, Down Dio Wills index; Martin, E., pers com; Edin Univ].

LOWRY, THEOPHILUS (*fl c* 1824), Dungannon, county Tyrone;
surgeon and apothecary, of Scotch Street and Irish Street, Dungannon c 1819 and 1824. [Bradshaw (1819); Pigot (1824)].

LOWTHER, WILLIAM (*fl c* 1838–45), Ballymena, county Antrim;
LRCS Edin; LAH Dub; surgeon and apothecary, of Ballymena c 1845; married Sidney — (who died 15 October 1838 at Ballymena). [*BNL* 23 October 1838 (d); Croly (1843–6); *Londonderry Sentinel* 27 October 1838 (d)].

LUKE, THOMAS DAV(E)Y (1873–1922), Matlock, Derbyshire, ship's surgeon, Edinburgh, Peebles, and Clevedon, Somerset;
born 13 June 1873 at Scorrier, Cornwall, son of Francis R. Luke, proprietor of copper mines, of Scorrier; educated at Truro Grammar School; studied arts and medicine at Queen's College, Belfast, from 1889; Malcolm Exhibition, Belfast Royal Hospital 1893; Coulter Exhibition 1894; MB BCh BAO (RUI) 1894; FRCS Edin 1902 MD (RUI) 1908; resident physician to Smedley's Hydro, Matlock Bridge, Derbyshire and Hazelwood Hydro, Grange-over-Sands; surgeon to the Union Steamship Company; assistant demonstrator in pathology at Queen's College, Belfast; anaesthetist to the Deaconess and Dental Hospitals, Edinburgh from c 1900; instructor in anaesthetics to Edinburgh Royal Infirmary and lecturer in anaesthetics at Edinburgh University, c 1905; of 6 Belford Terrace, Edinburgh c 1908; medical superintendent of Peebles Hydro from c 1910, of 'Esperanza' and 'St Ronan's', Pebbles; managing director of Ochill Hills Sanatorium, Kinross; surgeon-lieutenant RNVR c 1914–18; medical officer to Clevedon Cottage Hospital from 1920, of Emsworth House, Clevedon; author of *Guide to Anaesthetics* (2nd ed 1904, 4th ed 1908); *Anaesthesia for Dental*

Surgery (1903, 3rd ed 1910 and 4th ed 1918), *Manual of Natural Therapy* (2nd ed 1913), and various papers on anaesthesia, hydropathic treatment, etc; married Jane Thompson —; died 25 September 1922 at St Brenda's Nursing Home, Clifton, Bristol; probate Bristol 28 February 1923. [*Belfast Hosp, Ann Rep*; Kirkpatrick Archive; *Lancet* obituary (1922); Lond PPR, will cal; *Med Dir*; QCB adm reg].

LUNDIE, JOHN (1863/4–1917), Bailieborough, county Cavan;
born 1863/4; studied medicine at Queen's College, Galway, and the Royal College of Surgeons in Ireland; LKQCPI and LM, LRCSI and LM 1888; LM Coombe Hosp Dub; medical officer to Termon Dispensary District c 1890; medical officer, medical officer of health and registrar of births and deaths to Bailieborough Dispensary District from c 1892, of Orlando Lodge, Bailieborough; unmarried; died 28 June 1917 at Bailieborough; administration Cavan 19 October 1917. [Belf PRO, will cal; Dub GRO (d); *Med Dir*].

LUSK, SAMUEL FINLAY (1867/8–1944), Knockahollett and Ballymoney, county Antrim, and Loughbrickland, county Down;
born 8 May 1867, third son of James Wallace Lusk of Knockahollett, and Jane Brown; studied medicine at Edinburgh University and Surgeon's Hall; MB CM (Edin) 1895; general practitioner, of Knockahollett c 1905 and Linenhall Street, Ballymoney c 1910; temporary captain in RAMC during World War I; surgeon on plague duty, India; medical officer, medical officer of health and certifying factory surgeon to Loughbrickland Dispensary District from c 1912; medical officer to constabulary; married 12 February 1918 his fifth cousin Eleanor Moore Hanna (1888–1953), only daughter of William Hanna, merchant, of Ballymoney; father of Dr John Brown Hanna Lusk, RCAMC, of British Columbia; died 7 May 1944 at the Musgrave Clinic, Belfast; probate Belfast 13 October 1944. [Belf GRO (d); Belf PRO, will cal, will; Bennett (1974); Kirkpatrick Archive; *Med Dir*].

LUSK, THOMAS (1862–1913), Bury, Lancashire;
born 5 August 1862 at Glenarm, county Antrim, son of James Lusk, merchant, of Glenarm; educated at Larne Intermediate School; studied medicine at Queen's College, Belfast, from 1879; MD MAO (RUI) 1886; MCh 1887; general practitioner, of Mayfield, Walmersley Road, Bury; died 17 February 1913 at Nelson House, Nelson Street, Manchester; probate Manchester 7 March 1913. [Lond PPR, will cal; *Med Dir*; QCB adm reg].

LUSK, THOMAS GIBSON (1870–1940), New Brighton, Cheshire, Great Drifield, Yorkshire, and Monkseaton, Northumberland;
born 4 November 1870 at Larne, county Antrim, son of Robert Lusk, flour merchant, of Larne; educated at Larne Intermediate School; studied medicine at Queen's College, Belfast, from 1888; MD MCh (Edin) 1894; general practitioner, of Homewood, Seabank Road, New Brighton c 1895–1912; surgeon captain 1st Regiment (vol); general practitioner, of 26 New Road, Great Drifield, c 1912–25; honorary medical officer to Drifield Cottage Hospital; of 15 Balmoral Gardens, Monkseaton c 1925–8 and of Hoylake Road, Moreton, Cheshire, c 1928; deputy commissioner with Ministry of Pensions; retired c 1935 to Inver, Anstey Road,

Newtown Linford, Leicester; married —; died 4 May 1940 at Leicester General Hospital, Gwendolen Road, Leicester. [Lond GRO (d); *Med Dir*; QCB adm reg].

LUTHER HEINRICH WALDEMAR (or **WOLDEMAR**) (1819/20–96), Dublin, Cardiff, Cork and Belfast;
> born 1818/9, son of Dr Karl Wilhelm Waldemar; studied medicine at Berlin and Dresden; MD and LM (St Andrews) 1847 (by examination); founder and physician of the Homeopathic Dispensaries in York (1847) and Bath (1849); physician to the Irish Homeopathic Society, Dublin c 1850, of 111 Stephens Green West, Dublin; of 76 Harcourt street c 1860; of Melrose Cottage, Cardiff c 1865–70; general practitioner, of 19 Grand Parade, Cork c 1870; of Chlorine House, Malone Road, Belfast c 1880–96; married (1) —; (2) 12 February 1878 in University Road Methodist Church, Abbey A. Crawford, daughter of Alexander Crawford, merchant, of Belfast; died 22 February 1896; buried in Belfast City Cemetery; probate Belfast 22 June 1896. [Belf City Cem, bur reg; Belf PRO, will cal; *Med Dir*; Smart (2004); UHF database (m)].

LUTTEN, WILLIAM (d 1819), Hillsborough, county Down;
> surgeon and apothecary, of Hillsborough; died 13 September 1819 at Hillsborough. [*BNL* 17 September 1819 (d)].

LYLE, ALLAN ANDREW (1855–1923), Army Medical Service;
> born 20 May 1855 in Belfast, son of Andrew Lyle of Newington, Belfast; educated at Armagh Royal School 1870–72; studied medicine at Queen's College, Belfast, from 1872; LKQCPI 1876; LRCSI 1876; joined the Army Medical Service as surgeon 1878; surgeon major 1890; surgeon lieutenant-colonel 1898; retired 1898; worked subsequently at Aldershot 1915–18; married Catherine Elizabeth —; died 8 January 1923 at Douglas, Isle of Man; probate London 26 September 1923. [Ferrar (1933); Lond PPR, will cal, will; *Med Dir*; Peterkin and Johnston (1968); QCB adm reg].

LYLE, ROBERT PATON RANKIN (1870–1950), Dublin and Newcastle-Upon-Tyne;
> born 14 April 1870, at New Row, Coleraine, county Londonderry, son of Hugh Lyle, commission agent, of New Row, and Jane Rankin; educated at Coleraine Academical Institution; studied arts and medicine at Trinity College, Dublin, from 1888; BA (TCD)1893; MB BCh 1894; LM Rot Hosp Dub 1895; MD 1896; LRCPI 1897; MA 1899; MD (Durham, ad eundem) 1900; FRCOG 1929; DCh (*hon causa*) 1937; assistant master of the Rotunda Hospital, Dublin, 1897–9; gynaecologist to the Royal Victoria Infirmary, Newcastle; obstetrician to the Newcastle Maternity Hospital; lecturer in midwifery and diseases of women in Newcastle-upon-Tyne 1899–1908 and professor in the University of Durham 1908–35; founder of the Samaritan Free Dispensary for Women, in Newcastle and a new Maternity Hospital opened in 1923; JP for Newcastle; author of many papers on obstetrics; of Holmwood, Clayton Road, Newcastle; retired to 11 Osborne Terrace, Newcastle, c 1935, to Rose Villa, Archbold Terrace c 1938, and to Brightside, 16 Granville Road c 1949; married Mary —; died 1 February 1950; probate Newcastle-upon-Tyne 8 June 1950. [*BMJ* obituary (1950); Dub GRO (b); Kirkpatrick Archive; Kirkpatrick and Jellett (1913); *Lancet* obituary

(1950); Lond PPR, will cal; *Med Dir*; Peel (1976); TCD adm reg; *TCD Cat*, vols II (1896) and III (1906); *TCD Reg*].

LYLE, WILLIAM (1871–1949), Bacup, Lancashire, and Newtownstewart, county Tyrone;
born 30 March 1871 at Stonewold, Newtownstewart, son of Rev Leslie Alexander Lyle, minister of Ardstraw Presbyterian Church and — Scott of Dromore, county Tyrone;; educated at Newtownstewart Intermediate School; studied medicine at Queen's College, Belfast, from 1886; MB BCh BAO (RUI) 1893; general practitioner in Bacup c 1893–4; medical officer and medical officer of health to Newtownstewart Dispensary District, of Moyle View, Newtownstewart; medical officer to the post office and constabulary; retired 1936 to 'Moyle', Belmont Road, Belfast; MP in the Stormont Parliament for Queen's University 1942–5 and 1949–50; president of the NI branch of BMA; heavily involved in the order of Freemasons and Unionist party; married 8 June 1897 in St John's Presbyterian Church, Belfast, Sara Helena Fitzgerald, daughter of Joseph Edmund Fitzgerald of Ballylennan, county Tyrone; father of Dr John Scott Lyle, MB BCh BAO ((QUB) 1922, of Patterdale, Lancashire; Dr Leslie Alexander Lyle, MB BCh BAO (QUB) 1927 of Newtownstewart, and Dr William Fitzgerald Lyle, MB BCh BAO (QUB) 1926, of Heysham, Lancashire; died 2 August 1949 at 'Moyle', Belmont Road; administration (with will) Belfast 24 October 1949. [Barkley (1986); Belf PRO, will cal, will; *BMJ* obituary (1950); Kirkpatrick Archive; Lyle (1937); *Med Dir*; QCB adm reg; UHF database (m)].

LYNASS, JAMES (1864–1905), Belfast;
born 13 September 1864 in Belfast, son of William Lynass, manufacturer; educated at RBAI; studied medicine at Queen's College, Belfast, from 1883; MB BCh BAO (RUI) 1892; resident medical officer to the Belfast Infirmary 1893–7; general practitioner, of 89 Great Victoria Street and 20 Claremont Street, Belfast; assistant surgeon (and chloroformist) to the Belfast Hospital for Sick Children 1897–1900; first surgeon to the Belfast Infirmary 1900–05; largely self-taught as a surgeon and complained much for improvements in the operating theatre in the Infirmary; married Alice —; died 5 December 1905 (suddenly) at Belfast; administration Belfast 22 December 1905. [Belf PRO, will cal; *BMJ* obituary (1905); Calwell (1973); Craig (1974, 1985); Kirkpatrick Archive; *Med Dir*; QCB adm reg].

LYNCH, EUGENE (*fl c* 1760), Cavan;
from county Cavan; studied medicine at Rheims University; MD (Rheims) 1760. [Brockliss].

LYNCH, FRANCIS JOHN (1854/5–1930), Armagh;
born 1854/5; studied medicine at the Catholic University of Ireland; LRCSI 1875; LKQCPI and LM 1881; general practitioner, of Dobbin Street, Armagh; unmarried; died 15 December 1930 at Dobbin Street. [Belf GRO (d); *Med Dir*].

LYNCH, JOHN ANTONY (1860–c 1906), London and China;
born 17 January 1860 at Arva, county Cavan, son of John Lynch, farmer, of Arva; educated at St Patrick's College, Cavan; studied medicine at Queen's College, Belfast,

from 1881; MD MCh (RUI) 1883; general practitioner, of 42 Bloomsbury Square, London, c 1885; medical officer in Chinkiang, China, c 1895; died c 1906. [*Med Dir*; QCB adm reg].

LYNCH, OWEN (1853–94), Carndonagh, county Donegal;
born 17 March 1853 at Culmore, county Londonderry, son of James Lynch, farmer, of Culmore; educated at Foyle College, Londonderry; studied medicine at Queen's College, Belfast, from 1874; LRCP LRCS Edin 1879; general practitioner, of Mill Brae House, Carndonagh; married Mary —; died 1 December 1894 at Mill Brae House; administration Londonderry 24 December 1894. [Belf PRO, will cal; Dub GRO (d); *Med Dir*; QCB adm reg].

LYNCH, PATRICK (*fl c* 1804), Carrickmacross, county Monaghan;
LAH Dub 1804; apothecary, of Carrickmacross. [Apothecaries (1829)].

LYNCH, PATRICK A. (1811/2–64), Belfast;
born 1811/2; studied medicine at Glasgow University; MD (Glas) 1841; LAH Dub 1841; MRCSE 1853; medical assistant to Cholera Hospital, Belfast; general practitioner, of Donegall Street, Belfast; one of those who presented an inscribed gold box to Dr S.S. Thomson in 1834; unmarried; died 19 May 1864 at Ballycraigy, county Antrim, following a carriage accident; probate Dublin 5 July 1864. [Addison (1898); Belf PRO, will cal; Croly (1843–6); Dub GRO (d); *Med Dir*; Thomson box (1834)].

LYND, JOHN CHARLES (1862–1930), Limavady, county Londonderry;
born 15 September 1862 at Drumagosker, Limavady; educated at Coleraine Academical Institution; studied medicine at Queen's College, Belfast, from 1882; LRCP LRCS Edin 1893; LFPS Glas 1893; medical officer to Limavady Dispensary District and Workhouse Infirmary; retired c 1928; married Mary —; died 3 March 1930; probate Londonderry 19 May 1930. [Belf PRO, will cal; *Med Dir*; QCB adm reg].

LYNDON, GEORGE ERNEST (1854/5–94), Crossdoney, county Cavan, and London;
born 1854/5; studied medicine at Trinity College, Dublin, and the Royal College of Surgeons in Ireland; LRCSI 1876; LKQCPI and LM 1877; LM Coombe Hosp Dub 1877; MKQCPI 1880; general practitioner, of The Rocks, Crossdoney c 1878–90; JP for county Cavan; general practitioner, of 1 Pembridge Gardens, London; retired to Clonagonnell, county Cavan; married Selina Charlotte —; died 16 July 1894 at Clonagonnell; probate Cavan 6 September 1894 and London 20 September 1894. [Belf PRO, will cal; Dub GRO; Lond PPR will cal, will; *Med Dir*].

LYNDON, THOMAS (*fl c* 1793), Belfast;
LAH Dub 1793; apothecary, of Belfast. [Apothecaries (1829)].

LYNN, JOSEPH MARSHALL (1805/6–99), Markethill and Armagh, county Armagh;
born 1805/6; studied medicine at Glasgow and Edinburgh Universities, and at the Royal College of Surgeons in Edinburgh and Dublin; LRCS Edin 1829; MD (Glas)

1834; LRCSI 1840; LM RCSI 1843; acting staff surgeon to the Armagh Militia Regiment from 1832; medical officer to Markethill and Mountnorris Dispensary Districts and to constabulary 1846; surgeon to the Armagh Light Infantry from 1854; surgeon major 1876; of Melbourne Terrace, Armagh; author of various medical papers; married 23 July 1835 in Aghalee Church of Ireland Church, county Antrim, Anne Jane Chapman, eldest daughter of George Chapman of Tromra, county Antrim; died 10 October 1899 at Russell Street, Armagh; probate Armagh 24 November 1899. [Addison (1898); Aghalee Church of Ireland Marriage Register (PRO NI, T679/90); *BNL* 28 July 1835 (m); Belf PRO, will cal; Croly (1843–6); Dub GRO (d); *Med Dir*; QCB adm reg].

LYNN, ROBERT KERRISON (1808/9–73), Sligo;
born 1808/9 in county Down, son of John Lynn; educated by Mr Elliott; studied arts and medicine at Trinity College, Dublin, from 1824; BA (TCD) 1829; MB 1832; LM Dub Lying-in Hosp; general practitioner and medical officer to Sligo Dispensary and County Gaol, of Stephen Street, Sligo; married —; died 6 May 1873; administration Ballina 20 June 1873. [Belf PRO, will cal; Burtchaell and Sadleir (1924); Croly (1843–6); *Med Dir*].

LYNN, WILLIAM (*fl c* 1730), Fredericksburg, Virginia, USA;
born in county Donegal; emigrated to USA (with his sister Margaret, wife of John Lewis), to settle in Fredericksburg c 1730; qualified in medicine, probably in USA. [Kennedy (2005)].

LYNN, WILLIAM PARK (1855–1924), Manchester;
born 8 February 1855 at Galvally, Portstewart, county Londonderry, son of William James Lynn, farmer, of Galvally; educated at Coleraine Academical Institution; studied medicine at Queen's College, Belfast, from 1873; LRCP LRCS and LM Edin 1884; general practitioner, of 54 Delannays Road, Higher Crumpsall, Manchester c 1885, of 288a, 442 and 950 Ashton Old Road, Openshaw, Manchester from c 1890 and of 950 Ashton Old Road; married Jemima —; died 12 July 1924; administration London 12 August 1924. [Lond PPR, will cal *Med Dir*; QCB adm reg].

LYNN, — (d 1800), Randalstown, county Antrim;
'doctor'; United Irishman; hanged for his part in banditry following the rising, on 4 March 1800 at Randalstown. [Wilsdon (1997)].

LYON, RICHARD ST JOHN (CHINNERY) (1830/1–96), Scrabby, county Cavan, and Dalkey, county Dublin;
born 1830/1; studied arts and medicine at Trinity College, and the Carmichael School, Dublin; LAH Dub 1854; LRCS and LM Edin 1855; LM Dub 1855; LRCP Edin 1860; medical officer to Scrabby Dispensary District, medical officer to Robertstown and Kilmeague Dispensary District, Naas; general practitioner, of 3 Kent Terrace, Dalkey, c 1870 and 1 Temple Terrace, Dalkey c 1885; married —; died 2 November 1896 at Temple Terrace, Dalkey; administration Dublin 27 March 1897. [Belf PPR, will cal; Dub GRO (d); *Med Dir*].

LYONS, J.M. (*fl c* 1840), Markethill, county Armagh;
MD [?]; general practitioner, of Markethill; married —; twin children born 25 December 1839. [*BNL* 3 January 1840 (b)].

LYONS, ROBERT (1864–1935), London and Aberdeen;
born 16 January 1864 at Belfast, son of Robert Lyons, engine driver, of 64 Newtownards Road, Belfast; educated at RBAI; studied medicine at Queen's College, Belfast, from 1882; MB BCh BAO (RUI) 1890; general practitioner, of 25 Osnaburgh Street, London, c 1895–1910, of Bieldside, Aberdeen c 1910–20 and of Glengariff, 947 Finchley Road, Golder's Green, London, from c 1920; assistant medical officer to London County Council; retired to 60 Princetown Road, Bangor, county Down; married 12 February 1891 in Fortwilliam Presbyterian Church, Belfast, Elizabeth Moore, daughter of Patrick Moore, ship owner; died 21 July 1935; probate Belfast 15 January 1936. [Belf PRO, will cal; *Med Dir*; QCB adm reg; UHF database (m)].

LYONS, ROBERT WILLIAM STEELE (1859–1947), Indian Medical Service;
born 4 September 1859 at Coravalley House, county Monaghan, son of R. Lyons of Coravalley House; educated at the Modern and the Diocesan School, Monaghan; studied medicine at Queen's College, Galway, and from 1879, at Queen's College, Belfast; MD MCh (QUI) 1881; MAO (RUI) 1888; joined the Indian Medical Service (Bombay establishment) as surgeon 1882; surgeon major 1894; lieutenant-colonel 1902; colonel 1909; surgeon general 1914; Kaiser-I-Hind medal 1st class 1903; GSP 1914; KHP 1914; retired 1919 as major-general; lived later at Shierglas, Victoria Road, Fleet, Hampshire; married Miriam Isabel —; died 25 July 1947 at Shierglas; probate London 9 February 1948. [Crawford (1930); Kirkpatrick Archive; Lond PPR, will cal; *Med Dir*; QCB adm reg].

LYONS, SAMUEL (*fl c* 1819), Lurgan, county Armagh;
LAH Dub 1819; apothecary, of Lurgan. [Apothecaries (1829)].

LYONS, WILLIAM JOSEPH BENEDICT (1852–83), Merthyr Tydfil, Glamorgan, and Army Medical Service;
born 19 September 1852 at Rampark, Carlingford, county Louth, son of Michael John Lyons, science teacher, of Rampark, county Louth, Quay Street, Dundalk, and Rugeley, Staffordshire; educated at Dundalk Grammar School; studied medicine at Queen's College, Belfast, from 1869; MD (QUI) 1874; MCh Dip Mid 1875; general practitioner, of Dymoor Street, Merthyr Tydfil c 1875; joined the Army Medical Service as surgeon 1881; unmarried; died 30 April 1883 at Drolute Camp, Deolali, India; administration Armagh 5 May 1884 and London 7 June 1884. [Belf PRO, will cal; Lond PPR, will cal; *Med Dir*; Peterkin and Johnston (1968); QCB adm reg].

LYTLE, JOHN DOUGLAS (1843–71), Maghera, county Londonderry;
born 19 September 1843 at Maghera, son of James Lytle, grocer, of Maghera; brother of Dr Joshua Lytle (*q.v.*); educated at Garvagh Classical School; studied medicine at Queen's College, Belfast, from 1860; LRCS Edin and LM 1864; died 28 December

1871; administration Londonderry 26 June 1872. [Belf PRO, will cal; *Med Dir*; QCB adm reg].

LYTLE, JOSHUA (1855–1923), Shrewsbury, Shropshire;
born 21 February 1855 at Maghera, county Londonderry, son of James Lytle, grocer, of Maghera; brother of Dr John Douglas Lytle (*q.v.*); educated at Methodist College, Belfast, from 1870; studied medicine at Queen's College, Belfast, from 1872; MD MCh (QUI) 1878; house surgeon to Royal Albert Infirmary, Wigan; house surgeon to Rippon Dispensary and surgeon to the National Steamship Company; general practitioner, of 1 Wyle Cop, Shrewsbury c 1895; honorary surgeon to Shrewsbury Division of St John Ambulance Brigade; major RAMC in World War I; lived finally at 16 Coton Crescent, Shrewsbury; died 18 August 1923 at the Nursing Institute, Quarry House, Shrewsbury; administration London 29 February 1924. [Fry (1984); Lond PPR, will cal; *Med Dir*; QCB adm reg].

LYTTLE, JAMES SHAW (1853–1922), Pontypridd, Glamorganshire;
born 25 December 1853 at Ballynahinch, county Down; educated at Ballyhinch National School; studied medicine at Queen's College, Belfast, from 1878; MD MCh MAO (RUI) 1885; general practitioner, of Cilfynydd, Pontypridd, and surgeon to Albion Colliery c 1890–1912, of Dundela, Cilfynydd, Pontypridd; of Garthmore, Creigiar, Cardiff c 1912–21; retired c 1921 to Court Royal Hotel, Brighton; married Edith Mary —; died 13 August 1922 at 9 Easton Terrace, Brighton; memorial window erected to him in Cardiff Royal Infirmary by his widow; probate London 19 September 1922. [*BMJ* obituary (1922); Lond GRO (d); Lond PPR, will cal; *Med Dir*; QCB adm reg].

LYTTLE, LYNESS (1863–1926), Farnworth and Southport, Lancashire;
born 11 October 1863 at Hillsborough, county Down, son of William Lyttle, farmer, of Donacloney, county Down; MD MCh (RUI) 1887; general practitioner, of 41 Long Causeway, Farnworth c 1895 and of 57 Ash Street, Southport c 1905; retired c 1920 to 130 Sussex Road, Southport; married Margaret —; died 23 December 1926; administration London 27 January 1927. [Lond PPR, will cal; *Med Dir*; QCB adm reg].